# THE CONTINUUM DICTIONARY
## OF
## WOMEN'S BIOGRAPHY

# THE
# CONTINUUM
# DICTIONARY
# OF
# WOMEN'S
# BIOGRAPHY

## New Expanded Edition

### Compiler and Editor
### JENNIFER S. UGLOW

Assistant Editor on First Edition
(for Science, Mathematics and Medicine)

FRANCES HINTON

## CONTINUUM/NEW YORK

# For T., H., J. and L.

1989

The Continuum Publishing Company
370 Lexington Avenue
New York, N.Y. 10017

Printed in Hong Kong

**Library of Congress Cataloging-in-Publication Data**

The Continuum dictionary of women's biography: new expanded
edition of the International dictionary of women's
biography/compiler and editor, Jennifer S. Uglow.
     p.     cm.
  Bibliography: p.
  Includes index.
  ISBN 0–8264–0417–0
  1. Women – Biography – Dictionaries.   I. Uglow, Jennifer S.
  II. Continuum (Firm)   III. International dictionary of women's
  biography.
CT3202.C66 1989
920.72 – dc19
[B]                                        88-28224
                                           CIP

# Contents

# List of Illustrations

The Publishers wish to thank the following collections for permission to reproduce the illustrations: The BBC Hulton Picture Library 89 above right, 134 above right/below left, 275 below left, 329 below left/right, 403 below left, 512 above right. The Fawcett Library/City of London Polytechnic 37 above left, 242 below right, 403 below right, 512 below left. The Mansell Collection 37 below left, 89 above left/below right, 134 above left/below right, 188 above left/below left/right, 242 above left/below left, 275 above left/below right, 329 above left/right, 403 above right, 419 above left/right/below right, 482 above left/right/below left, 512 above left, 587 above right. The National Gallery, London 419 below left. The National Portrait Gallery, London 37 above right/below right, 89 below left, 188 above right, 242 above right, 275 above right, 403 above left, 482 below right, 512 below right, 587 below left/right. Popperfoto 587 above left.

# Foreword to First Edition

This Dictionary was compiled in response to two demands I encountered in teaching women's studies and in talking to friends about the lives and work of women. The first was simply for information; discussing the struggle to enter the medical profession raised practical questions: who were the women involved, where did they qualify, what did they go on to do? The second demand was less easy to define; a desire to look at women's strength in action, rather than (as is so often done) to lament their oppression as passive victims. It could be called a request for heroines. This book aims to meet the first demand on a quite unpretentious level, by providing basic biographical information about outstanding women in a variety of fields. Perhaps, in the process, it may go some way towards meeting the second.

There can be no such thing as an 'objective' biographical dictionary of women. First, how can one select from half the human race? Second, there is no accepted criteria of excellence implicit in the category itself as there is for artists, politicians or athletes. To some extent, therefore, selection is necessarily idiosyncratic, although the criteria for inclusion can be roughly defined as follows. Women, whose role in history, or whose contribution to society or use of talent would be remarkable regardless of their sex, are included. Some women are regarded as outstanding because their life or work affected the position of women directly – by their breaking into new occupational fields, or by leading campaigns to alter women's opportunities and status in law, politics, education, sexual freedom, marriage or employment. Others included have had an indirect effect – their embodying concepts of womanhood, good or bad, which condition the attitudes of both sexes (for example, witches, domestic science writers, film stars). Finally, a large number is included because they have become legendary figures, or because the imagination is caught by their courage, cruelty, gaiety, extravagance or sheer eccentricity.

The temporal and geographical scope of the book, which may seem arbitrary at first, is dictated by the wish to represent women's achievement in different fields. The majority of entrants come from North America, Europe and the British Commonwealth in the last two centuries. Particular social factors lead to a concentration of women in certain periods or areas – revolutionaries in Eastern Europe, Latin America or China in the 19th and 20th centuries, in contrast to leisured philanthropists and reformers in the USA and the UK. The lack or the inaccessibility of documentation may have led to an emphasis on Western rather than Eastern artists or feminist leaders. The depth of coverage must also vary; in certain spheres of activity, such as opera or film, it was necessary to select as fairly as possible from a large field, while in others, such as philosophy or finance, representative examples were more difficult to find. Finally, of course, cultural and personal bias in the evaluation of 'achievement' cannot be entirely ignored.

I became aware of how selection reflects

are seen in the 'boke of wikked wyves' much enjoyed by the last husband of the Wife of Bath in Chaucer's *Canterbury Tales*, in Boccaccio's *De claribus mulieribus* (1355–9), written deliberately to redress the poor picture presented of women in contemporary writings, and the *Cité des dames* of Christine de Pisan, 'the first European feminist', which lists women's virtues and achievements in order to combat the misogynistic views of popular writers like Jean de Meun.

Through the ages, biographies have been summoned as evidence in debates about the nature of women; and, as the grounds of debate shift, so do the examples. The heated arguments of the 16th and 17th centuries are reflected in works like Thomas Heywood's *Nine Bookes of Various Histories Concerning Women* (1640) which mixes entertainment and descriptions of public virtues with a safe didacticism: 'wives may reade here of chast virgins, to patterne their Daughters by, and how to demeane themselves in all Coniugale love towards their Husbands'. Two and a half centuries later, the burst of radical egalitarianism expressed in Mary Wollstonecraft's *Vindication of the Rights of Women* (1792) found its biographical counterpart in Mary Hays's six-volume *Female Biography* (1803) whose feminist purpose was explicit, 'My pen has been taken up in the Cause, and for the benefit, of my own sex.' At the end of the 19th century the struggle for suffrage resulted in a number of biographical collections by noted reformers, illustrating both women's capabilities and their part in serving 'the Cause'. It is interesting to note that women opposing suffrage also seized on biography as a tool, for example Sarah Josepha Hale, or Charlotte Yonge, whose *Biographies of Good Women* (1862) celebrated the more traditional virtues of self-sacrifice, 'Each lived unto God; and endeavoured to act as his faithful servant; and in this – whether her task were to learn, to labour, or merely to suffer – she proved her faith and obedience and shone forth as a jewel "more precious than Rubies".'

The New Feminism of the 20th century naturally produced a variety of approaches which reflect the trends within the movement. The traditional liberal feminism, which emphasises public virtue, is exemplified by two magnificent works, *Lexikon der Frau* (1953) which drew on the solidarity of the old suffrage movement, the average of contributors being around 80, and *Notable American Women* (vols i–iii, 1971; vol.iv, 1981). Radical feminism, which emphasises a separate female culture and therefore looks to representative symbols rather than to individuals who have broken into, and adopted, male criteria for success, is represented by the 39 guests and 999 women of achievement in Judy Chicago's impressionistic and stimulating exhibition and book *The Dinner Party* (1979). Socialist feminism, affected both by labour history and the growth of interest in oral history (the popular, word-of-mouth, rather than academic tradition), turns its back on the celebration of public figures and looks for heroines in ordinary workers, wives and mothers.

This Dictionary, despite its relatively straightforward educational aim, is influenced by its literary heritage, the patterns set by forebears and contemporaries. It remains a traditional work, looking to public recognition for a definition of success, but in writing it I came to realize that far from presenting a book which was representative of women's experience, I was compiling a book of deviants – independent, odd, often difficult women who had defied the expectations of their society as to what a woman's role should be. As these expectations come increasingly under attack it is important to remember the contribution of all those pioneering 'firsts', whether in engineering, politics or mountaineering.

Recent surveys have shown that despite increasing opportunities, women rarely reach the top of their chosen professions because they lack the 'thorough-going domestic support' available to men. (Do all successful careerists need a wife at home?) In presenting the biographies in this volume I have attempted to show how crucial their private life (the accepted women's sphere) has been, whether as an advantage or constraint in the extent of women's achievement. The influence of parents, the support of husbands, lovers, friends, the existence of close groups of women colleagues, the sudden turns of fortune which force women to become breadwinners and reveal hidden talents, have all been considered. The added energy so often required to combine the roles of career woman or campaigner and mother, or to face the ridicule and hostility which so often greeted their abandonment of traditional duties, has been given its due.

Every day I find more women whom I wish I had included, and much regret the constraints of time and space. Finishing the book has therefore been frustrating, but researching and writing it was immensely challenging and exciting. I hope that those who read and use it will find that they share some of that excitement, and will write to me with details of any women they consider overlooked.

J.U.
*18 May 1982*

# Acknowledgements to First Edition

The advice, assistance and criticism I have received from many people has made me feel, to some extent, that this is a collective work. I owe a special debt of gratitude to my Assistant Editor, Frances Hinton, who chose and wrote the entries on science and medicine, and who also contributed work on many athletes, explorers, mountaineers and aviators. I am also much indebted to the substantial contributions of Ruth Thackeray on musicians, Debbie Derrick on religious leaders and Richard Kwietnowski on film directors, and to Maureen Ritchie who checked and amended the Bibliography.

I would like to thank several other people who provided material on women in whom they were especially interested, notably: Maria Moore, Greek women; Derek Meteyard, actresses; Priscilla Sheringham, French authors; Melly Lewin, 20th-century British writers; Ann and Mike Caesar, Italian socialists; Sharmila Mukerjee, third world nationalists; Penny Brooke, contemporary Chinese leaders.

In addition, Frances and I would like to express our gratitude to everyone who responded so generously to our appeals for advice, including Hermione Lee, Hilkka Helevno, Roisin Batten, Autumn Stanley, Janet Sayers, Anne Seller, Thea Sinclair, Gaie Davidson, Jean Stockdale, Nanneke Redclift, Mary Woodman, Mike Driver and Alan Beck, and especially to David Doughan of the Fawcett Library.

There were, of course, a number of people involved in the thankless task of turning yards of scribbled manuscript into a book and I should like to thank them all, particularly Vivien Lucey, my typist, but also my Editor, Māra Vilčinskas, the copy editors, Audrey Twine and Alison Mansbridge, and the picture researcher, Juliet Brightmore.

Finally, there are two people whose unfailing practical and moral support carried me through times when the whole project seemed impossible: at Macmillan the hard-working and unshakeable Penelope Allport, and above all, always, Steve.

# Note on Second Edition

It was wonderful to be given the opportunity to amend and extend this Dictionary, but I have to admit that such a book could really be infinite. As I explored new areas and looked again at familiar ones, more and more names clamoured for entry and the problem of choice often seemed insurmountable. In the six years since the first edition was published, many excellent works have appeared which provide biographical information on women in particular fields, or particular subjects and so the sense of neglected lives has been partly assuaged. Yet I have still felt it necessary even in this broad survey, to include over two hundred and fifty more women – each one astonishing in different ways – while I have cut only a handful. Entries on contemporary women have been brought up to date so far as is possible and many historial entries have been revised in the light of fresh information. It is hard to compress a lifetime achievement into a few lines, but I hope that this book may be a starting point and that readers will have patience with its inevitable idiosyncracies, gaps and lapses and, above all, that they will find it as stimulating and enjoyable to use as I have found it to write.

J.U.
*16 March 1988*

# Acknowledgements for Second Edition

I am immensely grateful to all the friends, readers and reviewers who commented on the first edition and suggested amendments and additions. Particular thanks goes to Frances Hinton – my invaluable assistant editor the first time round – for her continuing interest and support, and to those who have checked and added to the entries in individual areas, notably Ruth Thackeray, classical music; Jane Bex, business and sport; Penny Brooke, Chinese women; Kimiko Shimoda, Japanese women, and Maureen Ritchie who updated the bibliography.

I would also like to acknowledge everyone who responded to our appeals for suggestions and corrections: their comments have been of great moral support as well as practical use. In this respect I owe a special debt to Susan Bassnett and Sybil Oldfield, and to all the following (listed alphabetically) who have contributed and enlarged the scope of the book in various ways: Margaret Alic, Harriet Anderson, Stephen Bourne, Chris Bratcher, Sarah Carter, Agnes Cardinal, Lorita Crowther, Angela Coutts, Sylvia Freedman, Jim Fyott, Richard Garnett, Debbie Gore, Lyn Innis, Annette Lawson, Hermione Lee, Kate McCluskie, Ravi Mirchandani, Hilary Rose, Margaret Rossiter, Autumn Stanley, Ruth Tomalin, Lisa Tuttle, Merryn Williams and Phyllis Willmot.

Further thanks go to Jacqui Dillon and Liz Cable for their typing assistance and to Margot Levy and (still unshakeable) Penelope Allport at Macmillan for their editorial enthusiasm and care. Finally, of course, I must thank my own family fot putting up so patiently (if irreverently) with the competing demands of two thousand other lives.

# Additional Reference Sources

## A. General Works

1. ENCYCLOPEDIAS
2. GENERAL BIOGRAPHICAL DICTIONARIES
3. NATIONAL BIOGRAPHICAL DICTIONARIES: HISTORICAL
4. NATIONAL BIOGRAPHICAL DICTIONARIES: CONTEMPORARY
5. ENCYCLOPEDIAS AND BIOGRAPHICAL DICTIONARIES BY SUBJECT
6. BIBLIOGRAPHIES AND INDEXES

## B. Biographical material on women

1. BIBLIOGRAPHIES AND INDEXES
2. INTERNATIONAL BIOGRAPHICAL DICTIONARIES
3. NATIONAL BIOGRAPHICAL DICTIONARIES
4. BIOGRAPHICAL DICTIONARIES BY SUBJECT AND COLLECTIVE BIOGRAPHIES BY SUBJECT

The notes below give a brief indication of the types of reference works which may act as starting points for readers seeking biographical information about individual women, or about women from particular countries or whose achievements fall into particular fields. Unfortunately a comprehensive bibliography of biographical collections and individual biographies of women does not yet exist and so one must look to a wide variety of sources. Section A notes general works which contain data on both sexes and Section B considers works on women alone.

## A. General Works

### 1. ENCYCLOPEDIAS

These obvious sources should not be overlooked if one needs quick information about women whose fame is already very well-established. To take two contrasting examples, the *Encyclopedia Britannica* (London, 15/1974) has entries ranging from a few lines to several pages, and while the single volume *New Columbia Encyclopedia* (New York, 4/1980) has extremely brief entries they are often accompanied by two or three useful bibliographic references. The multi-volume foreign language encyclopedias found in most large reference libraries are also useful initial sources.

### 2. GENERAL BIOGRAPHICAL DICTIONARIES

The well-known single-volume works, such as *Chambers' Biographical Dictionary*, (London, rev. 1974) or *Webster's Biographical Dictionary* (Springfield, Massachusetts, rev. 1972), are of limited use since their entries are brief, the people very well-known, and the proportion of women extremely low. Among the few multi-volume international biographical works published, the *McGraw–Hill Encyclopedia of World Biography* (New York and London, 1973) contains a number of articles on famous women in American and world history, with short bibliographies. The great

19th-century French *Biographie universelle* in 45 volumes edited by M. Michand (Paris, 1843–65) is still very useful, especially for information on 18th-century women.

### 3. NATIONAL BIOGRAPHICAL DICTIONARIES: HISTORICAL

Such works as the *Dictionary of National Biography* (London, 1885–1901; suppls., 1901–60), or the *Dictionary of American Biography* (New York, 1928–37; suppls., 1944–77), need no introduction. They are generally reliable, although the criteria for inclusion may seem idiosyncratic and earlier volumes should always be checked against more recent sources. Most large libraries have a selection of such dictionaries from different countries. The most useful of these are listed below in alphabetical order by country.

*Australian Dictionary of Biography* (Melbourne, 1966–)
*Dictionary of Canadian Biography* (Toronto, 1966–)
*Eminent Chinese of the Ching Period, 1644–1912* (Washington, DC, 1944)
*Biographical Dictionary of Republican China,* (New York, 1967–71; suppl. 1979)
*Dictionnaire de biographie française* (Paris, 1933–)
*Allgemeine deutsche Biographie* (Leipzig, 1875–1912)
*Neue deutsche Biographie* (Berlin, 1953–)
*Indian Dictionary of National Biography* (Calcutta, 1972–)
*Dizionario biografico degli Italiani* (Rome, 1960–)
*Japan Biographical Encyclopedia and Who's Who* (Tokyo, 1958–)
*Great Soviet Encyclopedia* (London and New York, 1973–)
*Biographical Dictionary of the Soviet Union 1917–1987* (London, Munich, New York, Oxford, Paris 1988)

Several countries also have concise one-volume works.

### 4. INTERNATIONAL AND NATIONAL BIOGRAPHICAL DICTIONARIES: CONTEMPORARY

The *International Who's Who* (London, 1935–) contains biographies of women prominent in politics, business and the arts. A more selective but far more detailed and livelier source is *Current Biography* (New York, 1940–). This is a monthly serial incorporating information drawn largely from the American press, with a bound annual cumulation. It contains over 300 biographies, and gives references for further information, but unfortunately is found only in very large reference libraries.

Many countries have an annual or biennial directory along the lines of *Who's Who* (London, 1849–) or *Who's Who in America* (Chicago, 1899–). The women they include tend to be of high birth, social position, political, cultural or scholarly status. These works and their retrospective *Who Was Who* collections (usually produced about every ten years) are useful for checking dates, educational qualifications, official positions, decorations etc.

### 5. ENCYCLOPAEDIAS AND BIOGRAPHICAL DICTIONARIES BY SUBJECT

These can provide helpful basic data, especially when accompanied by good bibliographies. Useful multi-volume works in particular areas include works such as *The New Grove Dictionary of Music and Musicians* (London, 1980) and the *Dictionary of Scientific Biography* (New York, 1970–80). There is also a proliferation of single-volume works, especially in literature, theatre, dance and film, which vary from very well-documented sources, like *Contemporary Artists* (New York, 1977) to those with only a scanty listing. Current directories, revised at irregular intervals, exist in a few areas, such as the single-volume, biennial *The Writer's Directory* (London, 5/1981) or *American Men and Women of Science* (New York, 14/1979)

6. INDEXES

A variety of comprehensive bibliographies and indexes are published, such as:

*Analytical Bibliography of Universal Collected Biography* (Detroit, 1980), [indexes 3000 works of collected biography]
*Anglo-American Historical Names Database* (Cambridge UK, Alexandria VA, 1986–xx)
*Bibliography of Biography* (London, 1985) A microfiche listing of biographical books published worldwide between 1970–1984, with name index and author-title list.
*Bio-base* (Detroit, 2/1981) [index to 'nearly 4 million citations to biographical entries appearing in 375 biographical dictionaries']
*Biographical Books 1876–1949* (New York, London 1983)
*Biographical Books 1950–1980* (New York and London, 1980). A listing of over 42,000 titles.
*Biographical Dictionaries and Related Works: an International Bibliography* (Detroit, 1967, suppls. 1972, 1978)
*Biography and Genealogy Master Index.* (Detroit, 2/1980)
*Biography Index* (New York, 1946–). A quarterly index covering current books, periodicals, obituaries etc with annual and three-yearly cumulations.
*Current Biography Cumulated Index 1940–1970* (New York, 1973)
*German Biographical Archive* (London, New York, Munich, Oxford, Paris 1982–5). A huge collection of biographical works on microfiche. Similar archives for France and Italy are currently being issued.

## B. Biographical Material on Women

1. BIBLIOGRAPHIES AND INDEXES

(*a*) The general bibliographies on women usually contain a section on biography, but in almost all cases this is disappointingly short. Among the more useful are:

S. Carter and M. Ritchie: *Women's Studies, an information profile* (Mansell, forthcoming)

*Resources for Feminist Research/Documentation sur la recherche féministe* (Toronto, 1972–) [until 1978 known as *Canadian Newsletter for Research on Women*]. An unparalleled resource guide covering research, recent publications, bibliographies, reports, periodicals etc.
S. Searing: *Introduction to Library Research in Women's Studies* (Boulder and London, 1985)
E. Stineman: *Women's Studies; a recommended Core Bibliography* (Littleton, Colorado, 1979) and C. Loeb, S. Searing and E. Stineman: *Women's Studies: a recommended core bibliography, 1980–85* (Littleton, Col, 1987)
*Studies on Women Abstracts* (Abingdon, UK 1983–xx)
*Women's Studies Abstracts* (Rush, N.Y., 1972–). Issued quarterly, it covers reviews of new books and a wide range of periodical literature.

(*b*) More specific bibliographies now abound. Some works which contain a large number of biographical references are:

D. Bachman and S. Piland: *Women's Artists: an historical, contemporary and feminist bibliography* (Metuchen, N.J., 1978)
S.F. Bailey: *Women and the British Empire: an annotated guide to sources* (New York and London, 1983)
P.K. Ballou: *Women: a bibliography of bibliographies*, 2nd ed. (Boston, 1986)
D. Bass and S.H. Boyd: *Women in American Religious History: an annotated bibliography and guide to sources* (Boston, 1986)
S. Chaff: *Women in Medicine: an annotated bibliography of the literature on Women Physicians* (Metuchen, N.J., 1977)
*Les Femmes: Guide Bibliographique* (Paris, 1974)
L. Frey, M. Frey and J. Schneider: *Women in Western European History: a select chronological, geographical and topical bibliography* (Westport, CT and Hassocks, UK, 1982)
L. Goodwater: *Women in Antiquity: an annotated bibliography* (Metuchen, N.J., 1978)
R. Green: *Native American Women: a contextual bibliography* (Bloomington Ind, 1983)

C. Harrison *et al: Women in American History: A Bibliography* 2 vols (Santa Barbara, 1980, 1986)

P. Hauck: *Sourcebook on Canadian Women* (Ottawa, 1979)

Hesung Chun Koh: *Korean and Japanese Women: an analytic bibliographical guide* (Westport CT, 1982)

D. Hixon and D. Henessee: *Women in Music: a bio-bibliography* (Metuchen, N.J., 1975)

S.E. Jacobs: *Women in Perspective: A Guide for Cross Cultural Studies* (Urbana, 1974)

M. Knaster: *Women in Spanish America: An annotated bibliography from Pre-conquest to Contemporary Times* (Boston, 1977)

M. Remley: *Women in Sport* (Detroit, 1980)

E. Tufts: *American Women Artists past and present: a selected bibliographic guide* (New York 1984)

K. Wei: *Women In China: a selected and annotated bibliography* (Westport CT, 1984)

M.C. Weitz: *Femmes: recent writings on French Women* (Boston, 1985)

*( c )* There is only one contemporary general index to biographical collections on women:

N.O. Ireland: *Index to women of the world from ancient to modern times: biographies and portraits*, (Westwood Mass, 1970). This surveys about 900 biographical collections and lists nearly 13,000 women, giving name, dates of birth, category (e.g. 'artist'), nationality and key to source. It is particularly useful for American history.

A useful earlier work is A. Ungherini: *Manuel de Biographie Bibliographique et de l'Iconographie des Femmes Célèbres* (1892–1905/R1968)

Some more specific works are:

P.K. Addis: *Through a Woman's I; an annotated bibliography of American Women's Autobiographical Writings 1946–1976* (Metuchen, NJ, 1983)

K. Herman: *Women in Particular: an index to American women* (Phoenix, AZ 1984)

D. Robinson: *Women novelists 1891–1920: an index to bibliographies and autobiographical sources* (New York 1984)

*(d)* Subject catalogues to specialist library holdings, document collections and archives are invaluable guides to biographical information. Examples include:

M. Barrow: *Women 1870–1928: A Select Guide to Printed and Archival Sources in the United Kingdom* (London, 1981)

*Bibliofem: the joint library catalogues of the Fawcett Library, London, and the Equal Opportunities Commission, Manchester, together with a continuing bibliography of Women* (1978–86), now sadly discontinued.

*Herstory: Microfilm collection of documents on women in history* (Berkeley, California and Chicago).

*The Gerritsen Collection of Women's History, 1543–1945* (Ann Arbor, Michigan, 1983). A 3 vol guide to material now mainly in the libraries of the University of Kansas, and of N. Carolina (Greensboro), but originally started in Amsterdam in the late 19th century. Contains much European material as well as American.

A Hinding & C.A. Chambers: *Women's History Sources* (New York, 1979)

*Women in Australia: An Annotated Guide to Records* (Canberra, 1977)

The huge G.K. Hall series of library catalogues includes a few special collections of women, for example that of the Schlesinger Library at Radcliffe College, the Sophia Smith Collection (Smith College) and the International Archive for the Women's Movement in Amsterdam. More and more libraries are producing lists of their women-related holdings, particularly in America, but also in the UK. Government department libraries can be contacted for latest compilations. The Feminist Library, Hungerford House, Victoria Embankment, London WC2, includes an accessions list in their newsletter, which is useful for modern material.

*(e)* Worth perusing for book reviews are the following:

*Belles Lettres: a review of books by women* (Arlington, VA 1985–xx)

*The Women's Review of Books* (Wellesley, Mass 1982–xx)

2. INTERNATIONAL BIOGRAPHICAL
DICTIONARIES

(a)  Pre-20th-century sources.

Not only are the earlier works fascinating for
what they reveal about the attitudes and
motivation of the compilers, but many 19th-
century collections are the result of
laborious research and contain information
not found elsewhere. Some examples of
these works, often written by dedicated
feminists, are:

H.G. Adams: *Cyclopedia of Female
Biography: Consisting of Sketches of all
Women who have been Distinguished by
Great Talents, Strength of Character,
Piety, Benevolence or Moral Virtues of
any Kind* (London, 1869). A
condensation of Hale (below).
*Biographium Femineum. The Female
Warriors: or Memoirs of the Most
Illustrious Ladies of All Ages and Nations*
(London, 1766)
W.H. Browne: *Famous Women of History:
Containing nearly 3000 Brief Biographies
and 1000 Female Pseudonyms*
(Philadelphia, 1895)
S.J. Hale: *Woman's Record, or Sketches of
All Distinguished Women from the
Creation to AD 1854* (New York, 1855)
M. Hays: *Female Biography: or Memoirs of
Illustrious and Celebrated Women of All
Ages and Countries* (London, 1803)
J.P. Proudhomme: *Répertoire Universel,
Historique, Biographique des Femmes
Célèbrées* (Paris, 1826–7)

(b)  20th-century works

*Biographical Encyclopedia of Women*
(Chicago, 1975)
J.C. Chiappe: *Le Monde au Féminin* (Paris,
1976)
*Contemporary Women* (Detroit, 1975)
V. Giglio: *Donne Celebri* (Milan, 1950)
R. Guimaraes: *Mulheres Celebres* (Sao
Paulo, 1960)
E. Kay: *Two thousand Women of
Achievement* (Totowa, N.J., 1970)
M.E. Kulkin: *Her Way: Biographies of
women for young people* (New York,
1976)
*Lexikon der Frau* (Zürich, 1953–4)

A. Weir & S. Raven: *Women in History*
(London, 1981)
M. Weiser and J. Arbeiter: *Womanlist* (New
York, 1981)
*The World Who's Who of Women* (Totowa,
N.J., 1973, 6/1982)

There are also some general works which are
not strictly biographical dictionaries but
which list women in terms of their
achievements in various fields. Examples
are:

J. Chicago: *The Dinner Party: A Symbol of
our Heritage* (New York, 1979)
J. & K. Macksey: *The Guinness Guide to
Feminine Achievements* (London, 1975)
L.D. O'Neill: *The Women's Book of World
Records and Achievements* (New York,
1979)

And lastly a dictionary of quotations:
E. Partnow: *The Quotable Woman: vol 1 From
Eve to 1799; vol 2 1800–1981* (New York
1982, 1985)

3. NATIONAL BIOGRAPHICAL DICTIONARIES

(a)  Historical.

O. Banks: *The Biographical Dictionary of
British Feminists*, vol 1 1800–1930 (Lon-
don, New York 1985). Vol 2 1930–present
forthcoming.
*The Europa Biographical Dictionary of British
Women: over 1000 notable women from
Britain's past* (London, 1983)
E.T. and J.W. James: *Notable American
Women, 1607–1950: A Biographical
Dictionary* (Cambridge, Mass., 1971)
B. Sickerman and C.H. Green: *Notable
American Women: the Modern Period,
1951–1975* (Cambridge, Mass., 1980).
An interesting earlier work is:
F. Willard and M. Livermore: *A Woman of
the Century: 470 biographical sketches
accompanied by portraits of leading
American women in all walks of life*
(Buffalo, 1893).

(b)  *Contemporary.* Current dictionaries of
the 'Who's Who' type have been produced
spasmodically for several countries but have
rarely had a long or continuous run. When

found they can be useful for checking detail. Examples from North America, Britain, Africa and India include:

*American Women: the Official Who's Who* (Los Angeles, 1935–9)

*Who's Who of American Women* (Chicago, 1960–)

*Woman's Who's Who of America: a biographical dictionary of contemporary women of the United States and Canada 1914–15* (New York, 1914)

*The Women's Who's Who* (London, 1934–5)

*The Lady's Who's Who* (London, 1938–9)

*Women's Who's Who* (Croydon, 1975–7)

*The Suffrage Annual and Women's Who's Who* (London, 1913)

*Directory of African Women* (New York, 1963)

*Who's Who of Indian Women* (Madras, 1977)

4. BIOGRAPHICAL DICTIONARIES BY SUBJECT, AND COLLECTIVE BIOGRAPHIES

The most common type of reference work on women is the collection of lives, ranging from 5–500 subjects, arranged around a particular theme, from women's wickedness to female heroism; or around a particular region or subject. Some collections are basic entertainments, but others are clearly didactic, or are offered as stirring examples of women's achievement. There are hundreds of examples, and selections can be found listed in N.O. Ireland, and in *Bibliofem* (see section B1 above) as well as in most general bibliographies on women. The lists below are intended to give a taste of the variety of such works, and in a few cases, the range of contents is noted as well as the title. Also included below are a few A–Z biographical dictionaries relating to special subjects. Other useful sources, which do not fall strictly within our brief, are general surveys or histories of women in individual countries, occupations or feminist movements.

(a) *General, moral, domestic themes*

W.H.D. Adams: *The Sunshine of Domestic Life* (London, 1891). Portraits to illustrate particular virtures include

Anne Askew, Elizabeth Inchbald, Lady Jane Grey, Jeanne d'Albret etc.

R. Armour: *It all started with Eve* (Boston, 1976). Satirical sketches from Eve to Mata Hari.

R. Baxter: *Guilty Women* (London, 1941)

L.M. Child: *Biographies of Good Wives* (Boston, 1850)

M.C. Clarke: *World-noted Women; or Types of Womanly attributes of All Lands and Ages* (New York, 1867)

N. Crouch: *Female Excellency; or the Ladies Glory* (London, 1728)

S. Dark: *Twelve More Ladies; Good, Bad and Indifferent* (Freeport, N.Y., 1932/ R1969)

A. Ewart: *The World's Most Wicked Women* (London, 1964)

H.K. Hosier: *Silhouettes: Women behind Great Men* (Waco, 1972)

E. Jenkins: *Ten Fascinating Women* (London, 1955)

C.E. Maine: *World-famous Mistresses* (Feltham, 1970)

D.S. Rosenfelt: *Strong Women* (Old Westbury, N.Y., 1978)

P.W. Sergeant: *Dominant Women* (London, 1929/R1964)

A. Vincent: *Lives of Twelve Bad Women: illustrations and reviews of feminine turpitude set forth by impartial hands* (Boston, 1897). Includes Moll Cutpurse, Elizabeth Chudleigh etc.

(b) *Historical: particular periods, countries, regions.*

J.M. Bannerman: *Leading Ladies, Canada 1639–1967* (Dundas, 1967)

E.O. Blackburne: *Illustrious Irishwomen from the earliest ages to the present* (London, 1877)

H. Buckmaster: *Women who shaped history* (New York, 1966). 19th-century biographies.

M. Cole: *Women of Today* (London, 1938)

E. Coxhead: *Daughters of Erin* (London, 1965)

L. Crane: *Ms Africa: Profiles of modern African Women* (Philadelphia, 1973)

H.S. Drago: *Notorious Ladies of the Frontier* (New York, 1969)

M.G. Fawcett: *Some Eminent Women of Our Time* (London, 1889)

M.L. Fava: *Cincuenta mujeres de nuestro tiempo* (Barcelona, 1975)

G. Frink: *Great Jewish Women* (New York, 1978)

G.A. Gollock: *Daughters of Africa* (New York, 1932/R1969)

M.E. Gridley: *American Indian Women* (New York, 1974)

H.A. Guy: *Women in the Caribbean* (Port of Spain, 1966)

M.S. Hartman: *Victorian murderesses* (New York, 1977)

J.D. Henderson: *Ten notable women of Latin America* (Chicago, 1978)

C. Hernandez: *Mujeres celebres de Mexico* (San Antonio, 1919)

P. Hogrefe: *Women of Action in Tudor England: Nine biographical sketches* (Ames, 1977)

M. Hume: *Queens of Old Spain* (London, 1906)

M.Q. Innis (ed.): *The Clear Spirit: Twenty Canadian Women and their Times* (Toronto, 1966)

G.F. Jackson: *Black Women, Makers of History: a portrait* (Sacramento, 1975)

A. Kempe Welch: *Of Six Medieval Women* (London, 1913)

E. Longford: *Eminent Victorian Women* (London, 1981)

B. Pusat: *Heroines of Indonesian History* (Jakarta, 1974)

E. Richey: *Eminent Women of the West* (Berkeley, 1975)

M. Roberts: *Select female biography: comprising memoirs of eminent British ladies. By the author of 'The Wonders of the Vegetable Kingdom displayed'* (London, 1829)

A. Rodrigo: *Mujeres de España* (Barcelona, 1979)

L. Samuel: *Les françaises célèbres* (Paris, 1972)

T.P. Saxena: *Women in Indian history: a biographical dictionary* (New Delhi, 1979)

H.B. Stowe *et al*: *Our Famous Women* (Hartford, 1888)

A. Volonterio: *Profili di donne svizzere* (Lugano, 1946)

C.D. Votow: *Puerto Rican Women: some biographical profiles* (Washington, 1978)

P.B. Watson: *Some Women of France* (Freeport, N.Y., 1936)

(*c*) *Public life, politics, religion, the professions etc.*

H.F. Blunt: *The Great Magdalens* (Freeport, N.Y., 1928)

*Women in Public Office: a Biographical Directory and Statistical Handbook* (New York, 1976, 2/1978)

J. Cahappell: *Noble Workers* (London, 1910). 19th-century reformers.

G. Evans: *Women in Federal Politics: a bio-bibliography* (Ottawa, 1975)

M.L. Goldsmith: *Seven Women Against the World* (London, 1935). Revolutionaries.

F.C. Griffin: *Women as Revolutionary* (New York, 1973). Social reformers.

R.A. Liston: *Women who Ruled: Cleopatra to Elizabeth II* (New York, 1978)

M. Hasan: *Daughters of Islam: short biographical sketches of 82 famous Muslim Women* (Lahore, 1976)

B.J. Love: *Foremost Women in Communications: a biographical reference work* (New York, 1970)

G.H. Macurdy: *Hellenistic Queens* (Baltimore, 1932)

E. Stineman: *American political Women; contemporary and historical profiles* (Littleton, Col, 1980)

M. Stern: *We the Women: career firsts of 19th-century America* (New York, 1963)

*Women Saints of East and West – Hinduism, Buddhism, Christianity and Sufism* (London, 1955)

*World Who's Who of Women in Education* (Ely, 1975)

(*d*) *Cultural Life*

J.R. Brink (ed.): *Female Scholars: a tradition of learned women before 1800* (Montreal, 1980)

G. Claghorn: *Women Composers and Hymnists: a concise biographical dictionary* (Metuchen NJ, 1984)

A. Cohen: *International Encyclopedia of Women Composers* (New York, 1981)

C. Galerstein: *Women Writers of Spain: an annotated bio-bibliographical guide* (Westpoet, CT and London, 1986)

W. and C. Jerrold: *Five Queer Women* (Norwood, P.A., 1929/R1976). 17th/18th-century writers.

L. Mainiero: *American women writers: a critical reference guide from colonial times to the present*, 4 vols (New York, 1979)

P. Migel: *The Ballerinas: From the Court of Louis XIV to Pavlova* (London, 1972)

J.W. Le Page: *Women composers, conductors and musicians of the 20th century: selected biographies* 2 vols, (Metuchen, NJ, 1980, 1983)

O.S. Opfell: *The Lady Laureates: Women who have won the Nobel Prize* (Metuchen, 1978)

A.I. Prather-Moses: *The International Dictionary of Women Workers in the Decorative Arts, from the distant past to the early 20th century* (Metuchen, 1981)

K. Petersen and J.J. Wilson: *Women Artists: Recognition and Reappraisal from the early Middle Ages to the Twentieth Century* (New York, 1976)

S. Smith: *Women who make Movies* (New York, 1975)

S. Stern: *Women Composers: a Handbook* (Metuchen, 1978)

E. Tufts: *Our Hidden Heritage: five centuries of women artists* (New York and London, 1963)

J. Todd: *A Dictionary of British and American women writers 1660–1800* (Totowa, NJ 1985)

A. Wallace: *Before the Bluestockings* (London, 1929)

V. Watson-Jones: *Contemporary American Women Sculptors* (Phoenix, AZ 1986)

E.R. Wheeler: *Famous Bluestockings* (New York, 1910)

(*e*)  *Science and medicine*

L. Haber: *Women Pioneers of Science* (New York, 1980)

C. Hacker: *The Indomitable Lady Doctors* (Toronto, 1974)

C.L. Herzenberg: *Women Scientists from antiquity to the present: an international reference listing and biographical directory of some notable women scientists from ancient to modern times* (West Cornwall, CT 1986)

E.P. Lovejoy: *Women Doctors of the World* (New York, 1954)

H.J. Mozans: *Woman in Science* (New York, 1913)

M. Ogilvie: *Women in Science: antiquity through the nineteenth century: a biographical dictionary with annotated bibliography* (Cambridge, Mass 1986)

L.M. Osen: *Women in Mathematics* (Boston, 1974)

T. Perl: *Maths Equals: biographies of women mathematicians and related activities* (Menlo Park, Calif., 1978)

P.J. Siegel: *Women in the Scientific Search: an American Bio-bibliography 1724–1979* (Metuchen, NJ 1985)

E. Yost: *American Women of Science* (Philadelphia, 1955)

(*f*)  *Sport, physical exploits, military adventures etc.*

E. de Beaumont: *Women and Cruelty* (London, 1905). Duellists and soldiers.

J. Graham: *Women in Chess: players of the modern age* (Jefferson, NC, 1987)

F.G. Gribble: *Women in War* (New York, 1917)

W. Hargreaves: *Women at Arms*

P. Hollander: *100 Greatest Women in Sport* (New York, 1976)

H.H. Jacobs: *Famous American Women Athletes* (New York, 1964)

J. Laffin: *Women in Battle* (London and New York, 1967)

H. Lanwick: *Heroines of the Sky* (London, 1960)

R. Markel: *For the Record: Women in Sports* (New York, 1985)

E. Nickerson: *Golf; a Women's history* (Jefferson, NC, 1987)

# A Note on Presentation

ENTRIES. In order to cover women's activities in a wide sphere in a single volume, entries are concise. They begin with a resume of basic facts – name, dates, nationality and reason for inclusion, followed by a brief biography. Many entries are accompanied by a reference to a biography or autobiography, or very occasionally to an article or collective work. Where an older source is cited this is because it remains the best, or the only complete book on the subject.

DATES. In a tiny proportion of cases it has proved impossible to check dates of birth or death. This is usually represented by (?) but for some contemporary women who appear to wish such information to remain private, the date has been omitted.

TITLES. Entries appear under the most familiar name, even if it is a pseudonym or nickname, with cross references from other titles. Parentheses and brackets in name headings have specific meanings. Parentheses enclose some forenames: where names are not normally used; where a maiden name is often incorporated into the usual form of address; where a nickname or shortened version is preferred. Brackets enclose the alternative form of a name; pseudonyms; maiden name.

As a very general principle, we have tried to place each entry where the majority of users of the Dictionary will expect to find it. Common sense and established usage are important factors. Unless there are reasons that dictate otherwise, names incorporating prefixes in the Romance languages are alphabetized under the prefix when it includes the definite article: thus, for French names, those beginning 'L', 'La' and 'Le' are placed under L and 'Du' under D, but those beginning 'De' are placed under the following word (as are many beginning 'D', though here established usage demands that some be under D). The reader of the Dictionary who looks in the wrong place will be led to the right one by a cross-reference.

SUBJECT INDEXES. These indexes have been limited to a few general categories for ease of reference but women may be entered in two or three categories if a single description is inadequate.

# A

**Abakanowicz, Magdalena** (1930–). Polish weaver. Abakonowicz is a sculptor in weaving, creating powerful, emotional structures which relate both to the world we live in and to the shape, ùnreliability and tensions of the human body.

She was born in Falenty, Poland, and attended the School of Fine Arts in Sopot, 1949, before spending five years at the Warsaw Academy of Fine Arts. In 1956 she married Jan Kosmowski and began working as an artist, concentrating on fibre and weaving during the 1960s. Her earlier works filled rooms with hanging ropes, mazes and enveloping forms, but she later turned to soft sculptures of rounded broken forms, wrapped heads, and grouped figures, which appear silent and waiting. Her most remarkable series include *Heads* (1975), *Seated Figures* (1974–9) and *Catharsis* (1985). Her work has been seen by some critics as a cultural response to state oppression, but she herself insists more on the organic, physical quality of weaving, its relationship to the body, and its place in craft and social history. She insists on shaping the materials by hand, and also works in burlap, wood, clay and bronze.

Abakanowicz has taught at the State College of Arts, Poznán since 1965, becoming Professor in 1979. She has received many honours in Poland and abroad, including the Grand Prize of the World Crafts Council, New York, and an honorary doctorate of the Royal College of Art, London (both in 1974), and has had one-woman exhibitions in several countries. Her work hangs in major national galleries including the Museum of Modern Art, New York, and the Pompidou Centre, Paris.

**Abbott, Berenice** (1898–). American photographer. Born in Springfield, Ohio, at the age of 22 she left to study sculpture in New York, Berlin and Paris where she worked as assistant to the photographer Man Ray from 1923 to 1925. During her stay in Paris her subjects included Joyce, Gide, Cocteau and MARIE LAURENCIN. In 1929 she returned to the USA and began to photograph New York City, its architecture, its people and the disappearing life of the old townscape, which was scheduled for demolition; this resulted in the publication of *Changing New York* (1937). From 1934 to 1958 she taught in New York at the New School for Social Research. Her other great interest has been the use of photography in illustrating the laws of physics, and several of her books concentrate on this highly specialized technical concern.

H. O'Neal: *Berenice Abbott* (1982)

**Abbott, Edith** (1876–1957). American feminist, economist and social reformer. From Nebraska where she was born, and where she graduated in 1901, Edith Abbott moved to Chicago, and took her PhD in 1905 with a study of unskilled labour in the United States from 1850. The following year she gained a Carnegie Fellowship to study the position of women in industry at the London School of Economics where she met Charles Booth and Sydney and BEATRICE WEBB. Then, after teaching at Wellesley, she joined the new Chicago School of Civics and Philanthropy as assistant to her life-long friend, Sophonisba Breckinridge. She became involved in campaigning, as well as research: for the rights of children and of immigrants; for education; for women's suffrage, industrial protection and unionization. Her essays on women's employment and on the development of opportunities for middle-class compared to working-class women, were collected in *Women in Industry: A Study in American Economic History* (1910). After

1920 she was a leading activist for social reform. In 1927, with Breckinridge, she started the highly influential *Social Science Review*, which she continued to edit until 1953. Edith Abbott was Dean of the School of Social Studies Administration at Chicago until 1942.

**Abbott, Maude (Elizabeth Seymour)** (1869–1940). Canadian cardiologist and promoter of medical education for women in Canada. Maude Abbott failed to gain admission to the medical school of McGill University, Montreal, from which she had her first degree, and instead trained at Bishop's College. Her goal, eventually achieved, was to join the medical faculty at McGill.

After three years in Europe, in 1898 she was appointed Assistant Curator of the medical museum at McGill. Here she developed the *Osler Catalogue of the Circulatory System*. In 1900 she became Curator, and in 1907 organized and edited the *Bulletin of the International Association of Medical Museums*. In 1923 she took a two-year appointment as Visiting Professor of Pathology and Bacteriology at the Woman's Medical College of Pennsylvania, returning as a Lecturer in Pathology to McGill. Among other works is her *Atlas of Congenital Cardiac Disease*. She received both an honorary MD and LLD from McGill.

**Abdel Rahman, Aisha** (*c*1920–). [pseud.: Bint-al-Shah]. Egyptian academic and writer. She was born at Damietta, an old port at the mouth of the Nile, from which she took her pen-name Bint-al-Shah (Daughter of the Beach). Educated at Cairo University, where she became an Assistant Lecturer in 1939, she then acted as Inspector of the teaching of Arabic language and literature for the Ministry of Education from 1942. From 1950 to 1957 she taught at Ain Shans University, where she was Assistant Professor (1957–62) and since then she has been Professor of Arabic literature at the University College for Women. She is best known for her literary criticism which includes *New Values in Arabic Literature* (1961) and *Contemporary Arab Women Poets* (1963), and she has also written novels and short stories, and six books on famous

women of Islam. Fascinated by Mohammed, her research into the women who surrounded him resulted in *The Wives of the Prophet* (1959), *The Daughters of the Prophet* (1963) and *The Mother of the Prophet* (1966).

**Abiertas, Josepha** (1894–1929). Filippina lawyer and feminist. Born in Capiz, Josepha and her brother became orphans at a very early age. She went to school in Capiz after which she enrolled to study law in the Philippine Law School. The first woman to graduate from the Law School, she delivered a speech called 'The New Age for Women', and actively campaigned for the vote. Josepha devoted her life to the welfare of her people, campaigning for better conditions for poor farmers, until she died of tuberculosis in 1929. After her death a welfare home, the Josepha Abiertas House of Friendship, was named after her.

**Abzug, Bella (Savitzky)** (1920–). American lawyer and politician. Born in New York, she is the daughter of Russian-Jewish émigré parents. She was educated at public schools in the Bronx, then Hunter College, New York, where she took her BA in 1942. As a student she protested against Fascism, and in support of the Republicans during the Spanish Civil War. In 1944 she married the businessman Martin Abzug (with whom she has two daughters), and a year later took her LLB at Columbia. She was admitted to the New York Bar in 1947 and practised in New York from 1944 to 1970. During the 1950s she defended civil rights cases in the South and writers accused of un-American activities. In the 1960s she was active in the peace, anti-nuclear and women's movements; founder and National Legislative Director of Women Strike for Peace (1961–70); and founder and former Chairman of the National Women's Political Caucus.

In 1971 Bella Abzug won a seat in the House of Representatives, and for six years campaigned tirelessly for welfare rights, full employment, job-producing public works programmes, consumer and environmental protection, and aid to Israel. She was also co-author of the *Freedom of Information and Privacy Acts*. Her flamboyant style won her the name 'Bellicose Bella', and in 1977 a hurricane was named after her. In 1976 she left Congress to run against Daniel Patrick Moynihan for a Senate seat, and after losing by a narrow margin, campaigned in 1977 for Mayor of New York. She is a member of many committees and pressure groups, including NOW, the American Civil Liberties Union and the Americans for Democratic Action. She is a commentator and writer on politics and women's issues, as well as a columnist for *Ms Magazine* (1979–), and author of *Gender Gap: Bella Abzug's guide to Political Power for Women* (1984).

B. Abzug: *Bella: Ms Abzug goes to Washington* (1972)

**Acarie, Barbe (Jeanne Avrillot)** [Marie de l'Incarnation] (1566–1618). French Carmelite and mystic. The daughter of wealthy, bourgeois parents, Barbe was educated at the Convent of Longchamps, where she showed signs of exceptional piety. She married Peter Acarie, Vicomte du Villemare, in 1584 in obedience to her parents although she wanted to become a nun. Known as 'La Belle Acarie', Barbe was popular and respected both in Paris society and by the poor and sick for whom she cared. When her husband had his property confiscated and was exiled she dedicated herself to the education of their six children.

Barbe was greatly impressed by the work of TERESA OF AVILA and believed she had a vocation to introduce the reformed order of the Carmelites into France: this she succeeded in doing in 1603. She also assisted Madame de Sainte-Beuve in establishing the Ursulines. After the death of her husband in 1613 she was received into the Carmel at Amiens, taking the religious name of Marie de l'Incarnation. Later she was transferred to Pontoise and died there, having acquired a reputation for holiness. Marie de l'Incarnation was beatified in 1794.

Her influence on this period of French Catholicism was enormous because of her social position, her personality and spirituality and her connections with the elite of the French religious establishment.

L.C. Sheppard: *Barbe Acarie, Wife and Mystic* (1953)

**Achurch, Janet** (1864–1916). English actress. Janet came from a theatrical family (her grandparents ran the Royalty Theatre, Manchester) and made her debut in 1883 in a farce, *Betsy Baker*. At twenty-one she joined Frank Benson's touring company, playing mainly Shakespearean leads. She is now chiefly remembered for being the first English actress to perform Ibsen, playing Nora in *The Doll's House* in 1889, and in 1896 producing *Little Eyolf* with herself in the part of Rita, and MRS PATRICK CAMPBELL as the Ratwife.

With other crusading actresses such as Florence Farr and ELIZABETH ROBINS she broke away from commercial theatre, portraying women who went against the grain of fashionable expectations. She managed the Novelty Theatre from 1889, and Bernard Shaw (to whom she gave the French source of *Mrs Warren's Profession*) was so impressed by her Nora, that he saw it five times, and later wrote *Candida* for her. In the same year (1900) she played Lady Cecily Wayneflete in *Captain Brassbound's Conversion*. Shaw thought her a tragic actress of genius, and he described the quality separating her from other actresses of the day: 'a more utter recklessness, not only of fashion, but of beauty, could hardly be imagined: beauty to Miss Achurch is only one effect among others to be produced, not the condition of all effects.' Yet the actor Richard Mansfield said he could never play a romantic part opposite her because she was the sort of woman who peeled onions, sat on the floor and combed her fingers through her hair.

She was married young, not altogether happily, to Charles Charrington, an actor. In childbirth she was administered morphine, and her subsequent addiction aggravated an existing alcoholic problem, which led to her retirement in 1913.

**Acosta de Samper, Soledad** (1833–1903). Colombian writer. Daughter of Joaquin Acosta, Colombian Ambassador to the United States and then Foreign Minister, and the English Caroline Kemble, Soledad was educated in Halifax, Nova Scotia and in Paris. In 1855 she married the politician and writer José Maria Samper, and travelled with him to Europe and Peru between 1858 and 1863, becoming known as a translator of French and English works (by Dumas and SAND) for his liberal newspaper *El Neo-Granadino*. She also sent home reports of European life and fashions for Bogotá papers. Within a Catholic framework, Soledad had pronounced feminist views, as shown in *La mujer en la sociedad moderna*, which advocates education, careers and freedom from the obligation to marry, and in the periodical *La mujer*, which she founded and edited from 1878 to 1881, the first of the four feminist journals she was to be associated with. While caring for their four daughters, she also wrote historical novels, heavily moralizing in tone, and then, in the 1880s, concentrated on biographies and history. After her husband died in 1888 she represented Colombia at the Quattrocentenary Congress of Americanists in Spain, was elected to several European and Latin American academies, and was a founding member of the Colombian Academy of History.

**Acton, Elizabeth** (1799–1859). English cookery writer. Born near Hastings, she was the daughter of a brewer. After an inconclusive engagement to a French officer, she began writing poetry, some of which was published during the 1820s and 1830s. She lived in Tonbridge, where she kept house for her mother. In 1845 Longman's published her *Modern Cookery* which became an instant classic, going through five editions in two years, much plagiarized in standard Victorian cookery books and continuing in print until 1914. She published her last book, *The English Bread Book*, in 1857.

**Adams** [née Smith], **Abigail** (1744–1818). American political figure and letter writer. Born in Weymouth, Massachusetts, Abigail was one of three daughters of a Congregational minister William Smith and his wife Elizabeth, a member of the influential Quincy family. A delicate child, she was educated largely by her grandmother at Mount Wollaston. In October 1764 she married John Adams, who sprang to the forefront of nationalist politics with his opposition to the Stamp Act the following year. They had five children and while John spent long periods in Philadelphia and then in Europe during the Revolution, Abigail ran the farm and brought up the family, describing their experience of siege, epidemic and daily life in vivid letters. An independent character, she supported the education of women and upheld the rights of wives in marriage.

After the Treaty of Paris in 1783 which ended the War of Independence, she joined her husband in Paris for eight months, and then in England where he was the American representative. Her letters from Europe are full of caustic comments on characters she encountered. After their return to the USA they shared many of the official duties after John was elected Vice-President in 1787 and then President in 1797. She was the First Lady in the White House after its completion in 1800, although the following year Adam was defeated and they retired to the family home at Quincy. A vehement Federalist, she was reputed to exercise considerable political influence over her husband, and over her son, John Quincy, who became a senator in 1803, and was eventually made President in 1824, six years after her death. The final years of her life were spent running the farm and acting as an informal political consultant. Her famous letters continued until her death from typhoid at the age of 74. Many were collected by her grandson Charles, and published in two volumes, *Letters of Mrs Adams* and *Familiar Letters of John Adams and his Wife during the Revolution*.

P. Levin: *Abigail Adams* (1987)

**Adamson** [née Gessner], **Joy** (1910–80). Austrian conservationist and writer. Born into a wealthy family in Troppau [now Opava], Silesia, and brought up in Vienna, she studied the piano. Unable to make a career as a concert pianist, she turned to crafts such as dressmaking, bookbinding and drawing; she was also interested in archaeology. She eventually decided to study medicine, but did not sit her examination to qualify for university entrance and in 1935 married Victor von Klarwill. In 1937 she met Peter Bally, a botanist, while travelling to Kenya. After her husband joined her there, they were divorced and she subsequently married Bally in 1938. She accompanied him on his field trips and painted over 700 studies of flowers, trees and shrubs. Their marriage also ended in divorce and she then married George Adamson, the British game warden in the North Frontier District.

Joy began painting illustrations of animals and people as well as plants, and was commissioned by the colonial government of Kenya to paint portraits of members of 22 tribes whose culture was vanishing. Her 600 paintings now belong to the National Museum of Kenya. In 1956 she began her association with Elsa, a tame lion-cub whom she was determined to teach to return to the wild. Her book on the experiment, *Born Free* (1960), was a worldwide success; it was followed by *Living Free* (1961) and *Forever Free* (1962). In 1964 she also retrained Pippa, a cheetah described in *The Spotted Sphinx* (1969), and worked with other animals. From the 1960s she was a leading conservationist, beginning with her launching of the World Wildlife Fund in the USA in 1962. In 1980 she was found dead in northern Kenya, supposedly mauled by a lion, but later a man was charged with her murder.

J. Adamson: *Autobiography* (1978)

**Adcock, Fleur** (1934–). New Zealand poet. Born in Papakura, Fleur Adcock grew up in New Zealand but spent the war years at various schools in England. On her return she went to Wellington Girls' College and graduated with a First Class degree in classics from the University of Wellington in 1955. She then worked as a lecturer and librarian at the University of Otago, Dunedin, from 1958–61, moving to the Alexander Turnbull Library in Wellington in 1962. In 1963 she went to London and worked as a librarian and then as head of the research department of the Foreign and Commonwealth Office until 1979. She has been married twice, and has two sons.

Although she had written poetry since her childhood her first collection, *The Eye of the Hurricane*, was not published until 1964. This was followed by *Tigers* (1967), *High Tide in the Garden* (1971), *The Scenic Route* (1974) and *The Inner Harbour* (1979). In 1982 she edited *The Oxford Book of Contemporary New Zealand Verse* and in 1983 her own *Selected Poems* appeared, as well as her verse translations of medieval Latin poems, *The Virgin and the Nightingale*. Much of her elegant, evocative poetry is concerned with the power of place, but her recent work has focused increasingly upon the lives of women.

**Addams, Jane** (1860–1935). American settlement founder and social reformer. She was born in Cedarville, Illinois, and brought up by her widowed father, a banker, state senator, abolitionist and friend of Abraham Lincoln. She was educated at Rockford Female Seminary until 1877, and after her father's death in 1881 she attended the Women's Medical College, Philadelphia, but withdrew due to severe spinal illness which reached a crisis in 1882. In 1883, while touring Europe with her stepmother, she described her reactions to urban poverty and on returning to the USA was baptized into the Presbyterian church, for which she undertook charity work. Unhappy and frustrated she paid a second visit to Europe in 1887. She then decided to found a settlement, taking Toynbee Hall, London, as an example, and in 1889 with Ellen Starr she bought Hull House in Chicago's immigrant 19th ward. Her aim to create a human community to offer protection against the anonymous city gradually changed into more active policies to overcome class barriers and campaign for social justice and equal rights. Hull House was instantly successful and by 1893 was running 40 local clubs, including a nursery, a dispensary, and a boarding house. The helpers included women like FLORENCE KELLEY, Grace Abbott, and ALICE HAMILTON.

In 1895 the *Hull House Maps and Papers* were published (a detailed study of local conditions), and the settlement exerted an influence both locally and nationally on protective legislation, union recognition, and treatment of juvenile crime in cities. During this period she wrote *Democracy and Social Ethics* (1902) and *The Spirit of Youth and the City Streets* (1909). In 1909 Addams became first woman President of the National Conference of Charities and Corrections, in 1911 first head of the National Federation of Settlements, and in 1912 she campaigned in support of Roosevelt. At the same time she was active in the suffrage movement, being Vice-President of the National American Women Suffrage Alliance (1911–14), and in the peace movement. During World War I she aroused hostility by speaking against American involvement. In 1915 she was Chairman of the Women's Peace Party and President of the first Women's Peace Congress at The Hague, and in 1919 presided over the second Women's Peace Congress in

Zurich, and raised funds for war victims. In 1920 she became a founder member of the American Civil Liberties Union. She continued to campaign on behalf of negroes, immigrants and disadvantaged groups and, although in the 1920s called 'the most dangerous woman in America today' by the Daughters of the American Revolution, she gradually won acclaim, sharing the Nobel Peace Prize in 1931.

J. Addams: *Twenty Years at Hull House* (1910)
M.J. Deegan: *Jane Addams and the Men of the Chicago School* (1986)

**Adelaide** (931–99). Italian queen and empress. The daughter of Rudolf II of Burgundy, after her father's death she was betrothed to Lothair, the son of her stepfather, Hugh of Arles, King of Italy. Three years after their marriage in 947 Lothair died and in the ensuing turmoil over the Italian succession in 951 Adelaide was imprisoned at Garda, then rescued by and married to Otto I of Germany. In 962 she was crowned Empress with him in Rome, and after his death in 973 her power was maintained. She remained influential for 20 years during the reigns of her son Otto II and grandson Otto III, sharing and eventually competing for power with her daughter-in-law Theophano until the latter's death in 991. She also helped her nephew Randolph III pacify the nobles during the rebellion of 999, just before her death. Towards the end of her life she turned from politics to devote herself to the monastery she had founded at Selz in Alsace. Her influence on monastic development, especially in supporting the spread of the Cluniac rite, was considerable. After her death the abbey became a place of pilgrimage and she was canonized in 1097.

M. Hopkirk: *Queen Adelaide* (1946)

**Adivar, Halide (Edib)** (1883–1964). Turkish nationalist. She was born in Istanbul into a traditional family. In 1901, after graduating from the American College for Girls at Üsküdar (Scutari), the first Muslim Turkish graduate, she worked in lycées as an inspector and teacher, and married the scholar Salih Zeki Bey. Involved in the formative years of the nationalist struggle, she wrote for the liberal paper *Tanine*. Her articles on women's emancipation, especially those advocating education, were met with bitter opposition by the

Conservatives so that when the Unionists were overthrown in 1909 Halide had to flee for her life. In 1910 she divorced her husband. At this stage she also began to write novels and autobiographies. She returned to Turkey and began a busy career lecturing and campaigning for the education of women. In 1912 she was the only woman to be elected to the Ojak, the Turkish nationalist club, with country wide organizations. In the same year she won fame with *Handan*, the love story of a young woman dominated by a socialist intellectual, and *Yeni Turan* which proclaimed her nationalist feelings. In 1918 she was elected to the Ojak council. During World War I she worked in Syria and Lebanon. She married a fellow activist Dr Adnan Adivar in 1917. She was one of the principal writers and translators attached to Mustapha Kemal Pasha's nationalist forces, first as a non-combative private and then as a corporal. After the war of independence the Adivars broke with Atatürk, retired from public life, and Halide dedicated herself to writing. Her *Memoirs* of her early life were published in 1926. They lived in England and France and did not return to Turkey until after Atatürk's death in 1938. Then Halide became Professor of English at the University of Istanbul and was a member of the Grand National Assembly from 1950 to 1954.

H. Adivar: *Memoirs* (1926)

**Aelgifu** (*c*1010–40). Saxon noblewoman, Regent of Norway. The daughter of a Northamptonshire nobleman, she became the mistress of Cnut of Denmark when he was raiding England as a young man, and remained his closest companion until his death, despite his formal marriage to Emma, Ethelred's sister. The eldest of their two sons, Sweyn, was made King of Norway, and Cnut appointed Aelgifu Regent. Her rule there was extremely harsh, and her reputation for tyrannical cruelty was unparalleled, eventually provoking an uprising which removed her from power in 1035.

When Cnut died she returned to England, and persuaded the nobles to recognize her other son Harold 'Harefoot' as King in 1037 but no records of her from then on have been found.

**Aethelflaed** [Lady of the Mercians] (*d* 918). Saxon queen. The daughter of King Alfred, she married a nobleman, Ethelred, ruler of West Mercia, and governed jointly with him until his death in 911, being effective ruler some years before this. She then continued to rule in her own name as Lady of the Mercians, protecting the interests of her kin. A shrewd commander, her deployment of the local armies helped her brother Edward, King of Wessex, to dominate the Viking forces in eastern England. She fortified strategic camps, repairing the walls of Chester and developing fortresses such as Warwick and Stafford which also became important centres of trade. Even more unusually she created around her a remarkable military household which she totally dominated. In 917 she and Edward began a major attack on the Danes and she led her army to the conquest of Derby and Leicester. Dorothy Stenton suggests that at the time of Aethelflaed's death, in Tamworth, she was planning campaigns further north and had already won the allegiance of York. She had also won authority over parts of Wales, and Northumbria. In 619 Edward took over her kingdom. An outstanding figure, her reputation endured until the Renaissance. Thomas Heywood included her as one of his English 'viragos' in his *Nine Books of various History concerning Women* (1624) and John Evelyn thought her worthy of commemoration when listing candidates for medals in 1697.

F.T. Wainwright: 'Aethelflaed, Lady of the Mercians', *The Anglo-Saxons*, ed. P. Clemoes (1959)

**Agassiz, Elizabeth (Cabot) Cary** (1822–1907). American scientist, and first President of Radcliffe College. Born in Boston, Massachusetts, the second of seven children of a cultured family, Elizabeth married the Swiss naturalist Jean Louis Agassiz in 1850. He was widowed, and she helped bring up three step-children and later grandchildren. Although not trained as a naturalist, she shared her husband's work, and they established a seaside laboratory on Sullivan Island. She published *Actaea: a First Lesson in Natural History* (1859), and *Seaside Studies in Natural History* (1866), two popular manuals. In 1856 she opened a select school for girls in Cambridge,

Massachusetts, and ran it for eight years.

In 1865 Elizabeth went with Louis to Brazil via Cape Horn, taking notes and careful records and learning Portuguese on the way (*A Journey in Brazil* (1867)). Later she went on two voyages on *The Hassler* and wrote articles on its deep-sea dredging. She helped develop the Natural History Museum at Cambridge and the Natural History School on Penikese Island. After the death of her husband in 1873, she wrote *Louis Agassiz, his Life and Correspondence* (1885).

In 1879, at a 'meeting about Harvard education for women' (her diary), she effectively founded the institution which was to become Radcliffe College. She was against co-education but believed that women should have the same educational opportunities as men, and with Arthur Gilman, Secretary of the group, worked hard to achieve this. She travelled to Oxford and Cambridge to gain ideas. From the College's independence in 1893 to her retirement in 1903 she was President, and during that time a scholarship and a student hall were endowed in her honour.

L.A. Paton: *Elizabeth Cary Agassiz: a Biography* (1919, reissued 1974)

**Agnesi, Maria (Gaetana)** (1718–99). Italian mathematician. Born in Milan to a wealthy and literate family, Maria was the eldest of 21 children. She was recognized as a child prodigy, speaking French by the age of five and Latin, Greek, Hebrew and modern languages by nine, at which time she delivered an hour-long *oratio* in Latin before a learned assembly on the right of women to study. As a teenager she tutored her younger brothers, acted as hostess at her father's gatherings of intellectuals, and studied mathematics. In character she was retiring and would have liked to enter a convent; instead she ran the household and studied at home.

In 1738 she published *Propositiones philosophicae*, essays and discussions on science and philosophy. By the age of 20 she had begun her major work, *Istituzioni analitiche*, one volume on algebra and geometry, the other on differential and integral calculus. This occupied her for ten years. Her scholarship and linguistic ability enabled her to bring together the work of authors writing in various languages, as well as formulating new mathematical methods. Although she is known particularly for her discussion of the *versiera*, a versed sine curve, this was in fact a minor component.

L'Académie Française admired her but did not admit her; the Bologna Academy of Sciences did, however, elect her, and she received other honours. Pope Benedict XIV recognized her and had her appointed Professor of Mathematics at the University of Bologna, but it is doubtful whether she took up the post.

After her father's death she converted her house to a small hospital, and spent the rest of her life serving the sick and poor. In 1771 the Pio Istituto Trivulzio was opened for the ill and infirm and the Archbishop asked Maria to take charge of it, which she did until her death at 81. It is ironic that owing to an early mistranslation of the term *versiera* as 'wife of the devil' instead of 'curve', Maria Agnesi was known in English for many years as the 'witch of Agnesi'.

**Agnes of Courtenay** (*c*1136–*c*1186). Crusader aristocrat. The daughter of Jocelyn II of Edessa, she first married a Crusader knight and after being widowed in 1149 moved to Jerusalem where she met Amalric, youngest son of Fulk and MÉLISANDE. They married in 1157 but the marriage was annulled on grounds of consanguinity, on the nobles' insistence, when Amalric became King in 1163. Agnes remarried twice, to Hugh of Ramleh who died in 1169 and Reynald of Sidon. After her husband's death she gradually regained influence since her son Baldwin was the only male heir, arranging marriages for her daughter and stepdaughters, raising great support among nobility and church leaders, securing appointments to key positions, and virtually ruling the country from 1180 to 1184. Finally, as her son became increasingly ill with leprosy she encouraged the coronation of her grandson by her daughter Sibylla, as Baldwin V. Her remarkable influence ceased with her son's death in 1185. Although criticized at the time as ruthless and mercenary, her policies had a decisive effect on the continuity of the Crusader kingdom.

B. Hamilton: 'Queens of Jerusalem', *Medieval Women* (1978)

**Agnes of Poitou** (1024–77). Holy Roman Empress. Descended from the royal houses of Burgundy and Italy, the daughter of William V of Aquitaine and Poitou, she became the second wife of the German king Henry III in 1043. They were crowned Holy Roman Emperor and Empress by Clement II in 1046. She bore a son in 1050, the future Henry IV, and then another son and three daughters. After her husband's death in 1056 Agnes acted as Regent for her son. She was not an experienced politician and was influenced by the nobility to part with the duchies of Bavaria and Carinthia, and entered into unwise alliances against the dominant reforming party in the Papacy. By 1062 discontent led to an uprising in which Anno, Archbishop of Cologne, took over the regency. Agnes retired to a convent where she remained until her death.

**Agnodice** (4th century BC). Greek; early woman gynaecologist. Dressed in men's clothing, she attended the medical classes of the famous doctor Herophilos and practised gynaecology disguised as a man. Other doctors, jealous of her fame, accused her of corrupting women. In court she was forced to reveal her sex in order to save her life. Then new charges were brought against her, of practising a profession restricted by law to men alone. Eventually she was acquitted by the Athenian court.

**Agrippina I** (14BC–33AD). Roman aristocrat. Agrippina was the daughter of Marcus Agrippa and Julia, and granddaughter of Augustus. She married Germanicus, the adopted son of Tiberius, with whom she had nine children and whom she accompanied to the Rhine (14–16AD) and the Eastern Empire (18–19AD). On his death in 19AD she proclaimed Tiberius responsible, and became the centre of an opposition group. Lacking in political talent and openly rebellious and arrogant, she relied on the popularity of her lineage but her ambitions to have her sons proposed as heirs to the Empire were countered by Sejanus, Tiberius' adviser. In 29AD she was arrested and banished to Pandateria, where she died of starvation.

H. Fasti: *Agrippa's Daughter* (1979)

**Agrippina II** (15–59AD). Roman empress. Eldest daughter of AGRIPPINA I and Germanicus, she was familiar from childhood with aristocratic intrigue and ambition, and made more ruthless by her mother's experience. In 28AD she married her cousin, Domitius Ahenobarbus; their son Nero was born in 37AD. Her brother, Caligula, was then on the throne, and after Domitius died, he accused her of adultery and treason, confiscated her estate and banished her. On the accession of Claudius she was reinstated, and married the wealthy Crispus Passienus. The subject of plots by VALERIA MESSALINA, she gradually acquired influence over Claudius, whom she married in 49AD. She then organized the succession for her son, relentlessly destroying rivals, and is believed eventually to have murdered Claudius himself with poisoned mushrooms (54AD). In the first years of Nero's rule her power increased, but she eventually lost support, and after fruitless intrigues was murdered at Baiae at Nero's command in 59AD.

E. Hamilton (ed.): *Memoirs of Agrippina* (1804)

**Aguilar, Grace** (1816–47). English author. She was born of Spanish-Jewish parents in Hackney, London, and educated at home. Her family moved to Devon in 1828. Always a semi-invalid, she began writing in childhood, her first poems being collected in *Magic Wreath* (1835). After her father's death she wrote for a profession, publishing her controversial attack on the formality of contemporary religion, *The Spirit of Judaism*, in 1842, followed by a more popular work, *The Jewish Faith* (1845), and a series of essays, *Women of Israel*. Her lasting popularity, however, came from her sentimental domestic novels which were mostly edited and published posthumously by her mother. Aguilar died, exhausted by work, at the age of 31, while visiting her brother in Frankfurt. Her novels include *A Mother's Recompense* (1850) and *Woman's Friendship* (1851). Her work was significant for its education of the general public about her faith, and for its concern for the position of women within Judaism.

**Agustini, Delmira** (1890–1914). Uruguayan poet. Born in Montevideo into a scholarly family, she had an unhappy childhood and then a tragic marriage. She published two collections of poetry which brought her fame throughout the Spanish-speaking world, *El libro blanco* (1907) and *Cantos de mañana* (1910), which were combined with some new work in *Los Calizes vacíos* (1913). In 1914 her husband, from whom she had separated, killed her and committed suicide.

Her poetry is remarkable for the period in its frank evocation of intense sexual relationships, with a brooding connection between the themes of love and death. Her great sensitivity and distress are revealed in her letters *Correspondencia íntima*, published posthumously in 1969.

**Ahern** [Wallace], **Lizzie** [Elizabeth] (1877–1969). Australian socialist. The daughter of an Irish gold-miner and radical, she was born at Ballaret, Victoria, left school at 14 and worked as a pupil-teacher and then as a cook in Melbourne, but her political commitment lost her her job. In 1905 she joined the Social Questions Committee which became the Victorian Socialist Party. One of the most eloquent orators in Australian politics, she moved huge crowds and became a prominent member of the Free Speech Campaign in Prahra, Melbourne. She was imprisoned in 1906 for defending the right to speak in public places. A dedicated feminist, she also helped to found the Domestic Workers' Union. In 1905 she married a fellow radical, Arthur Wallace, and in 1909 founded the Women's Socialist League. They then moved to Adelaide but in May 1916 returned to Melbourne and led the anti-conscription campaign during World War I, although Lizzie's own son enlisted and died of illness caught as a soldier. Wallace became an MP in 1919, and in later life Lizzie continued to work for the Australian Labour party and became a Justice of the Peace and Children's Court Magistrate. She remained interested in politics to the end of her life.

**Ahrweiler,    Hélène**    (1916–).    French academic. She was born in Athens, where she studied and taught middle-eastern and medieval history and archaeology before moving to France in 1950. She became an established Byzantine expert, specializing in social history, and in 1967 became the first woman head of the department of history at the Sorbonne. Three years later she became a Vice-President and was involved in splitting the Sorbonne into the two schools of humanities and social sciences. In 1976 she was elected President of the Sorbonne, the first woman in such a position in its 700-years history. She held the post until her retirement in 1981. She became Chancellor of the Universities of Paris in 1982 and has been Vice President of the Council of National Education since 1983. She also works with UNESCO and is on many official bodies, including the board of the Pompidou Centre.

**Aidoo, (Christina) Ama Ata** (1942–). Ghanaian writer. Born in the centre of Ghana, at Abeadzi Kyiakor, near Dominase, Christina attended Wesley Girls School, Cape Coast. She graduated from the University of Ghana at Legon in 1964, and became a research fellow there, at the Institute of African Studies. She went to Stanford, California to study creative writing, and began to write short stories which were published in leading magazines such as the Nigerian *Black Orpheus* and Ghanaian *Okyeame*. She has also written poetry and plays, among them *Dilemma of a Ghost*, first performed at the University of Ghana (1964), and *Anowa* (1970). In 1970 she also published a collection of short stories, *No Sweetness Here*, but since the 1960s she has written little, with the exception of her fine novel about the cultural shock when an African woman visits Germany, *Our Sister Killjoy: Reflections from a Black-eyed Squint* (1977). She sees her role as revolutionary, fighting for women's rights and self-expression: 'Clarity therefore becomes the only reliable companion and weapon for a fighting woman. For with such company, and thus armed, she can weather sexist disillusion and betrayal and thus move on.'

From 1970 Ama Ata Aidoo has been based as a lecturer in English at the University of Cape Coast. She has taught and lectured in East and West Africa, and in Europe and the United States, and is considered to be the finest living African woman author. In 1982 she was appointed Secretary for Education in Ghana.

**Aimée, Anouk** [pseud. of Françoise Sorya (Dreyfus)] (1932–). French film actress. The daughter of actors, she was born in Paris and

studied dance and drama at the Marseilles Opéra. She was classically 'discovered' walking with her mother along the rue du Colisée by Henri Calef, who cast the 14-year-old girl in his film *La maison sous la mer* (1947). Marcel Carné next directed her in *La fleur de l'âge* with ARLETTY, which was never completed, but he then wrote *Les amants de Vérone/The Lovers of Verona* (1949) as a vehicle for her. This drew her to the attention of Rank, who were seeking a French girl to play opposite Trevor Howard in *The Golden Salamander* (1950). For the next decade she remained in Europe, working with various New Wave directors, such as Philippe de Broca, Jacques Demy (*Lola*, 1960) and Federico Fellini (*La dolce vita*, 1960; *Otto e mezzo/8½*, 1963). Her most resounding success was in Claude Lelouch's *Un homme et une femme/A Man and a Woman* (1966). She has been married four times and did not act at all during her last marriage, to actor Albert Finney (1970–75). Since then she has appeared in films such as Lelouch's *Si c'était à refaire* (1976), *Mon premier amour* (1978), *Vive la vie* (1984) and *A Man and a Woman: Twenty Years Later* (1986).

**Ainianos, Aganice** (1838–92). Greek poet. Born in Athens, she grew up in an intellectual family environment steeped in liberal political ideals. She studied Classics, French and painting. After being involved in a democratic uprising of the people of mainland Greece against the tyranny of King Otto, Aganice fled into the countryside and lived for some years in hiding. She came to understand the country people and their struggle to survive. Her experience provided the context of her many poems about nature and beauty and especially about women at work, in poverty and misery and struggling for their daily bread. Her style, free of the pseudo-romanticism of her age, reveals a sense of realism and a remarkable awareness of social and national problems. She wrote in the Greek vernacular, contrary to the current tendency of writers to use the archaizing, 'pure' Greek (*katharevousa*). For these reasons she was despised by her fellow writers and dared not publish any of her work. It was only after her death that her talent became widely known and appreciated.

**'Ā'ishah Bint Abī Bakr** (613–78). Arabian Muslim leader. She was born in Mecca. Her father supported Mohammed and she became the Prophet's child bride after the battle of Bakr in 624. She was always his favourite and he defended her in palace disputes. He died when she was 18 and she was forbidden, as the Prophet's widow, to remarry. She emerged as a powerful force in the political turmoil that followed the death of Mohammed, who had left no male heir. She maintained her position of power through tremendous courage, intelligence and learning, and became an authority on Muslim tradition. She was very important for her active role in the civil war, but was defeated and captured in a battle near Basra in 656, called the 'Battle of the Camel', and only released on promising to abandon political life. Her religious teachings contributed to the emergence of the Sunni Muslims. 'Ā'ishah died at the age of 65 and she is an established name in the tradition of Islam.

**Akerman, Chantal (Anne)** (1950–). Belgian film maker who works with female technicians. She studied film in Paris and Brussels and made her first feature film in New York (*Hotel Monterey*, 1972). She now divides her time between Europe and America. First influenced by Godard and Snow, she soon became recognized as one of the most innovatory young film makers. Although her formal and thematic concerns are unique, she has increased her budgets and audiences without compromising. *Les rendezvous d'Anna* (1979) won Best Director awards at the Paris and Chicago Film Festivals (1980) and she is currently preparing a commercial film based on Isaac Bashevis Singer's *The Estate and the Manor*.

The intimacy conveyed by her films results from looking at things in a new way, without deception, through static space (long shots, often held after the character has left the frame), face-on angling and careful soundtrack. These weaken narrative and heighten the sense of process, rhythm and flow, and of the extraordinary in the mundane. *Jeanne Dielman, 23 quai du Commerce, 1080 Bruxelles* (1975), often described as the film crucial to a 'feminine aesthetic' in cinema, features three days in the life of a Belgian widow, fixed in the 'commerce' of being housewife, mother and afternoon prostitute to make ends meet. The murder which ends the film is registered on the same level as the detailed routine of housework. Crucial to her films is Akerman's relation to her mother (*News from Home*, 1976), and her treatment of female sexuality (*Je, tu, il, elle*, 1974). Her recent films include *Toute une nuit* (1982) and *Man with a Suitcase* (1984).

**Akhmadulina, Bella Akhatovna** (1937–). Russian poet. Born in Moscow of mixed Tartar-Italian descent, she graduated from the Gorky Literary Institute. In 1958 she married Yevtushenko, her second husband was the short story writer Nagibin and her third was Boris Messerer. Her first poems, published in the late 1950s, established her characteristic style, combining a lyrical, emotional tone with highly individual treatment of city life and imagery, using traditional Russian forms.

**Akhmatova, Anna** (1889–1967). Russian poet. She was born near Odessa, spent her childhood in Tsarskoe Selo, and studied in Kiev before moving to St Petersburg [now Leningrad]. She began publishing poetry in 1907 and with Gumilov, whom she married in 1910, launched the Acmeist movement which reaffirmed Russian traditions in reaction to contemporary Symbolism. The style is represented in her early collections *Evening* (1912), *Beads* (1914), and *The White Flock* (1917), concise, direct quatrains, with vivid evocation of settings and emotions. The marriage ended in 1918. Gumilov was shot for counter-revolutionary activity in 1921, and after the publication of *Anno Domini* in 1922 Akhmatova herself was forced into silence by official disapproval. She began publishing again in 1940, and continued writing when she was evacuated from Leningrad to Tashkent (1941–4) but in 1946 she was finally expelled from the Union of Soviet Writers. Although she was reinstated after Stalin's death, her tragic Christian tone did not achieve new popularity. Her great works, *Poem without a Hero* and *Requiem* (for the victims of Stalinism), were published abroad. She visited Italy in 1964 and received an honorary degree from Oxford University in

1965. In recent years she has been acclaimed as Russia's greatest woman poet.

A. Haight: *Anna Akhmatova: a Poetic Pilgrimage* (1976)

**Alakija, Aduke** (1921–). Nigerian lawyer. After her initial schooling in Lagos she went to the UK and finished her secondary education. She started studying medicine at Glasgow University, but decided to change to social science at the London School of Economics. She then went to Cambridge, where she formed the West African Students' Union. After working as a Welfare Officer in Nigeria, she returned to England to study law to become better equipped to fight for the rights of women and children. She was called to the Bar in 1953. A member of the Nigerian delegation to the United Nations (1961–5), and a trustee of the Federal Nigeria Society for the Blind and of the International Women's Society, she is also Adviser to the International Academy of Trial Lawyers, the first black African woman Director of Mobil Oil, and President of the International Federation of Women Lawyers (FIDA). In 1964 Columbia University conferred on her an honorary LLD.

**Alboni, Marietta** (1823–94). Italian contralto. A pupil of Rossini (one of the few he was prepared to teach), she made her debut in Pacini's *Saffo* (Bologna, 1842), making her first appearance at La Scala, Milan, in Rossini's *Le siège de Corinthe* the same year. One of the greatest exponents of classical Italian *bel canto*, she toured extensively in Eastern Europe, Germany and Italy, going to London for the performance of Rossini's *Semiramide* (as Arsace) that initiated the Royal Italian Opera's first season at Covent Garden. Her success was such that she not only rivalled JENNY LIND in popularity but her salary was voluntarily raised from £500 to £2000 for the season. In 1852 she made a highly successful tour of the USA, though her greatest triumphs were in Paris (where she made her debut, as Arsace, in 1847) and London. She sang at the premières of Gordigiani's *Consuelo* (Prague, 1846) and Auber's *La corbeille d' oranges*, as Zerlina (Paris, 1851), but she is mainly remembered for the flawless virtuosity she brought to Rossini and Donizetti roles. She and ADELINA

PATTI sang one of the duets from Rossini's *Stabat mater* at the composer's funeral (1868).

A. Pougin: *Marietta Alboni* (1912)

**Alcott, Louisa May** (1832–88). American novelist. Born in Germantown, Philadelphia, Louisa was the eldest of four daughters of the philosopher Bronson Alcott and was chiefly educated by her father although her other teachers included Thoreau, Emerson and Theodore Parker. After the failure of her father's school in Boston, and of the vegetarian community 'Fruitlands' in 1843, the family lived in great poverty, and she contributed to their income by sewing, schoolteaching, and domestic service. She also wrote for publication from the age of 16, producing magazine stories, especially revenge and romance thrillers. Her first book *Flower Fables* appeared in 1855.

In 1862 Louisa worked as an army nurse at the Union Hospital in Georgetown, Washington, DC, and *Hospital Sketches* (1863) based on her letters home brought her a national reputation. Her next novel, *Moods* (1865), was a passionate tale of doomed love, but after her trip to Europe in 1866 a publisher suggested she write about more familiar material, and *Little Women* appeared in 1868. It was an enormous success and she became sole earner for the family, working incessantly to produce a prodigious number of novels, stories, articles and poems (over 300 items). Her diary reveals the pressure of this output and the loss of her mother and sister in 1871. A vehement supporter of black rights and women's suffrage, she worked spasmodically at a feminist novel, *Success*, which appeared eventually as the quasi-autobiographical *Work: a Story of Experience* in 1873. Her own success relied on more domestic novels such as *Little Men* (1871) and her last work *Jo's Boys* (1886), although she took a break from what she described as 'moral pap for the young' with *A Modern Mephistopheles* (1877). She died in Boston, on the day of her father's funeral.

M. Saxton: *Louisa May: a Modern Biography of Alcott* (1977)

**Aleramo, Sibilla** [pseud.: Rina Pierangeli Faccio] (1876–1960). Italian writer and feminist. Born in Piedmont, she spent her childhood in Milan and married in 1892. While recovering from a breakdown in 1897 she read Darwin and Spencer, and was prompted to write on local social conditions. She rapidly established a national reputation and in 1899 edited briefly the new magazine *L'Italia femminile* ('Female Italy').

In 1902 she left her husband and son and began an independent literary life in Rome. Her most famous work, the semi-autobiographical *Una donna* ('A woman'), caused a sensation on publication in 1906. As Rina Faccio she was a political and social journalist and wrote literary criticism (especially on Ibsen, D'Annunzio, and GEORGE SAND). As Sibilla Aleramo she wrote novels including *Il passaggio* (1913), *Amo dunque sono* (1927), and *Il frustino* (1932). Her four volumes of poetry include *Momenti lirichi* (1920), *Si alla terra* (1935), *Il mondo e adolescente* (1949) and *Luci della mia sera* (1969). She was also an active social reformer and established teaching and medical centres around Rome. Although she was a member of the Fascist Artists and Writers Union for a brief period in the 1930s, she joined the Communist Party in 1946. In 1945 she published an account of the war years, *Dal mio diario* (1940–44). She remained an active and influential writer until her death.

**Alexander, Cecil Frances** (1818–95). British hymn writer. The daughter of a major in the Royal Marines, Cecil Frances Humphreys began writing poetry at the age of nine. As young women she and her friend Lady Harriet Howard were strongly influenced by the high-church Oxford Movement and wrote a series of much-admired tracts, Harriet providing prose and Cecil Frances adding poems: these were published from 1842 onwards and were collected in 1848. Her *Verses for Holy Seasons* (1846) was followed by the immensely popular *Hymns for Little Children* (1848). Marked by memorable rhythms and simple images, the collection contained such hymns as 'All things bright and beautiful', 'Once in Royal David's city', 'Jesus guides us o'er the tumult' and 'There is a green hill far away'. In 1850 she married the Rev. William Alexander who became Bishop of Derry and Raphoe in 1867 and, in 1896, Bishop of Armagh: they had two sons and two daughters. Mrs Alexander published

seven more volumes of poetry, mostly devotional but also including musical verse (admired by Tennyson) and Irish historical ballads such as 'The Siege of Derry' and 'The Irish Mother's Lament'. She also contributed to leading contemporary magazines. She died in the Bishop's Palace, Londonderry, but the hymns of 'Mrs C.F. Alexander' were sung, and continue to be sung, in Anglican communities and schools throughout the world.

**Aliberty, Soteria** (1847–1929). Greek teacher and feminist. She studied in Greece and Italy and taught in Constantinople [now Istanbul] in the Zappeion school for girls, the first of its kind in that city. She lived for some years in Romania where, together with the other women of the Greek community, she founded a school for girls. She wrote articles for the Greek newspaper of Bucharest and compiled the first 'Biographies of Distinguished Greek Women', which appeared in the *Women's Newspaper*, published in Athens. In 1893 she returned to Athens, where she devoted her time to various activities designed to raise women's consciousness. She founded the first women's association, Ergani Athena, and became editor of a literary journal, *Pleiades*. Her literary works include biographical studies of women and translations.

**Al-Khaizurān** (*d* 790). Arabian queen. A slave girl from the Yemen, she was noticed by the powerful Caliph of Baghdad, Al-Mansur, who took her to the household of his son Al-Mahdī. She bore Al-Mahdī two sons and a daughter, and after his accession to the Caliphate in 774 he freed and married her. She became a powerful influence at court, trying to control affairs totally during the year-long reign of her son Al-Hadī. When he died in 786 she was rumoured to have poisoned him and her second son Harun al-Rashid became Caliph: she continued to influence his government until her death.

**Al-Khansā** (600–670). Arabian poet. Born into a noble nomadic tribe, the Madar, Al-Khansā was one of the great poets of the period. Her life spans the early years of Islam. She refused to marry until she found the husband of her choice. Eventually she married three times and outlived all her husbands. Four of her sons were killed in the Battle of Qadasiyah, one of the decisive battles of early Islamic history. She took regular part in poetry competitions in a male-dominated environment and established an enduring reputation; her special genre was the elegy. The Prophet Mohammed was said to have been very impressed by her poetry.

**Al-Mala'ikah, Nazik** (1923–). Iraqi poet. She was born into a literary family in Baghdad; her father and grandfather were both poets. She assumed a leading role in the free verse movement through her poetry and her critical work. A graduate of Arabic literature from Baghdad University, she went to Princeton University to do an MA in Comparative Literature. The author of numerous collections of poetry, including *Ashiqat al-ayl* ('Lover of the night'), *Shadaya wa-ramad* ('Splinters and ashes'), *Qararat al-mawjah* ('The bottom of the waves'), and *Shajarat al-qamar* ('The moon tree'), and a former teacher at Baghdad University, Nazik Al-Mala'ikah now lives in Kuwait.

**Aloni, Shulamit** (1931–). Israeli government official. Born in Tel-Aviv of Russian parents, she was educated at the progressive Ben Shemers school. In 1948 she fought with Hagana units in the Jewish quarter of Jerusalem. After World War II she became a teacher but then took a law degree, graduating in 1956, and began broadcasting on a citizens' complaints programme. From 1965 to 1969 she was a Labour MP, and also chaired the Israeli Consumer Council from 1966. In 1973 she left the Labour Party and founded the Civil Rights Party which won three seats in the December elections (including one for MARCIA FREEDMAN, the Woman's Movement representative). In 1974 she was appointed Minister without Portfolio, and pressed for reforms such as the Civil Marriage Bill, but lost her position when Yitzhak Rabin allied with the National Religious Party. In 1977 she became the only Civil Rights MP in the Knesset.

Married to a civil administrator, she has three children, runs a free legal aid service and writes a column on civil rights. Her books include *The Citizen and his Country*,

*The Rights of the Child in Israel* and *Woman as a Human Being*.

**Al-Sa'īd 'Amīnah** (1914–). Egyptian writer. Born in Cairo, she came from the remarkable family of a progressive doctor who believed in the education of women. Her eldest sister, Karīmah, became a teacher and in 1965 was the first woman Minister of Education. Amīnah was one of the first small group of women who graduated from Cairo University in 1935 and has been advocating women's rights since her school days. She is the editor of *Hawā* ('Eve'), a women's weekly magazine, which has the largest foreign circulation of any Arabic paper. She is the first woman to be elected to the Egyptian Press Syndicate Executive Board; she is also a President of Dar al Hilal Publishing House (the oldest publishing firm in the Arab world) and a member of the Supreme Board of Journalism. She has delivered many lectures on Arab women at various international conferences, pointing out similarities and dissimilarities between Arab and Western women in the struggle for emancipation and in the social challenge their movement constitutes. A close colleague of President Sadat, she accompanied him on his famous visit to Jerusalem in 1977.

**Altwegg, Jeannette** (1930–). British ice-skater. Jeannette was British figure-skating champion four times between 1947 and 1950, and showed her wider sporting ability by also reaching the finals in the 1947 Wimbledon Junior lawn tennis championships. In 1951 she won the European and world figure-skating titles, showing her ability to remain unperturbed by the big occasion and to excel by her methodical approach in compulsory figures. In 1952 she again won the European title and also the Olympic gold medal at Oslo. This was so unusual for a British skater that her achievement was recognized by making her an OBE.

**Amaya, Carmen** (1913–63). Spanish dancer. Born in Barcelona, she was a member of a close gypsy family. Accompanied by her father on the guitar, she danced from the age of four, and appeared in Paris at the age of eight, before beginning regular per formances with the Raquel Meller Company in Paris in 1923. She appeared at the Barcelona International Exposition in 1919, and between 1930 and 1940 worked in Buenos Aires, where the Amai Theatre was specially built for her. She danced, with her successful family company, in New York in 1941 and in London in 1948, 1952 and 1959, and made the film of *La historía de los Tarantos* (a gypsy Romeo and Juliet) with Gades. A passionate, unsophisticated dancer, she showed superb talent for lively, complicated rhythms and precise timing. Just before her death she was awarded the Grand Cross of Isabella.

**Amina** (1560–1610). Nigerian queen. One of two daughters of a woman ruler Bakwa Turunku, she was accepted as a royal heir, and became a warrior, refusing all suitors and accompanying the chief Karama in his warfare. On his death in 1576 she took the throne, and over the next 30 years extended her territory by conquest south and west to the mouth of the Niger, dominated the northern cities of Kano and Katsina, and opened new east-west trade routes in addition to the Saharan routes. She took enormous quantities of tribute, and traditionally also took a lover in each city she conquered, beheading him the next morning. Her alleged habit of building a walled camp wherever she travelled has led to the ancient Hausa fortifications being called 'Amina's walls'. After her death her proverbial praise was sung, 'Amina, daughter of Nikatau, a woman as capable as a man'.

**'Anastasia'** (Manahan, Anna Anderson) (1901–84). Russian aristocratic claimant. 'Anastasia' claimed to be the only surviving child of Tsar Nicholas II, whose family were supposedly massacred with him in Ekaterinburg in 1917. According to her story she was pulled from among the dead by a soldier, Alexander Tchaikorski, who smuggled her to Romania. She alleged that they became lovers, and she had a child, but that he was murdered in Bucharest and she fled to Berlin. The known facts begin in 1920 when she was rescued, after a suicide attempt, from the Landwehr canal, Berlin. In a sanatorium a woman claimed to recognize her as Anastasia. For the rest of her life she tried to prove

this identity, and to claim the Imperial fortune from German banks. The case, opposed by the rival heiress Duchess von Mecklenburg, was tested in German courts from 1933 to 1970, when it was judged that neither case could be proved. Her opponents identified her as a Polish peasant, Franziska Schanzlavski, countering her 'recollections' of court life by pointing to her inability to speak Russian, and her Slav accent. She lived in Germany as 'Anna Anderson', but after a visit to America she married history professor John Manahan in 1969, and moved to the USA.

A. Anderson: *I am Anastasia, Grand-Duchess of Russia* (1958)

P. Kurth: *Anastasia: The Riddle of Anna Anderson* (1983)

**Anderson, Elizabeth Garrett** (1836–1917). Known as the first English woman doctor. Elizabeth was born in London, and grew up in Aldeburgh, Suffolk, in a family of ten children. Her father, Newson Garrett, supported her both financially and morally. Like ELIZABETH BLACKWELL, she began as a nurse in order to gain access to dissections and operations at the Middlesex Hospital, London, but after a year's training in 1860 she was refused admission to medical schools, as were all women at the time.

She studied at the London Hospital and St Andrew's, where she had to dissect cadavers in her own bedroom when denied access to dissecting rooms. She passed the apothecaries' examination so that she could be listed on the medical register as LSA.

In 1866 she opened St Mary's Dispensary for Women, which later became the New Hospital for Women and Children, and after her death was named the Elizabeth Garrett Anderson Hospital. While actively supporting the admission of women to the University of Edinburgh, in 1870 she achieved full professional respectability for herself in the form of an MD from the University of Paris.

While on a school board she met and married J.G.S. Anderson; they had three children, one of whom died of meningitis. Her daughter Louisa eventually became Chief Surgeon of Endell Street Military Hospital during World War I.

Elizabeth became a lecturer, and then Dean and President, at the London School of Medicine for Women. She had intended becoming a great physician to help women, and was also a pioneer in opening the medical profession to women. She was the first and only woman member of the British Medical Association from 1873 to 1892. She was linked with the women's suffrage movement through her sister MILLICENT GARRETT FAWCETT, and when elected Mayor of Aldeburgh in 1908 she became the first woman mayor in England.

J. Manton: *Elizabeth Garrett Anderson* (1965)

**Anderson, Dame Judith** (1898–). Australian-American actress. Born in Adelaide, she made her debut in Sydney in 1915, but emigrated to the USA in 1918. Her outstanding roles include Kelly's *Behold the Bridegroom* (1927), Lavinia in *Mourning becomes Electra* (1931), Gertrude in John Gielgud's *Hamlet* (1936), Lady Macbeth (1941) and Medea (1947). She won particular fame for her interpretation of evil roles in classical and modern drama and film, for example playing Mrs Danvers in the film *Rebecca* (1940). Her films include *A Man called Horse* (1970) and the Australian *Inn of the Damned* (1974). She was created DBE in 1960. In 1982 she returned to Broadway as the Nurse in Jeffers's *Medea.* In 1984 a Broadway theatre was named after her, and (at the age of 86) she signed a long-term contract for the soap-opera *Santa Barbara*.

**Anderson, Marian** (1902–). American contralto. Born into a poor black family in Philadelphia, she started singing at the age of six for the local Union Baptist Church, which raised money for her singing lessons. She graduated from the Philadelphia Southern High School and then went to New York, where she studied with Giuseppe Boghetti and came first out of 300 competitors for a prize in 1925. In 1930 she toured Europe, singing in London, Scandinavia and Germany, but did not make her New York debut until 1936. She was highly successful; her voice was noted for its range and rich tone. In 1939 she was barred from singing at Constitution Hall in Washington because of her colour and a protest group led by ELEANOR ROOSEVELT arranged for a separate concert at the Lincoln Memorial. She later sang at the White House and in 1955, at the age of 53, became the first black singer to appear at the Metropolitan Opera, as Ulrica in Verdi's *Un ballo in maschera*. A warm, energetic personality, she also worked for the civil rights movement and was a delegate to the United Nations in 1958. She retired from her concert career in 1965. Among the many tributes to her are a $10,000 award from the Box Foundation, with which she established the Marian Anderson Fellowship for young artists (1972), and the first Eleanor Roosevelt Human Rights Award (1984).

M. Anderson: *My Lord, what a Morning: an Autobiography* (1956)

**Anderson, Mary (i)** (1859–1940). American actress. Mary Anderson was born in Sacramento, California. Her family moved to Kentucky where she was educated at the Ursuline Convent in Louisville. Always determined to act, in 1874 she read for CHARLOTTE SAUNDERS CUSHMAN who suggested she train in New York. Her first appearance was as Juliet at the age of 16 in Louisville, and she then toured the cities of the South and West before making her New York debut in 1877 in *The Lady of Lyons*. After six years of triumphant tours she made her first London appearance at the Lyceum as Parthenia in *Ingomar* in 1883. Famous for her beauty and classical restrained style, she moved between England and the USA, playing many Shakespearean roles, especially Rosalind, Peridita and Hermione, and starring in several plays by W.S. Gilbert. In 1889 she retired after a nervous breakdown, and the following year married Antonio de Navarro and settled in Worcestershire. She never returned to professional theatre although she gave some charity concerts.

Mary Anderson: *A Few Memories* (1896)

**Anderson, Mary (ii)** (1872–1964). Swedish-American trade unionist. Born in Linköping, Sweden, at the age of 16 she emigrated to the USA with her sister and they washed dishes at a boarding house for lumberjacks in Michigan, before Mary found a job in an Illinois shoe factory. She joined the International Boot and Shoe Workers' Union in 1894 and became local branch President. In 1903 she joined the Chicago branch of the Women's Trade Union League (WTUL), having for some years experienced the difficulties of being the only woman on an all-male executive, and in 1910 she became the WTUL representative for the Garment Workers' Union, organizing, lecturing and investigating strikes for the WTUL until 1920. In 1914 she had become a research worker on a project studying women's war work and in 1920 her years of dedication were recognized when she was made first Director of the Women's Bureau of the Department of Labor, the first working woman to rise through union activities to a government position. She published vital evidence backing a series of reforming laws on working conditions and pay, and after her retirement in 1944 she continued to lecture, write and to co-operate with official investigations into labour issues.

M. Anderson: *Woman at Work* (1951)

**Andersson, Harriet** (1932–). Swedish film actress. Born in Stockholm, she began her career as a music hall dancer, then worked in revue and moved to serious stage roles at Malmö City Theatre in 1953. She appeared first on film in *While the City Sleeps* (1949). Her performance in *Trots/Defiance* (1952) caught the eye of Ingmar Bergman, who wrote *Monika* (1952) especially for her. Andersson has played in several of his films which explore the sensibility of women, notably *Smiles of a Summer Night* (1955), *Through a Glass Darkly* (1961), *All These Women* (1964), *Cries and Whispers* (1972) and *Fanny and Alexander* (1982). She has also worked with her husband, director Jörn Donnor, for example in *A Sunday in September* (1963), and *Anna* (1979), and with MAI ZETTERLING. She is regarded as one of Sweden's most expressive actresses.

**André, Valérie** (1922–). French army doctor. Born in Strasbourg, Valérie studied in Paris and graduated from the Faculty of Medicine in 1948. She was stationed in Vietnam as the Chief of Medicine of a women's infirmary, then as neurosurgery assistant at a military hospital. In 1950 she was commissioned as a helicopter pilot and flew 150 medical missions under combat conditions, notably during the siege of the fortress of Dienbienphu. She received nine decorations, including the Légion d' Honneur, Croix de Guerre and US Legion of Merit.

As Medical Chief of a helicopter squadron she participated in the Algiers campaign, and reached the rank of Colonel in 1970. She was Medical Technical Adviser to the commander of aerial transports, then Chief of Medical Service, before becoming the first French woman general. She married an air force officer.

**Andreas-Salomé, Lou(ise)** [Lelia] (1861–1937). Russian-German novelist, literary critic and psychoanalyst. Born in St Petersburg [now Leningrad], she was the fourth child of a family of French Huguenot origin, her father being an army officer. When she was 17 her father died and she entered a deeply religious phase, which led to her studying comparative religion at the University of Zürich. From then until her death she lived tumultuously, at the centre of central European intellectual life.

In 1880 her friend the idealist Malwida von Meysenburg introduced her to Paul Rée, the moral philosopher who became her constant companion; in turn he presented Friedrich Nietzsche, who fell in love with her beauty and incisive intelligence. He saw Lou as a pupil and she considered herself his 'free disciple', inspired by him to write essays, fiction, drama and diaries. *Im Kampf um Gott* (1884) presents a version of her experience with Nietzsche as a kind of morality play. She eventually turned down his proposal of marriage.

In 1887 she married the famous orientalist and philologist Frederick Andreas, a professor of Göttingen University. Their marriage was apparently unconsummated (although it lessened her association with Rée and Nietzsche) and her husband condoned her later love affairs. She subsequently separated from Nietzsche and Rée and published an account of Nietzsche's thought, *Friedrich Nietzsche in seinen Werken* (1894). From 1897 to 1901 she had an affair with the poet Rainer Maria Rilke, and visited Russia with him in 1899 and 1901 where they met Tolstoy and the poet Drozhzin. Her prolific literary output included a study of Ibsen's characters, *Henrik Ibsens Frauengestalten* (1892); the essay *Jesus der Jude* (1895); the novel *Ruth* (1895); and the fiction cycle *Im Zwischerland* (1902).

Although she knew nothing of the subject when she attended a conference on psychoanalysis in 1910, her constant fictionalization of her past and analysis of her experience gave her a basis for the 'deep and subtle understanding of analysis' which Karl Abraham found in her. She associated with Adler but turned against him through personal devotion to Freud, who was pleased with her essay *Anal-und Sexual* (1915) and the book-length manuscript *Ubw*, which endorsed some of his work on narcissism. From 1913 she took patients for analysis, seeing them at any hour and charging little. *Mein Dank an Freud* (1931) and *Grundriss einiger Lebenserinnerungen* (1933) are memoirs of her work as a confidante of Freud and an 'improved' version of her life experiences. She had continued to write essays and fiction, including *Rodninka* (1923), remarkable for its delicate subtle psychological understanding, but she was particularly well known during her lifetime for her books on Nietzsche (1899) and Rilke (1928). Her husband died in 1930. Lou was tended through diabetes and cancer by Mariechen, her husband's daughter by a maid. Her fascinating autobiography, *Lebensrückbild* ('A Backward Look at my Life'), was eventually published in 1951.

A. Livingstone: *Lou Andreas-Salomé* (1984)

**Andreini, Isabella** (1562–1604). Italian actress and writer. The first 'great actress' in Europe, Isabella Canali was born in Padua, and at 16 married the famous actor Francesco Andreini, a former soldier who had spent several years in slavery to the Turks. At this early age Isabella had already written her pastoral fable *Mirtilla*, which was published ten years later, in 1588, and went through several editions within the next thirty years. Francesco was leader of the commedia dell'arte troupe Il Gelosi, and Isabella acted with them, first appearing on stage in Florence in 1578. Praised by leading contemporary critics for her beauty, wit and talent, she created a 'type' (which was to feature in all the 'Isabella dramas' of the later commedia repertoire) in plays such as *La Pazzia di Isabella*, played at Florence in 1589 at the wedding of the Grand Duke Ferdinand. The troupe toured Northern Italy and France for many years, but Isabella died in childbirth in Lyons in 1604 on their journey back to Italy after four years in Paris. The Andreinis had seven children; their son Giovanni Battista is

known today as the author of *L'Adamo*, one of the reputed sources of *Paradise Lost*.

Isabella's poems, *Rime*, were published in Milan in 1601 and in Paris in 1603, and after her death Francesco collected more of her writings in *Lettere* (1607) and *Fragmenti di alcune scritture*, to which he wrote a preface in 1616 (published in 1620).

**Andrews, Julie (Elizabeth Wells)** (1935–). British singer and actress. Julie was born into a show-business family, in Walton-on-Thames, Surrey, and appeared in variety and radio shows as a child, making her first London stage appearance at the age of twelve in the revue *Starlight Roof* in 1947. In 1954 she performed in New York in *The Boyfriend*, but real fame came with the London and Broadway productions of *My Fair Lady* (1956–9), in which she played Eliza Doolittle. This was followed by *Camelot*, with Richard Burton. She moved into films with Disney's *Mary Poppins* (1964), for which she won an Academy Award, and the outstandingly popular *The Sound of Music* (1965), based on the life of MARIA VON TRAPP. Both showed her as brisk, good, almost saccharine sweet – a type she has found hard to live down. She went on to make *Thoroughly Modern Millie* (1967) and *Star!* (1968), and to star in her own television show.

Her 1959 marriage to Tony Walton ended in 1968; they had one daughter. In 1969 she married director Blake Edwards, and after two unsuccessful films together, they created a new persona for Julie, as a spirited comedienne in such films as *10*, with Dudley Moore (1979), *S.O.B.* (1981), the sophisticated dig at sexual stereotypes *Victor/Victoria* (1982), and *The Man Who Loved Women* (1983). Her recent films, which include *That's Life* (1985) and *Duet for One* (1986), have shown her to be an actress of charm, versatility and wit.

**Andzhaparidzi, Vera (Iulianovna)** (1900–). Georgian actress. Her father was a notary. After studies at Tbilisi she went first to the Rusthavelli Theatre (1920–26), progressing to several other theatres including the Moscow Realistic where she played the title role in Gorky's *Mother* (1932). Between 1957 and 1959, while director of the Mardzhanishvilli Theatre in Tbilisi, she gave an epic performance as the grandmother in

Kasson's *The Trees Die Standing*. Among her other outstanding roles are Cleopatra and Marguérite Gauthier. One of the founders of the Georgian theatre, she has 'a vivid creative individuality'. She has been awarded the Stalin Prize (1943, 1946 and 1952) and the Order of Lenin.

**Angela of Brescia** [Merici, Angela] (1474–1540). Italian saint and founder. Born at Desenzano, near Lake Garda, Angela was orphaned early in life. She joined the Franciscan tertiaries and began giving catechism lessons to the children in her village. Around 1506 she was told in a vision: 'before your death, you will found a society of virgins at Brescia', but it was not until 1516 that she had the opportunity to move there. In 1535 Angela and a number of younger companions formed the Company of St Ursula, the first teaching order of women to be established, especially devoted to the education of girls. Each member continued living in her own home and working among her family and neighbours. No formal vows were taken, but the primitive rule drawn up by Angela prescribed virginity, poverty and obedience. After her death this sisterhood was formally organized into a congregation according to the decisions of the Council of Trent.

P. Caraman: *St Angela* (1965)

**Angelou, Maya** (1928–). American writer. Maya Angelou was born in St Louis, Missouri, and when she was three, after her parents' divorce, was sent with her brother Bailey to live in Stamps, Arkansas, with her grandmother. There, at the age of eight, she was raped by her mother's boyfriend and became mute for five years: she was also later knifed by her father's mistress. In her teens she went with Bailey to California, graduating from school at 16 and giving birth to a son. The first volume of her autobiography describes the hardship of her early years during the Depression of the 1930s and in the 1940s. Angelou's career has been varied in the extreme: she has been waitress, singer, dancer, actress, teacher, black activist and writer. In her twenties she toured Europe and Africa in *Porgy and Bess*, and then settled in Harlem where she was a member of the Writers' Guild and established herself as a night-club singer and actress, her plays including Genet's *The*

*Blacks*. During the 1950s she became involved in the movement for civil rights and the black power struggle and for several years she lived in Ghana, where she edited the *African Review*. She became famous as a writer with *I Know Why the Caged Birds Sing* (1970), which was followed by four more volumes of autobiography: *Gather Together in My Name* (1974), *Singin' and Swingin' and Gettin' Merry Like Christmas* (1976), *The Heart of a Woman* (1981) and *All God's Children Got Travellin' Shows* (1986). An inspiring figure, with great presence and energy, she has also published several collections of poetry and made numerous television appearances. She became Reynolds Professor of American Studies at Wake Forest University, North Carolina, but continued to tour and give readings. In 1988 she directed Errol John's black classic *Moon on a Rainbow Shawl* at the Almeida Theatre, London.

**Anguissola, Sofonisba** (c1535–1625). Italian painter. Born in Cremona, she was the eldest of six daughters of a local nobleman who encouraged their artistic talents in case their inadequate dowries should force them to support themselves. Recognized as a child prodigy and brought to the attention of Michelangelo, she was apprenticed to the painter Bernardo Campi from 1546 to 1549, and several portraits of herself and her family date from before 1560. Her *Three Sisters Playing Chess* is an early example of portraits linked to social life. She taught painting to three of her sisters, who all showed remarkable talent, especially the short-lived Lucia (1540–65), and Europa who received many church commissions.

In 1559 Sofonisba was invited by Philip II to Spain, and remained in Madrid for many years as court portrait painter, until, between 1570 and 1580 she married a Sicilian nobleman, thought to have been Fabrizio de Mancada, and returned to Palermo with a lavish dowry provided by Ferdinand and Isabella. After her husband's death in 1584 she decided to return to northern Italy but married the captain of her ship, Orazio Lomellino, and lived with him in Palermo and Genoa.

Much of her work is lost, but the remaining pictures include court studies, such as *Philip II*, intimate studies such as *Husband and Wife*, and several self-portraits, emphasizing her role as artist, using symbols of literature and music as well as painting. The first internationally-famous Italian woman artist, her example is thought to have inspired successors such as LAVINIA FONTANA, Fede Galizia (1578–1630), an early still-life painter from Milan, and Barbara Longhi from Ravenna (1552–1638) who links traditional composition with intensity of feeling and innovative colouring.

**Anne** (1665–1714). Queen of Great Britain and Ireland. The second daughter of the Duke of York (later James II) and his first wife Anne Hyde, who died when she was six, she was brought up as a Protestant, by command of her uncle Charles II. A weak child she spent some time in France for her health when she was five, and illness dogged her all her life. At about the age of eight she was given as a companion Sarah Jennings, later Duchess of MARLBOROUGH, who had a lasting influence over her. Her lonely childhood and longing for affection made her cling to certain favourites all her life. In 1683 her marriage was arranged to Prince George of Denmark, and their relationship was very close until his death in 1708.

Anne supported the Protestant William of Orange, who had married her sister MARY, in the 'Glorious Revolution' of 1688 against her father, but she and Mary quarrelled over money and over Anne's favouritism to the Duchess of Marlborough and she was excluded from favour until her sister's death in 1694. She herself was heir, but had no surviving children to carry on the line, despite 18 pregnancies in as many years. When her last son died of smallpox at the age of 11 in 1700, she was distraught with grief, but agreed to the Act of Settlement, which passed succession from the Stuart to the Hanoverian line. She became Queen in 1702, and was accompanied by the Marlboroughs on her first public appearance, when she gave a speech in Parliament advocating the Union of Scotland and England. Marlborough led the troops to victory in the war of the Spanish succession, but Anne tired of the Duchess's support for the pro-war Whig ministers and in 1707 came under the influence of Abigail Masham, a relative of the Tory Robert Harley, later Earl of Oxford. Although the

Whigs returned to power in 1708 Anne finally used the unpopularity of the expensive war to recall Harley in 1710 and to dismiss the Marlboroughs in 1711. Harley remained in power until replaced by another Tory, Bolingbroke, in 1714. Soon afterwards Anne died, and final hopes for the restoration of the Stuarts were dashed by the succession of George I.

In all the political intrigues and parliamentary crises and factions Anne tried conscientiously to choose the best course, although she appears not to have had much foresight or imagination and was strongly dependent on her favourites and extremely obstinate once she had made a decision. She was uninterested in art, music or literature but she did patronize architects such as Wren and Vanbrugh. Her particular interest was in the Anglican Church; she supported legislation against dissenters in 1711 and 1714 and sponsored several clerical charities.

E. Gregg: *Queen Anne* (1980)

**Anne,** Princess Royal (1950–). British princess. Princess Anne was born in Clarence House, London where her parents, then the Duke and Duchess of York, lived until her mother became Queen ELIZABETH II, and the family moved to Buckingham Palace. She was educated by governesses (and was known as an unrestrained tomboy, nicknamed 'Ragtime Cowgirl Anne') until at the age of 13 she was sent to boarding school, a break with royal tradition, at Benenden School, Kent. After taking her A Levels, she chose not to go to university, but took a course at the Berlitz School of Languages.

Her first trips abroad were in 1969 and 1970, to the Pacific, Canada and the USA and to East Africa in 1971, as President of the Save the Children Fund. In the same year she became known for her horse-riding, winning the Raleigh Trophy at the European Three-Day Event at Burghley and being chosen Sportswoman of the Year. She continued to win numerous equestrian events after she married Captain Mark Phillips in 1973, including the European Silver Medal in 1975, and was a member of the British team in the Montreal Olympics (1976). Her children, Peter and Zara, were born in 1977 and 1981; the family live at Gatcombe Park, Gloucestershire. She has recently become interested in steeplechasing, winning her first race under National Hunt rules in 1987, and racing successfully in Europe and the USA.

Anne is one of the most hard-working members of the royal family, undertaking around 300 public engagements a year (second in number only to the Queen), and she is patron of over eighty charities, which she supports actively, working especially with the physically and mentally disabled. But her best-known work has been with the Save the Children Fund. Her gruelling tour in 1982 of six African countries, with its sixteen-hour days, left newsmen reeling, and she is now an acknowledged expert on the theory and practice of International Aid, abrasively impatient of obstructive bureaucracy and of the limited aid policies of the EEC and Western nations. Further tours have included West Africa in 1984 and of the Far East in 1987, and another African tour, in 1988.

In 1987 she was given the title of Princess Royal.

**Anne of Austria** (1601–66). Queen of France. The daughter of Philip III of Spain and Margaret of Austria, she was born in Valladolid, and married the young Louis XIII of France when they were both 14. She was lonely and homesick, ignored by Louis, and her position at the French court was made worse by her flirtation in 1625 with the Duke of Buckingham, who was passionately in love with her, and by the jealousy of Cardinal Richelieu from 1624. In 1626 she became involved with the intriguer Madame de Chevreuse in an attempt to assassinate the Cardinal, and in 1628, with her mother-in-law MARIE DE MÉDICIS, tried unsuccessfully to have him dismissed.

After the start of the Thirty Years War she came under suspicion because of her Catholicism and her loyalty to her brother Philip IV. She was accused of treason in 1637 and, although pardoned, Louis tried to prevent her obtaining the regency after his death. However, in 1643 Parliament ratified her powers, influenced by her lover and extremely able Chief Minister, Cardinal Mazarin. They overcame the revolts between 1648 and 1653 known as 'the Wars of the Fronde', inspired first by Parliament's resistance to their fiscal demands, and then by the resentment of the aristocrats led by the Prince de Condé. Her old ally Madame

de Chevreuse was now a bitter enemy. The Queen suffered setbacks in 1648 and in 1651 when Mazarin had to flee to Germany. In that year Louis XIV came of age and Anne's regency officially ceased. Mazarin was brought back in 1653, and Anne still retained enormous power over government, particularly in strengthening the alliance with Spain. After Mazarin's death in 1661 she was gradually excluded from state affairs. A passionate, clever woman, she is a central character in Dumas' novel, *The Three Musketeers* (1844).

H. Kleinman: *Anne of Austria: Queen of France* (1987)

**Anne of Beaujeu** (1461–1522). French princess. The eldest daughter of Louis XI, she was an extremely clever and politically-dexterous woman, who at the age of 22 was able to step in, with her husband Pierre de Bourbon, to control the unrest in the country which threatened the rule of the young King Charles VIII. She appeased the rebellious nobles and removed the old King's favourites, but refused the requests of the States General to control taxation, and became involved in civil war with Brittany and with the Duc d'Orléans, later Louis XII. The Bourbons won the undying hatred of ANNE OF BRITTANY, whose reluctant marriage to Charles they arranged in 1491. Pierre died in 1503 but Anne continued to govern the Bourbon domains which belonged to her daughter Suzanne. One of many powerful women of the period, at the end of her life she was engaged in disputes with LOUISE OF SAVOY over succession to the Bourbon lands.

**Anne of Brittany** (1477–1514). Breton duchess and French queen. Born in Nantes, the daughter of Duke Francis I of Brittany, she became Duchess at the age of 11, but just before this her land had been invaded by French troops who demanded that she should not marry without the consent of the crown. Afraid that Brittany would be absorbed into France, the young Duchess made an alliance with Maximilian of Austria (whom she married by proxy in 1490), Henry VII of England and Ferdinand II of Aragon, but eventually after a long siege, she was forced to marry the French king Charles VIII in 1491. After he died without an heir in 1498, Anne had to marry his successor Louis XII. But she insisted that Brittany should form a separate part of the inheritance, going to a second son or daughter, or to her own heirs.

Anne was a great patron of scholars, poets and artists, as witnessed by the famous *Book of Hours* created for her by Jean Baudichon. However her main effort was the preservation of the separate State of Brittany and she governed it well and efficiently. In the event, her plans to marry her daughter Claude to the future Charles V came to nothing, and Claude's marriage to Francis of Angoulême in 1514 led inevitably to the union of Brittany and France when Francis became king in 1532.

H.J. Sanborne: *Anne of Brittany* (1917)

**Anning, Mary** (1799–1847). British paleontologist. Born at Lyme Regis, Dorset, Mary caught the passion for paleontology from her father, a cabinet-maker who sold fossils to summer visitors. She continued the trade after his death in 1810. In that year her brother Joseph uncovered the head of a marine reptile on the foreshore between Lyme and Charmouth and a year later 12-year-old Mary painstakingly unearthed the complete remains of a 10-metre-long *Ichthyosaurus*. The discovery created immense excitement and led to a lifelong career of fossil hunting. In 1824 she discovered an almost perfect *Plesiosaurus* and in 1828 the first associated skeleton of a *Pterodactyl* of the small *Dimorphodon* genus. She supplied specimens to museums and individuals and achieved national celebrity – the tongue twister 'she sells sea-shells on the sea-shore' is thought to apply to her. Although she had no formal education she held court to scholars and enthusiasts and corresponded with experts from Britain and abroad. Mary never married and had a reputation for strong opinions, a love of controversy and great kind-heartedness. She lived in Lyme (where her shop was a notable tourist attraction), supported by a small government grant awarded by the Prime Minister, Lord Melbourne. She was made an Honorary Member of the Geological Society shortly before her death.

Mary is the best known of 19th-century women paleontologists, although others also made important discoveries, notably Mary Anne Mantell, who collaborated with her husband, Gideon Mantell, on *Fossils of the South Downs* and whose discovery of a strange tooth in Cuckfield Quarry, Sussex in 1820 led to the identification of the first *Dinosaur*.

**Anscombe, (Gertrude) Elizabeth (Margaret)** (1919– ). English philosopher. The most distinguished woman philosopher in the UK today, she was educated at Sydenham High School, won a scholarship to St Hugh's College, Oxford, graduating with a first class degree in classics and philosophy (Greats) in 1941. In the same year she married Peter Geach; they have seven children. She held research fellowships in Oxford and at Newnham College, Cambridge, from 1941 to 1944, and then became a research fellow at Somerville College, Oxford, in 1946, where she remained until 1970. She then moved to Cambridge, where she was Professor of Philosophy until 1986 and became a Fellow of New Hall.

Anscombe is known as a leading linguistic philosopher. Her chief works include *Intention* (1957), *An Introduction to Wittgenstein's Tractatus*, which she wrote with her husband in 1959, and *Three Philosophers* (1961). She is also the translator and co-editor of the posthumous works of Wittgenstein.

**Anthony, Susan B(rownell)** (1820–1906). American suffrage teacher. She was born in Adams, Massachusetts, into an old colonial family. Her father was first a farmer and then a mill-owner. Susan went to the Friends' Boarding School in Philadelphia (1837–8), before becoming a teacher herself, and eventually Head of the Female Department at Canahajorie Academy (1846–9). She left teaching to manage the family farm, and worked for the temperance and anti-slavery movements. With her sister she attended the first women's rights convention at Seneca Falls (1848), and in 1850 met her lifelong friend and collaborator ELIZABETH CADY STANTON.

In 1852 Anthony was prevented from speaking at a temperance rally because of her sex, and this led to the founding of the Women's State Temperance Society of New York under Stanton's presidency. During the 1850s she continued her temperance work, acted as agent for the American Anti-slavery Society (1856–61) and demanded equal voting rights and equal pay for women in the New York State Teachers' Association. From 1854 she organized canvassing and petitions for suffrage and for the passing of the Married Women's Property Act (1860).

After the Civil War she concentrated on the suffrage fight, leading exhausting campaigns in New York and Kansas. From 1868 to 1870 she edited *Revolution*, a radical crusading journal demanding suffrage, equal education, opening of employment opportunities, and encouraging women to form trade unions. To pay the debt incurred by the paper she undertook prodigious speaking tours to the Midwest and West Coast until 1876.

In May 1869, with Stanton, she formed the National Woman Suffrage Association, of which she became the driving spirit, although her view that black suffrage should be delayed until that of women, and her opinions on divorce, labour problems and campaign tactics caused later splits in the movement (*see* LUCY STONE). She was active in the successful campaign in Wyoming (1870), campaigned in California (1871), Michigan (1874), Philadelphia (1876) and Colorado (1877), and orchestrated a nationwide campaign in 1878. From 1881 to 1886 she wrote *History of Woman Suffrage* with Stanton and Matilda Gage, and in 1889 she called the meeting which founded the International Council of Women in London. In 1890 the National and American Woman Suffrage Associations were united; she succeeded Stanton as president in 1892 and in 1904, with CARRIE CATT, she founded the International Woman Suffrage Alliance in Berlin. Often impatient and demanding, Susan B. Anthony was an indomitable figure in the women's labour and civil rights movements and is honoured in America as a pioneering feminist.

K. Anthony: *Susan B. Anthony: Her Personal History and her Era* (1954)
H. Husted: *The Life and Work of Susan B. Anthony* (1969) [3 vols]

**Antonakakis, Suzana (Maria)** (1935–). Greek architect. Born in Athens and educated there, she attended the National Technical University School of Architecture from 1954 to 1959. In 1961 she married the architect Dimitris Antonakakis, with whom she had gone into partnership in 1959. She became Consultant to the Archaeological and Restoration Service (1961–3), and in 1965 founded with her husband 'Atelier 66'. One of the leading partnerships in Greece, involved in much development in tourist areas, they have won many awards. Their archaeological interest continued and in 1974 they published a six-volume work on identifying and recording important settlements in the Cyclades. She was President of the Department of Architecture, Technical Chamber of Greece in 1982–3 and has won numerous awards and prizes.

**Apostoloy, Electra** (1912–44). Greek communist activist and resistance fighter. While a 13-year-old schoolgirl she embraced communism and became a member of OKNE (the Greek Communist Youth Organization) during the dictatorship of Pangalos. She formed a small group of fellow schoolgirls who secretly arranged financial aid to exiled communists. Married to a communist doctor, she became an official member of the Communist Party, taking an active part in the 'working women's movement' by organizing classes on ideological education and by leading strikes. She was also Editor of the journal *Youth*, the instrument of the young communists. In 1935 she represented Greek women at the International Conference against Fascism in Paris. She also participated in many international conferences of the communist youth movement. In Greece she travelled all over the country organizing women's meetings and giving speeches, mainly about the imminent danger of fascism.

In 1936, during the dictatorship of General Metaxas, she was imprisoned for two years for disseminating anti-fascist propaganda. In prison she ran educational classes and managed to smuggle in newspapers. After a year of freedom she was again arrested for the same reason and was sent into exile, where her child was born. Transported to a prison hospital in Athens because of deteriorating health, she escaped and lived in hiding, working within the communist movement to mobilize young people into organized resistance against the

Germans. She formed EPON, the main group within the Greek Resistance movement. In 1944 she was arrested by the German-backed Greek secret police and tortured to death, but without revealing any information about her fellow comrades in the underground Communist Party.

**Applebee, Constance** (1883–1981). English hockey player. Born at Chigwell, Essex, and educated at home, she undertook physical education to improve her health and gained a diploma from the British College of Physical Education, London. In 1901 she went to Harvard for a year's track course and suggested field hockey as part of the training scheme. The first game of hockey in the USA was apparently played with ice hockey sticks on a concrete yard outside the Harvard gymnasium. From 1904 to 1928 she was Director of Outdoor Sports at Bryn Mawr, and she continued to coach in both England and the USA until 1965. Her zeal for the game even led her to run a hockey camp in Peru in 1923. In 1976 at the age of 94 she still attended the meeting of the International Federation of World Hockey Associations.

**Aptheker, Bettina** (1944–). American sociologist and feminist. The daughter of the Marxist historian Herbert Aptheker, she has been an important figure in the protest and feminist movements which emerged in the USA during the 1960s. She taught on the Women's Studies Programme at San José State University and at the University of California at Santa Clara, and was one of the directors of the American Institute for Marxist Studies. During the 1960s and 1970s her publications were related to protest, particularly within the academic world, for example *FSM* (Free Speech Movement), with Robert Kaufman and Michael Folson (1965), *Big Business and the American University* (1966) and the bibliography *Higher Education and the Student Rebellion in the United States* (1969); she later wrote a Marxist appraisal, *The Academic Rebellion* (1972). Deeply concerned with the more radical aspects of the civil rights movement, she collaborated with her father in *Racism and Reaction in the United States* and with ANGELA DAVIS in *If They Come in the Morning: Voices of Resistance* (both 1971).

She also wrote an account and analysis of Davis's trial, *The Morning Breaks* (1975). Her more recent historical studies include *Woman's Legacy: Interpretative Essays in US History* (1980).

**Aquino, (Maria) Corazon** (1933–). Filippina politician. The sixth of eight children of José and Demetria Cojuango, she grew up in affluence; her family owned a sugar and rice empire in Tarlac province. Her father was a Congressman, her grandfather a Senator. 'Cory' was educated at private Catholic schools, and from 1946 attended schools in Philadelphia and New York, before taking a degree in French and mathematics from the College of Mount St Vincent, New York. She intended to be a lawyer but gave up her legal studies in 1956 when she married politician Ninoy Aquino, who became leader of the opposition to the Marcos regime. In 1972 he was arrested on charges of murder and subversion and imprisoned for seven years, during which Cory acted as the link with his followers. After he was freed for heart surgery in the USA in 1980 they spent three years in exile in Boston. On his return, in August 1983 he was shot at Manila airport, the victim of a military conspiracy.

In 1984 Cory travelled the country on behalf of the opposition, and in 1985 gave in to constant demands that she should run for President. The election was almost sabotaged by Marcos supporters but Defence Minister Enrile and Lieut.-General Fidel Ramos, deputy chief of the armed forces, declared her the true winner, the citizens turned out to protect the rebel soldiers, and President Marcos and his wife fled the country. Aquino faced staggering problems: a vast foreign debt, a political system crippled by corruption, attacks from Marcos supporters and an on-going guerilla war. Although backed internally by the powerful Roman Catholic church and by a plebiscite endorsing her new constitution, and supported from without by the USA, her regime has seen constant unrest. In November 1986 she concluded the first ceasefire in 17 years of communist insurgency, but this has not been effective. In 1986 she sacked Defence Minister Enrile for plotting against the government and her power was apparently reinforced by elections in 1987, but an attempted coup in August was followed by several weeks of fighting. She won back the support of the army by allowing a drift to the right, and by the crackdown on communists and the arming of vigilante groups. Her party was successful in troubled, local elections, but her position was still regarded as precarious.

**Aquino, Melchora** [Tandang, Sora] (1812–1919). Filippina heroine. Known as the 'mother of the Philippine Revolution', she was involved in the successful attempt made in 1896 which gained the country freedom from Spain in 1898. She began her political career at the age of 83 when the rebel soldiers of Andres Bonifacio (who called themselves the Katipunan) made use of her store. The Spanish authorities caught her and she was imprisoned in Bilibid prison and then exiled to the Marianas Islands. She was set free when the Americans arrived in the Philippines. She lived to be 107 years old.

**Arányi, Jelly d'** (1895–1966). Hungarian-British violinist. A great-niece of Joachim, she was a pupil of Hubay at the Budapest Academy, giving joint recitals with her sister Adila (later ADILA FACHIRI) from 1908. In 1913 they settled in London, where their performances of Bach's concerto for two violins were much acclaimed; Holst wrote his *Double Concerto* for them (1930). Jelly gave the premières, with the composer, of Bartók's two violin sonatas (1922, 1923), both of which are dedicated to her, as are Ravel's *Tzigane* (1924) and Vaughan Williams's *Concerto accademico* (1925). She also inspired ETHEL SMYTH'S Concerto for violin and horn (1927). She formed a piano trio with Mme Suggia and Fanny Davies, and for over 20 years gave recitals with MYRA HESS.

J. Macleod: *The Sisters d'Arányi* (1969)

**Arber** [née Robertson], **Agnes** (1879–1960). English botanist. She developed her interest in botany at school in London, then at University College London, and at Cambridge University, where she worked on comparative plant anatomy. In 1909 she married E.A.N. Arber, Demonstrator in Paleobotany at Cambridge.

Agnes maintained few formal contacts with universities, preferring to pursue her work largely by herself. Her first book, *Herbals: their Origin and Evolution*, published in 1912 and rewritten in 1938, became the standard work about early printed herbals. From her 84 original papers, mainly on plant morphology, three major books emerged: *Water Plants: a Study of Aquatic Angiosperms* (1920); *Monocotyledons* (1925), and *The Gramineae: a Study of Cereal, Bamboo and Grass* (1934).

Her three later books reflected her consideration of science in relation to philosophy and metaphysics. She was the first woman botanist to be made a Fellow of the Royal Society and she received the Gold Medal of the Linnean Society in 1948.

**Arbus, Diane (Nemerov)** (1923–71). American photographer. Born into a prosperous Jewish family in New York City, she married Allan Arbus at the age of 18 and, after taking a short course with BERENICE ABBOTT, worked with her husband as a fashion photographer. She hated the work and abandoned it in 1957, and began to take pictures on the New York streets the following year. She had two daughters in 1945 and 1954; in 1960 she separated from her husband, and they eventually divorced in 1969. Throughout the 1960s she took a series of extraordinary photographs across the USA, disconcerting studies of ordinary people as well as studies of 'freaks', midgets, drag-queens and giants, which shocked and intrigued the public. She won two Guggenheim Fellowships, in 1963 and 1966, and taught at the Parsons School of Design (1965–6) and the Cooper Union (1968–9). She had many exhibitions, in New York (Museum of Modern Art, 1967), Chicago and Baltimore. She committed suicide in 1971. The following year she became the first American photographer to be included in the Venice Biennale.

P. Bosworth: *Diane Arbus: A. Biography* (1984)

**Arden, Elizabeth** [Graham, Florence Nightingale] (1884?–1966). Canadian beautician and businesswoman. She was born in Ontario and was the youngest of five children of a Scottish grocer. She received little education and worked at several jobs before setting off for New York. There she became an assistant in a cosmetics shop, then partner in a beauty salon before changing her name and going into business on her own on Fifth Avenue in 1909. In 1918 she married Thomas Lewis, who acted as her business manager until their divorce in 1935. He then went to work for her rival HELENA RUBINSTEIN as Arden had never allowed him to hold stock. In 1942 she married Prince Michael Evlonoff (divorced 1944). Elizabeth Arden invariably dressed in shades of pink, owned more than 100 exclusive salons in America and Europe and manufactured over 300 cosmetics products, basing her success on a prestigious image bolstered by high prices. She was a fiercely conservative and loyal Republican who felt that society was in decline. As a well-known racehorse owner she 'treated her women like horses and her horses like women', insisting that her own beauty preparations be used instead of horse liniment.

A. Lewis: *Miss Elizabeth Arden* (1973)

**Arenal, Concepción** (1820–93). Spanish social scientist and philanthropist. A specialist on penal science, international law and public education, she was a highly respected figure and influential journalist in late 19th-century Spain, winning the first prize from the Madrid Academy of Moral and Political Science for her essay on philanthropy *La beneficencia, la filantropía y la caridad*, which was published in 1861. Her other books included *Cortas a los delincuentes* (1865), and the two-volume *La cuestión social* (1880) and two books on women, *La mujer del parvenir* and *La mujer de su casa* (both published posthumously in 1895).

**Arendt, Hannah** (1906–75). German-American political philosopher. Born in Hanover into a Jewish family, she studied at Marburg, Freiburg and Heidelberg, where her teachers Jaspers and Heidegger initiated her interest in Existentialism. She completed her doctoral thesis on St Augustine's concept of love in 1928. In 1933 after a cursory arrest by the Gestapo, she moved to Paris, where she did social work among Jewish youth, arranging for the emigrations of orphans to Palestine [now Israel] with the Youth Aliyah. In 1940 she married the art historian Heinrich Bluecher and escaped to the USA, where she eventually became an American citizen.

In New York she worked as a publishers' editor, and was Research Director to the Conference on Jewish Relations from 1944 1946, before taking up academic posts. Her first important work, based on a series of articles, was *The Origins of Totalitarianism* (1951), in which she traced Nazi and Communist state theories to 19th-century nationalism, imperialism and racialism. She deplored the separation of moral thought from political action and this formed the basis of her attacks on the blindness of scientists developing weapons over which they could have no control, and on the liberal ideology which valued private over public virtues, which she explored in *The Human Condition* (1958). Sent to Israel by *The New Yorker* to cover Eichmann's trial, she wrote *Eichmann in Jerusalem, A Report on the Banality of Evil* (1961), which outraged some Zionists by presenting Eichmann as a bureaucratic tool of state evil, and which suggested that the lack of resistance among Eastern European Jews had been due to the absence of a political tradition. Her other books, *On Revolution* (1963) and *On Violence* (1970), stressed the idealistic, individualist nature of social change which she believed could not be linked to violent overthrow. Arendt was more drawn to anarchist, individual and collective, rather than centralist political theories and moved easily from theory to contemporary comment. She held posts in American universities, including Chicago, Berkeley and Columbia and was the first woman Professor at Princeton in 1959. Her last post was as Professor of Political Philosophy at New York City School for Social Research. At her death she left notes for a *Life of the Mind* of which two volumes, *Thinking* and *Willing*, were published in 1978, edited by MARY MCCARTHY, her friend and literary executor.

E. Young Bruehl: *Hannah Arendt* (1982)

**Arete of Cyrene** (mid-4th century BC). Greek philosopher. The daughter of Aristippus, the founder of the Cyrenaic school, she was taught philosophy by him and succeeded him as leading teacher after his death. She is credited with over 40 works, none of which survive. She taught her son, also called Aristippus, who developed the Cyrenaic theories of sensation as the means of physical knowledge and pleasure as the aim of all action. In a different 4th-century philosophical school, the Cynic, another woman, Hipparchus, was prominent, and is also reputed to have written tragedies and philosophical treatises.

**Argentenita, La** [Lopéz, Encarnaçion] (1895–1945). Spanish dancer. Born in Buenos Aires, she went to Spain as a child. She specialized in regional dance and chose her name in deference to LA ARGENTINA. In 1927 she founded the Ballet de Madrid with Garcia Lorca, and they toured the USA (1928) and Europe. In 1933 she collected famous veteran dancers and musicians to stage a traditional flamenco in *Las callas de Cadiz*, and in 1939 collaborated with Massin on *Capriccio espagnol*. Internationally respected, she appeared as a guest artist with the American Ballet Theatre before her early death in 1945. Her sister Pilar, also a dancer and a famous teacher (*b* 1912), then created the Ballet Espagnol.

**Argentina, La** [Mercé, Antonia] (1888–1936). Spanish dancer. Born in Buenos Aires, she studied under her father and made her debut at the age of nine in the Royal Opera House, Madrid, becoming *prima ballerina* at the age of 11. She enjoyed worldwide fame, first as a child prodigy and then as a concert artist, particularly in the regional dances of Spain. In 1925 she began her partnership with Escudero. She formed her own company in 1928, using traditional and modern Spanish music in works like *El amor brujo*, and in a series of one-act ballets. A great artist, she was especially famous for her individual castanet style.

**Ariyoshi, Sawako** (1921–84). Japanese novelist. Sawako Ariyoshi was the most popular writer in Japan at the time of her death. She wrote many novels on crucial social issues such as pollution (*Fukugo-ose*) and racial segregation (*Hishoku*). Her most famous novel, *Kokotsuno Hito* (*The Twilight Years*), deals with the problems of living with and caring for a senile relative. It sold an unprecedented two million copies when it appeared in 1972 and is now a modern classic in Japan. Her other works in English translation are *The River Ki* (1960) and *The Doctor's Wife* (1966).

**Arletty** [pseud. of Arlette-Léonie Bathiat] (1898–). French actress. Born in Courbevoie, a miner's daughter, she worked in a factory and then as a secretary and model before appearing in music hall revues. Her film career began with *Un chien qui rapporte* (1931), and her dark beauty led to frequent casting as a courtesan or prostitute, notably in *Hôtel du Nord* (1938) for Marcel Carné, with whom she also worked in *Le jour se lève/Daybreak* (1939). She played in films by Sacha Guitry but her greatest performance was as the courtesan Garance in *Les enfants du paradis/Children of Paradise* (1945).

After World War II Arletty was imprisoned as a collaborator because of a love affair with a German officer during the occupation of France. Her career went into decline, although the few roles she played in the 1950s included the lesbian in *Huis clos/No Exit* (1954) directed by Jacqueline Audry. She disliked working outside her own city: 'Etre loin de Paris, pour moi c'est l'exil'. During the 1960s she had several stage roles and, although her professional life was virtually ended by an accident which blinded her temporarily, she appeared in *Les volets fermés* in 1972.

**Armand, Inesse** (1874–1920). Russian revolutionary and feminist. Born Inesse Steffane, into an actor's family in Paris, her father died when she was very young, and she was brought up in Moscow in the home of the manufacturer Armand, eventually marrying A.E. Armand. She worked in Moscow with a philanthropic group helping prostitutes before joining the reformist Social Democrats, and then the Bolshevik party in 1904. Arrested after the 1905 uprising, she went into exile in Europe, lectured at the Party School at Longjumeau, near Paris, wrote for the journal *Rabotnitsa* (Woman Worker) from 1910, and spoke on women's rights to Russian groups abroad. In 1912 she was sent back to St Petersburg to work underground for the Party, and in 1915–16 represented the Bolshevik party at the International Women's Socialist Conference and at Internationalist Conferences at Zimmenwald and Kienthal. In 1916, in Paris, she translated the works of Lenin into French – his historically important letters to her are included in his *Complete Works*.

After the February 1917 revolution Inesse returned to Russia and helped to prepare for the armed October uprising. She was a member of the Moscow Bolshevik Party Committee and chaired the regional economic council. The founder and first director of the Women's Bureau Zhenotdel, in November 1918, with KOLLONTAI and SAMOILOVA she organized the first All Russian Conference of Women Workers and Peasants. She also directed the first International Conference of Women Communists. Inesse Armand died of cholera in 1920, and is buried in Red Square.

**Armstrong, Anne (Legendre)** (1927–). American politician. Born in New Orleans, and member of an old Creole family, she was educated in Virginia, and graduated with distinction from Vassar College in 1949. In 1950 she married Tobin Armstrong, moved to his Texas ranch, had five children and describes herself as 'never having a full time career'. She began as a volunteer campaigner for Truman in 1948, but turned to the Republican Party in 1952 and worked for the Eisenhower campaign. A staunch Republican local organizer, she rose to become first woman co-chairman of the National Republican Committee (1971–3) and in 1972 was asked to join the White House staff, to liaise between President Nixon and the Committee. She left in 1974 and was among the first to demand Nixon's resignation after the publication of the Watergate tapes. She was American Ambassador to London (1976–7), leaving after Ford's defeat in the presidential elections (at one stage she had been considered for vice-presidential running mate). She is on the board of directors of four large multinationals including American Express and General Motors, was a Trustee of the Guggenheim Foundation in 1980–84, and since 1977 has held academic posts in diplomacy and international affairs at Georgetown, Harvard and elsewhere.

**Armstrong** [née Hardin], **'Lil'** [Lillian] (1900–71). American jazz pianist and singer. Born in Memphis, Tennessee, she studied for three years at Fisk University before moving to Chicago with her family in 1917. She worked in a music store and then joined various groups before leading her own band at Dreamland, Chicago, in 1920 and working with King Oliver (1921–4). She became the second wife of Louis Armstrong in 1924, but they separated in 1931 and were finally divorced in 1938. During the 1920s they frequently worked and recorded together.

In 1928 she obtained a Teacher's Diploma at Chicago College of Music, and then a graduate Diploma in New York in 1929. She led an all-girl and then an all-male band in the 1930s, broadcasting regularly and also appearing solo in revues. In 1940 she moved to Chicago where she established herself as a club pianist, and toured Europe and England from 1952. She died on stage in St Louis, while taking part in a memorial concert for her ex-husband.

**Arnauld, (Jacqueline Marie) Angélique** (1591–1661). French abbess and Jansenist. Angélique was one of the 20 children of Antoine Arnauld, Advocate-General to Catherine de Medici, and Catherine Marian: the family whose members practically created the Jansenist party of 17th-century France. Her wealthy family had procured for her the abbacy of Port-Royal-les-Champs, near Versailles, a position she took up in 1602 at the age of 11. Angélique shared the worldly life of the convent until converted by a Capuchin friar in 1608. She promptly introduced drastic reforms – enclosure (she would only speak to her father through the grille), community of goods, abstinence and silence, and laid great emphasis on the inner discipline of the spirit. Reform was taken to many other foundations including Maubuissen, where Angélique spent five years. She was greatly influenced by St Francis de Sales and tried, unsuccessfully, to join his Visitation nuns. Mother Angélique returned to Port-Royal-les-Champs, which moved to Paris in 1626, but in 1630 was replaced as Abbess by her sister Agnes, although she continued to be influential and was instrumental in introducing Saint-Cyran as the convent's spiritual director. Under him the community became an enthusiastic upholder of Jansenist principles and practice; for example, Angélique would abstain from Communion for long periods. She was reappointed Abbess (1642–55) and was involved in the protest against Pope Innocent X's attack on Jansenism.

M.L. Trouncer: *The Reluctant Abbess* (1957)

**Arnould, (Magdeleine) Sophie** (1740–1802). French soprano. She studied singing with Marie Fel and made her debut at the Paris Opéra in 1757, becoming its leading soprano for over 20 years. She attracted particular attention in Rameau's *Castor et Pollux* and at the première of Monsigny's *Aline, reine de Golconde* (1766), in the title role, though her greatest triumph was the creation of Gluck's *Iphigénie en Aulide* (1774); she was less successful as Euridice in his *Orphée*. She was also an accomplished actress, trained by Hippolyte Clairon and much praised by Garrick. Her conversational powers and witty *bons mots* made her a lively figure in the salons of 18th-century Paris, though equally brought her considerable notoriety. A liaison with the Count of Lauragais, by whom she had three children, caused further scandal and probably contributed to the decline of her career. An edition of her memoirs was published in 1837, followed by a biography by E. and J. de Goncourt incorporating these with her correspondence (1857). Her colourful personality also inspired several stage works, including Gabriel Pierné's opera *Sophie Arnould* (1927).

**Artemisia of Halicarnassus** (5th century BC). Greek; the first woman sea-captain, mentioned by Herodotus. After the death of her husband she assumed command of his small fleet of five ships, taking part as an ally of Xerxes in his second war against the Greeks. She displayed great courage, skill and versatility – qualities which saved her life during the sea battle of Marathon. She even rescued the body of Xerxes's admiral brother from among the Greek ships. The Athenians promised a great sum of money to anyone who would capture her alive. She died tragically, throwing herself from a high cliff because of her unrequited passion for a younger man.

**Arwā** [Sayyidah] (1052–1137). Yemeni queen. A member of the Sulaihīd Dynasty in southern Arabia, she grew up at court in the care of Queen ASMĀ after her father's death and married the prince Al-Mukarram in 1065; they had four children. When Al-Mukarram became Sultan he virtually handed over power to his wife. An able ruler, she suppressed the constant tribal disputes of the country, revenged the murder of her father-in-law 'Alī al-Sulaihī, and then devoted herself to building up agriculture and trade, lowering prices and supervising tax collection. Her husband died in 1091, and Arwā's position was threatened, but after severe fighting she agreed to marry his successor Sabā, although they did not live together. She continued to rule, and her court was a centre of education and scholarship. She died in Jiblah, the new capital she had developed in the fertile plains replacing the old military stronghold of San'a, and her death heralded the end of Sulaihīd power in the region.

**Arzner, Dorothy** (1900–79). American film director. Her first contacts with film personalities were made in her father's Hollywood restaurant. After giving up her studies to become a doctor at the University of Southern California, she began typing scripts, then cutting, becoming Chief Editor in a Paramount subsidiary. After cutting 52 films, she edited Rudolph Valentino's *Blood and Sand* (1922) in which she also filmed part of the bullfight sequences. She then edited four films for James Cruze. Her first directing assignment was a chic melodrama, *Fashions for Women*, a star vehicle for Esther Ralston. Other silent films included *Get Your Man* with CLARA BOW. The first woman director of sound films, she was the only one working in Hollywood throughout the 1930s. Her 14 sound films include *Merrily we go to Hell* (1932), *Christopher Strong* (1933), with KATHERINE HEPBURN, *Nana* (1934), and *Dance Girl Dance* (1940). Her last film was made in 1943 for Columbia. She left the industry after a serious attack of pneumonia, and subsequently started the first film-making course at Pasadena Playhouse with very limited resources, taught film at UCLA for four years in the 1960s, and made over 50 television commercials for Pepsi Cola with Joan Crawford. Her work has recently received new acclaim within feminist film theory.

C. Johnston: *The Work of Dorothy Arzner – Towards a Feminist Cinema* (1975)

**Ashby, Margery Corbett** (1882–1981). English feminist. She was born into a wealthy progressive family. Her father was Liberal MP for East Grinstead, Sussex. Margery supported her mother in her work for women's suffrage and within the Liberal Party; as a girl she canvassed and made her first political speech at the age of 16. Educated by French and German governesses, she became a skilled linguist, later learning Italian and Turkish and acting as translator at international conferences. From 1900 to 1902 she read Classics at Newnham, Cambridge, and in 1904 accompanied her mother to the first International Suffrage Congress in Berlin. In 1907 she became Organizing Secretary of the National Union of Women's Suffrage Societies. She continued her feminist work after her marriage to the barrister Arthur Ashby in 1910. She represented the International Alliance of Women in the deputation to the Peace Conference at Versailles and the International Labour Organization and helped to secure equality of the sexes in their constitutions.

She became Secretary of the Alliance in 1920 and President in 1923, and lectured and campaigned in many countries. In the 1930s she was a British delegate to the disarmament conference in Geneva, which she found a deeply frustrating experience. After World War II and 42 years' involvement, she resigned from her post in the Alliance but continued to travel and to lecture as a pacifist and a feminist, as far away as India, Sri Lanka and Iran, until she was 80, and remained interested in the activities of the Alliance to the end of her life.

**Ashcroft,** Dame **Peggy** [Edith Margaret Emily] (1907–). English actress. Trained at the Central School of Drama, London, she made her debut at Birmingham Repertory Theatre in 1926. In 1930 she played Desdemona to Paul Robeson's Othello, and has played most of the great classical roles, being widely regarded as the finest Juliet of the century (1932 and 1935). In 1932 she played her first season at the Old Vic, and also starred in Komisarjevsky's production of *Fräulein Else* (1933) and *The Seagull* (1936). Later famous interpretations include Beatrice in *Much Ado About Nothing* (1950),

*Cleopatra* (1953) and Hedda in *Hedda Gabler* (1954), in which role she toured Norway, receiving the King's medal. In 1957 her performance in *The Hungarian*, about the moral dilemmas of the Russian invasion of 1956, typified the way she has stood up to her beliefs, sometimes at a cost to her career. Her Duchess of Malfi has been presented twice, once for Sir John Gielgud (1944–5) and once for the Royal Shakespeare Company (1960). She also gave a definitive performance of Margaret in the Shakespearian adaptation, *The Wars of the Roses*. In 1981 she triumphed with the Royal Shakespeare Company, in *All's Well That Ends Well*. Her potential for contemporary roles has often been underestimated, for example in Samuel Beckett's *Happy Days* (1975).

Peggy Ashcroft has made several films and won an Oscar for *A Passage to India* (1984), and has recently given outstanding performances in television drama, in *Caught on a Train* (1980), *The Jewel in the Crown* (1984) and *A Perfect Spy* (1987). She has been married three times: to Rupert Hart-Davis (in 1929); the Russian theatre director Theodore Komisarjevsky (in 1934) and to Jeremy Hutchinson (now Lord Hutchinson) in 1940, with whom she had a son and a daughter. In 1962 a theatre was named after her in Croydon, and she was created DBE in 1956.

**Ashford, 'Daisy' (Margaret Mary Julia)** (1881–1972). British writer. The famous child author Daisy Ashford was born in Petersham, Surrey, daughter of a retired War Office official. She was educated at home by a governess, and for one year (at 17) at the Priory Convent School, Haywards Heath. As a small child Daisy dictated stories to her parents, and at the age of nine, after the family moved to Southdown House, Lewes, she wrote her splendidly comic story of social life as seen by a child, *The Young Visiters, or Mr. Salteena's Plan*. She also wrote a play and other stories before she went to school.

As a young woman Daisy worked as a secretary. Sorting through papers after her mother's death, she unearthed *The Young Visiters*, which found its way to Frank Swinnerton, reader at Chatto & Windus, and was published with a preface by J.M. Barrie in 1919. It has been a great success ever since, enjoyed for its erratic spelling as much as its acute pinpointing of snobbery and pretension. In 1920 she modestly described her surprise at its reception in the preface to *Daisy Ashford: Her Book*, which contained her other childhood writings. In the same year she married James Devlin: they had four children, farmed in Norfolk and ran a hotel before settling down at Hellsdon, Norwich, in 1939. James died in 1956, but Daisy lived to see her work popular with yet another generation.

E.M. Malcomson: *Daisy Ashford: Her Life* (1984)

**Ashley, Laura** (1925–85). British designer and businesswoman. Born Laura Mountney in Dowlais, Glamorgan, South Wales, she was the daughter of a civil servant and was brought up as a strict Baptist. She was educated in London but was evacuated back to Wales at the start of the war and after finishing her schooling trained as a secretary; she worked for the War Office and the WRNS and then for the National Federation of Women's Institutes. In 1949 she married Bernard Ashley and in 1953, as a young housewife, during her first pregnancy, began printing fabric with a silkscreen put together by Bernard on the kitchen table of their Pimlico flat. Twenty scarves were sold to the John Lewis store and more were immediately ordered; soon Bernard Ashley left his City job to set up a business based on her design talent. Their first venture was the production of smocks and aprons, but by 1961 Laura was designing dresses, blouses and other clothes, and in 1967 they opened their first shop in Kensington. Laura Ashley collected designs and fabric patterns, particularly from the 18th and 19th centuries, from museums around the world, and her high-necked blouses, flowing skirts and floral patterns, using strong traditional materials, soon became an international vogue.

The Ashleys took over a disused railway station at Carno in Wales in 1963 as their base, and during the 1970s and 1980s opened many shops in Britain, Europe and America. The business expanded to furnishing fabrics and wallpapers and by the time of her death they owned eleven factories and 225 shops, employing over 4000 staff. Her son David developed the North American business and her son Nicholas designed dresses, while her daughter Jane contributed a contemporary collection. Laura herself dressed in Edwardian style and although they lived abroad, in a Picardy chateau and a Brussels town house, she maintained her insistence on simplicity of life-style. Called the 'Earth Mother of the Alternative Society', Laura Ashley died of her injuries a week after falling down stairs at her house, in 1985.

**Ashton-Warner, Sylvia** (1905–84). New Zealand teacher and novelist. Born in Stratford, New Zealand, she trained as a teacher in Auckland. She then married, and taught with her husband in Maori schools. Her extraordinarily powerful first novel, *Spinster* (1958), was about the teacher of a Maori infant class, a strong, frustrated passionate woman, driven to drink and to the edge of breakdown. Her other novels include *Incense to Idols* (1960), *Bell Call* (1963), *Greenstone* (1967) and *Three* (1970).

She is also famous as a teacher who introduced experimental educational techniques based on a belief in mutual response and she described these in *Teacher* (1963), in *Spearpoint: Teacher in America* (1972), and in her autobiography.

S. Ashton-Warner: *Myself* (1967)
        : *I Passed This Way* (1980)

**Askew, Anne** (1521–46). English Protestant martyr. She was born into an old Lincolnshire family, and was highly educated, showing particular interest in theological debate. She married a local squire, Thomas Kyme, and they had two children; after a dispute over religion they separated and she came to London, possibly to obtain a divorce. She became an attendant at the court of CATHERINE PARR and was criticized for her heretical religious views, which countered the severe Act of the Six Articles. After one examination in 1545 which failed to satisfy her accusers, she was arraigned again in June 1546, and tortured on the rack. On 16 July, so weak that she had to be carried in a chair, she was burnt at the stake at Smithfield. She showed extraordinary fortitude and calm throughout her ordeal, and was reverenced by Protestants as a martyr.

**Asmā** (*c*1028–84). Yemeni queen. A highly-cultured southern Arabian princess, she married 'Alī al-Sulaihī, her cousin, a lawyer and founder of the Sulaihīd Dynasty. He established the power of the Fatimid Caliphs in the Yemen, and also influenced the dominance of their Shī'ite doctrines in Mecca. Asmā herself was a famous patron of poetry and music. After a long period of rule, in 1080 'Ali al-Sulaihī was murdered on a pilgrimage to Mecca, and Asmā was taken prisoner. Two years later she was rescued by her son Al-Mukarram and ruled until her death, when her daughter-in-law ARWĀ took over control.

**Aspasia of Miletos** (5th century BC). Greek courtesan of striking beauty and intelligence. As a foreigner in Athens, she was not bound by the same laws and customs which confined Athenian women to their households. Her house was a place where philosophers, artists and politicians talked freely, thus giving her the chance to educate herself to a high degree by participating in conversations about philosophy, rhetoric, poetry and art. Socrates enjoyed talking with her and Plato mentions her as his teacher in the theory of love.

Pericles, the all-powerful ruler of Athens, fell deeply in love with Aspasia and married her. They were devoted to each other and Aspasia proved herself a worthy partner, both in his political ambitions to establish democracy in Athens and in his aspirations to adorn Athens with the greatest works of art and seal his own times as the golden age of literature. She inspired him in his great speeches and encouraged him in his struggle against the power of the aristocracy and the Areios Pagos ('High Court'), thereby bringing upon herself the hatred of his political enemies. They accused her in court of atheism and of procuring, but Pericles, in tears, defended her and she was acquitted.

Aspasia is also said to have influenced the social education of Athenian women; many men brought their wives to her to be taught how to run a happy household.

**Asquith** [née Tennant], **Margot** [Margaret] **(Emma Alice)** (1864–1945). Scottish political personality. The 11th child of Sir Charles Tennant, she was born in Peebleshire, Scotland, and educated by governesses until the age of 15 when she spent a few months at a London finishing school, and then in Dresden. She became a fashionable debutante and fearless huntswoman, and

was also a member of The Souls, a group of intellectuals and aesthetes who advocated greater freedom for women, particularly in self-expression and dress. Her wide circle of friends included Benjamin Jowett, Vice-Chancellor of Oxford, and William Gladstone, as well as writers such as John Addington Symonds and Alfred, Lord Tennyson.

In 1894 she became the second wife of Herbert Asquith, then the Liberal Home Secretary. She was a brilliant and devastatingly witty political hostess, and it became a mark of success to be included in the 'Margot set'. She exercised considerable influence but her flamboyance, passionate loyalties, love of intrigue and cruel tongue often aroused hostility. Asquith became Chancellor of the Exchequer in 1906 and was Prime Minister from 1908 to 1916, when he was forced to resign because of dissatisfaction with the nation's war record. He remained Liberal leader until 1926 and died in 1928. The Asquiths had seven children, but only two survived infancy.

After World War I Margot began to write, producing two volumes of autobiography, a travel book, *Places and Persons* (1925), essays entitled *Lay Sermons* (1927), an autobiographical novel, *Octavia* (1928), and two further books of reminiscences.

M. Asquith: *Autobiography* (1920–22)
———: *More Memories* (1933)
———: *Off the Record* (1943)
D. Bennett: *Margot: A Life of the Countess of Oxford and Asquith* (1984)

**Astell, Mary** (1668–1731). English polemicist. The daughter of a merchant in Newcastle-upon-Tyne and educated by a clergyman uncle, at the age of 22 she moved to London. In 1694 she published anonymously her *Serious Proposal to the Ladies for the Advancement of their Time and Greatest Interest*. The first demand for higher education for women, it proposed the foundation of an academic community, resembling a seminary, and in Part II (1697) Astell laid out detailed plans for study. The project was nearly put into effect but was countered by opposition from Bishop Burnet and by ridicule in journals such as *The Tatler*. Although disappointed, she continued to argue that women's apparent inferiority was a matter of education, not nature, and that education was also a necessary defence against mercenary marriages. Although advanced, her views were limited by sectarian and class prejudices. Her other writings are effective contributions to current philosophical and theological debates, the most notable being *The Christian Religion, as professed by a Daughter of the Church of England, 1705*.

R. Perry: *The Celebrated Mary Astell* (1986)

**Astor, Nancy (Witcher Langhorne)** [Lady Astor] (1879–1964). American-English politician. Born in Danville, Virginia, the daughter of a Confederate officer who became a tobacco auctioneer, her early years of poverty were followed by an adolescence surrounded by wealth. One of five beautiful sisters, she married Robert Gould Shaw II, a Bostonian, in 1897 and had one son. After her divorce in 1903 she visited England and in 1906 married Waldorf Astor, the son of an American millionaire who had been made a British peer. She became known as a society hostess at Cliveden, but they moved to Plymouth in 1910 when Waldorf was elected as a Tory MP. Nancy worked hard in the constituency, although she eventually had five children, and in 1919 after Waldorf's succession as Viscount, she was elected in his place. Her campaign, conducted in flamboyant style, attracted international attention and she entered the house as the first woman MP to take her place, with a 5000 majority (*see* CONSTANCE MARKIEWICZ).

The only woman MP from 1919 to 1921, her opening speech demanded stricter controls on drink, and she also spoke on issues affecting the family, women and children. She took an individual approach to policies, saying 'If you want a party hack, don't elect me'. Her stern moral stance and religious intolerance reflected her conversion to Christian Science in 1914. In 1931 she visited the USSR with George Bernard Shaw, but although she deeply disliked Communism she spoke out against later McCarthyite witch-hunts; similarly, although she supported appeasement in the 1930s she was not pro-Nazi, and vehemently attacked German policy in 1939. During the Blitz she won much affection by her continued visits to Plymouth, but by 1945 Labour opposition to her had grown and

Waldorf persuaded her to retire, a decision she took with some bitterness. She then withdrew from public life, particularly after Waldorf's death in 1952.

A. Masters: *Nancy Astor: a Life* (1981)

**Astorga, Nora** (1949–88). Nicaraguan revolutionary and diplomat. Educated at the Catholic University of Washington, Nora Astorga worked as a corporation lawyer with a leading Nicaraguan construction company before her brief but astonishing diplomatic career. She was married and divorced, with two children by her first husband and two by another union. The myths surrounding her are typified by the incident in 1978 (on 8 March, 'Women's Day') when the notorious General Perez Vegas of the Nicaraguan National Guard was murdered by the Sandinistas, having been lured to her bedroom. The CIA managed to block her appointment as ambassador to Washington, but in 1986 she became the Nicaraguan ambassador to the United Nations in New York, where she was known both for her fierce, logical argument and her highly feminine style – sending red roses with her diplomatic notes. She died at the age of 38, after a gruelling battle against cancer.

**Athaliah** (*d* 837). Queen of Judah. She was the daughter of Jehoram and Jezebel, and after the death of her son King Ahaziah she seized power, ruling alone for six years, the only recorded Queen of Judah. She is said to have massacred all the male members of the royal house except for a baby son of Ahaziah, Jehoash, who was concealed by her stepdaughter Jehosheba. Some years later Jehosheba and her husband, the priest Jehoiada, organized a successful coup to place Jehoash on the throne, during which Athaliah was killed. Her story is told in the Old Testament in II Kings, and II Chronicles, and forms the basis for Racine's *Athalie* (1691).

**Atwell, Mabel Lucie** (1879–1964). English children's book illustrator. Born and educated in London, she attended classes at Regent Street and Heatherley art schools, and began her career selling sketches to magazines such as *The Tatler*. Around 1900 she started illustrating books and some of her best work was carried out for Tuck's Raphael House Library of Gift Books, including *Mother Goose* (1908), *Alice in Wonderland* (1910) and the fairy stories of Andersen (1913) and Grimm (1925). In 1908 she married the artist Harold Earnshaw and after he was wounded in World War I she became the chief supporter of their three children. Highly professional, prolific and popular, her images of childhood and pictures of curly-haired infants dominated the 1920s and the *Lucie Atwell Annual*, started in 1922, endured, edited by her daughter, until ten years after her death.

**Atwood, Margaret (Eleanor)** (1939–). Canadian novelist and poet. Born in Ottawa, but brought up chiefly in the wilderness country of northern Ontario and Quebec (where her entomologist father ran forest stations), she graduated from the University of Toronto and then took an MA from Radcliffe College. She has lived and worked in Canada, Italy, England and the USA doing a variety of jobs, from being a waitress to lecturing in English at the University of British Columbia, Vancouver (1964–5), and at the Sir George William University, Montreal (1967–8). Atwood has written since she was a child and first made an international reputation as a poet. *The Circle Game* (1966) won the Governor-General's Award, and she has since published seven more collections including *Power Politics* (1971) and *You are Happy* (1974). Her short stories and articles have appeared in leading reviews, and in 1972 she published *Survival: a Thematic Guide to Canadian Literature*, which caused a lively critical debate. Atwood is now best known for her novels, which range from wild comedy to moving studies of breakdown and combine her major concerns for the environment, the rejection of mechanistic capitalism, the protection of Canadian culture from absorption by the USA and the need for women to assert their individual identities. Her novels include *The Edible Woman* (1969), *Surfacing* (1972), *Lady Oracle* (1976), *Life before Man* (1979), *Bodily Harm* (1981), *Unearthing Suite* (1983) and *The Handmaid's Tale* (1985), and her short stories are collected in *Bluebeard's Egg and other stories* (1986).

B. Rigney: *Margaret Atwood* (1987)

**Auclert, (Marie-Anne) Hubertine** (1848–1914). French feminist. Of middle-class origins, Auclert was a socialist who joined Leon Richter and MARIA DERAISMES in running the movement L'Avenir des Femmes in the 1870s. In 1878 she founded her own group, Droit de la Femme, which was renamed the Société de Suffrage des Femmes in 1883, demanding first the vote, then equal access to the professions, equal pay, civil rights and easier divorce. She spoke on her ideas at the socialist congress in Marseilles in 1878 and published works such as *Le Droit politique des femmes* (1878) and *L'égalité sociale et politique* (1879). She adopted unusually advanced protest tactics, such as street demonstrations, a shadow election of 1885, lobbies of deputies and withholding of taxes. In 1883 she attended a meeting in Liverpool which laid the foundations for an international movement; the participants included ELIZABETH CADY STANTON and SUSAN B. ANTHONY. Between 1881 and 1892 she edited the leftist journal *La citoyenne*, and contributed to other newspapers such as *Le radical*, *La libre parole* and *La fronde*. However, her campaign was weakened by bitter disputes with the moderates, such as Deraismes, and she was ousted from an effective role in the movement after she married Anotonin Levrier in 1888 and went to Algeria, where she lived with him until his death in 1892. She had quarrelled with her assistant Maria Martin, who closed *La citoyenne* and began her own paper.

After the 1890s she did little except write – her books included *Les femmes arabes en Algérie* (1900), *La vote des femmes* (1908) and *Les femmes au gouvernal* (1923). By the time she died she was embittered and isolated.

**Auerbach, Charlotte** (1899–). Scottish geneticist of German birth. Charlotte was born in Krefeld to a Jewish family with two generations of scientists on her father's side. In 1933 Nazism obliged her to leave Germany and she joined the Institute of Animal Genetics in Edinburgh where she obtained her PhD and was based throughout her career.

Charlotte was introduced to mutation research by H.J. Müller, and was the first to discover the deadly weapon of chemical warfare, mustard gas. She considered her most important work, however, to be the study in depth of mutagenesis as a biological process. She used the fruit-fly *Drosophila* and the fungus *Neurospora* to analyse the selective action of certain mutagens on certain genes.

*Mutation Methods* (1962) and *Mutation Research* (1976) were her main published works, but she was also interested in popularizing science, as in *Genetics in the Atomic Age* (1956, 1965) and *The Science of Genetics* (1962, 1969). In 1947 the University of Edinburgh awarded her a DSc and in 1967 a personal Chair. She also received several honorary degrees and awards, including medals from the Royal Society of Edinburgh and the Royal Society of London.

**Augspurg, Anita** (1857–1943). German feminist. She trained as a teacher, although she never practised as one, but went on the stage after the death of her parents, who had opposed a dramatic career. She then became a photographer and, driven by her concern for women's rights, took up the study of law. As the universities were still closed to women she went to Zürich where she met many radicals and political exiles, and also became involved with the European movement for the abolition of regulated prostitution.

In 1895, with MARIE STRITT and MINNA CAUER, she rose to the leadership of the Bund Deutscher Frauenvereine (Federation of German Women's Associations) and led a radical campaign against the new Civil Code's provision for women, holding huge public meetings in Berlin. By 1898 she had split from the moderate feminists and joined the Verband fortschrittlicher Frauenvereine (Union of Progressive Women's Associations), and in 1902, with Cauer, LIDA HEYMANN, Stritt and others, founded the Deutscher Verband für Frauenstimmrecht (German Union for Women's Suffrage) and became its first president. She accelerated the campaign for the vote, lobbied parliament deputies and wrote numerous pamphlets. In 1904 she was a founder and Vice-President of the International Woman Suffrage Alliance.

She achieved national fame as a militant suffragette after the Liberal bloc combined with the Conservatives in 1907. She moved with Heymann from Hamburg to Munich and organized new campaigns inspired by British militant tactics, abandoning the old suffrage union altogether in 1913 and forming yet another new organization, the Deutscher Frauenstimmrechtsbund (German Women's Suffrage League). As pacifists, during World War I their activities were suppressed, their propaganda censored and they lost most of their supporters. They continued to campaign for civil rights after suffrage had been granted, but represented a tiny radical faction whose ideals were embodied in journals such as *Die Frau im Staat*, and in the Women's League for Peace and Freedom and Bund für Mutterschutz and Sexualreform (League for the Protection of Motherhood and Sexual Reform). When the Nazis seized power, Augspurg and Heymann were on holiday in Italy; unable to return to Bavaria with Hitler in power, they emigrated to Switzerland in 1933 and lived with other German exiles in Zürich. Together they compiled their memoirs, *Erlebtes-Erschautes*, which were not published until 1972.

**Aulenti, Gae(tana)** (1927– ). Italian architect. Born in Udine province, she graduated from the Polytechnic Institute of Milan, Faculty of Architecture, in 1954, and has remained in Milan in private practice, while also holding visiting professorships in Venice (1960–62), Milan (1964), Barcelona, and Stockholm (1969–75). She was on the editorial staff of *Casabella* (1954–62), and a member of the Studies for Architecture movement (1955–61). She made her name with her inspired designs for the Olivetti showrooms in Paris and Buenos Aires in 1969, and during the 1970s her designs aroused great interest in Europe and the USA; they are related to her view that we must care about whole environments, such as cities, rather than individual 'units', if we are to have harmony between individual and collective life. As well as designing houses, schools and for industry, she has worked recently with theatre and stage design. In the 1980s she was responsible for transforming the Gare d'Orsay into a museum, the largest job of her career, involving thousands of drawings during six years of discussion.

**Auriol, Jacqueline (Marie-Thérèse Suzanne Douet)** (1917–). French aviator. Born in Challons, the daughter of a timber importer, in 1938 she married Paul Auriol (son of the future President of France); they had two children and were later divorced. At the age of 30 she took up flying out of curiosity, qualified as a tourist pilot in 1948 and started stunt flying. The following year she was severely injured when a seaplane in which she was a passenger crashed into the Seine, but after numerous operations she returned to flying and by 1950 had gained her licence as a military pilot. She then qualified at Brétigny as the world's first woman test pilot.

Her next interest was flying in jets, which involved quite different techniques, and in 1951, in one of the first Vampires, she broke JACQUELINE COCHRAN's speed record, by achieving 507 miles per hour. She was awarded the Légion d'Honneur and the American Harmon Trophy. In 1953 she was among the first to break the sound barrier, and ultimately held the women's world speed record five times between 1951 and 1964. Later she was one of the first to fly the supersonic Concorde.

Her more recent work was with the Ministère de la Coopération, using new remote sensing techniques to assist agricultural development, for example mapping crop species or locating water for irrigation. For this she was awarded the Ceres Medal of the United Nations Food and Agriculture Organization.

J. Auriol: *I Live to Fly* (1970)

**Austen, Jane** (1775–1817). English novelist. Jane Austen was born in Steventon, Hampshire, where her father was Rector, the youngest of seven children. She was educated both privately and at schools in Oxford, Southampton and Reading, learning languages, needlework and music, and also reading widely in classic and contemporary literature and history. In 1801 she moved with her family to Bath, visited Lyme in 1804, and after her father's death in 1805, moved with her mother and sister to Southampton. From 1809 until her last illness she lived with her brother at Chawton, Hampshire. She died in Winchester and is buried there.

Jane Austen began to write during her childhood, and completed her first full-length novel, *Pride and Prejudice*, between October 1796 and August 1797, at the age of 21. That autumn she began, but did not complete, *Sense and Sensibility*, based on an earlier rough work *Eleanor and Marianne*, and she wrote *Northanger Abbey*, her pastiche of the gothic romance, in 1798. It was apparently sold (as *Susan*) to a Bath publisher in 1803 for £10, but none of her work actually appeared in print until several years later. Then Egerton published *Sense and Sensibility* (1811), *Pride and Prejudice* (1813) and *Mansfield Park* (1814). Murray brought out *Emma* in 1816 and *Northanger Abbey* (which her brother Henry had bought back for £10) and *Persuasion*, posthumously in 1817. Between January and March 1817, when she became seriously ill, she was working on an untitled, unfinished novel, which we know as *Sanditon*.

In her lifetime her work appeared anonymously, and although it was reviewed in the *Quarterly* and she was invited to Carlton House by the Prince Regent, she received little fame and very little money. She was apparently delighted when *Sense and Sensibility* made a 'clean profit' of £150. Her gift of characterization, comic irony and acute rendering of contemporary values and enduring moral dilemmas have won her recognition as one of the finest English novelists.

J. Halperin: *The Life of Jane Austen* (1984)
D. Cecil: *Portrait of Jane Austen* (1978)

**Aveling, Eleanor.** See MARX-AVELING.

**Ayer, Harriet Hubbard** (1849–1903). American businesswoman and journalist. Born and educated in Chicago, she spent an unhappy childhood with her semi-invalid mother after her father's death in 1857. At the age of 16 she married Herbert Crawford Ayer. They had three children, the second of whom died as a baby in the Chicago Fire in 1871. Between 1866 and 1882 Harriet lived as a wealthy society matron, cultivating an intense interest in the arts which gradually led to an estrangement from her husband. They separated in 1882 when she moved to New York, and were divorced in 1886.

In 1883 Herbert Ayer's business failed, and to support herself Harriet worked as a

Jane Addams

Elizabeth Garrett Anderson

Sofonisba Anguissola

Jane Austen

saleswoman in prestigious furniture shops. In 1886 she began to manufacture and sell a facial cream, which she claimed to have discovered in Paris and which she publicized widely (and very successfully) as having been used by Madame RECAMIER. She was the first of many women to make a fortune from the cosmetics industry, but she lost everything due to a feud with one of her sponsors, the father-in-law of her daughter Harriet. He initiated litigation, claiming she was too unstable to manage the business, and eventually had her placed in a New York lunatic asylum in 1893. Although her lawyer obtained her release 14 months later, her business career was over.

Her final role was as a journalist, writing a beauty advice column for the *New York World* from 1896 until her death. Her daughter Margaret succeeded her. She published her best-selling book, *Harriet Hubbard Ayer's Book: a Complete and Authentic Treatise on the Laws of Health and Beauty*, in 1899.

M.H. Ayer: *The Three Lives of Harriet Hubbard Ayer* (1957)

**Aylward, Gladys** (1903–70). English-Chinese missionary. Born in Edmonton, London, Gladys worked as a parlourmaid when she left school at 14, but she was determined to become a missionary. After saving hard, in 1930 she bought a railway ticket to the North China port of Tientsin. Once there it was arranged for her to join an elderly Scots missionary, Miss Dawson, at her lone outpost at Yangzheng in southern Shanxi. Together they established 'The Inn of the Sixth Happiness' so that they could first attract local travellers and then teach them the gospel. Gladys succeeded in mastering the local dialect and winning the respect of the local Chinese. She made friends with the Mandarin and was appointed the area's official foot inspector, to enforce the new law prohibiting the ancient and crippling custom of female foot-binding. In 1931 Gladys became a Chinese citizen. War with the Japanese reached Yangzheng in 1938. The province of Shanxi was overrun and Gladys led 100 children on a long mountain march out of the occupied territory. Over the next few years she joined the Nationalists, fleeing from village to village and caring for the wounded. Gladys came back to England in 1948 to preach and lecture but returned to Taiwan in 1953 to work with refugees and orphans.

Known as 'The Small Woman' (she was 5ft tall), Gladys Aylward was made famous by the film *The Inn of the Sixth Happiness*, starring INGRID BERGMAN, which was based on her life in China.

A. Burgess: *The Small Woman* (1957)
G. Aylward and C. Hunter: *Gladys Aylward* (1970)

**Ayrton** [née Marks], **(Sarah) Hertha** (1854–1923). British physicist. She was born in Portsmouth, one of five children in a Jewish family. She read mathematics at Girton College and while there changed her name to Hertha. In 1885 she married W.E. Ayrton, whose first wife had been Mathilda Chaplin, a pioneer doctor; they had one child.

Hertha first invented a sphygmograph, but the work for which she is noted is on the motion of waves and formation of sand ripples, and the behaviour of the electric arc. In 1898 she was elected to the Institution of Electrical Engineers and was their only woman member. In 1902 she was nominated for fellowship of the Royal Society, but the council found 'it had no legal power to elect a married woman to this distinction'. In 1906 she won the Hughes Medal, the first medal ever awarded to a woman by the Royal Society. From 1905 to 1910 she worked for the War Office and Admiralty on standardizing the types and sizes of carbons for searchlights, and in World War I she invented the Ayrton Fan for dispersing poisonous gases. In 1920 she became a founder member of the National Union of Scientific Workers.

When MARIE CURIE visited England they formed a friendship. As a suffragette Hertha sheltered those who suffered under the 'Cat and Mouse Act' by alternate force-feeding in prison and release, followed by recapture as punishment for their militant feminist activities.

E. Sharp: *Hertha Ayrton: a Memoir* (1926)

# B

**Bâ, Mariama** (1929–81). Senegalese writer. Born in Senegal and brought up by her maternal grandparents, she attended a French primary school and then the Ecole Normale at Rufisque. After she married (although she had nine children before she divorced), she taught in a primary school, wrote journalism and worked with local women's organizations. She published her first novel at the age of 51. Translated as *So Long a Letter*, it won the French Noma award in 1980; she then completed a second novel, *Un chant écarlate*. Both novels deal with the problems of married women in Senegal, the first within Muslim polygamous marriage, the second in a mixed marriage, and with the conflict between tradition and self-fulfilment.

**Baarova, Lida** (1910–). Czech film actress. Born in Prague, Lida Baarova became one of the most important stars of the Czech avant-garde cinema after she made her first film, *The Career of Pavel Camrda*, at the age of 21. In 1934 she was signed up by the German UFA company, starring in roles such as Giacinta in *Barcarolle*. She continued to act in both Czech and German films, such as Vavra's *Virginia* and Krska's *A Fiery Summer*, but her career was threatened by her affair with Goebbels, the Nazi propaganda chief. In 1938 Hitler refused Goebbels permission to divorce his wife and marry Baarova: her films were banned and she was stopped from leaving Germany. She escaped to Prague, where she worked for an anti-Nazi spy ring, but after being expelled from Czechoslovakia in 1941 she went to Italy, where she made four films before being sent back to Prague by the Gestapo in 1945. She escaped again, but was then captured by US military intelligence, and spent two years in gaol.

In the 1950s she returned to her career, acting in major Italian and Spanish films such as Fellini's *I Vitelloni*, but in 1958 she moved to Salzburg, Austria, to work on stage throughout the 1960s. Before her retirement she appeared in Fassbinder's *The Bitter Tears of Petra von Kant* in 1970.

**Babanova, Maria Ivanovna** (1900–). Russian actress. She worked initially under Theodore Komisarjevsky until, in 1920, she was engaged by Meyerhold for his Theatre Workshop where she subsequently played leading roles. In 1922 she played Pauline in Ostrovsky's *Place of Profit* for the Theatre of the Revolution. While continuing to work in the Meyerhold Theatre she had her first experience of a Moscow Art Theatre director, A. Dikie, in Faiko's *The Man with the Portfolio*, again at the Theatre of the Revolution, where she subsequently became the leading actress. One of her most notable performances was that of Juliet in Popov's production of *Romeo and Juliet*. She received the Stalin Prize in 1941 for her performance as the heroine of *Tanya* by Arbuzov.

**Bacall, Lauren** [pseud. of Betty Joan Perske] (1924–). American actress. Born in New York City, she was brought up by her mother, and studied dancing for 13 years. After a term of training at the American Academy of Dramatic Arts, she was 'discovered' in 1943 by Howard Hawks's wife, who spotted her on the cover of *Harper's Bazaar*. Hawks tested her and offered her a seven-year contract. Her first film was *To Have and Have Not* (1944), in which she played opposite Humphrey Bogart. They married in 1945 and worked on some fine films together: *The Big Sleep* (1946), *Dark Passage* (1947), and *Key Largo* (1948). They were devoted to each other until Bogart's death in 1957, although Bacall has at times felt restricted by her identification with him. From 1961 to 1969 she was married to Jason Robards, Jr. She has three children.

Her screen personality was strong, cynical and independent, seen to advantage in the early films, and *How to Marry a Millionaire* (1952) with MARILYN MONROE and Betty Grable. Her career declined during the 1950s and 1960s until her return to the stage in *Cactus Flower* (1967), and *Applause* (1970) for which she won the Tony Award. In recent years she has continued to act in the theatre, for example in *Sweet Bird of Youth* (1985). She returned to the screen in *Murder on the Orient Express* (1974), *The Shootist* (1976), *Health* (1979), and *The Fan* (1981).

L. Bacall: *Lauren Bacall by Myself* (1978)
L. Quirk: *Lauren Bacall: Her Films and Career* (1986)

**Bacewicz, Grażyna** (1909–69). Polish composer and violinist. She studied in Łódź and Warsaw and was later a pupil of NADIA BOULANGER in Paris; she had violin lessons from Flesch and was also an accomplished pianist. During her early career she was acclaimed both as a performer and composer, being a prizewinner at the first Wieniawski Competition (1935) and touring widely in Europe in concerts of her own works. In the 1950s she decided to devote herself to composition, and her works received many awards, notably first prize in the International Composers' Competition for her Fourth String Quartet (1951) and the orchestral award at the International Rostrum of Composers for *Muzyka* (1958). She taught at the Łódź Conservatory (1934–5, 1945–6) and the Warsaw Academy (1966–9). Her music, mostly in a neo-classical idiom, includes three ballets, four symphonies, seven violin concertos, two cello concertos, seven string quartets and many violin pieces. She also wrote several novels and short stories, of which *Znak szczególny* ('Outstanding feature') was published in 1970; her television play *Jerzyki albo nie jestem ptakiem* ('Swifts, or I am not a bird') was produced in 1968.

**Bach** [née Wilcke], **Anna Magdalena** (1701–60). German musician. Her name is primarily associated with two volumes of music, popularly known as the 'Anna Magdalena Notebook', which were compiled for her instruction by her husband Johann Sebastian Bach. Dating from 1722 and 1725, they contain mostly simple keyboard pieces, though the second volume includes some songs. The daughter of Johann Caspar Wilcke, a court trumpeter, Anna Magdalena is known to have been a singer, appearing in chapel services. She married Bach in 1721, bearing him 13 children, 8 of whom died before the age of 5; she also took care of the 4 surviving children of Bach's first marriage.

**Bachmann, Ingeborg** (1926–73). Austrian writer. She grew up in a Protestant family, living in Klagenfurt after World War II. She then studied jurisprudence and philosophy at Innsbruck, Graz and Vienna, where she submitted her doctorate on Martin Heidegger in 1950. She lived in Italy between 1953 and 1957, was a visiting scholar at Harvard University in 1955 and became the first Professor of Poetics at the University of Frankfurt at the age of 33.

Her first volume of poetry, *Die gestundete Zeit* (1963), won an award from the German intellectual movement Group 47, and her second, *Anrufung des Grossen Bären*, appeared in 1956. In 1959 she was awarded the Prize of the War Blind for *Der gute Gott von Manhattan* (1958), a radio play. Her reputation as a leading innovator was confirmed by two radio plays and by her prose works: the short stories in *Das dreissigste Jahr* (1961) which won her the Berlin Critics Prize, the psychological novel *Malina* (1971) and the stories in *Simultan* (1973). She also collaborated with Hans Werner Henze on two operas, *Der Prinz von Homburg* (1960), and *Der junge Lord* (1965). Her work is concerned largely with the helplessness of women in a world of egotistic successful men. For the last ten years of her life Bachmann lived in Munich, Zürich and Rome, where she died in a fire in her home. A complete edition of her works was issued posthumously in 1978.

H. Pausch: *Ingeborg Bachmann* (1975)

**Backer-Grøndahl, Agathe (Ursula)** (1847–1907). Norwegian composer and pianist. A pupil of Kjerulf in Christiania [now Oslo], she went on to study with Kullak in Berlin

(1865–7), Bülow in Florence (1871–2) and later with Liszt in Weimar. Concert tours took her to England as well as throughout Scandinavia and Germany. However, she is chiefly remembered as a composer of songs; she wrote about 190, many of which have become a staple of the Romantic Norwegian vocal repertory. Her piano pieces, notably the sets of concert studies, give evidence of her remarkable technical skill as well as her strongly lyrical style. O.M. Sandvik's biography (1948) contains a complete catalogue of her works.

I. Hoegsbro: *Biography of the late Agathe Backer-Grøndahl* (1913)
O.M. Sandvik: *Agathe og O.A. Grøndahl* (1948)

**Baden-Powell, Olave** [Lady Baden-Powell] (1889–1977). English Girl Guide organizer. Born in Dorset, she was the daughter of an independently wealthy man whose restlessness resulted in Olave knowing 17 different homes in her childhood. In 1912 she accompanied him on a trip to the West Indies and found only one interesting person on board the cruise ship, Robert Baden-Powell 'the Scout Man'. They were married the same year and spent their honeymoon living under canvas in the Algerian desert. During World War I she began recruiting and organizing the Girl Guides in Sussex and in 1916 was made Chief Commissioner, re-titled Chief Guide in 1918. During the war years she also had three children, a son and two daughters.

During the 1920s she helped to build up the Scout and Guide organization, and in 1930 was elected Chief Guide of the World. She toured the world and was received by heads of state as well as by ordinary guide troops, and given constant press publicity because of her warm, charismatic personality. Between 1930 and 1970, when her doctor recommended that she should slow down, she flew 487,777 miles, and was called the world's most travelled woman. She was created DBE in 1932 and received numerous awards from other countries, including the Order of the White Rose from Finland and the Order of the Sun from Peru. At the time of her death the World Association of Girl Guides and Girl Scouts had 6.5 million members.

O. Baden-Powell: *Window on my Heart* (1973)

**Baez, Joan** (1941–). American folk and protest singer. Born in Staten Island, New York, she comes from a cultured middle-class family; both her grandfathers were ministers, her father was an academic physicist, and her mother taught English. Joan began singing in local choirs, and after graduating from high school in Los Angeles attended Boston University, abandoning her studies to sing in coffee houses, and in Club 47, Cambridge, Massachusetts. Her huge popularity began with her performances at the Newport Folk Festival in 1959 and 1960. In that year she recorded a traditional folk album, *Joan Baez*. After its success in the UK and the USA she began touring and produced a number of sequels including *In Concert*, vols I and II (1963–4). She became closely associated with the song 'We shall overcome', which she sang at the great civil rights marches and rallies of the early 1960s. She also introduced the unknown protest singer, Bob Dylan, at her concerts and they lived together from 1963 to 1965; her volume *Any Day Now* is composed entirely of his songs.

During the 1960s Baez became increasingly politically committed. An active pacifist, she founded the Institute for the Study of Non-Violence in Carmel Valley in 1965. Her Vietnam protests included the refusal to pay taxes, and many rallies and television appearances in the USA and Canada. She married student leader David Harris in 1968, and during his imprisonment for draft evasion in 1969 produced her *David's Album* and *One Day at a Time*. They separated in 1971. After several other protest albums, she made the highly commercial, and immediately successful *Diamonds and Rust* (1973), and began touring on a large scale, rejoining Bob Dylan in his concerts in 1975. Since then she has continued to sing in concert and to record, now for Columbia, and is one of America's most respected and famous entertainers, touring Europe and the UK regularly in the 1970s and 1980s and opening the American section of the Live Aid Concert in 1986.

Joan Baez is still a committed pacifist, has been a member of the advisory council of Amnesty International since 1974, and visited Hanoi in 1975. She was co-founder of

Humanitas, the International Human Rights Commission in 1979, and in the same year conducted a fact-finding mission in refugee camps in South-East Asia. She has also sung to Solidarnósc strikers in Poland and has worked with the mothers of the Disappeared in Argentina.

J. Baez: *Daybreak* (1968)
——— : *Coming Out* (1971)
——— : *And a Voice to Sing With* (1987)

**Bagryana, Elisaveta** (1893–). Bulgarian poet. While reading literature at Sofia University, Elisaveta began her published career with poems in *Savremenna misal* (1915). A Symbolist writer, whose poetry became increasingly emotional and topical in reference, she was a major contributor to the influential journal *Zlatorog* in the 1920s and 1930s. She published collections in 1927, 1932 and 1936, including the cycle *Seismograph of the Heart* which appeals for tenderness as opposed to mechanistic modern culture. Much of her work relates to the landscape of her homeland. She has travelled widely in Europe and Latin America, and her selected works were published in 1957.

**Bai, Lakshmi,** Rani of Jhansi (1835–57). Indian nationalist heroine. She was born in Jhansi, and after the death of her mother was brought up in a predominantly male household, learning riding and the martial arts. She married the Raja of Jhansi, an independent state over which the British took full control after the Raja's death, refusing to recognize his declared heir. During the Indian Mutiny in 1857, the 22-year-old Rani took the side of the rebellious sepoys, defending Jhansi against British attack and then fighting in defence of a neighbouring fortress. She was killed, still fighting in the midst of her troops, by a British soldier. In the independence movement of the 20th century she became a symbol of Indian patriotism.

**Bailey,** Lady **Mary** (1890–1960). English airwoman. Daughter of Lord Rossmore, she married the South African millionaire Abe Bailey in 1911. Awarded her pilot's licence in 1927, she was the first woman to fly across the Irish Sea. In 1928 when she was 38 years old, with 5 children, she made an epic solo flight from Croydon to Cape Town and back. She saw this act as a gesture of female independence and of faith in light aircraft. She also flew in many international competitions, and was awarded the Britannia Trophy and created DBE in 1930.

**Baillie, Joanna** (1762–1851). Scottish poet. Born in Lanarkshire, where her father was a Presbyterian Minister, Joanna suffered a repressed childhood before going to school in Glasgow in 1772. Her father, who had become Professor of Divinity at Glasgow University in 1776, died two years later, and she went first to her sister, then to her brother's house in London (1783) and finally moved to Hampstead (1791), where she lived with her sister after her mother's death in 1806.

Her first work, *Fugitive Verses* (1790), won the admiration of Robert Burns, but fame came with her series of ten blank-verse *Plays on the Passions*, published in three volumes between 1798 and 1812. Although intended for reading, one of these, *De Montfort*, had a successful run when produced by John Kemble and SARAH SIDDONS at Drury Lane. At first published anonymously, she soon accepted the popular acclaim and produced more verse and drama, collected in a three-volume edition in 1836. Sir Walter Scott, who was at first thought to be the author of her plays, became a lifelong friend, and she and her sister were the centre of a lively literary circle, until at the age of 89, she declared herself tired of life, went to bed, and died.

M. Carhart: *The Life and Works of Baillie* (1923)

**Bajer, Matilde** (1840–1934). Danish feminist. In 1871 she founded a feminist library and discussion group, and then organized the Danish Women's Association with her husband, Fredrik Bajer, who became an influential Member of Parliament. Largely inspired by their reading of John Stuart Mill's *Subjection of Women* (1869), they directed their campaigns towards such economic issues as financial independence for married women, and employment opportunities, opening a women's trade school in Copenhagen in 1872. During the 1880s Bajer was active in the social purity movement and the drive to abolish state-regulated prostitution, and began to believe that women could have no effective power as reformers unless they had the vote. Consequently she founded the Danish Women's Progress Association (1886), which was a precursor of the later suffrage movement. Among the Association's members were energetic social feminists such as the journalist, Caroline Testmann, Marie Rovsig, and Elizabeth Grundtvig, who edited the journal *Kvinden og Samfundet* ('Women and society'). Bajer continued to work with national and international feminist organizations until after World War I.

**Baker,** Dame •**Janet (Abbott)** (1933–). English mezzo-soprano. She has earned a reputation as one of the leading singers of the time, her achievement encompassing equally opera, oratorio and recital performances. She studied privately in England and at the Mozarteum, Salzburg. After joining the Glyndebourne Chorus, she won second prize in the Kathleen Ferrier Award in 1956, and that year made her operatic debut as Roza in Smetana's *The Secret* (Oxford University Opera Club). A noted champion of Handel, Purcell and early Italian composers, she made her debuts with both the English Opera Group and at Glyndebourne as Purcell's Dido (1962 and 1965 respectively), and at the English National Opera as Monteverdi's Poppaea. The role of her Covent Garden debut was Hermia in Britten's *A Midsummer Night's Dream* (1966); she has shown particular affinity with Britten's music, notably as Kate Julian in *Owen Wingrave*, a part written for her, and in *The Rape of Lucretia*, taken on the English Opera Group's Russian tour of 1964. She has also won acclaim for such roles as Dido in Berlioz's *Les Troyens*, Octavian in Richard Strauss's *Der Rosenkavalier* and the Composer in his *Ariadne auf Naxos*, Donizetti's Mary Stuart and Charlotte in Massenet's *Werther*. She made her farewell appearances in opera at Covent Garden in the title role of Gluck's *Alceste* (1981) and at Glyndebourne as his Orpheus (1982).

An equally wide-ranging repertory on the concert platform has included notable performances of Bach's oratorios and cantatas, Mahler's song cycles and Elgar's *Dream of Gerontius*. As a recitalist she has devoted much attention to French song as well as to German lieder and English music, including folksong.

She was created CBE in 1970 and DBE in 1976, and has received many honorary doctorates and international awards.

J. Baker: *Full Circle* (1982)

**Baker, (Sara) Josephine (i)** (1873–1945). American doctor and public-health worker. Family opposition strengthened her will to become a doctor, and she graduated from the New York Infirmary Medical College in 1898. She was appointed assistant to the Commissioner for Public Health of New York City, later heading the city's Department of Health in 'Hell's Kitchen' for 25 years.

Convinced of the value of well-baby care and the prevention of disease, in 1908 she founded the Bureau of Child Hygiene after visiting mothers on the lower east side, thus helping to decrease the death rate by 1200 from the previous year. Her work made the New York City infant mortality rate the lowest in the USA or Europe at the time. She set up free milk clinics, licensed midwives, and taught the use of silver nitrate to prevent blindness in newborns. She organized the Little Mothers' League and the first Federation of Children's Agencies in New York City, and in pursuit of her feminist interests lobbied President Wilson for the College Equal Suffrage League.

New York University did not admit women as postgraduate students, but after Josephine Baker refused a lectureship there for that reason the policy was changed.

S.J. Baker: *Fighting for Life* (1939)

**Baker, Josephine (ii)** (1906–75). American revue dancer. Born in St Louis, the daughter of a black American mother and Jewish father, she was educated in Philadelphia. She was always determined to dance, and although she was under age she persuaded a producer to give her a place in the chorus of the black revue *Shuffle Away*. She then danced at the Cotton Club in Harlem and in 1925, aged 19, appeared with the Révue Nègre at the Champs-Elysées; she remained in Paris for the rest of her life, apart from occasional trips to the USA. Her popularity was immense, with both the general public and avant-garde intellectuals; Picasso called her the modern Nefertiti and painted her portrait, and elsewhere her work was celebrated as 'très sauvage'. She starred in many revues at the Folies Bergères and the Casino de Paris during the 1930s, and also featured in films such as *La sirène des tropiques* (1927) and *Princesse Tam-Tam/ Moulin Rouge* (1935). She studied ballet with Balanchin, who choreographed dances for her, and returned to New York with the Ziegfeld Follies in 1936. Baker was witty, spontaneous and a superb stylist.

During World War II she worked for the French Resistance, and was later honoured with the Croix de Guerre, the Légion d'Honneur and the Rosette de la Résistance. After the war she campaigned for civil rights in America. Although she married 3 times, she had no children of her own but adopted 12 orphans of different races, which she called her 'Rainbow Tribe', living with them at her château at Bergerac in South West France. To support them she occasionally returned to the stage, acting in a vivid final performance at the age of 68 at the London Palladium in 1974.

L. Haney: *Naked at the Feast* (1981)

**Baker, Sarah** (1736–1816). English theatre proprietor. Daughter of an acrobatic dancer, Anne Wakelin, she married a dancer and theatre manager in her mother's company but was widowed in 1769 and left with three children to support. She turned to theatre management, taking responsibility for her mother's company (1772–7). Sarah Baker subsequently formed a new company to play a wide range of drama, including Shakespeare and Sheridan. Regular visits were made to Canterbury, Rochester, Faversham and Maidstone, as well as occasional journeys to other centres in Kent using a portable theatre. As her success increased, she had ten theatres built for her. Several famous actors appeared with her company early in their careers, including Edmund Kean and Thomas Dibdin.

**Balabanoff, Angelika** (1878–1965). Russian-Italian socialist. Born in Milan, she came from a Ukrainian family and was brought up in Russia, where as a girl she became concerned at the disparity between rich and poor. Ill-health led her parents to send her abroad and she lived in various countries,

developing contacts with socialist exiles. She studied in Brussels, Berlin, Leipzig and Rome. In Germany she met Bebel and CLARA ZETKIN, and in Switzerland befriended both Lenin and Mussolini. She then went to Italy, where she joined the executive of the socialist group Avanti, becoming one of Mussolini's fiercest opponents.

After the Revolution she returned to Moscow, becoming Commissioner for Foreign Affairs and liaising with Western socialist parties in Stockholm, but in 1921, after disagreement with the leadership, she asked to leave and went to Sweden, then to Vienna. She left the Communist Party and lived in Paris from 1926 to 1935, then went to New York, where several of her books were published, including her autobiography (1938), *Traitor or Fascist* (1942), *Conquest of Power* (1943) and *Tears* (1943). After the liberation she returned to Italy, supporting the policies put forward by Sargat, who later became President, and moving from the pro-communist Socialist Party to the new Social Democratic Party, but virtually retired from politics in the 1950s. She died in Rome.

A. Balabanoff: *My Life as a Rebel* (1938)

**Balas, Iolanda** (1936–). Romanian high jumper. She brought a new dimension to the high jump event, improving the world record 14 times, from 1.74 metres (5'8¾") (1956) to 1.84 metres (6'3¼") (1961). She won gold medals in both the 1960 and the 1964 Olympics, both times breaking Olympic records, and was the only competitor of either sex to win two gold medals for the high jump. She retired in 1965.

**Balch, Emily Greene** (1867–1961). American feminist and pacifist. The daughter of a successful lawyer, Emily Balch was born in Jamaica Plain, Massachusetts, and was a member of the first class to graduate from Bryn Mawr, in 1889. She went on to study economics and social sciences in Paris in 1890–91 (which led to her book *The Poor in France*), then at Harvard, the University of Chicago, and in Berlin (1895–6). From 1896–1915 she taught economics and sociology at Wellesley College, heading the department in 1913. An outstanding teacher who believed in practical investigation, she herself worked in a Boston social centre, and introduced the study of immigrant problems, studying the background of Slavic immigrants in America and Europe. A founder of the Women's Trade Union, she chaired the Massachusett's Minimum Wage Commission, and her work in Boston was greatly influenced by that of JANE ADDAMS.

In 1915 Balch was a delegate to the International Congress of Women at The Hague, where she was one of the founders of the Women's International Committee for Permanent Peace, ultimately the Women's International League for Peace and Freedom. She visited Russia and Scandinavia, and talked with President Wilson concerning points later incorporated in the League of Nations Covenant. Her pacifism lost her the job at Wellesley and at 52 she joined the staff of the radical *Nation* magazine and wrote her book *Approaches to the Great Settlement*. In 1919 she attended the WILPF Zurich conference and was Secretary-General of the international section in 1919–22 and 1934–5. She continued to work for WILPF between the wars and was influential in the withdrawal of US troops from Haiti, but in World War II her horror of Nazism led her to support the Allies despite her long pacifist alliances with groups such as the Quakers, the Fellowship of Reconciliation and the War Resisters' League. She then concentrated on international settlements for the post-war period such as shared defence bases, and also worked for refugees and for the rights of the interned American Japanese. In 1946 she received the Nobel Peace Prize for her lifelong dedication to the cause of peace and justice.

**Ballinger, (Violet) Margaret (Livingstone)** (1894–1980). South African politician. Margaret Hodgson was born in Scotland but her parents emigrated to South Africa when she was ten; she was educated in Port Elizabeth, Wellington, and at the University College of Rhodes. After obtaining her BA she won a Victoria Scholarship to Somerville College, Oxford, in 1914. From 1921 to 1938 she worked as a history lecturer at Witwatersrand University, and during the 1930s married William Ballinger, a Scottish trade unionist who had emigrated in 1928. Together they undertook influential studies of the protectorates, Swaziland, Bechuanaland and Basutoland.

In 1936 the Representation of Natives Act was passed and Margaret Ballinger was asked by leaders of the African National Congress to stand for one of the four seats designated for non-white voters. She won the Eastern Cape seat in September 1937 and remained in parliament for 22 years, being re-elected 5 times until her seat was abolished by the Bantu Self-Government Act, which ended representation of Africans in the House and Senate. As an MP she was a leading liberal, a founder member of the Liberal Party in 1953 and its first National Chairman. An eloquent attacker of racial discrimination, she fought continuously against apartheid after 1948.

When her parliamentary career ended, she lectured briefly at the Australian Institute of International Affairs, and during a period as a Nuffield Research Fellow, and on her return to South Africa, devoted herself to writing her major historical analysis, *From Union to Apartheid: a Trek to Isolation* (1968). She also served on various advisory bodies, founded a home for crippled African children, which was eventually closed by the Group Areas Act, and established scholarships for African students.

**Balthild** (*c*630–80). Frankish queen. Born in England, she was taken to Gaul as a slave and about 641 was bought by Erchinoald, mayor of the palace of Neustria, the western Frankish kingdom. Good-looking and clever, she caught the attention of Clovis II, son of Dagobert, who married her in 648. The future Lothair III was born in 649, and she had two more sons, Theoderic and Childeric, who also eventually became rulers. Balthild's influence during her husband's reign was considerable, since she controlled the court and the allocation of charity money, and had strong connections with Church leaders. After Clovis's death in 657 she became Regent for her son Lothair III and with her ministers embarked on a policy of unifying the Frankish territory by controlling Austrasia through imposing her son Childeric as Prince and absorbing Burgundy. This policy was fraught with difficulty, although presented by her early biographers as a crusade for peace. She lost her political power when Lothair came of age and was forced to retire to the convent of

Chelles, which she had founded and endowed with much of her personal wealth in 664 or 665. She had always been deeply involved with the new monasticism and had also founded the Abbey of Corbie in 657–61 and encouraged the expansion of religious cults. The resentment of some of the bishops may have contributed to her eventual downfall. She died in Chelles, after 15 years of a model life of religious humility.

**Bandaranaike, Sirimavo Ratwatte Dias** (1916–). Sri Lankan politician, the world's first woman Prime Minister. She belonged to an aristocratic family with a long record of service to the state, and her father was a member of the Senate. She was educated at an elite Roman Catholic convent, St Bridget's in Colombo, although she remained a practising Buddhist, and at the age of 24 her marriage was arranged to the much older politician Solomon Bandaranaike. She remained in the background, devoting herself to her family and supporting groups working to improve the position of women in Ceylon. Her husband became Prime Minister in 1956 but was assassinated by a Buddhist fanatic in 1959, and to the public's surprise Mrs Bandaranaike emerged from her retirement to tour the country, campaigning as his successor in highly emotional speeches on behalf of the Sri Lanka Freedom Party.

On a visit to England in 1961 she explained that she was formerly a reluctant politician, active only in her capacity as a wife: 'Mr Bandaranaike would never have been a happy husband if I had not thrown myself into politics'. She was elected Prime Minister in 1959 but her initial coalition with the Communists and Trotskyists proved unnecessary after her party won a substantial majority in the general elections three years later. Her progressive policies foundered on the problems of unemployment and poverty, and she was defeated in 1965, but returned in 1970 with an even greater majority. Several of her policies aroused controversy, in particular her making Sinhalese the official language, which outraged the Tamil population. In 1972 she declared Sri Lanka a republic; she also attempted to nationalize the press, and did nationalize the banks and tea plantations in 1975. She supported local industries and won great popularity in the rural areas, but her authority was weakened by the economic recession, and by charges of monopoly of power (she was also Minister of Planning and Economic Affairs, and of Defence and External Affairs) and of nepotism (her nephew, sons and two daughters held senior government posts). In 1977 her party was overwhelmingly defeated in the general election. In September 1980 she was convicted of misuse of power, was expelled from parliament and deprived of her civil rights.

**Bang, Nina** (1866–1928). Danish politician. In her early youth she joined the Social Democratic Party, and after graduating from university she joined the staff of the *Socialdemokraten*, the party newspaper in Copenhagen; she later married the editor, Gustave Bang. In 1903 she was elected a member of the Party's Central Board. Her public career began in local politics, as a member of the Municipal Council of Copenhagen (1913–17), and after the achievement of women's suffrage in 1918 she became the first woman to be a member of the Landsting (the Upper House) in Denmark's first Social Democratic government. In 1924 she became Minister of Education, and, as a former teacher, attempted a thorough re-organization of Danish public schools. She was also an economist, the author of a detailed work on *Trade Relations between Denmark and Great Britain*, and in 1926 was promoted to Minister of Commerce. Her other great interests were in the foundation of the League of Nations and in the improvement of the Danish National Museum.

**Bankhead, Tallulah** (1903–68). American actress. She was born in Huntsville, Alabama, and her uninhibited, rather disreputable public persona belied her staid establishment origins. Her father, William Brockman Bankhead, was Speaker of the House of Representatives, and Tallulah had a strict education. After winning a local beauty contest at the age of 15, she broke away from home and went to New York. She made her stage debut at the Bijou Theatre, and appeared in the film *When Men Betray* (1918). She then went to London, where she achieved many stage successes between 1923 and 1930, drawing attention by her rich laugh and harsh drawl. After returning to the USA in 1930 her stage performances included LILLIAN HELLMAN's *Little Foxes* (1939), and Thornton Wilder's *The Skin of our Teeth* (1943), for which she received the Drama Critics Award. She appeared in a few films, which did not do her justice except for Alfred Hitchcock's *Lifeboat* (1944). She was married for a time to actor John Emery.

T. Bankhead: *My Autobiography* (1952)
B. Gill: *Tallulah* (1973)

**Banti** [née Giorgi], **Brigitta** (1756 or 1757–1806). Italian soprano. Having been a street singer, she was taken to Paris, where the director of the Opéra arranged an appearance for her between the acts of a Gluck opera (1776). After some lessons from Sacchini she went to London (1778), where she succeeded Lucrezia Aguiari as principal soloist for the Pantheon concerts. As she could not read music, the terms of her contract specified that £100 a year be deducted for her musical education; several teachers apparently found the task impossible, and she was eventually dismissed. Audiences on the Continent, however, were enchanted by her voice, and she sang throughout Italy and in Vienna, Warsaw and Madrid, to increasing public acclaim. Her London success was reserved for her performance in Bianchi's *Semiramide* (1749), after which she became principal soprano in the King's Theatre, remaining there until her retirement in 1802. Her reputation is epitomized in Da Ponte's description of her as 'that cursed woman who terrified by her perverseness as much as she pleased with her voice'; admiration won through sufficiently for Haydn to compose for her his *Scena di Berenice* (1795). She is reputed to have donated her larynx, examined posthumously and proclaimed extremely large, to the city of Bologna, where her husband, the dancer Zaccaria Banti, had a monument erected in her memory.

**Ban Zhao.** *See* PAN CHAO.

**Bara, Theda** [pseud. of Theodosia Goodman] (1890–1955). American film star. Born in Cincinnati, Ohio, the daughter of a tailor, she began as a provincial actress and Hollywood extra before she achieved overnight success as a vamp in *A Fool·There Was* (1915). One of the first studio publicity campaigns promoted her as a sultry beauty of mystical power, and she made over 35 films between 1914 and 1919. Her list of *femme fatale* roles included Carmen, Salome and Cleopatra, offset against innocent roles such as Juliet, and the kind-hearted gypsy Esmeralda in *The Darling of Paris* (1916). The Fox Film Corporation was created around her films. After World War I her popularity waned. She worked on Broadway, and married director Charles Brabin, making a brief reappearance in films in *The Unchastened Woman* (1925) and *Madame Mystery* (1926). She then retired into obscurity until her death from cancer 30 years later.

**Barbara, Agatha** (1923–). Maltese politician and president. Born in Zabbar, Agatha was educated in Valetta, and then worked as a school teacher. During World War II she was an air-raid warden, and afterwards worked in various jobs, including managing the advertising for Freedom Press. She joined the Labour Party in 1946 and the following year became Malta's first woman Member of Parliament, remaining an MP for the next 35 years. She was Minister of Education from 1955 to 1958, and again from 1971 to 1974, when she was appointed Minister of Labour, Culture and Welfare. In 1982 she became President of the Republic of Malta. She has been highly influential in Maltese women's movements, within the Labour Party, and with the International Social Democratic Women's Group.

**Barbauld, Anna Letitia Aikin** (1743–1825). English poet, essayist and critic. Born in Kibworth, Northamptonshire, she was educated at her father's schools there and in Warrington. In 1723 her brother John arranged the publication of her poems, and she also collaborated with him in *Miscellaneous Pieces of Prose* (1774). Her family were radical dissenters, and when she married the Reverend Rochemont Barbauld in 1774 she helped him run his nonconformist boarding school in Palgrave, Suffolk, from 1774 until 1787. Dissatisfied with contemporary school books, she wrote *Lessons for Children* (1778) and *Hymns in*

*Prose* (1781), both of which won immediate popularity. Although conventional in private life, she wrote boldly on behalf of popular rights and religious toleration in her *Civic Sermons to the People* (1792), and *Sins of Government* (1793). Between 1792 and 1796 she contributed to her brother John's *Evenings at Home*, but then became increasingly engaged in criticism, editing Collins's *Poetical Works* (1797), her well-known *Selections from the Spectator, Tatler, Guardian and Freeholder* (1804), the 6-volume *Correspondence of Samuel Richardson*, and the 50-volume collection, *The British Novelists* (1810). In 1811 she edited a selection of prose for girls, *The Female Speaker*. Her achievement, which combines scholarship with idealistic personal commitment, is remarkable in its contradiction of her own advice to women to limit themselves to domestic life, 'Your best, your sweetest empire is to please'.

B. Rodgers: *Georgian Chronicle: Mrs Barbauld and Her Family* (1958)

**Bardot, Brigitte** (1934–). French film actress. Born in Paris, the daughter of a wealthy industrialist, she was educated at a ballet school and at the age of 15 posed for the cover of *Elle* magazine. During the 1950s she made several films, the best being René Clair's *Les grands manoeuvres/The Grand Manoeuvre* (1955). She married Roger Vadim in 1952 and his skill at exploiting women (later applied to CATHERINE DENEUVE and JANE FONDA) bore fruit in *Et Dieu créa la femme/And God Created Woman* (1956) in which Bardot shot to international stardom. From a spontaneous brunette she became a blonde product, 'B.B.', and was marketed to fuel the legend. Her private life was lived in public, reflecting the accepted image in temperamental outbursts, well-publicized affairs and suicide attempts. In 1957 she divorced Vadim, and has been married twice more, to Jacques Charrier, with whom she had a son, and Gunther Sachs, a millionaire playboy.

Her films are generally unmemorable, although they include Henri-Georges Clouzot's *La vérité/The Truth* (1960), and Louis Malle's *La vie privée/A Very Private Affair* (1962), and *Viva Maria* (1965). She was less an actress than a symbol of a child-woman, whose sexuality remained

unfettered by convention, as Pauline Kael called her, 'the distillation of all those irresponsible, petulant teenagers'. Since her rather ironic appearance in Vadim's *Si Don Juan était une femme/Don Juan* (1973) she has done little acting, but has worked strenuously for wild-life conservation organizations, opposing the Canadian seal hunts and campaigning against vivisection and tests on animals. She was created Chevalier, Légion d'honneur in 1985.

G. Roberts: *Bardot* (1985)

**Barnes, Djuna** (1892–1982). American poet, novelist and playwright. Born in New York State, she studied art at the Pratt Institute and the Art Students' League. She began writing for New York newspapers and as a founder member of the Theater Guild contributed to its magazine. Her early one-act plays were produced by the Provincetown Players (1919–20). She also established a reputation with the collection of poems and drawings *Book of Repulsive Women* (1915); *A Book* (1923), which also included plays; and *Ryder* (1928), a monologue concentrating on a man's relationships with his mother, wife and mistress, described as 'explosive' and issued in the USA in an expurgated edition. Her anonymous novel *Ladies' Almanack* was also published in 1928. For many years during this period she lived in Paris, where she was a friend of GERTRUDE STEIN and ANAÏS NIN, and also in the south of France and London. The *Ladies' Almanack* caused a sensation because it poked affectionate fun at lightly disguised lesbian socialites such as RADCLYFFE HALL and NATALIE BARNEY. She gained international fame in 1936 with *Nightwood*, a novel about five bizarre characters living in Paris. Described by T.S. Eliot as having a quality of horror approaching Jacobean tragedy, its atmosphere is doom-laden, claustrophobic and redolent of *fin de siècle* decadence, lightened by a macabre humour. After the 1930s she published little, with the exception of *Antiphon* (1958), a powerful poetic drama, and *Vagaries malicieux* (1974). Her work has aroused renewed appreciation in recent years for its bold treatment of lesbian relationships.

L.F. Kannenstine: *The Art of Barnes* (1977)

**Barnes,** Dame **(Alice) Josephine (Mary Taylor),** [Dame Josephine Warren] (1912–). British obstetrician and gynaecologist. The daughter of a Methodist minister and a musician, Josephine Barnes was the eldest of five children who all grew up in Oxford and went to the university and into professions. At Lady Margaret Hall she played hockey for the University and gained a first class degree, followed by scholarships to University College Hospital, London where she won two silver medals.

After qualifying as a doctor she married Sir Brian Warren; they had one son and two daughters, and the marriage was dissolved in 1964. Her various posts as a surgeon and consultant were mainly at University College Hospital, Queen Charlotte's Hospital, the Samaritan Hospital,London, and at the Radcliffe Infirmary, Oxford. She delivered babies and performed operations during the blitz, and from UCH ran an obstetric flying squad: an experience that convinced her that babies should be delivered in hospital. She has been labelled 'pro-abortion' but believes that the decision when to terminate should be left to doctors. Her other close medical concerns have been with infant mortality and cancer screening; she was President of the Women's National Cancer Control Campaign from 1974. She published widely and was even more active in committee work, being instrumental in promoting women's medicine from being 'the Cinderella of the profession'. In 1979–80 she served as the 139th, and first woman, President of the British Medical Association.

Her stamina allowed her to travel widely, lecturing and demonstrating past the normal age of retirement, and she has been awarded several honorary degrees. Of women she has said 'They have the satisfaction of being useful in the world.'

**Barney, Natalie (Clifford)** (1876–1972). American salon hostess. She was born in Dayton, Ohio, one of two daughters of a wealthy family; her mother, Alice Pike Barney (1857–1931), an artist who studied with Whistler, was a playwright and a philanthropist, and she took her daughters with her when she went to Paris to study painting. (She later exhibited at the Royal Academy, and designed and built ex-perimental cultural centres in Washington and on the West Coast.)

Natalie grew up in Washington, spending the summers in Maine and was educated by a French governess, at boarding school in Fountainebleau, where she became completely bi-lingual, and 'finishing' at Miss Ely's school for girls in New York at the age of 18. She then toured Europe, and studied the violin in Germany. Although she was a recognized society beauty and became engaged to a succession of eligible men, she was remarkably independent, frank and courageous and made an open declaration of her homosexuality. In 1898 she returned to Paris, where she became the centre of a famous lesbian group. Her affairs were well publicized and the subject of many novels, from Liane de Pougy's *Idylle sapphique* (1901), to DJUNA BARNES's *Ladies' Almanack* (1928).

She herself published a collection of love poems, *Quelques portraits-sonnets des femmes* (1900), which her mother illustrated, and continued to write poetry, drama, fiction and prose. From 1899 to 1901 she had a tempestuous affair with the poet Renée Vivien, and after Renée's death in 1909 gave an annual prize in her memory to a woman writer. Her Académie des Femmes, begun in 1920, was also designed to help new writers. Her salon at rue Jacob was justly famous, and is celebrated in the essays of the elderly Remy de Gourmont, published as *Lettres à l'Amazone* in *Mercure de France* (1912–13). Its witty repartee is evoked by Barney's own memoirs and her *Pensées d'une Amazone* (1920), and its habitués included Rilke, D'Annunzio, Valéry, Cocteau, Gide, Pound, Eliot, COLETTE, GERTRUDE STEIN and EDITH SITWELL.

Barney's lifelong companion was the painter ROMAINE BROOKS, but they became estranged after over 50 years together following a quarrel over another woman in 1969. The next year Brooks died, leaving Natalie distraught and ill, and her own death, at 95, followed within two years.

N. Barney: *Aventures de l'esprit* (1929)
———: *Souvenirs indiscrets* (1960)
———: *Traits et portraits* (1963)
J. Chalon: *Portrait of a Seductress: the World of Natalie Barney* (1976, Eng. trans. 1979)

**Barraine, Elsa** (1910–). French composer. She was a composition pupil of Dukas at the Paris Conservatoire and in 1929 won the Prix de Rome. She was active in the French Resistance, particularly in the Front National des Musiciens, and her sensibilities are reflected in such works as the symphonic poem *Pogromes* (1933). Her other orchestral works include three symphonies (1931, 1938 and 1947) and music for several ballets, including *Claudine à l'école* (1950) based on the book by COLETTE. She also wrote chamber music, notably *Atmosphères* (1967; for oboe and ten instruments), which incorporates rhythms derived from Indian music, and some works for voices and orchestra.

**Barry, Elizabeth** (1658–1713). English actress. When she was 10 years old, her father, a barrister ruined by the Civil War, put her in the care of Sir William Davenant, one of the two London theatre licensees. There she gained a good education, but was not at first considered a promising stage candidate. However, her lover, the Earl of Rochester, believed he could train her, and after a number of small parts she rose to fame in 1679–80, especially as Monimia in Otway's *The Orphan*. From then until shortly before her death, she played dozens of leading roles, both comic and tragic, Lady Touchwood in Congreve's *The Double Dealer*, Mrs Loveit in Etheridge's *The Man of Mode*, Roxana in Nathaniel Lee's *The Rival Queens* and Cassandra in Dryden's *Cleomenes*. But with Anne Bracegirdle as the leading comic actress, she increasingly concentrated on tragedy. Rochester had taught her to enter with passionate conviction into the feelings of the character; she played Belvidera in Otway's *Venice Preserv'd*, and of her Isabella in Southerne's *The Fatal Marriage* it was said she always 'forced tears from the eyes of her auditory, especially those who have any sense of pity for the distressed'.

In 1695, she and Anne Bracegirdle became co-managers with Thomas Betterton of a new company in Lincoln's Inn Fields. Her wealth (she had the highest salary in the company apart from Betterton), her shrewd business sense, and her many lovers, subjected her to vicious satirical attacks. But she remained a powerful leading lady until her retirement in 1708.

In 1677 she had a daughter (by Rochester) who died at the age of twelve; she never married. Among her bequests she left £200 to Anne Bracegirdle 'to save [her] harmless from any debt of the Playhouse'.

**Barry, James.** *See* STUART, MIRANDA.

**Barton, Clara** [Clarissa] **(Harlowe)** (1821–1912). American nurse and founder of the American Red Cross. Born in North Oxford, Massachusetts, Clara Barton was a timid child, the last of five. At 18, she began to teach in local schools, then attended the Liberal Institute at Clinton, New York. She founded one of New Jersey's first 'free' or public schools, but when a man was placed over her she resigned and took a clerkship in the Patent Office, becoming perhaps the first regularly-appointed woman civil servant. From 1854 she was based in Washington, DC.

With the outbreak of the American Civil War she advertised for provisions for the wounded and went to the front to distribute supplies by mule team, and to act as an unpaid nurse to the soldiers. She operated independently of the US Sanitary Commission and DOROTHEA DIX's division of female nurses, often spending her own money. In the later part of the war she was appointed Head Nurse in the two-corps Army of the James, and organized various corps hospitals in Virginia. She spent most of 1865 assembling information on missing men and marking graves. She became an effective speaker, describing her war experiences in more than 300 lectures, and was acclaimed a war heroine.

In 1868 she suffered a breakdown, and went to Europe to recuperate. In Switzerland, Clara learned of the International Committee of the Red Cross, formed in 1863 at a convention in Geneva, and she worked with the organization establishing military hospitals during the Franco-Prussian War. She returned to the USA determined to align her country with this effort to bring some humanity to the battlefield. Her campaign against the Government took five years and she appealed to the American people by including plans for the organized relief of domestic disasters such as floods, fires, accidents or epidemics.

In 1881 Clara organized the American Association of the Red Cross and was President until 1904. In 1881, the USA signed the Geneva treaty, including Clara's American amendment for relief in peacetime catastrophes. Clara rode mule wagons again as a nurse in the Spanish-American War, at the age of 77, but her later involvement in the Red Cross was criticized for lack of delegation. She received numerous medals and honours.

W.E. Barton: *Life of Clara Barton* (1922)

**Bashkirtseff, Marie (Konstantinovna)** (1860–84). Russian painter and diarist. Born in Poltava province she grew up abroad, travelling with her mother in Germany, Italy and in the South of France. Educated privately, she showed ability in Classics and in several modern languages. Her first ambition was to sing, but in 1877, after her voice failed, she studied painting with Robert Fleury and Bastien-Lépage in the women's class at the Académie Julien. She exhibited in the Salons of 1881, 1883 and 1884, and produced a remarkable body of work, including the well-known portrait of Paris slum children *The Meeting*.

Marie is, however, chiefly famous for her *Journal*, although the published version (1887) is actually a shortened edition of the much franker manuscripts which she wrote from the age of 12 until her death from consumption at 23. Her description of childhood feelings, fantasies and ambitions, and her later analysis of adolescent sensitivity give a vivid psychological self-portrait, and also a lively picture of studio life and the frustrations facing a female painter.

M. Bashkirtseff: *Journal* (1887)

**Bassi, Laura (Maria Caterina)** (1711–78). Italian physicist. Born in Bologna, Laura was outstanding in French, Latin, logic, metaphysics and natural philosophy. At the age of 21 she held a public disputation on philosophy against five scholars; fame, personal congratulations from Cardinal Lambertini, and a doctorate in philosophy followed. After a public examination she was appointed to the Chair of Physics at the University of Bologna, the first woman Professor of Physics in any university. She eventually married Dr Veratti, a physician and professor, and they had 12 children.

Laura published two Latin dissertations in the *Commentarius* of the Bologna Institute: *De problemate quodam mechanico* and *De problemate quodam hydrometrico*. Her publications were few; she was noted more for her teaching. She was also beautiful, was deeply religious, devoted to the poor, and wrote poetry. Her correspondents included Voltaire, who petitioned her for membership of the Accademia, which she secured for him. The Senate of Bologna coined a medal in Laura's honour, showing Minerva on the reverse.

**Batchelor, Joy** (1914–). English film animator and producer. Born in Watford, England, she studied art and entered films as a commercial artist. While working she met the Hungarian animator John Halas. They married, and in 1940 formed their own company, Halas and Batchelor Cartoon Films. They produced and directed cartoons for cinema, television, commercials, and promotional, scientific and instructional films. By 1962 their output included over 700 educational films, with a regular market in the USA, as well as experiments with puppets and three-dimensional films. Their own features include *Animal Farm* (1954), which took three years to make, and *Is there Intelligent Life on Earth?* (1963).

**Bateman [née Needham], Hester** (1709–94). English silversmith. She had no formal education. She married John Bateman, a worker in gold and silver who specialized in watch-chains, and they had five children. Her husband died in 1760 and in 1761 she took over the business and registered her own hallmark, 'H.B.'. She was helped by two of her sons, John and Peter, and an apprentice. After she had worked for other silversmiths for several years, her shop became known for its elegant domestic silver, especially coffee- and tea-pots, spoons and other table-ware, although she also produced some church plate and presentation pieces with fine, austere lines and decoration. She is now regarded as one of the greatest 18th-century silversmiths. She retired in 1790 and her son Peter and her widowed daughter-in-law Anne continued her very profitable business for many years.

**Bates, Daisy** (1861–1951). Australian welfare worker. Born in London, Daisy became a journalist before emigrating to Western Australia in 1899, prompted partly by a desire to investigate allegations of cruelty to the aborigine population. She remained among the aborigines for 35 years, living a nomadic life on the shores of the Great Australian Bight and eventually becoming respected as the *Kabbarli* ('Grandmother'). She was made a CBE in 1933. In 1935 she left her home in Ooldea for a camp on the Murray River, and wrote *The Passing of the Aborigines* (1939). Her detailed records were given to the archives at Canberra. In 1945 she finally left the outback because of ill-health.

E. Salter: *Daisy Bates: the Great White Queen of the Never Never* (1971)

**Bathory, Elisabeth, Countess Nadasdy** (1560–1614). Hungarian murderer. Born into a famous princely Transylvanian family, she was married at 16 to Count Nadasdy, and to distract her boredom while he was away at war she first took lovers and then turned to black magic. Famous for her beauty, she was haunted by visions of old age and took baths in blood, believing that this would preserve her youth. Between 1600 and 1610 she is alleged to have ordered the deaths of 500 virgins. Eventually one of her victims escaped and denounced her crimes. Her accomplices were mutilated and executed, but because of her noble birth she was spared execution, and instead was immured in a room in her castle. She lived there for four years, receiving her food through a slit in the walls.

H. Penrose: *Eliza Bathory, the Bloody Countess* (1962)

**Batten, Jean Gardner** (1909–82). New Zealand aviator. Born in Rotorua, Jean had an early ambition to fly, and particularly to fly solo from England to New Zealand. In 1929 she went to England to join the London Aeroplane Club and gained private and commercial licences by 1932. She found sponsors and after two unsuccessful attempts to fly solo to Australia her persistence was repaid in 1934 when she cut AMY JOHNSON's solo record by four days.

In 1935 Jean became the first woman to fly the south Atlantic from England to Brazil, establishing a new record speed for the flight. She had replaced her Gypsy Moth by a Percival Gull monoplane and in this she flew from London to New Zealand, establishing a solo flight record which was maintained for 44 years, as well as a new solo England–Australia record and one for the fastest crossing of the Timor Sea. Before tackling this dangerous stretch she instructed the station commander: 'If I go down in the sea no one must fly out to look for me . . . I have no wish to imperil the lives of others . . .' Her final record was for a flight from Australia to England in 1937, since when she has kept up an active interest in aviation. She has received many honours, including the Freedom of the City of London (1978) and Chevalier, Légion d'honneur.

**Bauld, Alison** (1944–). Australian composer. Born in Sydney, she studied at the National Institute of Dramatic Art and for two years pursued a career as an actress. She then studied music at Sydney University and in 1969 was awarded a scholarship to England, spending one year under the supervision of ELISABETH LUTYENS and another under Hans Keller, obtaining a DPhil from York University in 1974. Among the works she composed at this time are *On the Afternoon of the Pigsty* (1971; for female speaker, piano, alto melodica and percussion), *In a Dead Brown Land* (1971, rev. 1972; for two mime actors, two speakers, soprano, tenor and instruments) and *Pumpkin 2* (1973; for four actors and ensemble), all of which show her capacity for exploiting economical resources to maximum dramatic effect. *Egg* (1973; for tenor, flute, cello and percussion), written for the Aldeburgh Festival, is equally characteristic. Awarded a Gulbenkian Foundation grant, she then worked as a composer with several dance companies, producing such works as the tape for ballet *Inanna* (1975) for the Edinburgh Festival. In 1975 she was appointed musical director at the Laban Centre for Dance at Goldsmiths' College, University of London, a post she held until 1978. That year she returned to Sydney for a few months as composer-in-residence at the New South Wales Conservatorium. Notable Australian commissions include *Exiles* (1974; again for a combination of actors, singers and instruments), *The Busker's Story* (1978; for alto saxophone, bassoon, trumpet in C, violin and double bass) and *Monody* (1985; for solo flute). Having based herself in London, she has received several commissions from the BBC, notably *Richard III* (1985; for voice and string quartet) and *Once upon a Time* (1986; for five vocal soloists and chamber orchestra); the first performance of the latter included the soprano Jane Manning, who has given the premières of many of Bauld's vocal works, for instance *Dear Emily* (1973), *Mad Moll* (1973, rev. 1976) and *I loved Miss Watson* (1977), which was first performed at the Barcelona Festival.

**Baum, Vicki** (1896–1960). Austrian novelist. She was born in Vienna, and educated at the Hochschule für Musik und Darstellende Kunst. At the age of 18 she married a writer but they quickly separated and she moved to Germany, where she played the harp, taught music, and nursed during World War I. In 1916 she married the conductor Richard Lert, and gave up her musical career. Always a compulsive writer, her first book *Der Eingang zur Bühne/Falling Star* was published after a friend's accidental discovery of her manuscripts in 1920. She stopped writing until 1927, six years after the birth of her two sons, then in 1929 published *Helene Willfuer*, a study of a pregnant girl, and *Menschen im Hotel/Grand Hotel*. At the same time she was working as a magazine editor for *Ullstein*.

An international best-seller, *Grand Hotel* was made into a play and a film, starring GRETA GARBO and Joan Crawford. Visiting New York for two weeks to see the play, Baum stayed, brought her family over and settled in California, becoming a naturalized American citizen in 1938. She continued to write in German, but all her works were translated. A prolific, fluent writer, her novels and non-fiction works contain interesting studies of women in Europe and America. Her last books include *Hotel Shanghai* (1953) and *Ballerina* (1958).

V. Baum: *Autobiography* (1962)

**Baumer, Gertrude** (1873–1954). German feminist. Born in Hohenlimburg in Westphalia, she came from a family of evangelical priests and grew up in an atmosphere of social reform and discussion. From 1892 to 1898 she taught in Camnen and Magdeburg, where she was active in women's teachers associations, and went to Berlin to study at the university, where she met HELENE LANGE, becoming her secretary the following year. In 1900, at the age of 26, she was elected to the committee of the Bund Deutscher Frauenvereine

(League of German Women's Associations). Influenced by the philosophies of Friedrich Naumann, a collectivist, she adopted an ideology of nationalist liberalism as opposed to the individualist pacifism of other feminists. She wrote numerous pamphlets and books and in 1912 took over Naumann's journal *Die Hilfe* and collaborated with him on several works.

She was President of the German League from 1910 to 1919 and led the movement to more right-wing policies, causing a split with ANITA AUGSBURG, LIDA HEYMANN, MINNA CAUER and other radicals. During World War I she set up and worked in the Nationaler Fraudienst (National Women's Service) and in 1917 founded a Women's Socialist School. In 1919 she became a member of the National Assembly and she was a member of the Reichstag from 1920 to 1933, working in the Ministry of the Interior in 1920. She was a member of the first German delegation to the League of Nations and the representative on the Commission for the Protection of Children. She edited the League's journal *Die Frau* almost to the end of the Third Reich, although she was deprived of her Reichstag post on the Nazi rise to power in 1933. She remained in Germany, offering a 'Christian resistance' to the regime and was interrogated several times by the Gestapo. After World War II, however, the allies banned her publications until 1947, because of their 'militaristic nature'. With her old friend Marie Braun, she then started a party called the Christlich-Soziale Union (Christian Social Union), but her health was poor and she retired from active life some time before her death.

Baumer was also a popular critic and biographer, who wrote works on Goethe, Rilke, Fichte, Dante and RICARDA HUCH, and on historical figures such as Otto III and the Empress Adelaide.

**Bausch, Pina** (1940–). German choreographer and director. Born in the industrial town of Solingen, where her parents ran a restaurant frequented by many artists, actors and musicians, Pina Bausch went on from a local dance school to the Folkwangschule in Essen in 1955. There she was influenced by the Expressionist choreographer Kurt Jooss. In 1959 she received an award to study at the

Juilliard School in New York, where she also studied privately with Margaret Craske. She danced occasionally with the New American Ballet and joined the Metropolitan Opera Ballet for a season in 1960–61.

In 1962 Bausch returned to Germany, dancing in Kurt Jooss's company in Essen and touring internationally, and began to choreograph for the troupe in 1968. Her formal, emotionally intense pieces caught the attention of the director of the Wuppertal Opera Company, and she was asked to stage *Tannhäuser* for them in 1972. She was appointed a director of the Wuppertal Opera Ballet the following year, and revitalized the Company, broadening the repertoire, adding her own innovatory works such as *Ich bring dich um die Ecke* and *Adagio*, and adapting classical stories such as *Iphigenia in Tauris* and *Orpheus and Eurydice*. Her controversial ballet *Spring Sacrifice* drew international attention. She went on to choreograph Brecht–Weill plays and was recognized as a major force in contemporary ballet, with works such as *Legend of Chastity* (1979). Her recent works include *1980*, which examined children's games, fantasies and fears and their effect on adult life, and *Arias*, premièred in New York in 1985, which dramatizes sexual pretensions, male domination and the need for love. Her haunting, challenging work makes her one of the most exciting artists in world theatre today.

**Baylis, Lilian** (1874–1937). English theatre manager and the founder of the Old Vic and Sadler's Wells companies. A trained musician, she appeared in concerts with her parents who were both singers. She subsequently settled in Johannesburg as a music teacher until summoned to England by her aunt, Emma Cons, to help run the Victoria Theatre, London (then called the Royal Victoria Hall and Coffee Tavern), a temperance establishment managed by Emma Cons since 1880. Lilian took over the management in 1912 and rapidly became one of the leading managers in London for opera, drama and ballet, aiming to serve the widest possible public. She made the Old Vic a principal centre for Shakespeare and produced all his plays (1914–23). She rebuilt and opened Sadler's Wells in 1931, where outstanding productions of opera and ballet were staged with the assistance of Charles

Corri and NINETTE DE VALOIS, whom she appointed as head of the ballet company. Lilian Baylis was renowned for her belief in her theatres, her unstinting work for them, and her talent for inspiring enthusiasm in those who worked with her.

R. Findlater: *Lilian Baylis: the Lady of the Old Vic* (1975)

**Beach** [née Cheney], **Amy Marcy** (1867–1944). American composer and pianist. She was one of the first American composers to receive all her musical training in the USA, and her 'Gaelic' Symphony (1893) was the first symphony by an American woman to be performed there. In 1892 she was the first woman to have her music performed by the New York Philharmonic Society (the concert aria *Eilen de Wolken*) and by the Boston Handel and Haydn Society (*Mass in E flat*). During a tour of Europe (1911–14) her reputation was enhanced by performances of her symphony in Leipzig and Berlin, where she also played her own piano concerto. Her other compositions include an opera (*Cabildo*, 1932), many choral works (both with orchestra and *a cappella*), chamber music and piano pieces, though her songs brought her the greatest popularity. She was one of the founders of the Association of American Women Composers and became its first president, in 1926.

**Beach,** **Sylvia** (1887–1962). American publisher. Born in Baltimore, the daughter of a Presbyterian minister, she became determined to live in France at the age of 14, when her father was a pastor to American students there. During World War I she went with her sister Cyprian to work with the Red Cross in Belgrade and in 1919 used a legacy to open a bookshop, Shakespeare and Company, on the Left Bank in Paris. She combined this with a lending library and became friendly with many intellectuals then living in the city. She sold the works of GERTRUDE STEIN and in 1922 agreed to publish James Joyce's *Ulysses*, after it had been widely rejected elsewhere because of its avant-garde style and the potential for prosecution for obscenity. The process was slow, expensive and difficult because of the numerous mistakes of the non-English-speaking typesetters, but she was able to survive financially largely because of the help of Harriet Weaver (1876–1961), another independent American, who edited *The Egoist* and had published Joyce in London.

The shop survived until the German Occupation of Paris, when it was closed down, and Beach herself was interned for several months. After World War II she did not reopen it, but evoked its splendid past in *Shakespeare and Company* (1959).

**Beale, Dorothea** (1831–1906). English educationalist and feminist. Born in London, the 4th of 11 children of a Liberal surgeon, she was educated both at home and at a school in Shalford, Essex, and attended lectures at Gresham College. After a brief period in a Paris finishing school, which closed during the Revolution of 1848, she became one of the first students at Queen's College, Harley Street, at the same time as FRANCES MARY BUSS and ADELAIDE ANN PROCTER. In 1849 she began teaching mathematics there, and she was a senior teacher from 1854 to 1856. After she left in 1857, she became headmistress of the Clergy Daughters' School (the notorious Cowan Bridge School, attended by the BRONTE sisters) in Casterton, Westmoreland, but her demands for reform led her to resign after a few months.

In 1858, aged 27, she became Principal of Cheltenham Ladies College, which had opened in 1854. She transformed it into a famous and financially-secure school, increasing the number of pupils from 82 to 500 by 1880, with its own nursery school and a connected teacher training college, St Hilda's, named in honour of her heroine, St HILDA OF WHITBY. In 1892 she also established St Hilda's Hall, Oxford, to give trainee teachers a year at the University; it later became one of the University colleges. Her other major venture was the foundation of a College Guild, which maintained a settlement in Bethnal Green called St Hilda's East, which is still an active community centre. She was always involved in the public struggle for girls' education, giving evidence to the Royal Commission in 1864, writing an exposé in 1869 (a *Report on the Education of Girls*), acting as President of the Headmistresses' Association (1875–7) and co-authoring *Work and Play in Girls' Schools* (1898). A reserved, deeply religious woman, she was still an effective radical campaigner in education and a keen suffragette.

F.C. Steadman: *In the Days of Miss Beale: a Study of her Work and Influence* (1931)

**Beale, Mary** (1632–99). English portrait painter. Born in Suffolk, the daughter of a clergyman, she was influenced by the painters Walker and Lely. Her husband, the landowner and cloth manufacturer, Charles Beale, encouraged her work and kept detailed notebooks listing all the transactions relating to her painting. She established a studio in Covent Garden and became a popular portraitist, working particularly with intellectuals and churchmen including Abraham Cowley, Archbishop Tillotson, John Milton and even Charles II. A specialist in colour, her vigorous, expressive style could be seen in oil, water colour and crayon, and she made a substantial profit, charging £5 for a head, and £10 for half-length. The Beales left London to avoid the plague in 1665 but returned in 1670 and lived in Pall Mall. Mary continued to work until old age, but she suffered from the change of fashion after Lely's death. Her pupil Sarah Curtis was a successful portraitist, as were both her sons, although the eldest eventually became a doctor.

E. Walsh and R. Jeffree: *Catalogue 'The Excellent Mrs Mary Beale'* (1975)

**Beard, Mary Ritter** (1876–1958). American historian and feminist. Born in Indianapolis, a daughter of a reformist lawyer and a schoolteacher mother, she went to De Pauw University where she met Charles Austin Beard. She graduated in 1897 and after teaching German in schools she married Beard in 1900. A keen suffragist and trade unionist she went to England with her husband, who studied history at Oxford and was involved in the founding of the working-men's college, Ruskin Hall. In 1902 they returned to New York, where their daughter was born, and both enrolled at Columbia University in 1904.

After 1907, following the birth of her son, Mary became an organizer for the National Women's Trade Union League. From 1910 to 1912 she edited *The Woman Voter*, but left to concentrate on the more working-class movement, the Wage Earners' League.

She was a member of the militant faction led by ALICE PAUL from 1913 to 1919, but resigned in 1920 because she felt protective legislation to be preferable to an equal rights amendment. Her writing during these years included *Women's Work in Municipalities* (1915) and *A Short History of the American Labor Movement* (1920).

Mary went on to make a considerable reputation as a lecturer and writer, collaborating with her husband on their famous series of books about American history. Her feminist books included *Understanding Women* (1931) and her major work *Woman as a Force in History* (1946), written at the age of 70. Like another contemporary work, Viola Klein's *The Feminine Character* (1946), it lacked the backing of an active feminist movement, but although it aroused fierce criticism from the historical establishment at the time, during the 1960s it became recognized as a seminal work in defining 'women's history'. After her husband's death, Mary Beard moved to Arizona.

A.J. Lane: *Mary Ritter Beard: a Source Book* (1978)

**Beatrix (Wilhelmina Armgard)** (1938–). Queen of the Netherlands. Born in Baarn, she spent most of her infancy in Canada during World War II, moving to England in 1944 and returning to the Netherlands in 1945. She studied at universities at home and abroad, and in 1966 married the German-born diplomat Claus von Amsberg. Although he had Dutch nationality, the wedding provoked major riots in Amsterdam, linked to squatters' protests about the capital's 50,000 homeless; over 200 people were injured. In 1980 she succeeded to the Dutch throne on the abdication of her mother JULIANA. Further riots took place during the crowning ceremony, again linked to the housing shortage in the major cities of the Netherlands. Beatrix's role is merely formal and ceremonial.

**Beaufort,** Lady **Margaret** (1443–1509). English aristocrat, the mother of Henry VII. The daughter of John Beaufort, First Duke of Somerset, who died when she was five, she was carefully educated by her mother and became the ward of the Duke of Suffolk. In 1455, reputedly guided in her choice by a vision, she married Edmund Tudor, Earl of Richmond, who was half-brother to Henry

VI. In 1457 she was widowed and their son Henry was born. Around 1464 she married Sir Henry Stafford, who died in 1471, and in 1472 she took her third husband, the ambitious Thomas Stanley, who became First Earl of Derby. In 1470 her son Henry had been forced into exile, because his claim to the crown made him unpopular with the Yorkist Edward IV and Richard III, but in 1485, with Stanley's help, her forces defeated Richard's at Bosworth Field and Henry took the throne.

She then retired from political life and devoted herself to religion, charity and scholarship. She translated several devotional books and encouraged the new printing presses of De Worde and Caxton, who called himself 'Printer unto the most excellent princess my lady the King's grandame' in 1509. In 1501 she founded professorships of divinity at Oxford and Cambridge and in 1504 separated from her husband and took monastic vows, although she remained in her own palace at Woking rather than entering a convent. Greatly influenced by Bishop Fisher, she completed the endowment of Christ's College, Cambridge, begun by Henry VII in 1505, and in 1508 agreed to endow St John's College, leaving most of her fortune for this purpose when she died the following year. She also patronized several religious houses.

E.M.N. Routh: *Lady Margaret* (1924)

**Beauharnais, Josephine de.** *See* BUONAPARTE, JOSEPHINE.

**Becker, Lydia Ernestine** (1827–90). British suffragist. The Becker family went to Manchester from Thuringia a generation before Lydia was born there in 1827. The daughter of a manufacturer, she was educated at home and in Germany, with a short spell at boarding school in Liverpool. Convinced that women should study science, she gave talks at local girls' schools and published *Botany for Novices* (1864) and *Elementary Astronomy* (1866). She also founded the Manchester Ladies Literary Society, to which Charles Darwin sent a paper in 1867.

Lydia Becker did not become an active suffragist until she was nearly 40, influenced by Barbara Bodichon's paper to the Social Science Association on 'The Enfranchisement of Women' and then by the work of

Dr Richard Pankhurst in Manchester. She contributed an article 'Female Suffrage' to the *Contemporary Review* in 1867, and in the same year was a founder and the first Secretary of the Manchester Women's Suffrage Committee. In April 1868 she became the first British woman to speak publicly on women's suffrage, at the Free Trade Hall, Manchester; and from 1869 lectured throughout the north of England. In 1868, with Dr Pankhurst, she prepared the test case, which was tried as *Chorlton v. Lings*, claiming that women had the right to vote under older English law, and were included generically as 'men', but it was ruled that custom overruled this and new legislation would be required. She remained interested in education and in 1870 was one of the first women elected to serve on school boards in Manchester.

From 1870 until her death Lydia Becker edited the *Women's Suffrage Journal*, reporting on all Parliamentary speeches and events related to the cause. She was also treasurer of the Married Women's Property Committee, and from 1880 Secretary of the London Central Committee for Women's Suffrage. A clear and tenacious thinker, she was a crucial figure in the campaign for the vote, although her acceptance of a Suffrage Bill which excluded married women caused controversy within the movement.

**Beecher, Catharine (Esther)** (1800–78). American educator. The eldest of nine children of a Congregational pastor in Long Island, and the sister of HARRIET BEECHER STOWE, she was largely responsible for the upbringing of the family. She was educated first at home and from 10 to 16 attended a conventional private school in Litchfield, Connecticut. At 21 she began teaching in a girls' school in New London; when her fiancé Alexander Fisher, a Yale professor, died in 1823 she emerged from a severe depression determined to devote her life to education. She opened a school at Hartford, with an advanced academic curriculum, which became a great success. In 1832 she accompanied her father to Cincinnati and for five years ran The Western Female Institute, closing it in 1837 for financial and health reasons.

Her energy was then directed to campaigning for equal educational opportunities and to working with the Ladies' Society for Improving Education in the West, which recruited teachers and established colleges in Milwaukee and Wisconsin. She also wrote and lectured widely on the subject of higher education for women, and pressed for the inclusion of domestic science in the curriculum. She was, however, a dedicated anti-suffragist, believing that women should improve their minds only to be better wives and mothers, a view expressed in *Woman Suffrage and Woman's Profession* (1871). Her autobiography *Educational Reminiscences* appeared in 1874.

K. Sklar: *Catharine Beecher: a Study in American Domesticity* (1976)

**Beecher Stowe, Harriet.** *See* STOWE, HARRIET BEECHER.

**Beeton [née Mayson], Isabella** (1837–65). English cookery writer. She was born in Cheapside, London. Her father died when she was a baby and her mother married a widower, Henry Darling (a printer who became clerk of Epsom race course). He had four children, and together they had 13 more. Isabella seems to have enjoyed the large family and she was very well educated, learning French and German. In 1856 she married Sam Beeton, a publisher who came from another large London family. He published the *English-woman's Domestic Magazine*, the first of the popular women's magazines, combining cookery, house management and fiction, and a problem page with no questions but tantalizing answers on everything from fashion plates to a fiancé's responsibility for his prospective wife's debts. After the birth of her first child, who died young, Isabella became Assistant Editor, even travelling with Sam to Paris to collect the paper patterns, a great novelty. At the age of 23 she began to edit *Mrs Beeton's Book of Household Management*. It appeared in 30 monthly parts, containing over 3000 recipes and articles, often contributed by readers, with sections on medical, legal and other matters, commissioned from experts. Published in book form in 1861 it was an immediate best seller and went through many editions before the end of the century.

Sam and Isabella also managed to travel widely, to Germany, Ireland and France, but Sam was very improvident and after the death of their first two children and the illness of their third they moved from London to Greenhythe in the Thames valley. Isabella worked to keep the family finances going, correcting proofs right up to the birth of their fourth child. Attempting to return to work immediately, she neglected her health, contracted puerperal fever and died within a few days, at the age of 28.

S. Freeman: *Isabella and Sam* (1977)

**Behn, Aphra** (1640–89). English dramatist and novelist. She was born in Harbledown, near Canterbury, and little is known of her origins. She appears to have travelled from England with the family of the Governor of Surinam, staying with them until 1658, and drawing on childhood memories for her novel *Oroonoko* (1688). During the Anglo-Dutch War she was sent to Antwerp as a spy, passing on accurate but unheeded information about Dutch plans to sail in attack up the River Thames. Allegedly, she became engaged to a Dutchman who died of fever, was shipwrecked in the Channel, and had sundry other adventures.

Returning to England impoverished, she became the first Englishwoman to support herself wholly by writing. She was hardworking, inventive, witty, extremely prolific, and a shrewd careerist. After overcoming initial hostility she had two plays performed at the Duke's Theatre in 1671, *The Forc'd Marriage* and *The Amorous Prince*, followed by many others including *The Dutch Lover* (1673), *Abdelazar* (1676, *The Fop*, and her greatest success, *The Rover* (1677). Some of her plays were adaptations (*Sir Patient Fancy* (1678) is taken from Molière's *Le malade imaginaire*) but she could also be truly creative. In the 1680s her success continued and she wrote ten more plays, five novels, several long occasional poems and five translations from French. Her collected works were extremely popular at the start of the 18th century.

A. Goreau: *Reconstructing Aphra* (1980)

**Béjart, (Marie-)Madeleine** (1618–72). French actress. The leader of a famous family troupe of touring players, she made a considerable reputation playing the heroines of classical tragedy in the towns of Provence and Languedoc, and in 1643 met the young Molière, who reputedly became

an actor out of love for her. They joined together to form the Illustre Théâtre, but performed in Paris without success and so returned to the provinces for 13 years, amalgamating with a company under Dufresne, which Molière then took over. In 1658 their performance of Molière's *Le docteur amoureux* won the approval of Louis XIV, and the company remained at the Palais Royal for the next 13 years. Madeleine became one of France's first successful professional actresses, specializing in playing witty maids who make fun of their aristocratic mistresses, and creating many roles in Molière's comedies, such as Lisette in *L'école des femmes*, Frosine in *L'avare* and Dorine in *Tartuffe*. In 1662 Molière began his unhappy marriage to Armande Béjart, whom Madeleine had brought up, and who was thought to be her younger sister, or even her own child, since she had lost a girl child around the time of Armande's birth. But despite their financial difficulties and the scandals they provoked, Madeleine and Molière remained together, in what appears to have been a deeply-affectionate relationship, until her death, the year before his.

R. Gilder: *Enter the Actress* (1931)

**Belen.** *See* KAPLAN, NELLY.

**Bell, Gertrude (Margaret Lowthian)** (1868–1926). English traveller and political figure. Born in Washington Hall, County Durham, she was the only daughter of an iron magnate and landowner. Her mother died when she was three, and five years later her father married Florence Oliffe, a woman with influential diplomatic connections. Gertrude was educated at Queen's College in Harley Street, London, and went on to Lady Margaret Hall, Oxford, becoming the first woman to obtain first-class honours in history in 1888. She then led a rather restless life, travelling to visit her stepmother's relations, the Lascelles, who were posted to Bucharest and Tehran between 1888 and 1893. In Tehran she became engaged to a young diplomat, Henry Cadogan, who died shortly after her return to England. She continued living the life of a wealthy society woman and also taught herself Persian, publishing a volume of sketches, *Safar Nameh* (1894), and a translation, *Poems* *from the Divan of Hafiz* (1897).

In 1899 she set off for Jerusalem to learn Arabic and became fired with enthusiasm for the desert and archaeology. Returning to Europe she added yet another accomplishment, becoming famous as an Alpine climber in expeditions between 1901 and 1904. Eventually (1905) she began her travels in the Middle East: through Syria (*The Desert and the Sown*, 1907) and Asia Minor; then excavating Byzantine sites (*The Thousand and One Churches*, 1909) and journeying down the Euphrates, visiting Baghdad and returning through a Turkey disrupted by the Young Turks' rebellion (*Amurath to Amurath*, 1911); and then continuing her archaeological career (*The Palace and Mosque of Ukhaidir*, 1914).

She had always longed to explore central Arabia, like Lady ANNE BLUNT, and in 1913 she set off from Damascus but was stopped by political disturbances in Hail, finally retreating to Baghdad. She was the only European woman to penetrate so far into Arabia alone. In 1914 she joined the Red Cross, worked in France and then organized the London headquarters, concentrating on the service to trace missing men. In 1915 she was asked by the British government to join the new Arab intelligence bureau in Cairo, to collect information about northern Arabia for use in mobilizing the Arabs against Turkey. She first went on a liaison trip to India, returning via Iraq, where she became Assistant Political Officer in Basra and then moved to Baghdad. In 1917 she published *The Arab of Mesopotamia*. Her work in liaising between the British and the desert tribes was invaluable and her *Review of the Civil Administration in Mesopotamia* (1921) was extremely influential.

Gertrude Bell (like her friend T.E. Lawrence) had campaigned for independence for the Arabs, against the imperialist leanings of her superiors, and during 1920 and 1921 she was adviser to the British and to the newly-appointed Hashemite Emir Feisal, consolidating the new regime in Iraq and leading them through delicate political negotiations. After the position of Feisal seemed secure she concentrated on her work as Director of Antiquities and founded the national museum in Baghdad between 1923 and 1926. She died in the latter year, suddenly,

at the age of 58. An extraordinary character, who combined independence and forcefulness with great charm, affection and natural gaiety, her career continues to fascinate travellers and political observers.

G. Bell: *Letters* (1947)
H. Winstone: *Gertrude Bell* (1978)

**Bell, Laura (Eliza Jane Seymour)** (1829–94). Irish courtesan and missionary. Born in Antrim, Ireland, where her father was bailiff to the Marquis of Hertford, she worked in a Belfast shop before becoming a fashionable prostitute in Dublin. She then moved to London where around 1850 she was known as the 'Queen of London Whoredom'.

In 1852 she married the eccentric Captain Augustus Thistlethwayte and lived a shamelessly extravagant life in Grosvenor Square, London, but during the 1860s she completely changed her way of life. Now a fervent social missionary, she preached to large crowds with spell-binding eloquence as a 'sinner saved through grace' and worked with Gladstone in his rescue work with London prostitutes, although she still kept her mansion, jewels and fashionable dress. She became a highly respected figure. After her husband died in 1887 she retired to a cottage in Hampshire.

**Bell [née Stephen], Vanessa** (1879–1961). English artist. She was born in London, the eldest of four children of Sir Leslie Stephen and Julia Duckworth; her family also included four children from her parents' earlier marriages. She was the sister of VIRGINIA WOOLF, and the great-niece of the photographer JULIA MARGARET CAMERON. Educated at home, she studied art under Sir Arthur Cope, and then under John Sargent at the Royal Academy School (1901–04). After her father's death, she moved to Bloomsbury with Virginia and her brothers, and their house became a centre of artistic and intellectual circles. In 1905 Vanessa founded a discussion group, the Friday Club, which led to her friendship and marriage in 1907 to Clive Bell, the art historian. Their two sons were born in 1908 and 1910.

In 1911 she travelled to Turkey with Roger Fry, who was passionately devoted to her all his life, and the following year she exhibited four paintings in his Second Post-

Impressionist Exhibition, with artists such as Braque, Picasso, Derain, Matisse, Cézanne and Goncharova. Under their influence she became one of the first British Abstract painters, innovative but harmonious in her use of colour and tone. Between 1913 and 1919 she also contributed decorative art to Fry's Omega Workshops, and designed textiles, ceramics and book-covers for the Woolfs' Hogarth Press. In 1916 she moved to Charleston, Sussex, where she lived with Duncan Grant. Their daughter Angelica was born in 1918. Vanessa Bell returned to representational art, although formal relationships still dominated. She became a member of the London Group and exhibited with them, and on her own. She suffered a series of emotional blows: Fry died in 1934, her son Julian was killed in the Spanish Civil War in 1937, and finally Virginia Woolf drowned herself in 1941. She retreated to the country but continued to produce fine paintings, including a moving self-portrait of herself as an old woman in 1958.

F. Spalding: *Vanessa Bell* (1983)

**Belmont, Alva (Erskine)** (1853–1933). American suffragist. Born in Mobile, Alabama, into an old Southern family, Alva Smith was educated in France, where her family lived after the Civil War. In the 1870s they returned to New York, and she and her sisters were stars of Society. In 1875 she married William Vanderbilt, and was renowned for her lavish life-style and her $3 million mansion on Fifth Avenue. In 1895 she divorced Vanderbilt for adultery, and in the same year arranged the marriage of her daughter Consuelo to the Duke of Marlborough (allegedly against Consuelo's will).

After her second husband, Oliver Belmont, died (1908), Alva plunged into militant feminism, opening her mansion, donating thousands of dollars to the cause and writing numerous articles. Founder and President of the New York-based Political Equality League, she organized CHRISTABEL PANKHURST's American lecture tour in 1914. She later became a board member of ALICE PAUL's and LUCY BURN's Congressional Union. In 1917 this became the National Woman's Party and Alva was President in 1921. She also supported the Women's Trade Union League, and continued her feminist campaigns until 1930, although at the end of

her life she lived in France, where she had three houses: a 15th-century chateau, a Riviera villa and a Paris mansion. She died in Paris but was buried in New York.

**Belousova, Lyudmila (Yevgenevna)** (1935–). Russian ice-skater. Lyudmila was born at Ulyanovsk and at 16 came late to the sport for a future champion. Three years later she met Oleg Protopopov, who was serving in the Russian navy; he was the son of a ballerina. They married in 1955, and with him as partner Lyudmila developed a graceful, measured style to which their knowledge of ballet contributed. They won four European and four world pair-skating titles, and won gold medals in the 1964 Innsbruck Olympics and the 1968 Grenoble Olympics when he was 35 and she was 32. Protopopov's powerful build and height of 5'9" contrasted with her 5'3" to make them a striking pair and the most classical performers of the sport in the world. Their overhead lift was apparently effortless, and they are remembered too for the smooth, slow 'death spiral' in which Lyudmila swept the ice with her hair. They were widely acclaimed, particularly in the USSR, where they were made Honoured Masters of Soviet Sport.

**Benedict** [née Fulton], **Ruth** (1887–1948). American anthropologist. Born in New York, the daughter of a surgeon, she graduated from Vassar in 1909 and taught English in a Pasadena girls' school (1912–13). In 1914 she married the biochemist Stanley Benedict, wrote poetry and studied dance until 1918, when she became involved in the New School for Social Research. She then moved to Columbia to study anthropology, gaining her PhD in 1923. Over the next few years, during fieldwork with the Indian cultures of the South West and the northern Pacific islands, she developed her influential configurational concept of culture, which resulted in *Patterns of Culture* (1934). The following year she published *Zuni Mythology*.

From 1936 she worked as Assistant Professor at Columbia University and in 1940 attacked the bases of racism in *Race: Science and Politics*. During World War II she prepared cultural studies of Romania, the Netherlands, Thailand and Japan for the

Office of Information, publishing *The Chrysanthemum and the Sword: Patterns of Japanese Culture* (1946). In 1947 she became President of the American Anthropological Association, and also inaugurated a major international project, the Columbia University Research in Contemporary Cultures. Finally made a Professor at Columbia in 1948, she died on her return from Europe in September of that year.

M. Mead: *An Anthropologist at Work: Writings of Ruth Benedict* (1959)

**Benetton, Giuliana** (1938?–). Italian designer and businesswoman. Giuliana's father, a truck-driver from Treviso, near Venice, died when she was eight. At 13 she became a skein winder in a small knitting atelier in Treviso and in her teens, to help the family, she sewed sweaters for a local textile manufacturer and began making her own brightly coloured sweaters on a home knitting machine: Her brother, Luciano, sold these to local shops. In 1955 she founded her own business, and from her first collection of 18 pieces, the project gradually grew until she had a team of young women working for her in a small workshop. In 1960 they began to sell wholesale and in 1965 they opened a small factory in Treviso, followed by their first shop in nearby Bellino, three years later. Giuliana and her three brothers expanded their business in Italy during the 1970s and were soon operating throughout Europe and overseas. From 1983–6 they opened stores at a rate of one per day, reaching 4000 outlets in 54 countries by 1986. The company is now the world's largest manufacturer of knitwear and greatest consumer of virgin wool.

**Benjamin** [née Lange], **Hilde** (1902–). German lawyer and politician. She married Georg Benjamin in 1926 and worked as a lawyer until 1933 when the advent of the Nazi regime prevented her practising. She had joined the Communist Party in 1927. After World War II she became a state lawyer in Berlin, joined the Socialist Party and rose to become Vice-President of the Supreme Court (1949–53) and then Minister of Justice (1953–67). She later became a Professor of the History of Administration of Justice at the Akademie für Staats- und Rechtswissenschaft der DDR at Potsdam. Her many decorations include the Clara Zetkin Medal and the Order of Merit.

**Bennett, Louie** (1870–1956). Irish trade unionist. Born in Dublin, one of nine children of an Anglo-Irish businessman, she was educated in London, studied singing in Bonn, and wrote several minor novels. She helped to start the Irishwomen's Suffrage Federation in 1913, becoming Secretary in 1913, worked with Francis Sheehy Skeffington on the *Irish Citizen* and met James Connolly and James Larkin at Liberty Hall during the 1913 strike. She also co-founded the Irish Women's Reform League which tried to combine the suffrage issue with drawing attention to the problems of women workers. In 1914 she joined the Women's International League and campaigned for peace during World War I.

After 1916 she undertook the re-building of the Irish Women Workers' Union, beginning with the printing trade, where wages were nine shillings a week, then organizing laundresses and other trades, gradually creating a powerful organization, whose General Secretary she remained until her retirement in 1955. She was the first woman President of the Irish Trades Union Congress in 1931–2 and again (after HELENA MOLONY) in 1947–8. She was a Labour candidate in 1944 and a member of the Irish Labour Party administrative committee. In the troubled period before Independence she had also travelled to Washington, and had met Lloyd George to press the Irish cause.

**Benoist, Marie (Guilhelmine)**, Comtesse (1768–1826). French painter. Born in Paris, the daughter of an official, she was a pupil of MARIE ELISABETH LOUISE VIGÉE-LEBRUN, ADELAIDE LABILLE-GUIARD and Jacques Louis David. She was a close friend of the poet Demoustier, who acclaimed her beauty and talent in his best-selling *Lettres à Emilie* (1786–90). Her work, especially pastel portraits, was exhibited in the Exposition de la Jeunesse (1784–8), but during the 1790s she began to specialize in formal, historical and classical works. She then moved on to *genre* scenes with children, and portraits, undertaking numerous commissions for Napoleon, for which she received a gold medal in 1804. After her husband Pierre Benoist (whom she married in 1793) received the post of Conseiller d'Etat she had to withdraw from public exhibition. Her best-known work is *La négresse* (1800), a superb portrait which is thought to be a pictorial representation of the 1794 decree abolishing slavery.

M.T. Ballot: *La Comtesse Benoist, l'Emilie de Demoustier (1768–1826)* (1914)

**Berenice II** (*d* 80 BC). Egyptian queen. She was one of a succession of dominating queens called Berenice who ruled Egypt between 250 and 50 BC. She was the daughter of a Queen Cleopatra and *c*101 BC she married her uncle, Ptolemy X. She reigned with him as queen until he was expelled in an uprising in 89 BC and joined him in his violent and unsuccessful attempt to regain control of Alexandria until his death a year later. Berenice retained her power by marrying the reinstated Ptolemy IX, who had been deposed 20 years earlier. After he died, in 80 BC, she ruled alone. The Romans then tried to force her to marry her young heir Ptolemy Alexander, but her power and popularity made her reluctant to do so. Having survived violence and intrigue from her youth, she was now murdered on the young Ptolemy's command. In revenge, loyal Alexandrians killed him, the last heir of the Ptolemaic line.

**Berghaus, Ruth** (1927–). German theatre director. One of the leading directors in post-war German theatre, Ruth Berghaus was born in Dresden, and was choreographer of the Pauluccaschule, Dresden, and the Theater der Freundschaft from 1951 to 1964. She joined the Berliner Ensemble in 1964, and after a year as Deputy Director was the Ensemble's Director, 1971–7, then Director of the State Opera, 1977–9. In Berlin she produced numerous plays including works by Weiss, Brecht and Müller, and her later productions include *The Trojans* at Frankfurt (1986) and the surreal, psychoanalytic production of Berg's *Lulu* in Brussels, 1988. Described as 'East Berlin's most formidable producer', Ruth Berghaus has also been a member of the Berlin City Parliament since 1971.

**Bergman, Ingrid** (1915–82). Swedish actress. Born in Stockholm, she was orphaned young and brought up by relatives. In 1933 she joined the Royal Dramatic Theatre School and was taking leading parts within a year. Her performance in Gustaf Molander's *Intermezzo* (1936) led David O. Selznick to invite her to Hollywood to star in the American version of the film with Leslie Howard. Broadway successes followed, and a string of classic films such as *Casablanca* and *For Whom the Bell Tolls* (1943), *Gaslight* (1944), which won her an Academy Award, Alfred Hitchcock's *Notorious* (1946), and *Joan of Arc* (1948).

Studio publicity had lauded her Swedish 'wholesomeness' but in 1949 she left her husband, dentist Peter Lindstrom, whom she had married in 1937, for the Italian film director Roberto Rossellini with whom she fled to Europe. In 1950 they married and subsequently had three children. Her actions met with hysterical criticism, she was denounced in the US Senate and reviled as a free love cultist. Her films with Rossellini were neither critical nor commercial successes, although *Stromboli* (1949) and *Europa '51/The Greatest Love* (1952) are now much admired. The marriage was annulled in 1957 and in 1958 she married theatrical producer Lars Schmidt.

Her career revived with Jean Renoir's *Elena et les hommes/Paris Does Strange Things* (1956), followed by *Anastasia* for which she received her second Academy Award, and *Inn of the Sixth Happiness* (the life of GLADYS AYLWARD) (1958); the public seemed at last to have forgiven her. She also received a third Oscar for *Murder on the Orient Express* (1974), and was nominated for a fourth for Ingmar Bergman's *Autumn Sonata* (1978), in which her portrayal of a concert pianist echoed her own professional and private conflicts. After an eight-year fight against cancer, she died in London on her 67th birthday.

I. Bergman: *Autobiography* (1981)

L. Leamer: *As Time Goes By: The Life of Ingrid Bergman* (1986)

**Beriosova, Svetlana** (1932–). British ballerina of Lithuanian birth. She was born in Biržai and trained by her father, Nicholas Beriosov-Beržaitis, who was a ballet dancer with the state Opera and Ballet Theatre in Kaunas. The family emigrated to the USA and Svetlana studied ballet in New York at the Vilzak Scholler School. In 1947 she was accepted into the Grand Ballet de Monte Carlo. She danced with the Metropolitan Ballet in London between 1948 and 1949 and from 1952 she was a soloist with the Sadler's Wells Theatre Ballet. She has danced leading roles in the following ballets: *Designs for Strings* (Taras); *Fanciulla delle rose* (Staff); *Trumpet Concerto* (Balanchin); *Pastorale, The Shadow, The Prince of the Pagodas, The Lady and the Fool* and *Antigone* (all Cranko); *Rinaldo and Armida, Perséphone* and *Ondine* (Ashton); *Baiser de la fée, Diversions* and *Images of Love* (MacMillan); *Les sylphides, The Firebird, Checkmate* and *La fête étrange*. Her classical roles include *Swan Lake, The Sleeping Beauty, Giselle, Coppélia, Sylvia* and *Cinderella*. Beriosova has toured widely and is acknowledged for her superb technical and emotional dancing which is matched by her acting ability. In 1975 she retired from active dancing in order to teach.

A.A. Franks: *Svetlana Beriosova* (1958)

**Bernadette of Lourdes** [Soubirous, Marie Bernarde] (1844–79). French visionary and saint. Bernadette was the eldest child of an impoverished miller. At the age of 14 she claimed that on 18 occasions she had seen a young and very beautiful woman in a shallow cave on the bank of the River Gave. The lady, who finally identified herself as the Virgin Mary, asked that a new chapel be built, and gave Bernadette instructions which led to the rediscovery of a forgotten spring. It was here that seven cures occurred which the Catholic Church eventually accepted as the work of God. Bernadette's transfigurations were witnessed by thousands, and she suffered from both sceptical and over-enthusiastic publicity. The events of 1858 resulted in Lourdes becoming one of the greatest pilgrim shrines in the history of Christendom, but she herself took no part in these developments. In 1866 she was admitted to the convent of the Sisters of Charity at Nevers. She served as a nurse in the Franco-Prussian War and died of tuberculosis. She was canonized in 1933.

R. Laurentin: *Bernadette of Lourdes* (1979)

**Bernard** [née Ravitch], **Jessie** (1903–). American sociologist. She was born in Minneapolis into a Romanian-Jewish family. In 1920, aged 16, Jessie attended the University of Minnesota, where she later became research assistant to Luther Lee Bernard. They were married in 1925 and had three children. She became a graduate student at Washington University, obtaining her PhD in 1935, and with her husband co-authored *Sociology and the Study of International Relations* (1934) and *Origins of American Sociology* (1943).

In 1942 Jessie wrote *American Family Behavior* and in 1949, two years after the Bernards had moved to Pennsylvania State University, *American Community Behavior*. Her early positivism was now giving way to a functionalist approach. After her husband's death in 1951, she visited Europe, but returned to write *Remarriage: a Study of Marriage* in 1957. A year as Visiting Professor at Princeton, followed by a sabbatical, preceded her last two years of academic life at Pennsylvania from 1962 to 1964. After the publication of *Academic Women* (1964), a study of women's marginal position in academic life, she left to concentrate on research and writing. During the 1960s she moved towards the feminist position and adopted the challenging attitudes for which she is now best known, producing her most influential and popular books: *The Sex Game* (1968), *The Future of Marriage* (1972), *The Future of Motherhood* (1974), *Women, Wives, Mothers* (1975), and *The Female World* (1980).

J. Bernard: *Self Portrait of a Family* (1978)

**Bernhardt, Sarah** [pseud. of Henriette Rosine Bernard] (1844–1923). French actress. The illegitimate child of French and Dutch parents, she was educated in a convent but was always determined to work in the theatre and trained at the Paris Conservatoire from the age of 13. In 1862 she first appeared at the Comédie Francaise, in a small part in Racine's *Iphigenie*, but she then worked unsuccessfully as a burlesque singer before attracting attention in 1869 in Coppée's *Le passant* at the Odéon. After the Franco-Prussian War she returned to the Comédie Française, playing Cordelia in *King Lear* and the Queen in *Ruy Blas* (1872). During the next eight years she was a huge success, famous for her grace and beauty as well as for her legendary clear voice and expressive acting. Her roles included Cherubino in Beaumarchais' *Le mariage de Figaro*, Racine's Phèdre and Andromaque, Voltaire's Zaïre and Doña Sol in Hugo's *Hernani*. In 1879 she left the Comédie, complaining it lacked scope, caused a sensation with her Phèdre in London, and in 1880 had equal success in New York in *Adrienne Lecouvreur*. In 1881 she played her greatest role for the first time, Marguerite in *La dame aux camélias*.

She spent much of the rest of her life in London, where she enjoyed a long-lasting rivalry with ELEANORA DUSE, and in touring the USA, Australia, Europe, Russia and North Africa. She was also a painter and sculptor, and was equally renowned for her love life, although she was married only briefly, in her late 30s, to Jacques Damala. She had one son, Maurice, to whom she was devoted.

She went on to other triumphs after she took over the Théâtre de la Renaissance in 1893, renaming it the Théâtre Sarah Bernhardt. Her best-known parts were in Sardou's melodramas *Fédora*, *Tosca* and *Theodora*, in Rostand's *L'aiglon*, de Musset's *Lorenzaccio*, and in *Hamlet*. She also appeared in her own plays, which included *L'aveu* (1898) and *Un coeur d'un homme* (1909). Bernhardt continued to thrill audiences until her death, despite much personal unhappiness and misfortune. In her 70s, after the amputation of a leg, she appeared in seated parts.

S. Bernhardt: *Memoirs: My Double Life* (1907, 2/1968)

**Berry, Mary** (1763–1852). English writer. Born in Yorkshire, she lost her mother in 1767, three years after the birth of her sister Agnes, who was to be Mary's lifelong companion. Brought up by their grandmother until 1770, they then moved to Chiswick, London, and were educated by a governess until 1775. In 1783, on a long European tour with her father, Mary began her *Journals* which she kept for 70 years. Published after her death in 1865, they display the changing literary world from the 18th century to the time of Thackeray.

In 1788 the sisters met Horace Walpole, who called them his 'twin wives', bought a house for them in Teddington in 1788, and persuaded them to move into Little Strawberry Hill (Cliveden) in 1791. He wrote his *Reminiscences* for them and introduced them into literary society, but Mary did not accept his offer of marriage; she was briefly engaged to General O'Hara, Governor of Malta, in 1794. When Walpole died in 1797 Mary edited his works (nine volumes 1798–1825) and also the *Letters of Mme Defand* to Walpole and to Voltaire.

After her father's death in 1817 she became a professional writer, producing a biography of Lady Russell, a play (*Fashionable Friends*), and her major work, *Social Life of England and France, from Charles II to 1830* (1828–31). She was a brilliant personality, with a powerful intelligence, who remained at the centre of fashionable literary circles until her death at the age of 90.

T. Lewis, ed.: *Miss Berry's Journals* (1866) (3 vols)

**Berwick, Mary.** *See* PROCTER, ADELAIDE ANN.

**Besant, Annie** (1847–1933). English socialist and religious enthusiast. Born in London of Anglo-Irish descent, Annie Wood married the Reverend Frank Besant in 1867 and was legally separated from him in 1873. With Charles Bradlaugh she became the co-editor of the *National Reformer* and following her public declaration of atheism she was elected Vice-President of the National Secular Society in 1874. After the publication of a treatise called *The Fruits of Philosophy* (1875), advocating preventive checks to population, both Bradlaugh and Besant were prosecuted and sentenced to six months imprisonment and a fine of £200. The sentence was reversed on appeal, but Besant lost the custody of her daughter. She was also the author of *The Gospel of Atheism* (1877).

Converted to Socialism, she joined the Fabian Party in 1885, which brought about her estrangement with Bradlaugh, and became the chief organizer of the great Match Girls' strike in 1888 at Bryant and Mays in London's East End. She also sat on the London School Board (1887–90) as a member for Tower Hamlets, and contributed to the *Fabian Essays*, edited by George Bernard Shaw, in 1889. In the same year she was converted to Theosophy with dramatic suddenness under the influence of HELENA BLAVATSKY, left for India and in 1898 founded the Hindu College in Benares.

She learnt Sanskrit, translated the *Bhavagad Gita* and became keenly interested in Indian politics. In 1907 she was elected president of the Theosophical Society and left for Madras, where she advanced her demands for Indian Swaraj (self-government). She edited a daily paper in Madras called *New India*, instituted and directed the Home Rule India League (1916), and was interned on a hill station by the order of the Governor General in 1917 but released a few months later. Elected as the fifth president of the Indian National Congress from 1917 to 1923, she aided Srinivasa Sastri in the formation of the National Constitutional Convention (1924). In 1925 she vigorously advertised the merits of the Commonwealth of India Bill and won the backing of the Labour Party. She also travelled widely, supporting the messianic claims of Jidda Krishnamurti. She died in India.

A. Besant: *An Autobiography* (1893)
A. H. Nethercott: *The First Five Lives of Annie Besant* (1960)
———: *The Last Four Lives of Annie Besant* (1963)
R. Dinnage: *Annie Besant* (1987)

**Bess of Hardwick.** *See* TALBOT, ELIZABETH.

**Bethune, Louise (Blanchard)** (1856–1913). American architect. She was born in Waterloo, New York; her father taught mathematics and she was educated at home and at Buffalo High School. On graduating in 1874 she travelled and taught before becoming a draftsman in an architect's office. Here she met Robert Bethune, a Canadian. They became partners, opened an office and married in 1881. Louise designed a wide range of buildings, public and domestic, specializing in schools. The Bethunes' styles included 'Romanesque Revival' and the lavish 'French Renaissance', used for the Hotel Lafayette, Buffalo, in 1904. In 1886 Louise became the first woman elected to the American Institute of Architects, becoming a Fellow in 1889.

**Bethune, Mary McCleod** (1875–1955). Black American educator. Born in Mayesville, South Carolina, the 15th of 17 children of former slaves, she worked in the cotton fields, attending school between picking seasons, until she won a scholarship to Scotia seminary. After graduating at 18 she went to the Moody Bible Institute, Chicago. Unable to become a missionary in Africa she taught instead in several schools in Georgia and South Carolina, where she met Albertus Bethune in 1898. In 1904 she opened a school in Florida, starting with five girl pupils in an old frame house, financing the work by selling cakes and ice-cream to local building workers. She gradually acquired a staff and obtained sponsorship from the industrialist James Gamble in 1912. In 1923 the school merged with a boys' school, the Cookman Institute, Jacksonville, and eventually became the Cookman-Bethune College. She remained President, and at her retirement in 1942 the College had 1000 students.

She was also involved in running local insurance businesses, and, from 1940, a housing development programme, but her real effort was for black advancement. In 1932 she founded the National Council for Negro Women and in 1935 the National Association of Coloured People gave her the Springarn Medal. In 1936 Roosevelt appointed her Director of Negro Affairs in the National Youth Administration, where she served for eight years, working for better educational, recreational and employment opportunities; she was a close friend of ELEANOR ROOSEVELT.

E. Grenfell: *Mary McCleod Bethune* (1977)

**Bhutto.** Pakistani political family.
**(1) Begum Nusrat** (1934–). The widow of the former Prime Minister, Zulfikar Ali Bhutto, she was placed under arrest after his death in 1979 with her daughter **Benazir (2)**, and spent five months in solitary confinement, being released only when she became severely ill in 1981. She has since spoken out against the tortures inflicted on prisoners by General Zia ul Haq's regime. She is a leader of the left-wing Pakistan People's Party and has been involved with the Movement for the Restoration of Democracy since 1984.
**(2) Benazir** (1953–). Pakistani political activist. The daughter of the former President, and starting with an exceptional background in politics, she was President of the Oxford Union while an undergraduate, after which she returned to Pakistan (1977) to take up a diplomatic career. She found herself involved in the crisis that overtook Pakistan, during which her father was

overthrown by a military coup. He was subsequently put to death in 1979. Benazir became extremely active in opposing the military dictatorship of General Zia ul Haq. She was held under house arrest from 1977–84 with her mother, having previously spent several months in prison in Sind Province. In April 1985 she went into exile, but returned in 1986 as the charismatic leader of the Pakistan People's Party. After mass rallies and rioting she was arrested and imprisoned, but her campaign continued after her release. In 1987 she married wealthy landowner Asif Zardari. After an intense campaign the PPP gained the largest single block of seats in the elections of November 1988 and on 1 December Benazir Bhutto became the first woman Prime Minister of Pakistan.

**Billington-Greig, Teresa** (1877–1964). English suffragette. Born in Lancashire, the daughter of a shipping clerk, she was educated at a Blackburn convent and then through Manchester University extension classes. As a teacher, she helped to start the equal pay movement in 1904 and worked with the Ancoats University Settlement (1902–5).

She joined the Women's Social and Political Union in 1903, and acted as a national organizer (1905–6), before leaving to found the Women's Freedom League with CHARLOTTE DESPARD and EDITH HOW in 1907. In that year she married F.L. Greig, both partners taking their combined surnames. She contributed to *The Vote*, organized large-scale propaganda campaigns, and was twice imprisoned in Holloway. After 1911 she worked alone, criticizing the extremist tactics in *The Militant Suffrage Movement* (1911). Her other works included *Towards Women's Liberty* (1906), and *Women and the Machine* (1913). She was less prominent in public life after World War I.

**Bing Xin** [pen name of Xie Wanying] (1902–). Chinese writer. Born into a naval officer's family, Bing Xin grew up in a small fishing village, and trained as a medical student in Peking (now Beijing). She had begun writing as a girl and was encouraged by the 'May 4th Movement' in 1919 to publish her first story, *Two Families*; many more were to follow. Her subjects – the problems of youth and of being a woman, the depression of intellectuals, the suffering of peasants and soldiers, the oppression of a feudal society – immediately won her a wide following, and membership of the progressive Literary Research Society, and she became known as the first successful woman author of the century. She went to the United States to study at Wellesley College, 1923–6, and while in America published two collections of poems, *Numerous Stars* and *Spring Water*, and wrote her famous children's stories, *Letters to Young Readers* which were reprinted 20 times by 1935. In 1929 she married Wa Wencao, and in 1936 they again visited the USA, returning via Europe and the USSR in 1936. Bing Xin became a lecturer at Kunming University in 1937. She continued writing for children, and it is in this field that she is now best known, her later books including *Things Past* (1931), *After Returning Home* (1958) and *An Orange Lantern* and *We Awakened Spring* (both 1960). Second and third collections of her *Letters* were published in 1958 and 1978. In the 1940s and 1950s she was also active politically, as Deputy for Fuijan Province, and travelled widely, to Japan and Europe and the USSR, as representative of Chinese writers and also for the Women's Federation.

Bing Xin's work is especially notable for her love of nature and travel and her sensitive representation of the hopes, dreams and fears of ordinary people. Although her reputation suffered during the Cultural Revolution and she remained in disgrace from 1967 to 1972 she is now regarded as one of China's finest as well as most popular writers, and at 85 she began writing her autobiography. She became Vice-Chairman of the Chinese Federation of Literature and Art in 1979, in 1983 was elected a member of the Praesidium of the Central Committee and a member of the National Education Committee, and she has been Honorary President of the Prose Society since 1984.

**Bint-al-Shah**. *See* ABDEL RAHMAN, AISHA.

**Bird, Isabella**. *See* BISHOP, ISABELLA.

**Bishop, Elizabeth** (1911–79). American poet. She was born in Worcester, Massachusetts, but brought up by her grandparents in Nova Scotia and an aunt in Boston after the death of her father and her mother's committal to a mental hospital. By the time she graduated from Vassar College in 1934 she was already writing seriously, but she then spent 15 years in Brazil; her first acclaimed collection, *North and South* (1946), muses on the contrasts of cold and heat, reserve and passion, which are reflected in the contrasting restraint and extravagance of her own work. Her feeling for South America is evident also in the translation from the Portuguese of Alice Brent's *Diary of Helen Morley* (1956, a fictional journal of life there in the last century), in her collection *Directions of Travel* (1965), and in her contributions and translations in *An Anthology of Contemporary Brazilian Poetry* (1972).

In general,* however, her work, as illustrated in *The Complete Poems* (1969) and *Geography III* (1976), has a wider reference, identifying the strange elements in daily life and using bold imagery of weather, nature and household existence to illuminate the boundaries of shore and sea, of the experienced and the imagined world. Elizabeth Bishop lectured at Harvard from 1970 and also taught at other institutions; she won several major awards.

T.J. Travisano: *Elizabeth Bishop* (1988)

**Bishop, Isabella (Lucy Bird)** (1831–1904). English explorer and writer. Born in Yorkshire into a clerical family with strong evangelical leanings, she suffered from a spinal illness and learnt riding and swimming as a cure; many of her later expeditions were 'rests' for her delicate health. After an operation in 1854 she spent several months in the USA which resulted in *The Englishwoman in America* (1856). She returned there in 1857 to study the religious revival. In 1858 she moved to Edinburgh with her mother and sister, Henrietta, and became concerned with both urban and rural poverty, helping with emigration schemes to Canada (1862–6).

In 1873 she began a trip to Australia, New Zealand and the Pacific returning via the USA, an experience that is vividly evoked in *The Hawaiian Archipelago* (1875). *A Lady's Life in the Rockies* (1879) describes her friendship with 'Rocky Mountain' Jim, her 'dear desperado', who failed to persuade her to settle down with him. In 1878 she went to Japan, returning via Indonesia and the Middle East, again

publishing books on her travels. In 1881, after Henrietta's death, she married Dr John Bishop; after his death in 1886 she studied medicine in London and then left for India as a medical missionary. There she founded two hospitals in the Punjab and Kashmir, before travelling back through Afghanistan and Persia to the Black Sea. Now a famous character, courageous, exasperating, emotional, extreme ('I do not care for any waterfall but Niagara'), she addressed the British Association and became the first woman Fellow of the Royal Geographical Society.

Her final journey, from 1894 to 1897, was to China, via Canada, Japan and Korea. She travelled 8000 miles alone, penetrating through Szechwan to the Tibetan border and founding three hospitals. A keen photographer, her last book, *Chinese Pictures*, was published in 1900. She died in Edinburgh, with her trunk packed for yet another expedition.

P. Barr: *A Curious Life for a Lady* (1985)

**Björk, Anita** (1923–). Swedish actress. Born in Tällberg, Sweden, and trained at the Royal Dramatic Theatre School, Stockholm, she is both a stage and a screen actress. She was first seen in films at the age of 19 in Alf Sjöberg's *Himlaspelet/The Road to Heaven* (1942). She appeared in several more films before Sjöberg's *Miss Julie* (1951), in which her powerful performance has been regarded as definitive. Her other films include Ingmar Bergman's *Kvinnors Väntan/Secrets of Women* (1952), and *Adalen 31* (1969). She later worked at the Royal Dramatic Theatre in Stockholm and is regarded as one of her country's leading stars.

**Black, Clementina** (1853–1922). English trade unionist. The daughter of the Town Clerk of Brighton, at the age of 22 she was left in charge of her invalid father and 7 younger brothers, and not until several years later did she go to London to teach, study and write. Here she became involved with the problems of women's work and wages, and was appointed Secretary of the Women's Protective and Provident League (1886–8). She created a Consumers' League to pressurize low-wage-paying employers, supported the 1888 London Match Girls'

Strike and initiated the Equal Pay resolution at the Trade Union Congress of 1888.

After her resignation she joined the new Women's Trade Union Association and campaigned vigorously against sweat-shop labour. She was an original member of the Women's Industrial Council (1894) and later President, and became Vice-President of the National Anti-Sweating League, writing *Sweated Industry and the Minimum Wage* (1907), *Makers of Our Clothes: a Case for Trade Boards* (1909), and *Married Women's Work* (1915).

Clementina Black was also a keen suffragette, an early member of the National Union of Women's Suffrage Society, acting editor of the *Common Cause*, and inaugurator of the great suffrage petition of 1906. She also wrote five novels: *An Agitator* (1895), *The Princess Desirée* (1896), *The Pursuit of Camilla* (1899), *Caroline* (1908) and *The Linleys of Bath* (1911).

**Black** [née Munger], **Martha (Louise)** (1866–1957). Canadian politician and writer. Born in Chicago, Illinois, she was educated at St Mary's College, Notre Dame, Indiana. In 1887 she married William Purdy and they had three children. She and her husband separated in 1898 and Martha joined the Klondike Gold Rush and went with her children to the Yukon. After a return visit to the USA she went back to the Yukon in 1900, working her claim and managing a saw-mill. In 1904, now a widow, she married George Black who became Commissioner of the Yukon in 1912. During World War I she did war work in England, but returned to Canada, living in Vancouver and Ottawa, where her husband was an MP (1921–35 and 1940–49). During his long illness (1935–40) Martha was elected to represent the Yukon, the second woman after Agnes McPhail. She published the book *Yukon Wild Flowers* in 1936, but is famous for her autobiography, which tells of her change from fashionable wife, to mining pioneer, to politician.

M.L. Black: *My Seventy Years: as told to Elizabeth Bailey Price* (1938)

**'Black Agnes'.** *See* DUNBAR, AGNES.

**Blackburn, Helen** (1842–1903). Irish suffrage worker. Born in Knightstown,

Valencia Island, County Kerry, the daughter of a civil engineer, she moved with her family to London in 1859. She was Secretary of the National Society for Women's Suffrage between 1874 and 1895, when she gave up active work to care for her father, and acted as editor of *The Englishwoman's Review* from 1881 to 1890. During these years she was also Secretary of the West of England Suffrage Society, and in 1881 published a *Handbook for Women engaged in Social and Political Work*. She became increasingly interested in the position of women in industry, organizing an exhibition of women's industries in Bristol in 1885. She wrote *The Condition of Working Women*, with JESSIE BOUCHERETT in 1896, and *Women under the Factory Acts* in 1903. She also wrote a classic history, *Women's Suffrage: a Record of the Movement in the British Isles* (1902). She founded the Freedom of Labour Defence, which opposed protective legislation on the grounds that it lessened the earning capacity and personal liberty of women.

**Blackwell, Elizabeth** (1821–1910). English-American doctor, the first woman to gain a medical degree in the USA. Elizabeth was born in Bristol to a family of Liberal dissenters; among her nine surviving siblings were several other high achievers. The family emigrated to the USA in 1832, and after her father's death when she was 17 Elizabeth maintained a private school for four years with her mother and sisters. She eventually decided to study medicine, partly to place a 'strong barrier' between herself and matrimony, partly because she saw the 'great moral struggle' involved in gaining a medical degree, and partly to earn a living.

In 1847 she moved to Philadelphia, studied anatomy at private schools, and with the help of two Quakers, applied to medical schools. Geneva College, New York, accepted her when her application was put before the students who treated it as a joke. Her thesis was on typhus and hygiene. In 1849 she was awarded her MD, and 20,000 people watched her receive it. She sought further education in Europe; at La Maternité in Paris she had to enrol as a student midwife, contracted purulent ophthalmia from a baby and lost the sight of one eye. In 1850 she worked under Dr James

Paget at St Bartholomew's Hospital, London.

In 1851 she set up practice in New York, securing from the state a charter for a small hospital, The New York Infirmary for Indigent Women and Children, formally opened in 1857. With her sister EMILY BLACKWELL, she planned a medical college attached to this. It opened in 1868 after the Civil War, with Elizabeth as Professor of Hygiene, and functioned until 1899 when women medical students were accepted at Cornell. During this time Elizabeth gave and published lectures on hygiene, created a health centre and served as a health officer, appointed a sanitary visitor and otherwise practised her beliefs in preventive medicine. In 1854 she adopted Kitty Barry, a seven-year-old orphan, who became her companion and support.

Because she had practised in England before the Medical Act of October 1858, she appeared on the first Medical Register published in Great Britain in 1859. In 1869 she settled in England. She founded the National Health Society of London and helped form the London School of Medicine for Women, accepting the Chair of Gynaecology there in 1874. After meeting Charles Kingsley she converted to Christian Socialism. She fought the legal control of prostitution, and was opposed to vaccination and animal experimentation.

E. Blackwell: *Pioneer Work in Opening the Medical Profession to Women* (1895)
M. Grant: *Elizabeth Blackwell* (1974)

**Blackwell, Emily** (1826–1910). English-American doctor. Known mainly as the younger sister and co-worker of ELIZABETH BLACKWELL, Emily was better educated, did much administrative work in carrying out the projects which Elizabeth promoted, and was the first woman doctor to engage extensively in major surgery.

After being rejected by ten medical schools because of her sex, Emily was accepted at Rush Medical College, Chicago, in 1852, only to be turned away soon after when Illinois Medical Society vetoed the admission of a woman. Cleveland (Western Reserve) allowed her to study and she graduated in 1854. During two years postgraduate work in Europe she earned the testimony and respect of Sir James Simpson

while acting as his assistant in practising obstetrics and using chloroform.

In 1856 Emily returned from Europe and joined MARIE ELIZABETH ZAKRZEWSKA and Elizabeth in opening the New York Infirmary in the following year. All three shared the nursing and housework as well as medical and surgical work, and supported themselves by private practice. Emily was largely responsible for running the New York Infirmary for the next 40 years. Besides treating women patients, she trained many women medical students in the Women's Medical College of New York Infirmary, opened in 1868. Emily was Dean, and Professor of Obstetrics and Diseases of Women, and the College gained in reputation. For her last 18 years she lived and travelled with Dr Elizabeth Cushier.

E.R. Hays: *Those Extraordinary Blackwells* (1967)

**Blanche of Castile** (1188–1252). Regent of France from 1226 to 1234 and from 1248 to 1252. She was the daughter of Alonso VIII of Castile, and the grand-daughter of Henry II of England. She was born in Palencia, Old Castile, and in a dynastic treaty between France and England was betrothed at the age of 11 to the future Louis VIII; she was escorted to France in 1200 by ELEANOR OF AQUITAINE. In 1216 Blanche claimed the English throne, and bravely supported her husband Louis' hopeless attempt at invasion by organizing reinforcements from Calais. She then became involved in a war against the Cathar sect in southern France.

When Louis died he made Blanche Regent and guardian of their children. Louis IX was then 12 and Blanche ruled France alone from 1226 to 1234; dealing successfully both with a coalition of the powerful barons in 1226 – she rode into battle, dressed in white on a white horse, at the head of her troops – and with the attacks of Henry III in 1230; she was less successful with the student disturbances in Paris, which caused the university to leave the city from 1229 to 1233. She made clever alliances and expanded her territory, gaining Blois, Chartres and Sancerre by agreement with her ally Thibaut of Champagne, and Toulouse and Provence through skilful marriage treaties. A forceful character, she retained a powerful influence over Louis IX ('Saint Louis') after he came to the throne in

1236, with regard to both state affairs and religion. Her second regency lasted from 1248, when Louis set out (against her will) on a crusade, until her death four years later. With her third son, Alphonse, she maintained peace at home, despite the depletion of the country necessary to support the extravagant crusade, and negotiated personally for Louis' release after the battle of El Mansurah. She died in the Louvre in November 1252.

Her two daughters, Isabel of France and Marguérite of Burgundy, were also remarkable characters. Isabel was a pious humanist scholar who founded the Abbey of Longchamps and deliberately chose a life of humility in preference to a prestigious royal marriage. Marguerite established many schools and hospitals.

**Blankers-Koen, Fanny** [Francina] (1918–). Dutch athlete. Fanny Koen was born at Baarn; she had four brothers and her father participated in shot-putting and discus-throwing, but she did not take up athletics until she was 16, when she met Jan Blankers, the trainer, whom she married. At 17 she made her debut as an 800-metres runner. Always a superb competitor, between 1938 and 1951 she set world records in seven individual events: 100 yards, 100 metres, 220 yards, 80-metres hurdles, high jump, long jump, and pentathlon.

In 1946 she won gold medals in the 80-metres hurdles and the 4 × 100-metres relay, only six weeks after giving birth to her first child. It was in the 1948 Olympics in London, however, that she caused a sensation by her (then) unique achievement of four gold medals, particularly as she had been labelled 'too old' by the British press; these were the first modern Olympics since 1896 in which the focus swung to a woman. Her gold medals were in the 100 metres, 200 metres, 80-metres hurdles and 4 × 100-metres relay. The hurdles were the toughest race, against Britain's Maureen Gardner: her husband's reminder, 'Don't forget, Fanny, you are too old', just before the race, gave her the provocation she needed to win.

Fanny competed in the 1952 Olympics at Helsinki but without great achievements; as late as 1956, however, at the age of 38, she was timed at 11.3 seconds in a wind-assisted hurdles race, as compared with her 11-

second world record. She was possibly the greatest all-round woman athlete of the century, and was in demand at home and abroad.

**Blatch, Harriet Stanton** (1856–1940). American suffrage leader. The daughter of ELIZABETH CADY STANTON, she was born at Seneca Falls, educated privately and graduated in mathematics from Vassar College in 1878. She then spent a year at the Boston School of Oratory before travelling as a tutor. In 1881 she returned to rectify the bias towards the National Association in her mother's *History of Woman Suffrage* by writing the long account of the American Woman Suffrage Association in Volume ii.

In 1882 Harriet married William Blatch, an English businessman, and moved to Basingstoke, Hampshire, until 1902. Here she was impressed by the popular basis of the Women's Franchise League campaigns in the 1890s (the precursor of the PANKHURSTS' Women's Social and Political Union). She became a member of the Fabian Society, a friend of BEATRICE WEBB and her husband Sidney, George Bernard Shaw and Ramsay Macdonald. She helped Charles Booth with his *Village Life in England*, using her work as basis for an MA gained in 1894. On her return to the USA, she founded the Equality League of Self-Supporting Women, designed to attract women workers, and then the Women's Political Union in 1908. In 1910 she led the first big suffrage parade in New York City and she campaigned vigorously over the next few years for a constitutional amendment for women's suffrage.

After the death of her husband in 1913 she paid a visit to England (1915). On her return to the USA she merged her organization with ALICE PAUL's Congressional Union, but after the American entry into World War I she undertook war work for the Food Administration and the Women's Land Army, writing *Mobilizing Woman-Power* (1918). Her underlying pacifism is expressed in *A Woman's Point of View* (1920). In 1921 she was nominated as Socialist candidate for Comptroller of the City of New York. After World War I she identified herself with Paul's fight for an Equal Rights Amendment by the National Woman's Party. She advocated 'motherhood pensions' in recognition of female productivity and labour. Her own daughter, Nora, was the first American woman to graduate in civil engineering.

H.S. Blatch: *Challenging Years* (1940)

**Blavatsky, Helena (Petrovna)** (1831–91). Russian founder of modern theosophy. The daughter of Helena Hahn, a novelist who advocated the emancipation of women, Helena was born in Ekaterinoslav. At 17 she married a man much older than herself but soon left him. She travelled for many years, visiting Turkey, Greece, the Americas, India and Tibet, and became interested in spiritualism and the occult.

In 1873 Helena Blavatsky went to the USA and in 1875 helped set up the Theosophical Society. The Society assumed a continuity with the ancient traditions of occultism, transmitted through the ages by a brotherhood of mahatmas. She claimed to be in communication with a group of these adepts in Tibet.

Although the Society for Psychical Research demonstrated that many of Helena's miracles were fraudulent, she was estimated to have 100,000 followers at the time of her death. Towards the end of her life she wrote a number of books, including *Isis Unveiled* (1871) and *The Key to Theosophy* (1889).

C.J. Ryan: *H.P. Blavatsky and the Theosophical Movement* (1937)

**Blessington** [née Power], **Marguerite,** Countess of (1789–1849). Irish beauty, writer and salon hostess. The daughter of an Irish patriot and unsuccessful merchant, Francis Power, she was born at Knockbrit, near Clonmel, Tipperary. In order that her father's debts were paid, at the age of 15 she was forced to marry the fiery-tempered, sadistic Maurice St Leger Farmer. After three months she fled home, and over the next few years she became a famous Dublin beauty, her portrait being painted in 1807 by Sir Thomas Lawrence. In 1817 her husband died, falling from a window in King's Bench prison during a drunken brawl. She quickly remarried, becoming the second wife of the extravagant Charles Gardner, Viscount Mountjoy and Earl of Blessington.

The couple moved to London, where Marguerite achieved instant success and ran a dazzling salon in St James's Square. They also travelled in Europe, and stayed with their friend Lord Byron. By 1829 Blessington's fortune had vanished and Marguerite left him, returning to London with her lover, her step-daughter's husband, the Count d'Orsay. They lived openly together for the rest of her life. To support her family in Ireland and her own lavish lifestyle, Marguerite became a professional writer, publishing the novel *Grace Cassidy* in 1833, and editing the *Book of Beauty* from 1834. She also published witty sketches based on gossip and on her own journals, such as *Conversations of Lord Byron* (1834), *The Idler in Italy* (1839–40) and *The Idler in France* (1841). She became editor of *The Keepsake* and made a great deal of money by shrewd publishing deals, having her work serialized in *The Sunday Times*, and in 1846 becoming a highly-paid gossip writer of the *Daily News*. Her later novels included *Memoirs of a Femme de Chambre* (1846) and *Marmaduke Herbert, or The Fatal Error* (1847). Despite her success, she was continually in terrible debt, and to escape imminent arrest in April 1849 she fled with D'Orsay to Paris, where she died.

M. Sadleir: *Blessington d'Orsay: a Masquerade* (1933)

**Blixen, Karen (Christence)** [pseuds: Osceola, Pierre Andrezel, Isak Dinesen] (1885–1962). Danish writer. After studying art in Copenhagen, Paris and Rome she married her cousin, Baron Bron Blixen-Finecke, in 1914 and went with him to manage a coffee plantation in Kenya. After their divorce in 1921 she ran the plantation herself, becoming deeply involved with the country and local people, later describing this as an ideal independent existence, until a slump forced her to leave in 1931. Having begun to write for amusement in the rainy season, contributing to periodicals as Osceola, she now became a professional. Her first collection, *Seven Gothic Tales*, was published in English in 1934, a splendidly elaborate, witty and exotic book. Following a severe illness she wrote her moving memoirs, *Out of Africa*, in 1937, and during the Nazi occupation in 1944 published *Angelic Avengers*, an allegorical melodrama of the struggle against corrupt oppressors, under the pseudonym Pierre Andrezel. As

Isak Dinesen she continued to publish fiction (simultaneously in English and Danish), including collections of elegantly ironic stories from *Winters' Tales* (1942) to *Enraged* (1963).

F. Lasser and C. Svendsen: *The Life and Destiny of Karen Blixen* (1970)

**Bloom, Claire** (1931–). British actress. Claire Bloom was born in Finchley, and went to various schools including DORA RUSSELL's school in London. After spending 1940–43 as an evacuee in the United States, she trained at the Guildhall and Central schools between 1944 and 1946. In 1946 she appeared at the Oxford Playhouse and made her West End debut in *The White Devil* in 1947. In 1948 she joined the Royal Shakespeare Company, but became internationally known when Chaplin cast her in *Limelight* (1951) and when she toured the USA as Juliet in 1952. Her range is wide: she excelled as Shakespearean heroines but also as Helena in Osborne's *Look Back In Anger* (1959), and in plays such as *Rashomon* (1964), *A Doll's House* (1970), *A Streetcar Named Desire* (1974), *Rosmersholm* (1977) and *The Cherry Orchard* (1981). She has also continued to make films, such as *Always* (1984) and to work in television, for example in *Brideshead Revisited* (1981), winning the BAFTA Best Actress Award for *Shadowlands* (1985) and appearing in notable Shakespearean and also classical television productions such as *Oedipus The King* (1986). She has been married twice, to Rod Steiger, 1959–69, and to Hillard Elkins, 1969–76.

C. Bloom: *Limelight and After: the Education of an Actress* (1982)

**Bloomer, Amelia (Jenks)** (1818–94). American feminist. Born in Homer, New York, and educated locally, after six years of teaching she married a lawyer, Dexter Chamberlain Bloomer, in 1840. Bloomer was also a journalist and anti-slavery reformer and Amelia began contributing articles on temperance and social reform to his *Seneca Falls County Courier*. In 1848 she attended the Women's Rights Convention, but her real interest was in her temperance paper, *The Lily* (1849–55). Influenced by her fellow townswoman ELIZABETH CADY STANTON, she included articles on marriage, property law, women's education and suffrage. In 1851 the paper's support of Mrs

Miller and other women attacked for wearing pantaloons – a gesture against the physical restrictions of the crinoline – brought national notoriety. An earnest, argumentative personality, she adopted the dress herself, and in 1852 toured New York State and major northern cities as a lecturer.

In 1853 the Bloomers moved to Ohio, where Amelia continued to edit *The Lily*, employing female typesetters despite a strike by male printing staff, but she gave up the paper after they moved further west to Iowa in 1855. She continued as a lecturer, and organized relief during the Civil War. In 1871 she became President of the Iowa Woman Suffrage Society, and campaigned for the equal rights which were enshrined in the Iowa legal code of 1873.

D.C.Bloomer: *Life and Writings of Amelia Bloomer* (1895)

**Blow, Susan (Elizabeth)** (1843–1916). American kindergarten founder. Born in St Louis, Missouri, into a Presbyterian family, the daughter of a prominent businessman and politician, she was educated privately, attending school in New York at 16. In her late 20s she travelled widely in Europe and became interested in the pioneering teaching methods of Froebel. On her return to the USA in 1871 she discussed the possibility of creating infant schools within public education with William Harris, educational theorist, philosopher and superintendent of the St Louis schools, and after further study in New York, she eventually opened the first public kindergarten in the USA. In 1874 she established a training school, and her pupils gradually spread the movement across the country.

Susan appears to have been a difficult character, and her rigidly doctrinaire views, combined with her increasing reliance on Harris's idealist philosophy, caused a rift with her followers. She retired from the school in 1884, travelled, became increasingly depressed and left St Louis for Boston in 1889. After 1894 her health revived. She wrote a series of works on Froebel's teaching methods, spoke widely throughout the Midwest and taught at the Teachers' College, Columbia University, from 1905 to 1909. A conservative force in the International Kindergarten Union, she attacked progressive views in her book *Educational Issues in the Kindergarten* (1908).

A. Sugden: *Dauntless Women in Childhood Education* (1971)

**Blum, Arlene** (1945–). American mountaineer. Born in the Midwest, Arlene began climbing while at Reed College, Oregon, where she was studying physical chemistry. She gained a PhD and went on to teach and research in the area of environmentally hazardous chemicals. Of the almost 20 climbing expeditions in which she has taken part, some of the most notable are the ascent of Mount Pisco, Peru, in 1967, when she fell into a crevasse; the first all-woman climb of Mount McKinley, Alaska, in 1970, which she cites as her most satisfying climb; Noshaq in 1972; and the 1976 American Bicentennial Expedition to Mount Everest, a mixed expedition in which she and other women helped demonstrate women's stamina at high altitudes.

In 1978 came her greatest achievement to date, when she organized and led the American Women's Himalayan Expedition. Much of the $80,000 necessary was raised by the sale of T-shirts with the outline of a mountain and the slogan 'A woman's place is on top . . . Annapurna'. No woman and no American had climbed this avalanche-prone peak, the tenth highest in the world. Two women, Irene Miller and Vera Komarkova, with two sherpas reached the top, but in a second attempt two women died.

In 1980 she led the Indian-American Women's Expedition to the Gangotri Glacier, near the border of India and Tibet. She believes that 'our achievements in the mountains should speak for themselves'.

A. Blum: *Annapurna: a Woman's Place* (1980)

**Blunt** [née King], Lady **Anne** (1837–1917). British traveller. She was the daughter of ADA BYRON, Countess of LOVELACE; after an erratic education she married the poet and diplomat Wilfred Scawen Blunt in 1869 and had one daughter. Both spoke Arabic, and Lady Anne became the first Englishwoman to travel in and describe the Arabian peninsula. They went to Turkey, Algiers, and Egypt. In 1877 they made a desert journey from Aleppo to Baghdad, which is reported in *The Bedouin Tribes of the Euphrates* (1878). She wore a Kaffiya or Arab headdress over her tweed Ulster and was undaunted by desert raids; as Wilfred said, 'Afraid of nothing but the sea'. *A Pilgrimage to Nedj* (1881) describes further desert treks. In 1881 they bought an estate in Egypt where Lady Anne lived from 1906, and from where they began the trade and breeding of Arabian horses.

**Bly, Nelly.** *See* SEAMAN, ELIZABETH.

**Blyton, Enid** (1895–1968). English children's writer. Born and educated in Beckenham, she had an unhappy childhood, her father deserting the family in 1910. She showed early talent as a pianist but left music to take a Froebel teacher training course at Ipswich in 1916. She then became governess to a Surrey family before opening her own infants' school, at this point already writing for the magazine *Teacher's World* and soon contributing to the journal *Sunny Stories*. Her first poetry book, *Child Whispers*, was published in 1922. She married Hugh Pollock in 1924, and her daughter Gillian was born in 1931. During the 1920s and 1930s she continued to edit books on teaching and compiled a children's encyclopedia. After her divorce in 1942 she married Kenneth Darrell, a surgeon. At this point she was advised to try school stories for girls; these were an immediate success and from then on she wrote children's fiction for several different publishers. She ultimately produced over 400 titles which were translated into many languages, the most famous and commercially successful series being *Noddy*, *The Famous Five*, *The Secret Seven* and *Adventure Books*. At one time children's librarians imposed sanctions on her works because of her limited vocabulary, and the mean, potentially racist and class-biased attitudes of the central characters. Her furious reaction led to a heated public debate on the extent to which children's reading should be controlled. She continued to write into the mid-1960s, but suffered increasing mental confusion for the last two years of her life.

B. Stoney: *Enid Blyton* (1974)

**Boadicea.** *See* BOUDICCA.

**Bocanegra, Gertrudis** (1765–1817). Mexican freedom fighter. A patriot and philanthropist, she organized schools for Indian children in Mexico, and during the War of Independence (1810) she created an underground army of women. She was eventually taken prisoner by the government, tortured and publicly executed.

Bocanegra is typical of a long tradition of women freedom fighters in Latin America. Other examples are Baltazara Chuiza who led a revolt against the Spanish in Ecuador in 1778; Micaela Bastidas, who joined her husband Tupac Amaru in a rebellion in Peru in 1780, leading men and women in battle as well as recruiting, and organizing supplies; and Manuela Beltran, who organized the revolt against undue taxation in Colombia in 1780. In 1803 Lorenza Avemanay, an Indian from Ecuador, led the struggle against the Spanish in Guamote, while the guerilla wars in Bolivia between 1809 and 1825 revealed another outstanding woman leader, Juana Azurduy.

**Bochkareva, Mariya** [pseud.: Yashka] (1889–?). Russian Bolshevik soldier. The daughter of a former serf from Novgorod province, she began working at the age of 8, and from the age of 15 led a tumultuous life as a child prostitute, mistress and wife of a succession of men. In 1914, after her husband attempted to murder her, she abandoned this existence and became a fervent patriot. She enlisted as a woman soldier and became a much decorated heroine in front-line battles, famous for rescuing wounded comrades in the face of machine-gun fire. In 1917, on a visit to St Petersburg, she suggested the formation of a 'Women's Battalion of Death', a shock force which would challenge prevailing defeatist feeling. She made an emotional appeal for recruits: 'Our mother is perishing . . . I want to help save her. I want women whose hearts are pure crystal, whose souls are pure, whose impulses are lofty'. 1500 women enlisted that night, 500 the next day and 2 battalions were formed. But the rule of Bochkareva, known as 'Yashka', was so autocratic that many quickly withdrew. Her battalions were much applauded by prominent feminists such as Emmeline PANKHURST (who was then visiting ANNA SHABANOVA) who took their salute; and similar units were organized all over Russia.

They saw action in July 1917 with many casualties. In 1918 she was sentenced to death by the Bolshevik government but escaped and fled to the USA.

M. Bochkareva and I.D. Levine: *My Life as Peasant Officer and Exile* (1929)

**Bodichon** [née Leigh-Smith], **Barbara** (1827–91). English feminist. She was born in Watlington, nr Battle, Sussex. Her father, Benjamin Leigh-Smith, was a wealthy landowner who later became MP for Norwich (1838–47). He was a progressive educationalist, following the tradition of his father who had been a Liberal anti-slavery MP. This radical family also included FLORENCE NIGHTINGALE, Barbara's first cousin. Her mother died young, but instead of sending the children away to school Benjamin sent them to Westminster Infants' School, a pioneering 'ragged' school run by the eccentric Swedenborgian, James Buchanan. He also ensured that his daughters had the same financial independence that a boy would enjoy, and gave Barbara an allowance of £300 when she was 21. She then went to the newly-established Bedford College for women, London, in 1849, concentrating on art.

In 1852, having undertaken a thorough study of primary education in London she opened Portman Hall School in Paddington, an undenominational, unconventional school of mixed social class, which was run for ten years by herself and her friend Elizabeth Whitehead. She also campaigned for women's rights, collecting thousands of signatures for the Married Women's Property Bill in 1856 and writing *Women and Work* in 1857. In that year she married Eugène Bodichon, a French doctor whom she met in Algiers. He too was an unconventional reformer in his own field, and from then on she spent the winter with him in Algeria and the summer on her feminist campaigns in England.

In 1858 she helped to finance *The English Woman's Journal*, the major feminist voice for the rest of the century. She read the first paper on suffrage in 1865, supported the first suffrage petition in 1866 and then became Secretary of the Suffrage Committee in 1867. She was also active in fighting for higher education for women and was a keen supporter of EMILY DAVIES. She helped Davies open her college at Hitchin which moved to Cambridge in 1873 and became Girton College, and she financed individual students, founded scholarships, and tried to humanize the austere regime. She continued to campaign until the end of her life. In her youth she was very beautiful and her enthusiasm and single-mindedness supposedly made her the model for GEORGE ELIOT's *Romola* (1863).

H. Burton: *Barbara Bodichon* (1939)

**Bodley, Rachel (Littler)** (1831–88). American botanist and chemist. After attending her mother's private school, Rachel studied at the Wesleyan Female College of Cincinnati, then studied advanced chemistry and physics at Polytechnic College, and anatomy and physiology at the Woman's Medical College, Philadelphia, gaining her MD in 1879.

During her higher education she taught natural sciences, in 1865 becoming Professor of Chemistry at the Woman's Medical College, and then serving as Dean from 1874 onwards. She was the first female chemist on the staff. In 1865 she arranged and catalogued according to the latest methods a large collection of plants from the herbarium of James Clark, but although deposited in the Surgeon General's Library, it was not published.

**Bohra, Katharina von** (1499–1552). German Protestant; wife of Martin Luther. Placed in the Cistercian convent of Nimpsch in Saxony by her father, she escaped and fled with 11 other nuns to join Luther's Protestant movement. She married him in 1525 and encouraged and supported his campaign until his death, while caring for their five children. After Luther died in 1546, she enjoyed the patronage of the Elector of Saxony and the King of Denmark.

**Boivin [née Gillain], Marie (Anne Victoire)** (1773–1847). French obstetrician. Born in Montreuil, she was educated by nuns in a hospital and married in 1797. Soon widowed with a baby daughter, she became assistant to MARIE LOUISE LACHAPELLE at La Maternité, gained her midwifery diploma in 1800, and took up residence at Versailles. Her daughter was killed and, agonized, she

returned to work with Lachapelle. After 11 years, rivalry intervened and Marie resigned, accepting a servant's position at a hospital for unmarried mothers, despite other offers.

Her publications include: *Memorial de l'art des accouchements* (1812); *Nouveau traité des hemorragies de l'uterus* (1818); *Traité des maladies de l'uterus et des annexes* (1833); as well as minor works and translations. Her books were translated and used as textbooks in various countries. She invented a pelvimeter and a vaginal speculum, and was one of the first to listen to a foetal heart by stethoscope. In 1827 she was given an honorary MD from the University of Marburg, Germany, but no recognition from France. She died in great poverty.

**Boleyn, Anne** (1507–36). English queen; second wife of King Henry VIII and mother of Queen ELIZABETH I. She was the second daughter of Sir Thomas Boleyn, later Earl of Wiltshire and Ormond (who was descended from a family of rich London merchants), and Elizabeth Howard, daughter of the Earl of Surrey. The Boleyn sisters spent some time in France, probably attending the Princess Mary when she married Louis XII in 1514. Anne remained there until 1522, when she returned to the English court. She was extremely popular, but planned marriages to Piers Butler and then to Henry Percy were forestalled, and Henry VIII, who had previously made her sister Mary his mistress, made her an obvious favourite, granting honours and land to her father. In 1527 he began divorce proceedings against CATHERINE OF ARAGON, partly prompted by his desire for a male heir, but also by his genuine infatuation with Anne, revealed in his love letters to her. After 1530 they appear to have been lovers, and they married secretly in January 1533. In May, Cranmer pronounced the marriage with Catherine void and Anne was crowned in great splendour on Whit Sunday; in September, a daughter, the future ELIZABETH I, was born.

The dislike of the courtiers and people, the fact that the baby was a girl, and Henry's growing boredom with her made Anne's position precarious, and the situation worsened with a miscarriage in 1534 and a stillbirth in 1536. In May of that year, after the May Day tournament at which he claimed she gave a lover her favour, Henry had her imprisoned in the Tower, and accused of acts of adultery and incest extending over the three years of their marriage. The court of 26 peers unanimously found her guilty, although this has never been substantiated. Her five alleged lovers, including her brother, were executed on 17 May. On the same day an ecclesiastical court pronounced her marriage invalid and she was executed at Tower Green two days later. Henry married Jane Seymour within a fortnight, and went on to have three more wives: Anne of Cleves, Catherine Howard and CATHERINE PARR.

C. Erickson: *Anne Boleyn* (1984)

**Bol Poel** [née De Kerchove de Deuterghem], **Martha**, Baroness (1877–1956). Belgian feminist. Born into a distinguished Ghent family, she was educated at the Kerchove Institute, which had been founded by her grandfather. In 1895 she went to study in Paris, taking classes in painting at the Académie Julien. In 1898 she married the industrialist and politician Bol Poel, and founded one of the first maternity centres at his metal works at La Louvière. She was active in social reform, cultural and political circles until World War I, when she organized a secret correspondence service during the German occupation which led to her imprisonment in 1916. Seriously ill, she was exchanged for another prisoner in 1917 and exiled to Switzerland.

During the 1920s she became a leading figure in the Belgian women's movement, being elected President of the National Council of Women in 1934, and of the International Council of Women from 1935 to 1940. After the German invasion of Belgium in 1940 she was banned from all public activities, but was still involved with suppressed organizations. After World War II she retained her connection with the International Council of Women until her death.

**Bondfield, Margaret Grace** (1873–1953). English trade unionist and politician. Born near Chard, Somerset, the tenth of 11 children of a lacemaker with strong nonconformist and Radical sympathies, she taught in a local school at 13, became a draper's assistant in Brighton at 15, where she became interested in women's rights, and read widely under the influence of a Liberal woman friend. During the next 11 years she worked in shops in London and the provinces, living-in and working a 75-hour week for £25 a year. In 1894 she joined the Shop Assistants' Union, becoming the Assistant Secretary (1898–1908), and the first woman delegate to a Trade Union Congress (TUC) Conference in 1899. From 1896 she also worked with Sir Charles and Lady EMILY DILKE and GERTRUDE TUCKWELL through the Women's Trade Union League. She was a member of a Radical group which included George Bernard Shaw, BEATRICE WEBB and her husband Sidney, being first interested in the Social Democratic Federation, then moving to the Independent Labour Party (ILP) and Fabian Society.

In 1902 she met MARY REID MACARTHUR, who remained a close friend and associate until her death in 1921, and helped found the National Federation of Women Workers in 1906 (Secretary, 1914). She served on the ILP executive between 1908 and 1913 and lectured widely. She became organizing secretary of the Women's Labour League, and worked with the Women's Co-operative Guild, especially in their report on maternity. During World War I she took a pacifist stand, but was a member of Central Committee on Women's Employment and other advisory bodies. She was on the TUC General Council (1918–24, 1926–29); a delegate to conferences in Berne and Paris (1918), and to the American Federation of Labour convention in the USA; member of a delegation to the USSR (1920); and attended the first International Labour Organization conference in Washington DC in 1919 and five others to 1927, being British representative in 1924.

'Maggie' became chief woman officer when her union merged with the General Workers Union (1920–38), and was the first woman Chairman of the TUC in 1923. In that year she became Labour MP for Northampton, lost her seat in 1924, but returned as MP for Wallsend (1926–31). As Minister of Labour in 1929 (first woman Cabinet Minister) she became unpopular with the left for her increasing conservatism in relation to unemployment and treasury policies. She continued her trade union work until 1938, when she toured Mexico and the USA to study labour conditions. She became Vice-President of the National Council of Social Service in 1939, Chairman of the Women's Group on Public Welfare (1939–49), and lectured for the British government in the USA and Canada (1941–3).

M.Bondfield: *A Life's Work* (1949)

**Bonheur, Rosa (Marie Rosalie)** (1822–99). French artist. Born in Bordeaux, a painter's daughter, in 1829 she moved to Paris where the family shared a studio after her mother's death in 1833. Rosa refused to be apprenticed as a seamstress, persuading her father to send her to the same school as her brothers. From an early age she was making remarkable studies of animals, and in the Paris Salon of 1841 she exhibited her sculptures of rabbits, sheep and goats in bronze. Three animal paintings made in 1842 received great critical and public acclaim, and from then on she exhibited annually. In 1849 she took over from her father as Director of l'Ecole Impériale de Dessin, where her sister Juliette was also an instructor.

Bonheur inherited her father's Utopian Saint-Simonian views on the equality of women and was a great admirer of GEORGE SAND, but her dressing in men's clothes began as a device to enable her to observe anatomy by going to Paris slaughter houses. She eventually won official police permission to wear male dress in 1852. She deliberately avoided marriage, and in 1853 bought an estate at By, near Fontainebleau, where she lived with her friend Nathalie Micas for 40 years.

Her success had continued. *Plowing in Nivernais* (1849) was bought for the Louvre; *The Horse Fair* (1853–5) was so popular that Queen Victoria requested a private view; and in 1864 she received a personal visit from the Empress Eugénie who awarded her with the Légion d'Honneur. Fascinated by the Wild West, in 1889 she painted 'Buffalo Bill' Cody when he visited the Paris Exposition. She also received international awards, and was visited by royalty and by leading figures in society. Her detailed studies have a liveliness and romantic individualism which mirror her life. Her last companion, the young painter Anna Klumpke, later wrote her biography. On her death, she was buried beside her beloved Nathalie in Père Lachaise cemetery in Paris.

A. Klumpke: *Rosa Bonheur* (1908)

**Bonner, Yelena** (1923–). Russian dissident. Yelena Bonner's parents, both ardent members of the Communist Party, were arrested in a Stalinist purge in 1937, when she was 14. Her father was executed and her mother imprisoned until 1954. She lived in Leningrad with an aunt and uncle until they too were arrested, and then worked as a cleaner and clerk to support her studies. During the war she served at the front where her wounds caused severe eye problems, but in 1947 she entered the Medical Institute in Leningrad where she married Ivan Semyenov: they had two children. In 1953 she qualified as a doctor, and worked in the Soviet Union as a paediatrician, and as a foreign aid health worker in Iraq.

Although she had worked with the Komsomol youth organization during the 1940s, Yelena did not join the Party until 1965, when Stalinism was denounced. She later separated from her husband and was divorced, and in 1971 married nuclear physicist Andrei Sakharov. From 1975–80 she was allowed to travel to the West for eye treatment, and in 1975 was able to collect the Nobel Peace Prize on his behalf. She was a founder member of Moscow's Helsinki Human Rights Group in 1976. In 1980 Sakharov was sent to internal exile in the city of Gorky, and she joined him there in 1984, having been convicted of slandering the Soviet system. In 1985 Yelena was allowed to go to the USA for medical treatment for glaucoma and heart trouble. Although she had pledged to give no interviews, she was so outraged by videos showing Sakharov living in comfort in Gorky that she spoke openly against the Soviet regime and campaigned with other dissidents. After her return, at Christmas 1986, the Sakharovs returned from exile, and Andrei has since been noticeably reinstated in official favour, in the new climate of *glasnost*.

**Bonney, Anne** (*fl c*1718–20). Irish pirate. She was the illegitimate daughter of a prosperous lawyer in Cork who took her and her mother to Carolina to avoid his wife's fury and the town's disapproval. Her mother died soon after their arrival and Anne grew up to be independent and impetuous. She was cast out of her home when she married a penniless seaman, James Bonney, and they moved to New Providence, hoping to make a fortune from trading with the local privateers. She had a child, whose history is unknown, and became the mistress of one of the most famous pirates operating off the American coast and in the Caribbean, Captain Rackham ('Calico Jack'). She joined him in stealing a sloop from Providence, and was his partner in daring raids on the Spanish off Cuba and Hispaniolo. On board one of the ships captured was MARY READ, to whom Anne became passionately attached.

In October 1820 their sloop was attacked off Jamaica by a government ship, Anne and Mary apparently being the last of the defenders to remain fighting on deck. At Anne's trial in Jamaica her distinguished family and a false plea of pregnancy saved her from the death penalty, and Mary, although condemned to death, was also reprieved, but Rackham and the rest of the crew were hung. The rest of her life is obscure.

C. Gartner: *Anne Bonney* (1978)

**Booth** [née Mumford], **Catherine** (1829–90). English co-founder of the Salvation Army. Born in Derbyshire, Catherine was the daughter of deeply religious parents. Because of the ill-health which continued through her life, she was educated at home and thus learnt some theology. The family moved to London in 1844 and Catherine became an active member of the Wesleyan Methodist Church in Brixton; it was here that she met her future husband, William Booth, at a prayer meeting. Catherine persuaded him to leave the Methodists in order to pursue a life of evangelism among the urban poor. From preaching on street corners and the formation of a 'Hallelujah Band' from a number of converted criminals, the Booths began to build up what was to become known as the Salvation Army. Catherine devoted herself particularly to measures which improved the lot of women and children. She was a notable orator and a firm believer in the right of women to preach the gospel, a view

expressed in her pamphlet *Female Ministry* (1859). Her studies of scripture and theology led her to believe that the sacraments were not essential to salvation, a position that undoubtedly influenced the sacramental attitude of the Salvation Army.

All of Catherine's eight children became active Salvationists (*see* BOOTH, EVANGELINE). She died of cancer in 1890, and her funeral was attended by a gathering supposed to number 36,000.

W.T. Stead: *Mrs Booth of the Salvation Army* (1900)
C.H. Powell: *Catherine Booth* (1951)

**Booth, Catherine Bramwell** (1883–1987). British Salvation Army Leader. Grand-daughter of William and CATHERINE BOOTH, co-founders of the Salvation Army, Catherine grew up in a family of seven children in London's East End, where her parents, Bramwell and Florence, did welfare work: her mother ran a rescue home for prostitutes. In 1903 she entered the Salvation Army Training College, where she later taught, before becoming International Secretary for the Army in Europe (1917), and leading relief work for children after World War I (a task she undertook again in 1946). From 1926–37 she was leader of Women's Social Work, working with unmarried mothers and abused children. She continued to serve with the Army until her retirement, and also wrote biographies of her grandmother and her father. A vivacious, moving speaker, she was awarded the Best Speaker award by the Guild of Professional Toastmasters in 1978, and delighted British television audiences with her lively reminiscences, wit and warmth when her hundredth birthday was celebrated in 1983.

**Booth, Evangeline (Cary)** (1865–1950). English-American General of the Salvation Army. The seventh child of William and CATHERINE BOOTH, the founders of the Salvation Army, Evangeline was born in London. Always her father's favourite child, she inherited his sense of showmanship but learned to channel her histrionic talent through intense identification with the poor. Evangeline first worked in the slums of London where she was called 'The White Angel'. She advanced rapidly in the hierarchies of the Army, a sergeant at 15 and 2 years later a captain. After working in

English towns and on the Continent, she was placed in charge of all the Army's operations in London.

In 1895 Evangeline was sent to Canada and commanded the forces there for nine years. During this time she led a mission to the Klondike gold field, a venture fraught with danger and hardship. From Canada she was appointed Commander of the Salvation Army in the USA and expanded the Army's activities and resources until it became one of the country's main social service organizations. She also campaigned for increased democracy in the Army. In 1934 she was chosen as General of international forces. On her retirement in 1939 Evangeline returned to the USA where she was a naturalized citizen. Her publications include *The War Romance of the Salvation Army* (1919), and *Towards a Better World* (1928).

P.W. Consult Wilson: *General Evangeline Booth of the Salvation Army* (1948)

**Boothe-Luce, Clare** (1903–). American writer and politician. Born and educated in New York, Clare Boothe became secretary to the society hostess Mrs Belmont, through whom she met and married the tycoon George Tuttle Brokaw in 1923. They had one daughter but were divorced six years later, and Clare made a career as a journalist, becoming an editor on *Vogue* in 1930, and moving in 1931 to *Vanity Fair* where she was Managing Editor from 1933 to 1934. Meanwhile she had written her first novel, *Stuffed Shirts* (1933), and decided to work as a free-lance columnist and playwright. After *Abide with Me* (1935) her most successful play was *The Women* (1936), which made her a national reputation. Her other plays include *Kiss the Boys Goodbye* (1938), *Margin for Error* (1939) and *Child of the Morning* (1952).

In 1935 she married Henry Luce, the millionaire publisher of the Time-Life Group. During World War II she acted as a foreign correspondent. In 1946, after her daughter's death, she became a Roman Catholic and was the editor of *Saints for Now* (1952). However, the 1940s were years of political as well as literary achievement. She became the first woman elected to Congress from Connecticut (1943–7), and a popular speaker during the Republican presidential campaign in 1944. In 1953

Eisenhower appointed her Ambassador to Italy, the most important diplomatic post yet held by a woman, and in 1959 she was made Ambassador to Brazil, but resigned before taking up the post. Although often attacked for her arrogance, right-wing views and sharp tongue, she was widely decorated in the USA and abroad, and received the Hammarskjold Medal in 1966. She was a member of the President's Foreign Intelligence Advisory Board from 1982, and received the Medal of Freedom in 1983.

**Borden** [née Andrew], **Lizzie** (1860–1927). American alleged murderess. Born in Fall River, Massachusetts, she was accused of killing her father and stepmother at their home with an axe on 4 August 1892. She claimed to have been in the barn at the time. After her trial, which aroused nationwide publicity, she was acquitted. The case was never solved and Lizzie entered folk history and became a villainess of children's rhymes.

**Borgia, Lucrezia** (1480–1519). Italian noblewoman. She was the daughter of the Spanish cardinal Rodrigo Borgia; her mother was a Roman, Vanezza Catanei. In 1491 she was betrothed to two Spanish noblemen, but in 1493 married Giovanni Sforza of Pesaro. Her father had by now become Pope Alexander VI and needed this alliance with the Sforzas of Milan, but when he changed his allegiances and became friendly with Naples the marriage was no longer useful and was annulled in 1497. The following year Lucrezia was married again, to the young Alfonso of Aragon, the illegitimate son of Alfonso II. Her second husband, like the first, was forced to flee when her family changed their alliances and he was eventually murdered in 1500 on the instructions of her brother Cesare.

Lucrezia withdrew to the family estates and was the subject of scandal when she appeared with a child, acknowledged at first to be the illegitimate son of Cesare, then of Alexander; rumours of incest were fanned by her ex-husband Giovanni Sforza, especially as life at the Vatican was notoriously decadent. At the end of 1501 Cesare arranged her last marriage, to Alfonso d'Este, Duke of Ferrara (the brother of Beatrice and ISABELLA D'ESTE). Although this was yet another political marriage, Lucrezia was able to escape her family's intrigues, especially after Alexander's death in 1503, and she became a notable patron of the arts, her beauty and charm winning friends such as the poet Ariosto. After 1510 she became increasingly religious, although she never entirely shook off the aura of scandal before she died at the age of 39.

F. Gregorovius: *Lucrezia Borgia* (1903)

**Bose** [née Das], **Abala** (1865–1951). Indian educationalist. Abala Bose was the daughter of Durgahohan Das, the founder of the Sadharan Brahma Samaj and Brahmamoijee. The family moved to Calcutta in 1870 because they were ostracized by the community for advocating the remarriage of widows. Abala's mother died in 1875. Her father campaigned for higher education for girls and founded the Bethune Collegiate School for Girls. Abala and her sister Sarla attended the School and were amongst the first women to be permitted entry to Calcutta University. Abala then went to Madras for medical studies and married the renowned physicist Jagadish Chandra Bose in 1887. She travelled to Europe three times between 1896 and 1933, visiting various girls' schools to look at the aims and methods used in teaching. On her return she was elected as the Secretary of the Brahmo Balika Shikshalaya (School for Girls). For the next 26 years she devoted herself to the School where she attempted to provide girls with a varied education, including training in the art of self-defence by the revolutionary leader Pulin Das. She also introduced the MARIA MONTESSORI system of education in India. In 1919 she launched the Nari Shiksha Samiti in order to spread education amongst women all over the country. She established a home for widows in 1925 and started a Women's Industrial Co-operative Home in Calcutta in 1935. Later the home was converted into a relief and rehabilitation centre for women from East Pakistan [now Bangladesh]. She was founder of the Sister Nivedita Adult Education Fund and just before her death she set up the Sadhuna Ashram in Calcutta.

**Boserup, Esther Talke** (1910–). Danish development theorist. Educated at Copenhagen University, she married Mogens Boserup in 1931; they have three children. She worked for the Danish government from 1936 to 1947, and then for the next ten years was attached to the Research Division of the United Nations Economic Committee for Europe in Geneva. Since 1957 she has acted as a freelance author and a consultant on development; her projects have involved lengthy periods in India (1957–9) and Senegal (1964–5). She held various official posts, being a member of the United Nations Committee of Development Planning (from 1971), on the board of the Scandinavian Institute of Asian Studies (from 1978), and of the United Nations International Research and Training Institute for the Advancement of Women (from 1979). Her most influential publications are *Conditions of Agricultural Growth* (1965), *Women's Role in Economic Development* (1970), and *Population and Technological Change* (1981).

**Bouboulina, Laskarina** (1771–1825). Greek freedom fighter. She was the daughter of a sea captain from the island of Spetses. She married twice and had six children. Widowed for a second time at the age of 50, when the Greek War of Independence against Turkish occupation broke out, Bouboulina devoted her life and wealth to its purpose. She had four ships equipped for the war and maintained a small land army. She herself took part in the naval blockade of Nauplia, relieving many towns under siege by the Turks. In Tripoli, after a fierce battle, she was the first to enter the besieged town on horseback, and she controlled the rage of the Greek soldiers against the women of the harems. She used to ride in the countryside encouraging armed resistance. She died from a stray bullet during an argument with a relative over a family vendetta. Her heroic life and courage inspired many folk songs and literary poems.

**Boucherett, Jessie** (1825–1905). English feminist. She was born in Willingham, Lincolnshire, where her father was High Sheriff and an important landowner. Educated at Stratford, she became interested in the women's movement by reading HARRIET MARTINEAU's *Female Industry*, and *The English Woman's Journal* in 1859. She joined the Langham Place Group, and with BARBARA BODICHON and ADELAIDE ANN PROCTER founded the Society for Promoting the Employment of Women in 1860, advocating jobs such as farming, nursing, clerical work, engraving, and opening a day-school in arithmetic and book-keeping.

In 1866 she was a member of the first committee to present a petition for women's suffrage to Parliament through John Stuart Mill; she was editor of *The Englishwoman's Review* (successor to *The English Woman's Journal*) from 1866 to 1871. A staunch Conservative, and founder member of the Freedom of Labour Defence League against protective legislation, she collaborated with HELEN BLACKBURN in *The Condition of Working Women* (1896).

**Boudicca** [Boadicea] (*d* 62). Icenian rebel queen. Boudicca was the wife of Prasutagus, King of the Iceni, a tribe based in the region of modern Norfolk and Suffolk. After a brief revolt against the Romans in 50, Prasutagus kept his position as king but, hoping to protect his people's interest, he made the Romans co-heirs with his daughters. When he died in 60, the Romans claimed all the property and assaulted the family, enslaving some members and confiscating their land. Boudicca led the Iceni in revolt with the neighbouring Trinobantes, moving rapidly south, taking Camulodonum [Colchester] where they destroyed the temple of Claudius, then sacking Verulanium [St Albans] and Londinium [London]. Tacitus estimated that 70,000 Romans were massacred. Finally however, she was defeated in battle and took poison. The collapse of the revolt signalled the end of English resistance to Roman rule.

G.Webster: *Boudicca: the British Revolt against Rome, AD60* (1978)

**Bouhired, Djamila** (1935–). Algerian nationalist heroine. Born into a middle-class family, she was educated in a French school but became drawn into the nationalist struggle by her brother and during the Revolution worked as a liaison agent for the terrorist commander Saadi Yacef. She was captured in a raid and accused of planting bombs responsible for many deaths in French restaurants in Algiers. After considerable torture she was tried, convicted and sentenced to death in July 1957. The execution was postponed and in 1958 she was sent to the prison in Rheims. She became known internationally when Arnaud and Vergès defended her action in their book *Pour Djamila Bouhired* (1957) and was adopted as a national heroine in Algeria. After the Revolution (1962) she was a candidate for the first National Assembly. She worked with Vergès on the Communist journal *Révolution africaine* and toured many Arab countries.

**Boulanger, Lili** (1893–1918). French composer. She studied at the Paris Conservatoire and was the first woman to win the Prix de Rome, with her cantata *Faust et Hélène* (1913); she curtailed her studies in order to care for the families of musicians in war service. Dogged by ill health for most of her life, she nevertheless composed prolifically. Her most notable works are choral, including many psalm settings, *Pour les funérailles d'un soldat* for baritone, chorus and orchestra (1912) and *Vieille prière bouddhique* for tenor, chorus and orchestra (1917). At the time of her death she was working on an opera based on Maeterlinck's *La princesse Maleine*. She also wrote several orchestral works and some piano and instrumental pieces. NADIA BOULANGER is reputed to have turned her attention to teaching in recognition of her sister's more exceptional gifts as a composer, and did much to promote her music.

L. Rosenstiel: *The Life and Works of Lili Boulanger* (1978)

**Boulanger, Nadia** (1887–1979). French teacher, conductor and composer. She studied at the Paris Conservatoire, winning the second Prix de Rome with the cantata *La sirène* in 1908. Abandoning composition around 1912, she turned her attention increasingly to teaching, becoming one of the most influential teachers of the century and attracting students from all over the world. She taught at the Ecole Normale (1920–39); at the American Conservatory, Fontainebleau (from 1921), where she was appointed Director in 1950; and at the Paris Conservatoire (from 1946). While in the

USA in the 1930s and 1940s she also taught at Wellesley College, Radcliffe College and the Juilliard School. Her immense list of pupils includes many distinguished composers, among them Aaron Copland and Lennox Berkeley.

Boulanger was the first woman to conduct a symphony orchestra in London (1937), the first to give regular subscription concerts with the Boston Symphony Orchestra (1938) and New York Philharmonic (1939) and the first to conduct the Hallé Orchestra (1963). Through her many performances and recordings of Baroque and Renaissance vocal music, notably Monteverdi's madrigals, she played an important part in the early music revival. Among the most significant premières she conducted was that of Stravinsky's concerto for wind instruments, *Dumbarton Oaks* (Washington, DC, 1938). She received many honours and awards, including doctorates from Oxford and Harvard and a commandership of the Légion d'Honneur.

L. Rosenstiel: *Nadia Boulanger: a Life in Music* (1982)

**Boupacha, Djamila** (1942–). Algerian nationalist heroine. From a middle-class, French-educated background, like many other young women she joined the revolutionary terrorist movement. She was arrested in 1961 and accused of bombing a café near the University of Algiers. While in prison she suffered a series of atrocious tortures and sexual humiliation. She was released during the amnesty of 1962. Boupacha's case was the subject of a long legal battle, conducted by the lawyer GISELE HALIMI, and a 'Djamila Boupacha Committee' was set up, with many well-known French sympathizers including François Mauriac, SIMONE DE BEAUVOIR and GERMAINE TILLION.

After the Revolution she campaigned energetically for Algerian women to take a more prominent role in public life.

S. De Beauvoir and G. Halimi: *Djamila Boupacha* (Eng. trans., 1962)

**Bourgeois, Louyse** (1563–1636). French midwife. Brought up in the affluent district of Saint Germain, Paris, Louyse married Martin Boursier, assistant to the famous surgeon Ambroise Paré, a pioneer of obstetrics. In 1588 she fled the sacked suburbs during political disturbances and was reduced to supporting her three children by her embroidery. When able to return to Paris she studied midwifery under her husband and Paré, working among the poor for five years until she could join the guild of midwives. She then attended the nobility, including seven deliveries for Queen Marie de Médicis. The death from puerperal fever of the Duchess of Orleans, one of her patients, brought fierce criticism, to which she replied with a vehement attack on male doctors. By 1609 she was said to have attended over 2000 births.

In 1608 Louyse published her famous treatise, *Observations diverses sur la stérilité, perte de fruict, fécondité, accouchements et maladies des femmes, et des enfants nouveaux naiz*. Its many subjects included anatomy, the stages of pregnancy, position of the foetus, and perinatal mortality and among its insights were new observations about the detachment of the placenta and the identification of undernourishment as a cause of anaemia (she was the first to treat this with iron) and as a factor in premature birth. The second edition was accompanied by detailed clinical cases, a history of her own education and advice for her daughter, a trainee midwife. Numerous revised editions of this immensely influential work followed during the succeeding century and it was translated into German, Dutch, English and Latin.

M. Alic: *Hypatia's Heritage* (1986)

**Bourke-White, Margaret** (1904–71). American photo-journalist. She was born in New York City. Her father was a designer in the printing industry and her mother was involved in publications for the blind. She was at first interested in engineering and biology but at Columbia University she studied photography with Clarence H. White. In 1925 she married an engineering student, Everett Chapman, but they were divorced a year later and she returned to studying, working as a photographer to pay her way through Cornell University in 1927. Interested in technology, she specialized in work on architecture and industrial subjects and in 1929 Henry R. Luce asked her to do the cover for the first issue of *Fortune*, which she later joined as a staff photographer. In 1930 she made the first of several visits to the USSR, which resulted in her book *Eyes on*

*Russia* (1931). In 1936, working for Luce's *Life*, she was assigned to cover the Depression in the dust-bowl, with the writer Erskine Caldwell; they produced a tragic record of rural misery in *You have Seen their Faces* (1937). In 1939 she and Caldwell married, and in the three years before their divorce they collaborated in *North of the Danube* (1939) and *Say, is This the USA?* (1941).

During World War II she covered the German attack on Moscow in 1941 and became the first Army Air Force woman photographer in action in North Africa and Italy. In 1945, attached to Patton's Third Army, she was one of the first to enter camps such as Buchenwald, her stark photographs arousing world-wide outrage. After the war she worked in India, where she photographed Gandhi, and in South Africa and Korea, until the gradual escalation of Parkinson's disease forced her to leave her job at *Life* in 1957.

M. Bourke-White: *Portrait of Myself* (1963)
V. Goldberg: *Margaret Bourke-White* (1986)

**Bow, Clara** (1905–65). American film actress. She was born in Brooklyn, New York; her father was a waiter and her mother was mentally unstable. She escaped from extreme poverty at the age of 16 by winning a movie magazine beauty contest, the prize for which was a bit-part in a film. She signed a contract with independent producer B.P. Schulberg who took her with him when he became a staff producer for Paramount in 1925. There she appeared in films such as *Mantrap* (1926) and *It*, written by Elinor Glyn, in 1927. She was publicized as the 'It' girl, symbol of the flapper and the new freedom of expression and behaviour seized by American women of the 1920s who smoked, drank, wore daring clothes and were sexually brave.

In three years of immense popularity Bow worked for several directors, including DOROTHY ARZNER (*Get Your Man*, 1927; *The Wild Party*, 1929). By the age of 25 she had made 48 films but physical and mental frailty and scandal about her private life ended her career shortly after the advent of sound. She married cowboy star Rex Bell in 1931 and they settled on his Nevada ranch. Her attempt to return to the movies failed

and she spent most of her remaining years in various sanatoriums.

J. Morella: *The 'It' Girl: the Incredible Story of Clara Bow* (1976)

**Bowen, Elizabeth (Dorothea Cole)** (1899–1973). Anglo-Irish novelist and short-story writer. Born and brought up in Dublin and the family home at Bowen's Court, County Cork, she moved to Kent at the age of seven with her mother, who died six years later. She was educated at Harpenden Hall, Hertfordshire, and at Downe House School, Kent. At the end of World War I she worked in a hospital for the treatment of shell-shock in Dublin, and then moved to London, where she briefly attended the London County Council School of Art. She started to write short stories and her first volume, *Encounters*, was published in 1923, the year she married Alan Cameron, an educational administrator. Her first novel, *The Hotel*, came out in 1927, by which time she was moving in literary circles that included ROSE MACAULAY, David Cecil and, later, VIRGINIA WOOLF and Rosamond Lehman. During the 1930s she received critical acclaim for her novels, which explored with great delicacy and sensitivity moral dilemmas posed by contemporary society, for example, *To the North* (1932), *The House in Paris* (1935) and *The Death of the Heart* (1938). In all, she published more than 70 short stories, 10 novels and various non-fiction works. Her last novel, *Eva Trout* (1969), won the James Tait Black Memorial Prize.

She wrote *Bowen's Court* (1942), a history of the house which she inherited in 1928 and visited regularly; she lived there only after World War II, during which she was an air-raid warden. Her experience of wartime London bore fruit in the atmospheric settings of her short stories in *The Demon Lover* (1945) and her novel *The Heat of the Day* (1949). She had to sell Bowen's Court in 1960 and finally settled in Hythe, Kent, where she died. Her other writings include the history of the Dublin hotel *The Shelbourne* (1951), a travel book *A Time in Rome* (1960) and much literary journalism, some of which is included in *Collected Impressions* (1950).

V. Glendinning: *Elizabeth Bowen* (1977)

**Box, Betty (Evelyn)** (1920–). English film producer. She began work in film as assistant to her brother Sydney, helping to produce more than 200 propaganda and training films during World War II. She became a producer after a period in charge of production at Islington studios. Her films include *Dear Murderer* (1947), *Doctor in the House* (1954), *A Tale of Two Cities* (1957), *The 39 Steps* (1960), and *Percy* (1971). She was awarded an OBE in 1958 for her services to the British film industry. In 1949 she married Peter Rogers. She has been a Director of Welbeck Film Distributors (since 1958), and of Ulster Television (1955–85).

**Box, Muriel** (1905–). English playwright, script-writer and film director. After working as a continuity girl, secretary and production preparer, in 1933 she began a 30-year partnership writing for theatre and film with her future husband Sydney Box (brother of BETTY BOX). In 1946 they won an Academy Award for Best Original Screenplay for *The Seventh Veil*.

Muriel Box began directing documentary films in 1941, due to the wartime scarcity of male directors, and was prevented from directing her own script for a film about road safety for children by the Ministry of Information because the task was considered too unpleasant for a woman. She directed her first feature film, *The Happy Family*, in 1950 and considered herself accepted by artists and producers after the success of *Street Corner* (about policewomen), made in 1953.

M. Box: *Odd Woman Out: an Autobiography* (1974)

**Bracegirdle, Anne** (1663–1748). English actress. Unable to provide for his family, her father placed her as a child with the Betterton family in London. She began her career as Atelina in Mountford's *The Injured Lovers* in 1688. She subsequently appeared with Betterton at Lincoln's Inn Fields Theatre as Angelica in *Love for Love* (1695). She created the parts of Belinda in Sir John Vanbrugh's *Provoked Wife*, and Almeria in John Dryden's *Mourning Bride* (1967), and played Isabella, Portia, Desdemona, Ophelia, Cordelia and Mrs Ford in numerous Shakespearean adaptations. Her outstanding successes were in the comedies of William Congreve: she was the original Millamant in *Way*

*of the World*. She retired from the stage in 1707, equally admired by her fellow actors and the public. Anne Bracegirdle is buried in Westminster Abbey.

E. Robins: *Twelve Great Actresses* (1900)

**Braddon, Mary Elizabeth** (1837–1915). English novelist. Born in London, she was the daughter of a feckless solicitor and sports-writer; she was brought up by her mother, who left her husband taking Mary with her in 1840, and had a disturbed and impoverished childhood. She began writing in 1856, and in 1857 went on the stage as 'Mary Seaton' to support the family. In 1860 she became a full-time writer, and met the publisher John Maxwell, whose wife was in an Irish asylum. She lived with him until they were able to marry in 1874, looked after his five children and their own six (one of whom died as a baby), and made enough by her writing to pay off all their debts.

Financial pressures partly explain her prolific output: she wrote 20 novels between 1861 and 1871, and over 70 in all, as well as 9 plays, and some verse; she also edited several London magazines, notably *Belgravia* from 1866, and *The Mistletoe Bough* (1878–92). Her fourth book, *Lady Audley's Secret* (1862), was a best-seller and helped to inaugurate the vogue for the sensation novel, with lurid melodrama, sexual passion and criminal women; however, it has also been seen as a witty, subversive attack on the Victorian idea of the sentimental, asexual, passive woman. Many critics prefer later works such as the historical novel *The Infidel* (1900) and *The Rose of Life* (1905). Other sensationalists were Rhoda Broughton, author of *Cometh up as a Flower* (1867); Mrs Henry Wood, whose best-selling *East Lynne* appeared in the same year as *Lady Audley's Secret* (1862); and Helen Mathers, who wrote *Comin' thro the Rye* (1875).

R.L. Wolff: *The Sensational Victorian: the Life and Fiction of Braddon* (1978)

**Bradstreet** [née Dudley], **Anne** (c1612–72). American poet. Probably born at Northampton, daughter of Thomas Dudley, the steward to the Earl of Lincoln, she was privately educated, and well-read in Classical and contemporary European literature. She married the nonconformist

Simon Bradsteet in 1628, and they sailed to New England with John Winthrop in 1630. They settled in Ipswich (1635–45), and North Andover (1645–72), and had eight children. Simon became a judge and colonial administrator (later Governor of Massachusetts), and on her remote rural farm Anne wrote poetry. In 1650, without her knowledge, her brother-in-law published a collection of her poems in England, entitled *The Tenth Muse lately sprung up in America*, mostly allegorical poems influenced by Du Bartas, Spenser and Sidney. Lasting fame has come from the poems published after her death in 1678, which abandon literary models and deal directly with the life and landscape of New England, and with her love for her husband and children.

**Bradwell, Myra (Colby)** (1831–94). American lawyer. Born in Manchester, Vermont, into a distinguished family, she spent her childhood in New York State and Illinois, and was educated in schools near her married sister in Wisconsin, and in Elgin, Illinois. In 1852, after teaching in local schools, she married a poor law student, James Bradwell, against her parents' wishes. They moved to Memphis, Tennessee, where they taught and opened a private school, but in 1854 moved to Chicago, where James became a successful lawyer and judge. They had four children, two of whom died in infancy.

During the Civil War, Myra worked for the Northwestern Sanitary Commission, and later for various charities such as the Soldiers' Aid Society and the Illinois Industries School for Girls. She studied law with her husband, and in 1868 began publishing the *Chicago Legal News*. A special charter had to be granted to free her of her dependent status as a married woman so that she could act as a proprietor and manager independently. The paper, which published official court reports, was a tremendous success and the business expanded to include legal forms and the printing of the Illinois Revised Statutes. Although the office was gutted by fire in 1871, Myra still managed to publish the paper in Milwaukee.

She was a forceful, witty woman, who used her enormous influence in the legal world to encourage legislative reform, and to campaign for temperance, prison reforms and women's suffrage. Some of the state reforms she influenced included the right of women to their own earnings, the secure right of a widow to her husband's estate, a woman's right to hold public office on school boards, and equal custody rights over children.

In 1869 she qualified for the Illinois Bar but was vetoed as a woman, although in 1873 the Supreme Court decision decided to leave the issue to each individual state, and Illinois had already removed the sex disqualification. One woman who was admitted to the Bar in this year was Belva Lockwood (1830–1917) who became famous for her long battle to become the first woman to practise in front of the Supreme Court. Myra herself did not reapply until 1890. She managed the *Chicago Legal News* until her death, and her daughter, Bessie Bradwell, continued it until 1925.

H. Kogan: 'Myra Bradwell: Crusader at Law', *Chicago History* (1974–5)

**Bragina, Lyudmila** (1943– ). Russian runner. Born at Sverdlovsk, Lyudmila came to prominence only two months before the 1972 Olympics, and caused amazement at her first world record, in the 1500 metres, which was newly introduced as an Olympic event. In both semi-final and final she improved these records to 4 minutes 1.4 seconds, a speed faster than Albert Hill's 1920 gold medal performance by 1.4 seconds. Her lack of speed over shorter distances was compensated by tremendous stamina: her middle-distance running improved such that, at the 14th USA–USSR track meet in August 1976, she cut her own world record in the 3000-metres race by 18 seconds. This set a new women's record of 8 minutes 27.1 seconds.

**Brant, Molly** [Mary] (1736–96). American-Indian representative. Probably born in Mohawk valley, New York State, she became the mistress of Sir William Johnson, Superintendent of Indian Affairs for the Northern Colonies, with whom she had nine children after 1759. As his official hostess she was extremely influential in diplomatic relations with the Indian tribes. After his death in 1774 she ran a farm and business, but during the American Revolution she supported the British, sending intelligence and arms, and rallying tribes, particularly the Iroquois, to their support. Her brother, Joseph Brant, was a famous Indian warrior. Forced to move from her home, she was sent to Niagara, then to the St Lawrence River, and in 1783 settled in Ontario, receiving compensation and an annual pension in recognition of her services.

'Molly Brant, Mohawk Matron', *Ontario History* (1964)

**Braun, Eva** (1912–45). German mistress of Adolf Hitler. She was born into a bourgeois family, her father was a Lutheran and her mother a Catholic and she was educated at a school run by English nuns. She always retained both her piety and a love of English literature, her favourite author being Oscar Wilde. In her twenties she became sales assistant to the photographer Hoffmann, and it was in his studio that she met Hitler in 1929. In 1931 Hitler's niece Angela (known as Geli Rambal), who shared his house and of whom he was obsessively possessive, committed suicide. To help him overcome his distress Eva apparently slavishly imitated Geli's dress and behaviour. They became lovers in 1932. After he became Chancellor and then Head of State she continued to work for Hoffmann, and distraught at Hitler's indifference she attempted suicide several times. Eventually he bought her a house at Bogenhausen, where she worked as his secretary during most of World War II, but he never allowed her to be seen in public with him. She remained with him in Berlin jn the last days of the war and they are reputed to have married in the bunker at 11.45 pm on Saturday, 28 April 1945, and to have committed suicide 48 hours later. The bodies have never been identified.

G.B. Infield: *Eva and Adolf* (1974)

**Braun, Lily** (1865–1916). German writer and socialist. In 1893 she married the philosopher, Georg Gizicky, who died in 1895. She then married the socialist leader Heinrich Stammte. She taught and was a literary critic, writing *Aus Goethes Freundenkreis* in 1892. She became involved in socialist circles, but her strong feminist views, expressed in *Die Frauenfrage* (1901), alienated leaders such as CLARA ZETKIN who

believed women's issues should be subordinate to those of the working class as a whole. Lily was forced to leave the Social Democratic Party in 1901; she remained on the radical, militant wing of German feminism. Between 1909 and 1911 she published her *Memoiren einer Sozialistin*.

**Bremer, Fredrika** (1801–65). Swedish novelist. She was born in Abö, Finland, but her family moved in 1804 to a country estate near Stockholm; she was brought up in a sheltered and repressive household. In 1820–21 she made a tour of Europe, and on her return involved herself with charity work, publishing her *Sketches of Everyday Life* anonymously in 1828 to raise funds. Its success encouraged her, and after her father's death in 1830 she travelled and wrote, publishing many novels and short stories, including *The Neighbours* (1837), and *The House* (1843), winning a gold medal from the Swedish Academy in 1844. During the 1840s her novels, chiefly stories of family relationships, were translated into English by M. Howitt.

She was also actively involved in reform movements, organizing women's charity associations, and campaigning for rights to education and training, for the right to dispose of property, and for the establishment of an age of majority for unmarried women. In 1843 her appeal to women to form associations to help deprived city children was considered too radical, as it implied working outside the home. She herself nursed during the Stockholm cholera epidemic of 1853, founded an orphanage and also established a school to train women teachers. She visited the USA, England and Europe, studying the organization of social work, describing herself as a 'Christian Socialist'. In 1854, provoked by the Crimean War, she appealed to women internationally to found a peace movement, and in 1856 her feminist novel, *Hertha*, caused a national uproar. The first national women's association in Sweden was named after her in 1885. Her letters, *Fredrika Bremer's brev*, were published in four volumes (1914–15).

C. Bramer [Mrs Milow]: *Life, Letters and Posthumous Works of Fredrika Bremer* (1868)

**Brent, Margaret** (c1601–71). American colonist. One of 13 children of the Lord of Admington and Lark Stoke, Gloucestershire, Margaret was brought up as a Roman Catholic, and in 1638 emigrated with her sister and two brothers to the new Catholic colony of Maryland. With her sister she bought 70 acres in St Mary's, and in 1642 acquired 1000 acres on Kent Island from her brother. A powerful landowner, she was named as executor for Governor Calvert in 1647, when she restored calm and raised funds for mutinous soldiers by selling lands belonging to Lord Baltimore, 'The Proprietor'. She is represented as an early feminist because of her demand for two votes in the assembly, one for her freehold, another for her position as executor. In 1651 she followed her brother Giles to Virginia, naming her estate 'Peace'; they were highly influential in developing the colony.

**Brice, Fanny** (1891–1951). American comedienne and singer. Born in New York, as a girl she appeared in light stage shows in Brooklyn, moving on to vaudeville and burlesque shows, rising from the chorus to solo singing and dancing spots. She starred in nearly all of the Ziegfeld Follies from 1910 to 1923 and was as popular for her Brooklyn voice and earthy wit as for her singing. She starred in *The Music Box Revue* (1924–5), in several Broadway plays, and on radio. She was married first to gambler Nick Arnstein and then to producer Billy Rose. She also appeared in films, including *Night Club*, and *My Man* (1928), and *The Great Ziegfeld* (1936). The films about her life, *Funny Girl* (1968), and *Funny Lady* (1975), starred BARBRA STREISAND.
N. Katkov: *The Fabulous Fanny* (1953)

**Bridget** [Godmarsson [née Persson], Bridget] (*c*1303–73). Swedish saint and founder. The daughter of Birger Persson, Governor of Uppland, in 1317 Bridget married Ulf Godmarsson, who later became Governor of the province of Nercia. They had eight children, including Saint Katherine of Vadstena. When her husband died in 1344, Bridget retired to a life of penance and prayer near the Cistercian monastry of Alvastra. Here she dictated her revelations to the Prior. This book, chiefly about Christ's sufferings and future events, proved highly controversial and led theologians to disagree over the authenticity

and orthodoxy of her religious vision.

In one revelation, Bridget was commanded to found a new order, and after receiving papal permission in 1370 she began the Order of the Holy Saviour (Bridgettines). Apart from several pilgrimages, Bridget spent the last 23 years of her life in Rome, living very austerely, caring for the poor and sick, and ceaselessly working for the return of the Pope from Avignon to Rome.
J. Jorgensen: *Saint Bridget of Sweden* (Eng. trans., I. Lund, 1954)

**Brigid** (*c*450–*c*523). Irish abbess and saint. Although the ascertainable facts about her life are few, St Brigid, 'The Mary of the Gael', is Ireland's most revered saint after St Patrick. According to legend, she was born at Fochart in the present County Louth of a noble father and slave mother. While still a child, she was sold to a druid whom she later converted to Christianity. Her father then tried to marry her to the King of Ulster, who was so impressed by her piety that he freed her. It is known that she founded the first women's religious community among the Irish. The legends around Brigid give an impression of a strong, gay, compassionate character with a great concern to meet the physical and spiritual needs of her neighbours.
A. Curtayne: *St Brigid of Ireland* (1954)

**Brinvilliers.** *See* DE BRINVILLIERS.

**Brittain, Vera** (1893–1970). English writer. Born in Newcastle-under-Lyme, the daughter of a prosperous paper manufacturer, she was educated at St Martin's School, Kingswood, Surrey, and in 1914 won an exhibition to Somerville College, Oxford, leaving after a year to work as a voluntary nurse in London, France and Malta. In 1919 she returned, took her degree and became a journalist, and in 1925 married the political philosopher George Catlin. A compulsive writer since childhood, her first published novels were *The Dark Tide* (1923) and *Not Without Honour* (1926), but although she continued to write fiction, she achieved more success with her autobiographical trilogy: *Testament of Youth* (1933), which reflects her pacifism and feminism; *Testament of Friendship*

(1940), a tribute to Winifred Holtby; and *Testament of Experience* (1957).

Notable among her post-war books were the novels *Account Rendered* (1945), *Lady into Woman: a History of Women from Victoria to Elizabeth II* (1953), and *Radclyffe Hall: a Case of Obscurity* (1968).

Her outspoken views and allusions to contemporary figures caused much controversy. She contributed to many newspapers and periodicals, gave lecture tours in Canada, Germany, India, the Netherlands, Pakistan, Scandinavia, and the USA, was Chairwoman of the Married Women's Association, Vice-President of the Women's International League of Peace and Freedom, and Life President of the Society of Women Writers and Journalists. Her daughter, SHIRLEY WILLIAMS, became a prominent politician.

V. Brittain: *Testaments* (1933, 1940, 1957)

**Bronte.** English family of novelists. The Bronte sisters were the youngest three children of Patrick Bronte, the son of an Irish peasant who had won a Cambridge education and become Rector of Haworth, on the Yorkshire Moors near Bradford, in 1817. Their mother died of cancer in 1821, and the girls were brought up by their aunt Elizabeth, a stern remote figure, until 1842.

**(1) Charlotte** [pseud. Currer Bell] (1816–55). After her early education at home, Charlotte was sent to a boarding school for clergymen's daughters at Cowan Bridge, with her elder sisters Maria and Elizabeth and eight-year-old Emily. The elder girls both died of tuberculosis in the spring of 1825, aggravated by lack of food and insanitary conditions at the school, but Charlotte and Emily were removed during the following autumn in case they too fell ill.

Charlotte then spent several years at home, where, with her brother and sisters, she was encouraged to read widely and to discuss everything she wished, from world affairs with her father, to folk-lore with the elderly neighbours. During these years she, her brother Branwell, Emily and Anne, invented secret lands and wrote poetry, drama and prose sagas of extraordinary complexity, often inscribed in microscopic script in tiny sewn volumes. Mrs Gaskell's biography includes a list of 22 such works written by Charlotte between 1829 and 1831.

In 1831 she went alone to Miss Wooler's School at Roe Head, and then, after three more quiet years at Haworth, returned to Roe Head in 1835 as a teaching assistant, taking Emily with her for three months, and then Anne. She disliked the work and after a near-breakdown she left in 1836. In 1839 she tried to make a living as a governess, first with the Sidgwick family, whom she detested, later with the Whites, and then the sisters planned to open their own school. Branwell provided money for Charlotte and Emily to study at the Pensionat Heger in Brussels, where they spent February to November in 1842, but after receiving no enquiries concerning their school, Charlotte returned to Brussels as an English teacher in 1843; her misery and unrequited love for M. Heger are revealed in unsent letters published after her death, and in transmuted form in *Villette*.

Returning home in 1845, her discovery of Emily's poems and her organization of the publishing of *Poems by Currer, Ellis and Acton Bell* in 1846 initiated the intense period of the Brontes' literary activity. All wrote novels, and although Charlotte's *The Professor* was rejected several times, Smith & Elder's encouragement led her to offer them *Jane Eyre*, which was an overnight best-seller on its appearance in 1847. The sisters gave up their anonymity and Anne and Charlotte visited London to prove that all the Bells were not one person.

The following year brought the final decline and death of Branwell (September 1848), Emily (December) and Anne (May 1849). Now virtually alone, Charlotte wrote *Shirley* (1849) and *Villette* (1852). She visited London in 1849, 1850, 1851 and 1853, making considerable impact on literary circles despite her shyness. Having turned down three other proposals she married Arthur Bell Nicholls, her father's curate, in 1854, but died the next March during her pregnancy.

**(2) Emily** [pseud. Ellis Bell] (1818–48). Emily accompanied her sisters Maria, Elizabeth and Charlotte during their fatal few months at the Cowan Bridge school but after her return in 1825 she remained at home in Haworth until 1835 when she accompanied Charlotte to Roe Head. She hated the constraint, and returned home after three months. Between 1837 and 1838

*Sarah Bernhardt*

*Rosa Bonheur*

*The Bronte sisters*

*Catherine II*

she taught at a school at Law Hill, Halifax, and in 1842 went with Charlotte to the Pensionat Heger in Brussels. She again found the nine months of containment unbearable and refused to return as a music teacher when invited in 1843. She spent the rest of her life, apart from one trip to York with Anne, at Haworth.

In 1846 Charlotte persuaded her, against her will, to publish her passionate religious and nature poems in *Poems by Currer, Ellis and Acton Bell. Wuthering Heights* was published with Anne's *Agnes Grey* in 1847, but met with bewilderment and censure at its irregularity and power. After Branwell's death, Emily sickened, but continued her insistence on undertaking all the worst household work, and would not admit to pain, refusing all doctors and medicine, collapsing in December 1848 still adamant that she could stand alone.

**(3) Anne** [pseud. Acton Bell] (1820–49) had no formal education, apart from a few months at Miss Wooler's School at Roe Head in 1835. In 1839, like Charlotte, she worked as a governess, first with the Inghams at Blake Hall, and then with the Robinsons, where she remained from 1841 to 1845. She left after Branwell's obsession for Mrs Robinson led to his dismissal. Her poems were included in *Poems by Currer, Ellis and Acton Bell* (1846) and in the winter of 1846–7 she wrote *Agnes Grey*, published under the name of Acton Bell, with Emily's *Wuthering Heights*. This quiet semi-autobiographical novel was followed by the more melodramatic and successful *Tenant of Wildfell Hall* (1848). Tubercular since her youth, Anne's health collapsed after Emily's death and she died on a visit to Scarborough with Charlotte, in May 1849. She had hardly left home apart from her visit to York with Emily and her trip to London with Charlotte to confront their sudden fame.

Mrs Gaskell: *The Life of Charlotte Bronte* (1855)
W. Gerin: *Emily Bronte: a Biography* (1971)
————: *Anne Bronte: a Biography* (1975)

**Brooks, Gwendolyn** (1917–). American poet. Born in Topeka, Kansas, and educated in Chicago, she was Publicity Director for the National Association for the Advancement of Colored People in the 1930s. She married H.L. Blakeley in 1939 and they have two children. She became known as a fine lyrical poet on the publication of *A Street in Bronzeville* (1945), and won a Pulitzer Prize with her second volume, *Annie Allen* (1949). She taught poetry at various American universities and was a reviewer on leading journals. After two more collections of poetry, and a novel, *Maud Martha* (1953), her *Selected Poems* appeared in 1963. She continued to write, becoming increasingly militant in tone during the 1970s, and is recognized as a leading spirit in the movement to create a Black American aesthetic. She has published several collections since 1970, has received numerous awards and was named Poet Laureate of Illinois in 1969, and is a member of the National Institute and the American Academy of Arts and Letters.

G. Brookes: *Report from Part One* (1972)

**Brooks, Romaine (Goddard)** (1874–1970). English painter. Born in Rome, she spent an extraordinary childhood with her wealthy American mother in New York and Europe. After a scattered education and a period of training as a singer, she achieved financial independence and in 1896 went to study art in Rome. She had a studio there, moving to Capri in 1899 where she became a member of a group that included Somerset Maugham, Axel Munthe, Norman Douglas, and her future husband John Brooks. Both homosexuals, their marriage was one of convenience. After painting in London and Cornwall, Romaine, who had inherited the family fortune in 1902, eventually moved to Paris, becoming a prominent figure in society. She maintained a close relationship with NATALIE CLIFFORD BARNEY for over 40 years, and had many other affairs. Some of her most moving portraits are of eminent members of this lesbian group such as *At the Piano* (1920), *Una, Lady Troubridge* (1924), and *Renata Borgatti*.

She returned only once to the USA, in the 1930s, and spent the latter half of her life in Italy and in the South of France.

M. Secrest: *Between Me and Life* (1974)

**Brooks-Randolph, Angie (Elizabeth)** (1928–). Liberian lawyer and diplomat. She was educated locally, working her way through high school as a typist, then becoming a stenographer for the Justice Department. The first woman to be accepted as a legal apprentice, she was laughed at on her first appearance in court, and personally appealed to President Truman, who gave her a grant so that she could attend college in North Carolina. She went on to the University of Wisconsin, and then to University College, London (1952–3). She then returned to Liberia where she worked as a lawyer, becoming assistant Attorney-General 1953–8 and also doing some part-time teaching. From 1958 to 1972 she held the post of Assistant Secretary of State, but continued her legal work, and was President of the International Federation of Women Lawyers (1964–7). She was President of the 24th session of the United Nations General Assembly (1969–70, only the second woman after VIJAYA PANDIT), represented Liberia at the UN Plenary Session (1970–73), and was Permanent Representative to the UN (1975–7), during which period she was also Ambassador to Cuba. She has campaigned tirelessly for women's rights and professional status, and for better educational opportunities, and has herself taken care of 47 foster children. Angie Brooks-Randolph is on innumerable advisory bodies and committees, holds 18 honorary doctorates of law from various American universities, and has been awarded many honours by religious and civil organisations.

**Brough, (Alice) Louise** (1923–). American lawn tennis player. She was born in Oklahoma. Her tennis career, particularly the early part, was closely linked with that of Margaret Osborne, her friend, rival and doubles partner. They won the US Doubles in the years 1942 to 1950 and 1955 to 1957. Louise won the Women's Doubles at Wimbledon five times, and reached the finals three times, as well as winning French and Australian doubles and various mixed doubles.

Louise won the US Singles Title in 1947, but lost it to Margaret Osborne the following year. In 1948 an operation corrected the condition in her back which had caused her tendency to tire after two sets; in 1948 and 1950 she won all three titles at Wimbledon, and two of them in 1949. Her singles victories were interrupted by Doris Hart and 'LITTLE MO' CONNOLLY, but in a well-matched final against Beverly Fleitz in 1955, Louise's better tactics regained her the singles title in two sets (7–5, 8–6). In the Wightman Cup she won all 22 of her rubbers.

**Brown, Helen Gurley** (1927–). American journalist. Born in Green Forest, Arkansas, she studied at Texas State College and then at Woodbury College, graduating in 1942. For the next three years she was on the junior management staff of the Music Corporation of America, and then moved into advertising, working for a Los Angeles agency until 1958 as a copywriter. In 1959, aged 37, while working as an account executive for a Hollywood agency, she married David Brown. In 1962 her international best-seller, *Sex and the Single Girl*, thrust her into the limelight, seeming to encapsulate the new mood of independence and excitement which greater earning power had brought to many women. Three years later she published *Sex and the Office* and became the Editor-in-Chief of *Cosmopolitan*, making it into one of the five highest-selling magazines in the USA and creating the image of the 'Cosmo Girl'. Her other books include *Outrageous Opinions* (1966), *Sex and the New Single Girl* (1971) and *Having It All* (1982). Since 1972 she has also been Editorial Director of *Cosmopolitan*'s foreign editions. She has received several awards for journalism and has frequently been voted as one of the USA's most influential women. She won the New York Women In Communications Award (1985) and in the same year established the Helen Gurley Brown Research Professorship at Northwestern University.

**Brown, Rachel (Fuller)** (1898–1980). American biochemist. Born in Springfield, Massachusetts, Rachel grew up in Missouri where she was encouraged to collect specimens such as moths and butterflies. At Mount Holyoke College she studied history and chemistry, but the experimental method and exactness of chemistry appealed most and she gained her MSc in organic chemistry from the University of Chicago in 1921. She worked as a teacher before returning for her PhD in organic chemistry and bacteriology.

In 1926 she began work as a chemist for the New York State Department of Health and continued there for the next 42 years. Her work, before the days of antibiotics, was on the cause of pneumonia, pneumococcus bacteria, and the standardization of antiserums. After World War II there was some control of disease-causing bacteria, but not of fungi. Elizabeth collaborated with Elizabeth Hazen, a mycologist, on a research project, and in 1949 they isolated the first antifungal antiobiotic which they named *Nystatin*, after the New York State Laboratories. *Nystatin* is used in human fungus infections, and tissue culture, as well as in killing mildew on paintings and fighting Dutch Elm Disease. The income from it, about $12 million so far, they put in the Brown-Hazen Fund for grants and research. Rachel was the first woman to receive the Pioneer Chemist Award (1975) from the American Institute of Chemists, among other awards.

R.S. Baldwin: *The Fungus Fighters: Two Women Scientists and their Discovery* (1980)

**Brown, Rosemary** (1917–). English housewife and medium/composer. Rosemary Brown alleges that the spirits of dead composers dictate to her. She has written down over 400 works, especially in the styles of Liszt, Chopin, Beethoven, Brahms and Schubert, although she herself had little musical education and is not a technically accomplished musician. Most of the works are for piano. She has written two books, *Unfinished Symphonies* (1971) about her life as a medium and *Immortals at my Elbow* (1974) about her psychical philosophy. She has published several large collections of her 'received' works.

I. Parrott: *The Music of Rosemary Brown* (1978)

**Brown Blackwell, Antoinette-Louisa** (1825–1921). American reformer and priest. Born in Henrietta, Monroe County, New York State, she belonged to the Congregational Church and spoke at their meetings from childhood. She became a school-teacher at 16 and graduated in literature from Oberlin College in 1847 and theology in 1850. She was at first refused ordination because she was a woman and so preached in any church which would accept her until she became pastor of the Congregational Church in South Butler, New York (1852–4), becoming the first woman minister in the USA (she later became a Unitarian). She also campaigned for the abolition of slavery, for women's rights and temperance, and won

international publicity for her vociferous protests when refused permission to speak at the World's Temperance Convention (New York, 1853), although she was an official delegate.

In 1856 she married ELIZABETH BLACKWELL's brother Samuel, and thus also became the sister-in-law of LUCY STONE who married Henry Blackwell. They had six children, but she continued her crusade for the immediate emancipation of slaves. After the Civil War she devoted herself to fighting for prohibition and suffrage, and became well-known as a cogent and powerful public speaker. She also wrote several books clarifying her social and religious views, including *Shadows of our Social System* (1855), *The Sexes Throughout Nature* (1875) and *The Social Side of Mind and Action* (1915).

E.R. Hays: *Those Extraordinary Blackwells* (1967)

**Browning, Elizabeth Barrett** (1806–61). English poet. Born in Durham, the oldest of 11 children, she spent her childhood at Hope End, Herefordshire. A precocious child, reading Greek at 8, her *Battle of Marathon* was privately printed when she was 12. When she was 20 her mother died, and her father's financial difficulties made him move first to Sidmouth (1826–8), and then London, where he became increasingly jealous and tyrannical. Shocked by the drowning of her favourite brother, Elizabeth retreated into invalidism, writing verse, and articles for the *Athenaeum*. Her reputation was established with *The Seraphim* (1838), and *Poems* (1844), especially the moving pleas against social injustice such as 'The Cry of the Children'.

In 1846 Robert Browning came to the house, and although the relationship was fiercely opposed by her father, she evaded him and married Browning, escaping a week later to Paris. Her father never communicated with her again but after her marriage her health improved. The Brownings settled in Pisa (1846), then Florence (1847). Their son Robert was born in 1849. They became the centre of a literary circle, while Elizabeth was also deeply committed to the Italian nationalist cause. In 1851 she published *Sonnets from the Portuguese*, among the finest English love lyrics, and after other collections of verse, wrote the long narrative poem *Aurora Leigh* (1857). This combines an analysis of male domination in various guises, with a psychological romance ending in egalitarian love. It made a considerable impact, despite the polemical tone; in her time her reputation exceeded Browning's and she was considered as a potential Poet Laureate.

M. Forster: *Elizabeth Barrett Browning* (1988)

**Brundtland, Gro Harlem** (1939–). Norwegian politician, and the first woman Prime Minister of that country. Born in Oslo, where her father was a doctor and politician, later Defence Minister, she was educated at university there and at Harvard, and married Arne Olav in 1960; they have four children. (Her husband is a leading figure in the opposition Conservative Party.) A qualified doctor, with particular interest in public health, she became Consultant to the Ministry of Health and Social Affairs (1965–7), Medical Officer of Oslo City Health Department (1968–9) and Deputy Director of the Oslo School Health Services in 1970. At the age of 35 she was appointed Minister for the Environment, and in 1975 became Vice-Chairman of the Labour Party. In 1979 she left the government to concentrate on revitalizing the Labour Party organization, and then ran for President of the Party, receiving overwhelming support from local branches. In 1981, when Odvar Nordli resigned for health reasons, she took over at the head of the minority government for nine months. She is identified with the left wing of her party on social and economic policy, and is especially concerned about Norway's declining industries.

During the early 1980s she was also a member of the UN Commission on Disarmament and Security Issues, was Chair of the World Commission on Environment and Development (which produced the report *Our Common Future* in 1987) and in 1985 joined the board of directors of the 'Better World Society', Brundtland became Prime Minister of Norway for the second time in 1986. She heads a cabinet of eight women and nine men – the most female cabinet in history. The ruling she laid down within the Labour Party of 40% women candidates has led to 34% of Members of Parliament being women, more than anywhere else in the world.

**Brunhilda** [Brunehaut] (*d* 613). Frankish queen. A Visigoth princess, she was brilliantly educated, and became Queen of Austrasia, and a Catholic convert, when she married Sigebert I in 567. When her sister Galswintha, who had married Chilperic I, king of the western Frankish kingdom, was strangled at the instigation of FREDEGUND, she provoked her husband to demand compensation. This led to a long war which lasted until her death. Sigebert was murdered in 575 and Brunhilda was imprisoned in Rouen, where she managed to marry one of Chilperic's sons. Chilperic repudiated the marriage, but allowed her to return to Metz. Throughout the reigns of her young son, Childebert II, and of her two grandsons she continued her struggle against Fredegund, undeterred by Chilperic's death in 584; and in 592 she arranged the union of Austrasia and Burgundy. Her power was disputed after her son's death, and the Frankish nobles rebelled against her autocratic rule, appealing in 612 to her enemy, Fredegund's son Lothair II, for help. Brunhilda fled to Burgundy, but was betrayed and handed over to Lothair. He subjected her to three days of torture and public humiliation; she was tied to a camel in front of the army, before she was dragged to death by a horse. Her ashes were buried at the abbey of Autun, one of a number of religious establishments that she had founded.

Her reputation has always been ambivalent, although Gregory of Tours, who vehemently attacks Fredegund in the *Historia Francorum*, presents her as a model queen, and later historians have seen her as a great stateswoman, who maintained a consistent policy of supporting the throne against the aristocracy, at the same time exercising firm control over the development of the Frankish Church.

**Bryant, Hazel** (1939–83). American theatre producer. Hazel Bryant's father was a preacher in the African Methodist Episcopal Church, and she grew up in Ohio, Kentucky and Maryland. She studied music, graduating from Oberlin in 1962, then pursued her studies in Salzburg and at Columbia University, New York. Although her personal career was as a singer, touring in opera in the United States and Europe, her major work was the promotion of black theatre and music. In 1963 she founded the Afro-American Total Theater Arts Foundation, and in 1968 the Richard Allen Center of Culture and Art in New York. She became President of both the African-American Federation of Arts and the Black Theater Alliance, 1971, and was a major figure in the National Arts Consortium in 1977. Despite severe illnesses in 1967 and 1974, her energy went into funding organization and production, notably of the annual Arts Festival at the Lincoln Center. She produced over 200 musicals and plays, including the famous staging of Langston Hughes's *Black Nativity* and the all-black *Long Day's Journey into Night* (both in 1981). She died, aged only 44, before she could carry out still more ambitious plans for international black theatre programmes.

**Bryher** [legally adopted name of Annie Winifred Ellerman] (1894–1983). British writer. Bryher was born in Margate, Kent, the daughter of banker and shipbuilder Sir John Reeves Ellerman. She did not know until she was 24 that she was illegitimate, her parents having only married, secretly, when she was 15. Once she had discovered the fact she refused on principle to have her birth legitimized, insisting that their love was more important than legal marriage.

She had no formal education, but read widely, enjoying the classics and teaching herself Arabic. At 14 her restlessness made her parents send her, for a miserable year, to Queenswood boarding school. She wrote her first novel during World War I, when she began her lifelong friendship with the poet H.D. (HILDA DOOLITTLE), whose daughter Perdita she adopted. In 1921 she married the American writer Robert McAlmon, with whom she went to Paris: their circle there included writers and artists such as STEIN, Joyce and Picasso. She divorced McAlmon in 1926, and in 1927 married Kenneth McPherson. They divided their time between England and the Continent, and edited the film journal *Close-up*: she was the author of *Film Problems of Soviet Russia* (1929). In Berlin in the 1930s, Bryher helped many Jews and other members of persecuted groups to leave Germany, then joined a refugee committee in Switzerland where she lived from 1934 until 1940, when she returned to England, continuing to work with refugees. In 1947 she divorced McPher-

son and moved permanently to Switzerland.

Bryher published several collections of verse and sixteen novels, beginning with *Development* (1920). In later life she became known particularly for her historical novels, such as *Beowulf* (1948).

Bryher: *The Heart to Artemis: A Writer's Memoirs* (1962)
——— : *The Days of Mars: A Memoir 1940–46*

**Buck, Pearl S(ydenstricker)** (1892–1973). American writer. Born in Hillsboro, West Virginia, the daughter of Presbyterian missionaries, she spent a harsh early childhood travelling in China, where several of the family's other children died. The family settled in Chinkiang, on the Yangtse River, and she was sent at 15 to boarding school in Shanghai. At the age of 17 she travelled via Europe to Randolph-Macon College, Virginia, took a BA in 1914, and began teaching psychology. After returning to China to look after her mother, she married agriculturist John Lossing Buck, spent five years in the Northern Provinces, then taught English at Nanking University from 1921 to 1931.

Her first book, *East Wind – West Wind*, was published in 1929. She then wrote *The Good Earth* (1931). This saga of peasant life became an enormous success both as a book and film, and formed part of a trilogy with *Sons* (1932), and *The House Divided* (1935). In 1935 Pearl Buck finally returned to America. After her divorce she married publisher Richard Walsh, with who she co-edited the magazine *Asia* (1941–6). A prolific writer, Buck produced around 40 novels, most of which have Chinese themes, and several short-story collections. Her 50 non-fiction works include the classic biographies of her parents, *Fighting Angel*, and *The Exile* (both 1936). Her writing reveals liberal humanitarian attitudes also evident in her public actions, such as the founding of the East and West Association and the Wellcome House adoption agency for Asian-Americans in 1941.

She received the Nobel Prize for Literature in 1938, many other awards and honorary degrees, and was elected one of the two women life-members of the American Association of Arts and Letters in 1951.

P. Buck: *My Several Worlds* (1954)
J.F. Harris: *Buck: a Biography* (1969–71)

**Bunke, Tamara (Tania)** (?1940–68). Argentinian revolutionary. She was born in Argentina, where her German communist parents were living as refugees. They moved to Germany when she was a child, but she always retained an interest in Latin American nationalism. In 1961, a week after the attempted invasion at the Bay of Pigs, she left for Cuba. She worked with the Ministry of Education as a translator, studied journalism, and in the mid-1960s travelled as a liaison worker between Europe, Cuba and other Latin American countries, eventually becoming an undercover agent in Bolivia. She joined Che Guevara in the uprising there and was killed with eight comrades in 1968. Her memory is greatly revered in Cuba.

M. Rojas and M.R. Calderon: *Tania: the Unforgettable Guerilla* (1971)

**Buonaparte** [née Tascher de la Pagerie, Marie Josèphe Rose], **Josephine** (1763–1814). Empress of the French (1804–09). Born in Martinique, the daughter of a sugar planter, after a cursory education she was sent to Paris aged 15 to her aunt, where she met her childhood friend Alexandre de Beauharnais. Their marriage was arranged in 1779. Although she accompanied him to Paris, his indifference to his provincial wife was so profound that in 1785 she demanded a separation after retreat into a convent with her children. After three years in Martinique, she returned to Paris in 1789, her salon being a meeting place for Deputies of the Assembly, including her former husband. Alexandre was imprisoned and guillotined, and Josephine herself was interned in the Carmes, where she had a brief romance with General Hoche and met THÉRÉSIA DE CABARRUS TALLIEN.

After her liberation in 1795, she had a brief affair with Barras, a powerful member of the Directory, and then married Napoleon in a civil ceremony in 1796. She travelled to Italy with him, but remained in France during his Egyptian expedition, amassing a fortune through dealings for military contractors, which allowed her to buy the estate of Malmaison. Rumours of her extravagances and infidelities enraged Napoleon, but she regained his favour and was a zealous political supporter, reconciling the Republican old guard with the new Consulship and creating a court which attracted foreign ambassadors, artists and writers. In 1804 she persuaded Napoleon to re-marry her with full religious rites. She was married to Napoleon on the eve of their joint coronation as Emperor and Empress. She battled to keep her position until 1809, when she was finally divorced so that Napoleon could marry the Austrian archduchess Marie Louise. Created Duchess of Navarre, she kept the title and honours of Empress, and retired to Malmaison, where she died five years later.

N. Epton: *Josephine: the Empress and her Children* (1976)

**Burbidge** [née Peachey], **(Eleanor) Margaret** (1920–). English astronomer. Her father was a lecturer in chemistry, and she attended University College, London, then joined the University of London where from 1948 to 1951 she was Assistant Director, then Acting Director, and obtained a PhD in astrophysics. In 1948 she married Geoffrey Burbidge, also an astronomer and frequently a co-worker; they had one daughter.

She held research fellowships at the University of Chicago and the California Institute of Technology before moving to San Diego, where she became Professor of Astronomy in 1964; she is also Director of Astrophysics and Space Sciences. Her research in collaboration with William Fowler, Fred Hoyle and Geoffrey Burbidge, revealed how heavier elements are created by nuclear reactions in stars. In 1959 she was awarded the Warner Prize as a result of their famous research paper 'Synthesis of the elements in stars', in *Reviews of Modern Physics* (October 1957). Her work on the nature of quasars was published in *Quasi-Stellar Objects* (1967).

From 1972 to 1973, while on leave of absence, Margaret was the first woman director of the Royal Greenwich Observatory, but was denied the traditional honorary title of Astronomer Royal – typical of the professional discrimination she had encountered elsewhere. She was elected a Fellow of the Royal Society in 1964 and of the American National Academy of Sciences in 1978. She received many honorary degrees, and was the first woman to be President of the American

Astronomical Society (1976–8) and President of the American Association for the Advancement of Science (1981). She was appointed to the National Aeronautics and Space Administration (NASA) team to perfect a faint-object spectograph for the 1984 shuttle.

**Burdett-Coutts, Angela (Georgina)** (1814–1906). English philanthropist. Born in London, she was the grand-daughter of Thomas Coutts, banker to George III, whose vast fortune she inherited at the age of 23, from her step-grandmother the Duchess of St Albans. All the rest of the family, including four sisters, were cut out.

Now the richest heiress in England, pestered by offers of marriage, even from the 80-year-old Duke of Wellington, she became a lavish society hostess, received at all European courts, and a patron of the arts and theatre, friendly with Charles Dickens, William Macready and Henry Irving. She also undertook and managed innumerable philanthropic schemes, becoming known as 'The Queen of the Poor'. These included housing, church building, tax-free markets, female emigration, public-health works to African explorations, direct relief to victims of the Irish famine, and to Turkish refugees in the Russo-Turkish War.

At the age of 67 she married her 27-year-old American secretary, William Bartlett, despite suggestions from Queen Victoria and the Archbishop of Canterbury that she should adopt him instead, and they worked together on projects in Turkey and Africa. In 1893 she edited *Woman's Work in England*, not mentioning herself, and by her death she had given away almost three million pounds.

D. Orton: *Made of Gold: A Biography of Angela Burdett-Coutts* (1981)

**Burford,** Lieutenant **Harry.** *See* VELASQUEZ, LORETA JANETA.

**Burnett, Frances (Eliza) Hodgson** (1849–1924). English-American novelist and children's author. Born in Cheetham Hill, Manchester, England, she was the daughter of a hardware wholesaler who died in 1854. The family business was ruined by the depression in the cotton industry in Lancashire during the American Civil War, and they emigrated to live with an uncle in Knoxville, Tennessee, in 1865. After trying to run a private school Frances started writing stories, and at the age of 17 was selling them easily to local papers and journals. In 1873 she married Dr Swan Moses Burnett and moved with him to Europe in 1875, then to Washington in 1877. They had two sons, but the elder died when he was 16, leaving her desolate.

In 1877 she published four successful stories, including the realistic novel *That Lass O'Lowries*, set in industrial Lancashire. She had produced 16 novels by 1883, and in 1886 *Little Lord Fauntleroy* appeared, immediately becoming one of the best-sellers of the year. Her popularity, public appearances and tours, and new wealth estranged her from her husband, and they drifted apart, eventually divorcing in 1898. By this time Burnett had transferred much of her attention to writing for children, although she still produced adult novels. In 1900, while in Europe, she married Stephen Townsend, a young doctor and aspiring actor, but they separated almost immediately and were divorced in 1901. She then returned to the USA and settled near Plandrome Park on Long Island, where she wrote some of her best-known stories, including *The Little Princess* (1905) and *The Secret Garden* (1911).

In her later years Burnett was something of an eccentric, snobbish and escapist, inhabiting her own dream world and wearing elaborate wigs and clothes which won her the nickname of 'Frilly'; she also indulged in semi-mystical religions, while behaving like a minor tyrant to her family.

F.H. Burnett: *The One I Know Best of All* (1893)
A. Thwaite: *Waiting for the Party: the Life of Burnett* (1974)

**Burney, Fanny** [Frances] [Madame d'Arblay] (1752–1840). English novelist. She was born in King's Lynn and moved to London in 1760 where her father became a fashionable music teacher. Shortsighted, shy, considered 'plain' and stupid, she did not learn to read until 8 but at 10 began writing stories and plays, burning all her work in a fit of religious guilt on her 18th birthday.

In 1778 her brother Charles arranged the publication of *Evelina: or A Young Lady's Entrance into the World*. The mixture of sentiment, caricature, daring and sensitivity won critical and popular acclaim. Entering the literary world Fanny was introduced to Dr Johnson by Mrs Thrale and became his protegée. *Cecilia* (1782) met with equal success, but in 1785, at the urging of her father, she accepted a post as Second Keeper of the Robes to Queen Charlotte. Her diary describes her dreary and humiliating life, until she asked permission to retire in 1791. She received a pension and went to live in Chelsea, London.

Here she met French exiles, including Madame de STAEL, Talleyrand, and the impoverished General d'Arblay, whom she married in 1793. Now writing to support them, after the birth of her son in 1794, she published a blank verse tragedy *Edwig and Elgiva*, a one-night failure starring SARAH SIDDONS and John Kemble in 1795, and *Camilla* (1796). From 1802 to 1812 she was caught in France by the Napoleonic Wars, returning to publish her last novel, *The Wanderer*, in 1814. The following year she was in Brussels during the Battle of Waterloo, where d'Arblay was injured. He died in 1818 and Fanny, disconsolate at his death, remained in England, her only further work being a poorly received *Life* of her father (1832). Her *Letters and Diaries* were published in seven volumes between 1842 and 1846.

S. Kilpatrick: *Fanny Burney* (1980)

**Burrows, Eva** (1930–). Australian evangelist. Born in an Australian mining town, one of nine children of a Salvation Army officer, Eva rebelled against the ethos of the Army in her teens but rejoined as a student at the University of Queensland. There she took degrees in history and English and a graduate degree in education. After 17 years as an education officer in Rhodesia she left Africa in 1969 and returned to England as an administrator, becoming head of the women's social services for the Salvation Army in the mid 1970s, converting orphanages into refuges for battered women. She then worked as a territorial commander in Sri Lanka, Scotland and Southern Australia, where she was noted for initiating imaginative training schemes for unemployed youths. Described as a disciplined, single-minded, extrovert person totally devoted to her work, in 1986 she was chosen (in competi-

tion with six men) as Chief Commander of the Salvation Army world-wide, the first female leader since EVANGELINE BOOTH.

**Burton, Beryl** (1937–). English cyclist. Born in Yorkshire, Beryl was introduced to cycling by her future husband, Charles Burton, when they both worked as clerks for the local electricity board. Not only has she held the British woman's 'Best All-Rounder' title for cycling since 1959, but she was also the only woman to beat top-class male riders in open events. Her achievements in time-trialling are unsurpassed: in 1967 she covered 403.6 km (277¼ miles) in a 12-hour trial, 9.2 km (5¾ miles) more than the existing British men's record. In 1956 Ray Booty had brought the men's record for 160 km (100 miles) under 4 hours; in 1968 Beryl improved the record to 3 hours 55 minutes 55 seconds.

Although she preferred British competitions to the world championships, she had won seven gold medals by 1977, five in the pursuit event and two in the road race, a joint women's record with Yvonne Rijnders. Together with her four silver and three bronze medals in world championships, Beryl's overall success is approached only by Galina Ermolaeva of Russia. At Milan in 1960 she set a world record of 58.4 seconds for 20 km (12.427 miles), and holds more than 60 British titles. Her daughter Denise is now a cycling champion. Beryl works on a farm near Leeds.

**Burton** [née Arundell], **Isabel** (1831–96). English traveller. Although hardly a traveller in her own right, Isabel made an adventurous career of being the wife of Sir Richard Burton. Born in London of a Catholic family, she had a girlish passion for Richard, whom she identified at a chance meeting as her 'Destiny' with whom, according to a gypsy prediction, she would share a 'life all wandering, change and adventure. One soul in two bodies. . . .' She admired his explorations in India, Mecca, Harar and elsewhere, and shared his attraction to the East, though not his outstanding Oriental knowledge. While Burton led an expedition to discover the source of the Nile and Lake Tanganyika, Isabel undertook social work among London prostitutes. She nursed Richard on his return, and in 1861 they were married;

she could not go with him on his next consular post at the Spanish island of San Fernando Po, but two years later joined him in Santos, Brazil, undertaking much of the consular work, particularly during his long absences. Richard's appointment as Consul at Damascus in 1869 was the zenith of Isabel's life: they inaugurated inter-racial receptions, and undertook intrepid archaeological expeditions. Despite her constant support, Richard was publicly discredited on several occasions and in 1871 was recalled, sending Isabel a message: 'I am superseded. Pay, pack and follow.'

After mediating, the best Isabel could obtain for Richard was the consulate at Trieste. Their main activity, apart from diversionary European expeditions, was literature; Richard wrote over 80 books, and she several, among which *The Inner Life of Syria* (1875) was most successful. This financed a trip to India, including Goa and Suez. Although dying of cancer, she spent her last years in social and literary pusuit, writing the *Life of Sir Richard Burton*.

**Buss, Frances Mary** (1827–94). English educationalist. She was the daughter of an improvident painter-etcher, and her mother supported the family by running a school. She taught with her mother from the age of 14, and at 18 was running her own school at Clarence Road, Kentish Town, London. The school moved to Camden in 1850, becoming the North London Collegiate School. While teaching in the daytime, she attended courses at Queen's College, Harley Street, in the evening. Her school, which became a public school in 1871, was a democratic day school, with low fees and high academic standards, and she also founded and supervised the Camden School in Prince of Wales Road, which offered an education at even lower fees.

Frances Buss was an original member of the Council for Teacher Training, a founder of the Training College for Women Teachers which opened in Cambridge in 1886, and the first President of the Association of Headmistresses, whose opening meeting was held at her house. With DOROTHEA BEALE, the other famous headmistress of the period, she inspired a well-known rhyme, an early version being:

Miss Buss and Miss Beale
Cupid's darts do not feel,
They leave that to us,
Poor Beale and poor Buss.

J. Kamm: *How Different from Us: a Biography of Miss Buss and Miss Beale* (1958)

**Butler** [née Thompson], **Elizabeth (Southerden)** (1850–1933). English military painter. Born in Lausanne, she and her sister, the poet Alice Meynell, were educated by their father, a believer in travel and the learning of languages. She studied at the South Kensington School of Art from the age of 19 to 21, but also attended classes in Florence and Rome during vacations. Her first exhibit at the Royal Academy was *Missing* (1873), but the following year her *Calling the Role after an Engagement, Crimea* was a sensational success. Commissioned by a Manchester businessman, it was so popular that crowds had to be held back to protect it, and it was eventually bought by Queen Victoria. Other military scenes which followed this success included *Quatre bras* (1875), *Balaclava* (1876), *Scotland for ever* (1881), and *Steady the Drums and Fife* (1896). In 1879 Elizabeth Butler failed by two votes to be elected to the Royal Academy. Her work was universally admired for its precision, detail and sense of movement, and *Quatre bras* was described by Ruskin as 'Amazon's work'. She herself was reserved and very witty, a quality evident in her writing.

In 1873 she had become a Roman Catholic, and in 1877 married Colonel (later General) William Butler. Their travels to Israel, Egypt and Africa are described in her *Letters from the Holy Land* (1903), and *From Sketchbook and Diary* (1909). After his death in 1910, she lived at the home to which they had retired in Bansha, Tipperary, and finally with her daughter in County Meath.

E. Butler: *An Autobiography* (1922)

**Butler** [née Grey], **Josephine** (1828–1906). English feminist. She was born at Dilston, Northumberland; her father John Grey was a radical agricultural reformer and abolitionist. One of seven children, she was educated chiefly by her mother, a devout Moravian Christian, although she briefly attended school in Newcastle. In 1850 she met George Butler, a lecturer at Durham

University, and after their marriage in 1852 they lived in Oxford, where she suffered from the academic hypocrisy towards women. After a chest illness, they moved to Cheltenham, where George was Vice-president of the College. Here, in 1864, their five-year-old daughter died in a fall.

In the same year they moved to Liverpool, and Josephine countered her grief by working in the Bridewell, and establishing refuges for destitute and ill prostitutes. She was also drawn by ANNE JEMIMA CLOUGH into the educational struggle, acting as President of the North of England Council for the Higher Education of Women from 1868 to 1873.

In 1869 she ·was persuaded to take the leadership of the Ladies' National Association in the campaign against the state regulation of prostitution under the Contagious Diseases Acts (1866–9). She developed a new style of militant campaigning, taking direct action at the by-elections in Colchester (1870) and Pontefract (1872) at considerable physical risk. In 1871 in her evidence to the Commission, and in 1872 opposing the conciliatory 'Bruce's Bill', she made a determined stand on principle. In 1886 the campaign won repeal of the Acts.

Josephine also urged action on the Continent, visiting France, Italy and Switzerland (1874–5). In Brussels in 1880 her exposure of under-age prostitution eventually prompted W.T. Stead's article against the white slave trade in 1885. She was a founder member of the National Vigilance Association although she drew back from the social purity movements of the 1890s. After George's death in Winchester in 1890, she returned to Northumberland. She published many pamphlets, articles and books, continuing to edit her own periodicals such as *The Dawn* and *The Storm Bell* until her death.

J. Butler: *Personal Reminiscences of a Great Crusade* (1896)
————— : *Autobiographical Memoir*, ed. L. Johnson (1928)

**Butler-Sloss,** Dame **Elizabeth** (1923– ) British judge. Born Elizabeth Havers, the daughter of a High Court Judge and sister of Nigel (now Lord) Havers, the former Attorney-General and briefly Lord Chancellor, she decided to become a lawyer at the age of 12. Educated at Wycombe Abbey School, she entered barrister's chambers and was called to the Bar in 1955. At the age of 25 she married Joseph Butler-Sloss: they have three children. She also had political aspirations, and stood unsuccessfully as a Tory candidate in 1959, attracting much attention as her first baby was due on Polling Day.

Dame Elizabeth was a divorce registrar before her appointment to the Family Division of the High Court in 1979, the joint-third woman to be appointed. She was created a Dame in the same year, aged 46. In 1987 she chaired the difficult Cleveland Sex Abuse Inquiry, and at the end of that year was appointed to the Court of Appeal, the first woman judge to sit in that Court, at present holding the masculine title 'Lord Justice' Butler-Sloss.

**Butt,** Dame **Clara (Ellen)** (1872–1936). English contralto. She studied at the Royal College of Music, London, from 1890, and made her debut in 1892. Although acclaimed as Gluck's Orpheus, it was as a concert artist that she gained particular renown. She toured the USA in 1899 and 1913, and made a world tour with her husband, the baritone R. Kennerley Rumford, delighting audiences with her performances of English ballads. Elgar wrote his *Sea Pictures* (1899) for her, and she became strongly identified with his *Land of Hope and Glory*; her performances for war charities, notably *The Dream of Gerontius* in aid of the Red Cross, contributed to her being made a DBE in 1920. Her immensely powerful voice seemed made to match her height (6′ 2″).

W. Ponder: *Clara Butt* (1978)

**Byrne, Jane (Margaret Burke)** (1934– ). American politician. Born in Chicago into an American-Irish family, she was educated at Barnard College. She married William Byrne, a marine corps pilot, in 1956; they had one daughter but Byrne was killed in a crash in 1959. Jane became involved in politics during the Kennedy election campaign of 1960, and from 1964 to 1968 she worked with the Anti-Poverty Agency in Chicago. She then became Commissioner of Weights, Scales and Measures, enforcing the regulations despite pressure from large vested interests. After Mayor Daly died she protested about the amount of corruption under his successor Michael Bilandic, and initiated a police enquiry which led to his trial. He was acquitted and she lost her job. In 1979 she was persuaded to run against him as mayor, and in a surprise swing she was elected. She is a popular figure, adept at dealing with both crowds and committees. In 1978 she married again, Jan McMullen, a reporter on Chicago newspapers. She remained mayor of Chicago until 1983.

**Byron, Ada.** *See* LOVELACE, ADA BYRON

**Byron,** Lady **Noel (Anne Isabella)** (1792–1860). English philanthropist. She was born at Elmore Hall, Durham, the only child of Sir Ralph and Lady Milbanke. After the failure of her brief marriage to the poet, Lord Byron (1815–16), she became interested in reform, and friendly with Dr King, editor of *The Co-operator*. Her progressive but not radical views were expressed in her founding and sponsorship (1834–48) of an industrial and agricultural school, based on Fellenberg's ideas, at Ealing Grove. She also bought the Red House for MARY CARPENTER as a girls' reformatory in 1854, supported educational institutes, and co-operative ventures, and was a close associate of BARBARA BODICHON. Like other leisure-class Radicals she also supported the cause of American abolitionists and Italian Republicans. Her daughter, ADA BYRON LOVELACE, became a famous mathematician, and her granddaughter, ANNE BLUNT, a remarkable traveller.

E.C. Mayne: *Life and Letters of Anne Isabella, Lady Noel Byron* (1929)

# C

**Caballero, Fernán** [pseud. of Cecilia Boehl
von Faber] (1796–1877). German-Spanish
novelist. Of mixed German, Spanish and
Irish descent, the daughter of a German
Hispanic scholar who became consul in
Cadiz, Caballero was born in Morges in the
Vaud canton of Switzerland. She was raised
as a Catholic and at 19 married a Spanish
soldier, Antonio Planells, who died the
same year in Puerto Rico. In 1822 she
married the Marques de Arco Hermoso;
they lived in Seville and on their country
estate until his death in 1835. Her last
marriage, to Antonio de Ayala in 1837, was
less affluent, and in the 1850s she began to
publish her work to supplement their
income: studies of rural Andalusian life such
as *La gaviota* (1856) which appeared as a
periodical serial in 1849, *Cuadros de
costumbres populares andaluces* (1853),
*Lágrimas* (1853) and *La familia de Alvareda*
(1856). Her other novels include a study of a
woman's unhappy marriage, *Clemencia*
(1852), and the autobiographical *La Farisea*
(1853).

**Cable, (Alice) Mildred** (1878–1952). English
missionary and traveller. Born in Guildford,
the daughter of a draper, she acquired her
vocation for missionary work as a schoolgirl.
Planning to become a medical worker with
the China Inland Mission, she studied
science at London University, and shortly
after the Boxer Rebellion of 1900 she went
to join the well-known missionary
Evangeline French (1869–1960) in Shanxi
province. They ran a rapidly-expanding
school for girls, where they were joined by
Eva's sister, Francesca (1871–1960).

They became known as 'the trio' and in
1923 they received permission to preach to
the nomadic tribes of the Gobi Desert. They
travelled vast distances across Central Asia

during the next 15 years, crossing the Gobi
Desert 5 times, wearing Chinese dress,
learning local dialects and gaining the
respect and lasting devotion of the people.
They were observant and methodical
explorers as well as zealous preachers, and
on leave in England they lectured to learned
and scientific societies. Together with
Francesca French, Mildred wrote over 20
books, including *Through the Jade Gate and
Central Asia* (1927), *A Desert Journal* (1934)
and *The Gobi Desert* (1942). For this last
book Mildred received an award from the
Royal Central Asian Society.

After the Chinese Revolution in 1939,
the three friends returned to the UK and
lectured widely at home and in many
Commonwealth countries, working for the
British and Foreign Bible Society. Later
books by Mildred Cable and Francesca
French included *Dhina, her Life and her
People* (1946), and *A Journey with a Purpose*
(1950).

W.J. Platt: *Three Women* (1964)

**Cabrini, (Maria) Francesca (Xavier)** (1850–
1917). Italian-American saint and founder.
She was born in Sant' Angelo, Lombardy,
the youngest of 13 children. Her birth was
said to have been marked by a flight of white
doves round the house. She was determined
to become a missionary from the time of her
confirmation and first communion at the age
of 7, and from her twelfth year she took an
annual vow of virginity, which was made
permanent when she reached the age of 18.
Denied admission to the Daughters of the
Sacred Heart because of her delicate health
(she had caught smallpox while caring for
the sick), in 1874 she began to supervise an
orphanage which needed reform. After
three years she took religious vows, and was
then appointed Superior of the orphanage.

In 1880 she founded the Missionary Sisters of the Sacred Heart, acquiring an abandoned Franciscan convent as a mother house. Pope Leo XIII, who described Mother Cabrini as 'a woman of marvellous intuition and of great sanctity', told her to go 'west not east' when she expressed a wish to open a convent in China. In 1889 Francesca arrived in New York to work amongst impoverished Italian immigrants. The small mission was given a hostile reception by the local archbishop but, with papal support behind her, Mother Cabrini stayed. She became a naturalized citizen of the USA in 1909, and although plagued by ill-health succeeded in establishing 67 houses – one for each year of her life. She became the first American saint when she was canonized in 1946.

L. Borden: *Francesca Cabrini* (1945)

**Caccini, Francesca** (1587–?1640). Italian singer and composer. Daughter of the composer Giulio Caccini, she sang at the marriage of MARIE DE MEDICIS to Henri IV, King of France in Florence in 1600, her first professional appearance. She was officially admitted to the service of the Florentine court in 1607, and became one of the court's highest-paid musicians. She made several tours as a singer with her husband, to considerable acclaim. She was also an accomplished poet and instrumentalist, playing the lute, guitar and harpsichord. Most of the music she wrote is lost, but her opera *La liberazione di Ruggiero*, written in celebration of the future Polish king's visit to Florence in 1625, was given in Warsaw in 1682, marking not only Poland's first season of opera but also the first performance of an Italian opera outside Italy. *Il primo libro delle musiche* (1618), her only other surviving work, is an anthology of songs notable for the unusually florid writing for solo voice.

Her sister, Settimia (1591–?1638), was also a well-known singer in the courts of Florence and particularly Mantua; she sang Venus at the première of Monteverdi's *Arianna* (1608).

**Calamity Jane** [Cannary, Martha Jane] (1852–1903). American frontierswoman. She was probably born at Princeton, Missouri, where her parents farmed until moving West again in 1863. In the early 1870s she earned her living, dressed as a man, as a muleskinner in Wyoming, and at some point met James 'Wild Bill' Hickok, whom she later claimed was her husband and father of her daughter born in 1873. In 1875 she accompanied General George Crook's Sioux expedition but was sent back when found to be a woman. She settled with Hickok in the outlaw town of Deadwood, Dakota Territory, in 1876 but he was murdered the same year. In 1880 she left and wandered through the West before marrying C. Burke in California in 1891. They soon separated and she returned to Wyoming, gaining an increasing reputation for hard drinking and wild behaviour. She joined the Buffalo Bill Wild West Show and visited England (1893), toured Chicago, St Louis and Kansas City with the Palace Museum (1896), and starred at the Pan-American Exposition in Buffalo, New York, as a Western character (1901). Repeatedly fired for drunkenness, brawling and assaulting policemen, she kept returning to the West. She died of pneumonia at the Callaway Hotel, Terry, near Deadwood, and was buried next to Wild Bill Hickok, as she had requested.

M.C. Burke: *Life and Adventures of Calamity Jane: by Herself* (n.d.)
L. Jennewein: *Calamity Jane of the Western Trails* (1953)

**Caldicott, Helen (Broinowski)** (1938–). Australian paediatrician and anti-nuclear campaigner. Helen Caldicott was born in Australia, and her lifelong commitment to campaigning against the nuclear threat was spurred by a girlhood reading of Nevil Shute's novel *On the Beach* (1957), a post-holocaust tale with an Australian background. She studied at the University of Adelaide Medical School, qualifying as a general practitioner, and from 1966 to 1969 had a fellowship at Harvard Medical School. After 1972 she specialized in paediatrics, particularly concerned with cystic fibrosis. Her alarm at the threats to health posed by radioactivity drove her to lead the successful campaign against atmospheric nuclear testing by the French in the South Pacific, and a further campaign to stop Australian exports of uranium.

In 1977 Helen Caldicott emigrated to the USA to work at Harvard Medical School and

Boston Children's Hospital Medical Center. In 1978, the year in which she published her powerful book, *Nuclear Madness*, she joined the Society of Physicians for Social Responsibility and was its President until 1983, when she resigned over her opposition to all nuclear power, not just nuclear weapons. She is also one of the founders of the influential Washington-based lobby group WAND (Women's Action for Nuclear Disarmament), and published a second book, *Missile Envy*, in 1984.

**Caldwell, Sarah** (1924–). American opera impresario, conductor and producer. Born in Maryville, Missouri, she studied in Arkansas and then at the New England Conservatory. She showed early talent as a string player (violin and viola) and in that capacity spent several summers at the Berkshire Music Center (from 1946), where she also attended Koussevitsky's conducting classes and in 1947 staged Vaughan Williams's *Riders to the Sea*. Her attraction to the theatre was further nurtured by Boris Goldovsky, founder of the New England Opera Company; largely influenced by his policy of presenting economical but technically advanced opera productions, she became director of the Boston University opera workshop (1952) and in 1958 founded the Boston Opera Group (later renamed the Opera Company of Boston). The company has given the first American performances of many works, ranging from Rameau's *Hippolyte et Aricie* to Nono's *Intolleranza* as well as the world premières of operas by such composers as Gunther Schuller. Caldwell attracted internationally known singers for her productions, almost all of which she produced and conducted herself (an unusual professional combination, obviating the notorious disagreements that have characterized much of operatic history). During the 1960s and 1970s she became more widely known through tours of the USA, Europe and China. In 1975 she conducted the New York Philharmonic Orchestra at the Celebration of Women Composers Concert, whose programme spanned three generations of women composers, and in 1976 she was the first woman to conduct the Metropolitan Opera, in a performance of Verdi's *La traviata*. In 1982 her company began a collaborative venture to develop opera in the Philippines. Caldwell was appointed artistic director of the New Opera Company of Israel in 1983. Much of the attention she has received has focused on her lack of conformity, but it has been increasingly acknowledged that her success has been derived from an invincible personality combined with innate creative powers.

**Callas, Maria** (1923–77). Greek soprano She was born in New York, but left for Athens in 1937, becoming a Greek citizen in 1966. A pupil of Elvira de Hidalgo at the Athens Conservatory, and contracted to the newly founded Athens Opera during World War II, she gave her first important operatic performance in Ponchielli's *La gioconda* in Verona (1947). Her first appearances at the major opera houses (Aida at La Scala, Milan, 1950, and Norma at both Covent Garden, 1952, and the Metropolitan, New York, 1956) led to numerous international engagements and a reputation based as much on adulation as on notoriety for her altercations with managers: she would rather break a contract than appear below her best. Among her most acclaimed roles were Norma, Violetta, Tosca, Lucia and Cherubini's Medea. She created the title role in Peggy Glanville-Hicks's *Sappho* (San Francisco, 1965).

She was married to her manager Battista Meneghini from 1949 to 1959 and was later at the centre of much publicity through her association with Aristotle Onassis. She retired from the stage in 1965, but gave a highly successful series of master classes in New York (1971–2) and made extensive recital tours with Giuseppe di Stefano (1973–4). Although she was occasionally criticized for technical defects (mainly unevenness of register, which could be attributed to her minimal training), her interpretative powers ranked her as one of the greatest dramatic sopranos of the 20th century. Over 30 books have been written about her.

J. Ardoin: *The Callas Legacy* (1977, rev. 2/1982)
A. Stassinopoulos: *Maria Callas: the Woman behind the Legend* (1981)

**Callil, Carmen (Therese)** (1938–). Australian, publisher working in Britain. Born in Melbourne, a fifth-generation Australian of

Irish–Lebanese descent, Carmen was brought up by her mother after her father, a barrister and lecturer in French at Melbourne University, died when she was eight. Both her parents were voracious readers and Carmen read widely at home: she was educated at Loretto Convent, Toorak and Melbourne University.

In 1960 she went to London, working as a buyer's assistant at Marks and Spencer, then as editorial assistant at Hutchinson and at Batsford, before five years in publicity at Granada Books. As Publicity Manager, in 1970, she launched *The Female Eunuch* by her compatriot GERMAINE GREER. From 1970 to 1972 she worked at André Deutsch, then ran her own publicity company until 1976. In 1972 she also founded the feminist publishing house Virago (*OED*: 'a turbulent woman, termagant'). The company rapidly established its identity in the face of initial scepticism. With its apple logo, stylish design and strong political bent, as well as the Modern Classics Series and new writing by authors such as ANGELA CARTER, it has been a powerful force in modern British feminism. (The other notable feminist publisher, The Women's Press, was founded in 1978.)

In 1982 the company joined the publishing group of Chatto, Bodley Head and Cape. Carmen remained Chairman of Virago but also took the position of Managing Director of Chatto and Windus and The Hogarth Press. In 1987 Virago conducted a management buy-out and is now an independent company, while Random House Inc. bought the CBC group. Witty, intense and ferociously energetic, Carmen Callil is one of a new generation of women in top positions in British publishing. She has also been a Director of Channel 4 Television since 1985, and is a fellow of the Royal Society of Arts.

**Cameron, Agnes Deans** (1863–1912). Canadian traveller. Born in Victoria, British Columbia, she was a teacher and school trustee before making a 10,000 mile journey in 1909. *The New North* (1909) describes her trek from Chicago to the Arctic Ocean via Athabasca, the Great Slave Lake and Mackenzie River, returning by Peace River and the Lesser Slave Lake. Afterwards she lectured widely and wrote articles.

**Cameron** [née Pattle], **Julia Margaret** (1815–79). English portrait photographer. She was the third of seven daughters of Sir James Pattle, a member of the Bengal Civil Service, and was born and grew up in Calcutta. At the age of 23 she married Charles Hay Cameron, who was then a member of the Law Commission in Calcutta. A prominent member of society, known for her 'brilliant conversation', in 1846 she raised large sums of money in India for the victims of the Irish famine. Two years later the Camerons returned to England, where they educated their six children and Julia moved in the literary and artistic circles into which her sisters had married. She herself had translated Bürger's *Leonora* in 1847, and contributed many poems to *Macmillan's Magazine*. After living in London, they moved to Freshwater on the Isle of Wight in 1860, where they were Tennyson's neighbours; their hospitality there is recorded in many contemporary memoirs.

In 1863, when she was 48, Julia was given a camera by her daughter, and during the next two years she developed her hobby of photography into a fine art. She took portraits of all her friends and visitors, including Darwin and Sir John Herschel, Browning and Carlyle, and Tennyson and Trollope; she also took posed groups and romantic allegorical subjects, and even illustrated Tennyson's *Idylls of the King*. She achieved considerable fame in her own time, although she never worked as a professional, winning medals for her work in the USA, Austria, Germany and England, and exhibiting her portraits in London. In 1875 she went with her husband to Ceylon, and, although they revisited England in 1878, she returned to Ceylon and died there the following year.

**Campbell, Mrs Patrick** [née Tanner, Beatrice Stella] (1865–1940). English actress. The daughter of a contractor to the East India Company and his Italian wife, she was educated in London and Paris before running away at 19 to marry a city broker, Patrick Campbell (*d* 1900). Her second husband, whom she married in 1914, was George Cornwallis West. She made her first stage appearance in Liverpool in 1888 and subsequently toured with Ben Greet, appearing in London (1890) in *The Hunchback*, *School for Scandal*, and *As You Like It*. Following a season at the Adelphi came her outstanding performance as Paula in *The Second Mrs Tanqueray* at the St James's. Her later successes included Agnes in *The Notorious Mrs Ebbsmith*, Juliet and Ophelia to Forbes-Robertson's Romeo and Hamlet, Mélisande in English and French (the latter to the Pelléas of SARAH BERNHARDT) and several roles in Ibsen. She also played the role of Magda in *Heimat* by Suderman in London and New York, in which she was thought to be superior to ELEANORA DUSE. George Bernard Shaw wrote the part of Eliza Doolittle in *Pygmalion* for her and she created the role in 1914 and played in several revivals. At 68 she began a new career in films with *Riptide*.

Despite long absences from the stage, her remarkable beauty and scintillating wit made her a dominant figure in the theatre of her generation. Her correspondence with Shaw has been published.

Mrs P. Campbell: *My Life and Some Letters* (1922)

**Canal, Marguerite** (1890–1978). French composer, teacher and conductor. She studied at the Paris Conservatoire, where she became a teacher in 1919. Her orchestral concerts at the Palais de Glace (1917–18) were the first in France to be conducted by a woman. She went to Italy in 1920 as winner of the Prix de Rome (for her 'scène dramatique' *Don Juan*), resuming her Conservatoire appointment from 1932 until her retirement. She was a devoted teacher, and this has been put forward as one of the reasons why several of her compositions were never completed. Most notable as a song-writer (including settings of Verlaine, De Lisle, Baudelaire and Paul Fort, as well as poems of her own in the song cycle *Amours tristes*), she also wrote a Requiem (1921), the opera *Tlass Atka* (begun c1922; orchestration incomplete), some chamber music, a violin sonata and some piano pieces.

**Cannary, Martha Jane.** *See* CALAMITY JANE.

**Cannon, Annie Jump** (1863–1941). American astronomer. Born in Delaware, where her father became State Senator, Annie attended Wellesley and Radcliffe

Colleges. Under Edward Pickering, Harvard Observatory had already employed talented women astronomers; in 1896 Annie joined the staff and worked there for the rest of her life.

Her early work dealt with variable stars, but her greatest contributions were in the field of stellar spectral classification. Taking the opportunity to study astronomical photographs, she developed the definitive Harvard System of spectral classification and proved that the vast majority of stars represent only a few species. *The Henry Draper Catalogue* covering 225,300 stars, was published in 1924, followed by the *Henry Draper Extension*, and *Yale Zone Catalogue*, and *Cape Zone Catalogue*.

Annie was almost completely deaf unless she used a hearing aid, and it is suggested that this helped her great powers of concentration. She did not enter controversy and her classification work was dispassionate. From 1911 she was Curator of Astronomical Photographs at Harvard, and in 1938 became the William Cranch Bond Astronomer. Among her numerous honorary degrees was the first honorary doctorate awarded to a woman by Oxford University. She was an honorary member of the Royal Astronomical Society, and one of the few women ever elected to the American Philosophical Society. In 1931 the National Academy of Sciences awarded her the Draper Gold Medal, and in 1932 she received the Ellen Richards Research Prize, which was used to establish the Annie Jump Cannon Prize for women astronomers.

**Carlyle, Jane Welsh** (1801–66). English literary personality. She was the daughter of a prosperous doctor from Haddington, East Lothian, who was a strict disciplinarian and gave her a rigorous classical education from the age of five. Jane was a brilliant and imaginative student, who was writing gory five-act tragedies at the age of 13; she was also lively and charming. When she was 18 her father died and left her a considerable income. She met Thomas Carlyle in 1821, introduced to him by Edward Irving, who had taught them both. After five years of hesitation and delay, due to their temperaments and to Mrs Welsh's disapproval, they married in 1826. Their courtship is vividly evoked in the published *Letters*.

At first they lived on a farm belonging to Jane at Craigenputtock, Dumfriesshire, where Carlyle worked as a journalist and wrote *Sartor Resartus* ('The tailor retailored'), eventually published in *Fraser's Magazine* between 1833 and 1834. Jane found it desolate and lonely after literary life in Edinburgh. In 1834 they moved to Cheyne Row, Chelsea, London, and for a long time she endured Carlyle's irritability and melancholia, as well as their poverty, until he achieved acclaim in 1837 with the publication of *The History of the French Revolution*. A witty talker and good hostess, she became the centre of a circle of friends including John Stuart Mill, Harriet Taylor and Giuseppe Mazzini, and knew literary figures such as Charles Dickens, Alfred Tennyson, the Hunts and John Ruskin. Jane was known for her forthrightness and caustic remarks as well as for her emotional warmth. Her closest friend was GERALDINE JEWSBURY, to whom she was deeply attached.

The Carlyles lived at Cheyne Row from 1834 to 1866 but they were often apart, Thomas travelling abroad and Jane staying with friends. Their relationship when they were together was difficult and exhausting, particularly during the 1850s when Carlyle was associated with Lady Ashburton. Biographers, including Froude, a close friend, have suggested that sexual impotence may have caused much of the stress in their marriage. In the early 1860s Jane's health collapsed and she lived in terror of a mental breakdown. She returned to Cheyne Row after staying in Scotland in 1864, and after an apparent improvement, she died suddenly in April 1866.

T. Carlyle, ed.: *Letters and Memorials of Jane Welsh Carlyle* (1883)

**Carmen, Sylva.** *See* ELISABETH OF ROMANIA.

**Carney, Kate** (1868–1950). English music-hall entertainer. Although she began her career at the Albert in February 1890, singing Irish ballads, Kate Carney soon became a renowned interpreter of Cockney songs. Known as the 'Cockney Queen', she performed dressed in 'pearlies' and a vast hat crowned with feathers. She rivalled Albert Chevalier in her ability to combine sharp humour with the pathos of East End

life in London, and two of her most popular songs were *Liza Johnson* and *Three Pots a Shilling*. Just after the celebration of her golden wedding in 1935 (she married George Barclay, a music-hall comedian and step-dancer) she appeared in a Royal Variety Performance, singing two of her coster songs and leading the audience into enthusiastic participation. She continued to perform until shortly before her death.

**Carpenter, Mary** (1807–77). English philanthropist. Born in Exeter, she was the daughter of a famous Unitarian minister and teacher Lant Carpenter, and was educated in his Bristol school. In 1827 she went to work as a governess on the Isle of Wight, but in 1829 opened a girls' school in Bristol with her mother. Influenced by American philanthropist Joseph Tuckerman, in the 1830s she began working for poor children, founding her Working and Visiting Society in 1835. After her father's death in 1840 she took on some of his charitable work, and in 1846 opened a 'ragged school' in the Bristol slums. In 1851 her essay on reform schools (*Reformatory Schools for the Children of the Perishing and Dangerous Classes and for Juvenile Offenders*) prompted a conference in Birmingham but she disliked the punitive emphasis and in 1852 she opened her own reformatory for boys at Kingswood to publicize her more liberal ideas. Such schools were legally recognized by the Youthful Offenders Act 1854, and she soon opened a separate house for girls at Red Lodge. Tolerant, patient, with a buoyant sense of humour, Mary Carpenter then took up the cause of industrial schools, opening two herself, and lobbying Parliament over the passing of the Industrial Schools Acts 1857, 1861, and 1866. She also opened a workmen's hall and published a book on the convict system in 1864.

She had long been interested in India, and between 1866 and 1876 made four visits there, giving influential speeches and preparing reports on the education of women and on penal policy, pressing her proposals on her return to England where she founded the National India Association (1870). She also investigated European, American and Canadian reform systems, lecturing widely until her death. An advocate of higher education for women, by the end of her life she had overcome her youthful reservations about the involvement of women in public life. She remained single, but adopted a daughter in 1858.

J. Manton: *Mary Carpenter and the Children of the Streets* (1976)

**Carr, Emily** (1871–1945). Canadian painter. Born in Victoria, British Columbia, she studied at the Mark Hopkins School, San Francisco, and in 1899 went to the Westminster School of Art in England. She suffered from ill-health from 1902, and two years later returned to Canada, re-visiting Europe in 1910–11 when she studied at the Académie Colarossi, Paris. She was disillusioned by the lack of recognition for her work and abandoned painting for a few years, but from 1927 her work won increasing respect and in 1933 she joined the Canadian Group of Painters. Her vivid studies of nature, hauntingly individual, were deeply influenced by the many trips she made into the forests of British Columbia and by her interest in Indian culture.

After 1940 her poor health led her to turn from painting to writing, and she published a series of tales about Canadian life, *Klee Wyck* (1941), and also books about her childhood and her experiences of running a boarding house after 1910, *The Book of Small* (1942) and *The House of All Sorts* (1944). Her autobiography appeared after her death, and two other works, *The Heart of a Peacock and Pause: a Sketch Book* (about her stay in a British sanitorium) were published in 1953.

E. Carr: *Growing Pains: the Autobiography of Emily Carr* (1946)
———— : *Hundreds and Thousands: the Journals of Emily Carr* (1966)
P. Blanchard: *The Life of Emily Carr* (1987)

**Carreño, Teresa** (1853–1917). Venezuelan pianist. She took her first piano lessons from her father and from Gottschalk, giving a recital in New York at the age of eight and playing for President Lincoln at the White House in 1863; later she studied in Paris with Georges Mathias and Anton Rubinstein. In 1888 she gave the première of MacDowell's D minor Piano Concerto. Having made her Berlin debut in 1893 (she subsequently made Germany her base), she soon became renowned throughout Europe. One of the first to include Grieg's Piano Concerto in her repertory, she was noted for the immense power she brought to Beethoven's *Emperor*, Liszt's Concerto in E flat and the Tchaikovsky Piano Concerto. She toured Australia in 1907. The character of her colourful career changed with each of her four husbands: the violinist Emile Sauret, with whom she gave concerts, inspired an interest in string music which produced her String Quartet; the baritone Giovanni Tagliapietra formed an opera company which she managed for some years; the pianist and composer Eugen d'Albert influenced her piano playing to become less impetuous; and her second husband's brother, Arturo Tagliapietra, tamed her to settle with him until her death. Although remembered principally as a pianist (she was described as 'the Valkyrie of the piano'), her extraordinary versatility led her also to perform in opera (as the Queen in Meyerbeer's *Les Huguenots*, Edinburgh, 1874) and as a conductor (for the last three weeks of an opera season in Caracas). As a composer she wrote mostly piano pieces, including a waltz that gained considerable popularity (*Mi Teresita*), but she also produced a festival hymn for the Bolívar centenary (1885) at the request of the Venezuelan government.

I. Peña: *Teresa Carreño* (1953)

**Carriera, Rosalba** (1657–1757). Italian painter. Born in Venice, eldest of three daughters of a poor public official, she drew patterns for her mother, a lace-maker, but then turned to decorating snuff-boxes, and by 1700 was established as a miniaturist. By 1705 she was also working on pastel portraits, was elected to the Accademia San Luca in Rome, and soon collected distinguished patrons including Augustus of Poland, Maximilian II of Bavaria, Charles V and the Kings of Norway and Denmark. Her popularity was due to her subtle use of colour, precise detail and her ability to flatter most of her sitters. In 1719 at the invitation of the financier Pierre Crozat she visited Paris, where she was much fêted, painted Louis XV as a boy and was elected to the Académie Royale de la Peinture in 1720. Apart from visits to Modena in 1723 and to Vienna in 1730 she spent the rest of her life in Venice with her mother and her sister Giovanna, whose death in 1738 led to a severe depression. After that, although she took in helpers and apprentices, and her sister Angela came to assist her in 1741, she worked less and her melancholia was intensified by her loss of sight; despite operations for cataracts she was blind for the last seven years of her life.

E.W. Blachfield: *Portraits and Backgrounds* (1917)

**Carson, Rachel (Louise)** (1907–64). American ecologist and scientific writer. Born in Springdale, Rachel was educated at the Pennsylvania College for Women and then Johns Hopkins University, where her ambition to become a writer was overtaken by her interest in natural history. After working in genetics and zoology, she became Editor-in-Chief for the American Fish and Wildlife Services in 1949. She continued research into offshore life at the Marine Biological Laboratory at Woods Hole, Massachusetts.

Her controversial book, *Silent Spring* (1962), was not only against indiscriminate use of pesticides but also critical of an irresponsible industrial society. Other publications include *Under the Sea Wind*, *The Edge of the Sea*, and *The Sea Around Us*. Rachel's combination of scientific and literary achievement was reflected in many awards, including the Literary Award of the Council of Women of the USA (1956), the Schweitzer Prize for animal welfare (1963), and the Conservationist Award from the National Wild Life Federation.

P. Sterling: *Sea and Earth: the Life of Rachel Carson* (1970)

**Carter, Angela** (1940–). British writer. One of the most original of contemporary writers, Angela Carter was born in Eastbourne, Sussex, where her mother was evacuated from London during the war, but grew up in London. When she was 18 her father, a Scottish journalist, arranged for her to become an apprentice on the *Croydon Advertiser*, but she left at 20 to marry. In the years of her marriage she graduated in English from Bristol University, and began to write her unique fiction imbued with folk-lore, dream, sexuality and the possibilities of transformation. Her first published books were *Shadow Dance* (1965), *The Magic Toyshop* (1967, filmed 1987), *Heroes and Villains* (1969), *Love* (1971) and *The Infernal Desire Machine of Dr Hoffman* (1972).

In 1972 she went to live in Japan for two years. Her writing after her return to England was more overtly feminist and socialist, beginning with the futuristic fantasy *The Passion of New Eve* (1978) and two collections of short stories, *Fireworks* and *The Bloody Chamber* (both 1979). Also in 1979 she published *The Sadeian Woman*, an influential attack on the heritage of Sade's voracious heroines and 'feminine' victims, comparing them to Hollywood icons. Her selected journalism, published in 1983 as *Nothing Sacred*, revealed her as a trenchant critic of contemporary society. In 1984 she published *Nights at the Circus*, a long picaresque novel, whose heroine 'Fevvers', a winged woman performer, has strong echoes of MAE WEST as well as earlier ballet stars. This was followed by the short stories *Black Venus* (1985). She also wrote the screenplay for Neil Jordan's film *The Company of Wolves*, a version of Little Red Riding Hood based on her own short story.

Angela Carter has taught creative writing at Sheffield University and at the University of East Anglia. She has also been a Visiting Professor at Brown University and the University of Texas, and in Australia at the University of Adelaide. She lives in London, and has a son, born in 1984.

**Carter, Elizabeth** (1717–1806). English intellectual. Born in Deal, a clergyman's daughter, she was educated by him to be a Classical and Hebrew scholar, later learning Portuguese, Arabic, astronomy and history. She remained single, looking after her father's large family by his second wife. She began contributing to *The Gentleman's Magazine* in 1734 as 'Eliza'. She met Dr Johnson in 1738 after publishing *Poems upon Particular Occasions*, and started to contribute to *The Rambler*. Encouraged by her friend, Catherine Talbot, in 1749 she began a translation of the writings of Epictetus, which was eventually published to great acclaim in 1758, with four editions produced in her lifetime. She became a friend of the group of intellectual women known as blue stockings through ELIZABETH MONTAGU, and established her reputation by editing Mary Talbot's letters and essays. After her father's death in 1774 she remained in Deal, a highly venerated old lady.

A.C. Gaussen: *A Woman of Wit and Wisdom: a Memoir of Elizabeth Carter* (1929)

**Cartland, Barbara** (1904–). English writer. Her career as a novelist started at the age of 21 with the publication of *Jigsaw*. She married twice, in 1927 and 1936. As well as writing, she did a lot of charity work, particlarly with the St John's Ambulance Brigade and various nursing organizations. During World War II she was in the Auxiliary Territorial Services (ATS), and was the Lady Welfare Officer and Librarian to all services in Bedfordshire (1941–9). Her career has included many television appearances; she has become famous as an exponent of the virtue of health foods to maintain fitness and beauty in old age, becoming President of the National Association of Health in 1966.

An extremely prolific writer of romantic fiction, representative titles of her countless novels include *Kiss the Moonlight*, *The Wild Cry of Love*, and *Little White Doves of Love*. She has also written various advice books, such as *You in the Home*, *Woman the Enigma*, *Recipes for Lovers*, and some biographies of 'romantic' figures including *The Private Life of Elizabeth, Empress of Austria* and *Josephine, Empress of France*. There are five volumes of autobiography.

B. Cartland: *The Isthmus Years* (1943)
———: *The Years of Opportunity* (1947)
———: *I Search for Rainbows* (1967)
———: *We Danced all Night: 1919–1929* (1971)
———: *I Seek the Miraculous* (1978)

**Casarès (Quiroga), Maria** (1922–). French actress. She was born in Coruna, Spain, the daughter of a loyalist politician, and worked as a nurse in the Spanish Civil War before fleeing to France after Franco came to power. There she studied drama at the Paris Conservatoire, and, after making her debut in Synge's *Deirdre of the Sorrows* at the Théâtre des Mathurins, became the leading actress in early existentialist works such as Camus' *Le malentendu* (1944), and *L'état du siège* and *Les justes* (1948), and Sartre's *Le diable et le bon Dieu* (1951). She then rose to become a principal actress with the Comédie Française (1952–4), before working with the Théâtre National Populaire. In the 1960s she was involved in Barrault's Théâtre de France, her roles including the mother in Genet's *Les paravents* (1966). She is now considered one of France's leading actresses. During the 1940s she appeared in *Les enfants du paradis* (1945) and other leading films, including *La chartreuse de Parme* (1948). She also played La Mort in Cocteau's *Orphée* (1950) and in the *Testament d'Orphée* (1960).

M. Casarès: *Résidente Privilegiée* (1980)

**Caslavska, Vera** (1942–). Czech gymnast. She was born in Prague, and was a keen ice-skater, but when she was 15 she was selected for training during nationwide trials to find gymnastic talent. In 1958, at her international debut, she won a silver medal in the team event, and in 1959 a European title for her performance on the beam, a piece of apparatus on which she continued to show particular poise. At the Tokyo Olympics (1964), Vera overtook the current champion LARISSA LATYNINA to gain the individual title, as well as gold medals on the beam and vault. In both 1965 and 1967 she won gold medals in every event of the European championships, as Larissa Latynina had done before her; at the 1966 World Championships she narrowly beat the Russians for the combined exercises gold medal, and helped Czechoslovakia win the team championships.

The Mexico Olympics (1968) were overshadowed by Soviet suppression of the Czechoslovak bid for independence. Vera went into hiding and her only way of keeping fit was by carrying bags of coal. Thus, when she rounded off her career with four golds and two silvers, and with her 'Mexican Hat-dance' floor routine beat the Russian Natalya Kuchinskaya, the applause was rapturous: she represented Czechoslovak freedom. During the Games she married the Czech athlete, Josef Odlozil, and they later had two daughters.

On her return to Prague, Vera presented her medals to the Czechoslovak leaders Dubček, Černik, Svoboda and Smrkovsky, an act which later closed many jobs to her and her husband, but eventually she worked as a coach. Her World, Olympic and European titles totalled 22.

**Cassat, Mary** [pseud. May Stevenson] (1845–1926). American painter. Born in Allegheny City, Pennsylvania, she was inspired to be a painter by a visit to Paris and Germany with her family at the age of six. She attended the Pennsylvania Academy of Fine Arts but found the course too academic and decided to study abroad, arriving in Paris in 1866. She went back to the USA during the Franco–Prussian War (1870–72), via Rome, Parma, Spain and Antwerp, and on her return to Paris exhibited in the Salon of 1872–3 under the name of May Stevenson. In 1877 Degas invited her to join the Impressionist group Les Indépendents and they became great friends. Her family moved to Paris in 1877 and her sister Lydia became her favourite model in paintings such as *The Cup of Tea*, which was included in the Impressionist exhibition of 1881. She also painted many studies of her nephews and nieces and her favourite themes related to domestic life.

In 1882, with Degas, she left the Impressionist group. They influenced each other's work and her own pictures became clearer and more formal, especially after the Japanese Exhibition of 1890. In 1891–2 she designed a mural for the Woman's Building at the world's Columbia Exposition in Chicago. She then moved to the Château de Beaufresne in Oise. In 1895 her mother died and she revisited the USA, where exhibitions of her work had done much to influence taste in favour of the Impressionists. She continued to work, in paints and pastels, until 1912 when she developed cataracts in both eyes. During World War I she lived in Grasse in the south of France. She never recovered full sight, despite operations in 1921. Among her best loved paintings are *The Bath* (1891) and *Mother and Child* (1905).

N. Hale: *Mary Cassatt* (1975)

**Castle, Barbara** (1911–). English politician. Born in Chesterfield, Derbyshire, she was educated at Bradford Girls' Grammar School and won a scholarship to St Hugh's College, Oxford. During World War II she became an administrative officer at the Ministry of Food (1941–4) and then worked as a journalist on the *Daily Mirror*. In 1944 she married Edward Castle, later Lord Castle of Islington, who died in 1979.

Barbara Castle was involved first in local government, being one of the youngest members elected to the St Pancras Borough Council (1937–45) and a member of the Metropolitan Water Board (1940–45). An active Fabian, she undertook research which helped to influence the thinking behind the Beveridge Report in 1946. In 1945 she became Member of Parliament for Blackburn and remained in the House of Commons for 34 years. In July 1979 she became the member for Greater Manchester North, the European Parliament, where she is Vice-Chairman of the Socialist Group. While a British MP she was a member of the National Executive of the Labour Party (1950–79) and was party Chairman (1958–9). She acted as Minister of Overseas Development (1964–5), and as Minister of Transport (1965–8) was responsible for some radical legislation. This was followed by a difficult period as Secretary of State for Employment and Productivity (1968–70), during which she produced her controversial policy document *In Place of Strife*. In 1970 she carried the Equal Pay Act through parliament; it became effective in 1975.

After four years in the shadow cabinet, she returned to office as Secretary of State for Social Security (1974–6), and this period is the subject of her frank revelations in *The Castle Diaries* which created a lively debate on their publication in 1980 and 1984. Since 1979 she has been a member of the European Parliament, where she was Leader of the British Labour Group 1979–85 and Vice President of the Socialist Group. In 1987 she published a lively study of the British feminists CHRISTABEL and SYLVIA PANKHURST.

**Casulana** [Mezari], **Maddalena** (*c*1540–1583 or later). Italian composer and singer. The origin of her name remains obscure: 'Casulana' may be derived from her place of birth (Casola or Casole), though she was mainly active in Venice and Vicenza; she is occasionally referred to as 'Maddalena Mezari', possibly her married name. She composed an epithalamium that is known to have been conducted by Lassus at the marriage banquet of Wilhelm IV of Bavaria and Renée of Lorraine (Munich, 1568), but only its text survives; her extant works comprise 66 madrigals, most of them published in her own three volumes (1568, 1570 and 1583) and a few in collections by others. The dedications of her works imply that she had patrons in Verona, Florence and Milan.

The actor and poet Antonio Molino began taking music lessons from her in 1568 (apparently when he was over 70) and that year dedicated his *Dilettevoli madrigali* to her; she was also responsible for the publication of his second volume and was the dedicatee of Philippe de Monte's *Il primo libro de madrigali a tre* (1582). In 1582 she sang at a banquet in Perugia, when she was described as 'la Casolana famosa'.

**Catalani, Angelica** (1780–1849). Italian soprano. She received little musical education, but made her debut at La Fenice, Venice, in Mayr's *Lodoiska* aged 17, and in the next few years appeared at La Scala, Milan, and elsewhere in Italy. In Lisbon in 1804 she married Paul Valabrègue, who later became her manager. After her debut in London (1806), the King's Theatre virtually became her showcase. The manager Francis Gould engaged her at a fee of over £5000 (the maximum for other singers had been £500); the resultant increase in seat prices caused public protest but seems not to have affected her popularity. She was billed as 'Prima Cantatrice del Mondo', probably a justifiable claim at the time.

Best known for her singing of popular songs (even singing arrangements of virtuoso pieces for violin and flute), she also played both comic and tragic roles in operas by such composers as Cimarosa, Mayr, Nasolini and Paisiello; she was Susanna in the first London performance of Mozart's *Le nozze di Figaro* (1812), though she found Mozart's music inhibiting to her musical tastes. Her career lasted long enough for her extravagant vocal displays to become outmoded and harshly criticized.

From 1814 to 1817 Catalani directed the Théâtre Italien at the Salle Favart, Paris, though financial mismanagement caused her to abandon the enterprise and concentrate on singing once more. The composers Marcos Antônio Portugal and Vincenzo Pucitta wrote operas for her, the latter also serving as her accompanist during her tours of Scotland, Ireland and England, and in 1815 of the Netherlands, Belgium and Germany. She also toured Scandinavia, Poland and Russia.

**Catchpole, Margaret** (1773–1841). English-Australian pioneer and letter-writer. Probably born in Nacton, Suffolk, she became a servant and then nurse to the Cobbolds, an Ipswich brewer's family, where she learnt to read and write. After leaving them in 1795, allegedly out of love for William Laud, a smuggler, she was ill and out of work, and was eventually arrested for stealing her old employer's horse and galloping to London to meet Laud. Her death sentence was commuted to seven years transportation, but she scaled 20-foot walls to escape from gaol, and on being recaptured was eventually sentenced to transportation for life. Her lover, whom she had escaped to marry, was shot.

In 1801 she reached Sydney and worked as a cook, rising to the position of housekeeper and overseer for leading colonial families. Pardoned in 1814, she remained in Australia, keeping a shop and acting as midwife and nurse, until she died of influenza caught from one of her patients. She is remembered because of her letters, to relatives and to the Cobbolds, which give graphic accounts of daily life in the colony as well as of the aborigines and of major disasters such as the Hawkesbury River Floods. Her life became a legend after the letters were turned by Richard Cobbold into *The History of Margaret Catchpole* (1845), which added to her own life the successful married career of MARY REIBEY.

C.G. Carter: *Margaret Catchpole* (1949)

**Cather, Willa (Sibert)** (1873–1947). American novelist. She was born on a farm in Back Creek Valley, near Winchester, Virginia, and when she was ten moved with her family to Red Cloud, Nebraska. She was educated at the local high school, and then in Lincoln, where she attended the University of Nebraska from 1891 to 1895. As a student she was unconventional, wearing short hair and calling herself 'William'. She then became a journalist and joined the staff of the *Home Monthly* in 1896, moving the next year to the Pittsburgh *Daily Leader*; however, she was already writing short fiction, and in 1901 became a teacher to give herself more time. She taught Latin and English at local high schools. Her first book, *April Twilight* (1903), was a collection of verse, and her second, *The Troll Garden* (1905), a set of short stories in Jamesian style dealing mostly with the theme of the artist in society.

In 1906 Willa Cather became an editor on *McClure's Magazine* in New York. She published her first novel, *Alexander's Bridge*, in 1912, when she left journalism to be a full-time writer. The next year she began her marvellous series of novels dealing with life in the Nebraska of her youth, *O Pioneers!* (1913), *The Song of the Lark* (1915), *My Antonia* (1918), *One of Ours* (1922) and *A Lost Lady* (1923). With fame her life changed: she received the Pulitzer Prize in 1923, and her novel *The Professor's House* (1925) dealt with some of the problems this brought. Her later novels revealed an increasing range, and a deepening interest in the American Southwest, following her best-seller *Death comes for the Archbishop* (1927). Compassionate, energetic and vibrant, she always preferred the company of other women, and portrayed a series of independent women in her books. During the 1930s she was greatly respected and received several honorary degrees.

E.K. Brown and L. Edel: *Cather: a Critical Biography* (1953)

**Catherine II** [Catherine the Great] (1729–96). Empress of Russia. She was born Princess Sophia Augusta Frederika of Anhalt-Zerbst, in Stettin [now Szczeczin]. At the age of 15 she visited Russia, where her marriage was arranged to the 16-year-old Grand Duke Peter, after her formal conversion from Lutheranism to Russian Orthodoxy in 1745.

Intelligent, ambitious, energetic and diplomatic, she was a well-established figure when Peter succeeded in 1761, and his unpopularity allowed her to depose him with the support of the guards in June 1762. Rather than acting as Regent for her son, she proclaimed herself ruler; the death of Peter in prison, and of Ivan IV in 1764, secured the throne. Although she had influential ministers, lovers and favourites (Panin, Orlov, Potemkin) she exercised total authority throughout her reign.

Presenting herself as an enlightened ruler, corresponding with Voltaire and the Encyclopedists, she published a progressive *Instruction* (1767) which initiated reforms of the code of laws, and she also made plans to improve provincial and municipal administration (1775, 1785), and education (1786), but many of these measures were left incomplete. In reality, the nobility increased in power, serfdom was strengthened and, despite the creation of St Petersburg as a brilliant cultural centre, all intellectual protest was stifled.

In foreign policy Catherine's cautious start gave way to expansionist aims. She suppressed Polish nationalist agitation and divided the country with Austria and Prussia in three partitions of 1772, 1793 and 1794. Her aggression towards Turkey eventually resulted in the annexation of the Crimea (1783), and of parts of the Black Sea coast (1792, 1794), although she abandoned her dreams of taking Constantinople. During her reign, Russia became accepted as a leading European power.

J. Haslip: *Catherine the Great: a Biography* (1977)

**Catherine of Aragon** (1485–1536). First queen of Henry VIII of England. She was born at Alcalá de Henares, Spain, the youngest daughter of Ferdinand II of Aragon and ISABELLA I of Castile. After long negotiations she married Prince Arthur, eldest son of Henry VII, in 1501; at 16 she was 2 years older than her husband. He died the following year, and she was betrothed to his brother Henry, but diplomatic difficulties postponed the marriage until Henry became king in 1509. For many years the marriage was happy; both were lively, intellectual and cultured. She acted as a capable Regent during the French campaigns of 1511 to 1514, organizing the defence against the Scots which culminated in the Battle of Flodden in 1513. The chief sadness was the death of five of their six children, with only MARY I surviving. Catherine was a great patron of scholarship. She invited Louis Vives to come to England to supervise Mary's education, in the course of which he wrote *A Plan of Studies for a Girl*. She also had a splendid personal library, contributed to lectureships at Oxford and Cambridge, supported poor scholars there, and was friendly with leading scholars such as Thomas Linacre, John Colet, Thomas More and Richard Pace.

In 1527, prompted by his desire for a male heir and his infatuation with ANNE BOLEYN, Henry started negotiations to annul the marriage on the grounds of consanguinity because of Catherine's previous marriage to Arthur. Catherine appealed to Pope Clement VII, saying that her first marriage had never been consummated, and the Pope delayed a decision for seven years, because he could not afford to lose the support of her nephew, Charles V. Relations became increasingly strained, with Catherine refusing to give in and retire to a convent, and challenging the court hearing organized by Henry in 1529 under the cardinals Wolsey and Campeggio. In 1533 Henry secretly married Anne Boleyn and set up his own court under Cranmer; the court declared his first marriage invalid, and the Pope's decision on Catherine's behalf in March 1534 was too late. She was separated from her daughter Mary and never saw her again, though they managed to correspond secretly, and she was forced to withdraw from public life (since she had always been a great popular favourite and remained so until her death) and to live in virtual poverty on small estates such as Ampthill and Kimbolton Castle.

She always refused, despite threats, humiliations and cajolements, to take her title of Princess Dowager, or to acknowledge the Act of Succession or the Act of Supremacy. For the last two years of her life she was constantly ill, and there were frequent rumours that she had been poisoned.

G. Mattingley: *Catherine of Aragon* (1942)

**Catherine of Genoa** [Fieschi, Caterina] (1447–1510). Italian saint and mystic. Born of a noble Ligurian family, at the age of 16 Catherine made a marriage of convenience to the wealthy Julian Adorno. He proved to be spendthrift, inordinately pleasure-loving, bad-tempered and frequently unfaithful. She failed to find compensation in the gay life of Genoese society. In 1473 Catherine suddenly underwent a conversion and a few years later her new way of life also changed her husband. They agreed to live in continence, and their devotion to the sick in the hospital of Pammatane nearly resulted in Catherine's death from plague. She was Matron of the hospital from 1490 to 1496 and survived her husband by 13 years, though suffering severely from an undiagnosed illness in the last years of her life.

Catherine's spiritual life was very intense, and she underwent various contemplative and visionary experiences. She also showed great practical competence. Her spiritual doctrine is contained in *Vita e dottrina* (1551), although it is likely that she did not write it herself. This book is the source of *Dialogues on the Soul and the Body* and *Treatise on Purgatory*.

F. von Hugel: *The Mystical Element of Religion* (1908)

**Catherine of Siena** [Benincasa, Caterina] (1347–80). Italian mystic and saint. She was the 23rd child (a twin) of a Sienese dyer and his wife. As a young child she received visions which led her to vow her virginity to Jesus Christ, and when urged by her mother to care more for her appearance to increase her chances of marriage, Catherine cut her hair off. At the age of 16 she joined the Third Order of St Dominic and lived a life of prayer and service to the poor, subjecting herself to severe austerities. She continued to experience spiritual raptures which later culminated in the pain of the stigmata. Her extraordinary sanctity won a large band of followers which included many of noble rank.

Catherine's involvement with public affairs began in 1375, when she successfully implored Pope Gregory XI to leave Avignon and return to Rome. When Gregory's death led to the Great Schism, Catherine threw herself into the struggle on behalf of Urban VI, urging cardinals and monarchs to return to his obedience.

Many of Catherine's letters are extant, as well as the *Dialogo*, a spiritual work of some importance. She was canonized in 1461 and named a Doctor of the Church in 1970.

A. Curtayne: *Saint Catherine of Siena* (1935)

**Catt** [née Lane], **Carrie (Chapman)** (1859–1947). American suffrage leader. She initially worked as a teacher, school administrator, and journalist, in her home state of Iowa and then in San Francisco. After the death of her first husband, Leo Chapman, after two years of marriage in 1886, she returned to Iowa, married George Catt, an engineer, in 1890, and became actively involved in women's suffrage work. A superb administrator, she was Chairman of the Organization Committee of the National American Woman Suffrage Alliance (NAWSA) from 1895 to 1900, when she succeeded SUSAN B. ANTHONY as

President. She resigned briefly in 1903 but after George Catt's death in 1904 she became President of the International Women's Suffrage Alliance.

In 1912 Carrie Catt took control of the New York suffrage movement, organizing two major campaigns which eventually won the state vote for women in 1917. On becoming President of NAWSA, she imposed sweeping changes, drew up long-term plans, and lobbied tirelessly against enormous opposition until the Nineteenth Amendment was finally passed in June 1920. She then founded the League of Women Voters, and became involved in the Peace Movement, especially the Committee for the Cause and Cure of War.

Carrie Catt has been criticized for allowing her sense of expediency to compromise her stated principles. For example, she failed to combat racism within NAWSA, withdrew support for the militant feminists, and despite her pacifism, backed American entry into World War I. Her energy and political dexterity did, however, greatly benefit the suffrage movement. Her books included *Woman Suffrage and Politics* (1933), and *Why Wars must Cease* (1935).

M.G. Peck: *Carrie Chapman Catt* (1944)

**Cauer, Minna** [Wilhelmine] (1841–1922). German feminist. Cauer entered feminist politics in the 1880s. The widow of a left-wing educationalist, she led the new Kaufmannischer Verband für Weibliche Angestellete (Commercial Union of Salaried Employees). As an active member of the Verein Frauenwohl (Women's Welfare Association) she advocated social work for women and led the women's movement away from its conservative views of education as important to improve women in their role in the home. In 1900, with ANITA AUGSBURG, she founded the Verband fortschrittlicher Frauenvereine (Union of Progressive Women's Associations) and was involved in the campaign to abolish state regulated prostitution. In the early franchise movement she was a co-founder of the Deutscher Verband für Frauenstimmrecht (German Union for Women's Suffrage) (1902). She belonged to the militant wing of the movement, organizing the great street demonstrations of 1910, but had to resign

from the Union in 1912, after declining to insist on universal suffrage as opposed to limited suffrage. For many years she had been the leader of the radical feminists: she had tried to include working women in the movement and had been involved with the pacifist International Alliance of Women since its beginnings in 1904, so that, with LIDA HEYMANN, Augsburg and others, she became isolated from the women's movement by its swing to the right, characterized by the social purity and militaristic groups of World War I.

**Cavanagh, Kit** [Christian] ['Mother Ross'] (1667–1739). Irish soldier. Born in Dublin, daughter of a prosperous brewer, she married a servant, Richard Welsh. In 1692 he was forcibly conscripted into the army and in 1693 she disguised herself as a man and enlisted to find him. She served against the French with Marlborough in Holland and soon transferred to the cavalry, joining her husband's regiment the Scots Greys and remaining with them during the renewed fighting of 1702 and 1703. She was reunited with her husband but remained in the army. She was wounded at Ramillies and her sex was then discovered, but she was allowed to stay with the Dragoons as an officers' cook.

Richard Welsh was killed at the battle of Malplaquet, and soon after she married a grenadier with the Royal Greys, Hugh Jones, who was also killed, in 1710. In 1712 she returned to England, became an innkeeper and married a dissolute soldier named Davies. Eventually she was admitted to Chelsea Hospital where she died. She was buried with military honours.

D. Defoe: *The Life and Adventures of Mrs Christian Davies, commonly called Mother Ross* (1740)

**Cavell, Edith** (1865–1915). English nurse. The daughter of a clergyman, Edith worked as a governess then trained as a nurse, working through a typhoid epidemic before graduating at the London Hospital.

In 1907 she was appointed head of nursing at Belgium's first training school for nurses at the Birkendael Medical Institute in Brussels. When the Germans invaded Brussels the school became a Red Cross hospital. Edith treated all wounded soldiers regardless of their nationality, and also allowed the hospital to be used as an 'underground' stop for French and British soldiers going to the Netherlands: at one time 35 men were hidden there. Despite her good intentions, her Resistance work was not efficient; escaping soldiers had on occasion got drunk in Brussels, and eventually 11 of her co-workers were incriminated. Edith was arrested by the Germans in August 1915, court-martialled, and shot on 12 October 1915.

H. Judson: *Edith Cavell* (1941)
R. Ryder: *Edith Cavell: a Biography* (1975)

**Cavendish, Margaret,** Duchess of Newcastle (1623–74). English poet and essayist. The youngest of Sir Thomas Lucas's eight children, she was born near Colchester, and educated at home, before becoming Maid of Honour to Queen Henrietta Maria from 1643 to 1645. She disliked court life and left in 1645 when she married the Royalist Duke of Newcastle in Paris. They lived together in exile, apart from an 18-month period when Margaret returned, trying in vain to collect revenue from their estates. She wrote constantly, plays, poems and philosophy, and on their return to England at the Restoration found herself considered a court eccentric. Her first published works were *Philosophical Fancies*, and *Poetical Fancies* (1653), but her reputation at the time rested more on her *Playes* (1662), and her essays, such as *CCXI Sociable Letters* (1664). In 1662 her *Orations of Divers Persons* contained speeches by women arguing for freedom and equality, but concluded by accepting women's power to lie in romantic domination over men. Her interest now stems more from her vivid biography of her husband, written in 1667, and from her own autobiography, one of the earliest we have, written in 1655.

K. Jones: *A Glorious Fame: the Life of Margaret Cavendish, Duchess of Newcastle* (1988)

**Ceausescu, Elena** (1919–). Romanian scientist and politician. A chemical engineer, she was educated at the College of Industrial Chemistry and the Polytechnic Institute, Bucharest; she was an activist in the Union of Communist Youth, becoming a Party member in 1937. She married the rising politician Nicolae Ceausescu, with whom she had three children, but continued her scientific career. She has contributed to many learned journals, has published research on molecular compounds, has edited vols I and II of the *Encyclopedia of Chemistry* (1983, 1985) and is the author of *The Science and Progress of Society* (1985). Since her rise to political power she has received honorary awards from scientific institutes in many countries.

She herself did not become a full member of the Romanian Communist Party Executive Political Committee until 1973, but her husband became President in 1974 and she has long been considered the most influential political figure behind him. She became a member of the Party's Permanent Bureau in 1977 and headed the commission on cadres; in 1979 she became Chairman of the National Council on Science and Technology, after seven years on the executive committee. This was an office with ministerial rank, but in 1980 her seniority was increased when she was made one of three First Deputy Prime Ministers, and a member of the National Council for Socialist Democracy and Unity. She was made Deputy Chair of the Supreme Council on Socio-Economic Development in 1982, and has also chaired the National Council of Science and Education since 1985.

**Cecilia** (*fl* 2nd or 3rd century). Roman, Christian martyr and patron saint of music. Her life is chronicled, albeit unreliably, in The Acts of St Cecilia which date from around 500 AD. According to these she was a Roman aristocrat who vowed virginity as a child but was forced to marry the nobleman Valerian. In return for his agreement to respect her vow and to be baptized as a Christian, he and his brother Tiburtius (also a convert) were granted a vision of an angel. Shortly afterwards all three were martyred; in Cecilia's case, after unsuccessful attempts to suffocate or burn her, she was beheaded.

Later historians consider Cecilia may have been a devout matron who donated her house as a church, but she has also been identified with 'Bona Dea Restituta', a Roman goddess who heals blindness. She was venerated from the 5th century, but, ironically, was actually presented as disapproving of the secular enchantment of music until the 15th century, when she was adopted as patron by various musicians' guilds, possibly due to a misinterpretation of

The Acts. Since that time she has often been represented playing the organ in paintings. Her feast-day is 22 November.

**Cellier** [née Dormer], **Elizabeth** (*fl* 1680s). English midwife. She married a Frenchman, Peter Cellier, in London in the 1670s. She was a Catholic convert, and became involved in intrigue at the time of the Titus Oates conspiracy; she is said to have obtained the release of one of the conspirators in return for his promise to assassinate the king. He turned informer and declared that the plans for the plot could be found in a 'meal tub' in her house. In 1680 she was tried in connection with this 'Meal Tub' plot, but was acquitted. However, her pamphlet *Malice defeated; or a Brief Relation of the Accusation and Deliverance of Elizabeth Cellier* contained such an exposé of prison conditions at Newgate that she was tried for libel, sentenced to the pillory and ordered to pay £1000 fine.

She was equally bold in defending her profession. Deeply concerned with the scale of infant and perinatal mortality, she campaigned for the replacement of ecclesiastical licensing of midwives by a system that would ensure proper training and the maintenance of professional standards. She prepared a very detailed, practical proposal: *A Scheme for the Foundation of a Royal Hospital and raising a revenue of £5,000 or £6,000 a year by and for the maintenance of a corporation of skilled midwives and such foundlings or exposed children as shall be admitted therein* (1687). In her *Answer to Queries concerning the College of Midwives* (1687–8) she claimed that James II had agreed to unite the midwives with a corporation by Royal Charter, but no further steps were taken after his downfall in 1688.

Another contemporary midwife concerned about her profession was Mrs Jane Sharp, whose *The Midwive's Book* (1671) was the first textbook written by an English midwife.

**Centlivre, Susanna** (1667–1723). English dramatist. There is some confusion as to whether she was born in Holbeach, Lincolnshire, or County Tyrone where her father had a large land grant. Aged 15 she ran away from Ireland to Liverpool and while walking to London met Arthur Hammond, who persuaded her to go to Cambridge disguised as his valet. Their affair was happy but Susanna later left for London where she was married in 1684, possibly to a nephew of Sir Stephen Fox, who was soon killed in a duel. Her second husband, Carroll, whom she married in 1685, was also killed within a year by duelling. She then became a provincial actress, often appearing in her own plays.

Strikingly beautiful and accomplished (she spoke several languages), she turned to writing for the stage, and herself played the heroine in her first play, *The Perjured Husband* (1700). Before her death she wrote 17 comedies and several tragedies, her best known works being *The Gamester* (1705), *The Busie Body* (1709), *The Wonder! A Woman keeps a Secret* (1714), and *A Bold Stroke for a Wife* (1718). The lively dialogue, strong characterization and plotting provided fine acting parts and they were repeatedly performed in the 18th and 19th centuries. In 1707 Susanna married the Chef to George I and Queen Anne, Joseph Centlivre. They moved to London in 1712 and her house became a salon for well-known literary figures.

J.W. Bowyer: *The Celebrated Mrs Centlivre* (1952)

**Cerrito, Fanny** (1817–1909). Italian ballerina and choreographer. She studied under Blasis at La Scala, made her debut aged 15 in Naples in 1832, and secured instant recognition. Subsequently she toured Italy and Austria, was engaged at La Scala in 1838, and at Her Majesty's Theatre, London, in 1840. Here she was a great favourite, dancing in *Lac des fées*, *Alma*, *La vivandière*, and excelling in the *pas de l'ombre* in Perrot's *Ondine* in 1843. In that year she was asked by Queen Victoria to dance the *pas de deux* with FANNY ELSSLER at a Royal Command Performance, and the success inspired Perrot to stage his sensational *pas de quatre* in 1844 with MARIE TAGLIONI, CARLOTTA GRISI and LUCILLE GRAHN.

In 1845 Fanny married her regular partner, the dancer and choreographer Saint-Léon, and he created *La fille de marbre* in which she made a highly successful debut at the Paris Opéra in 1847. She left her husband in 1851 to become the mistress of the Marques de Bedmar, but remained at the Opéra, starring in Mazilier's *Orfa* (1852), and her own *Gemma* (with scenario by Gautier) in 1854. A supple, energetic, graceful dancer, Cerrito danced two seasons in Russia between 1855 and 1857, including an appcarance in the coronation celebrations for Alexander II. She retired in 1857, and lived in Paris until her death over 50 years later.

I. Guest: *Fanny Cerrito* (1956)

**Chadwick, Florence** (1919–). American swimmer. Born in San Diego, California, Florence was a good swimmer as a child, but never won national competitions nor reached the Olympic team. She studied law in college, married briefly, and then decided to emulate GERTRUDE EDERLE and swim the English Channel.

She raised money by working in Saudi Arabia, and in August 1950 she swam from France to England, the thirteenth woman to do so; her time of 13 hours 20 minutes was the fastest to date. In September 1951 she set a more important record as the first woman to achieve the more difficult swim from England to France, in spite of bad fog. The next year her target was the 21-mile channel between Catalina Island and Los Angeles, which she swam at her second attempt, in the fastest ever time; she was the first woman to conquer it. She began to earn money from swimming and in 1953 achieved a grand slam with four channel swims in five weeks, breaking records on each one. She repeated the England to France channel crossing, swam the Straits of Gibraltar, made a round trip across the Bosphorus and swam the Dardanelles.

Most of her records have now been superseded, partly because swimmers use radar to keep on course. Florence became a stockbroker, but continued to swim and to train others.

**Chaminade, Cécile (Louise Stéphanie)** (1857–1944). French pianist and composer. Her earliest compositions are some pieces of church music written when she was eight. A pupil of Godard, she made her debut as a pianist in 1875, attracting particular attention in recitals of her own works. She toured extensively and was especially popular in England, which she first visited in 1892. She wrote over 200 piano pieces, several of which she recorded, including the Scarf Dance from her ballet *Callirhoë*. Her other compositions include *Les amazones* for chorus and orchestra (*c*1888), a *Concertstück* for piano and orchestra (*c*1896), a Flute Concertino (1902), two piano trios and many songs.

**Champmeslé, Marie Desmares** (1642–98). French actress. Born in Rouen into a distinguished family, she was the granddaughter of a President of Normandy. As a young woman she began acting in local theatre, before her marriage to a Harfleur merchant, Monsieur Fleury. Soon widowed, she married the talented comic actor Charles Chevillet Champmeslé in 1666. They joined the Théâtre du Marais in 1669, and the following year moved to the Hôtel de Bourgogne. Marie soon outshadowed her husband and was much sought after by leading theatrical companies. At the Bourgogne she took the place of the leading actress Mlle Desoeillets in Racine's *Andromaque* in 1670. He was so impressed by her performance that he wrote the part of Bérénice for her the same year. She became especially associated with his plays, creating roles such as Atalida in *Bajazet* (1672), Ighigénie (1674), and Phèdre (1677). She was also the first Ariadne in Corneille's play (1673).

She became Racine's mistress, and commentators like Madame DE SEVIGNE said that his plays only succeeded because of her interpretation; they separated in 1679. The following year she and her husband became members of the new Comédie-Française, inaugurated by her performance in *Phèdre*. She remained there for the rest of her life, the most popular actress in France, and was responsible for initiating the chanting, declamatory style of French classical acting.

**Chanel, Coco** [Gabrielle] (*c*1883–1971). French couturier. Born into a poor rural family, Chanel was orphaned at an early age and went with her sister to work for a milliner in Deauville. She opened her first shop there in 1912. After acting as a nurse during World War I she founded a couture house in the rue Cambon, Paris, and lived in the Ritz Hotel nearby. During the 1920s the casual, liberating elegance of her clothes, which abandoned both the inner corset and outer formality, brought her popularity with the 'new women' of the era. In 1920 she introduced the chemise dress, in 1925 the collarless cardigan jacket, and then the bias-cut dress and other 'trademarks' such as floating neck scarves and heavy costume jewellery. By the late 1930s she was the wealthiest couturier in France, owning four businesses and factories making textiles, jewellery and perfumes.

E. Charles-Roux: *Chanel and her World* (1981)

**Chapman, Maria (Weston)** (1806–85). American abolitionist. Born in Weymouth, Massachusetts, she was educated locally and with relatives in London. Between 1828 and 1830 she taught at Ebenezer Barley's Young Ladies' High School, Boston, before marrying Henry Chapman, an active abolitionist. In 1832, as co-founder of the Boston Female Anti-Slavery Society she suffered abuse, social ostracism, even physical assault. A friend of the GRIMKÉ sisters, LYDIA CHILD and the visiting HARRIET MARTINEAU (whose biography she edited in 1877), Chapman worked with William Garrison in the Massachusetts Anti-Slavery Society and the Non-Resistance Society, helping to edit *The Liberator* and *Non-Resistant* (1839–42) and to launch the *National Anti-Slavery Standard*, becoming co-editor in 1844.

From 1848 to 1855 she lived in Europe, but returned to Massachusetts, and continued to work for the civil rights cause after the Civil War.

A. Lutz: *Crusade for Freedom* (1968)

**Chapone, Hester (Mulso)** (1727–1801). English essayist. She was born in Northamptonshire. Her precocious literary talent was discouraged by her mother, and she was largely self-educated, but after her mother's death in 1750 she became friendly with ELIZABETH CARTER, Samuel Richardson, and the blue stockings. In 1760, after a six-year struggle to win her father's approval, she married John Chapone, a lawyer, but he died within a year. She then lived alone, contributing to *The Gentleman's Magazine*, and writing her collection of essays. Her *Letters on the Improvement of the Mind*, written for her niece, were published in 1773, and proved so popular that three editions appeared before 1774,

and the book was still in print in the 1840s. The letters urge modesty, prudence, obedience, class exclusiveness, and the avoidance of scholarship.

**Charles, (Mary) Eugenia** (1919–). Dominican politician. Born in Pointe Michel, Eugenia Charles studied law, entered the Inner Temple, London, in 1947 and returned to the West Indies to practise in Barbados and the Windward and Leeward Islands and established a practice in the Dominican capital, Roseau. In 1968 she entered politics and was co-founder of the Dominica Freedom Party, becoming an MP in 1975 and leading the Opposition until 1980. After the election of that year she became Prime Minister, and also took the posts of Minister of Foreign Affairs, Finance and Development. She cracked down on corruption in government and the defence forces, and faced several emergencies, including a planned coup, in 1981. Although criticized for her reliance on US aid, in 1983 she persuaded President Reagan to stage his invasion of Grenada, after a left-wing coup. Re-elected as Prime Minister in 1985 she resumed all her former posts, adding those of Minister of Economic Affairs and Defence.

**Charpentier** [née Blondeau], **Constance (Marie)** (1767–1841). French painter. Born in Paris, and trained under Louis David and other artists, she exhibited in ten salons between 1795 and 1819, working particularly on family scenes of a rather sentimental kind. She was much admired and received a gold medal from the Musée Royale in 1819. Many of her paintings cannot be identified today and her most famous, an elegant portrait with an air of mystery, *Mademoiselle Charlotte du Val d'Ongres*, was attributed to David until the 1950s.

**Chase, Lucia** (1907–86). American ballet company manager. The third of five daughters, Lucia Chase was born in Waterbury, Connecticut. After graduating from St Margaret's School, Waterbury, she entered the Theatre Guild School, New York. In 1926 she married businessman Thomas Ewing, and did not return to the stage until his sudden death in 1933. She then studied ballet with Mikhail Mordkin, the former Bolshoy ballet-master, and joined his company, dancing leading roles in 1937. In 1940 she became a member and backer of the new American Ballet Theater, and was the principal dancer until 1960, especially acclaimed for her dramatic interpretations of ballets like Anthony Tudor's *Pillar of Fire* and *Dark Elegies*. After she retired she continued to dance, for example as the mother in Agnes de Mille's ballet based on the life of Lizzie Borden, *Fall River Legend*, and acted character parts well into her seventies. From 1945 to 1980, with Oliver Smith, she was co-director of the American Ballet Theater, producing classic works, but also encouraging new choreographers like TWYLA THARP. She was awarded the New York Handel Medallion in 1975, and the Medal of Freedom in 1980.

**Chattopadhyay, Kamaldevi** (1903–). Indian reformer and leader of a crafts movement. Born in Mangalore, she was educated locally, and then at Bedford College, London, and at the London School of Economics; in 1919 she married the progressive poet and dramatist Harindranath Chattopadhyay. She joined the Congress movement and was elected to the All India Congress in 1927, becoming organizing secretary and President of the All India Women's Conference, and suffering imprisonment in 1930, 1932, 1934 and 1942. After independence and partition she founded the Indian Co-operative Union in 1948 to help refugees, establishing the first co-operative at Chattarpur, near Delhi. She then helped in building the city of Fari Debad, for 300,000 refugees, established weaving and consumer co-operatives on a large scale, and then developed the highly-successful Cottage Industries Emporium as an outlet for the goods produced. In 1952 she became Chairman of All India Handicrafts Limited, and she helped to found the World Crafts Council of which she was senior Vice-president; she was also President of the Theatre Centre of India. She has received many national and international awards and has published books on Japanese, Chinese and American society, as well as on socialism and on Indian handicrafts. She was Vice President of the India International Centre in 1978–80.

**Chauviré, Yvette** (1917–). French ballerina and teacher. She was born in Paris and trained at the Opéra Ballet School, joining the Opéra Ballet in 1930. She was given major roles from an early age in Serge Lifar's ballets, from *Alexandre le Grand* (1937), to *Suite en blanc* (1943). She left the Opéra when Lifar died. From 1946 she worked with the Nouveau Ballet de Monte Carlo, interpreting several new roles in works such as Lifar's *Dramma per musica* (1946), and *Chota Rustaveli* (1947). For the following two years she returned to the Opéra, creating her famous *Mirages*, and returned again in 1953, becoming one of the great dancers of the 1950s, starring in classical ballets such as *Giselle* and *Sleeping Beauty,* and creating roles for choreographers including Cranko, Lander and Dolin.

Yvette Chauviré has an international reputation, having toured worldwide and appeared as a guest star with major companies such as the Royal Ballet, La Scala, and the Bolshoi. In 1963 she was appointed Artistic and Technical Advisor to the Paris Opéra, and in 1970 became Director of the International Academy of the Dance, Paris. In 1946 she was awarded the Légion d'honneur.

Y. Chauviré: *Je suis Ballerine* (1960)

**Chen Muhua** (?1940–). Chinese state leader. Little is known of her early life and career but she came into prominence and travelled abroad as Vice-Minister (1971) and then Minister of Economic Relations with Foreign Countries (1977). She became a member of the Chinese Communist Party Central Committee in 1973, and one of only two women of its Politburo in 1977. After 1978, when she was made Vice-Premier, she was responsible for China's health service and its birth control programme, and was in charge of the complex preparations for the population census of 1982. Chen Muhua became Minister of Foreign Trade in 1982 and has been President of the People's Bank of China, and Director of the State Treasury since 1985.

**Chen Tiejun** (1904–28). Chinese revolutionary and feminist. Daughter of a merchant, she joined the anti-imperialist student demonstrations of 4 May 1919, and in 1920 went to the new Jihua Girls' School which became a centre for revolutionary ideas. Forced to marry a merchant's son, she left after the ceremony, and entered a teacher training school. In 1925, she attended Zangshan University, was active in socialist and women's movements, and joined the Communist Party the following year.

When the university was besieged by Chiang Kai Shek's forces in 1927 she went underground, lived and worked with Zhen Wenjang, commander of the local workers' Red Guards, and organized a women's team to smuggle in weapons. Betrayed to the nationalists, she was arrested, tortured and executed in March 1928.

**Cheron, (Elisabeth) Sophie** (1648–1711). French artist. The daughter of a miniaturist, she worked as a portrait miniaturist in water colours and enamel, supporting her family after her father deserted them. Treated as a youthful prodigy she was unanimously elected to the Académie Royale in 1672, and was accepted also as a poet in 1676. She worked as a painter, engraver and enamellist, and enjoyed much patronage at court. To retain favour she and her sister renounced their Huguenot faith, while their brother fled to England. Sophie also had a reputation as a musician and society wit. In 1692 she married the King's Engineer, Jacques le Hay, but continued to work as an artist, being accepted into the Accademia dei Ricoverati in Padua in 1699. Among other works, she has left several fine self-portraits.

**Chiang Ch'ing.** *See* JIANG QING.

**Chibesakunda, Lombe Phyllis** (1944–). Zambian lawyer and diplomat. Her law studies began at the National Institute of Public Administration, Lusaka, in 1965. In 1966 she left Zambia to study law at Gray's Inn, London, where she lived till 1969. On her return to Zambia she became the first State Advocate in the Ministry of Legal Affairs, a post she held until 1973; she has held many other important positions. In 1973 she became the parliamentary candidate for the Matero constituency and also became Solicitor-General in the Ministry of Legal Affairs. She joined the diplomatic corps in 1974 and thus broke into a rigid male-orientated terrain. She was next appointed Ambassador to Japan (1975).

From 1977 to 1981 she was Zambian High Commissioner to the UK (1978) and concurrently Ambassador to the Netherlands and the Holy See.

**Chicago** [née Cohen], **Judy** (1939–). American artist. Born in Chicago, she studied at the University of California, Los Angeles (1960–64), and includes EMILY CARR, GEORGIA O'KEEFFE, BARBARA HEPWORTH and LOUISE NEVELSON among her chief influences. She married Jerry Gerowitz in 1961, but he died two years later. From 1963 to 1969 she taught external courses for the University of California. She then married Lloyd Hamrol and continued teaching in California and Washington State. She became increasingly involved with the feminist art movement and was one of the founders of Feminist Studio Workshop, Los Angeles. In addition to her own exhibitions in California, from 1966 she worked in films, making *Womanhouse* with Joanna Demetrakis in 1972, and she was influential in establishing the Women's Building, which developed from the original Studio Workshop. She always openly attacked taboos about female sexuality or femininity, shocking the public in such works as *Menstruation Bathroom* (1971).

The later 1970s were largely taken up with creating and mounting the extraordinary exhibition *The Dinner Party*. This eventually took the form of a triangular table, set with embroidered runners and ceramic plates, created to symbolize 39 guests who represented different aspects of women's history from the primordial goddesses to contemporary writers and artists, placed on a floor inscribed with the names of 999 women of achievement. It was a collective work, but accomplished largely through Chicago's driving energy. The exhibition drew huge crowds in Los Angeles, Chicago and New York but has yet to find a permanent home. It is described in two books: *The Dinner Party: A Symbol of our Heritage* (1979) (which concentrates on the ceramics, and on the women covered) and *The Dinner Party: Embroidering our Heritage* (1979).

J. Chicago: *Through the Flower: My Life as a Woman Artist* (1971)
———: *The Dinner Party* (1979)

**Chiepe, Gaositwe Keagakwa Tibe** (c1926–). Botswana diplomat and politician. She was born in Serowe, Botswana, and educated locally and at Fort Hare University, South Africa from 1944 to 1947; she later attended Bristol University (1955–7). In Botswana she worked as an education officer, gradually rising to become Director of Education (1968–9). In 1970 she was appointed High Commissioner to the UK and to Nigeria, and during these years she also held ambassadorial positions in several European and Scandinavian countries. From 1974–7 she was Minister of Commerce, from 1977–84 Minister of Mineral Resources and Water Affairs and Minister of External Affairs since 1984.

**Child, Julia** (1912–). American cookery writer. Julia McWilliams was born in Pasadena, California; she graduated in history from Smith College in 1934. After working as a clerk in New York she joined the OSS at the start of World War II, and was sent to Ceylon. There she met Paul Child, an artist making maps for the OSS, and both were assigned to China. Returning to California after the war, she enrolled in the Beverly Hills Cookery School before she married Child in 1946 and moved to Washington. Her husband joined the Foreign Service and from 1948 to 1954 they lived in Paris, where she studied at the Cordon Bleu School. With Simone Beck and Louise Bertholle she founded a cookery school, L'Ecole des Trois Gourmandes, which Julia continued during later diplomatic assignments, to Marseilles, Bonn and Oslo. Over the years, the three friends collaborated in the writing of *Mastering the Art of French Cooking*, which was published in 1961. In that year the Childs returned and settled in Massachusetts, and Julia began a new career as a television personality with her highly successful series *The French Chef*, which ran from 1963 to 1973. She subsequently hosted a cooking show based chiefly on native American cookery, *Julia Child and Company* (1978–9), and also wrote *From Julia Child's Kitchen* (1975) and *Julia Child and Company* (1978).

**Child, Lydia Maria (Francis)** (1802–80). American writer. Born and educated in Medford, Massachusetts, she became a teacher, before going to live with her brother in Maine, where she began writing her popular novels about New England life, *Habanok* (1824) and *The Rebels* (1825). In 1828 she married lawyer and reformer David Lee Child, and their stand on abolition of slavery led to ostracism from Boston society. During the 1830s she published several works on slavery including *An Appeal in Favour of the Class of Americans called Africans* (1833), and pamphlets such as the *Anti-Slavery Catechism* (1836), while from 1840 to 1844 she edited the weekly *Anti-Slavery Standard* with her husband. She also published works on domestic subjects such as the best selling *Frugal Housewife* (1829), the magazine *Juvenile Monthly* (1826–34), a *History of the Condition of Women* (1835), vivid *Letters from New York* (1843), and several biographies.

During the 1850s she became interested in religion, and wrote *A Progress of Religious Ideas* (1855) but was thrown back into controversy by her offer to nurse John Brown in prison. Her *Correspondence between Lydia Maria Child and Governor Wise and Mrs Mason of Virginia* (1860) sold over 300,000 copies. Still a versatile professional writer, she wrote several other pamphlets, studies such as *An Appeal for the Indians*, and novels like *A Romance of the Republic* (1867) before her final book *Aspirations of the World* (1878).
M. Meltzen: *Tongue of Flame* (1965)

**Chisholm** [née Jones], **Caroline** (1808–77). Australian philanthropist. Born near Northampton, England, the daughter of a prosperous farmer, she had an evangelical upbringing. She made it a condition of her marriage to Archibald Chisholm in 1830 that she be allowed to continue her charity work. He was a Captain in the East India Company and she went with him to Madras in 1832, where she founded the Female School of Industry for the Daughters of European Soldiers. During this period she became a convert to Roman Catholicism.

In 1838 they visited Australia and Caroline remained in New South Wales when Archibald returned to duty in 1840. Horrified at the plight of single immigrant women arriving in Sydney, she took many destitute girls into her own home and in 1841 pressured Governor Gipps to provide a building where she opened her Female.

Immigrants' Home. She wanted to find employment as well as accommodation, and so opened the first free labour registry. She then extended her service to all the unemployed, undertook a detailed survey of employment opportunities and arranged for immigrants to work on bush farms and properties, travelling with them herself all over the region. She started branches of the agency in several places and in the first year found work for 1400 women and 600 men. In 1845 her husband returned and together they promoted Caroline's 'family colonization' scheme. She wanted to bring emancipated convicts' families, and other families to Australia, instead of following the government policy of selective colonization which led to an imbalance of the sexes.

In 1846 the Chisholms took their campaign to London, virtually running an information service on Australia. Caroline eventually achieved all her aims, and with sponsorship founded the Family Colonization Loan Society in 1849. This loaned passage money, repayable when the emigrants had settled in Australia. One of the principal guarantors against loss was ANGELA BURDETT-COUTTS. The scheme was effectively publicized in Dickens's *Household Words* (1851–2), although he provides a rather unsympathetic caricature of Caroline in Mrs Jellyby in *Bleak House*. Eventually the discovery of gold in Australia ensured the success of the project. Caroline returned to Australia in 1854. The Chisholms were now famous but impoverished, and public and private funds were subscribed to set them up in business.

In her later years Caroline campaigned for land reforms, while giving public lectures and running a girls' school. She and her husband returned to England in 1866 and lived in relative obscurity in Liverpool and London. Although a firm believer that women's true role lay in marriage and family life, she eventually became a supporter of the suffrage movement.

M.L. Kiddle: *Caroline Chisholm* (1950)

**Chisholm, Shirley (Anita)** (1924–). American politician. She was born in Brooklyn, but spent most of her childhood in Barbados with her grandmother; she then attended Brooklyn College, where she graduated in sociology in 1946, and went on to take an MA in child education at Columbia University. From 1946 to 1952 she worked at the Mount Calvary Child Care Centre, and then ran her own nursery school, before directing the Hamilton-Madison Child-Care Center in New York and advising the city on day-care facilities. Several of her later awards have been for her service to early childhood education and to youth opportunities.

In 1964 she was elected a New York State Assemblywoman for the 55th District; one of her campaigns was to get domestic workers included in the minimum wage law. From 1968 to 1983 she was a Congresswoman for the 12th District, Brooklyn, the first black woman to be elected to Congress. She was on the Democratic National Committee in 1972 and 1976, and in 1972 ran for the Democratic nomination for President. In the Assembly and in Congress she has been an outspoken campaigner for the rights of women and of racial minorities, for improvement of employment and educational opportunities and for changes in inner-city conditions. She is a member of the League of Women Voters and the National Association for the Advancement of Coloured People (NAACP). Her concern for racial and sexual equality is evident in her books *Unbought and Unbossed* (1970), her autobiography to that date, and *The good Fight* (1973). Since 1983 she has held the Purington Chair at Mount Holyoke College, Massachusetts.

S. Brownmiller: *Shirley Chisholm: a Biography* (1971)

**Ch'iu Chin** (?1879–1907). Chinese revolutionary. She was the youngest child of a government lawyer. She received a classical education and became a talented poet. At the age of 18, after an arranged marriage to Wang T'ing-Chun, she moved to Peking. There she became involved in the opposition to the Manchu rulers following the failure of the Hundred Days Reform of 1898 and the Boxer Uprising of 1900. A conscious feminist who took JOAN OF ARC as her heroine, she openly opposed foot binding, started a girls' school and in 1904 left her husband and two children and went to study in Tokyo. There she joined a revolutionary group and the following year returned to China to work with her cousin,

Hsü Hsi-Lin. She helped to organize secret societies and achieved notoriety as a passionate public speaker. In 1906 she founded a women's journal in Shanghai and became Principal of the Ta'Tung College of Physical Culture.

Meanwhile, she and Hsü planned an uprising in HamKow but Hsü was forced to move too early and was captured and executed. Ch'iu Chin was taken prisoner but refused to confess under torture, writing only the seven Chinese characters 'The autumn rain and wind sadden us'. She was beheaded on 15 July 1907 and is revered as a martyr of the early revolutionary movement.

**Chojnowska-Liskiewicz, Krystyna** (1936–). Polish yachtswoman. The first woman to sail around the world solo, Krystyna was born in Warsaw and educated at the Polytechnical University in Gdańsk where she has been a shipbuilding engineer since 1960, the year in which she married Waclaw Liskiewicz. In March 1976 she set out to circumnavigate the globe in her single-handed yacht *Mazurek*, completing her voyage exactly two years later, in March 1978. The feat won her many decorations in Poland and abroad, and she described her adventure in *Pierwsza dook ola Swiata* ('The first one round the world', 1979).

**Chopin, Kate** [née O'Flaherty, Katherine] (1850–1904). American writer. She was the daughter of an Irish immigrant and a French-Creole mother in St Louis, Missouri. Her father died when she was young, and she was brought up by her mother, grandmother and great-grandmother. A member of the colourful Creole society, she was well-educated at the Sacred Heart Convent, spoke several languages and was beautiful, witty and popular. She was an insatiable reader, and was especially influenced by Maupassant and Flaubert. In 1870 she married Oscar Chopin and they moved to his plantation in Louisiana, living there and in New Orleans, and spending summers in the fashionable resort of Grand Isle, which was the setting for her most famous novel, *The Awakening*.

The failure of Oscar's business forced them to move to the Cane River district in Louisiana, a swampland region which Kate later brought to life in her short stories *Bayou Folk*. She continued to run the plantation there after Oscar died of swamp fever in 1882, to pay off his debts.

She then moved back to St Louis, and after the death of her mother began to write to support her six children. Her novel *At Fault* (1890) was followed by the stories that made her famous: *Bayou Folk* (1894) and *A Night in Acidie* (1897); she also wrote some children's stories and poems. But in 1899 she published *The Awakening*, an extraordinarily evocative tale of sexual passion, which ends with the heroine's suicide but without her repentance. The book's lack of condemnation outraged the public, and Chopin was insulted and ostracized; she was so disheartened that she never wrote again.

P. Seyersted: *Chopin: a Critical Biography* (1969)

**Christie, Dame Agatha (Mary Clarissa)** (1890–1976). English detective story writer. The daughter of a rich American expatriate, Frederick Miller, she was born in Torquay and educated privately and at home before going to Paris to study singing and the piano. In 1914 she married Archie Christie, an officer in the Flying Corps, and she worked as a VAD nurse in a Red Cross Hospital in Torquay during World War I. Archie was later made a colonel, but although they had a daughter, Rosalind, his alcoholism made the marriage a misery and they were divorced in 1928, two years after she apparently suffered a severe breakdown.

She began publishing detective stories in 1920 and was a success from her very first novel, *The Mysterious Affair at Styles*. By 1930 some of her best-known work had already appeared, including *The Murder of Roger Ackroyd* (1926) and *The Seven Dials Mystery* (1929). In that year she married Sir Max Mallowan, the archaeologist, and every year she joined him on his excavations in Iraq and Syria and in the Assyrian cities. During World War II this idyllic pattern of life was disrupted, and she worked in the dispensary of University College Hospital, but she never ceased to write.

Altogether she wrote over 70 books, plus some short stories and mystery plays like the long-running *The Mousetrap* (1952). Her plots are classic, maintaining suspense to the final page, her characters are sketchy but memorable, including the eccentric detective Hercule Poirot and Miss Marple, and her settings, whether the exotic Balkans or the English village, have acquired a rather dated charm.

Agatha Christie received many awards and in 1971 was made a DBE.

A. Christie: *An Autobiography* (1977)
J. Morgan: *Agatha Christie* (1984)

**Chudleigh, Elizabeth** (1720–88). English adventuress. The daughter of the Governor of Chelsea Hospital, she became Maid of Honour to Augusta, Princess of Wales, in 1743, and the following year secretly married John Hervey, before he left for two years in the West Indies. A son was born in 1747 but the marriage was unhappy. Meanwhile Elizabeth acquired a scandalous reputation at court, becoming mistress of the Duke of Kingston in 1759, and marrying him in 1765. In 1773 she inherited his estate, but was eventually tried for bigamy in 1776, after holding a banker at gunpoint in Rome to get money to return to England to defend herself. She fled to France to escape Kingston's heirs, then to Russia, where she was so popular with CATHERINE II, that she settled in St Petersburg [now Leningrad], and established a brandy distillery. Eventually she returned south, living in Paris, Rome and other capitals in outrageous luxury surrounded by admirers. She is reputed to be William Makepiece Thackeray's model for Beatrice in *Henry Esmond*, and Baroness Bernstein in *The Virginians*.

B.C. Browne: *Elizabeth Chudleigh* (1927)

**Chudleigh, Lady Mary** (1656–1710). English essayist. Born in Devon, unhappily married to a local landowner, she achieved fame for her pamphlet *The Ladies' Defence*, originally published anonymously in response to a sermon on conjugal duty, which caused much controversy. She also wrote poetry and published *Essays upon Several Subjects* (1710).

**Churchill, Caryl** (1938–). British playwright. Caryl Churchill's father was a political cartoonist for the *Daily Mail*, and in the late 1940s her family emigrated to Canada, settling in Montreal, where she was educated at Trafalgar School. In 1956 she returned to Britain to take a degree at Lady Margaret Hall, Oxford. She began writing as a girl and

her first plays, student productions at Oxford between 1958 and 1961, were followed by radio plays in the 1960s and early 1970s. She moved back into the theatre with *Owners*, for the Theatre Upstairs at the Royal Court in 1972, and *Objections to Sex and Violence* (1973). In 1976 she wrote two plays for radical theatre groups, both set in the 17th-century, *Light Shining in Buckinghamshire* (about the English revolution) for the Joint Stock Company, and *Vinegar Tom* (about witch-hunts) for the women's theatre group Monstrous Regiment. She continued to work with Joint Stock on *Cloud 9* (1979) and *Fen* (1983), which won the Susan Smith Blackburn prize. Her other plays include *Top Girls* (1982), *Softcops* (1984, influenced by her study of Foucault and based on the lives of two 19th-century French criminals) and the award winning comedy *Serious Money* (1986) about the after effects of the 'Big Bang' in the City of London which played to packed houses, mostly composed of stockbrokers. Most of her plays since 1979 have also been staged in New York and she is regarded as one of Britain's most provocative, witty and committed dramatists.

**Churchill, Odette.** *See* HALLOWES.

**Churchill, Sarah.** *See* MARLBOROUGH.

**Chytilová, Véra** (1929–). Czech film director. She studied architecture and philosophy and modelled fashions before entering the film industry as a script girl. She became an assistant director and won the right to make a feature film with her prize-winning short *Ceiling* (1962). Her most celebrated film *Daisies* (1966), an anarchic, surreal comedy intended to explode male values, was initially banned from domestic release. Making *Fruit of Paradise* in 1970 with Belgian money, she had to wait until 1977 to get Czech funding for another film, *The Apple Game*. More recent films include *The Panel Story* (1981) and *Calamity* (1982). Always personal projects, her films are seen as part of the Czech New Wave (led by Milos Formaň), with their emphasis on experiment, improvisation and formalism.

**Cibber** [née Arne], **Susannah** (Maria) (1714–66). English singer and actress. The daughter of a Covent Garden upholsterer, and the sister of the composer Thomas Arne, she made her debut at the Haymarket Theatre at the age of 18. In 1734 she married the theatrical manager of Drury Lane, Theophilus Cibber, who coached her in her first great success in Voltaire's *Zaïre* in 1736. Her life with him was far from happy: their two children died, he took all her wages, and he encouraged her affair with John Sloper so that he could claim £5000 damages for adultery to pay his debts. He was awarded only £10 but she withdrew from the stage for some years. She later returned and from 1753 to her death was Garrick's most famous partner and one of the leading tragediennes at Drury Lane.

She had first made her reputation as a singer, and she continued to perform in concerts and opera, singing in the first performances of Handel's *Acis and Galatea* and *Messiah*, in which the contralto solos were written especially for her. Greatly mourned by the theatrical world at her death, she was buried in Westminster Abbey.

M. Nash: *The Provok'd Wife: the Life and Times of Susannah Cibber* (1977)

**Cintron, Conchita** (1922–). American-Portuguese bullfighter. Her mother was Irish-American and her father Puerto Rican, and although Conchita was registered as an American citizen she grew up in Peru. It was not particularly unusual for a woman to be associated with bullfighting, and when she was 12 she made her first public appearance on horseback as a *rejoneadora*. In Spain, however, women were forbidden to fight as *toreras* on foot until 1973; Conchita began as a *torera* when she was 15, in Mexico, but struggled to be allowed to appear in Portugal, Spain and France – where she was summonsed for having 'mistreated a domestic animal', a charge which she said was insulting to the bull.

Conchita killed some 800 bulls from horseback and 400 on foot, becoming extremely popular in South America. In 1949 she celebrated her marriage to a Portuguese nobleman by appearing on horseback in a Spanish bull ring, and then defying the rules by dismounting, executing a perfect set of passes and dropping the sword, choosing not to kill the bull.

Although arrested, the crowd's demands secured her an immediate pardon. She retired to Lisbon, where she had six children and became a writer, a diplomatic attaché and a dog breeder.

L.V. Cintron: *Goddess of the Bullring* (1961)

**Cissé, Jeanne Martin** (1926–). Guincan diplomat. She began her career as a teacher in 1945, working as director of a school from 1954 to 1958 before moving into politics. In 1959 she became a member of the Democratic Party, working in the Federal Office of the Kinda Region. She was particularly active on behalf of women in this area, and worked on the National and Regional Women's Committees in the National Assembly, eventually becoming Secretary-General of the Conference of African Women (1962–72), and a member of the United Nations Committee on the Status of Women (1963–9). From 1972 to 1976 she was a permanent representative to the United Nations, being the first woman appointed as a delegate and the first to preside over the United Nations Security Council. In 1975 she was awarded the Lenin Peace Prize, and in 1976 returned to Guinea where she was Minister of Social Affairs until 1984. She is married with six children.

**Cixous, Hélène** (1937–). French academic, novelist and feminist. She was born in Oran, Algeria, into a Jewish family. Her father, a doctor, had a French colonial background and her mother was German. In her childhood she became aware of the pressures both of imperialism and of anti-semitism. Her father died when she was 11, but the family remained in Algiers, where her mother supported them by working as a midwife, and Hélène graduated from the Lycée Bugeaud there in 1954. In 1955 she went to France, married, and began teaching at a lycée in Sceaux; she took further degrees in English in 1957 and 1958. From 1959 to 1964 she taught in Arcachon, then spent two years in Bordeaux. In 1964 she separated from her husband and lived with her son and daughter in the south-west of France, before becoming an assistant lecturer at the Sorbonne in 1965. Moving to Nanterre in 1967, she became involved in the student uprisings of May 1968, and set up an experimental literature course at

Vincennes where she became a professor. She also submitted her doctorate on James Joyce. In 1969 she was a co-founder of a new review, *Poétique*.

She is particularly associated with exploration of the relation between psychoanalysis and language, and of the close involvement of writer and reader within the literary text. Her works include *Dedans*, about submerged memories, which won the Prix Médicis in 1969; *Le troisième corps* (1970); *Les commencements* (1970); *Neutre* (1972); *Tombe* (1973); and *Révolutions pour plus d'un Faust* (1975). Other publications include *Partie* (1976), *Angst* (1977), *La* (1979) and *Le Livre de Prométhéa* (1983). She has also written essays, prefaces and plays, and has taught in the USA and Canada. She is one of the most influential of contemporary French intellectuals.

**Claflin, Tennessee (Celeste)** (1846–1923). American feminist, journalist and financier. Her career is largely inseparable from that of her elder sister, VICTORIA WOODHULL. While acting in their clairvoyant show, she married John Bartels in 1866 but retained her maiden name. In New York, where they settled in 1868, she shared Victoria's activities in journalism and stockbroking but was less publicly involved in the women's rights movement. They both moved to London in 1877 and eight years later she met a wealthy merchant and art collector, Francis Cook. Tennessee remained a feminist and outspoken lecturer and writer on the emancipation of women, but she also became a leader of fashionable society.

**Clairon, Claire(-Josephe-Hippolyte de la Tude)** (1723–1803). French actress. Daughter of a seamstress, she experienced extreme poverty in her early childhood. At the age of 12 she joined the Comédie Italienne and went from them to La Noue at Rouen. Her outstanding singing voice took her to the Paris Opéra in 1743, and thence she transferred to the Comédie Française. As was customary, she was asked to choose the role for her debut and she selected the title role of Racine's *Phèdre*, then played by MARIE-FRANÇOISE DUMESNIL. Clairon was an instant success in this most challenging part (1743) and went on to play numerous major

tragic roles. Early in her career she made attempts to give historical authenticity to her costumes and in 1753 she abandoned the stilted declamatory style of acting of the period and adopted a freer more natural manner. Since her voice had innate tragic depth her new approach was successful. In 1765 Clairon, together with other members of the Comédie Française, refused to perform with an actor who had brought the company into disrepute and she never returned to the theatre. She took refuge with Voltaire, who had been one of her earliest admirers, and acted in his private theatre at Ferney. Returning to Paris, she appeared in private theatricals or at court until, aged 50, she was invited to the court of the Margrave of Anspach where she wrote her book *Mémoires et réflexions sur l'art dramatique* (published in 1799). On the death of the Margrave, and her pension having ceased with the outbreak of the French Revolution, she returned to Paris to live on the proceeds of her book.

**Clare of Assisi** (*c*1194–1253). Italian saint and founder. Born of a noble Assisi family, she refused two offers of marriage and finally under the influence of St Francis made up her mind to a religious vocation. Secretly leaving home at the age of 18, she went first to a Benedictine house, but when other women also wished to live in the Franciscan way, St Francis set up a separate community in Assisi with Clare as Abbess, a position she occupied until her death.

Clare's great concern was to persuade successive popes that her community of 'Poor Clares' be granted the 'privilege of poverty' and be allowed to live entirely on alms; the austerity of their order went far beyond any that women had previously undertaken. She also considered the penitential prayer life of the Clares to be a spiritually vitalizing force for the Church and society at large.

N. de Robeck: *St Clare of Assisi* (1959)

**Clark, Hilda** (1881–1955). British Quaker relief worker and pacifist. Hilda Clark was the youngest of six children of the owner of Clarks' Shoe Factory in Somerset. The family were active members of the Society of Friends, liberals, reformers and supporters of the women's suffrage movement. She was educated at home, then at school in Southport and at The Mount School, York. She then studied medicine in Birmingham (living with her aunt, a qualified doctor), but eventually obtained her degrees from London University. An advocate of the new tuberculin injection treatment, she became Tuberculosis Officer at Portsmouth, publishing *Dispensary Treatment of Pulmonary Tuberculosis* in 1914. She was also a keen suffragist and rode on horseback in the famous Pilgrimage of Women to London.

In 1914, with Edmund Harvey, she founded the Friends War Victims Relief, and was medical organizer of the first 'War Vics' team in France, whose members included EDITH PYE. In 1919 she went to Vienna, where two million were starving, and organized an elaborate scheme with Edith Pye, sending currency to the Netherlands and Switzerland to buy cows for farms outside the city and buying fodder from Croatia and Czechoslovakia: the farmers then gave free milk to Child Welfare centres, helping to fight rickets, TB and malnutrition. In the 1920s she concentrated on peace work in the League of Nations and the Women's International League, spending much time in Geneva and becoming Honorary Secretary of the Women's Peace Crusade. She also worked with Greek refugees from 1923 to 1930, helped Austrian refugees after the Ausschluss of 1938, and refugees from Nazi Germany. From 1938 to 1945 she was on the Board of Directors of the International Commission for Refugee Children, organizing relief work for Civil War victims in Spain and Southern France, and for children who escaped to France from the East at the beginning of the war. In her later years her work was necessarily nearer home, with the Soldiers', Sailors' and Airmen's Families Association in Kent. An inspiring leader for many years, she died at her home in Street, Somerset.

**Clark, Petula** [pseud. of Sally Olwen] (1934–). English singer and actress. She was born in Epsom, Surrey, and as a child singer entertained the troops during World War II. She had her own BBC radio series, *Pet's Parlour* (1943), and then made a series of films including *Medal for the General* (1944), *Here Come the Huggetts* (1948), *The Runaway Bus* (1953) and *That Woman Opposite* (1957). In the meantime she had established herself as a popular singer with many hit songs, which in the course of her career have earned her ten gold discs and two Grammy awards (for *Downtown* and *I Know a Place*). For many years she was regarded as the UK's leading woman pop singer, specializing in light-hearted sentimental ballads, but in 1959 her career spread to France, where her fame increased; she was named top female vocalist in 1962 and won an award for the outstanding woman in showbusiness in France in 1965. She has made innumerable concert and television appearances in Europe and the USA, and although she has made no films since *Finian's Rainbow* (1968) and *Goodbye Mr Chips* (1969), she is remarkable for her sustained popularity over 40 years and she came back to the stage in the *Sound of Music* (1981). In 1961 she married Claude Wolffe; they have two children and live in Switzerland, London and Paris.

**Clarke, Shirley** (1925–). American film maker. Educated at Johns Hopkins University and the University of North Carolina, she studied and performed with Martha Graham as a dancer. Without formal training in film she started making movies, mainly to do with dance, with a camera she received as a wedding present. She made her first feature film *The Connection* in 1962 which, with its 'real time' sequences, improvisations, and 360-degree camera turns, connected her with the *cinéma vérité* movement. Her second film *The Cool World* (1963) was the first ever to be shot in Harlem. In 1962 she co-founded the New York Film-makers' Co-operative with Jonas Mekas. *A Portrait of Jason* (1967) is a filmed interview with a male prostitute. In 1969 she appeared in AGNES VARDA's *Lion's Love*. During the 1970s she toured the USA giving video workshops and became Professor of Film at UCLA in 1975. She then concentrated on adapting theatre pieces for video, for example collaborating with Sam Shepherd on *Savage Love* in 1981.

**Claudel, Camille** (1864–1943). French sculptor. The sister of the poet and diplomat Paul Claudel, Camille was the daughter of a wealthy civil servant, who encouraged her study of art. In 1881 the family moved to Paris, where, as a student, she met the sculptor Auguste Rodin. She became his model and his lover, and worked with him closely for 15 years, to the fury of her own family and of Rodin's mistress Rose Beuret. Her work, expressive and emotional, has many similarities with his, and her best pieces include busts, such as the *Buste de jeune fille* (1887) and the portrait of Rodin himself (1892), and works based on classical sculpture such as *Le Jeune Romain* (1885) and larger mythological groups. After her relationship with Rodin ended Camille collapsed, became paranoid, and was placed in an asylum by her parents in 1913. For the rest of her life she remained in various institutions.

R.M. Paris: *Camille Claudel* (1984)

**Cleopatra VII** (69–30 BC). Egyptian queen. Born in Alexandria, she was the last ruler in the Macedonian Dynasty, founded by Alexander the Great's general, Ptolemy, which ruled Egypt from 323 BC until the Roman annexation in 31 BC. Her family was wholly Greek, although she did learn Egyptian and declared herself to be the daughter of the Sun God, Re, to enhance her status as a nationalist leader. Her childhood was marked by political intrigue, and although as his sister-bride she inherited the throne at 17 with her brother Ptolemy XII she was soon embroiled in civil war. She set out to win the support of Julius Caesar (allegedly being smuggled into his camp in a bed-roll), who arrived in Egypt in 48 BC, and he returned her to the throne with another brother, Ptolemy XIII, after severe fighting. After he left she bore a son, whom she named Caesarion.

After Caesar defeated Pompey, Cleopatra went to Rome, where she was treated as a royal personage and lived in one of Caesar's villas; officially she was there to negotiate a treaty. After his assassination in 44 BC she returned to Egypt, and saw her next opportunity to exploit the protection of Roman military power when Mark Antony invited her to meet him before his planned invasion of Persia. Her arrival by the Cydnus River to Tarsus forms the centrepiece of Shakespeare's portrayal of her in *Antony and Cleopatra*. She persuaded him to return to Alexandria, where they apparently lived in luxurious idleness. They had three children: the twins Alexander and Cleopatra in 40 BC, and a son Ptolemy in 36 BC after Antony had returned from three

years in Rome repudiating his conciliatory marriage with Octavia, sister of his rival Octavian (later Augustus). Cleopatra financed Antony's disastrous campaigns, the first of which, against the Parthians, was celebrated, despite its obvious failure, by a lavish triumph in Alexandria proclaiming Cleopatra, Antony and her children as rightful rulers of both the Egyptian and the Roman empires. Antony's will, exposed by Octavian, included plans to found a new imperial dynasty in Alexandria, rather than in Rome.

After a year in Greece, they found themselves committed to war with Rome and, deprived of the support of Herod of Judaea, whom Cleopatra's greed for territory had alienated, sent their fleets to meet Octavian in 31BC. Cleopatra abandoned the battle at Actium and fled to Egypt. After she had sent a message that she was dead, Antony committed suicide. She herself tried to win over Octavian but failed, and killed herself to avoid public humiliation, supposedly by an asp which was smuggled to her in a bowl of fruit. She and Antony were buried together. Although her political schemes to protect Egypt's power and her own had totally failed, she remains one of the most haunting figures of romance and ambition in history and literature.

H. Volkmann: *Cleopatra* (1953, Eng. trans. 1958)

**Cleopatra the alchemist** (*fl* 3rd or 4th century). Alexandrian alchemist. At this time alchemy was still a relatively new art and there were many women practitioners. Cleopatra, a woman scholar who hid her true identity under a pseudonym, is remembered because she was the author of a classic text, the *Chrysopeia* ('Gold making'), which survives in a manuscript of the 10th or 11th century. It contains many of the emblems which were developed in later Gnostic and Hermetic philosophy, such as the serpent of Eden, revered as a symbol of knowledge called Ouroborus, and the eight-banded star, as well as detailed descriptions of technical processes and drawings of furnaces. Cleopatra is mentioned with great respect in the Arabic encyclopaedia *Kitab-Fihrist* (988).

**Clifford,** Lady **Anne,** Countess of Dorset, Pembroke and Montgomery (1590–1676).

English aristocrat. The daughter of the Earl of Cumberland, she was born at Skipton Castle, educated at home and married at 19 to Richard Sackville, later Earl of Dorset. They had three sons who died young, and two daughters. The Earl died in 1624, and although Anne was badly disfigured by smallpox and determined not to remarry, she did in fact marry Philip Herbert, Earl of Pembroke, in 1630; he died in 1650. Neither of her two marriages was happy and she took refuge from the 'gay arbour of anguish' in books. In 1643, after 30 years of legal battles, she inherited all the Cumberland family estates and began the building and restoration programmes for which she is famous. She restored six castles – Skipton, Appleby, Brougham, Brough, Pendragon and Bardon Tower – living in each in turn and dispensing generous hospitality. Strong-minded, outspoken and witty, she lived to be 87. She kept scrupulous records, and at 63 wrote her autobiography, of which only an abridged third-person version survives.

G.C. Williamson: *Lady Anne Clifford* (1922)

**Clisby, Harriet (Jemima Winifred)** (1830–1931). Australian doctor and feminist. Born in London, she was the daughter of a corn merchant who emigrated to South Australia in 1838. Her family farmed until 1845 when they moved to Adelaide, and Harriet became a journalist. In 1847 she became a member of the Swedenborgian New Church and for the rest of her life she was concerned with the connection between moral and spiritual well-being and bodily health, adopting a vegetarian diet and practising gymnastics.

In 1856 she went to Melbourne and edited the *Southern Photographic Harmonia* from 1857, written entirely in shorthand. She also worked with CAROLINE DEXTER on the literary *The Interpreter*, published in 1861 and Australia's first journal produced by women. Around this time, having read ELIZABETH BLACKWELL's *Laws of Life* (1852), she decided to train as a doctor, and after two years tuition from a friend in physiology and anatomy, she went to England. Lacking a regular income she was unable to take ELIZABETH GARRETT ANDERSON's advice to train in the USA, and became a nurse at Guy's Hospital, London. Eventually a friend paid for her to study at the New York Medical College for Women, where she graduated in 1865. She lectured and founded the Women's Educational and Industrial Union in Boston (1871), remaining involved with its affairs and with other feminist and Christian groups for many years. In her old age she retired to Geneva, where she founded L'Union des Femmes.

**Clive** [née Raftor], **Kitty** [Catherine] (1711–85). English actress. The daughter of an Irish lawyer, she went on the stage partly to support her parents' large family. She became one of the great English comediennes, full of charm and vivacity, holding the London stage for 40 years. Her first appearances were in small parts at Drury Lane when she was 17, but she then gained popularity as a singer and was finally acclaimed as an actress after her appearance as Phillida in Cibber's *Love is a Riddle* in 1729. She worked mostly with Garrick at Drury Lane, although she fought with him constantly and deeply resented his (probably correct) determination not to let her play in tragedy. She was particularly good in farce, both as vulgar bourgeois married women and as boyish girls, and was much admired as Polly in Gay's *Beggar's Opera*. She herself wrote a burlesque and four farces.

She was passionate and outspoken and had many admirers, including Dr Johnson, Goldsmith and Walpole, although she remained single after the break-up of her early marriage, in 1733, to the barrister George Clive. When she retired in 1769 Walpole gave her a house on Strawberry Hill, Twickenham, known as 'Clive-den', where she held a fashionable salon.

K. Clive: *The Life of Mrs Clive* (1888)

**Clotilda** [Clotilde] (470–545). French queen and saint. The grand-daughter of King Gundovic of Burgundy, when her parents were murdered by an ambitious uncle, she took refuge with another of her father's brothers, Godegesil, in Geneva. Her marriage was arranged to Clovis, the Frankish king, and she devoted herself to converting him to Christianity. He was eventually baptized with all his warriors in 495 at Rheims, after a victory over his Germanic enemies, the Alamanni. His conversion proved politically expedient in appeasing the conquered people. After Clovis died in 511, the division of his kingdom between his four sons led to terrible family feuds; despite Clotilda's efforts to bring peace, one son, and two grandsons (whom she had adopted) were killed. She retired to Tours, and became famous for her holiness and charitable works. A strong but tragic character, she became a romantic figure in many later stories and is venerated as a saint.

G. Kurth: *Sainte Clotilde* (1912)

**Clough, Anne Jemima** (1820–92). English educationalist and feminist. She was born in Liverpool, the daughter of a cotton merchant, but spent much of her childhood in Charleston, South Carolina, and received an erratic education, although her brothers were sent back to English schools and universities. At 16 she returned with her family to England. She soon began teaching, at first at a school in Liverpool (1841–6), and then opening a school of her own in 1852, after she and her mother had moved to Ambleside in the Lake District. She became involved with progressive educational groups, and in 1866 organized the Liverpool branch of the Schoolmistresses Association, recently founded by EMILY DAVIES. She then organized with JOSEPHINE BUTLER and her husband George, Principal of Liverpool College, a series of lectures for women in Northern towns, which were given by James Stewart and met with enormous success. In 1867 they formed the North of England Council for Promoting the Higher Education of Women, with Josephine as President and Anne as Secretary, and began to press for women's examinations at university level. In this they met opposition from Emily Davies, who was fighting for women to have the same, not different, examinations. But in 1868 she was part of a group who petitioned Cambridge University, and they won a higher local examination for women in 1869.

She then became head of a house for female students, Merton Hall, Cambridge, for women who came to the town to attend the series of lectures which had been started, leading to the new examination. The house started with five students in 1871, but became Newnham Hall in 1875 and was incorporated as Newnham College five years later. Anne Clough was principal until her death, 21 years after the first house had opened.

B. A. Clough: *A Memoir of Anne Jemima Clough* (1897)

**Cobbe, Frances Power** (1822–1904). Irish reformer and feminist. The daughter of strict evangelical Protestants, she was educated at home, with two years schooling at Brighton. After her father's death in 1856 she travelled to Italy and Greece and became Italian correspondent of the *London Daily News*. She was involved in several welfare causes, advocating special care for the insane and the incurably sick, working with MARY CARPENTER in the Bristol 'ragged schools', and concentrating on reforms of workhouses and the care of working girls. She was also a keen anti-vivisectionist. An early suffrage campaigner, Power Cobbe is remarkable for her wit, the clarity of her theory, and for the radicalism of her view of women's position. Her articles appeared in many periodicals, and in anthologies. Independent publications include *The Theory of Intuitive Morals* (1855), *Broken Lights* (1864), *Studies of Ethical and Social Subjects* (1865), *Dawning Lights* (1868), *The Final Cause of Women* (1869), *Doomed to be Saved* (1874), and *The Scientific Spirit of the Age* (1888).

**Cochran, Jacqueline** (1910–80). American aviator. Born in Florida, she was adopted by a 'poor white' family and led a harsh life as a child. She worked in cotton mills, and then as a hairdresser. In 1932 she decided to learn to fly after meeting an aviator, Floyd Odlum, who later became her husband.

Her first flying experiment was in 1934 when she went up to over 30,000 metres in a biplane with canvas wings and an unheated, non-pressurized cockpit, trying to inhale oxygen through a tube which burst. For the next 30 years she preferred to try mainly for speed records, and held more of these than any other woman. She was the first woman to enter the trans-American Bendix Race in 1935, and won it in 1938 in an untried Seversky fighter. She was awarded the Harmon Trophy six times, as most distinguished aviator of the year, among other awards, and in 1971 became the only living woman in the American Aviation Hall of Fame.

During World War II Jacqueline served as director of Women Auxiliary Service Pilots (WASPS), directing more than 1000 women who by serving in transports freed men for combat duties. In 1977 she was among those who successfully lobbied Congress for veteran benefits for WASPS. From 1948 until 1970 she served in the Air Force Reserve, retiring with the rank of Colonel.

In 1953, in a Sabre Jet, she was the first woman to break the sound barrier, and continued to set jet speed records. In 1964 she logged a speed of 1429 mph, the fastest ever flown by a woman. She became active in politics, and was also correspondent for a national magazine, officer of several aeronautical associations and head of a cosmetic firm, in which capacity she was twice named Woman of the Year in business.

J. Cochran and M. Buckmann Brinley: *Jackie Cochran* (1988)

**Cole** [née Postgate], Dame **Margaret (Isabel)** (1893–1980). English socialist. She was born into a liberal family – her grandfather was the reformer John Postgate, and her father was a Cambridge Classics don. She was educated at Roedean School, and Girton College, Cambridge, where she obtained a first-class degree in Classics in 1914. She then taught for two years at St Paul's Girls' School, London. Her socialist leanings were intensified by her brother's imprisonment as a conscientious objector in World War I. She joined the Fabian Society Research Department, and in 1916 met G.D.H. Cole, author of *The World of Labour* (1913) and leader of the radical opposition to the Fabian leaders Sidney and BEATRICE WEBB. In 1918 they were married. They broke away to form the Labour Research Department, but abandoned it in 1925 after it became dominated by the British Communist Party, and moved to Oxford. In the late 1920s, reunited with the Webbs, they rejoined the Fabian Society. They influenced many future Labour leaders, such as Gaitskell, and organized a special strike committee in the 1926 General Strike.

In the 1930s Margaret organized classes for the Workers' Educational Association, for whom she taught from 1925 to 1949. She and her husband founded the New Fabian Research Bureau in 1935, which collected much of the data for the post-war Labour government's reforms, and they wrote *Review of Europe Today* (1933) and *The Condition of Britain* (1937). She was a member (1943–65) and alderman (1952–65) of the London County Council and was especially active on the Education Committee; from 1965 to 1967 she was with the Inner London Education Authority. She was President of the Fabian Society from 1963. From the 1940s onwards she produced many pamphlets and books (including *Makers of the Labour Movement*, 1948, and *Beatrice and Sidney Webb*, 1955), and edited two volumes of Beatrice Webb's diaries. In addition, she and Cole wrote over 30 very clever detective stories before his death in 1949. She was created a DBE in 1970.

**Coleridge, Sara** (1802–52). English writer. The daughter of Samuel Taylor Coleridge, she was influenced by him throughout her life. After a disorganized childhood, she educated herself with Robert Southey's help to a high level in Classics and modern languages, and her letters show a grasp of abstract philosophy. In 1829 she married her cousin Henry Coleridge, a lawyer, and lived in Hampstead, London, where she published some verse for children and the fairy tale *Phantasmian* (1837). After Henry's death in 1843 she devoted the rest of her life to the exhausting task of organizing, editing and annotating her father's works.

M. Wilson: *These were Muses* (1924)

**Colet, Louise** (1810–76). French poet. Contemporary criticism was divided about the merit of her work but despite much disparaging comment she obtained several literary awards. She met Flaubert in 1846 and their relationship lasted many years. They corresponded a great deal and it was to her that he confided his anguish in composing *Madame Bovary* – Colet was horrified by the realism of the finished product. For a while she set herself up as a champion of women and wrote *Le poème de la femme* (1856). Her novel *Lui* (1859), inspired by her affair with De Musset, contained, besides criticisms of Liszt and

Chopin, a virulent portrait of GEORGE SAND who had already published a novel, *Elle et lui*, about her own relationship with De Musset, and who had wounded Colet's pride by neglecting to praise her literary talent.

Colet's works include *Poésies* (1842), *Chant des armes* (1846), *Ce qui est dans le coeur des femmes* (1852) and *Les dévotés du grand monde* (1873).

**Colette, (Sidonie Gabrielle Claudine)** (1873–1954). French novelist. Born in Saint-Sauveur-en-Puisaye, a village in Burgundy, she was the daughter of a tax collector, and was educated in the village and at home, reading enthusiastically under the guidance of her mother, Sido. When she was 17 the family moved to the local town, where she met 'Monsieur Willy', the popular novelist and music critic Henri Gauthier-Villars. She married him in 1893 and they moved to Paris; he discovered her literary talent and forced her to write her first novels, which were published under his name: *Claudine à l'école* (1900), *Claudine à Paris* (1901), *Claudine en ménage* (1902) and *Claudine s'en va* (1903). Willy added *risqué* passages and the formula was an instant and slightly scandalous success.

In 1904 Colette left Willy and began writing some of her most characteristic works: animal stories, fictional reminiscences, and idylls of rural life, in which strong female characters such as her mother, gentle and sensuous, dominate the world of men. These works span 45 years, from *Dialogues des bêtes* (1904) to *Sido* (1929) and *Le fanal bleu* (1949), and during that time her life was colourful and varied. She divorced Willy in 1906, and at 33 became a music-hall dancer and mime artist, and the sporadic lover of the Marquise de Belbeuf ('Missy'); these years were described in her novel *La vagabonde* (1911). In 1912 her mother died and she married the editor of *Le matin*, Henri de Jouvenel, the father of her only child. During World War I she converted their St Malo estate into a hospital and nursed the wounded, a service for which she was made a Chevalier of the Légion d'Honneur in 1920. From 1913 to 1919 she was fiction editor of *Le matin* and also a columnist and critic in *Le figaro*, *Vogue*, *Demain* and other newspapers. She lectured, opened a beauty salon and wrote

novels, including the most famous, *Chéri* (1920) and *La fin de Chéri* (1926).

In 1925 she left De Jouvenel and after her marriage was dissolved, in 1935 (after a ten-year affair), she married Maurice Goudeket with whom she lived until her death. She remained an exotic and unconventional figure, symbolizing in her life and literature both the loneliness and the mysterious glamour of female sexuality. At the end of her life, crippled by arthritis, she held court in her apartment in the Palais Royal, where she died aged 81. Even her death caused controversy, since she was denied a Catholic funeral because of her marriages outside the church, and instead was given a state funeral attended by thousands of mourners. She received many honours, being elected to the Académie Royale de Belge in 1935 and chosen as the only woman in the Académie Goncourt in 1945, and she was made a Grand Officier of the Légion d'Honneur in 1953.

M. Sands: *Colette: a Biography*

**Collet, Clara (Elizabeth)** (1860–1948). British feminist and social economist. Daughter of the editor of *The Diplomatic Review*, Clara was educated at the North London Collegiate School and graduated from University College, London, in 1880, taking her MA in 1885, becoming the first woman fellow in 1896. After teaching for seven years in Leicester, she became Assistant Commissioner to the Royal Commission on Labour and worked with Charles Booth on his *Life and Labour of the People of London* (1889). In 1890 she was one of the founders of the Economic Club, at University College, later acting as secretary from 1905 to 1922. Her early work on women's employment had already been published in *The Economic Position of Educated Working Women* (1890). In 1893 she joined the new Labour Department of the Board of Trade as Labour Correspondent, concentrating on the earnings and employment of women as Senior Investigator for Women's Industries from 1903. Her work contributed significantly to government policy, notably through the Trade Boards Act of 1906; and she also continued to publish, with *Educated Working Women* (1902) and *Women in Industry* (1911). She retired in 1920 but continued to act on Trade Boards, and wrote the section on

Domestic Service for the *New Survey of London, Life and Labour*, edited by Llewellyn Smith in 1931. After her retirement she was a council member of the Royal Economic Society from 1920 to 1941, and of the Royal Statistical Society from 1919 to 1935.

**Collett [née Wergeland], (Jacobine) Camilla** (1813–95). Norwegian novelist. She was born in Kristiansand, the daughter of a clergyman. The family moved near the capital in 1817 and she was educated at home and at private schools. At the age of 17 she became infatuated with the poet Welhaven, a conservative involved in a bitter dispute with her revolutionary brother, the famous poet Henrik Wergeland. Although torn by the feud, and depressed by Welhaven's coolness, she did not leave him until 1836. Five years later she married Professor Jonas Collett, who encouraged her to write and supported her plans for *Amtmannens dötre* ('Daughter of an official'), which was eventually published after his death in 1855. It caused a national uproar, being an exposé of the injustices suffered by women within and outside marriage. The hostile reception intensified Collett's feminism, which is apparent in her collected stories (1861–73), although she remained an isolated figure, detached from the emergent women's movement in Norway.

**Collins, Joan** (1933–). British actress. To her own surprise, Joan Collins's image, in *Dynasty*, as the mature woman who can still be sexy, ruthless and powerful, has been acclaimed by many feminists as well as ardent soap opera fans. Joan was born in London, studied for two years at the Royal Academy of Dramatic Art and made her stage debut in *A Doll's House* in 1946. At 19 she made her first film, *I Believe in You* (1952), which was followed by nine films in the 1950s, in rapid succession, including *Our Girl Friday* (1953). She moved to Hollywood, and graduated from playing wayward girls to sultry glamorous women, with *The Girl in a Velvet Swing* (1955), *Island in the Sun* (1957), and several roles in the 1960s and 1970s, leading up to *The Stud* (1979) and *The Bitch* (1980). *Dynasty*, which made her an international television star, began in 1981, topping the US ratings in 1983–4. After a decline in its popularity in 1986–7, Joan

considered leaving the series to star in her own TV show.

She has been married four times, to Maxwell Reed, Anthony Newley, Ronald Kass and Peter Holm, whom she divorced amidst great publicity in 1987. She now divides her time between London and Los Angeles. Sister of novelist Jackie Collins, she herself has written *Past Imperfect* (1978), *The Joan Collins Beauty Book* (1980) and *Katy, a Fight for Life* (1982), describing her daughter's recovery from a post-accident coma.

R. Levine: *Joan Collins, Superstar: a biography* (1985)

**Colonna, Vittoria** (1490–1549). Italian poet. She was born in Naples of a Roman aristocratic family; her father was Constable to Ferdinand II. In 1509 she married the Marquis of Ferrara, to whom she had been betrothed as a child, and they lived in Ischia before he left to join the wars in northern Italy in 1511. He died in 1525 from wounds received at the Battle of Pavia. During the five years after his death she wrote over 100 elegiac poems to his memory, which reflect her grief and her gradual progress to religious consolation. She was friendly with leading intellectuals of the day including Bembo, Castiglione, and Tasso, and later with leading religious reformers such as Valdes and Ochino. In 1538 she moved to Rome where her long platonic friendship with Michelangelo began, resulting in a long exchange of sonnets and letters. Her verse had become highly spiritual and in 1540 she entered a convent, first at Orvieto, then Viterbo and finally St Anna di Funari, Rome.

M.F. Jerrold: *Vittoria Colonna* (1906)

**Colvin, Brenda** (1897–1981). British landscape architect. Born in Simla, India, she was educated in Paris before studying at Swanley Horticultural College around 1920. She worked with Madeline Agar on the War Memorial Garden in Wimbledon before going into private practice as a landscape architect in 1922. Although virtually self-taught, she was a pioneer in the field, and in 1929 was one of the founders of the Institute of Landscape Architects, later becoming Secretary (1941–8), Vice-President, and finally President (1951–3). By 1937 her profession was sufficiently recognized for

*Colette*

*Marie Curie*

*Simone de Beauvoir*

*Eleanora Duse*

her to lecture to the Architectural Association School.

After the war she wrote *Land and Landscape* (1947), which has become a classic in its field; she went on to undertake important contracts for the War Office, the Port of London Authority and the Electricity Generating Board, including her imaginative creation of a landscape based on waste ash at Gale Common in 1962. She received the OBE in 1973. She combined a romantic vision with a practical grasp of problems, and continued to practise from her Cotswold home into her eighties.


**Comnena, Anna** (1083–1153). Byzantine historian. She was the daughter of Emperor Alexius I and Irene Dukas. Her family had interests in learning and the arts, and she received an excellent education in philosophy, classics, astronomy, geography and probably in pharmacology and medicine as well. She tried, with her mother, to persuade her father to disinherit his son John in favour of her husband, the historian Nicephorus Byennius, whom she married in 1097. Following this unsuccessful attempt to seize the imperial throne she was forced to retire from court life, and after the death of her husband she withdrew into a convent and dedicated herself to writing. She continued his *Historia*, a chronicle of the house of Comneni. The result was the famous *Alexiad*, a long epic prose poem giving a history of her father's reign, in 15 books. Although it idealizes her father's character and achievements this work is a valuable source of information about her own time. Because of her involvement in court life and her access to state documents, she was able to give vivid accounts of persons, military expeditions, warfare and the intimate domestic life of her family. She did not hide her contempt for the lack of education and refinement of people from the Western Empire, and she was proud of the superiority of Byzantine civilization. The contemporary enthusiasm for ancient Greek culture is reflected in the language and style of her work. She is unusual in describing her personal views on women in detail, considering their chief role to be submissive and family-oriented, but admiring 'manly' characters like IRENE OF ATHENS. Her work is acknowledged as the most prominent work of medieval Greek historiography.

G. Buckler: *Anna Comnena: a Study* (1929)


**Compton-Burnett, Ivy** (1884–1969). English novelist. She was born in Pinner, a doctor's daughter, and was the eldest of seven children by his second wife; the household already contained five children from his first marriage. She received a classical education from the family tutor and took a degree in Classics at Royal Holloway College, London, in 1902. In 1905 she was made to act as governess to the younger children in her family, and after her mother's death became mistress of the house; her tyrannical attitude caused many conflicts. Repeated emotional blows included the loss of her favourite brother in 1908, the death of another in 1917 and the joint suicide of her two youngest sisters.

In 1919 she moved into the flat which she shared with the antique collector Margaret Jourdain for many years, and began to write again. An early sentimental work, *Dolores* (1911), is uncharacteristic; her series of 17 novels beginning with *Pastors and Masters* (1925) present a grimly humorous vision of parental tyranny, family misery, greed and battles for power and property in late Victorian and Edwardian upper-class England. Among the finest of her books are *Men and Wives* (1931), *A House and its Head* (1935), *Daughters and Sons* (1937) and *Parents and Children* (1941). Her later books include *A Heritage and its History* (1959) and *A God and his Gifts* (1963). All depend on stylized, ritualistic dialogue.

H. Spurling: *Ivy When Young* (1974)
————: *Secrets of a Woman's Heart* (1985)


**Connolly, 'Little Mo' (Maureen Catherine)** (1934–69). American lawn tennis player. She was born in San Diego, the daughter of a naval officer and began her career in tennis as ball-girl to the professional Wilbur Folsom, who helped her career. Eleanor 'Teach' Tennant coached her. Her first win against Ann Bissell in a minor tournament was perhaps her happiest, as thereafter Maureen developed a ruthless attitude and total involvement in any match. At 16 she won the US Singles title, and followed this by winning Wimbledon at her first attempt, in 1952, as well as both titles in the two following years. 1953 was her peak year: she achieved the 'Grand Slam', winning Wimbledon and the American, French and Australian titles, the first woman ever to achieve this. The 1953 Wimbledon final against Doris Hart and that of 1954 against LOUISE BROUGH are regarded as classic matches.

'Little Mo's' groundstrokes were her great strength, and she lost only four matches in the whole of her career after the age of 16, against Doris Hart, Shirley Fry and Beverley Baker Fleitz. She is regarded among the top few players of all time, even though her career was prematurely ended by a damaged leg in a riding accident in July 1954. She had to retire from competition, and married Norman Brinker, an Olympic horseman, with whom she had two children. Illness interrupted her work as a coach and she died of cancer on the eve of Wimbledon.
M. Connolly: *Forehand Drive* (1957)

**Conran** [née Pearce], **Shirley (Ida)** (1932–). English designer and writer. Trained at the Southern College of Art, Portsmouth, she started work as Press Officer for the jewellers Asprey Suchy in 1953. Two years later she became publicity officer for the Conran Group Companies for whom she organized and designed several kitchen and design exhibitions. In the same year she married Terence Conran and in 1956 became fabric designer and director of Conran Fabrics. She went on to become a member of the selection committee of the Design Centre in London from 1961 to 1969. Her marriage ended in 1962. Her two sons, Jasper and Sebastian, have become well-known, as fashion designer and inventor. Shirley worked for the *Daily Mail* as Home Editor from 1962 and in 1964 became the first Woman's Editor of the *Observer* Colour Magazine. She was even more successful as a journalist than she had been as a designer: in 1969 she became Women's Editor of the *Daily Mail* and from 1972 to 1974 was co-publisher and 'Life and Style' Editor of the young women's magazine *Over 21*. She has also been a columnist and feature writer for *Vanity Fair* and *Woman's Own*.

In 1975 she published her first book, *Superwoman*, a practical guide to how to juggle career and home successfully. An immediate best-seller, it was followed by almost annual sequels until 1979. Conran then decided to turn her hand to writing fiction and her first novel, *Lace* (1982), was an international best-seller. This was followed by *The Magic Garden* (1983) and *Savages* (1987). She is now married to John Stephenson. A woman of unbounded energy, her recreations include skiing, long-distance swimming and yoga.

**Cons, Emma** (1838–1912). British artist, housing reformer and founder of the Old Vic theatre. One of seven children of a London piano-maker, Emma studied at the Art School in Gower Street and then at Mrs Hill's school, where she became friendly with OCTAVIA HILL and met the reformers John Ruskin, Charles Kingsley and F.D. Maurice. When in 1851 her father's illness forced the children to find work she joined Mrs Hill's Ladies Art Guild, teaching toy-making in Ragged Schools. After the Guild closed she restored illuminated manuscripts for Ruskin, then with women friends opened a watch-engraving shop, which closed owing to intimidation from male watchmakers. Her next job was as first woman designer of stained glass windows for Powell's factory, which led to restoration work at Merton College, Oxford.

Through Ruskin and Octavia Hill Emma began managing restored slum property in central London, especially in Marylebone and in Drury Lane, where she opened a working men's teetotal club, a hostel for girls and the first of her 'Coffee Taverns'. An excellent manager, not above fixing roof slates herself, she also ran crèches and clinics for her tenants. In Lambeth, where she built model tenements such as Surrey Lodge, she took over the local music hall, the Old Vic, for the Coffee Palace Association; it re-opened on Boxing Day 1880, with a variety bill and Thursday ballad concerts. Financial problems were helped by donations and guarantees from the Martineaus, Lord Mount Temple and the textile manufacturer and MP Samuel Morley. Popular lectures at the theatre grew into regular classes, leading in 1899 to the foundation of Morley College for working people, with her friend Caroline Martineau as first Principal.

Emma's energy was boundless; she was Vice President of the London Society for

Women's Suffrage, an executive member of the Women's Liberal Foundation, a founder of the Women's Horticultural College at Swanley and, in 1899, one of three women on the first London County Council. She also went to report on atrocities in Armenia, established a silk factory for Armenian refugees in Crete and visited émigré tenants in Canada. In 1894 she became full-time manager of the Old Vic; on her death in 1912, her niece LILIAN BAYLIS took over the management. She lived until her death with her devoted sister and co-worker Ellen.

**Conway,** Lady **Anne Finch** (1631–79). English scientific theorist. Anne Finch was born in Kensington House, London, the daughter of Sir Henry Finch, Recorder of London and Speaker of the House of Commons. As a girl she studied classics and languages and was an early student and critic of Descartes, influenced by her brother John and his tutor, the Cambridge philosopher Sir Henry More, a lifelong friend. She continued her studies after her marriage, at 19, to Edward, Viscount Killulagh, later 1st Earl of Conway, teaching herself mathematics, astronomy and Euclidean geometry and in 1653, with More, she began a study of the mystic philosophy of the *Kabbala*.

From childhood Anne suffered severe ill health, even travelling to France where she asked for her skull to be opened to relieve her blinding migraines – a request refused by the surgeons. After the death of her small son in 1660 she was virtually confined to her home, Ragley Hall, Warwickshire. In 1670 she was visited there by Francis Mercury van Helmont, a famous Kabbalist scholar and healer, who became her constant companion and set up a chemistry laboratory at Ragley Hall. At the time Anne was developing her own theory of nature as an integrated material and spiritual organism consisting of individual 'monads', elementary matter linked by a Cosmic Order within a complex hierarchy in which lower forms could, potentially, develop into higher. Her spiritual interests were heightened when, against the advice of More, she joined the Quaker sect in the 1670s and thus became friendly with George Fox, William Penn and George Keith, with whom she and van Helmont collaborated on a treatise on the 'Doctrine of the Revolution of Human Souls'.

The notebooks outlining her vitalist scientific philosophy, written between 1671 and 1675, were eventually published in Latin by van Helmont in 1690, and retranslated into English in 1692 as *The Principles of the Most Ancient and Modern Philosophy, Concerning God, Christ and the Creation: that is, concerning Spirit, and Matter in General.* Her thesis challenged both Descartes and the new mathematical philosophy of Newton and influenced the central concept of Leibniz's philosophy of 'monadology'. Yet despite the full acknowledgement of Leibniz, Anne Finch Conway's radical ideas were constantly attributed to van Helmont himself.

M. Alic: *Hypatia's Heritage* (1986)

**Corbett Ashby, Margery.** *See* ASHBY, MARGERY CORBETT.

**Corday, Charlotte** [Corday d'Armont, Marie Anne Charlotte] (1768–1793). French political assassin. Born at Saint-Saturnin des Liguères, Normandy, she was educated in an exclusive convent. Her father was an impoverished aristocrat and staunch Royalist. Ambitious, reserved, convinced of a 'heroic destiny', after quarrelling with her father she went to live with her aunt at Caen, where the banned Girondins (Barbaroux, Petion, Guadet) took refuge in May 1793. She became closely associated with them, regarding their expulsion as the final collapse of the state. She determined to kill Jean Paul Marat, whom she saw as a regicide and murdering demagogue. She travelled to Paris, bought a kitchen knife, gained access to Marat by pretending she had news of a Girondin conspiracy, and stabbed him in the bath. Arrested on the spot and nearly attacked by the mob, she was tried by the Revolutionary Tribune and guillotined four days later. On the day of the assassination she explained her reasons in a highly rhetorical *Address to the French Friends of Law and Peace.*

M. Corday: *Charlotte Corday* (1931)

**Corelli, Marie** [pseud. of Mary Mackay] (1855–1924). English romantic novelist. Born in London, the daughter of the Scottish song-writer Charles Mackay, she was educated in a French convent. A brilliant pianist, she adopted her pseudonym and the story of her Italian parentage for her concert career, but her first novel, *A Romance of two Worlds* (1886) which was partly autobiographical, was such a huge success that she became a professional writer. Her 28 best-selling novels included *Thelma* (1887), *Barabbas* (1893), and *The Sorrows of Satan* (1895), which broke all previous sales records. Her wildly romantic fiction is characterized by an emphasis on spiritual power and universal love, as evident in *The Master Christian* (1900), *God's Good Man* (1904) and *The Secret Power* (1921). From 1901 she lived in Stratford-upon-Avon, in a house supposed to have belonged to Shakespeare's daughter. She remained unmarried, devotedly served by her friend Bertha Vyver. She was compulsively generous but engaged in constant disputes with neighbours and authorities. Convinced of her own genius, she hated criticism and refused to send her books to reviewers.

E.G. Coates: *Marie Corelli* (1977)

**Cori, Gerty (Theresa Radnitz)** (1896–1957). Czech biochemist. Born in Prague, Gerty wished to study chemistry and entered the medical school at the German University of Prague. She received her MD in 1920 and married a fellow student, Carl Ferdinand Cori, the same year.

She worked for two years at the Karolinen Children's Hospital in Vienna. In 1922 the Coris left Czechoslovakia for the USA, first settling at Buffalo and then joining the Washington University School of Medicine in St Louis. Their son was born in 1936. Gerty became Professor of Biochemistry in 1947.

Her work in the USA was at first on the metabolism of carbohydrates in animals, progressing to the isolation and characterization of individual enzymes. In 1947 the Coris received the Nobel Prize for Medicine, shared with Houssay, for effecting the first synthesis of glycogen in a test tube. Gerty was thus the third woman after MARIE CURIE and IRÈNE JOLIOT-CURIE, and the first woman doctor, to receive the Nobel Prize.

She subsequently made use of her chemical analyses to examine in detail the nature of glycogen storage diseases in children.

**Corner, Caterina** (1454–1510). Italian intellectual, and Queen of Cyprus. Born in Venice into an ancient and powerful family with large investments in Cyprus, she was educated at a Benedictine school and tutored by her learned brothers. In 1468 she was betrothed to James II of Cyprus, but he died a few months after their marriage in 1472. She found herself surrounded by intrigue; her son James III was taken from her by the Catalan Council of Regency, and her uncle and cousin were murdered. In 1474 she was restored to power but the child James died of malaria and she ruled alone for 14 years. Always vulnerable to the Venetian-Turkish power struggle, she was eventually forced to abdicate. She returned to Venice and was given large estates at Asolo, where she became a famous patron of the arts, her court a centre for humanist scholars, celebrated by Bembo in *Gli asolani* (1505). She also founded hospitals and initiated other humanitarian projects.

**Corrigan, Mairead** (1944–). Irish political campaigner. One of eight children, Mairead was educated at St Vincent's School, Belfast, and worked as a secretary from the age of 16. She was also involved with voluntary Catholic clubs for handicapped children and for teenagers. A previous republican sympathizer, outraged by the British Army's activities in Belfast, she was co-founder with BETTY WILLIAMS and Ciaran McKeaun of the Northern Irish Peace Movement in 1976. (Mairead was the aunt of the Maguire children whose deaths sparked off the movement.) She was jointly awarded the Nobel Peace Prize, with Betty Williams, in 1976 and travelled abroad campaigning for the cause, meeting President Carter in 1978. In that year she resigned from the Executive but continued to work for the popular movement, despite its disappointingly small impact on Northern Irish affairs. She became Chair of the Peace Movement again in 1980. That same year her sister Anne McGuire committed suicide and in 1981 Mairead married her brother-in-law Jackie McGuire.

**Coudreau, Octavie** (*c*1870–*c*1910). French explorer. Octavie travelled with her husband Henri to French Guiana (1894) and Pará in northern Brazil (1895–9). Together they published six volumes on their travels:

*Voyage au Tapajos*; *Voyage au Xingu*; *Voyage au Tocantius-Araguaya*; *Voyage au Itaboca et à l'Etacayana; Voyage entre Tocantius et Xingu*; and *Voyage au Yamunda*. While exploring the Trombetas, a tributary of the Amazon, Henri died, and Octavie completed the journey and published *Voyage au Trombetas*. From 1899 to 1906 she was employed by the Pará and Amazonas states to explore the Amazon area, and published *Voyage au Cuminá*, and *Voyage au Rio Curua, á la Mapuera, au Maycurú*. She wrote: 'The solitude of the virgin forest has become a necessity for me; it attracts me by its mysterious silence, and only in the great woods have I the impression of being at home'.

**Courtney,** Dame **Kathleen (D'Olier)** (1878–1974). British suffragette and pacifist. The daughter of Major D.C. Courtney of Milltown, Co. Dublin, Kathleen read modern languages at Lady Margaret Hall, Oxford. A keen suffragette, she was Hon. Secretary of the Oxford branch of the National Union of Women's Suffrage Societies from 1911–14. She attended the Women's Congress at The Hague in 1915 and was one of the founders of the Women's International League for Peace, chairing its British Section for ten years. During World War I she undertook relief work with Serbian refugees and worked with the Society of Friends in Austria, Poland and Greece. In 1928 she became an executive member of the British League of Nations Union, becoming its Vice-Chairman in 1939 During World War II she twice toured the United States, giving lectures on behalf of the Ministry of Information and in 1945 was in San Francisco for the drawing-up of the United Nations Charter. She became Vice-Chairman of the British branch of the United Nations Association and in 1949 took the posts of Chairman and joint-President, retiring as Chairman in 1951. *The Times* obituary mentions her skill as chairperson, her sternness, clear vision and gift for dispelling confusion 'like a knife cutting through butter'. A CBE in 1946 and DBE in 1952, Kathleen Courtney was an energetic, forceful person who enjoyed walking and travelling. She lived to the age of 96.

**Cousins, Margaret (Gillespie)** (1878–1954). Irish educationalist and feminist. Born at Boyle, County Roscommon, and educated locally and in Derry, she studied music at the Royal Irish Academy, Dublin, and taught in an infants' school before marrying a teacher, James Cousins, in 1903. In 1908 she became Treasurer of the Irish Women's Franchise League and went as a delegate to the 'Parliament of Women' in London in 1910, where she was briefly imprisoned for throwing stones at 10 Downing Street.

In 1908 James Cousins became a Theosophist, and in 1915 she accompanied him to India where he became editor of ANNIE BESANT's *New India*. She was the first non-Indian member of the Indian Women's University, Poona (1916) and was a founder member of the Indian Women's Association the following year. She was the first Head of the National Girls' School at Mangalore (1919–20) and she then became the first woman magistrate in India. In 1932 she was imprisoned for speaking against the Emergency Measures. She also wrote on various subjects, especially philosophy and education. After she became paralysed in 1943 she received financial support from admirers, from the Madras government, and later from Pandit Nehru, in recognition of her services to the Indian freedom struggle.
J. Cousins and M. Cousins: *We Two Together* (1954)

**Cox, Ida** (1889–1967). American jazz singer. Born in Toccoa, Georgia, she sang as a child in the local African Methodist Choir. At the age of 14 she began singing blues with minstrel groups in carnivals, clubs and bars, and ran away from home to tour with White and Clark's Minstrels. She turned solo in 1914 and during the 1920s and 1930s toured with her show 'Raisin' Cain', then led the Darktown Scandals. She began recording in 1923, producing *Ida Cox's Lawdy Lawdy Blues* and *I've got the Blues for Rampart Street*. Most of her life was spent in the South, but she appeared in New York in 1939. She remained on the road until 1945, when she suffered a stroke; she retired to Knoxville, Tennessee, four years later. In 1961 she made some final recordings, with all-star jazz backing.

**Craig, Isa** (1831–1903). Scottish feminist and poet. Born in Edinburgh, the only daughter of a hosier, she was orphaned as a child and was brought up by her grandmother. She left school at ten but began contributing poetry to *The Scotsman* and in 1853 joined the editorial staff. In 1857 she went to London and took up the position of Assistant-Secretary to the Social Science Association; her appointment was a revolutionary move which aroused much criticism. A year later she resigned to marry her cousin, the iron merchant John Knox, but she continued to campaign for the women's movement and was a member of the Ladies' Sanitary Association, founded in 1859 to educate people about hygiene and health care in areas where typhoid and fevers were epidemic.

Isa Craig was also a well-known author. She produced several volumes of poetry, including *Poems by Isa* (1856) and *Songs of Consolation* (1874), the novel *Esther West* (1870), and popular children's textbooks such as *Little Folk's History of England* (1872) and *Tales on the Parables* (1872 and 1877).

**Crawford, Cheryl** (1902–86). American theatre director. Cheryl Crawford was born in Akron, Ohio, and began to act as a schoolgirl and as a student at Smith College. After she graduated in 1925 she got a job with the Theatre Guild, rising from assistant stage manager to casting director by 1930. In 1932 with Harold Churman and Lee Strasberg she founded the Group Theatre, which developed Stanislavsky techniques, and the natural 'method' acting of the Moscow Arts Theatre. This eventually led to her establishing the American Repertory Theatre in 1945, with Eva Le Gallienne and Margaret Webster, and to founding the Actors' Studio in 1947 with Elie Kazan and Robert Lewis. During these years she produced an astonishing series of successful plays and musicals including the Broadway revival of *Porgy and Bess* (1942) and *Brigadoon* (1943), as well as productions of Tennessee Williams and Bertholt Brecht, and as late as 1975 she produced BARBRA STREISAND's *Yentl*.

C. Crawford: *My Fifty Years in The Theatre* (1977)

**Crawford, Joan** [stage name of Lucille Fay Le Suent] (1904–77). American film star. Joan Crawford was born in San Antonio, Texas. Before she entered show-business she worked in a variety of jobs, including being a laundress, a waitress and a shop assistant. She then won a Charleston contest and began to

dance professionally using her stepfather's surname, as 'Billie Cassin'. After nightclub work in Detroit and Chicago she was spotted in a Broadway chorus line by MGM and her stage name was chosen in a nation-wide movie-magazine contest. Many of her films in the 1920s emphasized her Charleston-dancing 'flapper' image, such as *Pretty Ladies* (1925), *The Taxi Dancer* (1927) and *Our Dancing Daughters* (1928). Her first talkie was *Untamed* (1929), but she took more serious roles in the 1930s as tough ambitious girls overcoming drawbacks, providing a lift for the Depression audiences, and gave fine performances in films like *Strange Cargo* (1940) and *A Woman's Face* (1941).

She was dropped by MGM in the 1940s, but her career took a new direction with Warner Brothers where she starred as a melodrama victim, winning an Oscar for her portrayal of the mother in *Mildred Pierce* (1945), and she then became the epitome of the 'glamorous older woman' in a string of films in the 1950s, and finally appeared in horror films from 1962–5, beginning with her brilliant performance opposite BETTE DAVIS in *Whatever Happened to Baby Jane?* (1962). She made only four more films in the 1960s; her last performance was in *Trog* (1970).

Joan Crawford was a Hollywood star for nearly 50 years, making over 50 films. One of the toughest and most dramatic of screen idols, she was married to actors Douglas Fairbanks Junior (1929–33), Franchot Tone (1933–9) and Philip Terry (1942–6). She adopted four children, and eventually married Alfred Steele, a Director of Pepsi-Cola, in 1956. After he died in 1959 she joined the Pepsi-Cola board as its first woman director and worked in Publicity. Her own memoirs were questioned by the harsh accusations of cruelty and neglect made by her adopted daughter Christina in *Mommie Dearest* (1978).

J. Crawford: *A Portrait of Joan* (1962)
——— : *My Way of Life* (1971)
A. Walker: *Joan Crawford, The Ultimate Star* (1983)

**Crawford Seeger, Ruth** (1901–53). American composer and educationist. Born in Ohio, she studied at the School of Musical Art in Jacksonville, Florida, and at the American Conservatory in Chicago. In 1929 she went to New York, where she studied composition with the eminent musicologist Charles Seeger (who later became her husband). The following year she went to Berlin and Paris on a Guggenheim Fellowship, the first American woman composer to receive this award.

Much of her music has come to be recognized as far in advance of its time. She was a contemporary of Berg and Bartók, and several of her pieces reflect their musical vocabulary, but some commentators have found traits that reach as far ahead as Ligeti and Lutosławski, particularly in her String Quartet (1931). Other notable chamber works include her Violin Sonata (1926) and the Suite for Wind Quintet (1952). Her Three Songs (settings of Carl Sandburg, a close friend), generally considered her finest vocal composition, were selected to represent the USA at the International Society for Contemporary Music in Amsterdam (1933).

Crawford's involvement in teaching was strongly linked to her interest in American folk music. This had been initiated by responding to Sandburg's request that she supply the accompaniments for his collection, *The American Songbag* (1927). On moving to Washington (1935), where she came into contact with John and Alan Lomax, she began transcribing, arranging and editing hundreds of folksongs from recordings held at the Library of Congress, many of which were published in the Lomaxes' collection, *Our Singing Country* (1941). She also published several of her own collections, designed for teaching, notably *American Folk Songs for Children* (1948). Of her four children, Mike Seeger (*b*1933) and Peggy Seeger (*b*1935) both became well-known as folk singers; Ruth was also influential in stimulating her stepson Pete Seeger (*b*1919) to embark on his highly successful career as a folksinger and songwriter.

M. Gaume: *Ruth Crawford Seeger: Memoirs, Memories, Music* (1986)

**Cross, Joan** (1900–). English soprano and opera producer. She was educated at St Paul's Girls' School, London, and studied at Trinity College of Music, London. In 1924 she joined LILIAN BAYLIS's opera chorus at the Old Vic, graduating to solo roles, and in 1931 she made her Covent Garden debut as Mimì in Puccini's *La bohème*. As principal soprano of Sadler's Wells Opera (1931–46), which she directed from 1943 to 1945, she appeared in wide-ranging roles, most notably at the première of Britten's *Peter Grimes* (as Ellen Orford) for the reopening of the theatre in 1945. She became closely associated with Britten through the English Opera Group (of which she was a founder member), appearing at the first performances of *Albert Herring* (Mrs Billows, 1947), *Gloriana* (Elizabeth I, 1953) and *The Turn of the Screw* (Mrs Grose, 1954). She also founded the Opera School (1948; renamed the National School of Opera, 1955) and was its director until 1964. Her productions include *Der Rosenkavalier* (Covent Garden, 1946), *La traviata* (Sadler's Wells, 1950) and several operas in Norway, the Netherlands and Canada. She was created a CBE in 1951.

**Crowe, Dame Sylvia** (1901–). English landscape architect. Born in Banbury, Oxfordshire, she was educated at Berkhamsted Girls' School, and went on to Swanley Horticultural College in Kent in 1920. During the 1920s and the 1930s she worked on many private gardens, and was for a time a pupil of the landscape architect Edward White. During World War II she served as an ambulance driver with the Polish Army in France in 1940, and then became a sergeant in the Auxiliary Territorial Service (ATS). After the war she went into private practice in London, and for many years shared an office there with another pioneer, BRENDA COLVIN. Like Colvin she worked for the Electricity Generating Board (1948–68), but her particular skills lay in designing New Town landscapes such as Harlow and Basildon. She was a founder of the International Federation of Landscape Architects, and was Secretary (1948–58) and Vice-President (1958–70). She published a series of influential books during the 1950s and 1960s, from *Tomorrow's Landscape* (1956) to the scholarly *Gardens of Moghul India* (1972). She was created a CBE in 1967, and a DBE in 1973.

**Cullberg, Brigit (Ragnhild)** (1908–). Swedish dancer and choreographer. She was born in Nyköping, and educated at the University of Stockholm before going to study under Jooss at Dartington Hall, England. She first appeared as a soloist with a small satirical dance group, and in 1946 co-founded the Svenska Dansteater. She made her reputation as a choreographer, particularly with her adaptation of Strindberg's *Miss Julie* (1950) which was performed at the Royal Theatre, and became choreographer to the Royal Swedish Ballet (1952–7), where her works included *Medea*. She then worked as a guest choreographer for the New York City Ballet, and for the American Ballet Theatre (1958–64) for whom she produced *The Lady from the Sea* (1960); she has worked with companies throughout Europe and the Americas. Since 1967 she has directed her own Cullberg Ballet at the Swedish National Theatre. Her works include *Dionysos*, *Eurydice is Dead*, *Romeo and Juliet*, *Revolt*, *Peer Gynt*, and *War Dances*. Cullberg is also a well-known lecturer and is deeply concerned with political and social issues and with the peace movement. She married Anders Ek in 1942 (they were later divorced), and their son is a leading dancer in Sweden.

**Cunitz, Marie** (c1600–64). German astronomer. Born in Silesia, Marie mastered seven languages including Latin, Greek, and Hebrew. She studied medicine, poetry, music and painting, and excelled in mathematics and astronomy. Around 1630 she married Monsieur de Lewen and shared her studies with him. He suggested that she should abridge the Rudolphine Tables. They were obliged to leave Silesia during the Thirty Years' War but Marie continued to compose astronomical tables in a Polish convent. Her husband prefaced and published her work, *Urania Propitia*, in 1651.

**Cunningham, Imogen** (1883–1976). American photographer. She was born in Portland, Oregon, and took her first photograph in 1901 in Seattle. She studied chemistry at the University of Washington, and then went to Germany to study technical aspects of print-making. In 1915 she married a photographer and print specialist, Roi Partridge, and her style was influenced by their close involvement with the realistic approach of the F/64 group based on the West Coast in the late 1920s. She continued to experiment, and became famous for her detailed studies of plants and for her portraits of Hollywood personalities and cultural figures such as MARTHA GRAHAM and GERTRUDE STEIN. She was a fellow of the American Academy of Arts and Sciences and received a Guggenheim Fellowship at the age of 87. Her last published book, *After Ninety*, was a collection of portraits of old people.

J. Dalch: *Imogen Cunningham: a Portrait* (1979)

**Cupis de Camargo, Marie-Anne** ['La Camargo'] (1710–70). French ballerina. Born in Brussels, daughter of an aristocratic Italian dancing master, she was a child prodigy, and took a season of special classes with Françoise Prévost in Paris at the age of ten. She joined the Brussels Opéra, taking her maternal grandmother's name Camargo. She made her debut with the Paris Opéra in 1726, gaining such immediate popularity that she was perceived as a threat by her former teacher Prévost and sent back to the *corps de ballet*. Her brilliant technique and vivacity ensured stardom, and from 1727 to 1735 she was rivalled only by MARIE SALLÉ. Between 1735 and 1740 she was absent from the stage, following the wishes of her lover the Comte de Clermont, the father of her two children, but she returned to become a leading star of the Paris Opéra. She is thought to be the first ballerina allowed to dominate a production, and the first to perform complicated steps like the *entrechat quatre*. Renowned for shortening her skirt to above the instep to display her virtuoso footwork, she was admired by Casanova and Voltaire. She retired at the height of her fame in 1751.

P. Migel: *The Ballerinas from the Court of Louis XIV to Pavlova* (1972)

**Curie, Marie** [Sklodowska, Maria] (1867–1934). Polish-French physicist; she discovered radium, polonium and the nature of radioactivity. Marie was the fifth and youngest child of a family of Warsaw intellectuals, disapproved of by the Russian authorities. Her father taught mathematics and physics. Marie read several modern languages, practised experimental work at a cousin's laboratory and participated in the activities of an underground Polish university. For six years from 1885 she took posts as a governess, to enable her sister Bronia to study medicine in Paris.

In 1891 she went to Paris, entered the Sorbonne with a scholarship, studied under conditions of privation, and passed the *licence* in physics and mathematics in 1893 and 1894, with high honours. She met Pierre Curie, a physicist, and they married in 1895. Their children Irène and Eve were born in 1897 and 1904.

Using the electrometer invented by Pierre and his brother, Marie measured the conducting power of rays from uranium compounds. Stimulated by Henri Becquerel's discovery of radioactivity in 1896, the Curies worked intensively on exacting experiments with pitchblende, culminating in the isolation of polonium (named after Marie's native country) and radium. This promoted new views of the nature of energy and matter. They received many joint awards for their discoveries, among them the 1903 Nobel Prize for Physics, shared with Henri Becquerel, and the Légion d'Honneur, which Pierre declined as it was awarded only to men. The Curies avoided both publicity and financial gain and were happy simply to continue their life and research together, until Pierre was killed in a street accident in 1906.

Marie took Pierre's place as a professor at the Sorbonne, the first woman to hold a chair there, just as she was the first woman to win the Nobel Prize. She developed methods of separating radium from radioactive residues in sufficient quantities to carry out detailed studies of its properties, isolating 22 mg of pure radium chloride to provide the International Radium Standard. In 1911 she became the first person to receive a second Nobel Prize, this time for chemistry.

During World War I she directed radiation therapy services with a corps of women doctor assistants. She gained a driving licence and went to the front lines with ambulances carrying portable x-ray equipment. After World War I she took up her post as Director of the Radium Institute in Paris, formed in 1914. The creation of the Curie Foundation (1920) allowed her to develop the medical uses of radium. Her health declined through exposure to high-energy radiation, and she died of leukaemia. She published *Pierre Curie* (1924), and her other main works were published posthum-ously as *Radioactivité* (1935), and *Oeuvres* (1954).

F. Giroud: *Marie Curie: A Life* (1986)

**Cushman, Charlotte Saunders** (1816–76). American actress and patron of the arts. She was born into a distinguished Bostonian family. Her father's death forced her to support herself and she studied opera, making her debut in *Le nozze di Figaro* (1835) before transferring to straight drama in New Orleans. She then left the South and made a successful career, joining the Park Company in New York in 1837 and becoming Stage Manager of the Walnut Street Theatre, Philadelphia (1842–4). Her greatest triumphs were as Meg Merrilees in *Guy Mannering* (1837) and as Nancy Sykes in *Oliver Twist* (1839); during 1843 and 1844 she played alternate nights in New York and Philadelphia with Macready in *Macbeth*.

In 1845 she went to London, where she was the centre of an expatriate cultural circle. She was a much-acclaimed star until 1849, and returned for a triumphal tour of the USA, acting male roles such as Hamlet and Romeo as well as female roles. She officially retired at the height of her fame in 1852 and lived in England and Rome until 1870. She then returned to the USA and concentrated on reading plays, although she gave some stage performances in America and England, including a famous season of her greatest roles, Meg Merrilees, Lady Macbeth and Queen Katherine at Booth's Theatre in 1874. She was ill with cancer for a long time before her death.

Cushman has been described as the USA's most powerful actress. Despite spells of illness and deep depression she was a forceful personality, and was extremely influential in helping younger actresses, artists, sculptors and musicians.

J. Leach: *Bright Particular Star: the Life and Times of Charlotte Cushman*

**Cynethryth** (*fl* 8th century). Saxon queen. She was the wife of Offa II, King of Mercia from 757 to 796, and acquired notoriety as a tyrannical queen. She was the only queen consort ever allowed to issue coins in her own name, and they carry vivid portraits, the earliest portrait of an Englishwoman. Her daughter, EADBURGH, acquired a still worse reputation.

# D

**d'Agoult, Marie (de Flavigny),** Comtesse [pseud.: Daniel Stern] (1805–76). French writer. Born in Francfort-sur-le Main, Marie de Flavigny was married in 1827 to the Comte d'Agoult who was 20 years her senior. She opened a salon in Paris and became well-known for her interest in new developments in literature and music. In 1835 she scandalized society with her decision to leave her husband and children because of her love for the pianist Franz Liszt. She and Liszt lived in Switzerland and Italy before returning to Paris, and they had three children, one of whom was to become COSIMA WAGNER. After separating from Liszt in 1844 Marie devoted herself to literature. Her novel *Nélida* (1846) was a fictional account of her relationship with Liszt and revealed her bitterness. This work was written under the pseudonym of Daniel Stern, which she continued to use for all her writing. She wrote moral and historical essays, political philosophy and numerous articles for journals. Her publications include *Essai sur la liberté* (1847), which shows her fervent Republican convictions; *Histoire de la Révolution de 1848* (1851): an unbiased and perceptive account enlivened by her knowledge of the leading participants on which Michelet congratulated her for achieving 'l'héroisme de l'impartialité'; a critical essay, *Dante et Goethe* (1866); and *Esquisses morales et politiques* (1849). She spoke many European languages and her close friends included prominent figures in 19th-century French intellectual life: De Vigny, Lamartine, Lamennais and GEORGE SAND.

C. Haldane: *The Galley Slaves of Love* (1957)

**d'Albret, Jeanne** (1528–72). Queen of Navarre and Protestant leader. The daughter of Henri d'Albret and MARGUERITE OF NAVARRE, she was educated by her mother and brought up in Normandy until she was ten. Her childhood was lonely and unhappy, and she was treated like a political pawn by her father and her cousin, Henri II of France. In 1548 her marriage was arranged to Antoine de Bourbon, Duc de Vendôme, a brilliant soldier, ambitious to become King of Navarre. In 1555 Jeanne succeeded to the Kingdom on her father's death, and she and Bourbon became involved in the religious reform movement. After 1561 Jeanne became one of the most prominent Protestant leaders, while Bourbon eventually returned to the Catholic party. At first she remained neutral, concentrating on establishing tolerance and improving local administration in her small Kingdom until 1572, but during the Third Civil War she committed herself as an active leader of the Huguenots and Calvinists, making her base in the stronghold of La Rochelle. She became an intransigent opponent of the Catholic Guise party. She reluctantly agreed, in March 1572, to a peace marked by the marriage of her son Henri (later Henri IV of France) to Marguerite de Valois. Jeanne died in June but her suspicions of the motives of the Regent, CATHERINE DE MEDICI, were subsequently proved correct by the massacre of St Bartholomew which followed the wedding.

Jeanne was a feminist and educationalist as well as a political and religious leader, and she influenced a remarkable circle of aristocratic women who later became highly influential. She was noted for her will-power, tenacity and powerful temper, and inspired respect rather than affection in her followers.

N.L. Roelker: *Queen of Navarre, Jeanne d'Albret* (1968)

**Dalida** (1933–87). Egyptian/French popular singer. Dalida was born in Cairo of Italian parents: her father was a violinist at the Cairo opera. She worked as a secretary in an import company until she won the 'Miss Egypt' competition at the age of 21, when, determined to become a film actress, she left for France under the protection of radio producer Lucien Morisse. Despite her sultry beauty her films were unsuccessful, but she had better fortune as a singer in music hall and cabaret, singing in French, Italian and other languages. Her great hits included *Bambino*, *Besame-mucho* and *Paroles, paroles* with Alain Delon, and she sold over 85 million records world-wide over the years, winning several awards (She made more successful films in the 1960s, such as *Parlez moi d'amour* (1960) and *Ménage a l'Italienne* (1964).) Her private life, however, was always troubled: her marriage to Morisse in 1961 ended after a few months; her friend Luigi Tenco, the Italian singer, overdosed on barbiturates in 1967, and she too tried to kill herself; her former husband shot himself in 1970, and the man she lived with for several years, Richard Camfray, known as the 'Comte de St Germain' gassed himself in 1983. For many years, despite her fame, she declared she found life intolerable and deeply regretted that she had no children. Although her professional life was a continuing success she died in Montmartre after an overdose of barbiturates at the age of 54. The tributes after her death included recognition of her talent by President Mitterand and Prime Minister Chirac.

**Dalrymple, Learmonth White** (1827–1906). New Zealand educator and feminist. Born in Port Chalmers, she became a progressive teacher and corresponded withe the British pioneers in girls' education DOROTHEA BEALE and FRANCES MARY BUSS. During the 1860s she campaigned for secondary education for girls and formed a committee in Dunedin, achieving the opening of the Otago Girls' High School (1871) which served as a model for later girls' schools, of which there were over 70 within a few years. She also fought for university education and in 1871, during the discussion about the founding of a University of New Zealand, launched a petition for the admission of women. This was supported by the Otago University Council, and the University of New Zealand's first woman graduate was Kate Edger, who graduated in mathematics in 1877. By 1893 over half the students in New Zealand universities were women. She also pressed for primary and pre-school education and wrote *The Kindergarten* (1879), an account of Froebel's ideas.

She was a member of the Women's Christian Temperance Union and an active suffrage worker, travelling abroad to meet other feminists during the franchise campaign.

**Daly, Mary** (1928– ). American feminist and theological writer. Born in Schenectady, New York, she studied at the College of St Rose, and has been teaching philosophy and theology since 1952 in the USA and, as part of a programme for American students, at Fribourg, Switzerland (1959–66). During the years at Fribourg she also obtained her doctorate in philosophy and theology (1965). Since 1966 she has taught at Boston College, a Jesuit institution in Chestnut Hill, Massachusetts.

Daly's writing presents a radical feminist perspective on patriarchal religions and on religion in contemporary society. She evokes a matriarchal past and advocates the rejection of contemporary religious expression in a search for new spiritual patterns. Regarded as an influential feminist theorist, she is the author of *The Church and the Second Sex* (1968), re-issued with *A new Feminist Post-Christian Introduction* (1975), *Beyond God the Father* (1973), *Gyn/Ecology* (1979), and *Pure Lust: Elemental Feminist Philosophy* (1984).

**Dame aux Camélias, La.** *See* PLESSIS, ALPHONSINE.

**Damer, Anne Seymour** (1749–1828). English sculptor. Only daughter of Field Marshal Conway, and grand-daughter of the Duke of Argyll, as a child she was a protegée of Horace Walpole. In 1767 she married John Damer, who shot himself in 1776 after contracting heavy debts. Anne became a professional sculptor and divided her time between England, Italy and Portugal. As well as the monumental work for which she is best known, she produced portrait busts, including studies of Fox, Napoleon, Nelson and George III. An executrix of Walpole's will, after his death she lived in Strawberry Hill from 1797 to 1811, and became friendly with MARY BERRY.

P. Noble: *Anne Seymour Damer* (1908)

**Dandolo, Giovanna** (*fl* 15th century). Venetian aristocrat and patron of printing. The wife of Doge Pasquale Malipero, she encouraged the printing industry, which had begun in Venice in 1441 and which flourished after the invention of new moulded types in 1469. Many of the early Venetian books bear expressions of gratitude to her. She also subsidised poor writers and was instrumental in developing and publicizing the lace industry in Burano. She earned two titles, 'Empress of Printing' and 'Queen of Lace'.

**d'Andrea, Novella** (*d* 1333). Italian lawyer and scholar. She was born in Bologna, where her father, Giovanni d'Andrea, was Professor of Canon Law at the University. He taught her and she gave lectures in his place when he was away. According to CHRISTINE DE PISAN, in her book *Cité des dames*, Novella sat behind a curtain to teach so that students would not be distracted by her beauty. She died young after her marriage to another lawyer, John Caldesimus, and her father called his commentary on the life of Gregory X the *Novellae* in her memory.

Her sister Bettina, who died in 1335, was also a lawyer and philosopher who taught at the University of Padua where her husband worked.

**Dandridge, Dorothy (Jean)** (1923–65). American film actress. The first black actress to be acclaimed as a star in American cinema, Dorothy appeared from the age of four in a song and dance act with her sister Vivien as 'The Wonder Children' and 'The Dandridge Sisters' and by her early teens was acting in Vaudeville and singing with the Jimmie Launceford Band. She had a small part in the Marx Brothers' *A Day at The Races* (1937), and minor Hollywood roles followed, including films for all-black production companies. During the 1940s and 1950s she made a name as a night-club singer, and after the all-black film *Bright Road* (1953) was the first black woman on the cover of *Life*. In 1955 she was nominated for an Oscar for *Carmen Jones* (1954), but her success was followed by mediocre films, typecasting her as 'sensuous and immoral' until in 1959 she made *Porgy and Bess*, her last screen appearance.

Her personal life was troubled: two disastrous marriages (to dancer Harold Nicholas, and to Jack Denison), bankruptcy, the collapse of her career and racial prejudice wore her down. In 1965, just when things were looking up, with offers of night-club engagements and new films, she died of a drug overdose, generally thought to be suicide.

**d'Angeville, Henriette** (1795–1871). French mountaineer. Although two other women had been hauled to the summit of Mont Blanc, Henriette was the first woman to organize and undertake her own climb. Her extensive list of provisions and clothing show her planning: her personal outfit included knickerbockers, an alpenstock and a veil. The climb took three days in September 1838, and a carrier pigeon was dispatched from the summit with news of success.

Henriette made 21 other ascents over the next 25 years, at the age of 69 climbing the Oldenhorn in the Alps in a crinoline. Eventually she went to live at Ferney, near Geneva, and died in Lausanne in the year the Matterhorn was first climbed by a woman.

**d'Angoulême (Marie Thérèse Charlotte de France),** Duchesse [Madame Royale] (1778–1851). French princess. The eldest daughter of Louis XVI and Marie Antoinette, her birth after their eight years of marriage was celebrated throughout France as proof of the royal couple's fertility. During the Revolution she was separated from her parents, and imprisoned in the Temple, and in 1795 was exchanged for prominent republicans held prisoner in Austria. She went into exile in Germany, and in 1799 married her cousin, the Duc d'Angoulême. They lived in England, returning to France at the Restoration. During the disturbances of 1830, between the abdication of Charles X and the Duc d'Angoulême's renunciation of the throne on the same day, she was Queen of France. Still known as 'Madame Royale' she returned to exile in England, never to see her country again.

**Danieli, Cecilia** (1943–). Italian industrialist. One of four daughters of Italian steel magnate Luigi Danieli, she grew up in the small village of Buttrio in north-east Italy, where she still lives. The steel company founded by her grandfather in 1914 was expanded greatly during the 1960s, and she started working there, as assistant to her father, in 1965. Danieli of Buttrio specializes in the construction and equipment of mini steel-mills, and has provided plants for 27 countries from the USA and USSR to Burma and Venezuela, making about half of the 250 such mills operating in the world. Since Cecilia took over complete control the revenues have doubled, production has been streamlined and customers now include firms such as Mitsubishi of Japan and Krupp of Germany. Known as 'Italy's first lady of steel', she is married to a lawyer and has three children.

**Danilova, Alexandra** (1904–). Russian ballerina. Born in Peterhof, she trained in Petrograd [now Leningrad], joined the Mariinsky [now Kirov] Theatre, and became a soloist in 1922–3. With Balanchin and other friends she left Russia for Paris in 1924 and joined Dyagilev's Ballets Russes, becoming ballerina with the Company in 1927. She created new roles in Balanchin's ballets such as *The Triumph of Neptune* (1926), and *Les dieux mendiants* (1927); her other roles included *Oiseau de feu, Boutique fantasque* and *Le beau Danube*. After Dyagilev's death in 1929 she danced with the Monte Carlo Opéra Ballet (1929–33) and then the Ballets Russes de Monte Carlo as their principal ballerina (1938–52). She created many leading roles for Balanchin, for example in their 1946 version of *Raymonda*. She gained a reputation as a charismatic performer with a wide technical and interpretative range, mistress of the economical, effective gesture.

During the 1950s, Danilova visited London, toured with her own company (1954–6), and staged ballets for various international companies, including the Metropolitan Opera, New York, La Scala, Milan, and the New York City Ballet. She then taught at the New York School of American Ballet. In the 1970s she staged several productions for the New York City Ballet, the Nijinsky Festival in 1975, and the Los Angeles Ballet. In 1977 she gave a moving performance as an aging dancer in the film *The Turning Point*. She has been married twice, to Giuseppe Massera and Casimir Kokitan, and has said 'I sacrificed marriage, children and country to be a ballerina and there was never any misunderstanding on my part – I knew the price'. She received the Capezio dance award in 1985.

A.E. Twysden: *Alexandra Danilova* (1945)

**d'Aragona, Tullia** (1510–56). Italian courtesan and scholar. Born in Rome, she eventually held a salon in Florence which was one of the most brilliant intellectual centres of the day, and won her the title 'priestess of humanism'. She was also noted for her lovers, who included writers and poets. Tullia was an accomplished poet; her *Rime* were published in 1547 and she also wrote *Dell'infinite di amore*, a treatise on the pains of love, and a narrative poem, *Il meschino d'il guerino*, which appeared in 1560.

**d'Arconville, Geneviève (Charlotte)** (1720–1805). French writer on medicine. Although primarily an anatomist, d'Arconville also wrote on chemistry, medicine, natural history and philosophy, a three-volume life of MARIE DE MÉDICIS, and a translation of Shaid's *Leçons de chimie* (1759). She illustrated Alexander Munro's *Osteology* with studies from her dissections. She published a study of putrefaction, including the action of acids on bile, and 16 medical works besides her major studies, for which she was highly regarded by her contemporaries.

**Darling [née Adams], Flora** (1840–1910). American founder of patriotic societies. Born in Lancaster, New Hampshire, in 1860 she married a southerner, who died during the Civil War. She returned from Louisiana to work as a clerk in Washington DC, later turning to writing short stories and society novels, expressing her pro-Southern views in *Mrs Darling's Letters, or Memories of the Civil War* (1883).

In the 1890s she became caught up in the vogue for nationalism, and women's heriditary clubs. She was first Vice-

President of the Daughters of the American Revolution (claiming to be the founder in her 1901 book) but resigned after a disagreement over organization. A political reactionary, anti-suffragist, and personal publicist, she later founded other societies, the Daughters of the Revolution, and US Daughters of 1812.

**Darling, Grace (Horsley)** (1815–42). English heroine. Born in Bamburgh, Northumberland, she was the seventh of nine children; her father had succeeded her grandfather as lighthouse keeper on the Farne Islands. From him she received a stern religious upbringing. In September 1838 the steamboat *Forfarshire* was wrecked, and in almost impossible seas father and daughter rowed out and managed to rescue five survivors who were clinging to a rock. The rescue caused a sensation. They received Gold Medals from the Humane Society, over £1700 was raised by subscriptions and invested, locks of Grace's hair and portraits were endlessly requested, and she was even asked to appear in Batty's circus. Despite her surprise fame Grace resisted offers of marriage and remained on the island until her sudden death from consumption at the age of 27.

**Dashkova,** Princess **Ekaterina (Romanovna)** (1743–1810). Russian princess and educationalist. Descended from the noble family of Vorontsov, she married Prince Mikhail Dashkov in 1759, and was widowed two years later. Through her contacts with her sister (the mistress of the future Peter III, husband of CATHERINE II), and her uncle, Chancellor to Empress ELIZABETH OF RUSSIA, she was able to warn Catherine of threats on her life in 1761. She intrigued for Catherine's rise to power, and dressed as a soldier led a band of troops to take part in the coup d'état which deposed Peter in 1762, but her subsequent request to be given command of the Imperial Guards was, not surprisingly, denied.

Despite her loyalty to Catherine, Dashkova was in favour of the limitation of royal power through a constitutional monarchy. Feelings cooled between them and she spent much of the next 20 years travelling abroad, educating her sons in England. She returned to Russia in 1782,

and in 1783 Catherine made her Director of the Academy of Arts and Sciences in St Petersburg and first President of the new Russian Academy, founded to preserve and study the Russian language. She supervised the production of a dictionary, edited a journal and wrote several plays. On the death of Catherine, she fell from favour and was forced to retire to a village, but was allowed to return to her estates in 1801. Her *Memoirs* were first published in England in 1840, and in Russian 19 years later.

Y. Dashkova: *The Memoirs of Princess Dashkov Written by Herself* (1840)
K. Fitzlyon: *Memoirs of Princess Dashkov* (1958)

**Daubie, Julie-Victoire** (1824–74). French feminist and educational pioneer. Born in the east of France, Julie was almost totally self-educated: after a basic primary education, she learned Latin and Greek with her brother, a priest. In 1860 she demanded to be allowed to take the *baccalaureat*, the principal qualifying examination, which had until then been reserved for men. After much debate, this was agreed by the government and she passed her examination before a jury from the Faculté des Lettres of Lyon. She later passed the advanced examination, the *licence* in 1871, but died three years afterwards. Her struggles to be admitted for the *baccalaureat* caused much controversy throughout France and were a significant step in the battle towards women's higher education. She herself wrote forcefully about her experience in *Du progrés dans l'instruction primaire: justice et liberté* (1862), *La femme pauvre au XIX siècle* (1866), and *L'émancipation de la femme* (1871).

**David, Elizabeth.** British cookery writer. Elizabeth David's books revolutionized British cooking in the mid-20th century, and are relished as much for their style, anecdotes and scholarship as for their recipes.

The daughter of MP Rupert Sackville Gwynne, she developed her passion for good cookery staying with a French family, while studying French history and literature at the Sorbonne. In 1944 she married Lt.-Col. Ivan David (the marriage was dissolved in 1960). When she returned to England in 1947, living first in London and then in Ross-on-Wye, she found herself craving for the south of France, the sun and the food, and not only taught herself French cookery, but also wrote her book *Mediterranean Food* (1950). In 1951 she published *French Country Cooking*, and in 1954, after spending a year in Italy, *Italian Food*. Her next books were *Summer Cooking* (1955) and *French Provincial Cooking* (1960), which is now an acknowledged classic. Elizabeth David has lived in France, Italy, Greece, Egypt and India, learning the local dishes. In the late 1960s she was involved in selling authentic regional kitchenware and utensils, but she broke her connection with the business in 1973 to concentrate on her writing. Her next interest was in native British cooking, as shown in *Spices, Salts and Aromatics in the English Kitchen* (1970), and after five years of research, visiting 'mills, museums, libraries, bakeries and local markets' all over the British Isles and in France, she published *English Bread and Yeast Cookery* (1977). In 1984 her selected essays and other writings appeared in *An Omelette and A Glass of Wine*, her nearest book to an autobiography. She was awarded the OBE in 1976 and the CBE in 1986, and in 1982 became a Fellow of the Royal Society of Literature.

**David-Neel, Alexandra** (1869–1968). French explorer. Born in Sainte-Monde, from 1893 she made a series of extraordinary journeys in Central Asia especially in the high plateaux of Tibet. At the age of 55 she disguised herself as a Tibetan beggar woman and was the first European woman to penetrate into the city of Lhasa. She wrote numerous books about her travels and about Buddhism, including *Voyage d'une Parisienne à Lhasa* (1930), *Mystère et magique de Tibet* (1929), and *Dans le coeur du Hind: le Népal inconnue* (1949).

**Davies, Mrs Christian.** *See* CAVANAGH, KIT.

**Davies, (Sarah) Emily** (1830–1921). English feminist and educational reformer. Born in Southampton, the daughter of a clergyman and a schoolteacher, she was educated at a local day school and at home, moving with her family to Gateshead, Co. Durham in 1840. Influenced by the efforts of ELIZABETH GARRETT ANDERSON and BARBARA BODI-CHON whom she met on a visit to London in 1859, she started a Northumberland and Durham branch of the Society for Promoting the Employment of Women. In 1861 after her father's death, she moved to London and became Editor of the feminist *English Woman's Journal*. From 1862 to 1869 she was Secretary of the committee aimed at opening the London Matriculation Examination to women. In 1863 she persuaded Cambridge University to hold an experimental examination for girls, and this was eventually made permanent. In 1866 Emily Davies also founded the London Schoolmistresses' Association, remaining its Secretary until 1888. In addition she managed to get girls' education included in the Government enquiry of 1864, wrote several papers on the subject, and after the 1870 Education Act was elected to the School Board for Greenwich.

Her main campaign, however, was for women's university education. In 1866 she circulated her ideas about a 'women's university', in 1867 formed a committee, and two years later opened her college at Benslow House, Hitchin, Hertfordshire, with five pupils, in order that women might take the Cambridge examinations by private arrangement with the examiners. The college moved to Cambridge in 1873, becoming Girton College in 1874. She was Mistress between 1873 and 1875 and remained Secretary for the next 30 years. In 1884 the University opened all its examinations to women but did not give full degrees until 1948. A tenacious, argumentative woman with conservative views about female behaviour, she clung to her own theories, fiercely opposing the separate educational development advocated by ANNE JEMIMA CLOUGH and others, which led to the foundation of Newnham College, Cambridge.

Davies was also a suffragette, and one of the organizers of the first suffrage petition presented by John Stuart Mill in 1866. In 1906, 40 years later, she led a deputation to Parliament demanding the vote. Her views are expressed in *Thoughts on some Questions Relating to Women 1860–1908*. At the age of 89 she made her last public appearance at the Girton jubilee in 1919.

B. Stephen: *Emily Davies and Girton College* (1927)

**Davies, Margaret (Llewelyn)** (1861–1944) English radical. Born in Marylebone, London, in her radical views and idea of public duty she was influenced by her father, a clergyman with Christian Socialist connections, and her suffragist mother. She was educated at Queen's College, London, and Girton College, Cambridge. While working as a sanitary inspector she joined the local co-operative society in 1886, becoming General Secretary of the Women's Co-operative Guild in 1889. She then moved to Kirby Lonsdale, and ran the Guild from there with Lilian Harris until 1921. She developed it into a pressure group supporting suffrage, minimum wage, and especially the rights of working women, wives and mothers. Her demands for such measures as equal laws and easier divorce in 1910 and her pacifism in 1914 met with opposition from male co-operators. She helped found the International Women's Co-operative Guild (1921), and was first woman President of the Co-operative Congress (1922). A supporter of the Russian Revolution, she was Chairman of the Society for Cultural Relations with the USSR (1924–8).

Her numerous publications include *The Women's Co-operative Guild 1883–1904* (1904), *Maternity: Letters from Working Women* (1915), and the anthology *Life as We have known It* (1930).

**Davis, Adele** (1904–74). American writer on nutrition. Born in Indiana, she attributed her interest in food to feeding difficulties as a baby, since her mother died soon after she was born. She attended a local high school, then went on to Purdue College and the University of California, Berkeley, where she took a BA in dietetics followed by an MsC in biochemistry from the Southern California Medical School. From 1931 to 1938 she acted as a consultant on diet and nutrition, and then became a freelance writer and lecturer. She was enormously influential after World War II, leading the movement for correct cooking and natural food in reaction to mass production and synthetic additives, and starting a vogue for vitamin counts and supplements. Her popularity increased with the vogue for alternative life-styles and the health craze of the 1960s and 1970s in the USA. Her most famous early book was *Let's cook it right* (1947), and later best-sellers include *Let's get well* (1965), *Let's have healthy children* (1972) and *You can get well* (1972), which sold over five million copies.

**Davis, Angela (Yvonne)** (1944–). American black radical. She was born in Birmingham, Alabama; her parents were schoolteachers and she herself proved a brilliant student, moving on to Brandeis University in 1961. She spent a year in Paris where she met many Algerian student radicals, and on her return to the USA her sense of political commitment was cemented by the deaths of the Sunday-school children in the Birmingham bombing. She became a civil rights activist and after the death of Martin Luther King in 1968 she moved to Los Angeles and joined the Communist Party, completing her Master's degree under Herbert Marcuse. In 1969 she was offered an appointment as Lecturer in Philosophy at the University of California, Los Angeles (UCLA), but her political affiliations made the California Board of Regents refuse to confirm it. The Board also objected to her association with the 'Soledad Brothers' – imprisoned black activists. In August 1970 after the shootings at Marin County courtroom, in which both brothers died, three of the guns used by Jonathan Jackson in the attempt to free his brother George were found to be registered to Angela Davis. She was charged with kidnapping, murder and conspiracy and was eventually apprehended in New York. Her trial (1971–2) lasted 13 weeks and received world-wide attention before she was eventually acquitted of all charges. Davis published her autobiography in 1974 and then returned to her political activities and to her teaching. She teaches ethnic studies at San Francisco University, and is married to another teacher there, Hilton Braithwaite. Her book *Women, Race and Class* appeared in 1980.

A. Davis: *Autobiography* (1974)

**Davis, Bette (Ruth Elizabeth)** (1908–). American actress and film star. Born in Lowell, Massachusetts, she was determined to work in films, but began as an actress in provincial stock companies, reaching Broadway in 1929 with the comedy *Broken Dishes*. She was hired by Universal in 1930 and appeared in *Bad Sister* (1931) and had three other small roles before she moved to Warner Bros. to play opposite George Arliss in *The Man who Played God*, her first success in 1932. Her years at Warner Bros. were marked by constant battles to escape limitation to supporting roles in thrillers and sentimental dramas, despite her magnificent performance in *Of Human Bondage* (1934) and the Academy Award she won the following year for *Dangerous*. In the end she refused to accept her roles, was suspended, went to London, and lost a ruinous court case, but her assertion of independence increased her popularity. Better roles came her way, *Jezebel* (1938), *The Sisters* (1938), *All this and Heaven too* (1940) and the film of LILLIAN HELLMAN's *The Little Foxes* (1941). After World War II her reputation waned. She left Warner Bros. and as a freelance made *All About Eve* (1950), which was much admired. But mediocre roles followed throughout the 1950s, until she achieved new fame portraying a neurotic, ageing woman in Robert Aldrich's films *Whatever Happened to Baby Jane?* (1962) and *Hush, Hush, Sweet Charlotte* (1964). In 1962 her autobiography revealed the will she had needed to struggle through the vicissitudes of her professional life and her four marriages.

Her recent films include *Family Reunion* (1981), *Hotel* (1983), *Murder with Mirrors* (1984), *As Summers Die* (1985) and *The Whales of August* (1988). In 1977 she was the first woman to be awarded the American Film Institute's Life Achievement Award; she has also won the Rudolf Valentino Life Achievement Award (1982) and the Women in Films Crystal Award (1983) and is a member of the American Academy of Arts (1983).

B. Davis: *The Lonely Life* (1962)
A. Walker: *Bette Davis* (1986)

**Davis, Rebecca (Blaine) Harding** (1831–1910). American novelist. Born in Washington, Pennsylvania, she was largely self-educated, living with her family in Alabama and then in Wheeling, West Virginia. She always wrote, although her literary ambitions were disapproved of by her family, and she developed a unique, realistic style. After the success of her story 'Life in the Iron Mills' in *Atlantic Monthly* (1861) she met and was encouraged by East Coast writers and intellectuals. Her first novel, *Margaret Howth: a Story of Today* (1862), painted the horrors of life for a poor single woman in an industrial town, despite its happy ending. In 1863 she married L. Clarke Davis, a journalist, and moved to

Philadelphia. They had a daughter and two sons, one of whom, Richard Harding Davis, became a famous journalist and successful novelist.

Rebecca now considered herself a professional writer, and she published ten more novels before 1900, as well as working on the editorial staff of the *New York Tribune* from 1869. She always wrote on current problems, such as poverty, the Civil War, racial prejudice and political corruption, as in *John Andross* (1874).

G. Langford: *The Richard Harding Davis Years: a Biography of Mother and Son* (1961)

**Davison, Emily (Wilding)** (1872–1913). English militant suffragette. Born in Blackheath of a Northumbrian family she graduated from London University and then obtained a first in English at Oxford, before taking several teaching jobs. In 1906 she joined the PANKHURSTS' Women's Social and Political Union (WSPU) and became a militant campaigner. She was imprisoned 8 times, went on hunger strike, and was forcibly fed 49 times. Her protests continued in prison; in Strangeways, Manchester in 1909 she barricaded herself in her cell and in 1911 she attempted suicide by throwing herself downstairs at Holloway to publicize the horror of forcible feeding. Her activities included stone-throwing, pillar-box arson and assaulting a Baptist Minister by mistake for Lloyd George at Aberdeen Station.

In 1913, wrapped in a WSPU flag, she threw herself under the King's horse during the Derby at Epsom, and died four days later. Her funeral was attended by vast crowds, including representatives of all the suffrage societies, and gas workers', dockers' and general labourers' unions. Emmeline Pankhurst was arrested under the 'Cat and Mouse Act' while joining the procession. Emily Davison's grave at Morpeth, Northumberland, is inscribed 'Deeds, not words'.

G. Colmore: *The Life of Emily Davison* (1913)

**Day, Doris** [pseud. of Doris van Kappelhoff] (1924–). American film star. Born in Cincinnati, Ohio, she trained as a dancer but was injured in a road accident at 15 and turned to singing for local radio stations. Her early life was hard, and she had two unhappy marriages, at 17 and 22 years of age. She became a successful band singer with Les Brown, joining Frank Sinatra on *Saturday Night Hit Parade* in the late 1940s. In 1948 she was used as a replacement in Warner Bros.' *Romance on the High Seas*, becoming an instant success in a series of musicals which included *Lullaby of Broadway* (1951), *April in Paris* (1952) and *Calamity Jane* (1954). Her blonde 'girl-next-door' look was copied throughout America.

Now much in demand and commanding huge fees, she worked in comedies such as *The Pajama Game* (1957), romances, and a series of innocent bedroom farces from *Pillow Talk* (1959), to *Do not Disturb* (1964), especially working with Cary Grant. The odd mixture of healthiness, respect for virginity and marriage, combined with salacious innuendo summed up for many the repressive nature of American sexuality in the 1950s. In 1952 she married producer Marty Melcher, who became her business manager and in the process either embezzled or mismanaged her entire fortune. After the revelation of this financial crisis at his death in 1968 she suffered a nervous breakdown, pulling herself back in 1970 to several years of success with *The Doris Day Show* on American television and in 1985 hosted her own chat show, *Doris Day and Friends*.

D. Day and A.E. Hotchner: *Doris Day: her own Story* (1975)

**Day, Dorothy** (1897–1980). American co-founder of the Catholic Worker Movement. The daughter of a journalist, Dorothy was born in New York, but spent much of her adolescence in California. After attending high school in Chicago, she won a scholarship to Urbana College, Illinois, and after completing her education became a journalist. Dorothy's earliest associates and ideas were of the left, and she joined the International Workers of the World, and worked for papers with a Marxist platform, such as *The Call*, *The Liberator* and *The Masses*, between 1917 and 1921. She was also involved with intellectual circles in Greenwich Village through a long affair with the playwright Mike Gold. Driven by a need to identify herself with the poor, she moved to a New York tenement and became a probationary nurse in Brooklyn during an influenza epidemic. She then travelled in Europe and entered a common-law marriage with Forster Batterham. In 1927 she had a daughter, Tamar Teresa, and was received into the Catholic Church, although she had earlier rejected Christianity because of its 'hypocrisy'.

She worked for the paper *Commonweal* until 1932, when she met Peter Maurin, a priest and professor of French turned itinerant workman, who proved to be the catalyst she needed to combine Communist idealism with American Catholicism. Together they launched the Catholic Worker Movement, with an accompanying newspaper. Using Dorothy's savings, the first issue of the *Catholic Worker* was published on May Day 1933. A year later, to help victims of the Depression who appealed to the paper, they founded St Joseph's House of Hospitality in New York, followed by numerous other houses and farms for the poor and homeless. Dorothy's book, *House of Hospitality* (1939), describes this period of her life. She carried on her work after Maurin's death in 1949. She was notoriously outspoken, often offending the Catholic community with her stand against fascism, nuclear weapons and the Vietnam war, and with her support for Chavez's unionization of migrant workers. Her last years were spent at a Catholic worker hospice, Maryhouse, on New York's lower East Side. A prolific writer, her works include *On Pilgrimage* (1948), *Loaves and Fishes* (1963) and *On Pilgrimage : the Sixties* (1972).

D. Day: *The long Loneliness* (1952)
W.D. Miller: *Dorothy Day: A Biography* (1982)

**Dean, Brenda** (1943–). British trade unionist. Brenda Dean was born in Salford, Lancashire, the daughter of a railway inspector. Educated in Eccles and Stretford, she worked in Salford as a secretary and joined SOGAT (the Society of Graphical and Allied Trades) in her teens, working as an administrative secretary from 1959 to 1972. She was Assistant Secretary of the Manchester Branch from 1972 and when the Secretary died suddenly during the Union Conference in Manchester, she took over, and the following year became a member of the National Executive Council. She also served on the Printing and Publishing Training Board, the Supplementary Benefits Commission (1976–80) and the Price Commission, and the

Occupational Pensions Board (since 1983). In 1983 Brenda became President of the Union and in 1984, at the age of 40, she was elected General Secretary when Bill Keays retired – the first woman General Secretary of a large trade union (and the youngest). She went to the United States to study the impact of the new technology, and was plunged into the forefront of the lengthy dispute in 1986–7 when Rupert Murdoch moved *The Times* and associated papers from central London to Wapping, at the cost of 6000 printing jobs, leading to a lengthy strike marked by mass picketing and aggressive policing.

**de Beauvoir, Simone** (1908–86). French philosopher, feminist and radical. She was born into a middle-class family on the boulevard Raspail, Paris. Her father was a lawyer. At the age of five she went to the Adeline Institute ('Le cours désir'). Her friendship there with 'Zara' (Elisabeth Mabille) and the latter's death in 1929 were major events in her youth. In 1925 she moved on to the Institut Sainte-Marie at Neuilly and also attended a mathematics course at the Institut Catholique in Paris. The following year she began a philosophy course at the Sorbonne, taking her final certificate in 1927 and in 1929 acquiring her Agrégation (a teaching diploma). In this year she came second to Jean-Paul Sartre, who was her close associate until his death in 1980; she rejected the idea of marriage on principle.

After teaching briefly in Paris, she moved to the Lycée Moulgrand in Marseilles, and then to the Lycée Jean d'Arc at Rouen, where she remained until 1936. For most of this period Sartre taught at Le Havre. In 1937 she began teaching at the Lycée Molière in Paris. She was already writing, although her first work *La primauté du spirituel* (1938) remained unpublished until 1979. During World War II she taught at various schools in Paris, remaining there during the Occupation and publishing her first novel *L'invitée/She Came to Stay* in 1943. She went on to write philosophical essays, developing an existentialist code of ethics in *Pyrrhus et Cinéas* (1944) and *Pour une morale de l'ambiguité/Ethics of Ambiguity* (1947); she also wrote two more novels, *Le sang des autres/The Blood of Others* (1945) and *Tous les hommes sont mortels/All Men are Mortal* (1946), and a play, *Les bouches inutiles* (1945). After the war she visited the USA, where from 1947 to 1950 she had an affair with the novelist Nelson Algren. In 1949 she published her massive two-volume study *Le deuxième sexe/The Second Sex*, which traces the nature of women's oppression, using myth, history, political theory and psychology. It caused an uproar on publication and has influenced feminist writers ever since.

The dilemmas facing politically-committed intellectuals in France during these years are portrayed in *Les mandarins/The Mandarins* (1954), as well as in her autobiography. Having been involved with the collective around *Les Temps Modernes* since its formation in 1945, de Beauvoir and Sartre became more sympathetic to the Communist Party, although not members. From 1952 to 1958 she enjoyed a close relationship with Claude Lanzmann, a young Communist journalist, and in 1956 she visited the USSR and China with Sartre, describing the latter country in *La longue marche/The Long March* (1957). In 1958 she began the series of four remarkable books (listed below) that make up her autobiography.

Her political involvement continued throughout the 1960s. She visited Cuba and the USSR (the latter frequently), as well as Japan, Egypt and Israel; she also attended the international Russell Tribunal on Vietnam with Sartre in 1967, and the following year participated in the student demonstration at the Sorbonne. She continued to write, however, producing with GISELLE HALIMI *Djamila Boupacha* (1962), an indictment of the Algerian war; a powerful account of her response to her mother's death in *Une mort très douce/A Very Easy Death* (1964); and fiction, *Les belles images* (1968) and *La femme rompue/The Woman Destroyed* (1968). In 1970 she published an extensive account of old age, *La vieillesse/The Coming of Age*.

De Beauvoir's feminism had become increasingly overt, and in 1971 she signed the *Manifeste des 343*, which appeared in *Le nouvel observateur*: a manifesto in which eminent women acknowledged having had abortions, as part of a campaign to liberalize the law. She also joined women's groups, such as Choisir, and constantly welcomed interviews from French and foreign feminist. From 1974 she was President to the League for the Rights of Women, pressing for active measures to aid battered wives, working women and single parents. In 1979, with Christine Delphy and MONIQUE WITTIG, she began a journal, *Questions feministes*. In 1981, following Sartre's death the previous year, she aroused new controversy in France by her book *Les cérémonies des adieux*, a frank and, some maintain, uncharitable account of the last years of his life.

S. de Beauvoir: *Mémoires d'une jeune fille rangée/ Memoirs of a Dutiful Daughter* (1958)
———: *La force de l'âge/The Prime of Life* (1960)
———: *La force des choses/Force of Circumstance* (1963)
———: *Tout compte fait/All Said and Done* (1972)

**Deborah** (*fl* 12th century BC). Israelite prophetess, judge and heroine. The story of Deborah is told in *Judges*, chapters 4 and 5; the 'Song of Deborah' is possibly the oldest section of the Bible, and although there are some inconsistencies between the two versions of the story, its factual basis is not disputed. Deborah was a keeper of the tabernacle lamps, a counsellor in disputes and a prophetess. When the Israelite settlements were threatened by a Canaanite advance, she told the Commander, Barak, to gather the tribes and attack. At the battle of Taanach, helped by a terrible thunderstorm which hindered the Canaanite charioteers, the Israelites were victorious, and the Canaanite leader Sisera fled, to be killed by Jael, the wife of a nearby Kenite leader, with whom he sought protection. Deborah's prophecy that victory would fall into the hands of a woman was therefore fulfilled. She is an unusual figure in the Bible because of her evident command over the male leaders of the tribe.

**de Brinvilliers, (Aubray, Marie-Madeleine Marguerite),** Marquise (1630–76). French poisoner. The daughter of the Civil Lieutenant of Paris, she married an army officer, Antoine Gobelin de Brinvilliers, in 1651. She soon took a lover, Gaudin de Sainte-Croix, but on her father's instigation he was imprisoned in 1663; he vowed revenge on his release. While in the Bastille he allegedly learnt about poisons from an Italian fellow-prisoner, and he managed to obtain materials from a royal apothecary. De Brinvilliers tested these potions on patients at hospitals she visited. She poisoned her father in 1666 and her two brothers in 1670, but failed to kill her husband. In 1672 Sainte-Croix died when his mask broke while he was engaged in experiments, and evidence in his papers revealed the murders. De Brinvilliers escaped to England and extradition was denied, but when she moved to Liège in Belgium she was forcibly taken over the border, tried, and executed in Paris in 1676. Her trial implicated numbers of prominent society members, including Madame DE MONTESPAN, and destroyed many people, including the alleged witch LA VOISIN. Madame de SÉVIGNÉ described her death in her letters. The poison used by de Brinvilliers, *aqua tofana*, was supposedly invented by TOFANA.

H. Stokes: *Madame de Brinvilliers and her Times* (1912)

**Decker-Slaney, Mary (Teresa)** (1958–). American athlete. Mary Decker was born in Bunnvale, a small community near Flemington, New Jersey, but in the late 1960s she and her family moved to Garden Grove, a suburb of Los Angeles. She started competitive running at the age of 11, when on a whim she decided to enter a local parks' department sponsored cross-country race. She won the race, in her own words, 'by a long ways', and 'After that, all I wanted to do was run.'

During the early 1970s her appetite for running was insatiable. She once competed in one week in seven races ranging in distance from a quarter of a mile to 26 miles. At 14, she delighted the USA by becoming the youngest ever US international. She came third at 1 mile indoors at Richmond, Virginia against the USSR in a race won by the Olympic champion, LYUDMILA BRAGINA. Later that year, still before her 14th birthday, she won at 800 metres, first at the Pacific Conference and then in the USA v. USSR match in Minsk. In 1974 Decker set her first world indoor record at 800 metres, and won again against the USSR both indoors and out. On the former occasion she gave vent to her anger when brushed past by her Russian opponent in a relay. Decker stumbled and then threw her baton at the Russian. She threw it again at the end of the race. Both teams were disqualified.

Although Decker had achieved considerable success her growing body could not take the strain of the schedule, and over the next few years she suffered a series of leg injuries.

Eventually her coach, the New Zealand runner Dick Quax, recognized that she was suffering from 'compartment syndrome', where the growing muscles have insufficient room within their sheaths of tissue. After operations on her calves in 1977 and 1978, she dropped out of her scholarship place at the University of Colorado to devote all her time to running.

She went on to win the 1979 Pan-American 1500-metres title and in 1980 set a world record at 1 mile and a US record at 1500 metres, although the US boycott meant that she had again to miss the Olympics, as she had through injury four years earlier. Further injuries made her miss the 1981 season. In the autumn of that year she married marathon runner Ron Tabb. They divorced in 1983.

In 1982 Mary Decker broke the world record at 1 mile again and also set world records at 500 metres and 1000 metres. She had a double triumph at the 1983 World Championships, winning the gold medal at 1500 metres and 3000 metres, but her long-held aspirations for Olympic success were shattered in 1984 when she fell in the 3000 metres, after tripping over Zola Budd. Nevertheless, the same year she broke the 2000-metres world record. 1985 was her greatest year so far, when she won all but one of her races from 800 metres to 5000 metres and set the 1 mile world record for the third time. She also won her overall Grand Prix title and ran six US records. In January of the same year she married British discus thrower Richard Slaney and her first baby was born in June 1986.

C. Henkel: *Mary Decker* (1984)

**de Erauzo, Catalina** (1592–?1650). Spanish soldier. The Basque Catalina de Erauzo, known as 'The Nun Ensign', escaped from a convent in San Sebastian at the age of 15 and lived a picturesque life, dressed as a boy, in northern Spain until 1610 when she sailed for South America. In Peru she retained her male disguise, and her numerous adventures included following the 500-mile mountain trail to Cuzco, fighting against the fierce Araucanian Indians in Chile, and frequent brawls. She was finally arrested for murder in 1623, but was reprieved when she revealed she was a woman, and a virgin. She was imprisoned in Huamanga convent, then in a Lima convent, before returning to Spain in 1624. There she petitioned King Philip, who granted her a pension, and in 1627 the Pope, in a special audience, gave her ecclesiastical permission to wear male dress. She returned to Latin America in 1630, settling in Mexico, where she spent the rest of her life profitably, as a muleteer on the Veracruz to Mexico City road.

**de Genlis, Stéphanie (Félicité du Crest de Saint-Aubin)** [Marquise de Sillery], Madame (1746–1830). French writer. She tutored the children of her lover, the Duke of Orléans (later known as Philippe Egalité). Her pupil Louis-Philippe (King of France, 1830–48) remembered her as systematic and severe. Despite her Republican sympathies, the Jacobins did not trust her and she was forced into exile. In 1800 she returned to France and in 1812 Napoleon honoured her with the post of Inspector of Primary Schools in Paris.

She wrote prolifically, and many of her works are connected with education: *Théâtre à l'usage des jeunes personnes* (1779), and *Adèle et Théodore ou Lettres sur l'éducation* (1782). She was hostile to the atheism of the *philosophes* and attacked them in *Deux réputations* (1784). Apart from this she wrote other essays and novels and also several volumes of memoirs.

V. Wyndham: *Madame de Genlis: a Biography* (1958)

**de Gournay, Marie le Jars** (1566–1645). French writer and feminist. The adopted daughter of Montaigne, she was a friend and correspondent of leading literary figures and a staunch defender of women's rights to education and campaigner against the idea of their 'natural' inferiority. She published an edition of Montaigne's *Essais* in 1595, three years after his death, and defended him and Ronsard against the attacks on their language launched by the precise school of grammarians such as Malherbe. Her pamphlets were collected in *L'ombre* (1626) and *Les advis ou les présens* (1634). She also translated Virgil, Ovid, Sallust and Tacitus. Her independence, plain appearance and refusal to adopt 'feminine' submissive manners won her the hostility and ridicule of the salon leaders of her day, but her works sold well and she was one of the first successful professional women writers. She specifically attacked hypocrisy towards women in her *Égalité des hommes et des femmes* (1622) and *Grief des dames* (1626).

M. Schiff: *Marie de Gournay* (1910)
M. Ilsley: *A Daughter of the Renaissance, Marie le Jars de Gournay* (1979)

**de Ibanez, Sara** (1909–71). Uruguayan poet. Born near Paso de los Toros in Chamberlain, a mountainous region of Uruguay, she became a notable poet in her thirties, using the complicated classical 'lira' structure (used by Juana de la Cruz), but influenced also by European modernist and surrealist verse, and by contemporary religious movements. Her works include *Canto* (1940), *Canto a Montevideo* (1941), *Hora Ciega* (1943), *Pastoral* (1948), *Artigas* (1952), *Las estaciones* (1957), *Apocalipsis* (1970) and *Canto Postumo* (1973). Her intense, mystical verse made her one of the most distinctive voices of her day, described by Pablo Neruda as a 'great, exceptional and cruel poet'.

**de la Sablière** [née Hessein], **Marguerite** (1630–93). French astronomer. Marguerite showed an early aptitude for science, and studied under Roberval. In 1654 she married a poet and financier and had three children. Although she had not yet published, she was famous by the age of 30 and was visited by such eminent people as Sobieski, the King of Poland, and La Fontaine. Her studies were the object of Boileau's *Satire contre les femmes*: he describes how, astrolabe in hand, she spent her nights making observations of the planet Jupiter, which, he says, weakens her sight and ruins her complexion. La Fontaine, however, said that she had 'beauté d'homme avec grace de femme'.

After an affair with the Marquis de La Fare she was converted to Catholicism. Although her studies were recognized by a pension of 2000 livres from the King, she moved to Les Incurables to tend the sick, and eventually died there.

**Delaunay, Sonia (Sophia Terk)** (1885–1979). French artist. Born in Ukraine, daughter of a Jewish factory owner, she was brought up by an uncle in St Petersburg [now Leningrad]. At first determined to be a mathematician, she then studied under the draftsman Schmidt-Reutte in Karlsruhe

(1903–4) and arrived in Paris in 1905. Inspired by Van Gogh, Gauguin and the Fauves she was recognized as a bold, innovative artist and became friendly with Picasso, Braque and Derain. In 1909 she married the art critic Wilhelm Uhde, and after their marriage of convenience was ended in 1910, became the wife of painter Robert Delaunay; their son was born in 1911. Together they developed the techniques of Orphism, and Simultanism, based on abstract harmonies of colour and design. A versatile artist, she illustrated the poems of Cendrars, exhibited paintings at the Salon des Indépendents, decorated pottery and, after the loss of her family fortune in the Russian Revolution of 1917, made a living by designing textiles, dresses and book-bindings. She was also associated with Dyagilev's Ballets Russes, and designed dresses with Heim for the Exposition des Arts Décoratifs in 1925.

During the 1930s the Delaunays concentrated on paintings, collaborating on vast murals for the Paris Exposition of 1937, and moving to the Auvergne in 1940. After Robert's death in 1941, Sonia lived with Hans and Sophie Arp and the Magnellis at Grasse and then at Toulouse. In 1953 she had her first solo exhibition since one which Uhde had arranged in 1916, and her works were then exhibited all over the world. During the 1970s many of her 1920s textiles were revived by major designers. She is the only woman to have had an exhibition at the Louvre in her own lifetime (1964).

J. Damase: *Sonia Delaunay, Rhythms and Colours* (1972)

**Deledda, Grazia** (1871–1936). Italian novelist. Born in Nuovo, Sardinia, where her father was mayor, she left school early but published her first novel, *Sangue Sarde*, when she was 17. After her marriage in 1900 to a civil servant, Palmiro Modesani, she moved to Rome, where she lived until her death. Most of her novels returned to the Sardinian setting of her youth. She was a regular and prolific writer, publishing a novel or collection of short stories almost every year. Her 33 novels are characterized by a direct style and flowing narrative, and are concerned with the inner dilemmas of apparently simple people, their obsessions, passions, fears and above all their haunting sense of guilt or sin. Women are often the strongest and most vividly portrayed characters. Her best known works include *Tesore* (1897), *Il vecchio della montagna* (1900), *Elias Portolu* (1903), *Conere* (1908), *L'incendio dell'oliveto* (1920) and *La madre* (1920). Her work became increasingly pessimistic, marked by a resigned fatalism. In 1926 she was awarded the Nobel Prize for literature.

**de Lenclos, Ninon** [Anne] (1620–1705). French courtesan. She was the daughter of an aristocratic scholar, Henri de Lenclos, Sieur de La Douardière, who fled from France after killing a man when she was 12. She grew up to be one of the most famous wits and beauties of her day; she had many influential lovers and friends, including Gaspard de Coligny, the Bourbon prince Louis de Condé, and the writers Saint-Evremond and La Rochefoucauld, and was admired by Molière and Scarron, Madame DE MAINTENON's husband. Since she was a proponent of a epicurean philosophy, the Queen Mother, ANNE OF AUSTRIA, ordered her to be sent to a convent for her lack of religious respect. On her release she defended herself in the book *La coquette vengée* (1659). In the next decade Madame de Maintenon used her influence to protect her.

She retired from life as a grand courtesan at the age of 51 and held entirely respectable salons, attended by writers such as De Boileau, Racine and MARIE LA FAYETTE, and by members of high society. In her old age she met the young Voltaire, whose father looked after her finances; she left him a small legacy to buy books. Her character formed the basis for Clarisse in MADELEINE DE SCUDÉRY's novel *Clélie*.

E.H. Cohen: *Mademoiselle Libertine* (1970)

**de Maintenon** [née d'Aubigné], **Françoise,** Madame (1635–1719). Second wife of Louis XIV of France. Her father was the son of Agrippa d'Aubigné, a Huguenot general and poet; at the time of her birth he was in prison for debt. She was born in the prison of Niort, Poitou, and until the age of seven was educated by her Calvinist aunt, Villette. After her father's release in 1645 the family spent two years in Martinique, where he had hoped for an official post. On his death in

1647 Françoise was raised by another aunt, the strict Madame de Neuillant, and became a fervent Catholic. When her mother died in 1652, her aunt sent her to the middle-aged and crippled poet Scarron, whom she married and nursed, meeting many influential aristocrats and writers at his literary salon. On his death in 1660 she went into a convent and lived with great dignity on the pension provided for her by ANNE OF AUSTRIA until 1668.

After her friend Madame DE MONTESPAN became the king's mistress, de Maintenon was employed as a nurse and governess to their illegitimate children; in 1674 she was able to buy the Château de Maintenon, and she was made a marquise in 1675. Her relationship with de Montespan grew worse as she increasingly won the king's favour, and in 1679 she was made a lady-in-waiting to the Dauphine. Finally, around 1680, she became Louis XIV's mistress. Queen Marie Thérèse remained devoted to her and died in her arms in 1683. Shortly afterwards Louis and Françoise were secretly married; their close relationship endured for 32 years.

Madame de Maintenon was highly influential at court in reducing the atmosphere of corruption and frivolity, and this at times won her the reputation of a prudish bigot. Her political influence was less important, although she was blamed for many of Louis's mistakes. She was particularly interested in education, and in 1686 founded the Maison Royale de Saint Louis, at St Cyr, a school for impoverished aristocratic girls. The school became fashionable and was admired throughout Europe; at first it was very progressive, the 250 pupils, aged between 6 and 19, studying literature, economics, music and other subjects. Many of de Maintenon's own fascinating letters and essays are concerned with education. In 1689 she asked Racine to write a sacred drama for the school, and he produced *Esther*, and two years later *Athalie*. Madame de Maintenon often escaped from the court to teach at St Cyr, but as she became increasingly devout she drastically altered the regime, turning it into an old-fashioned religious institution. After 1692 it became a regular Ursuline convent. When Louis died in 1715 she herself retired there for the last four years of her life.

C. Haldane: *Madame de Maintenon* (1970)

**de Marillac, Louise** (1591–1660). French founder and saint. Louise was born into a powerful family and she was well educated, but her childhood was unhappy; she was melancholy and suffered poor health. In 1613 she married an official of the Royal Court, Antoine le Gras and gave birth to her only child, Michel. After the death of her husband in 1625, Louise became more and more involved with the charitable work of St Vincent de Paul, who was her spiritual director. He realized that most aristocratic women were better suited to fund-raising than practical social work with the poor, but he recognised her qualities. In 1633 Louise set up a training centre in her home for young women, mainly of the peasant and artisan classes, which became the order of the Daughters of Charity whose 'convent is the sick-room, their chapel the parish church, their cloister the city streets'. The charitable activities carried out by the Sisters included the care of foundlings, galley slaves, the elderly, poor children and the insane.

Louise was canonized in 1934 and named universal patron of social workers by Pope John XXIII.

J. Calvet: *Louise de Marillac: a Portrait* (Eng. trans.: G.F. Pullen) (1959)

**de Medici, Catherine.** *See* MEDICI, CATHERINE DE.

**de Méricourt, (Anne Josephe) Théroigne** (1762–1817). French revolutionary. She was born in Marcourt, Belgium. Her father was a peasant and she left home early to escape her stepmother, going into service locally before becoming the companion of an Englishwoman, Mrs Colbert, in 1779. In London she became a singer, took a series of wealthy lovers and eventually returned to Paris where she made a fortune as a courtesan before progressing to Italy to train as a singer. In 1789 she returned to Paris and threw herself into the Revolutionary struggle, becoming a women's organizer and leader. She was among the first in the storming of the Bastille, dressed as an Amazon, and led the Women's March to Versailles in October. An inflammatory orator and journalist, she was constantly attacked by the Royalist press, and was reduced to destitution, giving all her wealth to the cause.

In 1790 Théroigne was forced to flee from the Royalists to Marcourt. She attempted to start a revolutionary journal in Liège, was arrested by the Austrians and sent first to the fortress of Kuffstein, then to Vienna. Eventually freed after an audience with Emperor Leopold, she returned to Paris in 1792. Idol of the clubs and at the height of her influence, she advocated an offensive war against the European monarchies. An outspoken feminist, she also organized women's clubs in the Faubourg St Antoine, which aroused opposition among male Jacobins. She took part in the storming of Les Tuileries and on the same day demanded and personally witnessed the death of the journalist Suleau who had lampooned her. In 1793 she became increasingly drawn into the party conflict between Gironde and 'Montaigne', lost popularity, and was publicly attacked and beaten by Parisian women when attempting to protect the Girondin Brissot. The shock affected her mind. Arrested in 1794, she was briefly imprisoned but eventually interned in the asylum of Salpétrière where she remained for the last 20 years of her life.

F. Hamer: *Théroigne de Méricourt: a Woman of the Revolution* (1911)

**Demessieux, Jeanne** (1921–68). French organist and composer. She became organist of the church of St Esprit, Paris, at the age of 12, and then trained at the Paris Conservatoire, where she won major prizes in harmony, piano, fugue and counterpoint (1937–40). She did not give a public recital until 1946, but after that toured widely in Europe, England and the USA. She became organ professor at the conservatory at Liège (1952), organist of the Madeleine (1962), and was the first woman invited to play in Westminster Cathedral and Westminster Abbey; she played at the inauguration of Liverpool Cathedral in 1967. She composed several works for the organ, from six *Etudes* (1946) to her last work, published posthumously: *Répons pour le temps de Pâques* (1968).

**de Montespan** [née de Mortemart] **(Françoise-Athenis de Rochechouart), Madame** (1641–1707). Mistress of Louis

XIV of France. She was the daughter of the Marquis de Mortemart and married the Marquis de Montespan in 1663; the following year she was appointed lady-in-waiting to Queen Marie Thérèse. In 1667 she became the mistress of Louis XIV, after LOUISE DE LA VALLIÈRE, and they had seven children; their first daughter died in 1672, but the next year Louis recognized the rest of the children and they lived openly with him at St Germain. Her three sons became, respectively, the Duc du Maine, the Comte de Vexin and the Comte de Toulouse. In 1668 the Marquis de Montespan had expressed his disapproval of his wife's liaison, and as a result was exiled to Guyana; they were legally separated in 1674.

At court Madame de Montespan encouraged such writers as Racine, Quinault and De Boileau, but she was considered haughty and arrogant and in 1680 was one of several leaders of court society to be implicated in the scandals which surrounded the exposure of the poisoner and alleged witch LA VOISIN. The king dismissed her, and subdued the splendour of the old Versailles luxury to save his reputation. But her dismissal was probably due as much to Louis's growing devotion to Madame DE MAINTENON. De Montespan nevertheless remained at court until 1691, when she returned to the Paris convent of St Joseph, where she eventually became Mother Superior.

H.N. Williams: *Madame de Montespan* (1903)

### de Montpensier (Anne-Marie-Louise d'Orléans), Duchess (1627–93). French princess.

She was the daughter of Gaston de France, Duc d'Orléans and brother of Louis XIII, known as 'Monsieur'; she herself was called 'La Grande Mademoiselle'. She was extremely wealthy, having inherited a fortune and vast estates from her mother, Marie de Bourbon Montpensier, and wanted to make a royal marriage, with either the future Louis XIV, Charles II or Ferdinand III. Instead she became embroiled in domestic politics, persuading her father to ally himself with the Prince of Condé during Mazarin's exile in the series of revolts known as the Fronde. In 1652 she overcame troops occupying Orléans and relieved the city, and three months later she opened the gates of Paris to Condé, after

ordering the cannons of the Bastille to be fired on the royal troops, rousing much admiration for her decisiveness and bravery. In October 1652, when Louis XIV returned to Paris, she went into exile with her father, returning for the years 1657 to 1662, but being banished again for refusing to marry Alfonso VI of Portugal.

At the age of 42 she fell in love with Lauzun, a Gascon captain in the king's bodyguard, and an obvious adventurer. The king granted permission for their marriage but then hastily withdrew it, and Lauzun was imprisoned for ten years. The duchess finally obtained his release and they married secretly in 1681. She showered land and riches on him but he was indifferent and cruel to her, and they separated only three years later. She spent the rest of her life in religious and charitable works, and in writing her *Memoirs* up to 1688. She also published two short novels, *La relation de l'île imaginaire* and *La Princesse de Paphlagonie*, which appeared under the name of Segrais, her secretary for 24 years.

G.H. Seely: *The Memoirs of Anne, Duchesse de Montpensier* (1928)
M. Buchan: *The Great Mademoiselle* (1938)

### Dench, Dame Judi (Judith Olivia) (1934–). British actress.

Judi was born in York, was educated at The Mount School and studied at the Central College of Speech Training and Dramatic Art. She first appeared with the Old Vic Company in Liverpool and London as Ophelia in 1957, and remained with the company touring Europe and North America until 1961, playing Shakespearean and Restoration roles and also Cecily in *The Importance of Being Earnest*. She then worked for a season with the Royal Shakespeare Company where her parts included Anya in *The Cherry Orchard* and Isabella in *Measure for Measure*. During the 1960s she undertook seasons at the Nottingham Playhouse (her main base) and the Oxford Playhouse, where she played St Joan in 1965, and appeared in films including *He Who Rides A Tiger* (1966). She returned to the RSC in 1969, taking leading roles such as the Duchess of Malfi, Beatrice in *Much Ado* and Lady Macbeth, joining the RCS tour to the Far East. She then starred in numerous West End as well as RSC productions, toured widely and also worked in television, including the award-winning series *A Fine Romance* with Michael Williams, whom she married in 1971.

In the 1980s she has performed a wide variety of roles in plays including *Pack of Lies* (1983), *Mother Courage* (1984), *A Great Deal of Laughter* (1985), *Mr and Mrs Nobody* (1986), in Di Trevis's production of *Yerma* (1987), and in *Anthony and Cleopatra* (1987), for which she won both the *Evening Standard* and the Laurence Olivier Actress of the Year awards. Her recent films are also notable, including *Wetherby*, *A Room with a View* and *84 Charing Cross Road*. Modest and unassuming off-stage, she is an actress of extraordinary power, vitality and presence. She was awarded the OBE in 1970, and the DBE in January 1988.

**Deneuve, Cathérine** (1943– ). French film actress. Born in Paris, the daughter of actors and younger sister of Françoise Dorléac, she first appeared in films when she was 13, adopting her mother's maiden name. She met Roger Vadim in 1961 while she was filming *Les parisiennes/Tales of Paris* and appeared in his *Le vice et la vertu/Vice and Virtue* (1963), based on de Sade's *Justine*. This was the first of many roles in which Deneuve's cool beauty has been set against suggestions of vulnerability, depravity or sexual fantasy, her finest performances in such parts being in Polanski's *Repulsion* (1965), Buñuel's *Belle de jour* (1967) and *Tristana* (1970), Deville's *Benjamin* (1968), and Aldrich's *Hustle* (1975). She first came to international attention in 1963 in *Les parapluies de Cherbourg/The Umbrellas of Cherbourg* and was one of the major stars of the 1960s. She acted with her sister in *Les demoiselles de Rochefort/The Young Girls of Rochefort* in 1967, just before Françoise's death in a car accident. In her private life she has insisted on independence – she had a child with Vadim in 1963 but refused to marry him, and her three-year marriage to the British photographer David Bailey finished in divorce in 1968. She had another child with Marcello Mastroianni in 1972. From 1971 to 1979 she was President and Director of Films de la Citronille, and in 1983 founded the Société Cardeva. Among her later films are *Le Choc* (1982), *Le bon plaisir* (1984) and *Paroles et musique* (1984).

F. Gerber *Cathérine Deneuve* (1981)

**Deng Yingchao** [Teng Ying-ch'ao] (1904– ). Chinese women's leader and stateswoman. Deng Yingchao's revolutionary career dates back to the 4 May Movement of 1919, a protest by students opposed to Japanese expansionism in China. After graduation she taught and became involved in women's activities. In 1924 she joined the Communist Party and married Zhou Enlai, one of its leaders and China's Premier for 26 years from 1949. From 1927 to 1932 she worked underground for the Party, mainly in Shanghai, and was one of only 35 women who made the Long March (1934–5). In 1945 she was one of only three women elected to the Party's Central Committee.

Deng was active in organization planning during the formation of the People's Republic of China and a major figure in the women's movement, but she did not rise to the highest political office until after her husband's death in 1976. She then became one of the senior members of the Chinese leadership, a member of the Central Committee 1978–85, and in recent years has undertaken a series of foreign visits, to Burma, Iran, Kampuchea, Japan and France.

**Denman, Gertrude (Mary), Lady** (1884–1954). English voluntary organizer. The daughter of W.H. Pearson (later Viscount Cowdray), she married Lord Denman at the age of 19 and had a son and a daughter before she was 23 years old. She served on the executive committee of the Women's National Liberal Federation (1909–10) but resigned in order to accompany her husband, Governor General of Australia (1911–14).

After their return in 1916, Lady Denman became Chairman of a sub-group of the Agricultural Organization Society which started the Women's Institutes (*see* ADELAIDE HOODLESS), and the following year became Assistant Director of the Women's Bureau of Food Production, continuing the work under the Ministry of Agriculture. In 1916 there were 24 Women's Institutes, 137 by 1917, and in the 1950s when the movement was reaching its peak there were 8000, with a membership of 450,000. She remained Chairman from 1917 to 1946, and in 1948 the Women's Institute residential centre in Berkshire was named Denman College in her honour.

She was also Chairman of the National Birth Control Council (later the Family Planning Association) from its foundation in 1930 until her death, and served on the committee of groups such as the Land Settlement Association (1934–9). From 1939 she was organizer of the Women's Land Army, resigning in 1946 when they were excluded from pension rights granted to other civil defence and service women.

G. Huxley: *Lady Denman* (1961)

**de Pisan, Christine** (1364–1430). Italian intellectual and feminist. She was one of the most outstanding women of the later medieval period. Christine was born in Venice, daughter of a scholar and councillor, who was invited to the court of Charles V as astrologer and physician. Christine and her mother joined him in Paris in 1369, and she was educated by him while living at court. At the age of 15 she married an official, Etienne de Castel, who died of the plague in 1389. She then supported her three children and her own family by writing for noble patrons such as the Earl of Salisbury and Philip of Burgundy. She wrote history, philosophy and poetry, produced a biography of Charles V, *Le livre des faitz et bonnes moments du sage Roy Charles* (1405), moral and didactic works such as the *Mutacion de fortune*, and poems bewailing the effects of the civil wars, such as *Le livre de la paix*. Very learned and enormously successful, she produced courtly lyrics, but also more personal songs and ballads, which reflect her loneliness and despair.

A firm defender of the rights of women, Christine attacked misogynistic writers such as Ovid or Jean de Meun (author of the *Roman de la rose*) in her *Epistre au dieu d'amour* (1399). She claimed women were free from political destructiveness and greed, and defended their right to education in *Le livre des trois vertus*. Her works record the deeds of famous women of the past (*Le livre de Duc des vrais amants* (1407); *La cité des dames*; *Trésor des dames*) and are found in English translations from the mid-15th century. Her views were invariably quoted in contemporary debates on the position of women.

After the French defeat at Agincourt, Christine retreated to a convent at Poissy.

Her last work was a song in honour of JOAN OF ARC (1429).

E. McCleod: *The Order of the Rose: the Life and Ideal of Christine de Pisan* (1976)

**de Poitiers, Diane,** Duchesse de Valentinois (1499–1566). Mistress of Henri II of France. She first came to the court of Francis I as a lady-in-waiting to LOUISE OF SAVOY and then to Queen Claude. She married the Sénéchal de Brézé. He died in 1531, when she was 37, and the 17-year-old Dauphin Henri fell passionately in love with her. Encouraged by his father, she became his mistress. Extremely conventional, dressed always in black out of respect for her husband, she became the dominant influence in his life, relegating the Dauphine CATHERINE DE MEDICI to obscurity. She was learned and cultured, the friend of Ronsard and of many contemporary writers and artists, and in art she led the 'French School', opposed to Catherine's 'Italian School'. At court she led the conservative Catholic faction whose influence on Francis I led to the terrible persecution of the Vaudois in 1545. She retained her influence over Henri II during his reign, and her power was attributed to magic, but on his death in 1559 Catherine forced her to restore the wealth he had given her and to retire from court. She spent the rest of her life at Anet, the château built for her by the great architect Delorme.

H.W. Henderson: *The Enchantress* (1928)

**de Pompadour,** Madame [Poisson, Jeanne Antoinette] (1721–64). French courtesan, the mistress of Louis XV. The daughter of a financial speculator who was forced to leave the country in 1725 after a scandal, she lived with her mother and sister under the guardianship of the family friend Le Normant de Tournehem. Her education was thorough, and she grew up cultured, witty and intelligent. She married De Tournehem's nephew Charles-Guillaume Le Normant d'Etioles, they had one daughter, and Jeanne became a prominent member of Paris society. After the death of the young Duchesse de Chateauroux in 1744 she became the King's mistress. She was legally separated from her husband and created Marquise de Pompadour.

She lived at Versailles, and became an

established figure at court, friendly even with the religious Queen Marie. By 1780, although she was no longer his sole mistress, she had achieved a secure position as lifelong confidante and adviser to the able but retiring Louis. She influenced appointments, such as that of the Duc de Choiseul and other ministers who encouraged the Austrian alliance and thus the costly Seven Years War. She also affected artistic and cultural life: with her brother the Marquis de Merigny she planned building developments such as the Place de la Concorde, the Petit Trianon and the Château de Bellevue; she patronized decorative craftsmen of all kinds; and encouraged the new royal porcelain factory at Sèvres. She was also a friend of Voltaire and the other authors of the *Encyclopédie* but could not rouse the same literary and philosophical interests in the king. Her later years were saddened by the disastrous Seven Years War and she died of cancer at the age of 43. She is credited with the famous remark to Louis XV 'Après nous le déluge!'.

N. Mitford: *Madame de Pompadour* (1964)

**Deraismes, Maria** (1828–94). French feminist. Born into a wealthy Republican family, she was extremely well-educated. She was financially independent and became a well-known writer, lecturer and anticlericalist during the 1860s. Her books included *Le théâtre chez soi* (1863), *Aux femmes riches* (1865), *Nos principes et nos moeurs* (1867), and *Eve contre M. Dumas fils* (1867). In 1866 she was a co-founder of the Société pour la Revendication des Droits de la Femme, with the journalist André Leo, PAULE MINK and LOUISE MICHEL. In 1870 she founded the Association pour le Droit des Femmes, one of the main moderate feminist organizations in France until the 20th century. She collaborated with Leon Richier until 1882, when he founded an even more conservative organization, La Ligue Française pour le Droit des Femmes. Together they organized several important national and international congresses during the 1870s and 1880s. In 1881 she founded the paper *Le Républicain de Seine et Oise*, and her later books included *Les droits des enfants* (1886), and *Eve dans l'humanité* (1891). Other important figures in the fight for women's rights in the late 19th century

included the teacher and trade unionist Marie Boneval (1841–1918) and Jeanne Schmail (1847–1915), campaigner for married women's property rights.

**Deren, Maya** (1908–61). American filmmaker. Born in Russia, the daughter of a psychiatrist who emigrated to America in 1927, she was educated in Switzerland, at New York University and Smith College. She trained as a dancer and became Secretary to the KATHERINE DUNHAM Dancers. After extensive recording of Haitian music she wrote *The Divine Horseman: the Living God of Haiti*. She made her first film in 1943 with her husband Alexander Hammid. Unable to obtain distribution she hired the Princetown Playhouse, Greenwich Village, for a screening of her first three films in 1946, and hired them out from her New York home. In 1946 she received the first John Simon Guggenheim Memorial Foundation Award of $2500 for further experimental work. She established the Creative Film Foundation and in the same year wrote her second book, *An Anagram of Ideas on Art, Form and Film*. An important figure in the development of American avant-garde films for her success with independent distribution and experiments with personal fantasy, her films include: *Meshes of the Afternoon* (1943), *The Witch's Cradle* (unfinished), *At Land* (1944), *Choreography for Camera: Pas de Deux* (1945), *Ritual in transfigured Time* (1946), *Meditation on Violence* (1948), and *Very Eye of Night* (1959).

**Deroin, Jeanne** (*c*1810–94). French feminist and socialist. One of the pioneers of feminism in France, Jeanne Deroin was a self-educated working woman who became a school-teacher and journalist. Earlier moderate women's rights journals had been published (for example the *Gazette des femmes* edited by Madame Poutret de Mauchamps from 1836 to 1837) but Jeanne linked the emancipation of women with the struggle of the working class. In 1832 she married Monsieur Desroches, but refused to change her name. She rose to prominence during the 1840s and argued, like FLORA TRISTAN, for a federation of all workers' associations. Although imprisoned for her views, she found little support from the male radicals with whom she worked. She edited a socialist women's paper *L'Opinion des femmes* and in 1848 wrote a bitter pamphlet, *Cours de droit social pour les femmes*, describing women's enslaved condition and consciousness. She was one of a number of women active in the revolutionary clubs in 1848, including Eugénie Niboyet, who founded another paper *La voix des femmes*; Désirée Gay, a campaigner for co-operative workshops; and Elisa Gremaille, a Saint-Simonian educationalist. Other notable women of this era included the feminist Pauline Roland, Léodile Champseix (who wrote under the name André Léo) and Suzanne Voilquin, editor of *Tribune des Femmes*. Jeanne Deroin was the first woman to stand as candidate for election to the National Assembly (1849), asserting in her address that an assembly entirely composed of men was incompetent to legislate for a mixed society. In 1852 she was exiled to London, where she published several works, including *Almanack des femmes* (1854) and *Lettre aux travailleurs* (1856). She died in London and William Morris delivered a graveside tribute.

**Desai, Anita** (1937–). Indian writer. Born in the hill station of Mussoorie, in Uttar Pradesh, Anita Mazumdar graduated from Delhi University in 1957, and a year later married businessman Ashvin Desai. Her early novels, written while her four children were growing up, include *The Peacock* (1963), *Voices in the City* (1968), *Bye-Bye Blackbird* (1968) and *Where Shall We Go This Summer* (1975). Already acclaimed by critics for her intense, atmospheric pictures of Indian life, she won international fame and popularity with *Fire On The Mountain* (1977) and *Clear Light of Day* (1980), and with the lyrically imaginative yet realistic stories of family tension *Games at Twilight* (1978). Her recent books include *In Custody* (1984).

**de Sévigné, (Marie de Rabutin-Chantal),** Marquise (1626–96). French letter-writer. She was born in the Place Royale, Paris, of an old Burgundian family; her grandmother was the religious leader Jeanne de Chantal. Orphaned at the age of six, she was brought up by her beloved uncle, Christophe de Coulanges, at the

Abbaye de Livry in Brittany. There she studied under the learned tutors Ménage and Chapelain, receiving an education usually reserved for boys, and developing a love of Latin, Italian and Spanish literature.

In 1644 her marriage was arranged with the Marquis de Sévigné, a profligate Breton nobleman who was killed in a duel in 1651. She brought up her son Charles, and her daughter Françoise-Marguerite to whom she was passionately devoted. Her daughter married the Comte de Grignan in 1669. Madame de Sévigné lived in Paris surrounded by a circle of close friends, including Madame de LA FAYETTE and La Rochefoucauld. She also spent time at Livry, on her estate Les Rochers, and with her daughter in Provence. Her 1500 surviving letters, mostly to her daughter, were written with wit, warmth and charm and reveal her humour and sensitivity. They provide a vivid commentary on the manners, intrigues, values and daily life of the reign of Louis XIV.

A.S. Megaw: *Madame de Sévigné: her Letters and her World* (1946)

**Despard** [née French], **Charlotte** (1844–1939). English suffragette and Irish patriot. She was born in Edinburgh, daughter of a naval commander who died when she was nine years old. She settled in London at the age of 18, and in 1870 married Maximilian Despard, an Irish merchant with whom she travelled to the Far East. In 1890, after the death of her mother, she decided to devote her life to the poor of London and moved to the slum district of Nine Elms, serving on poor law and education committees. She opened one of the first child welfare centres, in Currie Street, and founded a working men's club, joined the Independent Labour Party and spoke at many meetings. An idealist, she was also a Theosophist and a vegetarian.

Although a member of the Women's Social and Political Union, she disliked the despotic methods of the PANKHURSTs, and in 1907 she left to start the Women's Freedom League. She led demonstrations, launched a campaign against paying taxes ('no taxation without representation'), and toured the country in a caravan. After the vote for women was won, she stood unsuccessfully as a parliamentary candidate for Battersea,

London, in 1919, and she continued to demonstrate for Equal Suffrage until 1928.

Charlotte Despard's third great cause was Irish freedom. After her brother, Sir John French, became Lord Lieutenant of Ireland (1918–21) she worked with the rebel Sinn Fein as an active Republican speaker and she helped to found the Irish Workers' College in Dublin for the political education of workers. She continued to fight for such causes until her death; she spoke against General Franco during the Spanish Civil War, and at the age of 91 she addressed an anti-Nazi demonstration in Hyde Park. Regarded unjustly as an elderly eccentric, she was declared bankrupt at the age of 96.

A. Linklater: *An Unhusbanded Life: Charlotte Despard, Suffragette, Socialist and Sinn Feiner* (1980)

**de Staël (-Holstein [née Necker], Anne Louise Germain),** Madame (1766–1817). French novelist, literary critic, political writer and philosopher of history. Her mother was a strict Calvinist and her father, whom she greatly admired, was an eminent figure in French financial and political life and he encouraged her interest in politics. She received an intellectually rigorous education and her interest in literature was stimulated by her mother's famous literary salon. In 1786 her parents arranged for her to marry Baron Eric Magnus de Staël-Holstein, the Swedish ambassador in Paris. The marriage was an unhappy one and Madame de Staël had many love affairs, including a long-standing one with the Comte de Narbonne and a turbulent one with the writer Benjamin Constant. Before the French Revolution she opened a salon which became a meeting place for the liberal aristocracy. However her initial sympathy for the ideals of the Revolution soured and she escaped from Paris. She returned in 1795 and re-opened her salon which during the Consulat became a centre for opposition to Napoleon, who saw her influence as so dangerous that in 1804 he refused to allow her to live in France. She retreated to the family estate, Coppet, by Lake Geneva in Switzerland, and her home became a meeting-place for leading intellectuals. During the years in exile she travelled widely. She returned to Paris in 1814 after Napoleon's abdication and continued to be an influential figure in European politics until her death in 1817.

Her principal works include: *De l'influence des passions sur le bonheur des individuels et des nations* (1796) in which she developed one of the favourite themes, the impossibility of separating ideas from feelings; *De la littérature considérée dans ses rapports avec les institutions sociales* (1800); *De l'Allemagne* (suppressed by Napoleon in 1810 but published in London in 1813), a work that contributed greatly to awakening French intellectuals' interest in foreign literature.

Her two novels *Delphine* (1803) and *Corinne ou l'Italie* (1807) contain self-portraits and relate to her liaison with Constant. Madame de Staël was a pioneer of French Romanticism.

R. Winegarten: *Madame de Staël* (1985)

**d'Este, Isabella** (1474–1539). Italian princess. She was a member of the great and noble d'Este family, rulers of Ferrara and Modena, and received an excellent education in the classics, philosophy, Provençal, French and Spanish literature and music. When she was 16 she married Francesco Gonzaga, the Marquis of Mantua and a famous soldier and scholar; their court became one of the most brilliant of the Renaissance. Isabella in particular patronized artists, and her personal friends included Titian and Leonardo da Vinci, who both painted her portrait, Raphael and the writer Castiglione. Restless and flamboyant, she commissioned extravagant displays and entertainments, and was herself always lavishly dressed. She was also an efficient stateswoman, and used her constant pilgrimages and her family connections to construct an efficient system of military intelligence, since Francesco was perpetually involved in campaigns and in different alliances, with the Venetians, the French and the Papacy, in order to preserve Mantua's independence. She herself saved the city from invasion when he was captured in 1509, and continued to rule it herself after his death in 1519 on behalf of her son Frederico. Despite her independence, however, she was always both devoted and submissive to her stern husband and tolerant of his infidelities. Isabella's sister, the beautiful and scholarly Beatrice, who

married Ludovico Sforza of Milan, her brother Alfonso, the husband of LUCREZIA BORGIA, and her brother Ippolito, Cardinal d'Este, were also famous patrons of the arts.
J. Cartwright: *Isabella d'Este* (1903)

**de Suárez, Inés** (1507–72). Spanish/Chilean adventuress. Born into a noble Spanish family, Inés de Suárez sailed in search of her husband, who had left to seek his fortune in South America, in 1537. She traced him from Venezuela to Lima, Peru, and then to Cuzco, where she discovered he had died in a siege. There she lived alone, working a smallholding and becoming a nurse and well-known apothecary, before she became the mistress of Pizarro's lieutenant, Pedro de Valdivia. She obtained official status as nurse on his expedition to conquer Chile in 1539, crossing the mountains and the Atacama desert with his troops and becoming one of the founders of Santiago. Her influence was great, and she played a leading role in the terrible Indian attack of 1541, insisting on the beheading of the hostage Indian chiefs, killing the first herself. As peace was established, she was linked with Valdivia's extravagance and corruption, and when he was formally reprimanded in 1548, one of the conditions of his governorship was that Inés should be banished. Instead she married Rodrigo de Quirigo, and after Valdivia's death in 1553 became known as one of the most distinguished women of the colony, chosen to lay the foundation stone of the Church of San Francisco in 1572.

**de Tencin, (Claudine-Alexandrine Guerin), Marquise** (1685–1749). French novelist. The subject of many stories, she was a nun in her youth for a brief period, and then went to court after the death of Louis XIV, where she became the mistress of Cardinal Dubois, of the regent, the Duc d'Orleans, and of other leading political figures including Destouches, with whom she had a son who became the philosopher d'Alembert. At his birth, however, she allegedly abandoned him on a Parisian church doorstep. Her adventurous career continued when she was falsely accused of murder in 1726, and imprisoned in the Bastille until released through the influence of her brother Pierre, a prominent churchman. She then chose a more sedate life as a society hostess,

presiding over a salon noted for its freedom of speech and democratic views, attended by writers such as Fontenell, Marivaux and Montesquieu, whose works she helped to edit. She also wrote three romantic novels: *Les mémoires du comte de Comminges* (1735), a tale of doomed love set against a background of prisons and monasteries; *Le siège de Calais* (1739), a novel of the Middle Ages, widely acclaimed at the time despite an extravagant re-writing of history; and *Les malheurs de l'amour* (1747). De Tencin was a colourful, forceful character whose ruthlessness, greed and love of intrigue won her as many enemies as admirers.

**Deutsch, Helene** (1884–1982). Polish-American psychoanalyst. Born in Przemyśl, Galicia, Helene was the youngest of four children in a cultured family; her father was a lawyer. Her life was expected to be leisured and as a teenager she studied secretly; later, with another suffragette, she won the admission of women to law school. In 1907 she enrolled in the medical school of Vienna University; in her last year there (1912) she married Dr Felix Deutsch with whom she had one son. Having gained her MD, she undertook seven years' neurological and psychiatric training and in the absence of many men during World War I she headed the civilian women's section of the psychiatric department at Vienna.

In 1916 a new era in her life began with her discovery of Sigmund Freud and his *Interpretation of Dreams*. Helene was one of the first four women analysed by Freud and was the second woman admitted to the Vienna Psychoanalytical Society. From 1925 to 1933 she directed the Vienna Psychoanalytic Institute, but in 1933 was obliged to leave for the USA. *Psychoanalysis of the Neuroses* (1930) was one of her main works, but in her two-volume *The Psychology of Women* she broke new ground in constructing a comprehensive psychology of the life-cycle of women and exploring their emotional life.
H. Deutsch: *Confrontations with Myself: an Epilogue* (1973)

**de Valois, Dame Ninette** [Stannus, Edris] (1898–). Irish dancer, choreographer, and founder of the Royal Ballet. Born in County Wicklow, Eire, she attended theatre school in London and first performed with a touring children's theatre company. She studied under Legat and Cecchetti, became principal dancer with the British National Opera in 1918, and in 1922 danced with the companies of Massin and LYDIA LOPOKOVA. She became a soloist with Dyagilev's Ballets Russes in 1923.

On leaving Dyagilev in 1926 she opened the Academy of Choreographic Art in South Kensington, London, and persuaded LILIAN BAYLIS to let her stage dances for Old Vic performances. From 1926 to 1931 she was Choreographic Director to the Old Vic, the Festival Theatre, Cambridge, and the Abbey Theatre, Dublin, where she worked with W.B. Yeats. In 1931 she joined with Baylis in forming the Vic-Wells Ballet (later the Sadler's Wells Theatre Ballet). During this decade she created new works including *Job* for the Camargo Society (1931), *The Rake's Progress* (1935), *The Haunted Ballroom*, and *Don Quixote*. She encouraged young choreographers like Frederick Ashton, and staged memorable productions such as *The Sleeping Princess* (1939) with Robert Helpmann and MARGOT FONTEYN. Together with MARIE RAMBERT, Ninette de Valois is one of the creators of British ballet.

In 1947 de Valois founded the National School of Ballet in Turkey and later helped the ballets of Canada and Iran. Her ambition to create a British National Ballet was realized in 1956 with the granting of a charter to the Royal Ballet. After 32 years as Director, she retired in 1963, remaining a governor and an adviser to the School. In 1971 she retired from official duties but still supervised revivals of her own works, such as *Checkmate* (1975). She remained a highly influential figure.

In 1935 she married Dr A.B. Connell. She was awarded the CBE in 1947, the DBE in 1957 and in 1974 became the first woman to receive the Erasmus Prize Foundation Award.

N. de Valois: *Invitation to the Ballet* (1937)
———: *Come Dance with Me* (1957)
———: *Step by Step* (1977)

**Dexter** [née Harper], **Caroline** (1819–84). Australian feminist. Born in Nottingham, the daughter of a jeweller, she was educated in England and Paris, where she was friendly with GEORGE SAND. She married a painter, William Dexter, in 1843; he emigrated to Sydney in 1852 and she joined him three years later. After the failure of their art school they moved to Gippsland, and here Caroline produced her *Ladies' Almanack: The Southern Cross or Australian Album and New Year's Gift* (1857), an original wry and perceptive account of Australian domestic life and landscape, especially notable for its sympathy for aboriginal culture. She separated from her husband and moved to Melbourne where she became a dress-reform campaigner. She opened an Institute of Hygiene and in 1861 collaborated with HARRIET CLISBY in founding *The Interpreter*, a radical journal of literary and social comment.

William Dexter had died in 1860, and the next year Caroline married William Lynch, a wealthy lawyer, and established herself as a patron of artists and writers.

**d'Hericourt, Jenny** [Eugénie] (*fl* 19th century). French feminist. One of the first woman doctors in Europe, an energetic reformer and liberal, she visited Russia in the 1850s and was later regarded as one of the inspirers of the Russian feminist movement. She was the centre of a circle based on the Hôtel Molière in Paris, and a member of a Saint-Simonian group which formed around the journal *Revue philosophique*. She was the author of some influential work, including *La femme affranchie* (1880), which defended women against the attacks of Michelet in *L'Amour* (1858) and of Proudhon in *La justice dans la révolution* (1858).

**Diana**, Princess of Wales (1961–). British princess. Diana Frances Spencer, daughter of the 8th Earl Spencer, was born at Park House, Sandringham, Norfolk, and educated at Riddlesworth Hall Preparatory School, Norfolk, and at West Heath School, Kent, and then spent a short time at the Château d'Oex finishing school in Switzerland. She worked as a nursery school teacher in Pimlico, London from 1979 to 1981.

In July 1981 she married Charles, Prince of Wales, heir to the British throne. They have two sons, William and Henry, and two principal homes: Kensington Palace, London, and Highgrove, Gloucestershire. Diana has become associated with leading British fashion, but in recent years constant press coverage has focused increasingly on her private life, and the social life which she leads independently of Prince Charles. Since her marriage, Diana has been constantly in the public eye, with a heavy schedule of functions (in 1986 she had 176 engagements at home and 98 abroad) and of foreign tours, including those in Canada, and to the Australian Bicentennial celebrations in 1988. She is the patron of numerous bodies, ranging from the Welsh National Opera to the Pre-School Playgroups Association, Help the Aged to the National Hospital for Nervous Diseases, and is President of others, including the Welsh Craft Council, Dr Barnardo's and the Royal Academy of Music.

P. Junor: *Diana, Princess of Wales* (1983)

**Diane of France** (1538–1619). French princess. The illegitimate daughter of Henry II and the Italian Filippa Duc, she was legitimized in 1547. In 1553 she married Orazio Farnese, who died in battle the same year, and in 1559 François, eldest son of Constable Anne de Montmorency. Together they led the moderate Catholic Politique group. In 1579 François died, and three years later Diane was granted the Duchy of Angoulême for life. During the reign of Henry III she was highly influential in effecting reconciliation with Henry of Navarre, and when the latter became king her power increased. Cultured and sensitive, she was especially concerned to promote religious peace.

**Dickinson, Emily (Elizabeth)** (1830–86). American poet. She was born in Amherst, Massachusetts, into a famous New England family: her grandfather was founder of Amherst College, and her father, a leading lawyer, its treasurer. He was an autocrat, ruling the lives of Emily and her sister Lavinia long after they were adults, and even grudging them the freedom to buy books or choose their own friends. She was educated at Amherst Academy (1847–8), and then attended Mount Holyoke Female Seminary in South Hadley. After that, apart from visits to Washington and Philadelphia when her father was a Congressman in 1854 and a trip to Boston for eye treatment, she never left Amherst again, and saw no one

but her family and close friends. Her reclusive life and odd habits, such as always dressing in white and writing her poems on little scraps of paper, sewn into booklets with needle and thread and hidden in trunks and drawers, as well as the intensity of her verse, have given rise to much speculation about a hopeless passion for a man, or a woman, which led her to renounce the world, but the evidence is scanty and controversial.

She seems to have begun writing in the 1860s, and after an uncomprehending and patronizing reply from Thomas Wentworth Higginson, to whom she appealed for comment in 1862, kept her work to herself. Two poems were published in her lifetime, without her consent. Her style is unique – irregular, broken, tentative, exploring in images of startling originality and simplicity profound states of despair, awe and longing. An invalid for two years before her death from Bright's Disease, she asked for her manuscripts to be destroyed, but faced with over 1700 poems her sister was unable to burn them. They were edited in three volumes by Mabel Loomis Todd and Higginson during the 1890s.

R.B. Sewall: *The Life of Emily Dickinson* (1974)

**Didion, Joan** (1934–). American novelist. Born in Sacramento, California, she graduated from the University of California, Berkeley, in 1956 and worked as associate feature writer on *Vogue* until 1963. She has also been a columnist for the *Saturday Evening Post*, contributing editor of the *National Review*, and as a free-lance writer has published critical articles for most major American periodicals. In 1964 she married Gregory Dunne.

Her novels won immediate acclaim for their laconic, evocative portrayal of the unease of the contemporary American consciousness, and, almost indirectly, for their analysis of women's inner tension. Her books include *Run River* (1963), *Play It as it Lays* (1971), *A Book of Common Prayer* (1977), *The White Album* (1979), *Salvador* (1983), *Democracy* (1984) and *Miami* (1987). She is also the author of a book of essays, *Slouching Towards Jerusalem* (1968), and has collaborated on screenplays for films, including *A Star is Born* (1976).

**Dido** [Elissa] (*fl* *c*800 BC). Carthaginian queen. The sources for the history of Dido are literary rather than historical, but appear to have been based on fact. Reputedly she was the daughter of the Tyrian King, Mutton. After her husband Acerbas [Sychaeus in Virgil's *Aeneid*] was killed by her brother Pygmalion, she fled to North Africa where she bought land and founded the city of Carthage. To escape the matrimonial offers of a local chief, Iarbas, she committed public suicide by throwing herself on a pyre. In the *Aeneid* her death is presented as the result of desertion by Aeneas.

**Didrikson, Babe (Mildred Zaharias)** (1914–56). American athlete. Born in Texas, daughter of a Norwegian carpenter, she worked as an insurance clerk, but at the age of 15 broke two national records in Dallas, in javelin and basketball throw. She became the USA's greatest woman athlete, possibly the world's, with unparalleled success in all sports, including boxing, swimming, shooting, fencing, tennis and billiards. After winning gold medals at the 1932 Olympic Games she turned to professional golf, winning all major American and British titles when she returned to amateur status in 1946–47. Her professional career was cut short by cancer in 1953 but after a major operation she returned to win the American Women's Open Golf Championship for the third time in 1954.

**Dietrich, Marlene** [Maria Magdalene] (1901–). German-American film actress and singer. Born in Berlin, she was the daughter of an officer in the Royal Prussian Police who died when she was small. Her stepfather, a cavalry officer killed in World War I, provided a conventional upper-bourgeois home, but Marlene wanted to become a concert violinist until a wrist injury diverted her to the stage. She worked in revue and then trained with Max Reinhardt before beginning her film career in 1923 with *Der kleine Napoleon/So sind die Männer/Napoleons kleiner Bruder* and *Tragödie der Liebe/Tragedy of Love*. She made several films in Germany during the 1920s, and married the Czech production assistant Rudolf Sieber in 1924. Although the couple later drifted apart, especially after their

move to the USA, Marlene remained devoted to her daughter Maria, who was born in 1925.

Her transformation from a steady German actress to an international star was the work of Josef von Sternberg, who cast her as Lola, embodiment of cool sexuality, in *Der blau Engel/The Blue Angel* (1930). Dietrich followed him to Hollywood, where her exotic, mysterious screen image with its hint of cruelty and decadence was further developed by von Sternberg in *Morocco* (1930), *Dishonored* (1931), *Shanghai Express* and *Blonde Venus* (1932), *The Scarlet Empress* (1934) and *The Devil is a Woman* (1935). None of her later films has such power, although she has worked with directors such as Lang, Lubitsch, Wilder and Hitchcock.

Before World War II Dietrich was asked to work in Germany, and her refusal resulted in the banning of her films there. Instead she took American citizenship, and was decorated by the American and French governments for her tireless work entertaining troops, with classic songs such as *Falling in Love Again* and *See what the boys in the back room will have*. Although she continued to make films, during the 1950s she began a new career as an international cabaret star; her popularity and glamorous image still endure.

M. Dietrich: *My Life Story* (1979)

**Digby El Mezrab, Jane** (1807–81). English adventurer and traveller. Born in Norfolk, she was the daughter of an admiral, and lived mostly at her grandfather's home, Holkham Hall. Before she was 17 her marriage to Lord Ellenborough was arranged, but ended in the scandal of a divorce heard in the House of Lords. Her three other legal attachments made her successively Baroness Venningen, Countess Theotoky and the wife of Sheikh Abdul Medjuel El Mezrab, and involved elopements, a duel and a further divorce. She had six children by her first three husbands and by her first lover, the Austrian Prince, Felix Schwarzenberg, but was only attached to her last son, Leonidas Theotoky, who was killed when six years old. Her many other lovers included King Ludwig of Bavaria, and later his son King Otho of Athens. From being naive and passionate,

Jane finally developed into a witty and cultivated woman, commanding eight languages and interested in sculpture, painting and especially archaeology.

After living in Paris, Munich and Greece, Jane went to Syria when she was 46. Sheikh Medjuel was the guide to her camel caravan when she made a nine-day journey across the desert to see the archaeological remains at Palmyra, and after more journeys around Damascus and Baghdad they eventually married. He was an educated man and she spent 30 years with him, serving him but being respected as queen of the tribe, sometimes galloping into an inter-tribal war at the head of his horsemen, and retaining sufficient independence to defend the Christians during the massacre of 1859. They lived for half of each year in a house in Damascus and half in the black Bedouin tents as sheep- and horse-breeding nomads. Jane wore a traditional blue robe and yashmak, wore kohl round her eyes, went barefoot and smoked a hookah pipe [narghilyé]; she was revered among the Arabs for her excellent horsemanship and adventurous spirit. When cholera struck Damascus, she died of dysentery with Medjuel beside her.

**Dilke, Emily** [Emilia] **(Francis Strong)** (1840–1904). English trade unionist. She was born in Ilfracombe but the family soon moved to Oxfordshire, where her father was a bank manager, and she grew up in radical intellectual circles. From 1859 to 1861 she studied at South Kensington Art School, London, on the recommendation of John Ruskin, who deeply influenced her artistic and social theories. Her early religious mysticism developed, under the impact of Auguste Comte, into an ethical Christianity of duty and brotherly love. In 1861 she married Mark Pattison, Rector of Lincoln College, Oxford. Their circle included GEORGE ELIOT, who reputedly took them as models for Dorothea and Casaubon in *Middlemarch*. Emily became a critic, specializing in French art on which she published five major works, beginning with *The Renaissance of Art in France* (1879). On annual Continental tours between 1867 and 1884 she studied both art and contemporary politics.

A radical and a member of the Oxford Women's Suffrage Union, in 1876 she joined EMMA PATERSON's Women's Protective and Provident League, which was renamed the Women's Trade Union League (WTUL) in 1891. She was a particular advocate of technical education for women. In 1865, a year after Pattison's death, she married her close friend, the Liberal MP Sir Charles Dilke. From 1886 she took over the WTUL, becoming President in 1902, initiating enquiries into dangerous trades, organizing textile workers, arguing for equal pay, and defending workers' interests at Trades Union Congress meetings. She also worked with Dilke in his campaigns for shop assistants and against sweated trades. A passionate crusader for unionization she remained a Liberal, joining the Labour Party just before her death. In addition to her influential art criticism, she wrote many pamphlets for the WTUL and also published poetry and allegorical short stories in the 1890s.

B.E. Askwith: *Lady Dilke: a biography* (1969)

**Dinesen, Isak.** *See* BLIXEN, KAREN.

**Ding Ling** [Ting Ling] (1902–86). Chinese novelist. Born in Hunan province into a family of impoverished gentry, she was educated by her mother until 1917 when she went to study in Taoynan. As a student she adopted strong views on liberty and on the equality of women, and in 1919, after the events of the 4 May Movement, she ran away to join a co-educational school in Changsa, moving to Shanghai in 1921. From 1925 she lived with the well-known poet Hu Yeh-p'in and made her name as a short story writer from 1928 to 1930. Her new style heroine, independent but romantic, first appeared in *Sha-fei nu-shih te jih-chi* ('Diary of Miss Sophie', 1927). In 1930 she was active in the league of left-wing writers, and after the execution of Hu in 1931 her political commitment was intensified. She edited left-wing literary magazines, launched socialist-realist fiction with works like *Shuii* ('Flood', 1931) and joined the Communist Party in 1933. In the same year she was captured by Kuomintang agents and imprisoned, but in 1936 was released and escaped via Beijing [Peking] to join Mao Zedong's [Tse-Tung] forces in the liberated Yenan province, disguised as a Manchurian soldier.

She continued to write during the civil strife and the Sino–Japanese War, and published *Y'ing hsiung chuan* ('Stories of heroes') in 1946. Her saga of the struggle of the peasants against the rich farmers, *Sang-Kan-ho-shang* ('The sun shines over the Sangkan River') won the Stalin Prize in 1957. Her novels and short stories show women struggling for independence and sexual fulfilment, and are strongly critical of the old taboos. In the 1950s she married a film-script writer Chen Ming, held literary and academic posts and was Vice-Chairman of the Union of Chinese writers. She wrote a number of books and then joined the Hundred Flowers Campaign for greater literary freedom. In 1957 she was condemned by the Party as a reactionary, deprived of her rights as an author and expelled. She underwent a period of self-criticism and worked as a charwoman and peasant farmer in north-east China for 12 years. At the start of the Cultural Revolution in 1966 she was publicly humiliated, and in 1970 was sent back to a prison in Beijing where she spent five years in solitary confinement. In 1975 she was exiled to a mountain village in Shanxi Province, returning to the capital in 1978. In 1979 the Communist Party reversed its verdict and cleared her political reputation. Her work is now generally available and greatly admired in China, and after years of enforced silence she began to publish again.

**Dix, Dorothea (Lynde)** (1802–87). American nurse and social reformer. She was born in Hampden, Maine, where her father was a farmer and a lay preacher. She had an unhappy childhood, during which she often had to take responsibility for two young brothers, and from the age of 12 she lived with her grandmother. When she was 19 she began to run a school in her grandparent's Boston house; she wrote elementary science textbooks, a hymnbook, and other devotional works.

In 1836 she went to England to improve her health and met several social reformers. On her return in 1841 she began to teach Sunday school in the House of Correction, East Cambridge, and was horrified to find insane women were kept there in appalling conditions. She made a survey of prisons, almshouses and insane asylums, and in 1844 presented her report to the Massachusetts legislature. By this effort and through pamphlets and speeches, she secured massive funds for new facilities. Her priorities were to alleviate conditions for the mentally ill by having institutions for them separate from criminals and for ropes and chains to be removed. She played a direct role in the founding of 32 mental hospitals and was inspirational in founding many others with the result that the USA increased its number of asylums from 13 in 1843 to 123 in 1880. She called New Jersey's first mental hospital at Trenton 'my firstborn child'. Her humane policies laid the groundwork for psychotherapeutic work, although she would be criticized today for an undue emphasis on institutional as opposed to community care. When she was vetoed by the national legislature from trying to obtain the sale of public land for asylums, her disappointment drove her abroad, where she reformed prisons and hospitals in Scotland, the Channel Islands, France, Turkey and Russia.

With the outbreak of the American Civil War in 1861, Dorothea volunteered and was made Chief of Nurses for the Union Army. She developed the Army Nursing Corps, mobilizing thousands of women and turning public buildings into hospitals, but despite her high standards her appointment caused controversy. She had become imperious and autocratic, and would not accept members of religious sisterhoods or women under the age of 30. Her influence remained great, and workers for other causes such as helping the blind continued to seek her support. She spent her last days in the hospital she had founded at Trenton.

H.E. Marshall: *Dorothea Dix: Forgotten Samaritan* (1937)

**Dmitrieva, Elizabeth** (1851–1910). Russian-French socialist. The daughter of a Russian nobleman, she married an army officer in order to attend university in Switzerland. There she met other Russian radicals. She went to London and as a member of the Socialist International became a friend of Karl Marx. When she left England for Paris she sent him detailed analyses and descriptions of events in 1870. During the Commune of 1871 she organized the

Women's Union for the Defence of Paris as a branch of the Socialist International. When the communards were defeated, she escaped and returned to Russia, where she married a political prisoner who had been condemned to exile in Siberia. She lived with him there until her death.

**Dod, Lottie** [Charlotte] (1871–1960). British tennis player. She was tennis's first prodigy, known at 12 as 'the little wonder'. In 1887, at 15 years 10 months, she became the youngest-ever winner of the women's singles at Wimbledon, and retained the title in 1888, beating Blanche Bingley in the final. She did not compete again for two years, but then returned to win again in 1891, 1892 and 1893; only at their last meeting did Blanche Bingley (Mrs Hillyard) take a set from her. Her anticipation and powerful forehand were remarkable, and she added to this the ability to volley and smash effectively, which was rare in a Victorian woman.

Having lost interest in competitive lawn tennis, she became a hockey international (1899), a fine skater and tobogganner, British Ladies Golf Champion (1904) and won an Olympic silver medal for archery in 1908.

**Dodge, Grace (Hoadley)** (1856–1914). American welfare worker. Born in New York into a business family with a long humanitarian tradition, she was educated at home and at school in Connecticut (1872–4). From 1874 Grace taught in Sunday schools and in district schools of the Children's Aid Society, before working with her parents for the New York State Charities Aid Association. Deeply religious, she considered her work to be a full-time unpaid job rather than voluntary service. She ran a discussion group for factory girls (1881), which developed into a state and then a national Association of Working Girls' Societies, of which she became Director in 1896.

Grace Dodge was also involved in practical education schemes, working with the Industrial Education Association (IEA) from 1884, and the City Board of Education (1886–9). She was involved in the transformation of the IEA into the New York Teachers' College at the turn of the century. Her work with young girls involved

her in the popular social purity movements, and she founded the New York Travellers Aid Society in 1907. From 1906 until her death she worked as President of the Young Women's Christian Association National Board, resolving divisions between evangelical and liberal factions. In her will she left over $1½ million to various charities.

L. Stein and A. Baxter: *Grace H. Dodge: her Life and Work* (1974)

**Doi, Takako** (1928–). Japanese politician. Born in the Hyogo Prefecture, Japan, Doi Takako graduated in law from Doshisha university, where she lectured on Constitutional Law from 1958 to 1970. One of her chief concerns has always been the protection of international peace. She was first elected to the Diet, the national parliament, in 1969. In 1986, after the Japanese Socialist Party had performed disastrously in the national elections, the chairman Masahi Ishibashi resigned and Doi was elected to lead the party, winning 83% of the votes. Now head of Japan's largest opposition party, described as 'a political Joan of Arc' she is the first woman ever to become leader of a major-political party in Japan, and is renowned for her aggressive stance in opposition to the government. During 1987 she launched a campaign to recruit more members, particularly women, and to strengthen the party organization.

**Domitien, Elizabeth**. Central African Republic politician. She was closely connected with politics all her life, and joined the independence movement at the age of 20, proving a brilliant orator and leading the national women's organization for independence. She won the support of the women for Bokassa, a close friend who had been brought up in her father's house, before his coup in 1966. She accompanied him on his tours abroad and in 1975 he appointed her Prime Minister. Although she was a mere puppet in the newly-created post, she was removed from office and placed under house arrest when Bokassa declared himself Emperor in April 1976. Nevertheless, she remained vice president of the Mouvement d'Evolution Sociale de l'Afrique Noire (MESAN), the country's only political organization, from 1975 to 1979. After the coup which deposed

Bokassa in September 1979, Elizabeth Domitien was imprisoned and tried in February 1980.

**Doolittle, Hilda** [H.D.] (1886–1961). American poet. She was born in Bethlehem, Pennsylvania, the daughter of an astronomy professor, but her family moved to Philadelphia when she was nine, and she was educated there at Gordon School and the Friends' Central School; she then went on to Bryn Mawr College in 1904, until ill health forced her to leave two years later. Her first published works were children's stories, but on a visit to Europe in 1911 she came into contact with the Imagist group of poets, led by Ezra Pound, and feeling in sympathy with their attempts to give poetry a clear, precise diction able to express both inner moods and outer appearances she began writing herself. Her poems appeared in *Poetry* in 1913 and in that year she married the writer Richard Aldington. They began to make translations from Greek, which she continued in three collections in 1916, 1917 and 1919, and she took over the editorship of *The Egoist* from him (1916–17). In the 1920s H.D. produced several more volumes, then turned to fiction, with *Palimpsest* (1926), *Hedylus* (1928), *Kara and Ka* (1930) and *Nights* (1935). She also wrote two plays. Increasingly she identified human 'health' with the total empathy with the natural world expressed in Greek and Egyptian myth. She lived in Switzerland during this period, having separated from her husband whom she divorced in 1937.

After World War II H.D. wrote a verse trilogy linking themes of death and regeneration with the recent terrors: *The Walls do not fall* (1944), *Tribute to the Angels* (1945) and *Flowering of the Red* (1946). She continued to explore themes related to classical images until her death, her last collection being entitled *Helen in Egypt* (1961).

B. Guest: *Herself Defined* (1984)

**Dors, Diana** (1931–84). British actress. Born Diana Fluck, the daughter of a Swindon railway clerk, she studied at the Royal Academy of Dramatic Art, made her first film at 15, *The Shop at Sly Corner*, and was soon signed up with Rank, who were looking for British equivalents to Hollywood's glamorous blondes. But it was not until after 1951 when she married Denis Hamilton, a persevering publicist, that she became a national pin-up and also showed her real talent for acting, in Carol Reed's East End film *A Kid for Two Farthings* (1955), and *Yield to the Night* (1956). By then Britain's highest paid star, she separated from Hamilton, and after his death married Richard Dawson in 1959. Moving to Hollywood, she made several films during the 1960s but by 1968, back in England, divorced, and married to Alan Lake, her career seemed shattered when she was declared bankrupt and Lake was imprisoned for wounding a man in a fight.

Yet after years of small parts, and a close escape from meningitis, Diana Dors returned with a fine performance in *Craze* (1973), and re-established herself as a serious actress, winning enormous popularity in Britain, because of her warm, resilient personality, her nostalgic, comic memoirs, and her open, courageous struggle with cancer.

D. Dors: *For Adults Only* (1978)
———— : *Behind Closed Doors* (1979)

**Douglass, Dorothea** [Mrs Lambert Chambers] (1878–1960). British lawn tennis player. The daughter of a vicar, Dorothea was an all-rounder with a fine drop-shot, who despite her ankle-length dress showed such skill and energy that she was the most successful woman competitor before World War I. Her first major championship was the All England Badminton Ladies Doubles in 1903, followed by Wimbledon singles titles in 1903, 1904, 1906, 1910, 1911, 1913 and 1914. These seven wins surpassed Blanche Bingley Hillyard's previous record of six, and might have equalled Helen Wills's later record had not Wimbledon been closed for five years during World War I. In 1919 and 1920 she was beaten by the young SUZANNE LENGLEN in the final; the first match reached a higher standard than any previously seen, and Dorothea was within two match points of victory.

At an age when most women had long left tennis, she captained the victorious Wightman Cup team in 1925 and 1926, winning her singles and doubles in 1925. Aged 47, she ended that year seventh in the first authoritative ranking of the world's top ten women players ever issued. She turned professional in 1928, and remained fanatically interested in tennis until her death at the age of 81.

**Drabble, Margaret** (1939–). English novelist. She was born in Sheffield and educated at The Mount School, York, and Newnham College, Cambridge, where she took a double first in English. In 1960 she married Clive Swift, the actor; they had three children. She was divorced in 1975 and in 1982 married the biographer Michael Holroyd. The first of her novels was *A Summer Birdcage* (1963) and her third, *The Millstone* (1965), won the Llewellyn Rhys Memorial Prize in 1966. Her later works include *The Middle Ground* (1980) and *The Radiant Way* (1987). She has also written a biography of Arnold Bennett (1974) and *A Writer's Britain* (1979) and was Editor of the most recent *Oxford Companion to English Literature* (1979–84). Her influence on modern British fiction has been considerable and she is noted for her thoughtful, perceptive analysis of the problems and tensions of middle-class women in contemporary society.

In 1973 she received the E.M. Forster Award from the American Academy of Arts and Letters, and she has been Chairman of the National Book League since 1980.

**Draper, Ruth** (1884–1956). American monologuist. The seventh of eight children of an intellectual liberal New England family, her father was Professor of Clinical Medicine and her mother a musician. At eight she was a talented impersonator, and by the early 1890s was performing monologues at private New York functions and for charities. Her mother discouraged her becoming professional, although by 1913 her fame had spread to London, where she was recognized by society hostesses and even royalty. In 1915, a year after her mother died, she began touring, giving War Relief Benefits across the west and midwest USA. She became famous in *A Lady's Name* (1916) and in 1918 entertained American troops in France. In 1920, she became fully professional, and by 1927 was making $85,000 a year. Privately longing for marriage and domesticity, she wrote 'I have been captured, and am being led by the demands of this gift – so against my desires and longings I *must* work.' She wrote her own material, appearing alone on an empty stage, with a hat, shawl or fan to create character.

Her comic recitations such as 'Showing the Garden' or 'Opening the Bazaar' were brilliant social sketches, but she also had a gift for pathos and tragedy, with a perfect command of accent, intonation and mood.

In 1928, she fell in love with the poet Lauro de Bosis and considered marriage, but in 1932 after a series of anti-fascist, pro-monarchist escapades he committed suicide. For the rest of her life she devoted herself to her art, touring continuously until she died in her sleep, after a New York performance.

N. Warren (ed.): *The Letters of Ruth Draper* (1979)

**Drew, Jane (Beverley)** (1911–). English architect. She was born and educated in Surrey, and attended the Architectural Association School in London. Her first husband was the architect James Alliston but in 1942 she was married for a second time, to Edwin Maxwell Fry. From 1940 to 1945 she worked on her own, and in 1944 became adviser to the West African colonies on town planning, designing particularly in Ghana. In 1946 she and her husband formed a partnership with others and created important new developments in London and in Nigeria, where they designed Ibadan University College (1953–59). With Le Corbusier they also worked on designs for the New Capital City, Chandigarh, India. Drew's work is also found in Sri Lanka, France, Mauritius and Kuwait, in forms ranging from domestic interiors to schools and whole towns. The friend of artists such as Ben Nicholson, BARBARA HEPWORTH and Graham Sutherland, she has felt herself to be part of an aesthetic as well as a practical movement in architecture. Among her most important later works was the design of the Open University in Milton Keynes (1966–77). She has been a visiting professor at the Massachusetts Institute of Technology, at Harvard and at the University of Utah, and has been the focus of many exhibitions and received numerous awards. She has also written several books, especially on tropical architecture, and edited the *Architects' Yearbook* with Fry from 1946 to 1962.

**Droste-Hülshoff, Annette von** (1797–1848). German poet. She was born in Westphalia; her early interest in learning was discouraged by her mother, but she began writing poetry at the age of seven. The religious doubts of her early life are expressed in the intense devotional verses written between 1818 and 1820, which were completed in 1839 and eventually published in 1851 as *Geistliche Jahre*. She stopped writing for several years after an unhappy love affair, but after completing the epic *Das Hospiz am Grossen Sant Bernard* (1828) she travelled, and met other literary figures, the brothers Grimm, Feiligrath, Uhland and Schlegel. After her father's death in 1826 she lived with her mother and sister.

During the 1830s she wrote ballads, lyrics and prose pieces, and her finest poetry was written as she became increasingly devoted to her protegé, Levin Schucking, a writer 17 years her junior. She published her famous novella *Die Judenbuche* in 1841. After Schucking's rejection of her and marriage to another woman in 1843, she wrote no more poetry. Her work is characterized by both detailed natural realism, and by a preoccupation with the supernatural and demonic aspects of existence, and has a strange, haunted intensity.

M.E. Morgan: *Annette von Droste-Hülshoff* (1984)

**Drouet, Juliette** (1806–83). French actress. A successful actress in Paris, she met Victor Hugo when she acted in his *Lucrèce Borgia* in 1833. She became his mistress and remained totally devoted to him for the rest of their lives. During the 1850s she followed him into exile in the Channel Islands and acted as his secretary. She is the subject of many of his poems, notably *Tristesse d'Olympio*, one of his most famous lyrics.

**Drummond, Annabella** (*c*1350–1402). Scottish queen. The daughter of Sir John Drummond, she was born into an aristocratic Scots family. She married John Stewart of Kyle in 1367; he was the son of the Earl of Atholl, who succeeded to the Scottish crown in 1370. Due to his father's illness, Annabella's husband John was the effective ruler, and eventually became king in 1390, changing his name to Robert III. Annabella later helped her son David, Duke of Rothesay, during the invasion of the kingdom by Henry IV of England in 1399. Shortly after her death during the plague, Rothesay was murdered but her second son eventually became James I. She was remembered for her grace, beauty and kindness.

**Drummond, Flora** ['General Drummond'] (1869–1949). Scottish suffragette. Born in Scotland, she spent most of her childhood in the Highlands and later trained as a telegraphist but was disqualified from becoming a postmistress because of her lack of height, a fact which always rankled. In her teens in Glasgow she became involved in social reform, and when she moved to Manchester after her marriage she became a socialist. She took a factory job for experience, worked at the Ancoats settlement, and joined the Clarion Club and the Co-operative movement. She was finally drawn into the suffrage movement after Christabel PANKHURST's arrest in 1905. She became a Women's Social and Political Union organizer and was known as 'General Drummond' because she wore a uniform and led a drum and fife band on London marches. An exhilarating speaker, good with hecklers, small and very stout, she was the subject of many stories: she hired a launch to harangue MPs on the terrace of the House of Commons; she was imprisoned nine times; in 1914 she lay on the doorstep of Sir Edward Carson, an Ulster gunrunner, in protest that while thousands of women were imprisoned, public men were allowed to organize political violence. She later became more conservative and from 1928 was Commander-in-Chief of the Women's Guild of Empire, which opposed Communism and strikes.

**du Barry, (Marie Jeanne Gomard de Vaubernier) Comtesse** [Madame du Barry] (1743–93). French, mistress of Louis XV. Born in Paris, the daughter of a monk, du Vaubernier, and a dressmaker, Anne Bécu, she was educated in the convent of St Anne, Paris. She became a governess, an apprentice dressmaker and an inn-servant until she was taken up by Jean du Barry, an aristocratic gambler from Toulouse, who brought her to the attention of Louis XV in April 1769 after the death of Madame DE POMPADOUR. She was officially accepted at court after a marriage of convenience to Jean's brother, Guillaume du Barry. Her influence as the royal mistress was immense, but although she supported the ministers of the Triumvirate (d'Aiguillon, Maupeou, and Terray) she was more interested in the arts, encouraging the vogue for neo-classical art. Her genuine affection for Louis showed in her devoted nursing of him in his final illness, smallpox.

After Louis' death in 1774, du Barry was confined first to the Abbaye du Pont-aux-Dames and then exiled briefly to the Château of St Vrain. Eventually she was allowed to return to the palace at Louveciennes which Louis had given to her, where she lived in considerable luxury, enjoying a long affair with the Duc de Brissac. He was assassinated early in the French Revolution. Du Barry fled to England but rashly returned to France for a visit in 1793. Denounced by her negro servant Zemor, an ardent Republican, she appeared before the Revolutionary Tribunal, was imprisoned in St Pelagie, and executed by guillotine.

A. Stoeckl: *Mistress of Versailles: the Life of Madame du Barry* (1966)

**du Châtelet** [née de Breteuil], **Emilie,** Marquise (1706–49). French mathematician and physicist, known as much for her passionate affairs as for her knowledge, her spirited individuality enabled her to combine the two. She was born to a fashionable family and showed early aptitude for languages, Classics and mathematics. At 19 she married the Marquis du Châtelet, a colonel, and had three children. After various affairs she became Voltaire's companion from 1733 onwards, and lived with him at the du Châtelet family's Château de Cirey, while remaining married to the Marquis.

At Cirey Emilie and Voltaire established a laboratory. Both submitted studies on the nature of fire to a competition held by the French Academy of Sciences in 1738; although neither won the prize, their work was printed by the Academy and commended. Emilie anticipated later research by maintaining that heat and light have the same cause or are both modes of motion. She had private tutors and was visited by European scholars who were known as 'Emiliens'. Her time was spent in feverish intellectual activity despite festive interludes, many at the court of the former Polish King, Stanislas. *Institutions de physique*, published in 1740, is a physics textbook critically tracing the work of Leibniz, Newton, Descartes and others. She

was interested in critical deism and wrote a manuscript examining the Old and New Testaments, and contributed to moral philosophy with *Discours sur le bonheur*.

In 1749 she was still working on a translation from Latin to French of Newton's *Principia*, with a commentary, when she gave birth to another child by the Marquis de Saint-Lambert. She died a few days later and her best-known work, the translation of Newton, was published ten years later.

**du Coudray, Angélique (Marguerite le Boursier)** (1712–89). French obstetrician. Born in Clermont-Ferrand, Angélique had some training at the Hôtel Dieu School in Paris, and was licensed as a midwife or *accoucheuse* in 1740. She was among the French midwives who brought a scientific approach to medicine at a time when charlatans were common and methods crude. To provide her pupils with practice in delivery, she introduced the use of a model of the female torso and an actual foetus.

In 1759 she published *Abrégé de l'art des accouchements avec plusiers observations sur des cas singuliers*, an expansion and revision of a midwifery textbook written in 1667. She was given an annual salary by Louis XV to teach in all the provinces, and at once organized a class of 100 pupils in Auvergne. Altogether she trained 4000 pupils. In 1780 a course in practical obstetrics was established at the veterinary school at Alfort under her direction. Jealous surgeons were strongly opposed to her teaching, but such was her recognition that she was allowed by the Church to baptize babies, and was often summoned to assist at malpractice cases where the mother or child had been mutilated. In 1773 her *Oeuvres* were published, and she was granted a government pension in her old age.

**du Deffand, (Marie de Vichy-Chamrond)** Marquise (1697–1780). French salon hostess and intellectual. Educated in a Paris convent, she married her relation Jean Baptiste de La Lande in 1718 but separated from him four years later. She had a stormy, romantic youth, being a leader of the decadent court circle surrounding her lover, the regent Philippe II, Duc d'Orléans. She was later the friend of intellectuals such as

Voltaire and politicians such as Jean-François Henault, her companion until his death in 1770. She established a salon, which flourished between 1753 and 1780 and which became popular with Turgot, d'Alembert and the *philosophes*, although she remained hostile to the *Encyclopédistes* as a group. In 1754, now losing her sight, she employed JULIE DE LESPINASSE as a companion but ten years later dismissed her, jealous of her evident attractiveness, and her salon lost many of its leading members in the ensuing quarrel within the literary world.

Du Deffand then became close friends with the Duchesse de Choiseul and in 1766 she met Horace Walpole, to whom she became deeply attached, although he was 20 years her junior. When she died she left him her papers, and these, with her letters to Walpole and Voltaire, were edited in 1810 by MARY BERRY. Her letters reveal her independent, witty, cultured personality and provide a vivid account of contemporary society.

**Dudinskaya, Natalya (Mikhailovna)** (1912–). Russian ballerina. Born in Kharkov, she studied dance first with her mother Natalia Tagliori and from 1923 to 1931 at the Leningrad School of Choreography, where she was taught by AGRIPPINA VAGANOVA. In 1930 she entered the Kirov Ballet, dancing solo parts from her first season. Her repertoire included classic roles, especially Odette/Odile, Aurora, Raimonda, Giselle, and *Les Sylphides*. She has also created many new roles, including Krein's *Laurencia* (1936), Sergeyev's version of Prokofiev's *Cinderella* (1946), Paragna in Zakharov's production of Glière's *Bronze Horseman* (1949), Sarie in *Path of Thunder* (1957) and Titania in *A Midsummer Night's Dream*. In 1964 she appeared as Carabosse in Sergeyev's film of *The Sleeping Beauty*. She began her partnership with Sergeyev, whom she later married, during World War II and their association became regarded as one of the most outstanding in modern ballet.

In 1961 Dudinskaya retired from regular dancing to concentrate on her work at the Kirov Ballet School where she taught between 1951 and 1970. Since then she has taught at the Vaganova School and has been involved in choreographic work with Sergeyev, including *Hamlet* (1970), *Le Corsair* (1973), and *Beethoven's Appassionata* (1977). She has been awarded the honour of People's Artist of the USSR, as well as many other Soviet honours.

**Dugdale, Henrietta** (1826–1918). Australian feminist. Born in London, she emigrated to Australia with her first husband, Davies, and after his death married a clergyman, William Dugdale. Leader of the women's rights movement in Victoria, she was President of the first Women's Suffrage Society there in 1884. A radical, free-thinker and talented polemical writer, she campaigned for social and economic equality and educational opportunities, as well as on specific women's issues such as birth control, dress reform, sexual violence and hypocrisy. In her booklet, *A few Hours in a far-off Age* (1883) she attacked 'the greatest obstacle to human advancement, the most irrational, fiercest and powerful of the world's monsters – the only devil – male ignorance!'

**Dulac, Germaine** (1882–1942). French journalist and film-maker. After studying journalism she became a theatre critic and playwright. She made her first film, *Les soeurs ennemies*, in 1915, and consciously adopted the avant-garde influence in 1923 with *La souriante Madame Beudet*. She subsequently experimented with Impressionism, Dadaism and Surrealism. *La coquille et le clergyman/The Seashell and the Clergyman* (1927), written by Antonin Artaud (who denounced the film), was described as the first Surrealist film. It also provoked the famous comment from the British censor, 'If there is a meaning it is doubtless objectionable'. Her later films are 'musical accompaniments', to pieces by Chopin and Debussy. From 1929 she turned to making newsreels, for Pathé, Gaumont and Le Cinéma au Service de l'Histoire. As well as producing critical and historical writings on cinema, she was involved in the running of *Ciné Club*, a magazine created in 1921 by Louis Delluc and devoted to 'pure cinema' (a good description of her own work), emphasizing trick photography and Surrealist distortions of time and space.

**du Maurier, Daphne** (1907–). British writer. Daughter of the actor-manager Sir Gerald du Maurier, and grand-daughter of George du Maurier (author of *Trilby*), Daphne was educated at home with her two sisters and in Paris. She started writing as a girl and her first novel, the Cornish family saga *The Loving Spirit*, was published in 1931. The following year she married Lieutenant-General Sir Frederick Browning, and continued to write, publishing studies of her father and her family in the 1930s, as well as the best-selling novels *Jamaica Inn* (1936) and *Rebecca* (1938) (which was dramatized and later filmed). *Frenchman's Creek* (1942), *The King's General* (1946) and *My Cousin Rachel* (1952) confirmed her popularity and she has continued to write romantic, gothic and historical fiction. Since the 1970s she has concentrated on the short story, and has also written on the Elizabethan writer Sir Francis Bacon (1975, 1977) and published an autobiography and memoirs. She has lived for most of her life in Cornwall, where many of her novels are set.

D. du Maurier: *Growing Pains: The Shaping of a Writer* (1977)
———— : *The Rebecca Notebook and other Stories* (1981)

**Dumée, Jeanne** (*fl* 1680). French astronomer. Jeanne was born in Paris and was widowed at the age of 17. The manuscript of her book defending the theories of Copernicus, *Entretiens sur l'opinion de Copernic touchant la mobilité de la terre*, is in the Bibliothèque Nationale in Paris. She includes an apologia for writing it, challenging the long-held view that the brain power of women is inferior, owing to their smaller and lighter brains.

**Dumesnil, Marie-Françoise** (1713–1803). French actress. Born into a poor Parisian family, she joined the Comédie-Française in 1737 and became one of the principal interpreters of Voltaire's plays; she played in *Zulime* in 1740, in *Mérope* in 1743, in *Semiramis* in 1748, and was Clytemnestra in *Oreste* in 1750. She was remarkable for her passionate acting manner and, firmly resisting any move towards historical accuracy, always appeared in rich costumes of contemporary design and laden with jewels. She retired in 1775, and at the end of her life published a book of memoirs, which mainly refute, in a calm, dignified style, numerous injurious references made to her in Mademoiselle CLAIRON's *Mémoires*. Dumesnil and Clairon represented opposing sides of the argument about nature and art in acting, and a famous formal debate took place between them in 1787 at the Boule-Rouge.

M. F. Dumesnil: *Mémoires* (1823)

**Dunbar, Agnes,** Countess of ['Black Agnes'] (*c*1312–69). Scottish heroine. She was the grand-daughter of the Scots king, Robert Bruce, and daughter of the Earl of Moray. She married Patrick Dunbar, who was initially a supporter of the English king, Edward II, but later a keen ally of his cousins, Robert I and David II (apart from a brief change of sides in 1333–4). In 1337 he was campaigning against the English invaders, and left Agnes to defend the besieged castle of Dunbar, one of the few fortresses still remaining in Scottish hands. She directed the defence, jeered at the attackers from the battlements, and endured the extra hardships incurred by a blockade of the harbour for six months, until the English finally abandoned the siege. She became famous for her courage and her bravado. In later years the Dunbars acquired huge estates through inheritance, and their children (including a daughter Agnes, mistress of David II) continued the family's influence in the kingdom.

**Duncan, Isadora** (?1879–1927). American dancer. She was born into a large and very close Scottish-Irish family in San Francisco and brought up by her mother. In 1890 she danced at Augustin Duncan's San Francisco Barn Theatre. After four years of dancing lessons she left for Chicago, where she danced in a roof garden, and was engaged by Daly to appear in *A Midsummer Night's Dream* in New York. In 1899 she travelled to London, gave private recitals, and acquired a growing interest in classical art. Over the next two years she gave private concerts in Paris and Munich, where she met LOIE FULLER, and in 1903 gave a successful public performance in Budapest. In 1904 the Duncan family visited Berlin and then Athens, where they were inspired to build a modern arts commune in Mycenaean style, a rather expensive and brief experiment.

The following year she went on tour and

danced in Vienna, Berlin and St Petersburg. In Russia she met Dyagilev, Bakst, Benois and Stanislavsky. On her return she established a school in Grünewald with her sister Elizabeth, and met Gordon Craig. Her activity was slowed but not halted by the birth of her first child in 1906. She toured Russia, London and New York in 1907, revelling in popular and critical acclaim. On her return to Paris in 1909 she met the millionaire Paris Singer. Her continuing success was broken by the tragic accidental drowning of her two children in 1913.

In 1908 the Grünewald school moved to Paris, where it continued until 1919. During World War I Isadora continued to tour, visiting New York, California, and South America and always attempting to found further schools. In 1921 she was invited by the Soviet government to found a school in Moscow, and in 1922 she married the Russian poet, Sergey Essenin. He accompanied her to Europe and to the USA, where they attracted large audiences with Isadora's bold dancing and Sergey's 'Bolshevism'. He left her after their return to Russia in 1924, and committed suicide the following year.

Isadora out-faced convention in dance, attempting to replace classical form by free expression, developing new ideas of bodily movement, and of the relation of rhythm to gravity. She was equally unconforming in her private life. Although fat, depressed, and an alcoholic, she continued to sway audiences. She died in Nice in 1927 strangled by her silk scarf which was caught in the wheel of her car. A film of her life by Ken Russell, starring VANESSA REDGRAVE, appeared in 1971, and a ballet choreographed by Kenneth MacMillan was produced in 1981.

I. Duncan: *My Life* (1927)
F. Steegmuller: *Your Isadora* (1974)

**Duplessis, Marie.** *See* PLESSIS, ALPHONSINE.

**du Pré, Jacqueline** (1945–87). English cellist. After initial studies at the London Violoncello School, she attended the Guildhall School of Music, continuing her lessons with William Pleeth and later with Tortelier and Rostropovich. Her professional debut (at the Wigmore Hall, London in 1961) launched a career that soon established her international reputation. In 1967 she married the pianist Daniel Barenboim, with whom she gave many duo recitals and made many recordings. Her performances of concertos by Boccherini, Haydn, Dvořák, Schumann, Elgar and Delius were noted for their technical prowess and stylistic integrity. Alexander Goehr's *Romanze* for cello and orchestra was written for her, and she gave its first performance in 1968. Her performing career was interrupted in the early 1970s by the onset of multiple sclerosis, but she continued to give master classes, many of them televised. She was created an OBE in 1976.

**Durack, Fanny** (1894–1960). Australian swimmer. Born in Sydney, the daughter of a hotel keeper, Fanny became a member of the Ladies Amateur Swimming Association of New South Wales and an exponent of the new two-beat crawl. The Association's rules forbade women swimmers even to appear before men, but progressives managed to send Fanny and her rival Mina Wylie to the 1912 Olympic Games at Stockholm. The only swimming event open to women was the 100 metres freestyle in fresh water with no lanes nor turns. Fanny won this in world-record time. She set nine world records between 1912 and 1918, although further Olympic wins were denied by the wartime cancellation of the 1916 Games. Her two daily training sessions of 800 metres each helped her to set standards which other women took years to emulate, but years later when she met DAWN FRASER she was amazed at the intense level to which training had developed.

**Durand, Marguerite** (1864–1936). French feminist, actress and journalist. Born in Paris, she became an actress at the Comédie Française in 1881 and took several leading roles. She ended her acting career in 1888 to marry the journalist Georges Laguerre and worked with him on *La Presse*; they were later divorced. An extremely wealthy woman, she founded the first women's daily paper in the world, *La Fronde*, a social feminist paper directed largely towards working women which ran from 1897 until 1903, then monthly until 1905 and she then founded *L'Action*. She organized international congresses in 1900 and campaigned for temperance and social purity, better working conditions and legal rights as well as for suffrage. From 1908 until 1914 she was a co-director of Jacques Stern's *Les nouvelles*, a Parisian evening newspaper. She alienated many feminists by her patronizing manner. She was a candidate for the National Assembly in 1910, and led a flamboyant campaign accompanied by a tame lion called Tigre. During World War I she founded a women's driving organization for transporting the wounded. In 1922 she organized an exhibition of famous nineteenth-century women in Paris and in 1931 she donated to the city her unique collection of feminist archives [now known as the Bibliothèque Marguerite Durand].

**Duras, Marguerite** [pseud. of Marguerite Donnadieu] (1914–). French writer and filmmaker. She was born in Indochina, but left Saigon for Paris at the age of 17. She studied law and worked briefly as a civil servant before becoming a full-time writer. In 1942 she married Dionys Mascolo, the political philosopher and commentator; they have one son. Her first major novel, *Un barrage contre le Pacifique* (1950), reflects her opposition to colonialism, her attentiveness to socially-marginal and alienated individuals and her feeling for atmosphere. Subsequent novels (which include *Les petits chevaux de Tarquinia* (1953), *Le square* (1955), *Le ravissement de Lol V. Stein* (1964) and *Le vice-consul* (1966)) focus intensely on individuals, usually women, who are fascinated by a person or an incident which triggers a heightened awareness of themselves. *Moderato cantabile* (1960) was filmed by Peter Brook. Her semi-autobiographical novel *L'Amant* (1984) won the Prix Goncourt. More autobiographical material forms the basis for the stories in *La Douleur* (1986). In 1959 she wrote the screenplay for *Hiroshima mon amour*, a film by Alain Resnais which was widely acclaimed.

In the 1960s Duras turned towards the theatre, and in 1966 began directing films, but she has never ceased to write fiction; her creativity in all three fields draws on similar themes and she has frequently adapted her works from one medium to another. Plays by Duras include *La musica* (1966), *Des journées entières dans les arbres* (1965), *L'amante anglaise* (1967) and *L'Eden cinéma* (1977). The 11 films she has made

since 1969 have earned her an international reputation as an experimental film-maker. The films, which include *Détruire dit-elle/Destroy She Said* (1969), *Nathalie Granger* (1973), *India Song* (1975), *Le camion* (1977) and *Agatha* (1981), are made on fairly low budgets, outside the institutionalized cinema industry, and are remarkable for their narrative techniques, which often involve tension between images and soundtrack. *Les parleuses* (1974), a collection of interviews with the feminist critic Xavière Gauthier, reflects the considerable enthusiasm Duras's work has generated in some quarters of the women's movement. Although she is reluctant to be labelled a feminist writer, and stresses the broader existential and political ramifications of her work, Duras shares the convictions of contemporary feminism and has always placed women at the centre of her work.

M. Duras: *Marguerite Duras* (1987)

**Durocher, Marie (Josefina Mathilde)** (1809–93). French-Brazilian obstetrician. Born in Paris, she moved with her family to Brazil when she was eight. She married, was widowed young, and left with two children to support. At the age of 24 she began the obstetrics course at the newly-organized Medical School in Rio de Janiero, and in 1834 received the first diploma to be granted, and became one of the first women doctors in Latin America. Her professional life was influenced by the teaching of MARIE BOIVIN. She wore men's clothes, and practised for 60 years. In 1871 she was elected to titular membership of the National Academy of Medicine.

**Duse, Eleanora** (1858–1924). Italian tragedienne. Descended from two generations of travelling players, Duse went on stage at the age of four. Her first big success was in *Les Fourchambaults* (1878) and she achieved international fame when she toured as Erneste Rossi's leading lady in 1879. In 1881 she visited Russia, and in 1885 went to Latin America. She then founded her own highly successful company with Rossi. Her famous rivalry with SARAH BERNHARDT came to a head when both actresses played Magda in *Heimat* by Suderman in London in 1895.

Although married to actor Tebaldo Cecchi, by whom she had a daughter in 1882, Duse was credited with several lovers including D'Annunzio, whose poetic drama she promoted, bringing him fame with *La Gioconda* (1898), and *Francesca da Rimini* (1902). A statuesque, highly expressive actress, she excelled in modern tragedies, particularly Ibsen's *Hedda Gabler*, *The Doll's House*, *Rosmersholm* and *Lady from the Sea*, as well as classical roles. Her admirers included Shaw and Chekov (she is suggested as the model for *The Seagull*). She retired in 1914, but returned to the stage in 1921, making a final tour of the USA in 1923. She died in Pittsburgh, but was buried with great honour in Italy.

W. Weaver: *Duse* (1984)

**du Sousa** [née Soares], **Noemia (Carolina Abranches)** [pseud. Vera Micaia] (1927–). Mozambique poet. Born in Lourenço Marques, she wrote for national and Portuguese journals from 1951 to 1964, and also published in Brazilian and Angolan reviews. She married a Portuguese in Lisbon, but since her work was associated with the new militant Portuguese-African literature she was eventually forced into exile, and went to France, where she wrote under the name of Vera Micaia. Her poetry, which has gained her a wide international reputation, is strongly influenced by Black American and Caribbean writing, and the free-flowing rhythms echo those of negro spirituals and jazz blues.

# E

**Eadburgh** [Eadburga] (*fl* 800). Queen of the West Saxons. Daughter of Offa II, King of Mercia, she is first mentioned in records of the family in 787; she married Beorhtric, King of Wessex, in 789. She achieved great influence, engaged in ruthless court intrigues, and in 802 accidentally killed her husband, who drank the poison she had prepared for one of his favourites. She so alienated the people that future kings' wives were denied the title of queen and referred to simply as 'the Lady'. She fled with a large fortune to the court of Charlemagne, where she became a powerful abbess until she was expelled for her scandalous behaviour. For the rest of her life she lived in poverty and died, apparently a beggar, in Italy.

**Eady, Dorothy** (1904–81). English Egyptologist. She was born in London, and following a fall at the age of three she dreamed of a temple; after a visit to the British Museum a year later she insisted that the temple at Abydos was her true home. At the age of 29 she visited Egypt, married an Egyptian, and began working on the hieroglyphics at the Temple of Isis. She finally settled in Egypt in 1956, and remained the Keeper of the Temple, believing herself a re-incarnated minor priestess. She was a revered figure locally and an internationally-recognized expert on hieroglyphics.

**Earhart, Amelia** (1898–1937). American aviator. The daughter of a lawyer in Atchison, Kansas, she began her working life nursing casualties of World War I in Toronto, then went to medical school at Columbia University. Meanwhile, however, she had a trial flight at the California Air Show, and determined to become a pilot, taking lessons from the woman flyer Neta Snook.

In 1927 Lindbergh had made the first transatlantic flight; Amelia Earhart achieved instant fame in 1928 as the first woman to cross the Atlantic, this time as a passenger and log-keeper. She lectured and wrote, as well as flew, aiming to promote the aircraft industry and give women economic opportunities and independence; her husband, the publisher George Putnam, supported this but largely as a business partnership. On 20 May 1932 Amelia flew the small single-engine Lockheed Vega solo across the Atlantic in bad weather, carrying only a thermos of hot soup through the 15-hour flight.

Subsequent records included the first non-stop flight from Mexico City to Newark, New Jersey, and the first from Hawaii to California. She founded an American women's flying group, the Ninety-Nines, became an officer of the Luddington Line (the first airline to provide a regular passenger service between New York and Washington, DC), and was appointed at Purdue University to advise women students on careers.

In 1937 she set off in a Lockheed Electra on a round-the-world flight with navigator Fred Noonan. She documented the effects of prolonged flight on the human body and made mechanical tests on the aircraft. The journey was relatively uneventful until on the last stage of the flight the plane disappeared near Howland Island in the Pacific without trace. In a letter to her husband which he received only after her death, she wrote: 'Women must try to do things as men have tried. When they fail, their failure must be but a challenge to others.'

B. Davis: *Amelia Earhart* (1977)

**Eastman, Crystal** (1881–1928). American feminist and pacifist. Born in Marlborough, Massachusetts, Crystal was the third of four children. Her parents were both congregational ministers and her mother, Alice, a preacher and women's rights campaigner, was a dominant influence on her later feminism. Crystal gave her first paper on 'Woman' at the age of 15. She graduated from Vassar in 1903 and took a master's degree in sociology from Columbia in 1904. She then went on to study law and after her LLB (1907) and bar examinations she joined the Russell Sage Foundation, working on the 'Pittsburgh survey', examining over 1000 industrial accidents. She argued for changes in the law of compensation in *Work, Accidents and the Law* (1910), an aim achieved when she was secretary (and only woman member) of the New York State Employer's Liability Commission (1909–11).

After her marriage in 1911 to insurance agent Walter Benedict she moved to Milwaukee, where she joined the Political Equality League, fighting for women's suffrage. In 1913, with ALICE PAUL and others, she founded the Congressional Union for Woman Suffrage (later the National Woman's Party), and attended the first International Woman Suffrage Alliance conference in Budapest. Pressing for total equality of opportunities in education, employment and status, and economic independence, she opposed protective legislation for women, and argued against alimony. After her own divorce in 1916 she married Walter Fuller. The couple were active pacifists: Crystal chaired the Women's Peace Party in New York State, was executive director of the American Union against Militarism, and after 1917 helped conscientious objectors through the Civil Liberties Bureau and managed her brother Max's paper the *Liberator*. In 1919 she helped organize the first Feminist Congress in New York.

In 1921 the family moved to England, where Walter worked for the BBC and Crystal became involved in British women's campaigns, and contributed regularly to LADY RHONDDA's *Time and Tide*. From 1922 to 1927 she and her two children travelled between Britain and the USA, but soon after she returned to America, alone, in 1927, Walter died. She herself was already ill, and died the following year from nephritis, aged only 46. Tall, athletic, impulsive and determined, Crystal Eastman was one of the most charismatic and influential women of her generation.

**Eberhardt, Isabelle** (1877–1904). Russian traveller. Isabelle Eberhardt was born near Geneva: her mother, Nathalie de Moender had left her husband, a general at the court of Tsar Alexander II, and had fled to Switzerland with the children's tutor, Alexander Trophimowsky, an anarchist and friend of Bakunin. Trophimowsky brought up the illegitimate Isabelle as a boy and by the time she was 16 she spoke six languages, including Arabic. In late adolescence she was severely ill, probably anorexic, and often suicidal and began a lifelong dependence on narcotics and alcohol. In 1897 she went with her mother to Bone in West Africa, where they both converted to Islam: her mother died there. Isabelle wrote articles, which were published in Paris journals under a pseudonym, and developed a secret passion for all things Islamic. Fired by the romance of the desert, she began her forays into the Algerian Sahara disguised as an Arab student, returning with stories of drug-taking and sexual orgies. Although her bohemian life-style shocked the French settlers she was respected by the sheiks, yet despite her Arab sympathies she supported French rule in North Africa and worked as an agent of the Deuxième Bureau. In 1901 her notoriety increased when an attempt was made to assassinate her, followed by a famous trial. This led to her expulsion from Algeria but she was allowed to return after her marriage to Slimène Ehnni, a young arab sergeant. Their life for the next two years was one of poverty and harassment. In 1903 she was sent by an Algerian newspaper to report on General Lyautey's campaign in Morocco, and stayed for a time in a Moroccan monastery before returning to the military base at Ain Sefra, where she lay ill in hospital until she discharged herself: one day later she was drowned, in a flash flood, at the age of 27. After her death her writings were collected into five books: *Dans l'ombre chaude de l'Islam* (1906), *Notes de Route* (1908), *Pages d'Islam* (1920), *Cartes et Paysages* (1923) and *Au Pays de Sables* (1944). Her novel *Trimadeur* was translated by Annette Kobak as *Vagabond* (1988).

I. Eberhardt: *The Passionate Nomad: The Diary of Isabelle Eberhardt* (1987)
A. Kobak: *Isabelle* (1988)

**Ebner-Eschenbach, Marie** [Countess Dubsky] (1830–1916). Austrian writer. Born at Adislawitz Castle, Moravia, she grew up there and in Vienna, before marrying her cousin, an army officer and amateur scientist, in 1848. They moved to Vienna in 1863. As a girl she wrote lyric poetry, then experimented unsuccessfully with drama – *Maria Stuart in Schottland* (1860); *Marie Roland* (1867); *Das Waldfräulein* (1873) – before finding her metier in the novella form. Her stories are about peasant, bourgeois and aristocratic life, combining conservative views with sympathy for the poor. Among the best is *Das Gemeindekind* (1887), about a murderer's son's struggle to respectability. She was also famous for her pungent epigrams, published as *Aphorismen* (1880). Much honoured in her day, she was the first woman to be awarded an honorary doctorate by the University of Vienna in 1900. Her later works were autobiographical: *Meine Kinderjahre* (1906), and *Meine Erinnerungen an Grillparzer* (1916).
E.M. O'Connor: *Marie Ebner* (1928)

**Eddy, Mary (Morse) Baker** (1821–1910). American founder of Christian Science. Born into an old New England family, Mary was brought up a Congregationalist. Her first husband, George, died before the birth of her only son, and her second marriage, to a dentist, David Patterson, ended in divorce.

Personal unhappiness was exacerbated by constant pain from spinal illness. She received some help from P.J. Quimby, a mesmerist, but after his death the illness returned and a fall on ice in 1866 made her case seem hopeless. She turned to the New Testament and was suddenly healed; this she saw as the discovery of Christian Science, an idealist philosophy with a practical healing element.

After several lonely years in rented rooms, lecturing and writing, she published *Science and Health* (1875). Regarded by her followers as divinely inspired, in its revised form it formed, with the Bible, the scripture of the new faith. In 1876 she founded the Christian Science Association, the following year married Asa G. Eddy, one of her followers, and in 1879 the First Church of Christ Scientist was established. The movement grew rapidly, building churches, developing teaching programmes and publishing. The Church is governed by Mary's binding directives collected in *The Church Manual*. She also started three journals, and her other writings included *Retrospection and Introspection* (1892), *Unity of Good* (1908) and *Rudimental Divine Science* (1908).
R. Peel: *Mary Baker Eddy* (3 vols, 1971–7)

**Ederle, Gertrude (Caroline)** (1906–). American swimmer. She was one of swimming's early prodigies, and when at 12 she broke the 880 yards freestyle record with a time of 13 minutes 19 seconds, she also set a record for the youngest age at which any person had broken a non-mechanical world record.

She was a member of the New York Women's Swimming Association, which introduced the six-beat instead of the four-beat crawl in 1918, and set many world records in women's freestyle swimming. In the 1924 Olympic Games she won a gold and two bronze medals in the five racing events open to women. Her particular fame, however, comes from her swim across the English Channel, from Cap Gris-Nez in France to Dover, on 6 August 1926. She was the first woman to swim the Channel, and her time of 14 hours 39 minutes was then an overall record. She later became a swimming instructor and adviser on fashion.

**Edgeworth, Maria** (1767–1849). Anglo-Irish novelist. Born in Oxfordshire, the second of 21 children, after her father's second marriage in 1773 she accompanied him to Ireland, but was educated in Derby (1775–80) and in London (1780–82). As a child she suffered from poor health and from 'mechanical' efforts to increase her height. A good scholar, from 1782 she began supervising the education of 18 step-brothers and -sisters, helping with the business of the family estate, composing stories and also translating STEPHANIE DE GENLIS' *Adèle et Théodore*.

In 1793, provoked by criticism of her translating activities, she defended women's right to education in *Letters to Literary Ladies*, and in 1796 won popular success with the first part of *The Parent's Assistant* (six parts, 1800). In 1798 she published *Practical Education* with her father, modifying Rousseau's principles, which she also illustrated by the stories in *Early Lessons* and *Moral Tales* (1801). In 1800 she began writing adult novels, starting with *Castle Rackrent*, a novel of Irish life, published anonymously, and the only book not corrected by her father. *Belinda* followed, before her visit to France in 1802, during which she had an inconclusive romance with a Swedish officer, Edelkrantz, refusing his proposal out of family duty. She continued to write, producing several novels and earning substantial sums, especially from *Tales of Fashionable Life* (six volumes, 1809–12). Although overshadowed by her father on all trips outside the family home, she was overwhelmed by his death in 1817, and published his *Memoirs* in 1820.

Between 1819 and 1821 Maria visited London, Paris and Geneva but subsequently spent the rest of her life at Edgeworthston where she acted as estate manager from 1826. She continued to write – although at a *slower pace – short stories, novels such as Helena* (1834), and plays for children. At the age of 80 during the Irish Famine of 1846, she organized desperate relief measures for the local community.

M.S. Butler: *Edgeworth: a Literary Biography* (1972)

**Edwards, Sarah (Emma Evelyn)** (1841–98). American soldier. She grew up in New Brunswick, Canada, and was apparently greatly impressed in her youth by a novel called *Fanny Campbell, or the Female Pirate Captain* by M. Ballen, which first appeared in 1844. At 15 she left home, disguised as a boy, apparently to escape an unwelcome marriage and after working as a Bible salesman enlisted in the Union army as 'Franklin Thompson' at the outbreak of the Civil War. After two years, illness forced her to leave but her identity was never discovered. She published *Nurse and Spy in the Union Army* in 1865. It was widely publicized and very popular, with a best-selling combination of violence, sentimentality and religious moralizing.

In 1867 Sarah married Linus Seelye, a carpenter from New Brunswick, and after the deaths of their three children they adopted two boys. In old age, fearing poverty, she confessed her story, which was corroborated by other veterans, and in 1884 she was granted a government pension.

S.G.L. Dammett: *She rode with the Generals* (1960)

**Eisner, Lotte** (1896–1983). German film critic. Born into a cultured Jewish family in Berlin, Lotte studied art history and archaeology, obtaining a DPhil at Rostock in 1924. After a successful career as a literary journalist and art critic, she joined the daily *Film Kurier* in 1927, becoming Germany's first woman film critic, writing articles on the major Expressionist film makers. In 1933 she left Germany for Paris, working with Henri Langlois at his Cinémathèque Française and continued during the war under an assumed name, concealing banned pre-war films from the German authorities. From 1945 until the early 1970s she was curator of the Cinémathèque Française. One of the most famous of European critics, her major works were the classic study of German cinema *L'Ecran démoniaque* (1952), and her books on Murnau (1964) and Fritz Lang (1977).

**Eleanor of Aquitaine** (1122–1202). Duchess of Aquitaine, Queen of France and England. One of the most powerful women of her day, Eleanor inherited the vast Duchy of Aquitaine and Poitiers from her father William X when she was 15, and at once married Louis VII and became Queen of France. In their 15 years of marriage, during which she had two daughters, she influenced many state decisions and from 1147–9 accompanied Louis on the second crusade taking a company of 300 women, both to fight and to tend the wounded. Her closeness to her uncle Raymond of Antioch aroused Louis' jealousy during the campaign and although they were briefly reconciled, their marriage was finally annulled in 1152.

Overwhelmed by suitors, she married Henry of Normandy two months after the annulment; he became King of England in 1154. As queen for 50 years, she bore him 8 children and was engaged in constant political intrigues. In 1173 she supported her sons, Richard and John, against her husband, was captured attempting to return to Aquitaine and imprisoned for fifteen years until Henry's death in 1189. On her release she made a triumphal progress, granting amnesty to prisoners and ensuring the country's loyalty to her son, Richard the Lion Heart. She ruled as Regent during his absence on the crusades and personally arranged his ransom and release when he was imprisoned. After his death she ensured the succession of her other son, John. Although nearly 80, she protected Plantagenet interests, arranged and supervised the marriage of her grand-daughter BLANCHE OF CASTILE, to the future Louis VIII of France, and defended Anjou, Aquitaine and Mirabeau against the forces of Arthur of Brittany. After this last campaign in 1021, she retired to the Abbey of Fontrevault, where she died.

Eleanor was as influential in cultural as in political life, and established a brilliant court in her city of Poitiers, where she acted as patron to the troubadours and to the authors of the Breton romance cycles. She gathered together the finest poets, musicians and scholars and founded educational and religious establishments in both France and England. The marriages of five of her daughters created alliances with several ruling houses, so that, like Queen VICTORIA centuries later, she earned the title 'Grandmother of Europe', while her other daughter, Marie de Champagne, continued her mother's patronage of art and courtly love and literature in France.

A. Kelly: *Eleanor of Aquitaine and the Four Kings* (1950)
M. Meade: *Eleanor of Aquitaine* (1978)

**Eliot, George** [pseud. of Mary Anne Evans] (1819–80). English novelist. Born in Warwickshire, where her father was agent to a large landowner, she spent five years at local boarding schools and from 1832 to 1835 went to school at Coventry. She showed early intellectual prowess, was a talented musician and, at this stage, deeply religious. After her mother's death in 1836 she took charge of the household, and became involved in local charities. She moved with her father to Coventry (1841–9), where she met the free-thinker Charles Bray and his wife Caroline and sister-in-law Sarah Hennell. Resulting religious doubts led to a rift with her father. From 1843 to 1846 she worked on the translation of Strauss's *Life of Jesus* and then began translating Spinoza's

*Tractatus theologico-politicus*. After her father's death in 1849 she spent several months in Geneva before moving in with the Brays at Rosehill.

In 1850 she began contributing to *The Westminster Review*, and in September 1851 moved to London, acting as Assistant Editor until 1854, when her translation of Feuerbach's *Essence of Christianity* appeared. Her interest in Positivism led her into an acquaintance with Herbert Spencer and with George Henry Lewes, with whom she lived from 1854. Their position was difficult since Lewes's wife refused to divorce him and they also had the financial burden of his family. In 1856, with Lewes's encouragement, she started writing fiction, beginning with 'Amos Barton' (1857), which was collected with 'Mr Gilfil's Love Story' and 'Janet's Repentance' in *Scenes from Clerical Life* (1858). Critical success was followed by popular acclaim after the publication of *Adam Bede* (1859), *Mill on the Floss* (1860) and *Silas Marner* (1861), and the historical *Romola* (1862–3) which is allegedly based on the character of BARBARA BODICHON.

In 1863 she moved with Lewes to The Priory, Regent's Park, and her Sunday receptions there are described in many memoirs of the time. The novels of her second period include *Felix Holt* (1866), the great portrayal of provincial life in *Middlemarch* (1871) and *Daniel Deronda* (1876), in which her sensitivity to the gap between aspirations and achievements is linked to an interest in Jewish idealism. She also wrote poetry: *How Lisa loved the King* (1867), the dramatic *Spanish Gipsy* (1860), *Armgart* (1870) and *The Legend of Jubal* (1870); her final work was the satire *Impressions of Theophrastus Such* (1879). The royalties from her books relieved financial pressure, and she and Lewes were able to travel on the Continent until his sudden death in 1878. In 1880 she married an old friend, John Cross, but died in December of the same year.

G. Haight: *Eliot: a Biography* (1968)

**Elisabeth of Romania** [pseud.: Carmen Sylva] (1843–1916). Queen of Romania and writer. A German aristocrat, her childhood was overshadowed by family illnesses, but she was educated at home and travelled to Russia and England. In 1869 she married Prince Charles of Hohenzollern-Sigmaringen, who was established as Prince and (in 1881, after the Russo-Turkish War) as King of Romania. Elisabeth became deeply involved with her new country, particularly as a consolation after the death of her adored four-year-old daughter Marie in 1874, learning the language, establishing schools and other institutions, translating school books, and nursing the war-wounded.

She also began writing, publishing translations and original poems in the 1880s, continuing with short stories, novels, aphorisms collected in *Pensées d'une reine* (1888) and popular fairy stories such as the *Fairy Tales of Pilesh*, which sold over a million copies. She died in Bucharest during World War I.

**Elizabeth,** Queen Mother (1900–). British Queen. The ninth of ten children, Elizabeth Angela Marguerite Bowes-Lyon was born at St Paul's Waldenbury, Hitchin, Hertfordshire. Her aristocratic Scottish family, descended from Robert the Bruce, owned a castle at Glamis, Scotland, where she spent most of her childhood. She was educated at home by her mother and governesses, and helped to care for patients when Glamis became a hospital during World War I.

In 1920 she met Prince Albert ('Bertie') Duke of York, and after an initial refusal in 1921 agreed to marry him two years later. They were married in 1924, and their two daughters, Elizabeth and Margaret, were born in 1926 and 1930. The Yorks went on international tours, for example to East Africa and Australia, but they cherished their quiet domestic life until the abdication in 1938 of Edward VIII (for which Elizabeth never forgave WALLIS, DUCHESS OF WINDSOR), which meant that the Duke became King, taking the formal name George VI. She became a much-loved public figure, refusing to leave London during the Blitz and visiting the bombed-out areas of the city; when Buckingham Palace was hit she said 'I'm glad we've been bombed. I can now look the East End in the face.' Her popularity has continued to grow since the King's death and the accession of ELIZABETH II in 1953, when she was given the title 'Queen Mother'. She has continued to make innumerable public appearances and international tours, notably to Canada, well into her eighties. In 1979 she became the 160th Warden of the Cinque Ports, the first woman to hold this position for 900 years.

**Elizabeth I** (1533–1603). Queen of England and Ireland from 1558 to 1603. Elizabeth was born at Greenwich, the daughter of Henry VIII and ANNE BOLEYN, whom he had secretly married after the divorce from CATHARINE OF ARAGON. Anne was executed in 1536 and Elizabeth declared illegitimate. Although her place in the succession, after her younger half-brother Edward and her older half-sister MARY I, was restored by Parliament in 1544, her childhood was clouded by political intrigue. In 1554 during the Catholic Mary's reign, she was imprisoned after Sir Thomas Wyatt's plot, because she formed a rallying point for the Protestant opposition. She did, however, receive an excellent education, her tutors including Roger Ascham and other famous scholars, and she was encouraged by her learned step-mother, CATHERINE PARR, to learn French, Italian, Greek and Latin as well as mathematics and science. Her own court was later a great centre of learning.

In 1558 she succeeded to the throne, and her first task was the appeasement of the Catholic population, through a tolerant religious settlement, the Acts of Unity and Supremacy of 1559, which lasted until 1570 when she was excommunicated by Pope Pius V after the vicious suppression of a rebellion in the North of England. Thereafter the penal laws grew harder, especially after the arrival of Jesuit missionaries in 1580. At her succession, England was threatened with an impoverished economy and her government instituted currency reforms, employment laws (Statute of Artificers, 1563) and measures for poor relief (1563–1601), which may have hastened the end of the close medieval community, but allowed capitalist agriculture and commerce to expand.

Elizabeth's foreign policy was complicated and delicate, and many diplomatic moves revolved around the possibility of her marriage. In 1559 she ended Mary's war with France, and refused the offer of marriage of Philip II of Spain. For the next 30 years she kept an uneasy peace with both countries, while supporting the Huguenots in France and the campaign of the Duc d'Alençon (another suitor) against Spain in the Netherlands. She supported the Protestants in Scotland, and after MARY, QUEEN OF SCOTS was forced to abdicate in 1568 gave her 'refuge' in England for 19 years, despite innumerable plots. Finally, however, with such deep reluctance that she suffered a hysterical breakdown, she allowed Mary to be executed after the Babington plot in 1587.

This execution heightened the determination of Philip of Spain to take the English throne. Infuriated by the Cadiz raid, by the lengthy pillaging of Drake and others and by Elizabeth's Dutch policy, he launched the Armada to bring the Spanish army from the Low Countries to invade England in 1588. The fleet was defeated off the west coast, but in the meantime Elizabeth had collected an army at Tilbury to resist the invasion. Her moving speech there is justifiably famous: after promising to live or die with them, she offers 'to lay down for my God, and for my Kingdom, and for my people, my honour and my blood, even in the dust. I know I have the body of a weak and feeble woman, but I have the heart and stomach of a King, and a King of England too.' The threat was removed, but a lingering war dragged on until her death. Her last great problem was Ireland, which was always the scene of rebellion, the final great uprising of her reign being that of Hugh O'Neill, Earl of Tyrone, in 1598, which was suppressed between 1600 and 1603. In the course of this Robert Devereux, Earl of Essex, the Queen's favourite, furious at the cold response to the failure of his own expedition, rose against the Queen and was executed in 1601.

Essex had come to be favourite after the death of Robert Dudley, Earl of Leicester, Elizabeth's friend from childhood and possibly the only man she ever loved. Arguments over her status as virgin queen see her refusal to marry as a political move, as the result of childhood traumas, or the only way to maintain power as a woman. After Dudley's wife Amy Robsart died in 1560 in mysterious circumstances, marriage may have seemed unwise, although in 1569 Parliament begged her to marry whosoever she wished.

Her rule lasted 45 years, and she outlived most of her loyal friends and counsellors, such as William Cecil, and Sir Francis Walsingham. She not only saw the rise of England as a secure European power and commercial force, but also, in projecting a charismatic royal image, encouraged the ebullient nationalism which is evident in the flourishing culture of her time.

C. Erickson: *The First Elizabeth* (1984)

**Elizabeth II** (1926–). Queen of the United Kingdom of Great Britain and Northern Ireland. The first child of the future King George VI, then known as Prince Albert, Duke of York, she was christened Elizabeth Alexandra Mary. She was not considered as a likely heir to the throne, and she and her sister Margaret were educated privately, mostly by governesses and at a small school at Windsor Castle. She particularly enjoyed history, languages and music. In December 1936 her life was dramatically altered when Edward VIII abdicated in order to marry Wallis Simpson (see Duchess of WINDSOR), and her father became King. She was subjected to many more restrictions, but persuaded her parents to let her train as a driver in the Auxiliary Territorial Service in 1944 during World War II.

In 1947 she became engaged to Lieutenant Philip Mountbatten, a distant relative (formerly Prince Philip of Greece and now Duke of Edinburgh), and they were married in Westminster Abbey in November 1947. A year later her son Charles was born, then other children, Anne (1950; see ANNE, PRINCESS ROYAL), Andrew (1960) and Edward (1964). From 1951 Elizabeth represented her ailing father on state occasions abroad, and in 1952, in Kenya, she learnt of his death and her accession to the throne. She was crowned in June 1953. One of the most widely-travelled of contemporary monarchs, she has undertaken numerous tours in the Commonwealth and other parts of the world, and her 'walkabouts' have become a traditional part of such occasions. As Queen she is also Head of the Anglican Church and of the British Commonwealth. She takes a particular interest in Commonwealth Affairs, and intervened directly (an extremely unusual step) in the aftermath of the coup in Fiji in 1987.

R. Lacey: *Elizabeth II and the House of Windsor* (1977)

*George Eliot*

*Elizabeth I*

*Millicent Garrett Fawcett*

*Loie Fuller*

**Elizabeth of Hungary** (1207–31). Hungarian saint and princess. The daughter of King Andrew II of Hungary, Elizabeth married the Landgrave of Thuringia, Ludwig IV, when she was only 14 years old. Although this marriage had been arranged for political reasons, it was also a love match. Ludwig died while on crusade and Elizabeth was driven out of the court by her brother-in-law on the pretext that her charitable activities were exhausting the state finances. Having provided for her three children, she joined the third order of St Francis and devoted herself to the care of the poor and sick.

Elizabeth had put herself wholly under the direction of her confessor, Master Conrad of Marburg, a learned, able but harshly insensitive man. His treatment of her was ruthless, at times brutal, but although she admitted how much she feared him, he did not break her spirit. Until her health failed Elizabeth was tireless in serving the wants of those in need. She was canonized in 1235.

J. Ancelet-Hustache: *St Elizabeth of Hungary* (1964)

**Elizabeth of Portugal** [Isabella] (1271–1336). Portuguese queen. The daughter of Peter III of Aragon, she married King Dinis of Portugal when she was 13, but her strict and devout upbringing (she was named after her great-aunt ELIZABETH OF HUNGARY) made it difficult to fit into his decadent court. She helped the poor and sick, and founded hospitals and convents. Known as 'The Peacemaker', she reconciled her husband to their rebel son Alfonso. She settled other court disputes and died on her way to the battlefield, where she hoped to make peace between Alfonso, now king, and Alfonso of Castile. After Dinis died in 1325, she retired to the convent of Poor Clares she had founded at Coimbra. She was canonized in 1625.

**Elizabeth of Russia** [Yelizaveta Petrovna] (1709–62). Russian empress. The daughter of Peter I, she was intelligent, charming and vivacious. She was persuaded to stage a coup d'état in 1741 to depose the infant Ivan IV and his regent Empress Anna. She abolished the cabinet system of government and reinstated the more democratic Senate, but in fact left affairs of state to her advisers. She remained unmarried and was thus sole ruler

of Russia for 20 years. She devoted herself to making the court a centre of fashion which could compete with other European capitals, and promoted education, founding the University of Moscow and the Academy of Arts at St Petersburg [now Leningrad]. She also fostered economic growth through a system of banking, and encouraged the development of Eastern Russia, but her policies with regard to landowners led to some unrest. During her reign Russia's foreign policy was notably successful, in the war against Sweden (1741–3) and in the alliances with France and Austria against Prussia in the Seven Years War (1756–63), although these alliances were dissolved on the accession of her heir, Peter III.

T. Talbot Rice: *Elizabeth, Empress of Russia* (1976)

**El Saadawi, Nawal** (1930–). Egyptian feminist. Born in Cairo, she graduated from the university there in 1955, and later studied at Columbia University, New York, in 1966. A qualified physician, she worked on the staff of Cairo University Hospital, as a doctor in rural areas and then as a psychiatrist. Her psychosocial study *Women and Sex* (1972) caused enormous controversy when it was first published, since it openly discussed such issues as chastity and the taboos dominating women's position in Arab society, and called for revolutionary changes in the position of women within the family and as wage-earners. A Director in the Ministry of Health, and Editor of the government *Health* magazine, Nawal el Saadawi lost her post because of her outspoken views.

Her feminism found expression in her writing. She is the author of seven novels, four collections of short stories, and of five non-fiction books including *The Hidden Face of Eve: Women in the Arab World* (1979); all are concerned with women's struggle for equality in Arab society. In 1978 she wrote a novel, translated as *Woman at Point Zero*, about a woman condemned to death for killing a pimp and imprisoned in the notorious Qanatir Prison. In 1981, with several other women, she was arrested on the orders of President Sadat for publishing a feminist magazine, *Confrontation*. She herself was imprisoned in Qanatir. On her release in 1982 she founded a new Pan-Arab Women's Organization.

**Elssler, Fanny** [Franjziske] (1810–84). Austrian dancer. Her father was a copyist and valet to Haydn, and she grew up in a large, poor family, and began her dancing career as a child with her sister Thérèse. She left Austria aged 14 to dance in Italy and at 16 was pressured into a liaison with the Prince of Salerno. On her return to Vienna she came under the protection of the elderly publicist and intellectual Baron von Gentz, for whom she retained a lasting affection. She later had two children but deliberately remained unmarried in order to safeguard her independent career.

After dancing in London and Berlin (1830–4), Fanny and Thérèse were engaged at the Paris Opéra by Veron. Fanny made her debut in Coralli's *La Tempête* and from that time Veron capitalized on the contrasting styles and professional rivalry between her and MARIE TAGLIONI. She achieved fame in Coralli's *Le diable boiteux* (1836), Mazilier's *La gypsy* (1839), and Coralli's *La tarentule* (1840). In 1843 Queen VICTORIA requested Elssler and FANNY CERRITO to dance a *pas de deux* at a Command Performance. Elssler's style was described by Gautier as 'pagan' and her dramatic, passionate presence was contrasted with Taglioni's ethereality.

In 1840 she became the first great ballerina to tour the USA, with sensational success; Congress adjourned for lack of a quorum when she danced in Washington. Delaying her return, and sued for damages by the Paris Opéra, she performed in London to avoid arrest, appearing in Perrot's productions of *Giselle* and *La Esmeralda*. In 1848 she appeared at La Scala, Milan, where her Austrian nationality drew hisses from the audience. After visiting St Petersburg (1848–50) and Moscow (1850–51) she gave her last public performance in Vienna in 1851.

I. Guest: *Fanny Elssler: the Pagan Ballerina* (1970)

**Elstob, Elizabeth** (1683–1756). English Anglo-Saxon scholar. Born in Newcastle, she was educated by her mother, who died when she was eight, and then sent to live with her uncle, the Reverend C. Elstob, in Canterbury. Although he discouraged her studies as unnecessary for a girl, she studied and read several languages. From 1702 to 1715 she lived in London with her brother William, a clergyman and also an Anglo-Saxon scholar. Here she edited several texts, in 1708 publishing a translation of MADELEINE DE SCUDERY's *Essay on Glory*, and in 1709 the *Anglo-Saxon Homily on the Nativity of St Gregory*, with an English translation. In the preface she defended the right of women to study, and also engaged in a theological dispute about the organization of the Old English Church. She planned to produce a complete edition of Aelfric's *Homilies*, and obtained support from scholars and eminent patrons such as Lord Oxford, but although printing was begun the work never reached publication. In 1715 she produced *Rudiments of Grammar for the English-Saxon Tongue, first given in English; with an Apology for the Study of Northern Antiquities.*

Her learning and her precise editorial skills were remarkable for the age, but after her brother's death financial difficulties put an end to scholarship. In 1718, after leaving London because of debts, she opened a small school in Evesham, Worcestershire, and subscriptions from friends brought her a small annuity. Eventually, in 1738, she became governess to the children of the Duchess of Portland, Lord Oxford's daughter, and remained there until her death.

M. Green: 'Elizabeth Elstob: "The Saxon Nymph"', *Female Scholars*, ed. L. Brink (1980)

**Emecheta, Buchi** (1944–). Nigerian novelist. Buchi Emecheta was born in Nigeria, and went to England with her student husband at the age of 27. After they separated she brought up her five children alone, while writing, getting a degree in Sociology, and later a PhD. Her early novels *In the Ditch* (1972) and *Second-Class Citizen* (1974) are based on her own experience. She then began to write about women's problems in Nigeria, set in the context of history and social change and civil war: *The Bride Price* (1976), *The Slave Girl* (1977), *The Joys of Motherhood* (1979), and *Destination Biafra* (1982). Her other works include *Adah's Story* (1981) and *The Rape of Shavi* (1983). She has written several books for children, and her work has been crucial in drawing attention to black women writers in Britain.

**Emerson, Gladys Anderson** (1903–). American biochemist and nutritionist. Born in Caldwell, Kansas, she graduated from Oklahoma College for Women in history and English, and chemistry and physics. She chose history for her master's degree at Stanford, then after teaching won a Berkeley fellowship in nutrition and biochemistry.

She worked at Göttingen, and then returned to Berkeley. Dr Herbert Evans had identified and named Vitamin E, but Gladys isolated it in its pure crystalline form from wheat germ oil. Moving to the Merck Pharmaceutical Company in New Jersey in 1942, she investigated the connection between Vitamin B-complex deficiency, and diseases such as arteriosclerosis. For a two-year period at the Sloan-Kettering Cancer Research Institute she similarly pursued the possible relationship of nutrition and cancer. In 1956 she became Professor of Nutrition at the University of California, Los Angeles (UCLA), and Chairman of the department of home economics. She was Vice-Chairman of the department of public health until her retirement in 1970 and prominent in the 1969 White House Conference on Food, Nutrition and Health. Merck presented UCLA with 29 rhesus monkeys to aid her research.

**Enheduanna** (*fl c*2200 BC). Sumerian poet. The daughter of the ruler Sargon, she became a high priestess of the moon god, Inanna, in whose honour she wrote a famous *Exaltation*. Her religious verse was an influential model for later writers and she was held in great reverence for generations.

**Enoki, Miswo** (1939–). Japanese feminist. A qualified pharmacist, she led the most radical wing of the Japanese feminist movement during the 1970s, known as the Pink Panthers. They organized large demonstrations with a series of campaigns related to abortion, equal opportunities, equal pay, and legal rights in marriage and divorce. In the 1977 general elections she formed a Japan Woman's Party, but polled only a small fraction of the vote.

**Enters, Angna** [Anita] (1907–). American mime-actress. Born in New York, she began as a social dancer, turning professional when invited to partner Michio Ito. She made her first appearance in New York in 1924, and in London in 1927, subsequently returning on numerous occasions. She devised her own one-woman show comprising wordless mime and dance-sketches of her own composition, wearing appropriate costume, the most famous of which has been *Moyen âge*, created in 1926. She created a repertoire of approximately 200 items (notable among them *The Queen of Heaven*, *Pavana* and *Pierrot*), and her range of vividly expressive gesture was particularly wide. She was also an accomplished painter, was a screenwriter during the 1940s and wrote a number of books including *Artist's Life* (1957), describing her theatrical experience, and *Angna Enters on Mime* (1965).

**Erinna** (early 3rd century BC). Greek poet. She came from the Dorian island of Tetos, and successfully imitated SAPPHO's style, writing in her local Doric dialect. Her best-known poem, *The Distaff*, describes in 300 verses and with deep feeling the joys of childhood and games played with her friend Baucis. She also wrote epigrams. She died when she was only 19.

**Erxleben** [née Leporin], **Dorothea (Christiana)** (1715–62). German doctor. With her brother, she studied Latin, basic science and medicine with their father, a physician of Quedlinburg in Prussia. The ability shown in her petition that her brothers and father should avoid military service attracted the attention of King Frederick I, who allowed Dorothea and her brother to be admitted to the University of Halle in 1741.

In 1742 she was obliged to withdraw because of her father's last illness. She subsequently married a widower with four children, had four of her own, and was herself widowed. Meanwhile she practised medicine among the poor, but was challenged by three local doctors who accused her of quackery. Permission for her to attend medical school at Halle had not been rescinded so she resumed her studies, gained her doctorate, and in 1754 her graduation was authorized by the King.

Her first book, *Rational Thoughts on Education of the Fair Sex*, was published in 1749. She practised successfully in

Quedlinburg for eight years, possibly dying of a tubercular haemorrhage.

E. Kraetke-Rumpf: *The Physician of Quedlinburg: a Biography of Germany's first female medical Doctor* (1939)

**Esau, Katherine** (1898–). American botanist. Born in Russia, Katherine moved with her family in 1919 to Germany, where she took her degree. In 1922 the family emigrated to the USA.

Her work on the effects of viruses on plants began when she was employed by the Spreckels Sugar Company in California to develop sugar-beet strains resistant to the virus disease called curly top. This work was transferred to the University of California where she obtained her PhD in 1931. She then taught and continued her research, becoming Professor Emeritus in 1975.

Katherine contributed to botany in three areas: by using ultra-structural research methods to determine the specialization of certain viruses in relation to plant tissue; by distinguishing primary from secondary vascular tissue in healthy plants, thus establishing a base for work on differentiation in plants; and by clarifying developmental features of phloem or food-conducting tissue. Her five main books include *Plant Anatomy* (1953, 1965), *Vascular Differentiation in Plants* (1965), and *Plants, Viruses and Insects* (1968).

In 1957 she was elected to the American National Academy of Sciences, and in 1971 to the Swedish Royal Academy of Sciences.

**Espert, Nuria** (1935–). Spanish actress and director. Nuria was born in Barcelona and began her professional career in the theatre as an actress at the age of 12, playing Juliet at 16 and Medea three years later. In 1959 she founded her own company, with her husband Armando Moreno. The Nuria Espert Company has toured through Europe, the USSR, the United States and South America since 1969 and has become internationally known for its exhilarating productions of modern plays, including O'Neill's *Mourning Becomes Electra*, Brecht's *The Good Person of Setzuan*, Sartre's *Huis Clos* and Genet's *The Maids*. The repertoire also included classical drama (Nuria played the lead in *Hamlet*), 19th-century plays like Wilde's *Salomé*, and many productions of major Spanish dramatists

such as Lope de Vega, Calderón de la Barca and Garcia Lorca. Her powerful tragic performance in Lorca's *Yerma*, directed by Victor Garcia, was acclaimed as a triumph in London in 1971, and was repeated at the 1986 Edinburgh Festival.

Nuria Espert directed at the National Theatre in Madrid from 1980 to 1981. In 1986, in London, she directed the award-winning production of *The House of Bernarda Alba*, and in 1987 made her first venture into opera for the Silver Jubilee of Scottish Opera with a radical new production of *Madama Butterfly*.

**Espin, Vilma** (1930–). Cuban revolutionary and feminist. She was born in Santiago de Cuba, of a Cuban father and French mother, and studied to be a chemical engineer. In her fourth year as a student (1952), she became a political activist after Batista's pre-election coup which ended democratic government, joining the big street demonstrations. After graduating from the University of Oriente, she went as a post-graduate to Massachusetts Institute of Technology, eventually returning to Cuba via Mexico, where she met the exiled Fidel Castro. She then worked to form the first aid brigades and women's units in preparation for the abortive revolution of November 1956, and afterwards liaised with the rebels in hiding in the Sierra. In 1959, after Castro came to power, she took a delegation to the Congress of the International Federation of Democratic Women in Chile, and in 1960 they established the Federation of Cuban Women, to fight illiteracy, organize workshops and employment, and to gain their political participation. Vilma Espin became its head, and also rose to become a member of the central committee of the Cuban Communist Party, while working in the Ministry of Food, in the Chemical Engineers Office. She married Raiul Castro, Fidel's brother, who was Chief of the Army, and had four children.

**Essipoff, Annette** [Esipova, Anna Nikolayevna] (1855–1937). Russian pianist. She was a pupil of the great teacher Leschetizky at the St Petersburg Conservatory, and was married to him from 1880 to 1892. Based in Europe for most of her concert career (1871–92), she toured extensively, making her London debut in 1874 and being particularly acclaimed in Paris (1875) and the USA (1876). Her technical mastery and poetic insight made her an ideal interpreter of Chopin. Shaw described her as 'truly an astonishing – almost a fearful player', drawing attention to her facility and precision. She became pianist to the Russian court in 1885. Among her pupils at the St Petersburg Conservatory, where she taught from 1893 to 1908, were Prokofiev and Borovsky; Prokofiev's exceptional piano technique is attributed to the influence of Essipoff in Israel Nestyev's biography of the composer, though he later spurned the romantic inclinations of her schooling.

**Estaugh** [née Haddon], **Elizabeth** (c1680–1762). American Quaker. She was born in Southwark, London, the eldest daughter of well-to-do parents; they were staunch Quakers who had been tried on a number of occasions for persistently attending meetings. John Haddon, Elizabeth's father, had purchased a tract of land in New Jersey, but circumstances prevented his emigration. In 1701 Elizabeth went in his stead to establish a home for travelling ministers. After her marriage to a young preacher, John Estaugh, Elizabeth managed the plantation, ministered to the sick and fulfilled her vocation of hospitable hostess. A village developed at Haddonfield and a monthly meeting was established. Elizabeth served as clerk of the women's meeting for over 50 years. She lived on at Haddonfield for 20 years after the death of her husband, surrounded by the children of her adopted son, Ebenezer Hopkins.

**Eugénie (Marie Eugénie de Montijo de Guzman)** (1826–1920). French empress. Born in Spain, she married Napoleon III in 1853. Famed for her beauty, she became a leader of fashion and maintained a brilliant court. She was an ardent supporter of the papacy and it was through her influence that a French garrison preserved the pope's rule in Rome after the unification of the rest of Italy. When the emperor abdicated after defeat in the Franco–Prussian war she lived with him in England and remained there after his death. Their son, the Prince Imperial, was killed fighting for the British in the Zulu War (1879).

**Evans,** Dame **Edith** (1888–1976). English actress. She was the unrivalled mistress of comedy, both in classical and commercial theatre, and her most significant contributions to the repertoire included Millimant in *The Way of the World* (1924), Lady Bracknell in *The Importance of being Earnest* (1939), the Nurse in *Romeo and Juliet* and Rosalind in *As You Like It*. She was very successful in Shaw's plays, while her successes in commercial theatre included a remarkable portrayal of Mrs Lancaster in *Waters of the Moon* (1951). She was created DBE in 1946.

B. Forbes: *Ned's Girl: the Authorised Biography of Dame Edith Evans* (1977)

**Ewing, Winifred Margaret** (1929–). Scottish politician. Born and educated in Glasgow, she became a practising solicitor in 1956 and married Stewart Ewing in the same year: they have three children. She was Secretary of the Glasgow Bar Association 1961–70, and President in 1970. In 1967 she was elected MP for Hamilton, and the following year became Vice-President of the Scottish Nationalist Party, a formidable campaigner and organizer on their behalf ever since. From 1974 to 1979 she was MP for Moray and Nairn, and since 1975 has been the Euro MP for the Highlands and Islands of Scotland. In 1984 Winnie Ewing was made Vice-President of the European Democratic Alliance.

**Exter** [née Grigorovich]**, Alexandra** (1882–1949). Russian artist and designer. Born in Bielostock, near Kiev, she studied at the School of Fine Arts in Kiev, and exhibited with avant-garde artists both in Moscow and in her own city. She then married her cousin, Nikolai Exter, and visited Paris, where she met Picasso, Braque and Apollinaire, studying briefly at the Académie de la Grande Chaumière. Over the next few years she visited Paris regularly, and exhibited with the Futurists in Russia, establishing a studio school in Kiev in 1916. In 1920, after the Revolution, she married her second husband, the actor George Nekrassov. Although teaching art at the Ukhutemas school in Moscow, she became increasingly interested in stage design, creating integrated settings and costumes which revolutionized theatrical design. From 1924 she also worked on films, and her early work includes her science fiction masterpiece *Aelita*. After the authorities ceased to support experimental art, Exter emigrated to France in 1924, and taught at Leger's Académie de l'Art Moderne and in her own studio. She worked on ballet, stage and film designs for Paris, London and Rome and also designed furniture, china, textiles and lights, and illustrated books during the 1930s for Editions Flammarion. She rarely exhibited after the 1930s and, although interest in her work has revived recently, she died in obscurity at her home in Fontenay-les-Roses where she had settled in 1928.

Lissim *et al: Alexandra Exter: Artist of the Theatre* (1975) [catalogue]

# F

Faber, Cecilia Boehl von. *See* CABALLERO, FERNÁN.

Fabiola (?*d* 399). Roman nurse and doctor. The daughter of a patrician family of Rome, Fabiola was converted to Christianity at the age of 20 after an unhappy marriage. She was married a second time and was widowed, and to expiate her early life she followed the teachings of her contemporary St Jerome and devoted herself to medical charity. In 390, with her friend Paula and Paula's son-in-law Pammachius, she founded a hospital at Ostia at the mouth of the Tiber. She probably practised surgery and was noted for her reading of Homer and of Hebrew, her Christian pursuits and her attention to patients.

Fachiri [née d'Arányi], Adila (1886–1962). Hungarian–British violinist. She was a pupil of Hubay at the Budapest Academy, making her debut in Vienna (1906) with Beethoven's Violin Concerto. Joachim, her great-uncle, left her a Stradivarius violin of 1715. She and her sister JELLY D'ARÁNYI formed a famous partnership in Bach's concerto for two violins, particularly in London, where they settled in 1913. Holst's *Double Concerto* was written for them, while Somervell and R.O. Morris wrote concertos for Adila, who shared her sister's fiery temperament but was technically less gifted.
J. Macleod: *The Sisters d'Aranyi* (1969)

Faithful, Emily (1835–95). English feminist printer. The youngest daughter of the Rector of Headley, near Epsom, Emily had a conventional but liberal education, and began to be interested in the lack of career openings for women. Having heard of the role of women in the 15th-century printing industry, she decided to set up her own firm employing women only in 1857. Two years later she became Secretary of the first Society for Promoting the Employment of Women, and founded the Victoria Press in Great Coram Street, London, in 1860. She solved problems of fatigue by introducing stools for women compositors and employing men to move the heavy chases, but this mixed workshop met with enormous hostility from the print unions, ostensibly because it encouraged immorality. In 1862, however, Emily earned the title of Printer and Publisher in Ordinary to the Queen, and moved to a steam printing office in Farringdon Street, finally settling in Praed Street, Paddington, where she remained from 1873 to 1881. In 1876 a Women's Printing Society was started to find apprenticeships and skilled work.

She was herself involved in the publications produced by her firm, including the feminist *English Woman's Journal*, the *Victoria Magazine*, of which 206 numbers in 35 volumes appeared between 1863 and 1880, and the reports of the Social Science Congress. But she also lectured, starting in Hanover Square, London, and touring the USA very successfully (1872–3, 1877 and 1882–3); she gave dramatic readings and founded an International Musical, Dramatic and Literary Society. She was also a writer, publising some occasional poetry and prose in 1863 and a novel, *Change upon Change*, in 1868. Her life seems to have been less active after 1880, but her firm continued after her death in Manchester.
W.P. Fredeman: 'Emily Faithful and the Victoria Press', *The Library* (1964)

Fallaci, Oriana (1930–). Italian writer and journalist. She was born in Florence, and educated at the Liceo Galileo Galilei before attending medical school. She began her journalistic career in her teens, becoming a special correspondent for an Italian paper in 1950. Since 1967 she has also acted as a war-correspondent, in Vietnam, for the Indo-Pakistan War, in the Middle East and in South America; she is International Correspondent for *L'Europeo*. Fallaci is especially famed for her confrontational interviews, such as that with Henry Kissinger, and for the persistent and ingenious ways she has used to persuade 'inaccessible' subjects to talk to her, including the Ayatollah Khomeini.

She has twice won the St Vincent Prize for journalism in Italy, and has also written non-fiction books, including *The Useless Sex* (1960), *The Egotists* (1965) and the autobiographical *Interview with History* (1974). Her novels include *Un uomo/A Man* (1979; Eng. trans., 1981), a powerful portrait of the Greek resistance fighter, Alexander Panagoulis.

**Fanshawe, Lady Anne** (1625–80). English Royalist. The daughter of Royalist Sir John Harrison, she was 15 when her mother and brother died, her father was imprisoned and the family fortune was lost. In 1644 she married Sir Richard Fanshawe; of her many children only five survived. Her life was adventurous and courageous; after Richard's imprisonment at the Battle of Worcester she obtained his bail, later accompanied him to France and the Netherlands where he acted as Secretary to Charles II in exile, and, after the Restoration, went with him to ambassadorial posts in Portugal and Spain. On his death in Madrid in 1666 she refused offers to remain at the Spanish court, brought his body back to England, and devoted the rest of her life to her family and her memoirs. It is for these that she is now chiefly remembered.

*The Memoirs of Anne, Lady Fanshawe* (1907)

**Farmer, Fannie Merritt** (1857–1915). American cookery writer. Born in Boston, Massachusetts, into a poor family, her left leg was paralysed by a stroke when she was 16, but on leaving school in Medford she was able to help in housekeeping. In 1887 she enrolled at the Boston Cooking School, where she took a two-year course; she stayed on as Assistant Principal, and was made Head in 1894. Her publishers asked her to pay for the first edition of her *Boston Cooking School Cook Book* (1896), but in fact it was immediately successful, full of clear recipes and innovative in its methodical use of directions, timing and measurement; it has sold millions of copies since. She herself was very shy and avoided the publicity which the book brought her.

In 1902 she founded the Miss Farmer School of Cookery, and then began giving courses on nutrition to nurses and school children, as well as advising on diets for Harvard Medical School. In 1904 she published *Food and Cooking for the Sick and Convalescent*. She suffered from poor health herself but, as well as writing a cookery page in the *Woman's Home Journal* for ten years, continued to lecture from her wheelchair after two strokes; she gave her last talk ten days before her death.

**Farrar, Geraldine** (1882–1967). American soprano. She was born in Melrose, Massachusetts, the daughter of a leading baseball player, and was encouraged to sing by her parents. From an early age she gave impersonations of JENNY LIND. She studied in Boston and New York, and then with Trabadello in Paris. Finally she worked with LILLI LEHMANN, and made her first appearance as Marguerite in *Faust* with the Royal Opera, Berlin, in 1901. After five years' singing with major European companies she sang with Enrico Caruso in *Rigoletto* in Berlin, the start of 'the strongest box-office combination of operatic history'.

Farrar returned to New York in 1906 and joined the Metropolitan Opera company in Gounod's *Romeo and Juliet*, where she was one of their principal stars until 1922. Among the roles she created were the Goose Girl in Humperdinck's *Königskinder* (1910), Louise in Charpentier's *Julien* (1914) and the title role in Puccini's *Suor Angelica* (1918). Beautiful, dark-haired, with a clear, precise voice, she gave fine performances in roles varying from Cherubino to Carmen, and was particularly popular as Madam Butterfly (which she sang 96 times). Adored by the public, she was forgiven her fiery temperament and frequent clashes with directors and conductors. She also made several films, including *Joan of Arc* and *Carmen*, and from 1916 to 1918 was married to the Dutch actor Leon Tellegen. She retired from opera at the age of 40, receiving a rapturous ovation from huge crowds after her farewell appearance in Leoncavallo's *Zazà*, but continued to appear in concert performances until 1931. She lived quietly in retirement at Ridgefield, Connecticut, until her death.

G. Farrar: *Such Sweet Compulsion* (1938)
E. Nash: *Always First Class: the Career of Geraldine Farrar* (1982)

**Farrell, Suzanne** (1945–). American ballet dancer. Born in Cincinnati, Ohio, she studied at the Cincinnati Conservatory of Music and won a scholarship to the School of American Ballet in New York before joining the New York City Ballet at the age of 16. Her first solo role, in *Serenade*, came the next year (1962), and she went on to dance many roles created by Balanchin, such as Dulcinea in *Don Quixote* (1965). She left the company in 1968 and the following year married Paul Meija. From 1971 to 1975 she danced with the Béjart Ballet of the 20th Century in Brussels, creating many new roles. Since her return to the New York City Ballet in 1975 she has become recognized as a leading interpreter of Balanchin's work. Her many awards include an Emmy award for outstanding individual excellence in the ballet *Eight by Adler* (1985).

**Farrow, Mia (Maria de Lourdes Villiers)** (1946–). American actress. The daughter of actress Maureen O'Sullivan and film director John Farrow, Mia was born in Los Angeles and educated in convent schools in Madrid and London. She began acting in repertory theatre at 17, before becoming known in the part of Alison Mackenzie, the waif-like girl in the television soap-opera *Peyton Place* in 1968. In 1969, after several small film parts, her leading role in Polanski's *Rosemary's Baby* brought wide recognition.

Mia married singer Frank Sinatra in 1966, but they were divorced two years later and in 1970 she married conductor André Previn: they had twin boys. They moved to London, where Previn directed Mia in Honegger's play *Jeanne d'Arc*, and she acted frequently in British theatres during the 1970s, including a season with the Royal Shakespeare Company in 1975–6. She also continued to appear in films, for example as Daisy in *The Great Gatsby* (1974). The Previns were divorced in 1979, and in 1981 she began to work with Woody Allen, her constant companion over the next few years; their first child was born in 1988. Allen gave her far more demanding roles than her usual vulnerable, boyish innocents, in films such as *Broadway Danny Rose* (1984), *The Purple Rose of Cairo* (1985), *Hannah and Her Sisters* (1986) and *Radio Days* (1987). An independent, interesting woman, disturbed by social problems, she has established her own individual space in modern cinema.

**Farrukhzad, Furugh** (1935–67) Iranian writer and film maker. Born in Teheran, she was educated in girls' public schools and never received a high school diploma. At the age of 13 she began composing poetry in the traditional *ghazal* form. She married Parviz Shapur at the age of 16 and published the first edition of *The Captive* in 1952, which was reissued in 1955 with some modifications. Her son Kamyar was born in 1953; soon afterwards she was divorced and lost custody of her child. On republication *The Captive* met with public outcry over its 'immorality' and 'scandalous' candour; it gained further notoriety when details of Furugh's private life became known. *The Wall*, her second collection of poems, appeared in 1956. On returning from travels in Europe in the summer of that year, she wrote her impressions in *Firdawsi* magazine. *Rebellion*, Furugh's third collection, appeared in 1957, followed by *Another Birth* in 1961. In 1959 she went to England to study film production. Films with which her name is associated include *The Firs* (1959), *Courtship* (1960), *Water and Heat* (1961), *A Fire* (1961), *The House is Black* (1962), *Another Birth* (1963) and *Brick and Mirror* (1964). A selected anthology of her poems was published in 1964. In 1965 UNESCO produced a film about her life and in the same year Bernardo Bertolucci produced a film biography. She was intending to make a film in Sweden when she was killed in an automobile accident.

**Fatimah** [Al-Zahrā] (c606-632). Arabic religious figure, the daughter of the prophet Mohammed. She was born in Mecca and brought up in a household which included her cousin and future husband 'Alī, Mohammed's devoted disciple. She accompanied her father during his years of persecution and fled with him from Mecca to Medina in 622. Shortly afterwards she married 'Alī. Passionately devoted to her family, she had two sons and two daughters; legends present her as the perfect housewife, 'with blistered hands from grinding corn', seeking her father's help against her husband's infidelity and occasional cruelty. She nursed Mohammed in his final illness, but after his death, when the succession fell on Abū Bakr, 'AISHAH BINT ABI BAKR's father, rather than on 'Alī, she entered into a dispute with the rest of the family.

Fatimah's importance is due to the reverence accorded her within Islam, especially by the Shī'ite sect, where she is the subject of many legends, especially because she alone of Mohammed's children produced a long line of descendants, some of whom, the Fatimids, laid claim to the caliphate in the 10th and 11th centuries on the basis of this relationship.

**Faucit, Helena** (1817–98). English actress. Born Helena Saville into a theatrical family, she first appeared at Covent Garden in 1835 as Shakespeare's Juliet, soon after as Julia in Sheridan Knowles's *The Hunchback*, and Belvedera in Otway's *Venice Preserv'd*. In 1837 she joined William Macready's management at Covent Garden as his leading lady, an association strained by her hopeless love for him (Macready was already married), and by professional rivalry. The partnership ended bitterly in 1844–5 in Paris, where the critics clearly regarded Helena as the greater artist. During these years, besides roles from Shakespeare and the 18th-century repertory, she interpreted new parts in the plays that Macready encouraged from modern authors, such as Pauline in Bulwer Lytton's *The Lady of Lyons*, Clara Douglas in his *Money*, Helen Campbell in Serjeant Talfourd's *Tragedy of Glencoe*, and Mildred Tresham in Browning's *Blot on the 'Scutcheon*.

Tall and graceful, she was declared by many contemporaries the best actress since Sarah Siddons, though others insisted that, apart from her appearance, she was merely competent. Many saw her as exemplifying

their ideal of womanhood, a task which, at a moral level, she herself took very seriously: 'whatever gifts I had as an actress were regarded by me as a sacred trust for widening and refining the sympathies of my audiences' (*On Some of the Female Characters of Shakespeare*, 1885). In practice this meant making even unpromising characters more 'womanly' than actresses before her.

In 1851, she married Theodore Martin (later Sir Theodore), official biographer of Prince Albert. She continued to act although her health was precarious, but after 1865 she preferred readings. The Queen was a particular admirer, and the Martins were frequent guests at Osborne and Windsor; they were themselves visited by Victoria in 1889 at their house in Llangollen.

Sir Theodore Martin: *Helena Faucit* (1900)

**Faustina, Anna Galeria** (*c*125–76). Roman empress. The daughter of Emperor Antoninus Pius and Faustina (the elder), she was first betrothed to Lucius Verus, but in 139 her father promised her to Marcus Aurelius, whom she married in 145. She accompanied him on his northern campaigns (170–4) and during the Danube Wars received the title of Mater Castrorum. In 175, after a revolt led by Avidius Cassius, the imperial couple set out to visit the eastern provinces, but she died suddenly on the way. She was much maligned by ancient writers as a faithless immoral wife who may even have conspired with Cassius, but these rumours seem to be groundless. Marcus Aurelius was devoted to her and he founded a school, the Puellae Faustinanae for daughters of the poor, in her memory, just as Antoninus had done in honour of her mother.

**Fawcett,** Dame **Millicent Garrett** (1847–1929). English leader of the constitutional suffrage movement. Born in Aldeburgh, Suffolk, the daughter of an East Anglian merchant, her only formal schooling was at Blackheath, London (1859–62). She was involved from an early age in the women's movement through her sister ELIZABETH GARRETT ANDERSON and her friend EMILY DAVIES. In 1867 she married Henry Fawcett, Professor of Economics at Cambridge and Radical MP for Brighton, and their daughter Philippa was born the following year. His blindness necessitated her learning to work as his political secretary, and in 1870 she published *Political Economy for Beginners*.

Her real effort was always devoted to women's rights. She was on the first suffrage committee in 1867, and also worked for the Married Woman's Property Act, while her house in Cambridge was the base for the women's lecture scheme from which Newnham College developed. After Henry's death in 1884 she became more involved, working for social purity with the Vigilance Society, and founding a separate suffrage society with Lydia Becker in 1886. In 1897 she reunited the movement, becoming President of the National Union of Women Suffrage Societies (NUWSS). During these years she was also known as a national political figure, a member of the Liberal-Unionist group (1887–1903), a frequent visitor to Ireland and speaker against Home Rule, and leader of a women's commission to investigate concentration camps in South Africa in the Boer War.

After the Boer War, interest in the suffrage question was revived with the PANKHURSTs' militant campaigns, and Millicent strengthened the constitutionalist campaign with tireless national speaking tours, parliamentary lobbying, and party alliances. At the outbreak of World War I in 1914, although opposed by pacifists in the NUWSS, she urged the membership to devote its energies to the war effort; but in 1916 she pressed again for enfranchisement, which was recommended by a Parliamentary Conference (1917) and passed by both Houses (1918). She then resigned her presidency but continued to campaign for full suffrage (1928) and for professional opportunities and legal rights. She wrote several books on famous women, including *Life of Queen Victoria* (1895), a history of the movement, *Women's Suffrage* (1912), and *Women's Victory and After* (1918). Her last work was a biography of JOSEPHINE BUTLER (1927). She was created DBE in 1925.

M. Fawcett: *What I Remember* (1924)
R. Strachey: *Millicent Garrett Fawcett* (1931)

**Fell,** Dame **Honor (Bridget)** (1900–86). British cell biologist. She graduated from Edinburgh University in 1922 and took her PhD in 1923 and her DSc in 1930. She

became assistant to T.S.P. Strangeways at the Cambridge Research Hospital and in 1929, after his death, was made Director.

Using the organ culture method, largely developed at Strangeways Laboratory, she studied the effect of excess vitamin A on explanted limb bones of foetal mice and found that intercellular material disappeared from both cartilage and bone. These responses demonstrated that organ cultures could be used for biochemical study of vitamins and hormones and applied to a range of physiological problems. In 1970 she began using post-foetal tissues to examine the pathogenesis of arthritis.

For many years she was a member of the Royal Society's research staff, and became a Fellow of the Royal Society in 1952. In 1963 she received the OBE, and in 1965 a prize from the Académie des Sciences de l'Institut de France. She retired from the directorship of the Strangeways Research Laboratory in 1970 but continued to work in immunopathology at Cambridge.

**Fell** [née Askew], **Margaret** (1614–1702). English Quaker. Born into a land-owning family, Margaret married Judge Thomas Fell; they had nine children. A deeply pious person, Margaret opened their house, Swarthmore Hall, to all religious people. During the winter of 1652, George Fox, leader of The Society of Friends, took advantage of this open invitation and as a result converted Margaret and most of the family to his views. Following the death of her husband in 1658, Margaret became much more active in the affairs of the Quakers, writing frequently to Charles II and gaining a number of interviews with him to plead the cause of imprisoned Quakers, including on occasion Fox himself.

In 1663 Margaret was arrested for refusing to take the Oath of Allegiance; she was imprisoned and her estates given to her son. Following her marriage to George Fox in 1669 she was again arrested and later fined on a number of occasions for allowing meetings to take place at Swarthmore. After Fox's death in 1691, Margaret continued to take an interest in the Quakers but does not appear to have been actively employed on their behalf. From the time of her conversion Margaret wrote extensively, including a work called *Women's speaking*

*Justified, Proved and Knowed of the Scriptures* (1666).

I. Ross: *Margaret Fell, Mother to Quakerison* (1949)

**Fenwick, Ethel (Gordon)** (1857–1947). English nurse and politician. Ethel Manson's father was a doctor who died when she was three; her stepfather was an MP. She spent a year as a lady-pupil at a Nottingham children's hospital, two years as a sister at the London Hospital, and six as Matron of St Bartholomew's Hospital, London, before marrying Dr Bedford Fenwick in 1887.

Ethel was the leader of a group of lady-pupils in a move to form a professional association. They eventually formed the British Nurses' Association (BNA), with Ethel as President. It contained 'the elite of the profession', as the group thought higher standards of nursing could be achieved if nurses were drawn from the higher social classes. In 1893 the BNA was granted a Royal Charter, but in the election which followed Ethel was deposed. In opposition she and her husband founded the British College of Nurses in 1926.

In 1894 she started the Matrons' Council of Great Britain and Ireland for matrons who wanted state registration, and she lobbied Parliament for registration bills between 1904 and 1914. These measures were opposed by FLORENCE NIGHTINGALE. Partly as a platform for the campaign, the Fenwicks bought *The Nursing Record*, later called *The British Journal of Nursing*.

When the International Council of Women met in London in 1899, Ethel took the opportunity, through the Matrons' Council, to organize an International Council of Nurses, the first such organization among health professions, or professional women. She became its first President.

**Ferraro, Geraldine Anne** (1935–). American politician. Born in Newburgh, New York, she was educated at Marymount College, Fordham University and New York University Law School. Married to John Zaccaro in 1960 (she has two sons and one daughter), she continued to study law at night school, was called to the New York bar in 1961 and practised in New York from 1961 to 1974. She was Assistant District Attorney for Queens County in 1974–8, and joined the bar

of the US Supreme Court in 1978. A Democratic member of the House of Representatives from 1981 to 1985, she was the first woman from a major party to be a candidate for Vice-President, as Walter Mondale's running mate in 1984. The campaign collapsed amid allegations of tax fraud in her husband's real-estate dealings. She then faced an inquiry lasting two years into the funding of her Congressional campaign, complicated by other scandals involving her family. She remained in political retirement, and decided not to run for a New York senate seat in 1986.

G. Ferraro: *Ferraro: My Story* (1985)

**Ferrier, Kathleen** (1912–53). English contralto. Ferrier's potential greatness as a singer was recognized comparatively late; she had won prizes as a pianist and began by earning her living as a telephone operator. Through her activities with local choral societies she was eventually heard by Malcolm Sargent, who advised her to go to London for study with Roy Henderson; she also had lessons with J.E. Hutchinson. She was soon recommended to Britten for the première of *The Rape of Lucretia* (Glyndebourne, 1946), having already become much in demand as a concert artist. Tours of Europe and the USA assured her international reputation. She became particularly associated with the music of Elgar and Mahler, her performances of *The Dream of Gerontius* (with Barbirolli) and *Das Lied von der Erde* (with Bruno Walter, most notably at the first Edinburgh Festival, 1947) being distinguished by her dignity and intensity; she was similarly acclaimed for her interpretations of Bach and Handel as well as of English folksong. Britten wrote his Second Canticle with Ferrier in mind for the alto part, and Bliss's scena *The Enchantress* was written for her. Besides Lucretia, her only operatic role was Gluck's Orpheus, which she sang first at Glyndebourne in 1947. The four scheduled performances of this work at Covent Garden (1953) had to be reduced: few were aware of the resources that Ferrier had had to call on in order to sing the first two. She was taken from the opera house on a stretcher and died eight months later. Memorial funds in aid of cancer research were immediately established, contributions arriving from all over the world in tribute to a much-loved woman and a supreme artist. Annual scholarships for young singers are awarded in her memory by the Royal Philharmonic Society, whose gold medal Ferrier received in 1953, the year she was created CBE.

W. Ferrier and N. Cardus: *Kathleen Ferrier: her Life and a Memoir* (1959)

**Ferrier, Susan Edmonstone** (1782–1854). Scottish novelist. Susan Ferrier was the daughter of the clerk of Sessions in Edinburgh, the youngest of ten children. Her father's friends included Sir Walter Scott, later a great supporter of her writing, and the Duke of Argyll, with whose niece Charlotte Clavering she collaborated on the first part of *Marriage*.

She became housekeeper to her father at the age of 15, and wrote *Marriage* in 1810, publishing it anonymously in 1818. Shrewd, humorous, closely based on the society she knew, it was an immediate success. She went on to write *The Inheritance* (1824) and *Destiny* (1831), but although now a successful author she gave up writing fiction after a conversion to Evangelicalism. A member of the Free Church, she devoted her later life to charity works and to campaigning for the temperance cause and the abolition of slavery. Her other published works include short memoirs, an account of a visit to Scott, and her letters (1898).

**Feuillère** [née Cunati], **(Caroline Vivette) Edwige** [pseud.: Cora Lynn] (1907–). French actress. She studied drama in Dijon and Paris and began her Paris career as Cora Lynn in light comedies. In 1931 she joined the Comédie-Française, appearing there as Suzanne in Beaumarchais' *Le mariage de Figaro*, but frustration at the limited roles she was given made her leave to go into films in 1933. Four years later she achieved fame with her performance in Becque's *La parisienne* and Dumas' *La dame aux camélias*. Her other notable appearances included performances in Giraudoux's *Sodome et Gomorrhe* (1943), Cocteau's *L'aigle à deux têtes* (1946), Molière's *Amphitryon* (1947) and Claudel's *Partage de midi* (1948). In 1947 she worked with Jean-Louis Barrault and MADELEINE RENAUD. She toured widely and played frequently in London during the 1950s and 1960s, appearing with her own company. For many years she was one of the leading actresses of the French stage, with a charismatic personality and a fine voice. She made a number of films including *Topaze* (1933) and *L'aigle à deux têtes* (1948). Her recent stage roles include *Cher menteur* (1980) which was also filmed, and *Leocadia* (1984–5). She is a Chevalier of the Légion d'honneur and received the César award of the French Academy in 1984.

**Field, (Agnes) Mary** (1896–1968). English film producer. Born in Wimbledon, London, and educated locally and at Bedford College, London, she gained an MA at the Institute of Historical Research, with distinction in Commonwealth History. After a period of teaching and research, her work checking films on the Commonwealth led to her joining British Instructional Films in 1926. She moved to Gaumont in 1934, and during these years produced the famous documentary series *Secrets of Nature* (1928), and *Secrets of Life* (1934). In 1944 she established and became Executive Producer of the Children's Film Division of J. Arthur Rank, and in 1951 became Executive Head of the Children's Film Foundation, helping to create the well-known children's matinées. Beginning in the 1950s she also undertook advisory work, touring the Commonwealth countries in 1954, North America in 1960, and acting as consultant to the UNESCO Centre of Films for Children. In 1952 her book, *Good Company*, analysed the children's responses. Mary Field was married to Gerald Hankin, a Ministry of Education official. She was made a CBE in 1951, and at one stage was President of the British Federation of Business and Professional Women.

**Fields, Dame Gracie** [Stansfield, May] (1898–1979). English singer and comedienne. Born in Rochdale, Lancashire, she was a talented child performer and appeared professionally in music hall entertainments from 1910. From 1915 to 1925 she toured the country in revues produced by the comedian Archie Pitt, whom she married in 1923. She appeared successfully and she made the first of her nine Royal Command Performances in 1928. She soon became known for comic songs such as *The Biggest Aspidistra in the*

*World* and sentimental ballads like *Sally*. Her greatest fame came when she starred in English film comedies of the 1930s such as *Sally in our Alley* (1931), *This Week of Grace* (1933), *Queen of Hearts* (1936), *Keep Smiling* (1938), and other popular songs which defied the Depression gloom. In 1938 she was described as the world's highest-paid star.

After divorcing Pitt in 1940, she married the actor/director Monty Banks. He was declared an alien in the UK because of his Italian birth. They went to Hollywood where she made films such as *Holy Matrimony* (1943), and *Molly and Me* (1945); she also toured widely entertaining British troops. Banks died in 1950 and two years later she married the film director Boris Alperovici and spent the rest of her life with him on the island of Capri. Despite almost 40 years abroad 'Our Gracie' retained her popularity in Britain and received rapturous tributes when she was created DBE in 1979.

G. Fields: *Sing as We Go* (1960)

**Fiennes, Celia** (1662–1741). English traveller. Between 1685 and 1702, she undertook a series of journeys with a few servants, travelling ostensibly in pursuit of health but also in a 'spirit of pure curiosity'. Her diary vividly records the journeys and she hoped that in reading it women would make a 'study of those things which tend to improve the mind'. In 1698 alone she travelled more than 1,000 miles, most of it, as with her other tours, on horseback. She observed crafts and industries, explored coal mines and caves as well as grand houses; her comments on Dissenters and others also recorded the varied cultural life of the 17th century.

C. Mair, ed.: *The Illustrated Journeys of Celia Fiennes* (1982)

**Figes, Eva** (1932–). British feminist writer of German birth. Born in Berlin in 1932, she came to England at the age of seven and was educated in London, graduating in English from University College. After working as a publisher's editor and a translator, she became a full-time writer in 1967. Her novels include *Equinox* (1966), *Winter Journey* (1967), *Konek Landing* (1969), *B* (1972), *Days* (1974), *Nelly's Version* (1977)

and *Waking* (1981). She has also written non-fiction, such as *Tragedy and Social Evolution* (1976).

She is also a well-known journalist and reviewer. In 1970 her book *Patriarchal Attitudes: Women in Society* examined the ideology of women's subordination in religious thought, liberal philosophy, capitalist economics, psychoanalysis, and popular custom. With GERMAINE GREER'S *The Female Eunuch* (1970), it provided a descriptive base for the ideas of the emerging women's movement in the UK. She has remained interested in the feminist debate, and has written a study of the lives of British women writers, *Sex and Subterfuge: Women Novelists to 1850* (1981).

E. Figes: *A Child at War* (1978)

**Figner, Vera (Nikolayevna)** (1852–1942). Russian populist revolutionary. She was the eldest of six children in a prosperous Kazan family and had a happy childhood, being educated at home and then at the Rodionovsky Institute in Kazan. She married a lawyer, Aleksei Filippov, in 1870, and in 1872 they went with her sister Lidiya to Zürich. Lidiya joined the radical Fritsch discussion group and Vera soon followed. Many of the students returned to Russia in 1875–6 and joined the group *Zemlya i Volya* ('Land and liberty'), but Vera went on to medical school in Berne, and had nearly finished her course when she received a message that she was needed in Russia, since many of her friends had been arrested.

In Moscow she obtained a licence to work as a paramedic, divorced her husband and went to work in the countryside. She joined the terrorist branch of the movement *Narodnaya Volya* ('People's Will') after a split in the movement in 1879, and became their agent in Odessa, contributing propagandist articles, establishing links with the army and navy, and planning attempts to blow up the Czar's train (1879–80). After his assassination in 1881 and the arrest of SOFYA PEROVSKAYA and her other colleagues, she became the acting leader of the *Narodnaya Volya*, working in Khar'kov in southern Russia. She was eventually arrested in 1883 and condemned to death the following year. For a year she was imprisoned in the Peter-Paul prison in St Petersburg [now Leningrad] and then spent 20 years in the terrible Schlisselburg island fortress in the river Neva. Here she wrote her memoirs *Kogda chasy zhizni ostanovalis* ('How the clock of life stopped'), published in 1921. In 1904 she was released into exile to Archangelsk in Siberia, and made her way abroad in 1906. She lived in Switzerland but returned to Russia in 1914, having joined the Russian Socialist Revolutionary Party. After the Revolution she became a chairman of the Amnesty Committee and helped many released political prisoners. She became a legendary heroine in the USSR, and her collected works were published in seven volumes (1929–32).

V. Figner: *Memoirs of a Revolutionist* (1927)

**Figuero, Ana** (1908–70). Chilean feminist. Born in Santiago in 1928, she graduated from the University of Chile and became a teacher until World War II broke out, after which she went to the USA to study at Columbia University and Colorado State College. She was always a feminist, being President of the committee which obtained women's suffrage, and after directing the national secondary school system from 1947 to 1949 she was put in charge of the Women's Bureau in the Ministry of Foreign Affairs. In 1951 she became Chile's special envoy to United Nations; as Head of the Social, Humanitarian and Cultural Committee she was the first woman to head a UN Committee of the General Assembly. In 1952 she became the first woman on the Security Committee, and broke a final barrier in 1960 when she became the first woman Assistant Director General of the International Labour Organization. She retired from the ILO in 1967.

**Filosova, Anna (Pavlovna)** (1837–1912). Russian feminist. Born Anna Diagileva in St Petersburg, into a rich, noble family, she was educated at home. After 1859 she became involved in philanthropic work with MARIYA TRUBNIKOVA and NADEZHDA STASOVA: known as 'the triumvirate' they organized housing and employment for unmarried women and campaigned for higher education for women. This led to the establishment of the first general education courses for women in St Petersburg in 1872 and the Bestuzhev Advanced Courses in 1878. Filosova later became active in the international movement

and was Vice-President of the International Council of Women in 1899. During the 1905–7 Revolution she sided with the Constitutional Democrats and advised against women joining the revolutionary movement. She also chaired the first All-Russian Women's Congress, in 1908.

**Fini, Leonor** (1908–). Argentinian-French artist. Born in Buenos Aires, from 1919 to 1937 she lived in Trieste with her mother's family and during the 1930s met Surrealist painters in Milan and Paris, where she settled in 1937. Her friends included Paul Eluard, Man Ray, Salvador Dali and especially Max Ernst and Leonora Carrington. Although never a member of the Surrealist group, she exhibited her work alongside theirs. During World War II she lived in Monaco, and then in Rome with the artist Stanislau Lepri, before returning to Paris in 1947. During this period she designed stage sets and costumes and has worked for La Scala, the Paris Opéra and on films. Her book illustrations include Sade's *Juliette* (1944), Shakespeare's *Sonnets* (1949), Genet's *La galère* (1950) and Poe's *Tales of the Grotesque* (1953).

Her paintings have a strange power, endlessly exploring archetypal myths of woman, sexuality and fertility; from goddesses to sphinxes, through morbid and erotic fantasies to more explicit, clear images such as the castration symbols in *Capital Punishment* (1960), or studies of the subconscious such as *The Lesson on Botany* (1974)

C. Jelenski: *Leonor Fini* (1968)

**Finnbogadottir, Vigdis** (1930–). President of Iceland. The daughter of a wealthy engineer, she studied at the University of Iceland and then went on to Grenoble and the Sorbonne. Before her work in theatre she taught French at junior colleges and was the Head of Guide Training for the Iceland Tourist Bureau. While working as a translator she produced a version of Feydeau's *A Flea in her Ear*, which was a national success; it inaugurated a theatrical career which culminated in her becoming a director of the Reykjavik Theatre Company in 1972. She also taught Icelandic drama at the University of Iceland and worked for state television. From 1976 she was a member of the Advisory Committee on Cultural Affairs in Nordic Countries and became Chairman in 1978.

In 1980 she was persuaded to run for President and after obtaining just over a third of the total vote became the world's first democratically-elected woman Head of State, a formal rather than executive position. Her own political sympathies are left-wing. Her popularity has increased considerably during her period of office.

**Firestone, Shulamith** (1945–). Canadian feminist. Born in Ottawa, she studied at the Art Institute of Chicago, and came to feminism through her involvement as a student in the civil rights and anti-Vietnam War movements. She sprang to prominence in the women's movement in 1970 with the publication of her daring and vigorously argued book *The Dialectic of Sex: the Case for Feminist Revolution*.

Regarded as a pioneering radical feminist writer, she was also a co-founder and Editor of the journals *Redstockings* in 1969 and *Notes from the Second Year*, 1970, and remained active in the New York feminist movement.

**First, Ruth** (1925–82). South African writer and revolutionary. Ruth First's parents were Jewish immigrants from the Baltic, and were members of the International Socialist League. She herself joined the Communist Party at Witwatersrand University, was actively involved on behalf of black workers in the miners' strike of 1946 and campaigned against the appalling conditions of African farm workers. Secretary of the Party Central Offices in Johannesburg, she edited journals such as the *Guardian* and *New Age* (which were later banned by the government) and the literary *Fighting Talk*. In 1949 she married lawyer and labour organizer Joe Slovo; both were tried and acquitted at the Treason Trial of 1956. Their friends included leaders like Walter Sisulu and Nelson Mandela: they were to be among the first white members of the African National Congress. In 1963 her book *South West Africa* appeared and in the same year Ruth was arrested and held in solitary confinement for six months under the 90-day Law.

She left South Africa on her release, and she described her experiences in prison in *117*

*Days* (1965). She went first to Kenya and then she and her husband moved to London; Ruth became a Research Fellow at the University of Manchester in 1972 and from 1973 to 1979 taught on the sociology of underdevelopment at the University of Durham. Her later books include *The South African Connection: Western Involvement in Apartheid* (1972), *Libya: the Elusive Revolution* (1974) and *Olive Schreiner* (1981). From 1979 until her death she taught at the Centre of African Studies in Mozambique; her book *Black Gold: The Mozambiquan Miner* was published posthumously in 1983. She was killed by a letter bomb in August 1982.

**Fisher, Mary Frances Kennedy** (1908–). American food writer. Born in Michigan, she grew up in Whittier, California, where her father was a newspaper editor and writer, and she describes herself as 'a fifth generation writer'. She was educated at Illinois College, Occidental College, the University of California at Los Angeles, and the University of Dijon in France. Her first book, *Serve It Forth*, appeared in 1937, followed by *Consider the Oyster* and *How to Cook a Wolf*. She lived for several years in Switzerland, and translated Brillat-Savarin's *Physiology of Taste*. During the 1950s and 1960s she became a stalwart champion of native American food and wine. Her 17 books include writings on food such as *The Gastronomical Me*, *With Bold Knife and Fork*; on travel, such as *Two Towns in Provence*; one novel, *Not Now But Now*, and collections of essays and autobiographical pieces that include the memoir of her childhood years in the Quaker community of Whittier, *Among Friends* (1970). She has been married three times, has two daughters, and now lives in the Sonoma Valley, California.

**Fiske** [née Davey, Marie Augusta], **Minnie Maddern** (1865–1932). American director and actress. The daughter of a theatrical agent in New Orleans, before she was five she started as a child performer but retired from the stage on her marriage to Harrison Grey Fiske in 1890. She returned to acting in 1893 in socially conscious plays, including Ibsen's *The Doll's House* and an adaptation of *Tess of the d'Urbervilles*. Together with her husband she managed the Manhattan Theatre, staging a series of outstanding plays, including a number by Ibsen which she directed. Her acting was instinctively natural, and from 1893 onwards she was a determining force in the battle for realism on the New York stage. Unequalled in comedy parts she also had vast talent as a director and encouraged young playwrights.

A. Woodcott: *Mrs Fiske* (1917)

**Fitzgerald, Ella** (1918–). American jazz singer. Born in Newport News, Virginia, she was brought up in an orphanage in Yonkers, New York, and was spotted by the band-leader Chick Webb in a talent contest at the age of 16. She sang with him and after his death in 1939 took over his band until 1942. During the 1940s she became a cabaret singer and developed her highly individual 'scat-singing' technique, which was shown to perfection in songs like *Lady be Good*, using her voice like an instrument that can compete with the fastest jazz improvisation; she also excelled at slow 'white' ballads such as *My Heart belongs to Daddy*. From 1946 she was associated with Granz's 'Jazz at the Philharmonic' tours, and travelled all over North America, Europe and Japan. Between 1956 and 1967 she also made superb records devoted to single composers such as Cole Porter, Duke Ellington, Richard Rodgers, George Gershwin and Irving Berlin, in a 19-volume series of 'Song Books' containing nearly 250 songs. She has been married twice, to Bernie Kornegay (from 1941 until 1943) and to Ray Brown of the Oscar Peterson Trio (from 1949 to 1953), with whom she had a son.

**Fitzgerald, Zelda** (1900–48). American literary personality and writer. The sixth child of an Alabama Supreme Court judge, Zelda Sayre was born in Montgomery, Alabama. She was educated at home and at the local high school, and grew up to be a pampered Southern belle. In July 1918 she met Francis Scott Fitzgerald, who was then in the army and stationed in Montgomery. They fell in love, and although Zelda broke off their engagement while Scott was trying to establish himself as a writer in New York, they were eventually married in 1920, at the same time as his novel *This Side of Paradise* was published. The book was an immediate success and Scott and Zelda found themselves treated, in Ring Lardner's words, like the 'prince and princess of their generation'. Their daughter, christened Frances Scott

[Scottie] was born in October 1921. They feared the pressures of their fame and popularity and in 1924 retreated to live with the expatriate American community in the South of France.

In the late 1920s Scott began to drink heavily and Zelda became obsessed with the idea of a career in ballet, practising night and day in her room. She was eventually offered the chance, which she did not accept, of joining the San Carlo Opera Ballet in Naples. She also started writing, producing a series of six sketches about the lives of young women, isolated heiresses and ballerinas, during the winter of 1928–29. Although she wrote them herself five were published under the Fitzgeralds' joint names in *College Humour*, and one appeared only under Scott's name in *The Saturday Evening Post*.

In 1930 Zelda suffered a severe mental breakdown, followed by another in 1932. She continued to write stories. Her novel, *Save me the Waltz*, appeared in October 1932, and an exhibition of her paintings and drawings was held in New York in 1933. She spent the next few years in and out of clinics, becoming increasingly confused, and was finally sent to Highland Hospital, Asheville, where she remained, apart from short holidays, until March 1940. In December of that year Scott, who was living quietly in Hollywood with Sheila Graham, collapsed and died of a heart attack. Zelda lingered on, with bursts of intermittent illness, working on a second novel, *Caesar's Things*, which remained unfinished at the time of her death. Her final collapse came in November 1947; she returned to Asheville and died with nine other women in a fire at the hospital in 1948.

N. Mitford: *Zelda* (1970)

**Flagstad, Kirsten (Malfrid)** (1895–1962). Norwegian soprano. One of the greatest Wagnerians of the 20th century, she showed her affinity with his music in the remarkable feat of memorizing the part of Elsa in *Lohengrin* at the age of ten. She made her debut as Nuri in Eugen d'Albert's *Tiefland* at the National Theatre, Oslo, in 1913; her career was restricted to Scandinavia until 1933, when she was recommended to Bayreuth. She appeared there in small roles at first, then as Sieglinde and Gutrune. Her New York debut followed at the

Metropolitan in 1935, as Sieglinde; four days later she sang Isolde there, and by the time she appeared as Brünnhilde in the same season she had secured a position of supremacy. At Covent Garden (1936–7, 1948–51) she aroused similar excitement, her roles including Isolde, Brünnhilde, Senta and Kundry.

Her second husband, Henry Johansen, caused her considerable embarrassment by joining the Norwegian Nazi (Quisling) party while she was in the USA during the early stages of World War II; she persuaded him to resign, and further manifested her view (despite her reputation for political naïveté) by accepting invitations to sing only in neutral countries. She was nevertheless treated with suspicion, especially in the USA, where some of her later appearances were greeted by protests and picketing. She showed unusual resilience in dealing with this hostility and managed a successful comeback; her final American appearance was in the title role of Gluck's *Alceste* in 1952.

In London she gave the first performance of Richard Strauss's *Vier letzte Lieder* (1950) and made her last operatic appearance as Purcell's Dido (1953). After her retirement from the stage she turned her attention to directing the newly-formed Norwegian State Opera (1958–60).

E. McArthur: *Flagstad: a Personal Memoir* (1965)

**Fleming, Amalia,** Lady (1909?–1986). Greek–British physician and political activist. Amalia Coutsouris was born to Greek parents in Constantinople (now Istanbul), Turkey. In 1914 the Turkish authorities confiscated her father's laboratory and the family home, and her family fled to Greece: a first encounter with the political turmoil which intermittently disrupted her life.

She studied medicine at the University of Athens, specializing in bacteriology. After completing her degree in 1938 she worked at the city hospital in Athens. Shorty after the outbreak of World War II she joined the anti-Nazi underground movement. Eventually she and forty others were betrayed by a colleague and she was sentenced to death, spending six months in gaol before being released by the advancing Allied troops. She and her estranged husband, Manoli Voureka, a Greek architect, found their house destroyed, and,

deeply discouraged, she went abroad. In 1946 she joined the Wright–Fleming Institute in London, working with Sir Alexander Fleming, discoverer of penicillin, and Robert May, on a study of streptomycin.

In 1951 she took up a post as chief bacteriologist at the Evangelismos Hospital in Athens. Meanwhile, Fleming, whose wife had died the year before, had fallen in love with her; he proposed to her during a visit to a UNESCO conference in Athens in 1952: they were married the following year. In 1955 Fleming died at the age of 73. Lady Fleming continued her research in London until 1967, when she returned to Greece.

Appalled by the oppressive military regime which followed the April 1967 coup, she started a campaign of outspoken opposition. The authorities were reluctant to arrest her as she held dual Greek–British citizenship. Lady Fleming worked to aid political activists and their families and to publicize the situation in Greece. The junta attempted to silence her by threats and finally in August 1971 they arrested her and sentenced her to 16 months in prison. She refused deportation, despite her failing health, saying, 'I am a Greek and I intend to stay.' In November 1971 she was literally pushed on board a plane bound for London. Defiantly, she refused to leave the plane when it arrived in London and told the press that she would 'walk back to Greece' if necessary. But meanwhile the junta had illegally taken away her Greek citizenship. She fought on 'with the only weapon I have – talking', fund-raising and lobbying the American government to cease supporting the Greek regime. When the military regime fell in 1973 she returned to Athens and became the head of the Greek Committee of Amnesty International and a member of the European Human Rights Commission. At the time of her death she was a member of both the Greek and European Parliaments.

**Fleming, Williamina (Paton Stevens)** (1857–1911). Scottish-American astronomer. Born in Dundee, the daughter of a craftsman, Williamina married James Orr Fleming at 20 and emigrated to Boston a year later. Soon afterwards the marriage broke up and she was obliged to support herself and her baby by doing domestic work for Edward Pickering, Director of the Harvard College

Observatory. She progressed to working in the Observatory and frequently collaborated with Pickering. By studying an enormous number of stellar spectra plates she found 10 of the 24 novae ever recorded up to 1911, and more than 200 variable stars. Her most important work was the classification into 17 categories of 10,351 stars in the *Draper Catalogue of Stellar Spectra*, published in 1890.

In 1898 Williamina was appointed Curator of Astronomical Photographs, supervising a team of about 12 women. She had become the leading woman astronomer of her time, and in 1906 was made an Honorary Member of the Royal Astronomical Society. Some accounts (*Nature* 86, 1911) credit her, rather than Pickering, with the discovery of the duplicity of Beta Lyrae.

**Flèsche, La.** *See* TIBBLES, SUSETTE.

**Fletcher, Alice Cunningham** (1838–1923). American anthropologist. Born in Cuba, she was privately educated and she travelled widely, eventually settling near Boston. She worked for the Peabody Museum at Harvard in the 1870s and became interested in North American ethnology and archaeology. In 1886 she officially joined the museum staff. She undertook several field trips among the Plains Indians, producing her best-known work, *The Omaha Tribe*, in 1911. She became concerned for the plight of the Indians, but her solution was to recommend integration and privatization rather than retaining the separate collective culture, and in the 1880s she encouraged the disastrous policy of dividing the reservations into small farmsteads. She became President of the Women's Anthropological Society in 1893, of the Anthropological Society of Washington in 1903, and Vice-president of the Association of American Anthropological Societies in 1895. In 1905 she was also made President of the American Folklore Society.

**Florentino, Leona** (1849–84). Filippina poet. She was born in Vigan, Ilocos Sur, into a wealthy family, and was the cousin of the patriot, José Rizal. Leona wrote her first poem at the age of ten. She was denied any secondary or higher education, and studied by herself, learning English from the parish priest at Vigan, who encouraged her to write. Although most of her poems were lost during the Revolution (1896) some still survive, including *To a young Woman on her Birthday*, *Castora Benigna*, and *Leon XIII*. They depict the lives of the people of the Ilocos province. A statue in her honour has been erected in Vigan. Her work is known outside the Philippines and was included in the International Exposition of Paris in 1887.

**Flynn, Elizabeth Gurley** (1890–1964). American radical and labour organizer. She was born in Concord, New Hampshire; her father was a Socialist engineer and her mother an Irish nationalist and feminist. In 1900 the family moved to the South Bronx and there Elizabeth was educated, began attending Socialist meetings and met the anarchists EMMA GOLDMAN and Berkman. She made her first speech when she was 16, to the Harlem Socialist Club on 'The Subjection of Women under Socialism'. Her dramatic appearance enhanced her eloquence and she became a popular speaker, leaving school and joining the International Workers of the World (IWW) in 1906. Two years later she married a miner, John Jones, but after the birth of her daughter (1909) and son (1910) she returned to political work, eventually divorcing her husband in 1920.

In 1909 she had led successful free speech fights against the banning of IWW speakers, and from 1910 in New York became involved in strike organization. At this time she worked with the Italian anarchist Carlo Tresca, and she remained deeply attached to him although their long affair ended in 1925. In 1916 and 1917 she opposed the war and was indicted for espionage with other IWW leaders, although the charges were dropped. In 1918 she founded the Worker's Defence Union to help immigrants threatened with deportation in the post-war purge of radicals, and in 1920 was one of the founders of the American Civil Liberties Union (she was later expelled, in 1940, for her Communist affiliations.)

In 1926 her political work was stopped by a serious heart illness, and she spent ten years in virtual retirement in Portland, Oregon. But in 1936 she returned to New

York and finally joined the Communist Party, to which she had applied ten years before. She organized, lectured and wrote on women's issues, demanding both equal pay and protective legislation, in the *Daily Worker*. In 1941 she was elected to the Party's Central Committee, and the following year ran for Congress, campaigning in New York State largely on women's issues. After the war she formed part of the American delegation to the Women's Congress in Paris. As anti-Communist feeling grew she organized the defense of radicals, but was herself arrested in 1951 for conspiring to overthrow the American Government, and was sentenced to three years' imprisonment. She continued to work for the party after her release and became the first National Woman Chairman in 1961. Although she disliked the Soviet dominance of the party she visited the USSR and eastern Europe in 1960 and died in Moscow, of gastro-enteritis. She was given a state funeral in Red Square.

E. Gurley Flynn: *The Rebel Girl* (rev. edn 1973)

**Follett, Mary Parker** (1868–1933). American social psychologist and management scientist. Born in Quincy, Massachusetts, Mary Follett was educated at the Thayer Academy, Braintree, Mass., until 1884 and then used an inheritance to pay to study political economy with the Society for Collegiate Instruction of Women associated with Harvard University (1880–90). This was followed by a year at Newnham College, Cambridge, and sporadic study at Radcliffe in the 1890s. She eventually received her degree in 1898, and by then had already published an innovative study, *The Speaker and the House of Representatives* (1896). During the next 20 years she was an active voluntary community worker in Boston, leading the committee on school community centres of the Women's Municipal League from 1908 to 1920. Her work on neighbourhood groups led to criticisms of contemporary democratic institutions in *The New State* (1918) and *Creative Experience* (1924). She became increasingly interested in industrial relations, serving on several wage boards, and in 1924 began to lecture on industrial management, which took her to Oxford in 1926 and to the League of Nations and the ILO in Geneva in 1928. Her great contribution was her belief in group power

rather than hierarchical structures, and in the need for participation in decisions by people at all levels within an organization. Many of her extremely influential lectures were published in *Dynamic Administration* (ed. Metcalf and Urwick, 1941) and *Freedom and Co-ordination* (ed. Urwick, 1949). She returned to London in 1929, to live with her friend Dame Katharine Furse, the Red Cross leader, and lectured at the London School of Economics in 1933. She died on a visit to Boston in December of that year.

**Fonda, Jane** (1937–). American film star and political activist. The daughter of the actor Henry Fonda, she lived in California until she was ten and then moved to Greenwich, Connecticut. She left Vassar College to study art in Paris, and on her return modelled for *Vogue*, and under the influence of Lee Strasberg began working at the Actors' Studio. In 1960 she appeared on Broadway and played in Logan's *Tall Story*, making other promising appearances in films before leaving for France in 1964. Here she met and married Roger Vadim, whose efforts to mould her into another BRIGITTE BARDOT resulted in films such as *La ronde/Circle of Love* (1964), and *Barbarella* (1968). She also appeared in American films such as *Cat Ballou* (1965).

Shaking off the images imposed by her father and husband, Fonda emerged in the late 1960s as a committed political activist, whose opposition to the Vietnam War led her to form the Anti-War Troupe with Donald Sutherland, shown in *Free the Army* (1972), and to visit North Vietnam, filmed in *Introduction to the Enemy* (1974); the aftermath of that war is the subject of *Coming Home* (1978). Her later films have usually been tied to her feminism – as in *A Doll's House* (1973), *Julia*, the story of LILLIAN HELLMAN (1977), and *9 – 5*, about office life (1980) – or her politics as in the prophetic anti-nuclear film *The China Syndrome* (1979). She has also toured the USA with her second husband Tom Hayden (whom she married in 1973), lecturing on their political theory of Economic Democracy. In 1981 she appeared in *On Golden Pond* with her father and KATHERINE HEPBURN. She arranged the production of the film which she called 'a present to my father'. Her recent films include *Agnes of God*

(1985) and *The Morning After* (1986). She has written several books on exercise, and *Women Coming of Age* (1984).

M. Freedland: *Jane Fonda* (1987)

**Fontana, Lavinia** (1552–1614). Italian painter. She was the daughter of Prospero Fontana, a prominent Bolognese painter and teacher whose home was a centre of artistic and intellectual life; she studied with him, and worked on paintings in his workshop. By 1570 Lavinia was recognized as an artist in her own right and became a popular portrait, group and narrative painter. In 1577 she married Zappi, a painter from Lucca, but they continued to work in her father's house. Lavinia bore 11 children, of whom all except three died before her. Her range of work is illustrated by her *Portrait of a Noblewoman* (1580), the *Gozzadinci Family* (1584), *The Visit of the Queen of Sheba*, and the fine religious work *Noli me tangere* (1581). In the 1590s she began to produce superb altarpieces, such as the *Holy Family with the Sleeping Christ Child* for the Escorial. Admired by Pope Gregory XIII and later patronized by Clement VIII, she was official painter to the papal court, and after her father's death in 1600 she moved to Rome. Here she undertook large-scale commissions, such as the altarpieces *The Stoning of Stephen* for St Paul's Without the Walls. She operated as a prolific independent master, with workshops in Rome and Bologna, enjoying fame and considerable wealth, and like SOFONISBA ANGUISSOLA, she encouraged and inspired many later women artists by her example.

**Fonteyn** [née Hookham, Peggy], Dame **Margot** (1919– ). English ballerina. The daughter of a mining engineer, she spent her childhood in China, the USA and South East Asia, but managed to pursue an early interest in dance, with teachers such as Goncharov in Shanghai. She joined the Vic-Wells Ballet School in 1934, first appearing as a Snowflake in *Casse noisette*, but establishing herself as a soloist in 1935, as Young Tregennis in de Valois' *Haunted Ballroom*. She danced Odette in 1935, full Odette/Odile in 1937 and Aurora in 1939. During the 1930s she also studied with the great Russian teachers in Paris, such as Olga Preobrajenska and MATHILDE KSCHESSIN-SKAYA.

Over the next 30 years, Fonteyn established her reputation as a great dancer; her notable performances included Swanilda in *Coppélia* (1943), an appearance with Massin in his revival of *Le tricorne* (1947), and guest performances with the Roland Petit Ballet in Paris in *Les demoiselles de nuit* (1948). She appeared at the Paris Opéra, in Copenhagen, at La Scala, and toured the USA in 1949 and in 1950–1 when she danced in Balanchin's *Ballet Imperial*. Known as a superb interpreter of classic roles, she was also identified with new choreographers, especially Frederick Ashton, in *Symphonic Variations* (1946), *Daphnis and Chloë* (1951), and *Ondine* (1958), which was described as a 'concerto for Fonteyn'.

In 1954 she became President of the Royal Academy of Dancing and in 1959 Guest Artist to the Royal Ballet. She appeared to be withdrawing slightly from performance, but in 1962 she began her decade-long partnership with Rudolf Nureyev, which drew new heights of achievement and was acclaimed on several international tours. In 1981, aged 62, she was still dancing, appearing as Lady Capulet in Nureyev's *Romeo and Juliet* at La Scala, Milan. Fonteyn's appeal was dependent not only on her harmonious musical style and exquisite line but also on her unassuming personal charm. She was very influential in popularizing ballet, for example in the British television series *The Magic of Dance* (1980). Her book *Pavlova Impressions* was published in 1984.

In 1955 she married the Panamanian politician Dr Roberto Arias and was created DBE in the same year. She was the first ballerina of international stature to be trained and developed in England.

M. Fonteyn: *Margot Fonteyn* (1975)
———: *A Dancer's World* (1978)

**Forbes, Joan Rosita** (1893–1967). English traveller and journalist. Born in Lincolnshire, and privately educated, she acquired an 'obsession for maps'. At the age of 17 she married Colonel Ronald Forbes, visited India, China and Australia, left her husband (divorced 1917) and travelled back alone through Africa. After driving an ambulance in World War I, she travelled to the Far East with a woman friend, 'Undine', and wrote *Unconducted Wanderers* (1919). She then worked as a journalist in Paris, and was commissioned to write on French colonialism in North Africa. Her travels there and in Arabia, her commitment to Arab nationalism and her visit to the remote Moslem Senussi sect are described in *Secret of the Sahara Kufara* (1922), and in the novel *The Jewel in the Lotus*. She had married again in 1921 but embarked on a new expedition to western Arabia and Morocco. Her later expeditions resulted in the books *Red Sea to Blue Nile* (1925) and *Conflict* (1931) about the Middle East; *Eight Republics in Search of a Future* (1933) about South America; *Forbidden Road, Kabul to Samarkand* (1937), and *India of the Princes* (1939). She also described the people she met in *These are Real People* (1937), and *These Men I Knew* (1940). All her works reflect her interest in politics and social conditions. At the end of her life she lived and wrote in the Bahamas.

J.R. Forbes: *Appointment in the Sun* (1949)

**Fossey, Dian** (1932–85). American zoologist. Born in San Francisco, Dian Fossey trained as an occupational therapist, and in 1956 began work at a children's hospital in Louisville, Kentucky. She had always longed to go to Africa and in 1963 set out on a seven-week safari to the Olduvai Gorge in Tanzania, where she met Louis and MARY LEAKEY, and then to the mountains of Zaire to see the gorillas. In 1966 she was persuaded by Mary Leakey to return again to Tanzania, visiting JANE GOODALL for advice, and setting up a work station in the Virunga mountains. She founded the Karisoke Research Centre in the forests of Rwanda, and remained there studying and living with the gorillas for 18 years, becoming increasingly reclusive: she was known locally as 'Nyiram acibili', 'the woman who lives alone in the forest'. Her moving plea for conservation, *Gorillas in the Mist*, appeared in 1983. The day after Christmas 1985 she was found dead, murdered by machete blows. The poachers whose raids she had long struggled to stop were suspected, although her assistant Wayne McGuire was initially accused of her death, allegedly motivated by an attempt to steal her scientific research.

H. Hayes: *The Dark Romance of Dian Fossey* (1988)

**Fowler, Lydia Folger** (1822–79). American doctor. Lydia came from a distinguished family, her cousins including MARIA MITCHELL, Benjamin Franklin and LUCRETIA MOTT. Lydia married at 22, then attended Rochester Eclectic Medical College, one branch of the Central Medical College of New York. She gained her MD in 1850, becoming the first American woman to receive that degree.

The following year she became the first woman to hold a chair at a legally authorized school when she was appointed Professor of Midwifery and Diseases of Women and Children at Rochester. She practised preventive medicine through writing and lecturing on medico-social subjects and also held a private practice in New York City.

In 1858 the Folgers went to England for the sake of her husband Lorenzo's phrenology practice. Lydia was limited to volunteer practice in the slums and promoting preventive medicine through lectures. She died of pneumonia.

**Frame, Janet** (1924–). New Zealand novelist. Born in Oamaru, nr Dunedin, she was educated at Otago University and after a period as a teacher became a nurse-companion. Her first short stories were collected in *The Lagoon* (1951). After suffering a severe mental breakdown she spent several years in and out of hospital, transmuting her experience into the extremely moving novel *Faces in the Water* (1961), which presents the world of the 'sane' as possibly more cruel and strange than that of the hospital inmates. In 1956 she left New Zealand and lived for some years in London.

Her novels, from *The Owls do Cry* (1957) and *The Edge of the Alphabet* (1961) to *Intensive Care* (1970) and *Living in the Maniototo* (1979), deal with problems of personal vision, communication and language in a style whose surface simplicity masks considerable sophistication. She has recently published three remarkable volumes of autobiography: *To the Is-land* (1982), *An Angel at My Table* (1984) and *The Envoy from Mirror City* (1985).

**Francis, Clare (Mary)** (1946–). English sailor. Born in Surbiton, Clare was able to begin sailing when on holidays in the Isle of Wight. She was educated at the Royal Ballet School and then took a degree in economics at University College, London.

After six years in marketing she rose to a challenge to make a solo trip across the Atlantic, which she did in 37 days in a 32-foot boat she bought for £7000. In 1974 she was sponsored in the Round Britain Race, and came third. In 1975 she sailed to the Azores and back singlehanded, and sailed in *L'aurore* in 1975 and 1976.

In 1976 she was one of four women among 125 participants in the Royal Western Singlehanded Transatlantic Race. She was the only woman to finish, and in spite of battering by massive waves and of encroaching icebergs she set a women's transatlantic record of 29 days from Falmouth to Newport, Rhode Island, in her Ohlson 38 *Robertson's Golly*. Sponsorship easily followed success and she became the first woman skipper in the Whitbread Round the World Event (1977–8); she and the crew of 11 came fifth.

In 1977 she married a yachtsman, Jacques Redon; they have one child. In 1978 she was created an MBE, and in 1981 co-presented a television series, *The Commanding Sea*. She has since become a best-selling novelist with *Night Sky* (1983), *Red Crystal* (1985) and *Wolf Winter* (1987), but in 1987 she was diagnosed as suffering from the mysterious, fatiguing disease myalgic encephalomyelitis (ME) which has severely affected her work.

C. Francis: *Come Hell or High Water* (1977)
——–: *Come Wind or Weather* (1978)

**Franco, Veronica** (1546–91). Italian poet. Born in Venice, Veronica Franco was married briefly to Paolo Panizza, a doctor, but left him and embarked on a series of love affairs, principally with poets Marco and Domenico Veniaro, and also with the king of France, Henri III. Her scandalous love life, combined with unusual independence and poetic skills, led in 1580 to an accusation being brought against her by the Inquisition of practising witchcraft to make men fall in love with her. The trial was abandoned for reasons unknown, and in the same year she suggested the idea of opening a refuge for women of the streets. The first such refuge was opened in 1591, the year of her death.

Her poems, mainly epistolary letters in *terza rima* and some sonnets, were collected and published in an edition of 1575, entitled *Terze Rime*. Her letters were published in 1580, and their moral tone appears to suggest that she underwent some kind of religious conversion in later life. The tone of her poetry is remarkable, full of energy and explicit sexual language. She asserts her own right to love independently and to choose men on her own terms. Her plans for a women's refuge, however, show her concern for the plight of women abandoned by men and the need for sisterly solidarity.

Like many other major women poets of the Renaissance, Veronica Franco's work was neglected for centuries. In 1912 the *Terze Rime* and sonnets were reissued and in 1946 the great Italian critic Benedetto Croce edited a volume of her letters. The love poems between Veronica Franco and Maffio Venier included in *Il libro chiuso* were published in 1956. There is no biography of Veronica Franco in English and very little has been written about her.

G. Masson: *Courtesans of the Italian Renaissance* (1975)
G. Tassini: *Veronica Franco, Celebre poetessa e cortigiana del secolo XVI* (1988)

**Frank, Anne** (1930–45). Jewish martyr. She was born in Germany, but her family escaped to Amsterdam after the Nazi rise to power in 1933. When the Germans occupied the Netherlands in 1941, Anne had to move to a Jewish school, and as the persecution increased her family took refuge with four other Jews in the back rooms of the office and warehouse behind their grocery business, being cared for and brought food by a Dutch family who lived below. They remained there until an informer denounced them in 1944. During these years, Anne wrote stories and also kept a diary in which she recorded her hopes, ambitions and early romantic and sexual longings, conscious of the desire to live and of the imminent threat of death. She died of typhus in Belsen shortly after her deportation. The rest of her family also perished, except for her father who was in the camp hospital at the time of the liberation of Auschwitz. A friend gave him all Anne's writings, which she had carefully hidden. He published an edited version of her diary in 1947 as *Het achterhuis* (translated as *Diary of a Young Girl* in 1953). It has been translated into 30 languages and been adapted for stage and cinema. The house in Amsterdam is preserved in memory of all the young Jews who suffered and died in the war.

**Frankenthaler, Helen** (1928–). American painter. After studying at Dalton School and Bennington College, Vermont, she went to New York in 1946 where she studied at the Art Students' League and privately with Wallace Harrison and Hans Hofman. Fascinated by abstract art since high school, from 1951 she developed her technique of 'stain and soak' influenced by Jackson Pollock, creating lyrical colour compositions. During the 1950s she travelled widely in the USA and Europe, married Robert Motherwell in 1955, taught at New York University (1958–9), and won the first prize at the Paris Biennale (1959). In later years she has taught occasionally at Yale, Princeton and elsewhere. Since early exhibitions such as 'Fifteen Unknowns' (1951) and '9 Women Painters' (1953), her work has been shown across the USA and Europe and is included in many collections. Deliberately ambiguous, merging form and abstraction, her later work is more neutral and geometric. A major retrospective exhibition was held at the Guggenheim Museum, New York in 1985–6.

H.C. Goosen: *Helen Frankenthaler* (1969)

**Franklin, Aretha** (1942–). American singer. Born in Memphis and brought up in Detroit, one of five children of a famous preacher and gospel singer, she began singing in the choir of the New Bethel Baptist Church as a child, singing solos on her father's evangelical tours from the age of 14. At 18 she signed a contract with Columbia records, but real success did not come until 1966 when she signed for Atlantic and immediately made the classic *Never loved a Man* (1967). She continued to produce best-selling soul and blues music until 1970. Never fiercely ambitious, shy and overshadowed by her fame, she then withdrew from the limelight for a year or two. After her return she recorded a pure gospel album, with her father and a huge choir, *Amazing Grace* (1972). She has made over 30 albums including *Young, Gifted and Black*

(1972), which includes largely autobiographical songs of her own composition, *Almighty Fire* (1978) and *Love All the Hurt Away* (1981). She has played to audiences throughout the USA and Europe, winning the title of 'Lady Soul'. Her two sisters are also well-known, Carolyn as a song-writer, and Erma as a soul singer. She was first married to Ted White, with whom she had three children, and after their divorce married Glynn Turman in 1978.

**Franklin** [née Griffin], **Jane** [Lady Franklin] (1791–1875). English reformer and traveller. Born in London, the daughter of a silk weaver, in 1828 she became the second wife of the explorer Sir John Franklin, accompanying him when he was made Governor of Van Diemen's Land in 1836. Forceful and idealistic, in eight years she turned Tasmania into the cultural centre for the Australian colonies, persuading Franklin to found a scientific society in 1839, buying land for a botannical garden and natural history museum which housed her collections until 1853, and establishing an agricultural settlement. She spent much of her personal fortune on reform. In 1843 she started the Tasmanian Society for the Reformation of Female Prisoners, corresponding on the subject with ELIZABETH FRY, and founded a State School, Christ's College, in 1840, which she endowed with large estates. She then became embroiled in the political disputes which led to Franklin's recall in 1843.

A determined traveller, she explored New Zealand and Australia as well as Tasmania, being the first woman to climb Mount Wellington and to travel overland from Melbourne to Sydney. In 1845 John Franklin set off on a voyage of Arctic exploration. When no news was received, Jane organized her own expeditions to find him, fitting out five ships between 1850 and 1857, the last of which, *The Fox*, revealed that he had discovered the long sought North-West Passage, since traces of his ships and equipment had been found in King William's Land. During these anxious years, Jane herself travelled widely, from Japan and India to the USA and Hawaii. Her own journeys and the expedition of her ships contributed greatly to contemporary knowledge, and in 1860 she was awarded the

Founder's Medal of the Royal Geographical Society. She continued to travel, and to pursue her scientific interests, and at the age of 83, at the end of her life, fitted out the yacht *Pandora*, which she sent to try to break through the North-West Passage, where her husband had died.

F.J. Woodward: *Portrait of Jane* (1951)

**Franklin, (Stella Marian Sarah) Miles** (1879–1954). Australian writer. Born in Talbingo, New South Wales, into an old pioneer family, she was educated at home and at a local school. Her parents farmed unsuccessfully and in 1915 moved to Sydney. As their poverty increased she worked as a governess in 1897, and this and her bush childhood are described in her defiant novel *My Brilliant Career*, published in the UK in 1901. Her fame brought difficulties, but through ROSE SCOTT she became involved in feminist circles in 1902 and was then drawn into Christian Science. She rejected a marriage proposal and set off for California in 1906, continuing to Chicago where she met the American feminists JANE ADDAMS and MARGARET DREIER ROBINS, and for several years worked as a secretary for the Women's Trade Union League. In 1915 she moved to London, worked as a cook and continued to write – as she had all through these eventful years. In 1917 and 1918 she worked with a Scottish Women's Hospital unit in Macedonia. After World War I she remained chiefly in London, then returned to Australia in 1927 and revisited London in 1931.

A professional writer and promoter of Australian literature, she published *Old Blastus of Bandicoot* (1931), *Bring the Monkey* (1933), and completed her six-volume cycle of pastoral novels, originally published under the name of *Brent of Bin Bin*. Her prize-winning book *All that Swagger* appeared in 1936. During World War II she rejected the prevalent right-wing nationalism. A further autobiographical novel, written years earlier about her youth and called *My Career goes Bung*, appeared in 1946. Her last lectures on Australian literature, given at the University of Western Australia in 1950, were published in 1956 as *Laughter, Not for a Cage*.

M. Barnard: *Miles Franklin* (1967)

**Franklin, Rosalind (Elsie)** (1920–58). English scientist; a researcher in physical chemistry and molecular biology. After graduating from Cambridge in 1941, Rosalind Franklin stayed on to investigate gas-phase chromatography under Ronald Norrish. From 1942 to 1953 she held successive posts with the British Coal Utilisation Research Association, the Laboratoire Central des Services Chimiques de l'Etat, Paris, the Medical Research Council Unit at King's College, London, and Birkbeck College, London. Her studies involved the physical structure of coals and carbons, using X-ray diffraction techniques, which in her later posts she applied to the problems of the structure of DNA and then of viruses.

She is known widely for her controversial part in the race to explain the helical structure of DNA; J.D. Watson's *The Double Helix* gives most of the credit to Watson and Crick, but A. Klug's article 'Rosalind Franklin and the discovery of the structure of DNA' in *Nature*, 219 (1968) describes her crucial contributions and the thoroughness of her inductive approach. She died of cancer.

A. Sayre: *Rosalind Franklin and DNA* (1975)

**Fraser, Dawn** (1937–). Australian swimmer. She was born to a large, poor family in Sydney. Her career as a top-class swimmer was comparatively long: she won the 100 metres freestyle gold medal at the Olympic Games of 1956, 1960 and 1964, the only competitor to win the same title at three successive Games. She was not only the first woman to swim 100 metres and 110 yards in under one minute, but also broke the 100 metres record 9 successive times, as well as breaking 30 other world records.

Dawn's training was more gruelling than that of previous competitors. She estimates that in 10 years she swam 10,000 miles (c16,000 kilometres). She achieved great popularity and publicity, and was awarded the OBE, but she also aroused controversy, and in 1965 was suspended from competitive swimming, with three others, for three years.

During this time she was briefly married to Gary Ware, a bookmaker, and had a daughter.

**Fredegund** (*d* 597). Frankish queen. While working as a servant, she became the mistress of Chilperic I, the Merovingian King, and influenced him to reject his wife Audovera, and then to murder his second wife, Galswintha, in 568. She then became his wife. The hatred of BRUNHILDA, Galswintha's sister and the wife of King Sigebert, and Fredegund for each other led to almost 40 years of war between their two Frankish kingdoms of Neustria and Austrasia. In the course of the war Fredegund engineered the deaths of Sigebert and of her own step-children, Audovera's sons, one of whom she accused of killing her own three sons who had died of the plague.

When Chilperic was murdered, in mysterious circumstances, in 584, Fredegund seized his wealth and fled to sanctuary in Paris with her remaining son Lothair II. She persuaded the nobles to accept him as legitimate heir, and acted as Regent, continuing her power struggles first with the kings of Burgundy, Guntram (561–92) and Childebert II (593–5), and then with Brunhilda again, who supported her own grandsons' claim to the throne. In 597 she finally defeated her old opponent but died in Paris a few months later. Her reputation as an indomitable, ingenious and atrociously cruel woman was enhanced by Gregory of Tours in his *Historia Francorum*.

**Frederick, Pauline** (*c*1920–). American news analyst. She was born in Galitzin, Pennsylvania, and educated at George Washington University, where she obtained an MA in International Law. She began as a free-lance journalist for various newspapers and radio stations, visiting China in 1945, before becoming a news commentator for ABC (1946–53). She had an early morning radio show and sometimes worked on the evening television news, the only woman working on 'hard news' broadcasting, and in 1948 the first to cover a national political convention; in 1950 she covered the United Nations Security Council meetings at the start of the Korean war.

In 1953 she moved to NBC, and, as their United Nations correspondent, covered the crises in Suez, the Congo, Hungary, Cuba, Cyprus, Vietnam and the Middle East, until 1974. In 1976 she acted as moderator in the election campaign debate between Carter and Ford. Since then she has been an international affairs analyst for National Public Radio. She has received numerous awards for journalism, and honorary degrees.

**Freud, Anna** (1895–1982). Austrian-English psychoanalyst, the youngest daughter and sixth child of Sigmund Freud. Anna left school early, and after teaching at primary school became her father's secretary, companion and pupil. In 1922 she became an active member of the International Psychoanalytical Association and began practice; in 1925 she was Secretary of the Vienna Training Institute, headed by HELENE DEUTSCH. Over the next two years Anna gave a series of lectures on observing normal childhood behaviour, which led to the establishment of the *Kinderseminar*. Her child analysis differed from that of MELANIE KLEIN's; it was of the 'Continental' school which believed that adult analysis must be modified.

Her book *The Ego and the Mechanisms of Defence* (1937) extends Sigmund Freud's work of ten years before on anxiety as a signal function of ego. Of her many works (later collected in seven volumes), this is probably her most significant theoretical contribution.

In 1938 the threat to Jews in Austria obliged Anna to emigrate with her father to England, where he died in 1939. During World War II she directed Burlingham which afterwards became the Hampstead Child Therapy Clinic, with Anna as Director from 1952. She aimed to create a developmental profile of a child, rather than laying too much stress on obscure pre-verbal periods. The many aspects of her work extended to family law in which she stressed the psychological importance of the parent to the child.

Her first return to Vienna was not until 1971, when she was given a standing ovation at the 27th International Psychoanalytical Congress. In 1972 Vienna University awarded her an honorary MD, and she also received similar honours elsewhere. For many years she edited the annual volume *Psychoanalytic Study of the Child*.

U.H. Peters: *Anna Freud: A Life Dedicated to Children* (1984)

**Friedan, Betty** (1921–). American feminist writer and organizer. Betty Goldstein was born in Peoria, Illinois, the daughter of a Jewish jeweller and a mother who had left a career as a journalist for marriage; she saw both these factors as influencing her later fight for minority rights. She took courses in psychology and sociology at Smith College and at the University of California, Berkeley, and was herself a journalist, later training as a psychologist. In 1947 she married Carl Friedan, a theatrical producer, and left work to look after her three children. She lived the life of a suburban housewife until 1963, when *The Feminine Mystique* was published. This defined 'the problem that has no name' as the American woman's pressure to conform to the role of housewife and mother, with any other self-expression being considered deviant. It immediately met with an enormous response, and Friedan has been called 'the mother of the new feminist movement'.

In 1966 she organized the National Organisation for Women (NOW) which still remains the most powerful lobby group for women's rights in the USA, and she was its first President, until 1970. She also helped found the National Women's Political Caucus in 1971, led the National Women's Strike for Equality, convened the International Feminist Congress in 1973 and helped found the First Women's Bank the same year. Divorced in 1969, she became increasingly radical in outlook during the 1970s and in 1977 edited an anthology of articles on the movement, called *It Changed my Life*. Since the late 1970s she has campaigned actively for the Equal Rights Amendment, but her more reformist stance in *The Second Stage* (1981) disconcerted many feminists.

**Frink, Dame Elisabeth** (1930–). English sculptor. Born in Thurlow, Suffolk, she was educated at a convent in Exmouth, and then studied at Guildford and Chelsea schools of art between 1947 and 1953. She then taught at Chelsea (1953–60) and at St Martin's School of Art (1955–7). She lived in France between 1967 and 1972, and later lived and worked in Dorset. She has been married three times, to Michael Jamnet (1956–62), Edward Pool (1968–74) and Alex Csaky (from 1975).

Elisabeth Frink has exhibited regularly, especially in the Waddington Galleries, since 1955. She creates strong individual figures in landscape, usually in movement, and her particular interest in the male head can be seen in a succession of series since the 1950s, from warriors to soldiers, to victims of suffering. Among her public works are the Kennedy Memorial in Dallas and the lectern of Coventry Cathedral. She also paints, and has published etchings illustrating *Aesop's Fables* (1967), *The Canterbury Tales* (1971), and the *Odyssey and Iliad* (1974–5). She was made a CBE in 1968 and DBE in 1982 and was elected to the Royal Academy in 1977.

E. Frink: *The Art of Elisabeth Frink* (1972)

**Frith, Mary** [Moll Cutpurse] (c1590–1659). English thief and transvestite. Moll dressed as a man, wore a sword, and was reputed to be a highway robber. Middleton and Dekker made her the heroine of *The Roaring Girl, or Moll Cutpurse* (1611), and there are many other literary references to her. She was put in the Clink in 1610 for stealing money and jewels, and in Bridewell in 1611 for making lewd speeches and singing a song on stage at the end of *The Roaring Girl*. On Christmas Day 1611 she was arrested for wearing men's clothes in St Paul's Cathedral, but when she came to do penance at St Paul's Cross she was maudlin drunk. She married Lewkner Markham in 1614, though she was reputed to be a hermaphrodite. In 1621 she was involved with the constable of St Bride's in a racket for recovering stolen goods. Her impudent high spirits appealed to her contemporaries, and there are many legends about her: that she robbed General Fairfax on Hounslow Heath, that she was an ardent royalist and made the gutters run with wine in honour of Charles I, and that her verse epitaph was written by Milton. Like her autobiography (1662), they are probably apocryphal.

**Fry** [née Gurney], **Elizabeth** (1780–1845). English prison reformer. Born in Norfolk, the daughter of a banker, and a member of a famous Quaker family, she began visiting the sick and teaching poor children under the influence of the American evangelist Savery. She herself became an Anglican at the age of 18, but in 1800 married another Quaker, Joseph Fry. They had ten children. After the death of her father in 1809 she became a Quaker minister, noted for her effective public speaking, and in 1813 became interested in conditions in Newgate Prison, London, especially the appalling plight of women and children. She visited, preached, established a school and founded a prioners' aid society in 1817. She gave forceful evidence to the 1818 Royal Commission, and lobbied vigorously for improvements in conditions for prisoners transported to Australia. During the 1820s she toured the country inspecting prisons, demanding reform, and founding women's associations and pressure groups. She also toured Europe and was sympathetically received at the courts of France, Prussia and Russia. During this period she also campaigned for employment and housing schemes for the London poor. After her husband's bankruptcy in 1828 her public activities were curtailed but she continued her personal visiting.

J. Rose: *Elizabeth Fry* (1980)

**Fry, (Sarah) Margery** (1874–1958). British penal reformer. The daughter of an eminent judge, Sir Edward Fry, Margery came from a remarkable family: her brother Roger Fry, with whom she lived for many years, was a famous art critic; her sister Agnes a distinguished scientist, and her sister Isabel a pioneering educationist. Margery was educated at Roedean School and Somerville College, Oxford, where she worked as Librarian from 1898 to 1904. She then became warden of a students' hostel at Birmingham University, later University House, until 1915 when she left to work with the Quakers' War Victims Relief Mission in France.

She later devoted herself to prison reform, becoming Hon. Secretary of the Penal Reform League in 1919 and overseeing its amalgamation with the Howard Association, to form the Howard League. One of the first women magistrates in 1921, she was also the first education adviser at Holloway. After she resigned as Secretary of the Howard League in 1926 she was Principal of Somerville College for five years, but then returned to her reform work, travelling and lecturing in China, the United States and elsewhere, representing Britain at the International Penal and Penitentiary Congress of 1946, and presenting a paper to UNESCO on human rights the following year. A committed opponent of the death penalty since the 1920s she campaigned vigorously for changes to the law. A noted public speaker, who cared passionately for her cause, she was immensely persuasive and influenced public opinion, as well as the official policy of such bodies as the Home Office Advisory Council on the Treatment of Offenders. In addition to many pamphlets she wrote one book, *Arms of the Law* (1951).

E. Huws Jones: *Margery Fry* (1966)

**Fuller, Loie** [Louise] **(Mary)** (1862–1928). American dancer. She was born in Illinois and began her career in vaudeville, and as a circus artist and actress (1865–91). In 1891 she developed her skirt dance, using light effects on yards of swirling silk in the *The Fire Dance*, *Serpentine Dance*, and *Rainbow*. She took her act to Paris in 1892, and her brilliant complicated staging, rather than dancing ability, brought recognition from avant-garde art movements, inspiring work by Lautrec, Rodin and Roone, among others. Some dances were based on natural forms, for example *Butterfly* (1892), *Clouds* (1893) and *Holy and Fire* (1895), and others on ensemble movements creating many landscapes, such as *Bottom of the Sea* (1906) and *Ballet of Light* (1908). In 1921 she developed outside performances, using the natural stage effects of light and wind. The school which she founded in 1908 and her troupe of girl dancers continued after her death.

Loie Fuller was imaginative, and genuinely interested in the scientific basis of her light effects, developing machines in her own laboratory (she created a *Radium Dance* in honour of MARIE CURIE). She was also an energetic business woman, impresario and amateur politician.

L. Fuller: *Fifteen Years of a Dancer's Life* (1913)

**Fuller, Margaret.** *See* OSSOLI, MARGARET FULLER.

**Furtseva, Ekaterina** (1910–74). Russian politician. She was born in the textile town of Vyshni Volochek in the Kalinin region, where she became a weaver. She was admitted to the Young Communist League at the early age of 14, achieving membership of the Party at 20. A hard worker and a good organizer and speaker, she became

Secretary of the Crimea Area Committee and between 1937 and 1942 studied at the Moscow Institute of Chemical Technology. Long acquainted with Krushchev, after Stalin's death her power increased. She became Second Secretary of the Moscow Party (1950), Chairman (1954), and one of three women members of the 133-strong Party Central Committee. Her husband, Firyabin, was also a leading politician. In 1956 Furtseva was elected as the first woman member of the Praesidium, becoming Minister of Culture in 1960, despite her disapproval of 'decadent' modern art.

**Furujhelhm, Annie** (1860–1937). Finnish suffragette. The daughter of an admiral, she began her career as a journalist, editing the monthly *Nutid* and the women's magazine *Astra*. An early supporter of the feminist movement, she took a leading role in the struggle for the franchise and was a member of the Finnish Diet under the Russians from 1914 to 1919, and then of the independent parliament (1922–9), where she pressed for many social reforms. She then left politics to devote herself to her work for the International Alliance of Women and the Finland Swedish Women's Union.

# G

**Gaidinliu, Rani** (1915–). Indian freedom fighter. Rani Gaidinliu was born into a poor farming family. She joined the freedom movement at the age of 13. In 1931, at the age of 16, she took up leadership of the movement amongst the Nagas in Assam and the Naga Hills, and headed a well-organized and trained band of guerillas fighting British rule. The British Government in India used an entire contingent of the Assam Rifles to defeat her guerillas and Rani Gaidinliu was arrested and sentenced to life imprisonment. She remained in gaol for 14 years and was released by Nehru in 1947 after Indian independence. Retired from active political life, she was later involved in social work in Nagaland. She also composed songs and was a specialist in weaving.

**Galindo, Beatriz** [La Latina] (1474–1534). Spanish scholar. A famous humanist scholar and professor of philosophy, rhetoric and medicine at Salamanca, she was known as 'La Latina' and became tutor and possibly adviser to Queen ISABELLA I. She wrote poetry, in Latin, and commentaries on Aristotle and on classical authors as well as founding schools and hospitals in many parts of Spain. Her husband, Francisco Ramirez, was a soldier and secretary to King Fernando V.

**Galla Placidia** (?390–450). Roman aristocrat. She was the daughter of Theodosius the Great (*d* 395). During her childhood increased Visigoth threats to the Empire led to the removal of the imperial residence to Ravenna. She was taken prisoner by Alaric after the siege of Rome as part of his booty; after his death she married his brother Ataulf in 414. Their son died in Barcelona in 415, Ataulf was murdered, and Galla Placidia was handed back to the Roman general Constantius; in 417, against her will, she was married to him. Her close relationship with her brother Emperor Honorius gave rise to scandal, but in 421 she was made Augusta, and as 'Augustus' Constantius became co-Emperor. After her husband's death, Galla Placidia alienated her brother by pressing for agreements with the Goths and supporting Boniface as military leader; she was exiled to Constantinople to the court of her nephew Theodosius II. After Honorius's death (423) her son Valentinian was crowned Emperor of the West (425), but in her last years her influence decreased.

Galla Placidia was a generous patron of the arts. Her mausoleum is still an impressive feature of Ravenna.

*Galla Placidia Augusta: a Biographical Essay* (1968)

**Gandhi, Indira** (1917–84). Indian politician. The only child of Jawaharlal Nehru and Smt Kamla Nehru, and the niece of VIJAYA LAKSHMI PANDIT, she was in a volatile political arena from the time of her birth in Allahabad. At the age of 13 she founded the Bal Chakha Sangh and was part of the Vanas Sena, the children's organization which ran messages to help the Congress Party or Freedom Movement during the non-cooperative movement. But despite her family's nationalist views she was sent to England to school, attending Badminton and Somerville College, Oxford, and also spending some time in Switzerland.

Indira joined Congress in 1938 and was imprisoned for 13 months in 1942 by the British. In that year she married Feroze Gandhi, a journalist; they had two sons, Feroze and Sanjay. Indira, however, remained with her father, who became Prime Minister after Independence, and acted as his hostess and close supporter from

1947 to 1964. Under Gandhi's instructions she worked in the riot-affected areas of Delhi in 1947. Associated with numerous organizations, she was Chairman of the Central Social Welfare Board (1953–7), member of the Congress Working Committee and Central Election Committee from 1955 and the Central Parliamentary Board from 1956, and President of the All India Youth Congress from 1956 to 1960. On Nehru's death in 1964 she was elected to Parliament in his place. After acting as Minister of Information and Broadcasting (1964–6), Indira Gandhi became Prime Minister on the death of Lal Shastri in 1966, having toured India, drawing enormous crowds in her campaign, a practice her father began and which she has always continued. Her opponents in the party caused a split, but her 'Ruling Congress' was determined to institute radical policies such as the nationalization of banks and land reform. In 1971 she called a general election to seek public support and won by an enormous margin.

Despite her declared aim of attacking poverty, her period in office was marked by severe economic troubles, especially following the war with Pakistan over Bangladesh. In 1974 there were huge demonstrations and in 1975 she declared Emergency Rule, imprisoning thousands of political opponents and imposing fierce press censorship. Her unpopularity was increased by her son Sanjay's ambitious commercial plans and his introduction of a campaign of compulsory sterilization for men to control the ever-growing population. She called an early election in 1977 but lost heavily and came under the onslaught of public censure and criticism, facing charges of corruption and authoritarianism. Sanjay was briefly imprisoned, she herself was expelled from Parliament, imprisoned and released in 1978. She then resigned from the Congress Party and became leader of the India National Congress, winning a seat through a by-election. Her tours across the continent and endless public appearances won back her followers and in 1980 she was re-elected as Prime Minister by an overwhelming majority. Sanjay, on whom she had grown increasingly reliant, was killed in a plane crash the same year.

Indira Gandhi was remarkable for her ambition for personal power, her endurance and political tenacity. On a world front she insisted on India's independence, gradually loosening the ties with the USSR developed in the early 1970s when China seemed menacing, and was a forceful spokeswomen for the rights of poorer nations. Her ruthless and autocratic methods were often at variance with her democratic principles and she continued to face determined opposition in India, especially in 1983 and early 1984 when in response to disturbances among Sikhs in the Punjab she sent in government troops, who sacked the Golden Temple of Amritsar. She was assassinated in the garden of her official residence in New Delhi by two Sikh bodyguards, and India was plunged into sectarian violence, during which over 1000 people died. Her son Rajiv Gandhi was immediately sworn in as Prime Minister.

N.P. Saghal: *Indira Gandhi's Emergence and Style* (1978)

**Garbo, Greta** [pseud. of Greta Louisa Gustafsson] (1905–).. Swedish-American film actress. She was born in Stockholm into a poor labouring family and her childhood was dominated by poverty and unemployment. After her father's death, at the age of 14 she worked in a barber's shop, then as a salesgirl, where her appearance in a publicity film led to other short roles, and to her entering the Royal Dramatic Theatre School. She was chosen by Mauritz Stiller for *The Story of Gösta Berling* (1924), which was a European success. Stiller coached her and managed her career, as Josef von Sternberg was to manage that of MARLENE DIETRICH, with whom she played in Pabst's *The Joyless Street* in Berlin (1925).

Stiller was given a Hollywood contract by Louis B. Mayer in 1924 and insisted on taking Garbo who at once became a great star, in the silent film *The Torrent* (1926). Stiller returned to Sweden and died in 1928, but Garbo remained to make ten silent films, before her first talking part in *Anna Christie* (1930). Her other great films of the decade include *Mata Hari* and *Grand Hotel* (1932), *Queen Christina* (1933), *Anna Karenina* (1935), *Camille* (1936) and *Ninotchka* (1939). After the failure of *Two-Faced Woman* (1941) she suddenly retired from films, perhaps sensing that her appeal would not survive World War II. Frequent attempts to make her return have been in vain, although in 1954 she was awarded a special Academy Award for her performances. She has never married, despite rumours of attachments to John Gilbert, Reuben Mamoulian, Gaylord Hauser and Cecil Beaton. Garbo's withdrawal into the life of a recluse in Switzerland, France and New York, echoing the lonely ending of many of her films, has merely added mystery to her legend.

**Garden, Mary** (1874–1967). American-Scottish soprano. She was taken to the USA as a child and studied singing in Chicago and from 1895 in Paris. Having been contracted to the Opéra-Comique, she was scheduled to make her debut as Micaela in Bizet's *Carmen* in October 1900, but in April was able to replace Marthe Rioton, who had collapsed in mid-performance, in the title role of Charpentier's *Louise*. The role with which she is primarily associated, however, is Debussy's Mélisande, which she created in 1902 despite the objections of the librettist Maeterlinck. The association with Debussy continued the following year, when they began recording many of his songs together. Having impressed Massenet with her interpretations of his *Manon*, she gave the first performance of his *Chérubin* (1905); she also gave the American première of his *Thaïs* (Manhattan Opera House, 1907), a production controversial for her choice of costuming. She defied convention too in singing the tenor role of Jean in his *Jongleur de Notre Dame*. Other notable roles included Carmen and Salome, which she danced herself.

After her appearance as Mélisande at the Chicago Grand Opera in 1910, she became that company's leading soprano for the next two decades, and was its Director for the 1921–2 season.

M. Garden and L. Biancolli: *Mary Garden's Story* (1951)

**Gardner, Isabella Stewart** (1840–1924). American art collector. Born into a wealthy family in New York, Isabella was privately educated, and in 1856–8 she visited Italy and attended a finishing school in Paris. In 1860 she married John Lowell Gardner, a Boston businessman and financier; the loss of her two-year old son in 1865 threw her into a severe depression. After a visit to Europe to recuperate she became a notable society hostess, entertaining on a lavish scale, befriending writers and musicians and beginning her art collection. A world tour in 1883 influenced her to become a collector of Oriental art, but her major acquisitons were European Old Masters, and modern Impressionist artists. In 1891 her father died, and, with the aid of her protégé Berenson, her whole inheritance was spent on art. On Gardner's death in 1898, he left over $2 million to found a museum, and Isabella personally supervised the building of the extravagant rococo Fenway Court, Boston, which was opened to the public in 1903. She spent the rest of her life there and continued her purchases until 1921.

L.H. Thorp: '*Mrs Jack*' (1965)

**Garland, Judy** [pseud. of Frances Gumm] (1922–69). American singer and film actress. Born in Grand Rapids, Michigan, the daughter of vaudeville performers, at the age of three she appeared on stage with her two older sisters in 'The Gumm Sisters Kiddie Act'. When she was nine they changed their stage name to 'Garland' and the following year she became 'Judy'. At the age of 13 she was signed up by Louis B. Mayer for MGM, appearing in *Every Sunday* (1936), making headlines with *Broadway Melody of 1938*, and starring in a succession of films with Mickey Rooney. Her greatest success was in *The Wizard of Oz* (1939) for which she won a special Academy Award. Constantly under pressure, she made seven more films before 1943, and was by then largely dependent on drugs. In 1941 she married the band-leader David Rose, and in 1945 Vincente Minnelli, with whom she made *Meet me in St Louis* (1944), *The Clock* (1945), *Ziegfeld Follies* (1946) and *The Pirate* (1947). Their daughter Liza was born in 1946 and they were divorced in 1951.

Increasingly unhappy and temperamental, she was fired from MGM in 1951 and attempted suicide. Her third husband Sid Luft, with whom she had two children, helped her by organizing triumphant concert appearances in London and New York. In 1954 she made the unforgettable *A Star is born*. The late 1950s were years of more breakdowns and lawsuits and despite her magnificent concert in Carnegie Hall in 1961 Judy made only four more films including *I could go on Singing* (1963). She was married to Mark Herron briefly (1965), and to Mickey Deans in 1968. She was booed when attempting a cabaret season in London, and the following year died from an overdose of sleeping pills.

A. Edwards: *Judy Garland* (1975)

**Garnett, Constance** (1861–1946). British translator of Russian. Constance Black was born in Brighton, where her father was town clerk. At the age of 17 she won a scholarship to Newnham College, Cambridge, and in 1883 took a first in Classics. After working as a governess for three years she was appointed librarian at the People's Palace in the East End of London. In 1889 she married Edward Garnett, a publisher's reader who became an influential critic, particularly of Joseph Conrad, John Galsworthy and D.H. Lawrence. In 1892, recovering from a difficult childbirth, she learned Russian and began translating the classics. Her editions of Turgenev (1894–8), Tolstoy (1901–4), Dostoevsky (1912–20), Chekhov (1916–22) and Gogol (1922–8) introduced them to English readers and remained the standard versions for half a century. Promoted by her husband's critical writings they had a great influence on English literature. Her descriptive passages are masterly, but she was less successful with dramatic dialogue. She was a rationalist and agnostic and for much of her life a socialist, being on the executive of the Fabian Society in 1895–6. Her son was the novelist David Garnett.

C. Heilbrun: *The Garnett Family* (1961)
R. Garnett: *Constance Garnett* (in preparation)

**Garrison, Lucy McKim** (1842–77). American slave-song collector. In 1862 she spent three weeks in the South Carolina Sea Islands, where she was profoundly impressed by the songs of the freemen. Her work in notating these, with William Francis Allen and Charles Pickard Ware, resulted in the publication of *Slave Songs of the United States* (1867). This collection, the first of its kind, remains one of the most important sources of slave music of the Civil War.

**Gaskell, Elizabeth (Cleghorn Stevenson)** (1810–65). English novelist. Born in Chelsea, London, the daughter of a Unitarian minister, she was a year old when her mother died and was brought up by her aunt in Knutsford, Cheshire. From 1825 to 1827 she attended Avonbank School, Stratford. After the death of her brother, then of her father in 1829, she stayed with various relatives and lived briefly in Edinburgh with her friend Ann Turner, before marrying William Gaskell, a Unitarian minister and teacher of English at the Working Men's College, in 1832.

Elizabeth Gaskell's early years in Manchester were chiefly domestic: she had five children and her only writing was the poem *Sketches among the Poor*, written with her husband in 1837. She began to write as a consolation for her grief at the death of her baby son William from scarlet fever in 1845, and the resulting novel was *Mary Barton* (1848), an indictment of contemporary employment conditions. Its success led her to contribute to several magazines including Dickens's *Household Words*, in which *Cranford* began to appear in 1851. Her next work, *Ruth* (1853), caused a storm because of its sympathetic picture of a seduced girl who bears an illegitimate child, but after *North and South* (1855) she turned to biography and spent two years researching the life of her friend Charlotte BRONTE, whom she had met in London in 1850 and visited at Haworth in 1853. Her winters were now spent writing, keeping house and helping in the parish, and her summers in travelling, especially to Paris and Italy. In the 1860s she published collections of short stories as well as the historical novel *Sylvia's Lovers* (1863); *Wives and Daughters* was unfinished at her death. In the autumn of 1865 she collapsed of heart failure at the new home in Hampshire that she had bought as a Christmas surprise for her husband. Her novels reveal careful attention to realistic detail and character, enlivened by a dislike of all hypocrisy, from employer's cant to the double standard of Victorian morality.

W. Gérin: *Gaskell: A Biography* (1976)

**Gauhar Shad** (*c*1378–1459). Persian-Afghan Timurid queen. In 1391 she married the son and successor of Tamburlaine (Timur), Shah Rukh who ruled from 1404–47. Their court was a centre of a great cultural renaissance, encouraging science, literature, art and especially architecture, and their two sons became famous, one as an astronomer and the other as a calligrapher. Gauhar Shad herself built two magnificent mosques in Meshed and Herat, in the north-west of Afghanistan, with attached theological colleges. The buildings in Herat stood until 1885 when they were destroyed, probably at British command, to stop a Russian invasion, but her mausoleum and those at Meshed remain.

After Shah Rukh's death during a journey in Persia [now Iran], she became involved in the terrible quarrels within the family. Her influence remained consider-able and in 1459 she was executed for sup-porting her great-grandson against an opposing prince ʻAbu Saʼid.

**Gauthier, Xavière** (1942–). French feminist. A teacher at the University of Paris I, she founded the journal, *Sorcières*, in 1976. Concerned to establish a new mode of writing, consistent with a female- rather than male-oriented aesthetic, she is the author of *Surréalisme et sexualité* (1971); *Les parleuses* (1974), with Marguerite Duras; *Rose saignée* (1974); and *Dire nos sexualités – contre la sexologie* (1977). She has also written a study of the artist LEONOR FINI, published in 1979.

**Genée,** Dame **Adeline (Anina Jensen)** (1878–1970). Danish dancer and teacher. Born at Hinnerup, Denmark, Adeline's early interest in dance was encouraged by her uncle, the ballet master Alexandre Genée, and his Hungarian wife Antonia Zimmer-man. She took her uncle's surname and changed her first name to Adeline (after ADELINA PATTI). Trained in the classical French style, she made her debut in Christiania [now Oslo] at the age of ten. She joined her uncle's touring company and danced in Berlin and Munich where she gave her famous interpretation of Swanilda in *Cöppélia* for the first time in 1896.

In 1897 Genée was engaged at the Empire Theatre, London, where her six-week contract was extended to ten years. Dancing classical solos and lighter 'character' pieces, her virtuosity, charm and humour made her one of the most popular Edwardian stage figures: 'A most intel-ligent, most delightfully human actress' (Beerbohm). As guest dancer she visited Denmark (1902), the USA (1908 and later

tours), Australia and New Zealand (1913). In 1910 she married the businessman Frank Isitt and gradually withdrew from ballet after 1914, retiring from regular perform-ance in 1917. Her last appearance was with Dolin in charity performances of *The Love Song* (1932–3).

In 1920 she became the first President of the Association of Operatic Dancing, which became the Royal Academy of Dancing in 1935. She retired from the presidency in 1954 and was succeeded by MARGOT FONTEYN, but she retained an active interest. In 1967 she opened a theatre named after her in East Grinstead, Sussex. She was created DBE in 1950.

I. Guest: *Adeline Genée: a Lifetime of Ballet under six Reigns* (1958)

**Genlis.** *See* De GENLIS.

**Gentileschi, Artemisia** (1593–c1653). Italian painter. The daughter and pupil of Orazio Gentileschi, Artemisia was the subject of a lengthy rape case brought by her father against Agostino Tassi in 1612. Although she married after the case, the notoriety apparently encouraged a spirit of defiant independence.

In 1614 she moved to Florence and at the age of 23 she was made a member of the Florentine Accademia del Disegno. Her work was commissioned by Michelangelo for the ceiling of Casa Buonarroti, and her fine *Judith and Holofernes* and *Judith and her Maidservant* date from the same period. From 1620 to 1626 she worked in Rome, establishing a reputation for portraits and narrative paintings such as *Esther and Ahasuerus*. Many of her paintings feature other famous women, such as CLEOPATRA VII, Lucretia, Mary Magdalene, and Bathsheba. Her female nudes are particularly strong and vigorous. For the rest of her life she lived in Naples, apart from a brief visit to England to join her father in 1639 at the request of Charles I (a self-portrait hangs at Hampton Court).

Gentileschi received many commissions, including paintings for the choir of Pozzuoli Cathedral, but despite her considerable fame she appears to have died in poverty.

**Geoffrin, Marie-Thérèse Rodet de** (1699–1777). French salon hostess. Born in Paris, the daughter of a valet, she married a rich bourgeois merchant who had made his fortune producing ice-cream. Although not formally educated, her interest in cultural affairs and her natural sensitivity made her a popular figure in literary society. After the death of Madame DE TENCIN in 1749 she inherited her salon and made it into a famous international meeting-place for artists such as Boucher and La Tour, and writers such as Fontenelle, Walpole, Marivaux, Marmontel and Helvétius. Sainte-Beuve called this well-organized, highly respectable salon, where discussion of religion and politics was forbidden, 'one of the institutions of the 18th century'. Marie-Thérèse helped to sponsor the *Encyclopédie*. She was a correspondent of CATHERINE II of Russia and a friend of King Stanislaw of Poland, whom she visited in 1766. Hers was the leading salon of the Paris bourgeoisie, rivalling in influence that of the aristocratic Madame DU DEFFAND.

J. Aldis: *Madame Geoffrin* (1905)

**Gerin-Lajoie** [née Lacoste], **Marie** (1867–1945). French Canadian feminist. Born in Montreal, the daughter of a leading lawyer and politician, she married Henri Gerlin-Lajoie, the son of a famous journalist, in 1887. She used her privileged position to press effectively for women's suffrage and legal rights in Quebec, and published two influential treatises, *Traité de droit usuel* (1902) and *La femme et le code civil* (1929).

**Germain, Sophie** [pseud: Le Blanc] (1776–1831). French mathematician. While growing up in Paris at the time of the fall of the Bastille and during the Reign of Terror, Sophie studied alone in her father's library. She was fascinated by the geometry of Archimedes and ardently pursued the subject. Her parents objected, and denied her light and heat in her room; she then worked secretly with a quilt round her and with hidden candles. Finally they relented and she spent her life studying.

In 1794 the Ecole Polytechnique opened in Paris, and although women were not admitted, Sophie collected professors' lecture notes, particularly those of Lagrange. Under the pseudonym Le Blanc she submitted a paper which impressed him: he discovered her identity, and continued to encourage and sponsor her. She corresponded with Gauss, who did not suspect her identity for several years. She became interested in Chladni's work on the vibration of elastic surfaces, and in 1811, 1813 and 1816 submitted papers to the Académie Française competition for the best essay on the mathematical laws of elastic surfaces compared with experimental data. Despite her lack of formal training her third attempt won the prize, and she was publicly acclaimed and welcomed at the Institut de France. Gauss recommended to the University of Göttingen that she be given an honorary doctorate but she died of cancer before it could be awarded.

Sophie published other memoirs on the theory of elasticity and important work on the theory of numbers. She was interested in philosophy, and her paper *Considérations sur l'état des sciences et des lettres aux différentes époques de leur culture* propounds a theme of unity of thought.

When the Eiffel Tower was constructed, using in part her knowledge of the elasticity of materials, her name was not included among those of 72 *savants* inscribed there.

**Gertrud von Helfta** [Gertrud die Grosse; Gertrude the Great] (1256–1302). German nun and mystical writer. At the age of five she was entrusted to the nuns of the Cistercian abbey of Helfta, nr Eisleben in Saxony. She studied secular subjects such as Latin and philosophy until a vision of Christ in 1281 led her to devote her life to her sacred writings. An influential mystic, she described her visions in the *Exercitia spiritualia septem* and the *Legatio divinae pietatis*; her works were translated into German in the 14th century. Her mentor and friend at the convent was Mechtilde von Hackeborn, also a mystic, and together they initiated the cult of the adoration of the Sacred Heart.

Gertrud von Helfta was at one time confused with another scholarly nun of the same period, Gertrud von Hackeborn (1241–98) who was the abbess of Helfta when she was brought there as a child and recorded Mechtilde's visions in the *Liber specialis gratiae*.

**Gibson, Althea** (1927–). American tennis player. Brought up in Harlem, New York,

Althea began by playing paddle tennis and progressed to serious lawn tennis at the age of 13. Her ambition was to be 'the best woman tennis player who ever lived'. She left school and supported herself working as a chicken cleaner and in a factory, but support from a prominent Southern black family enabled her to continue at school, improve her game and take a college degree in physical education.

In 1950 she was the first black invited to play in the American Lawn Tennis Association championships, and came close to beating LOUISE BROUGH, the reigning Wimbledon champion. Althea's game, notable for strength and aggression, improved steadily: in 1956 she won the French and Italian singles titles and Wimbledon doubles, and in 1957 and 1958 dominated women's lawn tennis, becoming the first black to win at Wimbledon and going on to win the American championship at Forest Hills. Her only setback was a defeat by Christine Truman, then 17, in the Wightman Cup in 1958. After retiring from competitive amateur tennis, she became a night-club singer, then a professional golfer.

A. Gibson and R. Curtis: *So Much to Live For* (1968)

**Gilman, Charlotte (Anna) Perkins (Stetson)** (1860–1935). American feminist economist. She was born in Hartford, Connecticut; her father deserted the family, providing little support, and her mother deliberately withheld affection to save later disillusionment. At the age of 18 she went to Rhode Island School of Design, and then worked as a teacher and commercial artist. She married a painter, Charles Stetson, in 1884. Suffering deep depression after the birth of her daughter, she separated from her husband in 1888, but was not divorced until 1894. She moved to California, where she lectured on women's issues, labour and social policy and wrote stories, including the account of her breakdown in *The Yellow Wallpaper* (1892), and poetry, *In This our World* (1893).

At the 1895 California Women's Congress she met JANE ADDAMS, spent some months in Chicago, then in 1896 attended the International Social and Labour Congress in London. At the end of that year she rapidly wrote *Women and Economics*

(published 1898) which received immediate acclaim, was translated into seven languages, and won her applause at the International Council of Women in London (1899) and Berlin (1904). It has since become a feminist classic. Based on her lectures it attacked women's financial dependency, advocating centralized nurseries and co-operative kitchens, themes later developed in *Concerning Children* (1900), *The Home* (1903) and *Human Work* (1904). In 1902 she married her cousin, the New York lawyer George Gilman. From 1909 to 1916 she wrote features and stories for her own journal *The Forerunner*, including *Herland* which envisages a separatist Utopia with reproduction by parthenogenesis. Increasingly convinced that women must assert their nature, which is peaceful and co-operative, to counteract male destructiveness, she wrote *Man-made World* (1911) and *His Religion and Hers* (1923). In 1932 breast cancer was diagnosed, and she decided to end her life when the disease could no longer be arrested.

C.P. Gilman: *The Living of Charlotte Perkins Gilman* (1935)

**Ginzburg, Natalia Levi** [pseud.: Alessandra Tornimparte] (1916–). Italian novelist and essayist. Born into an intellectual Jewish family in Palermo, she grew up in Turin where her father was a professor from 1919, and their house became the centre of an anti-fascist group. In 1938 she married a Slavic scholar and socialist Leone Ginzburg, who was imprisoned for his underground political activities in 1940, and who died four years later.

Natalia began publishing after his imprisonment, at first under the pseudonym Alessandra Tornimparte with *La strada che va in città* (1942). She published a series of fine short novels, dealing with marital unhappiness, politics, the Italian Resistance and life during the war. In 1964 she won the prestigious Strega Prize for *Lessico famigliare*, an autobiographical narrative treating her own family. Her novels include *Caro Michele* (1973) and *Famiglia* (1977). Her simple style disguises psychological subtlety, and her nameless heroines embody a bitter but humorous perception of alienation and loneliness.

**Giovanna I** (1326–82). Queen of Naples, Countess of Provence. At 16 she married her cousin Andrea, a Hungarian prince, and in the same year succeeded her grandfather, Roberto, as ruler of Naples. Two years later, distrust of the Hungarian influence at court led her to approve a plot in which her husband was assassinated. She then married Louis of Taranto (1347). The following year, Andrea's brother, King Louis of Hungary, led a raid of vengeance on Naples and Giovanna fled into exile in Provence, remaining there for four years. During this period she sold Avignon to the papacy, in return for their declaration of her innocence. Her second husband died in 1362, and she then married James III of Majorca, although they rarely lived together, allegedly because he feared for his life. After his death in 1375 she married a soldier, Otto of Brunswick. Giovanna established the Angevin rule in Naples and ended a feud with the Aragonese of Sicily but in the last years of her life she became embroiled in the politics accompanying the split in the papacy. She supported the anti-pope in Avignon and the French King Charles V. She disinherited her heir, Charles of Durazzo; with the help of the Pope in Rome, he led an army against Naples in 1381, captured Giovanna and eventually suffocated her in the castle of Muro.

Giovanna I is often confused with her namesake, Giovanna II of Naples (1371–1435), who was Queen of Naples 40 years later (1414–35), led an equally turbulent life, with a succession of husbands and powerful lovers, and was similarly prone to cause chaos by adopting and then disinheriting her heirs. She was the last Angevin to rule in Naples before the dominance of the Aragonese.

**Gippius, Zinaida Nikolayevna.** *See* HIPPIUS.

**Gipps, Ruth** (1921–). English composer and conductor. Having had a piece of music published at the age of eight, she studied at the Royal College of Music, London, where her teachers included Vaughan Williams, whose influence is discernible in most of her early compositions. During her early career she worked as an orchestral oboist, also appearing as a concert pianist. From 1948 to 1950 she was Choirmaster of the City of Birmingham Choir, after which she turned her attention increasingly to conducting. As Musical Director of the London Repertoire Orchestra (from 1955) and of the Chanticleer Orchestra, which she founded in 1961, she has devoted a great deal of energy to a profession tackled by remarkably few women. In 1967 she was appointed a Professor at the Royal College of Music and was Chairman of the Composers' Guild of Great Britain. Her works include five symphonies (1942, 1945, 1965, 1972, 1980), concertos for violin (1943), piano (1948), violin and viola (1957) and horn (1968), several choral works, and chamber music. She was made an OBE in 1981.

**Giroud, Françoise** (1916–). French journalist and politician. Born in Geneva, of Turkish descent, she left school at 15 and during the 1930s mixed with literary and artistic groups and worked as a script girl, for example with Renoir on *La grande illusion/ Grand Illusion* (1937). During World War II she was imprisoned, and following the birth of her son during the German occupation suffered a period of intense depression. She was married briefly later, but devoted herself to a career in journalism. She became Editor of *Elle* from its foundation in 1945 with HÉLÈNE GORDON-LAZAREFF, until 1952; a co-founder and Editor of the weekly *L'Express* (1953–71) with Jean-Jacques Servan-Schreiber; and Director and President of *L'Express-Union* (1970–74).

In 1974 she was appointed the first Secretary of State for Women's Affairs, and then became Secretary of Culture in 1976; she was also Vice-President of the Parti-Radical (1975–6). In 1977 she was not reappointed by Giscard d'Estaing and returned to media work, becoming Director of *Revue de temps libre* in 1979. She has always maintained her interest in the cinema as well as in journalism, publishing *La nouvelle vague: portrait de la jeunesse* (1958), and writing several films: *Antoine et Antoinette* (1947), *L'Amour, Madame* (1951), *Julietta* (1953), *Le Bon Plaisir* (1984) and *Le quatrième pouvoir* (1985). In 1984 she became President of Action International contre le Faim.

F. Giroud: *La comédie de pouvoir* (1977)

**Gish** [de Guiche], **Lillian (Diana)** (1896–). American actress. Born in Springfield, Ohio, she performed with her mother and her sister Dorothy as a child actress, contributing to the family income after they were deserted by their father. In 1912, while visiting their friend MARY PICKFORD, the Gish sisters were introduced to D.W. Griffith at the American Biograph Company in Manhattan. He immediately gave them and their mother parts in *An Unseen Enemy*. During the next two years Lillian made 20 short films, and then left Biograph with Griffith, appearing in his numerous films including *Birth of a Nation* (1915), *Intolerance* (1916), *The Greatest Thing in Life*, *Broken Blossoms* and *Take Heart Susie* (all 1919) and *Orphans of the Storm* (with Dorothy) (1921). She established herself as a frail, innocent but determined heroine, and the aura of virginal austerity was to remain a lasting image.

After breaking with Griffith over a salary dispute she worked for Inspiration, and then joined MGM in 1925. She insisted on the right to vet scripts and directors and appeared in several remarkable films, notably *La Bohème* (King Vidor, 1926), *The Scarlet Letter* (Sjöstrom, 1926) and the prairie tragedy *The Wind* (1928). She refused to adapt to the more hedonistic mood of the 1920s and after making two more films for other companies she left Hollywood. During the 1930s she had several Broadway successes including *Camille*, and Ophelia in Gielgud's *Hamlet*. She continued to act, to appear on television, undertake lecture tours of Europe and America (1969–70) and to appear in occasional film roles. She kept her extraordinary beauty in old age. Her last stage roles were in *Uncle Vanya* in New York (1973) and *A Musical Jubilee* (1975). She continued to make films in her eighties, and now nineties: *A Wedding* (1978), *Hambone and Hillie* (1984), *Sweet Liberty* (1986) and *The Whales of August* (1988), her 106th feature film, made at the age of 92.

L. Gish: *The Movies, Mr Griffith and me* (1969)
———— : *Dorothy and Lilian Gish* (1973)

**Glanville-Hicks, Peggy** (1912–). Australian-American composer. After studying at the Melbourne Conservatorium (1927–31), she furthered her musical education at the Royal College of Music, London, under Vaughan Williams, and later in Vienna under Wellesz and in Paris with NADIA BOULANGER. In 1938 she married the English composer Stanley Bate; they founded the ballet company Les Trois Arts in London in 1940. Based in New York from 1942 to 1959 (she became an American citizen in 1948), she applied herself to the cause of new music in many ways: she was co-founder (with Carleton Sprague Smith) of the International Music Fund, which helped to re-establish European artists after World War II; she was a Director of the New York Composers' Forum; she organized concerts of contemporary music at the Museum of Modern Art, the Metropolitan Museum and Central Park; in 1958 she founded the Artists' Company, which has been crucial in promoting American opera; and she played an influential role as music critic of the *New York Herald Tribune* between 1948 and 1958. Having settled in Athens in 1959, she returned to Australia in 1976.

Her compositions reflect similarly wide-ranging energies: her Choral Suite, conducted by Boult in London (1938), was the first Australian work to be performed at a festival of the International Society for Contemporary Music. Commissions from the Louisville Orchestra and the Ford Foundation resulted in two of her most important operas: *The Transposed Heads* (1953), based on Mann's novella, which shows her developing interest in oriental sonorities (further stimulated by her studies of Aegean demotic music since living in Athens, an influence also reflected in her opera *Nausicaa*, 1961, whose libretto she prepared with Robert Graves); and *Sappho* (1965), a setting of Durrell's text. Besides ballet music (notably *The Masque of the Wild Man*, 1958, commissioned for the first Spoleto Festival) and film scores, she has written several orchestral works and songs; her instrumental music, especially of the 1950s, shows a lively concern for expanding the repertories for percussion and harp.

**Glasgow, Ellen (Anderson Gholson)** (1874–1945). American novelist. Born in Richmond, Virginia, into an affluent family, because of her delicate health she was educated at home and in private school. She took a degree in politics at the University of

Virginia, although her hearing had deteriorated from the age of 16, and she eventually went deaf. In 1896 she visited London, where she met Henry James, and later visits to Europe introduced her to other leading writers. She began writing in 1896, publishing *The Descendant* in 1897 and *Phases of an inferior Planet* in 1898. Her first two novels, realistic in tone, were set in New York, but in 1900 she began a cycle of novels running from *Voice of the People* (1900) to *One Man in his Time* (1922), which followed the history of Virginia from the Civil War to World War I, tracing the social changes which had destroyed the myths of old Southern culture. Her greatest novel came still later: *Barren Ground* (1925), which describes the grim life of a poor country woman. In her later work superb comedies of manners such as the *The Romantic Comedians* (1926) were followed by increasingly pessimistic pictures of the South such as *The sheltered Life* (1932), *Vein of Iron* (1935) and *In This our Life* (1941). For most of her life she remained in Richmond, living in the centre of the town, and. becoming revered as an urbane, sophisticated 'grande dame'. This conventional exterior was at odds with her unconventional novels, with their enduring feminist and radical demand for an end to hypocrisy. She received several awards, and became a member of the American Academy of Arts and Letters in 1938. Her autobiography was published nine years after her death.

E. Glasgow: *The Woman Within* (1954)

**Glasse** [née Allgood], **Hannah** (1708–70). English cook. Born in Holborn, London, into a Northumbrian family, she married a solicitor, Peter Glasse, before 1725 and had eight children, four of whom died in infancy. She attained great popularity with *The Art of Cooking made Plain and Simple*, which was probably the first guide to cooking and meal planning written for the English housewife. It reached a fourth edition by 1751, and a tenth by 1784, remaining in print until 1824. The style and organization were unusally clear for the day, although she was attacked for extravagance and credited with the opening line for a recipe, 'First catch your hare . . .' Her other books included *The Compleat Confectioner* (?1770) and *The Servant's Directory or Housekeeper's Companion*. Details of her life are sparse but she seems to have been a businesswoman, being 'Habit Maker' to the Princess of Wales in Covent Garden, and possibly listed as bankrupt in 1754. She died in Newcastle.

**Glover, Jane (Alison)** (1949– ). British conductor. Britain's leading woman conductor, Jane Glover was educated at Monmouth School for Girls and St Hugh's College, Oxford, where she stayed on to take a DPhil, and where she was made a Junior Research Fellow in 1973, was Lecturer in Music from 1976 to 1984, and Senior Research Fellow in 1982. At Oxford she has also been attached as a lecturer to St Anne's and Pembroke Colleges, and she has been on the Open University Faculty of Music since 1979.

Her instrument is the piano but her real fame has come as a conductor. She made her professional debut at the Wexford Festival in 1975 and since then she has conducted at numerous festivals, has worked with most of the leading British orchestras and has done a considerable amount of work for the BBC. She joined the music staff of the Glyndebourne Festival Opera in 1979, becoming Director the following year, and Festival Conductor in 1984. As part of her Glyndebourne work she has toured widely and has been particularly influenced by her visits to China, teaching singers at the Central Conservatory about Western opera technique. In addition to her conducting Jane Glover has written books on Cavalli and Monteverdi, and has made and produced several programmes for British television including *Orchestra* (1983) and *Mozart* (1985). She has also been Musical Director of the London Choral Society since 1983 and Artistic Director of the London Mozart Players since 1984. A Governor of the Royal Academy of Music, she holds several awards and honorary degrees.

**Glyn, Elinor** (1864–1943). British writer. Born Elinor Sutherland, in Jersey, the younger daughter of a Scottish civil engineer who died when she was three months old, Elinor spent her early years in Canada with her mother and her aristocratic French grandmother, whose notions of court life, privileges and duties influenced her greatly. In 1871 her mother remarried and Elinor rebelled both against her tyrannical stepfather and the sequence of governesses who taught her after the family's return to Jersey, preferring to dream and read widely on her own. A striking beauty with red hair and green eyes she found herself the centre of extravagant attention, but did not marry until 1892, choosing the landowner Clayton Glyn. They had two daughters.

Her first novel, *The Visits of Elizabeth* (1900), first serialized in *The World*, showed her amused, acute observation of country-house society, but her later works reflected her inner fantasies, with improbable plots featuring high-bred heroines and dominating heroes. The scandalous *Three Weeks* (1907) dealt with an affair between a young Englishman and a much older woman, a Balkan queen, and included the famous 'tiger-skin episode'. After 1908 Clayton Glyn's debts forced Elinor to write for money although her high life-style continued; a winter at the court of St Petersburg provided material for *His Hour* (1910). Her romantic longings and craving for knowledge led to fixations on men of action such as Lord Milner, Lord Curzon and F.D. Maurice: the latter two appear disguised in *Halcyone* (1912). Glyn's success was sealed by works like *The Man and the Master* (1915) and *The Career of Katherine Brown* (1917). In 1920 she moved to Hollywood as a scriptwriter, where her own novels *Three Weeks* and *It* (1927) were also filmed (the star Clara Bow was dubbed the 'It girl'). In 1929 she returned to England, and resumed writing after a short attempt at film production. Her personal outlook is expressed in *The Philosophy of Love* (1923) and in her autobiography *Romantic Adventures* (1936).

**Godiva** [Godgifu] (c1040–80). Anglo-Saxon heroine. She is famous for a legendary ride, naked but hidden beneath her long hair, through the streets of Coventry. The story is recorded in the chronicles of Roger of Wendove in the 13th century; he stated that she agreed to take up the challenge after her husband, Leofric, Earl of Mercia, had announced in answer to her repeated protests that this was the only action which would make him lift the heavy taxes imposed on the people of the city. The only citizen to look through the shuttered windows was nicknamed 'Peeping Tom'. Godiva was also known as a generous benefactor, who endowed several monasteries, especially Coventry, which she and her husband founded.

**Godwin, Mary Wollstonecraft.** *See* WOLLSTONECRAFT, MARY.

**Goegg, Marie** (1826–99). Swiss feminist and pacifist. Marie Pouchoulin was born into a Geneva family, descended from French Huguenot refugees. At 13 she went to work in the shop of her father, a clockmaker. She married at 19 but was divorced in 1856, and then married the revolutionary exile Armand Goegg, who had fled to Switzerland to escape a life sentence in Germany in 1849. He adopted her son by her first marriage and they had two more sons.

Marie became involved in the International League of Peace and Freedom, founded in Geneva in 1867, of which her husband was one of the organizers. Her call, in the League's journal, for a separate international body for women, and her insistence that there must be equality for women in revolutionary movements, if such movements are not to become as authoritarian as the regimes they oppose, illustrate her boldness and clear thinking. She created and ran the Association International des Femmes in 1868 (renamed Solidarité in 1870, after the international links were disrupted by the Franco-Prussian War). She also campaigned successfully for the opening of the University of Geneva to women in 1872, and continued to play a major role in the League of Peace and Freedom until her old age.

**Goeppert-Mayer, Maria** (1906–72). German-American physicist. Born at Kattowitz [now Katowice, Poland], Maria was descended from six generations of university professors. She received her doctorate from Göttingen in 1930 and married Joseph Mayer, an American physical chemist, in the same year. They had two children.

She emigrated to the USA in 1931 and worked successively at Johns Hopkins University, at Columbia University on the separation of uranium isotopes, and in 1945 went to the newly-finished Institute for Nuclear Studies at the University of Chicago. Under Enrico Fermi she became interested in nuclear physics. In 1948 she suggested that the atomic nucleus consisted of protons and neutrons arranged in shells, hence some nuclei are more stable than others. She thus proposed a model of nuclear structure analogous to that of electrons in the outer atom.

For this major discovery Maria shared the Nobel Prize for Physics in 1963 with J.H.D. Jensen, who had advanced the same theory independently, and Wigner. She was the first woman to win this prize since MARIE CURIE in 1903. In 1960 she became a professor at the University of California. In 1956 she was elected to the National Academy of Sciences.

**Goldman, Emma** ['Red Emma'] (1869–1940). American anarchist. Brought up in Königsberg in East Prussia, her family moved in 1882 to St Petersburg, where she worked in a glove factory and became influenced by prevailing populist and nihilist ideas. In 1885 she emigrated to the USA with her half-sister Helena, and lived in Rochester, New York, where she found a job in a clothing factory. Three years later she married Jacob Kershner (later obtaining a divorce on the grounds of his impotence). Her interest in socialism was fired by the trial of the Haymarket Anarchists in 1886, and in 1889 she moved to New York, where she met Alexander Berkman, her life-long associate. She began speaking in public, and became involved in plans to assassinate the steel magnate Henry Frick during the Pittsburgh Steel Strike of 1892. Berkman's attack failed and he was sentenced to 22 years' imprisonment, but he was eventually released in 1916.

She herself acquired the nickname 'Red Emma', and was imprisoned for a year for incitement to riot. In prison she worked as a nurse and on her release (1895) went to Vienna to train further, meeting Austrian anarchists and LOUISE MICHEL in London. After her return to the USA she organized meetings and lectured brilliantly against oppression and injustice, but her talks also included discussions of Shaw, Ibsen and Strindberg which were eventually published in *The Significance of Modern Drama* (1914). In 1899 she was arrested again, in connection with the assassination of President McKinley. From 1906 Emma Goldman edited *Mother Earth*, an anarchist

monthly, advocating wide social changes, especially in the position of women in relation to marriage, child rearing and sexual fulfilment, and her pronouncements on birth control led to further imprisonment. In 1911 she published *Anarchism and other Essays*. She opposed American entry into World War I, and in 1917 was sentenced, with Berkman, to five years' penal servitude for opposing conscription.

On their release after two years, they were deported to Russia, but they left in 1921, horrified by the centralism of the government which Emma attacked in *My Disillusionment in Russia* (1923). Two years later, hoping to return to the USA with British citizenship, she married James Cotton, a miner, but she was allowed only a brief visit in 1934. She lived, travelled and lectured in England and Canada, publishing her autobiography in 1931. Berkman committed suicide in 1936 but Emma fought on, undertaking speaking tours on behalf of anti-Franco forces in the Spanish Civil War. She died in Toronto after a stroke and was buried beside the Haymarket martyrs in Chicago.

E. Goldman: *Living my Life* (1931)
R. Drinnan: *Rebel in Paradise : A Biography of Emma Goldman* (1970)

**Goldmark, Josephine** (Clara) (1877–1950). American social reformer. The daughter of Czech immigrants, whose lives she described in *Pilgrims of '48* (1930), she graduated from Bryn Mawr College in 1898, then enrolled at Barnard College where she was a tutor (1903–5). Becoming Research Director to Florence Kelley's National Consumer's League in 1903, she researched the background to the famous 'Brandeis briefs', presented by her brother-in-law Louis Brandeis (later Supreme Court Judge) in Miller *v.* Oregon (1908), which helped to establish the constitutional validity of protective legislation in industry. She wrote *Child Labour Legislation Handbook* (1902), campaigned for the ten-hour law with Felix Frankfurter and Brandeis, was co-author of *Fatigue and Efficiency* (1912), and was a member of the team investigating the deaths of 146 women in the Triangle Shirt-waist fire (1912–14). She also prepared test-cases on the New York law against nightwork for women, and published *Women in Industry* (1916).

After virtual retirement from public life Goldmark conducted a survey of health resources in Cleveland in 1919, and then became Secretary to the Rockefeller Committee, who produced the highly influential 1923 report, *Nursing and Nursing Education in the United States*. She also worked with FLORENCE KELLEY on health and safety campaigns during the 1920s. A typical reformer of the Progressive era, her liberal philosophy is made clear in *Democracy in Denmark* (1936) and in her biography of Florence Kelley (published in 1953).

**Goldstein, Vida** (1869–1949). Australian feminist. Born in Portland, Victoria, and educated at Melbourne Presbyterian College, she was interested in social work and political affairs from an early age, and during her twenties campaigned against slum poverty and sweated labour and opened a co-educational school with her sister in St Kilda, Melbourne. She then began to study sociology and economics to back up her impressions of the causes of poverty and women's oppression, and eventually gave up her school to devote herself full-time to the women's movement. She campaigned for property rights in marriage, divorce reform and improvement of working conditions for shop assistants, and from 1899 ran a monthly paper, *The Australian Woman's Sphere*, which covered local issues and also reprinted material from LUCY STONE'S *Woman's Journal*, thus keeping in touch with an international movement. She was also influenced by Dr Charles Strong, of the Australian Church, whom she helped in his campaigns for slum clearance.

When the federal vote was gained in 1902 she stood as Independent candidate for Victoria, polling a large number of votes and arousing enormous press hostility. She stood unsuccessfully four times before 1917. In 1902 she represented Australia and New Zealand at the Women's Suffrage Conference in Washington, DC, and in 1903 founded the Women's Federal Political Association. Votes for women were finally obtained in Victoria in 1908 and the following year she launched a new paper, *The Woman Voter*. With ROSE SCOTT she opposed party politics, arguing that women should act independently of party interests, lobbying every political group. While she remained a strong feminist, her views on social issues became increasingly repressive; she supported restraint rather than birth control as a means of reducing family size, advocated social purity, opposed assisted immigration, supported a white Australia policy and demanded an Australian navy to safeguard national independence. In 1911 she went to England where she enjoyed a triumphal speaking tour, and remained in Europe working for the peace campaign. She then returned to Australia and gradually withdrew from politics, devoting the last 20 years of her life to Christian Science.

**Goncharova, Natalia (Sergeyevna)** (1881–1962). Russian painter. Born in Ladyzhino, Tula, into a family of artistic, but impoverished aristocrats, she studied in Moscow in 1892. In 1898 she entered the school of painting there and met Larionov in 1900, beginning a close and enduring relationship that eventually led to their marriage, on her 74th birthday. Together they travelled around Russia and created the Rayonnist movement in 1909. Their work was included in all the major post-Impressionist and Futurist exhibitions between 1906 and 1915. The works shown in her individual exhibitions in Moscow (1910, 1913) and Petrograd [now Leningrad] (1914) startled the public with their primitive forms and brilliant colours which adapt Cubist and Fauve techniques to traditional Russian styles. Her work was also shown in London and Paris.

In 1914 Goncharova had begun to work for the theatre, designing the set for *Le coq d'or*. In 1915 she moved to Geneva with Larionov and designed for Dyagilev's Ballets Russes, touring Spain and Italy with the company before settling in Paris. She returned to Russia and collaborated on a magazine with ALEXANDRA EXTER, but went back to Paris in 1921. She created sets for *Les noces* (1923) and *The Firebird* (1926) and after Dyagilev's death in 1929 she also designed for other companies. Goncharova continued to paint and exhibit until her death. She took French nationality in 1938.

M. Chamot: *Natalia Goncharova* (1972)

**Gonne, Maud.** *See* MACBRIDE, MAUD.

**Goodall, Jane** (1934–). English zoologist.
Born in London and educated in
Bournemouth, she had a traditional middle-
class upbringing and took secretarial
courses, followed by a series of jobs.
However, she was always fascinated by
animals and was a keen amateur naturalist.
At the age of 23 she went to Kenya on
holiday with a friend, where she met the
anthropologist Louis Leakey. She became
his secretary at the Museum of Natural
History and then one of several researchers
whom he inspired to work on the study of
primates in their natural surroundings.

In 1960 she began her lengthy study of
chimpanzees, which eventually resulted in
her being accepted by a particular group
with whom she lived on the shores of Lake
Tanganyika. She described them as
intelligent, social, hunting animals, with
complex systems of communication and
games, and the ability to use tools. Her study
was not completed until 1966, and in the
meantime she was accepted by Cambridge
University, where she prepared her work for
a Doctorate in Ethology. In 1964 she
married the Dutch naturalist and
photographer Baron Hugo von Lawick and
they had a son in 1967. They became joint
Directors of the Gombe Stream Research
Centre in Tanzania, on the site of Jane's
former project. In 1970 they published a
joint study of wild dogs, jackals and hyenas,
*Innocent Killers*, and in 1971 Jane published
*In the Shadow of Man*, her popular work on
the chimpanzees, illustrated by Hugo's
pictures.

After the von Lawicks were divorced,
Jane married Derek Bryceson, a Tanzanian
administrator who had been in charge of
the National Parks before becoming a
politician. She has since continued her work
as a zoologist.

**Goodbody, Buzz (Mary Ann)** (1946–75). British theatre director. Buzz Goodbody was
educated at Roedean and Sussex University,
where she directed a prize-winning adaptation of Dostoevsky's *Notes from Underground*. In 1967 she joined the Royal Shakespeare Company as John Barton's personal
assistant, and in 1971 directed Trevor Grif-
fiths's *Occupations* at The Place, London, an

RSC experiment with small theatre. In the
same year she helped to start the Women's
Street Theatre Group, taking part in its first
production, *Sugar and Spice*. In 1973 she was
invited by Trevor Nunn to become the first
artistic director of The Other Place, Stratford.
Her first season there in 1974, a sell-out, was
marked by a vitality and freedom that had
often been lacking at the main house. For her
second season she directed Ben Kingsley in a
much-acclaimed modern-dress *Hamlet* and
brought in Howard Davies to direct Brecht's
*Man is Man*. Four days after the opening
night, on 12 April 1975, she committed
suicide.

She was the only female director in the
Company, and the only one to bridge the two
worlds of mainstream and fringe theatre. She
was also a feminist and member of the
Communist Party. Her death was entirely
unexpected, but it is thought that her special
position imposed considerable strains.

**Gordimer, Nadine** (1923–). South African
writer. Born in Springs, Transvaal, she was
educated at a convent school and the
University of Witwatersrand, Johannesburg. She married G. Gavran in 1949 and
published her first collection of short stories
in the same year, entitled *Face to Face*,
followed by another collection *The Soft
Voice of the Serpent* (1952). In 1954 she
married Reinhold Cassirer, a Jewish refugee
from the Nazi regime. They have two
children.

Her first novel was *The Lying Days*
(1953), in which the heroine has to fight to
free herself from the prejudices of her
mining background and from the simplistic
intellectuals she meets, and learn how to
deal with her guilt at the racial hatred she
sees. One of her later works, *Berger's
Daughter* (1978), deals with a similar feeling
of obligation and tension, as the daughter
of committed Communist parents reluctantly
recognizes her duty to fight oppression. In
between, Gordimer has produced a series of
works which chronicle the stresses and ironies
of life in South Africa for English and
Afrikaans-speaking whites and for blacks,
and which expose its cruelty and hypocrisy.
Her novels are also remarkable for the evocation of the landscape which encloses the
action. Many of her books are banned in
South Africa, but widely read elsewhere and

she has been a visiting lecturer at numerous American universities since 1961. Gordimer has published several volumes of short stories and novels, including *A World of Strangers* (1958), *Occasion for Loving* (1963), *The late bourgeois World* (1966), *A Guest of Honour* (1970), *The Conservationist* (1974), *July's People* (1981) and *A Sport of Nature* (1987).

**Gordon-Lazareff, Hélène** (1909–88). French journalist of Russian birth. She was born in Rostov on the Don River, but after the Russian revolution her family fled to Turkey and then to Paris. She studied ethnology, was associated briefly with surrealism, but eventually became a journalist. During World War II, in the United States, she worked for major American women's magazines, and on her return in 1945 she founded the magazine *Elle* with FRANÇOISE GIROUD and acted as Director. She remained as Editor from then until 1973, a leader of the international fashion press. Her grand style and complete self-assurance won her the nickname 'Czarina'. She was married twice: to Paul Radnitz, with whom she had one daughter, and to Pierre Lazareff, Editor of *France-Soir*, the father of her second daughter and co-author with her of *USSR in the Time of Malenkov*. From 1965 she was on the French television advisory council.

**Gouges, Olympe de** [pseud.: Marie-Olympe Gouze] (1748–93). French feminist and revolutionary. Born in Montauban, she was the daughter of a butcher although she claimed to be the bastard of an aristocratic poet, Le Frère de Pompignan. At the age of 16 she married an officer, Louis Yvres Aubury; they separated two years later and Olympe left for Paris where she became famous for her beauty, her love affairs and for her writing. She wrote several successful comedies including *Le Mariage inattendu de Chérubin* (1786), *Molière chez Ninon* (1788) and *Le Couvent ou Les voeux forcés* (1792), and oriental tales such as *Le Prince philosophe* (1792).

In 1789 she became a fierce supporter of the Revolution, founding the Club des Tricoteuses in 1790, and writing the feminist polemic *Déclaration des droits de la femme et de la citoyenne* (1791). A vehement opponent of Robespierre, she was arrested after protesting at the death of Louis XVI, and was sent to the guillotine in 1793.

**Gourd, Emilie** (1879–1946). Swiss feminist. She did not become prominent in the pacifist and women's movement until her mid-thirties, when she founded the paper *Le mouvement féministe*, which she continued to edit until her death and which campaigned for suffrage, education, legal rights and changes in public attitudes. Despite the intransigent attitude of the Swiss authorities she continued to organize plebiscites asking for support for women's suffrage during cantonal and national elections. From 1914 to 1928 she was President of the Swiss Women's Association, and in 1923, at the Rome conference, became Secretary of the International Alliance of Women. Among her many activities she edited a yearbook of Swiss women and wrote a life of SUSAN B. ANTHONY (1920).

**Gournay.** *See* DE GOURNAY.

**Grable, Betty** [Elizabeth] (1916–73). American film star. Betty Grable may not have been one of America's great screen actresses, but her roles in musicals, and as the GIs' favourite pin-up during World War II, have given her an enduring place among Hollywood idols. She was born and educated in St Louis, Missouri and later attended the Hollywood Professional School. A child vaudeville singer and dancer, she made her first film appearance (arranged by her mother) in *Let's Go Places* in 1929, but the studio contract was cancelled when it was discovered she was only 13. In 1930 Sam Goldwyn hired her and during the next decade she played small ingenue parts in comedies like *Follow The Fleet* (1936), sang with Ted Fiorita's band, and was tossed back and forth between studios like RKO and Paramount. After she married Jack Coogan in 1937 (they were divorced in 1941) they worked together in variety, and in 1940 she made her stage debut in *Du Barry was a Lady*. Her second marriage, to musician Henry James in 1943, also ended in divorce, in 1965.

Her real break in films came with 20th Century Fox when she replaced an ill Alice

Fay in *Down Argentine Way* (1940) and went on to star in numerous Technicolor musicials such as *Tin Pan Alley* (1940), *Moon over Miami* (1941), *Song of the Islands* (1942), *Coney Island* (1943), *Sweet Rosie O'Grady* (1943), *Pin-Up Girl* (1944) and *Diamond Horseshoe* (1945). All were box-office hits and the famous photographs of Grable with white bathing suit and long legs were stuck on the sides of bombers, and pinned up in barracks, ships and submarines throughout the war. In the 1950s her star faded, and was replaced by that of Marilyn Monroe, with whom she appeared in 1953 in *How to Marry a Millionaire*. Grable made only two more films, but took up her stage career again in the 1960s in shows like *Guys and Dolls* (1962), *High Button Shoes* (1964), *Hello Dolly* (1965–7) and *Belle Star* (1969).

D. Warren: *Betty Grable: The Reluctant Movie Queen* (1981)

**Grace (Kelly),** Princess (1929–82). American film star, princess of Monaco. Grace Kelly was born and educated in Pennsylvania. She attended the American Academy of Dramatic Art (1947–9), supporting herself by modelling and appearing in television commercials. In 1949 she made her stage debut in a play written by her uncle, George Kelly, and in the same year appeared on Broadway in Strindberg's *The Father*. Her first film, *Fourteen Hours*, was made in 1950. After studying with Sanford Meisner at the Neighbourhood Playhouse, New York, she moved to Hollywood. Stardom was instant: *High Noon* (1952) was followed by three films which won her Academy Awards for Best Actress: *The Country Girl* (1953) and Hitchcock's *Dial M for Murder* and *The Rear Window* (both 1954). After a further Hitchcock film, *Catch A Thief* (1955), she played Princess Alexandra in *The Swan* and starred in *High Society* (1956). That year she moved into high society herself, by marrying Prince Rainier III of Monaco: they had three children. She never acted in a film again, although she did contribute to occasional documentaries.

As a film star Grace Kelly was notable for the suggestion of sexual fire beneath a cool blonde beauty, and of vulnerability beneath controlled elegance. She played the part of Princess with equal professionalism, until her death in a car accident in 1982.

J. Spader: *Grace: The Secret Lives of a Princess* (1987)

**Graham, Katharine** (1917–). American newspaper proprietor. Born in New York, the daughter of a banker, Eugene Meyer, she was educated there, then at Vassar College and the University of Chicago, before becoming a reporter on the *San Francisco News* (in 1938) and then moving to the *Washington Post* (in 1939), which her father had bought in 1933. She worked intermittently for the *Washington Post* until 1945, while her husband, the lawyer Philip Graham, was away on war service. They married in 1940 and had three sons and a daughter.

After World War II Philip Graham became publisher of the *Washington Post* and in 1948 he and Katharine bought it from Meyer for a token $1. The empire flourished, incorporating *Newsweek* in 1961. In 1963, after her husband's suicide, Katharine took over as President of the company, and since 1973 has been Chairman of the Board, Chief Executive Officer and Publisher. She also controls paper-mills, associated papers and television companies, but although a forceful personality, she is admired for the responsibility (and high pay) which she gives to her editors. A courageous and independent figure, she has resisted political pressure and encouraged the investigative journalism which led to the publication of the 'Pentagon Papers' in 1971, and the exposé of the Watergate scandal between 1972 and 1974. Within the world of the Press she is admired for her financial acumen which has made her company an astounding commercial success. She became co-Chairman of the Board of the *International Herald Tribune* in 1983, and (since 1982) is also a member of the Brandt Commission on Development Issues.

**Graham, Martha** (1894–). American dancer and choreographer. Born in Allegheny, Pennsylvania, the daughter of a doctor, she attended the Denishawn School, Los Angeles (1916–23), where she showed a particular liking for primitive dance; her abandoned performance in ballets such as *Serenata Morisca* and Shawn's Aztec *Yochitl* attracted wide attention. From 1923 to 1925 she danced with Greenwich Village Follies, and taught at the Eastman School of Music, Rochester, N.Y. In 1926 she made her debut as an independent dancer in New York, going on to explore themes of mood in works like *Lamentation* (1930) and *Primitive Mysteries*, and also experimenting with theories about the architectural and expressive properties of the body. 1928–38 was also a decade in which she choreographed works of protest: *Revolt, Immigrant, Four Insincerities, Heretic*. Her distinctive style based on contraction and release, episodic choreography, brilliant staging, use of specially written scores and her collaboration with brilliant designers such as Noguchi, all contributed to her impact.

In a 'middle period' begun by the famous *Frontier* (1935) she explored her American heritage (*Salem Shore, Appalachian Spring, American Document*), especially the experience of women, moving to specific characters such as Emily Dickinson in *Letter to the World*. Her interest in great women is illustrated by other work on characters such as the Brontes, Herodias, Joan of Arc and Mary, Queen of Scots, and can be felt behind her use of Greek mythology in her later phase which culminated in the great *Clytemnestra* (1958). During the late 1960s Martha Graham's power as a performer declined and in 1973, after a severe illness, she became a full-time teacher, lecturer and Director of the Martha Graham Dance Company. She has received many honorary degrees, awards and decorations, including the Medal of Freedom (1976). Her more recent works include *Phaedra's Dream* (1983) and *Song* (1985).

E. Sodelle: *Deep Song* (1984)

**Grahn, Lucille** (1819–1907). Danish ballerina. Born in Copenhagen, Lucille insisted on a ballet career from the age of four, and her first public appearance was as Cupid in 1826. She was taught by Larcher at the Royal Danish Ballet School, and then became Bournonville's protégée. She created the title role in his version of *La Sylphide* at the Royal Theatre in 1836. Having established her reputation in Copenhagen with *Don Quixote* (1837), she applied for leave and studied in Paris under Blasis while still under contract to the Royal Theatre. She was engaged at the Paris Opéra (1839–42) and then visited St Petersburg [now Leningrad] and London, where she took part in the famous *Pas de quatre* with TAGLIONI, FANNY CERRITO and CARLOTTA

GRISI in 1845. Lucille Grahn's international career continued until 1856, when she married the Austrian tenor Friedrich Young and retired from the stage. She was Ballet Mistress at Leipzig (1858–61) and at Munich (1869–75) where she choreographed for operas, including Wagner's *Tannhäuser*. On her death she left her fortune to the poor of Munich.

I. Guest: *The Romantic Ballet in Paris* (1966)

**Graine Mhaol.** *See* O'MALLEY, GRACE.

**Grand, Sarah** [pseud. of Frances McFall] (1854–1943). British novelist. Born in Donaghadee, County Down, Northern Ireland, she was the daughter of a naval officer, and after her father's death in 1861 she moved to live with her mother's family in Yorkshire. An unhappy adolescence both at home and in repressive boarding schools provoked her decision to marry a widower, surgeon Major David McFall, when she was 16. She travelled with him to Hong Kong, and the Far East and then returned to England where they lived in Norwich and Warrington.

In 1888 Sarah's first novel, *Ideals*, appeared. She left her husband and child and moved to London, where she was drawn into feminist circles. Her next book, *The Heavenly Twins* was a fervent plea for emancipation which shocked the public and became an immediate best-seller. Her most enduring work, *The Beth Book: Being a Study from the Life of Elizabeth Caldwell Machure, a Woman of Genius* (1897), was a quasi-autobiographical novel about the frustrations experienced by an intelligent woman in seeking education, work and sexual freedom.

In 1898, after her husband had died, she went to Tunbridge Wells, where she became President of the local branch of the National Union of Women's Suffrage Societies. In 1920 she moved to Bath where her fame led to her election as mayor in 1927. The rest of her life was uneventful and she died in Bath aged 88.

G. Kersley: *Darling Madame: a Portrait of Sarah Grand* (1982)

**Grasso** [née Tambussi], **Ella** (1919–81). American politician. Born in Windsor Locks, nr Hartford, Connecticut, she was the only daughter of Italian immigrants. She won scholarships to Chaffee School and then to Mount Holyoke College, Massachusetts, where she graduated with distinction in 1940 and obtained an MA in sociology and economics. In 1942 she married the schoolteacher Thomas Grasso, and from 1943 to 1946 worked as Assistant State Director of Research for the Federal War Manpower Commission in Connecticut. She had two children and before the youngest was two years old she became a Democratic candidate for the State Assembly. In 1952 she won a seat in the legislature, became floor leader in 1955 and Secretary of State in 1958, turning her office into an open 'people's' lobby. She retained this post until 1970 and also became active on the Democratic National Committee, collaborating in the minority report opposing American policy in Vietnam, which was presented at the 1968 Chicago Convention. In 1970 she ran for Congress, and her record there showed her to be a reluctant feminist, although ambivalent on such issues as abortion and nursery provision.

In 1974 she won the Governorship of Connecticut in a landslide victory, and at once took very unpopular but successful measures to demolish the huge state debt. Her popularity was restored during the 1978 blizzard, when she personally organized massive emergency relief and in 1978 she won more than 75 per cent of the towns in the state. She was the first woman Governor elected in her own right rather than in succession to a husband, and *Time* described her as a combination of a 'tough, back-slapping politician' and a 'disarmingly rumpled matron'. After the discovery that she had cancer she ran the state government from her hospital room for several weeks, eventually resigning on New Year's Eve, 1980. She died two months later.

**Gray, Eileen** (1879–1976). Irish designer and architect. Born at Brownwood, Enniscorthy, County Wexford, she was educated privately before studying painting at the Slade School, London (1898–1902). She was apprenticed to the Japanese lacquerist Sugawara (1907–14) in Paris, where she designed furniture and carpets, and drove an ambulance during World War I. With Sugawara she ran a studio in London and then in Paris. From 1926 she owned a gallery in the Faubourg St Honoré, becoming famous for her handmade furniture, and in the mid-1920s designed two houses which anticipated modern design in their use of space and their exciting interiors. One was decorated by Le Corbusier, the other was later bought by Graham Sutherland. She was also a daring pilot and balloonist. During World War II she was interned as an enemy alien and afterwards lived in France virtually as a recluse, although continuing to design with innovative materials: steel, glass, and plastics. In the 1970s her reputation was revived and she was made Royal Designer for Industry, Royal Society of Arts (1972), and Fellow of the Royal Institute of Irish Architects (1973). In 1976 she was the subject of a retrospective exhibition at the Victoria and Albert Museum, London.
S. Johnson: *Eileen Gray: Designer 1879–1976* (1979)

**Green, Anna Katherine** (1846–1935). American mystery writer. The author of *The Leavenworth Case* (1878), considered to be the first detective story written by a woman, Anna was born in Brooklyn, New Jersey, the daughter of a well-known criminal lawyer, and was educated at Ripley Female College in Poultney, Vermont. She married Charles Rohlfs, a furniture designer and manufacturer, and they lived in Buffalo, New York, with their three children. *The Leavenworth Case*, her first book, was an instant and continuing best-seller, combining melodrama and sentiment with skilful plotting. (It was later adapted for the stage, and was filmed twice, in 1923 and 1936.) The detective Ebenezer Gryce appeared in several more of her novels, sometimes with his assistant Amelia Butterworth. She also invented another female detective, Violet Strange. As well as her 40 mystery novels, written before 1923, she published two volumes of poetry and a verse drama in the 1880s.

**Green, Hetty** [Henrietta] **(Howland Robinson)** (1834–1916). American financier. She was born at New Bedford, Massachusetts, into a Quaker family; her father made a fortune in whaling and in trade with China. She was educated on Cape Cod and in Boston, and after her mother's death in 1860 she went with her father to New York. In 1865 she inherited her father's millions, and after a complicated legal battle also won an interest in the fortune of her aunt who had virtually brought her up.

In 1867 she married Edward Green, a silk merchant trading with the Philippines, and after the birth of their daughter they entered a contract guaranteeing each other's financial independence. On her return to the USA Hetty began playing the Stock Exchange and lending money on Wall Street. A shrewd investor, she survived the crash of 1907, and held massive interests in railways, government bonds and city properties. Known as 'the witch of Wall Street', and alleged to be the richest woman in the world, she turned her inherited $10 million into $100 million. Her meanness became the subject of many newspaper articles; she wore old clothes and lived frugally in a Hoboken apartment. It was reported that she took her son to a free clinic rather than pay a doctor, and this resulted in an unnecessary leg amputation. Towards the end of her life she withdrew entirely from the public gaze.

B. Sparker and S.T. Morse: *Hetty Green, a Woman who loved Money* (1930)

**Greer, Germaine** (1939–). Australian feminist critic. Born in Melbourne, she was educated at a convent and after taking a degree in Education at Melbourne University in 1959 she went on to Sydney University, where she did post-graduate work and taught until 1964. She then went to Cambridge as a Commonwealth Scholar and obtained her PhD on Shakespeare's comedies. From 1967 to 1973 she was a lecturer in English at the University of Warwick. For three weeks in 1968 she was married to journalist and building worker Paul de Feu.

She obtained overnight fame, or notoriety, with the publication of *The Female Eunuch* in 1970, a lively survey of the forms of women's subordination. She became a familiar figure in the British media, and was a *Sunday Times* columnist. Since then she has been a freelance writer and lecturer and has lived chiefly on her farm in Italy. Her other publications include *The Obstacle Race: the Fortunes of Women Painters and their Work* (1979), a substantial piece of research.

In 1979 Greer became a Director of the Tulsa Centre for the Study of Women's Literature, in Oklahoma. She divides her time between Italy, London and the USA, although in 1981 she spent three months in India researching a book on the politics of human fertility, work which influenced her next controversial book, *Sex and Destiny: The Politics of Human Fertility* (1984). She has continued to write in numerous journals, and to appear on television and her recent books include *Shakespeare* (1985) and the collection of essays *The Madwoman's Underclothes* (1986).

**Gregory** [née Persse], **(Isabella) Augusta** (1852–1932). Irish playwright. Born at Roxborough, County Galway, she was educated privately and married Sir William Gregory, a nearby landowner at Coole Park, in 1881; Sir William died in 1892. After meeting W.B. Yeats in 1895 she became a patron of Irish artists and grew increasingly interested in national folklore. With Yeats and Edward Martyn she founded the Irish Literary Theatre (1899) (which later became the Abbey Theatre), and Coole Park became the centre of the 'Irish Renaissance'. She learned Gaelic and published English translations of old sagas, *Guchulain of Muirthemne* (1902) and *Gods and fighting Men* (1904). In 1904 she became co-director with Yeats and Synge of the newly-opened Abbey Theatre (built by ANNIE HORNIMAN), which after 1909 she managed for the rest of her life, proving a tireless administrator and fund-raiser. She also revealed a talent for play-writing, eventually producing over 40 plays, mainly comedies of Irish rural life but also local adaptations of Molière, Goldoni and other writers. All her works combine natural dialogue with a simple effective structure; some of the earliest plays are among her most successful: *Spreading the News* (1904), *The Rising of the Moon* (1907) and *The Workhouse Ward* (1908). She was dedicated to restoring Irish culture and political independence and this is reflected in her drama, memoirs, biographies, political and economic pamphlets, and books for children. In 1914 she published *Our Irish Theatre: A Chapter of Autobiography*.

H. Adams: *Lady Gregory* (1973)
C. Smythe, ed.: *Seventy Years: Being the Autiobiography of Lady Gregory* (1975)

**Grey, Beryl (Elizabeth)** (1927–). English ballerina. Born in London, she was educated at theatre schools, entering the Sadler's Wells Ballet School at the age of nine, and was taught by NINETTE DE VALOIS and Vera Volkova. In 1941 she joined the Sadler's Wells Ballet Company and danced *Swan Lake* for the first time on her fifteenth birthday, followed by *Giselle* (1944) and *The Sleeping Beauty* (1946). Her repertoire has included a wide range of classical and modern ballets from *Les Sylphides* to *Ballet Imperial*, and she has created many new roles, a memorable example being the Winter Fairy in Ashton's *Cinderella*. She danced with Royal Ballet in all parts of the world.

In 1950 Beryl Grey married Dr Sven Svenson, and has since made many guest appearances in Sweden. In 1957 she left the Royal Ballet, but was Guest Ballerina until 1963, and also in 1957 became the first foreign ballerina to be a guest artist at the Kiev, Bol'shoi and other Russian ballets. In 1964 she was the first to dance with the Peking and Shanghai ballets; these experiences are described in her books, *Red Curtain Up* (1958) and *Through the Bamboo Curtain* (1965). She was appointed Director of the Arts Educational School, London, in 1966 and from 1968 to 1980 was Artistic Director of the London Festival Ballet. She produced and staged *Giselle* in Australia (1984) and *The Sleeping Beauty* in Stockholm (1985).

**Grey, Lady Jane** (1537–54). English claimant to the throne. She was the daughter of the Marquis of Dorset, the granddaughter of the Duke of Suffolk, and the niece of Henry VIII. An acknowledged beauty, distinguished for youthful learning, she was a member of CATHERINE PARR's household from the age of nine until the Queen's death in 1548. She then became the subject of intrigues to marry her to Edward VI, as a result of which her guardian Thomas Seymour (Catherine Parr's second husband) was executed. Now aged 15 she returned to her family, studying with her tutor Aylmer. Ascham records her as being very proficient in Greek, Hebrew, Latin, Italian and French.

After her father became Duke of Suffolk in 1551 she moved to Court and in 1553 reluctantly married Guildford Dudley, fourth son of Suffolk's ally the Duke of Northumberland. The Dudley family's ill-treatment of her caused severe nervous illness. Victim of her father's ambitions, she was named successor to the throne by the Privy Council on Edward's death and established in the Tower of London, but was forced to stand down in the face of overwhelming national support for MARY I. Confined to the Tower, she was arraigned for treason in November 1553; she pleaded guilty and was sentenced to death. Any chance of mercy was forestalled by Suffolk's involvement with Wyatt's uprising and she and her husband were beheaded on Tower Hill on 12 February 1554. She was a staunch Protestant, and possibly a Calvinist.

A. Plowden: *Lady Jane Grey* (1985)

**Grimké.** American sisters, abolitionists and feminists. Born in Charleston, South Carolina, the daughters of a judge and slave-owner, they were educated at home. Their later careers, which defied contemporary expectations of women, were inextricably intertwined.

**(1) Sarah Moore** (1792–1873) moved to Philadelphia in 1821, unable to remain in the South because of her hatred of slavery. She became a Quaker in 1823. Joined by her sister Angelina in 1829 she began to campaign for abolition, challenging the theological defences of slavery in her *Epistle to the Clergy of the Southern States* (1836). They then moved to New York, becoming the first women lecturers for the American Anti-Slavery Society. They graduated from female to mixed audiences, provoking the disapproval of the press, the conventional public and even the dissenting clergy of Massachusetts. Sarah countered this criticism in *Letters on the Equality of the Sexes* and *The Condition of Women* (1838). After 1838 she lived with Angelina who was now married, and they continued to campaign, their *American Slavery as it is: Testimony of a Thousand Witnesses* (1838) being especially influential. They later moved to Massachusetts where they taught until their retirement in 1867.

**(2) Angelina Emily** (1805–79) joined Sarah in Philadelphia in 1829 and provoked their public career by a letter to the *Liberator* in 1835, followed by a passionate appeal asking women to defy the slavery laws in *Appeal to the Christian Women of the South* (1836) and *Appeal to Women of the Nominally Free States* (1837). She moved to New York with Sarah and replied to criticisms of their boldness in lecturing to mixed audiences in her *Letters to Catharine Beecher* (1838). In the same year she married Theophilus Weld; they had one child. Sarah joined their household at Fort Lee and then at a communal settlement, Rariton Bay Union, in New Jersey. They campaigned, wrote and taught together there and in Massachusetts until their retirement in 1867.

G. Lerner: *The Grimké Sisters of South Carolina* (1967)

**Grimshaw, Beatrice** (1871–1953). Irish traveller and writer. She was born in Cloona, County Antrim, and educated at Caen, at Victoria College, Belfast, and Bedford College, London. She became a journalist in London and, as an 'emancipated woman', was a keen cyclist, setting a new 24-hour world record. Always longing to travel, she obtained sponsorship from shipping companies in return for promised press coverage, and in 1906 set out for the South Pacific. Over the next few years she travelled extensively among the islands of South East Asia, including Fiji, New Hebrides, Solomon Islands, and the Moluccas, and explored the hinterland of Papua New Guinea; she was the first woman to go up the notorious Sepik River and Fly River.

Her experiences were recorded in nearly 40 travel books, short stories and novels beginning with *From Fiji to the Cannibal Islands* and *Vaiti of the Islands* in 1907, and she also became a recognized authority on tropical colonization. She retired to Australia in 1939.

**Grisi.** Italian singers. They were cousins of the ballerina CARLOTTA GRISI.

**(1) Giuditta** (1805–40), mezzo-soprano. She studied at the Milan Conservatory and made her debut in Vienna in Rossini's *Bianca e Faliero* (1826). The role of Romeo in Bellini's *I Capuleti e i Montecchi* (1830)

was written for her, and she also appeared in his *Il pirata* and *La straniera*. Her comparatively few performances outside Italy included visits to London and Paris (1832, in *La straniera*) and to Madrid (1834, as Romeo and Norma). She retired in 1838.

**(2) Giulia** (1811–69), soprano. She had singing lessons from her sister Giuditta as well as from Marliani in Milan and Giacomelli in Bologna, where she made her debut in the 1828–9 season in operas by Rossini and Cordella. She was Juliet to her sister's Romeo at the première of *I Capuleti e i Montecchi*, other roles written for her by Bellini including Adalgisa in *Norma* and Elvira in *I puritani* (1835).

Giulia left Italy in 1832 and did not return in a professional capacity, largely because of her attempt to break her contract at La Scala. That year she made her debut in Paris, in the title role of Rossini's *Semiramide* (which she repeated at the opening of the Royal Italian Opera at Covent Garden, 1847). After her London debut in 1834, as Ninetta in Rossini's *La gazza ladra*, she alternated between Paris and London each season for over a decade in astonishingly diverse roles, though excelling as an interpreter of Donizetti; she created Norina in *Don Pasquale* (Paris, 1843), and at the London première of *Lucrezia Borgia* (1839) she sang opposite the tenor Giovanni Mario, initiating a lifelong partnership both on and off the stage (she was unable to secure a divorce from her husband Gérard de Melcy), including tours to St Petersburg [now Leningrad] (1849) and New York (1854). Her official farewell performances were in 1861, though several had been billed as such since 1849; an isolated performance of *Lucrezia Borgia* in 1866 stood testimony to her characteristic determination.

**Grisi, Carlotta** (1819–99). Italian ballerina. Born in Visinada, nr Mantua, she studied at La Scala ballet school, Milan, where she made her debut in 1829 and achieved acclaim as a child star. She toured major Italian cities and in 1833 was seen in Naples by Jules Perrot. She became his protégée and he took her to Paris, coached her and choreographed her dances. She appeared in Paris in 1836 and 1837 but was not engaged at the Opéra until 1841, when she partnered Lucien Petipa in Donizetti's *La favorite*.

Success came with her creation of the title role in the Coralli–Perrot *Giselle*, with scenario by Gautier who became her lifelong friend. He described her dancing as having 'a childlike artlessness, a happy and infectious gaiety'.

In 1843 Grisi created *La Péri*, notorious for her daring leap from a high platform into Petipa's arms. Other successes included Mazilier's *Le diable à quatre* and *Paquita* (1846). From 1842 to 1851 she was a regular visitor to London, where she enjoyed great popularity. In 1850 she danced Giselle at the Bol'shoi Theatre, St Petersburg [now Leningrad], spent the next three years in Russia where she worked with Perrot again, and danced in Warsaw in the 1854 season. She then retired and spent the rest of her life at St Jean, nr Geneva.

S. Lifar: *Carlotta Grisi* (Eng. trans. 1947)

**Grøndahl, Agathe.** See BACKER-GRØNDAHL.

**Groza, Maria** (1918–). Romanian economist, feminist and politician. Born in Déva and educated at the Bucharest Academy of Economics, after World War II she became a civil servant, working in the Ministry of Foreign Affairs from 1948 to 1955 and also teaching at the Academy of Economics, where she became a full-time lecturer in 1955. She wrote extensively on the position of women in Romania, and on educational issues; she was Secretary of the National Council of Women (1958–64) and Vice-President (1965–75). She is now a Deputy Minister of Social Affairs, and a member of the influential Council of Front of Socialist Democracy and Unity.

Groza confirmed her international reputation during the 1960s and 1970s when she was a UN delegate and attended and chaired many UNESCO and UN conferences on social issues, her offices including Rapporteur-Général at the World Conference for International Women's Year in 1975. She became Deputy Minister of Foreign Affairs in 1980.

**Guertes, Dolores Adios.** See MENKEN, ADAH ISAACS.

**Guest, Lady Charlotte (Elizabeth)** (1812–95). Welsh author. The daughter of Albemarle Bertie, the 9th Earl of Lindsey,

she was born at Uffington House, Lincolnshire. Her father died when she was six, and her mother married the Reverend Peter Parsons in 1821. Although her stepfather discouraged education for girls, she read widely and learned modern and classical languages, Hebrew and Persian with her brothers' tutors. In 1833 she married a middle-aged widower, Josiah John Guest (later Sir), an iron-master of Dowlais in Glamorgan, South Wales. Charlotte learned Welsh and produced a classic translation and edition of the famous collection of old Celtic tales, *The Mabinogian*, which was published in Llandovery between 1838 and 1849. She was helped with the translation by a Welsh bard, John Jones 'Tegid' and she also became a keen promoter of the newly-revived Welsh festivals, the eisteddfods.

When her husband died in 1852, in addition to looking after his ten children, she became manager of the huge ironworks, having previously been its accountant. She ran the business herself until she married Charles Schreiber, a Cambridge academic and former MP in 1855. During their marriage she became an avid collector, first of china and ceramics, of which she presented a superb collection from Europe and the Middle East to the South Kensington Museum on her husband's death in 1884; she gave an equally impressive collection of fans to the British Museum in 1891, and at her death left the museum a collection of playing cards.

M. Guest: *Lady Charlotte Guest, Extracts from her Journals* (1950)

**Guggenheim, Peggy** (1898–1980). American art collector. The niece of Solomon Guggenheim, who founded the Museum of Modern Art in New York, she had a luxurious but lonely childhood and after finishing school went to Paris, where she lived a bohemian life, married to the artist Laurence Vail. They had two children, but the marriage was unhappy and after the death of her lover John Holms she turned to a career as an art collector.

In 1934 she opened the avant-garde gallery Guggenheim-Jeune with the help of her friend Marcel Duchamp, to exhibit Surrealist and Expressionist works. It is said that as the exhibitions rarely sold she bought a piece from each show to encourage the artists, which included Miró, Cocteau, Kandinsky, Klee, Braque and Picasso. The gallery closed in 1938 and in 1940 she took her large collection to the USA, where she married the artist Max Ernst and opened another gallery called Art of This Century, showing then unpopular artists such as Motherwell, Rothko, Tanguy and Pollock (the last two, as well as the writer Samuel Beckett, were reputed to be among her numerous lovers). She returned to Europe after World War II, showing her collection in a special pavilion at the Venice Biennale, and in 1951 she opened a permanent exhibition in her 18th-century palace, the Venier dei Leoni on the Grand Canal; she eventually gave the collection to the city of Venice.

P. Guggenheim: *Out of this Century* (1946)
————: *Confessions of an Art Addict* (1980)

**Guyard, Marie** (1599–1672). French missionary. She was the daughter of middle-class parents, her father being a master-baker. In obedience to her parents' wishes, Marie married Claude Martin, a silk worker, in 1617, despite her attraction to the religious life. Her husband died three years later and in 1632, after working as housekeeper for her sister and brother-in-law, she entered the Ursuline Convent at Tours, leaving her son in her sister's care. Marie received a number of revelations concerning the Incarnation, the Sacred Heart and the Trinity and in 1635 she had a dream which hinted at her missionary vocation. Four years later she joined Madame de la Peltrie and two other sisters in accepting an invitation of the Jesuit mission to form a convent in Quebec. They immediately opened their first school for daughters of both settlers and Indians and despite sickness, poverty and Indian persecution, the school grew and in two years needed to move to a larger place. In 1648, when Iroquois hostilities endangered Quebec, Marie was advised to return to Europe, but she and her nuns chose to remain.

Marie's works, published posthumously, include *Retraites* (1682) and her letters (1681) which are an important source for the early history of French Canada. She also composed cathechisms in Huron and Algonquin, and a dictionary of French and Algonquin. In 1911 she was pronounced Venerable by Pius X.

A. Repplier: *Mère Marie of the Ursulines* (1931)

**Guy-Blaché, Alice** (1875–1968). French film director. She was the first woman film director. While she was secretary to the French film pioneer Léon Gaumont, she made the short *La Fée aux Choux* in 1896 with a friend. This is reputedly the first fiction film. She directed all Gaumont productions in 1905, including some experimental sound films with synchronized cylinder rolls. She moved to the USA after her husband, a cameraman from London, Herbert Blaché-Bolton, was made head of Gaumont's New York office. Returning to film production after the birth of their daughter, she founded her own studio and production company Solax in 1910, with herself as President and Director-in-Chief, erecting the two-foot high sign 'Be Natural', for the benefit of her players. In the four years of Solax's existence, she directed over 100 films, and supervised many more. She closed down her very successful company to work in her husband's studio, directing Bessie Love in *The Great Adventure* (1918), and several films with the British-born Olga Petrova. She gave a series of lectures on film-making at Columbia University in 1917. She made her last film in 1920, turned down the offer to direct *Tarzan of the Apes*, and returned to France in 1922 after separating from her husband. Unable to return to film production in the late 1920s, she worked mainly as a translator, living with her daughter in France, Belgium and the USA.

**Guyon, Jeanne Marie (de Bouvier de la Mothe)** (1648–1717). French Quietist author. Her father was old and her mother neglectful and Jeanne Marie spent most of her childhood in various convents. At the age of 16 she was married to Jacques Guyon de Chesnay, an invalid over twice her age. He died after 12 unhappy years of marriage. Jeanne Marie had always been attracted to the inner life of prayer and now she developed her own version of Quietism, teaching complete indifference, even to eternal salvation: a heretical view to orthodox eyes.

Setting her children aside, Madame

Guyon travelled through Europe with the Barnabite Father François La Combe, in order to spread the word. Suspicion about her doctrine and the possiblility of immorality between the two led to their arrest in Paris in 1687. With the assistance of Madame DE MAINTENON, the unacknowledged wife of Louis XIV, Jeanne was freed, became influential in the royal circle and won a powerful follower in Abbé François Fénelon, later Archbishop of Cambrais. His support for her led him into a great dispute with Bossuet, Bishop of Meaux. In 1695 Jeanne Marie demanded a theological commission to clear her but the resulting Commission of Issy condemned her and she was again arrested. Released in 1702, she spent the rest of her life in Blois.

Jeanne Marie Guyon has been called half saint, half lunatic, good in heart but weak in mind. Her chief mystical writings include *Moyen court et très facile de faire oraison* (1685) and *Le Cantique des Cantiques* (1688).

R.A. Know: *Enthusiasm* (1950), 319–52

**Gwyn, Nell (Eleanor)** (1650–87). English actress. Initially an orange-seller at the Theatre Royal, Drury Lane, London, her first roles are uncertain, but were possibly the 'breeches part' of Melina/Pedro in *The Siege of Urbino* or the courtesan Paulina in Killigrew's *Thomasso* in the 1664–5 season. After the plague in 1665 more reliable records show her to have played several comedy parts, such as Lady Wealthy in *The English Monsieur*, Caelia in *The Humorous Lieutenant* and Florimel in *Secret Love* (in which she was famously attractive in breeches). In 1667 she played Cydaria in Dryden's *Indian Emperor*. She continued at the Theatre Royal till 1671, and later played other theatres before returning to Drury Lane in the early 1680s. Although illiterate, through her charm and vivacity she was particularly effective in comedy. She became the mistress of Charles II, ousting her rival the Duchess of Portsmouth and retaining royal favour till his death. One of her two sons by the king was created Duke of St Albans in 1684 and tradition has it that it was owing to her influence that Chelsea Hospital was founded. Her portrait was painted by Lely.

A. Dasent: *Nell Gwynne* (1924)

**'Gypsy Rose' Lee.** *See* LEE, 'GYPSY ROSE'.

*Elizabeth Fry*

*Nell Gwyn*

*Caroline Herschel*

*Dolores Ibarruri (La Pasionaria)*

# H

**'Hachette', Jeanne Laisne** [Fourquet] (*fl* 1470). French heroine. Jeanne won her lasting fame during the Burgundian siege of Beauvais in 1470 when she led a body of women, armed with hatchets, who drove off the attackers and captured their flag. She was rewarded by Louis XI for her bravery. She later married Collin Pillon, and she and her descendants were exempted from taxation. The town of Beauvais held an annual march in her memory, in which the women walked in front of the men, a tradition which lasted until the late 19th century.

**Hadewijch** (*fl* late 12th or early 13th century). Dutch mystic and poet. Little is known of her life except that she was of noble birth and led a group associated with the lay religious communities, the beguines. She lived in Brabant. Her intense mystical poetry is outstanding in mediaeval literature for its devotional power, clarity of neo-Platonic thought and great beauty of expression. Much of her poetry, later collected in *Strophische Gedichten*, uses Provençal courtly forms and may have been set to music. She also wrote didactic verse and prose letters, which brought her a great reputation in Europe as a teacher.

**Hainisch, Marianne** (1839–1936). Austrian feminist. She was born and brought up in Vienna. After her family interests were affected by the collapse of the cotton trade during the American Civil War, she observed the inability of middle class women to support themselves financially and she began to campaign for higher education, demanding schools which could prepare women to enter universities and to take up professions. In 1870, at a meeting of the Women's Employment Association she appealed for a concerted educational campaign, and subsequently wrote *Die Brötfrage der Frau* (1875), about the question of women's ability to earn a living. Charming, eloquent and determined, she founded her own public school in Vienna but still continued to press for women's rights, especially for the vote. As founder and President of the Allgemeiner Österreich-ischer Frauenverein (General Austrian Women's Association) in 1899 she fought for reform of the marriage laws, improvement of the position of illegitimate children, and the abolition of legalized prostitution. She later wrote *Frauenarbeit* (1911), *Die Mutter* (1913), and contributed to many feminist journals. A pacifist, she campaigned against World War I and later became Vice-President of the Austrian Red Cross. She was an indomitable but friendly personality, determined and daring to the end of her life. Her son Michael served two terms as President of the Austrian Republic.

**Hale, Sarah Josepha (Buell)** (1788–1879). American journalist. Born in Newport, New Hampshire, and educated at home, from 1806 to 1811 she ran a small private school and wrote articles for the local newspapers. In 1813 she married a lawyer who encouraged her writing, but on his death in 1822 she opened a millinery shop to support her five children. During this decade she published poetry, *The Genius of Oblivion* (1823), and a novel *Nortonwood* (1827), and in 1828 began editing the new *Ladies' Magazine*, writing half the journal herself. A conservative feminist, she campaigned for women's education but in the belief that this would make them better wives and mothers, not as a step towards equality with men.

In 1837 her journal was bought by Louis Godey and she became editor of *Godey's*

*Lady's Book*, a long-running and highly influential magazine, which mixed domestic hints, fashion and etiquette tips with short stories and poems. It had a very patriotic tone and, like the *Ladies' Magazine*, took a cautious feminist line, stopping short of supporting the suffrage movement. By 1841 Sarah Hale had moved to Philadelphia, where she became involved in several philanthropic groups, and was one of the organizers of the Ladies' Medical Missionary Society in 1851. Among her other publications was the *Women's Record: or Sketches of all distinguished Women, from the Creation to AD 1654* (1855), containing over 1000 biographies.

R.E. Finley: *The Lady of Godey's: Sarah Josepha Hale* (1931)

**Halimi** [née Taieb]**, Gisèle (Zeiza Elisa)** (1927–). French lawyer and feminist. Born in La Goulette, Tunisia, she was educated at a lycée in Tunis and then at the University of Paris, graduating in law and philosophy. In 1948 she qualified as a lawyer, and has practised at the Paris bar since 1956. She acted as counsel for the Algerian National Liberation Front, most notably for the tortured activist DJAMILA BOUPACHA in 1960, and wrote a book in 1961 (introduced by SIMONE DE BEAUVOIR) to plead her cause. She has also defended Basque terrorists, and has been counsel in many cases related to women's issues, such as the Bobigny abortion trial of 1972 which attracted national publicity.

In 1971 she founded the feminist group Choisir, to protect the women who had signed the *Manifeste des 343* admitting to having illegal abortions. In 1972 Choisir formed itself into a clearly reformist body, and the campaign greatly influenced the passing of the laws on contraception and abortion carried through by SIMONE VEIL in 1974. Halimi is the author of *La cause des femmes* (1973) and instigator and contributor to the collective work *Le programme commun des femmes* (1978). This outlined women's chief needs: legal, medical, educational and professional, and suggested solutions which should be demanded by women voters. In 1981 she was elected to the National Assembly, as an Independent Socialist, and was Deputy for Isère until 1984. Since 1985 she has been French delegate to UNESCO. She has been twice married, to Paul Halimi, and to Charles Faux, and has three sons.

**Halkett, Anne (Murray)** [Lady Halkett] (1622–99). English Royalist and writer. She was the daughter of Thomas Murray (*d* 1625), tutor to Charles I and Provost of Eton College, and Jane Drummond, governess to the younger royal children. Her mother supervised her education, which was very conventional with a strong religious element, but she also studied medicine and surgery, later gaining a considerable reputation for healing. After her mother's death in 1646 her involvement with Joseph Bamfield led to many adventures: aiding the escape of the Duke of York, joining Charles II in Scotland in 1650, and nursing Royalist sick and wounded until 1654. Finally convinced that Bamfield's wife was alive and that he would never marry her, Anne married Sir James Halkett in 1656.

Despite her loyalty to the Stuarts she received no compensation from the Treasury at the Restoration for her lost estates, and after Halkett's death in 1676 took pupils at her Dunfermline home. Her religious writing filled 20 manuscript books but the most interesting work is her fascinating *Autobiography*, which was attached to her writings on their publication in 1701.

*Autobiography of Anne, Lady Halkett* (1875)

**Hall, (Marguerite) Radclyffe** (1883–1943). English novelist and poet. Born in Bournemouth, she was educated at King's College, London, and in Germany. She became financially independent at the age of 21 and took up a literary career. At first she wrote poetry, publishing her first volume *Twixt Earth and Stars* in 1906. This was followed by three more volumes of poetry, then eight novels and some short stories. She won the Prix Femina Vie Heureuse and the James Tait Black Memorial Prize for *Adam's Breed* (1926), but her most infamous novel was *The Well of Loneliness* (1928), a deliberately explicit portrayal of lesbianism. The novel was put on trial for obscenity and suppressed, despite the fact that writers such as VIRGINIA WOOLF and E.M. Forster were willing to testify to its literary merits.

From 1907 to 1916 she lived with Mrs Mabel Batten, through whom she met Una, Lady Troubridge, her lover and companion for the rest of her life. They lived in London, Sussex and Paris, where they frequented the same café society as COLETTE, NATALIE BARNEY and other lesbian socialites. She was a member of the PEN club, the Council of the Society for Psychical Research, and a fellow of the Zoological Society. In 1930 she received the Gold Medal of the Eichelbergher Humane Award.

M. Baker: *Our Three Selves: a Life of Radclyffe Hall* (1985)

**Hallowes, Odette (Marie Céline)** (1912–). French wartime agent operating from Britain. 'Odette' is one of the most famous British agents in wartime France. Born in France, she was educated at a convent in Amiens. In 1931 she married Roy Samson and the following year went to Britain. She was recruited in 1942 to work with the French Resistance and for the Special Forces in France. In 1942 she landed by felucca on the French Riviera, and joined Peter Churchill's network 'Spindle' as a courier. In 1943 the group moved to Annecy, but was penetrated by the Germans; Odette and Churchill were captured by the Gestapo and sentenced to death. To save him, she said that they were married and that she had forced him to come to France. She was tortured intensively, but refused to betray other colleagues and was sent to Ravensbrück concentration camp until 1945, when the camp commandant, believing she was Winston Churchill's niece by marriage, drove her to the Allied lines. After her first husband's death she married Captain Peter Churchill (who died in 1947) and in 1956 married Geoffrey Hallowes. She holds several positions, such as Vice-President of the Women's Transport Services (FANY), and was awarded the Légion d'honneur in 1950.

**Halprin, Ann** (1920–). American modern dancer and choreographer. Born Anna Schumann in Winneteka, Illinois, Ann trained at the Humphrey Weidman studio. She married architect Lawrence Halprin, and in San Francisco co-founded an experimental dance workshop and studio with Wellard Lathrop in the late 1940s. From 1953 her summer schools were attended by leading modern choreographers and composers. She created exciting, large-scale works such as *The Prophetess* (1955), *Birds of America* (1957) and *Four-Legged Stool* (1961), and after 1964 made the choreography into a collective venture with dancers and technicians. Her innovative works in the 1960s included *Parades and Changes* (1967), which caused a storm because of the nudity involved. She has continued to work in California, with productions such as *Dance by the People of San Francisco* (1976) and remains one of the most influential leaders in post-modern dance.

**Hamer, Fannie Lou** (1918–77). American civil rights leader. Born in the state of Mississippi, the grand-daughter of a slave and the youngest of 20 children, she worked as a labourer on the plantation where she grew up until 1961, when she started to help the Student Non-Violent Co-ordinating Committee. In 1962, infuriated by the lack of control over her life that she experienced when she was given a hysterectomy without her consent while undergoing hospital treatment, she tried to register as a voter, and her protest lost her her job. She became more involved with the civil rights movement, helping to organize a network of contacts in the state, and in 1964 she ran as a candidate for Congress. She also became a committed feminist and an opponent of American military policy, and was elected to the Central Committee of the National Women's Political Caucus in 1971. A stirring orator and tireless organizer she remained undeterred by physical or verbal assaults.

**Hamilton, Alice** (1869–1970). American doctor of industrial medicine. Born in New York City, Alice was one of five children and was taught at home. She was influenced by her grandmother, a friend of SUSAN B. ANTHONY. At medical school at the University of Michigan, Ann Arbor, she was interested in pathology, and gained her MD in 1893.

On her return from a year's work in Germany, she heard JANE ADDAMS speak, and worked with her at Hull House, Chicago, for the next 22 years. She also taught at Women's Medical College, Northwest University, and was active in the birth control movement.

In 1902, during an outbreak of typhoid fever she began public pressure which discovered a contaminated drinking water supply. Her interest in 'dangerous trades' began, and in 1909 she made public the conditions of work of matchmakers which led to 'phossy-jaw'. She frequently had to challenge not only medical ignorance but the protectionist interests of management. In 1910 she headed the Occupational Disease Commission which studied lead poisoning in, for example, hat making, the enamelling of bathtubs, and work on the inside of Pullman cars, and presented her case to the officials. During World War I she investigated the high-explosives industry, where deaths were frequently cited as from natural causes or heart failure, instead of the nitrous-fume poisoning which she discovered caused similar symptoms.

In 1919 she was invited to become a Professor of Industrial Medicine at Harvard Medical School, on condition that she promised not to use the Harvard Club, a male faculty stronghold. A visit by invitation to the USSR impressed her with their concern for industrial hygiene. Her last detailed study was of the artificial silk (viscose rayon) industry, in which carbon disulphide caused mental disease, loss of vision and paralysis. Some examinations had to be made secretly, but when her results were published a compensation law was passed in Pennsylvania. Some of her findings on the employment of women in the dangerous trades were published in a Department of Labour Bulletin, *Women Workers and Industrial Poisons*.

In 1935 Alice retired to Hadlyme, Connecticut. She was the first woman to receive the Lasker award from the American public health department, among other honours.

A. Hamilton: *Exploring the dangerous Trades* (1943)
M. Grant: *Alice Hamilton: Pioneer Doctor in Industrial Medicine* (1967)

**Hamilton, Edith** (1865–1963). American classical scholar. The child of a wealthy family, she grew up in Fort Wayne, Indiana, and was educated privately before studying at Bryn Mawr College. She had developed a love of the Classics early in life and in 1895 went to Munich University to do research. In 1930 she wrote *The Greek Way* and in 1932 *The Roman Way* which won her widespread popular acclaim. In the next decade she wrote four more books and numerous articles. She moved to Washington, DC, in 1943.

D. Reid: *Edith Hamilton: an Intimate Portrait* (1967)

**Hamilton** [née Lyon, Amy], **Emma** [Lady Hamilton] (1761–1815). English beauty; mistress of Admiral Horatio Nelson. She was born in the village of Great Neston, Cheshire, the daughter of the local blacksmith. Her early life is obscure although she seems to have worked as a nursemaid, shop assistant, barmaid, and prostitute. She already had two children when she became the mistress of Sir Henry Fetherstonehaugh in 1780. From 1781 to 1785, calling herself Emily Hart, she lived a quiet, domestic life as the mistress of the young Charles Greville in Paddington Green, London. She was a great beauty who modelled several times for her friend Romney during these years, and later also sat for Reynolds, Lawrence and several Italian artists. In 1784 she met Charles's uncle, Sir William Hamilton, who agreed to pay his nephew's debts if Emma and her mother would accompany him to Naples, where he was ambassador. They arrived in Naples in 1786 and, after initial reluctance, Emma became Hamilton's mistress before she eventually persuaded him to marry her in 1791. She was an extremely popular figure in Neapolitan high society, and a friend of the Queen of Naples, Maria Caroline.

Lady Hamilton and Nelson first met in 1793 and on his second visit to Naples in 1799, after the successful battle of the Nile, they became lovers. She and her husband joined Nelson on his triumphal tour of England in 1800, and her daughter Horatia, always believed to be Nelson's child, was born in 1801. After Sir William Hamilton's death in 1803 she lived with Nelson at Merton, Surrey, until he was killed at the Battle of Trafalgar in 1805. The substantial fortunes left to her by both men were soon absorbed by her luxurious style of living, and after years of debt, during which she tried in vain to obtain pensions from the governments of Britain and of Naples, she was eventually arrested as a bankrupt and spent a year (1812–13) in the King's Bench Prison. An alderman, Joshua Smith, obtained her release and helped her escape to Calais, where she died in 1815.

N. Lofts: *Emma Hamilton* (1978)

**Hamnett, Katherine** (1952–). British fashion designer. Katherine's father was a British Air Attaché and her childhood was spent between European air bases and embassies. She attended Cheltenham Ladies College and studied fashion design at St Martin's School of Art, made a 'disastrous' marriage (she has two sons), and founded her first company in 1969 with Anne Buck, designing under the Tuttabankmen label, which went bankrupt in 1974. She then worked freelance in London, Paris, Rome and New York and for a sportswear company in Italy, while making and selling her own designs from home. In 1979 she started a new company with a £500 bank loan. The company, which achieved sales of £20 million in 1987 and predicted £30 million in 1988, is backed by Danish fashion entrepreneur Peter Bertelson. She also has a shop in the Brompton Road, London. She follows the Buddhist faith, and her social concern is made clear on T-shirts with slogans such as 'Education not Missiles', 'Heroin-free zone', 'Choose Life': her anti-establishment views are uncompromising, and deeply felt. She works in utilitarian fabrics such as cotton drill or lining silk and is known for loose simple lines and fine, witty details, and is 'possibly the most copied designer working today' (*Observer*). In 1988 she received the BKCEC (British Knitting and Clothing Export Council) award for outstanding achievement in export: almost 80% of her clothes sell overseas.

**Hancock,** Dame **Florence** (1893–1974). English trade unionist. Born in Chippenham, Wiltshire, one of 14 children of a weaver, she worked from the age of 12 in a café and a condensed milk factory. In 1913 she joined the Workers' Union, rising to District Officer for Wiltshire and Gloucestershire by 1917. 12 years later, after the merger with the Transport and General Workers' Union (TGWU), she went to Bristol as a Women's Officer, remaining in this post until she became Chief Woman Officer of the TGWU in 1942. From 1935 to 1958 she was on the general council of the Trades Union Congress, of which she became President in September 1947. She

fought for many years for equal pay in industry, better provision for domestic workers, youth employment, child care and aid for married women workers, and also advised the Ministry of Labour on women's war work from 1941 to 1945. A reserved, energetic organizer she also worked on several government commissions during the 1950s and was a Director of Remploy and Governor of the BBC. She was made a DBE in 1951.

**Hani, Motoko** (1873–1957). Japanese educationalist and journalist. Born in Aomori Prefecture, into a former samurai family, Motoko was baptized a Christian in 1890. She first worked for an educational magazine but later joined the newspaper *Hochi shimbun*. Starting off as a copy editor, in 1897 she became the first full-time woman reporter, covering women, education, and religion. In 1901 she married a colleague, Soshikazu Hani, and together they started a magazine, *Fujin no Tomo* ('Woman's Friend'), advocating that women be self-reliant members of society. The Friends' Association, a nationwide association of loyal readers of this magazine, which was founded in 1930, is still active and has over 30,000 members.

In 1921 they founded a private school, Jiyu Gakuen, renowned for its liberalism, based on both Protestant and traditional Japanese ethics. During World War II the school remained largely independent of state control, and has provided outstanding graduates. Their two daughters, the social critic Setsuko (wife of a famous sociologist, Goro Hani, and mother of film director Susumu Hani), and the educationalist Keiko (who succeeded her mother as principal of the school), have both followed in Motoko's footsteps.

**Hansberry, Lorraine (Vivian)** (1930–65). American playwright. The daughter of a financier and slum property owner, who founded a black bank in Chicago, she was educated locally, at the Chicago Art Institute, and the University of Wisconsin, Madison, graduating in 1948. She worked as a journalist and editor and married theatrical director Robert Nemiroff in 1953. In 1959 her play *A Raisin in the Sun* was produced on Broadway, the first major popular and critical success in New York for a black woman. It analysed the frustrations of life in a black ghetto. Her next play was *The Sign in Sidney Brustein's Window*, which considered prejudice in the context of anti-semitism and local politics. It was being produced on Broadway by her husband, whom she had divorced the previous year, at the time of her death. Hansberry was not directly involved in racial-political activism but she did write *The Movement: Documentary of a Struggle for Equality* in 1964. She died of cancer at the age of 34.

L. Hansberry: *To be young, gifted and black* (1971)

**Hao Tianx'u** (1934– ). Chinese politician. Born in Qingdao, the daughter of a mule-cart driver, after liberation of the province in 1949 she worked in a state textile mill, developing new working procedures for spinning, which were introduced nationally in 1951. Aged only 16 she was commended as a model worker, received by Mao, and then studied at the Hua Dong Textile Engineering Institute (1953–62). In 1965 she became a mill director and improved working conditions but was labelled a 'capitalist roader' during the Cultural Revolution. After the collapse of the Gang of Four she was elected to the Party Central Committee, and in June 1979 appointed Vice-Minister of the textile industry, unusually young for such a post in China.

**Harlow, Jean** [pseud. of Harlean Carpenter] (1911–37). American film actress. Born in Kansas City, Missouri, a dentist's daughter, she eloped at the age of 16 with a local tycoon, and they settled in Los Angeles. Here she got small parts in films such as *Love Parade* (1929) and Chaplin's *City Lights* (1931) and worked in several Laurel and Hardy comedies. She was divorced in 1929 and in 1930 got her first big break in Howard Hughes's *Hell's Angels* (1930) as a witty, sexy, independent woman. Under contract to Hughes, she was loaned out for several films, the most successful being *The Public Enemy* and *Platinum Blonde* (both 1931).

In 1932 she joined MGM. Here she married Paul Bern, a production director, and was harshly attacked when he committed suicide shortly afterwards amid rumours of his impotence. Her own films, such as *Red-Headed Woman* (1932), *Red Dust* (1932), *Bombshell* (1933), *Reckless* (1935) and *Saratoga* (1937), all emphasized

her sexual glamour but also showed she was a controlled, subtle and sympathetic actress. She was married to the director of photography Harold Rossen from 1933 to 1934, and then became engaged to William Powell. She was only 26 when she died of cerebral oedema.

C. Brown: *Jean Harlow* (1977)

**Harper, Frances (Ellen)** (1825–1911). American abolitionist. Frances Watkins's parents died before she was three and she was brought up by her uncle, a preacher, free schoolteacher and abolitionist. After 1839 she worked as a maid and seamstress in Baltimore, continuing to study and write, and publishing a collection, *Forest Leaves*, in 1845. She then taught sewing, but from 1853 became increasingly caught up in the abolitionist movement, especially after her successful lecture 'Education and the Elevation of the Coloured Race' (1854). She then travelled and lectured for the Maine Anti-Slavery Society until 1860, appearing in many states. She also wrote poetry, and became the most famous black poet since PHILLIS WHEATLEY.

From 1860 to 1864 Frances farmed with her husband in Columbus, Ohio, but he died after four years and she resumed her lecturing career, pleading for education and civil rights and denouncing white racism – although she joined with white suffrage workers during the 1870s and 1880s. She published more volumes of poetry, her later collections including *The Martyr of Alabama* (1894), and also the popular novel *Iola Leroy* (1892). During the 1880s she was active in the Temperance Union, and in the 1890s in youth movements, and was an organizer of the National Association of Colored Women in 1896.

**Harper, Ida A.** (1851–1931). American journalist and suffragist. Born in Fairfield, Indiana, Ida Husted left Indiana University after a year in 1869 to become a high school principal at the age of 18. Two years later she married Thomas Harper, a lawyer, and settled in Terre Haute, where their friends included the railway union leader Eugene Debs. Ida secretly wrote articles for the local paper under a male pseudonym and then, despite her husband's disapproval of paid work, wrote her own column 'A Woman's

Opinions', and edited a woman's page in Debs's *Locomotive Firemen's Magazine* from 1884 1893. After the Harpers divorced in 1890 she became briefly Editor of the *Terre Haute Daily News*, and then joined the *Indianapolis News*.

Involved in the suffrage movement since the 1880s, Ida moved to California and became a close associate of SUSAN B. ANTHONY, with whom she lived from 1897, editing her papers and writing her three-volume biography (2 vols, 1898; 1 vol., 1908). The two women travelled the United States on lecture tours, and attended conventions in London (1899), Berlin (1904) and elsewhere. Ida also continued her feminist journalism, writing women's columns in the New York *Sunday Sun* (1899–1903) and *Harper's Bazaar* (1909–13) as well as syndicated articles for many other papers. In 1916 she took charge of publicity for the Leslie Bureau of Suffrage Education, which lobbied fiercely for the passage of the federal amendment. She then completed the final two books of the six-volume *History of Woman Suffrage* (having worked on the fourth with Anthony), which were published in 1922. Still an active campaigner, she lived in Washington until her death at the age of 80.

**Harris, Patricia Roberts** (1924–85). American lawyer and politician. Born in Mattoon, Illinois, the daughter of a Pullman waiter and a schoolteacher, she proved a brilliant student and went on to study at Howard University, the University of Chicago and the American University, Washington, and later qualified at the George Washington University Law School. As a student she organized a sit-in to force desegregation of a Washington cafeteria, and after graduation she became Programme Director for the Young Women's Christian Association (YWCA) (1946–9) before taking a job as Assistant Director of the American Council on Human Rights (1949–53).

In 1955 she married William Harris, but continued her career, returning to law as a Trial Attorney for the US Department of Justice (1960–61), and then teaching at Howard University Law School. A staunch Democrat, from 1965 to 1967 she was Ambassador to Luxembourg and she was a delegate to the UN in 1966. While acting as Dean at Howard University, clashes with

students led her to retire and become a partner in a Washington law firm, specializing in litigation until 1977. She continued to campaign for civil rights, being on the Executive Board of the National Association for the Advancement of Coloured People (NAACP) Legal Defence Fund from 1967 to 1977. As a member of the National Commission on the Causes and Prevention of Violence, she filed a minority report supporting the idea of non-violent civil disobedience as a possible prevention rather than contributory cause of confrontation.

In 1977 Patricia Roberts Harris was appointed Secretary of Housing and Urban Development, the first black woman in the Cabinet, and in 1979 she became Secretary of Health, Education and Welfare.

**Harrison, Jane (Ellen)** (1850–1928). English classical scholar. Born in Yorkshire, she was educated at home, in Cheltenham, and at Newnham College, Cambridge, where she became a Fellow. She was Vice-President of the Hellenic Society from 1889 to 1896 and eventually became Director of the British School of Archaeology in Rome. She used archaeology in an innovative and highly influential way in the interpretation of Greek religion, on which she wrote several books. Her publications included *Myths of the Odyssey in Art and Literature* (1882), *Introductory Studies in Greek Art* (1885), *Prologomena to the Study of Greek Religion* (1903), *Themis* (1912), *Ancient Art and Ritual* (1913) and *Epilogomena to the Study of Greek Religion* (1921). In later life she found an additional interest in the study of Russian with her friend Hope Mirrlees, with whom she published three books on Russian language and literature including a series of translations, called *The Book of the Bear* (1927). She received numerous academic awards.

J.G. Stewart: *Jane Harrison: a Portrait from Letters* (1959)

**Hart,** Dame **(Constance Mary) Judith** (1924–). English politician. Born in Burnley, Lancashire, Judith Ridehalgh was educated locally and at the London School of Economics. In 1946 she married Dr Anthony Hart and had two sons. Although always involved in politics she did not become a member of Parliament until 1959 when she was elected Labour MP for Lanark. In the Labour adminstration of 1964–70 she held several ministerial posts: Joint Parliamentary Under-Secretary of State at the Scottish Office (1964–6), Minister of State for Commonwealth Affairs (1966–7), Minister of Social Security (1967), and Paymaster-General (1968). Her greatest impact was made as Minister of Overseas Development, an office she held in 1969–70, 1974–5 and 1977–9, where she was outspoken in her expression of the UK's moral responsibilities to the Third World. Her ideas on this subject are explored in *Aid and Liberation : A Socialist Study of Aid Policies* (1973). She was a member of the Labour Party National Executive from 1969 to 1983, and Chairman of the Party 1981–2.

**Haskil, Clara** (1895–1960). Romanian pianist. Born in Bucharest, she made her debut there at the age of nine and then studied in Vienna and Paris. In 1910 she began her concert career, and was a brilliant interpreter of Mozart, Beethoven and Schubert. She was recognized as a performer of international stature.

**Hatshepsut** (1503–1482 BC). Egyptian queen. The daughter of Thutmose I, she married his successor, her half-brother Thutmose II, becoming his major queen and a powerful political influence. On his death she became Regent for his heir, 6-year-old Thutmose III, the son of a minor wife. In the second year of his reign she assumed the title of Pharaoh, becoming the first woman ruler for 2000 years. Statues and reliefs show her ruling jointly with Thutmose III whom she married to her daughter Meritha, or alone, usually depicted as a man but always described as a woman in the text. At the start of her reign she seems to have been involved in military campaigns, fighting with her troops in Nubia and elsewhere, but she is generally associated with peaceful prosperity and cultural life. Her beautiful mortuary temple at Deir el-Bahri in west Thebes shows scenes of her miraculous birth and of achievements such as bringing huge obelisks to the temple at Karnak, and the expedition she sponsored to Punt on the Red Sea which brought back exotic cargoes of spices, ebony and ivory, animals and strange plants.

When she died Thutmose continued to rule. He removed many of her followers and at the end of his reign a campaign was begun to detract from her memory; her statues were smashed and her tomb in the Valley of the Kings was left unfinished.

**Hatzimichali, Angeliki** (1895–1956). Greek writer and folklorist. Daughter of a professor of Greek literature, she particularly loved Greek traditonal culture, both Byzantine and modern folk. Realizing that modern life in Greece would soon eclipse traditional art for ever, she spent much of her life among the peasants in the countryside, painstakingly observing and recording customs, handicraft techniques and embroidery designs. Through her efforts, many professional schools for the preservation of traditional crafts were founded, as well as workshops which offered facilities to emigrant women from Asia Minor for continuing their customary crafts. In 1921 she organized the first exhibition of folk art in Greece. Some of her numerous writings on folk art, crafts and local guilds have been published both in Greece and abroad in journals devoted to folk art. The bulk of her work, however, remains unpublished.

**Hawkes, Jacquetta** (1910–). British archaeologist. The daughter of Nobel prize-winner Sir Frederick Hopkins, Jacquetta was born in Cambridge and educated there, at the Perse School and Newnham College. In 1931 she began her lifelong work in archaeology, working in Britain, Ireland, France and Palestine. In 1933 she married the archaeologist Christopher Hawkes. Her first book, in 1939, was on the archaeology of Jersey, and in 1944, with her husband, she published the influential *Prehistoric Britain*, followed by *Early Britain* in 1945. After working with the Post-War Reconstruction Secretariat she joined the Ministry of Education, and was also secretary of the UK Commission for UNESCO (1943–9). In 1949 she became Vice-President of the Council for British Archaeology and advised on the archaeological coverage at the 1951 Festival of Britain, for which she wrote her evocative book *The Land* and the *Guide to Prehistoric Monuments and Roman Monuments*. She has since held many other official positions, for example as a Governor of the British Film Institute (1950–55) and a member of the Central Committee of UNESCO (1966–79).

Jacquetta Hawkes's numerous books have been of great significance in popularizing archaeology in Britain. She has also written poetry and plays, as well as joint works with her second husband, the novelist J.B. Priestley, whom she married in 1953. In the 1970s she was Editor of the *Atlas of Ancient Archaeology* (1974) and the *Atlas of Early Man* (1976) and has since written *A Quest for Love* (1980), a biography of Sir Mortimer Wheeler (1982), and the new *Shell Guide to British Archaeology* (1986).

**Hayashi Fumiko** (1904–51). Japanese novelist. Hayashi Fumiko emerged from a background of poverty, her father being described as a travelling pedlar. Determined to write, she kept up her education until 18, then lived precariously while establishing her reputation. Her novels are not overtly political but present realistic pictures of deprived urban communities. They include the semi-autobiographical series *Horoki* ('Journey of a vagabond') (1922–7); *Shita-Machi* ('Tokyo'); and *Ukignomo* ('The floating cloud') (1951).

**Hayes (Brown), Helen** (1900–). American actress. She was born in Washington, DC, where she first appeared on stage at the age of five. She acted on Broadway in 1909, but her best known youthful roles were Pollyanna (1917–18), and Margaret in *Dear Brutus* (1918). She transferred to adult parts with *To the Ladies* (1922) and her successes included Shaw's Cleopatra in 1925 and the extraordinary performance from childhood to old age in *Victoria Regina* (1935–8). Other famous roles are Portia (1938), Amanda Wingfield in *The Glass Menagerie* (1948), and Mrs Antrobus in *The Skin of our Teeth* (1955). She has also appeared in films, winning an Academy Award for *Airport* (1970); subsequent films include *Candleshoe* (1978). Widely regarded as the USA's most outstanding actress, the Fulton Theatre, New York, was renamed in her honour in 1958. She married the playwright Charles

MacArthur in 1928 (*d* 1956) and has one son.

H. Hayes: *On Reflection* (1969)
——— : *Our Best Years* (1984)
——— : *Loving Wife* (1987)

**Hays, Mary** (1760–1843). English feminist. A friend of MARY WOLLSTONECRAFT, she and her sister had already been feminists for several years when they wrote their *Letters and Essays Moral and Miscellaneous* (1793), and the anonymous *Appeal to the Men of Great Britain on Behalf of the Women* (1798), arguing for greater freedom for women in marriage, ownership of property and sexual relations. Hays was also a novelist. She published *The Memoirs of Emma Courtney* (1796), the story of an independent and educated woman, and described the misery of an illegitimate orphan girl in a *Victim of Prejudice* (1799). In 1803 she published a six-volume *Dictionary of Female Biography*.

A.F.Weld, ed.: *The Love Letters of Mary Hays* (1925).

**Haywood** [née Fowler]**, Eliza** (1693–1756). English novelist and playwright. The daughter of a London tradesman, she married Valentine Haywood in 1717, but he abandoned her and their two small children in 1721. A writer from childhood, she had also acted in Dublin and London, and from 1721 became a professional writer. Her first play was *A Wife to be Left*, performed at Drury Lane in 1723 and she later collaborated on an adaptation of Fielding's *Tom Thumb*, but her real métier was fiction. Between 1719 and 1730 she wrote nearly 40 novels beginning with *Love's Excess*, mostly on the trials of virtue, often based (like MARY MANLEY's work) on current society scandals, the most notorious being *Memoirs of a certain Island* (1725). These sexual melodramas brought considerable commercial success. She published little in the 1730s and 1740s, but her last works in the new fashion of domestic realism, *The History of Miss Betty Thoughtless* (1751) and *The History of Tommy and Jenny Jessamy* (1753), remained popular throughout the century. A thorough professional, she also wrote for periodicals such as *The Tea Table* and published *The Female Spectator*, the first periodical for women edited by a woman.

G.F. Whicher: *The Life and Romances of Haywood* (1915)

**Hayworth, Rita** [pseud. of Margarita Carmen Cansino] (1918–87). American film actress and dancer. Her father was a Spanish dancer, her mother a Ziegfeld girl, and her cousin was the dancer Ginger Rogers; she herself first appeared dancing in Mexican night-clubs at the age of 13. During the early 1930s she had small dancing parts with Fox, but after the merger with 20th Century lost her job. In 1937 she married an older man, William Judson, who managed her career, obtaining a contract with Columbia and turning her into a red-haired beauty with a new name. She gradually won better parts, for example in *Only Angels have Wings* (1939), *Blood and Sand* (1941) and dancing with Astaire in *You'll never get Rich, You were never Lovelier* (1941–2) and with Gene Kelly in *Cover Girl* (1942), becoming the most famous pin-up of the day by the time she made *Gilda* (1946). The subsequent decline of her career was aggravated by the exposé of her as a predatory adventuress by her second husband Orson Welles in *The Lady From Shanghai* (1948), and by her elopement and marriage to Ali Khan in 1949. Her films became increasingly mediocre, her fourth and fifth marriages failed and her alcoholic breakdowns made her yet another Hollywood casualty.

J. Morella and E. Epstein: *Rita* (1983)

**H.D.** *See* DOOLITTLE, HILDA.

**Head, Bessie** (1937–86). South African novelist. Bessie Head was born in Pietermaritzburg, South Africa, the daughter of a white mother and a black father. As a 'coloured' she was brought up in a foster home and she became a teacher. In her early twenties she left her husband, fleeing across the border to Botswana, where she was accepted for citizenship 14 years later. Her powerful, haunting novels are set in Botswana and they include *When Rain Clouds Gather* (1969), *Maru* (1971) and *A Question of Power* (1973). She lived in the village of Serowe, where she collected the material for her short stories in *The Collector of Treasures* (1977) and in 1981 she published a history and a vivid evocation of the complex life of the community in *Serowe: Village of the Rain Wind*. One of modern Africa's most famous novelists, she died in 1986, aged 49.

**Head, Edith** (1907–86). American costume and fashion designer. Born in Los Angeles, the daughter of a mining engineer, she was brought up in the mining camps of Nevada and Arizona, but went on to study languages at the University of California, Los Angeles, and then obtained an MA from Stanford University. She studied at the Otis Art School and the Chouinard Art School in Los Angeles, while teaching French, Spanish and art at the Hollywood School for Girls and Bishop's School, La Jolla. In 1923 she began making fashion sketches for Paramount and soon became their head designer, working on cowboy films, musicals, classical dramas and modern comedies. In 1938 she was appointed Chief Designer, the first woman to hold such a post, and for the next 5 years worked on about 35 pictures each year. One of her earliest triumphs was the dressing of MAE WEST in *She Done Him Wrong* (1933) but she won her first Academy Award with *The Heiress* (1949), followed by others for *All about Eve* (1950), *Samson and Delilah* (1950), *A Place in the Sun* (1951), *Roman Holiday* (1954), and *The Facts of Life* (1960). She moved to Universal City Studios in 1967 and won yet another Academy Award for the costumes in *The Sting* in 1973.

E. Head: *Fashion as a Career* (1966)
P. Calistro: *Edith Head's Hollywood* (1983)

**Heath, Sophia** (1896–1936). American aviator and sports administrator. In 1922 Sophia founded the Women's Amateur Athletic Association, and spoke before the Olympic Committee in Prague to solicit the participation by women in Olympic athletics. This was allowed in 1928, and the UK joined in in 1932.

In 1919 the International Commission for Air Navigation had banned women from taking part in commercial navigation; Sophia overcame the ban by qualifying in all the medical and aptitude tests. She became the first airline pilot employed by the Royal Dutch airlines, and made it her first concern to improve air safety and reliability. In 1928 she was the first woman to fly solo from South Africa to England, and another record she made was in taking off and landing at 50 different airfields and 17 'likely landing fields' in England in a single day, with six refuellings. She suffered serious injury in an air crash.

**Heathcoat-Amory.** *See* WETHERED, JOYCE.

**Hedwig.** *See* JADWIGA.

**Heilbron, Dame Rose** (1914–). English lawyer. Educated at Belvedere School and Liverpool University, where she graduated with first-class honours in 1935, she then won a scholarship to Gray's Inn, took her LLM in 1937 and was called to the Bar in 1939. She married Dr Nathaniel Burstein in 1945 and they had one daughter. Her legal career advanced rapidly; she became a Queen's Counsel and was the first woman Recorder in the UK in 1956, holding this position in Burnley until 1974. In that year she was created DBE and became the second High Court Judge after Elizabeth Lane, on the Northern Circuit in the Family Division. In 1975 she was appointed Chairman of the Home Secretary's Advisory Group on Rape. She was Presiding Judge of the Northern Circuit from 1979 to 1982, and became Treasurer of Gray's Inn in 1985.

**Hellman, Lillian (Florence)** (1907–84). American playwright. Born into a Jewish family in New Orleans, she described her childhood in *An Unfinished Woman*. She was educated at New York University (1923–25), and then spent a year at Columbia University. In 1925 she married the writer Arthur Kober, but they divorced seven years later. While a student she had become a reader for the publishers, Horace Liveright, and she worked for the *New York Herald Tribune* as a reviewer (1925–28), and for MGM in Hollywood as a reader of plays (1927–30) and then scripts (1930–32). Restless and dissatisfied, already a feminist and socialist, she met Dashiel Hammett, with whom she had a close and constant, if difficult, relationship until his death in 1966.

Hammett encouraged her to write, and her first play *The Children's Hour* (1934), a study of the tragic results of accusations of Lesbianism in a girls' school, revealed her daring and talent. It was followed by *Days to Come* (1936), and *The Little Foxes* (1939), a devastating analysis of family and political tension with a Southern capitalist family. Hellman visited Spain during the Civil War,

and undertook an extraordinary and exhausting trip to Russia in 1944. During World War II she also wrote the anti-fascist plays *Watch on the Rhine* (1941), and *The Searching Wind* (1944). During the McCarthy era both she and Hammett suffered for their left-wing sympathies, and were questioned by the Un-American Activities Committee in 1952. This ordeal and Hammett's imprisonment are described in *Scoundrel Time*. She wrote several more plays, most notably *The Autumn Garden* (1951) and *Toys in the Attic* (1960), ambiguous studies of power struggles within personal relationships. She also wrote the scripts for the musicals *Regina* (1949) and *Candide* (1957) (with DOROTHY PARKER, a friend of many years), and several film-scripts.

Her three autobiographical works brought her added acclaim. Tough, provocative, sensitive both to large-scale social injustice and to the nuances of personal suffering, Hellman was one the most remarkable women writers of her period.

L. Hellman: *An Unfinished Woman: a Memoir* (1969)
———: *'Pentimento': a Book of Portraits* (1973)
———: *Scoundrel Time* (1976)

**Héloïse** (1101–64). French abbess. Her love for Abelard has become legendary and her contribution to literature consists of her letters to him (*Lettres d'Abelard et d'Héloïse*, first published in Latin; Paris, 1616). Héloïse's uncle was a canon called Fulbert who encouraged her remarkable intellectual gifts at a time when it was rare for women to be educated. She met Abelard, a leading French scholastic philosopher, when he taught her at the University of Paris. They had a passionate love affair and were married secretly after their son was born. The marriage was meant to appease Fulbert but after quarrels and a serious misunderstanding his revenge was vicious – his servants broke into Abelard's room at night and castrated him. Abelard entered the Abbey of St Denis and persuaded Héloïse to take the veil, although she had no vocation. She became the Abbess of Paraclete, a Benedictine convent founded by Abelard, and after 12 years of monastic life she was brought by chance the *Historia calamitatum Abaelardi* (an autobiographical work in the form of a letter in which Abelard recounts to a friend the story, among other things, of his tragic love for Héloïse). The first letters from Héloïse in the ensuing correspondence reveal her passion for Abelard and her despair and longing for him during her early days at the convent. In his letters Abelard tries to turn her towards the peace of God, and after the sixth letter the correspondence focuses on questions of monastic discipline. The letters, which are admired for their style, reflect the Classical learning of the correspondents and their intense interest in questions of faith and morality.

While Héloïse was Abbess, the Paraclete grew to be one of the most distinguished convents in France and Héloïse was revered both for her learning and for her administrative skill.

E. McCleod: *Héloïse* (1971)
B. Radice (ed.): *The Letters of Abelard and Heloise* (1971)

**Hemans** [née Browne], **Felicia (Dorothea)** (1793–1835). British poet. Born in Liverpool, the daughter of a merchant, she moved with her family to Wales in 1800 after their business collapsed and she was educated privately at home by her mother. Her first book, *Poems*, was published in 1808; despite severe criticism from older writers two more collections had appeared by the end of 1812. That year she married an Irishman, Captain Alfred Hemans. They lived with her parents and had five sons, but in 1818 Captain Hemans suddenly deserted her and went to live in Italy and they never saw each other again. She then began to support herself by writing. During her marriage she had published *The Restoration of the Works of Art to Italy* (1816) and *Modern Greece* (1817), and she subsequently produced one or two volumes a year until her death. Very prolific and versatile, she dealt with classical, legendary and folk themes, and produced religious and nature verse, sentimental love lyrics and children's poetry. She had a fine lyrical style, often verging on the sentimental, and is typical of the 'picturesque' Romantic movement. She also wrote magazine stories and a play, *The Vespers of Palermo* (1823). She went to live with her brother, a well-known literary figure in Dublin, but her health gradually deteriorated and she died,

exhausted and disillusioned, at the age of 38.

She was a popular figure, and her poetry is often quoted in contemporary novels, her close friends and admirers including Shelley, Scott, Byron, Wordsworth and JOANNA BAILLIE. She is remembered today for her poem *Casablanca*, better known as 'The boy stood on the burning deck'.

P. Trinder: *Mrs Hemans* (1985)

**Hemessen, Caterina van** (1528–87). Flemish painter. She was born in Antwerp. Her father was an artist, and under his tuition and then alone after 1545 she worked on religious paintings and portraits, such as the *Portrait of a Lady* (1551) now in Rijksmuseum, Amsterdam. In 1554 she married Chrétien de Morien, organist of Antwerp Cathedral. In 1556 they were invited to Spain, under the patronage of Queen Mary of Hungary, former Regent of the Netherlands, who left them a pension when she died in 1568. They then returned to Antwerp, but Caterina seems to have painted far less than she did before her marriage. Her portraits are sympathetic and straightforward, although small and very formal in composition. She is the first Flemish woman artist whose works are recorded.

E. Tufts: *Our Hidden Heritage* (1974)

**Henje** [Henie], **Sonja** (1910–69). Norwegian-American skater and film actress. Norwegian champion at the age of 11, after winning her first of ten World Championships in 1927, she became Olympic gold medallist in 1928, 1932 and 1936. She then went to Hollywood where she starred in 11 films, earned more than any athlete had done before, and in 1938 was one of the ten most lucrative box office attractions. Her films included *One in a Million*, *Thin Ice* and *My Lucky Star*.

Sonja became an American citizen in 1941. She was married three times, and with her third husband, the Norwegian shipowner Niels Onstad, she built up a large collection of Impressionist and post-Impressionist art. The Sonja Henje-Niels Onstad Art Centre was opened in Oslo in 1968, 14 months before Sonja's death from leukaemia.

S. Henje: *Wings on my Feet* (1940)

**Henry, Alice** (1857–1943). Australian socialist, feminist and journalist. Born in Richmond, Victoria, she published her first article in 1884 and went on to be recognized as one of Australia's leading journalists, contributing to *The Argos* and *The Australasian*, usually under a pseudonym. She also lectured, campaigned for women's trades union movements, protective legislation, women's suffrage and proportional representation. She was involved in charitable projects such as the Queen Victoria Hospital and a number of the radical women writers' clubs founded in 1902. In 1905 she left Australia for the USA, where she became a prominent feminist organizer and writer. She visited Australia for two years between 1924 and 1926 and returned finally in 1933.

A. Henry: *Memoirs of Alice Henry* (1944)

**Hepburn, Audrey** [pseud. of Edda Hepburn van Heemshra] (1929–). English film actress. Born in Brussels of wealthy Irish-Dutch parents, she was educated in the Netherlands and in England, and trained in ballet. She worked in England, dancing, modelling and acting until 1951 when a meeting with COLETTE led to her taking the lead in the stage version of *Gigi* (1952). This was followed by a move to Hollywood, where she won an Academy Award for *Roman Holiday* (1953). She married Mel Ferrer in 1953 and appeared in several of his films. Her most popular performances were in *War and Peace* (1956), *The Unforgiven* (1960), *Breakfast at Tiffany's* (1961), *Charade* (1963) and *My Fair Lady* (1964). After her divorce in 1968 she married an Italian psychiatrist, retired to Rome, and virtually ceased acting except for *Robin and Marian* (1976), *Bloodline* (1979), *They all Laughed* (1980) and the television film *Here a Thief* (1987).

I. Woodward: *Audrey Hepburn* (1984)

**Hepburn, Katharine** (1907–). American actress. She was born in Hartford, Connecticut, into a distinguished New England family; her mother was a suffragist and birth-control campaigner and her father was a surgeon. On graduating from Bryn Mawr College in 1928 she became an actress, appearing in summer stock and on Broadway, and married a rich broker, Ludlow Ogden Smith; they were divorced in 1934. In 1932 she accepted a film contract with RKO and was an immediate success in *A Bill of Divorcement*, directed by George Cukor. During the 1930s she made many films including *Morning Glory* (1933) which won her her first Academy Award, and *Little Women* (1933), but her most memorable were the comedies with Cary Grant, such as *Bringing up Baby* (1938). She was not, however, popular with the general public and her independent character led her to return to Broadway, choosing her own material, and playing in the immensely successful *Philadelphia Story*.

During the filming of *Woman of the Year* (1942) she met Spencer Tracy, and their love affair, lasting 27 years, became a respected 'open secret' in Hollywood. They appeared together in nine films, the last being *Guess Who's Coming to Dinner*, released a few weeks before Tracy's death in 1967. Hepburn's film career, meanwhile, had highlights such as *The African Queen* (1951), *Suddenly Last Summer* (1962), and *Long Day's Journey into Night* (1962). The latter and *The Lion in Winter* (1969) provided two more Academy Awards. She also starred on stage in several Shakespearian roles during the 1950s such as Rosalind, Katharine in *The Taming of the Shrew*, and Portia. In 1970 and 1971 she toured with the musical *Coco*, based on the life of COCO CHANEL. In 1981 she appeared in *On the Golden Pond* with Henry and JANE FONDA and won another Academy Award. Her recent films include *The Ultimate Solution of Grace Quigley* (1984) and *The Whales of August* (1988). Hepburn's career is remarkable for the independence and strength she revealed on screen, for her dealings with the studios, and for the protection of her private life.

A. Edwards: *Katharine Hepburn* (1986)

**Hepworth, Dame Barbara** (1903–75). English sculptor. The daughter of a Yorkshire county surveyor, she was educated at Leeds College of Art (1920–21) and then at the Royal Academy of Art, London (1921–4), after which she won a travelling scholarship to Italy, married the sculptor John Skeaping and shared a joint exhibition with him at the Beaux Arts Gallery, London, in 1928. Both were members of the radical artists' group, the

Seven and Five Society. In 1930 she aroused attention by her exhibition at Tooth's Gallery, which included works such as a stone *Mother and Child*.

Her early stylized figures gave way to more abstract forms. After 1931 she worked with the painter Ben Nicholson, whom she married after her divorce in 1933. They exhibited together at the Lefevre Gallery, and worked with abstract groups such as Unit One (1933–4) and Abstraction-Creation (1933–5). In 1939, they moved to St Ives, Cornwall, and here Hepworth developed her characteristic style, resembling that of her friend Henry Moore but more demonstrative and sensual. During the 1950s she suffered personal unhappiness – her marriage was dissolved (1951) and her eldest son Paul was killed in Malaya (1953). But she also achieved international eminence with her *Figures in a Landscape* and was made CBE in 1958 and DBE in 1965. Later commissions included *Single Form* for the UN Building, New York (1964), and the Dag Hammerskjöld Memorial. One of her last monumental works was the nine-piece group *Family of Man* (1972). She died in a fire at her studio in St Ives.

A.M. Hammacher: *Barbara Hepworth* (1968)

**Herbert, Mary**, Countess of Pembroke (1561–1621). English aristocrat and scholar. Born in Worcestershire, the niece of Robert Dudley, Earl of Leicester, and younger sister of the poet Sir Philip Sidney, she grew up in Ludlow Castle, where her father Sir Henry Sidney was based as president of Wales. She received a thorough classical education. After the deaths of her three sisters, she moved to the court of Queen ELIZABETH I in 1575, and in 1577 she became the third wife of Henry Herbert, Second Earl of Pembroke. She lived at Wilton, where her brother Philip joined her when in disfavour at court, and at her suggestion wrote *The Countess of Pembroke's Arcadia* between 1580 and 1583. They also worked together on a metrical version of the Psalms. After the death of their parents, and of Philip in 1586, she devoted herself to editing his works, and became the patron of a circle of scholars and poets which he had formed, including Spenser and Daniel. Her collected editions of the *Arcadia* appeared in 1593 and 1598. She also translated Plessis du

Mornay's *Discourses of Life and Death* (1593) and Garnier's *Antonie* (1592). She was greatly admired by the poets of the next generation such as Nashe and Donne. Her literary life may have caused some estrangement from her husband; after he died in 1601 he left her hardly any inheritance. She lived with her son at Wilton in London and after 1615 at Ampthill Park, granted to her for life by James I, where she built the splendid Houghton House. She is buried in Salisbury Cathedral.

F.B. Young: *Mary Sidney, Countess of Pembroke* (1912)

**Hernandez, Angela** [Angelita] (1949?–). Spanish bullfighter. In 1973 Hernandez caused a furore in her native country by insisting on competing in the previously all-male sport of bullfighting. In 1908 a law was passed limiting women's participation to fighting on horseback. At the age of 24, Hernandez wanted to enter the ring in Higuera Real as a *torero*, but although the Madrid labour court upheld her right to fight on foot the Ministry of the Interior refused to grant her a licence. During her training on a bull-ranch near Seville she is quoted as saying, 'These damned men. What do they think they are doing? Women fly planes, fight wars and go on safaris; what's so different about fighting bulls?'

**Herrade of Landsburg** (*d* 1195). German abbess and artist. As Abbess of Hohenburg in Alsace, between 1160 and 1170 Herrade collected a set of improving readings for her nuns, which were copied onto 324 parchment sheets. Superbly illustrated with vivid miniatures and called the *Hortus deliciarum*, it contained information on everything from the seven deadly sins to gardening tips. Tracings were made in 1818 but the original was destroyed when Strasbourg Library was burned in the 1870 siege.

**Herschel, Caroline (Lucretia)** (1750–1848). English astronomer of German birth. Born in Hanover, she was taught little beyond violin playing and housework. Her elder brother William took her to England to become his housekeeper at Bath. William helped her to train and perform as a singer as well as to assist with his astronomical observations, but soon astronomy demanded all her time and they worked together for the next 50 years.

At first they built and sold telescopes to finance their own huge ones. After William discovered Georgium Sidus, now known as Uranus, he was appointed Astronomer Royal at £200 a year; Caroline was pleased to become his assistant at £50. When not working for William she spent her time 'minding the heavens' and discovered 14 nebulae and 8 comets.

Two of her works were published by the Royal Society: *Catalogue of 860 stars observed by Flamsteed but not included in the British Catalogue*, and *A General Index of Reference to every Observation of every Star in the above-mentioned British Catalogue*. For *The Reduction and Arrangement in the form of catalogue, in zones, of all the star-clusters and nebulae observed by Sir W. Herschel in his sweeps* she was awarded a gold medal by the Royal Astronomical Society in 1828. She received medals from the Kings of Denmark and Prussia, and in 1835, at the age of 85, was elected with MARY SOMERVILLE as an honorary member of the Royal Astronomical Society; they were the first women to be given this honour. The Royal Irish Academy also elected her.

After William's death in 1822 she returned to Hanover and continued her meticulous work. Shortly before her death at the age of 97 she received a copy of her nephew Sir John Herschel's *Cape Observations* which satisfactorily completed her life's work. Caroline was, however, suspicious of progress in science which might detract from William's reputation. She observed 'All I am, all I know, I owe to my brother'.

C.A. Lubbock: *The Herschel Chronicle* (1933)

**Hess,** Dame **Myra** (1890–1965). English pianist. She won a scholarship to the Royal Academy of Music, London, at the age of 12, and was a pupil of Tobias Matthay. She made her debut in 1907 with a performance of Beethoven's Fourth Piano Concerto (conducted by Beecham), a work with which she became closely identified, along with her transcription of the chorale from Bach's cantata no. 147 under the title 'Jesu, joy of man's desiring'. Equally renowned for the insight she brought to Schumann's piano music and to all Mozart's piano concertos, she had a repertoire ranging from Domenico Scarlatti to Debussy; she occasionally included contemporary music in her programmes, giving the first performances of Howard Ferguson's Piano Sonata (1940) and Piano Concerto (1951). She also played much chamber music, and formed a piano duo with her cousin Irene Scharrer. Tours of Europe and the USA (from 1922) assured her as much affectionate esteem abroad as she enjoyed in England.

Her name is inextricably linked with the series of daily lunch-time concerts she organized at the National Gallery, London, during World War II, when all concert halls were closed. Engaging soloists, chamber ensembles, orchestras and choirs, she performed herself at many of the concerts, and in 1941 was created DBE in recognition of her services as a public benefactor. She received honorary doctorates from Cambridge, London and several other universities.

M. McKenna: *Myra Hess* (1976)

**Hesse, Eva** (1936–70). American sculptor. Born in Hamburg, into a Jewish family, she was separated from her parents until they all escaped to the USA in 1939. Many of her relatives died in World War II and tragedy followed her to the USA, where her parents separated, her brother died, and later her own marriage collapsed three years before her early death from a brain tumour.

A brilliant Expressionist sculptor, she studied at the Pratt Institute, New York (1952–3), at the Art Students' League, and at the Cooper Union (1954–7). After her marriage to Tom Doyle in 1962, she lived for some time in the Federal German Republic. On her return to the USA she travelled to Mexico and taught at the New York School of Visual Art. She had many individual and group exhibitions during the 1960s and 1970s, and her witty, iconoclastic, erotic sculptures reflected her perpetual search for a sense of 'self' and identity as a woman. She wrote, 'I cannot be something for everyone . . . woman, beautiful, artist, wife, housekeeper, cook, saleslady, all these things. I cannot even be myself or know what I am.'·

L. Lippard: *Eva Hesse* (1976)

**Heyhoe Flint, Rachel** (1939– ). English cricketer. After taking a diploma in physical education at Dartford, Kent, Rachel taught in various schools, coached the American Field Hockey Association in 1964 and 1965, and was a journalist with various newspapers in the Wolverhampton area and for the *Daily Telegraph*. She was Independent Television's first woman sports reporter in 1972.

Between 1960 and 1977 and from 1979 she was a member of the England women's cricket team, which she captained for 11 years. Under Rachel's captaincy England won the first Women's World Cup in 1972. In 1971 she married Derrick Flint with whom she had one son in addition to three stepchildren. She also represented England at hockey and was a county squash player. From 1981–6 she was Vice-Chair of the Women's Cricket Association and since 1982 she has worked as a marketing and promotions consultant for a number of organizations, including Wolverhampton Wanderers Football Club.

**Heymann, Lida (Gustava)** (1867–1943). German feminist. She was born in Hamburg into a rich Protestant merchant family. On the death of her father she inherited a fortune, and in the 1890s was an active charity worker, founding a day nursery, the first progressive kindergarten in Germany, a lunch club for single women, an actresses' society, a women's home and a society for women office workers. She also established a school to train women as apprentices and clerks. In 1898, influenced by MINNA CAUER, she led a campaign against regulated prostitution with a committee for the women's movement which became the very radical Verein Frauenwohl (Women's Welfare Association) in 1900, even taking legal action against the police, who banned her meetings.

In 1902 she was one of the 13 founders of the Deutscher Verband für Frauenstimmrecht (German Union for Women's Suffrage), together with Cauer and ANITA AUGSBURG, with whom her career was to be inextricably entwined for the rest of her life. They campaigned for the vote and in 1907 moved to Munich where they adopted more militant tactics, organizing demonstrations and marches and joining the aggressive Deutscher Frauenstimmrechtsbund (German Women's Suffrage League) in 1913, when divisions within the movement caused them to abandon the Union for Women's Suffrage. During World War I their pacifist stance lost them many supporters; they had led demonstrations for peace from as early as 1899 and had been prominent members of the International Woman Suffrage Alliance from its foundation in 1904 until 1909. In 1915 they went to the first congress of the Women's League for Peace and Freedom at the Hague, but in 1916 their suffrage league was closed down by the authorities and in 1917 Heymann was officially expelled from Bavaria, remaining in hiding for the rest of the war.

In 1919 she became Vice-President of the League for Peace and Freedom and worked to organize the German section, although during the 1920s she and Augsburg represented only a small section of the women's movement, which became increasingly nationalistic. In 1918 they had started the periodical *Die Frau im Staat*, which lasted until they were forced from Germany by the Nazi rise to power in 1933. They moved to Zürich, wrote their memoirs (*Erlebtes-Erschautes*; published 1972) and worked within the international women's movement until their deaths.

**Hicks, Amie (Amelia Jane)** (1839 or 1840–1917). English trade unionist. The daughter of a Chartist, she married and emigrated to New Zealand where she worked as a ropemaker, returning to England in the early 1880s with her husband and children. In 1883 they joined Hyndman's Social Democratic Federation, and Amie lectured, especially on free education, and took part in labour demonstrations. She worked as a midwife, was a member of the Ladies' Medical College, and campaigned against state regulation of prostitution before the repeal of the Contagious Diseases Act (1886). After the London Dock Strike, she helped form the Women's Trade Union Association, where she worked with CLEMENTINA BLACK; she was Secretary of the East London Ropemakers' Union (1889–99); a founder member of the Women's Industrial Council, which promoted investigations into labour conditions (1894–

1908); and President of the Clubs Industrial Association from 1898, encouraging the education of working girls in industrial law. A tireless campaigner, with a direct, motherly manner, she greatly influenced women of the succeeding generation, such as Margaret Macdonald and MARGARET BONDFIELD.

**Hicks, Sheila** (1934–). American weaver. Born in Hastings, Nebraska, she wanted to be a painter and studied at Syracuse University and then Yale, graduating in 1957. She began weaving in 1955 and was influenced by her travels on a Fulbright Scholarship to Chile, Venezuela, Colombia, Ecuador, Peru, Bolivia and Brazil between 1957 and 1959. In 1958 she obtained her Master of Fine Arts degree at Yale, and in 1959 married Henrik Schlubach, with whom she had one daughter. They divorced and she married Enrique Zanartu in 1965; they have one son. During this period she taught in England and the USA and established her studio in Paris, where she finally settled in 1965.

Hicks has always been involved with innovative craft schemes in different countries: in 1964 she founded a workshop at the Wuppertal factory in Germany, making huge braided and wrapped rugs; in 1966 she went to India to advise the weavers of Kozhikode on designs that would appeal to the West; in 1968 she organized a weaving workshop using local materials in Huagen, Chile; in 1970 she provided advice and assistance to the Moroccan rug industry. While in Morocco she was influenced by traditional Muslim designs and created a series of prayer rugs. In 1972 she worked in Mexico with the architect Luis Barragan. She has since concentrated chiefly on her own work, producing a number of major commissions, often for new buildings. Her works hang in many of the world's major museums.

**Hilda of Whitby** (616–680). English saint and abbess. Descended from the Northumbrian royal line, Hilda was baptized when she was 13 by Paulinus, Archbishop of York. At the age of 33 she wished to become a nun at Chelles, in France, like her sister Hereswith, but was recalled by Aidan, Bishop of Lindisfarne. He first placed her in a small nunnery on the River Wear, but shortly afterwards she was made Abbess of a religious house at Hartlepool, Durham. Ten years later Hilda made a foundation at Streaneshalch (later named Whitby by the Danes), on land given her by King Osiwin. The monastery housed both men and women in adjoining quarters, and among her subjects were St John of Beverley and Caedmon, the first English religious poet. Five of the inmates during her time became bishops.

At the Synod of Whitby (664), Hilda sided with Aidan in his defence of Celtic customs, but submitted to the king's decision in favour of adopting the Roman Easter usage. Bede is enthusiastic in his praise of Hilda, saying: 'all who knew her called her mother, such were her wonderful godliness and grace'.

**Hildegard of Bingen** (1098–1178). German abbess, visionary, scholar and saint. Entering a Benedictine convent at the age of 7, Hildegard took vows at 14, although her visions and revelations did not begin until she was 32. In 1136 she became Abbess of Diessem, and later moved her expanding community to Bingen. She also founded several other convents.

Hildegard described and illustrated her visions in *Scivias* (i.e. sciens vias Domini: 'the one who knows the ways of the Lord'); she wrote hymns, poetry and a morality play and was an accomplished artist and musician: her beautiful and original hymns are thought to be the earliest surviving Mass music composed by a woman. Known as 'the Sibyl of the Rhine', her learning extended to science and medicine. Her natural-history writings include remarkably advanced and precise studies of plants, minerals, elements and animals, and the medical topics range from circulation of the blood to mental instability. Her scientific works, some of which may have been prepared by groups working under her direction, include the *Liber subtilitatem*, and *De simplicines medicae*. Her last work was the *Liber divinorum operum*.

A persuasive speaker and writer, Hildegard gave advice (often unsought) to contemporary rulers, including Henry III, Frederick Barbarossa and Pope Eugenius III, and in conjunction with Bernard of

Clairvaux mobilized public support for the Second Crusade.

B. Newman: *Sister of Wisdom* (1987)

**Hill, Octavia** (1838–1912). English housing reformer. Born in Wisbech, Cambridgeshire, the daughter of a corn merchant and banker, she was influenced by her father's interest in penal reform and the work of her grandfather Thomas Southwood Smith on fever and sanitation. Educated at home, in 1852 she went to London to work at the Ladies' Guild, a Christian-Socialist co-operative association managed by her mother, where she met John Ruskin and Frederick Maurice. She taught slum children, and earned money by copying pictures.

In 1856 she became Secretary of the women's classes at Maurice's Working Men's College, and also established an intense friendship with SOPHIA JEX-BLAKE, with whom she shared a house briefly in 1862. Sophia left after a disagreement and the Hills started a school for poor girls.

In 1864 Ruskin sponsored her proposal to improve three local houses, acquiring capital by managing the schemes as a five per cent investment. Her schemes expanded rapidly, their success due to the knowledge of building, finances, rates and legal matters with which she backed her idealism. She trained her sister Miranda and several other assistants, but overwork led her to take a long Continental tour in 1877. From 1884 she was appointed by the Church Commissioners to manage their property in Southwark and elsewhere.

Octavia Hill also campaigned for the preservation of open space and recreation areas and was a co-founder of the National Trust in 1895. She worked with the Charity Organization Society, but preferred voluntary to official schemes, and refused to join the Royal Commission on Housing in 1889. She did, however, serve with the young BEATRICE WEBB on the Poor Law Commission (1905–8). Her written works include *Homes of the London Poor* and *Our Common Land*.

E.M.Bell: *Octavia Hill* (1942)

**Hind al Hunnud** (*fl* 7th century). Arabian leader. Known as 'the Hind of Hinds', she was a member of the Quraish tribe and lived in the Kingdom of Kindah. Her people had been in power at Mecca and she led their opposition to Mohammed, engaging in battle with him in 624 at the Battle of Badr, where her uncle, father and brother were killed. With her husband, Abū Sūfyan, she directed a campaign of vengeance, but eventually submitted to Mohammed and became a Muslim convert. A devotee of the cult of the 'Lady of Victory', she led groups of women in chanting songs to inspire the warriors in battle, and was known as a brilliant, ruthless woman.

**Hippius** [Gippius], **Zinaida** (Nikolayevna) (1869–1945). Russian writer. Born in Tula, she married the poet Dmitry Merezhkovsky in 1889, and they held a salon in St Petersburg which was a centre for leading writers and intellectuals of the Silver Age. She prompted the foundation of the journal *Novy Put* in 1903, which reflected her metaphysical ideas. In 1905 she was sympathetic to the populist uprising but bitterly opposed the Bolshevik Revolution of 1917. Two years later she and her husband emigrated to Poland and finally settled in Paris, becoming powerful figures in émigré circles.

She was a versatile writer, producing several collections of intense poetry, influenced by the Symbolist movement, with philosophical themes of love, death and transcendence, which look to salvation in the final submergence of man's divided self in the sexual symbol of androgyny. Her poems are collected in *Sobraniye stikhov* ('Collected Poems') (1904 and 1910) and *Siyaniya* ('Radiances') (1938). She also wrote short stories, a play, witty literary criticism and some superb memoirs *Zhivye litsa* ('Living Faces') (1925) which contain portraits of characters such as Rasputin, Blok, and Rozanov.

T. Pachmuss: *Zinaida Hippius: an Intellectual Profile* (1971)

**Hiratsuka, Raicho** (1886–1971). Japanese feminist. Born in Tokyo, in her early days she was influenced by Western culture, especially English literature and Western philosophy. She became well known to the public through an incident involving an attempted double suicide with another writer in 1908, and became a focus of those young women in Japan who wanted to express their roles within the liberal climate of the period (1912–26). In 1914 she founded the 'Seitosha' (Bluestocking Society) and published the magazine *Seito* ('Bluestocking'), in which she printed the famous manifesto entitled 'In the Beginning Woman Was the Sun'. Later she went to live with a painter, H. Okumura, and had two children, but their life was dogged by poverty. She was also influenced by the Swedish feminist ELLEN KEY and in 1918 started a public debate on the protection of motherhood. Subsequently, with FUSAE ICHIKAWA and other feminists she founded Shin Fujin Kyokai (New Women's Association), and engaged in a campaign for the reform of the social and legal position of Japanese women. The group achieved the first political success of the women's movement with the amendment of the Public Order and Police Law, thus making it legal for women to participate to some degree in political activities. After World War II, she remained active in such areas as pacifism and democracy and continued her campaign for peace as president of the Federation of Japanese Women's Societies, as well as a member of various international organizations, until her death.

**Hobbs, Lucy** (1833–*c*1900). American dentist. The first woman graduate in dentistry, she was born in Ellenberg, New York. Her mother died when she was a child, and at the age of 16 she became a teacher, although she studied medicine with a doctor in Michigan for a short time. In 1859 she applied for admission to the Eclectic Medical College, Cincinnati, but was refused on the grounds of her sex and advised to try dentistry. No local dentist would accept her as a student trainee, but the Dean of the Ohio Dental College eventually allowed her to work in his office while she looked for a tutor. Finally she found a place with a Dr Samuel Wardle, supporting herself by sewing at night. In 1861 she was refused entry to the Ohio Dental College, and instead opened an office in Cincinnati, moving to Iowa at the outbreak of the Civil War. In 1865 the Iowa State Dental Society accepted her as a member, and formally supported a final, successful application to the Ohio Dental College, where she graduated the following year, coming top of the final examinations. In 1867 she began to practise in Chicago.

Although she was the first graduate dentist, other women had practised dentistry unofficially, including Eveline Roberts James, who acquired her skills from helping her husband, continuing his practice in Connecticut on his death in 1855.

**Hodgkin** [née Crowfoot]**, Dorothy (Mary)** (1910–). English biochemist. Dorothy was born in Cairo while her father was in the Egyptian ministry of education. She graduated from Oxford and obtained her doctorate from Cambridge, where her work was on the x-ray diffraction of crystals of the digestive enzyme pepsin. Although her scientific achievements were very wide-ranging, this work determined the use of x-ray diffraction as the focus for later work.

In 1937 she married Thomas Hodgkin and had three children; the family travelled widely and frequently pursued individual interests.

During World War II Dorothy worked on the structure of penicillin, making the first use of a computer in tackling a biochemical problem. She also worked out the structure of vitamin B12. In 1964 she became the third woman to receive the Nobel Prize for Chemistry, and decided to use the money for a scholarship and for the cause of peace and the relief of famine. Her next work was to find the structure of insulin.

Among many honours, she was elected to the Royal Society in 1947 and received their Royal and Copley Medals. She was awarded the Order of Merit in 1965, the only woman to be so honoured since FLORENCE NIGHTINGALE. From 1960 to 1977 she was the first Wolfson Research Professor of the Royal Society. Her other honours include membership of the Russian Academy of Science (1976) and the Dimitriou Award (1984).

**Hodgkins, Frances** (1869–1947). New Zealand painter. Born in Dunedin, Frances was taught water-colour painting by her father, and studied with the Italian painter G.P. Berti before going to Dunedin Art School in 1895. She gave piano lessons to save for a trip to Europe and from 1901–4 she toured Italy, France, the Netherlands and Morocco. She went back to Wellington but left again in 1906, finding no success in New

Zealand as a painter. Settling in Paris in 1907 she taught at Colarossi's and then opened her own water-colour school, chiefly for women. In 1912–13 she gave a series of notable exhibitions in New Zealand and Australia and returned to Paris before moving to St Ives, Cornwall on the outbreak of war in 1914. There she began painting in oils. After 1918 Frances moved around England, giving sketching classes, and in the mid-1920s, following a brief period in Paris, she worked in Manchester as a designer for the Calico Printers Association and joined the Manchester Society of Modern Painters. Her fortunes turned in 1928 when an exhibition at Claridges Gallery, London, containing major new work, was received with great critical acclaim and in 1929, aged 58, she was invited to join the Seven and Five Society, a group of progressive painters much younger than herself including Winifred and Ben Nicholson, David Jones and Cedric Morris. During the 1930s she travelled in Europe, particularly in Spain, but eventually settled in Dorset. Frances Hodgkins's later work, contrasting in style with the early, subtle post-impressionist water-colours was strong and stylized, marked by a poetic freedom and expresive, rich use of colour. Forgotten for some years after her death, she is now recognized as one of the most original painters of her day. She received a Civil List Pension in 1942 and died five years later at Herrison, Dorset. A Centenary Exhibition of her work was held in Auckland City Art Gallery in 1969.

**Hoffman, Malvina** (1887–1966). American sculptor. Born in New York, Malvina Hoffman studied painting and sculpture in New York and Paris, where Rodin taught her for four years and persuaded her to attend dissection classes at a local medical school to learn anatomy. In the years before World War I she was a member of a circle of well-known artists and performers, many of whom were her subjects, especially dancers like her friend ANNA PAVLOVA.

In 1929 she was commissioned by the Field Museum of Natural History in Chicago to travel around the world for two years and sculpt the different racial types. When she returned the Museum opened a special exhibition hall, called 'The Hall of Man', containing 105 sculptures in bronze. (About 50 remain in Chicago today.) Her book

*Heads and Tales* (1936) gives a fascinating account of the world-wide quest which she made with her husband, musician Samuel Grimson. She then published a work on sculptural technique, *Sculpture Inside and Out* (1937), and continued to work as a sculptor until late in her life.

M. Hoffman: *Yesterday Is Tomorrow: A Personal History* (1965)

**Ho Hsiang-ning** (1879–1972). Chinese revolutionary feminist. Born into a famous merchant family, partly educated in Hong Kong, she married Liao Shung Kai in 1897 and they both studied in Japan where they joined the group led by Sun Yat-Sen in 1905. After the first revolutionary attempts of 1911–13, she returned to Japan until 1923, when she became one of the three women members of the Kuomintang Congress. She took an active role in feminist politics in the 1920s, being one of the first to bob her hair as a gesture of independence. Her husband was assassinated in 1925 and she gave up her job as Head of the Women's Department of the Kuomintang after the Communists broke with Tsiang Kai-Shek in 1927. She then went to Hong Kong with Soong Ching' Ling, maintaining a critical attitude towards the nationalist government. In 1949, after the Revolution, she returned to Peking and was Head of the Overseas Chinese Affairs Commission until 1959. In 1960, at the age of 80, she became Honorary Chairwoman of the China Women's Federation.

**Holden, Joan**. American mime producer. Joan Holden first began to work with the San Francisco Mime Theatre in 1967, adapting Goldoni's *L'amante militaire*, and she was one of the original twelve members when the theatre re-formed as a collective in 1970. She has been one of their major writers, primarily known for her exciting Marxist political mimes of the 1970s, which were taken on tour, playing mostly in parks and other outside venues, until the company 'moved indoors' in the early 1980s. Their best productions include *Electrobucks*, *Hotel Universe, Steeltown* and *1985*, a re-write of Dickens's *Christmas Carol*. Although recent work suggests both a growing political disillusionment and a greater interest in individual consciousness, Holden stands out for her personal and artistic commitment, demonstrated, for example, in *Spain/36* the masked mime musical about the Spanish Civil War which is the company's biggest ever production, much praised for its boldness, scope and vitality.

**Holiday, Billie** [Eleanora] (1915–59). American jazz singer. Born in Baltimore, Maryland, she was the daughter of a professional guitarist. After a childhood of hardship she became a prostitute in New York and served a short spell of imprisonment. She started singing in Harlem bars in 1931. An instant local success, she began recording with Benny Goodman in 1933, toured Canada, sang in New York and Chicago clubs, and worked with Count Basie in 1937 and Artie Shaw in 1938 before becoming a solo cabaret star in 1940. During these years she made a series of recordings, mostly with the saxophonist Lester Young. She was briefly married to the trumpeter Joe Guy, with whom she toured (1945) before her first solo concert at New York Town Hall in 1946. She also appeared in films such as *Symphony in Black* (1935) and *New Orleans* (1947).

Her private life was tempestuous and unhappy, and after 1947 she was subject to increasing spells in hospital and imprisonment on narcotics charges. However, she returned from prison to give a triumphant concert at Carnegie Hall in March 1948, and worked for another ten years throughout the USA, although she was banned by law from appearing in New York clubs. Early in 1954 she toured Europe, where her intense dramatic interpretation and the instinctive 'instrumental' flexibility of her voice won her rapturous receptions in eight countries. Eventually defeated in her struggle against heroin addiction she was admitted to hospital; although dying, she was arrested for possessing illicit drugs. She died in the Metropolitan Hospital, New York.

B. Holiday and W. Dufty: *Lady Sings the Blues* (1956)
B. James: *Billie Holiday* (1984)

**Holland, Agnieszka** (1948–). Polish film director. The daughter of Polish–Jewish parents (her father's entire family was killed during the war), she grew up in Poland but studied at the Film Academy in Prague. She returned to Poland in 1971 and worked as assistant director to Krzystof Zannussi, while also directing in the theatre and making films for television. Her first feature film was in 1974, and she became widely known with *Provincial Actors* (1978), *The Fever* (1980), *A Woman Alone* (1981) and *The Story of a Bomb* (1981). This last film, about Polish resistance to the Tsar, was censored under the martial law of December 1981. A supporter of Solidarity, she left Poland, directed documentaries for French television and collaborated with Andrej Wajda on *Danton*. Her recent film *Angry Harvest* (1988) was made in Germany and deals with a peasant's growing awareness of his part in the Nazi persecution of Polish Jews.

**Hollingworth, Leta Stetter** (1886–1939). American educational psychologist. Daughter of a migrant farmer, she spent a childhood in Nebraska before studying English at the University of Nebraska, where she met a psychologist, Harry Hollingworth, whom she married. She worked as a preacher and then studied psychology at Columbia University and at Bellevue Hospital, New York, where she gave mental tests. Her PhD in 1916 submitted theories of male superiority to scientific investigation. With her husband she marched in suffrage parades in 1915 but thought the reform of attitudes more important than the vote.

Later she moved to the educational rather than clinical field, particularly studying mental and emotional abnormality. Among her many books were *Psychology of Subnormal Children* (1920), *Gifted Children* (1926) and *Psychology of the Adolescent* (1928). She was co-author of *The Problem of Mental Disorder* (1934). In 1937 she was appointed Director of Research at the experimental Speyer School. She received an honorary LLD from Nebraska University before she died of cancer.

**Holm, Hanya** (1895–). German dancer, teacher and choreographer. She was born at Worms, Germany, and attended the Dalcroze schools at Frankfurt and Dresden. Deciding to dance rather than be a musician, she joined MARY WIGMAN, becoming head teacher at her school and principal dancer in 1928. In 1930 she remained in New York to open a school after the Wigman company's tour of the USA. She taught in New York from 1931 to 1967, and developed a lecture-demonstration technique which introduced the Central European style to the USA. Her major works of the 1930s and 1940s include *Trend* (1937), *Tragic Exodus*, *Metropolitan Daily* and *Windows*, and she also created dances for Broadway shows, including *Kiss me Kate*, *My Fair Lady* and *Camelot*.

W. Sands: *Hanya Holm* (1976)

**Holm, Jeanne (Marjorie)** (1921–). American Air Force officer. Born in Portland, Oregon, she joined the Women's Army Auxiliary Corps in 1942 and was commissioned as a Second Lieutenant in 1943. By the end of World War II she was a Captain in charge of a women's training regiment, but after returning to civilian life she rejoined the services in 1948 and was transferred to the Air Force, advancing through the grades to become a Major-General in 1973, the highest rank achieved by any woman in the American armed forces. Her postings included supervising manpower needs at the Headquarters of the Allied Air Forces for Southern Europe in Naples (1957–61) and in Washington (1961–5). From 1965 to 1972 she was Director of Women in the Air Force. Here she implemented great changes in career opportunities, assignments and the abolition of discriminatory rules. Her last two years before retirement were spent as Director of the Secretariat of Air Force Personnel. She remained active and worked as adviser to the Defense Manpower Commission, and to the President (1976–7), and was a member of the Advisory Committee on Women in the Services until 1980. She is a strong supporter of women's rights, a member of the National Women's Political Caucus, and founder and first Chairperson of Women in Government. She also writes and lectures.

**Holtby, Winifred** (1898–1935). English feminist. She was born in Rudstone, Yorkshire, and became a member of the Women's Auxiliary Corps in the World War I, and then went to Somerville College, Oxford, where she met VERA BRITTAIN. After they graduated, they shared a flat in London. Winifred became a prolific journalist, writing for the *Manchester Guardian*, *News Chronicle*, and *Time and Tide*, of which she became a Director in 1926. She was also involved in feminist and pacifist groups and later lectured for the League of Nations Union.

Her first novel, *Anderby Wold*, was published in 1923, followed by *The Land of Green Ginger* (1927), *Poor Caroline* (1931), the satirical *The Astonishing Island* (1933), *Mandea! Mandea!* (1933) and her most popular book *South Riding*, which appeared posthumously in 1936. She also wrote poetry, short stories, a critical book about VIRGINIA WOOLF (1932) and an analysis of women's position in contemporary society, *Women and a Changing Civilisation* (1934).

V. Brittain: *Testament of Friendship: the Story of Winifred Holtby* (1940)

**Hoodless** [née Hunter], **Adelaide** (1857–1910). Canadian welfare worker. The youngest of 12 children on a farm in Brantford, Ontario, at the age of 24 she married a rich businessman, John Hoodless. After the death of their fourth son from contaminated milk, she campaigned for health education for mothers, and for better home conditions. The authorities regarded her demand for training in scientific nutrition, sanitation and housekeeping as unreasonable so she herself taught at Hamilton Young Women's Christian Association (YWCA) in 1889. She organized a household science class (1890) and as President of the YWCA (1892) opened a school of domestic science. Having appealed unsuccessfully to the Ontario government, she obtained funds from Sir William Macdonald, a tobacco magnate, and opened a separate Macdonald Institute attached to the Ontario Agricultural Institute at Guelph in 1904. To build up a support network in the community she founded the first Women's Institute for farm women at Stoney Creek, Ontario, in 1897. She died on a lecture platform while campaigning for more funds for home economics.

R. Howes: 'Adelaide Hunter Hoodless', *The Clear Spirit*, ed. M. Imris (1966)

**Hopkins, Thelma** (1936–). Irish sportswoman. Thelma was an outstanding all-round athlete, and an international player in hockey and squash rackets. As a high jumper, she won a silver medal at the

1956 Olympic Games, broke the world record, and won gold medals at both the Empire Games and European championships of 1954. She held the British record for pentathlon, and won medals as a long jumper. As a hockey player, she won 40 caps, scoring in her first international match; she was versatile as an attacker. She joined the first British touring hockey team in 1965, visiting the USA. She also represented Ireland at squash.

**Hopper** [née Murray], **Grace (Brewster)** (1906–). American mathematician, naval officer and computer pioneer. Born in New York, Grace attended Vassar College then Yale University, receiving her PhD in mathematics in 1934. In 1930 she married Vincent Hopper (they were divorced in 1945). While lecturing at Vassar she joined the military section of the Women Accepted for Voluntary Emergency Service (WAVES) and as a Lieutenant was assigned to develop operating programmes for the Mark I computer. This was the first automatically sequenced digital computer, the forerunner of the electronic computer, but she still termed it a calculator.

While remaining in the US Naval Reserve, Grace served in five different universities, her last being George Washington University (from 1971). She held posts in several industrial companies, including the Eckert-Mauchly division of Remington Rand and the Universal Automatic Computer (UNIVAC) division of Sperry Rand. Here she did her most recognized work on the first compiler. She developed the concept of automatic programming from which the first English language compiler system was incorporated into the widely-used Common Business Oriented Language (COBOL).

When she became a Fellow of the Institute of Electrical and Electronic Engineers (IEEE) she was one of only two women, and one of five elected to the National Academy of Engineers. She was also awarded other distinguished memberships and honours including the Legion of Merit. She thought her most important contribution to be in training others and in interpreting computers to people, together with serving in the Navy. Although she retired in 1966, she was recalled the following year to direct Training and Technology in the Naval Data Automation Command (NAVDAC). In 1973 she was promoted to Captain while on the retired list, a precedent in the Naval Reserve.

**Hopper** [née Furry], **Hedda (Elda)** (1890–1966). American journalist. Born into a Pennsylvanian Quaker family, she began her career as a chorus girl and was then an actress on Broadway. After marrying DeWolf Hopper, who named her Hedda, she went with him to Hollywood in 1916, and played occasional bit parts in films. In 1935 she appeared on stage in Los Angeles in *Dinner at Eight*, and worked for the Elizabeth Arden salon. From 1936 she wrote a Hollywood column for the *Chicago Tribune*, *New York Daily News* and others. She appeared monthly in the Art Linklater TV show and toured as an entertainer to servicemen in World War II. In 1960 she was the only columnist to refuse to attend a luncheon honouring Nikita Krushchev as part of his tour of Hollywood. She wrote two autobiographical volumes: *From under my Hat* (1952) and *The whole truth and nothing but* (1963).

**Horne, Lena** (1917–). American singer and actress. Born into the black middle class, Lena always admired her grandmother Cora Calhoun Herne, an active campaigner for women's and black rights from the 1890s to the 1930s. She went to the Ethical Culture School and the Girls' High School, Brooklyn. Her mother encouraged a career in show business and at 16 she joined the chorus line at Harlem's Cotton Club. In 1934 she made her broadway debut in *Dance With Your Gods* and from 1936 sang with Noble Sissle's band and later with Charlie Barnet. In 1937 she married Louis James, but they were divorced in 1944. In 1947 she married the musician Lennie Hayton (he died in 1974). In 1942, a singer in a Hollywood night club, she became the first black artist to be given a long-term contract by MGM. Her first feature film was *Panama Hattie* (1942). Refusing to be cast as a 'Latin-American' or to play stereotyped maid roles, she starred in the all-black musicals *Cabin in the Sky* (1942) and *Stormy Weather* (1943) and made guest appearances in other musicals – although her scenes were often cut in Southern states. Despite her talent, prejudice affected her career, and she lost the role of Julie in *Show Boat* (1957) to Ava Gardner because the part involved marrying a white man.

Lena's politics, as well as her colour, worried Hollywood. A friend of Paul Robeson, she was accused of Communism during the McCarthy era, but never officially charged. In the late 1950s she left Hollywood, making only three later films, including *The Wiz* (1978, made by Sidney Lumet, husband of her daughter Gail Jane) with DIANA ROSS and Michael Jackson. But her successful theatrical and singing career continued, culminating in the longest running one-person show in Broadway history in the 1980s. During the 1960s she worked for the Civil Rights Movement and has always been outspoken about politics and discrimination.

G. Lumer Buckley: *The Hornes: An American Family* (1987)

**Horney** [née Danielson], **Karen (Clementine)** (1885–1952). German-American psychoanalyst. Born in Hamburg, Karen decided at the age of 12 to study medicine, although her father, a Norwegian sea captain, did not approve of education for women. She went to medical school at the University of Freiburg and then to Göttingen where she met Oscar Horney, who was studying law; they were married in 1909. She graduated from Berlin in 1911 and gained her MD in 1915, with a thesis on traumatic psychoses. She gave birth to three daughters, in 1911, 1913 and 1915.

Horney worked at the Berlin Sanitorium and the military neuropsychiatric hospital during World War I. After the war she moved to the Berlin Psychoanalytic Institute where she established her reputation. She challenged Freud's pessimistic view of human nature and he replied. She herself underwent therapy with Karl Abraham, and her interest began to focus more on feminine psychology. She thought that women do not really envy the penis but the superior position of men in society. She produced papers on the distrust between the sexes, and young girls and maternal conflict. She separated from her husband in 1926 and in 1932 went to the USA.

The second phase of Karen's work developed a theory of personality and new concepts of neuroses. *The neurotic personality of our time* (1937) advanced three strategies for coping with anxiety: moving towards others, or against others, or withdrawing. Integration of all three is normal behaviour. She suggested that clinging to one parent did not demonstrate the Oedipus complex but a disturbed parent-child relationship. *New ways in psychoanalysis* (1939), re-interpreting Freudian concepts, resulted in uproar and her resignation from the New York Psychoanalytic Society in 1941. The same year she founded the Association for the Advancement of Psychoanalysis and the American Institute of Psychoanalysis, and was also Editor of the *American Journal of Psychoanalysis*.

Karen was a teacher, therapist, and prolific writer; a neo-Freudian, humanist and feminist, with wide interests and a full social life. One of her last journeys was to Japan to pursue an interest in Zen Buddhism. Before she died of abdominal cancer she learnt that the Karen Horney Clinic was about to be opened in New York.

L. Rubins: *Karen Horney: gentle rebel of psychoanalysis* (1978)
S. Quinn: *A Mind of Her Own: the life of Karen Horney* (1988)

**Horniman, Annie (Elizabeth Fredericka)** (1860–1937). English theatre manager and patron. She was born in Forest Hill, London, the daughter of a wealthy Victorian tea merchant; at 14 she developed a lifelong passion for the theatre, disapproved of by her Quaker family. She studied at the Slade School of Art, and on holidays she travelled abroad. In Germany she saw the plays of Ibsen for the first time and realized the importance of subsidized theatre. She went to Ireland in 1903, where she sponsored the building of the Abbey Theatre, Dublin, which opened in 1904 and which she financed until 1910. For a time she also acted as unpaid secretary to W.B. Yeats. She bought and reconstructed the Gaiety Theatre, Manchester, and ran her own repertory company there (1907–17), staging the plays of George Bernard Shaw, the classics, and plays of the Manchester school, including Harold Brighouse and Allan Monkhouse. The venture proved financially unsuccessful; the company was disbanded in 1917 and the building was sold in 1921.

Annie Horniman was a principal supporter of the Irish theatre movement and a founder of the English repertory theatre. She was a forceful personality, always dramatically dressed, and brandishing a monocle. On her retirement she gave her library of plays to the British Drama League. She had the satisfaction of seeing her pioneer work imitated by other principal cities in the UK, and various actors and actresses who began their careers with her reaching the top of their profession, including SYBIL THORNDYKE and Lewis Casson.

J.W. Flannery: *Miss Annie F. Horniman and the Abbey Theatre* (1970)

**Hosmer, Harriet** (1830–1908). American sculptor. She was born in Massachusetts. Her mother, sister and brother died while she was a child, and to strengthen Harriet her father instituted a rigorous programme of outdoor physical activity. She was sent to school in Boston and, determined to become a sculptor, she arranged for private anatomy classes from a friend at a St Louis medical school, because the subject was then thought improper for women. She was also an intrepid climber and Mount Hosmer, Missouri, is named after her. After travelling alone along the Mississippi she returned to Massachusetts. In 1852 her father introduced her to CHARLOTTE CUSHMAN, who offered to sponsor her in Rome, where she became a pupil of the sculptor John Gibson. She stayed on after her family fortune was lost, earning commissions and achieving fame with the whimsical *Puck* (1857). She exhibited in London (1862) and the USA (1864) and became known for her monumental works such as *Zenobia*. Regarded as an extraordinary, independent woman, she wore men's clothes for working and employed several stone-cutters in her studio. A friend of ANNA JAMESON and ELIZABETH BARRETT BROWNING, she worked less after 1880 and spent much of her time in England. Her last great work was a statue of Queen ISABELLA, commissioned by the city of San Francisco and unveiled in 1894. The most successful woman sculptor of her day, she finally returned to the USA in 1900.

H. Hosmer: *Letters and Memories* (1913)

**Howard, Mabel** (1893–1972). New Zealand politician. Her first political activities were as Secretary of the General Labourers' Union in Canterbury and as a member of Christchurch City Council. Elected to parliament in 1943, she became the first woman cabinet minister in New Zealand and the Commonwealth, when appointed Minister of Health and Child Welfare (1947–9) by the first Labour government. She campaigned for social security, housing provision and consumers' rights and was a tough, witty and colourful speaker. Not an overt feminist, she fought with determination for the rights of women and children.

**How-Martyn, Edith** (1880–1954). English suffragette. After obtaining a DSc in economics from London University, she became a mathematics lecturer at Westfield College. She was Secretary of the Women's Social and Political Union from 1906 to 1907, when she left to found the Women's Freedom League with CHARLOTTE DESPARD; she was Secretary until 1911, then head of the 'political and militant department'. As candidate for Hendon in the 1918 election she lost her deposit, but the following year became the first woman member of Middlesex County Council.

After suffrage she turned to birth-control and was Honorary Director of the Birth Control International Information Centre. She travelled to India with MARGARET SANGER, lecturing around the world, and wrote *The Birth Control Movement in England* (1931). She also founded the first play centre, in Hampstead Garden Suburb. In 1939 she moved to Australia, where she lectured on women's rights. She died in Sydney after several years of illness.

**Hrotsvitha** [Roswitha] **of Gandersheim** (*c*935–72). Saxon writer. She was a canoness and a member of an intelligentsia of nobly-born Saxon women in a Benedictine nunnery. She was the author of six plays (*Gallicanus, Dulcitius, Callimachus, Abraham, Pafnutius,* and *Sapientia*). Her plays and poetry in Latin distinguish her as the first female German writer and, if the plays were performed (though this is doubtful), as the first European dramatist after the disappearance of the Classical theatre. The plays centre on the theme of Christian virgin martyrdom, with gruesome torture scenes, typical of early hagiography. Scenes depicting the conversion of Roman prostitutes are particularly touching, and for such material, Hrotsvitha claimed the influence of Terence, the ancient Roman comedy writer.

The manuscripts were discovered around the year 1500 by Conrad Celtis. Hrotsvitha also wrote narrative poems, legends of the saints, a life of the Virgin Mary, and verse histories of Otto I and of the convent of Gandersheim from its foundation in 856.

**Hua Mu-Ian** (5th century). Chinese heroine. Although her memory endures only in folktales, legends and popular songs, she probably lived under the Tartar Wei dynasty, which ruled from 386–557. According to legend she took the place of her invalid father when he was conscripted to fight for the government and after 12 years in the army disguised as a man, she returned home to her ordinary life. She is credited with fierce fighting courage, the power of leadership and an ability to inspire her fellow warriors in the defence of their villages.

**Huch, Ricarda** [pseud.: Richard Hugo] (1864–1947). German novelist and historian. Born in Braunschweig into a well-known Protestant merchant family, she was the sister of the novelist Rudolf Huch and a cousin of Friedrich Huch. She went to Zürich in 1887 to study history, receiving a doctorate in 1891, and remaining there as a teacher in a girls' school. Her student experiences are described in *Frühling in der Schweiz* ('Spring in Switzerland'). There she wrote her first poetry, *Gedichte* (1891), and the quasi-autobiographical novel *Erinnerungen von Ludolf Ursleu dem Jüngeren* (1893; Eng. trans. 1913–15). In 1897 she returned to Germany and after an unhappy romance with a married cousin, Richard Huch, she moved to Vienna where she married a dentist from Trieste, Ermanno Ceconi, in 1899 and had a daughter. She began spending part of the year in Munich and in 1907 divorced her husband and married the cousin whom she had loved ten years before. During this period she had written several works, including the critical studies *Die Blütezeit der Romantik* (1899)

and *Ausbreitung und Verfall der Romantik* (1902) about the Golden Age, and the expansion and decline, of Romanticism. She also published stories about life in a Trieste slum, *Aus der Triumphgasse* (1902) and the novel *Vita somnium breve* (1906).

Her second marriage ended unhappily in 1910 and she lived in Munich, frequently returning to Trieste, and continuing to write. She produced historical studies about Garibaldi, *Die Geschichten von Garibaldi* (1906), the Thirty Years War, *Der grosse Krieg in Deutschland* (1912–14), Luther (1916) and the Holy Roman Empire (3 vols 1934,1937,1939). Greatly respected, she was the first woman admitted to the Prussian Academy of Literature in 1931, but left it in 1933 in protest against Nazi policies, and the Academy's expulsion of Jewish writers. Ostracized and impoverished, she lived in Jena, remaining there during World War II. In 1947 she was elected President of the first congress of German writers in Berlin. She died soon afterwards on her way to join her daughter in the West. Throughout her life Huch was a feminist, and a leader of the intellectual circles in the German women's movement. Thomas Mann called her 'Deutschlands erste Frau' ('the First Lady of Germany').

M. Baum: *Leuchtende Spur: das Leben Ricarda Huchs* (1950)

**Hugonnai-Wartha, Vilma** (1847–1922). Hungarian doctor. The daughter of a count, Vilma married György Szillassy in 1865. The death of their child at the age of six promoted her interest in paediatrics and in 1872, while living in Zurich, she began studying medicine. First she had to matriculate in Latin and mathematics; she then became Nursing Assistant to a professor at the medical school.

Vilma published two papers, on tracheotomy in diphtheria and on the treatment of burns. The oral for her MD was in February 1879, but as a woman she was allowed only a midwife's certificate. She returned to Budapest and became assistant to Professor Vince Wartha, whom she later married.

In 1897 the Ministry of Culture recognized her Zurich degree and she began an intensive practice, making major research progress in Hungarian medicine as well as improving women's status. Until 1913 it was possible for a woman to practise medicine in Hungary only in association with a male doctor.

**Humphrey, Doris** (1895–1958). American dancer and choreographer. She danced in a variety of styles from the age of eight, attended Denishawn School (1917–27), and first experimented with choreography in the unaccompanied *Tragica*. She broke with Denishawn in 1926. With her partner Charles Weidman, she established a school and began work on abstract dances: *Colour Harmony*, *Water Study* (1928) and *Dance of Motion* (1931). In the 1930s she explored psychological themes, for example in her passionate trilogy *Theatre Piece*, *With my Red Fires* and *New Dance* (1935).

During the 1930s and 1940s she also made several social protest dances for her own company, such as *Inquest*. After 1944, when arthritis forced her to retire from performance, she created powerful works for the company of her protégé José Limon, including *Lament for Ignacio Sanchez and Mejias* (1946), and *Day on Earth* (1947). She continued to teach, developing her theory of movement and dramatic expression, and directed workshops at Connecticut College and the Juilliard School. She wrote *The Art of Making Dances* (1959).

S.J. Cohen: *Doris Humphrey: An Artist First* (1972)

**Hunt, Harriot (Kezia)** (1805–75). American doctor. Born in Boston, Massachusetts, Harriot became a schoolteacher but the illness of her sister Sarah led both to study anatomy and physiology with Dr and Mrs Mott. Encouraged by their mother, they set up in practice in 1835. Sarah married and withdrew from the practice but Harriot tried repeatedly to add a degree to her practical experience by applying to Harvard University. Her correspondence with the Dean, Oliver Wendell Holmes, is preserved, and he accepted her as a student at the same time as accepting three blacks. The students, however, rioted at these admissions, objecting particularly to the 'sacrifice of her modesty', and she was obliged to withdraw.

In 1843 Harriot organized a Ladies' Physiological Society and gave talks, and in 1849 she gave a free course of public lectures in Boston on physiology and hygiene. She became interested in mental illness after observing 'physical maladies growing out of concealed sorrows'. She tried to combat women's nervous diseases by helping them towards self-esteem. In 1853 the Female Medical College of Pennsylvania made her an honorary MD after she had practised for 18 years.

Harriot was outspoken over women's and civil rights. For 20 years she accompanied her own tax payment with a protest at not having the vote, and championed women's rights to education and careers, including remuneration for domestic labour. She spoke against slavery and racial inequality. Together with campaigners such as LUCRETIA MOTT, LUCY STONE and ANTOINETTE BROWN-BLACKWELL, she attended the Women's Rights Convention at Worcester, Massachusetts, in 1850.

H.K. Hunt: *Glances and glimpses: or 50 years social, including 20 years professional life* (1856)

**Huntingdon, Selina** [Countess of Huntingdon] (1707–91). English founder of a theological college. Selina married the Earl of Huntingdon in 1728 and was converted by her sister-in-law to Methodism some ten years later. A Calvinist-Methodist, she supported the preacher George Whitefield and his work in North America. After her husband's death in 1746, Selina devoted herself to social and religious work, and became the chief medium for introducing Methodism to the upper classes. Using her right as a peeress, she appointed evangelical clergymen as chaplains and built chapels in fashionable towns such as Brighton and Bath. However, this method of supporting Methodist ministers was disallowed by the Consistory Court of London in 1779. In order to save her chapels, Selina registered them as dissenting places of worship under the Toleration Act.

In 1768 she established Trevecca College in Brecknockshire for the training of evangelical clergymen after six theological students had been expelled from Oxford under the suspicion of Methodism. After her death the college was moved to Hertfordshire and finally to Cambridge.

S. Tytler: *The Countess of Huntingdon and her circle* (1907)

**Huo Xuan Huong** (*fl* late 18th century). Vietnamese poet. She is regarded as the finest Vietnamese poet for her depiction of daily life in verse of great simplicity and delicate rhythms; she is unusual in her frankly erotic and sexual description, which was contrary to the Confucian code of her day, and for her forthright defence of women.

**Hurst** [née Berney], **Margery** (1914– ). English businesswoman. Born in Southsea, Hampshire, she was educated at Kilburn High School, London, and went to Minerva College and the Royal Academy of Dramatic Art before working for her father Sam Berney, a builder of cinemas. In 1943 she joined the Auxiliary Territorial Service (ATS) but was invalided out in 1944. After World War II she began her own business in Brook Street, Mayfair, an agency supplying temporary secretaries on a daily basis. The Brook Street Bureau became one of the most reputable employment agencies for secretarial staff, concentrating on very careful selection of employers and jobs, and the number of branches expanded to over 200 in the UK, USA, Australia and Hong Kong. Margery Hurst soon became a millionaire and her company went public in 1965. She also established schools and colleges for administrative and secretarial workers and in 1960 founded the non-profit making Society for International Secretaries. She was awarded the Pimms Cup for Anglo-American business friendship in 1962 and from 1967 to 1970 was on the American Committee of the British National Economic Commission. In 1970 she became one of the first women members of Lloyds Underwriters. She retired as Managing Director of Brook Street Bureau in 1976, but remained joint-Chairman with her husband, the lawyer Eric Hurst, whom she married in 1948. They have five daughters. She was awarded the OBE in 1976. In 1981 she became the first woman member of the Worshipful Company of Marketers and was made a Freeman of the City of London.
M. Hurst: *No Glass Slipper* (1967)

**Hurston, Zora Neale** (1901–60). American author. One of the most influential of black American writers, celebrated by ALICE WALKER in *In Search of Our Mothers' Gardens*, Zora was born in Eatonville, Florida. When she was nine her Baptist preacher father remarried, and her later girlhood was spent in different kinds of occasional work, including sometimes working on the costumes for an itinerant theatre group. She had little formal education, but eventually attended the Morgan Academy, Baltimore, and then, 1918, studied part-time at Howard University, Washington. She wrote essays and short fiction, and was already a recognized new writer when she moved to New York in 1925, soon gaining a scholarship to study Cultural Anthropology at Barnard College, graduating in 1928.

From 1928 to 1932 she researched into Southern folklore, financed by a Rosenwald grant, and in the next two decades published a series of remarkable novels: *Jonah's Gourd Vine* (1934), *Their Eyes Were Watching God* (1937), *Moses, Man of the Mountain* (1939) and *Seraph on the Sewanee* (1948). She also published two folklore collections, *Mules and Men* (1935) and *Tell My Horse* (1938), while her own early childhood was evoked in *Dust Tracks on the Road* (1942).

In 1936–8 she had a Guggenheim Fellowship to do research in Haiti and Jamaica and she then became Professor of Drama at the North Carolina College for Negroes. She was one of the first widely acclaimed black writers to assimilate folk tradition into modern literature. During the 1950s her work was limited to essays and her standpoint on the necessity for preserving black culture, which led to her opposition to integration, aroused much hostility. Ill and poor, she was increasingly ignored until her death in Florida in 1960.
R. Hemenway: *Zora Neale Hurston: A Literary Biography* (1986)

**Hutchinson, Anne** (1591–1643). American religious radical. Born in Lincolnshire, England, the daughter of a clergyman, Anne emigrated to Boston with her family in 1634. In America her nursing ability and intellectual insight won a following among laymen and clergy to her unorthodox religious views. Anne advocated redemption through faith rather than deeds, a doctrine known as Antinomianism. She started to hold meetings and denounced the Massachusetts clergy as being with few exceptions 'under the covenant of works, not of grace'. These actions split the Colony, with the Governor and his Deputy taking opposite sides. At an election the Deputy-Governor ousted her supporter, the Governor, the issue hingeing upon a threat to the state since some of her followers refused to take up arms in its defence. Anne was charged with heresy and sedition, and was banished in 1638. The Boston Church excommunicated her. After banishment, she and her friends acquired territory from the Narragansett Indians in Rhode Island, where they set up a community on the principle that no-one was to be accounted a 'delinquent for doctrine'. After the death of her husband, Anne moved to Long Island and then to Pelham Bay, where she was killed in an Indian uprising.

W.F. Rugg: *Unafraid: a Life of Anne Hutchinson* (1930)
N. Shore: *Anne Hutchinson* (1988)

**Hutton, Ina Ray** (1918–84). American band-leader. The leader of an all-female band in the 1930s, Ina Ray Hutton grew up in show business. She sang and danced at nine, at New York's Palace Theatre, and continued to appear in review, playing with great band-leaders like Harry James and Artie Shaw until at the age of 17 she put together her own band, The Melodears, giving it the glamour of Hollywood with her blond hair, sleek dresses and deliberately sexy movements. Soon she was labelled 'The Blond Bombshell of Swing', but her star status was also backed by a talent for arrangements and skill as a conductor. The band toured relentlessly until 1940 when she left to take over an all-male band which she led until 1950, re-establishing a female orchestra with great success for her California television show in the 1950s.

She married four times, and in the 1960s after her marriage to businessman Jack Curtis she gradually retired from the limelight.

**Hypatia** (c370–415). Greek mathematician and philosopher. The daughter of the mathematician, Theon, who became Director of the University of Alexandria, she was brought up with careful attention to a full education which included encouragement to think and question rather than to accept formal dogmatic religions. She established her reputation as a mathematician while studying at Athens under Plutarch the Younger and his daughter Asclepegeneia. On her return to Alexandria she was invited to teach mathematics and philosophy at the university. She taught geometry, astronomy, and the new science of algebra. She became a popular teacher and was considered an oracle and known simply as 'The Nurse' or 'The Philosopher'.

She is known to have written a number of works, but none has survived intact. She wrote a commentary on the *Almagest*, Ptolemy's astronomical canon, and with her father was co-author of at least one treatise on Euclid. Her commentary on the *Astronomical Canon* of Diophantus (which may have been part of the *Almagest*) probably included original problems, while her geometrical work on the Conic Sections of Apollonius of Perga became of interest to mathematicians from the 17th century. Her most significant work was on algebra, a commentary on the *Arithmetica* of Diophantus.

The source of much knowledge of Hypatia is a number of letters from one of her pupils, Synesius of Cyrene, asking her for scientific advice. From the letters we learn that she invented an astrolabe, or planisphere; apparatus for distilling water, and measuring its level; and a hydroscope or aerometer for measuring the specific gravity of liquids.

The neo-Platonic school of thought to which she belonged embraced a scientific rationalism which was counter to the doctrinaire beliefs of Christian religion, and Cyril, Patriarch of Alexandria, systematically opposed it. Although Hypatia had already received enormous acclaim, Cyril incited a mob to drag her from her chariot and torture her to death.

# I

**Ibarbourou** [née Fernandez Morales], **Juana** [Juanita] **de** (1895–). Uruguayan poet. Born in Melo, Uruguay, she was educated at a convent. At the age of 18 she was married to a soldier and went to live in Montevideo. In 1919 she published her first book of nature lyrics, *Las lenguas de diamante*, which was followed by the prose poem *El cantaro fresco* (1920), *Raíz salvaje* (1922) and *La rosa de los vientos* (1930). By 1929 she had become so popular that she was given the title 'Juana de America'. She also wrote books and plays for children, religious books and her *Autobiografía* (1957). In 1950 she became President of the Uruguayan Society of Authors. She published two more poetry collections, *Perdida* (1950) and *Oro y tormento* (1956).

**Ibarruri Gómez, Dolores** [pseud: La Pasionaria] (1895–). Spanish Communist and politician. Born in Gallarta, Vizcaya, the daughter of a Basque miner, she worked as a servant before joining the Partido Socialista in 1917 and writing for a worker's newspaper under the pseudonym La Pasionaria ('the passion flower'). She took part in the formation of the first Communist groups in Spain and joined the Party in 1920, becoming leader of her local branch. Her husband Julian Ruiz, a miner, was also an active Party member. (They had six children.) In 1930 she became a member of the Cortes, and of the Political Committee of the Party in 1932. She continued to work on the newspaper *El Mundo Obrero* and founded a women's group, Agrupación de Mujeres Antifacistas, in 1934.

In 1936 she was elected to Parliament, and was released from a current spell of imprisonment. She helped to establish the Popular Front Government and proved a brilliant and moving orator. After the outbreak of the Civil War she was one of the most inspiring of the Loyalist leaders, proclaiming '*no pasaran!*' ('they shall not pass!'). In 1939, after Franco won power, she left Spain and remained in exile in the USSR, where she was Secretary-General of the Spanish Communist Party from 1942 to 1960 and President from 1960. In May 1977, after Franco's death, she returned to Spain, to a tumultuous welcome, and in June, aged 81, she was re-elected to Parliament in the first elections for 40 years. She was honorary Vice-President of the International Democratic Federation of Women and has received many awards, including the Lenin Peace Prize.

D. Ibarruri: *They shall not pass: the autobiography of La Pasionaria* (1967)
——— : *Pasionaria: Memorias* (1985)

**Ichikawa, Fusaye** (1893–1981). Japanese feminist and politician. She began her career as a teacher in a country village, and later jobs included that of stockbroker's clerk, journalist and labour organizer. In 1918 she was a co-founder of the New Women's Association, which asserted the right of women to take part in political life, at a time when they were forbidden to attend meetings, and in the 1920s she directed a Women's Committee for the International Labour Organization. During the 1930s she campaigned against totalitarianism and women's issues until, after the Japanese surrender, she was elected head of the New Japan Women's League, which fought first for suffrage and then for the rights of women voters.

During the 1950s she led campaigns against regulated prostitution, and in 1952 she was elected to the Upper House of Councillors in the Japanese Diet. She remained a member of Parliament for 18 years, and after a three-year absence was returned again in 1974 with massive support from women's and radical groups.

**Ichiyo, Higuchi** (1872–96) [pseud. of Higuchi Natsuko]. Japanese novelist. Higuchi Ichiyo was born in Tokyo. After the death of her father when she was 15 her mother was forced to live in the cheap down-town area of the city, where the family ran a paper shop. Ichiyo had little time to pursue her desired career as a writer, held back by poverty and ill health, yet she succeeded during her brief life in creating some of the most acclaimed works of her generation. In the year before her death she published over twenty short stories, such as *Takekurabe* ('Growing up'), *Nigorie*, *Wakareaichi* and *Jusanya* ('The thirteenth night'), and was particularly known for her portrayal of the emotions of women and children. She died from tuberculosis at the age of 24 but remains a landmark in Japanese literary history, the only woman represented in the Museum of Contemporary Literature in Yokohama.

R.L. Danby: *In The Shade of Spring Leaves* (1981)

**'Iffat** (1910–) Saudi Arabian queen. Although born and brought up in Istanbul, she came from the family of Sa'ud, rulers in central Arabia. Her grandfather had gone to Istanbul as a prisoner of the Ottoman Empire and her father returned to Riyadh as adviser to the King during World War I, although he married a Turkish wife. In 1931 his cousin the Crown Prince Faisal visited 'Iffat and her mother in Turkey, and took them back to Riyadh. He married 'Iffat, and they lived much of the time in Mecca and at Jidda on the Red Sea. They attempted to modernize the ancient state, and were especially concerned with education. Their own nine children were educated in England and Switzerland.

In 1942 'Iffat started a government boys' school, but was unable to open one for girls until 1956. Dar al Hanam ('the House of Affection') had expanded from 15 orphans to 1200 pupils by 1979, and adult education centres and an Institute of Management and Administration for Women are planned. In 1967 'Iffat also started a girls' College of Education for teacher training, and women are now admitted to universities. Queen Sita, the wife of Khalid who succeeded

Faisal in 1975, is also concerned to improve the condition of women.

**Ikasia**. *See* KASIA.

**Inchbald** [née Simpson], **Elizabeth** (1753–1821). English actress and writer. Born in Bury St Edmunds, the daughter of a farmer, she ran away to join her brother George on the stage. In 1772 she married Joseph Inchbald, a painter and actor. She played with him in the provinces and in London, and became a popular figure although her acting was marred by a speech defect. She became a close friend of Tate Wilkinson, Dorothy Jordan and SARAH SIDDONS.

After her husband's death in 1779 Elizabeth did not remarry, despite many offers, allegedly including one from William Godwin after the death of MARY WOLLSTONECRAFT. In 1789 she retired from acting to write. One of the earliest women playwrights, she produced successful comedies, sentimental and moralizing, based on French and German models. They include *I'll tell you What* (1785), *Lovers' Vows* (1798) and *To Marry or Not to Marry* (1805). She was also a journalist, contributing to the *Edinburgh Review*; a novelist, author of *A simple Story* (1791) and *Nature in Art* (1796); and the Editor of *The British Theatre* (1806–9), a 25-volume collection of earlier dramas. Contemporary memoirs present her as a strong, witty, affectionate woman of great integrity and of liberal political and economic views. She was also thought to be a great beauty, a combination of 'a milkmaid and a Duchess'.

R. Manwell: *Elizabeth Inchbald* (1988)

**Inglis, Elsie (Maude)** (1864–1917). British doctor. Born on a Himalayan hill station while her Scots father was in the Indian civil service, Elsie eventually followed her seven siblings to England for her education. She attended the Edinburgh School of Medicine for Women, founded and run by SOPHIA JEX-BLAKE, but found the organization high-handed and defected to Glasgow where, with her father's support, she promoted a rival Medical College for Women, and won the right to study surgery with men.

In 1892 she passed the Scottish Triple Qualification and in 1899 gained her MD from Edinburgh. With Jessie MacGregor, she founded the only maternity centre run by women in Scotland, which became the Elsie Inglis Hospital. She gained experience visiting clinics in Germany, Vienna, New York, Chicago and the Mayo Clinic in Minnesota. Her father also encouraged her suffragist views, and she lectured throughout Scotland; she was Honorary Secretary of the Federated Women's Suffrage Societies of Scotland from 1906 to 1914.

In 1914 at the outbreak of World War I she showed her great organizing capacity by raising £25,000 in one month and founding and leading the Scottish Women's Hospitals (SWH), whose teams were entirely female. The British War Office did not take the organization seriously, but the French sent two SWH units to France, and Elsie Inglis's unit to Serbia. After dealing with a typhus epidemic, she and her team decided to stay when Austrians and Bulgars invaded the camp; from November 1915 they served as prisoners in the military hospitals at Krusevac caring for Serbian and Austrian wounded. Sent back to England in February 1916, she soon organized the return of her team via an indirect sea route in order to care for the Serbs, who were now part of the Russian army, since the Bolshevik Revolution. She sent two members of her unit to the British Foreign Office with a memorized report, so that a gap in medical coverage at the Mediterranean Greco-Serbian front could be serviced by an SWH unit. She was worn and ill when sailing back to England in November 1917; she made the effort to come on deck on the last day to say goodbye to her Serbian staff, and was able to walk from the ship when it docked in Newcastle but she died the next day, 26 November.

Elsie Inglis exercized to the full her 'two passions' of 'suffrage and surgery', and her name is remembered through the Elsie Inglis Unit of the Scottish Women's Hospitals, a children's home in Yugoslavia and a wing of the Royal Infirmary of Edinburgh.

F. Balfour: *Dr Elsie Inglis* (1918)

M. Lawrence: *Shadow of Swords: a Biography of Elsie Inglis* (1971)

**Iragaray, Luce** (1939–). French feminist psychoanalyst. A practising psychoanalyst, follower of the reinterpretation of Freud by Lacan, and of the theories of Derrida, she has been very influential in feminist theory in Europe. Her best known works have been: *Le Langage des déments* (1973); *Speculum de l'autre femme* (1974), which attempts to 'psychoanalyse philosophical and psychoanalytic texts, working backwards from Freud to Plato'; the essays *Ce sexe qui n'en est pas un* (1977); *Et l'une ne bouge pas sans l'autre* (1979); and *Amante marine* (1980). She is concerned with the repression of the female libido, 'la jouissance feminine', through the acceptance of identity defined by 'single' male linguistic structures as opposed to structures which would reflect the hiddenness and duality ('the two lips') of female sexuality.

**Irene of Athens** (*fl* 8th century). Byzantine empress, the wife of Leo IV. She was the first women to rule the Empire alone, and was thus addressed as *Basileus* ('King'). She had a personality of great force and ambition: not satisfied with her role as co-ruler and Regent during the adolescence of her feeble son, Constantine VI, she eventually had him blinded, and ruled alone autocratically for five years (797–802). Her reign was a period of religious unrest, inherited from the previous Emperor. The clergy and the people were split into two factions: those who were against any presentation and veneration of holy images (iconoclasts), and those who favoured the use of images in churches and for private worship (iconodules); the latter group were persecuted because of the current official policies. In 787 Irene summoned the Seventh Ecumenical Council (of Nicaea), which restored the practice of venerating icons officially, thus bringing peace and stability to a divided Empire.

Irene was less successful in managing the economics of the Empire. Costly military expeditions and her support for free trade weakened the imperial treasury and eventually brought about the rebellion of her ministers. She was deposed in 802 and died, in exile, the following year.

**Isaacs** [née Fairhurst], **Susan (Brierley)** (1885–1948). English child psychologist. She graduated from Manchester University in 1912, worked as a research fellow in

*Elizabeth Inchbald*

*Gwen John*

*Helen Keller*

*Alexandra Kollontai*

Cambridge, and lectured in Manchester and London. She ran an experimental progressive school, Malting House School, Cambridge, from 1924 to 1927, during which time she was secretary of the British Psychological Society Committee of Research in Education. In 1933 Susan was appointed to take charge of the Department of Child Development at the London Institute of Education, and this she made one of three main centres of child psychology. She followed MELANIE KLEIN's theories and criticized Piaget's dating of developmental stages. She remained there until 1943, when she became a member of the Training Committee and of the Board of the London Institute of Psychoanalysis. She was assistant editor of the *British Journal of Psychology* from 1921 and on the editorial boards of the *British Journal of Educational Psychology* (1931–48) and *Medical Psychology* (1936–48).

Although a progressive educator with an emphasis on spontaneity, her books *Intellectual Growth of Young Children* (1930) and *Social Development of the Young* (1933) criticized exaggerated notions of freedom; a child needed 'a settled framework of control and routine, and definite help along personal paths . . .'. She wrote 14 books in all, the later ones largely about the effect of war and of family breakup, such as *The Family in A World at War* (1942) and *Troubles of Children and Parents* (1948).

**Isabella I** of Castile (1451–1504). Queen of Spain. She was the daughter of Juan II of Castile and Isabella of Portugal. Her father died when she was three and she was brought up by her mother, but taken to the court of her half-brother Enrique IV when she was 13. She became the focus of opposition in the corrupt court, but managed to avoid conspiracy and was eventually recognized as heir to the throne. The subject of many diplomatic marriage proposals, she insisted on her own choice and without Enrique's formal agreement married Ferdinand of Aragon in 1469, so that she and her husband were joint rulers of the whole of Spain. This led to disagreements about the succession, but in 1474, on Enrique's death, she rapidly arranged to be crowned Queen instead of Juana, his illegitimate daughter and final

choice as heir. The King of Portugal invaded to support Juana but was finally defeated in 1479, the same year in which her husband succeeded to the throne of Aragon as Ferdinand II.

They each governed independently, and Isabella embarked on a programme of reform, reducing the power of the rebellious nobles and reviving medieval laws which allowed her to take over their land, restoring the currency, and codifying the law. At court she encouraged scholarship, founding a new palace school, and patronized musicians and artists from both Flanders and Spain. She also, after much prevarication, supported Columbus on his voyages of exploration.

One of the most controversial aspects of her reign was her religious policy. Intensely pious, she allowed the Inquisition to be established in Andalusia in 1480; this led eventually to the expulsion of over 170,000 Jews, an inhumane act which deprived Spain of valuable skills in commerce, learning and art. She also united with Ferdinand in the wars to conquer the Kingdom of Granada, which had been under Muslim rule for centuries. After ten years of campaigning, in which she herself took part, always travelling with her five children, Granada fell in 1492. But despite her respect for the Roman Catholic faith she herself insisted on filling the key bishoprics in the Spanish Church. Having virtually achieved the unification of Spain, she eventually left the throne of Castile to her daughter Joan, since her eldest son Juan and daughter Isabella died before her.

**Isabella, Leonarda** (1620–1700 or later). Italian composer. She was born in Novara, where she entered the convent of S Ursula in 1636. The *maestro di cappella* of Novara Cathedral was Gasparo Casati, whose *Terzo libro de sacri concenti* (1640) includes two of Isabella's compositions. By the end of her remarkably long life she had published 20 of her own collections, containing over 200 works: these are mostly solo motets, many of them settings of her own texts, though she also wrote masses, psalms and other sacred pieces, several with instrumental accompaniment. After 50 years at the convent she became mother superior (1686) and then provincial mother superior (1693). Her last collection, comprising 14 motets, was published in 1700.

# J

**Jaburkova, Jozka** (*d* 1944). Czechoslovak feminist and patriot. A successful journalist, she edited a women's magazine *Rezsevacka* ('The Disseminator'), and was a leader of the women's progressive movement and the pacifist group. She wrote three novels about working women and was also a children's author. A member of Prague City Council, she joined the Communist Party and during the 1930s campaigned for employment for women, better wages, nurseries and schools. In the early days of the German occupation she was sent to Ravensbrück, where she organized an international resistance movement before her death. After World War II she was acclaimed as a national heroine; many schools bear her name and a statue was erected to her memory in Prague in 1965.

**Jackson, Glenda** (1936–). British actress. The eldest of four daughters, her father a bricklayer, her mother a home help, Glenda was born in Birkenhead. In 1939 the family moved to Hoylake, Cheshire, and she was educated at West Kirby Grammar School for Girls. In 1951, aged 15, she was inspired by seeing Donald Wolfit as Shylock at Stratford, and when she left school the next year, to work at Boots the chemist, she took elocution and dance lessons and joined an amateur theatre group, winning a scholarship to RADA in 1954. During her first professional season at Worthing in 1957 she met and married actor Roy Hogden. They have one son, and were divorced in 1976. After intermittent parts in repertory and an appearance in the film *This Sporting Life* (1963) she joined the Royal Shakespeare Company in 1964, making a stunning debut as Charlotte Corday in Peter Brook's production of Weiss's *Marat Sade*, which was taken to Broadway in 1965. She also played Ophelia to David Warner's

Hamlet (1965). Her reputation grew in the theatre with performances such as Masha in *Three Sisters* at the Royal Court (1967) and she then moved into films, where she is one of only eight actresses to win two academy awards, for Gudrun in *Women in Love* (1971) and for the comedy *A Touch of Class* (1974). She continued to play in the theatre, with remarkable performances in Edward Bond's adaptation of *The White Devil* (1976) and as Hedda Gabler, Phaedra, and Cleopatra. In 1978 she was awarded the CBE. Over the years she also won British hearts with television appearances, ranging from Elizabeth I to the zany comedy of the Morecombe and Wise show.

In 1983 Glenda Jackson produced plays for the new United British Artists, of which she is a director, and helped to form the Women's Playhouse Trust. A committed socialist and member of the Labour Party since the age of 16, she was asked to contest the labour seat of Bridgend in 1983, but declined. In 1984 she lectured at Oxford and Pennsylvania, before returning to the London stage in plays such as *Strange Interlude* (1984), *Phaedra* (1984–5) and *The House of Bernarda Alba* (1986). She has also continued to make films, notably *The Return of the Soldier* (1982), *Great and Small* (1983), *The Turtle Diary* (1985) and *Business as Usual* (1987). Outspoken, witty, a formidable perfectionist in everything she does, she remains one of the leading actresses of the British stage.

I. Woodward: *A Study in Fire and Ice* (1987)

**Jackson, Helen (Maria Fiske) Hunt** (1830–85). American reformer and writer. She was the daughter of an Amherst professor, and was educated in Ipswich, Massachusetts. In 1852 she married a military engineer, Edward Hunt, but he was killed in 1863 and both her sons died as children. She first published poetry and prose in 1865 and became a prolific reviewer and contributor to journals such as the *Atlantic Monthly*, *The Century* and *Hearth and Home*. During the 1870s she published poetry and three novels including *Mercy Philbrick's Choice* (1876), supposedly based on her life-long friend EMILY DICKINSON. In 1875 she married a banker, William Sharpless Jackson, and settled in Colorado Springs. There she became involved in the campaign for Indian rights, stirred by accounts of the sufferings of the Ponca Indians, and in 1881 she published *A Century of Dishonour*, a weighty history of the Indian wars, which she sent to all members of Congress. A brilliant, impetuous woman, she remained devoted to the Indian cause for the rest of her life.

In 1882, with Albert Kinney, Hunt was appointed special commissioner to investigate the condition of Mission Indians in Colorado, and she wrote a deliberately conscious-raising novel about them, *Ramona* (1884), which has endured as a popular historical romance. She died the following year, and her later poetry, reminiscences and short stories were published in 1886 in *Sonnets and Lyrics*, *Glimpses of Three Coasts* and *Between Whiles*.

R. Odell: *Helen Hunt Jackson* (1939)

**Jackson, Mahalia** (1911–72). American gospel music singer. Born in New Orleans, she was the grand-daughter of a slave, and the daughter of a stevedore who was also a minister in the local Baptist church. She sang in the choir at the age of five, and as she grew older was inspired by the nearby Holiness Church, and the 'profane' blues singers of whom her family disapproved: BESSIE SMITH, MA RAINEY and IDA COX. Several members of Mahalia's family were in vaudeville, but her father would not countenance such a career, and she herself retained an intense piety which prevented her from singing the blues and from performing in clubs and bars. At 16 she went to Chicago where she sang professionally for the choir of the Greater Salem Baptist Church and from 1932 with the Johnson Gospel Singers. She began recording in the mid-1930s but reached the height of her fame ten years later with *Move on up a little*

*higher* (1947), which sold a million copies, and *Let the Power of the Holy Ghost fall on me* (1949). She toured Europe in 1952. After 1954 she began singing with choruses and large orchestras; the film *Jazz on a Summer's Day* includes her singing her gospel songs. She sang at most of the great rallies of the civil rights movement in the 1960s, and after the funeral of Martin Luther King in 1968 moved vast crowds with her performance of *Precious Lord, Take my Hand*. She collapsed while on tour in Munich in 1971 and died the following year.

M. Jackson and E.M. Wylie: *Movin' on up* (1966)

**Jacobi, Mary (Corinna) Putnam** (1842–1906). American doctor. She was born in London, the daughter of the publisher, George Putnam; the family emigrated to New York City when Mary was five. She studied chemistry and pharmacy and graduated from the New York School of Pharmacy in 1863, but was determined to become a doctor; she graduated from the Women's Medical College of Pennsylvania in 1864. To improve her medical experience, which she regarded as inadequate, and to gain a more widely recognized qualification, she went to study in Paris. Between 1866 and 1868 she made repeated attempts to enroll at the all-male Ecole de Médécine, and was finally admitted by ministerial permission.

In 1871 she returned to the USA with her Paris MD to become a faculty member of the struggling Women's Medical College of the New York Infirmary. Here she was Professor of Materia Medica and Therapeutics for 25 years, and was known both for her teaching and clinical abilities in voluntary work in the slums and in private practice. She was cited by Dr William Osler as the most brilliant medical woman in the world.

Mary applied for membership of the Medical Society of the County of New York in 1873 and met its President, Abraham Jacobi. He was twice-widowed, and already well-known as the first recognized paediatrician. They married in the same year, had two children, and much of their work towards social progress was continued together. Out of concern for the quality of medical education received by women, in 1872 Mary founded the Association for the Advancement of the Medical Education of

Women. With ELIZABETH and EMILY BLACKWELL, she was basically opposed to the 'separate but equal' policy in medical schools, and was happy to close the Women's Medical College when Cornell University eventually offered places to women. Mary also organized the first consumers' organization in America, the National Consumers' League, which worked towards the abolition of sweatshops.

She produced nearly 100 medical articles, and among other subjects examined what would now be known as psychosomatic complaints of women; she maintained that boredom can cause breakdowns and that rest can cause menstrual pain in healthy but indolent women. In 1876 she won the Boyleston Prize, sponsored by Harvard University, for *The Question of Rest for Women during Menstruation*. She observed that celibacy increased menstrual pain, and added that celibacy implied social failure; she recommended more practical meaningful experiences for the patient. An address she gave in 1894 became the book *Common Sense applied to Woman Suffrage*, and she also wrote several stories.

Mary was the first woman to be elected to the New York Academy of Medicine (1880), and later became Chairman of its neurology section. She diagnosed her own brain tumour, the cause of her death.

R. Putnam: *Life and Letters of Mary Putnam Jacobi* (1925)

**Jacobs, Aletta** (1851–1929). Dutch doctor and birth control campaigner, The eighth of 11 children of a country doctor with progressive views, as a child she was determined to have a medical career. Educated at home and at the local school, followed by a brief and unhappy spell at a finishing school, she found the university medical schools barred to her, but managed to qualify as an apprentice dispenser. She then wrote to Thorbecke, the Prime Minister of The Netherlands, who replied that if her father consented she could attend the University of Groningen. She studied there from 1874, with a short period in Amsterdam because of ill-health, and was one of the first women to attend Dutch universities, as well as becoming the first qualified woman doctor. In 1879 she met with enormous hostility from men, who advised her to confine herself to midwifery, but joined her father's practice and then worked on her own, running a free surgery for the poor, with courses on hygiene and child care. In 1882 she started the world's first birth control clinic in Amsterdam, and persevered with her efforts despite opposition from the medical establishments during the next 30 years.

At the same time she was involved in many other campaigns to improve the position of women and of society in general, including shorter working hours, protective legislation about safety at work, education about venereal disease, the abolition of regulated prostitution, the extension of sexual knowledge and counselling, penal reform and reform of the marriage laws. She married the reforming journalist and politician Carel Victor Gerritsen in 1892, having tried for several years to keep up a 'free union', since they both felt the current marriage laws were humiliating to women. Their only child died aged one day, and in 1905 Carel died, to Aletta's enduring grief.

She was an active suffragist from her student days, and virtually alone during the 1880s, when her attempt in 1883 to have her name entered on the voting list simply moved the government to add 'male' to the voting regulations. In 1894 she started the Association for Women's Suffrage, whose membership grew to 6500 by 1909 and 14,000 by 1913. She was also an initiator of the international suffrage movement in Washington, DC (1902), and in Berlin (1904). A hard-working committee member, able to keep peace between the different personalities and adored by the younger generation, in 1903 she became President of the Dutch Association. In 1911 she toured the world with CARRIE CATT and during World War I she led the Peace Movement with JANE ADDAMS. After suffrage was achieved in The Netherlands in 1919, she worked for the International Alliance of Women and was particularly concerned about the position of women in Asia.

**Jacquet de la Guerre, Elisabeth-Claude** (c1666–1729). French composer and harpsichordist. The daughter of an organist and harpsichord maker, she was an extremely talented child, regarded as a prodigy in Paris in 1677 and called 'the marvel of our century'. Louis XIV placed her in the protection of his mistress, Madame DE MONTESPAN, and encouraged her career. She married the organist, Marin de la Guerre, some time before 1684, but after the death of her son, and of her husband in 1704, she remained a professional musician in Paris, winning an international reputation for her technical virtuosity and imaginative improvisations. It is known that she composed harpsichord pieces and ballet music in the 1680s and 1690s, but her first extant work is the opera *Cephale et Procris* (1694). Several later books of music for harpsichord, violin sonatas and biblical cantatas also survive. She was so famous that after her death a commemorative medal was struck in her honour.

E. Borroff: *An Introduction to Elisabeth-Claude Jacquet de la Guerre* (1966)

**Jadwiga** [Hedwig] (1374–1399). Polish queen. The daughter of Louis d'Anjou, King of Hungary and Poland, she was betrothed at the age of four to Duke William of Hapsburg. She succeeded to the Polish crown after the death of her father in 1384, her sister Maria becoming Queen of Hungary. Her early betrothal was broken and after a treaty promising the union of the countries Poland and Lithuania, the conversion of Lithuania to Christianity and the payment of substantial damages to the rejected Austrian duke, she married the Grand Prince of Lithuania, Jogaila [Polish Jagiello] who took the Christian name of Wladyslaw II, in 1386. He was 20 years her senior and together they ruled for nineteen years, until Jadwiga's death in childbirth in 1399.

Her reign saw the start of the famous Jagiellian dynasty and the greatest 200-year epoch of Polish history. She was also an influential patron of learning and the arts, especially church music, and re-established the University of Kraków.

C. Kellog: *Jadwiga: Poland's Great Queen* (1932)

**Jakubowska, Wanda** (1907–). Polish film producer and director. She was a student of fine art in Warsaw, and went on to co-found the radical Society of the Devotees of the Artistic Film (START) (1929–30). Before World War II she made documentary films, and in 1948 she made *The last Stop*, a film

about her experiences in Auschwitz and Ravensbrück during the war. In 1955 she was made Artistic Director of START, and she became an important presence in the growing Polish film industry. Her own films include *Soldier of Victory* (1953) and *It happened Yesterday* (1960).

**Jameson** [née Murphy], **Anna (Brownell)** (1794–1860). Irish author. She was born in Dublin, the eldest of five daughters of an Irish miniaturist. In 1798 the family moved to Cumberland, and then to London, and after receiving a mediocre education Anna became governess to the Marquis of Winchester, at the age of 16. Her first engagement to Robert Jameson was broken in 1821, but after a spell as a governess in Italy she married him in 1825; the marriage was unhappy from the start. Her fictionalized novel cum journal, *The Diary of an Ennuyée* (1826) was a great success, and started her on her writing career; among her most successful works were *Characteristics of Women* (1832), essays on the women in Shakespeare's plays, and *Sacred and Legendary Art* (in four volumes, 1848–60).

In 1829 and 1833, Robert Jameson had posts abroad, and after 1836 they separated; Anna's writing then supported her mother, sisters and niece. Her wide circle of friends included FANNY KEMBLE, ELIZABETH BARRETT BROWNING, JANE WELSH CARLYLE, BARBARA BODICHON and, especially, Lady NOEL BYRON. In 1855 and 1856 she lectured on the work of the Sisters of Charity and on the role of women as reformers and educators, a topic she raised again at the Social Science Association Congress in 1859.

C. Thomas: *Love and Work Enough: the Life of Anna Jameson* (1967)

**Jameson, (Margaret) Storm** (1891–1983). British writer. Storm Jameson was born into an old seafaring family in Whitby, Yorkshire. Educated privately, then for a year in the Municipal School, Scarborough, she won a County Scholarship to Leeds University and in 1912 gained a research scholarship to London University, eventually obtaining an MA for her work on modern drama in Europe. She went back to Leeds and had one son by her first husband, but returned to London in 1919, working first as an advertising copywriter, then editing the *New Commonwealth* magazine, and finally representing Knopf publishers in 1923–5 and managing their British firm until 1928 with Guy Chapman (whom she married in 1925 and who later became Professor of Modern History at Leeds).

Her first novel, *The Pot Boils*, was published in 1919 and she said that her early books were 'written in London, largely while pushing prams'. Over the next 60 years she wrote 44 more novels: well-known works include *The Clash* (1922), the three novellas *Women against Men* (1933–7) and the trilogy *Company Parade* (1934), *Love in Winter* (1935) and *None Turn Back* (1936). She was the first woman president of the British section of International PEN, 1939–45, and worked unceasingly for refugee writers. She continued to write after the war and travelled widely with her husband until his death in 1972. For the later years of her life she lived in Cambridge.

**Jamison, Judith** (1943– ). American dancer. She was born in Philadelphia, and studied at the Judimar School there, but her first real chance came when her teacher Agnes de Mille gave her the role of Mary Seaton in *The Four Marys* in 1964. The following year she joined the black troupe, the Alvin Ailey American Dance Theatre, and she has toured the USA and Europe with them, remaining their soloist until 1980, although she also worked with the Harkness Ballet (1966–7). She attended the First World Festival of Negro Arts in Dakar, Senegal, and in 1972 was the first woman, the first dancer and the first black artist to be elected to the Board of the National Endowment for the Arts. In 1981 she starred in the Broadway show *Sophisticated Ladies* and the following year received awards from New York City and Harvard University. She is now with the Maurice Hines Dance School. She is particularly admired for her statuesque presence and her passionate intensity. She is married to a Puerto-Rican dancer, Miguel Godreau.

**Janauschek, Francesca (Romana Maddalena)** (1830–1904). Czech actress. Two years after making her debut in Prague (1846) she became the leading lady at the Frankfurt Stadttheater. After some years there she moved to Dresden. She toured Europe and the USA and in 1873 played a number of Shakespearean and other roles in English. One of the last of the great tragic actresses on the grand international scale, she was renowned for her powerful interpretations of parts like Iphigenia, Mary Stuart and Lady Macbeth. She spent her later years in USA, where she died four years after a stroke which paralysed her.

**Jebb, Eglantyne** (1876–1928). English philanthropist. Born in Ellesmere, Shropshire, into an affluent family she was educated at home before going to Lady Margaret Hall, Oxford, in 1895. She graduated in 1898 and trained as a teacher, but after teaching for a year in Marlborough, Wiltshire, ill-health forced her to return to live with her mother in Cambridge. Here she plunged into social work, producing a register of town charities. She also travelled, especially to Italy, and wrote poetry. After World War I she worked in Macedonia and became an organizer of relief for the Balkan countries. Her chief project was to obtain aid for the four or five million children left destitute in Europe. Her first Fight the Famine Council became the Save the Children Fund, founded in 1919 against great hostility. The fund expanded rapidly, since she was a forceful publicist, and she raised enormous sums. Direct aid was administered as well as the provision of hospitals, homes and schools. Jebb's next victory was the adoption by the UN of her Children's Charter, at the Declaration of Geneva in 1924. The following year she joined the UN Council for the Protection of Children. She remained based in Geneva for the last three years of her life and died there, aged only 52, apparently exhausted and ill from the physical and emotional strain of her work.

F.M. Wilson: *Eglantyne Jebb, Rebel Daughter of a Country House* (1967)

**Jekyll, Gertrude** (1843–1932). English horticulturalist. Born into a wealthy family, she had little formal education, but showed a versatile artistic talent, studying painting and working with silver, woodcarving and embroidery. She travelled widely and moved in high society, and her decorative schemes included one for the house of the Duke of Westminster. In her late thirties her eyesight began to fail and she turned from detailed work to gardening. She met the 20-year-old architect Edward Lutyens in 1889; they became close friends and she designed many of the gardens for his houses, combining bold planning with blends of colour influenced by the French Impressionist painters. She was also inspired by the English cottage gardens with their 'simple and tender charm', using many native plants, especially scented but not flamboyant flowers such as honeysuckle, pinks and mignonette. She was responsible for many new trends, such as 'wild' gardens, trailing climbers through old trees, silver and white borders, herb gardens and above all for replacing the standard 'bedding out' of formal Victorian gardens by varied herbaceous borders. Her ideas were expressed not only in her gardens but also in a series of popular books.

B. Massington: *Miss Jekyll: Portrait of a Great Gardener* (1966)


**Jesenská, Miléna** (1890–1944). Czech journalist and humanist. Jesenská was the daughter of a renowned Czech professor and novelist. A rebellious, brilliant girl, defiant of all conventions, she horrified her father by her scandalous behaviour (which allegedly included stealing gold from him to give to her lovers) and he had her interned in a mental clinic near Prague. She was released after 18 months and married Ernst Polak, a German-speaking Jewish writer, with whom she moved to Vienna where Polak was a member of the neo-positivist Vienna circle. She began working as a correspondent for Czech papers, and, being interested in Kafka's works, in March 1920 wrote to him asking if she might translate them. This grew into a regular correspondence, which deepened into love. Kafka described her as 'a living fire – extremely tender, courageous, bright'. She refused to leave her husband, despite marital unhappiness, and spent only a few days with Kafka (four days in Vienna and later an unsatisfactory weekend) but she is generally accepted as the model for Frieda in *The Castle*. Kafka was already severely ill with tuberculosis and gave her his diaries when she visited him in hospital in Prague in 1921, and her obituary of him was the only one in the Czech papers to recognize his

stature. His *Briefe an Miléna* were published in 1952

Miléna pursued a distinguished career as a journalist. Briefly a member of the Communist Party, she was later known for her defiant stand against Nazism, and was sent to Ravensbrück in 1942 for putting on a Yellow Star, although she herself was not a Jew. Margaret Buber Neumann, her fellow prisoner there until Miléna's death (after a kidney operation in 1944) described her as humane, sane and brave, saying 'It was worth being sent to Ravensbrück in order to meet Miléna.'


**Jewett, Sarah Orne** (1849–1909). American novelist. Born in South Berwick, Maine, and educated locally, she accompanied her father, a doctor, on his visits to the rural communities along the coast, and at 19 published her first story of Maine life in the *Atlantic Monthly*. The series of sketches which followed were collected in *Deephaven* (1871) and were an immediate success. Her life was uneventful, except for her deep relationship with her friend Annie Fields, a prominent figure in Boston literary society, with whom she travelled to the West Indies and to Europe. Her books continued to describe New England in a romantic, nostalgic style, often incorporating memories of life before the Civil War. They include *A Country Doctor* (1884), *A Marsh Island* (1885), *A White Heron* (1886), and a series of precise, evocative sketches, *The Country of the Pointed Firs* (1896). She also wrote *The Life of Nancy* (1895), and a historical novel, *The Tory Lover* (1901). Her *Letters* were collected by Annie Fields in 1911 and her stories were edited by WILLA CATHER in 1925.

R. Camay: *Sarah Orne Jewett* (1962)


**Jewsbury, Geraldine (Endsor)** (1812–80). English novelist. She grew up in Measham, Derbyshire, where her father was a businessman. After her mother's death she was educated by her elder sister Maria (1800–33), who was also a talented writer (*Three Histories*, 1829). Geraldine remained at home after Maria married in 1932 as housekeeper to her father, then, after his death in 1840, to her brother. During this time she wrote three novels, *Zoe* (1845), *The Half-Sisters* (1848) and *Marian Withers* (1851), her best work being her realistic descriptions of working-class life. After her brother married in 1853 she moved to London to be near her friend JANE WELSH CARLYLE; there she contributed to literary periodicals and wrote further novels, such as *Constance Herbert* (1855), *The Sorrows of Gentility* (1856), and *Right or Wrong* (1859). She moved to Sevenoaks in 1866.

S. Howe: *Geraldine Jewsbury* (1935)

**Jex-Blake, Sophia** (1840–1912). English doctor. After a privileged upbringing by high-principled parents, Sophia progressed from private education to holding a tutorship in mathematics at Queen's College, London. Her father did not allow her to receive 'compensation' for this, so she appreciated being a wage earner at her next teaching job, in Germany. When she was 25 she sailed to Boston to see how teaching was carried out in the USA; her impressions are recorded in *A Visit to some American Schools and Colleges* (1867).

Sophia was not committed to teaching, and in Boston she volunteered at the New England Hospital for Women and Children. She found medicine 'a cause worth fighting for, a way of life and a field of service that should be open to all women'. She was rejected, as a woman, from Harvard Medical School and from others in England, and instead became the first woman to register at the Women's Medical College of New York Infirmary; however, she returned to England on the death of her father. With four other women she gained acceptance at Edinburgh Medical School in 1869, but hostile factions prevented the group from graduating.

In 1874 Sophia founded the London School of Medicine for Women. In 1877 she graduated from the University of Bern, with a thesis on puerperal fever, then passed the examinations of the King's and Queen's College of Physicians: 12 interrupted years of medical study had passed before she gained the right to practise in England.

Sophia's personality was forceful, and a clash of views with ELIZABETH GARRETT ANDERSON caused her to leave the London School and return to Edinburgh in 1878, where she opened a dispensary which in 1886 became the Edinburgh Hospital for Women and Children. She was the first woman doctor in Scotland. Two years later

she opened her own medical school for women in Edinburgh, and a great ambition was achieved when the Edinburgh Medical School, though her influence, admitted women in 1894. Her school closed because no longer needed, and in 1899 she retired to the south of England.

M. Todd: *Sophia Jex-Blake* (1918)

**Jezebel** (*c*9th century BC). Israeli queen. According to the Old Testament Jezebel was the daughter of the Phoenician Ethbaal, King of Sidon, and married Ahab, heir to the Kingdom of Israel. Strong-willed and dominating, she encouraged the worship of the Phoenician gods Melkaart (Baal) and Ashtaroth (goddess of fertility). She established a large priesthood, endorsing shrines and temples, and eliminated Israelite priests who opposed her. The leader of the priests' resistance was Elijah, who defeated her followers in a battle on Mount Carmel, escaping before Jezebel could take her revenge. Their next confrontation was over Jezebel's command for the false arrest and stoning of Naboth, whose vineyard (next to the royal palace) Ahab had desired. Eventually she was assassinated by the army commander Jehu. She met her death with proud defiance, ordering her servants to hurl her from the window rather than be captured. Allegedly only her skull was found, and Elijah's curse that she would be eaten by dogs, was apparently fulfilled.

**Jhabvala, Ruth Prawer** (1927–). Indian writer. Ruth Prawer was born in Cologne, Germany, of Polish parents who emigrated to England in 1939. She was educated at Chiswick High School and Queen Mary College, University of London, graduating with an MA in English Literature. In 1951 she married a visiting Indian architect, Cyrus Jhabvala, and returned with him to live in India: they have three daughters. An acute observer of her adopted country, she published her first novel, *To Whom She Will* (as 'Amrita'), in 1955. Among her other books are *The Nature of Passion* (1956), *A Backward Place* (1965), *An Experience of India* (1971), *Heat and Dust* (1975), *In Search of Love and Beauty* (1983) and *Out of India: Selected Stories* (1986).

In 1963 she began her association with producer Ismail Ivory and director James Merchant, with an adaptation of her 1960 novel *The Householder* and the screenplay for the famous *Shakespeare Wallah* (1965), an account of an old-fashioned English theatre troupe travelling in India. She has worked with Merchant Ivory on over 13 productions for cinema and television, including *The Europeans* (1979), *Quartet* (1981), *Heat and Dust* (1982), *The Bostonians* (1984) and the award-winning *A Room With A View* (1986). Her writing for the screen, like her fiction about India, is rich and subtle, often exploring misunderstandings and clashes of culture. She now divides her time between India and New York.

**Jiang Qing** [Chiang Ch'ing] (1914–). Chinese political figure. She was born in Shandong Province, China. She had some drama training in her teens and later went to Qingdao University where she studied literature and first came in contact with left-wing ideas. She acted in films and played stage roles, such as Nora in Ibsen's *A Doll's House*, in Shanghai in the mid-1930s. In 1936 she left Shanghai for Yenan, the headquarters of the Chinese Communist Party (CCP). There she began formal study of Marxist-Leninist theory, received some military training and met the Communist leader Mao Zedong. Mao, 20 years her senior, married Jiang Qing (his third wife) allegedly on the condition of his fellow party leaders that she would not be involved with politics. Either because of this embargo, or because of ill-health, Jiang Qing rarely appeared in public during the first dozen years of the People's Republic.

In the 1960s she took up an interest in art and literature, attacking feudal and bourgeois influences and encouraging the creation of new works with proletarian and revolutionary themes, such as *The Red Detachment of Women*. In 1966 she was appointed Cultural Adviser to the People's Liberation Army, and became increasingly involved in the politics of the Cultural Revolution, later becoming one of its major leaders. In 1969 she was elected to the Politburo of the CCP, in recognition of the power she now wielded both in her own right and as the apparent spokeswoman for the aging Mao Zedong. In October 1976, ten days after Mao's death, she was arrested (with three other leaders) and from that time reviled as the leader of the 'Gang of Four'.

She was finally brought to trial in December 1980, charged with subverting the government and with framing, torturing and gaoling many innocent people. She was given a death sentence, suspended for two years, in 1981, commuted to life imprisonment in 1983.
R. Witke: *Comrade Chiang Ch'ing* (1977)

**Jinnah, Fātima** (1893–1967). Pakistani political figure. Born in Karachi, after the death of her father, when she was eight, she went to live in Bombay with her brother, Ali Jinnah, who was 18 years her senior. She attended a mission school, and later studied dentistry. In 1929 she attended a Round Table Conference in London with her brother, and they remained in England for four years. On their return in 1934, she joined the revitalized Muslim League, opposing the conservative orthodox attitudes to women, and beginning her work for the social emancipation and welfare of women. She led the All-India Muslim Women's Committee after its formation in 1938. She toured India, founded branches and student federations, and inspired the establishment of industrial schools, collectives and other organizations. She also founded the Fātima Jinnah Women's Medical College, Lahore.

Fātima rarely left Ali Jinnah's side and became his hostess when he was made the first Governor General of the newly-created Pakistan in 1947. The following year he died and she went into retirement. She emerged in 1954, campaigning for the Muslim League, and by the early 1960s was an outspoken critic of the totalitarian regime in East Pakistan. She was persuaded to stand against Ayub Khan in the presidential elections, as candidate for the combined opposition parties (1964–5). Although the attempt failed, her fierce sincere campaign met with tumultuous receptions everywhere. She became known as Madar-i-Millat ('Mother of the Country'). This support was reflected in the riots which took place during her funeral in Karachi.

**Joan**, Pope (*d* 858). German-English Pope. The story of Pope Joan is thought to be largely apocryphal, although it may have some foundation in fact. According to late mediaeval chronicles, she was a brilliant scholar and notary; her birthplace is sometimes placed in England, Germany or Ireland. She disguised herself as a man and went to Athens, either to follow a Benedictine monk with whom she was in love, or to obtain a degree in philosophy. She was made a cardinal by Pope Leo IV and on his death in 855 she was elected Pope. She was discovered to be a woman when she gave birth to a child, allegedly in the middle of a procession through Rome, and was immediately stoned to death outside the city. Her existence was accepted until 1601 when the whole story was declared to be mythical by Pope Clement VIII. It has been suggested that the story of a woman pope is connected to the power wielded by Theodora the Senatrix and her daughter Marozia, who completely controlled the elections of the popes from 901 to 964, and whose sons and grandsons kept the papacy in the family's possession.

**Joan of Arc** [Jeanne d'Arc; St Joan] (?1412–1431). French heroine. She was born into a peasant family in Domrémy, Lorraine; when she was 13 she had visions of St Michael, St Catherine and St Margaret, who told her that her mission in life was to free France from the English and ensure the coronation of Charles VII. In 1429, áfter three attempts and examination by priests, she persuaded de Baudricourt, Captain of nearby Vaucouleurs, to escort her to Charles at Chinon; the townspeople gave her men's clothing, arms and a horse. Joan is recorded as volatile, brave, sympathetic and overwhelmingly persuasive. Having proved her doctrinal soundness, she was sent as a Captain with the army which raised the siege of Orléans, the key to Charles's continued hold over his territory south of the Loire. He was crowned in her presence at Rheims.

Although accepted as an inspired soldier, Joan could not persuade Charles to continue hostilities against the English and the Burgundians near Paris. His negotiations forced her to remain at court until April 1430, when she took a party to the defence of Compiègne. There she was captured by the Burgundians and ransomed by the English, who made her undergo a lengthy interrogation and trial on charges of witchcraft and fraud. The records show her to have been forthright and humorous under great pressure, and she was eventually convicted only of wearing male clothes, an offence against the Church. She signed an 'abjuration' but recanted two days later, and so could be convicted as a relapsed heretic. She was burned in Rouen marketplace in May 1431.

In 1456 the judgement was reversed by an ecclesiastical commission, and her legend gradually grew: she acquired the name 'd'Arc' in the 16th century, became a popular patriotic heroine in the 19th, and was eventually canonized in 1920.

M. Warner: *Joan of Arc: the Image of Female Heroism* (1981)

**John, Gwen** [Gwendolen] (1876–1939). Welsh artist, the elder sister of the painter Augustus John. She was born in Haverfordwest, Pembrokeshire, but her mother died when she was seven and the family moved to Tenby to escape their puritanical aunts. Here they supposedly learnt by imitating the beach painters, and in 1895 Gwen was allowed to follow Augustus to the Slade School, where she studied figure drawing under Henry Tonks, winning the Nettleship Prize. In 1898 she went to Paris with Gwen Salmond and Ida Nettleship, her future sister-in-law, and studied at Whistler's Académie Carmen. In 1900, in London, she began exhibiting with the New English Art Club, and shared an exhibition with Augustus at the Carfax Gallery, but in 1903 she returned to France for good. In 1906 she became first a model for, then lover of, Auguste Rodin; she was also a close friend of Rainer Maria Rilke. She was influenced by the work of the Post-Impressionists. Her interest in mysticism was strong, and in 1913 she became a Catholic, moving to Meudon the following year, and spending much time with the Dominican Sisters there. Her life focused on religion, and on her deep love for Vera Oumancoff, who lived in the nearby household of the philosopher Jacques Maritain and for whom she produced innumerable drawings and water-colours. As her life became more reclusive, so her paintings became more austere, the colours more restrained and the figures elongated and still.

M. Taubman: *Gwen John* (1985)

**Johnson, Amy** (1903–41). English aviator.

Born in Hull, Amy was the daughter of a fish merchant. She gained a BA in Economics at Sheffield University before taking a badly-paid secretarial job, and soon used her money to take flying lessons. Despite their misgivings, her parents encouraged her to become a commercial pilot, and in order to help cover her expenses she also became a capable mechanic, the first woman to pass the test for the British Ground Engineers' Licence.

In May 1930, with only 50 hours of flying behind her, she persuaded a backer to sponsor her, converted a De Havilland Moth to a monoplane and made the first woman's solo flight from London to Australia, taking 17 days. *The Manchester Guardian* wrote: 'certainly she ran very great risks in passing over savage countries, and risks to a woman are greater than the risks run by a man'. She became a celebrity and was in demand as a lecturer and newspaper writer. She made solo flights from London to India and to Tokyo and back, and was the first woman to fly the Atlantic from east to west.

Amy married Jim Mollison, another top-ranking pilot, in 1932. Soon after, she made the London to Cape Town flight, which cut 10 hours off the 4 day 17 hour record previously held by her husband. They felt that competition might strain their marriage so the next record flights, across the North Atlantic in 1933, and from England to India and England to Cape Town in 1936, were made together. Pressure of publicity told particularly on Jim Mollison, and they divorced in 1938.

When World War II broke out Amy volunteered in the Women's Auxiliary Air Force, ferrying planes and dispatches around England. She disappeared over the Thames Estuary and is thought to have drowned when bad weather forced her down.

C. Babington Smith: *Amy Johnson* (1967)

**Joliot-Curie, Irène** (1897–1956). French physicist. Born in Paris, the elder daughter of Pierre and MARIE CURIE Irène spent much of her childhood with her grandfather, a doctor, and was influenced by his free-thinking socialist ideas. Marie and her Sorbonne colleagues took charge of her science education, and she took the *licence* in physics and mathematics in 1920.

During World War I Irène served as an army nurse, and assisted her mother as a radiographer. In 1918 she became an assistant at the Radium Institute, and worked on her doctoral thesis, a study of the alpha rays from polonium. In 1926 she married Frédéric Joliot; they had two children. They collaborated in work culminating in the discovery of artificial radioactivity, for which they shared the Nobel Prize in Chemistry in 1935. However, her own lesser-known work on the radioelements produced by the irradiation of uranium with neutrons was sufficient to establish her as a great modern scientist.

As an anti-Fascist, Irène served as Under-Secretary of State in the Popular Front Government in 1936. As a feminist she appeared before the Académie des Sciences to argue the right of women to become members. She was appointed Professor at the Sorbonne in 1937. With Frédéric she worked on the basis of nuclear fission, and after World War II they were two of the four scientific commissioners establishing the French atomic energy project, until 1951. In 1946 she was made Director of the Radium Institute, but she also spent much time working for pacifist movements until her death from radiation-induced leukaemia.

**Jones, Mary (Harris)** ['Mother' Jones] (1830–1930). American labour leader. She was born in Cork, Ireland, but her family emigrated in 1835 to Toronto, where her father was a railway worker. After teaching in a Michigan convent, she became a dressmaker in Chicago, but by 1861 was a schoolteacher in Memphis, where she married. Her husband and four children died in a yellow fever epidemic, and after returning to Chicago as a seamstress, and losing all her possessions in the 1871 fire, she became involved in the labour movement, helping in the Pittsburgh railroad strike in 1877, and travelling, organizing and running educational meetings during the 1880s. After 1890 she worked mainly with coal miners, becoming an organizer for United Mine Workers. She went to Virginia in 1900, leading marches of strikers' wives and taking a deputation of children from Pennsylvania to Roosevelt's home in Long Island. After the strike settlement of 1903 she organized workers in Arizona and Colorado, resigning in protest when the Colorado strike was ended by the Union. She had helped to found the Social Democratic Party in 1898, although never a consistent theoretician, and was present at the founding of the International Workers of the World in 1905. Meanwhile she opposed the Women's Movement as a diversion from the class struggle.

By 1911 she had returned to West Virginia, and was sentenced to 20 years' imprisonment for conspiracy to murder, after the 1912 strike; and after her reprieve she moved on to organize Colorado strikes against the Rockefeller mines. She was present in New York in the city-wide strikes of 1915 and 1916, and in the 1919 steel strike in Pittsburgh. In 1921, at the age of 91, she attended the Pan-American Federation of Labor meeting in Mexico. She died in Maryland, but was buried near the graves of strike victims in the coalfields of southern Illinois.

M. Jones (ed. M. Parton): *The Autobiography of Mother Jones* (1925)

**Jong, Erica (Mann)** (1942–). American novelist and poet. She was born and educated in New York City, and after graduating from Barnard College in 1963 and gaining an MA at Columbia in 1965 she became a teacher at the City University, New York. From 1967 to 1969 she taught in Europe, for the Overseas Division of the University of Maryland, and then returned to City University for another year. She had been writing poetry for some time and her first two collections, *Fruits and Vegetables* (1971) and *Half Lives* (1973), won several awards. She has since published more volumes of poetry including, *Loveroot* (1975), *Edge of the Body* (1979) and *Ordinary Miracles* (1983).

In 1973 Erica Jong achieved world-wide fame with her novel *Fear of Flying*, a picaresque account of the sexual adventures and literary ambitions of its heroine, Isadora Wing. With Lisa Alther's *Kinflicks* (1975), Rita Mae Brown's *Rubyfruit Jungle* (1973) and Marge Piercy's *Woman on the Edge of Time* (1976), it embodied the new physical freedoms of American women. Her next novel, *How to Save your own Life* (1975), was also a success, and in 1979 she published

*Fanny*, a parody of an 18th-century novel, about the 'real' Fanny Hill. In *Witches* (1981) she analyses the myth of the witch in sexual terms. Her recent books include *Parachutes and Kisses* (1984) and *Serenissima* (1987).

She divorced her first husband, Allan Jong, in 1975 and married writer Jonathan Fast in 1977.

**Joplin, Janis** (1943–70). American rock singer. She was born and brought up in Port Arthur, Texas, and was first influenced by the great blues singers, including BESSIE SMITH, but in the 1960s began singing with a small country-and-western band. In 1962 she enrolled briefly at the University of Texas, but then went out to the West Coast to join the band Big Brother and the Holding Company. She caused a sensation at the Monterey Festival in 1967 with her raw, powerful and passionate performance, and the album *Cheap Thrills* sold a million copies in 1968. The following year she went solo, performing with different backing groups, and creating an impact with her outrageous behaviour and heavy drinking, as well as with her voice. In 1970 she formed a new group, but after finishing recording an album which bore the title of her own nickname, *Pearl*, she was found dead from an overdose of heroin in a Hollywood hotel room. After her death a collection of her *Greatest Hits* appeared in 1972, the documentary *Janis* in 1974 and the film based on her life, *The Rose*, in 1979.

M. Friedman: *Buried alive* (1975)

**Joyce, Eileen** (1912–). Australian pianist. Born in Zeehan, Tasmania, she was educated at Loreto College, Perth, and studied at the Leipzig Conservatory before moving to London, and making her debut at a Promenade Concert under Sir Henry Wood. Immediately acclaimed for her technical virtuosity, she built up a repertoire of well-known works which won her popularity with a wide audience. During World War II her concerts with the London Philharmonic Orchestra helped to ensure its survival, and over the next 20 years she played with leading orchestras throughout the world, from Australia (1948) to India (1962). She expanded her repertoire to include such composers as John Ireland and Shostakovich and also became a proficient harpsichord performer; she even played sound tracks for some films, including *Brief Encounter*, and appeared in others, including the autobiographical *Wherever she goes*.

**Juana, Iñes de la Cruz** [de Asbaje y Ramirez de Santillana] (1651–95). Mexican poet, playwright, feminist and nun. She was born near Mexico City, and brought up by her maternal grandparents. Although largely self-educated, she had acquired such a reputation for scholarship by the age of 14 that she was invited to court as lady-in-waiting to the viceroy's wife, the Marquesa de Mancera. Two years later she spent three months in a strict Carmelite convent, and in 1669 she entered the Order of St Jerome. Her motivation has puzzled many later scholars, who suggest unhappy love affairs, disgust at court life and unease with her social position, but she claimed it was from total dislike of the idea of marriage and a desire for peace to study.

Between 1669 and 1690 she studied avidly, collecting the largest library in South America, and wrote poetry, plays and prose. Her early poetry is sensuous and perceptive, with sonnets and ballads celebrating a mystic love, but she also wrote comedies, such as *Love, the Greater Labyrinth* (1689), and sacramental plays such as *The Divine Narcissus*, which combined Aztec with Greek and Christian religious symbolism.

In 1690 she became involved in a dispute with the Bishop of Puebla, which provoked her moving *Reply to Sor Filueta* (1691), which is a defence of women's learning and an attack on repression by the Inquisition and oppression by men in society, as well as being an intellectual autobiography. After the ensuing controversy, Juana sold her 4000 books, instruments and other possessions and gave the proceeds to the poor, and re-affirmed her religious vows in her own blood. She died while nursing during a plague epidemic.

**Juhacz, Marie** (1880–1956). German socialist and feminist. Born in a village near Brandenburg, the daughter of a carpenter, she began working in a factory at 14, then went to Berlin as a seamstress. She was active in the suffrage movement and joined the Social Democratic Party, founding the Workers' Welfare Organization and becoming a member of the National Assembly in 1919. She was a member of the Reichstag from 1923 until 1933, when she was forced to leave the country by the Nazi rise to power. She lived in France, Martinique and America before returning to Germany in 1949, and continuing her social and political work with the Welfare Organization.

**Julia**. A powerful female dynasty of two sisters, and two daughters, who held control in the 3rd century AD in Rome. Julia Domna and Julia Maesa were daughters of a Syrian high priest, Bassianius from Emesa.

**(1) Julia Domna** (*d* AD 217). She was the second wife of the Roman Emperor Septimius Severus, who ruled from 293 to 211 AD. She was a patron of learning, and gathered a circle of scholars around her, including Galen and Philostratus. From 200 to 205 her undoubted influence was overshadowed by that of the Prefect Plautianus, but at his fall she regained her power. When Septimius died, her two sons Caracalla and Geta became joint emperors but, despite her efforts to reconcile them, Caracalla murdered his brother in her presence and ruled alone until 217, leaving Julia in virtual control of the Imperial administration. He was murdered in 217 and she allegedly starved herself to death in Antioch.

**(2) Julia Maesa** (*d c* 226). The sister of JULIA DOMNA, she married a Syrian senator Julius Avitus, and had two daughters, Julia Soaemias and JULIA MAMAEA, who became the mothers of the Emperors Elagabaeus and Alexander Severus. During their reigns, (218–22 and 222–35) she wielded great influence over the government.

**(3) Julia Mamaea** (*d* 235). The daughter of JULIA MAESA, she controlled the Empire in the reign of her son, Alexander Severus, who became Emperor at the age of 14, holding power particularly after the death of her mother. She ruled effectively as Regent with a council of senators, but her peaceful policies may have resulted in the Roman defeat in the campaign against Persia in 232. This alienated the army and she and her son were murdered by Roman soldiers in 235.

**Juliana** (1909–). Former Queen of the Netherlands. She was brought up in the

Netherlands, and in 1937 married Prince Bernhard; they had four daughters. She escaped to Canada during the German Occupation, returning to the Netherlands via England in 1944. On her mother WILHEL-MINA'S abdication in 1948 she became first Princess Regent and then Queen. She herself abdicated in 1980, in favour of her daughter BEATRIX.

**Julian of Norwich** (1342–1443). English mystic. Little is known of her life except that she probably lived as an anchoress, outside the walls of St Julian's Church, Norwich. In 1373 Julian suffered a serious illness which was ended by a series of 16 revelations; she received these in a state of ecstasy and together they lasted five hours; one other vision followed the next day. These visions were chiefly concerned with the Passion, the Holy Trinity and the Virgin Mother. Her later contemplations on their spiritual meaning led her to write (or dictate) *XVI Revelations Divine Love* some 20 years after the original experience. The account of the visions is interwoven with reflections on the mysteries of faith, prayer and, especially, the divine love of God. Julian's *revelations* are regarded as one of the most remarkable documents of medieval religious experience.

P. Molinari: *Julian of Norwich* (1958)

# K

**Kael, Pauline** (1919–). American film critic. Born in northern California, she was raised on a farm until this was lost in the Depression and her family moved to San Francisco. At Berkeley, Kael worked her way through college, graduating in Philosophy and English in 1940. As a young woman in San Francisco she wrote notes for local film societies, and reviewed for local radio and for local magazines like *City Lights*. During the 1950s (capturing typical notoriety for her review of *Limelight* as 'Slimelight'), she contributed to *Sight and Sound*, *Partisan Review*, *Film Culture* and *Film Quarterly*. From 1955 she ran the Berkeley Cinema Guild Theatre, with many revivals, and became known for her fine, original film notes. In 1965 her hard-hitting pieces were collected in *I Lost It At the Movies*, a best-seller which took her to the east coast as reviewer for McCalls – a family magazine which sacked her for a harsh review of *The Sound of Music*. Her second book, *Kiss Kiss Bang Bang*, appeared in 1968. She worked briefly on the *New Republic* then moved to *The New Yorker* where her highly personal, forthright, learned reviews made her enormously influential, on critics, audiences and film-makers. At one point she left to become a Hollywood producer, but returned angry and disillusioned to *The New Yorker*. Kael's later criticism, collected in books such as *Going Steady*, *Deeper Into Movies*, *When the Lights Go Down*, *Taking It All In* and *State of the Art* have made her the most outstanding critic in the history of American cinema.

**Kaffka, Margit** (1880–1918). Hungarian writer. Born in Nagykaroly, she became the first great Hungarian woman writer. After her father's death in 1886 she was brought up by nuns in an orphanage, and then became a teacher. She began publishing poems in literary reviews, was a member of the intellectual circle which formed around the journal *Nyugat* after 1908, and was a close friend of the poet Endre Ady, who influenced her aesthetic views.

From 1912 she started writing novels and short stories, which were pioneering works in Hungarian fiction, being impressionistic, episodic narratives which reveal the inner psychology of the protagonists. Her heroines are women who reject their traditional position yet are frustrated in their search for new roles. She herself was an active feminist and pacifist. Her best known works, which remain very popular in modern Hungary are: *Szinek és évek* ('Colours and years') (1912); *Mária évei* ('Mary's years') (1913); *Allomasók* ('Stations') (1914); *Hangyaboly* ('Anthill') (1917); *Kétnyár* ('Two summers') (1916).

Kaffka was married twice, to Bruno Fröhlich in 1904, and to Ervin Bauer in 1914. She died in the great influenza epidemic after World War I.

**Kahlo, Frida** (1910–54). Mexican painter. She was born in Coyoicoán, Mexico City, one of five children of a Mexican mother and a German-Jewish father. Her early ambition was to become a doctor, but while recovering from a road accident (which left her with life-long pain) she began painting and sent her work to Diego Rivera, with whom she had been infatuated since the age of 13. They met, and eventually married in 1929, but it was a stormy relationship, upset by Diego's infidelities, their divorce and re-marriage, and by Frida's obsessive yearning for the child she could not have. All this is recorded in her 'primitive', highly-stylized, brilliantly-coloured paintings, with an unnerving power and honesty. Well-known works include *The Broken Column*, *Portrait of Diego* (1949) and *The Birth of Moses*.

During the 1930s the Riveras spent much time in the USA, to escape political persecution, and lived for a time in San Francisco. The Surrealist painter André Breton promoted her work in 1938, but she did not have a major independent exhibition in her own country until 1953, when she was already extremely ill. After her death Diego donated their house as the Frida Kahlo Museum.

**Kairi, Evanthia** (1797–1866). Greek educationalist and feminist pioneer of the enlightment in Greek thought following the modern liberation of Greece from Turkish rule. Broadly educated under the guidance of her scholarly brother, she soon employed her talents in various intellectual, social, political and national activities for the emancipation of the newly-liberated nation of Greece. To this end she translated into Greek French works concerning education and counselling of young women. For many years she was the Head of a famous girls' school in Kydonies (Asia Minor), where she taught Classics and history.

With the outbreak of the Greek Revolution against the Turks, she appealed to women's organizations in Europe for help. Through her personal contacts and her intellectual influence she created a strong philhellenistic movement in Europe and the USA among women intellectuals. After the Greek Independence she settled in her native island of Andros, where she founded a home to provide a good education for war orphans.

X. Koula: *Evanthia Kairi: a Historical Monograph* (1956)

**Kalthum, (Ibrahim) Um** [Kulthum, Ibrahim Umm] (1908–75). Egyptian singer. Born into a traditional family in a small village on the Nile Delta, she first began singing in religious celebrations. With the guidance of the famous singer Shaykh Abu aj-'lla, she went to Cairo in 1922, where she struggled to gain fame and recognition; her first successful concert was in 1926. She was influenced by the poet Ahmad Rami, and sang more than 250 of his songs. She became famous for her mastery of the microtonal intervals involved in the *maqām* (modes). Most of her concerts were given in the open air, to huge crowds, and lasted for several hours. Her last concert was given in 1973, in Cairo. She was known as 'the mother of Middle-Eastern music', and at her death Cairo Radio broadcast the chanting of the *Koran*, an honour usually reserved for heads of state; many dignitaries from the Arab states were present at her funeral, together with millions of other mourners who knew and loved her music.

**Kalvak, Helen** (1901–84). Canadian Inuit artist. Helen Kalvak lived all her life in the wild Northwestern Territories of Canada. She began to draw in her late sixties, creating over 3000 drawings which convey in vivid detail the life of the Copper Inuit, people of the Canadian arctic, who by the time of Helen's birth numbered only 800. divided into 50 regional bands, subsisting on seal-hunting in the winter, living on the ice, and trapping and hunting the musk-oxen and caribou in summer. Her drawings are also concerned with the spiritual life, legends and ceremonies of the community, and with the linking of human and animal worlds. At the end of her life her work was acclaimed internationally, and she was elected a member of the Royal Canadian Academy of Arts in 1975.

**Kang Keqing** [K'ang K'o-ch'ing] (1912–). Chinese revolutionary fighter and women's leader. Born of peasant stock, she joined the Chinese Communist Party's revolutionary activities in her teens. In 1929 she married General Zhu De [Chu Teh], one of the founders of the Red Army, who was 24 years her senior. She was one of the few women to make the epic Long March (1934–6) when the Red Army had to abandon its base in the South and travel 800 miles to the Northwest. During World War II she worked in the women's movement and also had important political responsibilities in the Red Army's headquarters. After the setting up of the People's Republic in 1949, she was one of the senior leaders of the Chinese women's movement, becoming President of the All-China Women's Federation in 1978. She is also Chair of the National Committee for the Defence of Children, and a member of the Presidium of the sixth National Peoples' Congress (1986).

**Kaplan, Nelly** [pseud.: Belen] (1931–). French script-writer, journalist and film director. Of Russian extraction, she was raised in Buenos Aires. She abandoned university and went to Paris when she was 18; there she worked in film journalism. An invitation to watch Abel Gance shooting began a ten-year collaboration with him, working as his assistant director on three films. She was also closely involved with André Breton and the Surrealist group. She published collections of erotic/Surrealist short stories under her pseudonym, and made several art documentaries, one of which, *Le regard Picasso*, won the Golden Lion award in Venice (1967). She also filmed a tribute to Gance. In 1968 she directed her first feature film, *La fiancée du pirate*, which Picasso compared with the work of Luis Buñuel and described as 'tender and ferocious . . . with insolence raised to a fine art'. Other feature films include *Papa les petits bateaux* (1971), *Néa* (1976), adapted from the Emmanuelle Arsan novel, and *Charles et Lucie* (1979), which became the second most successful foreign film ever released in the USA. Her two films released in England, *La fiancée du pirate/A Very Curious Girl* and *Néa* were sold as soft-core pornography. It has been suggested that this is because her films are too entertaining to be considered 'art cinema' (containing comic-strip situations, bizarre humour, frank eroticism, violence and parodies of Hollywood genres), but too anarchistic and provocative (dealing with prostitution, adolescent sexuality and female immorality) to be considered commercial.

**Karatza, Rallou** (*c*1778–1830). Greek freedom fighter. As a daughter of a Greek prince in Walachia, Romania, she was acquainted with the arts and culture of Europe. Particularly interested in the theatre, both ancient and modern, she was the first Greek woman to form a group, recruiting amateur players from the Greek School in Bucharest. After being initiated into the secret society known as 'Philiki Etaireia' which organized the Greeks to fight against the Turks, Rallou used her theatre for propaganda purposes. The revolutionary plays and ethnic dramas expressing ideas of freedom boosted the national morale of local Greeks and later contributed to the uprising of 1821.

Rallou translated works from the international repertoire, many of which she directed herself. She even provided scholarships for actors to go to Paris to study drama. As a result her theatre was changed from a place of popular entertainment into a centre for didactic performances. After the Independence of Greece (1829) she moved to Athens, where she died.

**Karinska, Barbara** (1886–1983). Russian costume designer. Born in the Ukraine, eldest of ten children of a wealthy businessman, Karinska began by designing costumes for family entertainments. After studying law in Moscow she married, and in 1928 emigrated to Paris where she began embroidering scarves for Liberty, and made costumes for the Comédie Française. In 1932, in Monte Carlo, she met George Balanchin and created the costumes based on Christian Bernard's designs for his *Cotillon* for the Monte Carlo Ballet. Her career took off on her return to Paris, where she worked on designs by Chagall, Matisse and Dali for companies such as the Ballet Russe. In 1938 she went to work in Hollywood, creating costumes for films such as *Kismet* and *Gaslight*, and the historically authentic, hand-dyed costumes for INGRID BERGMAN's *Joan of Arc* (for which she won an Academy Award in 1948). In 1940, she had established her own design business in New York, and in the 1950s provided costumes for stage, opera, and Broadway shows. But her major work, between 1949 and 1977 was her legendary collaboration with Balanchin and the New York City Ballet. Noted for her flamboyance, her daring use of colour, her imaginative choice of materials and her precise attention to detail, she received the Capezio Dance Award in 1961 for outstanding services to dance, the only designer ever to win this award.

**Karsavina, Tamara (Platonovna)** (1885–*c*1955). Russian ballerina. She was born in St Petersburg [now Leningrad], and studied at the Imperial Ballet School there; she graduated into the company as a soloist in 1902 and became a ballerina in 1909. In 1905, with ANNA PAVLOVA, Fokin and others, she challenged the dictatorial Mariinsky management. She took part in all the early Dyagilev seasons and appeared in Paris in 1909 and 1910, joining the company in Monte Carlo in 1911. She was a highly expressive and intelligent dancer, and the supreme interpreter of Fokin's choreography in *Les sylphides* (1908), *The Firebird* (1910), *Carnaval, Petrushka* and *Le spectre de la rose* (all 1911).

In 1915 Karsavina returned to St Petersburg for the birth of her child, and then danced again with the Mariinsky. After divorcing her first husband, Vasily Mukhin, she married the British diplomat Henry Bruce in 1917 and left Russia. In 1919 she rejoined Dyagilev, dancing the Miller's Wife in Massin's *Le tricorne* and starring with Lifar in BRONISLAVA NIJINSKA's *Romeo and Juliet* (1926). She remained in London, becoming Vice-President of the Royal Academy of Dancing, and appearing as guest artist during the Ballet Rambert's opening season in 1930. A much-loved ballet personality, she passed on her knowledge of Mariinsky and Dyagilev interpretations to younger dancers and choreographers such as Frederick Ashton and MARGOT FONTEYN. She is the author of a classic ballet autobiography, *Theatre Street* (1930).

**Kartini,** Raden **Adjeng** (1879–1904). Javanese princess and educator. She was the daughter of the Regent of Djapara in Java and was born on the coastal area of Central Java. Her brothers attended Dutch schools but the girls were forbidden by law (*Adat*) to leave their own homes from the age of 12 to 14 until their marriage. Her brothers sent her books, and she read widely; in 1899, after reading a Dutch feminist magazine, she placed an advertisement asking for a correspondent. Her letters to her pen-friend Stella Zeehandelaar ·vividly portray the society in which she grew up, and her longing for independence, equal education and the right to earn a living. She also wrote to the wives of the Javanese Minister of Education and to prominent members of Parliament, pleading for more opportunities for girls. The Education Minister, Abendanon, encouraged her to start her own school in her house in 1903.

Kartini herself begged to be sent to college in Jakarta, and was at last allowed to go, but was then ordered to return to marry the powerful Regent of Renbang in Central Java. He supported her progressive views and they started another school, but she died shortly after the birth of their son, at the age of 25.

A.L. Symmers, ed.: *Letters of a Javanese Princess* (1921)

**Kasia** [Ikasia] (*fl* 9th century). Byzantine poet and hymnographer. She was the daughter of a nobleman, and took part in a 'bride show' for the Emperor Theophilus; unfortunately, her sharp reply to his caustic jibe about all evil coming from women cost her the throne. She founded a convent where she devoted herself to writing epigrams and composing hymns, many of which are in liturgical use in the Orthodox Church.

Her work reveals her strong character, deep religious feelings, rich emotions and original thought. Krumbacher (a writer on Byzantine literature), who studied her poems, remarked that 'she was a wise but singular woman, who combined a fine sensitiveness and a deep religiousness with an energetic frankness and a slight tendency to feminine slander'.

**Kauffman, Angelica** (1741–1807). Swiss painter. The daughter of a portrait and ecclesiastical painter, she was recognized as having precocious talent, and received her first commission, a portrait of the Bishop of Como, when she was only 11. She was determined not to be limited to the 'femine genres' of portraits and still-lives, but to work on serious historical pictures. With her father she travelled to Florence in 1762 and then to Rome, where she painted a portrait of the art historian Johann Winckelmann. Her interest in his view of neoclassicism is evident in her *Bacchus and Chloë* (1764), and in her later work.

After visits to Naples (1763–4) and Rome, where she was elected to the Accademia di San Luca, she reached Venice in 1765, where the wife of the British Ambassador, Lady Wentworth, persuaded her to come to England. Despite her reputation for vanity and flirtation, and the scandal which attached to her friendships with other artists such as Dance, Fuseli, Ryland and even Reynolds, her London life was one of austerity and hard work. She became famous for her portraits and also for historical and allegorical paintings such as the *Interview of Hector and Andromache* (1769) and *Vortigern and Rowena* (1770). A founder member of the Royal Academy, her work was included in every exhibition there from 1769 and 1782, and she also decorated the Academy's new lecture rooms in Burlington House.

During this time, Angelica Kauffman secretly married in 1767 the adventurer 'Count van Horn', and the revelation of his bigamy led to her public humiliation. In 1781, after his death, she married the decorative painter Antonio Zucchi, and left for Italy. She enjoyed the patronage of European royalty and nobility, eventually establishing her studio in Rome, where she received many honours and was a leading member of society. In 1786 she formed part of the 'Goethe circle' there. She continued working until her death, although her output lessened after Zucchi died in 1795. Kauffman's work has been called 'essentially feminine', but within the conventions she was an original colourist and her graceful compositions were highly influential.

D. Mayer: *Angelica Kauffman, R.A. (1741–1807)* (1972)

**Kautsky, Luise** (1864–1944). Austrian socialist and feminist. Born in Vienna, she became the wife of the Marxist theoretician Karl Kautsky and collaborated with him in his writings. She was active in the socialist movement and was friendly with ROSA LUXEMBURG and CLARA ZETKIN, and from 1910 she was also a leading suffragette. She continued to work for the Communist Party between World War I and World War II. She died in Dachau in 1944.

**Kawakubo, Rei** (1942–). Japanese fashion designer. Kawakubo is the founder of the so-called 'raven fashion'. Born in Tokyo, a graduate of Keio University, Kawakubo briefly worked in Asahikasei Textile Co. before establishing her own brand 'Comme des Garçons' in 1973. Unlike most fashion designers she ignored couture-orientated methods and introduced concepts hitherto alien to fashion design; asymmetry, use of holes, a rug-like look and austere clothes based on monks' garments. Her 1981 Paris collection caused a commotion in the conservative European fashion circle and her designs received both critical acclaim and criticism alike. Her work is seen as the antithesis to traditional fashion and her strik-ing creations, with their original ideas have brought both commercial success and international fame. The uncompromising minimalist attitudes of her own life-style seem to permeate into her design and she is considered to be one of the most influential fashion designers of today.

**Kehajia, Kalliopi** (1839–1905). Greek educationalist and feminist. After training as a teacher in London, she worked as the headmistress of the Hill School for girls in Athens. At the same time she made a great impact in society because of her social and intellectual activities. She was the first person to use open lectures as a means of education, and gave a series of 80 lectures over 2 years on classical literature and on social problems, mainly concerning women. Being a woman of open mind and progressive ideas, Kalliopi worked systematically for the improvement of the social and intellectual status of Greek women.

In 1872 she founded The Society for Promoting Women's Education, an organization which provided educational classes and practical training in crafts, and in 1874 she visited France to study the latest educational systems and to establish contact between Greek women abroad and at home. A year later she was invited to Constantinople [now Istanbul] to organize the Zappeion School for girls; she remained there as Head for 15 years. In 1888 she travelled to the USA, visiting educational institutes, orphanages and women's organizations. Thrilled by her experience in the West, on her return she published a series of newspaper articles about women's achievements and position in the USA, hoping to alert the public to the deprived and inferior position of women in Greek society.

**Kehew, Mary Morton (Kimball)** (1859–1918). American feminist and unionist. She was the daughter of a Boston banker, and her maternal grandfather had been Governor of Massachusetts. Educated privately and in France, Germany and Italy, in 1880 she married a Boston merchant; they had no children. In 1886 she joined the Women's Educational and Industrial Union, became Director in 1890 and was

President from 1892 to 1913, and from 1914 to 1918. She forced the Union into a more active role, expanding the advice and training schemes, but also emphasizing social research and legislation. She worked for the new schools of dressmaking (1895), housekeeping (1897) and salesmanship (1905) to be established; she was also a trustee of Simmons College for Women and a member of numerous local reform bodies and State Commissions.

With Mary Kenney, a former Hull House worker, she founded the Union for Industrial Progress, organizing bookbinders, laundry and tobacco workers and women in the clothing trades between 1896 and 1901. In 1903 she became the first President of the National Women's Trade Union League, with JANE ADDAMS as Vice-President. One of her sharpest moves was the organization of a research team which backed up campaigns for legislation, in areas from loan finances to sanitation, old age pensions to minimum wage, with detailed reports and statistics. Her effectiveness as a campaigner depended not on public appearances, which she avoided, but on establishing a broad base of support from shop-floor workers to society leaders.

**Keller, Helen (Adams)** (1880–1968). American campaigner for the blind. Born in Tuscumbia, Alabama, she became blind and deaf after scarlet fever at the age of 19 months. Her mother and father were convinced of her ability although she behaved like an 'untamed creature', and when she was seven they employed Anne Sullivan, who, with amazing perseverance, taught her a manual alphabet. Helen made rapid progress, learning braille, able to 'listen' by touching the speaker's throat and developing speech. She eventually went to Radcliffe College where she proved an outstanding scholar, with all lectures tapped out in her hand by Sullivan. She typed perfect examination papers, spoke fluent French and German, studied Classics and philosophy, and also learnt to ride and swim. At the age of 23 she published her first book, *The Story of my Life* (1903).

Keller and Sullivan campaigned on behalf of the American Foundation for the Blind, successfully reaching their personal target of $2 million through coast-to-coast tours and lectures. A socialist, and later a Swedenborgian, conscious of the value of each human spirit, determined on equal achievement, Keller resented all forms of condescension to the disabled. Her worst crisis was Sullivan's death in 1936, movingly described in *Helen Keller's Journal* (1938). She maintained an equally close relationship with Polly Thompson, who was her secretary from 1914 to 1960. Her earlier life is also described in *The World I live in* (1909) and *Song of the Stone World* (1910).

**Kelley, Florence** (1859–1932). American reformer and feminist. Born in Philadelphia, the daughter of a congressman, she graduated from Cornell University in 1882. After being refused admission to Pennsylvania University to study law because she was a woman, she studied law and economics at Zürich (1883–5). Here she met many exiled East European radicals, joined the Socialist Party and married Vishnevetzky in 1884. Her translation of Engel's *Condition of the Working Class in England in 1844* was published in 1887.

After some years back in the USA, Kelley left her husband and took her three children to Chicago, where from 1891 to 1899 she worked at the Hull House Settlement. Her projects there resulted in the *Hull House Maps and Papers* (1895), and as the first woman factory inspector for Illinois she pushed an anti-sweatshop bill with an eight-hour clause through the state legislature. In 1895 she also obtained a law degree from Northwestern University.

In 1899 she moved to New York, where she lived in the Henry Street Settlement and became General Secretary of the National Consumers' League, campaigning especially for protective legislation for women and children in her first book *Ethical Gains through Legislation* (1905) and in *Modern Industry* (1913). She continued this work until the late 1920s. In 1910 she was a founder member of the National Association for the Advancement of Coloured People. Although a pacifist, during World War I she worked on the Board of Control of Labor Standards for army clothing. In 1919 she was a delegate to the International Congress of Women for Permanent Peace, at Zürich.

J. Goldmark: *Impatient Crusader* (1953)

**Kelly, Petra (Karin)** (1947–). German politician. One of the best-known leaders of the Green movement in Germany, Petra Kelly was born in Gunzburg, Bavaria. She was educated in Germany but then moved with her family to the United States, where her stepfather John Kelly was an officer in the American Army hospital service. They moved to Columbus, Georgia, in 1960 and from 1966 to 1970 Petra studied politics and international relations at the American University, Washington. As a student she was a volunteer on the electoral campaigns of Senators Hubert Humphrey and Robert Kennedy and was involved in demonstrations against the Vietnam War and American nuclear defence policy. In 1970, after the death of her 10-year-old sister, she founded a group for research into children's cancer.

In 1970 Petra returned to Europe to undertake a year's research into European Integration at the Europa Institute, Amsterdam, and the following year began her career with the EEC in Brussels, where she continued her research on postwar European political movements. Her work for the EEC Economic and Social Committee dealt particularly with environmental protection, health and education. In 1972 she joined the West German Association of Environmental Protection Action Groups and for the next seven years was also a member of the German Social Democratic Party, which she left in 1979 in protest against their policies on nuclear defence, health and women. She then founded the Green Party with several friends, becoming their leading national candidate in the European elections. The extraordinary success of the radical Green movement made her an international figure and she was awarded the Alternative Nobel Prize in 1982 and the American Peace Woman of the Year Award in 1983. In that year she became one of 17 Green members of the West German Parliament. She takes a moderate stand in the current debates within her party. Her books include *Fighting for Hope* (1984) and *Hiroshima* (1985).

**Kemble, Fanny [Frances] (Anne)** (1809–93). English actress, writer and abolitionist.

The daughter of the actor-manager Charles Kemble, and a niece of SARAH SIDDONS, she appeared with outstanding success as Juliet to her father's Mercutio at Covent Garden in 1829; her performance saved her father and his company from bankruptcy. Fanny Kemble was equally at home in tragedy and comedy, and her notable roles included Lady Macbeth, Portia, Beatrice, Constance, Mariana and Queen Katherine. She made her first visit to the USA in 1833. In 1834 she married Pierce Butler, a Georgia planter, whom she divorced in 1849. She had resumed acting after her initial separation from Butler in 1845 and had one season with Macready at the Princess' Theatre in 1848. In the same year she began a series of Shakespearean readings, and between 1849 and 1868, and 1873 and 1878 she lived in the USA. She published several poetical-dramatic writings but is now best remembered for her autobiographical works – flamboyant and indiscreet, she often offended people by her lack of tact but was also greatly admired for her intellect, humour and boundless energy. Her work includes *Poems* (1844), *Plays* (1863), *Journal of a Residence on a Georgian Plantation* (1863), and *Records of Girlhood* (1878), *Records of Later Life* (1882) and *Further Records* (1891).

**Kempe, Margery** (*c*1373–after 1438). English mystical writer. The daughter of the Mayor of Lynn, Norfolk, she married John Kempe, a burgess of the town; they had 14 children. The failure of her attempts at trade (a brewery and a horsemill), together with an attack of 'madness' suffered after the birth of her first child, led her to prayer and penance. The attack of madness was ended by a vision of Christ and in gratitude she and her husband made a pilgrimage to Canterbury. Her fervent denunciation of all pleasure aroused strong opposition and accusations of Lollardy. In 1413 Margery and John took vows of chastity to enable her to live a religious life. She visited many English shrines and holy people, including JULIAN OF NORWICH, and then set out for the Holy Land. On her return she spent six months in Italy, where the Italians seemed more tolerant of her 'boystrous' crying, exclusively religious conversation and habits of rebuking her neighbours' faults. Margery continued to travel, although she spent six years nursing her husband. The *Boke of Margery Kempe* is the oldest extant autobiography in English; it was set down between 1431 and 1438. It is a vivid and frank account of her travels and mystical experiences and of her deep compassion for sinners. Margery Kempe is a controversial figure – considered by some a victim of religious mania, and by others a genuine mystic.

K. Cholmeley: *Margery Kempe; Genius and Mystic* (1947)

**Kendrick, Pearl Luella** (1890–1980). American microbiologist and doctor. Born in Wheaton, Illinois, she attended Syracuse then Johns Hopkins universities. After teaching in New York State, she joined first the New York then the Michigan Department of Health, holding the post of Associate Director of Laboratories, Western Michigan from 1920 until her retirement. Working in very basic conditions, she developed with her colleague Dr Grace Eldening a pertussis (whooping cough) vaccine which by 1939 was available for mass production. From this she evolved the standard DPT (diphtheria, whooping cough and tetanus) immunization which virtually eradicated some of the major childhood diseases from the western world. She refused publicity, however, and did not name the vaccine after herself.

She was at various times a consultant to WHO and UNICEF, wrote many articles on communicable diseases, particularly for the *American Journal of Public Health*, and was a Fellow of the American Public Health Association and Vice President in 1944.

**Kenney, Annie** (1879–1953). English trade unionist and suffragette. She was born in Springhead, near Oldham, the fifth of twelve children; she attended village school, went to work part-time in the mill when she was 10, and by the age of 13 was a full-time card and blowing-room operative. Inspired by writings of Robert Blatchford in *The Clarion*, Annie started a union, and organized in other mills. The first woman in textile unions elected to the District Committee, she used her fees to become a correspondence student of Ruskin College, Oxford.

In 1905, through the Clarion Vocal Union, she met Christabel PANKHURST and became a speaker for the Women's Social and Political Union (WSPU). At the Liberal Party meeting to endorse candidacy of Winston Churchill at the Free Trade Hall, Manchester, they challenged Sir Edward Grey on his suffrage policy, unfurled their banner and were ejected and arrested. Their short prison sentence, the first in the suffrage campaign, caused a national sensation. In 1906 Annie was arrested again for interrupting the Prime Minister, Campbell Bannermann; in the same year, she helped Keir Hardie's campaign, and became London organizer for the WSPU. Between then and 1912, she also organised in the West Country, was imprisoned, and went on hunger-strike several times. She was a witty, vigorous and persuasive speaker, and in 1912 took over the WSPU while the Pankhursts and EMMELINE PETHICK-LAWRENCE were imprisoned; the following year she was arrested and sentenced to 18 months' imprisonment. During her releases and recapture under the 'Cat and Mouse' Act she attempted, unsuccessfully, to claim sanctuary at Lambeth Palace. In 1914 she joined Mrs Pankhurst in her recruiting drive. In 1921, she married James Taylor and moved to Letchworth; despite her former militancy, she took no further part in public life.

Her younger sister, Jessie Kenney, a child mill-hand, also became a suffragette, joining Christabel Pankhurst in Paris in 1912, and touring the USA with Emmeline Pankhurst from 1914 to 1918. She visited Russia, worked for the American Red Cross and was the first woman to qualify as a radio officer. Later she returned to London where she joined the Rosicrucian Order, becoming master of the London Chapter.

A. Kenney: *Memories of a Militant* (1924).

**Kettle,** Dame **Alice.** *See* KYTELER, ALICE.

**Key, Ellen** (1849–1926). Swedish social feminist. Born in Sundsholm, in southern Sweden, she was educated at home; she subsequently taught in the village school and founded a local library. In 1867 a present of Ibsen's plays dramatically altered her social theories. The following year, when her father became a member of the Riksdag, the family moved to Stockholm, and Ellen began contributing to the periodical *Idun*. The family fortune was lost and at the age of

30 she started teaching in Stockholm, and then lecturing at working men's clubs on social reforms, and economics, and running classes for women in history and literature. In the 1880s she began publishing works on the property rights of women, and biographical studies of her friends. In 1895 she published *Individualism och Socialism*, followed the next year by *Missbrukad Kvinnokraft* ('The strength of women misused'). This caused a furore, and was attacked by conservatives as advocating free love and atheism, although Key's view of the position of women was dominated by a fundamental belief in the sanctity of motherhood. In 1900 her most famous book appeared, *Barnhets ahrundrade*, soon translated into English as *The Century of the Child*, which reviewed theories of education and attacked conventional expectations of marriage and sex roles. Now internationally famous, Key undertook several lecture tours abroad between 1903 and 1909, and continued to write, producing 30 books on a variety of topics. Her study of the women's movement, *Kvinnororeisen*, appeared in 1909.

L.H. Nystrom: *Ellen Key: her Life and Work* (1913)

**Khadijah** (*c*564–619). Arabian first wife of Mohammed. Khadijah became an eminent businesswoman, twice-widowed, in the leading Meccan tribe of Quraish, employing agents and managers and sending out caravans. Mohammed became one of her agents and she married him, when she was apparently 40 and he 25; they had six children. She supported him after his first vision in about 610 and encouraged his mission wholeheartedly. Although he had 11 more wives, including A'ISHA-BINT ABĪ BAKR, he remained faithful to her during her lifetime and always revered her memory. She was the mother of FATIMAH.

**Khan,** Begum **Liaquat Ali** (1905–) [née Ra'ana Pant]. Pakistani politician and women's leader. She was a member of an aristocratic Muslim family, educated at the universities of Lucknow and Calcutta, and at the age of 26 left her hill town in Almora in the United Provinces of North India and joined the faculty of Indraprastha College for Women in New Delhi, where she taught economics. In 1939 she married Liaquat Ali Khan, a member of the United Provinces Legislature, and two years later submitted as her MA thesis plans for a Women's Association, which was eventually founded after another 18 years.

In 1947, after partition, her husband became Prime Minister, but four years later he was assassinated in Rawalpindi. During the troubles following partition the Begum had formed a National Organization of over two million women to act as nurses, teachers and administrators, and in 1949 this received formal status as the All Pakistan Women's Association. The first office was originally situated in her own house, but at a conference three years later it was decided to change the organization in status from an emergency rehabilitation body to a major women's movement. A vital force in involving women in the political life of the country, it founded schools, hospitals and craft industries. She herself remained active in political circles after her husband's death and became the first Muslim woman ambassador when posted to Belgium and the Netherlands in 1954; she has also been Ambassador to Italy and to Tunisia. Her work has also encompassed United Nations committees and studies for the International Labour Organization. In 1973 she became the first woman to govern a province, that of Sind, and she is Chancellor of the University of Karachi. In 1978 she received the Human Rights Award of the United Nations.

**King** [née Moffit], **Billie-Jean** (1943–). American tennis player. She won her first tournament when she was 13, and later met the former American champion Alice Marble, who offered to coach her. Billie-Jean's keen tactical sense is borne out by the large number of doubles titles she holds, beginning with her first Wimbledon title when she was 17, playing with Hantze against Lehane and Margaret Smith. In all she has won 20 Wimbledon titles – a record total, they comprise 6 singles, 10 doubles and 4 mixed doubles titles, won between 1961 and 1979. Her singles victories include Forest Hills in 1967, 1971 and 1972, Paris in 1972, Rome in 1970 and Australia in 1968, as well as Wimbledon in 1966 to 1968, 1972 and 1973 and 1978. Her game is of the service and volley style.

She had always objected to men's prize

money so exceeding women's, and campaigned to equalize it by organizing a boycott of women players against official American Lawn Tennis Association tournaments. She furthered her case at Houston in 1973 by beating Bobby Riggs, men's champion at Wimbledon in 1939, in a much-publicized match. Billie-Jean became the first sportswoman to earn $100,000 in a single year. In 1975 she established both the World Team Tennis League and the Women's Professional Softball League, and helped to launch a magazine called *Woman Sports*. In 1962, while studying history at Los Angeles State College, she met a law student, Larry King, whom she married in 1965.

B.-J. King: *Billy-Jean* (1982)

**King, Coretta Scott** (1922–). American Civil Rights leader. Born in Marion, Alabama, she was educated at Antioch College, Ohio, and in 1951 moved to Boston to study singing at the New England Conservatory of Music. There she met Martin Luther King, a philosophy and theology student, and they married in 1953. They returned to Montgomery, Alabama, and had four children. In 1955 King led a year-long boycott of public transport after Rosa Park had been arrested for refusing to move to the back of the bus, and Coretta became involved with him in the civil rights movement. In particular she gave concerts across the USA and in India; she also worked for the anti-nuclear lobby and the protest movement against the Vietnam War.

When King was assassinated in 1968 she planned a centre in his memory for 'non-violent social change' which was opened in Atlanta in 1971, received many peace awards and honours on his behalf, and became an activist herself, leading a protest in Charleston in 1969. She has continued her 'work ever since. In 1986 she met WINNIE MANDELA during a visit to South Africa, which was notable for her boycott of a meeting with President Botha.

C.S. King: *My Life with Martin Luther King* (1969)

**Kingsley, Mary** (1862–1900). English explorer. The niece of the writer Charles Kingsley, Mary's first 30 years were unremarkable. She had little formal education but an aptitude for the practical use of knowledge. Both her parents died in 1892,

and Mary then decided to finish some anthropological work begun by her father George Kingsley, who had travelled widely.

After a trip to the Canary Islands she travelled throughout West Africa for two years, mostly as a trader to gain the confidence of the bush Africans: she was agnostic and did not encourage missionaries. She studied seamanship on her voyage to Africa and became adept. *Travels in West Africa* (1897) begins with her colourful observation of 'fish and fetish'. In spite of heavy black skirts, a high-necked blouse, various head-dresses and an umbrella, she travelled extremely rough, ate 'native chop' (manioc), and mixed freely with cannibals and dangerous tribes-people. On her second journey she explored the Calabar and Ogowe rivers, paddling her canoe through mangrove swamps and encountering hippopotami, crocodiles and gorillas. Of the lively Fan tribesmen who accompanied her she said 'we each recognized that we belonged to that same section of the human race with whom it is better to drink than to fight'. Having survived a fall into a spiked game pit and waded up to her chin through a swamp, emerging with a neck frill of leeches, she returned to become the second climber to reach the top of Mungo Mah Lobeh (Cameroon Mountain), the highest point in West Africa.

In England in 1896 she became a celebrity. She had collected and deposited in the British Museum insects, reptiles and fish, three of which were named after her. While keeping house for her younger brother she wrote *West African Studies* (1899); the Negro, she said, was not a lawless savage but 'lived by precise and binding rules which the white man disturbed at his peril'. From an archetypically tough explorer she had progressed to pioneer anthropological work, then to political judgements, which led her to champion African causes. She indicted the British government and addressed the British Association on the inappropriate hut tax imposed on the Sierra Leone protectorate. The Colonial Secretary Joseph Chamberlain invited her suggestions, and she proposed that West Africa be administered mainly by traders, side by side with Africans. She approved of neither the bicycle nor women's suffrage, but volunteered during the Boer War and nursed prisoners. She died in South Africa of enteric fever, at 38, and was buried at sea.

**Kirch** [née Winkelmann], **Marie (Margaretha)** (1670–1720). German astronomer. She was born at Panitzsch, near Leipzig, and in 1692 became the second wife and pupil, then co-worker with, the Berlin astonomer Gottfried Kirch. In 1702 she discovered a comet. She was a friend of Leibnitz and was presented by him to the court of Prussia. After her husband's death in 1710 she continued their work, and in 1713 wrote a work on the forthcoming conjunction of Jupiter and Saturn; it contained astronomical calculations as well as the more fashionable astrological observations. Her daughters calculated an *Almanac* and *Ephemeris* for the Berlin Academy of Sciences.

**Kirchgessner, Marianne (Antonia)** (1769–1808). German glass harmonica player. Left blind by an illness contracted when she was three, she was encouraged to develop her musical talents from an early age. She studied the glass harmonica with J.A. Schmittbauer in Karlsruhe and made the first of many concert tours in 1791. After hearing her in Vienna, Mozart wrote some music for the glass harmonica, including a quintet with flute, oboe, viola and cello. On a visit to London (1794) a new instrument was made for her by Fröschel, and Salomon wrote a sonata for her. She was befriended by Goethe shortly before her death (apparently caused by the debilitating acoustic qualities of the glass harmonica).

**Kitzinger** [née Webster], **Sheila (Helena Elizabeth)** (1929–). English childbirth educator. Born in Somerset, she was educated at Bishop Fox Girls' School, Taunton, and then studied to be a drama teacher. After attending Ruskin College, Oxford, she went on to St Hugh's College where she took a BLitt in social anthropology. From 1951 to 1953 she undertook research on race relations in the UK at the University of Edinburgh. In 1952 she married Uwe Kitzinger, an economist; they have five daughters.

From 1958, when she became a member of the Advisory Board of the National Childbirth Trust, she has developed a psychosexual approach to childbirth, and her pioneering teaching of the reduction of fear and pain through relaxation and knowledge has been highly influential; her first book was *The Experience of Childbirth* (1962). She then became a National Childbirth Trust teacher and has lectured all over the world. She has produced a series of books including: *Education and Counselling for Childbirth* (1977); *Women as Mothers* (a cross-cultural study) (1978); *Giving Birth: Emotions in Childbirth*, *Birth at Home*, *The Experience of Breastfeeding*, *The Good Birth Guide* (all 1979); *Pregnancy and Childbirth* (1980). In addition to her work in the UK she is also on the Board of Consultants of the International Childbirth Education Association of the USA.

**Klein** [née Reizes], **Melanie** (1882–1960). Austrian child psychoanalyst. She was born in Vienna and trained as an analyst in Budapest and Berlin, with the encouragement of two Freudians, Ferenczi and Karl Abraham. In 1926, at the invitation of Freud's biographer and friend Ernest Jones, she settled in London with the youngest of her three children.

Melanie studied problems of character and personality by analysis of progressively deeper levels of the unconscious, and was the first to apply the psychoanalytic technique to small children. The youngest child she analysed was under three: she used play-techniques now adopted in child guidance clinics. She believed human nature is determined largely by the result of a struggle occurring in the first four months of life between life instinct and innate envy of the mother. Her aim was to integrate various aspects of the child's personality by rendering conscious the child's unconscious. *The Psychoanalysis of Children* was published in 1960. Clinically, the most important aspect of her work may be that concerning the origins of more severe mental disorders: psychosis, paranoid-schizoid illness and depression. Her understanding of these conditions extended the range of patients who can be psychoanalysed.

Melanie was a member of the Training Committee of the British Psychoanalytic Society, and of the International Psycho-analytical Association. Her other work included research in the psychological bases of ethics, thinking, group relations and aesthetics.

**Klumpke, Dorothea**. American astronomer. She was born in San Francisco. Dorothea's family were distinguished: her sister Anna became an artist (the close friend and biographer of ROSA BONHEUR), Julia a violinist, and Augusta a doctor of nervous diseases, and the first female intern in a Paris hospital. In Europe Dorothea became proficient in languages, mathematics and astronomy.

She applied as a student to the Paris Observatoire and was the first woman to be allowed to work there, as well as the first woman to gain a doctorate in mathematics there, producing a thesis which completed SONIA KOVALEVSKY's work on the rings of Saturn. Her other work was on the spectra of stars and on meteorites. She was appointed head of a bureau within the Paris Observatoire for measuring photographic plates to be used in a large catalogue of stars for the International Astronomical Congress. Dorothea was the first woman elected to the Astronomical Society of France.

**Knight,** Dame **Laura** (1877–1970). English painter. She was born at Long Eaton Derbyshire, educated locally, and studied at Nottingham School of Art. In 1903 she married the painter Harold Knight and they moved to Newlyn, Cornwall. The Knights' circle of friends included Bernard Shaw, T.E.Lawrence, Alfred Mannings, Augustus John, and later ANNA PAVLOVA, whom she recorded in distinctive portraits. Her painting first caught public attention with *Daughters of the Sun* (1910), a study of girls bathing.

After World War I she became fascinated by the circus, spending years travelling with big tops and painting studies of life in and out of the ring; in the 1920s she also travelled with gypsy bands. A well-known exhibitor, she was made Associate of the Royal Academy of Art in 1927 and DBE in 1929. In later years she was known for her landscapes, and for her studies of ballet life such as *Bolshoi Ballet Rehearsing* (1958).

Although Dame Laura had been President of the Society of Women Artists, had had a major retrospective exhibition in 1965 and had been a full member of the Royal Academy since 1936, she was only allowed to attend the annual member's banquet for the first time in 1967.

J. Dunbar: *Laura Knight* (1975)
L. Knight: *Oil Paint and Grease Paint* (1936)
——: *A Proper Circus Drive* (1962)
——: *The Magic of a Line* (1965)

**Knight, Margaret** [Mattie] **E.** (1838–1914). American inventor. She was born in York, Maine, and later said of her childhood, 'the only things I wanted were a jack knife, a gimlet and pieces of wood'. She is said to have thought of her first invention when she was 12 while watching her brothers at work in a cotton textile mill; this was a stop-motion contrivance to stop the steel-tipped shuttles from falling out and injuring people. Margaret then worked in a shop and invented a machine for making square bottomed paper-bags, for which she took out a patent in 1870.

Her next three inventions were domestic: a dress and skirt shield, a clasp for holding robes, and a spit. In Framingham, Massachusetts, where she lived for the rest of her life, she invented and patented several machines for shoe-cutting from 1890 onwards. After inventing a window frame and sash and a numbering mechanism, she moved on to rotary engines and motors, where her special contribution was the sleeve-valve engine. Margaret is notable for the range and number of her inventions and for their concern with heavy machinery.

**Knipper-Chehkova, Olga (Leonardovna)** (1870–1959). Russian actress. Born in Glazov, the daughter of an engineer, she studied drama at the Moscow Philharmonic Society from 1895 to 1898, and made her debut in 1898 at the Moscow Art Theatre under Nemirov-Danchenko, her former teacher. She appeared in Chehkov's plays, as Arkadina in *The Seagull* (1898), Helena Andreyevna in *Uncle Vanya* (1899), Anna Petrovna in *Ivanov* (1901), and made a particular impact as Masha in *Three Sisters* (1901), giving a convincing performance of a passionate spirit stifled by bourgeois life. She was known as a poetic, lyrical actress but one who avoided sentimentality.

She married Chehkov in 1901, and after his death three years later she remained one of the principals at the Moscow Art Theatre. After the Revolution she added more comic parts to her repertory, and also played in two films during the 1920s. In 1943 she appeared as Madame Ranevsky, a role she had created in 1904, in the 300th performance of *The Cherry Orchard*. A People's Artist of the Soviet Union, she died in Moscow aged 79.

H.J. Pitcher: *Chekov's Leading Lady* (1979)

**Koch, Marita** (1957–). East German athlete. Koch has been described as the 'athlete of the decade' and a strong candidate for the best woman athlete of all time. Born in Wismar, she is a student of paediatric medicine and a member of the Sports Club Empor Rostock. At her first top athletics meeting in the 1975 European Junior Championships in Athens she won a gold in relay and silver in the 400 metres. She was unbeaten at 400 metres from 1977 (World Cup, in which she came second to Irena Szewinska) until Jarmila Kratochvilova beat her once at the 1981 World Cup in Rome. She was also brilliant at shorter distances, the world's best at 200 metres (21.71 secs), challenging Marlies Gohr, her team-mate, at 100 metres and setting the fastest ever 60 metres (7.04 secs) indoors. She was the first woman to break 49 seconds for 400 metres and 22 seconds for 200 metres and set 16 world records outdoors and 14 world bests indoors. She has three times been voted best female athlete in the world (1978, 1979 and 1982).

In 1985 at the World Cup in Canberra Koch regained the world record, which Kratochvilova had set at 47.99 seconds in 1983, and reduced it to 47.60, matching the time of Eric Liddell's world record at the Paris Olympics of 1924. Despite Achilles tendon problems, she continued to compete in 1986 but after the 400 metres Grand Prix final in Rome decided to retire. She planned to complete her medical studies and to marry her coach, Wolfgang Meier.

**Kogan,    Claude**    (1919–59).    French mountaineer. She lived in Nice, where she ran a swimwear factory. She became a distinguished climber in the Ardennes and the Alps and subsequently climbed in the Andes. Here her climbs included a first ascent, with a party, of Sakantay (19,951 ft) in Peru's Cordillera Vilcabamba in 1952. Her husband Georges died after their return from the Andes.

From 1953 she tackled the Himalayas. First she led a first ascent to the 23,410 ft summit of Nun in the Pubjab's Nun-Kun

massif. Then in 1954 she reached what remains the highest point for a European woman of nearly 25,000 ft on Cho Oyo. The next year she made a first ascent of Ganesh Himal (24,300 ft). She was made an honorary member of the Ladies' Alpine Club and lectured on her climbs at an unprecedented joint gathering of this and the Alpine Club in London. In July 1959 she began leading the Expédition Feminine au Nepal, an international all-women party, to Cho Oyo (26,700 ft). In October she and three others were lost in an avalanche near Camp IV.

**Kollontai, Alexandra (Mikhaylovna)** (1872–1952). Russian revolutionary, feminist and politician. She was born in St Petersburg [now Leningrad] into an aristocratic liberal family: her father was a general in the Imperial army, but her mother was the daughter of a Finnish wood merchant, who already had three children by a previous arranged marriage. Alexandra, much younger, was brought up largely by servants at the family homes in St Petersburg and Finland, educating herself through reading. When she was 16 she refused to become a conventional debutante, and although she was not allowed to study abroad, she was permitted to travel through Europe. Her first encounter with socialism was in Berlin. When she was 20 she married a cousin, Vladimir Kollontai; they had a son, Misha, and she soon began writing short stories reflecting her rebellion against domesticity.

In 1896 she accompanied Vladimir on an inspection of a large textile factory and was enraged by his view that the appalling conditions could be bettered by small improvements, turning for support to the new Marxist Union of struggle for the working class. She had already read Marx and Engels and now worked among factory women; she took time off to study economics in Zürich in 1898, where she became interest in the views of Kautsky and ROSA LUXEMBURG. On her return she wrote *On the Question of the Class Struggle* (1905) and *The Social Basis of the Women's Question* (1908). After the publication of a pamphlet on Finland she was harassed by the police and went into exile in Germany, leaving her son behind.

In exile she was an ardent pacifist and

opponent of conscription, touring Europe and being briefly imprisoned in Germany and Sweden in 1914. In 1915 she rejoined the Bolsheviks, and toured the USA making impassioned pleas against participation in World War I, and for international socialism. She returned to Russia after the February Revolution in 1917 and was in the party which met Lenin and other émigrés on their return. She became Commissar for Public Welfare in the first Bolshevik government (the only woman) and campaigned for reforms in domestic life, such as the acceptance of free love, simplification of divorce and collective child-care. In 1920 her disillusionment with the democratic New Economic Policy led her to join the Workers' Opposition, which was banned in 1921. This, and her affairs with the seamen Pavel Dubenko and Alexander Shlyapnikov (both of whom died in the purges of the 1930s), roused the disapproval of Party Central Committee, although the general membership refused to expel her.

Instead, Stalin removed her from the centre of activity by making her trade delegate, then Minister, to Norway (1923–5), to Mexico (1925–7), to Norway again (1927–30) and to Sweden (1930–45), where she became Ambassador in 1943. Virtually an exile, her main achievement was the armistice negotiations ending the Soviet–Finnish war in 1944. In her last years she was adviser to the Russian Foreign Ministry.

While she was posted abroad her collection of stories *Love of Worker Bees* was published (1923) as part of a series, *Revolution in Feelings and Morality*. It aroused great controversy because of its frankness in dealing with sexuality, and ambivalence towards children and the place of women in the economy, subjects she had treated directly in previous books, articles and pamphlets such as *Communism and the Family* (1920) and *The New Morality and the Working Class* (1918). Her *Autobiography*, (1926) remained unpublished in Russia. In the 1970s almost all her writings were issued in English editions.

A. Kollontai: *Autobiography of a Sexually Emancipated Woman* (Eng. trans., 1972)
C. Porter: *Alexandra Kollontai* (1981)

**Kollwitz** [née Schmidt], **Käthe** (1867–1945). German graphic artist and sculptor.

She was born in East Prussia, into a liberal household, the daughter of a Free Congregation preacher. She studied in Königsberg, then at art schools in Berlin and Munich until 1890. In 1891 she married a medical student, Karl Kollwitz, and they moved to Berlin where he worked as a doctor. In 1892, influenced by Gerald Hauptmann's play *The Weavers' Uprising* about an industrial revolt in Silesia in the 1840s, she produced a series of etchings which were exhibited in Berlin in 1898, but the proposed gold medal was vetoed by the Kaiser. She taught in an art school and despite some time spent abroad, studying sculpture in Paris in 1904 and in Florence in 1907, her permanent home for 50 years was Berlin. Between 1902 and 1910 she produced other great cycles: *The Peasants' War* and *Images of Wretchedness*.

Bitterly opposed to World War I, especially after the death of her son Peter in 1914, she produced passionate woodcuts on the subject of war, death and poverty in two series in the 1920s, *War* and *Proletariat*. She worked for many years on the sculpture *Father and Mother*, a tribute to Peter showing his mourning parents, which was unveiled as a war memorial in 1933. Her last great print cycle was a series of eight lithographs, *Death* (1934–5).

Kollwitz was elected Professor of Graphics at the Prussian Academy in 1928, but forced to resign by the Nazis in 1933; she then retired from public life. She was widowed in 1940, and lost her grandson on the Russian Front in 1942. She died at Moritzburg, near Dresden.

Kollwitz was a magnificent graphic artist, whose work combines emotion, strength and a terrible beauty. Among her most powerful works were her political posters, dealing with hunger, such as *Vienna is Dying! Save its Children!* (1920), and with alcoholism, abortion, safety at work and, above all, war. Perhaps the best known of these are *Bread!*, created to raise money for strikers in Berlin in 1920, and *Never Again War!* (1924).

Kollwitz, H., ed.: *Diaries and Letters of Käthe Kollwitz* (1955)
M. Keans: *Käthe Kollwitz: Woman and Artist* (1976)

**Kolstad** [née Lundegaard], **Eva** (1918–). Norwegian politician. Born in Halden, she became a teacher of book-keeping and commercial skills in 1938 and gradually qualified in accountancy, becoming an independent chartered accountant in 1944. She married Ragnar Kolstad in 1942. An active feminist, she worked for the International Alliance of Women and served on the board from 1949 to 1958, from 1961 to 1968 and in 1973. She was also President of the Norwegian Association for the Rights of Women (1956–68) and a member of the UN Committee on the Status of Women (1969–75). For 15 years, from 1960, she was also a member of Oslo City Council. She then moved into national government as a Member of Parliament (1958–61 and 1966–9). She became Minister of Consumer Affairs (1972–3), President of the Liberal Party (1974–6) and leader of the Government Council on the Equal Status of Men and Women (1977–8). Since 1978 she has held the post of Ombudsman.

**Konie, Gwendoline** (1938–). Zambian diplomat. Born in Lusaka, she was educated locally and then studied in Wales, at University College, Cardiff, and in the USA, at the American University, Washington, D.C. In 1961 she began working in the Ministry of Local Government and Social Welfare, and she became a member of the Legislative Council in 1963 before moving to the Ministry of Foreign Affairs in 1964. She worked in the Presidential Office in 1972 and then, from 1974 to 1977, was Zambian Ambassador to Sweden, Norway, Denmark and Finland. For the next two years she represented her country at the United Nations where her duties included chairing the UN Council for Namibia. Since 1979 she has been a Permanent Secretary in the Zambian Civil Service. She has undertaken many other advisory and consultancy roles and is on the executive boards responsible for adult education and family planning.

**Korbut, Olga** (1955–). Russian gymnast. The youngest of four daughters of an engineer in Grodno, Olga attended gymnastics school from the age of nine. When she was 14 she came fifth in the Soviet National Championships, and at the age of 16, she took 3 gold medals at the 1972 Munich Olympics. Here she was the first person in competition to demonstrate a backward somersault on uneven parallel bars, and the only female to do a backflip on the balance beam; she showed great originality and grace in the floor exercises. It was not, however, simply her daring routines that were influential, but her appealing and sometimes emotional personality: she finished only seventh overall at the Olympic Games, yet it was she who particularly delighted spectators and television audiences, and caused many thousands of girls to join gymnastics clubs to emulate her.

In 1973 she took the Russian and World Student Games titles, then took part in the European Championships in London. She won a silver medal in the combined exercises, coming second to LUDMILA TURITSCHEVA, but then injured her leg and withdrew from individual apparatus events. She retired from competition in 1977 and from gymnastics in 1978, and subsequently married Leonid Bortkevich, a folk-rock singer, and had a child.
Smith, J.H: *Olga Korbut* (1974)

**Kovalevsky** [née Korvin-Krukovsky], **Sonya** [Kovalevskaya, Sofya Vasilyerna] (1850–91). Russian mathematician. She was born in Moscow, to an aristocratic family whose social circle included Dostoevsky. During the 1880s Sonya described her early life in *Recollections of Childhood* (or *The Sisters Rajevsky*), disguising it as a novel for political reasons. Her literary career continued, although from the age of 14 it was subordinated to her interest in calculus.

While studying at St Petersburg [now Leningrad], she belonged to a young people's movement to promote the emancipation of women in Russia. When she was 18 she married Vladimir Kovalevsky, a palaeontologist, in order to leave with him to study in Heidelberg, under Konigsberger, Kirchoff and Helmholtz. Recommended by Konigsberger to his master Karl Weierstrass, she moved to Berlin while her husband returned to Russia. Weierstrass became her mentor and lifelong friend. She was refused admission to university lectures because she was a woman, so he tutored her privately for four years. Three papers on partial differential equations, Abelian integrals, and Saturn's rings, qualified her for a doctorate *in absentia* from the University of Göttingen.

Unable to gain an academic post, she returned to Russia, lived with her husband and had a daughter, 'Foufie', in 1878. She resumed mathematical studies and after her husband's suicide in 1883 was appointed, through Weierstrass's influence, to a lectureship in mathematics at the University of Stockholm. In 1889 she became a life Professor. Her most important work was done here: in 1888 *On the Rotation of a Solid Body about a Fixed Point* won the Prix Bordin of the French Académie, with the usual prize of 3000 francs raised to 5000 in recognition of the quality of the work. In 1889 she won a prize from the Swedish Academy of Sciences, and was elected to membership of the Russian Academy of Sciences. Her name is also remembered through the Caucy-Kovalevsky theorem of partial differential equations. She died at the height of her career, of influenza complicated by pneumonia.

A.C. Leffler: *Sonya Kovalevskaya* (1895)

**Kovalskaya, Elizaveta** (1850–1933). Russian nihilist. The daughter of a landowner and a woman serf, she spent her childhood in poverty but was later educated as a gentleman's daughter and left a legacy. She then established a radical educational centre in the house she inherited in Khar'kov, organizing study groups for working women and political discussions. This was closed by the police in 1869. In 1870 she and her friend SOFYA PEROVSKAYA were among the first group of women to extend the public lectures, known as the Alarchinskii courses, in St Petersburg [now Leningrad], and in 1872 she went to study in Zürich, where she met many other young revolutionary students. On her return to Russia she undertook propaganda work among factory workers and briefly joined the Black Repartition group, then, with Saltykov Shchedrin, she established the Union of Russian Workers of the South, in Kiev in 1880. Together they developed a programme of 'economic terror' directed against landlords, local authorities and factory owners which met with a huge response from the local people. In 1881 she was arrested and sent to Siberia (she escaped on the way there but was re-arrested); she remained there for 20 years.

On her release in 1903 she went to Geneva, joined the Socialist Revolutionary Party and then the maximalist group, which demanded the socialization of all means of production. She returned to Russia just before the October Revolution of 1917, and worked in the state archives, becoming a respected historian of the revolutionary movement.

**Krasner, Lee** (1908–84) American painter. Krasner was born in Brooklyn, New York and studied at the Women's Art School of Cooper Union (1926–9), the Art Students' League (1928), the National Academy of Design (1929–32), and with Hans Hoffman in New York (1933–40). During the 1930s she worked for the Public Works of Art Project, and then for the Federal Arts Project in various capacities from 1935 to 1942. She was already recognized as an artist when she married Jason Pollock in 1945, although her first exhibitions did not take place until the 1950s. For several years she was overshadowed by Pollock's fame, and after his death in a car accident in 1956 she became known as a fierce guardian of his reputation, often engaging in sharp controversy. Her paintings, collages and huge murals of the late 1950s were notable for their bold style and during the 1960s she achieved even greater freedom with exceptional use of colour and form. As interest in 'women's art' grew in the 1970s she was recognized as one of the finest American abstract expressionists, with her work included in numerous group exhibitions and as individual shows in America and overseas, culminating in a series of major retrospectives from 1983 to 1985.

B. Rose: *Lee Krasner* (1983)

**Kreps** [née **Morris**], **Juanita** (1921–). American economist and politician. She was born in Lynch, a coalmining town in Harlan County, Kentucky, where her father was a mine manager. She was educated at Berea College and received an MA from Duke University in 1944. In that year she married the economist Clifton Kreps, with whom she had three children. From 1945 to 1950 she taught economics at Denison College, and after holding two other posts returned to Duke University in 1958; there she was made a Professor in 1967 and Vice-President of the University (the first woman) in 1973. She had also just become the first woman Director of the New York Stock Exchange in 1972, and from 1977 to 1979 was the first female Secretary of Commerce, appointed by Jimmy Carter, one of only five women to hold a cabinet post by that date. She was particularly concerned with labour and manpower problems and with racial and sexual equality in business. As an economist, after co-authoring a text on *Principles of Economics* (1962), she has concentrated on women's employment and on economic problems related to age, as is evident from her publications *Lifetime Allocation of Work and Income* (1971), *Sex in the Marketplace: American Women at Work* (1971), *Women and the American Economy* (1976) and (as editor) *Technology, Manpower and Retirement Policy* (1966). An astute business woman, she is on the board of some prominent companies, including Eastman Kodak and United Airlines.

**Kristeva, Julia** (1941–). French literary theorist. Born in Bulgaria, she has worked in France since 1966 and teaches at the University of Paris VII. She has not been associated with any particular feminist group, but has used elements of Marxist, Freudian-Lacanian and post-structuralist method in several influential works on the philosophy of language, on contemporary literature, and cultural history. Her works include: *Semiotikè: recherches pour une sémanalyse* (1969); *Le texte du roman* (1970); *La traversée des signes* (1974); *La révolution du langage poétique* (1974); *Les chinoises* (1974) (her best-known work abroad); *Polylogue* (1977); *Folle vérité* (1979); *Pouvoirs de l'horreur: essai sur l'abjection* (1980), *Histoire d'amour* (1983) and *Soleil noir: depression et mélancolie* (1987). Many of her works have been translated into English. She has also been on the editorial board of the journal *Tel quel.*

**Kristiansen** (née Christensen), **Ingrid** (1956–). Norwegian athlete. Born in Trondheim, Norway, she began running competitively early in life. At 15 she took part in the European Championships in the 1500-metre heats. Her first successes were in cross-country skiing, in which she competed at the 1976 Olympic Games and 1978 World Championships. But it is as a long-distance runner that Kristiansen has been internationally successful. She is the only athlete to set world records at 5000 metres (1981 and 1984), 10,000 metres (1985) and the marathon (1985), and was third in 1982 at the European Championships and fourth in the 1984 Olympics.

In 1986, possibly her best year, Kristiansen was undefeated. She broke two world records, the 10,000 metres in Oslo in July with a time of 30 minutes 13.74 seconds and in August in Stockholm she ran 5000 metres in 14 minutes 37.33 seconds. She is married and has a son, Gaute, born in 1983.

**Kschessinskaya** [Kschessinska] **Mathilde (Maria-Felixovna),** Princess Romanovsky-Krassinsky (1872–1971). Russian ballerina and teacher. She was the daughter of a Polish character dancer who had been invited to the Mariinsky as an expert in the mazurka. Mathilde was born at Ligovo, and trained at the Imperial Ballet School in nearby St Petersburg [now Leningrad], graduating in 1890. She became a ballerina in 1895, and was immediately acclaimed for her brilliance. She was the first Russian ballerina to perform the 32 *fouettés* and the first Russian to dance Aurora. She was renowned for her superb technique, energy and charm, and eventually gained the title of *prima ballerina assoluta* (1895). She excelled in the great classical ballets but also enjoyed dramatic roles like *La Esmeralda*. Although she became a star of the Mariinsky company, she danced with the Dyagilev Ballets Russes in 1911, in London, Budapest and Monte Carlo.

Kschessinskaya was famous for her private as well as for her professional life; while at the Imperial Ballet School she became the mistress of the future Czar Nicholas II, and on his marriage he gave her a palace as a farewell present and she later came under the protection of Grand Duke Mikhailovich, who helped promote her career. She had a capricious, gay, generous character. During the Revolution she fled with Grand Duke André, father of her son, to the south of France and later took the title Princess Romanovsky-Krassinsky. In 1929 she opened a studio in Paris, teaching several great dancers of the 1930s and 1940s and continuing until 1963.

M. Romanovsky-Krassinsky: *Dancing in Petersburg: the Memoirs of Kschessinska* (1960)

**Kuan, Fu-Jen** (1262–1319). Chinese painter and calligrapher. She was born in central China into a prosperous family in Zhejiang province, and married the artist Zhao Meng, who agreed to take an official post under the Mongol invaders in 1286. Together they went north to the new frontier capital of Beijing which had been established by Kubla Khan in 1263. Kuan accompanied her husband on all his provincial tours, although they eventually had nine children. She was a traditional artist who worked on compositions of bamboo, blossoms and birds, and she quickly became a court favourite, receiving many honours as her husband rose in status. In 1319 she became ill with beriberi and although allowed to return to her home province she died on the way in Shandong.

**Kulisclov, Anna** (1854–1925). Italian socialist. Born at Simferopol in the Crimea. She studied at Zürich Polytechnic in 1871, where through contacts with Russian émigrés she came under Bakunin's influence. On her return to Russia her political activities led to her exile in 1877. In 1878 she moved to Florence and was promptly arrested; from then until her death she was active in Italian politics. From 1877 to 1885 she lived with Andrew Coska and supported him in his move away from Bakuninist internationalism to the foundation of a revolutionary Socialist Party. About 1884 she became interested in Marxism and moved to northern Italy, where she qualified in medicine and practised among the Milanese working-classes. At that time she was living and working with Filippo Turati. In 1890 she organized a conference, *Il monopolio dell'uomo*, in which she tackled the question of women's economic and social inferiority. She launched and edited with Turati the journal *Critica sociale* and took part in the Socialist League of Milan and the first socialist congress in Genoa.

She split with ANNA MARIA MOZZONI,the other great protagonist in the fight for women's emancipation, over the issue of Socialism and feminism (Mozzoni had doubts as to whether working-class victory would bring personal freedom for women). Kulisclov went on to battle for a law protecting women and children at work, causing controversy among feminists and revolutionaries, and in 1901 opposed Turati and the majority of the Socialist Party in demanding that the party made a woman's right to vote one of its demands. In 1912 she helped build the Unione Femminile Nazionale Socialista and edited a paper for working-class women, *La digesa delle lavoratrici*. She was active as a socialist and feminist until her death in Milan.

**Kyo, Machiko** [stage name of Motoko Yano] (1924–). Japanese film star. Born and educated in Osaka, Kyo first appeared on stage with the Shockiku Girls' Opera Company at 12, and was famous as a dancer before she moved into films. Her remarkable glamour and the sensuality and eroticism of her performances made her a leading star of the Daiei studio, which she joined in 1949, but she broke free of such type-casting in 1950 as Masago in Kurosawi's *Rashomon* and as Kimicho in Yoshimura's *Itshweraru Seiso*. In 1957 she made a film in America with Marlon Brando, *The Teahouse of the August Moon*. Since then she has become known internationally through her work with Yoshimura and Yamamoto. In over 80 films she has developed into an actress whose range extends from comedy to powerful tragedy.

**Kyteler** [Kettle], **Alice** (*fl* 1324). Irish reputed witch. The wealthiest lady in Kilkenny, she married four times, her first three husbands dying in mysterious circumstances. She was accused of witchcraft by the Bishop of Ossory, the indictments including heresy, animal sacrifice, prophecy through demons, parody of religious ceremonies, the making of charms from sinister ingredients 'all boiled in the skull of a beheaded robber over a fire of dark wood' and sexual relations with a spirit, Robert Artisson. The charge may have been inspired by a dispute over property, as her children accused her of robbing their inheritance through magic.

Dame Alice defied and even imprisoned the Bishop, despite being excommunicated. Helped by local nobility she fled to England, but others of her coven were punished, and her maid Petronilla was burnt at the stake. Her trial was a forerunner of the later witch-trials held in Europe and Britain.

T. Wright, ed.: *Proceedings against Dame Alice Kyteler* (1843).

# L

La Argentenita. *See* ARGENTENITA. LA.

La Argentina. *See* ARGENTINA. LA.

**Labé, Louise** (*c*1524–66). French poet. Born near Lyons, which was one of the principal Renaissance centres of France, she received a thorough education, in imitation of Italian noblewomen of the time. Her studies included Latin, Italian and music, and she was a skilful and daring horsewoman. Around 1550 she married Ennemond Perrin, who died in 1560. It was a marriage of convenience; her subsequent amorous adventures (real or fictitious) have elicited much comment, but it would appear that her real love was for the poet Olivier de Magny (*c*1531–61). She played a prominent part in the intellectual circle which centred on the poet Maurice Scève (*c*1510–60) and which brought together some of the leading writers of the time. She believed fervently in the intellectual potential of women and wanted to see them equal or surpass men. In 1555 her *Oeuvres* were published. They include a *Débat de folie et d'amour*, 3 elegies and 23 sonnets. The sonnets, all of which take love as their theme, show Petrarch's influence. They are admired for their formal perfection, originality of style and powerful evocation of passionate love.

F. Farrell: *Louise Labé: Complete Works* (1986)

**Labille-Guiard, Adelaide** (1749–1803). French artist. The last of six children of a merchant, she was first taught by the miniaturist François Elie Vincent. In 1769 she married Louis Guiard, a clerk, but they separated ten years later. She continued to study, learning the art of pastels from Quentin de la Tour, and exhibiting her work at the Académie de San Luc in Paris in 1774. She then began studying oils with the son of

her old teacher, François André Vincent, and his portrait was included in her work exhibited in the Salon de la Correspondence in Paris (1782). In 1783, after undertaking a series of portraits of leading academicians, including her masterpiece the pastel *Portrait of the Sculptor Pajou*, she was accepted into the Académie Française, on the same day as her rival, MARIE VIGÉE-LEBRUN.

She took many women pupils at her studio, including the two shown in her self-portrait, which was hung in the Académie Salon of 1785 as a silent protest against the new quota of only four women members; one of them was Marie Gabrielle Capet, who remained a close friend until her death. They exhibited as a group, meeting with hostility from critics. In 1795 she managed to obtain an apartment in the Louvre, which had previously been the terrain of male artists and students.

Recognized as a leading portrait painter, she remained in Paris during the Revolution, painting the Deputies of the National Assembly instead of the aristocrats who had formed her earlier subjects; she also presented a scheme to Tallyrand asking for state-subsidized art education for women. A determined professional and feminist, she campaigned continuously for greater opportunities for women artists. At the end of her life, in 1800, she married her old friend François André Vincent.

A. M. Passez: *Adelaide Labille-Guiard (1749–1803)* (1973)

**Lachapelle** [née Dugés], **Marie** (**Louise**) (1769–1821). French obstetrician. Both her mother and her grandmother were influential midwives. In 1792 Marie married Lachapelle, a surgeon, but he died three years later. At her mother's death Marie was appointed Head of Maternity at the Hôtel

Dieu, where Baudelocque was teaching obstetrics. They respected each other but were opposed over several matters: she insisted that instruments should be used as little as possible, and never merely for the sake of shortening labour, and in classifying positions of the foetus she reduced his 94 positions to 22. Her great published work was the *Pratique des accouchements* (1821–5) in three volumes, covering 40,000 cases. The second volume concentrated on extraordinary cases and their treatment, and the third on the new operation of symphysiotomy.

She studied further in Heidelberg under Naegele, and on her return organized a maternity and children's hospital at the Port Royal, where she trained many midwives for other parts of Europe and instituted such innovations in patient care as the immediate repair of a torn perineum, and dilation plus version to save both mother and child in cases of *placenta praevia*.

**Lacombe, Claire** ['Red Rosa'] (1765–?). French revolutionary. Born in Pamiers, she spent her early youth as a tragic actress, appearing in provincial theatres in Marseilles and Lyons with a travelling company of players. Increasingly fired by the Revolution, she went to Paris in July 1792, visited the Convention and Jacobin Club, and was named the 'Heroine of August 10th' for her part in the storming of the Tuileries. In April 1793 she founded a working women's organization, the Republican Revolutionary Society. This became closely associated with the extreme left-wing group, the Enragés, and Lacombe was friendly with the leadership, especially Jacquet Roux and Théophile Leclerc, with whom she lived for some time before his marriage to PAULINE LÉON. The club arranged debates, took part in Revolutionary campaigns and petitioned for the right of women to vote and participate in councils of the Revolutionary Committee. This militant feminism was attacked by Robespierre in the Assembly, and although Lacombe defended its activities fiercely the club was finally suppressed in November. In March 1794 she was arrested, while trying to leave Paris to start a new acting career in Dunkerque, and was imprisoned until the

coup in 1795. Nothing is known of her later life.

**La Dame aux Camélias**. *See* PLESSIS, ALPHONSINE.

**La Fayette, (Marie Madeleine Pioche de la Vergne), Comtesse de** (1634–93). French writer. Born into a family of the lesser nobility, she satisfied her ambitious mother by marrying the Comte de La Fayette, a widower 18 years her senior, in 1655. After bearing two sons Madame de La Fayette spent most of her time in Paris while her husband remained on his estates in the Auvergne. In Paris she obtained an appointment in the entourage of the King's sister-in-law, Henrietta of England, whose biography she was to write.

Her interest in literature had been awakened early by her tutor, the Abbé Ménage. She became friendly with the poet Ségrais, with Mme DE SEVIGNÉ, the famous letter writer, and with the moralist La Rochefoucauld. Her first novel, *La Princesse de Montpensier*, was published anonymously in 1662, and it is thought that Ménage collaborated with her on this work. In 1678 her most important novel, *La Princesse de Clèves*, was published anonymously and enjoyed an immediate success. It has become a classic in French literature.

Mme de La Fayette died in 1693, having suffered from ill-health most of her life. Three works were published posthumously, including *L'histoire de Mme Henriette d'Angleterre* (1720).

J. Railt: *Madame de La Fayette and 'La Princesse de Clèves'* (1981)

**Laforet (Díaz), Carmen** (1921–). Spanish novelist. Born in Barcelona, she was brought up in Las Palmas in the Canary Islands, and returned to mainland Spain at 18 to study humanities and law. Moving to Madrid, she married a journalist, Manuel González Cerezales. In 1944 she published a novel, *Nada*, a powerful semi-auto-biographical work examing the growth of a young girl's sensibilities during a youth surrounded by misunderstanding, super-stition, family conflict and prejudice. A haunting story of a struggle against inevitable destinies, it won the Premio

Nadal, and brought her instant fame. Her later novels include *La isla y los demonios* (1952), and a series of stories concerning the impact of religion on women's lives, following her own conversion to Roman Catholicism in 1951, such as *La muyer nueva* (1955), and the trilogy written during the 1960s, *Tres pasos fuera del tiempo*. Four of her short novels have been collected in *La Clamada* (1954).

**Lagerlöf, Selma** (1858–1940). Swedish novelist. Born at Mårbacka, the small family estate in Värmland, Sweden, Selma Lagerlöf listened to folk tales in her childhood, and much of the power of her later work derives from her fascination with the oral tradition of the countryside. The only great novelist in the Swedish literary renaissance of the 1890s, she published her first novel, *Gosta Berlings Saga*, a vivid portrait of local rural life, in 1891. Her next novel, *Antikrists Mirakler* (1897, 'The Miracles of Anti-Christ') dealt with the problems of modern society, and was set in Italy. Her critical standing was ensured when she published *Jerusalem* (two vols, 1901–2). A lighter side of her work is seen in a magical story of a small boy who flies over the whole country as a goose, *The Wonderland of Nils* (1906, trans. 1907). She was awarded the Nobel Prize for Literature in 1909 and used the money to buy back the Värmland estate. Selma Lagerlöf's later novels include *Korkarlen* (1912), a social problem novel set in folk-tale form, and *Bannlyst* (1918, 'The Outcast') on the evils of World War I. In the 1920s she wrote her powerful Lowenskolds trilogy, translated in 1931 as *The Rings of the Lowenskolds*. In her later years she described the beauty of her childhood home and her career as a writer in three volumes of autobiography.

S. Lagerlöf: *Marbacka* (1922)
———— : *Memoirs of my Childhood* (1934)
———— : *The Diary of Selma Lagerlöf* (1936)

**'La Gran Contessa'.** *See* MATILDA.

**Laine, Cleo (Clementina Dinah)** (1927–). English jazz and popular singer. Born in Southall, Middlesex, she became a popular singer and joined the Dankworth Orchestra in 1953. Her recording successes were enhanced by concert television performances and in 1958 she won a Moscow Art Theatre Award for an acting performance in *Flesh to a Tiger*. During the 1960s she began singing the works of modern composers and appeared in various singing roles in London and at the Edinburgh Festival, beginning with Brecht/Weill's *The Seven Deadly Sins* in 1961. Her rich voice, versatility, superb command of phrasing and extraordinary range of over four octaves make her equally suited both to jazz 'scat' singing and to works like William Walton's *Façade*, and to the blues tradition of BILLIE HOLIDAY. She attains the highest recorded note reached by the human voice on the recording of 'Being Alive' by Stephen Sondheim on *Cleo's Greatest Show Hits*. Cleo Laine continues to tour the USA, Europe and elsewhere, and her stage appearances in the 1980s have included *Colette* (1980), *A Little Night Music* (1983), and *Edwin Drood* (1986), for which she won several awards.

She was married to George Langridge in 1947 but the marriage was dissolved in 1957. In 1958 she married the musician John Dankworth, who has composed and arranged many of her finest songs.

**Lal-Ded** (*fl* late 14th century). Indian mystic and poet. Born during the reign of Sultan Ala-ud-din, near Srinagar, she was married as a child to a young boy and cruelly treated by her stepmother. She became a disciple of Sidh, propounded a Siva-Yoga philosophy, and wrote verse in Kashmiri, known as *Lal-Wakhi* ('The Songs of Lal'). She preached in the surrounding countryside, singing and dancing without clothing as a demonstration of her spiritual nakedness. Although widely mocked, she became famous for her ecstatic dance of Śiva. She lived to a very old age, the subject of numerous stories, and died a respected hermit, at Bijbehara.

Another great woman poet of the period was Mahadevija Kka, who also worshipped Śiva and was a member of the unorthodox Virasaivist Hindu movement.

**Lamb,** Lady **Caroline (Ponsonby)** (1785–1828). English writer. She was the daughter of the third Earl of Bessborough. Educated in Italy until 1794, she was always considered a 'highly-strung' child, and was brought up by her aunt, the Duchess of Devonshire. At the age of 16 she married

William Lamb, later the Prime Minister Lord Melbourne. Despite his devotion it proved a difficult marriage, dominated by Caroline's obsessive passion for Lord Byron, with whom she had a brief affair in 1812. Her novel *Glenarvon* (1816) is a fictional exposé of his behaviour. She is more famous for her tragic, hectic decline than for her novels, which also include *Ada Reis* (1823). In 1824 the sight of Byron's funeral procession led to a final breakdown and she separated from Lamb, although returning to live at their country house, Brocket, until her death.

E. Jenkins: *Lady Caroline Lamb* (1974)

**Landowska, Wanda** (1879–1959). Polish harpsichordist. She was a pioneer in the 20th-century revival of the harpsichord, an instrument to which she was increasingly drawn through her research into 17th- and 18th-century music. Having played the piano since the age of four, she studied at the Warsaw Conservatory, and in 1896 became a composition pupil of Heinrich Urban in Berlin. After her first harpsichord recital, in 1903, she toured widely in Europe and the USA, also teaching and giving master classes. She founded the Ecole de Musique Ancienne at St-Leu-la-Forêt (near Paris) in 1925, though this had to be abandoned – along with her valuable collection of instruments and books – in 1940, after which she lived in the USA.

Harpsichord concertos were written for her by Manuel de Falla (1926) and François Poulenc (*Concert champêtre*, 1928). She is primarily associated, however, with the 17th- and 18th-century repertoire, and especially with the music of J. S. Bach; her performances of his *Well-Tempered Clavier* and *Goldberg Variations* demonstrate the vitality of her approach (she recorded the former at the age of 70). She received decorations from both the French and Polish governments.

B. Gavoty and R. Hauert: *Wanda Landowska* (1957)

**Lane** [née Culborn], **Dame Elizabeth** (1905-1988). English lawyer. She was educated at Malvern Girls College and privately, and in 1926 married Henry Lane; they had one son. At the age of 35 she became a Barrister at the Inner Temple, and in 1948, in addition to her court work, was a member of the Home Office Committee on Depositions in Criminal Cases. From 1953 to 1961 she held the position of Assistant Recorder of Birmingham, and then became Recorder of Derby (1961–2), and Commissioner of the Crown Courts at Manchester and a Circuit Court Judge (1962–5). In 1965 she was created DBE and became the first woman judge in England, attached to the High Court in the Family Division, remaining there until her retirement in 1979. She was also Chairman of the Committee on the Abortion Acts (1971–73).

E. Lane: *Hear the Other Side* (1985)

**Lange, Dorothea** (1895–1965). American documentary photographer. Born in Hoboken, New Jersey, she trained as a photographer with Clarence White and began her career as a society photographer in San Francisco in the 1920s. She abandoned this work in the 1930s, unable to face the gulf between the world she was recording and the misery caused by the Depression. In 1934 she began photographing the food queues and soup kitchens, and from 1935 to 1942 recorded the poverty, migrant workers, tent camps and starving children of the Oklahoma Dust Bowl for the Federal Resettlement Administration. Her famous study of *The Migrant Mother*, holding a baby while two children lean on her shoulders, was published worldwide to raise funds for medical supplies. In 1939 her work appeared in *An American Exodus: a Record of Human Erosion*.

During World War II she photographed Japanese-American internees, and later turned to studies of Shaker communities and other aspects of the vanishing rural life; she also took contrasting pictures of delegates to United Nations conferences. She died of cancer just before her one-woman show opened at the Museum of Modern Art in New York.

N. Meltzer: *Dorothea Lange: a Photographer's Life* (1979)

**Lange, Helene** (1848–1930). German conservative feminist. She was born into a merchant family in Oldenburg. Her mother died when she was young, and she grew up in a conservative but evangelical home. She rejected the idea of marriage, and became a teacher in Berlin, publishing a plea for higher education for girls in 1878. From the mid-1880s she became active in the General German Women's Association. An energetic, dominating and opinionated conservative, she demanded education not for individual fulfilment but so that women could become superior wives and mothers. In 1889 she founded the German Women Teachers' Association.

In 1894, in the course of a heated dispute with the more radical supporters of MINNA CAUER, Lange formed the Berlin Women's Association. She led the moderate wing of the movement during the 1890s and was highly influential in the Federation of German Women's Associations, together with her secretary and assistant GERTRUDE BAUMER. They also worked to persuade the Progressive Party to give active support to female suffrage. During World War I Lange emphasised women's duty to perform voluntary service, preparing the way for Baumer's National Women's Service.

For many years from its foundation in 1893, Lange was associated with *Die Frau*, the main journal of the movement. With Baumer, she also edited the *Handbuch der Frauenbegung*, which appeared in five volumes between 1901 and 1906. A selection of her polemical writing is included in *Kampfeitzen* (1928) [2 vols]. She died in Berlin.

**Langer, Susanne Knauth** (1895–1985). American philosopher. Born in New York City, she graduated from Radcliffe College in 1920 and obtained a PhD in 1926. She wrote *The Practice of Philosophy* in 1930, then held various teaching posts; she lectured at Columbia University from 1945 to 1950 and became Professor of Philosophy at Connecticut College from 1945 to 1962, continuing afterwards as an emeritus professor. Influenced by Alfred North Whitehead, her chief works have been on linguistic analysis and aesthetics, notably *Philosophy in a new Key: a Study in the Symbolism of Reason, Rite and Art* (1942). She elaborates the distinction between the modes of art and science, 'non-discursive and discursive symbols', in other works such as *Feeling and Form* (1953) and *Mind: an Essay on Human Feeling* (1967–72) [2 vols].

Her other books include *An Introduction to Symbolic Logic* (2/1953), *Problems of Art* (1957), and *Philosophical Sketches* (1962).

**Langtry** [née le Breton, Emilie Charlotte], **Lily** (1853–1929). English actress. Because of her outstanding beauty she was known as the Jersey Lily (she was the daughter of the Dean of Jersey). At the age of 22 she married Edward Langtry (*d* 1897), a wealthy Irishman. She became a dazzling leader of London society and was an intimate friend of Edward VII, then Prince of Wales. She made her stage debut as Kate Hardcastle in *She Stoops to Conquer* at the Haymarket in December 1881: her beauty and social standing attracted more attention than her acting ability, which was never more than pleasingly competent. She organized her own company, which she ran efficiently, playing in London, where she managed the Imperial Theatre, the provinces and in the USA. She married a second time, to Hugo de Bathe in 1899 (he became a baronet in 1907), and lived extravagantly, maintaining a large racing stable at Newmarket, Suffolk. In 1925 she wrote her autobiography,

L. Langtry: *The Days I Knew* (1925)
J. Birkett: *Lily Langtry* (1979)

**Lansing, Sherry (Lee)** (1944–). Film company executive. Sherry Lansing was born in Chicago, and after her father's early death was brought up by her mother, a Jewish refugee from Nazi Germany, who later married Norton Lansing. She attended a school for gifted children, the University of Chicago Laboratory High School, and in 1966 graduated brilliantly in theatre from Northwestern University. The same year she moved to Watts, Los Angeles, to teach in high school, but left to become a freelance model, obtaining minor glamour parts in a couple of films: she describes herself as 'a terrible actress'. Fascinated by the business, she took film courses at UCLA and the University of Southern California and began reading scripts, soon becoming an executive story editor for Warner International, and then, in 1975, for MGM, where she became 'vice-president of creative affairs' in 1979. In November of that year she moved to Columbia, where she was in charge of production of successful films including *The China Syndrome* (with JANE FONDA), and *Kramer v.*

*Kramer* (with MERYL STREEP). At the beginning of 1980 she was appointed president of the feature-film division of Twentieth Century Fox, with a salary of $300,000 plus bonuses, the first woman to be put in charge of production at a major studio. Tough, energetic, notoriously hard-working, she is still an addict of the movies, saying 'I like to stand on line, buy my popcorn, and see a picture with the people.' She remained at Fox until 1983, when she founded her own company, Jaffe–Lansing productions.

**La Pola.** *See* SALAVARRIETA, POLA.

**La Saragossa.** *See* SARAGOSSA, LA.

**Laskaridou, Aikaterini** (1842–1916). Greek educationalist and feminist. She was typical of the rich, educated middle-class women who at this period were ambitious to improve the intellectual status of Greek women. Education was the only sphere in which such women could work effectively and achieve some of their objectives. Laskaridou went to Western Europe to study educational systems, which she then tried to apply in her own country, spending her entire personal fortune on the subject. She opened the first nursery schools in Greece and trained teachers to work in them. It was in response to her ideas that gymnastics were introduced into girls' schools, and workshops created where poor women could obtain a basic training.

Among her many writings are treatises on education for girls and on child rearing. She also published a few short stories.

**Lathrop, Julia** (1858–1932). American reformer. Born in Rockford, Illinois, the daughter of a keen suffragist, she was educated in the local high school and graduated from Vassar College in 1880. She then worked as a secretary in her father's law office and in local businesses before joining JANE ADDAMS's Hull House Settlement, Chicago, in 1890. Here she remained for 20 years, working on the Illinois Board of Charities from 1893 to 1901 and from 1905 to 1909, and arguing especially for separate relief schemes for children and for the insane. She also studied mental-health care in Europe, and in 1909 became a member of the National Committee for Mental Hygiene. Another interest was the professional training of social workers, and she was connected with the Chicago School of Philanthropy from 1908 to 1920.

In 1899 she had been part of a group pressing successfully for the establishment of juvenile courts and probation systems, and in 1912 she was appointed first Head of the Federal Children's Bureau. The Bureau investigated infant mortality, produced pamphlets on child care and enforced the child-labour laws in 1916. In 1921 she retired due to illness, but remained President of the Illinois League of Women Voters (1922–4), and from 1925 to 1931 worked on the Child Welfare Committee of the League of Nations. Lathrop was an unusual, unconventional woman, whose concern with organized welfare never blinded her to individual misery and injustice.

**Latina, La.** *See* GALINDO, BEATRIZ.

**Latynina, Larissa (Semyonovna)** (1935–). Russian gymnast. Larissa Latynina has been the most successful gymnast of all time, male or female, in terms of the medals she won between 1956 and 1964. She began her public achievement by overtaking the Hungarians at the 1954 World Championships to win the combined exercises and four other gold medals. At the 1955 European Championships and the 1958 World Championships she won a record five gold medals at each competition.

In the course of three Olympic Games (1956, 1960 and 1964) she won more Olympic medals than anyone else in any sport, although her count of six individual golds was exceeded by her champion successor in gymnastics, VERA CASLAVSKA. Larissa won three golds as a team member, plus five silver and three bronze medals, making an unsurpassed total of eighteen.

At the 1964 Olympic Games Larissa was beaten into second place in the combined exercises by Vera Caslavska. By 1966 she had ceased to win individual medals but helped Russia to achieve second place in the team event of the world championships. She retired in that year, having modernized the sport, and continued to influence it with her advanced techniques by becoming a coach. She also had two children during her career and worked as a city councillor for Kiev for several years.

**Lauder, Estée** (1908–). American business-woman. Born Josephine Estée Mentzer, Estée Lauder is the subject of a classic American success story. The daughter of poor Jewish parents from Eastern Europe, she grew up in the Corona section of Queens, New Jersey. After 20 years of slow hard work in the cosmetics industry, starting by selling a face cream made by her Hungarian uncle, she brought out her Youth Dew scented bath oil, which was an enormous success in the 1950s and 1960s. Innovative, with a talent for adapting, marketing and promotion, she built up an estimated $1 billion a year business, bringing in scent-free hypo-allergenic cosmetics ('Clinique'), and 'Aramis' cosmetics for men. Her husband and partner Joe Lauder died in 1982 and their son Leonard now runs the company. She is also renowned for her lavish life style, inveterate socializing and flamboyant likeable personality.

E. Lauder: *Estée: A Success Story* (1986)

**Laurence, (Jean) Margaret** (1926–86). Canadian novelist. Born Jean Margaret Wernyss, she grew up in the small prairie town of Neepawa, Manitoba, during the Depression. Its harsh Scots Presbyterianism gave the background for her later 'Manawaka' novels. She decided to become a writer as a girl, and after graduating from United College, Winnipeg, worked as a reporter for the trade-union-backed *Winnipeg Citizen*.

In 1947 she married an engineer, moving first to England and then, in 1950, to Somalia and Ghana, until 1957. In 1954 she published a collection of translations from Somali poetry and folk tales, and East Africa gave her settings for *This Side Jordan* (1960) and the stories in *The Tomorrow Tamer* (1963). After five years in Canada she returned to England in 1962 and wrote the Manawaka books, which include *The Stone Angel* (1964), *A Jest of God* (1966, filmed as *Rachel, Rachel*), *The Fire-Dwellers* (1969), the story-cycle *A Bird in the House* (1970) and *The Diviners* (1974). This last novel was banned in Canadian schools because of its explicit sexual scenes, a fact which angered her greatly, but it won the Governor General's Award, as *A Jest of God* had done previously. She later returned to Canada. An open-hearted, friendly woman, she was writer in residence at Toronto University (1969–70) and went on to write stories, children's books, and

a study of African literature. She was completing a volume of memoirs when she died.

**Laurencin, Marie** (1886–1956). French painter. Born in Paris, an illegitimate child, she was brought up in relative prosperity, educated at the Lycée Lamartine and studied drawing at the Académie Humbert. She was friendly with Braque and Picasso, and had a lengthy and tumultuous affair with Apollinaire from 1908; he included her in his work on *Les peintres cubistes* (1913). She first exhibited in the Salon des Independents (1907) and then at the Galerie Barbazouges (1912). Her impact at this time is described in GERTRUDE STEIN's *Autobiography of Alice B. Toklas*. In 1914 she married the German artist Otto von Waerjen, and forced into exile by World War I they escaped to Barcelona. There she contributed poems and articles to Picabia's Dadaist periodical *391*. She continued to correspond with Apollinaire until his death in 1918, and by 1920 was divorced and had returned to Paris.

Increasingly famous, she had exhibitions in Paris, London and other cities, and turned her hand to oils, lithography, water colours, dress design for the famous art-deco designer Poiret, and wallpaper and textiles for André Groult. She also wrote poetry (*Petit bestiaire*, 1926), illustrated books and designed the sets and costumes for BRONISLAVA NIJINSKA's *Les biches*, performed by the Ballets Russes in 1924. She continued to paint portraits, and is especially well known for her elongated, stylized society women.

C. Gere: *Marie Laurencin* (1978)

**Lavin, Mary** (1912–). Irish writer. Mary Lavin was born in East Walpole, Massachusetts, but her parents returned to Ireland when she was nine and settled in County Meath. She went to the Loreto Convent in Dublin, and became an MA of the National University in Ireland in 1937. After a visit to America she began writing fiction, publishing a short story in *Dublin Magazine* in 1938. Her first collection, *Tales from Bective Bridge* (1942), won the James Tait Black Memorial Prize, and the short fiction has been the form in which she excels. Thirteen more collections have since appeared, up to *A Family Likeness* (1985); her selected stories appeared in 1984. She has also written two novels, *The House in*

*Clewe Street* (1945) and *Mary O'Grady* (1950).

In 1942 Mary Lavin married William Walsh and they had three daughters. He died in 1954 and in 1969 she married Michael Macdonald Scott. She still lives in Bective, County Meath. One of Ireland's leading contemporary authors, she has received numerous awards, was President of Irish PEN in 1964–5 and President of the Irish Academy of Letters in 1971–3.

**Lavoisier** [née Paulze]**, Marie (Anne Pierrette)** (1758–1836). French chemist. Although not an original scientist, she contributed greatly to science by her translations and by her assistance to her husband, Antoine Lavoisier, 'founder of modern chemistry'. Marie, the daughter of a farmer-general and friend of Lavoisier, married when she was 14. They had no children and she spent the next 23 years collaborating with him in his laboratory work on combustion and respiration. They developed the law of conservation of matter in chemical changes, coined the word 'oxygène' (oxygen) in 1777, and established the basis of chemical nomenclature.

Marie learned Latin and English, which Lavoisier did not read, and translated the chemical works of Henry Cavendish and Priestley, and Kirwan's *Essay on Phlogiston*. She studied art with the painter David and became a skilled draughtswoman and engraver, illustrating Lavoisier's *Traité de chimie*. Most of the work was carried out at a laboratory Lavoisier established at the Paris Arsenal.

After Lavoisier's and her father's death on the guillotine in 1794, Marie edited her husband's *Mémoires de chimie*. He had planned eight volumes; she produced two, and distributed them, unsold, to eminent scientists in 1805. There followed a four-year marriage to an American-born wit and scientist, the Count of Rumford, which ended in separation. Marie continued to hold a salon frequented by eminent scientists until her death.

**Lawrence** [née von Richthofen]**, Frieda (Emma Johanna Maria)** (1879–1956). German-English literary personality. She was born in Metz, the daughter of Baron Friedrick von Richthofen, a former army officer and the new civil governor of the city where Frieda spent her childhood. At the age of 17, after spending a year in Berlin high society, she returned to Metz, met Professor Ernest Weekly, and came to live in Nottingham after their marriage in 1898; they had three children. In 1910 she fell in love with D. H. Lawrence, one of her husband's pupils. They left together for Germany in 1912 and were married in 1914.

Frieda inspired Lawrence by her unconventional behaviour, beauty, gaiety and sensuality. They both had volatile personalities and their relationship was often fiery, but she left him only once, unable to bear his religious quest in Mexico, and then they were reunited in Europe. After his death in 1930 she settled in New Mexico, and in 1952 married the artist Angelo Ravagli.

F. Lawrence: *Not I, but the Wind* (1936)

**Lawrence** [née Berg]**, Mary (Georgene Wells)** (1928– ). American advertising executive. She was born in Youngstown, Ohio, the daughter of a furniture salesman. In 1944 she graduated from the Carnegie Institute of Technology; while there she had married Burt Wells, and they later adopted two daughters. She worked in her home town as a copywriter at McKelvey's, a local department store, for a year before moving to Macy's, New York, in 1952 to manage their fashion advertising. She then moved into advertising herself, working for McCann-Erikson and other big New York agencies for 13 years. Her biggest account, undertaken with Rich and Greene, was the complete 'repackaging' of Braniff Airlines, demanding re-styling down to the last detail. In 1966 she is said to have turned down a 10-year million-dollar contract, instead starting her own company, Wells, Rich, Greene Inc., of which she has remained Chairman and Chief Executive. She took it rapidly to the top of the league of agencies, and in the 1980s is reputed to be the most powerful woman in the industry as well as the highest-paid executive in the USA. In 1965 she divorced Wells, and in 1967 married Harding Lawrence, the Chairman of Braniff Airlines.

**Lawson, Louisa** (1848–1902). Australian feminist. Born at Guntawang, New South Wales, at 18 she married gold-digger and ex-seaman Peter Larsen (anglicized to Lawson). Their first child, the writer Henry Lawson, was born in 1867 in a tent on a digging near Grenfell, New South Wales. She became involved in politics in 1876 when she began campaigning for a local school but was not allowed to attend meetings because she was a woman. After separating from her husband in 1883 she took the children to Sydney, and earned her living as a seamstress. Becoming involved in radical and feminist politics she founded a discussion group, the Dawn Club, in 1888, and edited the newspaper *The Dawn* from 1889, insisting that it would be produced entirely by women, despite opposition from the typographical unions. Her club's interests were defined as 'health, temperance, suffrage, social purity, education, dress reform and physiological matters'. She brought out *The Dawn* for 17 years, and her other activities as a feminist included the founding of the Darlinghurst Hostel for Working Girls. In her last years she grew increasingly isolated and embittered, but she lived to see the achievement of the vote for women in New South Wales in 1902.

**Leakey** [née Douglas], **Mary** (1913–). English archaeologist. She was born in London and educated privately. In 1936 she married the anthropologist and archaeologist Louis Leakey; they had three sons. While working with Leakey in Tanganyika [now Tanzania] in 1959, it was Mary who noticed the skull in Olduvai Gorge which became known as the famous 'missing link', demonstrating that man had evolved in different branches and about a million years earlier than had been thought. After Louis' death in 1972 Mary remained in Tanzania, and continued work as Director of the Olduvai Gorge excavations. She has contributed to many learned and scientific journals, establishing herself quietly as a leading authority on prehistoric technology and the culture this implies. In 1983 she published *Africa's Vanishing Art: The Rock Paintings of Tanzania*, and then two volumes of autobiography, *Disclosing the Past* (1984) and *Lasting Impressions* (1985).

**Lease** [née Clyens], **Mary (Elisabeth)** (1850– 1933). American politician. The daughter of Catholic Irish immigrants, she grew up on a farm on the border of Pennsylvania and New York State. Her father died in the Civil War in 1864, and after she graduated from St Elizabeth Academy, Allegheny, she became a teacher. Then, in 1870, she went to work in Kansas, where she married Charles Lease, a pharmacist, three years later. After ten unsuccessful years of farming, Mary and her four children moved to Wichita. She formed a women's discussion group, spoke in public on behalf of the Irish National League (1885), and became an active member of the Union Labor Party, supporting the small farmers. In 1888 she edited the *Union Labor Press*, and on a visit in 1889 helped found the *Colorado Workman*.

From 1890 to 1894 she gained a wide reputation as a powerful, dramatic, spontaneous orator for the Farmer's Alliance and the People's Party, campaigning throughout the South and West. Under the populist state government of 1893–4 she was for a short time President of the Board of Charities; her dismissal after an argument with the Party led to prolonged litigation. She then wrote *The Problem of Civilization Solved* (1895), which tackles everything from colonization to protective tariffs. After her divorce in 1902 she retired to New York where she lectured, campaigned for women's suffrage and was President of the National Society for Birth Control.

R. Stiller: *Queen of Populists*

**Leavitt, Henrietta Swan** (1868–1921). American astronomer. Born in Lancaster, Massachusetts, she had a puritanical upbringing as one of seven children. She studied astronomy at Radcliffe College and received an AB in 1892. After travelling, she volunteered as a research assistant at Harvard College Observatory and rapidly advanced to a permanent position as Head of the Photographic Photometry Department.

Edward Pickering, the director, planned to establish a standard photographic sequence based on stars near the North Celestial Pole, and Henrietta carried out this work meticulously. Her most famous discovery was the periodical luminosity relation of the constellation Cepheid (variable stars). Although not bringing her much publicity, this work was extremely valuable in making possible investigations of the Milky Way galaxy. Her more obvious contribution to astronomy was the discovery of 2400 variable stars, about half of those known at the time.

Like ANNIE JUMP CANNON, Henrietta was very deaf. She was deeply religious, and devoted to her work and family, living with her mother after her father's death. She died of cancer.

**Le Blanc.** *See* GERMAIN, SOPHIE.

**Le Blond** [née Hawkins-Whitshed], **Elizabeth** [Mrs Aubrey] (1861–1934). British mountaineer. She was brought up mainly in Ireland. While married to Fred Burnaby, a soldier, she climbed Mont Blanc and the Grandes Jorasses in 1882. After being widowed she bicycled to Italy. During her second marriage, as Mrs Main, she travelled in China but she was again widowed, and after her third marriage, to Aubrey Le Blond, she achieved fame as a mountaineer.

She made long winter and spring ascents, and was the first woman to lead guideless parties at this time. In Italy she climbed Piz Sella, Piz Zugo and the Disgrazia (among others), and her ascent of Piz Palu in 1900, with Lady Evelyn McDonnel, was probably the first 'women's rope'. Over her breeches she wore a skirt which she removed on the higher stretches, and she had a lady's maid to accompany her as far as possible. After 1895 she climbed mainly in Norway, but in 1907 she became the first President of the new Ladies' Alpine Club and was elected for a second term in 1932.

**Lecouvreur, Adrienne** (1692–1730). French actress. The daughter of a poor hatter, she began acting in amateur productions at the age of 14, but was helped by the actor-dramatist Legrand, and eventually joined the Comédie-Française. In her 13 years with that company her natural style of acting prevailed over the academic diction of her rivals; she also advocated historically accurate costumes. She excelled in tragic roles and is associated with the first productions of plays by Crébillon, La Motte and Voltaire. Her fame and energetic love-life inspired plays like *Adrienne Lecouvreur* by Scribe (1849). She was for some time the mistress of Maréchal Saxe. After her sudden

death she was refused Christian burial (apparently because she had not renounced her acting profession), and was interred secretly at night in a corner of the rue de Bourgogne. Voltaire, who was with her when she died, subsequently wrote a poem criticizing the Church's attitude.

**Lee, 'Gypsy Rose'** [Hovick, Rose Louise] (1914–70). American stripper. Born in Seattle, Washington, she joined her mother and sister June on a vaudeville circuit when she was four, and by the age of six was a regular performer in the act 'Dainty June and her Newsboy Songsters'. When she was 16, in Kansas City, she took lessons from Tessie the Tassel Twirler, who gave her the famous advice, 'You've gotta leave 'em hungry for more. You don't dump the whole roast on the platter'. She achieved stardom at once, moving from Minsky's Republic Theatre to the Ziegfeld Follies in 1936. Her act was suggestive yet decorous, and sprinkled with intellectual references. She retired from stripping in 1937 and went to Hollywood where she made *Ali Baba Goes to Town* (1937) and other undistinguished films in the late 1930s and the 1940s. She gave occasional stage performances later, including *Gypsy Rose Lee and Her American Beauties* (1949), *Auntie Mame* (1960) and *The Threepenny Opera* (1961). Her last appearance was in the film *The Stripper* (1963). She also wrote thrillers, such as *The G-String Murders*, and her autobiography, *Gypsy* (1957), was made into a Broadway musical (1959) and a film (1962).

**Lee, Jennie** [Baroness Lee of Asheridge] (1904-1988). Scottish politician. Daughter of a Fifeshire miner, she was born in Lochgelly, Fife, and won scholarships from her local school to the University of Edinburgh, where she went on to obtain an MA in Education in 1926 and an LLB in 1927. While a student, she worked at the strike headquarters in the city during the 1926 General Strike. For two years she worked in mining areas as a teacher, but in 1929 she was persuaded to stand as Independent Labour Party Candidate for North Lanark in the by-election. When she became an MP, at the age of 24, she was the youngest member of the House of Commons. Over the next two years she visited Austria and the USSR; she lost her parliamentary seat in 1931. Three years later she married the politician Aneurin Bevan (d 1960). She continued her involvement with the Labour Party, lecturing extensively in the USA, Europe and the USSR, and over the next decade published *Tomorrow is a New Day* (1939) and *Russia our Ally* (1941). During World War II she supervised shop-floor conditions for the Ministry of Aircraft Production. In 1945 she was returned as MP for Cannock, retaining her seat until her retirement in 1970. A left-winger, she was Director of *Tribune*, and was on the National Executive Committee of the Labour Party from 1958 to 1970, being Chairman from 1967–1968. She was Parliamentary Secretary, Ministry of Public Building and Works (1964–5), Under-Secretary of State for Education and Science (1965–7), and Minister of State (1967–70). In 1970 she was created Baroness Lee of Asheridge. Her books include *This Great Journey* (1963) and the vivid autobiographical and political memoirs *My Life with Nye* (1980).

**Lee, 'Mother' Ann** (1736–84). American religious leader. Born in Manchester, England, the daughter of a blacksmith, she started work young and never learned to read or write. In her early 20s she joined the Shaking Quakers, or Shakers, whose worship centred on the open confession of sin. She married Abraham Standerin, a blacksmith, and they had four children, all of whom died in infancy. As a child, Ann had urged her mother to withstand her father's lust, and the deaths of her children and her mother strengthened her repugnance for marriage and she became convinced of the sin of sexual relations.

In 1774 a vision directed Ann to go to the USA, which she did with a small party of friends and relatives. After a severe illness, her husband renounced his Shaker principles and left her, so she joined the Shaker community at Watervliet, near Albany, New York. 'Mother' Ann continued to have visions and revelations concerning the conduct of her Church and she, herself, was regarded by her followers as the second appearance of Christ, Jesus having been the first, and both being

necessary for the complete revelation of the Father–Mother God.

From 1781 to just before her death, 'Mother' Ann and some of the elders toured New England holding meetings for the increasing numbers of Shakers and preaching a practical message of simple honesty, frugality and industry.

H. Desroches: *The American Shakers from Neo-Christianity to Presocialism* (1971)

**LeFanu, Nicola (Frances)** (1947–). English composer. The youngest daughter of the composer ELIZABETH MACONCHY, she studied music at Oxford University as a pupil of Egon Wellesz and at the Royal College of Music, London. In 1968 she was awarded a scholarship to attend a series of Goffredo Petrassi's master classes in Siena and in 1973–4, on a Harkness Fellowship to Harvard and Brandeis universities, continued her studies with Earl Kim and Seymour Shifrin. Also active as a teacher, she was appointed a lecturer at King's College, London, in 1977, a post she later shared with her husband, the Australian composer David Lumsdaine; they have directed several composers' seminars together, notably in 1979 as joint composers-in-residence at the New South Wales Conservatorium, Sydney.

LeFanu is primarily associated with her music theatre pieces, initiated by *Antiworld* (1972; for dancer, soprano, baritone, alto flute, clarinet and percussion), which incorporates poems by Russian dissidents, and *The Last Laugh* (1972), written for the Ballet Rambert as a result of winning a Gulbenkian Dance Award. She produced her own libretto for the chamber opera *Dawnpath* (1977), based on American Indian myths of creation and death. The monodrama *The Old Woman of Beare* (1981), which received its première at the 50th-anniversary series of the MacNaghten Concerts, was inspired by an Irish poem of the 9th or 10th century; LeFanu's handling of the instrumental writing here reflects her concern to exploit dramatic effect without losing the lyrical quality that characterizes her most effective chamber music, for instance *Deva* (1979), an octet with solo cello. Among her most notable orchestral works are *The Hidden Landscape* (1973), commissioned by the BBC and first performed at the Proms, and *Columbia Falls* (1975). Other important commissions include the song cycle *The Same Day Dawns* (1974; Fromm Foundation), first performed in Boston, and the radiophonic opera *The Story of Mary O'Neill* (1986; BBC).

**Lefaucheux** [née Postel Vinay], **Marie-Hélène** (1904–64). French feminist. Born in Paris, she studied music and attended the Ecole du Louvre, then went on to become one of the first women students at the Ecole des Sciences Politiques. She married a lawyer and civil engineer, Pierre Lefaucheux. During World War II they became prominent members of the Résistance, and in 1944, Pierre, now leader of the Parisian Résistance, was arrested, but she managed to get him released from Buchenwald. After the war she was awarded the Croix de Guerre and Rosette de la Résistance.

Her husband then became President of Renault and she became a Deputy in the Assembly in 1945, and Vice-President of the Paris Municipal Council. From 1946 to 1948 she was a member of the Senate (Conseil de la République), and she then represented metropolitan France in the Assembly of the French Union, becoming Vice-President from 1959 to 1960. She was also a founder of the Association des Femmes de l'Union Française, particularly concerned with the welfare of African and Algerian students. A member of the French delegation to the First General Assembly of the United Nations, and to many subsequent UN and UNESCO conferences, she represented France on the UN Commission on the Status of Women from its inception, being President in 1947 and acting on behalf of the Status of Women Commission on the Commission of Human Rights.

She was President of the National Council of Women from 1954 and then elected President of the International Council of Women in 1957, retiring in 1963. The following year she was killed in a plane crash in the USA.

**Le Fort, Gertrud (Petrea), Baroness von** (1876–1971). German poet and novelist. The daughter of a Prussian army officer, Gertrud was educated at home in a devout Protestant family, and then studied philosophy and theology at the universities of Heidelberg, Marburg and Berlin: the only woman student in her classes. She did not publish her poetry until 1924, when the religious cycle *Hymnen aun die Kirche* appeared. In 1926 she converted to Roman Catholicism, and was to become known as Germany's leading Roman Catholic novelist, with works such as *The Veil of Veronica* (1928), the historical *The Pope from the Ghetto* (1930) and *Song at the Scaffold* (1931). This last novel became the basis of Poulenc's opera *The Carmelites* (1956) and her novels of the 1930s seemed to many a protest against contemporary German oppression as well as a study of earlier persecutions. Her own family estates were confiscated by the Nazis. She continued to write fiction and poetry, and her work has remained highly regarded.

**Legh, Alice Blanche** (1855–1948). English archer. Archery was the first sport to have been taken up with any real success by women, and Alice Legh held an amazing record of 23 British championships spanning 41 years (1881–1922). Between 1882 and 1885 Alice's own mother, Mrs Piers Legh, won the championship from her, and World War I prevented the event from being held between 1915 and 1918. Alice held two record runs of seven and eight consecutive titles, ending in 1892 and 1909 respectively.

**Lehmann, Lilli** (1848–1929). German soprano. She spent her childhood in Prague, studying singing with her mother, Marie Loewe; she made her debut there in 1865 as the First Boy in *Die Zauberflöte*. After appearing in Danzig [now Gdańsk] and Leipzig, in 1870 she joined the Berlin Opera, breaking her contract in 1885 to go to the USA. Recognition had come slowly, her first important engagement (albeit in small parts) being in 1876, when she was invited to sing in the first Bayreuth Festival, as Woglinde, Helmwige and the Woodbird in the première of *The Ring*. Having made her London debut (as Violetta in *La traviata*) in 1880, she sang Isolde at Covent Garden in 1884, a role she repeated for the first American production of *Tristan* in 1886. She had made her Metropolitan debut as Carmen the previous year, singing Brünnhilde (*Die Walküre*) and several other leading roles in the same season; in 1889 she sang in America's first complete *Ring* cycle. On her return to Germany that year, the

Kaiser banned her from operatic performances as a penalty for having overstayed her leave; the ban was lifted in 1891. She returned to Bayreuth in 1896 and to Covent Garden in 1899, her final season there including Isolde and Bellini's Norma. Although remembered primarily as a Wagnerian, she had an astonishingly wide range of roles (at least 170, in about 120 operas), excelling particularly in Mozart. She sang at the Salzburg Festival between 1901 and 1910 and was for a time its artistic director. After her retirement from the stage she continued to give concert performances (until 1920) and was active as a teacher. She published *Meine Gesangskunst* (1902) and *Mein Weg* (1913; Eng. trans. as *My Path through Life*, 1914).

**Lehmann, Lotte** (1888–1976). German–American soprano. She studied singing in Berlin with Mathilde Mallinger. Having been associated with the Hamburg Opera since 1908, she made her solo debut there as Aennchen in Nicolai's *Merry Wives of Windsor*. Based in Vienna from 1916 to 1938, when the implications of the *Anschluss* caused her to leave, she attracted an exceptionally warm following in England and the USA, as well as in Austria. Her first London appearance, in 1914, was as Sophie in Richard Strauss's *Rosenkavalier* – she was the first to appear successively in all three soprano roles, her Marschallin being virtually unsurpassed. Strauss chose her for the premières of *Die Frau ohne Schatten* (Vienna, 1919) and *Intermezzo* (Dresden, 1924), and she also had notable success in *Ariadne auf Naxos* and *Arabella*. Although primarily associated with his music and Wagner's, notably as Sieglinde in *Die Walküre* (the role of her American debut, 1930), she was much acclaimed for her interpretations of Leonore in Beethoven's *Fidelio* and for her lieder recitals; her earlier career included roles in operas by Massenet, Tchaikovsky and Puccini.

An accomplished painter, she further demonstrated her versatility by publishing several autobiographical works, books on interpretation, a novel and some poetry; she continued to teach and give master classes after her retirement from the stage.

G. Beaumont: *Lotte Lehmann* (1987)

**Lehmann, Rosamond (Nina)** (1901–). English Writer. Born and brought up in Buckinghamshire, she was one of four children of the Liberal MP R.C. Lehmann and his spirited New England wife; her sister Beatrix became a famous actress and her brother John a well-known writer and publisher. After a private education she won a scholarship to Girton College, Cambridge (she was made an Honorary Fellow in 1986). Her first novel, *Dusty Answer* (1927), written after her short, unhappy marriage to Leslie Runciman and a miserable period in the north of England, was a huge success, bringing notoriety as well as fame, since it dealt with the passionate feelings of a young society girl. After her second marriage, to the artist the Hon. Wogan Phillips, she published *A Note in Music* (1930), which also caused a stir because it dealt with homosexuality. *An Invitation to the Waltz* (1932) was followed by its sequel *The Weather in the Streets* (1936) which (despite its romantic bent) confirmed her reputation for controversy by raising the issues of unhappy marriage, adultery and abortion. Her post-war novels included the semi-autobiographical *The Ballard and the Source* (1944) and *The Echoing Grave* (1953), and her war-time short stories for John Lehmann's *New Writing* were collected in *The Gipsy's Baby* (1946). She wrote no further fiction until *A Sea-Grape Tree* (1970).

A turning point in her life was the tragic death of her daughter Sally in 1958, which led to her subsequent belief in spiritual contact after death; she is now President of the College of Psychic Studies. She also remains involved in the literary world, as an International Vice-President of PEN and a member of the Council of the Society of Authors. Among other distinctions, Rosamond Lehmann was awarded the CBE in 1982. She lives near Aldeburgh, Suffolk.

**Leigh, Vivien** [pseud. of Vivian Mary Hartley] (1913–67). English actress. She was born in Darjeeling, where her father was in business, but went to England in 1920 and was educated at the Convent of the Sacred Heart, Roehampton, until she was 13; she then attended schools and convents in France, Italy and Bavaria. At the age of 18, already a noted society beauty, she went to the Royal Academy of Dramatic Art, and although she married a barrister, Leigh Holman, in 1932, she returned to the stage after the birth of their daughter, in 1934. Her success in *The Mask of Virtue* (1935) led to a five-year contract with Alexander Korda, who cast her with Laurence Olivier in *Fire over England* (1937). She also played Ophelia in Olivier's Elsinore production of *Hamlet*, and after her sensational success as Scarlett O'Hara in *Gone with the Wind* (1939) their respective marriages were dissolved, and they were married in California in 1940.

During 1942 she appeared on stage in *The Doctor's Dilemma* and toured North Africa entertaining the services. After the war her success continued with *The Skin of our Teeth* (1945), a tour of Australia and New Zealand (1947–8), and her interpretations of Antigone (1949) and of Blanche in *A Streetcar named Desire*; she won her second Oscar for the film version in 1951. During the 1950s she took several classical roles at Stratford-upon-Avon, but began to suffer from nervous problems. In 1960 she risked her reputation when she stood up in the balcony of the House of Lords to protest the demolition of St James's Theatre, and led a march through London. The same year her marriage to Olivier ended, and although she continued to act she suffered several severe breakdowns before her death from tuberculosis in 1967.

J. Russell Taylor: *Vivien Leigh* (1985)

**Leigh-Smith, Barbara.** *See* BODICHON, BARBARA.

**Lejeune, Caroline Alice** (1897–1973). British film critic. Born in Didsbury, Manchester, C.A. Lejeune was the youngest of eight children; her father died when she was a year old. She was educated at Withington Girls' School and although she passed the Oxford entrance examination she decided to stay at home, first working as a secretary and then studying English at Manchester University, obtaining a first-class degree in 1921. She began to review opera for the *Manchester Guardian*, and then, from the age of 24, concentrated on film. At that time there were few film critics, and she had to move to London, combining her work with study for a PhD. Her regular film column in the *Guardian* first appeared in 1922. In 1925 she married the journalist Roffe Thompson and

they moved to Middlesex, where their son was born in 1928.

C.A. Lejeune was a distinguished, original critic, alert to new developments such as the coming of sound, and (although she herself did not travel abroad) keen to introduce new foreign directors to British audiences. Her friends in the film world included Korda and Hitchcock, and her work remained highly influential until her retirement in 1960. Her written works include *Cinema* (1931), the selected reviews *Chestnuts in Her Lap* (1947) and her autobiography *Thank You for Having Me* (1964).

**Lemel, Nathalie** (1827–1921). French socialist. Originally a bookbinder, she became involved in radical politics in the strikes of the 1860s. She separated from her husband and became a member of the Socialist International. In the Commune of 1871 she founded a workers' restaurant with another bookbinder, Varlin. She was active in the popular clubs which the International organized on the Left Bank and in the central arondissements, and helped ELISABETH DMITRIEVA from the Women's Union for the Defence of Paris. After the fall of the Commune, she was deported with LOUISE MICHEL and other leading women communards. She later returned to France and took part in feminist and socialist groups until World War I.

**Lenclos.** *See* DE LENCLOS.

**Lenglen, Suzanne** (1899–1938). French lawn tennis player. In all-time ratings of women tennis players, Suzanne is generally ranked first. In 1914 she won the international Clay Court Championship at St Cloud, then from her first Wimbledon title in 1919 until 1926 when she turned professional, she dominated both the game – losing only one match, to Molla Mallory – and the public. Her poor background and her parents' ambition added to her own desire for victory, and her high emotion and glamour, as well as her graceful tennis, proved appealing. Her shorter, more daring style of dress, and particularly her striped bandeau, were copied slavishly.

She won the French championship seven times, missing the event in 1924 when she was ill with jaundice. She achieved great consistency with the rhythm and sweep of her strokes and rarely dropped more than a few games; an exception was to her friend and rival Elizabeth Ryan in the French championship, to whom she lost the middle set in a 6–2, 6–8, 6–4 victory. In the year of her first win at Wimbledon she had never played on grass before; she won there five more years before quarrelling with a referee, and then turned professional. She also ran a coaching school in Paris.

Thereafter her tennis was not notable. She had, however, already made women's tennis popular and professional in approach, and when she died of pernicious anaemia, on the eve of Wimbledon, her funeral was a national event; she was awarded a post-humous Cross of the Légion d'Honneur.

**Lenngren** [née Malmstedt], **Anna Maria** (1754–1817). Swedish poet. She was the daughter of the academician Malmstedt, and in 1780 she married Carl Lenngren, who became councillor at the Royal Board of Commerce. Her first poems, published in periodicals, included *The Conseillen* (1777), a satire on woman's triviality. She then began writing for the *Stockholms-Posten*, co-edited by her husband and the influential critic Johan Kellgren. Her work ranges from elegant satirical attacks on the upper classes to realistic idylls of country life; in later years she became more reactionary, warning women not to abandon traditional roles in favour of acquiring learning or public positions.

**Lenormand, Marie (Anne Adelaide)** (1772–1843). French fortune-teller. Born in Alençon, she went to Paris, where she became known as 'The Sybil of the Faubourg Saint-Germain'. A skilful clairvoyant, she rose to fortune during the French Revolution when her anxious clients included Danton, Desmoulins, Marat, Saint-Just, and even Robespierre. She survived the Terror and found an equally profitable role under the Directoire and then the Empire. Napoleon allowed her to visit JOSEPHINE BUONAPARTE at Malmaison, where she predicted accurately their eventual divorce. Her other clients included the painter David and Madame de STAEL.

**Lenya, Lotte** (1898–1981). Austrian–American singer. She studied ballet and drama in Zürich from 1914 to 1920, after which she left for Berlin, turning her attention increasingly from dancing to acting; her reputation stems from the distinctive vocal style that she made her own. Through the playwright Georg Kaiser she established a friendship with Kurt Weill, whom she married in 1926. Weill's musical collaborations with Brecht bear the imprint of Lenya's characterizations: she took part in the première of their *Mahagonny* (1927), though their greatest and most enduring success came with *Die Dreigroschenoper* (1928), in which Lenya played Jenny. In 1933 she and Weill left for the USA. Weill wrote his choral ballet *Die sieben Todsünden* (1933) as a vehicle for Lenya, and in New York (where she and Weill settled in the 1930s) she created the roles of Miriam in *The Eternal Road* (1937) and the Duchess in *The Firebrand of Florence* (1945). Her inimitable style, captured on many recordings and in Pabst's film of *Die Dreigroschenoper*, recalls the atmosphere of Berlin during the 1920s and 1930s, which she captured with her individual blend of coolness, passion and musical insight.
H. Marx, ed.: *Weill–Lenya* (1976)

**Léon, Léonie** (1838–1906). French; the mistress of Léon Gambetta. Part Creole and part Jewish, attractive and well educated, she became the mistress of an imperial official, by whom she had a son. In 1868 she met the statesman Léon Gambetta and in 1872 became his mistress. Although he wanted her to marry him in 1879 she did not consent until 1882, and he died before the marriage took place. After his death she lived in retirement. She seems to have had a limited restraining influence on his political career.

**Léon, Pauline** (1758–?). French revolutionary and feminist. Born in Paris, the daughter of a chocolate manufacturer, after his death she helped her mother run the business and raise the five younger children. She welcomed the Revolution with enthusiasm and in 1791 she joined the Jacobin Société des Cordeliers, and addressed the National Assembly on behalf of Parisian women, requesting authorization for a women's militia, claiming that they were as essential as men to the armed defence of the Revolution. In July of that year she was one of the signatories of the petition at the Champs de Mars, where the crowds were violently attacked by Lafayette's cavalry. Léon was one of the principle founders of the Société des Révolutionaires Républicaines with CLAIRE LACOMBE and became its President in 1793. She married the leader of the Enragés party, Théophile Leclerc, in November 1793, and they criticized the hypocrisy and terror of the Jacobin regime. In 1794 she and her husband were arrested and spent some time in the Luxembourg prison. The rest of her career is obscure.

**Leonora Christina,** Countess Ulfeldt (1621–98). Danish writer. The daughter of King Christian IV and Christine Munk, she was born in the Royal Palace, Copenhagen, but brought up by her grandmother on the Isle of Flyn. A precocious student and gifted writer, she married Chancellor Count Corfitz Ulfeldt when she was 15; they had been betrothed since she was nine. Ulfeldt became Royal Seneschal in 1643, but after the death of Christian he became involved in treasonous intrigues in Denmark and Sweden. He was imprisoned and released, and sentenced to death *in absentia*; he died in 1668. By then Leonora had been captured in Dover, while on her way to reclaim a loan made to Charles II, who was in exile. She was imprisoned in the Blue Tower in Copenhagen for 22 years without sentence, until the death of her enemy the Dowager Queen Amalia Sofia. She wrote religious works and hymns, but is remembered for her brilliant, vivid and proud autobiography *Jammers Minde/Misery of the Imprisoned Countess Leonora Christina*, which was not discovered and published until 1869.

S. Birket-Smith, ed.: *Memoirs of Leonora Christina* (1872)

**Leontias, Sappho** (1832–1900). Greek writer and educationalist from Constantinople [now Istanbul]. She studied Classics and French and German literature, and for many years worked as a headmistress in girls' schools in the islands of Samos and Smyrna [now Izmir].

Sappho was one of the few enlightened women of her time who saw the importance of education for women as a means of improving their status in Greek society. She struggled for equal opportunities for women in education and gave open lectures on the subject. She published her own literary journal, *Euridice*, encouraging women to contribute to it and inviting works written in the Greek vernacular. Language was a burning issue among scholars of her time in Greece; they were divided into two camps, the one advocating the use of the sophisticated language of literary tradition, known as *katharevousa* (pure Greek), and the other encouraging the use of the naturally-evolved spoken language of the people. Sappho was in favour of the vernacular in schools and of the introduction of Greek Classics in modern translation into school curricula. She translated Aeschylus's *The Persians* into modern Greek, and Racine's *Esther* from the French. She wrote many works on educational topics, gave many lectures and took part in open debates on the language controversy, always impressing her audience with her vast knowledge and her pragmatic approach to various problems.

**Lepaute, Nicole-Reine (Etable de la Brière) Hortense** (1723–88). French astronomer. Her father was attached to the court of the Queen of Spain. She married Jean-André Lepaute, the royal clockmaker. She investigated the oscillations of pendula of different lengths, and her results were included in her husband's book, *Traité d'horlogerie* (1755).

In 1757 Lalande, the Director of the Paris Observatory, employed her and the mathematician Clairaut to determine the extent of the pull Jupiter and Saturn had on Halley's Comet. Clairaut was impressed with her work and called her 'La savante calculatrice', but did not acknowledge her contribution through jealousy.

She made calculations for the eclipse of 1762 and for the annular eclipse of 1764, including a table of parallactic angles which were published by the French government. Her monograph on the transit of Venus was published in 1761. Between 1759 and 1774 she helped Lalande with the annual *Connaissance des temps* for the Académie des Sciences. From 1774 to 1783 she worked on the seventh and eighth volumes of the

*Ephemeris*, in which calculations for the sun, moon and planets extended to 1784 and 1792 respectively. In old age her eyesight became poor. A Japan rose was named *Lepautia* in her honour, but was later renamed *Hortensia*.

**Lespinasse, Julie (Jeanne-Eléanore) de** (1732–76). French salon hostess and letter writer. The illegitimate child of the Comtesse d'Alban she was educated in a convent and then became governess to her legitimate half-sister, the Marquise de Vichy. Here she met Madame DU DEFFAND the brilliant leader of one of the most famous Paris salons. Du Deffand was growing blind, and in 1754 asked Julie to become her companion and reader in Paris. Over the next ten years Julie's charm, keen intelligence and emotional warmth made her extremely popular, and in 1764 she was dismissed by her jealous patron after a quarrel. She set up her own salon, attracting many of Du Deffand's intellectuals, and writers of the *Encyclopédie*, such as Turgot, Condorcet, and the philosopher and mathematician Jean d'Alembert. D'Alembert was devoted to her, but although she cared for him and they lived together she had other lovers, including the Spanish Marquis Gonsalvo de Mora, who died in 1774, and the flamboyant Comte de Guibert. Her passionate letters to Guibert, published in 1809, written in the last three years of her life, are a classic of unrequited love and despair. An interesting portrait of her is given by Diderot in *Le rêve de d'Alembert*, where she is shown to veer between intelligent frank sensitivity and a conventional prudery which leaves her shocked at her own actions.

J. Bouissonnouse: *Julie de Lespinasse* (trans 1962)

**Lessing, Doris** (1919–). Rhodesian novelist and short story writer. Born in Kermanshah, Iran, where her father was a British Army Captain, she lived with her family in Southern Rhodesia [now Zimbabwe] from 1924 to 1949, when she came to England. Her early months in England are described in *In Pursuit of the English* (1960). She was married twice, from 1939 to 1943 to Frank Wisdom, and to Gottfried Lessing from 1945 to 1949, and has three children.

Her first novel, *The Grass is Singing* (1951), reflects her racial concern, and much of her subsequent work such as *Martha Quest* (1966) is set in Southern Africa. A Communist in her youth, in her early novels she analysed the dilemmas of intellectuals and political activists with clarity and subtlety, and also explored the problems of women's independence, themes which are linked in her most famous work, *The Golden Notebook* (1962). Her short stories, collected in *A Man and Two Women* (1965) and *The Story of a Non-Marrying Man* (1972), are particularly perceptive. Her disillusionment with Communism is expressed in the tetralogy *Children of Violence* (1952–69). After her 'spiritual autobiography', *Memoirs of a Survivor* (1974), her work tended towards the moral mysticism apparent in the four books of the *Canopus in Argos Archives* (1979–82), but her recent books have moved away from the fantastic, for example *The Good Terrorist* (1985), and *The Fifth Child* (1987).

**Leverson** [née Beddington], **Ada** (1862–1933). English novelist. Born in London, the daughter of a couple moving in high society, and educated privately, she married Ernest Leverson when she was 18; they had a son, who died as a child, and a daughter. She began writing in 1885 and during the 1890s contributed sketches and parodies to periodicals such as *The Yellow Book* and *Punch*. Intelligent and sophisticated, she was the centre of a literary circle which included George Moore, Max Beerbohm and Oscar Wilde, whose loyal friend she remained throughout his trial and imprisonment, and who called her 'the wittiest woman in the world'. Her six novels, the first published when she was 45, all appeared between 1907 and 1916. They are brilliant and very funny comedies of manners, unusual in that they deal with the tensions of married life rather than of courtship. Three of them – *Love's Shadow* (1908), *Tenterhooks* (1912) and *Love at Second Sight* (1916) – are about the same couple, the Ottleys. Leverson continued to write occasional pieces as the women's columnist 'Elaine' for *The Referee* and for *The Criterion* (1926). In later years she became very deaf and divided her time between London and Italy, where she stayed with the Sitwells. Her daughter, Violet

Wyndham, based the title of Ada's biography on Wilde's name for her, 'my dear Sphinx'.

V. Wyndham: *The Sphinx and her Circle: a Biographical Sketch of Leverson* (1963)

**Levi-Montalcini, Rita** (1909–). Italian-American biologist. A brilliant young biologist, Levi-Montalcini was driven from Italy by the fascists just before World War II. She managed to continue her pioneering work on the nervous system, using makeshift equipment in her bedroom. Invited to work in America after the war, she discovered proteins which govern the development of cells essential to growth and recovery. In 1951 she suggested that the signals which allowed organs to link with developing nerve cells came from growth-stimulating chemicals, and in 1952 observed nerve fibres on single nerve cells. In 1953 she met Stanley Cohen, a biochemist, at Washington University, and their work together led to vital developments in the treatment of burns and of diseases such as cancer. They were awarded the joint Nobel Prize in 1986. She now works for the National Council of Scientific Research in Rome.

**Levin, Rahel.** *See* VARNHAGEN VON ENSE, RAHEL.

**Lewald, Fanny** (1811–89). German novelist. Born into a Jewish family in Königsberg [now Kalingrad], she became a Lutheran convert in order to marry a young theologian in 1828, but his sudden death occurred before the wedding could take place. In 1845 she met the schoolmaster and novelist Adolf Stahr, with whom she lived until they were free to marry, following his divorce in 1854. During these years she often travelled abroad, and published accounts of her visits to Italy, England and Scotland. When she met Stahr, Fanny Lewald was already a well-known novelist. Her first novels, *Clementine* (1842), *Jenny* (1843) and *Eine Lebensfrage* (1845) deal with the problems of marriage and of social injustice. In 1847 she wrote *Diogena*, parodying a novel by the writer Idavon Hahn-Hahn, followed by the novel *Prinz Louis Ferdinand* (1849) whose central character was the saloniste RAHEL VARNHAGEN VON ENSE. Her later books were realistic family sagas, *Von Geschlecht zu Geschlecht* (1863–5) and *Die Familie Darner*

(3 vols, 1887). Her autobiography, *Meine Lebensgeschichte*, was published in 1861.

**Lewis, (Mary) Edmonia** (1845–? after 1909). American sculptor. Born near Albany, New York, of Afro-American-Indian parentage, and brought up by her mother's tribe, the Chippewa Indians, she was orphaned as a child. From 1859 to 1862 she attended Oberlin College, but in her final year was accused of poisoning two white school friends. After a triumphant acquittal she travelled to Boston, and with the help of Lloyd Garrison received training from the sculptor Edmund Brackett. Her first works, a medallion of John Brown and a bust of Colonel Robert Gould Shaw, were so popular that the sale of copies paid for her trip to Rome in 1865.

In Italy Lewis met CHARLOTTE CUSHMAN, HARRIET HOSMER, MARY WATSON WHITNEY and other expatriots, and made her name with portraits and with paintings of emotional groups of slaves or Indians, such as *Forever Free, Hiawatha's Wedding, Indian Arrowmaker and his Daughter. Hagar in the Wilderness* (1868) expressed her sympathy for women in struggle. In 1873 her work was exhibited in San Francisco, and in 1876 in the Centennial Exposition in Philadelphia. But by the 1880s she had returned to Rome, where she became a Catholic. Her fame waned and the date of her death is uncertain.

**Leyster, Judith** (1609–60). Dutch artist. She was the daughter of a brewer and was born in Haarlem. She showed early artistic talent and, after a brief period in Utrecht in 1628, she lived in Haarlem, where she was associated with the family of Frans Hals. By 1633 she had been admitted to the painters' Guild of St Luke, and took pupils, even suing Hals for taking one of her apprentices. In 1636 she married the artist Jan Miense Molenaer and the following year they moved to Amsterdam. Judith had three children and produced noticeably less work after her marriage. Her best works are genre pictures, especially scenes and incidents from everyday life such as *The gay Cavaliers* (1628–9) and the *Flute Player* (1631), and she is unusual in painting women and children in the home, in fine works such as *The Proposition* (1631), which turns a convention of painting men making sexual suggestions into an understanding portrayal of unwanted harassment.

E. Tufts: *Our Hidden Heritage* (1974)

**Lillie, Beatrice** (1898–). Canadian–British revue artist. The daughter of English and Ulster immigrants, she was educated at St Agnes College, Belleville, Ontario, and went to England from Toronto with her mother and her sister Muriel, a talented musician, to make a career as a serious singer. She failed until André Charlot spotted her comic potential and engaged her for *Not Likely!* (1914). Throughout World War I she sang in Charlot's many revues, guying the sentimental songs of the period, very often (being small and slight) in top hat and tails.

In 1920 she married Robert Peele, later Sir Robert. A son, Bobbie, was born the following year, but English aristocratic life did not suit her and money was desperately needed to maintain the family seat, so she returned to the stage in *Nine o'clock Revue* (1922) and then, with Gertrude Lawrence, in the successful *Charlot's Revue of 1924* on Broadway. Dressed as Britannia in the show-stopping patriotic song *March with Me* she was compared with Charlie Chaplin, who called her his 'female counterpart'.

For the next 40 years she travelled between London, New York, Chicago and California, earning sometimes as much as $8000 a week, appearing in Charlot's, or C.B. Cochran's revues, and in Noel Coward's *This Year of Grace* (1928) and *Set to Music* (1939). During World War II she entertained the troops. Her husband had died in 1934 and her son was killed in action. After the war she appeared in her own show *An Evening with Beatrice Lillie* on Broadway and in London (1952–6) and in *Auntie Mame* (1958). Her songs included *Rotten to the Core*, *Come into the garden Maud* (getting more and more solemnly drunk with each verse), *There are fairies at the bottom of my garden* (long pearls whirling centrifugally round her neck), *Wind round my heart* (a tragic song about indigestion), and *Mad dogs and Englishmen*, which Noel Coward wrote for her. She also appeared in films from *Exit Smiling* (1927) to *Around the World in 80 Days* (1956) and *Thoroughly Modern Millie* (1967). Kenneth Tynan called her 'the most achingly funny woman on earth', and the embodiment of 'the spirit of unreason, of anarchy and caprice'.

B. Lillie: *Every Other Inch a Lady* (1972)

**Lind, Jenny** (1820–87). Swedish soprano. She studied at the Royal Opera School, Stockholm, having made her first stage appearance at the age of ten and subsequently singing in vaudevilles. Her true operatic debut was in 1838, as Agathe in Weber's *Der Freischütz*. Within a few years, before she was 21, her technique was being hampered by over-strain, and she was sent to Paris for lessons with Manuel García. After a recommended period of rest, she studied with him for ten months and returned to Stockholm in 1842, appearing in the title role of Bellini's *Norma* with her voice in markedly better repair. While in Paris she had met Meyerbeer, who engaged her to sing at the Berlin Opera, where she appeared in the 1844–5 season to increased acclaim. Her visits to London (1847 and 1848–9) were still more sensational: not only were audiences delighted by her singing, but further attention was focussed on her through a law-suit caused by signing a contract with Her Majesty's Theatre when already contracted to the Drury Lane Theatre. The damages (of £2500) were borne by Her Majesty's, where she made her debut as Alice in Meyerbeer's *Robert le diable*; she made her final operatic appearance there in the same role (1849).

In 1850 she was engaged for a tour of the USA; her initial accompanist was the conductor Julius Benedict, but he was replaced the following year by Otto Goldschmidt, whom she married in 1852 (she later assisted him in founding London's Bach Choir).

Lind's operatic career outside Sweden was virtually confined to Germany and England and was of comparatively short duration. Besides Norma, the roles for which she is remembered are Amina in Bellini's *La sonnambula,* Alice in *Robert le diable* and Marie in Donizetti's *La fille du régiment*. Meyerbeer wrote *Ein Feldlager in Schlesien* with Lind in mind for the part of Vielka (though she did not sing at its première), and she created the role of Amalia in Verdi's *I Masnadieri*. After her retirement from the stage she sang mostly for charities; she became Professor of

Singing at the Royal College of Music, London, in 1883.

Admired to distraction by many contemporaries (Hans Christian Andersen was among her unsuccessful suitors), the 'Swedish Nightingale' also achieved posthumous distinction, in being the first woman to be represented in Westminster Abbey's Poets' Corner.

J. Bulman: *Jenny Lind* (1956)

**Linley, Elizabeth (Ann)** (1754–92). English soprano. One of 12 children born to Mary Johnson and Thomas Linley (composer, harpsichordist, concert director and teacher), she had singing lessons from her father and was soon appearing in concerts at Bath and Bristol. Her London debut (Covent Garden, 1767) was in *The Fairy Favour*, a masque by Thomas Hull, after which she sang regularly in the oratorio seasons in London (1769–73) and at the Three Choirs Festival (1770–73), gaining a reputation as the finest English soprano of her day. Her career was interrupted by her marriage to Sheridan (1773), with whom she had eloped to France in 1772; his association with the family resulted in the comic opera *The Duenna* (sub-titled *The Double Elopement*, 1775; music by Thomas Linley, father and son). Reynolds and Gainsborough painted portraits of her.

M. Bor and L. Clelland: *Still the Lark: a Biography of Elizabeth Linley* (1962)

**Linton, Eliza Lynn** (1822–98). English novelist and anti-feminist journalist. The twelfth child of the Vicar of Keswick, in the Lake District, she was largely self-educated, since her tyrannical father disapproved of learning for girls. Her book *The Autobiography of Christopher Kirkland* (1845) describes her own childhood surroundings. In her late teens she developed a passion for religion and for republicanism, forcing herself to the verge of breakdown by her austere habits and by her intellectual experiences which eventually led to a total loss of faith. She left home in 1855 and set off to become a professional writer in London. Living in poverty, she wrote her novels *Azeth the Egyptian* (1846) and *Amynone* (1848). She then met Walter Savage Landor, obtained a job on the *Morning Chronicle* and was a member of a radical free-thinking

group which contained intellectuals such as G.H. Lewes.

In 1858 she married W.J. Linton, a poor engraver and communist writer. They settled in London, where Eliza attempted to hold a literary salon, but eventually the marriage collapsed and Linton emigrated to the USA although they remained close friends for life. In 1866 she began writing for *The Saturday Review*, which was already well known for its vehement opposition to women's emancipation of any kind, and with her famous article 'The Girl of the Period' in March 1868 she launched her own bitter anti-feminist campaign, attacking the 'modern phases of womanhood – hard, unloving, mercenary, ambitious, without domestic faculty and devoid of healthy natural instincts', as 'a pitiable mistake and a grand national disaster'. She continued to pour out such articles (although she supported divorce reform and protective legislation) until her death, and became the accepted mouthpiece of conservative views on the 'feminine nature' and woman's role.

E.L. Linton: *My Literary Life* (1899)
H. van Thal: *Eliza Lynn Linton* (1929)

**Lioba** [Truthgeba] (*d* 782) Anglo-Saxon abbess and saint. Born in Wessex, of a noble family, she was baptized Truthgeba, but was called Liobgetha, of which Lioba 'dear one' is a contraction. Educated first at the nunnery of Minster-in-Thanet and then at Wimborne in Dorset, Lioba took a great delight in literature. Writing to her mother's relation Boniface, she concluded the letter with a poetic passage and asked him to correct her writing. As a result of the ensuing correspondence, some of which survives, 30 nuns including Lioba were sent to join Boniface in Mainz. She was made Abbess of the Convent of Tauberbischofsheim, which she made into one of the great centres of Christianity, and many daughter-houses were established under her direction. After 28 years as Abbess, Lioba retired to Schornsheim; from there she visited Charlemagne's Court at the invitation of Queen Hildegard. She died soon afterwards and was buried near Boniface's tomb at Fulda. *The Life,* by Rudolf of Fulda, written about 50 years after her death, paints an attractive portrait of an accessible, intelligent and kind woman.

C.H.Talbot: *Anglo-Saxon Missionaries in Germany* (1954; contains a translation of *The Life*)

**Lisiewska, Anna (Dorothea)** (1721–82). German artist. She was born in Berlin; her father was a Polish painter and probably her first teacher. Before her marriage to the innkeeper and artist Ernst Therbusch, she painted elegant scenes of courtly life, and in 1761 when her children were grown up she returned to painting; she worked at the courts of Stuttgart and Mannheim between 1761 and 1764. The following year she visited Paris, but it is suggested that she lacked the beauty and social graces to ingratiate herself, although she was elected to the Académie and exhibited in the 1767 Salon. She was also elected to the Bologna and the Vienna academies in 1776. She painted genre scenes and elaborate historical and mythological works, although after her return to Berlin in 1771 she concentrated on portraits. Her own self-portrait of 1780 shows a remarkably sympathetic, down-to-earth looking middle-aged woman with a determined expression. Her sister Rosina (1713–83) was also a talented artist, and a member of the Dresden Academy.

**Lispector, Clarice** (1925–77). Brazilian novelist. She was born in the Ukraine but her family emigrated to Brazil when she was a baby and she grew up in Recife and Rio de Janeiro. She studied law, graduating in 1943, and married a diplomat, Mauri Gurges Valente, living abroad for many years including eight years in the USA. After her divorce in 1959 she returned to Brazil and was soon recognized as one of the country's leading writers. She wrote six novels (the first was published when she was only 19) and a number of short stories. In recent years her work has been translated into several languages: her books now in English include *The Apple in the Dark*, *Family Ties*, *Foreign Legion: Chronicles and Stories* and *The Hour of the Star*. Lispector's work is remarkable for its rich symbolic style and its powerful exploration of identity, isolation and doubt, brilliantly expressed in her highly experimental and personal style.

**Littlewood, Joan (Maud)** (1914–). English director, and the founder and manager of the Theatre Workshop. Born in London of working-class parents, she won a scholarship to the Royal Academy of Dramatic Art, where she did well. She then went to work in radio in Manchester and founded with her husband, the singer and writer Ewan McColl, an amateur group, the Theatre Union, followed by the Theatre of Action, which quickly gained a reputation for its productions of experimental plays. The group broke up with the declaration of war in 1939, but was reformed in Manchester in 1945. In 1953 they leased the Theatre Royal, Stratford, London, which was the base for the Theatre Workshop and for a series of productions that influenced English and Continental directors. Joan Littlewood worked to her own individual methods, though influenced by Stanislavsky and Brecht in encouraging audience participation. She was responsible for successes like *The Quare Fellow* (1956), *A Taste of Honey* (1958) and *Fings ain't wot they used t'be* (1959), which all subsequently transferred to the West End. Such transfers upset the harmony of the company, and Littlewood left in 1961, but returned in 1963 to produce *O what a lovely War!*, which also transferred to the West End, and to Broadway. She was one of the most original stage directors working in England after World War II.

Her only film to date, *Sparrows can't Sing*, was made in 1962, using a cast from her Theatre Workshop, and taking as its plot the story of an East End community under threat from council planning. The film is remarkable for its inclusion of almost every notable British TV 'sit-com' figure to emerge in subsequent years.

Theatre Workshop was disbanded in 1964 and Littlewood became involved in cultural projects in Tunisia (1965–7) and Calcutta (1968), and in mixed media and children's projects in Stratford East, London. The company re-formed under her direction in the early 1970s but in 1975 she left to work in France, living in Vienne. She remained active in occasional British productions, and in 1985 was again in the headlines as editor of *Milady Vine*, the autobiography of Philippe de Rothschild.

**Liubatovich, Vera** (1854–1917). Russian revolutionary. She came from a rich,

*Käthe Kollwitz*

*Jenny Lind*

*Rosa Luxemburg*

*Carry Nation*

cultivated family, her mother's father being the owner of a gold-mine and her father an engineer, and after an education in Moscow she went with her sister Vera to study medicine in Zürich in 1871. There she became involved in radical circles and returned to Russia as a member of the Pan-Russian Social Revolutionary Group. One of many women activists at this time, she was arrested as a propagandist while working in a factory and in 1877, in the 'Trial of the 50', was sentenced to nine years' hard labour; the sentence was reduced to banishment to western Siberia, where she acted as a medical worker in the local community. In 1878 she escaped by staging a mock suicide. Back in St Petersburg [now Leningrad], she joined the group Narodnaya Volya (People's Will), and was smuggled to Geneva to escape police harassment. In 1879 she returned, and after a split in the party joined the small extremist group with her lover Nikolai Morozov, who proposed grass-roots democracy as opposed to centralism, and a programme of systematic terror. In 1880 they fled again to Geneva where Vera had a baby daughter, but after Morozov was arrested while returning to Russia she left her child to search for him. After months of hopeless wandering she was arrested in November 1882 and banished to Irkutsk in eastern Siberia for 20 years. She returned to Russia in 1905 and wrote her moving *Memoirs* in 1906.

B. Engel and C. Rosenthal: *Five Sisters: Women against the Tsar* (1975)

**Livia, Drusilla** [Julia Augusta] (*c* 55 BC–29AD). Roman empress. The daughter of Marcus Livius Drusus Claudianus, she married her cousin Tiberius Claudius Nero in 43 or 42BC, but was ordered by Octavian (later Augustus) to divorce her husband and marry him instead. She had two sons, Tiberius and Nero, by her first marriage. She was a beautiful woman, enormously powerful, and ambitious and her political intrigues became notorious. She was devoted to Augustus, and acted as counsellor to him. Under his will she was adopted into the Julian family and renamed Julia Augusta in 14AD. She was ruthless in obtaining the succession for her son Tiberius, and may have been responsible for the assassination and poisoning of many of his rivals, including Agrippa and Germanicus. After the accession of Tiberius, he resented her continuing ambition and it is suggested that he left Rome for Capri largely to avoid her. Her grandson Claudius later deified her, a tradition which Tiberius deliberately omitted.

**Lloyd, Christine (Marie) Evert** (1954–). American tennis player. Born in Fort Lauderdale, Florida, Christine Evert played amateur tennis until the age of 18, when she turned professional. She quickly rose to the top position in the sport, winning Wimbledon singles titles in 1974 and 1976, the French and Italian Championships in 1974 and 1976 and holding the American Women's title every year from 1975 to 1978, and acting as President of the Women's Tennis Association in 1975–6. Since 1979, when she was World Champion, she has continued to be a dominating player, winning Wimbledon in 1981 and adding four more French championships, and two American. A member of the USA Wightman Cup team from 1971 to 1982, she has an unbeaten record in singles, and is an extremely popular figure both with crowds and the media although, now that she is a senior player, rumours of her retirement abound.

In 1979 she married the British tennis player John Lloyd. Their book *Lloyd on Lloyd* appeared in 1985, but the strains of separation on the professional circuit led to their divorce in 1987.

**Lloyd, Marie** [pseud. of Matilda Alice Victoria Wood] (1870–1922). English music-hall singer. The daughter of a waiter, she was the eldest of 11 children. She first appeared at the Grecian Saloon, then known as the Royal Eagle Music Hall, in 1885 under the name of Bella Delmere, but she soon adopted the stage name of Marie Lloyd. Her first success was at the Old Mo with Nellie Power's song *The Boy I love sits up in the Gallery;* a year's engagement at the Oxford followed. She was then selected as principal girl in the Drury Lane pantomime (1891–93). Marie Lloyd went on to triumph in all the leading music halls in England, and toured the USA, South Africa and Australia. In 1920 her 50th birthday was celebrated by a special performance at the Bedford, and she continued stage work until a few days before her death two years later. Her most famous songs were *Oh Mr Porter*, *My Old Man said Follow the Van*, and *I'm one of the Ruins that Cromwell knocked abaht a bit*. Although she had a reputation for vulgarity, it was unfounded: she simply gave some lines of her songs daring implications.

Marie Lloyd was married three times: to Percy Courtney in 1887 (divorced 1904); to Alec Hurley, the Coster King, who died in 1913; and to Bernard Dillon, the jockey. Despite her success, popularity, and a legendary reputation that continues to grow, her life was hard, but she faced all difficulties with courage. She has a claim to be the greatest of all female stars of the music hall.

D. Farson: *Marie Lloyd* (1972)

**Lockwood, Belva (Ann)** (1830–1917). American lawyer, feminist and pacifist. Belva Bennett was born in Royalton, Niagara County, New York, and at the age of 15 left school and taught for four years before marrying a local farmer, Uriah McNall. When he died in a saw-mill accident in 1853 Belva began teaching again to support her small daughter and took a degree in 1857. As head of the Lockport Union School she introduced progressive ideas: gymnastics, nature walks, public speaking, and at a teachers' institute met SUSAN B. ANTHONY. In 1866 she opened her own co-educational school in New York, and later ran it with Frederick Lockwood, whom she married in 1868. She then studied law at the National University Law School (after being rejected, as a woman, by Columbia, Georgetown and Harvard universities), obtained her diploma in 1873 and was admitted to the District of Columbia Bar. After being refused permission to plead in the Court of Claims and the Supreme Court, she campaigned for a change in the law and in 1879 became the first woman admitted to practise before the Supreme Court.

From 1867 she had been a leading suffragist, a founder of the Washington Universal Franchise Association, and an active member of the National Woman Suffrage Association, drafting resolutions and bills, circulating petitions, and campaigning successfully for the 1872 equal pay act for women government employees. She supported VICTORIA WOODHULL and in 1884, as a member of the National Equal Rights Party, campaigned for President, her platform including demands for equal rights for women, American blacks, Indians and immigrants and for reform in the marriage and divorce laws. Although this independent stand alienated the organized suffrage movement, she continued to campaign, making annual lecture tours. Increasingly, however, she devoted her attention to world peace, as a forceful member of the Universal Peace Union and, after 1893, with the International Council of Women. During these years, with the help of her daughter Laura, she built up a substantial legal practice in Washington. Her successful cases included winning a damages award from the government of $5 million for the Eastern Cherokee Indians, but after Laura's death in 1894 her financial fortunes collapsed, and her last years were spent in ill health and relative poverty.

**Loden, Barbara** (1934–80). American film actress and director. Born in Asheville, North Carolina, the daughter of a barber, she described herself as a 'hill-billy's daughter', growing up in the poverty of the Appalachians. After local high school she sought glamour in New York in modelling, night-club dancing and television walk-on parts, until in 1957 she began to get parts in films and plays, working with the Lincoln Center Repertory (1960–4) and eventually winning an award for her performance as Maggie in Miller's *After the Fall* (1964). She then faded from sight, marrying Elia Kazan in 1967; she had divorced her first husband, film producer Laurence Joachim, with whom she had two sons in 1961 and 1963.

Loden re-appeared in the film world as director of *Wanda* in 1970, an extraordinary study of a poor woman from the coalfields of her own childhood. Made on a tiny budget, with hand-held cameras and edited in her own home, her film won the International Critic's Prize in Venice in 1970 and has since become a classic statement of the need for women's liberation (and for opportunities for women film directors). She died of cancer, aged 46.

**Loeb, Sophie Irene** (1876–1929). American social reformer. Sophie Simon was born into a Jewish family in Rovno, Russia; the family went to the USA in 1882. Her father died ten years later, and to support her mother and five younger siblings she taught and wrote for a Pittsburgh paper. In 1894 she married an older man, Anselm Loeb, but was divorced in 1910 and moved to New York as a reporter for the *Evening World.* Her articles on slum children aided the campaign for state assistance and for community rather than institutional care.

In 1913 Loeb was appointed to the New York State Commission for Relief of Widowed Mothers, and after a study tour of Europe joined the State Welfare Board from 1915 to 1922, securing a considerable amount of welfare legislation on housing, maternity care and schools and influencing public opinion by her book *Everyman's Child* (1920). In 1924 she became President of the Child Welfare Committee of the USA, and was also adviser in this field to the League of Nations. Her other campaign was on behalf of Zionism, about which she wrote *Palestine Awake* (1926) after being sent to the Middle East by the *Evening News.*

**Long, Marguerite (Marie Charlotte)** (1874–1966). French pianist. She studied at the conservatories of Nîmes and Paris, going on to teach at the latter from 1906 to 1940 (as Professor from 1920). As a performer her reputation rests chiefly on her interpretations of early-20th-century French music: she gave the premières of Ravel's *Tombeau de Couperin* (1919) as well as of his Piano Concerto in G (1932), with the composer conducting; they later recorded it together. She also published authoritative books on Debussy (1960), Fauré (1963) and Ravel (posthumously, 1971), interspersing lucid studies of their piano music with personal anecdotes. In 1943 she and Jacques Thibaud founded the international piano and violin competition that bears their names.

J. Weill: *Marguerite Long: une vie fascinante* (1969)

**Lonsbrough, Anita** (1941–). English swimmer. After competing successfully at freestyle in various clubs, at the age of 16 Anita began to specialize in breaststroke, and within months won her first Commonwealth title at Cardiff in 1958. At a time when the UK had few winners in swimming, she won a gold medal at the 1960 Rome Olympics for 200 metres, became European champion in 1962, then in the Commonwealth Games held the 220 yards and 110 yards breaststroke titles and the 440 yards medley. She was awarded the MBE and married Hugh Porter, an international cycling champion.

**Lonsdale,** Dame **Kathleen Yardley** (1903–71). Irish-English crystallographer, physicist and chemist. Kathleen was the youngest of ten children of a postmaster's family in Newbridge, Ireland. The family moved to England, and Kathleen won scholarships through which she entered Bedford College, London, when she was 16 to read mathematics and physics. She headed the University of London list and was invited to join W.H. Bragg's research team to work on the crystal structure of organic compounds by X-ray analysis.

Her work was carried out at University College, London, and the Royal Institution, apart from three years in Leeds after her marriage to Thomas Lonsdale in 1927. She had three children, travelled widely, had many interests and was an active member of the Society of Friends. Her scientific work ranged through the theory of space groups, organic crystal structures, divergent beam X-ray photography of crystals and diffuse X-ray reflection by single crystals, and these many advances contributed to the development of X-ray crystallography.

She received many honours. In 1945 she became the first woman Fellow of the Royal Society, in 1956 she was created CBE, and in 1957 she received the Davy Medal of the Royal Society. At different times she held a Chair in Chemistry and was Vice-President of the Royal Society, President of the International Union of Crystallography, and President of the British Association.

**Loos, Anita** (1893–1981). American screenwriter and novelist. She was born in California and started writing for her father's paper at the age of ten; she then worked as a child actress for touring companies in San Francisco. Her film scripts were accepted and produced by D.W. Griffith between 1912 and 1916, and she also wrote screenplays for films with Douglas Fairbanks. She claimed to have invented 'talking' titles for silent films (conveying only dialogue) and she wrote the sub-titles for Griffith's *Intolerance* (1916). In 1919 she married the film director John Emerson, with whom she collaborated on scripts, stage plays and books. She retired and wrote the novel *Gentlemen prefer Blondes* in 1925; the story has since been through over 85 editions, and has been turned into a play (1951), a musical and a film (1953). Loos returned to film-writing for sound films, including *San Francisco* (1936) with Clark Gable and Spencer Tracy.

A. Loos: *A Girl Like I* (1966)
——— : *Cast of Thousands* (1977)

**Lopéz, Encarnación.** *See* ARGENTENITA, LA.

**Lopez, Nancy** (1957–). American golfer. Of Mexican-American descent, Nancy Lopez was born in Torrance, California, but the family soon moved to Roswell, New Mexico. She began playing golf with her father as a child, winning her first tournament at the age of 9, and the first of three state women championships at 12. In her senior year at high school she finished second in the US Women's Open. She won an athletics scholarship to the University of Tulsa, but after becoming intercollegiate champion she dropped out to play as a professional, winning her first championship, the Bent Tree Classic, in 1978. Later that year she won a record five consecutive tournaments, and also won the European Ladies title. The leading prize-winner in 1979, she went on to confirm her form in major tournaments in the 1980s, winning the Ladies Professional Golf in 1985, when she also set a record for official prize money: over $416,000.

N. Lopez: *The Education of a Woman Golfer* (1979)

**Lopokova, Lydia (Vasilievna)** (1892–1981). Russian ballerina. She was born in St Petersburg [now Leningrad] and made her first stage appearance at the age of nine; she graduated from the Imperial Ballet School to the corps de ballet of the Mariinsky in 1909. She joined Dyagilev's Ballets Russes

in 1910 and created the role of Columbine in *Carnaval*, going on to replace TAMARA KARSAVINA in *The Firebird* (1911). That year she left to dance in the USA, occasionally appearing as an actress in New York. In 1916 she returned to Dyagilev in London, taking the lead in Massin's *Les femmes de bonne humeur* (1916) and appearing as the Can Can Dancer in *La boutique fantasque* (1919) and the Lilac Fairy in the 1921 revival of *The Sleeping Princess*.

In 1921 Lopokova married the British economist Maynard Keynes, and together they founded the Arts Theatre, Cambridge. An influential supporter of British ballet, she danced in Ashton's *Façade* for the Camargo Society in 1931, and in *Coppelia* for the Vic-Wells Ballet in 1933. From 1933 to 1937 she took several stage roles at the Old Vic, including Olivia in *Twelfth Night*, Nora in *A Doll's House*, Hilda in *Master Builder* and Celimène in *Le misanthrope*. She lessened her public involvement with the ballet after her husband's death in 1946, but from 1946 to 1949 was a member of the Arts Council of Great Britain.

M. Keynes: *Lydia Lopokova* (1983)

**Lorde, Audre Geraldin** (1934–). American feminist poet. Audre Lorde's parents were immigrants from the West Indies living in New York City. She went to Hunter High School and Hunter College, publishing her first poem in *Seventeen* while still at school. In 1961, she obtained a master's degree in Library Science, and in 1962 married a lawyer, Edwin Rollins: they had two children and were divorced in 1970. After working in librarianship Lorde taught in high school in New York, but she was already becoming known for her powerful poetry, with its political force and strong lesbian themes. She has since taught at several American colleges, and has been Professor of English at Hunter College since 1981.

An increasingly important force in the women's movement and in the development of black and feminist women's writing and theory, Lorde challenges all sexism and racism, yet emphasizes the importance of sexual difference and polarity, and the value of the erotic. She has published several collections, including *The First Cities* (1968), *Cables to Rage* (1970), *Coal* (1976) and *Chosen*

*Poems Old and New* (1982). She has also written a moving account of her mastectomy in *The Cancer Journals* (1980), and the autobiographical *Zami. A New Spelling of My Name* (1982). She is an active campaigner in writers' organizations and arts councils, has served on the editorial board of magazines such as *Chrysalis, Black Box* and *Black Scholar*, and was a co-founder of Kitchen Table-Women of Color Press. Several of her influential essays and lectures appeared in *Sister Outsider* (1984).

**Loren, Sophia** [pseud. of Sofia Scicolone] (1934–). Italian actress. She was born in Rome, an illegitimate child, and brought up in poverty in Naples, until she won a prize in a beauty contest at the age of 14. With her mother she then went to Rome, where in 1949 they worked as extras in *Quo vadis* (1951). She won more beauty contests and modelled for magazines. When she was nearly 15 she met Carlo Ponti who gave her a contract, coached her and made her a star in Italy before she was 25, in films such as *Aida* (1953), *L'oro di Napoli/Gold of Naples* (1954) and *La fortuna di essere donna/Lucky to be a Woman* (1956). She then went to Hollywood where her warm, generous beauty and personality were vulgarized in her treatment as a sex goddess in such films as *Desire under the Elms* (1958) and in the self-parodying *The Millionairess* (1960) with Peter Sellers. After retiring to Italy she won the Cannes Film Festival Award for *La ciociara/Two Women* (1960) by De Sica, who also directed her in *Ieri, oggi e domani/Yesterday, Today and Tomorrow* (1963) and *Matrimonio alla italiana/Marriage Italian Style* (1964) with Mastroianni. She also later appeared in LINA WERTMULLER'S *Revenge* (1979).

Sophia Loren and Carlo Ponti were eventually married in 1957, but as his earlier divorce was not recognized in Italy they were charged with bigamy, and had to annul their marriage in 1962; in 1966 they became French citizens so that they could legally marry. Her memoirs deal openly with her childhood, her marriage and her longing for children; she now has two sons. Her book *Women and Beauty* brought her into the public eye again in 1984.

A.E. Hotchner: *Sophia – Living and Loving: Her Own Story* (1979)

**Los Angeles, Victoria de** (1923–). Spanish soprano. She studied at the Barcelona Conservatory, making her operatic debut in 1945 as the Countess in Mozart's *Le nozze di Figaro*. Her Covent Garden debut, as Mimì in Puccini's *La bohème,* launched a highly successful decade of regular appearances there, mostly in operas by Puccini, Wagner and Verdi, but notably also in the title role of Massenet's *Manon*. Equally acclaimed at New York's Metropolitan Opera, she also appeared during the 1950s at La Scala, Milan, at Bayreuth in 1961 and 1962, and in Buenos Aires in 1965. After 1969 she abandoned opera to concentrate on recital programmes; the fiery sensuality she brought to her interpretations of Spanish song have assured her enduring international reputation.

P. Roberts: *Victoria de Los Angeles* (1982)

**Loughlin, Dame Anne** (1894–1979). English trade unionist. She was born in Leeds, eldest daughter of an Irish boot- and shoe-worker. Her mother died when she was 12 and she went to work in a garment factory while looking after the family, becoming a shop steward in her teens and an organizer for the Tailors and Garment Workers Union in 1915 (which had a membership of 10,000) at the age of 21. A tireless worker and fiery speaker, the next year she took part in the famous Hebden Bridge strike of 6000 clothing workers. She served on nine different Trade Boards, settling reasonable hourly rates, and on becoming a national organizer in 1920 she travelled the country negotiating, organizing and settling disputes. By 1948 when she became General Secretary (the first woman head of a mixed union) the membership had risen to 100,000.

In 1929 Anne had been elected to the General Council of the Trades Union Congress, becoming the first woman President in 1943, and receiving the DBE in the same year. She also served on Royal Commissions and government committees concerned with holidays, equal pay, safety and unemployment insurance. She retired as General Secretary of her Union in 1953 because of ill health.

**Louise of Savoy,** Duchesse D'Angoulême (1476–1531). French queen. The daughter of the Duke of Savoy and Marguerite de

Bourbon, she was orphaned young and brought up as a 'poor relation' by the powerful ANNE OF BEAUJEU, who betrothed her at the age of two to the Count of Angoulême. She married him when she was 12, although he refused to abandon his mistress Jeanne de Polignac. They had two children: the daughter became MARGUERITE OF NAVARRE and the son, Francis, became heir to the French throne in 1498. After her husband died she presided alone over an extravagant but scholarly and artistic court, refusing to remarry, and was a devoted and indulgent mother. At this time she was engaged in fierce rivalry with ANNE OF BRITTANY, who had opposed Francis's marriage to the Princess Claude. On Francis's succession in 1515 Louise became highly influential in state affairs; she was created Duchess of Angoulême, and acted as Regent during Francis's expedition to Italy (1515–16). Her other passion at this time was for Charles de Bourbon, the Constable of France, and after he rejected her she was determined to avenge herself. She claimed the estates of her niece Suzanne, Bourbon's wife, on her death in 1521 and this provoked him to open revolt in 1523.

In 1522 a scandal occurred when the money for the Italian wars was said to have been diverted to Louise's own funds. She denied this and the treasurer Samblançay was executed for corruption in 1527. In 1525–6 Francis again left her as Regent; she formed an important alliance with Henry VIII, arranged for Francis's release from imprisonment in Spain after the battle of Pavia and with Margaret of Austria negotiated the Treaty of Cambrai (known as the 'Ladies' Peace') between him and Charles. In 1531, after the final celebrations of the peace, a comet appeared and Louise, always fascinated by astronomy, insisted on watching it; she caught a chill and died. She was found to have a personal fortune of 1.5 million gold coins.

D.M. Mayer: *The Great Regent* (1966)

**Love, Bessie** [stage-name of Juanita Horton] (1898–1986). American film star. Born in Midland, Texas, Bessie travelled with her parents through Arizona, New Mexico and California before they settled in Los Angeles. She attended Los Angeles High School, and in 1915 was 'discovered' by D.W. Griffith. Her first films included *Intolerance* (1916), and *Nina and the Flower Girl* (1917) and in 1919 she formed Callaghan Productions with Andrew J. Callaghan. An effervescent, natural actress, immensely versatile, she made 87 films before leaving America for Great Britain in 1935, the most famous being *Broadway Melody* (1929). She also acted in theatre, and in a variety act in New York. In 1929 she married William Hawks, brother of director Howard Hawks. (They were divorced in 1935.)

From 1935 she continued her career in Britain, working for the American Red Cross during World War II, and for BBC radio, and touring army bases in Europe during 1945–6. Well known on the British stage, and on television, she also wrote her own play *The Home Coming* (1958). Her later work included remarkable cameo-performances in films such as *The Barefoot Contessa* (1954), *The Greengage Summer* (1961), *Sunday Bloody Sunday* (1971) and *Reds* (1981).

B. Love: *From Hollywood with Love* (1977)

**Lovelace, (Augusta) Ada Byron,** Countess of (1815–52). English mathematician. The legitimate daughter of Lord Byron, Ada was never allowed to meet him but was instead dominated by her autocratic, mathematically-minded mother, Lady NOEL BYRON. She taught herself from Paisley's *Geometry* and was instructed in astronomy and mathematics by William Frend, then in 1833 met Charles Babbage, inventor of the calculating machine or 'difference engine'; he became her correspondent and friend. In 1842 Ada translated from Italian and annotated a paper by Menabrea on the difference engine, thus showing her understanding of the principles of the programmed computer. She was also known for her grasp of symbolic logic, but such pursuits were thought to produce dangerous tensions of mind in a woman.

In 1835 Ada had married Lord William King; they had three children (her daughter, ANNE BLUNT, became a famous traveller). She was still heavily supervised, and dominated by ill health. Her mathematical skills were now mainly employed in a secret gambling system, but this did not prevent her falling into debt before her early death from cancer of the uterus. She was belatedly honoured by the naming of the high-level universal computer programming language (ADA), of which the development was begun by the American Department of Defence in 1977, although her claims to pioneering work have lately been questioned by Stein's biography, which shows the difficulty she had in grasping basic scientific concepts.

D. Stein: *Ada, A Life and a Legacy* (1986)

**Lowell, Amy Lawrence** (1874–1925). American poet. She was born into a leading and immensely wealthy New England family in Brookline, Massachusetts; she was educated privately, and accompanied her parents on long trips to Europe. One of her brothers became President of Harvard, and another a noted astronomer. Before she was 30 her parents died and she bought the family estate 'Sevenals', where she lived until her death. In her twenties she threw herself into local politics as a reactionary Republican. She suffered a glandular disorder which made her very fat, and her appearance enhanced the effect of eccentricity since she swore and smoked cigars but wore exaggeratedly 'feminine' clothes.

From 1902 she dedicated herself to poetry. Her first book, *A Dome of Many-coloured Glass* (1912), was very conventional but, influenced by Pound, whom she met in England, she became the leading American exponent of the 'Imagist' style from about 1912. Her poems convey a mystical sense of transcendent power, often through idealized landscapes, standing in painful contrast to human inadequacy and the rejection of love. She published five more collections, including most of her best work, before 1921, and was influential in explaining Imagism as a lecturer and reader. In 1921 she published versions of Florence Ayscough's translations from Chinese poetry. Her later work returned to more conventional forms. Lowell was also an accomplished critic, producing scholarly works such as *Six French Poets* (1915) and a major biography of John Keats in 1925.

She was the subject of many stories – she slept in the day and worked at night, covered all her mirrors, subjected her guests to the attention of a pack of untrained dogs, and so on. She was also devoted to the theatre, and

among her most passionate poetry of idealized love are six sonnets to ELEANORA DUSE. Lowell's unconventional life and art led her to be often misunderstood in her life and neglected after her death.

A. Gregory: *Lowell: Portrait of the Poet in Her Time* (1958)

**Lowell, Josephine Shaw** (1843–1905). American social reformer. Born into an old Boston family, she moved to New York in 1847 and was educated there and in Europe. Her family friends included LYDIA MARIA CHILD and Margaret Fuller. As radical abolitionists they supported the Union cause in the Civil War; her brother Robert Gould Shaw led the Black regiment from Boston until his death in 1863, and Josephine joined the Women's Central Association of Relief. In October 1863 she married Colonel Charles Lowell, who was killed a year later, just before the death of her daughter Carlotta. She flung herself into welfare work and fund raising, first for the National Freedman's Relief Association, then for the New York Charities Aid Association (1872), where her outspoken report on city paupers in 1875 led to her appointment as the first woman member on the State Board of Charities. Her investigations and exposures led to many reforms, and she tried to develop principles for state relief, especially in *Public Relief and Private Charity* (1884).

Perceiving the effect of low wages and bad working conditions, she retired in 1889 to concentrate on labour problems. As President of the first Consumer Council (1890–96), she worked with the unions and wrote *Industrial Arbitration and Conciliation* (1893). She also organized the Women's Municipal League as a political lobby group and campaigned against aggressive foreign policy. Her career embodies the shift from patrician philanthropy to 'preventive' social policies.

W.R. Stewart: *The Philanthropic Work of Josephine Shaw Lowell* (1911)

**Luders, Marie-Elizabeth** (1888–1966). German feminist and politician. Born in Berlin, one of seven children of a civil servant, she took courses in housekeeping but was determined to have a career and after demanding private lessons in Classics, she became one of the first women to obtain a doctorate in political science and economics in 1912. With GERTRUDE BAUMER and others she founded the National Women's Service during World War I, and in 1916 became head of a war office department dealing with female labour. In 1919 she joined the Democratic Party and became a member first of the National Assembly, then of the Reichstag. During the 1930s she campaigned openly against Nazi policies, her women's organization was disbanded, she was briefly arrested by the Gestapo in 1937 and spent the war in exile. On her return to Berlin in 1947 she became a member of the senate, and was the senior member of the Bundestag in 1953. She was made Honorary President of the Federal Democratic Party in 1957 but retired in 1961.

**Lukens** [née Pennock], **Rebecca Webb** (1794–1854). American industrialist. Born in Coatesville, Pennsylvania, she was the daughter of Isaac Pennock who had founded the Brandywine Rolling Mill, the first in America which made boiler plate. After a conventional education she married a doctor, Charles Lukens, in 1813; they had three children. Her husband took over the mill, but died in 1825 and Rebecca became the first woman manager in the iron industry. She left the daily running of the mill to an overseer and concentrated on expanding her market, dealing with major distribution problems, and with the transport of coal for her furnaces. She achieved such a reputation for high quality plate that she even exported it to England, to be used in early railway engines, and at her death she left a greatly enlarged business to her two sons-in-law. In 1890 the mill was renamed Lukens Mills in her memory.
R. Wolcott: *A Woman in Steel – Rebecca Lukens* (1940)

**Lundequist, Gerda** (1871–1959). Swedish actress. Born in Stockholm, she trained in drama at the Stockholm Academy of Music, graduating at the age of 15. In 1889 she made her debut in Strindberg's *Mäster Olof*. During the 1890s she played in Göteborg, but she returned to the capital in 1896, establishing herself as a great tragic actress in works like the adaptation of Tolstoy's *Resurrection* and Maeterlinck's *Monna Vanna*. After 1906 her range increased to include classic roles such as Lady Macbeth, Antigone and Mary Stuart, but she also appeared in modern parts such as Anna Karenina and as Mrs Alving in Ibsen's *Gengangere/Ghosts*. Noted for her sensuality and for her thrilling voice, which won her the reputation of a 'Swedish Bernhardt', she continued to appear on stage until 1940. She also appeared in films, including a powerful performance in the early Stiller classic *The Gösta Berling Saga*, which saw the debut of GRETA GARBO. Her last film was *Giflas* (1955).

**Lupino, Ida** (1918–). English-American film director and actress. She had a theatrical background (her father and cousin were comedians), and received formal training in acting at the Royal Academy of Dramatic Art. In 1932 she met Allan Dwan, who gave her a leading role in his film *Her First Affaire* (1933). She went to Hollywood a year later, and signed up with Paramount. In 1940 she signed up with Warner Bros., and specialized in playing the 'moll' in gangster films. After being suspended by Warner Bros. she worked first in radio, and then formed her own production company with Collier Young: Film Makers. With Young she wrote the script for its first production. When the director had a heart attack, she finished the directing, and she co-wrote, produced and directed each subsequent film. The company was notable for choosing controversial topics (unmarried mothers, career women etc), with fast-shooting schedules, low budgets and new talent; it collapsed after moving into the field of distribution. She was talked into acting for television by David Niven, but after three years returned to directing, at Joseph Cotten's request, for *The Trial of Mary Surratt*. She began directing for television, and established a reputation as an action director. She always refused to direct herself.

Lupino's films as an actress include *They Drive by Night* (1940), *High Sierra* (1941), *The Big Knife* (1955) and *While the City Sleeps* (1956), and as a director, *Hard, Fast and Beautiful* (1951), *The Bigamist* (1953) and *The Trouble with Angels* (1966).
J. Vermilye: *Ida Lupino* (1977)

**Lutyens, (Agnes) Elisabeth** (1906–83). English composer. Daughter of the architect Edwin

Lutyens, she studied at the Ecole Normale in Paris in 1922 and then at the Royal College of Music, London. In 1931 she was one of the co-founders of the Macnaghten–Lemare Concerts, which fostered the work of such composers as Britten and Rawsthorne. Although she subsequently withdrew most of her own music written at this time, including the ballet performed as her major compositional debut (*The Birthday of the Infanta,* 1932), it was this series that first drew Lutyens to public attention. Nevertheless, she was only slowly recognized as one of Britain's leading composers, and her stylistic development reflects a single-minded pursuit of techniques that were spurned, or at least regarded with suspicion, in England until the early 1960s. One of her most remarkable works is the First Chamber Concerto (1939), among the earliest examples of serialism in music by a British composer. She was extremely prolific (over 140 opus numbers), though with each new work responded to the demands of the medium with a fresh approach. Several of her stage works, including *Infidelio* (1954), *Time Off? – Not a Ghost of a Chance!* (1968), *Isis and Osiris* (1970) and *The Goldfish Bowl* (1975), were written to her own librettos. Among her most important orchestral works are the *Concertante* (1950) and the three sets of *Music for Orchestra* (1955, 1962, 1963). Many of her instrumental and chamber pieces have resulted from commissions. The texts for her vocal works were drawn from a wide range of sources, e.g. Rimbaud (in *O saisons, o châteaux!,* 1946), Wittgenstein (*Motet 'Excerpta tractatus-logico philosophici',* 1952), Chaucer (*De amore,* 1957), Japanese poetry (*The Valley of Hatsu-se,* 1965), Quasimodo (*And Suddenly it's Evening,* 1966; *Dialogo,* 1972), Joseph Conrad (*Vision of Youth,* 1970) and African verse (*Counting your Steps,* 1972). She was created CBE in 1969.

E. Lutyens: *A Goldfish Bowl* (1972)

**Lutz, Bertha** (1899–1976). Brazilian feminist. The founder of the Brazil Federation for the Advancement of Women (1922), she was its President until her death. She was also permanent delegate of Brazil to the Inter-American Commission of Women.

She studied biology at the Sorbonne and entered the National Museum in Rio de Janeiro, winning her post against ten men and thus opening government service to women. She organized and led the fight for the vote for women, which was won in 1931. In 1936 after much campaigning she set up a government department dealing with the specific problems facing women, and she represented Brazil at many international congresses, including the first United Nations meeting in San Francisco where she succeeded in having the word 'sex' added to the proposed list of 'non discrimination on the grounds of . . .'. Bertha Lutz also succeeded in getting a United Nations Commission on the Status of Women. For many years she taught zoology at the University of Rio de Janeiro.

**Luxemburg, Rosa** (1870–1919). Polish-German socialist, feminist and pacifist, the founder of the German Communist Party. She was born into a Jewish family in Zamosc, Russian Poland, but when she was three her family moved to Warsaw, where her merchant father was a member of leading intellectual circles. The youngest of five children, she grew up lame, very tiny, and apparently fragile, but never lacked self-confidence. As a girl she was keenly interested in politics, influenced by the first Polish socialists in the 'Proletariat' organization, which she joined in 1887. When a small, illegal discussion club which she ran at her school was discovered in 1889 friends smuggled her across the border to Zürich. There she studied philosophy, economics and law, and after presenting a thesis on *The Industrial Development of Poland* in 1896 she married a German anarchist, Gustav Lubecks, so that she could obtain German citizenship. During this period she studied European labour movements and became friendly with Karl and LOUISE KAUTSKY, and especially with Leo Jogisches. With him she founded the Social Democratic Party of Poland in 1893.

From 1897 to 1899 she was in France, and she then moved to Berlin, where she joined the staff of *Vorwärts,* the daily socialist paper. In 1904 she was briefly imprisoned and in 1905, on a false passport, she returned to Poland, organizing workers' revolts in Warsaw with Jogisches. After returning to Germany, via Finland, she advocated whole-scale workers' action in her extremely influential pamphlet *The Mass Strike*. She broke with Jogisches in 1906 and the next year was appointed Instructor of Economics at a school for Party officials; she produced an economics text-book in 1912, and her most famous work, *The Accumulation of Capital*, in 1914.

Rosa had consistently opposed nationalism, because she felt it destroyed international workers' solidarity, and she was appalled when German socialists supported the war in 1914. She spent most of the next four years in prison, from where she organized the radical Spartacus League with Liebknecht and CLARA ZETKIN. After the war this became the German Communist Party, opposing the new moderate socialist régime. Although she advocated a gradualist strategy, she supported her followers in the abortive Spartacist uprising of January 1919, especially through editorials in *Die rote Fahne*. Once their hiding place was discovered, she and Liebknecht were arrested, but were then taken from the police by soldiers, interrogated, beaten and shot. Luxemburg's body was thrown into the Landwehr Canal. Her murderers were acquitted.

P. Nehi: *Rosa Luxemburg: a Biography* (1966) [2 vols]

**Lyn, Gillian.** British choreographer. One of the most successful choreographers of contemporary musicals, Gillian Lyn learnt to dance in the 1940s with the Royal Ballet, where she was principal soloist from 1944 to 1951 and studied under NINETTE DE VALOIS. She then began working in the cinema and acting in repertory theatre, and also starred in revue at the London Palladium (1951–3). She continued to dance both classical and revue during the 1950s and 1960s and in 1963 she conceived the dance *Collages* for the Edinburgh Festival. She began work as a professional choreographer, and choreographed three shows on Broadway for David Merrick: *Roar of the Greasepaint*, *Pickwick*, *How Now Dow Jones* in 1966–7. She has since choreographed, and often directed, over 30 West End shows, including *Cats*, *Phantom of the Opera* and *Cabaret* (which she also directed). She has also worked in television, and on 11 major films. In 1980 she married the young dancer Peter Lord, whom she had directed in *My Fair Lady*.

**Lynn** [née Webb], **Loretta** (1935–). American country singer. Born into a mining family in Butcher's Hollow, Kentucky, she began singing as a girl at local functions. Just before her 14th birthday she married Oliver 'Moonshine' Lynn. In the 1950s they moved to a farm in Custer, Washington, and after the birth of four daughters Lynn began singing, forming a small band which included her younger brother. She wrote and made the record *Honky Tonk Girl* in 1960, touring with her husband to promote it on all the small local radio stations. An instant hit, it enabled her to go to Nashville from where she toured with Patsy Cline. In 1967 she made the aptly-named *Success*, and since then she has been one of the most successful country-and-western woman singers, with nearly all her releases, including her famous duets with Conway Twitty, reaching the Top Ten.

During the 1960s and 1970s Loretta was unusual amongst country musicians for her stand against the Vietnam war and her support of black and native American causes (her mother is part Cherokee). Recently her songs have shown the impact of the women's movement, for example in *We've come a long Way, Baby* and *The Pill*. She suffered a breakdown at one stage from the pressure of work and publicity. She had six children, was a grandmother at 32, owned a large video production company, a talent agency and the whole of her home town of Hurricane Mills, Tennessee.

Her best-selling autobiography, *Coal Miner's Daughter* (1976), was made into an equally successful film in 1980.

**Lynn** [née Welch], **Dame Vera (Margaret)** (1917–). English singer. Brought up in East Ham, London, she first sang in public at the age of 7, joined a dancing troupe at 11 and from 15 was involved in running a small dancing school. In 1935 she began recording with Joe Loss and joined the Charlie Kunz band. After singing from 1937 to 1940 with the Ambrose Orchestra she was so popular that she went solo, having been voted the top singer in a competition run by the *Daily Express* newspaper the previous year. Golden-haired, slim, with a charming smile and soft voice, she was named the 'Forces' Sweetheart' during World War II. In the war years she sang to the troops, visiting Burma in 1944, while her own show, *Sincerely Yours*, ran from 1941 to 1947. In the 1950s she appeared on radio and television, and in cabaret and variety shows in the USA, Europe, South Africa and Australia, and appeared in seven Royal Command performances. She became the first British artiste to reach the top of the American hit parade, and her most famous song, *Auf Wiederseh'n*, has sold over 12 million copies. Vera Lynn has received many honours including the DBE in 1975, the Freedom of the City of London in 1978 and the Burma Star in 1985.

V.Lynn: *Vocal Refrain* (1975)

**Lyons, Enid (Muriel)** (1897–1981). Australian politician. Born in Leesville, and brought up in Tasmania, she was educated at the State School and at Hobart Teachers' Training College. When she was 17 she married Joseph Lyons, a considerably older man who was the Minister of Education and who became Prime Minister of Australia. After his death in 1939 she entered politics, becoming the first woman member of the House of Representatives for Darwin, Tasmania (1943–51), and Vice-President of the Executive Council (1949–51) – the first woman member of a Federal Cabinet. From 1951 to 1961 she was a member of the Board of Control of Australian Broadcasting; she also worked as a newspaper columnist. She

remained active in political and reforming circles. She had 11 children: 5 sons and 6 daughters.

E. Lyons: *So We Take Comfort* (1960)
——: *Among the Carrion Crows* (1973)

**Lytton,** Lady **Constance (Georgia)** (1869–1923). English suffragette. She was born in Vienna, daughter of the Earl of Lytton, Viceroy of India, and lived a retired life with her mother until an inheritance brought them independence in 1906. She became involved with the suffragette movement through her aid to working girls, joined the Women's Social and Political Union and was imprisioned several times for miltant protests. When on hunger strike she was always released on health grounds, so in 1911 she disguised herself as a working woman, 'Jane Wharton', a seamstress. After her arrest for inciting people to stone the house of the Governor of Walton Gaol, Liverpool, she was passed as fit, forcibly fed, and became so severely ill that she suffered a stroke and remained partially paralysed. She published an account of her sufferings in *Prisons and Prisoners: some Personal Experiences by C. Lytton and Jane Wharton, Spinster* (1914). Although she became a permanent invalid, she continued to work for the suffrage movement by writing articles and organizing petitions.

B. Balfour, ed.: *Letters of Constance Lytton* (1925)

# M

**McAliskey** [née Devlin], **(Josephine) Bernadette** (1948–). Irish politician. Born into a poor Catholic family, she was brought up with her five brothers and sisters in Dungannon, County Tyrone, by her mother. She won a scholarship to Queen's University, Belfast, in 1966 to read psychology, and joined the student protest movement, People's Democracy. In 1969 she was elected Member of Parliament for Mid-Ulster by the Independent Party; at 21 she was the youngest member of the House since William Pitt. Her style was unconventional; called the 'five-foot firebrand', she attacked British policy in her maiden speech, was arrested for leading Catholic rioters in the Battle of the Bogside, and was sentenced to nine months' imprisonment for incitement to riot (she served four months). The birth of her illegitimate daughter in 1971 lost her much Catholic support, and in 1974 she did not stand in the General Election. She had married the teacher Michael McAliskey in 1973 and after her unsuccessful attempt to win a seat in the European Parliament in 1979 she seemed to stand back from active involvement.

But in 1980 she re-emerged in demonstrations in support of the IRA hunger strikers, and in January 1981 she and her husband were shot while getting their three children ready for school. After her recovery she decided not to stand as a candidate for Parliament but continued to campaign on behalf of the hunger strikers, making a dramatic appearance in Spain (where she had been declared an undesirable alien for inciting terrorism), and being smuggled out of the country after the meeting. She remained the Chairman of the Independent Socialist Party of Ireland of which she was co-founder in 1975. She later unsuccessfully contested a Dublin seat for the People's Democracy Party in 1982.

B. Devlin: *The Price of my Soul* (1969)

**Macarthur** [née Veale], **Elizabeth** (1767–1850). Australian pioneer and wool merchant. Born in Devon, she came from a prosperous farming family and received a good education. In 1788 she married John Macarthur, a soldier, and the following year accompanied him when he transferred to the New South Wales Corps, posted to Botany Bay. They took their small son Edward, but a daughter born on the voyage died. Her letters home give a vivid account of life aboard the convict ship.

Elizabeth was the first cultured woman in the colony, and for 20 years dominated military and administrative circles. She also had seven more children before 1808. Her husband's arrogance had led to rifts with Government House, but he gradually acquired a fortune, as paymaster, inspector of public works and entrepreneur. In 1793 he acquired land grants and stock with which he built up Elizabeth Farm, the first great Australian estate, complete with elegant mansion and gardens, founding the colonial wool trade and being nicknamed 'hero of the fleece'. Involved in the rebellion against Governor Bligh he was forced to leave Australia in 1809, and for eight years Elizabeth ran the business in correspondence with her husband in London. A brilliant and industrious businesswoman she built up the merino flocks, travelling throughout Australia, expanding sales into the English market and establishing New

South Wales as a wool producing area. She retired as manager when John returned in 1817, and his increasing melancholia and violent jealousy created great personal problems until his death in 1834. Her sons, under her guidance, then developed the family wool empire.

M.H. Ellis: *John Macarthur* (1955)

**MacArthur, Mary (Reid)** (1880–1921). Scottish trade unionist. Born in Glasgow, the daughter of a prosperous Conservative draper, she was educated at Glasgow High School, then spent a year in Germany (1896) before joining her father's business in Ayr as a clerk. In 1901 she became a member of the Shop Assistants' Union, rising quickly to become President of the Scottish National District. In 1903 she moved to London where, through her friendship with MARGARET BONDFIELD and GERTRUDE TUCKWELL, she became Secretary of the Women's Trade Union League, which she completely revitalized. She increased the membership, and worked to establish trade boards, organize strikes, and negotiate minimum wages. In 1904 and 1908 she was delegate to the International Congress of Women in Berlin and the USA, in 1906 she founded the National Federation of Women Workers and in 1907 the popular journal *Woman Worker*. Her most notable campaigns concerned sweated trades (1906), home-workers (1907) and the chain-makers, whom she led in a famous strike in 1910. From 1909 to 1912 she was also on the National Council of the Independent Labour Party.

During World War I she protected women's interests on the Central Committee of Women's Training and Employment, striking up an unexpected friendship with Queen Mary. A Labour left-winger, she supported the Russian Revolution and allegedly refused a DBE. In 1918 she was narrowly defeated as Labour candidate for Stourbridge. In 1919, although distraught at the death of her husband, the politician W.C. Anderson, she continued to campaign, attending ILO conferences in the USA and in Geneva. She died of cancer at the age of 41. All Labour histories emphasize her energy and charm, analysed by Beatrice Webb as combining an 'exuberant and contagious joy of life with a consistently held social purpose'.

M.A. Hamilton: *Mary Macarthur: a Biographical Sketch* (1925)

**Macaulay** [née Sawbridge], **Catharine Graham** (1731–91). English historian. Born in Wye, Kent, she was educated privately and as a girl passionately admired the idea of liberty she discovered in her reading of Greek and Roman history, adopting a stern republican ideology. She began working on her massive eight-volume *History of England* in her twenties, and the first volume appeared in 1763, three years after her marriage to a doctor, George Macaulay. The work immediately aroused controversy because of her clear sympathies.

Her husband died in 1766, but she continued her work, gaining a considerable reputation and becoming the centre of an intellectual and political circle in Bath, where she moved in 1774. She visited Paris in 1775 and 1777 and was acclaimed as a leading figure in British culture. She was also an extremely lively and fashionable figure and at the age of 47 shocked society by marrying the 21-year-old William Graham. She moved with him to Berkshire, and continued the *History*, which was completed in 1783 and which eventually covered the years from 1603 to the accession of the Brunswick line. She had also published several pamphlets on political philosophy, and her sympathy for the colonists in the War of Independence led her to visit America in 1784, where she and her husband became close friends of George Washington. She was greatly admired by MARY WOLLSTONECRAFT, who called her 'the woman of the greatest abilities that this country has ever produced'.

**Macaulay**, Dame **Rose** (1881–1958). English writer. Born in Rugby, Warwickshire, she spent eight years of her childhood near Genoa in Italy. She went to Oxford High School and then Somerville College, where she read history. She then moved to London and became a prominent figure in literary society. During World War II (in which she suffered personally and materially) she was a voluntary part-time ambulance driver. She was made DBE in 1958.

She published the first of her 23 novels, *Abbots Verney*, in 1906. Her early novels were somewhat naive social satire, which had become more sophisticated by the 1920s (*Potterism*, 1920; *Going Abroad*, 1934). She won the Prix Femina Vie Heureuse for *Dangerous Ages* (1921) and her last novel *The Towers of Trebizond* (1956) won the James Tait Black Memorial Prize. She contributed to many journals and newspapers of varying degrees of seriousness, and published volumes of essays including *Personal Pleasures* (1935). After World War II she wrote a number of travel books, such as *They went to Portugal* (1949).

R. Macaulay: *Letters to a Friend* (1961)
———: *Last Letters to a Friend* (1962)
———: *Letters to a Sister* (1964)

**MacBride [née Gonne], Maud** (1866–1953). Irish actress and revolutionary. The daughter of an Anglo-Irish army officer and his English wife, who died when Maud was very young, she was educated in France and at the age of 16 accompanied her father to Dublin. On a return visit to France, convalescing from tuberculosis, she was inspired by the journalist, Lucien Millevoye, with whom she fell in love, to return to Ireland and to organize protests on behalf of evicted tenants and political prisoners. Her relationship with Millevoye deepened after 1890, and they had two children (1893 and 1895), but at the end of the decade she left him in order to devote herself entirely to the Irish cause. She had already raised funds by lectures in France, Britain and the USA, had briefly edited *L'Irlande Libre* in Paris, and she founded a women's group, Inghinidhe Na Eireann (Daughters of Ireland) in 1900.

She was capable of arousing personal and patriotic devotion in others, notably W.B. Yeats, who met her in 1889, proposed marriage ten years later, and never entirely recovered from his hopeless love for her. Maud took the title role in his play *Cathleen Ni Houlihan* in Dublin in 1902. (Yeats unsuccessfully proposed marriage to her daughter Iseult in 1917.)

Maud became a Catholic convert. In Paris in 1903 she entered into a disastrous marriage with the revolutionary, John MacBride, who was executed after the Easter Rising of 1916. He had long since separated from Maud, who remained in Paris until 1917. She returned to Dublin to take part in the Republican movement. She spent six months in Holloway Prison in 1918,

was an active relief worker during the Troubles and continued to demand total Irish independence after the Anglo-Irish Treaty of 1921, organizing the Republican Women's Prisoners' Defence League in 1922.

She remained a passionate devotee of the Republican cause for the rest of her life. Her son Sean MacBride (1904–87) was Irish Minister for External Affairs from 1948 to 1951. Maud's memoirs, *A Servant of the Queen* (1938), give a lively account of her early life.

S. Leverson: *Maud Gonne* (1977)

**McBride, Patricia** (1942–). American ballerina. Born in Teaneck, New Jersey, she studied at the School of American ballet and made her professional debut at 15 with André Eglevsky's Petit Ballet Company. She joined the New York City Ballet in 1959, working up from a member of the *corps de ballet* to principal dancer. A virtuoso performer with dazzling technique, she is especially known for her character parts, but she has danced classical roles as well as modern works such as Balanchin's *Harlequinade* (1965), *Jewels* (1967) and *Who Cares?* (1970), and Robbin's *Dybbuk Variations* (1974). She is married to the dancer Jean-Pierre Bonnefous.

**McCarthy, Mary (Therese)** (1912–). American writer. Born in Seattle, Washington, and educated first at the Forest Ridge Convent there, she was orphaned at the age of six when her parents died in the great influenza epidemic of 1918. She and her brother were brought up by relatives. A clever child, she went to school in Tacoma, Washington, and suffered from a repressive and jealous régime at home. Her grandfather paid for her to go to Vassar College, and after graduating in 1933 she married Harold Johnsrud, an actor. After he died in a fire she married the critic Edmund Wilson in 1938, but following the birth of her son Revel they divorced the same year. Meanwhile she had been working since 1936 as an editor with Covici Friede, the New York publishers, and had moved on to become an editor on the *Partisan Review*, remaining their drama critic until 1962. Her opinionated, often biting theatre criticism is collected in *Sights and Spectacles 1936–56* and *McCarthy's Theatre Chronicles* (1962).

Wilson, who is portrayed in *A Charmed Life*, encouraged her to write fiction and her first novel, *The Company she keeps* (1942), an episodic picture of Greenwich Village life, was a great success. After World War II she became a teacher at Bard College, Annandale (1945–6), and at Sarah Lawrence College (1948), and married Bowden Bowater. Three novels appeared, *The Oasis* (1949), *The Groves of Academe* (1952) and *A Charmed Life* (1955), followed by her vivid autobiography *Memories of a Catholic Girlhood*, two travel books, *Venice Observed* (1956) and *The Stones of Florence* (1959), and a collection of stories and several essays. In 1961 she visited Poland and a meeting there led to her separation from Bowater and marriage to Jim West, an information officer. Her most famous novel *The Group*, about a generation of women graduates, appeared in 1963, and another, *Birds of America*, in 1971. She has since written several non-fiction works. McCarthy's writing is full of searching social comment and keen wit, which has reflected her hatred of hypocrisy and commitment to radical causes.

M. McCarthy: *Memories of a Catholic Girlhood* (1957)
———— : *How I Grew* (1987)

**McClintock, Barbara** (1902–). American geneticist. A doctor's daughter, Barbara McClintock was born in Hartford, Connecticut, but in 1908 the family moved to Flatbush, Brooklyn, where her fascination with science began at Erasmus Hall High School. Her parents were alarmed by her 'unfeminine' interests and her mother opposed her going to college, so in 1918 she went to work in an employment agency, studying at nights and weekends until in 1919 she was allowed to enrol at Cornell University in the College of Agriculture. She gained her BSc in 1923, followed by an MA, then a PhD in 1927. At Cornell she and two fellow students, Marcus Rhoades and George Beadle (later also famous geneticists), began their work on maize chromosomes and cytological markers, submitting a famous pioneering paper in 1931. For the next two years, Barbara worked in various laboratories on a National Research Council fellowship and in 1933 on a Guggenheim Fellowship travelled to Germany, returning swiftly, because of her horror of Nazism. Eventually, after a period at Cornell and four years

teaching at the University of Missouri, she found a permanent position at the Cold Spring Harbor Laboratory on Long Island. Her pioneering work was recognized when she was made president of the Genetics Society in 1944, and became only the third woman nominated to the American Academy of Science.

Her great discoveries followed, notably 'jumping genes' – the realization that chromosomes were not stable, but that genetic material could shift unpredictably over generations – a discovery that directed the way to understanding cell differentiation. In 1951 this seemed like heresy and she was ignored for years; she has acknowledged that 'they called me crazy, absolutely mad at times', despite the apparent support that the discovery of the structure of DNA gave to her ideas. However, in 1965 she was given a chair at Cornell, and new developments in genetic engineering validated the original vision which had been reached by her unique combination of an intuitive sense of structure and painstaking observation and analysis. Many awards followed, including the National Medal of Science in 1970, the Albert Lasker Basic Medical Research Award, and the Columbia University Horwitz Prize in 1982. Finally, in 1983, at the age of 81, she was awarded the Nobel Prize for Medicine and Physiology.

E. Fox Keller: *A Feeling for the Organism: The Life and Work of Barbara McClintock* (1983)

**McCullers** [née Smith], **(Lula) Carson** (1917–67). American novelist. Born in Columbus, Georgia, as an adolescent she had severe rheumatic fever which led to the invalidism and paralysing strokes of her later life. From the age of 13 she was determined to become a concert pianist, but at 16 also began to write plays to be acted by her family, her first effort *The Faucet* being a sensational drama based on O'Neill. In 1934 she went to New York to study at Columbia University and the Juilliard School, financed by the sale of family jewels. Immediately losing all her money on the subway she was forced to work at odd jobs during the day and study creative writing at night, living first at the Parnassus Club and then at the Three Arts Club.

In 1935, while working on the *Columbus Ledger*, she met Reeves McCullers and after two more years in New York, during which she had two pieces published in *Story*, she married him and they moved to Charlotte, North Carolina. By 1940 the marriage was near collapse. Carson had published *The Heart is a Lonely Hunter*, which portrays the desperate devotion of a group of odd characters in a Southern town for its deaf-mute hero; it won instant recognition for her original talent. The McCullers moved to Greenwich Village and were soon divorced. *Reflections in a Golden Eye* appeared in 1941, and in 1942 Carson obtained a Guggenheim Fellowship and spent time at' the Yaddo Artist Colony in Saratoga, where she met KATHERINE ANNE PORTER and to which she frequently returned for the rest of her life.

She always remained close to Reeves and in 1945 they remarried and stayed uneasily together, through his alcoholism and her nervous illness, until 1948. In 1946 *The Member of the Wedding* was published and on a second Guggenheim Fellowship they visited Paris but returned when Carson suffered a stroke followed by a long illness and attempted suicide. Her life was later largely dedicated to seeking treatment for a paralysed arm, but in 1950 she dramatized *Member of the Wedding* which became a long-running Broadway hit and successful film, winning her two drama awards. In 1951 she published *The Ballad of the Sad Café*, and visited England, staying with ELIZABETH BOWEN. Another close friend of her later years was EDITH SITWELL. Her last book, a final ironic, comic look at the South, was *Clock without Hands* (1961). For much of her time she was confined to a daybed or wheelchair; she died at the age of 51, having been in a coma for 47 days after a stroke.

V.S. Carr: *The Lonely Hunter: a Biography of McCullers* (1975)

**McGill, Helen** (1871–1947). Canadian feminist and lawyer. She was born in Hamilton, Ontario, and her mother, a pioneer suffrage worker, encouraged her academic ambitions. She graduated from University of Trinity College, Toronto, in 1888, the only woman in her class, and became a journalist, her assignments including a trip to Japan to write about social conditions there. On her return she married a Dr Flesher and moved to California where

she and her mother ran two papers, *The Searchlight* and *Society*, before they moved to Minneapolis where Helen became a professional journalist. Her husband died in 1900 but she remained in the USA, working as an editor for a St Paul's daily newspaper and campaigning for protective legislation, penal reform and equal rights for women. In 1902 she married J.H. McGill, and moved to Vancouver, where she began to practise law.

In 1917 she was appointed to the juvenile bench in British Columbia, where she served until 1929, and again from 1934 until 1945. She was a member of the Minimum Wage Board (1918), Chairman of the Mother's Pension Board (1920–21), a founder of the Vancouver Women's Building, and a campaigner for reforms in welfare laws. A member of the International Council of Women, she was also active in the International Association of Women Lawyers. Her daughter became the first qualified woman aeronautical engineer in Canada.

E.G. McGill: *My Mother the Judge* (1955)

**McKinney** [née Crummy], **Louise** (1868–1933). Canadian suffragette and politician. Born in Franksville, Ontario, she worked as a teacher in North Dakota and then settled in Claresholm, Alberta, after her marriage. After 1916 she became a leading member of the Non-partisan League, an agrarian movement advocating public ownership of grain stores and flour mills, and was elected in the Alberta legislature as a candidate for the League in 1917. She thus became the first woman member of any legislative body in the British Empire. She was, however, defeated in 1921 and did not run again. She was not only a progressive politician, but a senior member of the Canadian Temperance Movement and a feminist who fought for suffrage, and was also one of the signatories in 1927 of EMILY MURPHY'S appeal against the decision of the Supreme Court of Alberta that women were not legally entitled to membership of the Canadian Senate.

**MacLaine, Shirley** (stage name of Shirley Maclean Beaty) (1934–). American film actress. Born in Richmond, Virgina (the sister of actor Warren Beattie), Shirley studied at

Washington School of Ballet and attended high school in Arlington, Virginia. When she graduated in 1952 she had already appeared in the chorus line of *Oklahoma* (1950) and *Me and Juliet* (1952). Her first screen role was in Hitchcock's *The Trouble with Harry* (1955), but her early reputation was based on her comic skill, as shown in *Around the World in 80 Days* (1956), and on wayward waifs like Ginny in *Some Came Running* (1958), qualities combined in *The Apartment* (1960), *Irma La Douce* (1963) and *Sweet Charity* (1968).

In 1970 MacLaine began playing different, more powerful roles, starting with *Two Mules for Sister Sara*, and revived her singing and dancing career as a night club star. In the same year her 1954 marriage to Steve Parker ended in divorce: they had one daughter. She stands out in Hollywood for her strong political stance, and her mystical religious views, as well as for her dramatic performances in recent films such as *The Turning Point* (1977), *A Change of Seasons* (1980) and *Terms of Endearment* (1983), for which she won an Academy Award.

S. MacLaine: *Out on a Limb* (1983)
———— : *Dancing in the Light* (1985)

**McLaren, Agnes** (1837–1913). Scottish doctor. Agnes did not begin her medical studies until the age of 38, in Edinburgh, where she became a friend of SOPHIA JEX-BLAKE and was associated with suffragist activities. In 1878 she received her degree from the University of Montpellier with her thesis *Flexions of the Uterus* and began to practise in Cannes.

20 years later she was converted to Catholicism, joined the Third Order of Dominicans and began her major work in providing women doctors for Catholic missions. Women in religious orders were forbidden under Roman Catholic canon law to become doctors at this time – a ruling not rescinded until 1936 – but Agnes helped achieve the appointment of several, among them Elizabeth Bielby, to Rawalpindi in India. In 1909, at the age of 72, Agnes visited Rawalpindi Open Hospital. Her work was continued by the Austrian Anna Dengel, who with Joanna Lyons founded the Society of Catholic Medical Missionaries in 1925.

K. Burton: *According to the Pattern: the Story of Dr Agnes McLaren and the Society of Catholic Medical Missionaries* (1946)

**Macmillan, Chrystal** (1871–1937). Scottish feminist, pacifist and lawyer. She was born into a prominent Edinburgh family and was educated at St Leonard's School, St Andrews, and Edinburgh University, where she obtained a first class degree in mathematics and natural sciences, before undertaking further study in Berlin. She was active in the Scottish suffrage campaign; in 1908 she became the first woman to address the House of Lords when she appealed for her right as a graduate to vote for the parliamentary candidates for the Scottish Universities seat. The case was defeated after a seven-day hearing. She joined the National Union of Suffrage Societies, led by MILLICENT GARRETT FAWCETT, and remained a leader of the Union (which became the National Union of Societies for Equal Citizenship in 1924) until she eventually resigned because she opposed their support of protective legislation. In 1923 she founded the Open Door Council which campaigned for the removal of legal restraints on women. She had qualified as a lawyer herself, and was called to the Bar in 1924,·although she never practised. In 1929 she became President of the Open Door International for the Economic Emancipation of the Woman Worker. She was also deeply involved in another campaign concerning the legal status of women, the fight for women's right to retain their nationality on marriage to a foreigner.

Chrystal Macmillan's other great cause was pacifism. She was one of the chief organizers of the International Women's Congress at The Hague in 1915, which led to the foundation of the Women's International League for Peace and Freedom. She was also Secretary of the International Alliance of Women from 1913 to 1923. Her last public fight was as the unsuccessful Liberal candidate for Edinburgh in the 1935 election.

**McMillan, Margaret** (1860–1931). British educationalist. Margaret and Rachel McMillan, both pioneers in British education, were born into a Scottish family in New York. After their father died in 1865, they returned with their mother to Inverness, and went to Inverness High School. Intending to be a governess Margaret then studied music in Frankfurt and languages in Geneva and

Lausanne, before going to work in London in 1883. She was an active member of socialist groups and of the suffrage movement in London and in 1893 was invited north to Bradford, where she became one of the first members of the new Independent Labour Party, and in 1894 was elected to the Bradford School Board. In 1899 she instigated the first recorded government-backed school medical inspection, in Bradford.

In 1902 she joined her sister Rachel (who had become a teacher of hygiene) in London, and campaigned for wider school health care, and in 1904 published *Education through the Imagination*. The first children's clinic was opened at Bow, followed in 1910 by one in Deptford which was soon supported by government grants for dental, eye and ear care. The sisters also set up camps for deprived children, and in 1913 founded a local infants' school with a large garden. Embodying Rachel's ideas on child health it was finally completed in 1917, and was called the Rachel McMillan Open Air Nursery School.

Margaret McMillan continued her work in Deptford, her campaigns for improvement in children's education, and her support for socialism, through the Labour Party. She was made a CBE in 1917, and a Companion of Honour in 1930.

**Macnaghten, Anne (Catherine)** (1908–). English concert promoter and violinist. She studied at the Leipzig Conservatory, having had private lessons from JELLY D'ARÁNYI and continuing her tuition with several other violinists. In 1932 she formed a string quartet, consisting entirely of women, which gave many concerts and broadcasts. Disbanded between 1939 and 1947, the quartet (with different membership) went on to encourage music-making in schools through teaching and coaching as well as concerts.

She is primarily associated, however, with the series of concerts that she founded (with Iris Lemare and ELISABETH LUTYENS) in 1931 to promote contemporary music, especially British. The first Macnaghten–Lemare Concert took place at the Mercury Theatre (then known as the Ballet Club) and included the premières of music by Imogen Holst and Lutyens. Britten, Alan Rawsthorne, Richard Rodney Bennett and later Peter Maxwell Davies are among the composers whose works have had first performances through the society. During the 1960s it became more international in scope, incorporating such composers as Berio and Stockhausen in the first concert of electronic music in the UK. The society has survived many vicissitudes (mostly financial) and continues as the New Macnaghten Concerts, and many composers have dedicated their works to its founder. The 50th anniversary series of concerts included the première of *The Old Woman of Beare* (1981) by NICOLA LEFANU.

**Maconchy, Elizabeth** (1907–). English composer of Irish origin. She was a pupil of Charles Wood and Vaughan Williams at the Royal College of Music, London, and then had a short period of study with Jirák in Prague, where her first large-scale composition, the Piano Concertino (written 1928) was performed in 1930. In the UK her early work became known through the Macnaghten–Lemare Concerts, while on the Continent her music was included in the festivals of the International Society for Contemporary Music held at Prague (1935), Paris (1937) and Copenhagen (1947), and was favourably received in Belgium, Hungary and Poland. She succeeded Britten as president of the Society for the Promotion of New Music, and in 1959 she became the first woman to chair the Composers' Guild of Great Britain.

Her reputation rests chiefly on her chamber music, especially her technical mastery of the string quartet (she produced her twelfth in 1979). She wrote her first opera, *The Sofa*, to a libretto by Ursula Vaughan Williams, in 1957; Anne Ridler and Maconchy herself supplied the librettos for her later stage works, many of which are written for children, resulting in the accessibility that characterizes much of her output. Her vocal works include the dramatic cantata *Héloïse and Abelard* (1979) and settings of Gerard Manley Hopkins and Anacreon, the latter translated by her husband William LeFanu. They have two daughters, the younger of whom is the composer NICOLA LEFANU. Maconchy won the Cobbett Medal for chamber music in 1960 and was made a CBE in 1977. Her eightieth birthday was marked by several concert series and a documentary film.

**Mcphail** [née Campbell], **Agnes** (1890–1954). Canadian suffragette and politician. Born in Grey County, Ontario, she was educated at Stratford Normal School and became a school teacher. She was involved with the suffrage movement and also with radical groups and in 1921 was elected MP for the United Farmers of Ontario, for South-east Grey. She thus became Canada's first woman MP, retaining her seat until 1940. At first she voted with the Progressive Party but in 1924 broke away with several other MPs known as the 'Ginger Group', which eventually formed the Co-operative Commonwealth Foundation in 1932. From 1943 to 1951 she was a member of the Ontario legislature.

M. Stewart and D. French: *Ask no Quarter: a Biography of Agnes McPhail* (1959)

**McPherson, Aimée Semple** (1890–1944). Canadian evangelist and founder of the International Church of the Foursquare Gospel. Aimée was born near Ingersoll, Ontario, and her family were active members of the Salvation Army. In 1908 marriage to Robert Semple, a pentecostal evangelist, took her to Asia as a missionary. Following his death in 1910, Aimée returned to the USA with her daughter and devoted herself to revival work across the continent. She married again in 1921 (to Harold McPherson) and for a third time in 1931; both marriages ended in divorce.

In 1923 Aimée established a permanent home for the Foursquare Gospel movement in Los Angeles. The movement's theology was built around the four roles of Christ as Saviour, Baptizer, Healer and Coming King; faith-healing was also important. Much of the movement's success was due to Aimée's skill in publicity and her flamboyant style. On 18 May 1926 she disappeared while swimming in the Pacific Ocean and reappeared a month later claiming to have been kidnapped, but her story was inconsistent in its details. This episode caused disaffection within the leadership but the majority of her followers remained loyal. The movement continued to grow despite financial difficulties in the 1930s. Aimée died from what was ruled as an accidental overdose of sedatives. Her most important autobiographical writings are *This is That* (1923) and *The Story of my Life*

(1951), which was compiled after her death.

L. Thomas: *Storming Heaven* (1970)

**Madame Royale**. See D'ANGOULEME.

**Madison** [née Payne], **Dolley** [Dolly; Dorothea] (1768–1849). American political personality. Born into a Quaker family in Guilford County, North Carolina, she moved to Philadelphia in 1783. In 1790 she married John Todd, who died in the yellow fever epidemic of 1793. They had one surviving son. The following year she left the Society of Friends and married James Madison, a politician nearly 20 years her senior. When Madison became Secretary of State in 1801, Dolley acted as hostess for President Jefferson, who was a widower. Charming and tactful, she established an atmosphere of open friendliness but her hospitality became increasingly magnificent after Madison became President in 1809. He retired in 1817 and they lived on their plantation at Montpelier, Orange County; when he died she returned to Washington, DC, and took her place again as a leading political hostess. Despite the financial embarrassment of her final years, she was greatly honoured and remained one of the most colourful and popular figures in political life.

E. Thorne: *Dolley Madison: her Life and Times* (1970)

**Magnani, Anna** (1908–73). Italian actress. Born in Alexandria, the illegitimate child of an Italian mother and Egyptian father, she spent a poverty-stricken childhood in Rome, where she was educated at a convent before entering the Academy of Dramatic Art. She worked as a night-club singer, then as a variety performer and repertory actress. In 1927 she toured Argentina in a play and appeared in the silent film *Scampolo*, but she returned to the stage. In 1935 she married the director Alfredo Alessardis who discouraged her film career, but she made a brief appearance in 1941 in De Sica's *Teresa Venerdì/Doctor Beware*. The following year she had a son by the actor Massimo Serato, and much of her time was later spent nursing her child after he contracted polio. Her marriage was dissolved in 1950.

In 1945 she made her real debut in Rossellini's film *Roma Città aperta/Open City*, in a performance of outstanding passion and force, almost equalled by *L'Amore/Ways of Love* (1948). During the 1950s she worked in Italian and American films, winning an Academy Award for *The Rose Tattoo* (1955). Her roles sometimes degenerated into a caricature of the overbearing Italian mother, but she was recognized by many directors as one of the greatest actresses of her day. She worked on stage and television during the 1960s. She died of cancer at the age of 65.

**Mahler** [née Schindler], **Alma** (1879–1964). Austrian; wife of Gustav Mahler. Daughter of the distinguished painter Anton Schindler, she was brought up in one of the most highly-cultivated intellectual and artistic circles of Vienna. Mahler, almost 20 years her senior, first met her in 1901; they were married within a few months. Herself a composition pupil of Zemlinsky and an extremely gifted pianist, she was an astute critic of Mahler's music (and devoted much time to copying scores for him); Pfitzner, Zemlinsky and Schoenberg equally admitted to benefiting from her advice. Despite the inevitable strain imposed on a marriage between equally strong-willed partners (Mahler's friendship with Freud developed out of a matrimonial crisis), his recognition of her is expressed, for instance, in the comments left in the manuscript of his unfinished Tenth Symphony; and a theme in the first movement of his Sixth Symphony was conceived as a 'portrait' of her. Her edition of his letters was published in 1924 and her memoirs in 1940, both remaining fundamental source material.

Of their two daughters, Maria Anna (*b* 1902) died at the age of four, and Anna Justina (1904–88) became a successful sculptor and wife, successively, of the composer Krenek, the publisher Szolnay and the conductor Fistoulari.

**Maintenon.** *See* DE MAINTENON.

**Makarova, Natalia** (1940–). Russian ballerina. Born in Leningrad, she graduated from the Vaganova School (1959) and joined the Kirov Ballet. In 1961 she made a triumphant appearance in *Giselle* at Covent Garden, London, and toured the USA. Her roles in the USSR included the great classics such as Aurora and Odette–Odile. In 1970

she defected after a European tour and joined the American Ballet Theatre in New York, dancing classical roles and modern ballets such as Tudor's *Jardin aux lilas*, *Dark Elegies*, *Pillar of Fire* and *Romeo and Juliet*. She has made guest appearances in the USA and UK, dancing in Macmillan's *Manon*, and *Das Lied von der Erde*; in the revival of BRONISLAVA NIJINSKA'S *Les biches*; as the Black Queen in NINETTE DE VALOIS' *Checkmate*; and was guest artist of the London Festival Ballet in 1984. She combines classical finesse with a mysterious, haunting stage presence.

N. Makarova: *A Dance Autobiography* (1980)
——— : *On Your Toes* (1984)

**Makeba, (Zensi) Miriam** (1932–). South African singer. Miriam Makeba was born in Prospect township, outside Johannesburg, a member of the Xhosa people. She began singing in the choir at her Methodist school, and gave her first solo performance when a girl, on the visit of George VI to South Africa. After leaving school she worked helping her mother, a maid in wealthy white Johannesburg houses, singing as an amateur at weddings and funerals until 1954, when she joined the travelling group the Black Manhattan Brothers, touring for three years throughout South Africa, Rhodesia and the Congo. A well-known artist in South Africa, in 1959 she played Joyce, a shebeen-owner in the all-black jazz opera *King Kong*. Her personal life was troubled. Her first husband was a policeman by whom she had a daughter (who later died in childbirth); her second was the South African ballad singer Sonny Pillay; she then married trumpet player Hugh Masekela, also a star of *King Kong*.

In 1958, Makeba had starred in the American anti-apartheid film *Come Back Africa*, and she left South Africa when it was shown at the Venice Film Festival in 1959, going on to London (where she met Harry Belafonte, who was later to help her career considerably) and then to America, where she appeared on television and began singing in Greenwich Village night clubs. In the 1960s she became one of the best-known singers in the USA, making national and international tours with Belafonte, and having several major record hits, notably with *The Click Song* and *Wimeweh*, an allegory of opposition to the 'lion' of South Africa. (Four of her relatives had died in the Sharpeville massacre of 1960.) In 1963 she attended conferences in Ethiopia, and testified before the UN Committee on Apartheid. In the late 1960s, her marriage to Masekela having ended, she married Stokely Carmichael, the black militant activist, and her connection with the Black Panthers led to the cancellation of many contracts and concerts.

Makeba then left the United States and settled in the former French colony of Guinea, at the suggestion of President Sekou Touré. Until 1984 she combined her concert and recording work with cultural and diplomatic missions. She has addressed the United Nations, and performed at many African official celebrations. She still lives in Guinea and is now married to Bageot Bah. In 1986 Makeba was a special guest on Paul Simon's *Graceland* tour, which has brought her renewed international fame.

M. Makeba: *Makeba, My Story* (1988)

**Makin, Bathshua (Pell)** (1608–75). English educator. She was born at Southwick, Sussex, the daughter of the local Rector; her brother John became an eminent mathematician and Ambassador to Holland. Little is known of her early life or marriage, but during the 1640s she tutored the daughters of Charles I, particularly Princess Elizabeth, teaching her Greek, Latin, Hebrew, mathematics, French, Italian and Spanish. After the interregnum she kept a school at Tottenham High Cross, and here she wrote her *Essay to Revive the Antient Education of Gentlewomen* (1673), for which she is best remembered. She held radical views by contemporary standards, advocating a wide range of knowledge in arts and sciences, and technical skills. She was a correspondent of ANNA VAN SCHURMAN.

J.R. Brink: 'Bathshua Makin', *Female Scholars* (1980)

**Malakhovskaya, Natalia** (1947–). Russian feminist. She graduated from the faculty of letters in Leningrad in 1973 and worked as a teacher, but became involved in the underground feminist movement as editorial secretary and contributor to the review *37*, and formed the Club Maria, an illegal women's organization. With other women, including the artist Tatyana Mamanova and the poet Julia Voznesenskaya (who had already been sen-

tenced to two years in Siberia), she wrote the *samizdat* publication *Women and Russia*, which was smuggled out in 1980 and which speaks out against domestic oppression and inadequate state provision for maternity and childcare. A few months later she and the other leaders of the group were exiled to Vienna, and other members were later banished in 1982.

**Malibran** [neé García], **Maria(-Felicia)** (1808–36). Spanish mezzo-soprano. A daughter of the celebrated tenor Manuel García, from whom she received her initial training (and a great deal of harshness), she created a vocal legend in a lifespan of only 28 years. Her sister became equally famous as the mezzo-soprano PAULINE VIARDOT. Having been immersed in the theatre as a child, Maria made her formal operatic debut at the King's Theatre, London, as Rosina in Rossini's *Il barbiere di Siviglia* (1825). Following this success, García took his opera company, consisting mostly of his family, to New York, resulting in the first season of Italian opera in the USA. The repertoire included five Rossini operas, Mozart's *Don Giovanni* and two works by García, with Maria in the leading roles. While on this tour, she married Eugène Malibran, mostly as a means of escape from her father, leaving him a matter of months later. She returned to Europe in 1827, making her Paris debut the following year in Rossini's *Semiramide*; she spent the next period, until 1832, alternating between Paris and London to ever-increasing acclaim. She then embarked on the most triumphant part of her career, in Italy, where she appeared in all the major opera houses, most notably in the title roles of *Norma* (and other Bellini roles) and Donizetti's *Maria Stuarda*, an opera whose early history is marked by bitter wrangling among prima donnas (Malibran herself was not in good voice for the première, but persisted in singing because of the fees involved). Many contemporary composers, including Chopin, Mendelssohn and Liszt, succumbed to her vocal artistry, casting aside criticisms of excess in her acting. Her marriage to Malibran was eventually annulled, though not before she had borne a son to the violinist Charles de Bériot, whom she married in 1836 a few months before her death as a result of injuries sustained in a riding accident.

A. Fitzlyon: *Maria Malibran: Diva of the Romantic Age* (1987)

**Malina, Judith** (1926–). American theatre director and actress. Born in Kiel, Germany, Judith Malina studied at the Dramatic Workshop of the New School for Social Research and made her acting debut in 1945 in *By Any Other Name* at the Cherry Lane, New York. She continued to act at the Cherry Lane, and it was there, in 1947, that she founded The Living Theatre with Julian Beck, whom she married in 1948: one of their early productions was GERTRUDE STEIN's *Ladies Voices*. They concentrated on 'uncommercial' plays, and Judith herself began directing in 1951 with *The Thirteenth God*. In that year the theatre acquired its own base on lower Sixth Avenue, and its productions became increasingly bold, both in political content and staging, including plays by T.S. Eliot, Pirandello, Cocteau, Picasso, Arturo Ui, as well as unknown playwrights, such as the innovative study of drug addiction, Jack Gelber's *The Connection* (1959).

The Living Theatre first toured Europe in 1961. Despite their huge European success and many awards, trouble faced them in America – political, critical, legal and financial – and they closed the company there in 1963. They came to London with *The Brig* in 1964, and remained in Europe playing in West Berlin, Brussels and Rome until 1968, when they returned to America. They have since made other tours including a visit to Brazil in 1971 with *The Legacy of Cain*, a collection of 100 short plays performed over two weeks in open village sites. In 1975 the Becks settled with their troupe in Bordeaux, France, where their plays have included *Masse Mensch* (1980).

**Mandela, Winnie (Nomzano)** (1934–). South African political activist. She was born in Pondoland, part of what is now Transkei, a member of the Tembu royal house. After her matriculation she went to Johannesburg, obtained a social science diploma and became a social worker, attached to the Baragwanath General Hospital. In 1958 she married Nelson Mandela, a lawyer and a member of the national executive of the African National Congress (ANC). They have two daughters. She has been arrested, imprisoned and banned many times since first being arrested in 1958 for taking part in a women's anti-pass demonstration. She joined and became very active in the Women's League of the ANC which was declared an illegal organization in 1961. Nelson Mandela then went underground but was captured in 1962 and sentenced to life imprisonment on Robben Island. Winnie Mandela was banned and severely restricted but came to be accepted as the spokeswoman for the ANC in Nelson's absence. In 1966 she was imprisoned for nearly 12 months for breaking her banning order and between 1969 and 1975 she was rearrested many times on the same charge. Altogether she has served over 16 months in solitary confinement. After the 1976 Soweto uprising Winnie was banned to the outskirts of the Orange Free State town of Brandforth where she was forced to live in primitive conditions. She was charged again in 1978 for breaking her ban and given a suspended sentence. She broke the ban after her home and clinic were burned in 1985, and in 1986 returned to live in Soweto. In 1985 she won the Third World Prize and she has become a symbol of heroism, dignity and resistance, the representative of her imprisoned husband.

W. Mandela: *A Part of my Soul went with Him* (1985)
N. Harrison: *Mother of a Nation* (1985)

**Mandelstam, Nadezhda** (1899–1980). Russian writer. Born in Saratov on the Volga, Nadezhda Khazina was educated by English governesses, learning French and German as well as English. After attending school in Kiev she studied art, with the painter Alexandra EXTER, and there, in 1919, she met the poet Osip Mandelstam, whom she married in 1921. After living in the Caucasus they settled in Moscow, working as translators, but in 1934 Mandelstam was arrested (in the presence of their close friend AKHMATOVA) for his satire against Stalin, and the couple spent three years in exile and extreme poverty in the Urals and in Voronezh, harassed by the GPU and under constant threat of deportation. After a brief return to Moscow, Mandelstam was once again arrested and sentenced to forced labour, dying in a labour camp in 1938.

Nadezhda survived by working in factories and teaching English in a series of provincial towns, and devoted her life to preserving and memorizing her husband's poems, smuggling them out of Russia. In 1956 she was allowed to return to Moscow, where she gained her doctorate and wrote her famous memoirs, *Vospominaniya* (*Hope Against Hope*, 1970) and *Vtoraya Kniga* (*Hope Abandoned*, 1974).

**Mangolte, Babette** (*c*1945–). French film technician. She first became interested in the visual side of cinema when she saw foreign films without subtitles at the Cinémathèque Française, Paris, while taking a degree in mathematics and physics at the Sorbonne. She passed the Institut des Hautes Etudes Cinématographiques examination, but was refused entry because she was a woman. However, she was accepted by the more technically-oriented Ecole Nationale de la Photographie et de la Cinématographie. She edited two short films by Marcel Hanoun, and worked on five films for industrial firms, but chose to work for individuals after the events of May 1968. In 1970 she moved to New York and took photographs of the live performing arts. She was the Director of photography for YVONNE RAINER's first two films and for five CHANTAL AKERMAN films, and taught 16mm film-making at the Pratt Institute, New York. At the 1975 Toulon Film Festival she won the Prix de la Lumière for photography in Rainer's *Film about a Woman who . . .* and for her own first film *What Maisie knew* (1975), which is based on the Henry James Novel and related the child's point of view to the subjective film camera. She has since made several short films and a second long one, *The Camera: Je/ La Camera: Eye* (1977)

**Manley, Mary (de la Rivière)** (1663–1724). English novelist and polemical writer. She was born in Jersey, the daughter of a Royalist hero who was later Governor of Jersey. After her father's death in 1688 she was inveigled into a bigamous marriage with her cousin John Manley, who subsequently deserted her. After a short time with the Duchess of Cleveland she travelled around England until 1696, when her letters were published and two plays, *The Lost Lover* and *The Royal Mischief*, were produced in London. Her struggles are fictionalized in *The Adventures of Rivella* (1714).

She became famous for her love affairs as well as for writing spicy narratives of current gossip thinly disguised as fiction, such as *The Secret of Queen Zarah* (1705), which was about the Duchess of Marlborough. However, her major work was *The New Atlantis* (1709), a denunciation of Whig corruption and intrigue which led to her arrest for libel. From 1710 she collaborated with Swift on Tory pamphlets and succeeded him as Editor of *The Examiner* in 1711. Her last work was *The Power of Love* (1720), whose main theme was the corruption of female innocence by male lust. She was one of the first English professional women writers.

**Manning, Olivia** (1908–80). British writer. Olivia Manning was a naval officer's daughter, born and brought up in Portsmouth. She trained at art school and then went to London, where she had a variety of jobs and began to write, publishing her first novel, *The Wind Changes*, in 1937. In 1939 she married R.D. (Reggie) Smith. Their experiences in Bucharest, where he was a British Council lecturer, formed the background to her Balkan Trilogy: *The Great Fortune* (1960), *The Spoilt City* (1962) and *Friends and Heroes* (1965), while the time following their evacuation to Athens, and Egypt, where Olivia was Press Officer to the United States Embassy, gave her the setting for the Levant Trilogy: *The Danger Tree* (1977), *The Battle Lost and Won* (1978) and *The Sum of Things* (1980).

From 1941 to 1945 she worked in Jerusalem as a Press Assistant and for the British Council. Returning to London she reviewed, wrote journalism and won increasing acclaim as a novelist with 11 novels between 1949 and 1980, while her husband pursued a career as a radio producer and, later, an academic. She was made a CBE in 1976.

**Mansfield, Katherine** [pseud. of Kathleen Beauchamp] (1888–1923). New Zealand short-story writer. Born in Wellington, New Zealand, she went to London in 1903, and apart from the period 1906–8 spent the rest of her life in Europe. She spent some time at an academy in Harley Street, London. On her return to London in 1908 she started to make a literary career for herself. In 1909 she married George Bowden but left him the next day. She also published her first short story in that year, and during the next became associated with A.R. Orage's *The New Age*. She was also introduced to feminism, and her work reflected her feminist concern more overtly during this period than later. She became friendly with other writers, including VIRGINIA WOOLF, D.H. Lawrence and most importantly his friend John Middleton Murry. They became lovers, though they did not marry until 1918, and she started to write reviews for his literary paper *The Athenaeum*. Her first collection of short stories, *In a German Pension*, came out in 1911. In 1915 her brother Leslie visited her; he was later killed in a military accident. This had a profound effect on her, and later that year she went to the South of France for the sake of her health. Her most famous work, *Prelude* (a first publication of the Hogarth Press in 1917), re-creates the New Zealand of her childhood, as many of her stories were henceforth to do. In the last two years of her life, while desperately seeking a cure for tuberculosis, she produced some fine work, including *Bliss and other Stories* (1920) and *The Garden Party and other Stories* (1922). Her last collection, *Something Childish* (1924), came out after her death at the Gurdjieff Institute near Paris. Her *Journals* (1927) and *Letters* (1928) were edited by Middleton Murry.

A. Alpers: *The Life of Katherine Mansfield* (1980)
C. Tomalin: *Katherine Mansfield: A Secret Life* (1987)

**Manton, Sidnie (Milana)** (1902–79). English zoologist. After taking a degree at Girton College, Cambridge, Sidnie studied arthropods. Her work on crustacean embryology set new standards, and her demonstration that *onychophora* are related to *arthropoda* led to beautifully-illustrated work on how centipedes and millipedes walk. An expedition to the Great Barrier Reef in 1929 supplied further data on crustacea. Until this work, knowledge of invertebrates was very slight compared with that of vertebrates.

From 1935 to 1942 she was Director of Studies in Natural Science at Girton College, Cambridge; her subsequent appointments were at London University and as an honorary worker at the British Museum Natural History section, where her husband John Harding, whom she married in 1937, became Keeper of Zoology. They

had a daughter and adopted a son.

In 1948 she was elected Fellow of the Royal Society, and was awarded the Linnaean Gold Medal in 1963. She was co-author of *Practical Vertebrate Morphology* (1930, 4th edn 1969), and her book *Arthropods* appeared in 1977.

**Manus, Rosa** (1880–1942). Dutch feminist. The daughter of a businessman, she was educated in Amsterdam and became involved in the suffrage struggle there at the age of 24. After suffrage was achieved in The Netherlands she toured Europe and South America with CARRIE CATT and became Vice-President of the International Federation for Women's Suffrage in 1926. She also organized peace conferences in Dresden and Berlin, and mounted a major exhibition of women's work in Amsterdam. In 1935 she organized an International Women's Congress in Istanbul.

After the German invasion of the Netherlands, Manus was arrested and in 1941 sent to Scheveningen, and then to Ravensbrück and finally to Auschwitz.

**Manzolini** [née Morandi], **Anne** (1716–74). Italian anatomist. Born in Bologna, Anne was brought up to lead a domestic life. At the age of 20 she married Giovanni Manzolini, who at 24 was Professor of Anatomy at the university and an expert in making anatomical models from wax. Five years later Anne was the mother of six children and also very skilful at making the anatomical models, which she sold to help support the family.

Anne also studied anatomy and was invited to lecture in her husband's place during his illnesses. She was appointed a lecturer in her own name on his death (an unusual distinction), then in 1760 became Professor of Anatomy with the additional title of *modellatrice*.

She was patronized by the royalty of Europe – the Emperor Joseph II of Austria bought several wax models – and elected to membership of the Russian Royal Scientific Association and the British Royal Society. Milan offered her a blank contract to work there but she refused to leave Bologna. The collection of anatomical models which she made for her own use was left to the Medical Institute of Bologna after her death.

**Marcet, Jane** (1769–1858). British scientific writer. The daughter of a wealthy Swiss merchant, Anthony Haldimand, Jane was born in Geneva but grew up chiefly in London. At the age of 15, after her mother's death, she took charge of the house and younger children. At this stage her main interest was art, which she studied with Sir Joshua Reynolds and Thomas Lawrence. In 1799 she married Alexander Marcet, a Swiss doctor and enthusiastic experimental chemist, later a Fellow of the Royal Society. The Marcets' social circle included the historian Henry Hallam, Thomas Malthus, HARRIET MARTINEAU and MARIA EDGEWORTH. Jane attended the popular lectures on chemistry given by Humphrey Davy at the Royal Institution and later became his student. Her first book, *Conversations on Chemistry; intended more specially for the female sex*, published in 1805 in two volumes, was intended to provide background knowledge for the women who went to such lectures. It took the form of conversations between a teacher and two girl pupils and gave lively descriptions of experiments illustrated by the author's own woodcuts and drawings. Instantly popular, the book went through 16 British and 15 American editions, taking account of all new developments in the subject. Michael Faraday, who was introduced to electrochemistry when he bound the book as an apprentice bookbinder in 1810, became a close friend.

Her most famous work, *Conversations on Political Economy* (1816), inspired the young Harriet Martineau when she read it in 1827. Although designed for women, it was admired by leading historians and economists and also went through numerous editions. Marcet's other works included *Conversations on Natural Philosophy* (1824) and *Conversations on Vegetable Physiology* (1829). From 1830 to 1858 she wrote primarily for children: her determination to make science, history and economics accessible to women was linked to her belief in the importance of mothers in the education of their family. She died in London at the age of 89.

**Margaret** (1353–1412). Queen of Denmark, Norway and Sweden. The daughter of King Valdemar IV of Denmark, at the age of six she was betrothed to Haakon, King of Norway and son of Magnus Eriksson of Sweden and Norway, as part of a dynastic treaty. Delayed by an intermittent war with Magnus, the couple were eventually married in 1363. Haakon lost the Swedish crown in 1364 but remained King of Norway, and Margaret therefore grew up at the Norwegian court, soon showing great skill as a scholar and also as a stateswoman. Their son Olaf was born in 1370 and five years later, after the death of her father, Margaret persuaded the Danes to accept Olaf as King, under her regency. When Haakon died, in 1380, she also became Regent for Olaf in Norway, and continued to press his claim for the Swedish crown. After Olaf's sudden death in 1387, Margaret adopted her nephew, Erik of Pomerania, as heir and continued to rule. Two years later, having formed an alliance with the Swedish nobles, and been proclaimed the rightful queen, she defeated the unpopular King Albrecht of Mecklenburg in battle, imprisoning him until 1395.

Now the ruler of all three Scandinavian states Margaret consolidated her position by crushing the opposition of the nobles, culminating in the coronation of Erik as king at Kalmar in 1397. A tentative plan for union was proposed. She herself retained considerable power, centralizing her authority, building up a strong treasury through taxation (despite bitter resentment), and establishing a network of provincial sheriffs, often operating out of their native territory, to strengthen loyalty to the crown rather than the region. She also firmly dominated the ecclesiastical establishment and the appointment of bishops. Her dual aims, of creating a unified kingdom and maintaining Scandinavian power in the face of German territorial and commercial expansion were largely realized. The tri-partite union was never firm, and finally ended in 1523, but the union of Sweden and Norway endured for over 400 years, until 1814.

M. Hill: *The Reign of Margaret of Denmark* (1898)

**Margaret of Anjou** (1430–82). English queen. The daughter of René I of Anjou, titular King of Naples, she was brought up by her energetic and scholarly mother Isabella of Lorraine, and then by her grandmother Yolande of Aragon. In 1445 her marriage to Henry VI was arranged as part of agreements for the Truce of Tours during the Hundred Years War, and she was eventually crowned in Westminster Abbey. Beautiful, intelligent, and as fond of excitement in politics as in hunting, she soon allied herself with the 'King's Party' (led by Suffolk and then Somerset against the opposition of Richard, Duke of York), and successfully negotiated for an extension of the French truce. She also took over much administration, raising taxes and making matches for the aristocracy, and founded Queen's College, Cambridge, in 1448. Ruthless to her opponents, she was the centre of rumour and scandal, and her fiercely partisan attitude, especially after Henry became insane and after the birth of her son in 1453, partly provoked Richard's open opposition which led to his victory over the Lancastrians at St Albans in 1455.

Margaret managed to regain control, nominally for Henry, in 1456, but the struggle continued. She outlawed Yorkist leaders in 1459, refused to accept York as Henry's heir and eventually killed him in 1460, freeing Henry from captivity the following year. Her army was then defeated by the future Edward IV, York's son, and she was forced to flee to Scotland. After two years of resistance, during which she was reduced to begging for food, she sailed to France, remaining there until 1471. Then an alliance with an old rival, the Duke of Warwick, who had deposed Edward IV in 1470, enabled her to return, but Warwick was killed and she herself defeated in battle at Tewkesbury where her son died. Soon afterwards her unstable husband was murdered in the Tower of London. Margaret remained in custody until ransomed by Louis IX in 1475, when she returned to France, eventually dying in poverty and isolation among her childhood surroundings in Anjou.

J.J. Bagley: *Margaret of Anjou, Queen of England* (1948)

**Margrethe II** (1940–). Queen of Denmark. Educated at the universities of Copenhagen, Århus and Cambridge, the London School of Economics and the Sorbonne, Margrethe became a keen archaeologist and often contributes to archaeological journals. In 1967 she married Count Henrik, Count de Monpezat and they have two children. The Danish throne has only a ceremonial and

official role; the right of female succession was established only in 1953 and when she succeeded in January 1972 she became Denmark's first Queen for over 1000 years. She is also an artist and has illustrated books such as *The Lord of the Rings* (1977–8), *Norse Legends* (1979) and *Bjarkemaar* (1982).

**Marguerite of Navarre** (1492–1549). French aristocrat and intellectual. She was the daughter of Charles d'Orléans, Count of Angoulême, and the learned and independent LOUISE OF SAVOY; her brother became Francis I. She was educated by her mother in Hebrew, Latin, Italian, German and Spanish, and by special tutors in philosophy, history and theology. In 1508 she made a great impression at the court of Louis XII, but the following year married the Duke of Alençon and disappeared into provincial obscurity until Francis's succession to the throne. She then became his hostess, and in 1517 he gave her the Duchy of Berry, which included the powerful University of Bourges. She attracted leading scholars, developed new subjects, and became increasingly interested in reform in the Catholic Church.

During Francis's imprisonment in Spain in 1525 she took a dominant role, and negotiated his release and the subsequent Treaty of Cambrai. Also in 1525 Alençon died and in 1527 she married Henri d'Albret, King of Navarre. Her isolation from the French court is shown in her passionate letters to Francis, but she helped her husband initiate economic and legal reforms, and established a court at Nérac which became a refuge for religious reformers and persecuted intellectuals. She herself wrote religious verse such as *Le miroir de l'âme pécheresse* (1531), condemned by the orthodox theologians of the Sorbonne, and other verse collected in *Les marguerites* (1547). Her best-known work, the *Heptameron*, a collection of short stories after Boccaccio, was published after her death in 1558.

Marguerite was the centre of a remarkable group of gifted, reformist noblewomen, including Renée of France (1528–75) and Marguerite, Duchess of Savoy (1523–74). Her daughter JEANNE D'ALBRET became a Huguenot leader.

**Maria Antonia Walpurgis,** Electress of Saxony (1724–80). German princess and patron, composer, singer and writer. The daughter of the Elector Karl Albert of Bavaria and Archduchess Maria Amalia of Austria, she married Friedrich Christian (later Elector of Saxony) in 1747. She was instructed in music in Munich by Giovanni Ferrandini and Giovanni Porta, and in Dresden by Porpora and Hasse. Conscious of the decline of artistic activity at the Dresden court brought about by the Seven Years War, she committed herself to reviving it through involving herself as a patron, composer and performer. Hasse, Porpora and Naumann were among the composers to benefit from her support. She wrote two operas, both to her own texts, singing the leading roles at their first performance (*Il trionfo della fedeltà*, 1754; *Talestri, regina delle amazoni*, 1760). Her other works include arias and intermezzos; her name on some manuscripts indicates ownership rather than authorship.

She was also a painter and poet; her poetry was set to music by such composers as Hasse (for whom she also supplied the libretto of the oratorio *La conversione di Sant'Agostino* and several cantatas), Naumann and Ferrandini. She was a member of the Arcadian Academy in Rome from 1747, and some of her published works appear under the name 'ETPA' (Emmelinda Talea Pastorella Arcada).

C. von Weber: *Maria Antonia Walpurgis, Churfürstin zu Sachsen* (1857)

**Maria the Jewess** (1st century AD). Alexandrian alchemist. Maria, referred to sometimes as Mary or Miriam, lived at the time of Alexandria's highest renown for scientific research. Her work as an alchemist, aiming to transmute base metals into gold, drew on elements of Gnostic science as well as practical experimentation. The science was strongly connected with women, holding the goddess Isis as its founder, and Maria, according to current practice, wrote under the title of a prophetess as 'Miriam, sister of Moses'. Her theory was based on the premise that metals were living beings, male and female, and that the chemical process was one of sexual linking and reproduction. Her writings survive only in fragments, but it is for her practical contribution that she is best remembered. She designed apparatus which remained in use for centuries, such as the three-part still, the *kerotakis* process for the condensation and reflux of vapours (originally for sulphur, mercury and arsenic vapours to treat metal alloy), and the water-bath, or double boiler, to maintain substances at a constant temperature – which is still called a 'bain-marie'. These and other significant inventions gave her a lasting reputation as one of the founders of chemistry.

**Maria Theresa** (1717–80). Austrian empress; Archduchess of Austria and Queen of Bohemia. She was born in Vienna, the eldest of three daughters of the Holy Roman Emperor Charles VI and his wife Elizabeth. After the death of his son, Charles VI, who was the last Habsburg prince, passed a special act known as the Pragmatic Sanction which allowed the female line to succeed. In 1736 he married Theresa to Francis Stephen, son of the Duke of Lorraine, who became Duke of Tuscany. Their union was described as a marriage of love rather than convenience and they had 16 children, 10 of whom survived to adulthood including MARIE ANTOINETTE.

After Charles's unexpected death in 1740, the 23-year-old Maria Theresa, then expecting her fourth child, immediately assumed control. Her initial impetuosity and love of frivolity gave way to a stern, autocratic and rather puritanical style. She ensured that her husband was crowned Emperor in 1745 and instituted severe taxes and levies to pay for an army to defend her right to the throne, which was challenged by Frederick the Great of Prussia in the War of the Austrian Succession. To do so she limited the power of the nobles, enlarged the central administration, reformed the treasury, implemented sweeping changes in the civil service and the universities, and, despite her piety, brought the Church more strictly under state control.

In 1745 she ceded Silesia to Russia and in 1748 the war ended, but she was determined to recover her territory and in 1756, having cut off her alliance with England, she made treaties with France and Russia, initiating the Seven Years War. The whole campaign was disastrous and expensive, but she continued in her efforts to regain Silesia, instigating a new war the year before her death.

After Francis's death in 1765, Maria Theresa engaged in a new round of social reforms, less immediately geared to efficient fund-raising and administration: reforming the law and harsh penal policy, developing a poor law system and introducing compulsory primary education. Her policy of centralization also encouraged the architectural, social and cultural development of Vienna as a great European capital. Her relations with her many children were often strained, especially with her son Joseph, co-ruler since Francis's death; only under pressure from him did she agree to the partition of Poland with Russia and Prussia in 1772. For much of this later period she was ill, very fat and very weak, living in her own palace of Schönbrunn, a converted hunting lodge on the outskirts of the city, but she remained able and powerful until she died, a far-seeing ruler who had achieved a remarkable unification between the diverse areas of her Austro-Hungarian Empire.

R. Pick: *Empress Maria Theresa* (1966)

**Marie Antoinette** (1755–93). Queen of France. The eleventh daughter of the Holy Roman Emperor Francis I and MARIA THERESA, she was married at the age of 15 to Louis, the dauphin, as part of an Austro-French alliance, but her arrival in France was not happy, because of traditional dislike of Austria, and because of Louis' indifference. By 1774, when Louis became King, she had taken refuge in a small, dissolute clique led by Yolande de Polignac and her extravagance became notorious. Rumours of her love affairs came to a head in the 'Affair of the Diamond Necklace' (1785–6) in which she was unjustly accused of an affair with Cardinal de Rohan, in a complex plot arranged by Madame de la Motte. Her relations with members of the palace guard were also questioned, and the scandals increased the unpopularity of the monarchy.

The Queen became less frivolous after the birth of her son, but she had a poor understanding of economic reality (the famous remark 'let them eat cake' is probably apocryphal, but she had little sympathy for the hungry poor). She became increasingly influential in the Royal Councils, and in 1789 was instrumental in

Louis' decision not to implement the reforms, such as the abolition of feudalism and restriction of the royal prerogative, demanded by the National Guard. Her unpopularity was at its height when she was brought with the King to Paris from Versailles (October 1789). In 1791 she was seized at Varennes when the royal family attempted to escape. Having earlier negotiated with Mirabeau, who was now dead, she entered secret talks with Barnave, who persuaded Louis to accept the Assembly's new constitution. She weakened this step by trying to get Austria to intervene on behalf of the Bourbons. Her Austrian intrigues prompted the final storming of the Tuileries in 1792, during which she and Louis were captured and accused of treason. Louis was executed in January 1793; Marie Antoinette was placed in solitary confinement in the Conciergerie, was tried, as 'Widow Capet', before the Revolutionary Tribunal on 14 October and guillotined on 16 October. Their first son had died in 1789, their second son, now Louis XVII, died in prison in 1795.

P. Huisman: *Marie Antoinette* (trans., 1971)

**Marie de France** (c1140–1200). French poet. Little is known of the life of Marie de France although it is thought that she lived in England, probably at the court of Henry II. The most famous of her works are the *Lais* (which are thought to be written before 1180), short narrative poems inspired by the ancient lays of Breton harpists but treated in a very personal way: magical and fantastic elements are interwoven with both heroic and simple human deeds. *Le lai de Lanval* is often considered her masterpiece and throughout the collection her skill as a storyteller is evident. She made the narrative *lai* popular in France and its influence extended throughout medieval European literature. She also translated and adapted fables which were published under the title *Isopet* (c1180) – a collection of 103 moral fables with traces of satire written in verse. She also wrote *L'espurgatoire Seint Patriz* (c1190), a translation from a Celtic source about the adventures of a knight called Owen. Marie de France is often referred to as France's first woman poet.

During the same period there were many famous women troubadours, the greatest being Beatriz Contessa de Die, about whose life little is known. Others included a woman called Fibors, Almucs de Castlenau, and Maria de Ventadorn, while a celebrated travelling poet of the next century was Barbe de Verrue.

**Marie de l'Incarnation.** *See* ACARIE, BARBE.

**Marillac.** *See* DE MARILLAC.

**Marina** [Malintzin, Malinche] (c1501–50). Mexican Indian princess. In 1519 she was among a group of women given by the Tabascan Indians to Cortes's Spanish force. She became Cortes's mistress and her work as guide and interpreter are considered to have been of crucial importance in his conquest of Mexico, since she knew both Mayan, spoken along the coast, and Nahuatl, the language of the interior. She became a Christian convert, and some time after bearing Cortes's son Martin, she married another soldier, Juan de Jaramillo. Togther they visited Spain where Doña Marina was greatly honoured.

**Markham, Beryl** (1902–86). Kenyan aviator and race-horse trainer. Born in Melton Mowbray, Leicestershire, Beryl went to Kenya at the age of four with her father, Captain Clutterbuck. Her mother and brother remained in England and Beryl grew up on the farm created by her father, learning to speak Swahili, Nandi and Masai. She became apprenticed to her father, who trained and bred racehorses, but when the farm was lost in a financial crisis following a drought, the Captain left for Peru, leaving her one horse, Pegasus. At 18 she became the first woman in Africa to be granted a race-horse trainer's licence and the following year one of her horses won the Kenya St Leger.

A noted beauty, with many admirers, her first husband was the Scots International rugby player Jock Purves, but they were divorced after two years and in 1927 she married Mansfield Markham: their son was born in 1929. During their marriage the Duke of Gloucester, visiting Kenya with the Prince of Wales, became infatuated with her: Markham threatened to sue and was bought off with substantial damages. They soon separated, but were not divorced until 1942.

In the 1920s Beryl learnt to fly and in 1931 became a pilot, ferrying mail and passengers all over East Africa and pioneering the scouting of game from the air. In 1936, in appalling weather, she became the first woman to fly the Atlantic from east to west (apparently upside down for part of the way, not realizing this until it was revealed by a bolt of lightning). After crash-landing in Nova Scotia she was given a ticker-tape welcome in New York. She then went to California where she married the writer Raoul Schumacher, who helped her write *West with the Night* (1942) and also later wrote short stories under her name. *West with the Night*, which describes her bush-flying and love of Africa as well as the Atlantic crossing, has been compared to KAREN BLIXEN's *Out of Africa* and was thought by Ernest Hemingway to be 'bloody wonderful'.

Beryl was divorced again in 1947 and in the early 1950s returned to Africa, training horses in Kenya, Rhodesia and South Africa. She won the top trainer's award five times and had six Kenyan Derby winners. At the end of her life she lived in a bungalow on the edge of Nairobi race course, a legend in Kenyan society.

**Markiewicz** [née Gore-Booth], **Constance** [Countess Markiewicz] (1868–1927). Irish nationalist politician. Born in London, the sister of the trade unionist Eva Gore-Booth, she was educated by governesses on the family estate at Lissadell, County Sligo, until her presentation at court in 1887, when she became a well-known society beauty. In 1893 she went to study art at the Slade School in London; she then went to Paris where in 1899 she married Count Casimir Markiewicz, a Polish painter. After spending some time in Paris and the Ukraine, they returned to Dublin in 1903. Constance became involved with the cultural and national renaissance in Ireland, joining the Gaelic League and the Abbey Theatre, helping to found the United Arts Club (1907), joining Sinn Fein and MAUD GONNE's Daughters of Ireland (1908), and founding the youth movement Na Fianna (1909).

Known as 'Madame' and the 'Red Countess', she was an active participant in the 1913 Dublin Strike and the 1916 Easter Rising. She led 120 Republican soldiers, garrisoning the Royal College of Surgeons for three days. On surrender, dressed in the green uniform of the Irish Citizens' Army, she kissed her revolver before handing it' over. Condemned to death, but subsequently committed to life imprisonment, she was held in Aylesbury prison until the 1917 amnesty. In the 1918 General Election, she was elected MP for a Dublin constituency, while still in prison, the first woman MP in the UK, but with other Republican MPs, as a Nationalist protest, she refused to go to Westminster. In 1919 she was Minister for Labour in the outlawed Irish parliament, Dail Eireann. After the 1921 Treaty she continued to fight, sharing in the storming of the Four Courts (1922), and raising funds for the Republic, although elected MP for Dublin South (1923). She was repeatedly imprisoned and went on hunger-strike. In 1926 she joined De Valera's Fianna Fail party and was re-elected in 1927, but died in Dublin the same year.

S. O'Faolain: *Constance Markiewicz* (1954)
D. Norman: *Terrible Beauty* (1987)

**Markova,** Dame **Alicia** [Marks, Lilian Alicia] (1910–). English ballerina. She was born in London, and she made her first professional appearance in *Dick Whittington* at the Kennington Theatre in 1920. She was trained by Princess Astafieva and appeared with the Legat Ballet Group in 1923, and was engaged by Dyagilev the following year, aged 14; she also studied under Cecchetti. She danced the title role in Balanchin's *Le rossignol* in 1926. After Dyagilev's death in 1929 she danced with the Blum company at Drury Lane, London, then at the Metropolitan Opera House, New York. A delicate classical dancer she was the first *prima ballerina* of the Vic-Wells Ballet (1933–5), and was partnered by Dolin; she also danced with the Rambert Ballet Club. From 1935 to 1938 she toured with her own Markova–Dolin Ballet, the first group to undertake large provincial tours.

In 1938 Markova joined the Ballet Russe de Monte Carlo, creating roles for Massine in *Seventh Symphony* and *Rouge et Noir*. She danced with the American Ballet Theatre in New York from 1941 to 1944, at the height of her career, creating leads in Massin's *Aleko* and Tudor's *Romeo and Juliet*. During the 1940s she appeared as a guest artist all over the world, and toured from Mexico to the Philippines, returning to give guest performances with Dolin at Sadler's Wells. In 1950 she was a co-founder of the London Festival Ballet and became Vice-President of the Royal Academy of Dancing in 1958.

Markova retired from dancing in 1963 and began a new career as a producer and teacher. From 1963 to 1969 she was Director of the New York Metropolitan Opera Ballet and in 1970 became Professor of Ballet at the University of Cincinatti Conservatory of Music. She continued to give master-classes in London, Paris and elsewhere and held a 'Masterclass' series on BBC Television in 1980. She was made CBE in 1958 and DBE in 1963, and was appointed Governor of the Royal Ballet in 1973 and President of the London Festival Ballet in 1986.

A. Markova: *Giselle and I* (1960)
——— : *Markova Remembers* (1986)

**Marlborough,** Duchess of **(Churchill** [née Jennings], **Sarah)** (1660–1744). English aristocrat. Born near St Albans, she joined the household of Mary of Modena, then Duchess of York, as attendant to her step-daughter Princess ANNE, and the two girls became close friends. In 1676 she met John Churchill and they married secretly in 1678, against his parents' wishes. A distinguished General, he was created Baron Churchill in 1682 by James II, and the following year Sarah became Lady of the Bedchamber to her friend Anne and a close confidante. Churchill transferred his allegiance to William of Orange and was made Lord Marlborough the following year, but then began intriguing with the exiled James and lost royal favour from 1692 to 1698. Sarah managed to maintain her close relationship with Anne and in 1702, on Anne's accession, she was given important positions: Groom of the Stole, Mistress of the Robes and Keeper of the Privy Purse.

Sarah promoted her husband's career as Commander-in-Chief during the War of the Spanish Succession, but her support of the Whig party alienated Anne, and. After 1705 her influence on the queen was taken over by Abigail Masham, a Tory sympathizer. In 1710 Anne dismissed the Whig Ministry, and the Churchills lost their positions the following year and went abroad in 1713, returning to live quietly in retirement at Blenheim until John's death in 1722.

Sarah spent the last 20 years of her life completing Blenheim Palace and carrying on an endless series of quarrels and lawsuits with the architect Sir John Vanbrugh and with her own family, and in arranging her own and Marlborough's papers for publication.

D. Green: *Sarah, Duchess of Marlborough* (1967)

**Marsden, Kate** (1859–1931). British traveller and nurse. Born in Edmonton, Kate was the daughter of a solicitor and the youngest of eight children, many of whom died of tuberculosis. She trained as a nurse at Snell's Park and Tottenham Hospital, moving to the new Tottenham community which put its evangelical mission first and nursing second. This satisfied both aspects of Kate's desire to serve, and she was glad to have a chance to travel to Bulgaria in 1877 to tend Russian soldiers wounded in the Russo-Turkish war. Here she first came across lepers. Back in England she worked in Westminster Hospital, then at a convalescent home; visiting New Zealand with her mother in 1884, she stayed to become Lady Superintendent of Wellington Hospital.

After what was probably a mental illness, she returned to England and in 1890 was invited to St Petersburg to receive a medal from the Russian Red Cross. With official introductions to help her she began to inquire about lepers and gained permission to enter the northern wilds with a Russian-speaking friend, Anna Field. After a three-month adventure by sledge, visiting prisons on the way and dispensing tea, sugar and the Gospel, she rode the last 1000 miles with Cossacks to Viluisk, encountering bears, mosquitoes, subterranean fires and bats and spending nights in the open. At Viluisk she visited leper settlements where some wore hopeless expressions and could hardly crawl for food. She returned to Yakutsk, riding in stages of 70 miles a day and was so exhausted she had to be nursed during the last part of the journey to Moscow.

She reported her journey to the Venereological and Dermatological Society in Moscow, then raised 32,000 roubles by writing and lectures which opened a hospital at Viluisk in 1897. This throve until the 1950s when it had accomplished its purpose and had no lepers to serve. *On Sledge and Horseback to Outcast Siberian Lepers* (1893) publicized her venture, but she was criticized as a traveller and administrator, so in 1921 published *My Mission to Siberia: A Vindication*. The Royal Geographical Society included her in its list of 'well qualified ladies' elected in 1892, and she was made a Free Life Fellow in 1916. For her last 30 years she was an invalid in England.

H. Johnson: *The Life of Kate Marsden* (2nd edn, 1895)

**Martin, Emma** (1812–51). British socialist, feminist and free-thinker. Born in Bristol, Emma Bullock rejected the conventional religion of her mother and step-father and joined the Particular Baptists. She set up her own Ladies Seminary at 18, and in 1831 married Isaac Martin, a brick and tile maker, continuing to run the school with her sister; the Martins had three daughters. In 1835 Emma began editing the *Bristol Literary Magazine* and three years later gave her first public lecture, on education.

During 1839 she continued as a lecturer (one of her subjects being 'Woman') and became gradually drawn into Owenite circles. She moved to London, where her daughters joined her and she became one of the leading speakers in the Owenite Halls of Science and Social Institutions. Her feminist talks included demands for education and political rights, and attacks on the contemporary marriage system as a product of 'market relationships'. She also attacked religion, engaging in fierce controversy, and gave lecture tours from 1840 to 1845, drawing large crowds in the Midlands, the North and Scotland, as well as in London: several of her lectures and essays were published. Exhausted, she decided to settle in London and qualified as a midwife at the Royal Adelaide Hospital, practising in Long Acre, near Covent Garden, and publishing a treatise on *The Most Common Female Complaints* in 1848. In the 1840s she also published translations, of the maxims of Guiccardini, and of Boccaccio, and wrote a novel, *The Exiles of Piedmont*. In her later years she lived with an engineer, John Hopkins, and their daughter Manon Roland (named after MANON ROLAND) was born in 1847. Equal in prominence to FRANCES WRIGHT as a socialist feminist, she died of tuberculosis at the age of 39.

**Martindale, Hilda** (1875–1952). English civil servant. She was born in London. Her father was a city merchant and her mother a Liberal suffragette. She was educated in Germany, at Brighton High School, and at Royal Holloway College and Bedford College, London, where she studied hygiene and sanitary sciences. In 1900 she went on a world tour with her mother and sister, studying state schemes for children, and in 1901 entered the Home Office as a factory inspector under Adelaide Anderson. She began by prosecuting on behalf of London dressmakers. In 1903 she supported GERTRUDE TUCKWELL's campaign against lead poisoning, and in 1905 conducted an exhaustive enquiry into Irish labour conditions.

She gradually rose to become Deputy Chief Inspector of Factories in 1925, and in 1932 moved to the Treasury as Director of Women's Establishments, despite her objection that separate treatment vitiated the principle of equal opportunity. Reserved but persistent, she championed women's interests on many committees. She also advised government delegations at ILO conferences, and was a member of the Industrial Health Research Board (1933–7). After she retired in 1937 she wrote her memoirs, *Women Servants of the State, 1870–1938* (1938) and *Some Victorian Portraits* (1948). She was made CBE in 1935.

H. Martindale: *From one Generation to Another* (1944)

**Martineau, Harriet** (1802–76). English novelist, political economist, and children's writer. She was born into a Huguenot family which had settled in Norwich in the 17th century; her father was a textile manufacturer. She had a strict puritanical upbringing, and her good education was marred by her nervousness and increasing deafness. In 1819, after a visit to a schoolmistress aunt in Bristol, she became intensely religious and her first works were *Devotional Exercises for the use of Young Persons* (1823) and *Addresses for the Use of Families* (1826). In 1826 her father went bankrupt and within a short space of time her father, brother and fiancé all died; from then on she was determined to become independent as a professional writer.

In 1831, after winning prizes for essays in the *Unitarian Journal*, she visited her brother in Dublin. On her return, influenced by the work of Jane Marcet, she decided to write a series of stories illustrating principles of political economy, which was then a new subject. She began publishing her *Illustrations of Political Economy* (1832–4) in which ideas taken from Mill, James and Ricardo formed the basis of short tales. The series was an instant success. Similar series on reform issues were *Poor Laws and Paupers Illustrated* (1833–4) and *Forest and Game-Law Tales* (1845–6). Harriet now established herself as a London journalist. She visited the USA (1834–6) where she attended abolitionist meetings, publishing *Society in America* in 1837.

At the end of the decade she fell ill, and from 1839 to 1844 was an invalid at Tynemouth. During these years she wrote her children's stories, collected in *The Playfellow* (1841), and two novels, *Deerbrook* (1839) and *The Hour and the Man* (1841), about Toussaint l'Ouverture. Her cure coincided with hypnotic treatment and she became a devotee of mesmerism and wrote *Life in the Sickroom* (1844) and *Letters on Mesmerism* (1845). On her recovery she moved to Clappergate, Westmorland [now part of Cumbria], where she became a friend of the Wordsworth family. In 1846–7 she visited Egypt and Palestine [now Israel]. She was a contributor to the *London Daily News* from 1852 to 1866, her radical articles covering diverse subjects, from agricultural economics to the evils of licensed prostitution. She also supported the Married Women's Property Bill in 1857 and wrote a critical article on women's employment, 'Female Industry', in 1859. In 1849 she had become Secretary of Bedford College for Women, London. In 1851 she described her rationalist philosophy in *Letters on the Laws of Man's Nature and Developement* (with H.G. Atkinson) and in 1853 published a translation, *The Philosophy of Comte*.

In 1854 she was again told she was incurably ill, and she was prompted to write her brilliant and courageous *Autobiography*, which was not published until her death in 1877. She continued to write and, although her output diminished, remained a frank, outspoken commentator on her society.

F. Miller: *Martineau* (1972)

**Martínez de Perón, Isabelita.** *See* PERÓN. ISABELITA.

**Marx-Aveling, Eleanor** (1856–1908). English socialist. The youngest daughter of Karl and Jenny Marx (*see* VON WESTPHALEN, JENNY), she was renowned as a child for her generous, impetuous personality. She was devoted to her father; she helped him with his work and accompanied him on visits to Germany. In 1870 she also visited Paris during the Commune to help her sister Laura, who had married the French socialist Paul Lafargue. In 1872 she became passionately attached to Lissagaray, a Communard journalist 14 years her senior, arousing her parents' fierce disapproval. She then took a teaching post in Brighton. Eventually they allowed her engagement to Lissagaray which lasted until 1882; she translated his *Histoire de la Commune de Paris* in 1876. She became very frustrated at her lack of a career and in 1881, having rejected a proposal of marriage from the Russian populist Leo Hartmann, she succumbed to a severe nervous depression, which she tried to overcome by attempting a career in the theatre; she was a talented actress with the New Shakespeare Society, a friend of Shaw, Dolly Maitland and other theatrical people, and later a translator of Ibsen.

In the summer of 1882 she met Edward Aveling, a socialist and secularist, and a long-standing associate of ANNIE BESANT and an acquaintance of friends of Eleanor's such as OLIVE SCHREINER and Havelock Ellis. After Marx's death in 1883, Eleanor and Aveling became lovers and from 1884 to her death she lived with him openly. During these last 15 years she worked constantly for different socialist sects, often changing her allegiance at the behest of her old friend Friedrich Engels, or because of Aveling's unreliability with funds and the subsequent bitter disputes. They were at first committed members of Hyndman's Socialist Democratic Federation (SDF), then briefly formed their own Socialist League, where Eleanor edited the *International Record*. In 1886 and 1887 they toured the USA, speaking out against the treatment of the 'Haymarket martyrs' in Chicago. Eleanor also attacked Bebel in her influential article 'The Woman Question' in the *Westminster Review* of 1885, which called for social and physical liberation rather than a mere vote. She translated, wrote articles and reviews, taught literature, lectured, and toured the country, tirelessly speaking at working men's clubs and union meetings. In the 1890s she rejoined the SDF and campaigned for protective legislation and the eight-hour day. Her greatest affiliations were to the unions such as the gasmakers' and the dockers', and to the Second Socialist International. Her private life was unhappy: she worried about her childlessness and about Aveling's affair with a younger woman, and was devastated by Engels's death-bed revelation that her dear friend Freddy Demuth was not his illegitimate son, but her father's. In despair, she asked Aveling to obtain prussic acid for her and she committed suicide at the age of 42.

Y. Kapp: *Eleanor Marx* (1974, 1977) [2 vols]

**Mary** [The Blessed Virgin]. The mother of Jesus Christ. Nothing is known of Mary beyond the words of the New Testament, so her parentage and place of birth are unknown. Both her divine maternity and her virginity are clearly stated in the gospels in the accounts of the events leading up to the birth of Christ. During Christ's public ministry Mary is heard of only occasionally, most noticeably at the wedding-feast in Cana; but at the time of the Crucifixion she is standing by the cross. After Christ's ascension she is with the Apostles at the time of Pentecost.

From these few biblical mentions have arisen a series of theological statements on the one hand and the development of devotion to Mary on the other. It is Roman Catholic belief that Mary was without sin from the moment of her own conception (her 'immaculate conception') and that at the end of her earthly life she was taken body and soul into heaven (her 'assumption').

M. Warner: *Alone of all her sex: the Myth and Cult of the Virgin Mary* (1979)

**Mary,** Queen of Scots (1542–87). Scottish queen, claimant to the English throne. Born at Linlithgow, West Lothian, she was the only child of James V of Scotland and the French Mary of Guise. She became Queen when she was six days old, and her mother betrothed her to the French dauphin (later Francis II) and sent her to France at the age of five to be brought up at the court of Henry II and CATHERINE DE MEDICI. Her childhood was happy and she received an excellent education, learning Latin, Italian and Spanish, and a little Greek, and speaking French as a first language. She married Francis under a treaty whereby a male heir would unite the two thrones. In the same year ELIZABETH I's succession to the English throne was challenged by Mary's Catholic supporters. Francis was crowned in 1559 but died in 1560, and the young widow returned to Scotland in 1561.

Diplomatic and charming, she took pro-English counsellors, her illegitimate brother James and William Maitland, and overcame hostility to her Catholicism by her policy of tolerance, accepting the Presbyterian Church but continuing to attend Mass herself. Her marriage in 1565 to Henry Stewart, Earl of Darnley, an equal claimant to the English throne, caused a political crisis, and his jealous murder in her presence of her confidential secretary Rizzio made life intolerable. After the birth of their son James she became involved with James Hepburn, Earl of Bothwell, and when Darnley was found murdered in January 1565, he was suspected but acquitted. Three months later Bothwell abducted Mary, rapidly divorced his wife and married her. The Scots rebelled and by June Bothwell was exiled (he died in prison in 1587), and Mary was banished to Lochleven Castle and deposed in favour of James. Her supporters were defeated the following year and she fled across the border.

In England she found refuge, but Elizabeth's fears of Mary's rivalry to the throne led her to keep Mary in virtual captivity for the next 19 years, allegedly in connection with Darnley's murder. Bored and ill, Mary worked ceaselessly for her release, by pleas to her cousin, then by encouraging a series of conspiracies. Many plots, involving Spanish help, were discovered and Parliament demanded her execution. Elizabeth refused until 1587, when the revelation of Babington's plot (and the promise that the Scots would not take revenge) persuaded her to sign. Mary was executed at Fotheringay at the age of 44. She

has remained a potent and mysterious figure in history and literature.

A. Fraser: *Mary Queen of Scots* (1969)

**Mary I** [Mary Tudor; Bloody Mary] (1516–58). Queen of England. The daughter of Henry VIII and CATHERINE OF ARAGON, she was born at Greenwich Palace, and was given a superb education by her mother and by scholars such as Linacre and Vives, but even as a child she was a political pawn, with bids for her hand coming from France, Austria and other sources. Eventually she was betrothed to Charles V, the Holy Roman Emperor, but the match did not take place. In 1525 she was made Princess of Wales, but two years later Henry began his divorce negotiations and Mary, remaining loyal to Catherine and to Catholicism, began a life of misery. In 1534, when Henry broke with Rome, she was separated from her mother, whom she never saw again, and she was declared illegitimate in 1536 and made to act as Lady-in-waiting to the baby ELIZABETH I. Charles V finally persuaded her to acknowledge her illegitimacy and renounce the Church, and she was reconciled with her father and eventually (1544) granted succession rights after Edward.

During Edward VI's reign (1547–53) Mary challenged possible execution by continuing to celebrate the banned Latin Mass, and at his death was forced to flee to the country during the brief seizure of power by supporters of Lady JANE GREY. Finally, aged 37, she ascended the throne, the first woman to rule in her own right in England. Rashly she determined on two unpopular courses, a marriage with the 26-year-old Philip of Spain (1554) and the restoration of Papal supremacy. This provoked Sir Thomas Wyatt's uprising which Mary suppressed successfully, and she went on to fulfil her wishes regarding her marriage and her faith. She also re-introduced the laws against heresy in 1555, unleashing three years of persecution in which countless rebels were hanged and over 300 heretics burned at the stake, including the famous clerics Ridley, Rogers, Latimer and Cranmer. She was personally blamed for the cruelty, formerly unknown in England but common to Catholic Europe, and gained the title Bloody Mary. Finally, Philip II, who had left Mary in 1555, frustrated by Parliament's refusal to crown him king, drew England into the war between Spain and France, which lost Mary Calais and won her the increased hatred of her people. She herself was lonely, ill and childless, and made wretched by Philip's absence and a series of false pregnancies. She died in London at the age of 42.

H.F.M. Prescott: *Mary Tudor* (2/1953)

**Mary II** (1662–94). Queen of England. Mary was the daughter of the Catholic Duke of York (later James II) but she was educated as a Protestant with her sister ANNE. In 1677 she married her cousin, the Dutch Protestant leader, William of Orange. They lived in Holland until 1668, when Mary supported her husband in his invasion of England and the deposition of James II, events which later became known as 'The Glorious Revolution'. After her father fled, Mary came to London, and although she was the successor to the throne she insisted that she and William be crowned as joint sovereigns. She proved an efficient ruler during William's absence on campaigns in Europe and Ireland but withdrew from active involvement in government when he returned. She was a modest, intelligent woman, interested in science, geography and theology. She enjoyed great popularity in both Holland and England. Her personal life seems to have been unhappy because of her childlessness, her husband's infidelities, and her quarrels with her father and her sister Anne. She died of smallpox aged only 32.

E. Hamilton: *Mary II* (1972)

**Masham** [née Cudworth], **Damaris** [Lady Masham] (1658–1708). English scholar. The daughter of a Cambridge scholar, Rolf Cudworth, she married Sir Francis Masham of Oates, in Essex, and was a close friend of John Locke, who lived with them from 1691 to his death in 1704. She was a firm believer in the education of women (though chiefly so that they in turn could educate their children) and she resented the contemporary view that scholarship would create 'a danger of not finding husbands'. These unfashionable thoughts and her general philosophy are expressed in *Occasional Thoughts in Reference to a Christian Life* (1694) and *Discourse concerning the Love of God* (1696).

**Masina, Giulietta** [Giulia] **(Anna)** (1920–). Italian actress. Born near Bologna, the daughter of a schoolteacher, she began acting while a student in Rome and joined the Ateneo Theatre Group there. She worked for radio as the wife in a series, *Cico e Pallina*, written by Federico Fellini, whom she later married (1943). For three years she did not act, then returned to the stage, and appeared briefly in Rossellini's *Paisà/Paisan* (1946). But her real debut was as the confidante Marcella in Lattuada's *Senza Pietà/Without Pity* (1948), for which she won the Italian Critics' award. She appeared in several films, often in the role of understanding mistress or friend, but her brief international success was due to Fellini's *La Strada* (1954) and *Le Notti di Cabiria/The Nights of Cabiria* (1956), in which her plaintive, clowning wistfulness was exploited to the full. Since then her career has declined, with occasional notable films such as *Giulietta degli Spiriti/Juliet of the Spirits* (1965), and *Frau Holle* (1985).

**Mašiotene** [née Brazauskaité], **Ona** (1883–1949). Lithuanian feminist. Born in Slavenae, in the county of Utena, she studied science at the Advanced School of Moscow, where she became interested in Western European feminist movements. Returning to Vilnius, in 1905 she was a founder of the Lietuvos Moterŭ Susivienijimas (Alliance of Lithuanian Women) which she represented at the Russian National Women's Congress. She was active in local and national women's organizations and from 1911 to 1914 taught in a high school in Vilnius. During World War I she moved to Moscow and in 1917 became involved in the ˇnationalist movements. She organized the Lithuanian Women's Freedom Association, on whose behalf she attended the conference in Petrograd which pressed for Lithuanian independence. In 1918 she ran a girls' school in Vilnius and organized adult evening classes.

After the war Mašiotene founded and became President of the Council of Lithuanian Women (1929). She published a history of the political and national role of women, *Moteru politnis ir valstybiniai tautiskas darbas* (1907–37).

**Massevitch, Alla Genrikhovna** (1918–). Russian astronomer. One of the Soviet Union's most distinguished astronomers, Alla Massevitch was born in Tbilisi and educated at the Industrial Institute of Moscow University. She married in 1942 and had a daughter, and in 1946 joined the department of Astrophysics at Moscow University, becoming a Professor in 1948 and specializing in the internal structure of stars and stellar evolution. She became Vice-President of the Astronomical Council of the Soviet Academy of Sciences in 1952 and was closely involved with the space research programmes of the next two decades, and as the official in charge of the tracking of space vehicles, through visual, photographic and laser ranging techniques, she headed a series of major committees. She has been President of Section Satellite Tracking for Geodesy since 1978 and became Deputy General Secretary of UNISPACE in 1982. During the 1960s she was also involved in the Institute for Soviet-American relations, and is a member of the Royal Astronomical Society and the International Academy of Astronautics. She was awarded the USSR State Prize in 1975.

**Mata Hari** [pseud. of Margaretha Geertruida Macleod [née Zelle]] (1876–1917). Dutch dancer, courtesan and spy. She was the daughter of a wealthy hatter, and originally trained to be a teacher in Leiden. In 1895 she married Captain Rudolph Macleod, a Dutchman of Scots descent in the Dutch Colonial army. After living in the East Indies from 1887 to 1902, and in Europe, they separated. She became a professional dancer in Paris, known first as 'Lady McLeod', and then as 'Mata Hari', a Malay name meaning the sun. Her quasi-oriental dances, exotic scanty costumes and statuesque beauty gained her instant fame and many lovers. In 1907 she allegedly joined the German secret service, and during World War I travelled between The Hague and Paris, passing on secret information gained from high-ranking allied officers among her admirers. She herself claimed to be a double agent, simultaneously working as a spy for the French in Belgium. In February 1917 she

was arrested in Paris, tried for espionage and executed by firing squad five months later. Her guilt has always been a matter of controversy.

S.Wagenaar: *The Murder of Mata Hari* (1964)

**Matilda,** Countess of Tuscany ['La Gran Contessa'] (1046–1115). Italian noblewoman. Born in Lucca, she was the daughter of Boniface, Lord of Canossa, who was assassinated in 1052. After the death of her older brother and sister, Matilda became heir to the richest estate in Italy. In 1054 her mother, Beatrice of Bar, married Godfrey of Lorraine. In 1055 mother and daughter were taken as hostages for a year by Henry III, the Holy Roman Emperor. Beatrice supervised Matilda's education; she eventually spoke French, Italian and German, corresponded fluently in Latin, built up a large library and supervised an edition of Justinian's *Pandects*.

In 1069 she married her step-brother, Godfrey the Hunchback. After the death of their baby she left Lorraine and returned to Italy, ruling jointly with her mother until the latter's death in 1076. She controlled Tuscany, parts of Umbria and Emilia-Romagna, and built up the economic strength of the powerful Florentine guilds. A supporter of the papacy against the Empire, she received Henry IV when he came to visit Pope Gregory VII as a barefoot penitent in 1077 at Canossa, but later engaged in warfare with him and financed the papal troops.

In 1089 she married the 17-year-old Wolf V of Bavaria but they soon separated and their quarrels became intertwined with her feud against Henry IV. In 1093 she supported Conrad, son of Henry IV, in his bid to seize the Italian throne from his father, but eventually made peace with the new Emperor, Henry V (1010–11). She then willed her territories to him, but as she had already given them to the Holy See in 1102 this action led to confusion. After her death territorial struggles were renewed between Emperor and Pope. Called 'La Gran Contessa', Matilda was one of the most powerful and revered rulers of mediaeval Italy.

**Matto de Turner, Clorinda** (1854–1909). Peruvian writer and feminist. Clorinda Matto de Turner is famous for her championship of Peruvian women, and also for her work for the Andean Indians, among whom she lived in the village of Tinto for ten years after her marriage. She began writing as a journalist, founding a periodical for women, *El Recreo*, in 1876, and then, under the pseudonym 'Carlote Dimant', editing *Los Bolsa*. In 1884 she wrote a guide to reading for women, *Elementos de Literatura. Para el uso de bello sexo*. She became known for her short stories and also for her impassioned speeches; in 1886 she joined the Circulo Literario of Lima, and the following year continued her crusade on behalf of the Indians, founding the weekly *El Peru Illustrado*. Her most famous novels are on this theme, notably *Aves sin Nido ( 1889, 'Birds without a nest')*, which has been compared to *Uncle Tom's Cabin*; *Indole* (1891) and *Herencia* (1895). As a feminist, she retained a belief in the supreme role of motherhood but she also advocated education for women and full participation in social affairs. Towards the end of her life her views led to excommunication and public outcry and she was forced to flee to Argentina, where she made a series of powerful speeches, and then to Europe. She was one of a group of distinguished women writers including Mercedes Cabello de Carbarera and others, who presented a radical, controversial picture of Peruvian society in their day.

**Matute, (Ausejo) Ana Maria** (1926–). Spanish novelist. Born in Barcelona, she suffered severe ill-health as a child and had an unhappy education in a French-run college. In 1943 she wrote *Pequeño teatro* (published 1954), then *Los Abel* (1948). In the late 1950s her novel of the Civil War, *Los hijos muertos* (1958), won an award, and brought her national acclaim, although her sympathies are clearly with the poor and destitute rather than with the successful party. During the 1960s her reputation was confirmed by her trilogy, *Los mercaderes,* which describes the psychological crises of a young girl from the beginning of the Civil War to the 1960s; the work was completed in 1969. She continued to publish during the 1970s, her best known work being *Olvidado Rey Gudu* (1974). She has also written short stories and some fine children's fiction. She has spent several periods as a visiting writer at American universities and is the winner of many literary prizes.

M.E.W. Jones: *The Literary World of Ana Maria Matute* (1970)

**Maury, Antonia (Caetana de Paiva Pereira)** (1866–1952). American astronomer. Antonia Maury was a niece of Henry Draper, and a grandaughter of John William Draper, a pioneer in the application of photography to astronomy. Her father was a minister, a naturalist, and the editor of a geographical magazine; her sister Carlotta became a palaeontologist, and Antonia was also an ornithologist.

After graduating from Vassar College, Antonia became an assistant at Harvard College Observatory, and carried out her most creative research in the next eight years. Edward Pickering had just discovered that the spectral lines of the star Mizar were double on one photographic plate but single on others, and Antonia determined its period (104 days). In 1889 she discovered the second such spectroscopic binary, Beta Aurigae, with a period of about four days.

When WILLIAMINA FLEMING'S *Draper Catalogue of Stellar Spectra* was published in 1890, Antonia undertook more elaborate study of the brighter stars and devised detailed classification for them. Although Hertzsprung used and admired her system, the simpler Draper classification as extended by ANNIE JUMP CANNON continued to be generally accepted.

Antonia was temperamentally unsuited to continuous observatory routine and although she was sometimes a research associate and sometimes undertook teaching she chose not to stay at Harvard fulltime. After retiring in 1935, she served for several years as Curator of the Draper Park Museum at Hastings-on-Hudson, New York.

**Mavrogenous, Manto** (*d* 1848). Greek freedom fighter. She belonged to an old and distinguished family. When the Greek revolution against the Turks broke out in 1821, Manto went to Greece from Trieste, settling on the island of Mykonos. She bought two ships and had them specially equipped to chase the pirates away from the Greek islands. She organized a body of guerilla fighters which she maintained at her own expense and led it in many successful campaigns against the Turks in the Peloponnese. She spent all her personal fortune in contributing to the maintenance of the small official Greek army and providing ammunition for its expeditions. She was given the title of Lieutenant-General in recognition of her services. Her appeals and personal letters to women in England and France for moral and financial support in the Greek struggle for independence stirred up great sympathy for the Greek people.

After Greece gained independence, political intrigues forced Manto to withdraw from active life and to live in solitude on a small pension granted to the war-widows by the State. She died poor and completely forgotten. But the personality and physical beauty of this Greek heroine survive in many portraits painted by contemporary artists and in poems and legends created while she was alive.

**Mavrokordatou, Alexandra** (1605–84). Greek intellectual. An educated Greek from Constantinople, she was the first to introduce the literary salon in Greece, an idea later taken up by other women and artists.

After two unhappy and adventurous marriages she focused her interests on studying the Classics, history, literature and philosophy, turning her house into a meeting place for both Greek and foreign literati, diplomats and artists. Many talented artists and famous politicians emerged from her salon; her personality acted as a catalyst in the creating of new ideas about education, culture and languages. She died in prison, where she had been held because her son, a diplomat in the Turkish government, was suspected by the Turks of betraying their interests in the Vienna siege of 1683.

**Mayreder, Rosa** (1858–1938). Austrian feminist, writer, artist and pacifist. Rosa first entered public life by joining the radical wing of the Austrian women's movement in 1893, making her mark by outspoken attacks on compulsory health inspections for prostitutes, which she considered as supporting the double standards of patriarchal morality. After formally leaving the organized women's movement in 1903, she continued to campaign on feminist issues and was a leading member of the small Austrian feminist pacifist movement during and after World War I.

Her main achievement, which earned her international recognition, is her contribution to feminist theory in the essays in *Zur Kritik der Weiblichkeit* (1905; trans as *A Survey of the Woman Problem*, 1913) and *Geschlecht und Kultur* (1923). In these she stresses the importance of acknowledging individual variation independent of sex and critically assesses leading intellectual figures such as Freud and Weininger. Her theoretical work extended to pacifist writings on women and war, sociology and a Christian-evolutionist theodicy, writings which display a fascinating feminist reception of thinkers such as Kant, Darwin, Goethe, Schopenhauer and Nietzsche.

Mayreder also wrote two novels, a drama, a collection of novellas, sketches and poetry, while as an artist she exhibited in Vienna and in the World Exhibition in Chicago (1893), and was co-founder of an art school for women in Vienna in 1897. From 1900, Mayreder was a significant intellectual figure in Vienna, where she spent all her life, a close friend of Rudolph Steiner and the composer Hugo Wolf, writing the libretto for the latter's only opera. She married the architect and city planner, Karl Mayreder; they had no children, and the marriage was strained by Karl's mental illness from 1912 until his death in 1935. The recent publication of Mayreder's work and of her extensive diaries has aroused great interest in this feminist thinker.

H. Anderson (ed.): *Rosa Mayreder: Tagebücher 1873–1937* (1988)

**Maywood, Augusta** (1825–76). American ballerina. She made a successful debut in Philadelphia at the age of 12, went to study at the Paris Opéra and was engaged there in 1838. Her first performances drew critical acclaim; Gautier described her as having 'sinews of steel, legs of a jaguar, and an agility approaching that of circus clowns'. In 1840 she eloped with and married her partner Mabille, left the Opéra and danced with her husband in Marseilles, Lyons and Lisbon. She left her husband in 1841 and led a stormy personal life, developing an independent career, dancing in Vienna and Italy. In Italy she was acclaimed as *prima ballerina e prima mima assoluta*, and she made a fortune before retiring to a villa at Como. A racy, vivid character, she was the first American dancer to win international fame.

**Mbogo, Jael** [Mama Jael] (1939–). Kenyan social worker and politician. Born in the Rift Valley Province of Kenya into a working-class family, she went to school in Nyanza Province and then undertook a correspondence course and qualified as a stenographer. She was the first woman shorthand typist to join the Nairobi City Council, in the late 1950s. She went to the USA to study economics and on her return to Africa in 1963 she joined her husband and six children in Tanzania. She worked closely with Umoja wa Wanawake wa Tanzania, the women's wing of the party. The Mbogos returned to Nairobi in 1965 where Jael joined the Maendeleo wa Wanawake, the women's social and cultural organization. She has since become the Secretary General of Freedom from Hunger, an offshoot of the Food and Agricultural Organisation (FAO) of the UN. She ran for the Bahati constituency seat in the 1969 parliamentary elections and was very narrowly defeated. Many poor people and women fondly refer to her as 'Mama Jael'.

**Mead, Margaret** (1901–78). American anthropologist. Born in Philadelphia, the eldest of five children, she spent a happy childhood in Pennsylvania. Her father was a professor of finance at Wharton School, University of Pennsylvania; her mother, a teacher and sociologist, was a feminist and suffragist and Margaret was chiefly educated at home by her grandmother, also a qualified teacher. She credited them all with great influence both on her values and on her ability to memorize detail.

In her senior year at Barnard College she studied under Franz Boas, whose insistence on studying 'whole cultures' in comprehensive detail is reflected in her early writing, and she met his research assistant RUTH BENEDICT, who was to become one of her closest friends. After graduating in 1923 she married Luther Cresswell, a fellow student, and went on to complete an MA in psychology at Columbia in 1924. The following year she undertook her first field trip to Samoa and on her return met Reo

Fortune, a New Zealand anthropologist. They were married on board ship in 1928 on the way to study the Manus tribe in the Admiralty Islands. Five years later she met the English biologist and anthropologist Gregory Bateson in New Guinea. They married in 1935, their daughter Mary was born in 1939 and after working together, especially in Bali, they were divorced in 1945, ending Mead's long period as a 'collaborating wife'. She had also been working independently for the American Museum of Natural History since 1926. In 1948, after Ruth Benedict's death, she became Director of the Columbia University Research in Contemporary Cultures. In 1954 she became an adjunct professor at Columbia, and in 1965 was made Curator Emeritus of Ethnology at the museum.

Margaret Mead wrote over 40 books, 18 with other people, and over 1000 monographs and articles, and built up a valuable collection of notes, tapes, films and objects. Her influence was enormous, but perhaps her greatest contribution was that she made anthropology accessible and important to ordinary people in understanding their own society. Her earliest books, *Coming of Age in Samoa* (1928) and *Growing up in New Guinea* (1930) were best-sellers, and *Sex and Temperament in Three Primitive Societies* (1935) showed the social basis of women's position by offering a cross-cultural perspective. During World War II she studied her own society, first for the US Committee on Food Habits, and secondly as a lecturer smoothing cultural mis-understandings between American troops and the British communities in which they were based.

Mead was always a pioneer in technique and subject, one of the first anthropologists to exploit film and photography, especially with Geoffrey Bateson in the remarkable *Balinese Character* (1942), and one of the first to study child-rearing and to link it to overall societal patterns. In 1949 *Male and Female* balanced an examination of biological differences with the social factors which determine gender roles. During the 1950s and 1960s she became increasingly concerned with the rift between generations, which she dealt with in *Culture and*

*Commitment* (1970) and she took a radical position with regard to many social issues, such as the legalization of marijuana.

In the 1970s she frequently returned to New Guinea, where she had opened a large exhibition hall (the Hall of the People of the Pacific) at the museum. She received many awards and was President of the American Association for the Advancement of Science in 1976. On her death from cancer in 1978 she was mourned throughout the world.

M. Mead: *Blackberry Winter: My Earlier Years* (1962)
——— : *Letters from the Field 1925–1975* (1977)
J. Howard: *Margaret Mead: A Life* (1984)

**Mead, Sylvia Earle** (1935–). American marine biologist. Born in Gibbstown, Sylvia grew up on a small farm in Florida and learned scuba diving in the Gulf of Mexico while studying botany at Florida State University. She held research fellowships and taught zoology. In 1964 she joined the International Indian Ocean Expedition as a diver. She was the only woman among 60 men. It was a long-term operation and four more cruises followed.

When the Mote Marine Laboratory was established in 1966, she became Director. She married Giles Mead, an icthyologist, moved to Cambridge, Massachusetts, and brought up their children. In 1970 she led the only all-woman team (among 17) to live underwater for 2 weeks on the Tektite II project. Swimming outside their habitat for several hours a day, her team observed 35 species of fish and 154 of marine plants, 26 never before observed in the area. When they emerged, the women were given lunch at the White House and received the Conservation Service Award, experiencing what Sylvia termed 'reverse discrimination'.

In 1972 she made expeditions to the Galapagos and Cocos Islands and continued projects in the USA, her chief research interest being the inter-relationships between marine plants and animals. In 1973 she visited China as the representative for American Women for International Understanding.

**Mechtild of Magdeburg** (1210–82). German mystic. Born in Saxony of noble parents, Mechtild had her first mystical experience at the age of 12, when she felt that she was greeted by the Holy Spirit. Desiring to live wholly for God, she became a Beguine at Magdeburg in 1230, and under Dominican direction lived a life of intense prayer and austerity for 40 years. Mechtild's extraordinary spiritual experiences and severe criticism of the clergy aroused great hostility and she was forced to leave Magdeburg. Ailing and partially blind, she found refuge in the Cistercian convent at Helfra in 1270.

Mechtild's writings have been collected under the title *Das fliessende Licht des Gottheit*, a phrase supposedly spoken to Mechtild by Christ, who said that she was to be a witness to the 'light of my divinity flowing into all hearts that live without guile'. Her work, written in a forceful and poetic style, deeply influenced German medieval mysticism. It is also thought that she influenced Dante and is the Matelda referred to in *Purgatorio* (cantos 27–33).

A. Kemp-Welch: *Of Six Medieval Women* (1913)

**Medici, Catherine de** (1519–89). French queen. Born in Florence, the daughter of Lorenzo, Duke of Urbino, and Madeleine de la Tour d'Auvergne, she was orphaned early and educated under the supervision of her uncle, Pope Clement VII. In 1533 she married Henri, Duke of Orléans, who succeeded to the throne in 1547. After his death she acted as Regent for her sons, the 15-year-old François (1559), and 10-year-old Charles (1560), and remained influential during the reign of her third son Henri (1574–89), her authority declining only during the last year of her life. She was an immensely ruthless politician, but despite her deservedly harsh reputation most of her intentions were for reconciliation between individuals, families, religious sects, and (through dynastic marriages) between nations.

Her aim was the consolidation of royal power, and the appeasement of the opposing Catholic and Protestant factions of Montmorency, Guise and Bourbon which threatened national unity. She tried to bring about religious reconciliation through a conference of theologians, the Colloquy of Poissy (1561), and the January Edict (1562) which recognized Protestantism in France. In 1564 a suspected alliance with Spain led the Protestant Condé to attempt a coup and limited toleration was only re-established in

1570. The fragile peace was shattered by the massacre of St Bartholomew, on the occasion of her daughter Marguerite's marriage to Henri of Navarre in 1572. This nationwide persecution, which Catherine had allowed as a means of crushing Huguenot pressure for war with Spain, precluded any marital alliance with ELIZABETH I, and ensured the continuance of the religious wars until the assassination of Henri III which followed her own death, in 1589.

P. Van Dyke: *Catherine de' Medici* (1923)

**Médicis, Marie de** (1573–1642). Queen of France. The daughter of Francesco de' Medicis, Grand Duke of Tuscany, she married Henri IV of France in 1600 after he divorced his wife Margaret, and brought him a large dowry. She had nine children within as many years but the marriage was full of tension, owing to Henri's love affairs and her own favouritism towards the Florentine Concini. When Henri was assassinated in 1610 she became Regent for her son, Louis XIII, and she reversed Henri's policies, forming marriage alliances with the Habsburgs of Austria and Spain (traditional enemies), dissipating the treasury in court extravagance and appeasing the nobility with pensions. She maintained power until 1617, three years after Louis' majority, but then her adviser Concini was assassinated and she was exiled to Blois.

In 1619 and 1620 she led insurrections but was reconciled to Louis in 1622, persuading him to make her favourite, Richelieu, first Cardinal and then Chief Minister. Richelieu, however, did not uphold Marie's favoured policies and returned France to its old alliances. In 1630 she demanded his dismissal, but in 1631 she was banished to Compiègne, from where she fled to the Netherlands, never to return; she died in poverty 11 years later. Her daughter Henrietta Maria married Charles I of England. She is known not only for her political intrigues but as the builder of the Luxembourg Palace, which Rubens decorated with scenes from her life in the 1620s.

J. Pardoe: *Marie de Médicis* (1890) [3 vols]

**Meer, Fatima** (1929–). South African academic and activist. She has taught sociology at Natal University since 1959 and is the highest-ranking black academic in white South Africa. She participated in the Defiance Campaign and founded the Women's Federation but was banned from 1952–1954. During the 1960s she published a number of books and lectured abroad, vehemently opposing the policy of apartheid. In 1975 she was elected as President of the Black Women's Federation, which was subsequently banned. The government refused to renew her passport in 1976 and she was detained under the Internal Security Act. After her release, although she was allowed to teach, she was prevented from travelling, engaging in any political activity or publishing any material.

**Meinhof, Ulrike (Marie)** (1934–76). German political activist. Descended from an old bourgeois family from Württemberg, she was born in Oldenburg, where her father was Assistant Director of the State Museum. They moved to Jena in 1936; her father died in 1940, and her mother in 1948. Her foster mother, Renate Riemecke, was a university lecturer, and in 1950 they spent a year in England. At 18 she went to the Gymnasium Philippinum in Hesse, took her *Abitur* examination in 1955 and went first to Marburg University, and then to Münster in 1957. She became involved in the anti-nuclear movement and edited a student paper *Das Argument*. In 1959 she became Foreign Editor and later Editor of the leftist journal *Konkret*, and lived with the communist activist Klaus Rainer Röhl. They married in 1961, and in 1962 she had twin girls. (In the same year she had a serious brain operation, and x-rays of her skull were used to prove her identity 10 years later.) In 1968 she divorced her husband and became drawn into more radical circles in Berlin with Jan-Carl Raspe.

In 1970 Ulrike helped to free Andreas Baader in Dahlem, and was forced to go underground. After a stay in Jordan with Baader, Gudrun Ensslin and Horst Mahler, she returned to Germany where she took part in bank robberies and planted bombs especially aimed at large industrial groups such as Springer and at American bases. She became a leader of the Röte Armee Fraktion which was known as the Baader-

Meinhof Gang, and was their chief propagandist. She was arrested in June 1972, but sentenced to only eight years imprisonment for her part in the freeing of Baader. She was tried in a special court at Stannheim with Baader, Ensslin and Raspe. She committed suicide in prison on 9 May 1976 and the others also died apparently by their own hands 18 months later, after the failure of the hijack at Mogadishu ended their hopes of release.

J. Becker: *Hitler's Children* (2/1978)

**Meir** [née Mabovitch, Goldie; Myerson], **Golda** (1898–1978). Israeli politician. Born in the Jewish quarter of Kiev, Ukraine, in 1906 she emigrated with her family to join her father in the USA. They settled in Milwaukee, where she trained as a teacher and became an active Zionist campaigner. She married Morris Myerson, whom she persuaded to emigrate to Israel in 1921 as a condition of their marriage, and they worked on a kibbutz for two years. They then moved to Tel-Aviv, where Golda worked as a clerk and took in washing to supplement the family income, since Morris's health was poor and they had two children. She began to work within the labour movement, becoming Secretary of the Women's Labour Council by 1928 and attaining a high position in the Histradut, the labour federation, representing them at international conferences. She was then elected as delegate to the World Zionist Congress and undertook missions to the USA and UK during the 1930s.

When the British Mandate was enforced in Israel in 1946 she joined the Jewish self-government organization and in May 1948 she was one of the signatories of the Declaration of Independence, becoming the first Israeli minister to the USSR that September. In January 1949 she was elected to the Knesset ('parliament') as a Mapai ('Labour') representative, and she became Minister of Labour and Social Insurance under Ben Gurion. In 1956 she was made Minister of Foreign Affairs. During these years she was the only woman in the administration. When she was widowed in 1956 she changed her name to Meir, the Hebrew form.

She also chaired the Israeli delegation to the United Nations from 1953 to 1966 and was Secretary-General of the Labour Party from 1965 to 1968. She then retired, but on the death of Levi Eshkol in March 1969 she was asked to act as interim Prime Minister, and went on to win the office in the October elections. She held the post, dominating the Knesset and demonstrating toughness combined with a general warmth of personality as an international stateswoman. She eventually resigned in 1974 during the heart-searching and disputes which followed the war of October 1973.

G. Meir: *My Life* (1975)

**Meitner, Lise** (1878–1968). Austrian mathematical physicist. Born in Vienna into a large Jewish family, Lise was brought up as a Protestant. Her interest in physics began early, and after a good general education she received her doctorate from the University of Vienna in 1906. After studying the new subject of radioactivity in Vienna she moved to Berlin to study with Planck in 1907. There was difficulty in doing experimental work as Emil Fischer allowed no women in his laboratories, but she met Otto Hahn and together they equipped a carpenter's workshop for radiation measurement. This began a lifelong association.

In 1912 Lise joined the Kaiser-Wilhelm Institut für Chimie. During World War I she served as a radiographer and nurse with the Austrian army, but during their leaves she and Hahn continued to measure radioactive substances and by the end of the war announced the discovery of a new element, protactinium.

In 1918 Lise became head of the physics department at the Kaiser-Wilhelm Institut, and in 1926 Professor of Physics at the University of Berlin. She worked towards clarifying the relationships between beta and gamma rays. In 1938 she was helped to leave Nazi Germany and went to the Netherlands. She was soon invited to work at the Nobel Institute in Stockholm. Here she published her most famous contribution to science, a paper (with her nephew Otto Frisch) that described nuclear fission.

In 1947, after visiting the USA as a professor, she retired from the Nobel Institute. The Swedish Atomic Energy Commission established a small laboratory for her. In 1960 she retired to Cambridge, UK.

She was the first woman to receive a Fermi Award from the Atomic Energy Commission (1966). When invited to join a team working on the nuclear fission bomb she refused, stopped working on nuclear fission, and hoped the project would prove impossible.

E. Yost: *Women of Modern Science* (1959)

**Melba** [née Mitchell, Helen], Dame **Nellie** (1861–1931). Australian soprano. She studied the piano and organ in Melbourne (the city from which she derived her stage name). In 1882 she married Captain Charles Porter Armstrong. She went to Paris in 1886 for training with Mathilde Marchesi. She made her operatic debut the following year in Brussels, as Gilda in Verdi's *Rigoletto*. In 1888 she appeared at Covent Garden, London, in the title role of Donizetti's *Lucia di Lammermoor*; she sang there regularly from 1889 to 1914 and sporadically thereafter until her farewell performance in 1926. Meanwhile she travelled widely, scoring particular success in Paris (1889 and 1890) as Gounod's Juliet and Marguerite, and making her debuts both at La Scala, Milan, and the Metropolitan, New York, in 1893. During 1897–8 she toured the USA. On return trips to Australia she organized three operatic seasons (1911, 1924 and 1928). She was made a DBE in 1918 and a GBE in 1929.

The roles with which she is primarily associated include Gilda, Mimì, Violetta and Marguerite. Her many recordings (about 150) testify to the brilliance she brought to these demanding coloratura roles as well as to the roundness of tone of her maturity. The esteem in which she was held at Covent Garden is exemplified by the fact that she was one of the few singers allowed to dictate casting for the operas in which she appeared. Her name has been bequeathed to Pêche Melba and Melba toast.

T. Radic: *Melba: the Voice of Australia* (1986)

**Mélisande** (c1105–60). Queen of Jerusalem. The eldest daughter of Baldwin II of the Frankish court of Edessa and his Armenian wife Morphia, she began to reign with her father at the end of his life and in 1129 married Fulk V of Anjou; their son, the future Baldwin III was born in 1130. In 1131 they became joint rulers of Jerusalem, but Mélisande was less powerful and rumours of her adultery with the rebel Hugh II estranged her from her husband. She roused her supporters and they were reconciled in 1136. During this period Mélisande was a lavish patron of the arts and religion, founding a huge abbey at Bethany. After Fulk's death in 1143 she became Regent for her son, then effective Queen; they were in fact crowned together. She clung to power after he came of age, although in 1152 their rivalry became so intense that they divided the kingdom, Mélisande ruling Judaea and Samaria and Baldwin the north. After a brief period of war they ruled together again from 1154 until her death in 1160 at the convent of Bethany.

B. Hamilton: 'Queen of Jerusalem', *Medieval Women* (1978)

**Melmoth, Charlotte** (1749–1823). American tragic actress. In her youth she ran away with an actor named Courtney Melmoth; they soon separated but she continued to use his name, becoming well known in Dublin, Edinburgh and on other provincial stages. She appeared at Covent Garden, London, in 1774 and at Drury Lane in 1776. In 1793 she had a great success as Euphrasia in the *Grecian Daughter* (a favourite role of SARAH SIDDONS) with the American Company at the John Street Theatre, New York. Her powerful acting, particularly as Lady Macbeth, caused the American Company to add more tragic parts to their repertoire. When the Park Theatre, New York, opened she became a leading actress there, but left after a row with Dunlap, the manager, in 1802. She returned the following season but after Dunlap's bankruptcy she went to the Chestnut Street Theatre, Philadelphia. Her final New York appearance was in 1812. She later opened a school of English elocution. Throughout her career in the USA, Charlotte Melmoth was one of the shaping influences of the early American stage.

**Menchu, Rigoberta** (1951–). Guatemalan activist. A Quiche Indian from the remote northern highlands, her father was a leading member of the committee for peasant unity, organizing against the purchase, oil-prospecting and exploitation of peasant-owned land in the 1970s. Rigoberta left her village, learnt Spanish and became a CUC activist. Her younger brother and both parents were killed by the Garcia regime, and two other members of her family have 'disappeared' – like 38,000 other Guatemalans. In 1981 Rigoberta left the country to speak for the CUC, and for the United Representation of the Guatemalan Opposition, throughout Latin America, Europe and at the United Nations. She returned to Guatemala in 1983 for a year, working in the mountain villages opposing the government's forced resettlement schemes. Her autobiographical account of the struggle, published in 1984, drew international attention to the plight of her people. Since then she has married, but continues to campaign officially, and unofficially, for the Guatemalan cause.

R. Menchu: *I . . . Rigoberta Menchu* (1984)

**Mendelssohn (-Bartholdy), Fanny (Cäcilie)** (1805–47). German pianist and composer. The sister of the composer Felix Mendelssohn, she is considered by many to have been equally talented; her musical precocity was exemplified in her ability to play Bach's 48 Preludes and Fugues from memory at the age of 13. After initial training from her mother, she studied in Berlin with Ludwig Berger (piano) and Carl Zelter (composition), and in 1816 with Marie Bigot in Paris. In 1829 she married the painter Wilhelm Hensel, with whom she travelled in Italy during 1839–40. On her mother's death in 1842 she returned to the Mendelssohn home in Berlin, where she organized local concerts and occasionally appeared as a pianist. Her published music, stylistically similar to her brother's, includes songs, piano pieces and a piano trio, though most of her compositions remain in manuscript; six of her songs appeared under Felix's name in his two sets of Twelve Songs opp. 8 and 9. Her son Sebastian wrote a family biography based on her diaries and correspondence (1879).

**Menetewab** [Mentuab] (c1720–70). Ethiopian empress. Christened Welleta Georgis, a prophetic name, in her youth she was known as Berhan Magass, 'Glory of Grace'. She married the Emperor Bakaffa in the 1720s and during his reign was made 'Iteghe', being given the name Menetewab, with the right to act as regent. On Bakaffa's death in 1729 she became Regent to her son Iyasu II; as he grew up interested in little except hunting and art collecting she controlled the government until his death in 1755. She is held responsible for weakening the old empire, since her nepotism aroused the hostility of the nobles and she had insufficient power to crush the resulting rebellions. In 1755 she managed to have her grandson Ioas made Emperor but she was gradually overtaken in influence by her daughter-in-law's family and on Ioas's death in 1769 her power ended. James Bruce, the Scottish traveller, recorded her life story when he met her in retirement in Cusquam still plotting to set up a rival candidate for the throne.

**Menken, Adah Isaacs** [pseud. of Dolores Adios Fuertes] (1835–68). American actress and poet. Probably born in Milneburg, a New Orleans suburb, she was orphaned at 13, and became a dancer. In 1856 she married the musician Alexander Isaacs Menken and appeared with him throughout the South. She also published her poems in local and New York papers. After her New York debut in 1859 she left her husband and married the prize fighter John Heenan; the revelation of her bigamy, the ensuing scandal, divorce, and desertion by Heenan, and the death of her small son apparently made her increasingly determined to succeed alone. In 1861 she appeared with sensational success in *Mazeppa*, as the hero of Byron's poem, playing in California, New York and then in London (1864), where she was much admired by Dickens, Rosetti, Swinburne and other literary figures. The play's impact seems to have rested largely on her appearance, bound to the back of a horse, 'in a state of virtual nudity'. In 1861 she married Robert Newell, and was arrested as a self-declared secessionist in Baltimore. By 1865 she had divorced Newell and married James Bailey, whom she left within three days. She had a child and lived in Paris, where her friend GEORGE SAND was her son's godmother and the elderly Alexandre Dumas her infatuated admirer. She had persevered in her writing, her second volume of poems, *Infelicia* (1868), showing a marked degree of talent and feeling. A romantic, impulsive, melancholic character, she died in Paris aged 33.

W. Mankowitz: *Mazeppa* (1982)

**Mentschikoff, Soia** (1915–84). American lawyer. Born in Moscow, the daughter of a Russian aristocrat businessman who had become an American citizen, Soia returned with her family to New York before the Revolution. She attended Hunter College and Columbia Law School, and then became a specialist in labour relations. In 1944 she was made a partner of Spence, Windells, Waller, Hotchkiss & Angel, the first female partner on Wall Street. She had continued to work for Professor Karl Llewellyn on his Universal Commercial Code, and they married in 1946. In that year she also became the first woman to teach at Harvard Law School.

In 1950 Llewellyn and Mentschikoff moved to Chicago Law School, although regulations meant that she could not be given tenure, or be made a professor, until after her husband's death in 1962. There, too, she was the first woman teacher. At Chicago she also directed the Commercial Arbitration Project, and worked on the Commission on the Rights, Liberties and Responsibilities of American Indians. From 1974 to 1982 she was an innovative and energetic Dean of the University of Miami Law School, and from 1980 was also on the Panel of Arbitrators of the International Center for the Settlement of Investment Disputes. She was the first woman president of the Association of American Law Schools, and the recipient of many academic awards and honours.

**Mentuab.** See MENETEWAB.

**Mercéni, Antonia.** See ARGENTINA, LA.

**Mercouri, Melina** (1923–). Greek film actress and politician. She was born in Athens, into a prominent political family, her grandfather being Mayor of Athens, and her father Deputy Mayor and Minister of State. At the age of 17 she went on the stage, against her parents' wishes, and made her first film *Stella* with Michael Cacoyannis in 1955. She married American director Jules Dassin, and reached international stardom in his films, being nominated for an Academy Award for *Never on Sunday* (1960), and making a version of *Phaedra* in 1962. She made several more films before 1978, but her main energy was devoted to campaigning against the military junta who took power in Greece in 1967. She lived in exile in Paris and the USA, was declared an enemy of the state, deprived of her passport, and all her films were banned.

In 1974, after the fall of the colonels, she returned to Greece, and stood unsuccessfully for parliament. She finally obtained a seat in 1978 for Piraeus, from 1981–5 was Minister of Culture and Sciences in Papandreou's Panhellenic Socialist Movement Government, and has been Minister of Culture, Youth and Sports since 1985.

M. Mercouri: *I was born Greek* (1971)

**Merian, Maria Sibylla** (1647–1717). German botanical and entomological illustrator. She was born in Frankfurt. Her father was an etcher and book publisher who died when she was three. Her stepfather, Jacob Marrel was a flower painter, one of whose pupils was Johann Graff, who became Maria's husband in 1665. One of her chief sources of inspiration was the volume of engravings of flowers published by her father in 1641. Maria began her botanical and entomological work after she moved to Nuremberg in 1670, and in 1675, 1677 and 1680 published her three-part work the *Neue Blumenbuch* ('New Book of Flowers'), and in 1679 and 1683 the two parts of *Der Rampen wunderbare Verwandelung und sondebare Blumennahrung* ('The miraculous transformation and unusual flower-food of caterpillars'). She kept live specimens, a wholly new approach, and showed moths, butterflies and other insects at each stage of their development, recorded with almost surrealist clarity and precision.

During the 1680s Maria separated from her husband, returned with her children to Frankfurt and became a member of the Labadist sect (like MARIA VAN SCHURMAN), joining their colony, of which her elder half-brother had been a member, in a castle in west Friesland. In 1690 she moved to Amsterdam, learned Dutch and studied the collections of insects brought back from the East and West Indies. In 1699 she went with her daughter Dorothea to a Labadist mission in Suriname, where her eldest daughter Johanna was living. Partly sponsored by the Amsterdam civil authorities, she explored the territory and studied the daily life of the people as well as the tropical flora and fauna, and completed a series of detailed, brilliantly formalized paintings. Weakened by yellow fever she returned to Holland and in 1705 published her work, with 60 plates engraved from watercolours, in *Metamorphosis insectorum surinamensium*. She then returned to her work on European insects, publishing a third volume and a Dutch edition of *Der Rampen*. She suffered a stroke in 1714 and died in poverty three years later. Her scientific work is recognized in a number of insects and plants which bear her name.

**Merici, Angela.** *See* ANGELA OF BRESCIA.

**Méricourt, Théroigne de**. *See* DE MERICOURT, THÉROIGNE.

**Merman, Ethel** (1908?–84). American singer and actress. One of the greatest Broadway stars, she was born Ethel Zimmerman in Queens, New York, and got her first show-business contacts while working as secretary to the tycoon Caleb Bragg, who gave her an introduction to producer George White. She turned down Bragg's offer of a chorus-line job and began singing in night clubs, and also took a short contract with Warner Brothers. She changed her name while appearing in Vaudeville in 1929, and her real break came in 1930 when she was cast in Gershwin's *Girl Crazy* with Ginger Rogers, and sang the hit song *I Got Rhythm*. Her 14 Broadway shows included *Anything Goes* (1934), *Stars In Your Eyes* (1939), *Annie Get Your Gun* (1946), *Call Me Madam* (1950), *Gypsy* (1959) and *Hello Dolly* (1970), and she launched a host of famous songs, such as *I Get a Kick Out of You, You're the Top* and *There's No Business like Show Business*, written by Gershwin, Cole Porter, Irving Berlin and many others. Her powerful, untrained voice could cope with the most complex arrangements, and her sheer professionalism and stamina were a by-word in musicals. Merman appeared in several films based on her musicals but her greatest triumphs were on Broadway, where she reigned as undisputed queen. She was married, and divorced, four times.

**Messalina, Valeria** (22–48). Roman empress. The daughter of a patrician family, in 39 or 40AD she became the third wife of Claudius, her second cousin, who became Emperor in 41. They had two children, Octavia (who married the emperor Nero) and Britannicus. She was notorious at court for her sexual behaviour and for her endless and violent intrigues. The gentle and ingenuous Claudius remained unaware of these scandals; he was even influenced by her to remove senators, such as Appilus Silanus, who had rejected her, and many others were executed at her instigation. In 48 she caused the death of Polybius, one of Claudius's secretaries. His colleague, Narcissus, also a freedman secretary, caused her downfall by revealing to the emperor that she had actually gone through a marriage ceremony with Caius Silius, with whom she was conspiring against Claudius. Narcissus ordered her execution before Claudius could recover from the shock and reverse his order.

**Mészarós, Márta** (1931–). Hungarian film director. Born in Hungary, Márta moved with her family to the USSR in 1936, but her father, a sculptor, disappeared during the Stalinist purges, her mother died and she returned to Hungary in 1946 to live with an aunt. She was awarded a scholarship to study at VCIK (Film School) in Moscow, and in the 1950s worked in Romania. In 1959, after divorcing her Romanian husband, she returned to Budapest and at the Newsreel Studio made over 100 short science films and documentaries. In the mid-1960s she joined Mafilm Group 4, where she met and later married Hungary's best known film director Miklós Jancsó. *The Girl* (1964) was the first of several feature films such as *Adoption* (1975), *Nine Months* (1976), *Two Women* (1979) and *Silent Cry* (1982). *Diary for My Children* (1982, released 1985) tells the story of her early life and is the first of a projected autobiographical trilogy.

**Metzger** [née Bruhl], **Hélène** (1889–*c*1944). French chemist and writer on the history of science and philosophy. Hélène showed outstanding early promise and studied mineralogy at the Sorbonne, receiving her *Diploma d'études supérieures* in physics for her *Etude cristallographique du chlorate de lithium*.

In 1913 she married Paul Metzger, a professor of history and geography, but in September 1914 he was reported missing in one of the first battles of World War I; from then on she devoted herself to research. Her doctoral thesis showed the evolution of crystallography (*La genèse de la science des cristaux*) and she then applied her historical methods to the whole of chemistry. In 1925 she won the Prix Bordin in philosophy for *Les concepts scientifiques* and she continued to seek out the philosophical bases of science in later work. This was interrupted by the German occupation of Paris and she moved to Lyons and worked at the Bureau d'Etudes Israëlites on a study of Jewish monotheism. She was arrested in February 1944, deported to Drancy, then sent to Auschwitz.

From 1939 she had been in charge of the library of the history of science at the Centre Internationale de Synthèse and through published work and personal contact she exerted considerable influence among historians of science.

**Mew, Charlotte Mary** (1869–1928). English poet. Born in London, the daughter of an architect, she was educated privately and spent some time in Paris, and her writing suggests that she suffered at some time from a profound but hopeless love. She began writing short stories, poems and critical articles in the 1890s, publishing them in journals such as *The Yellow Book*, *The English Woman*, *Temple Bar* and *The Egoist*. She also undertook voluntary social work in the poorer parts of London. After her father died in 1897 the family were left in poverty, but she and her sister Alice renounced marriage because of the fear of hereditary insanity. Eventually Alice and a brother were confined to a mental hospital where they died.

Charlotte's few poems, powerful and haunting, often deal with love, renunciation and death. They were published in leading reviews and in 1916 Harold Monro published a brief collection, *The Farmer's Bride*. Through this she met Thomas Hardy, who became a firm friend and with John Masefield and de la Mare obtained a Civil List pension in 1922 to keep her from starvation. Following the death of her mother and then of her remaining sister Annie in 1927, she too became seriously ill; although she recovered she felt unable to continue and poisoned herself in March 1928. Another collection, *The Rambling Sailor*, appeared in 1929, *Collected Poems* in

1953, and *Collected Poems and Prose* (1982).
P. Fitzgerald: *Charlotte Mew* (1984)

**Meynell** [née Thompson], **Alice (Christiana Gertrude)** (1847–1922). English poet and essayist. She was born in Barnes, London. Her father was a scholar, her mother a concert pianist, and her sister became the famous military painter ELIZABETH BUTLER. She was educated at home by her father and spent much of her childhood in France, Switzerland and especially Italy. As a girl she was converted to Catholicism, her mother's faith. Her first volume of poems, *Preludes*, was published in 1875 to much praise from Ruskin, Rossetti and GEORGE ELIOT; all her life she was a favourite of other artists and writers. Through the Catholic poet Francis Thompason she met the author and journalist Wilfrid Meynell, whom she married in 1877. They had eight children and little income and supported themselves by journalism, Alice contributing to numerous periodicals and helping Wilfrid edit the *Weekly Register* and *Merry England*. From 1893 to 1898 she wrote a weekly column for *The Pall Mall Gazette* and was its Art Critic in 1902–5. During these years, despite the family and constant migraine she also undertook charity work, was an active suffragette and held a salon for writers such as Patmore and Moore at her home in Palace Court.

Between 1893 and her death she had more time to write and published eight volumes of poetry, mostly in a lyrical, semi-mystical vein but with a very precise choice of language. After Tennyson's death she was proposed as Poet Laureate. She also published many volumes of essays, biographies of Holman Hunt (1893) and Ruskin (1900), several editions of other writers including Patmore, Blake and Johnson, and three translations.
K. Michalik: *Meynell: Her Life and Works* (1934)

**Michel, Louise** (1830–95). French socialist and revolutionary. Born at Vroncourt, near Domrémy, Louise Michel was the illegitimate daughter of a local landowner; her mother was a servant. Brought up by her grandfather, a kindly egalitarian man, she studied widely and became a promising poet. On her grandparents' death her father returned to the estate and Louise, resented by his wife, was sent to school at Chaumont. She then became a teacher, but lost her post for outspoken criticisms of the Second Empire in 1852. In 1856 she went to Paris, taught, took courses in chemistry and physics and joined secret Republican clubs associated with Blanqui. She also wrote several novels, all with themes of social protest; they included *Le bâtard impérial, La claque-dents, Les microbes humains.*

During the siege of Paris in the Franco–Prussian War (1870) she took part in the Committee of Vigilance of the 18th district and, influenced by her lover Théophile Ferré, became increasingly militant. During the Commune, she took charge of social and educational policies, and fought fiercely on the barricades, being among the last defenders in Montmartre cemetery in May 1871. She gave herself up in place of her mother, to whom she was devoted, and after being imprisoned in Versailles was tried in December and sentenced to life imprisonment in New Caledonia. Ferré was executed. Louise remained in the penal colony until the 1881 amnesty, studying botany, teaching, and writing poetry.

On her return to France she immediately renewed her political activities, speaking at meetings across the country. She was imprisoned in 1882, and in 1883 sentenced to six years' imprisonment for inciting a mob to break into bakeries during a food riot. After the death of her mother in 1885 she suffered severe depression, but on her release in 1889 resumed political work. In 1890 she led strikes in the Vienne district; she was arrested but fled to London to escape plans to certify her insane. She lived in East Dulwich, with her friend Charlotte Vauvalle, and raised funds for European revolutionary groups. She was a member of the Fabian society and of various anarchist groups, and was visited by many activists, including EMMA GOLDMAN. In 1896 she returned to France, lectured on new developments in Russia, and worked at an exhausting pace until her death in Marseilles in 1895.

E. Thomas: *Louise Michel* (1971)

**Midler, Bette** (1945–). American comic and singer. Born in New Jersey, she was brought up in Hawaii and always wanted to be an actress, having been named by her mother after BETTE DAVIS. In 1965 she left for Los Angeles, then New York, working in a series of poorly-paid jobs while trying to find parts in plays and musicals. She was in the cast of *Fiddler on the Roof* (1966–9), *Salvation* (1970) and *Tommy* with the Seattle Opera Company in 1971. Her first individual success as a singer, in 1970, came in the odd setting of a cabaret at the Continental Baths in New York, a homosexual Turkish baths. Camp, satirical, brazenly witty, she quickly became a cult figure. National fame followed television appearances, concerts and records such as *The Divine Miss M*, and *Songs for the New Depression* (1975). She has since become recognized internationally as one of the funniest and most eccentric contemporary entertainers, her albums including *Broken Blossoms* (1979) and *Midler Madness* (1980). Recent screen appearances have brought her a new public, in films like *Down and Out in Beverly Hills* (1985), *Ruthless People* (1986) and *Outrageous Fortune* (1987). In 1985 she married Martin von Haselberg, an Argentinian commodities dealer.

**Mihr-ur-Nisa.** *See* NURJAHAN.

**Mill, Harriet.** *See* TAYLOR, HARRIET.

**Millay, Edna St Vincent** (1892–1950). American poet. Born in Rockland, Maine, she was educated there and in Camden and went to Barnard College and then to Vassar College. As a student her poem *Renascence* was published in *The Lyric Year* in 1912, and when she graduated in 1917 her first volume of poetry appeared. She moved to Greenwich Village, at its height as a centre for bohemian artists, and achieved an enormous and controversial reputation with the publication of *A Few Figs from Thistles* in 1920. The poems it contained, although traditional in form, seemed typicl of 'rebellious youth' and the 'emancipated women' in their demands for free thought, free love, equality and freedom from conventional taboos. She published two more collections before winning the Pulitzer Prize for *The Harp Weaver and other Poems* (1923). She was also associated with the early days of the Provincetown Players and wrote three verse plays in 1921. Later, in 1927, she wrote the libretto for Deems

Taylor's grand opera *The King's Henchman*, and a final play in 1932, *The Princess marries the Page*. In 1923 she married Eugen Jan Boissevain; they moved from the city to upper New York State and travelled in Europe. She also gave reading tours in the USA.

Millay continued to publish collections every two or three years, but her poetry of the 1930s turned from personal defiance to concern for human and social suffering, particularly in volumes such as *Conversation at Midnight* (1937). She remained an emblem of feminist revolt but as she became more reclusive she was labelled as arrogant, whimsical and self-absorbed, while her lyrical sonnets seemed outmoded in an age of free verse. In recent years her reputation has been revalued and after her death she became a heroine of the emerging women's movement.

T. Gould: *The Poet and her Book: A Biography of Millay* (1969)

**Millett** [née Murray], **Kate** [Katherine] (1934–). American feminist. She was born in St Paul, Minnesota. Her mother sold insurance and supported the family after her father left in 1948. She went to a local school and then to the University of Minnesota, graduating in 1956. She then took a first class degree at St Hilda's College, Oxford, in 1958 and later went on to do a PhD at Columbia in 1970. Her early career was as a sculptor, and she lived in Greenwich Village and then in Japan from 1961–1963. There she met the sculptor Fumio Yashima who returned to New York with her, and whom she married in 1965. She worked as a teacher, and became a member of the English department at Barnard College (1964–8). During the 1960s she was actively involved in the civil rights movement, and was one of the early committee members of the National Organization for Women (NOW) in 1966.

In 1970 she published *Sexual Politics* which has become a seminal work in the women's liberation movements in the USA and the UK. She propounded a radical feminism, demanding changes in personal and sexual attitudes as well as the greater opportunities claimed by liberal feminists such as BETTY FRIEDAN, and backed up her analysis of patriarchy by discussion of religion, psychoanalysis and particularly literature. In 1971 she moved on to make a film about women, *Three Lives*, and published *The Prostitution Papers*, and she has since explored the meaning of liberation in her own life in her autobiography *Flying* (1974) and in the account of her love affair with another woman *Sita* (1977). Her other books include *The Basement: Meditation on a Human Sacrifice* (1979). Throughout the 1970s she was also involved in active feminist politics, particularly in demonstrations for the Equal Rights Amendment, and in 1979 she visited Iran to press for women's rights after the revolution, but was expelled by Khomeini's government. She subsequently wrote *Going to Iran* (1981). She also continued to work as a sculptor, having several one-woman shows in New york, and exhibiting in The Woman's Building in Los Angeles in 1977.

**Milner, Marion** (1900–). British psychoanalyst. Marion Milner's first ambition was to be a naturalist. She graduated in psychology and physiology from London University and after working in industrial psychology continued her research in America on a Rockefeller fellowship. Her first published works (under the pseudonym Joanne Field) were *A Life of One's Own* (1934) and *An Experiment in Leisure* (1937), which considered the freeing of the subconscious through writing a journal. Her next book, *The Human Problem in Schools*, was based on observation of girls' schools in England. Her growing interest in psychoanalysis led her to train with the British Psychoanalytic Society and her later studies often illuminate problems of self-expression and control, particularly through art – her own difficulties with drawing and formal rules in *On Not Being Able To Paint* (1950) and analyses of the drawings of Susan, a schizophrenic patient over 20 years, in her famous book *The Hands of the Living God* (1969). In recent years her work has collected a greater following, and her two early books have been reissued while their sequel, *Eternity's Sunrise, A Way of Keeping a Diary*, which describes her travels in Greece, India and Israel, was published for the first time in 1987. Marion Milner practises as a psychoanalyst in Hampstead, London, and her other recent books include *The Suppressed Madness of Sane Man* (1987).

**Mink** [née Mekarska], **Paule (Paulina)** (1839–1900). French socialist feminist. Born at Clermont-Ferrand, she was the daughter of Polish nobles who had fled to France after taking part in the 1830 revolution. In her teens she moved to Paris, taught languages, worked as a seamstress and joined Republican and feminist societies. In 1868 she founded a women's mutual aid society, and gave public lectures on women's work with MARIA DERAISMES. The following year she founded *Les mouches et l'araignée*, a Republican paper which was soon suppressed. She organized the defence of Auxerre during the Franco-Prussian War, and worked in Paris and in the provinces in 1871 trying to raise support for the Commune. Afterwards she fled to Switzerland.

She returned to France in 1880 after the amnesty, and worked in various socialist groups. Between 1891 and 1896 she contributed articles and stories to the journal *La question sociale*. In 1893 she became a member of the Comité Révolutionnaire Central, founded in 1889, and continued to act for women's interests. In 1884 she had spoken against a narrow concentration on women's suffrage in opposition to HUBERTINE AUCLERT but during the 1890s she was persuaded by EUGÉNIE POTONIE-PIERRE to change her views, and joined the organization La Solidarité in 1893. In the same year she stood as one of five woman candidates for the National Assembly. She was also Editorial Secretary of the journal *La question sociale*, from 1894 to 1897. She became the effective leader of the Socialist Women's Movement in France from 1896 until she died. At her funeral there was a mass popular demonstration in memory of her as a communard heroine with crowds kept under control by 1300 troops.

**Minnelli, Liza** (1946– ). American singer and film actress. The daughter of JUDY GARLAND and film director Vincente Minnelli, Liza was born in San Francisco and appeared as a child with her mother in *In the Good Old Summertime* (1949), and also acted with her in New York in 1953. She acted at school and made her first appearances on Broadway as a teenager in *Best Foot Forward* (1963) and at the London Palladium, again with Garland, in 1964. She had already recorded professionally, and began a career in cabaret in 1965, but then turned to films, with *Charlie Bubbles* (1969) and *The Sterile Cuckoo* (1969), which won her an Academy Award nomination for her performance as Pookie Adams. Her greatest international success, however, was as Sally Bowles in *Cabaret*, although she has continued to appear in films, for example in her father's production *A Matter of Time* (1976) and Scorsese's *New York, New York* (1981) which exploited her powerful voice and her dramatic range.

For a time her career appeared to be in decline: two marriages, to Peter Allen in 1967 and Jack Haley, Jr. in 1974, had ended in divorce before she married Mark Gero, and she experienced problems with drink and drugs. However, after a cure at the Betty Ford Clinic she returned triumphantly, with roof-raising concerts at the Carnegie Hall, in 1987, and in London.

**Mira Bai** (1498–1547). Indian poet. The details of her life are obscured by later legend, but she is believed to have been born in Merta, and brought up at the court of her grandfather in the worship of the Hindu god Vishnu. At 18 she was married to the Prince of Mewar, but retained her devotion to Krishna, instead of her husband's favourite goddess, the destructive Kali. After his death she became a temple poet and drew persecution upon herself because of her betrayal of caste in caring for the poor. She died in Dwarka.

U. Nilsson: *Mira Bai*

**Mistinguett** [pseud. of Jeanne-Marie Bourgeois] (1873–1956). French actress, dancer, and music-hall singer. She began her career in 1890 at the Casino de Paris as a singer under the name Mistinguett. She became popular after 1910, first at the Moulin-Rouge (of which she was part-proprietor for some years) and at the Folies Bergère, where she was partnered by Maurice Chevalier in 1917 and in the same year performed spectacular dances in her own *Revue Mistinguett*. Renowned for her beautiful legs (insured for 1,000,000 *francs*) and her extravagant hats and costumes, Mistinguett was a comedienne of outstanding originality who became the queen of Parisian revue. She was also an outstanding comedy actress, giving perhaps her best performance in Sardou's *Madame Sans-Gêne* in 1921. Mistinguett retired in 1951 and wrote her reminiscences, *Toute ma vie* (1954).

Mistinguett: *Mistinguett, Queen of the Paris Night* (1954)

**Mistral, Gabriella** [pseud. of Lucila Godey Alcaya] (1889–1957). Chilean poet. She was born in Vicũna, northern Chile, and brought up by her mother, a school teacher. She studied education, child welfare and labour problems and in 1904 began teaching in rural and secondary schools. In 1912 she became Director of the Liceo de Los Andes, Punta Arenas, in southern Chile and soon attracted notice by her poems *Sonetos de la Muerte* (1914). In 1922 her collection *Desolaçion* was published, and she was also sent on a government mission to Mexico to study educational and library systems. She was honoured on her return in 1924 for her 'outstanding cultural work'. In that year she also published *Ternura*.

In 1925 she began a new career as a diplomat, being Chilean delegate to the United Nations, acting as head of the Cultural Committee and of the Committee of the Institute of International Intellectual Co-operation in Paris (1926–39). At the same time she was Chilean Consul in Madrid (1934), and after being made a unique 'life consul' chose posts in Lisbon, Nice, Rio, and Los Angeles. In 1944 she was diagnosed as diabetic and moved to the USA for her health, and served there as delegate to the United Nations.

After a long break she had returned to poetry in 1938, publishing *Tala*, and *Lagar* (1954). She also wrote novels on Chilean life, and in 1945 was awarded the Nobel Prize for Literature. Haunted by personal grief, from the suicide of her first love in 1909 to that of her nephew who was also her adopted son, her poetry celebrated deep private emotions, yet she managed to become a symbol of the nationalist aspirations of her country.

M.A. de Vazquez: *Gabriella Mistral: The Poet and her Work* (1964)

**Mitchell, Joni** [pseud. of Roberta Joan Anderson] (1943–). Canadian singer and song-writer. Born in McCleod, Alberta, and educated in Saskatoon, Saskatchewan, she intended to become a commercial artist and studied at Alberta College of Art, Calgary. She taught herself to play the ukelele and the guitar and in 1964 went to Toronto where she sang in local coffee houses. In 1965 she married Chuck Mitchell and moved to Detroit, separating from him soon afterwards. A successful performer, she went on to New York. Her own recording success was preceded by her popularity as a song-writer for other singers and groups, but in 1967 she made *Songs to a Seagull*, for Reprise, and then *Clouds*. She moved to California where she became deeply involved with singer Graham Nash, and then made her series of fine, reflective records, often largely autobiographical in content, including *Blue* (1971), *Ladies of the Canyon* (1972), *Court and Spark* (1974) and *The Hissing of Summer Lawns* (1975). Her musical accompaniment has become increasingly more sophisticated, evidenced by the prize-winning jazz album *Mingus* (1979), *Shadows and Light* (1980) and *Dog Eat Dog* (1986).

**Mitchell, Juliet** (1940–). British feminist. She was born in New Zealand, but moved to England in 1944 with her family, and was educated at King Alfred School, Hampstead, London, and then at St Anne's College, Oxford, where she took a degree in English. After postgraduate study at Oxford, she became a lecturer at the University of Leeds(1962–3) and the University of Reading (1965–70). Since 1971 she has been a free-lance writer, broadcaster and lecturer. A committed socialist and feminist, she has at different times been on the editorial boards of *New Left Review*, *Social Praxis* and *Signs*. Her first books, *Women: the Longest Revolution* (1966) and *Women's Estate* (1972), analysed the liberation movement in Marxist terms, relating it to other social protests of the 1960s, but her disillusionment with the analysis of women's position in socialist theory led her to re-evaluate fundamental patriarchal structures in *Psychoanalysis and Feminism* (1974). She is also co-editor with

ANNE OAKLEY of *The Rights and Wrongs of Women* (1976), a selection of essays.

**Mitchell, Maria** (1818–89). American astronomer. Maria was the third of ten children, educated chiefly by her father William Mitchell. As a child she helped him with chronometer ratings of whaling ships, and in 1831, during an annular eclipse of the sun, helped in timing the contacts he used to determine the longitude of their home town, Nantucket, Massachusetts.

At the age of 18 she was appointed Librarian of Nantucket Atheneum and held the post for 24 years. Meanwhile she made astronomical observations, in the course of which she discovered a new telescopic comet on 1 October 1847. Her discovery brought her fame, and a gold medal from the King of Denmark.

From 1849 she was employed by the US Nautical Almanac Office to compute ephemerides of the plant Venus. She was a faculty member at Vassar Female College from its founding in 1865, and in 1868 resigned from her post at the Nautical Almanac Office when her duties as Professor of Astronomy and Director of the college observatory demanded full attention.

Maria Mitchell was the first woman to be elected to the American Academy of Arts and Sciences. She also belonged to the American Philosophical Society and to the American Association for the Advancement of Women, of which she was President in 1870, then Chairman of its Committee on Women's Work in Science.

P. Mitchell Kendall: *Maria Mitchell, Life, Letters and Journals* (1896)
H. Morgan: *Maria Mitchell: First Lady of Astronomy* (1977)

———

**Mitchison, Naomi (Mary Margaret)** (1897–). British writer. Born in Edinburgh, the daughter of the scientist John Scott Haldane, she grew up in Oxford, attending the Dragon School and become a 'home student' at the college which later became St Anne's. After working as a VAD nurse in London, she married the lawyer G.R. Mitchison, later a Labour MP. She too became involved in politics, standing as a Labour candidate in 1935.

Naomi Mitchison's energy was as remarkable as her talent. After her first novel, *The*

*Conquered* (1923), she wrote over 70 books, including the well-known novel of the pre-Christian Greece, *The Corn King and the Spring Green* (1931), and many other equally popular works such as *The Big House* (1950), *Cleopatra's People* (1972) and *Not by Bread Alone* (1975). She also wrote children's books, short stories, travel, history, poetry and three volumes of autobiography.

In 1937 the Mitchisons moved to Argyll and she became increasingly concerned with Scottish affairs, being a member of Argyll County Council for 20 years, from 1945 to 1965, and of the Highland Panel (1947–65) and the Highlands and Islands Advisory Council (1966–75). She also travelled widely and in 1963 was made Tribal Adviser and Mother to the Bakgatla of Botswana, one among many honours. She has continued to write all her life and her later works, as a great-grandmother, include *Are You Taking Notes?* (1985).

**Mitford, Jessica (Lucy)** (1917–). English-American author. She was the sixth of the seven children of the 2nd Baron Redesdale, an aristocratic eccentric who disapproved of formal education for girls. Her sisters included Pamela Unity, who became a close friend of the German Nazi leaders in the late 1930s, Nancy who became a famous novelist and biographer, with decided left-wing preferences, and Diana, who married the British fascist leader, Sir Oswald Mosley, and Deborah, who became the Duchess of Devonshire. Her only brother, Tom, was killed on active service.

Jessica eloped at 20 with another upper class rebel, a nephew of Sir Winston Churchill, Esmond Romilly, who joined the Communist Party and went to Spain with the International Brigade. In 1939 they moved to the USA, where their daughter Constancia was born, but Romilly was killed in action in 1942. The following year she married a lawyer, Bob Treuhaft, and became an American citizen in 1944. They have one son, Benjamin. As they were associated with the American Communist Party, they suffered considerable harassment during the McCarthy era. Jessica continued to fight for her beliefs, and during the 1950s was secretary of the local Civil Rights Congress in Oakland, California. In 1960 she published an account of her early life, *Hons and Rebels*, but her best-known books have all been masterpieces of investigative journalism: *The American Way of Death* (1963), an exposé of the funeral business; *The Trial of Doctor Spock* (1969); *Kind and Usual Punishment: the American Prison Business* (1974); *A Fine Old Conflict* (1977); and a collection of essays and articles, *The Making of a Muckraker* (1979). She also lectures widely in the USA, and in 1981 went to London to give a lecture for International Human Rights Day, sponsored by the Cobden Trust. In 1984 she published a memoir of Philip Toynbee, *Faces of Philip*.

**Mitford, Nancy (Freeman)** (1904–73). British novelist. Nancy Mitford was the eldest of six daughters of Lord Redesdale (see JESSICA MITFORD). Her eccentric father, who appears in her novels as 'Uncle Matthew', gave his daughters no formal education except French, but allowed them to read as they wished in the large library at Swinbrook, the family house in the Cotswolds. When Nancy was a debutante in London she moved in literary circles which included her friend Evelyn Waugh. Her first novel, *Highland Fling*, appeared in 1931; this was followed by other light-hearted comedies, *Christmas Pudding* (1932), *Wigs on the Green* (1935) and *Pigeon Pie* (1940), and in the 1930s she also edited two volumes of letters of her mother's family, the Stanleys of Alderley.

In 1937 she married Peter Rodd, son of Lord Rendell. She spent much time in France and after the Spanish Civil War worked in a French refugee camp for refugee republicans. During World War II she opened her house to many of the Free French led by General de Gaulle, whom she greatly admired. Her first best-seller was *The Pursuit of Love* (1945), followed by its equally successful sequal *Love in a Cold Climate* (1949). These and the later novels, *The Blessing* (1951) and *Don't Tell Alfred* (1960), were closely based on her own past and contained extremely funny yet poignant portraits of bohemian upper-class society.

After the war Nancy Mitford settled in France, first in the Faubourg St Germain, Paris and then in Versailles. Here she wrote her acclaimed biographies: *Voltaire in Love* (1957), *Madame de Pompadour* (1954), and *Frederick the Great* (1970). Her other work

included essays and translations, and she also edited *Noblesse Oblige* (1956), in which A.S.C. Ross developed the witty code of social acceptability of 'U' and 'non-U' outlined the year before in *Encounter*.

S. Hastings: *Nancy Mitford* (1985)

**Mnouchkine, Ariane** (1939–). French theatre director. The daughter of a French film producer, Ariane became involved in drama while studying at Oxford University and formed a student theatre group on her return to Paris in 1961, directing *Ghenghis Khan* among Roman ruins. In 1964, after travelling to study alternative theatre she founded the famous collective Théâtre du Soleil, with 40 amateur student actors. Their first productions built on Gorki in *Les petits Bourgeois*, and Gautier in *Captain Fracasse*. She studied at Jacques Lecoq's mime school, passing her lessons on to the troupe. This approach, plus intensive study in a Paris restaurant, bore fruit in the acclaimed realistic production of Wesker's *The Kitchen*. In 1968 the group began studying other theatrical traditions – Chinese, Greek, commedia dell'arte – to be used in *Clowns* (1968) and in the great political collage *1789*. After their Milan success in 1970 the French government gave them a disused munitions warehouse, La Cartoucherie, which became their permanent base. Later productions have included *1793*, the spectacular satire *L'Age d'or* (1975), the film *Molière* (1978), *Mephisto* (1979), the Kabuki-Shakespearean experiments of the early 1980s and Hélène Cixous' play *L'Indiade*, a large-scale political drama about the conflicts surrounding the independence of India and partition. Mnouchkine remains one of Europe's leading directors, and the company is still organized on its original egalitarian lines.

**Modersohn-Becker, Paula** (1876–1907). German painter. She was born in Dresden. Her family moved to Bremen in 1888 and at the age of 16 she went to stay in London where she attended art school. She returned to complete a two-year teacher-training course but then continued her art studies at the School for Women Artists in Berlin. In 1897 she visited the village of Worpswede, where an artists' and writers' colony propounding rural as opposed to industrial values had been established, and she settled there the following year, becoming a pupil of the figure painter Mackensien. Her first exhibition (1899) met with a hostile response and in 1900 Paula went to Paris, spending some time at the Académie Colarossi and the École des Beaux Arts, but she returned to marry Otto Modersohn in 1901. France and Worpswede offered rival attractions, and she returned to Paris four times between 1903 and 1907. She had admired the Breton symbolists, especially van Gogh and Gauguin, and her magnificent studies of country women, such as *Old Peasant Woman* (1904), reveal their influence. Her last works were largely inspired by Cézanne whose work, she said, 'struck me like a thunderstorm'.` She painted still-life, landscapes, portraits such as that of her close friend Rilke (1906), and studies of women and children which are at once realistic and powerfully symbolic. Some of her own self-portraits continue the theme of maternity; tragically, after Otto had persuaded her to return to Worpswede in 1907 she gave birth to a daughter but died of a heart attack within a month. Her bold, solid paintings were regarded as crude and shocking in her lifetime but she has since become recognized as one of the most powerful figure painters of the 20th century.

G. Perry: *Paula Modersohn-Becker* (1980)

**Modjeska** [Modrzejewska], **Helena** (1844–1909). Polish-American actress. The daughter of a musician, she ran away from home in 1860 and formed a theatrical company with her husband Gustave Zimajer. She also appeared in provincial repertory and in 1868 joined a Warsaw company in Scribe's *Adrienne Lecouvreur*. In the same year she married a Polish aristocrat, Charles Chlapowski. She dominated Polish theatre in classical, contemporary and Shakesperian roles until 1876, when she and her husband emigrated to the USA. After attempting in vain to make a living on a ranch she returned to the stage. She learned English, toured the USA and revisited Poland in 1878–9. She starred in Schiller's *Maria Stuart*, in *Romeo and Juliet* and in other plays in London in 1881, and worked for much of the time in the UK until 1900. She played Shakespeare (whose plays she promoted in Poland and

elsewhere) in English, and was noted for her Ophelia and Lady Macbeth.

After a short visit to Poland she retired from the stage in 1903, giving a final farewell performance at the Metropolitan Opera House, New York, in 1905. A rival of ELEANORA DUSE and SARAH BERNHARDT, she was one of the finest tragediennes of the 19th century.

H. Modjeska: *Memoirs and Impressions* (1910)

**Moillon, Louise** (1615–75). French still-life painter. Born into a Protestant artist's family in Paris, she began painting while very young, probably under the tuition of her father (*d* 1619) and stepfather. An early specialist in studies of fruit and vegetables, her work is elegant and restrained, displaying a superb sense of composition with a lush use of colour. She occasionally included figures, as in *The Fruit Seller* (1629) or *At the Greengrocer* (1630). Although she is thought to have returned to painting late in life, after her three children had grown up, most of her work dates from before her marriage in 1640 to the merchant Etienne Girardot.

**Moll Cutpurse.** *See* FRITH, MARY.

**Molony, Helena** (1884–1967). Irish trade unionist. She joined the Nationalist movement, becoming a member of Maude Gonne's Daughters of Ireland in 1903; in 1908 she edited *The Irishwoman*, which had a policy of 'militancy, separatism and feminism'; and in 1909 she helped CONSTANCE MARKIEWICZ found the youth movement Na Fianna. For the next ten years she was also a member of the Abbey Theatre Company. In 1915 she became Secretary of the Irish Women Workers' Union and edited the national Labour journal. In 1916 she joined the Citizens' Army, taking part in the attack on Dublin Castle, for which she was imprisoned in Aylesbury gaol. After the treaty of 1921, like Maude Gonne, she took the Republican side. She became a union organizer and was President of the Irish Trade Union Congress until ill-health forced her to retire in 1945.

**Môme Moineau** [pseud. of Lucienne Benitz-Reixach] (1905–68). French cabaret singer. Born in a caravan, the daughter of travelling market-sellers, she was famous as a child flower-seller at Fouquet's on the Champs Elysées, Paris. In the 1920s the couturier Paul Poiret launched her as a cabaret singer and she acquired the name 'Môme Moineau' ('kid sparrow'), perhaps because her personality was more striking than her talent. Her meeting with her future husband was typically bizarre; feeling exhausted while visiting Coney Island, New York, she entered an unlocked car and fell asleep, ordering the owner on his return to take her back to the city. He was a wealthy Puerto Rican engineer, who not only drove her back but later married her. After her last show-business appearance in 1930 she lived in abandoned extravagance in Paris and the South of France. 'She tossed her hat into the crater of Etna, offered five million dollars to the man who would find a lock of hair during a cruise, challenged Onassis to a yacht race, and became cultural attaché at San Domingo' (*Times*, Obituary).

**Monroe, Marilyn** [pseud. of Norma Jean Baker] (1926–62). American film actress. Born in Los Angeles, she was the illegitimate daughter of Gladys Baker, a film-negative cutter who was often hospitalized for mental illness during Marilyn's childhood. Marilyn lived unhappily in various foster homes and orphanages, and was married at the age of 14. During World War II her husband, Jim Dougherty, was posted overseas and she worked in a munitions factory. She began posing for pin-up photographs for the armed forces and by 1946 was divorced and working as a successful model, appearing in national magazines. She was offered a screen test by Howard Hughes, but signed up with 20th Century-Fox for a year, was dropped, then took acting lessons and in 1948 moved to Columbia. She struggled on in small parts in 'B' feature films, moved back to 20th Century-Fox in 1950 and very gradually made a national reputation. Her new agent and devoted friend Johnny Hyde obtained parts for her in *The Asphalt Jungle* (Huston; 1950) and *All About Eve* (1950).

During the next four years she made over 20 films, which emphasized her husky voice, her figure and her blonde sexiness. The best were *Niagara* (1953) and *How to Marry a Millionaire* (1953). When she married the baseball star Joe di Maggio in 1954 and visited troops in Korea on their honeymoon and divorced him nine months later, she was treated as a temperamental goddess. She was already having problems at the studios, being constantly late, extremely nervous and dependent on her acting coaches. After making *The Seven Year Itch* (1955) she went to New York, where she studied at the Actors Studio. She was persuaded to return to Hollywood and made some of her best films: *Bus Stop* (1956), *The Prince and the Showgirl* (1957) and *Some Like it Hot* (1959). In 1956 she was converted to Judaism, before marring the playwright Arthur Miller. He wrote *The Misfits*, her last film, for her, but during its filming she was suffering from exhaustion ands intense depression, mixing alcohol and pills in a desperate attempt to keep going. She divorced Miller just before the film's opening in 1961, and soon collapsed in a psychiatric hospital. In 1962 Marilyn returned and tried to start work again on *Something's Got to Give*, but she was found dead from an overdose of sleeping pills in August. Her life and death have since been the subject of rumour, mystery, and commercial explitation and over 50 books, but her mixture of confident exhibitionism and childlike vulnerability defies analysis.

G. Steinem: *Marilyn* (1986)

**Montagu** [née Robinson], **Elizabeth** (1720–1800). English intellectual. Born in York, she was brought up by her grandmother, whose second husband was Librarian of Cambridge University. A precocious, unusually well-educated girl, she became a member of the literary group surrounding the Duchess of Portland. In 1742 she married Edward Montagu, 30 years her senior, and after the death of their only son in 1744 devoted herself to literary life. She gave informal parties (allowing 'blue stockings' rather than formal black silk), which developed into famous salons, at her home first in Hill Street, then Portman Street. After her husband's death in 1775 she became a noted patron of young writers and artists. Her only published works were three dialogues in Lyttleton's *Dialogues of the Dead* (1760), and an anonymous essay on the *Writings and Genius of Shakespeare*, replying to Voltaire, in 1769.

R. Blunt (ed.): *Mrs Montagu, 'Queen of the Blues', Her Letters and Friendships from 1762–1800* (1923)

**Montagu, Lady Mary Wortley** (1689–1762). English traveller, writer and feminist. The daughter of the 5th Earl of Kingston and his wife Lady Mary Fielding (sister of the novelist Henry Fielding), she rebelled against an arranged marriage and eloped with a Whig MP, Edward Wortley Montagu, accompanying him to Turkey when he was appointed Ambassador there from 1716 to 1718. After her return she wrote a series of brilliant letters based on her diary and correspondence, full of sympathy and interest in Turkish life and culture, which were published in 1763.

Back in England she held a salon in Twickenham, and was recognized as an elegant poet among her friends who included Alexander Pope and John Gay. She also wrote a play, *Simplicity*, in 1735. From 1736 to 1742 her life was dominated by her infatuation for the Italian scholar Francesco Algarotti, but after a disillusioning reunion with him in 1741 in Turin, she settled in Avignon for five years. She then lived in Brescia with her lover, Count Ugo Palazzi, until 1756, and only returned to England, following her husband's death in 1761, after a further five years in Venice.

She is remembered not only for her flamboyant and daring manner, and for her writing, but also for the introduction of the smallpox inoculation to England, learnt during her stay in Turkey.

R. Halsband: *The Life of Lady Mary Wortley Montagu* (1956)
———: *The Complete Letters of Lady Mary Wortley Montagu* (1965–7) [3 vols]

**Montespan.** *See* DE MONTESPAN.

**Montessori, Maria** (1870–1952). Italian educator. Born at Chiaravalle, Ancona, she was supported in her desire for education by her mother, against the wishes of her father, who was an army officer. She went to Rome in 1882 and enrolled for mathematics and engineering classes in 1884, but decided to study medicine, becoming Italy's first woman MD from the University of Rome in 1894.

After teaching in the university psychiatric unit, where she developed an interest in educating backward children, she was appointed Director of the Schola Ortofrenica in Rome, and managed to enter 'idiot' 8-year-olds for State examinations with superb results. From 1901 to 1904 she was engaged in research and held the Chair of Hygiene at the Scuola di Magistero Femminile. From 1904 to 1908 she was Professor of Anthropology at Rome University and also a government school inspector and practising doctor. In 1907 she took charge of the Casa dei Bambini, a crèche founded as part of improvements in the San Lorenzo slum district. Here she developed her methods of free discipline, with the teacher supplying materials and guiding children through a spontaneous learning process without formal rewards or punishments, in defiance of contemporary educational theories.

Her methods were described in *Metodo del pedagogica scientifica* (1909) and *Autoeducazione* (1912), and were tried with success in the UK, USA and elsewhere. During the 1920s and 1930s Maria travelled, lectured and organized training courses and colleges. Since her death her humane methods have become increasingly popular.

R. Kramer: *Maria Montessori* (1983)

**Montez, Lola** [pseud. of Maria Dolores Eliza Rosanna Gilbert] (1818–61). Irish dancer and adventuress. The daughter of a British army officer stationed in Limerick, she was educated at Montrose, Scotland, and in Paris. At the age of 19 her marriage to an elderly judge was arranged, but she eloped with Captain Thomas James whom she divorced five years later. Having studied dancing briefly, she appeared as a Spanish dancer in London, in other European capitals and at St Petersburg [now Leningrad]. In 1847 her dancing caught the attention of the elderly King Ludwig of Bavaria, who showered wealth upon her and made her Countess of Lansfield. She was highly influential and her liberal reforms caused great controversy; she was eventually banished in 1848.

Lola Montez continued to dance and to lecture, touring the USA and Australia. Credited with several lovers, she also married a Lieutenant Heald in 1849 and after his death a Mr Hull of California. Eventually she settled in New York and devoted the last two years of her life to charitable work.

L. Montez: *Lectures, including her autobiography* (1838)
A. Darling: *Lola Montez* (1972)

**Montpensier.** *See* DE MONTPENSIER.

**Montseny, Federica** (1905–). Spanish politician. A follower of Bakunin's theories, she was a fierce anti-royalist and anti-cleric in the 1930s and with Oliver, Peiro and Ascana became one of the most respected Anarchist leaders. After the establishment of the Government of the Popular Front in February 1936, she became Minister of Health, despite reservations on the part of President Azana, and she proved to be a highly competent minister. She continued to dominate the anarchist groups and during the confrontations on the streets of Barcelona between Communists and anarchists in May 1937, her appeals prevented any outbreak of violence. After the victory of Franco in 1939, she went to live in Toulouse, where she organized the anarchists in exile.

**Moodie, Susanna** (1803–85). Canadian pioneer writer. Susanna Strickland was born in Bungay, Suffolk. She and her sister began to write early, partly to support the family after their father's death in 1818. Their work appeared in ladies' journals, and Susanna's sketches of country life *La Belle Assemblée* appeared in 1827–8. In 1831 she moved to London, where she met her husband Lieutenant John Moodie, through their mutual work for the Anti-Slavery Society. She herself published the abolitionist tracts *The History of Mary Prince, a West Indian Slave* and *Negro Slavery Described by a Negro* (both 1831), and in the same year a volume of poems, *Enthusiasm*.

In 1832, with the first of their six children, the Moodies emigrated to Canada, where her brother Samual Strickland, who had worked for the Canada Company since 1825, was now a pioneer farmer near Douro. They settled first on a farm near Cobourg in Upper Canada, moving two years later to the backwoods area of Douro, where they cleared land and created a farm. After John Moodie helped to put down the 1837 Rebellion

he was appointed Sheriff, and in 1840 the family moved to Belleville. For the next four years Susanna wrote for the *Literary Garland*, including many sketches of pioneer life which later appeared in her famous book *Roughing it in the Bush; or, Forest Life in Canada* (1852) and in *Life in the Clearings versus the Bush* (1853), which described her changed life after the move to Belleville. She also wrote fiction, including the novel *Flora Lyndsay* (1854), and earlier, in 1847–8, she co-edited with her husband a popular, but high quality literary magazine for working people the *Victoria Magazine*.

Her sister, Catharine Parr Traill, also married a 'half-pay officer' and emigrated in 1832, to settle near Douro. She too became famous for her accounts of pioneer life, her *Female Emigrant's Guide*, and her works on natural history and plant life of the forest.

**Moody, Helen N. Wills** (1905–). American lawn tennis player. Helen's father, a doctor, taught her tennis and at the age of 14 she joined Berkeley Lawn Tennis Club and emulated William Johnston's heavy forehand drive. At 16 she entered the National Singles Championships; her defeat by Molla Mallory only sharpened her urge to succeed, which was always strong. The following year (1922) she gained the American singles title.

Between 1926 and 1938 she dominated the major tournaments at Wimbledon, Forest Hills and Paris, her 31 titles in these being challenged as a record only by Margaret Court, and her 8 Wimbledon singles wins standing as an all-time world record for either sex. Helen met SUZANNE LENGLEN, whom she had succeeded, only once; she lacked Suzanne's popular appeal but was imperturbable and expressionless, showing remarkable concentration and determination. In 1929 she married Fred Moody.

Great controversy was aroused in the 1933 Forest Hills final when her rival Helen Jacobs led 8–6, 3–6 and 3–0, and Helen Wills Moody abruptly withdrew from the match with an injured leg. Her next major championship was not until 1935 when she beat Helen Jacobs in a close Wimbledon final; in 1938 they met again at Wimbledon, where a similar injury situation was reversed but Helen Jacobs limped on to lose. Helen

Wills Moody then retired from major tennis and spent her time as a painter.

**Moore, Marianne** (1887–1972). American poet. Born in Kirkwood, Missouri, she was brought up in the home of her grandfather, a Presbyterian minister, and was educated at the Metzger Institute, Carlisle, Pennsylvania, and at Bryn Mawr College, graduating in 1909. After a course at Carlisle Commercial College, she taught stenography there until 1919. She then moved to New York, where she worked as a secretary until 1921, and as a librarian in 1921–5. She had met Pound, Williams and other imagist poets and contributed to *The Egoist* from 1915, her work appearing in several magazines and anthologies before the publication of *Poems* (1921), which was printed without her knowledge. Her *Observations* appeared in 1924, and from 1926 to 1929 she worked as acting Editor of *The Dial*, making it into an international and successful journal.

From the mid-1930s to the 1960s she published several collections, such as *Selected Poems* (1935), *The Pangolin* (1936), *What are Years* (1941), *Nevertheless* (1944), *Collected Poems* (1957), *O to be a Dragon* (1959), *The Arctic Ox* (1964) and *The Complete Poems* (1967). She also published essays and translated fairy-tales and French fables. Her verse is marked by precise, unexpected use of language and structure, by sharp observation of nature, and by a strong moral concern.

E. Phillips: *Marianne Moore* (1982)

**Morante, Elsa** (1918–85). Italian writer. Elsa Morante was born in Rome, where she lived for most of her life. She was married in 1941 to the author Alberto Moravia; they separated in 1962. Her first publication was a series of essays *Il Gioco Segreto* (1941), and her first novel, *Menzogna e Sortilegio* ('House of Liars') appeared in 1948, a tragic family saga of southern Italy, rich in symbolism, and written in an intensely poetic style. Her other novels include *L'Isola di Arturo* (1957), and *La Storia* (*History*, 1974), which is regarded as one of the major modern Italian novels, a passionate plea on behalf of the poor and oppressed, set in Italy during World War II. Her last novel, *Aracoeli* (1982), was a sensitive treatment of male homosexuality, and was also about a woman suffering from brain disease, based on her own illness of hydrocephalus at the end of her life. Morante also published short stories, and collections of poetry including *Alibi* (1958) and *Il Mondo Salvato dai Ragazzini* (1968).

**Morata, Olympia Fulvia** (1526–55). Italian scholar. The daughter of the scholar Pellegrino Morata, at the age of thirteen she was chosen by Duchess Renée of Ferrara to be the companion of Princess Anna, aged eight. She then went on to teach the other princesses, instructing them in Classics, geometry and geography as well as literature. After being persecuted at Duchess Renée's court because of her independent religious views, she fled to Germany with a Bavarian student of theology and philosophy and began teaching Classics at Heidelberg. Her Greek and Latin dialogues were published in the year of her death.

Morata was one of many humanist scholars who were prominent in Italy and Spain during the 16th century, including Tarquinia Molza (1542–1617), Isabella Cortesi (*d* 1561); Cassandra Fidele of Venice, and other better known figures such as ISOITA NOGAROLA, GASPARA STAMPA, VITTORIA COLONNA, and TULLIA D'ARAGONA.

**More, Hannah** (1745–1835). English poet, playwright, and religious writer. Born at Fishponds, Bristol; the fourth of five daughters of a schoolteacher, she was first a pupil then a teacher at her sisters' school. After an engagement lasting six years she received £200 annual allowance as compensation from her reluctant fiancé, a Mr Turner and went to London, where she became a hugely successful tragedian and a friend of Garrick. Her plays include *A Search after Happiness* (1762), *The Inflexible Captive* (1774), *Percy* (1777) and *The Fatal Falsehood* (1779). At one time she was engaged in a long dispute with another remarkable woman playwright Hannah Cousley (1743–1809), who accused her of plagiarism. She also became a friend of ELIZABETH MONTAGU and the 'Blue Stockings'. Her work gradually became more serious, with the *Sacred Dramas* (1782), the poems in *Bas Bleu* (1786) and the essay *Estimate of the Religion of the Fashionable World* (1790). She then turned to writing moral tracts for the poor, such as *Village Politics by Will Chip* (1793) and the *Cheap Repository Tracts* (1795–8), whose success led to the founding of the Religious Tract Society.

At William Wilberforce's suggestion she and her sister started a school in the rough mining district of the Mendips, Somerset, but she continued to write, producing a didactic novel *Coelebs in Search of a Wife* (1809) and *Moral Sketches* (1819). Although concerned to improve the standard of education for girls, in *Strictures on the Modern System of Female Education* (1799) her views on the position of women were conservative and she rejected MARY WOLLSTONECRAFT's approach as inappropriate to women.

M.A. Hopkins: *Hannah More and her Circle* (1947)

**Moreau, Jeanne** (1928–). French actress and film director. She was born in Paris, where her mother was a revue star. Jeanne trained at the Paris Conservatory of Dramatic Art and became a successful actress with the Comédie Française from 1948 and later with the Théâtre National Populaire. She made a few films in the early 1950s before her work for Louis Malle in *Ascenseur pour l'Echafaud/Frantic* (1957) and *Les Amants/ The Lovers* (1958) brought parts suited to her mobile talent. She then made *Les Liaisons dangereuses* for Vadim (1959), *Moderato Cantabile* for Peter Brook (1960), *La Notte* (Antonioni; 1961), *Jules et Jim* (Truffaut; 1961) and *La Baie des Anges/Bay of the Angels* (Demy; 1962). All were outstanding portraits of independent or isolated women. During the last 20 years she has starred in many films, including Welles's *Falstaff/Chimes at Midnight* (1966), MARGUERITE DURAS' *Nathalie Granger* (1973), Kazan's *The Last Tycoon* (1976) and Losey's *The Trout* (1982), *Pastoquet* (1986) and *La Nuit de L'Océan* (1987). She has also occasionally directed: *La Lumière* (1975) and *L'Adolescente/The Adolescent* (1979).

**Morgan, Robin** (1941–). American feminist, writer and theorist. Robin Morgan comes of a Jewish family: her father died when she was born and she was brought up by her mother. She describes herself as influenced in her teens by the Civil Rights movements of the 1950s, and she herself became involved in the protest campaigns and the movement to create alternative life-styles in the 1960s. In the mid-1960s she worked as a lexicographer for a publishing house and also did freelance editing and proof-reading. She then married the poet Kenneth Pitchford. An early member of the Women's Liberation Movement, Robin Morgan edited *Sisterhood is Powerful* in 1970, an anthology of writings from the movement which was to have an international impact. She also wrote poetry, notable for its militancy, publishing collections such as *Monster* (1972) and *Lady of the Beasts* (1976). In 1978 she published *Going too Far: the Personal Chronicles of a Feminist* and then *The Anatomy of Freedom* (1982).

Robin Morgan was one of a generation of radical feminists in America in the 1970s, remarkable for their energy and the diversity of their approach. They include MARY DALY, Jo Freeman (writer of *The Bitch Manifesto*, 1970, and *The Politics of Women's Liberation*, 1975), Andrea Dworkin (*Woman Hating*, 1974, and *Pornography*, 1981), Ti-Grace Atkinson (*Amazon Odyssey*, 1974), Charlotte Bunch (editor of *The Furies*, 1971, and founder of *Quest: A Feminist Quarterly*, 1974), Susan Brownmiller (*Against Our Will*, 1975), and Susan Griffin (*Woman and Nature*, 1978; *Rape*, 1979; *Pornography and Silence*, 1981). Robin Morgan herself has focused less on issues of sexuality and separatism than on active politics and solidarity internationally, as shown in her anthologies *The New Woman* and *Sisterhood is Global* (1984). Her first novel, *Dry Your Smile*, was published in 1987.

**Morgner, Irmtraud** (1933–). East German writer, socialist and feminist. She was born in Chemnitz (now Karl-Marx-Stadt), the daughter of a train-driver. It was her third novel, *Hochzeit in Konstantinopel* (1968), which established her reputation, particularly in West Germany, as one of the most promising young writers of the Democratic Republic. Her subsequent writings increasingly abandoned the portrayal of contemporary socialist reality in favour of tales of lucid imagination and subversive fantasy, and thus heralded a new era in GDR literature. In her sixth novel, *Leben und Abenteuer der Trobadora Beatriz* (1974), acclaimed as the most important German-language novel of the 1970s, as well as in a further novel *Amanda. Ein Hexenroman* (1983), she enfolds her exuberant tales of wondrous events within a proliferation of formal devices, complex viewpoints and linguistic experimentation in such a way as to place her firmly in the vanguard of international modernism and feminism.

**Morison, Harriet** (1862–1925). New Zealand feminist and labour movement leader. The daughter of an Irish tailor, she began work in the garment trade in Dunedin, and helped to found the first women's union in 1889, the Tailoresses' Union, becoming its Secretary the following year, and campaigning for improved pay, conditions and social and medical services. At the same time she prompted the foundation of a short-lived Domestic Servants' Union. She was also a keen suffragette and temperance worker. She became a factory inspector in 1906, and worked for the Labour Department as head of the Women's Employment Bureau (1908–13). As well as working with the labour movement, she was deeply involved with the Unitarian Church, being chairwoman of the church committee for many years, and one of the first women to preach in New Zealand.

**Morisot, Berthe** (1841–95). French painter. Born in Bourges into a family of the upper bourgeoisie, encouraged by her mother she took drawing lessons as a child and, with her sister Edma, studied under the painter Guichard in 1858 and Corot after 1861. She exhibited her landscapes and portraits in the Salon of 1864–74. In 1868 she met Edouard Manet. They influenced each other's work: she encouraged his use of lighter colours and persuaded him to work outdoors; he influenced her to a firmer outline and brushwork. But she at times resented his patronage and in 1874, when she married his younger brother Eugène, she went against his advice and that of Guichard, and exhibited in the Impressionist exhibition of that year. She continued to identify her approach with the Impressionists and although critics persisted in describing her and MARY CASSAT as 'feminine Impressionists' she was a leading spirit in the movement. Her letters to Edma, who gave

up painting after her marriage in 1869, reveal the independence and courage she required to reconcile her roles as woman, mother (she was devoted to her daughter Julie) and artist. Her work was shown throughout the 1880s in Paris, London, Brussels and Boston and she held a major solo exhibition in 1892, the year of her husband's death.

D. Rouart: *Berthe Morisot and her Circle* (1952)
——: *The Correspondence of Berthe Morisot* (1957)

**Morris, Jan** (1926–) British historian and travel writer. Jan Morris was born James Morris, but after education at Oxford, service in the British Army and experience as a foreign correspondent on the London *Times* and *The Guardian*, completed a change of sexual role and has lived since 1974 as a woman. Her best-known books, written either as James or as Jan Morris, include the *Pax Britannica* trilogy about the decline of the British Empire, *Venice, Oxford, Spain, The Matter of Wales, Manhattan '45, Hong Kong,* the autobiographical *Conundrum,* six volumes of collected travel essays and the fictional *Last Letters from Hav,* which was short-listed for the Booker Prize in 1986. She is a Fellow of the Royal Society of Literature and lives in Wales.

**Morrison** [née Wofford], **Toni (Chloe Anthony)** (1931–). American novelist. Born in Lorain, on the Ohio uplands, she was educated at Howard University (1949–53) and obtained an MA from Cornell University in 1955. She then taught literature at the Southern University (1955–57) and at Howard University until 1965, when she moved to New York and became a publisher's editor with Random House. She has remained in publishing but continues to take seminars and to teach, and was an Associate Professor of the State University of New York (1971–72). Morrison's novels deal with the dreams and tensions within black communities and cliques, poor people living on the borders of the South as in *The Bluest Eye* (1970) or *Sula* (1973), northerners seeking their past as in the best-selling *Song of Solomon* (1976), or rich New Yorkers with connections in the Caribbean, as in *Tar Baby* (1979). Her latest novel, *Beloved* (1987), returned to history, set immediately after the emancipation of the slaves. Her style is dense, allusive, idiomatic, witty but often shocking in the cool depiction of violence and inner turmoil. She is married with two sons.

**Moses** [née Robertson], **Anna (Mary)** (Grandma Moses) (1860–1961). American painter of Scottish-Irish descent. Born on a farm in Washington County, New York State, one of ten children, she worked in the county as a 'hired girl', and in 1887 married Thomas Moses. They farmed in Virginia, returning to New York State in 1905; they had ten children, of whom five died in infancy.

After Thomas died in 1927 'Grandma Moses' began painting as a hobby. Her work was discovered by a New York collector who was touring the area in 1938 and included in an exhibition, 'Contemporary Unknown American Painters', at the Museum of Modern Art in 1939. In 1940 she had her first solo exhibition, and her vivid, precise studies of country life brought her international fame. She received numerous awards and exhibited in over 20 shows in the USA, Canada, and Europe, including the UK. Credited with around 2000 pictures, she continued to paint until her death.

A.M. Moses: *My Life's History* (1952)

**'Mother Ross'.** *See* CAVANAGH, KIT.

**Mott, Lucretia (Coffin)** (1793–1880). American reformer and feminist. Born in Nantucket, Massachusetts, where her father was master of a whaling ship, after moving to the mainland in 1804 she was educated in a Quaker school at Poughkeepsie, NY, where she later taught. In 1811 she married James Mott and moved to Philadelphia, and at the end of the decade became a Quaker minister. An active abolitionist, she founded the Philadelphia Female Anti-Slavery Society in 1833 and attended the Anti-Slavery Convention in London 1840, where the refusal to allow women delegates a seat brought her into contact with ELIZABETH LADY STANTON. During the next few years she founded and ran the Philadelphia Association for the Relief and Employment of Poor Women, and in 1848 joined Stanton in organizing the first women's rights convention in Seneca Falls.

The most prominent woman in the abolition movement, she sheltered fugitive slaves, organized aid during the Civil War, and continued to fight for freedmen's rights after it ended. During the 1860s she also continued her fight for women's rights, presiding over the 1866 Equal Rights Convention. She attempted to reconcile the different wings of the suffrage movement until her death.

M. Bacon: *Valiant Friend* (1980)

**Mozart** [née Weber], **Constanze** (1762–1842). She is remembered as the wife of Mozart, whom she married (against strong opposition) in 1782; after his death she played a considerable role in ensuring that his reputation would endure. She and her two sisters (Aloysia and Josepha WEBER) were all sopranos, and Constanze was also a pianist. She bore Mozart six children, of whom only two survived beyond infancy. Their last years together were difficult and impoverished, but on a pension of one third of Mozart's salary she managed to improve her position through arranging performances of his works, singing in several of them herself. Further business acumen is evident in her negotiations with the publisher André, to whom she sold Mozart's manuscripts in 1800, resulting in the groundwork for the catalogue on which subsequent Mozart scholarship has been based. In 1809 she married Georg Nikolaus Nissen, who began a biography of Mozart the following year. On his death she was left to see it through to publication (1828); it remained the main source of Mozart studies for many years.

**Mozzoni, Anna Maria** (1837–1920). Italian socialist and feminist. Born in Milan of wealthy, upper-class parents, she came from a liberal, patriotic and secular background. From the 19th-century nationalist Risorgimento she developed her own concept of the *risorgimento delle donna* ('the renaissance of women'). After a period with the Mazzinian movement she left to join the developing socialist and workers' movement.

Mozzoni emerged as an early theoretician and activist in the construction of a women's movement in Italy. She founded a league in defence of women's interests, La Lega promotrice degli interessi femminili, in Milan; she argued that paid work was fundamental to the development of women; she fought against all manifestations of discrimination; and she argued that the women's question should be a part of the working-class movement. Concerned for women's legal status, she noted that the new Italian state denied women the civil rights won for them in the 1789 revolution, and as a result she drew up an 18-point reform which incorporated work, education, family and political rights. She fought for the right to vote, presenting her last petition in 1907. She also wrote and campaigned on matters concerning public morality – particularly prostitution, education and culture. Mozzoni argued that women were the one protection humanity had and would continue to have against men's periodic thirst for blood and destruction. She died in Rome. Her writings included *La liberazione delle donne* and *L'indegna schiavitù*.

**M'rabet, Fadéla** (1935–). Algerian feminist. Born in Constantine, Algeria, she came from a very religious family with a long tradition of relationship to the *'ulama* or elders of Islam. Her father was involved in Algerian radio and she went to work there after graduating from the University of Algiers; she was in charge of a woman's programme. In her first book, *La femme algérienne*, she wrote about the reactions of women she had interviewed immediately after the revolution and the subsequent granting of independence. The book appeared in 1962 and *Les algériennes* appeared shortly afterwards. *L'Algérie des illusions* was published in 1973. An active spokeswoman on feminism, she later lived in Paris.

**Muir, Jean (Elizabeth)** (?1931–). English designer. Educated in Bedford, Jean Muir began her career as a sales girl and sketcher at Liberty's in 1950 and in 1956 moved to Jaeger where she became responsible for the dress and knitwear collections. In 1961 she started a new company, Jane and Jane, but left in 1966 to work under her own name with her husband Harry Lenckert, whom she had married in 1955, as her co-director and financial manager. Her elegant, gentle, flowing designs have continued to win awards. She opened an office in New York in 1974. In 1985 Jean Muir joined the Coats Viyella group of factories. She has served on several design committees, including the Design Council since 1983, and in 1984 became a Trustee of the Victoria and Albert Museum. Winner of the Chartered Society of Designers Medal 1987, she remains Britain's most distinguished woman designer, recognized as such in Europe and America.

**Muller, Mary** (1820–1902). New Zealand feminist. A pioneer in the women's rights movement, Mary Muller was married to a magistrate in Nelson, and related to the local newspaper proprietor. She wrote anonymously, as 'Femina' in the Nelson paper, her passionate articles in favour of emancipation being reprinted nationally, and in 1869 she published *An Appeal to the Men of New Zealand*, which demanded 'Why, when the broad road of progress is cleared for so many human beings, is the Juggernaut car of prejudice still to be driven on, crushing the crowds of helpless women beneath the wheels?'

She was congratulated by J.S. Mill, who sent her a copy of *On the Subjection of Women*, but so disapproved of by her husband that she had to work in secret. She became a corresponding member of a London suffrage society, campaigned for reforms such as the 1884 Married Women's Property Act, and tried, through personal persuasion, to influence leading politicians of the day. When suffrage was eventually achieved in 1894, she wrote to KATHARINE SHEPPARD, saying that her life had 'not been all in vain'.

**Munter, Gabriele** (1877–1962). German Expressionist painter. Born in Berlin, she studied art at Düsseldorf Ladies' Art School, and after visiting the USA for three years she attended the Munich School for Women Artists in 1901, and then the progressive Phalanx School, run by Kandinsky with whom she lived until 1917. They exhibited together in Paris, and travelled across Europe, eventually settling in Murnau in the Bavarian Alps. They were co-founders of the New Artists Association of Munich in 1909, and two years later they both exhibited in the first 'Blue Rider' show organized by Kandinsky and Marc which illustrated their theories of the expressive potential of colour. Accepted, though attacked, as part of the German avant garde, during World War I they left for Switzerland and then Stockholm. Kandinsky returned to the USSR, where he married. Munter turned from her brilliant colour-work to develop her portrait style, concentrating on studies of women. She continued to paint, developing a new, meditative style during the 1930s, but her most original work was done in her early period.

**Murasaki, Shikibu** (*c*978–1030). Japanese novelist, diarist and poet. Her father, a member of the ruling Fujiwara family, was a government official and a provincial governor. She studied with her brother, although this was unusual for a woman, and about 998 she married her cousin Fujiwara no Nobutaka, a member of the Imperial guard. She had children and was happy, but her husband died and when her father was posted far from the Kyoto Court he found her a position with the Empress Akiko.

Her chief work is the world's earliest surviving long novel, the famous *Genji monogatari* ('The Tale of Genji'), in 54 books. Probably written over several years for reading aloud at court, it retails the romantic and adventurous life of a prince, and then of his son, in a reflective, poetic style. It has been called the finest work of Japanese literature and one of the greatest novels of the world. She also wrote a diary of court life between 1007 and 1010, full of lively descriptions of contemporaries, and was well known as a poet.

A.E. Omori and K. Doi: *Diaries of Court Ladies of Old Japan* (1920)

**Murdoch,** Dame **Iris (Jean)** (1919–). British novelist and philosopher. Although born in Dublin, she was educated in London at the Froebel Educational Institute, then at Badminton School and at Somerville College, Oxford. She was an Assistant Principal at the Treasury from 1942 to 1944, and an Administration Officer with UNRRA from 1944 to 1946. She took a philosophy studentship at Newnham College, Cambridge and became a Fellow and Tutor in Philosophy at St Anne's College, Oxford in 1948. In 1956 she married the scholar and critic John Bayley.

Her first publication was philosophical: *Sartre, Romantic Rationalist* (1953), but beginning with *Under the Net* (1954) and *The Flight from the Enchanter* (1955) she started to write novels, most of which could best be described as 'gothic intellectual'. Many, such as *A Severed Head* (1961) or *A Fairly Honourable Defeat* (1970), deal with problems of commitment and loyalty in an apparently irrational world. She has received several awards and in 1978 she won the Booker Prize with *The Sea, the Sea*. Her recent works include *The Philosopher's Pupil* (1983), *The Good Apprentice* (1985) and *The Book and The Brotherhood* (1987). She has continued to write philosophical works such as *The Sovereignty of Good* (1970) and *Acastos* (1986) and has had some plays performed, including *Art and Eros* which was produced at the National Theatre in 1980.

**Murphy** [née Ferguson], **Emily (Gowan)** (1868–1933). Canadian feminist, lawyer and writer. Born in Cooksville, Ontario, into a leading family, she was educated at Bishop Strachan School, Toronto. In 1887 she married Arthur Murphy, Rector of Chatham, Ontario, and a travelling missionary, and they had two daughters. In 1904 they moved to Swan River, Manitoba, and then to Edmonton, Alberta, where Emily became a leading social reformer, campaigning against drunkenness and rural poverty, and working for the suffrage movement, especially for the legal rights of women and for the establishment of a special court to hear women's evidence in 'difficult cases' such as divorce or sexual assault. In 1916 the Women's Court was established in Edmonton and she became the first woman magistrate in the British Empire, attached to the juvenile court. Alice Jamieson was then appointed to a similar position.

When she came to pass sentence on her first case the defence lawyer challenged her authority, claiming 'you are not even a person', since under a British act of 1876 women were vulnerable to legal penalties but did not have legal rights or privileges. Her position was however upheld by the Supreme Court of Alberta in 1916 and she then campaigned for women to be admitetd to the Senate. After a quorum of five women including Nellie Mcclung and LOUISE MCKINNEY had petitioned the Government, the Supreme Court finally decided in 1928 that 'women, children, criminals and idiots are not legally "persons"'. In 1929 a final appeal to the British Privy Council resulted in the ruling that 'persons' covers both sexes and that women were eligible for seats in the Senate. In 1931 she resigned her judicial post, but remained a supervisor of Alberta's prisons and asylums.

Emily was also a writer, keeping a diary on which she based *Janey Canuck Abroad* (1901), a satirical account of the splendours of England and Germany, detailing slum conditions and exploitations as well as European affectations. She also provided vivid accounts of life in Manitoba, *Janey Canuck goes West* (1910), and Alberta, *Open Trails* (1912) and *Seeds of Pine* (1914), and in 1922 wrote a study of drug addiction in *The Black Candle*.

B.H. Saunders: *Emily Murphy, Crusader* (1945)

**Murray** [Lindsay], **Lilian** (1871–1959). English dentist. Born in London, educated at Camden School for Girls and the North London Collegiate School, she defied the insistence of her teacher, FRANCES MARY BUSS, that she should become a teacher of the deaf and dumb, and left school in 1889. Mrs Buss apparently threatened to stop her entering any other career, to which she replied without thinking 'You cannot prevent me from being a dentist'. She was apprenticed for three years in London, but was not even allowed to enter the building of the National Dental Hospital. The Dean, who interviewed her in the street, suggested she try the Edinburgh Dental Hospital, and despite considerable prejudice against her she became the first British woman licentiate in dentistry, in 1895.

Ten years later she married her teacher, the dentist Robert Lindsay, and they practised jointly in Edinburgh. She was the first woman to be a branch president, and the first to be Presient of the British Dental Association, and was a regular contributor to the *British Dental Journal*.

**Murray, Margaret (Alice)** (1863–1963). British scholar. She was born in Calcutta into an Anglo-Irish family with a long family connection with India; her father was a merchant, and her mother a missionary. She was educated in England, lived in Bonn between the ages of 10 and 16 and went back to India several times before she was 23. When she was 17 she was the only white woman nursing in Calcutta General Hospital. In 1886 she returned to England permanently and became a keen feminist and suffragette.

In 1894 she became a student of Egyptology at University College London under Sir Flinders Petrie. Her ability was so apparent that she was immediately assigned research on property inheritance in the early period and in 1895 she took over the teaching of elementary hieroglyphics. She became a lecturer for Oxford University extension courses in 1899 and catalogued antiquities in leading museums. After the death of her mother she settled permanently in London. She taught at University College from 1902, becoming assistant in 1909, lecturer in 1921, and Assistant Professor in 1922. Although she joined Petrie briefly at Abydos and later excavated in Malta, she was effectively in charge of the teaching in London while he was abroad.

Margaret Murray was also interested in folklore and her influential, and now controversial, studies *The Witch-Cult in Western Europe* and *The God of the Witches* were published in 1921. She became a Fellow of the Royal Anthropological Institute in 1926. In 1932 she retired from University College, undertook excavations in Palestine and devoted herself to writing. She published numerous books and articles on Egypt including *The Splendour that was Egypt*, written when she was 86. From 1953 to 1955 she was President of the Folklore Society. She worked until her death, her last books, *The Genesis of Religion* and her autobiography, appearing in 1963.

M. Murray: *My First Hundred Years* (1963)

**Murrell, Christine** (1874–1933). English doctor. Christine Murrell was the first woman to be elected to membership of the General Medical Council of Great Britain (1933). She gained her MD in 1905 from London University and went into general practice, becoming a member of the St Marylebone Health Society. During World War I she served in the Women's Emergency Corps. In 1924 she was elected to the Council of the British Medical Association and became President of the

Medical Women's Federation in 1925. Her book *Womanhood and Health* was published in 1923. She opposed the Factories Bill of 1927 which provided protective measures for women workers.

C. St John: *Christine Murrell, M.D.* (1935)

**Musgrave, Thea** (1928–). Scottish composer and conductor. She studied at Edinburgh University (1947–50) and then went to Paris for further instruction from Nadia Boulanger; during her student years she was awarded the Donald Francis Tovey Prize and the Lili Boulanger Memorial Prize. From 1958 to 1965 she taught in the extramural department of London University. She has since lectured at many British and American universities, including a period as Visiting Professor at the University of California at Santa Barbara (1970). Her activities have extended to serving on many committees, for example the music panel for the Arts Council of Great Britain and the executive committee of the Composers' Guild. In 1973 she was made an honorary Fellow of New College, Cambridge. In 1987 she became a lecturer at Queen's University, New York.

Her music has reached a wide public through many broadcasts and performances at major international music festivals. As a conductor she has worked with orchestras in the UK and the USA, giving the premières of several of her own works. Many have been specially commissioned, notably the operas *The Voice of Ariadne* (1973, Royal Opera House, based on Henry James's *The Last of the Valerii*); *Mary, Queen of Scots* (1977, Scottish Opera); *A Christmas Carol* (1979, Virginia Opera), for which she herself adapted Dickens's novel as libretto; and *Harriet, the Woman Called Moses* (1985, Royal Opera House and Virginia Opera), based on the life of HARRIET TUBMAN. Commissions from the BBC include the Viola Concerto (1973) and *Orfeo* (1975) for flute and pre-recorded tape (or flute and 15 strings), with optional solo dancer, and *An Occurrence at Owl Creek Bridge* (1981), a half-hour radio opera. Earlier works, such as the ballet *A Tale for Thieves* (1953) and the chamber opera *The Abbot of Drimrock* (1955), are eclectic in style; since the 1960s her music has progressed through serial techniques (as in *Triptych*, 1960, for tenor and orchestra) to

a personal idiom that she has described as 'dramatic-abstract', exemplified in the orchestral *Night Music* (1969), the concertos for clarinet (1967) and horn (1971) and such chamber and instrumental pieces as *Space Play* (1974) for wind quintet and string quartet. She collaborated with Richard Rodney Bennett on *Moving into Aquarius* (1984), an occasional piece written as an 80th birthday tribute to Michael Tippett.

She is married to Peter Mark, who has presented several of her works with the Virginia Opera Association, of which he is conductor and general director.

**Mussey, Ellen Spencer** (1850–1936). American lawyer. Born in Ohio, the tenth of 11 children, she was expected to teach in the school on her family's farm from the age of 12. After her father's death she was educated at various schools, living with different brothers and sisters and eventually settling in Washington, DC, where she worked in her brother Henry's Spencerian Business College. In 1871 she married an older man, General Reuben Mussey, and during his illness in 1876 she began helping in his law office, remaining there permanently. In 1892, after Reuben's death, she applied unsuccessfully to study law at the National University and at Columbia, but was admitted to the Bar by oral examination in 1893. She became an expert in commercial and international law, being counsel to the Norwegian and Swedish legations for 25 years. With two other women lawyers she started a class for women pupils in 1896, and after her students were refused admission by Columbia she opened her own Washington College of Law. She was a member of leading women's suffrage organizations and influenced the passing of legislation on property rights and equal guardianship. In 1910 she joined the North American Women's Suffrage Association. Her last work before retirement through ill-health was as Chairwoman of the National Council of Women, on the committee on the legal status of women (1917) and in drafting the bill on citizenship rights passed in 1922.

M. Rottier: 'Ellen Spencer Mussey', *Maryland Historical Magazine* (1974)

**Myerson, Bess** (1924–) American politician.

The daughter of Russian immigrants to the Bronx, Bess was the first Jewish girl to win the Miss America contest, in 1945, winning a scholarship to study classical music. Her experience of anti-semitism at college led to a speaking tour for the Anti-Defamation League. After a brief career as a concert pianist, including a performance at Carnegie Hall, she made her name in television. She married the wealthy lawyer Arnold Grant, (she has since re-married and divorced), and in 1969 was appointed New York Consumer Affairs Commissioner by Mayor John Lindsay, surprising many by her legal expertise, and winning support for tough local legislation. She campaigned for Mayor Koch in 1977, stood unsuccessfully as a Democratic candidate for Senate in 1980 and went on to become Cultural Affairs Commissioner for New York in 1982, showing herself a formidable campaigner for the arts. In April 1987 she resigned, after refusing to testify against construction boss, Andy Capasso, her constant companion.

**Myrdal, Alva** (1902–86). Swedish politician. She was born in Uppsala, where she was educated and took a degree before attending other universities in Stockholm and Geneva. Her early studies of population problems and economic conditions were translated into English as *Nation and Family* and *Women's Two Roles* (written with Vida Klein). In 1936 she founded the Social Pedagogical Institute, Stockholm, which she directed until 1948, promoting progressive educational theories and reforms in child care. At the same time she headed a government commission on women's work and was Chairman of the Federation of Business and Professional Women. In 1949, a member of the International Civil Service, she went to New York as Principal Director of the Department of Social Sciences at Unesco.

From 1955 to 1960 she acted as Swedish Ambassador to India, Burma and Ceylon, and then worked for the foreign office. She was elected to the Swedish Upper House in 1962, heading the delegation to the UN Disarmament Committee. She became a cabinet minister in 1962, being Minister for Disarmament 1966–73 and for Church affairs 1969–73, and lectured widely. Her books include *The Game of Disarmament* (1976) and *War, Weapons and Everyday Violence* (1977). She married the economist Gunnar Myrdal in 1924. Together they won the German Peace Prize in 1970, Alva was awarded the Albert Einstein Peace Prize in 1981, and she shared the Nobel Prize for Peace in 1982.

# N

**Naidu** [née Chattopadhyaya], **Sarojini** (1879–1949). Indian poet, feminist and politician. Born in Hyderabad into a Brahmin family noted for its learning, she passed the matriculation examination for the University of Madras at the age of 12. She was sent to England at 16 and studied at Kings College, London, and Girton College, Cambridge, also travelling in Europe, especially Italy. In 1898 she married Dr G.R. Naidu, against family disapproval because this broke the Brahminical caste. He became Principal Medical Officer and in 1908 she worked with him in organizing flood relief in Hyderabad.

A writer from the age of 11, she achieved fame with her lyrical poetry published in the collections *The Bird of Time* (1912), *The golden Threshold* (1916) and *The broken Wing* (1917). During these years she also toured India as a lecturer. She became increasingly involved in the independence movement. In 1924 she went to investigate the condition of Indians working in East and South Africa and in 1925 she was the second woman to be President of the Indian National Congress, the first being ANNIE BESANT. In 1928 she visited the UK and the USA, where she was received as 'The Nightingale of India' and spoke on behalf of the nationalist campaign. The same year she chaired the All India Conference for Educational Reform. In 1930 she took over the Anti-Salt Law campaign when Gandhi was imprisoned, and was arrested after leading a raid on a salt depot on the Gujerat coast. She was imprisoned again in 1932 and 1942 after years of campaigning, and in 1946 she took part in the discussion about independence with the British Cabinet mission. She died three years later, at Lucknow.

P. Sengupta: *Sarojini Naidu: a Biography* (1966)

**Nandi** (c1760–1827). Zulu queen. A member of the Langeni tribe, she became pregnant by the Zulu chief Senzangakhoma, and her son Shaka, named in disgrace after an intestinal beetle (since the couple were within forbidden degrees of kinship), was to become one of the greatest Zulu chiefs. After six years she left the Zulu and returned to her own tribe who received her reluctantly, and then evicted her during the 1802 famine. She then stayed with the Mtetwa people until 1815, when Shaka claimed the Zulu chieftainship on his father's death. Nandi then ruled as Queen Mother, known as Ndlorukazi ('The Great She Elephant'), exercising considerable power.

When Nandi died Shaka instituted a terrible period of public mourning, which involved hysterical scenes in which summary executions were followed by the general massacre of an estimated 7000 people. Her young handmaidens were placed with her in the grave, and 12,000 soldiers were set to guard it for a year. Shaka decreed that no crops were to be planted, milk was to be poured away and all pregnant women were to be killed. After three months Nandi's old friend Mnkabayi, Senzangakhoma's sister, engineered a coup by which another of her nephews, Dingane, overthrew Shaka.

Nandi and Mnkabayi were typical of the powerful Zulu princesses of the period. A further example is another sister of Senzangakhoma, Mawa, who acted as a royal representative during the reigns of Shaka and Dingane, but after supporting an unsuccessful coup in 1840 fled to Natal with several thousand Zulus and arranged their permanent settlement there.

**Naqi'a.** *See* NITOCRIS.

**Nation, Carry (Amelia Moore)** (1846–1911). American militant temperance reformer. She was born in Garrard County, Kentucky. Her father lost most of his fortune in the Civil War and her mother suffered increasing delusions. Lacking formal education, she was deeply impressed by the evangelical crusade of the Church of the Disciples of Christ, and also by the beliefs of the negro slaves among whom she grew up.

In 1867 she married a doctor, Charles Gloyd, and settled in Montana. A chronic alcoholic, he died within a year. She then lived with her baby daughter and mother-in-law, working as a school-teacher until in 1877 she married an older man, David Nation. In 1879 they moved to Texas, where David unsuccessfully tried to run a plantation and engage in local politics. Living in Medicine Lodge, Carry plunged into philanthropy and developed a strange, unique religious creed. Her experience with Gloyd had left her with a hatred of alcohol and in 1892, as co-founder of the local branch of the Women's Christian Temperance Union, she launched a powerful emotional campaign which closed down all the town's illicit saloons. Her campaign spread across the state, her tactics including weeping, hymn-singing, and smashing bottles and furniture with an axe, which she called the 'hatchetation of joints'. She was frequently arrested but extended her activities to New York, Washington, Pittsburgh, San Francisco and other large cities, financing her mission by lecturing and selling souvenir hatchets, and by stage appearances, pamphlets and the sale of her autobiography written in 1904. Increasingly ridiculed and internationally notorious, she toured the UK in 1908. Her husband eventually divorced her for desertion. At the end of her life she became mentally confused and retired to a farm in the Ozark Mountains in Arkansas.

H. Ashbury: *Carry Nation* (1929)

**Navratilova, Martina** (1957–). Czechoslovakian American tennis player. Martina's childhood in Pornice, near Prague, was a disturbed one: her father left home when she was very young, and later committed suicide. She grew up extremely independent and determined, becoming one of the young stars of the Czech Tennis Federation. Resenting their restrictions on travel and earnings, she defected at the age of 18, while competing at the US Open in New York in 1975. She was awarded American citizenship in 1981 and has returned to Czechoslovakia only once, with the American team in 1986. Since turning professional Martina has won all the major titles in the USA, Australia and Europe, becoming world champion in 1980, setting the professional women's record for consecutive wins in 1984, winnng her 100th title in 1985 and equalling the record of eight Wimbledon singles titles held by HELEN WILLS MOODY in 1987. She has been almost equally successful in women's and mixed doubles, and was President of the Women's Tennis Association from 1979 to 1980.

Her close relationship with novelist Rita Mae Brown from 1978 to 1981 caused a furore, and led her to a brave open stand on lesbian issues. Her private life seemed at one point to arouse as much interest as tennis, and attention still focuses on her large entourage, her intensive fitness training and her vast earnings – she has won over $9 million in prize money, more than any other athlete, male or female. Much of this went towards establishing the Martina Foundation in 1983, for under-privileged children worldwide. A keen skier, she was featured in the skiing film *Steep and Deep* (1985).

M. Navratilova: *Being Myself* (1985)

**Nayar, Shushila** (1914–). Indian doctor. Born in Gujarat, Pakistan, she was educated at Lahore College for women, Lady Hardinge Medical College, Delhi, and at the Johns Hopkins University in the USA. A supporter of Mahatma Gandhi, and his medical attendant, she was a member of the Independence movement and was imprisoned from 1942 to 1944. After Independence she continued to work as a senior Medical Officer, but became increasingly interested in politics and was Minister of Health, Rehabilitation and Transport in Delhi State, and Speaker of the Delhi Legislative Assembly from 1952 to 1956. In 1957 she became a member of the Lok Sabha (the lower house of the Indian parliament), and was later appointed Minister of Health (1962–7). She lost her seat in 1971. She remained a highly influential figure in the medical world of India and from 1969 was Director of the Mahatma Gandhi Institute of

Medical Sciences, where she was Professor of Preventive and Social Medicine. She was also Secretary of the Leprosy Board of the Mahatma Gandhi Memorial Trust and worked at the Kasturba Hospital, New Delhi.

**Nazimova, Alla** (1879–1945). Russian actress. Trained in Moscow, she became the principal actress of a St Petersburg [now Leningrad] theatre in 1904, and then toured Europe and the USA. In 1906 she played her first English-speaking part, in Ibsen's *Hedda Gabler* in New York. She remained there, specializing in Ibsen roles, and established her own Nazimova Theatre in 1910. A passionate, subtle performer, she also worked in films such as *Salome* (1923), but returned to the theatre, acting with the Civic Repertory and the Theatre Guild in plays by Ibsen, Chekhov, Turgenev and O'Neill.

**Necker, Suzanne** (1739–1817). Swiss writer and philanthropist. Born at Crassier, in the Vaud, the daughter of a Protestant minister, Suzanne Curchod married the banker and politician Jacques Necker in 1764. In Paris she established a famous salon, frequented by leading writers and poetical thinkers such as Diderot, Buffon, Marmontel and Grimm, where her daughter, later MADAME DE STAËL, shone precociously. A strict Calvinist, Suzanne Necker was also an active, energetic reformer. She visited Paris hospitals and studied medicine and architecture in order to improve the appalling conditions. In 1776 she converted a convent into a 120-bed hospital, clean and efficiently administered, in the rue de Sèvres. The hospital took her name in 1820 and remained an important centre of paediatric medicine and research. She proved that the exercise was cost-effective as well as humanitarian in her book *Mémoire sur l'établissement des hospices* (1786), and she also wrote other works on different subjects but with equally strong opinions, including *Des inhumations precipitées* (1790) and *Réflexions sur le divorce* (1794).

**Nefertiti** (*fl* 14th century BC). Egyptian queen. The daughter of Queen Tiy and Amenhotep III and wife of Akhenaton (who raised her to considerable power) she first promoted and then rejected the new religion propounded by her husband, which elevated the sun-god Aten. She brought up and educated her young half-brother Tutankhamen and after her husband's death ensured the continuance of her power by arranging his marriage and having him crowned at Karnak. He then re-instated the old religion of the sun-god Amon. She is usually remembered for her great beauty, as shown in a sculpture of the time.

**Negri, Pola** (1894–1987). Polish film actress. Born in Janowa, Poland, and described as the daughter of a gypsy violinist who died in exile in Siberia, she married when she was a dancer in St Petersburg [now Leningrad]. She made a number of films in Warsaw between 1913 and 1917 and then went to Berlin to play in Max Reinhardt's production of *Sumurun/One Arabian Night* (1920) and became a star of German cinema. She was especially outstanding in the historical films produced by Lubitsch, such as *Carmen/ Gypsy Blood* (1918), *Madame du Barry/Passion* (1919), *Medea* (1920) and *Die Flamme/ Montmartre* (1922). In 1922 she was invited to Hollywood, the first European star to be, and made a succession of exciting films such as *The Charmer* (1925) and *Loves of an Actress* (as the French actress RACHEL; 1928), built around her gloomy sensual image. She achieved notoriety for her passion for Valentino and her aristocratic marriages. Her heavy accent kept her out of films after the coming of sound and in 1934 she returned to Germany. She re-assumed her role as a popular star but during World War II she went to France, and then to the USA in 1943. Her last, brief appearance was in *The Moon-Spinners* (1964).

P. Negri: *Memoirs of a Star* (1970)

**Nesbit, Edith** (1858–1924). British writer. Born in London, the daughter of John Collis Nesbit, an agricultural chemist who died when she was three, Edith was the youngest of six children. She was educated in France, Germany and Brighton and as a girl, through her elder sister Mary, met the Rossettis, Swinburne, and William Morris; her first poem was published in the *Sunday Magazine* in 1876. In 1880 she married the journalist Hubert Bland. Both were founder members of the Fabian Society in 1884, with a circle of friends which included H.G. Wells (who caricatured their unconventional private life in his *Experiment in Autobiography*) and Bernard Shaw. They had two sons and two daughters, but Hubert was a notorious womanizer and Edith included his illegitimate children in their sociable, generous household. His financial troubles and poor health forced her to turn from poetry to popular fiction and she wrote the first stories of 'the Bastable family' in 1898. *The Story of the Treasure Seekers* (1899) was rapidly followed by such successful children's novels as *The Would-be Goods* (1901), *The Five Children and It* (1902), *The Phoenix and the Carpet* (1904), *The Railway Children* (1906) and *The Enchanted Castle* (1907). Her writing combined realism, based on her own childhood memories, with magic and fantasy: she also wrote several excellent ghost stories, such as *Man-sized in Marble* and *The Violet Car*. Hubert died in 1914 and Edith married Terry Tucker, an engineer. She wrote little after World War I, but her last novel, *The Lark*, appeared in 1922. Nesbit's other published work includes early collections of poetry, political verse such as *Ballads and Lyrics of Socialism* (1908) and a study of childhood, *Wings and the Child* (1913).

J. Briggs: *A Woman of Passion* (1987)

**Neuber** [née Weissenborn], **Frederika (Carolina)** (1697–1760). German actress-manager. As a child she suffered from the treatment of her tyrannical father, and at 19 eloped with Johann Neuber, a clerk. After they married they acted for ten years with companies in Weissenfels, before forming their own company which was licensed to play at Leipzig fairs. She was known as 'Die Neuberin' and appeared in adaptations of French classical tragedies and comedies. She worked in association with Johann Gottsched, the critic and writer, who wanted to reform German traditional theatre which was dominated by folk dramas and farces. Her efforts to develop dramatic theatre led to the banishment of the old comic figure 'Hanswurst' from the theatre, and to his symbolic burning in Leipzig in 1737. She was an extremely efficient actress-manager, one of the earliest and most famous, training her company precisely and looking after their welfare, and was devoted to improving the standard of her art. By 1739 she had tired of Gottsched's rigid neo-classical views and broke up their collaboration. In 1740 she

toured Germany and Russia with her husband but her popularity had noticeably declined. The Neubers' company broke up, and they struggled to make a living, being finally reduced to destitution during the Seven Years War.

**Neuman, Theresa** (1898–1962). Austrian religious figure. The eldest daughter of a sailor, she grew up in a Bavarian village and suffered severe injury in a fire in 1918 which left her paralysed, eventually blind and deaf. On the day of the beatification of Thérèse of Lisieux in 1923 she recovered her sight, and on the day of the canonization in 1925 she was completely cured. After a vision of Christ's passion in 1926 the stigmata appeared on her body, recurring periodically during her life, especially during Holy Week. Her 'miraculous' existence, thought (but never proven) to be fraudulent was made even more baffling by the fact that she took no solid food and existed solely on the daily communion wafer and sip of water. She lost no weight, but was never subjected to rigorous medical tests. Her village of Könnersreuth became the centre of numerous pilgrimages, which continued even during the Third Reich.

**Nevelson** [née Berliawsky], **Louise** (1899–). American sculptor of Russian birth. She was born in Kiev and her family emigrated to the USA in 1905 and settled in Maine. In 1920 she married Charles Nevelson and moved to New York; they had one son, Myron. Always fascinated by sculpture, she began studying at the Art Students' League in 1929, and after separating from her husband went to work under Hans Hofman in Munich in 1931. The following year she worked on a mural with Diego Rivera in Mexico. She had already begun collecting African and Amerindian art, and returned many times to Central and South America. During the 1930s she worked as an art teacher and in the 1940s began exhibiting her extraordinary solid sculpture at the Karl Dierendorf Gallery, New York. She moved from terracotta and ceramic ware to large assemblies, often of cheap wooden materials such as boxes or broken furniture as in *Sky Cathedral* (1958). These were often painted black until 1963, then gold, or white. Recently her work has become less austere, incorporating glass, mirrors and other materials.

Recognition came during the 1950s and at the end of the decade she worked for other artists as President of Artistic Equity for New York (1957–9) and for the USA (1962–4), and was also a member of other organizations such as the National Association of Women Artists. She has won several major awards and her work has been seen throughout North America and Europe in solo and group exhibitions, including a personal retrospective at the Whitney Museum, New York. In 1979 she was elected to the American Academy of Arts and Letters, and in 1985 was awarded the National Medal of Arts.

A.B. Glimchen: *Louise Nevelson* (1972)

**Ngoyi, Lilian** (1911–80). South African activist. Educated in the Transvaal, she married John Ngoyi in 1936, and they had three children. Moved by the sight of young people going to gaol during the Defiance Campaign, Lilian Ngoyi joined the Women's League of the African National Congress in 1952; she was then a widow aged 40. Her whole life was a struggle against the poverty and degradation black people undergo in South Africa. A brilliant public speaker, she found herself in the front ranks of political activity and in 1953 was elected President of the Women's League. In 1956 she was elected President of the Federation of South African Women. She was arrested in 1956 and charged with treason after an elaborate trial that lasted for more than four years. During that period she had to undergo solitary confinement. She was acquitted in 1961, but from that time was confined to her home in Orlando Township under severe bans and restrictions.

**Nguyen Thi Binh** (1927–). Vietnamese politician. She was born in Saigon, Vietnam. Her family were middle-class and French educated but both her father (a civil servant) and her grandfather, the legendary Phan Chan Trinh, were Nationalist leaders. Her father became a resistance worker and after her mother's death she took care of the rest of her family. She became a teacher, and was a student political leader in Saigon, organizing the first anti-American

demonstration there in 1950. From 1951 to 1954 she was imprisoned by the French authorities; she was released after the Geneva Treaty. She then married a farmer from the Mekong Delta and they had two children. She and her husband worked constantly for the underground opposition to President Diem. From 1963 to 1966 she was a Council Member of the Union of Women for the Liberation of South Vietnam, organizing and recruiting peasant women, and she then became a member of the Central Committee of the National Liberation Front (NLF), leading the delegation to the Peace Conference in Paris in 1968. In 1969 she was appointed Foreign Minister of the NLF's Provisional Revolutionary Government, and she signed the agreement ending the Vietnam War in 1973.

When the country was re-unified, she was made Minister of Education of the Socialist Republic of Vietnam (1976–87), in Hanoi, and Vice-President of the Vietnamese Women's Union. She became a member of the Council of State in 1981.

**Nhiwatiwa, Naomi** (1940–). Zimbabwe politician. One of the three women in the 36-strong Mugabe government, she is the Deputy Minister for Posts and Telegraphs. A psychology graduate who was active in the struggle for the creation of Zimbabwe, she is now concerned with fighting for women's rights. She campaigns particularly for abolition of the practice of *lobola* (arranged marriages for a bride-price).

**Nhongo** [née Mugari], **Joice** (1955–). Zimbabwe guerilla fighter. One of nine children of peasant parents, she ran away from her village to join 'the boys in the bush'. At the age of 18 she became a member of ZANLA's General Staff and at 21 was appointed Camp Commander of Chimoio, the largest guerilla-cum-refugee camp in Mozambique. She met and married Rex Nhongo, who was deputy head of the ZANLA forces. Known by the name of Mrs 'Teurai Ropa' Nhongo ('Spill-blood' Nhongo), she became the most famous guerilla in Robert Mugabe's forces. She was hunted by the Rhodesian security forces who were very keen to capture her for propaganda purposes. In 1978 the Rhodesian air force attacked the camp when Joice was pregnant. Two days after the raid, during which Joice carried on fighting, she gave birth to a girl. A month later her daughter, Priscilla Rungano, was sent to live in Zambia with friends and Joice did not see her for two years: they were united only after the creation of Zimbabwe. She now has three daughters. In 1980 she was briefly Minister of Youth, Sport and Recreation, and in 1981 became Minister of Community Development and Women's Affairs.

**Nicole.** *See* PARTURIER, FRANÇOISE.

**Nielsen, Asta** (1883–1972). Danish film actress. Born in Copenhagen, the daughter of a washerwoman, she trained at the children's school attached to the Royal Theatre. She was already a well-known stage actress when she caught the attention of August Blom, who directed her in three Danish films during 1910 and 1911. She then married Urban Gad and in 1911 they went to Germany where he directed her in 30 films, including *Das Mädchen ohne Vaterland* (1912), *Die Suffragetten* (1913) and *Zapatas Bande* (1914). A passionate, disciplined actress, her formal power made her a great artist in the contemporary expressionist cinema. After her divorce from Gad in 1916 she worked with several other directors. She formed her own company with her second husband Svend Gade as director, and in 1920 took the title role in *Hamlet*. Some of her best performances were in classic dramatic roles such as *Fraülein Julie/Miss Julie* (1922) and *Hedda Gabler* (1924). After the arrival of sound she made only one film, *Unmögliche Liebe* (1932). When the Nazi regime began in 1933 she returned to Denmark, despite flattering offers from Goebbels. She continued to act there until the outbreak of World War II and then lived in retirement, honoured by the Danish government. She married for the third time two years before her death. Her beauty and theatrical strength have made her one of the legendary stars of the silent film era.

A. Nielsen: *The Silent Muse* (1946)

**Nightingale, Florence** (1820–1910). English nurse and administrator. The second daughter of wealthy parents who were travelling in Florence when she was born,

Florence was taught Classics and mathematics by her father as well as learning modern languages. She visited the poor and sick with her mother, but when she was 24 her parents would not allow her to become a nurse at Salisbury Hospital. Influenced by visits to the Lutheran hospital at Kaiserwerth, Germany, she used her £500 allowance from her father to run an Institution for Sick Gentlewomen in London, gaining her first experience of committees and administration.

In 1854 the Crimean War was in progress and after reading an account in *The Times* of the conditions at Scutari she volunteered to go there; her friend, Sidney Herbert, now Secretary of War, invited her to lead a party of nurses. Accompanied by 38 nurses, she attacked the filthy and verminous conditions and established medical organization in the British army. As Superintendant of the female nursing establishment in the war zone, within a few months she had reduced the death rate from 42 per cent to 2.2 per cent. She dealt with supplies and the welfare of the men.

The 'Lady with the Lamp' returned to England in 1856 as a popular heroine. She used the principles of hygiene she had practised in public health work. She was adviser to the first district nursing service, established in Liverpool, and organized the appointment of women health commissioners. Her analyses of medical statistics were innovatory.

In gratitude to Florence Nightingale for her achievements in the Crimea, the British public raised £44,000, which she used to endow the Nightingale School of Nursing at St Thomas Hospital. She appointed Mrs Wardroper as Matron, and under their strict guidance, 'character', technical ability and professionalism, combined with ward hygiene, established standards in nursing which raised it from its former menial status. *Notes on Nursing* (1859) incorporates many of the principles. Her missionary purpose in nursing enabled her to bring her methods into use in many hospitals, workhouse infirmaries, and district nursing areas in the UK and Europe.

Increasing ill-health made her an invalid, but did not decrease her intellectual influence, and probably allowed her to expand her vast output of correspondence.

Her radical reform of the British Army Medical Corps in particular led her to be widely consulted on administrative matters. She became a political expert on imperial India and architect of the massive Indian Sanitary Commission. She was the first woman appointed to the Order of Merit, by Queen VICTORIA.

C. Woodham-Smith: *Florence Nightingale* (1951)

**Nijinska, Bronislava** (1891–1972). Russian choreographer. Born at Minsk, the daughter of professional dancers, she studied at the Imperial Ballet School in St Petersburg [now Leningrad], and was taught by Cecchetti, Fokine and Legat. In 1908 she graduated with distinction, became a soloist with the Mariinsky company and danced in the early Dyagilev seasons in Paris from 1909. In 1911 she resigned from the Mariinsky after her brother Nijinsky's dismissal and joined the Dyagilev Ballet. During 1914 she appeared with Nijinsky's company in London at the Palace Theatre.

During World War I Nijinska remained in Russia and started a school in Kiev. In 1921 she returned to Dyagilev's Ballets Russes, alternating as the Lilac Fairy with LYDIA LOPOKOVA in *The Sleeping Princess*. She was Dyagilev's only woman choreographer, becoming Principal Choreographer after Massine left, and creating eight ballets, including her masterpieces *Les noces* (with music by Stravinsky and designs by NATALIA GONCHAROVA, 1923), *Les biches* and *Le Train Bleu* (1924).

In the late 1920s Nijinska worked at the Colón Theatre, Buenos Aires, and choreographed *Le baiser de la fée* and *La Valse* for the Ida Rubinstein company. From 1930 to 1934 she was Ballet Mistress of the Opéra Russe in Paris, and in 1932 formed her own company, creating and dancing the lead in *Hamlet*. She also choreographed *Les cents baisers* and *Danses Slaves et Tziganes* (1935–6) for de Basil, and worked for the Markova-Dolin company in 1937. From 1938 she worked mainly in the USA, establishing a school in California and working freelance for different companies including the Ballet Russe de Monte Carlo, the de Cuevas Ballet and American Ballet Theatre. In 1964 she was persuaded by Ashton to stage a revival of *Les biches* and then of *Les noces* (1966) for the Royal Ballet. She was married twice, to the dancers Kochetovsky and Singaevsky.

B. Nijinska: *Early Memoirs* (1982)

**Nin, Anaïs** (1903–77). American diarist and novelist. She was born in Paris. Her father was the Spanish musician Joachim Nin; her mother was Danish. She spent her childhood travelling with her father until he left them in 1914 for another woman and the family emigrated to the USA. Her diary seems a lifelong plea for his return. She had some elementary-school education in New York, but was then largely self-taught. From 1918 to 1920 she worked as a fashion model. In 1920 she married Hugh Guiler and they soon moved to France, where she continued modelling and worked as a dancer, mixing with intellectuals and writers. She studied psychoanalysis and practised in Europe under Otto Rank and briefly, but not very successfully, in New York. From 1930 to 1940 she remained in Paris, writing professionally from 1932 and establishing Siana Editions in 1935. Her first novels were *House of Incest* (1936) and *Writer of Artifice* (1939), discursive collections of impressions largely based on the diary portraits, on dreams and on her response to her experience. In 1940 she left for the USA where she produced many more fictional exercises over the next 20 years, such as *A Spy in the House of Love* (1954), and became a well-known figure in the Greenwich Village intelligentsia. Her diaries were published between 1966 and 1976 and have been taken up by that part of the feminist movement which sympathizes with her belief in psychoanalysis and in the ineffable mystery and difference of 'masculine' and 'feminine' natures.

A. Nin: *The Diary* (6 vols.) (1966–76)

**Nitocris** [Naqi'a] (?7th century BC). Assyrian queen. There is considerable doubt as to her historical authenticity, but she is mentioned by Herodotus and is tentatively identified with Naqi'a, wife of Sennacherib, who ruled from 704 to 681 BC and was mother of his successor Esarhaddon (680–669 BC). She allegedly dominated the reigns of her son and grandson, and may have gained her reputation from involvement in the reconstruction of Babylon, which had been

*Florence Nightingale*

*Caroline Norton*

*Annie Oakley*

*Emmeline and Christabel Pankhurst*

flooded by the River Euphrates. Later her life story became merged with that of SAMMURAMAT.

**Noce, Teresa** (1900–). Italian socialist. Born in Turin, she became a militant socialist and feminist at an early age, influenced by the struggles of other women workers in Turin. First a laundress and dressmaker, she became a turner for Fiat Brevetti during World War I. In 1919 she joined the Socialist party and in 1921 the Communist party. She also became a journalist, writing for *Il grido del popolo* and *Ordine nuove*. After the mass arrests at the beginning of 1923 she was responsible for a while for the Communist Youth Federation and their periodical *La voce della gioventù*. She led the women's section of the party in France, returned to Italy and was active in the important anti-facist strikes of the women workers in the rice fields in the early 1930s. In 1934–6 she participated in the organization of initiatives which were conducted by the international women's movement against war and fascism. She promoted and edited a number of periodicals, including *La voce della donne* (an anti-fascist periodical founded in 1934 by women).

During World War II Noce was active in the French Résistance after escaping from a concentration camp, but she was captured in 1944 by the Gestapo and sent to Ravensbrück. She returned to Italy in 1945. A member of the central committee of the Communist party, she worked for the creation of the Italian Republic. For many years she was secretary for the Federazione Impiegati Operai Tessili and in 1947 she founded *La voce dei tessili* ('The voice of the textile workers'). In 1938, in Paris, she published *Gioventù senza sole*, a novel based on her experience as a young worker. Her later work includes *e domani fara giorno* (1952), about the concentration camps, and *Rivoluzionaria di professione* (1974).

**Noddack** [née Tacke], **Ida (Eva)** (1896–). German chemist. She was born at Lackhausen-bei-Wesel and obtained her doctorate at Berlin in 1921. She worked in Siemen's laboratory and then with Walter Noddack whom she married in 1926. Together they searched for the missing elements 43 and 75. They discovered the

latter which was named rhenium after the River Rhine, near which Ida was born.

The Noddacks continued to work together, mainly at Freiburg, Strasbourg and Bamberg. In 1934 when Fermi reported his first observations in the neutron bombardment of uranium, Ida suggested the possibility of fission. Her idea was ignored at the time but credited five years later.

**Noether, Emmy** [Amalie] (1882–1935). German mathematician. She was born in Erlangen, where her father was a professor of mathematics at the university. Emmy had a conventional upbringing. Both she and her younger brother Fritz shared their father's interests and she was tutored by Paul Gordon, a family friend. In 1907 she wrote her doctoral thesis, *On complete systems of invariants for ternary biquadratic forms*, under Gordon's tutelage. Occasionally Emmy lectured at the university as a substitute for her father.

After the retirement of Gordon and her father and the death of her mother, Emmy was persuaded by David Hilbert to move to Göttingen and continue research there on mathematical formulation of the theory of relativity and the axiomatic method in mathematics. She had no formal appointment because the staff was opposed to admitting women, but Hilbert supported her and she gave lectures which were announced under his name. After World War I, opinion changed and in 1922 she was allowed to lecture, but at a low salary. As co-author of a paper on differential operators she began to be recognized as a force in modern abstract algebra. With Hasse and Brauer she investigated the structure of non-commutative and cyclic algebras, and was also known as a stimulating teacher.

She lived quietly and after 1918 she was a firm pacifist. As a Jew, an intellectual and a Liberal, she was dismissed from her appointment during the Nazi rise to power in 1933, but was welcomed as a Professor at Bryn Mawr College in the USA. After 18 months she died unexpectedly after an operation.

**Nogarola, Isotta** (1418–66). Italian scholar. Born into a noble family in Verona, she proved a brilliant student and at 18 was already famous: she was called 'The Divine

Isotta' and praised by leading humanist scholars for her classical knowledge and eloquence in Latin debate. Her sister Ginevra was also a fine classical scholar. In 1438 she, her brother and her sister Bartolommea were charged by an anonymous accuser with promiscuity, homosexuality and incest. Deeply distressed, she moved to Venice for two years and in 1441 decided to abandon her humanist studies and devote herself to sacred learning. She lived in total seclusion in her mother's household. As a sacred scholar, she won great admiration and was particularly encouraged by her close friend the Venetian noble and scholar Ludovico Foscarini. In her religious writings she reveals a preoccupation with male and female expectations of roles, defending Eve's part in the fall from grace in *De pari aut impari Evae atque Adae peccato* (1451). She also wrote a treatise on Saint Jerome, *Oratio in laudem beati Hieronymis* (1453).

**Noor Al-Hussein** (1951–). Jordanian queen. Lisa Najeeb Halaby was born in Washington, DC and brought up in California. The eldest daughter of the President of Pan American Airways, she went to study architecture and urban planning at Princeton University in 1969, a member of the first class to admit women to professional courses. After graduating in 1974 she worked on urban planning projects in Australia, Iran and Jordan and was converted to Islam during 18 months spent in Amman, where she was developing an organizational structure for Alia, the Royal Jordanian Airline. She met King Hussein in Amman and became his fourth wife in 1978; they have four children. Deeply involved with Jordanian issues and with the problems of planning in the New Third World, she has lectured widely in America on the plight of the Palestinians. She established the Noor Al-Hussein Foundation for educational and environmental projects and heads the National Committee for Public Buildings.

**Norman, Jessye** (1945–). American soprano. Born in Augusta, Georgia, one of five children in a black middle-class family, she began singing with the nearby Baptist church, and learned to love opera by listening to Sunday afternoon radio recitals. At 16 she was awar-

ded a scholarship to Howard University, and in 1965 won first prize in a vocal competition from the National Society of Arts and Letters in Washington. Two years later, after a term at the Peabody Conservatory, she went on to train at the University of Michigan, existing on scholarships and part-time teaching until, while on a tour of South America run by the State Department, she heard that she had won a scholarship to enter the International Music Competition in Munich. She won first prize, and on her return began giving public recitals. Her velvet-toned, heavy voice delighted critics in America, but in 1969 she signed a three-year contract with the Deutsche Opera Berlin. Her recording career began in London in the early 1970s, and she made her operatic debuts in 1972 at La Scala, Milan, the Royal Opera House, Covant Garden, and the Hollywood Bowl. Her operatic successes included Aida in Berlin and Milan, and Berlioz's *The Trojans* at Covent Garden (both 1972). Her reputation grew on both sides of the Atlantic, particularly in recitals; she sang at numerous festivals, and toured North and South America, Europe, the Middle East and Australia. In the 1980s she has become acknowledged as one of the finest contemporary performers in opera, not only for her superb voice but for her dramatic and expressive power, as shown in the 1987 production of *Ariadne auf Naxos*.

**Normanton, Helena (Florence)** (1883–1957) English lawyer. Born and educated in London, she obtained a first class honours degree in history at London University, and also studied at Dijon, France, obtaining qualifications in French language, literature and history. She was the second woman (after Dr Ivy Williams) to be called to the Bar in England, entering the Middle Temple in 1919 (the first woman accepted by the Inns of Court) and being called in 1922. In 1921 she married Gavin Clark, but retained her maiden name. She practised chiefly in the Central Criminal Court, and won a reputation for earnestness and learned quotations. She was one of the first women to be made a King's Counsel in England (1949), and the first to be elected to the General Council of the Bar (although a woman had previously been co-opted). *The Times* Obituary notes that she would be principally remembered at the Old Bailey for re-organizing the Bar Mess 'especially as regards the cooking'. She lectured in Glasgow and London, and contributed to the *Famous Trials Series*.

Helena Normanton was influential in the International Society of Women Lawyers, and in the International Federation of Business and Professional Women, two of her books being *Sex Differentiation in Salary* and *Everyday Law for Women*. She became President of the Married Women's Association, and in that capacity caused controversy by her memorandum to the Royal Commission on Marriage and Divorce, which she regarded as not representing the principle of 'equal partnership' (1952). Her subsequent resignation led to a split which resulted in the formation of a separate Council of Married Women.

**Noronha, Joana Paula Manso de** (*fl c* 1850). Argentinian-Brazilian feminist. Born in Argentina, she married a Portugese violinist and composer, but separated from him and moved to Rio de Janeiro where she became a journalist and literary critic. In 1852 she founded an extremely progressive feminist paper *O jornal das senhoras*, presenting the examples of progress she had found in the USA during her visit in 1846. She persevered with the paper, despite considerable hostility, but after six months she was forced by financial constraints to hand over to Violante Atabalipa de Bivar e Vellasco, who later founded her own paper *O domingo* (1874). *O jornal das senhoras* ceased publication in 1855 but its influence remained. Later, more radical feminist journals were *O sexo femminiso* which began in 1873 and *A familia*, founded by Josephina Alvares de Azevedo in 1888.

J.E. Hanner: 'The 19th Century Feminist Press in Brazil', *Latin American Women*, ed. Lavrin (1978)

**North, Marianne** (1830–90). English traveller and painter of flowers. Born in Hastings into a well-to-do family, Marianne had little formal education, but a cultured environment. She travelled with her father through Austria, Turkey, Syria and Egypt until his death in 1869, and kept households in Hastings and London.

In 1871 she undertook her first long journey, via Canada, the USA and Jamaica to Brazil, often spending whole days in painting flowers. After 18 months she returned to England, visited Tenerife, and in 1875 went with friends to Japan via the USA. Alone she visited and loved the redwood forests and the Yosemite Valley. After the cold of Japan she recovered from rheumatism in Sarawak and discovered the largest of all pitcher plants. She found Java a 'garden of luxuriance'. In 1877 she visited Ceylon, India and the Himalayas. At Charles Darwin's suggestion she went to Australia in 1880 to render her botanic collections more complete.

In 1879 she displayed her paintings in a small gallery and in 1882 achieved her scheme of housing them permanently at Kew Gardens when she opened the North Gallery. The quality and quantity of her paintings demonstrate her great industry. In 1883 she travelled to the Seychelles and found a hitherto unclassified capucin tree, which was later named *Northia seychellana*. In spite of deafness and increasing health problems she went to Chile to find a monkey-puzzle tree, also discovering the beautiful 'great blue puya'. She retired to Alderley, Gloucestershire, and created a fine garden. Her books *Recollections of a Happy Life* (1892) and *Further Recollections of a Happy Life* (1893) were abridged and edited by Mrs Addington Symonds.

**Norton** [née Sheridan]**, Caroline (Elizabeth Sarah)** (1808–77). English novelist and campaigner for married women's rights. The grand-daughter of Richard Brinsley Sheridan, and one of the seven children of Thomas Sheridan, a civil servant, she was brought up by an aunt and after her father's death in 1817 went to school in Surrey. In 1827 she married the barrister George Norton, who was an MP at the time. Financial difficulties led her to publish her verse, *The Sorrows of Rosalie* (1829). In 1831 she became Editor of a court magazine *La Belle Assemblée* and then of the *English Annual* (1834–8). Her novel *The Wife and Woman's Reward* appeared in 1838.

In 1836 Norton brought a suit against Lord Melbourne for alienating Caroline's affections. She could not be represented in the trial, having no legal status. The suit failed, but she then began the battle for custody of her three sons and her pamphlet

*A Plain Letter* influenced the passing of the Infant Custody Bill in 1839. She was reunited with her children, but the youngest died in 1842.

From 1845 she lived alone and wrote, but in 1853 Norton brought a new suit against her for debt and took all her copyright interests, prompting her to write in favour of the Divorce Bill and the first Married Women's Property Bill in her *English Laws for Women in the Nineteenth Century* and *A Letter to The Queen* (1855). After her husband died in 1875 she retired from writing and in 1877 married an old friend, Sir William Stirling Maxwell, but she died suddenly a few months later. Meredith modelled *Diana of the Crossways* on her life story.

A. Acland: *Caroline Norton* (1948)

**Nur Jahan** [Mihr-ur-Nisa] (1571–1634). Moghul Indian empress. Originally named Mihr-ur-Nisa, she was the daughter of a Persian official of the Moghuls and married another Persian with whom she had one daughter. They lived in Bengal, but after her husband's death she came to court as Lady-in-waiting to the stepmother of the Emperor Jahangir, who fell in love with her. They married in 1611, when she was 40, and she became his favourite wife and at once raised her relations to high positions. Her brother became chief minister and her niece Mumtaz (whose mausoleum is the Taj Mahal) married the heir to the throne. She formed a clique with her family, with Asaf Khan and with Jahangir's third son Prince Khurram (later Shah Jahan). Devoted to her husband, she modified his addiction to drink and opium, but he virtually handed over authority to her and she took over most of the administration of the Empire, issuing decrees and becoming the only woman ruler of India to issue coins in her own name. She greatly increased the splendour of the Moghul court, enjoying spectacles, playing polo, hunting tigers and patronizing learning, art and scholarship.

A great factionist, she upset political stability by first supporting Khurram, then, after her daughter married Jahangir's second son Prince Shahryar, transferring her allegiance to Shahryar; this led Khurram to rebel, provoking a civil war from 1623 to 1626. She concluded peace on her terms but,

jealous of the rising power of the Imperial General Mahabat Khan, she ordered him to Bengal to face charges of disloyalty. This caused another rebellion in which Mahabat Khan abducted the Emperor and captured Nur Jahan. Eventually they regained power but on Jahangir's death in 1627 Khurram took the throne, crushing opposition. He gave Nur Jahan a generous pension and she retired into private life, after 16 years of almost total power.

**Nwapa, Flora** [Florence] (1931–). Eastern Nigerian novelist. An Ibo from Oguta, a district renowned for independent women, Florence Nwapa was educated in Lagos and at University College Ibadan, and received a Diploma in Education at Edinburgh in 1958. She has worked as an education officer in Callabar, and as a teacher and administrator at Lagos University. She wrote first about village life, and her published works include *Efuru* (1966), which portrays the dilemma of an educated woman attempting to readjust to simple rural life; *Idu* (1970); *This is Lagos* (short stories, 1971); *Emeka* (1975) and *Never Again* (1981). Her writing has received critical acclaim in Africa and abroad. After the civil war in 1974 she received a commission from the Lands, Survey and Urban Development Board in her state to set up a publishing company and printing press to produce children's books, novels and stories about local life.

**Nyembe, Dorothy** (1930–). South African activist. She joined the African National Congress (ANC) in her early 20s and became a women's organizer in the party. She served two years in prison during the Defiance Campaign. Dorothy Nyembe led the Natal women who protested against the pass laws in 1956. She was endorsed out of Durban in 1959 and during the 1960 State of Emergency she was detained for five months. In 1962 she represented the Women's Federation in the South African Congress of Trade Unions conference. She was arrested in 1963, charged with furthering the aims of the ANC and sentenced to three years' imprisonment. She was banned in 1963 and again in 1968. In 1968 she was once again detained and in 1969 charged under the Terrorism Act and the Suppression of Communism Act, after which she was sentenced to 15 years' imprisonment. She was released in 1984.


**Nzinga, Mbande** [Dona Ana de Souza] (c1582–1663). Angolan queen. She was Queen of Ndongo (1624–6) and of Matamba (1630–63), and leader of the national struggle against the Portuguese. In 1622 Nzinga, an influential figure, was sent by her brother the King of Ndongo to negotiate with the Portuguese. She persuaded them to recognize the independence of their rich, slave-trading state and received Christian baptism as Dona Ana de Souza. She renounced her Christianity but is reported to have returned to it before her death.

On her brother's death in 1624 she became Queen, and two years later was driven east by the Portuguese, who tried to install a new ruler. 30 years of inconclusive warfare followed as Nzinga organized a powerful army, conquered and imposed rule on Matamba, developed alliances and controlled the slave routes. In the 1640s an alliance with the Dutch forced the Portuguese to retire briefly, but the war did not finally end until 1654. A charismatic and shrewd leader, she continued to rule in relative stability until 1663.

# O

**Oakley, Ann** (1944–). British feminist sociologist. Born in London, she was educated at a girls' grammar school and then at Chiswick Polytechnic, before taking a degree at Somerville College, Oxford, and obtaining a doctorate from London University on the subject of women's attitudes to housework. Her first book, *Sex, Gender and Society* (1972) was a lucid survey of the evidence from biology, psychology, sociology and anthropology used in arguments about the position of women and has become a classic introductory text. Her next two books, which radically influenced contemporary ideas about women in the home, were *Housewife* and the more academic *The Sociology of Housework* (both 1974). In that year she became Research Officer at Bedford College, University of London, and in 1976, with Juliet Mitchell, edited the collection of essays *The Rights and Wrongs of Women*. She has also written on motherhood (she herself has three children) and this interest led her to become a Consultant to the National Perinatal Epidemiology Unit, Churchill Hospital, Oxford, and to publish *Becoming a Mother* (1979) and *Women Confined* (1980). Her other books include *Subject Women* (1981), the autobiographical *Taking It Like a Woman* (1984) and *Telling the Truth about Jerusalem* (1986).

**Oakley** [Mozee; Moses], **Annie** [Phoebe Anne] (1860–1926). American markswoman. She was born in a log cabin in Ohio. Her parents were Quakers and she remained a devout Fundamentalist. After her father's death in 1870 she shot game to help support the family. In 1879 she won a shooting match against Frank E. Butler at the Cincinnati Coliseum; she married Butler the following year and they toured together giving demonstrations – shooting moving glass balls and playing-cards thin edge on. In 1884 Butler stepped out of the act to become her manager, and after working briefly for the Sells Brothers Circus they joined the Buffalo Bill Wild West Show (1885), touring the USA, Canada, England (they were presented to Queen Victoria in 1887) and Europe (where Annie shot a cigarette from Kaiser William II's mouth in 1889). A train crash at Lexington in 1901 temporarily paralysed her and she left the show, but she played the lead in the melodrama *The Western Girl* in 1902 and continued to tour. In 1917 she rejoined Bill Cody for his farewell season, and from 1915 to 1917 she taught trapshooting; in 1918 she demonstrated marksmanship to the American troops. She retired to Florida in 1922, but returned to Dayton, Ohio, just before her death in 1926. In contrast to another Western character, CALAMITY JANE, she had a reputation for modesty, kindness and philanthropy.

A. Swartout: *Missie: an Historical Biography of Anne Oakley*

**Oates, Joyce Carol** (1938–). American novelist. Born in Lockport, New York, she graduated from Syracuse University in 1960 and obtained an MA at the University of Wisconsin the following year. She married Raymond Smith in 1961, and from 1961 to 1967 taught English at the University of Detroit. Since then she has been Professor of English at the University of Windsor in Ontario. Her first stories were published in 1963, and novels, collections of short stories and volumes of poetry have followed, at a rate of two or three publications a year, ever since. Her work is varied and offers an acute analysis of American contemporary life and mores, and a strong awareness of the pressure of history. Recently her novels, such as *Angel of Light* and *Unholy Loves* (both 1981) have become increasingly experimental in style.

**Ocampo, Victoria** (1890–1978). Argentinian writer and literary editor. Born in Argentina into a wealthy family, Victoria was educated to speak several languages fluently and was married in accordance with the desires of her family, but she left her husband and lived independently, establishing herself at the centre of a literary salon in Buenos Aires. She was responsible for introducing the work of numerous international writers into South America, most notably Rabindranath Tagore and Virginia Woolf, with whom she had a close friendship. Passionately concerned with expanding the frontiers of South American letters, she was also involved with feminism and became a champion of the rights of women and the promotion of women's writing. In 1931 she founded the literary journal *Sur* that was to have much influence on generations of Latin American writers. During the Perónist regime she was in opposition and despised Evita Perón's reactionary feminism. As a publisher she pioneered translations of a great number of overseas writers and also encouraged new South American writers.

Victoria Ocampo once said that if she could have a magic lamp that would enable her to write like Shakespeare, Dante, Goethe or Cervantes she would reject it, because what she most wanted to do was to write like a woman in some new, unknown way. Her advanced ideas prefigured contemporary feminist views on art and creativity. Although remembered principally for her criticism and her literary salon, she is also remembered as a gifted, creative woman in her own right. Her younger sister, Silvina, became an important writer of short stories in the developing Latin American genre of the Fantastic.

D. Meyer: *Victoria Ocampo: Against the Wind and the Tide* (1978)

**O'Connor, (Mary) Flannery** (1925–64). American writer. Born in Savannah, Georgia, she was brought up as a Roman Catholic among Fundamentalist Southern Protestants, and her fierce unpitying stories of grotesque or poor Georgian people desperately seeking for a spiritual meaning to their lives reflects this background. She lived on her mother's farm but went to the Women's College of Georgia [now Georgia College] at Milledgeville, graduating in 1945 and then taking a Master's degree at the University of Iowa. When young she developed lupus, an inherited and incurable disease which crippled her and led to her early death. She wrote of her disease and of her sense of death or release in her fiction. She began contributing stories to Southern journals, and although she wrote two novels – *Wise Blood* (1952) and *The Violent bear it away* (1960) – the short story remained her true métier. Two collections were published in her lifetime, *A Good Man is hard to find* (1957) and *Everything that Rises must Converge* (1965), and these brought her several grants and honours before she died. Her letters shed further light on her philosophy and her attitude to writing and to the society around her.

F. O'Connor, S. Fitzgerald, ed.: *The Habit of Being: Letters* (1978)

**O'Connor, Sandra (Day)** (1930–). American Supreme Court judge. Born in El Paso, she grew up on the Lazy B Ranch on the New Mexico–Arizona border, which had been in the family since 1881. Since there were no local schools, she spent much time with her grandmother in El Paso, attending Radford School and later the public high school. By the age of ten she could drive a truck and tractor, and she wrote of her childhood 'We played with dolls, but we knew what to do with screwdrivers and nails' (Time, July 1981). She went on to Stanford, where she graduated *magna cum laude*, and then won a place on the *Stanford Law Review*; she married a fellow law student, John O'Connor, in 1952. After graduation she tried to obtain work in a private law firm in Los Angeles, but prejudice against women led her to become a Deputy County Attorney in San Mateo, California. After three years in Frankfurt, where her husband worked for the army legal service and she acted as civilian lawyer for the Quartermaster Corps, they returned to the USA, moving to Phoenix in 1957. She briefly ran her own law firm, then spent five years as a full-time housewife with three sons. In 1965 she went back to work as an Assistant

Attorney General in Arizona, and ran successfully for the State Senate in 1970 and 1972; she was elected Majority Leader, the first woman to hold such a post, in 1972. In 1974 she returned to the law, winning a place on the Maricopa County Superior Court Bench, and in 1979 she was appointed to the Arizona Court of Appeals. Although a staunch Republican, her nomination to the Supreme Court by Ronald Reagan in July 1981 was opposed by the New Right because her record in Arizona was considered to show support of abortion and of the Equal Rights Amendment. She is the first woman judge of the Supreme Court in the history of the USA.

**Ogot, Grace** (1930–). Kenyan novelist. Grace was born in the central Nyanza District of Kenya and educated at Ng'iya Girls' School and Butore High School. From 1955 to 1959 she trained as a nurse and midwife in Uganda and England, and worked as a script-writer and announcer for the BBC in London. Her other jobs have included Community Development Officer in Kisumu, nursing at Maseno Hospital, and public relations work for Air India in Nairobi. In 1959 she married the historian Bethwell Ogot; they have three children.

Grace Ogot, published her first novel, *The Promised Land*, in 1966, the story of a young couple driven from their new farm in Tanzania by witchcraft-induced illness. Her interest in magic and folklore also appears in the short stories of *Land Without Thunder* (1968). A further collection *The Other Woman* (1976) was followed by a novel dealing with contemporary issues, *The Island of Tears* (1980), and the novella *The Graduate*, (1980).

**Okamoto, Ayako** (1951–). Japanese professional golfer; winner of the 1986 American women's professional golf tournament, the 'Elizabeth Arden Classic'. Born in Ehime prefecture, she began as a pitcher in the local baseball team and later joined a softball team of the Yamato Textile Company, where she worked. After her success in Japan she moved to the United States. Her record of 17 under par over the three-day tournament entered the *Guinness Book of Records* and she is one of the most promising young golfers today,

having won 26 titles in Japan and 6 international tournaments, including the British Open.

**O'Keeffe, Georgia** (1887–1986). American artist. Born on a farm at Sun Prairie, Wisconsin, she was a member of a large family. As a child she was a gifted musician, but she also showed early artistic talent. She was educated at a convent in Madison, then studied at the Art Institute, Chicago, from 1905 to 1906, and at the Art Students' League from New York in 1907 to 1908. She then worked as a commercial artist designing lace and embroidery in Chicago from 1908 to 1910, and in the summer of 1912 took a course in design at the University of Virginia, Charlottesville, which led her to teach progressive theories of design in Texas schools, for which she also studied at the Teachers' College, New York, in 1914. At the age of 30 she resolved to create her own original style, and her drawings were exhibited without her knowledge at Alfred Stieglitz's Gallery 291 in 1916. Stieglitz encouraged her and exhibited her work, and in 1924 they were married; before his death in 1946 he photographed her over 500 times.

In 1929 O'Keeffe visited New Mexico, returning numerous times and eventually settling there in 1949. An inveterate traveller, she covered most of North America, and in the 1950s and 1960s visited Europe, the Middle East, Asia and the Pacific Islands. Her early work was formal and abstract, although using natural forms such as flowers or shells as a base; she then moved on to rural paintings, for example of barns and Mexican-Indian buildings. But she is best known for her precisely painted, heavily symbolic studies – for example of flowers, in *Black Iris* (1926), and of the desert, in *Cow's Skull* (1931) and *Pelvis with Blue* (1944). Her work is frequently interpreted in relation to female sexuality. O'Keeffe continued to produce challenging work although in her nineties; among the greatest contemporary American artists, she had several major retrospective exhibitions after 1963, in Chicago, New York and Texas, and was elected to the American Academy of Arts and Letters in 1963, and of Arts and Sciences in 1969.

G. O'Keeffe: *Georgia O'Keeffe* (1980)

**Okwei, Omu** (1872–1943). Nigerian merchant. In West Africa, particularly Nigeria and Ghana, women have traditionally dominated the marketing side of the economy, selling surplus produce from their land and home crafts, and often rising to be considerable entrepreneurs. The white colonialists, unable to understand this structure, often caused violent resistance through their attempts to bring economy into line with Western patterns, for example provoking an uprising among 160 women traders over taxation in 1929. Contemporary governments are still trying to suppress the market women, as recent studies from Ghana have shown.

Omu Okwei came from Ossonaria in Nigeria and after making a large fortune was elected Market Queen, Chairwoman of the Council of Mothers. She is known as the last merchant queen, because the British afterwards transferred supervision of retailing from the Council of Mothers to the city authorities.

F. Ekejiuba: 'Omu Okei: a biographical Sketch', *Journal of the Historical Society of Nigeria*, iii (1967)

**Olga** (890–969). Russian princess and saint. The widow of Prince Igor I after his assassination in 945, she became Regent of the principality of Kiev for his son Svyatoslav. She first instituted an atrocious revenge for her husband's murder, scalding the leading rebels to death and executing hundreds of others who had complained against Igor's heavy taxes for his raiding expeditions against Byzantium in 941. During her regency Romanus I of Constantinople tried to improve relations with Russia by diplomatic and trading exchanges. In 957 Olga was baptized, and during the reign of Constantine VII paid a state visit to Constantinople. She remained Regent until 964 and her influence allowed the spread of Christianity within Russia; the mass conversion of the people was eventually achieved by her grandson Vladimir during the 990s. She became the first Russian saint of the Orthodox Church.

**Oliphant** [née Wilson], **Margaret** (1828–97). Scottish novelist. She was born at Wallyford, Midlothian; her father was a customs official in Edinburgh. Her first novel of Scottish life, *Mrs Maitland of Sunnyside*, was published when she was 21, and she wrote three more before her marriage in 1852 to her cousin Francis Oliphant, a stained-glass designer. They lived in Liverpool and then in London, but Francis died in Rome in 1859, leaving Margaret with a young son and daughter, and expecting a third child. She became a professional writer to support her family, pausing only briefly at the death of her daughter in 1864. Her output was astonishing, mostly contributions to *Blackwood's Magazine*, but also stories, reviews, articles and numerous novels, of which the most popular were the series of studies of religious life in an English country town, Chronicles of Carlingford (1863–76), including *Miss Marjoribanks* and *Phoebe Junior*. Her work is often compared to that of Anthony Trollope and George Eliot. Contemporaries describe her as a kindly, warm figure, but her autobiographical works reveal sadness and strain.

H. Coghill, ed.: *M. Oliphant: the Autobiography and Letters* (1899)
M. Williams: *Margaret Oliphant: A Critical Biography* (1986)

**Olsen** [née Lerner], **Tillie** (1913–). American feminist author. She was born in Nebraska. Although she had little formal education she was a promising writer in her youth, but marriage to Jack Olsen, the care of their four children and the need to earn a living stopped her writing, a situation which spurred her to write *Silences* (1978) many years later. In her forties she began to write again, publishing the prize-winning short story collection *Tell me a Riddle* in 1962 and *Yonnondio: From the Thirties* in 1974 – 40 years after the first chapter had appeared in *Partisan Review*.

During the 1970s she taught as a visiting lecturer and was writer in residence at a number of American universities, including Amherst (1969–70), Stanford (1972), Massachusetts (1973–4) and San Diego (1977); she won many awards including a Guggenheim Fellowship for 1975–6. She also wrote *Rebecca Harding Davis: Life in the Iron Mills* (1973) and her recent books include *The Word Made Flesh* (1984) and *Mother to Daughter: Daughter to Mother* (1984).

**O'Malley, Grace** [Graine Mhaol] (c1530–c1600). Irish leader. Probably born in County Mayo, she belonged to a famous family of sea-rovers and spent her childhood among the western isles. Known as Graine Mhaol ('Grace of the cropped hair'), she married first O'Flaherty of Galway, and then Richard Burke of Mayo, known as 'Richard of the iron'. She was known as a bold leader of many expeditions at sea, but although she made an alliance with Sir Henry Sidney in 1576, she was held in Dublin in 1577, and continued to plot rebellion. She is said to have visited London and to have negotiated with ELIZABETH I on equal terms. In 1586 she was arrested on a charge of plunder, and gallows were built for her execution, but she was released on her son-in-law's surety and fled to O'Neill in Ulster, forfeiting all her fleet. She was pardoned by the queen, but eventually died in poverty in Connaught. She later became immortalized in many Irish tales and ballads.

R. Macdonald: *Grace O'Malley: Princess and Pirate* [Eng. trans., R. Machray] (1898)

**Onassis, Jacqueline Lee Bouvier Kennedy** (1929–). American, widow of President John F. Kennedy. Born in Southampton, Long Island, into a wealthy New York family, Jacqueline Bouvier was educated at Vassar and George Washington University and studied at the University of Paris. She began work as a photographer for the *Washington Times Herald* in 1952, and the following year married John Kennedy. They had a son and a daughter; a second son died soon after birth. When Kennedy became President of the United States in 1961 Jackie became an international trend-setter. Her complete re-decoration of the White House caused national controversy, and her glamour, clothes and style were copied worldwide. She undertook constant public engagements and represented her husband on a tour of India in 1962, but this world was shattered by Kennedy's assassination in Dallas, Texas in 1963. Fives years later she married the Greek shipping millionaire Aristotle Onassis. After his death in 1975 she returned to New York where she worked as consultant to the publishers Viking. In 1977 she joined Doubleday & Co., becoming a full editor there in 1982.

**Ono no Komachi** (c810–c880). Japanese poet. Little is known of her life, but she is believed to have been a great courtesan with many lovers. According to legend, in old age she became ugly, living as a beggar and dying in poverty to atone for her wild youth. Her poetry is in the Japanese court style, full of witty word play and conceits, but also very moving in the delineation of sexual tone and the onset of age. Her work was included in the *Kokinshū*, an anthology of 'Six Poetic Geniuses' compiled for the Imperial Court.

**Oppenheim, Meret** (1913–). Swiss artist born in Germany. She moved with her family from Berlin to Wiesenthal in 1918, and was educated in Germany and Switzerland until 1930. In 1932 she went to Paris, where she met dancers, intellectuals and artists, including Giacometti, SOPHIE TAUBER-ARP and Hans Arp, and was invited to exhibit with the Surrealist group at the Salon des Surindépendents in 1933. She took part in their major exhibitions, such as Cubism-Surrealism (1935) and the great International Surrealist Exhibition of 1936, in which her *Déjeuner en fourrure* (*The Fur Tea Cup*) caused a sensation. She worked in Paris until 1937, and then went to Basel, where she studied at the Kunstgewerbeschule (1938–40); she then moved to Bern. She has lived there, or in Paris, ever since, and in 1949 married Wolfgang La Roche (d 1967).

Her work is always startling, often because of its sexual undertones and her interest in the subconscious; she underwent a long period of Jungian psychoanalysis during the 1940s. She has also worked in other media, writing poetry, designing costumes for a Picasso ballet in 1956 and organizing the symbolic *Banquet* in 1959, with a nude woman as centrepiece. Her reputation increased during the 1960s and 1970s, and she is now recognized as an artist of international stature.

**Orzeszkowa** [née Pawlowska], **Eliza** (1841–1910). Polish novelist. Born in Mil-kowszczyzna, and educated in Warsaw, she married Pietr Orzeszkowa when she was 16, but they were driven from their estates by the Russians in the uprising of 1863, and moved to Grodno. She began writing novels in 1866, writing with sensitivity and feeling about the oppression of women, their lack of education and employment opportunities and their arranged marriages, for example in *Marta* (1872), about the struggles of a young widow. She also wrote about the racial and religious intolerance faced by the Jewish community (*Eli makower*, 1874, *Meir ezofowicz*, 1878) and about the Polish peasantry (*Cham*, 1889). Her work is imbued with patriotic, anti-Russian, feeling and with appeals for a more democratic society; both themes are found in her complex study of regional life *Nad Neimnem/On the Banks of River Neman* (1886).

**Ossoli, Margaret Fuller** (1810–50). American transcendentalist writer and feminist. She was born in Cambridgeport, Massachusetts, the eldest of nine children. She was greatly influenced by the rationalist views of her domineering father, who was a lawyer and politician. He gave her a rigorous classical education which almost ruined her health before she was sent to a local school at the age of 14. In the 1820s she was regarded as a brilliant prodigy in Harvard society, but in 1833 her father retired from public life and Margaret went back to live in the country, helping to bring up the younger children and studying privately. After his death in 1835 she became involved in the intellectual circles around Emerson in Concord and Bronson Alcott in Boston, and following a brief period as a teacher she moved to Jamaica Plain, near Boston, where she held her famous Conversations. These meetings to discuss issues such as art, education, philosophy and women's rights were attended by many transcendentalist theorists and by women reformers like LYDIA MARIA CHILD and SOPHIA PEABODY. In 1840 she joined Emerson in producing the journal *The Dial* which she edited until 1842.

Margaret Fuller was a formidable thinker and a vivid, passionate writer and talker. In 1844 she published her first book, *Summer on the Lakes*, and then went to New York as literary critic for the *New York Tribune*. The following year her classic work appeared, *Woman in the 19th Century and Kindred Papers relating to the Sphere, Condition and Duties of Woman*, which became one of the most influential feminist texts. She published *Papers on Literature and Art* in 1846 and then left for a visit to Europe, where she was feted in London (she was a close friend of HARRIET MARTINEAU) and in Paris, before travelling to Rome in 1847.

In Italy she met and fell in love with a radical aristocrat, Giovanni d'Ossoli, with whom she lived for two years before their marriage and the birth of their son, Angelo, in 1849. She took an active part in organizing relief during the siege of the newly-proclaimed Roman Republic by the French in 1849, and after the Republic was overthrown she and Ossoli fled to Florence. There she became friendly with ELIZABETH BARRETT BROWNING and wrote her history of the Roman Revolution. In 1850, partly to escape police harassment, she sailed for America with her husband and child, but shortly before reaching New York the ship was wrecked in a storm. Her body was never found.

P. Blanchard: *Margaret Fuller: Transcendentalist to Revolutionary* (1987)

**Otero, La belle** [Puentovalga, Caroline] (1868–1965). Spanish courtesan. She was born in Cádiz, and was allegedly abducted by a cabaret dancer at the age of 13; when she was 14 she married an Italian tenor and made her debut as a night-club singer in Monte Carlo. She soon became one of the famous courtesans of the 'Gay Nineties', acquiring a large fortune and hoards of jewels, all of which she gradually lost in gambling sessions in her later years. Her lovers reputedly included Edward VII, the Kaiser, Alfonso XIII of Spain, the French Prime Minister Aristide Briand, Gabriele d'Annunzio and many others, and at the height of her fame she visited St Petersburg [now Leningrad] and toured the USA, drawing rapturous reviews for her beauty and sensuality. She died in relative poverty in Nice.

C. Cash: *La belle Otero: the last great Courtesan* (1981)

**Otto-Peters, Luise** [pseud.: Otto Stern] (1819–95). German pioneer feminist. Her parents died when she was 16 and after studying history, literature and politics she became known as a social novelist, under the pseudonym Otto Stern, with books such as *Ludwig der Kellner* (1843) about class prejudice, and *Kathinka* (1844), an idealist work about the emancipation of women. In 1848 she took an active part in the unsuccessful liberal revolution, during which she demanded full equality for women, including the vote. From 1848 to 1850 she edited her own newspaper and in 1851 met the poet and revolutionary August Peters whom she married seven years later. He died in 1864.

By 1865 she had become more cautious, and, as President of the newly-founded General German Women's Association and editor of the journal *Neue Bahnen*, she declared it was too early to fight for the franchise or to engage in political activity. However, in 1876 and 1888 the Association petitioned for a reform of the highly-discriminatory marriage laws. Despite this moderate approach Otto-Peters is regarded as the founder of the German women's movement, although another, more radical pioneer of 19th-century feminism in Germany was Louisa Aston (1814–55). Other notable figures were Malwida von Meysenburg (1816–1903), radical feminist and educationalist and friend of Herzen; Louise Buchner (1821–77), sister of the playwright George Buchner, one of the founders of German nursing; Hedwig Dohm (1833–1901), radical feminist and suffragist, and Franziska Tiburtius (1843–1927), the first German woman doctor.

**Ouida** [pseud. of Marie Louise de la Ramée] (1839–1908). English novelist. She was born at Bury St Edmunds, of a French father and an English mother; she was educated locally and in Paris. In 1857 she settled in London, and in 1860 began writing for *Bentley's Miscellany*. Her fantastic novels of glamorous life, such as *Held in Bondage* (originally *Granville de Vigne*, 1863) and *Chandos* (1866), and about the Brigade of Guards, in *Under Two Flags* (1867), were enormously popular. Her vivid imagination and strong views challenged Victorian conventions, and in 1875 she moved to Florence, where she began to live in the grand style of her novels. She continued to write, and became interested in Italian life; her novel *A Village Commune* (1881), about the struggle against centralized bureaucracy, caused a furore. In 1894 she moved to Lucca, but her flamboyant habits were checked by increasing poverty. She died at Viareggio after a long illness.

E. Bigland: *Ouida: the Passionate Victorian* (1950)

# P

**Palli, Angeliki** (1798–1875). Greek-Italian writer. She lived among the Greek community of Livorno, Italy. The daughter of a rich and intellectual family, she received a very good education in languages and European culture and was a close friend of famous poets and artists of her time. She wrote tragedies and lyrical dramas, short stories and poems. In 1851 she published *Discorso di una donna alle giovani maritote del suo paese*, a work addressed to young mothers and full of admonitions aiming at their education and emancipation. Although she wrote in Italian, most of her works have a patriotic content referring to the struggles of the Greek people for their independence from the Turkish yoke. She also wrote some romantic novels and translated into Italian works by Shakespeare, Victor Hugo and French and Greek poets. Her last work, *Epiro e Thessalia*, is a passionate patriotic sonnet about Greece, the country she never lived in, but considered as her own.

**Palm, Etta Aelders** (1743–after 1793). Dutch feminist. Born in Holland, she married a student, Lodovyk Palm, and went to Paris in 1774. In 1791 she was the leader of the women's deputation to the legislative assembly, where she made a famous speech for the rights of women in education, politics, law and employment. She was also active in the revolutionary women's clubs, but after 1793 she returned to Holland.

**Panajiotatou, Angeliki** (1875–1954). Greek scientist. She and her sister were the first women to be accepted as students at the Medical School of Athens University. After further studies in Germany she returned to Greece and was appointed a lecturer in the same medical school. Her first appearance created great upheaval, the hostile students shouting 'back in the kitchen, back in the kitchen'. They refused to attend her classes, and she was forced to resign, despite her acknowledged merits.

She went to Egypt where she accepted a professorship at Cairo University. For 30 years she was the Director of the general hospital in Alexandria. As a microbiologist, with a special interest in tropical diseases, cholera and typhus, she undertook laboratory experiments which revealed ways of eliminating lethal epidemics, announcing her results at international medical conferences. In Alexandria she was a respected figure in the Greek community because of her cultural interests and literary occupations; Greek and foreign artists and intellectuals met frequently at her home. She returned to Greece in 1938, and was appointed Professor at Athens University.

**Pan Chao** [Ban Zhao] (*c*45–115AD). Chinese scholar and historian. She was born in Fufang, in modern Shanxi. Her family had distinguished connections, and her aunt was a member of the harem of the court of Cheng Ti. She was educated by her father Pan Pioq, a magistrate, and by her brother, Pan Ku; both were historians. Her other brother was a military commander in Central Asia. She married Tsao Shi-shu at the age of 14 and had several children, but when she was widowed continued to work as a writer. Her father died when he was 52, in the middle of writing his great *History of the Han Dynasty*, and her brother took over the work. When he died in prison, accused of plotting against the new Emperor Ho in 92, Pan Chao was ordered to complete the work. She also taught the young Empress Teng, and was known as an astronomer, mathematician and poet. Her lasting fame is partly due to her *Nu Chien* ('Advice for Women'), a Confucian moralistic work advocating submissiveness and domesticity as essential virtues; it was used as a moral text for centuries. She also wrote 16 books of poems, narratives and essays. She died after an arduous journey accompanying her son to his post as a provincial magistrate.

N.L. Swann: *Pan Chao: Foremost Women Scholar of China* (1932)

**Pandit, Vijaya (Lakshmi)** (1900–). Indian politician. She was the sister of Pandit Jawarharlal Nehru, and married Ranjit Pandit in 1921. A follower of Gandhi, she joined the Non-co-operative Movement and was imprisoned for a year in 1931. During the following decade she rose to influential positions in local government in Allahabad and in the Uttar Pradesh government (1937–9); she became the first woman minister in 1946. A member of the Congress Party, she served three further terms of imprisonment – in 1932, 1941 and 1942, when she was detained for a year.

Following Independence, Vijaya Pandit was leader of the Indian Delegation to the United Nations (1946–51), and she was later President of the United Nations General Assembly (1953–4). She has also held ambassadorial posts: to the USSR (1947–9), the USA (1949–51) and as High Commissioner to the UK and Ambassador to the Irish Republic (1955–61). After her return to India she acted as Governor of Maharashtra (1962–4). During the period of Indira Gandhi's Emergency Powers she left the Congress Party to join Congress for Democracy (1977), which is now part of the Janata Party. Her memoirs, *The Scope of Happiness* (1979), describe her remarkable political career.

**Pankhurst.** English family of suffragettes. Emmeline Pankhurst (often simply referred to as Mrs Pankhurst) came from Manchester to London in 1905 and led the militant Women's Social and Political Union before World War I. Her three daughters, Christabel, Sylvia and Adela, were born in Manchester and initially educated at home and at Manchester High School. They all joined their mother in the early activities of the Women's Social and Political Union

(WSPU) but their lives took increasingly divergent paths after 1910.

D. Mitchell: *The Fighting Pankhursts* (1967)

**(1) Emmeline** [née Goulden] (1858–1928). She was the eldest of ten children of a prosperous Manchester calico printer. Her parents were radical reformers, and she attended her first suffrage meeting with her mother at the age of 14. She was educated at boarding schools in Manchester and Paris. In 1879 she married Dr Richard Pankhurst, a progressive barrister, and both worked for the Manchester Women's Suffrage Committee and Married Women's Property Committee, Dr Pankhurst drafting the 1882 Bill. Their circle of friends included ANNIE BESANT, Kier Hardie, Charles Dilke and William Morris. Active Liberals until Gladstone's omission of women's suffrage from the 1884 Reform Act, they joined the Fabian Society and then the Independent Labour Party (ILP) in 1893. In 1885 they had moved to London but Richard was too radical for success at the bar, so Emmeline ran a shop in the Tottenham Court Road. In 1898 Dr Pankhurst died, and to support the family she became Registrar of births and deaths in Rusholme, a working-class district of Manchester.

In 1903 she resigned from the ILP and with her daughter (2) Christabel formed the WSPU. After two years of local campaigning, the publicity given to the arrest of Christabel and ANNIE KENNEY in 1905 launched the party into the militant stage. Emmeline went to live with (3) Sylvia, then an art student in London, where she recruited, organized, led marches and deputations, becoming increasingly autocratic but inspiring many by her brilliant oratory. Her first arrest in 1908 accelerated the campaign which now adopted illegal tactics such as window-smashing. She made fund-raising tours to the USA in 1909 and 1911. In 1912, with the PETHICK-LAWRENCES, she was convicted of conspiracy, and after her release she and Christabel assumed full control of the WSPU. In 1913 she was re-arrested for incitement to violence, and under the 'Cat and Mouse Act' was imprisoned, went on hunger and thirst-strike, was released when her condition became critical, then re-arrested 12 times, but appeared on public platforms even on a stretcher. She joined Christabel in France, before visiting the USA, where her detention on Ellis Island caused an uproar.

With the outbreak of World War I in 1914, the WSPU ceased campaigning and Emmeline threw herself into the recruitment drive, taking no part in the final negotiations for suffrage before 1918. After the war she adopted four orphans. She toured Canada speaking on social purity and child welfare, and on her return in 1926 joined the Conservative Party and was prospective candidate for Whitechapel. She was able to celebrate full women's suffrage just before her death.

E. Pankhurst: *My Own Story* (1914)
S. Pankhurst: *Life of Emmeline Pankhurst* (1935).

**(2) Christabel** (1880–1958). Educated at home, Manchester High School and Switzerland (1896), after her father's death (in 1898) she helped her mother as Deputy Registrar. In 1901, while studying law at Victoria University, Manchester, she was a member of the North of England Society for Women's Suffrage and of the Manchester Women's Trade Union Council, establishing a close relationship with Eva Gore-Booth from 1902. Growing impatient with the Independent Labour Party, (1) Emmeline and Christabel decided to form a women's branch, founding the WSPU in 1903 with the slogan 'Votes for Women'. After two years of local campaigning, she caused a sensation when arrested with ANNIE KENNEY after their protest at a Liberal election meeting in Free Trade Hall, Manchester; the *Daily Mail* newspaper coined the term 'suffragette'. Her militancy had been further inflamed by the refusal of Lincoln's Inn to accept her in 1904 because she was a woman. In 1905 she won a prize for International Law and came joint first in the LLB (1906).

In 1907 Christabel moved to London, for the next six years acting as organizer and courageous orator for the WSPU. Arrested several times, at her trial in 1908 she called as witnesses the Home Secretary (H. Gladstone) and the Chancellor of Exchequer (Lloyd George). Threatened with a conspiracy charge in 1912 she escaped to Paris, joining the Lesbian feminist group around the Princesse de Polignac. She broke with the PETHICK-LAWRENCES but directed the English campaign through *The Suffragette*. Using strong separatist rhetoric, she attacked sexual as well as political oppression, winning new recruits with her long articles on venereal disease and prostitution, re-issued as *The Great Scourge*. She stopped her work for suffrage to help Emmeline in the recruiting drive in 1914. In 1918 she was narrowly defeated at Smethwick, after propounding a vision of industrial salvation through collectivism and automation. After 1920, politics gave way to Christian polemics as she preached the Second Advent through a series of best-selling tracts. She settled in California in 1940. Her book, *Unshackled: the Story of how we won the Vote*, was eventually published a year after her death, in 1959.

D. Mitchell: *Queen Christabel* (1977)

**(3) (Estelle) Sylvia** (1882–1960). After leaving school, she attended the Municipal School of Art, Manchester, where she won medals and a travelling scholarship which enabled her to take a diploma at the Accademia, Venice, before taking up a National Scholarship at the Royal Academy of Art. A founder member of the WSPU, she devoted her art to producing banners, posters, murals, the 'Holloway Brooch' and the 'Suffragette Tea Service'. She also painted superb studies of women at work. She is described as 'essentially an artist, drawn into the unsuitable and unsympathetic political machine' by HELENA SWANWICK. She founded WSPU branches in the East End of London (1912–13), which became the separate East London Federation. She was imprisoned 13 times and forcibly fed on hunger strike.

In 1914 her violent opposition to World War I led to a final break with her mother, (1) Emmeline. She founded the pacifist socialist journal *Worker's Dreadnought* (1914–24), ran clinics, a Montessori school, cheap restaurants and a co-operative toy factory; she was fined for anti-war propaganda. In 1920 she stowed away on a Finnish ship bound for the USSR and met Lenin. She published *Soviet Russia as I saw it* (1921) and was a prominent member of the British Communist Party until expelled for refusing to hand over the *Worker's Dreadnought*. She continued her feminist socialist campaigns and in 1928 refused to

*Adelina Patti*

*Evita Perón*

*Madame de Pompadour*

*Adelaide Ristori*

name her son's father (Italian socialist Silvio Orto) in protest against persecution of unmarried mothers. She published *The Suffragette Movement* (1931) and *Life of Emmeline Pankhurst* (1935).

During the 1930s she protested against Italian fascism and became deeply involved in the Abyssinian struggle, editing *Ethiopian News* (1936–56), writing several books and pamphlets, and finally settling in Ethiopia in 1956. She was editor of the *Ethiopian Observer* when she died.

R. Pankhurst: *Sylvia Pankhurst: Artist and Crusader* (1979)
P. Romero: *E. Sylvia Pankhurst* (1987)

**(4) Adela Constantia** (1885–1961). She campaigned with her mother and sisters for the WSPU but after a disagreement with Emmeline she emigrated to Australia. She first joined Vida Goldstein's separatist feminist group in Victoria, which became the Women's Peace Army in 1914, and then organized opposition to World War I. She published her pacifist booklet, *Put up the Sword*, in 1915. In 1917 she resigned and joined the Victoria Socialist Party as an organizer. She toured Western Australia, wrote a five-act play, *Betrayed*, edited a newsletter, *The Dawn*, suffered fines and imprisonment, and married the militant socialist Tom Walsh. They moved to Sydney in 1919 with her son and three stepdaughters, and she helped Walsh's efforts to mobilize the Seamen's Union, of which he was President (1921–25). Although they had taken part in the early discussions which led to the founding of the Australian Communist Party, by 1928 they were campaigning against communist involvement and sabotage tactics, and Adela was speaking in favour of industrial peace, national unity and the virtues of family life. In 1929 she launched the Australian Women's Guild of Empire, editing the *Empire Gazette* until 1939. Then she became involved with the Australia First Movement, visiting and recommending an alliance with Japan. She resigned after Pearl Harbour but was interned in 1942. After Tom Walsh's death in 1943 she became a nurse for retarded children. Just before her death she was received into the Roman Catholic Church. As with all the Pankhursts her life reveals both deep commitment and startling changes of direction.

**Paradis, Maria Theresia von** (1759–1824). Austrian composer, pianist, organist and singer. Blind from an early age, she had a wide-ranging musical education in Vienna from several distinguished musicians, including Salieri and Kozeluch. She was soon in demand as a concert pianist, also giving private performances in aristocratic homes (her father was the Viennese Imperial Court Secretary). In 1783–4 she made her first tour, being particularly acclaimed in Paris, where she also appeared as a singer, and in London. A device invented by Riedinger enabled her to write her compositions down, and she wrote letters by means of a specially made hand-printing machine. Her works include the Singspiel *Der Schulkandidat* (1792), a cantata on the death of Louis XVI (1793), several piano sonatas and songs. In 1808 she founded an institute for music education in Vienna. Mozart was so impressed by her playing that he wrote a piano concerto for her (probably no. 18 in B flat, K 456), and she was the dedicatee of an organ concerto by Salieri.

**Pardo Bazán, Emilia**, Condesa de (1851–1921). Spanish novelist. She was born into an ancient Spanish family in La Coruña, Galicia, and at the age of 16 married an older man, Señor de Quiroga, and moved to Madrid. Her interest in philosophy, science and literature is reflected in her early essays and first novel, *Pascual López* (1879), about the life of a medical student. In the preface to her novel *Un viaje de novios* (1881), and in the essays in *La cuestión palpitante* (1883), she argued for the introduction of French Naturalism and the treatment of social problems into Spanish realistic fiction; her views provoked a fierce debate. She undertook detailed research for *La tribuna* (1882), a novel about a revolutionary woman tobacco worker, but her greatest achievements were the studies of decadent Galician aristocracy in *Los pazos de Ulloa/ The Son of the Bondswoman* (1886) and *La madre naturaleza* (1887). After 1890 realism gradually gave way to Christian idealism, and her final novels *Sirena negra* (1907) and *Dulci dueno* (1911) are marked by a mystical spiritualism.

Pardo Bazán was also an influential critic, drawing attention to Russian, as well as

French, writers in the 1880s, and running a famous literary salon in Madrid. She acted as a counsellor on public education, and in 1916 was made Professor of Romantic Literature at the Central University of Madrid, a post never previously held by a woman. She was a life-long feminist.

W.T. Pattison: *Emilia Pardo Bazán* (1971)

**Parker** [née Rothschild], **Dorothy** (1893–1967). American wit, poet and writer. Born in New Jersey, she spent an unhappy childhood in New York with her father and stepmother, and was educated first at a convent and then at Miss Dana's School, Morristown, New Jersey. After her father's death in 1912, she moved to live alone in New York, working as a pianist in a dancing school. She was witty, ambitious, an eccentric dresser, a supporter of the suffrage movement, and a determined 'independent' woman, and after having a poem published in Crowninshield's *Vanity Fair* (1916), she got a job on *Vogue*, which he also owned, writing captions.

In 1917 she married Edwin Parker, a Wall Street businessman, but after his return from the war they separated; they were divorced in 1928. In the meantime Dorothy had become drama critic of *Vanity Fair* in 1919, had been fired in 1920 for an over-caustic review, and had achieved national success with her verse, published in *Enough Rope* (1926) and *Sunset Gun* (1928). She had also experienced a drink problem, a series of sad affairs, and two suicide attempts, in 1923 and 1925. Her public success continued with verse (*Death or Taxes*, 1931; *Not so Deep as a Well*, 1936) and with her bitter-sweet short stories in *Scribner's* and *The New Yorker*, collected in *Laments for Living* (1930) and *After Such Pleasures* (1933).

In the early 1930s she moved to Hollywood with Alan Campbell, whom she married in 1933, divorced in 1947, remarried in 1950, was separated from in 1953, and was finally reunited with from 1956 until Campbell's death in 1963. In California she worked on many scripts, including her great friend LILLIAN HELLMAN's *The Little Foxes* (1941). Always outspokenly anti-fascist, she reported from Spain during the Civil War. Her last play was *Ladies of the Corridor* (1953), a study of widows in an hotel on New York's upper East Side. She herself lived as a virtual recluse at the Volney Hotel towards the end of her life. She left the bulk of her estate to Martin Luther King.

Parker's stories expose loneliness, cruelty and the isolation of women, and she was also an influential reviewer. But she is remembered best for her wit, from *Vogue* captions such as 'Brevity is the Soul of Lingerie' to the typically self-deprecating reply to 'Are you Dorothy Parker?' – 'Yes, do you mind?'.

L. Frewin: *The Late Mrs Dorothy Parker* (1987)

**Parr, Catherine** (1512–48). Sixth and last queen of Henry VIII of England. She was the daughter of Sir Thomas Parr, a Westmoreland baron who was Master of the Wards and Controller of the Household of Henry VIII. He died when Catherine was five, and she was raised with her brother and sister by her young mother, who remained unmarried and gave the children an excellent education. Catherine became a notable scholar, fluent in Latin, capable in Greek and modern languages. Her first marriage was to the elderly Edward Borough who died in 1529; she then became the third wife of John Neville, Lord Latimer. He died in the winter of 1542–3, leaving her large estates in Worcestershire, and she planned to marry Sir Thomas Seymour. But (apparently to her terror at first) she was proposed to by Henry VIII and eventually married him in July 1543, becoming his sixth and final wife.

Catherine was calm and tactful: she nursed and entertained her irascible and often ill husband, and undoubtedly modified some of his policies, such as the persecution of Roman Catholics under the Act of the Six Articles. When Henry was away in France in 1544 she acted as Regent in his absence. She had a particular influence on the lives of MARY I and ELIZABETH I, supervising their education in detail, and indirectly influencing the scholarly aspirations of women in the 16th century. Roger Ascham addressed her as 'learned Queen', and she herself wrote prose and religious poetry such as the *Lamentation or Complaint of a Sinner* (1547), published in Elizabeth's reign. She also arranged for the translation and publication of the first part of Erasmus's *Paraphrase of the Gospels*, and edited

*Prayers and Meditations*, which became known as the *Queen's Prayers*. Interested in theology, and supporting Protestant reformers like Miles Coverdale and Nicholas Udall, her independence of view allegedly almost caused Henry to authorize her arrest.

After Henry's death in 1547 she did not obtain the Regency, but she and her brother retained influence at court, and she managed to obtain Edward's consent to her marriage to her former suitor, the ambitious Thomas Seymour, now Baron Seymour of Sudeley. She retired to Sudeley Castle for the birth of her only child, a daughter, but died of puerperal fever a few days later.

A. Martienssen: *Catherine Parr* (1974)

**Parra, Teresa de la** [Anna Teresa Sanojo] (1895–1936). Venezuelan novelist. Born into a wealthy family, she was educated in Paris and returned to Caracas as an adolescent. Her works, which are all fictionalized autobiography, won immediate popularity. They include *Diario de una señorita que se fastidia* (1922) and *Ifigenía* (1924), which took the form of a long letter from a disillusioned 18-year-old returning from Paris who finds herself faced with the rigid conventions and hypocritical attitudes to women of Venezuelan society. Her later work, *Memorías de mama Blanca* (1929), is based on her memories of an idyllic childhood on a family estate. She was an innovatory writer, who wrote with sensitivity about women's desires and psychological make-up. She never married, despite her many admirers, and in the last years of her life she returned to Europe seeking a cure for tuberculosis in various sanitoriums.

T. de la Parra: *Mama Blanca's Souvenirs* (Eng. trans. 1959)

**Parren, Kalliroe** (1861–1940). Greek pioneer of feminism and journalist. She trained as a teacher and for ten years was headmistress in various girls' schools, but gave up teaching to dedicate herself to journalism. In 1888 she became Editor of her own newspaper, *The Women's Newspaper*, the first ever to address itself to, and be run exclusively by, women. Apart from standard news items, it carried articles and reports about social problems, especially those relating to women. It became an instrument of her struggle to raise the intellectual and social status of Greek women and to take the concern about women beyond charitable relief work or social and cultural functions.

Parren did much to direct public awareness to women's rights. She took part in international women's conferences and founded the Union for the Emancipation of Women and the Union of Greek Women (in 1894 and 1896 respectively). She ran classes and schools where educated women gave basic instruction in reading and writing; through her efforts many women's institutes, as well as homes for widows and war orphans and special hospitals for incurable diseases, were founded. Her campaigns also influenced government policies: laws for the protection of children and working women were enacted, the first women were permitted to study at the University and the Polytechnic of Athens, and women doctors were appointed to women's prisons.

In 1911 she founded the Lyceum of Greek Women, an association which supported women in the fields of education, home economics, child care and job orientation. She even demanded the vote for women, though this was not to come about until long after her death. Her pioneering work prepared the ground for the more organized movement which followed. Parren also wrote four novels, a feminist play and two studies: *The History of Woman* and *A History of Greek Women from 1650 to 1860*.

**Parton, Dolly (Rebecca)** (1946–). American country singer. Born in Locust Ridge, Sevier County, Tennessee, the fourth of 12 children of a mountain farmer, she had become a child radio performer by the age of ten, and made her first record at 13. After leaving high school in 1964, she went to Nashville, working as a songwriter until 1967 when the records *Dumb Blonde* and *Something Fishy* established her as a singer. She went on to make a series of best-selling duets with Porter Wagoner, touring with his road show until 1974, when she began working as a solo star, with hits such as *Jolene* (1974) and *All I can do* (1976). She now runs her own company and continues to tour, as well as to record and appear on radio and television. In 1980 her natural talent as a comedienne was revealed in an effervescent performance in the film *9 to 5*, with JANE FONDA. In 1981 she recorded two major albums, *Love is like a Butterfly* and *9 to 5 and Odd Jobs*. She has since made more films, such as *The Best Little Whorehouse in Texas* (1982) and *Rhinestone* (1984), and her recent albums include *Real Love* (1985) and *Portrait* (1986). She has been married to Carl Dean since 1966.

J. Keeley: *Dolly Parton* (1979)

**Parturier, Françoise** [pseud.: Nicole] (1919–). French journalist. Born in Paris, the daughter of a doctor, she studied at Paris University and in 1947 married Jean Gatichon. She taught contemporary literature in the USA (1950–51), and then became a professional journalist and writer. A regular contributor to *Figaro* from 1956, as 'Nicole' she collaborated on three books with Josette Raoul-Duval before writing under her own name from 1959. She is one of the more direct and popular of contemporary French feminists, and her works include *L'amant de cinq jours* (1959), *Marianne m'a dit* (1963), *Lettre ouverte aux hommes* (1968), *L'amour?*, *Le Plaisir?* (1968), *Lettre ouverte aux femmes* (1974), *La lettre d'Irlande* (1979) and *Les Hauts de Ramatuelle* (1983). With Honoré Damier she also wrote *Les intellectuels, les bas bleus (1844) et les femmes socialistes (1849)* (1974).

**Pasionaria, La.** *See* IBARRURI, DOLORES.

**Pasta** [née Negri], **Giuditta (Maria Costanza)** (1797–1865). Italian soprano. She was a pupil of Giuseppe Scappa in Milan, where she made her debut in his *Le tre Eleonore* (1815). Engagements followed in Paris (1816, in Paer's *Il principe di Taranto*) and London (1817, in Cimarosa's *Penelope*); the benefit of a further year's study was evident in a slightly more successful appearance in Venice (1819, in Pacini's *Adelaide Comingo*). Her first triumph, however, was as Desdemona in Rossini's *Otello* (Paris, 1821), a role she repeated in London (1824), *Semiramide* following soon after, both with the composer conducting. The roles with which she is particularly associated are Amina in Bellini's *La sonnambula* (1831) and the title roles of *Norma* (1831) and Donizetti's *Anna Bolena*, all of which were written for her. Other roles she created include the title parts of Pacini's *Niobe* (1826) and Bellini's *Beatrice di Tenda* (1833). The esteem in which she was held was based as much on the intensity of her acting as on the brilliance of her voice, which became increasingly uneven towards the end of her career.

M. Ferranti-Giulini: *Giuditta Pasta e i suoi tempi* (1935)

**Paston, Margaret** (1423–84). English countrywoman. Margaret Paston is one of the liveliest correspondents in the famous Paston letters, which give a vivid account of life in England in the 15th century. She was the daughter of John Mautby, of Mautby in Essex, who arranged her marriage to John Paston, a nearby landowner, farmer and prosperous merchant. She remained at their home in Norfolk, looking after his interests, when he was elected to parliament in 1460. Life was turbulent and made precarious by intermittent civil war. In 1450 a neighbour who claimed the property had attacked it with a gang of men and in 1465 Margaret had to defend the house against another claimant who led 60 armed men against her. She also transacted deals in her husband's malt and wool business, dealt with the lawyers and courts at Norwich, ran a large household, and ruled her own family with an iron hand.

N. Davis, ed.: *Paston Letters and Papers of the Fifteenth Century* (1971)

**Paterson** [née Smith], **Emma (Anne)** (1848–86). English trade unionist. Born in London, she was encouraged to study by her father, a schoolteacher. At first an apprentice bookbinder, after her father's death she worked as Assistant Secretary at the Working Men's Club and Institute Union (1866–72). Here she met Thomas Paterson, whom she married in 1873, after a brief spell as Secretary of the Women's Suffrage Association. Together they visited the USA, where Emma found the models she had been seeking for women's industrial organizations in the Parasol and Umbrella Makers' Union and the Women's Typographical Union. On her return home in April 1874, she published her idea for a general union of women workers in *Labour*

*News*, and in July founded the Women's Provident and Protective League and began organizing women in different trades, first bookbinding, and then dressmaking, millinery and upholstery. In 1875 she was the first woman to attend the Trade Union Congress, at Glasgow, and she continued to attend until her death. She fought particularly for women factory inspectors but opposed protective legislation in the 1870s (like many other suffragists) because it might jeopardize women's employment to the benefit of men.

From 1876 she edited the monthly *Women's Union Journal* which extended its coverage to suffrage, educational and legal rights and dress reform. In the same year, following the example of her friend EMILY FAITHFUL, she taught herself printing and founded the Women's Printing Society. Despite ill-health (she was diagnosed a diabetic in 1885), she continued to organize and write until her death. Lady EMILY DILKE then took over the League, which became the Women's Trade Union League in 1891.

H. Goldman: *Emma Paterson* (1974)

**Patil, Smita** (1955–86). Indian film star. Smita Patil's career started with a theatre group in Poona. In 1972 she began working as a television newscaster in Bombay, where she was 'discovered' by the director Shyam Benegal, who gave her a leading role in *Nishant* (1975) and made her a national star over night. After her success in Benegal's *Bhumika* (1978), based on the life of a famous Marathi actress harrowed by alcoholism and disastrous love affairs, she was recognized as an actress of considerable stature, as well as glamour. She was said to embody the 'ideal modern woman' of the new, realistic Indian cinema, and her notable films include Benegal's *Bhumika* (1978) and *Mandi* (1983), which also starred the other great contemporary Indian film star Shabana Azmi, and *Raowan* (1984).

**Patterson** [née Abraham], **(Constance) Marie** (1934–). English trade unionist. She was educated at Pendleton High School and Bedford College, London, and became a staff member of the Transport and General Workers' Union in 1957. In 1960 she married Thomas Patterson (*d* 1976). Marie was Woman's Officer of the union from 1963 to 1976, and made her reputation as a calm, tough negotiator. From 1963–84 she was a member of the General Council of the Trades Union Congress (TUC), and was Chairman of the TUC from 1974 to 1975 and in 1977. Other positions have included a place on the Executive of the Confederation of Shipbuilding and Engineering Unions from 1966–84 (President 1977–8) and membership of various industrial training boards, of the Equal Opportunities Commission (from 1975–84) and of the Central Arbitration Commission (from 1976–84) and she was also a Director of Remploy from 1966–87. She was awarded the OBE in 1973 and created CBE in 1978.

**Patti, Adelina** (1843–1919). Italian soprano. Both her parents were professional singers, and her mother is reputed to have appeared as Bellini's Norma the night before Adelina was born. The family went to New York in 1844, and Adelina made her first public appearance there, in a charity concert, at the age of seven. She studied singing with her brother-in-law, Maurice Strakosch, and, having toured the USA with such musicians as Ole Bull and Louis Gottschalk, made her formal operatic debut as Donizetti's Lucia (New York, 1859). Soon afterwards she was invited to Covent Garden (1861, as Amina in Bellini's *La sonnambula*, a role she repeated for her debuts in Paris, 1862, and Vienna, 1863), subsequently appearing there in 25 consecutive seasons in over 30 roles, notably in the first London performance of *Aïda* (1876); her final performances there were in 1895. Meanwhile her tours extended as far afield as St Petersburg [now Leningrad] and Buenos Aires, and wherever she went her audiences were captivated – as much by such encores as *Home, Sweet Home* as by her operatic repertoire. She brought to such roles as Amina, Lucia and Violetta a purity of tone and astonishing technique that earned her reputation as the 'Queen of Song' (as well as her fortune amassed through being the best paid singer of the day: some of her American performances were at a fee of £1000 each). When Rossini died in Paris in 1868, Patti and MARIETTA ALBONI sang a duet from his *Stabat mater* at his funeral.

Patti was married first to the Marquis de Caux, whom she divorced in order to marry the tenor Ernest Nicolini in 1886; he had sung opposite her in *La traviata* on the occasion of her debut at La Scala (1877). A year after his death she married Baron Rolf Cederström.

Her career spanned a legendary 45 years, and 'farewell performances' were legion. She made her final American tour in 1903, having given her last operatic performances in France in 1897. After her final London concert (1906) she made a tour of the provinces, coming out of retirement for charity concerts until 1914. She died at her castle in Wales and was buried in Paris.

H. Klein: *The Reign of Patti* (1920)

**Pauker, Ana** (1893–1956). Romanian socialist. She was the daughter of a Jewish ritual butcher from northern Moravia, and after attending local schools she taught in a Jewish primary school in Bucharest during World War I. An early member of the socialist underground movement, she and her husband Marcel, whom she met while studying medicine in Zürich, helped to found the Romanian Communist Party in 1921. On a secret mission to Bucharest following a major railroad strike in 1934 she was arrested; she was imprisoned until Antonescu exchanged her for two Romanian politicians who had been arrested by the Russians in 1940.

In World War II Pauker organized a Romanian prisoners' division of the Red Army and afterwards acted as liaison between the national party and the occupying forces. She was credited with an enormous, and sinister, power, and although she opposed Stalinist policies she rose by 1947 to become Minister of Foreign Affairs, the world's first woman in such a post, and Vice-Premier. In 1952 she was purged on charges of deviationism, and she spent the rest of her life in obscurity, although still influential in the Party.

**Paul, Alice** (1885–1977). American feminist. Born in Mooretown, New Jersey, into a Quaker family, she was educated at Swarthmore College and then the New York School of Philanthropy; she later received a PhD from Pennsylvania University, and published *The Legal Position of Women in Pennsylvania*. In 1907 she came to England to continue her studies at Birmingham and London universities. She worked in settlements and became involved with the PANKHURSTS' Women's Social and Political Union; she was arrested six times and imprisoned three times after suffrage demonstrations in 1909. She went on hunger-strike and was forcibly fed.

Paul returned to the USA in 1912 and, with HARRIET STANTON BLATCH, organized massive suffrage parades in New York. In 1913 she became head of the congressional committee of the National American Woman's Suffrage Alliance (NAWSA), but left to form her own more militant Congressional Union, which became the Women's Party in 1916. Fanatically determined, a charismatic speaker and brilliant propagandist, she used tactics which brought many new recruits but also wide hostility, especially after her nationwide tour of 1915, when she attacked the Democratic candidates for not supporting suffrage, and her demonstrations against the war in 1916. After the franchise was won in 1918 Paul mobilized the National Woman's Party to fight for the Equal Rights Amendment, campaigning vigorously throughout the 1920s. In 1927 she became Chairwoman of the Women's Research Foundation, and in 1928 she founded the World Party for Equal Rights for Women. She continued to organize in the USA and in Geneva for equal rights, for pacifism, and for a wider public role for women.

**Pavlova, Anna** [Pavolvna] (1882–1931). She was born into a poor family in St Petersburg [now Leningrad] and her father died when she was two. Although she was a sickly child, she became determined on a dancing career after seeing a performance of *The Sleeping Beauty* at the Mariinsky Theatre. In 1892 she entered the Imperial Ballet School. She first danced *Giselle* in 1903 and achieved ballerina status in 1906. The following year Mikhail Fokin created 'The Dying Swan' for her. She toured Denmark, and Sweden where she was awarded the Order of Merit and her carriage was pulled through the streets by admirers. In 1908 she danced Aurora and visited Leipzig, Prague and Vienna. She appeared with Nizhinsky in Fokin's *Pavillon d'Armide* in 1909 during her only season with Dyagilev's Ballets Russes in Paris. Partnered by Mordkin, she appeared in London in *Coppélia* in 1910, returning in 1911 to dance in *Giselle*, *Cleopatra*, *Petrushka*, and *Les sylphides*. In 1912 she bought Ivy House, Hampstead, London, which became her base for the rest of her life.

Pavlova resigned from the Mariinsky Theatre in 1913 and formed her own company. The next decade was filled with international tours managed by her reputed husband, Victor Dandré; they had no children. It is estimated that the company travelled 300,000 miles, giving nearly 3600 performances, taking ballet to provincial areas as well as capital cities and introducing it to countries such as Egypt, Japan, China and India. Pavlova's fame and earnings reached a peak in 1915 and in 1916 she went to Hollywood to mime *The Dumb Girl of Portici*. Her repertoire was conservative but her immense dedication, superb technique and magnetic appeal in performance won her admirers throughout the world. In 1930 she danced *Giselle* for the last time in the UK; the next year she died suddenly from pneumonia after catching a chill on the way to The Hague to begin yet another tour.

O. Kerensky: *Anna Pavlova* (1973)
K. Money: *Pavlova* (1982)

**Paxinou, Katina** (1900–73). Greek actress. She was born into a wealthy family in Piraeus; her sister, Maria Ralli, became a well-known poet. Katina was educated at a French-Greek school and then in Switzerland, before going on to study music in Berlin, Geneva and Vienna. Her first appearance in Athens, at the age of 20, was in Maeterlinck's *Sister Beatrice*. In 1916 she married a rich Greek from Romania, but they separated after having two children. During the 1920s and 1930s her reputation increased and she was the leading actress of the Greek National Theatre for many years. From 1940 to 1950 she lived in the USA and in England, where she earned great popularity for her personal and passionate interpretation of the leading roles in classical and modern dramas, from Clytemnestra in the *Oresteia* to Abbie in Eugene O'Neill's *Desire under the Elms*. Among her most famous roles were Mrs Alving in Ibsen's *Ghosts* and Bernarda Alba in Lorca's *La casa de Bernarda Alba*. In 1944 she was awarded an Academy Award for her role as

Pilar in the film *For Whom the Bell Tolls*. Her other films included *Mourning becomes Electra* (1947) and *The Miracle* (1959).

When she returned to Greece she acted only in classical tragedies performed in ancient theatres, her special talent attracting massive audiences.

**Payne** [née Moore], **Sylvia (May)** (1880–1974). English psychoanalyst. The daughter of a clergyman, she was educated at the London Hospital School of Medicine, qualifying in 1906. She married J.E. Payne, a surgeon, and they had three children.

During World War I, Sylvia was Commandant and Medical Officer in charge of the Torquay Red Cross Hospital, for which she was created CBE in 1918. She then became a psychiatrist at the London Clinic of Psychoanalysis. Psychoanalysis was a controversial subject, and Sylvia helped establish it as a useful contribution to psychotherapy. She became Chairman of Directors of the Institute of Psychoanalysis, President of the British Psychoanalytical Society, and Fellow of the British Psychological Society.

**Peabody, Elizabeth Palmer** (1804–94). American educator. She was born in Billerica, Massachusetts, and educated at her mother's schools in Salem and Lancaster, where she worked as a pupil teacher. She organized private schools and acted as secretary to the Unitarian teacher Ellery Channing (1825–34), who influenced her educational theory, as did Bronson Alcott, with whom she worked in the Temple School, Boston (*Record of a School*, written in 1835, records her experiences there). From 1839 to 1845 she ran a bookshop and a publishing business, which carried a selection of European books and produced works by her brother-in-law Nathaniel Hawthorne and her friend MARGARET FULLER; it became a centre for the Transcendentalist Club. In connection with the movement she also published the journal *The Dial* (1842–3).

After 1845 she returned to teaching, briefly edited the journal *Aesthetic Papers* (1849), and wrote several texts, including her *Chronological History of the United*

*States* (1865). Increasingly interested in infant education, she organized progressive nursery schools, including the first publicly-funded kindergarten, in Boston, and in 1867 travelled to Germany to see Froebel schools in action. On her return she lectured widely and published the *Kindergarten Messenger* (1873–5). After 1880 she also campaigned for American-Indian education, continued to write, and taught in the Concord School of Philosophy.

R.M. Baylor: *Elizabeth Palmer Peabody: Kindergarten Pioneer* (1965)

**Pechey-Phipson, (Mary) Edith** (1845–1908). English doctor. She was born near Colchester, the sixth of seven children; her father was a minister. After working as a governess, in 1869 she helped initiate the struggle for medical education for women in Britain by being admitted, with SOPHIA JEX-BLAKE and three others, to the University of Edinburgh. In her first year she won the Chemistry Prize, but both it and the Hope Scholarship of £250 were denied her because she was a woman, and this caused a furore. Since Edinburgh would not give medical degrees to women, she transferred to Bern University and gained her MD there; she was granted a licence to practise by the Royal College of Physicians of Ireland on the same day as Sophia Jex-Blake in 1877.

After practising in Leeds, in 1883 she went to India through the Medical Women for India Fund. She directed the new Cama Hospital, Bombay, for women and children, ran a dispensary and started a private practice in 1884. Five years later she married Herbert Phipson, the Secretary of the Fund. She advocated improved health services for women and the banning of child marriages. She learnt Hindustani, and was thus able to establish a nursing school. In 1881 she became the first woman elected to the Senate of the University of Bombay; later she fought bubonic plague in Bombay for five years. She was a member of the Royal Asiatic Society.

In 1905 she returned with her husband to England via Australia and Canada. After her retirement she was an active speaker, addressing the Suffrage Association of Leeds, among others, and leading the 'Mud March' of 1907. She founded and endowed the Pechey-Phipson Sanitorium for women

and children near Nasik in India before dying in Folkestone of breast cancer.

E. Lutzker: *Edith Pechey-Phipson, M.D.: the Story of England's Foremost Pioneering Woman Doctor* (1973)

**Peck, Annie (Smith)** (1850–1935). American mountaineer. She was born in Providence, Rhode Island. She read Classics at the University of Michigan, then taught in schools and colleges. After further study in Germany she travelled to Greece in 1885 to be the first woman admitted to the American School of Classical Studies in Athens.

On her travels in Europe she had been intrigued by the sight of the Matterhorn. After a few practice climbs she achieved celebrity by climbing the Matterhorn in 1895, dressed in knickerbockers, a tunic and a felt hat tied by a veil. She followed this with Popacatapetl and Orizaba in Mexico and the Jungfrau in Switzerland, among others. She gave lectures on climbing and in 1902 was one of the founders of the American Alpine Club. In 1904 she made the first ascent of Mt Sorata (6489 metres) in Bolivia, and another in 1908, of the south peak of Huascarán in the Peruvian Andes. This she estimated at 7291 metres and claimed it as a female altitude record, but FANNY BULLOCK WORKMAN challenged this and at her own expense sent French engineers who triangulated it at 6626 metres – still a remarkable feat without oxygen, and an American record in the Western hemisphere. Her books include *A Search for the Apex of America* (1911; published in the UK as *High Moutain Climbing in Peru and Bolivia*, 1912) and *The South American Tour* (1913).

In 1911, at the age of 61, she climbed Mt Coropuna (6455 metres) in Peru, planting a 'Votes for Women' sign at the summit. She described herself as a firm believer in the equality of the sexes: '. . . any great achievement in any line of endeavour would be an advantage to my sex'. Other publications include *Flying over South America – 20,000 miles by air* (1932), on the feasibility of commercial aviation there. Her last climb was of Mt Madison, New Hampshire, when she was 82. In 1927 the Lima Geographical Society named Huascarán's north peak Cumbre Ana Peck in her honour.

**Pedersen, Helga** (1911–). Danish lawyer and politician. Born in Taarnborg, she was educated at Copenhagen University and at Columbia University, New York, and then worked in the Department of Justice for ten years from 1936. After World War II she became a Judge in a Copenhagen District Court, and in 1950 she was elected a Member of Parliament. She was at once appointed Minister of Justice (1950–3). She remained an MP until 1964, but was also a District Court Judge (1953–6) and an Appeal Court Judge (1956–64); in 1964, when she left Parliament, she was appointed a Judge of the Supreme Court. She has served on many important Danish committees, for example on higher education and on copyright, and has been a delegate to international conferences, including the United Nations Commission on the Status of Women. In 1971 she became the first woman Judge at the European Court of Human Rights. Her particular causes have been prison and penal reform, and improvement in the legal status of women.

**Peeters, Clara** (1594–after 1657). Dutch still-life painter. Born in Antwerp, she appears to have painted remarkable still-lifes, among the earliest examples of the genre in the Netherlands, before she was 20. She preferred scenes of food and tableware to the more usual flower and fruit arrangements, and specialized in reflected light on goblets or jewellery against dark backgrounds, or in simple meals of cheese, bread and wine. Her latest dated work is 1657, but the only relatively certain biographical information known is that she married one Henrik Joossen in Antwerp in 1639.

**Pelletier, Madeleine** [Anne] (1874–1939). French feminist. Christened Anne, she later adopted the name of Madeleine; she was born into a *petit-bourgeois* Paris household, and became a flamboyant militant feminist, dressing in men's clothes complete with tie, bowler hat and cane. She managed to train as a doctor and in 1899 became the first woman appointed to the staff of the Assistance Publique, and in 1906 the first woman allowed to qualify to work in mental hospitals. She was also one of the first women freemasons.

In the late 1890s she joined the suffrage movement, and edited the journál *La suffragiste*. She was a militant campaigner, adopting the law-breaking tactics of the PANKHURSTS' Women's Social and Political Union (WSPU) and became Secretary of Le Groupe de la Solidarité des Femmes in 1905. She was also an active member of the Socialist International, La Section française de l'Internationale Ouvrière, but failed to win the full backing of the communists for women's suffrage. In 1910 she was a candidate for the Parti Feministe of La Solidarité in the campaigns for the National Assembly, but received very few votes. She soon left the Communist Party to join the anarchists, whose policies were more egalitarian. At the end of her life she campaigned for women's right to birth control and legalized abortion, and openly practised abortions herself until her arrest in 1939. She had been paralysed by a stroke in 1937 and the judge ordered her to be interned in an asylum. Her physical and mental health rapidly deteriorated and she died within the year.

Her publications included *La femme en lutter par ses droits* (1908), *L'emancipation sexuelle de la femme* (1911), and *L'education feministe des filles* (1914). She also wrote a novel, *La femme vierge* (1933).

**Pereira, Irene (Rice)** (1907–71). American artist. She was born in Chelsea, nr Boston, but her family moved to Brooklyn in 1916, and after her father's death in 1922 Irene helped to support the family by working as a stenographer. Meanwhile she took night-school classes in design, and from 1927 to 1930 studied at the Art Students' League. She married Humberto Pereira, a commercial artist, in 1929. Two years later they visited Europe and North Africa, and she was strongly, and permanently, influenced by her experience of the light and space of the Sahara. In 1933 she had her first solo exhibition at the ACA Gallery, New York, and showed there in successive years. She joined the innovatory Design Laboratory, and her work became increasingly abstract. In the 1940s she became interested in surface texture (using glass or parchment) and light refraction, as in *Three White Squares* (1940), *Undulating Arrangement* (1947) and *Shooting Stars* (1952). In

1953 she had a major exhibition with Loren McIver at the Whitney Museum, and she continued to paint and exhibit until her death in Marbella, Spain. She was also a poet and connected her artistic experimentation with a quest for transcendental unity, writing several books on art and philosophy, including *Light and the New Reality* (1951), *The Nature of Space* (1956), *The Crystal of the Rose* (1959) and *The Evolution of Cultural Forms* (1966).

**Perey, Marguerite (Catherine)** (1909–75). French physicist. Born in Villenoble, Marguerite was educated in Paris, where she was a brilliant scholar and gained a DSc. From 1929 she was a member of MARIE CURIE's staff, and from 1958 Director of the Nuclear Research Centre at Strasbourg University. In 1939 she discovered a natural radioactive element she called 'francium' (actirium K).

She was awarded the Légion d'Honneur and L'Ordre Nationale du Mérité et des Palmes Académiques, but her outstanding honour came when she was made the first woman member of the Académie des Sciences in 1962, after this had been closed to women for 200 years. She received their *lauréat* in 1950 and 1960, and the Lavoisier Silver Medal of the French Chemical Society. From 1949 she was Honorary Professor of Nuclear Chemistry at Strasbourg. Her death was caused by exposure to radiation.

**Perkins, Frances** (1882–1965). American politician and the first woman cabinet member. She was born in Boston but brought up in Worcester, where she attended the Worcester Classical High School and then Mount Holyoke College (1898–1902), majoring in physics and chemistry. Influenced by her study of economic and labour history, and by a speech of FLORENCE KELLEY, she became a teacher. She was also a voluntary worker for the Congregational Church and a helper at the Addam's Hull House settlement. From 1907 to 1909 she was Secretary to the Philadelphia Research and Protective Association, helping immigrant working girls, but she then returned to studying economics and sociology, first at the

University of Pennsylvania, then at Columbia; she gained her MA in 1910. As Executive Secretary of the New York Consumers' League (1910) she lobbied for industrial reform and for women's rights. Appalled by scenes during the Triangle Shirt-waist Company Fire of 1911, in which 146 workers (mostly young girls) died, she became an investigator for the State Factory Committee, and then Secretary of the New York City Committee on Safety (1912–17). During this period she married an economist, Paul Wilson; they had a daughter in 1916. Wilson became severely depressive after financial trouble and was frequently in hospital, but Frances cared devotedly for him until his death in 1952.

After her co-campaigner Alfred E. Smith became Governor of New York in 1918, she joined the State Industrial Commission, and in his second administration (1923) administered important reforms such as the Workmen's Compensation Act. In 1926 she became Chairman of the Commission, and in 1929, under Roosevelt's governorship, was made Commissioner. After Roosevelt became President in 1933 she became Secretary of Labor, the first woman in the Cabinet. A vigorous and efficient administrator, she also drafted New Deal legislation such as the Social Security Act (1935), the National Labor Relations Act (1935), and the Wages and Hours Act (1938). Although she was dismissive of Communist policies, her support of organized labour provoked right-wing hostility. She resigned in 1945, but remained on the Civil Service Commission under Truman until 1952. She then lectured, and was appointed Professor at Cornell School of Industrial Relations in 1956. Her numerous publications include *People at Work* (1934) and *The Roosevelt I knew* (1946).

G.W. Martin: *Madam Secretary: Frances Perkins* (1976)

**Perón** [née Duarte], **Evita** [Eva] **(Maria)** (1922–52). Argentinian political leader. She came from a humble family in Buenos Aires. Her early history is obscure, but by the age of 20 she was an established stage and screen personality, known especially for her portrayal of self-sacrificing patriotic heroines in historical radio dramas. In his campaign to gain a popular footing for the military regime after 1943, Colonel Juan

Perón, then Minister of Labour, asked for the help of 'Señorita Radio' in an earthquake appeal. Soon after their marriage Perón was ousted from power and arrested (1945), and Evita roused the unions to strike for his release and to support his presidential bid in 1946. She collaborated in his tight control of labour, organizing women workers and also instigating educational and welfare reforms, campaigning for suffrage and fiercely attacking all opponents of the regime. The basis of her considerable power and popularity was the gigantic Social Aid Fund, which financed much public spending.

A charismatic speaker, Evita exploited both her working-class origins and her obvious glamour and wealth. In 1951 her candidacy for the vice-presidency was violently opposed by the army, and she made a dramatic broadcast publicly renouncing the office. In the same year she described her political and social ideals in *La razon de mi vida*. Her health collapsed, and her last public appearance, after an operation, was at the ceremonies installing Perón for his second term in 1952. He was deposed in 1955.

W. Harbinson: *Evita* (1981)

**Perón, Isabelita** [María Estela Martínez de] (1931–). Argentinian dancer and politician. Born in La Rioja province, she became a member of a company of travelling folk-dancers and worked in cabaret across South America. In 1961 she married Juan Perón, who had been President of Argentina from 1946 to 1955, and whose first wife had been EVITA PERÓN. They lived in Spain until 1973, when he returned to Argentina as President; she assumed the position of Vice-President. On his death in 1974 she took over as President, but her hopeless incompetence was the excuse for a military coup in 1976. She was imprisoned for abuse of public property and was released in July 1981 after five years of detention. She settled in Madrid, and although she is permitted to return to Argentina, she is banned from holding office and from making political statements. She continued to chair the Perónist party until 1985.

**Perovskaya, Sofya (Lvovna)** (1853–81). Russian conspiratorial revolutionary. She came from a distinguished noble family, her grandfather having been Governor of the Crimea. Her father was Governor-General of St Petersburg [now Leningrad], and the family lived in the Ministry of Internal Affairs building at the time of her birth. When she was 13, following an attack on the Czar, her father lost his position and they retreated to family estates in the Crimea. She taught herself during her three years in the country and in 1864 decided to enrol in the new Alarchinskii courses at St Petersburg, to study mathematics. She was encouraged by her brother but opposed by her father and she left home to live with her friend Alexandra Kornilova. Sofya became the leader in the radical Chaikovsky discussion group and from 1872 to 1873 she taught and worked as a nurse in the countryside, gradually building up contacts with revolutionary groups. In 1874, with many others, she was arrested and brought to trial but released for lack of evidence. She then worked in the capital and in Khar'kov to obtain the release of prominent prisoners; she obtained a false passport and joined the Zamlya i Volya ('Land and Liberty') group. After the split in the movement in 1879 she became a leading member of the terrorist wing, involved in assassination attempts with VERA FIGNER and others, including her lover Zhelyabov. In February 1881 she organized and directed the successful assassination of the Czar. Zhelyabov had already been arrested and Sofya became totally careless of her own safety; she was captured in March, tried with five others, and sentenced to death. She was hanged just before Zhelyabov, on 3 April, aged 28.

**Peters, Mary (Elizabeth)** (1939–). British athlete. Born at Halewood, Lancashire, Mary competed in the pentathlon for 17 years before achieving fame at the Munich Olympics in 1972. In the 1964 Olympics she was placed fourth, and she was only ninth in the 1968 Olympics, partly because of an injured ankle. She rested in 1969 and in 1970 her form improved; she won gold medals in both the shot and the pentathlon while representing Britain at the Fourth Commonwealth Games. Her pentathlon score was 5148 points (4524 in the new tables).

Between 1971 and 1972 she was able to improve this score dramatically by changing her high-jump style from the straddle to the Fosbury flop, which brought her jumping alone close to world class. Her shot-putting never quite reached this. Prior to the Olympics, she raised the British pentathlon record to 4630 points, ranking her fifth among pentathlon contenders.

Her cheerful perseverance paid off when, aged 33 and appearing in her third Olympics, she continued the tradition of MARY RAND and Ann Packer, the only previous British champions, and won the Olympic gold medal with a world record pentathlon score of 4801 points. She was created MBE as a result.

**Pethick-Lawrence** [née Pethick], **Emmeline** (1867–1954). English social worker and suffragette. Born in Bristol, she was educated at private schools in England, France and Germany. She worked for the West London Mission as a 'sister of the people' from 1890 to 1895, co-founded with the Esperance Club for working girls, initiated the first holiday scheme at Littlehampton in 1898, and started a co-operative dress-making firm (the Maison Esperance) with an eight-hour day, a minimum wage and annual holidays. She was a long-standing member of the Suffrage Society, and in 1906 Keir Hardie introduced her to Emmeline PANKHURST, as a result of which Pethick-Lawrence agreed to act as Treasurer of the Women's Social and Political Union, raising over £134,000 in six years.

In 1907 she started *Votes for Women* with her husband Frederick Lawrence; they had married in 1901, and both took the joint name Pethick-Lawrence. A generous, tireless and imaginative worker, largely responsible for the pageantry and symbolism of militant demonstrations, she was arrested several times. In 1912, following release from imprisonment for conspiracy after window-breaking demonstrations, the Pethick-Lawrences were unexpectedly repudiated by Emmeline and Christabel Pankhurst, and they joined the United Suffragists. Emmeline went to the USA to represent the Women's International League for Peace in 1912, and in 1915 was present at the Women's Peace Congress at The Hague. In 1918 she stood in the first election open to women, as Labour candidate for Rusholme, Manchester, and she continued for many years as President of the Women's Freedom League after CHARLOTTE DESPARD.

R. Pethick-Lawrence: *My Part in a Changing World* (1938)

**Pfeiffer, Ida** (*d* 1858). Austrian traveller. Between 1842 and 1848 Ida covered about 200,000 miles making botanical, mineralogical and entomological collections for the British Museum and elsewhere. A friend of Alexander von Humboldt, she was made an honorary member of the Geographical Society of Berlin and received a gold medal from the King of Prussia.

**Philips** [née Fowler], **Katherine** [pseud.: Orinda] (1631–64). English poet. Born in London, into a merchant's family, she was educated at Mrs Salmon's School, Hackney. At the age of 17 she married a Welshman, James Philips; they had two children. After her marriage she divided her time between her husband's home at Cardigan and London. She established a literary salon called the Society of Friendship, which included Abraham Cowley, Jeremy Taylor and Henry Vaughan. Her translation of Corneille's *Pompée* (1663) was successfully produced in Dublin, and her poems were published after her death in a smallpox epidemic. She was known to her contemporaries as 'the Matchless Orinda'. Her letters to Sir Charles Cottrell, published as *Letters from Orinda to Poliarchus* (1705), give a vivid impression of her character.

P.W. Suners: *The Matchless Orinda* (1931)

**Phillips, Marion** (1881–1932). British socialist. Born in Melbourne, Australia, the daughter of a lawyer, she graduated from Melbourne University and then obtained a scholarship to England to do a doctorate at the London School of Economics on colonial autocracy. She moved in socialist and feminist circles, working on the Poor Law Commission with BEATRICE WEBB, becoming Secretary of the National Union of Women's Suffrage Societies, and a Fabian. In 1911 she became a full-time worker for the new Labour Party and was chief woman officer from 1918. She was also one of the first women Justices of the Peace. In the 1926 General Strike she was the chief organizer of the Women's Committee for the Relief of Miners' Wives and Children. She won a parliamentary seat for Sunderland in 1929 but lost it in the general election two years later, shortly before her early death aged 51.

**Phryne** (365–410 BC). Greek artist's model. Her exceptional beauty provided the model for *Aphrodite Emerging*, a masterpiece by the painter Apelles, and inspired the love of the sculptor Praxiteles, who immortalized her perfect figure in his two famous statues of Aphrodite (those of Cos and of Cnidos). It was because the perfection of her physical features was seen as a divine gift that Phryne was the first woman ever granted permission to dedicate a golden statue of herself at Delphi.

**Piaf, Edith** [pseud. of Edith Giovanna Gassion] (1915–63). French singer. Born in Paris, the daughter of a famous acrobat, Jean Gassion, and a café singer, she suffered temporary blindness as a child. After attending the Ecole Primaire Bernay she became a street singer at the age of 15, graduating to music-hall and cabaret. Nicknamed 'La môme Piaf' ('the kid sparrow') by a night-club owner in 1935, she became a cult figure in intellectual circles. She made her debut on radio in 1936. Her direct, plaintive tone, full of nostalgia, made her famous with songs like *Mon légionnaire*, *L'accordéoniste*, *Non, je ne regrette rien*, *Milord* and *C'est l'amour*. Although she used material by Prévert and other writers, she created many of her own songs, including *La vie en rose* and *C'était un jour de fête*. She acted in *Le bel indifférent*, written for her by Cocteau in 1940, and after World War II made several films including Renoir's *French Cancan/Only the French Can* (1955). After 1947 she toured Europe and the USA. Her personal life was troubled and intense, but she fought to retain her fame as a performer. After a long period of severe illness she returned triumphantly in 1961 in her own show, which was forced to close after a long run because of her total physical and nervous collapse. She married Theo Sarapo in 1962. She wrote two

volumes of memoris, *Au bal de la chance* (1958) and *Ma Vie* (1964).

M. Lange: *Piaf* (1982)

**Pickford, Mary** [pseud. of Gladys Marie Smith] (1893–1979). American film star. She was born in Toronto. Her father, a labourer, was killed at work when she was five, and through her mother's theatrical lodgers she got work as a child actress, touring as 'Baby Gladys'; she found work also for her younger brother and sister. When she was 14 she starred in a Broadway play, and when she was 16 she started working for D.W. Griffith at Biograph. Here she became a leading player, appearing in 75 two-reelers before 1912; she was known to the public as 'Little Mary', a high-spirited and lovable character. She was equally talented as a businesswoman, moving to the Independent Motion Picture Company in 1910, then to Majestic, and back to Biograph, ending up in 1912 with Adolph Zukor's Famous Players Company. By moving she had increased her salary from $40 to $500 a week in three years, and by 1916 it had risen to $10,000; when she moved to First National the following year she was able to ask for, and get, $350,000 a picture. She was able to choose her pictures and directors, and increased her sentimental appeal in films like *Tess of the Storm Country* (1914), *The Foundling* (1916), *The Poor Little Rich Girl*, *Rebecca of Sunnybrook Farm* and *The Little Princess* (1917). Known as 'America's Sweetheart', she toured the USA selling war bonds.

In 1919, with Charlie Chaplin, Griffith and Douglas Fairbanks, she formed the United Artists Corporation, to control their own distribution. After divorcing the alcoholic Owen Moore, whom she had married in 1911, she married Douglas Fairbanks. Their mansion was called 'Pickfair', and although their marriage was unhappy, it seemed the epitome of screen romance until they divorced in 1936. She continued to play child roles, such as *Pollyanna* (1920), and appeared as both mother and son in *Little Lord Fauntleroy* (1921), but her work declined in quality and audiences refused to let her escape her 'little girl' roles, although she tried to in *Coquette* (1929), *The Taming of the Shrew* (with Fairbanks, 1929), *Kiki* (1931) and *Secrets* (1933). The last three were all failures. She retired in 1933 and gave radio broadcasts, wrote books, founded a cosmetics company (1937), and after her divorce married actor 'Buddy' Rogers (1937). She and Chaplin sold United Artists in 1953. In 1975 she won a special Academy Award for her services to the film industry.

M. Pickford: *Sunshine and Shadow: the Autobiography of Mary Pickford* (1956)

**Pinckney** [née Lucas], **Eliza** [Elizabeth] (1723–93). American agricultural pioneer. The daughter of an English army officer, she was probably born in Antigua, in the West Indies, but was educated in England and moved to South Carolina with her family in 1738. Her father bought a plantation near Charleston, and Eliza was left in charge when he had to return to the West Indies. She experimented with a variety of high-yield crops suitable for upland cultivation and for export: ginger, cotton and alfalfa, and by the mid-1740s she decided that indigo had the greatest potential. She used seeds sent by her father from the West Indies, and with the help of a man from Montserrat produced an export crop for England. During the 1740s the colony developed indigo growing and dye-making and it remained a staple industry until the late 19th century.

In 1747 Eliza married Charles Pinckney, and on his plantation she continued to experiment, cultivating flax, hemp and silk. In 1753 she went to England when her husband became the agent for South Carolina, but after five years in London they returned to the USA for a holiday, during which Charles died. Eliza then resumed the job of plantation manager until her death. She left a journal and letters which provide a fascinating picture of 18th-century plantation life.

H.H. Ravenal: *Eliza Pinckney* (2/1967)
H. Harry, e.d.: *E. Pinckney: Diaries and Letters* (1926)

**Pinkham, Lydia E(stes)** (1819–83). American medicine seller. The tenth of 12 children of a shoemaker, she was born in Lynn, Massachusetts, where she lived for most of her life. Educated in the local academy, she became a schoolteacher, a founder member of the town Female Anti-Slavery Society and a prominent reformer. Her enthusiasm encompassed causes from phrenology to temperance and women's rights and, later, spiritualism. In 1843 she married Isaac Pinkham and devoted herself to him and their 5 children for the next 30 years. In 1873 Isaac lost all his money in a financial crash, and Lydia decided to combat their terrible poverty by selling her home-made herb medicine, advertising it as 'Mrs Lydia E. Pinkham's Vegetable Compound', in 1875. She circulated leaflets through the town, took the medicine to druggists in Salem, Boston and Providence and her son Daniel won orders in Brooklyn and New York. In 1876 she patented it and began a big advertising campaign which reached its height 20 years later when the Compound was the most publicized medicine in America. Lydia herself supervised production, wrote the advertising copy and answered an enormous fan mail. She ran the business until her death, despite her grief at the death of her two younger sons from tuberculosis in 1881. There is no evidence that the Compound had any medicinal power but it apparently worked as a placebo. Since her death it has become a comic legend of American entrepreneurial enterprise.

C. Washburn: *The Life and Times of Lydia E. Pinkham* (1931)

**Pintasilgo, Maria de Lourdes** (1930–). Portuguese politician. Born in Abrantes, she showed an early interest in music and literature but decided to take courses in chemical engineering, which she regarded as a feminist challenge. She became President of the Catholic student organization Pax Romana, and was a proficient public speaker with a reputation for feminist and left-wing views. She became Head of the Documentation Centre, Companhia Uniano Fabril, and was a member of the Department of Politics and General Administration, Corporative Chamber (1969–74), and of the mission to the United Nations (1971–2).

In the first two provisional governments after the 1974 revolution she was Secretary of State for Social Security, and then Minister for Social Affairs; she was responsible for establishing a committee on the status of women, and for legislation on women's rights. From 1975 to 1979 she was Portugal's Ambassador to UNESCO, and she acted as Caretaker Prime Minister from July to December 1979. She remained Adviser to the President until 1985, and has also been a member of the World Policy Institute since 1982, and of the UN University Council and the Interaction Council of Former Heads of Government since 1983.

She has written extensively on international affairs and issues relating to the development and position of women. In 1980 she published *Les nouveaux féminismes*, and in 1985 *Dimensâo de mudança*.

**Pisan.** *See* DE PISAN.

**Pizzey [née Carney], Erin (Patricia Margaret)** (1939–). British campaigner for battered wives. Born in China, the daughter of a diplomat, Cyril Carney, she and her twin sister had an itinerant childhood, living in South Africa, Beirut, America and Iran. However, they were sent back to England to be educated at a strict convent school. A rebellious child, Erin left without any educational qualifications. In 1961 she married John Pizzey and they had one son and one daughter. She later started working at a community centre in Chiswick, London, giving social security advice; this gradually led to the opening of a refuge for battered women and the foundation of Chiswick Women's Aid in 1971. Determined to pursue an open-door policy she attracted much publicity for the cause by her frequent prosecutions for overcrowding and by her book *Scream Quietly or the Neighbours will Hear* (1974). A dominant personality, she has often clashed with other campaigners and feminists. Since 1979 she has extended her field to include general problems of violence in the family, as Director of Chiswick Family Rescue. Her first marriage was dissolved in 1979 and the following year she married Jeffrey Shapiro, with whom she wrote *Prone to Violence* (1982). In the 1980s she has also written a series of popular novels such as *The Watershed* (1983) and *First Lady* (1987).

E. Pizzey: *Infernal Child* (1978)

**Plamnikova, Franciska** (1875–1942). Czech feminist and politician. A teacher and school inspector, she founded the earliest substantial Czech feminist organization, the Women's Club of Prague (1901), and the Committee for Women's Suffrage (1905). Both were strongly nationalistic organizations, whose members joined with other Liberals and independent groups to harass the Imperial Austrian Diet. She led the campaign before World War I and from 1923 was the first Chairwoman of the Czech Council of Women, then Vice-Chairman of the International Council of Women. In 1918 she was elected to the Municipal Council of Prague; in 1925 she became a member of the Legislative Assembly and in 1929 was elected a Senator. She campaigned for equal status for women in all professions, including their eligibility as judges. In 1939 she visited the UK, pleading with the government to intervene on behalf of Czech women social workers in danger from occupying German forces. She was arrested with many others three weeks after her return, as retaliation for the death of Heydrich. Her property was confiscated and she died in a concentration camp in 1942.

**Planinc, Mila** (1925–). Yugoslav politician. Born in Croatia, she joined the Communist Youth League in 1941, and fought with Tito's partisans during World War II. After 1947 she settled in Zagreb, graduating from the Zagreb Higher School of Administration. She then rose through the Party bureaucracy to become head of the League of Yugoslav Communists in Croatia, and as a member of the National Parliament established a reputation as a tough politician. In January 1982 it was announced that she would take over the post of Prime Minister in May, following the policy inaugurated by Tito of rotating senior posts in turn to nationals of the various provinces. She was the first woman Prime Minister of a Communist country. She is married to an engineer and has two children and one grandchild.

**Plater, Emilija** (1806–31). Lithuanian soldier. She was born in Vilnius and from an early age she was an ardent patriot, yearning for an armed confrontation with the Russians, who had ruled Lithuania since 1795. Taking JOAN OF ARC as her model, she studied military subjects and learned the use of weapons. When the insurrection broke out she and a group of cadets at the military academy of Daugavpils (Latvia) began plotting to seize that strategically important garrison town. With the help of her cousin Cezaris, she organized an insurgent unit from the area around their estate, consisting of 60 mounted nobles, 280 mounted riflemen and several hundred peasants armed with scythes. When they approached Daugavpils they were met and routed by the Russians. After this defeat, she joined another rebel unit and participated in the capture of Ukmerge. A subsequent attempt to dislodge the Russians from Vilnius failed. Later, when the insurgents were organized into regular military units, Emilija was appointed company commander with the rank of Captain.

After taking part in the battle of Kaunas, where she barely escaped being captured, her regiment was compelled to retreat to Šiaulenai. On its way it was surprised and defeated at Šiaulenai. While the insurgent army eventually crossed the border into Prussia and laid down arms, Emilija refused to give up and, disguised as a peasant woman, attempted to reach Poland, where the fighting was still going on. She fell ill en route and died at Justinava, near Kapčiamiestis.

**Plath, Sylvia** (1932–63). American poet. She was born in Boston. Her father was a professor of biology who had moved to the USA from Germany in his youth and her mother had been a teacher of English and German. After the long illness and death of her father in 1940, events which attained deep significance in her poetry, Sylvia's mother supported the family by teaching medical secretaries' courses at Boston University and they moved from the coast into the city in 1942. In 1950 she graduated from Bradford High School and in 1953 won a scholarship to Smith College endowed by the writer Olive Higgins Prouty, who helped her considerably during her later breakdown. A fiercely competitive student, in 1953 she won a prize to be guest editor in New York on *Mademoiselle* and then suffered a deep depression, which led to shock treatment, a suicide attempt and a long period of hospital care before she returned to Smith College in 1954. On graduation she won several prizes, and was awarded a Fulbright scholarship to study at Newnham College, Cambridge. There she took a degree in English and met the poet

Ted Hughes; their dramatically intense involvement led to marriage in 1956. By this time she had published some short stories and was writing poetry, influenced by her reading of Graves, Roethke, Lawrence, Auden and VIRGINIA WOOLF.

After taking her degree in 1957, she and Ted Hughes returned to Boston, she to teach at Smith College and he at the University of Massachusetts, and it was during this period that she became friendly with the poet ANNE SEXTON. In 1960 she and her husband returned to London; her first collection, *The Colossus*, appeared, drawing cautiously interested reviews, and her daughter Frieda was born. In 1961, after a miscarriage, they moved to an old manor house in Devon, where she wrote her only novel, *The Bell Jar* (1961), about her student collapse. After the birth of her son Nicholas she wrote little poetry, but produced the radio play *Three Women*, set in a maternity home, which was broadcast in 1962. Hughes's poetic reputation was now considerable. He was often in London and after Sylvia discovered his affair with another woman he asked for a divorce. Her violent response initiated a period of intense writing in which she explained her own spiritual development and desolation, linking it to crises in the 20th century. In December she returned to London, but after three months of illness and anxiety committed suicide by putting her head in the gas oven. The powerful poems of her last few months caused a sensation when published in *Ariel* (1965) and she was treated as a legendary victim, romantic poet and female martyr. Between 1971 and 1973 six more collections appeared and a definitive *Collected Poems*, edited by Ted Hughes, was published in 1982.

A. Plath, ed.: *Letters Home* (1975)
L. Wagner-Martin: *Sylvia Plath* (1988)

**Plessis, Alphonsine** [Duplessis, Marie] [La Dame aux Camélias] (1824–47). French literary figure, the original Dame aux Camélias. Born in poverty in the small Normandy village of Saint-Germain-de-Clairefeuille (Orne), Alphonsine was brought up by a relative after her mother had left her drunken father when she was a small child. She later joined her father in Paris and by the time of his death, in the winter of 1839–40, she had already had a varied career as an apprentice laundress, mistress of an elderly bachelor, servant in an inn and child prostitute. She gradually acquired the patronage of wealthier clients, including restaurant owners, aristocrats and diplomats. At the age of 18 she entered fashionable society, gambling at the German resort of Baden-Baden, riding in the Bois de Boulogne in Paris, and attending first nights at the Opéra, where she always wore a corsage of fresh camellias. She was even allowed to assist at a charity bazaar patronized by respectable duchesses, and the varied admirers and guests at her salon in the rue de Madeleine included the Russian Ambassador, LOLA MONTEZ and Franz Liszt.

In 1845 she met two other characters who were also re-created in Dumas' novel about her: an elderly Duke who wished to adopt her because she resembled his dead daughter, and the young Comte de Perregaux, who squandered his whole fortune on her, and whom she married in Kensington Registry Office in 1846. After the wedding she returned to Paris and Baden-Baden, and saw little of her now impoverished husband. She lived a life of hectic gaiety, but debt and consumption eventually reduced her to lonely despair, and she died in poverty in February 1847. Her husband and the elderly Duke both attended her funeral. The following year her life was immortalized in the character of Marguérite Gauthier in the young Alexandre Dumas' first successful novel, La Dame aux camélias. It was turned into a play in 1849 and provided the basis for Verdi's libretto for the opera La traviata in 1853.

**Pocahontas** (1596–1617). American Indian heroine. She was the daughter of Powhatan, Chief of the Algonquin confederacy of Indian tribes in Virginia. Her personal name was Matoaka, 'playful'. She allegedly saved the life of John Smith when he was attacked by her tribe in 1607, and then helped to establish trade and interceded for Indian prisoners with the English in Jamestown. In 1613, after two years of difficult relations, she was captured by the English and held for exchange for prisoners and stolen goods. While held in the English colony she was baptized (as 'Rebecca') and met John Rolfe,

a tobacco grower, whom she married in 1614. Powhatan gave the couple land, and the link ushered in eight years of peace. In 1616 Rolfe and Pocahontas visited England, where she was presented to James I, but on the eve of their return she died of pneumonia or tuberculosis, at Gravesend. The 'legend' of Pocahontas's rescue of John Smith for love began in the 18th century and formed the subject of Davies's novel Captain Smith and Princess Pocahontas (1805) and many subsequent works.
J. Fritz: *Pocahontas* (1983)

**Poitiers.** See DE POITIERS.

**Pollard, Marjorie** (1899–1982). English hockey player. Marjorie played hockey for England from 1921 to 1928 and from 1931 to 1936. She was always an outstanding goal-scorer, in 1926 scoring 13 goals against Wales in a 20–0 win, and all 8 goals against Germany in another match, as well as 5 against Scotland, 7 against Ireland and 5 against South Africa in other years. She also played for the Midlands, Northants and Peterborough, and founded the North Northants team.

Marjorie had considerable influence on women's hockey: as acting President of the All-England Women's Hockey Association, as a sports journalist writing for leading newspapers such as The Times, The Guardian and Morning Post from 1926, and as Editor of the journal Hockey Field from 1946 to 1970. She was also a notable cricket player and was a founder member of the England Women's Cricket Association.

**Pompadour.** See DE POMPADOUR.

**Ponselle** [Ponzillo], **Rosa** (1897–1981). American soprano. She studied in New York, having appeared in vaudeville and in film theatres, often singing duets with her sister Carmela. At Caruso's suggestion she sang Leonora in the first Metropolitan production of La forza del destino (1918), her first operatic appearance; she performed there regularly until 1937 as the leading soprano in operas ranging from Mozart to Weber, being particularly well suited to the coloratura repertoire of Meyerbeer, Rossini and Verdi; she also made a significant contribution to the revival of rarely performed operas by such composers as Breil, Montemezzi and Romani. Her Covent Garden debut was in 1929, as Bellini's Norma, one of her most successful roles. After her retirement from the stage, at the height of her vocal powers, she moved to Baltimore, becoming director of the Civic Opera and a celebrated teacher.

**Popova** [née Eding], **Liubov (Serbeevna)** (1889–1924). Russian artist. She was born near Moscow and educated at two exclusive schools there; she studied painting privately from 1907. She visited Italy in 1910, and France in 1912, becoming interested in Cubism. On her return to Moscow she became a leading figure in the Suprematist group, holding Futurist exhibitions in Petrograd [now Leningrad] and in the 'Jack of Diamonds' and 'The Shop' exhibitions in Moscow (1914–16). During the Revolution she designed posters, and in 1918 she became involved with the Constructivist group, showing her work (with ALEXANDRA EXTER) in the famous '5×5=25' exhibition in Moscow in 1921. She believed art should be as accessible to analysis as science, and therefore concentrated on structural and spatial values rather than on subjective qualities.

After 1917 Popova taught at the Vkhutemas Art Training School, and at Gvitma and Proleckult, working on street decorations and mass spectacles and eventually designing for the populist theatre of Vsevolod Meyerhold (1922) and Sergei Tretyakov (1923). In the last two years of her life she deliberately submerged individualism in the interests of social commitment, like Nadezhda Udaltsova, and designed textiles at the First State Textile Factory, Moscow. After her early death the artist Kasimir Malevich stitched and carried her funeral banner.

**Popp, Adelheid** (1869–1939). Austrian trade unionist. Despite opposition from her family and ridicule from male unionists, she edited a socialist women's paper, *L'Opinion des femmes*, in 1849 and during the 1880s she became a militant trade union leader and rose to lead the Austrian Socialist Women's Movement and edit its paper *Arbeiterinnen-Zeitung* from 1892. In 1893 she founded the discussion group Libertas to enable women to gain experience in political debate, and in 1896 tried to get the Austrian Trade Union Congress to back an official women's organization, failing by one vote. In 1893 she had also led the first women's strike of 600 women in a clothing factory near Vienna.

She remained leader of the movement after the turn of the century, concentrating increasingly on the demand for women's suffrage, and for equal pay, equal legal rights, protective legislation, divorce reform and nursery care. She eventually became an Austrian government-elected official before the dominance of the Nazis in the 1930s.

A. Popp: *Autobiography of a Working Woman* (1912)

**Porter, Katherine Anne (Maria Veronica Callista Russell)** (1890–1980). American novelist. She was born in Indian Creek, Texas, the fourth of five children. Both her parents were descended from early settlers and she wrote that the family were brought up with a 'sense of their own history', being related to Daniel Boone and to the short-story writer O. Henry. Her mother died when she was two, and she was brought up by her grandmother (who appears in many of her stories) near Kyle, Texas. After her grandmother's death she went to convent schools in Texas and Louisiana, but when she was 16 she ran away to get married. However, she was divorced by the time she was 19, and worked as a reporter, actress and entertainer. She joined the *Rocky Mountain News* in Denver, and nearly died from the great influenza epidemic of 1918 which killed her soldier lover. She then moved to New York, where she lived in Greenwich Village and worked in theatrical journalism. She went to Mexico during the Obregón Revolution (1920–2) and helped to organize a large Amer-Indian art exhibition. On her return to New York she became involved in radical politics, especially in the defence of Sacco and Vanzetti, the anarchists, who were executed in 1927.

In 1928, after writing privately for 15 years, she published her first collection of stories, *Flowering Judas*, which won her a Guggenheim Fellowship; this enabled her to travel again to Mexico, and then to Europe. In Paris she married a consular official, Eugène Pressly, translated French *chansons* and wrote her novel *Hacienda* (1934). By 1938 she was divorced, and she returned to the USA, where she married Albert Erskins, a professor of English. They too divorced, within four years. In 1939 *Pale Horse, pale Rider: Three Short Novels* confirmed her high reputation, with its wistful evocation of the old South. During the 1940s and 1950s she published many more stories and essays, taught at various American universities such as Stanford, Chicago, Michigan and Virginia, and spent a year in Belgium (1954–5). However, most of her energies were devoted to writing the massive novel *Ship of Fools* which eventually appeared in 1962, arousing lasting controversy. After revisiting Mexico as a lecturer and teaching in California, Porter settled in Maryland. She wrote no more fiction, although her *Collected Stories* won a Pulitzer Prize in 1967 and her last book, *The Never-Ending Wrong* (1977), returned to her youth and the trial of Sacco and Vanzetti.

J. Givner: *Katherine Anne Porter: A Life* (1984)

**Post, Emily** (1873–1960). American writer on etiquette. Born into a well-established Baltimore family, the daughter of an architect, she travelled widely in Europe and was educated in New York. She married in 1892, and had two children, but was later divorced and became a society journalist. In 1922 her book *Etiquette: the Blue Book of Social Usage* was published; in it she attempted to simplify the elaborate order of manners, covering everything from the use of knives and forks to the manner of addressing royalty. An immediate success, it was revised ten times in her lifetime. The Emily Post radio programme (1931) was followed by a syndicated column, and in 1946 she founded the Emily Post Institute for the Study of Gracious Living. A kindly woman, who hated affectation, she also wrote novels and short stories.

E. Post: *Truly Emily Post* (1961)

**Poston, Elizabeth** (1905–87). English composer, pianist and broadcaster. She studied at the Royal Academy of Music, London, and was a piano pupil of Harold Samuel. Having continued her studies in Europe, where she nurtured an interest in folksong, especially Italian, in 1940 she joined the music department of the BBC, becoming Director of the European Service;

although she resigned this post in 1945, she maintained her links (after a period in the USA and Canada) in an advisory capacity when the Third Programme was initiated and also continued to broadcast. Among her most notable lecture-recital series was that on the songs of Peter Warlock. She was president of the Society of Women Musicians (1955–61). Her compositions include incidental music for radio and films, notably *Howards End* (1970), several chamber works and much vocal music; she published her first songs in 1925, and the choral *An English Kalendar* (1969) and *An English Day Book* (1971) were commissioned by the Farnham Festival. She preferred miniature forms and also wrote for early instruments. She is best known, however, for such publications as the *Penguin Book of American Folksongs* (1964), two collections of Christmas carols, also in the Penguin series (1965, 1970), *The Cambridge Hymnal* (1967) and *The Faber Book of French Folksongs* (1972).

**Potonie-Pierre, Eugénie** (1844–98). French feminist. An active feminist with Léon Richer and MARIA DERAISMES in the 1870s, she was a co-founder of the Union des Femmes in 1880 with Léonie Rouzade (novelist, socialist, and the first woman to stand for municipal election in France in Paris 1881) and Marguerite Tinayre (a collaborator of LOUISE MICHEL both as a novelist and communard). She married pacifist historian, Eduard Potonie, in 1881 and thereafter became a less radical socialist. In 1889 she founded La Ligue Socialiste des Femmes and in 1891 Le Groupe de la Solidarité des Femmes with Maria Martin, then editor of *Le journal des femmes*. In 1892 she united eight Parisian feminist groups as the Federation Française des Societées Feministes, but soon left and concentrated on La Solidarité. This was largely a charitable organization to aid working women but it also campaigned for women's rights, demanded the franchise, and in 1893 fielded five candidates for the National Assembly, including Potonie-Pierre, Maria Pognon (an eminent social feminist who was president of La Ligue des Droits de Femmes) and PAULE MINK. By 1896 she was the undisputed leader of the Socialist Feminist movement, and led the

French deputation to the feminist congress of Brussels in 1897, but she died suddenly of a cerebral haemorrhage.

**Potter, (Helen) Beatrix** (1861–1943). English illustrator of children's books. Born in South Kensington, London, the daughter of a wealthy lawyer and heir to a Lancashire cotton magnate, she was educated by governesses. She began to draw her precise studies of plants and animals during childhood holidays in Scotland and the Lake District. She also managed to smuggle a variety of pets, including bats, mice, frogs and a rabbit, into her London nursery.

She began to write at the age of 27, producing a series of illustrated letters to a sick child. Her first book, *Peter Rabbit*, was published privately in 1900; it was followed by *The Tailor of Gloucester* (1902). Over the next 30 years the publisher Frederick Warne, who became a close friend, produced 24 of her books. Beatrix continued to live with her autocratic parents until the age of 39, when she became engaged, against their wishes, to Warne's son, Norman. He died a few months later, but she still proceeded to leave home, and moved to Sawrey, in the Lake District. In 1913, now 47, she married William Heelis, an Ambleside solicitor, although her parents again strongly objected. She ceased to write and devoted her last 30 years to becoming an extremely successful hill-farmer.

M. Lane: *The Tale of Beatrix Potter* (1968)

**Power, Eileen (Edna Le Poer)** (1889–1940). English historian. Born in Altrincham, Cheshire, the eldest daughter of a London stockbroker, she was educated in Bournemouth and at Oxford High School before obtaining a first in history at Girton College, Cambridge, in 1910. She was awarded a research fellowship and studied in Paris and Chartres before moving to the London School of Economics (1911–13). From 1913 to 1921 she was Director of Studies at Girton College, and then she was a lecturer, Reader (1924) and Professor of economic history (1931) at the London School of Economics.

Eileen Power was determined to research the economic position of women in the Middle Ages. Her fascinating study of community life *Medieval English Nunneries*

*c.1275–1535* was published in 1922. Her interest is also evident in *Medieval People* (1924) and in her translation of *Le ménagier de Paris* (1928), a medieval book of advice compiled by an elderly bourgeois husband for his young wife. During the 1920s she also worked with R.H. Tawney on *Tudor Economic Documents* and on the history of the wool trade, and helped to plan the medieval sections of the *Cambridge Economic History of Europe* and to found the *Economic History Review* (1927). Another of her interests, evident in the study of Marco Polo in *Medieval People*, was the Far East, which she visited in 1921 and 1929.

Power's lectures on the position of women were edited by her husband Michael Postan after her early death, and were published as *Medieval Women* in 1975. With her other works, they link her with Alice Clark (*The Working Life of Women in the 17th Century*, 1919) and Ivy Pinchbeck (*Women Workers in the Industrial Revolution*, 1930) as one of the pioneers of women's history in Great Britain.

**Press, Tamara (Natanova)** (1937–). Russian shot-putter and discus thrower. A formidable muscle-woman and accomplished athlete, Tamara set 12 world records between 1959 and 1965, improving her distance for the shot from 56'7½" to 61', and for the discus, 187'6" in 1960 to 195'10½". She began her awards with a bronze medal in the 1958 European shot, and gold in the European discus, followed by a gold at the 1960 Olympics for shot-put and a silver for discus. In the 1962 European championships she won gold medals for both shot and discus; she did the same in the 1964 Olympics. She won six major championships, while her sister Irina Press also won two. She retired in 1965 and worked for the All-Union Council of Trade Unions from 1967.

**Preston, Ann** (1813–72). American doctor. Born at Westgrove, Pennsylvania, she spent her early life caring for her Quaker family, as her mother was an invalid. She gained her MD at the Female Medical College [Women's Medical College] of Pennsylvania in 1851, at the age of 39, with a graduation thesis against purging and bloodletting, proposing ideas about psychosomatic medicine: 'multitudes have been depleted for visceral lesions whose primary disease was anguish of spirit'.

In 1855 Ann became Professor of Physiology at the Female,Medical College. In 1859 the Pennsylvania Medical Society resolved not to recognize the school; the Civil War intervened, and Ann became the college's champion, changing tactics from passive resistance to written attacks. In 1861 she founded the Women's Hospital, Philadelphia, and in 1866 her appointment as Dean at the Female Medical College made her the first woman dean of a medical college; she held the post until her death. She was noted for introducing medical ethics into her lectures. Among the 138 students who graduated under her were many medical missionaries. She saw the education of women in medicine as 'established in the fitness of things and in the necessities of society'.

**Price, (Mary Violet) Leontyne** (1927–). American soprano. The first black American woman to achieve international acclaim in opera, Leontyne Price was born in Laurel, Mississippi: her father worked in a saw-mill and her mother was a midwife. As a girl Leontyne joined the choir of the Methodist church where both her parents sang, and was inspired with ambition to be a singer when she heard MARIAN ANDERSON at a concert in Jackson, at the age of nine. She graduated from high school and studied music at the College of Education, Wilberforce, Ohio, and then won a scholarship to the Juilliard School of Music, New York, in 1949. While a student she sang Alice Ford in Verdi's *Falstaff* and shortly thereafter was chosen by Virgil Thomson to appear on Broadway in a revival of his opera *Four Saints in Three Acts* (1952). This led to her being engaged to appear with William Warfield (to whom she was married, 1952–72) in the title role of Gershwin's *Porgy and Bess*; the all-black cast toured Europe in 1952–3 and was largely responsible for rescuing the work from its precarious beginnings to become the first substantially successful American opera. A televised performance in the title role of *Tosca* (1955) brought her still wider acclaim. She is primarily associated with Verdi roles: it was as Aida that she made triumphant debuts in Verona, Vienna, Covent Garden (all 1958) and at La

Scala, Milan (1960), and as Leonora in *Il trovatore* at the Metropolitan, New York (1961). Roles that she has created include Cleopatra in Samuel Barber's *Antony and Cleopatra* (1966), with which the new Metropolitan Opera House at Lincoln Center was opened. Her repertory also extended to Handel, Mozart (notably Donna Elvira in a performance of *Don Giovanni* at the Salzburg Festival, 1960), Puccini and Tchaikovsky. She retired from the stage in 1985, giving *Aida* at her last performance at the Metropolitan, but has continued to give concert performances. Among her awards are the Presidential Medal of Freedom (1965) and the National Medal of Arts (1985), as well as several honorary doctorates.

**Primus, Pearl** (1919–). Trinidadian dancer. Born in Trinidad, she studied anthropology at Columbia University before taking up dance as a career; she made her first appearance as a soloist in 1941. In 1943 she formed her own group and produced dances related to social and racial problems, such as *Strange Fruits* (1943). In 1948 she went to Africa, and studied dance there and in the Caribbean for many years with her husband Percival Borde. Her choreography is very ritualistic and her best-known works include the dances for her own compositions, such as *Fanja* (1949), for which she was awarded the Star of Africa by the President of Liberia, and *The Wedding* (1961). She is Director of the Art Centre of Black African Culture in Nigeria, but continues to choreograph for many different groups and also teaches at Hunter College, New York.

**Pritchard, Hannah** (1711–68). English actress. Born Hannah Vaughan, she was brought up in the neighbourhood of Drury Lane, where her father was a stay-maker, but did not begin to act until she was 21 and already married to an actor. Her first success was in burlesque and ballad opera at the St Bartholomew and Southwark fairs, from where she quickly graduated to the theatres royal in London, Bristol and Bath. During the 1730s and 1740s she played roles in all genres, from Ophelia and Phaedra to Dol common in Jonson's *The Alchemist*, Lucy in *The Beggar's Opera* and Lady Townley in Colley Cibber's *The Provok'd Husband*. She rejected the old sing-song school of declamation long before Garrick, and when he became lessee of Drury Lane in 1747 she joined him there, now one of the leading actresses of her generation.

Dr Johnson blamed her for the failure of his play *Mahomet and Irene*, in which she played Irene, and dismissed her as 'an idiot'. However, she was without good looks and extremely corpulent, and it was precisely the intelligence of her interpretations that audiences admired. In an age when actors usually specialized, she was remarkable for her versatility; the only Beatrice of her age (in *Much Ado about Nothing*, full of 'spirit, vigour, whim and fancy') yet also a trascendent Lady Macbeth (after her retirement Garrick, her constant partner, never performed Macbeth again).

Her private life was entirely respectable, so much so that in 1761 she was appointed Dresser to the Queen. And in spite of much professional overlap she maintained a close friendship with Kitty Clive, who, it was said, retired shortly after her 'to follow her example'.

A. Vaughan: *Born To Please: Hannah Pritchard* (1979)

**Procter, Adelaide (Ann)** [pseud.: Mary Berwick] (1825–64). English poet and feminist. Born in London, the daughter of the poet Bryan Procter, she was a precocious student and began publishing verse as Mary Berwick in Dickens's *Household Words* in 1853. A two-volume collection of her poetry, *Legends and Lyrics*, appeared in 1858.

A dedicated feminist and a student of Queen's College, London, she worked on two Social Science Association committees on women's work in 1859, and helped BARBARA BODICHON and JESSIE BOUCHERETT to found the Society for Promoting the Employment of Women. Her anthology of miscellaneous poems *Victoria regia* was produced by EMILY FAITHFUL's Victoria Press in 1861, and her own collection *A Chaplet of Verse* (1862) was sold on behalf of a homeless women's night refuge. In her time, her poetry was as popular as Tennyson's.

**Pulcheria** (399–453). Byzantine empress and saint. A woman of uncommon ability and deep piety, Pulcheria was the daughter of the Emperor Arcadius and the elder sister of Theodosius II. From 414 to 416, despite her youth, she was made regent for her weak-minded brother, and ran the imperial palace at Constantinople [now Istanbul] on strict and ascetic Christian principles. After her brother's marriage in 421 Pulcheria found life at court increasingly difficult, partly because of theological intrigues, but also because Theodosius's wife proved strong-willed. Pulcheria succeeded to the throne in 450 and ruled as joint sovereign with the capable General Marcian; their marriage was nominal as she maintained a vow of celibacy made as a young woman. A stalwart supporter of orthodoxy, Pulcheria induced Theodosius to condemn Nestovius, and as empress arranged for a General Council to meet at Chalcedon in 451.

A.B. Telgen: *The Empress Pulcheria* (1907)

**Pye, Edith** (1876–1965). British Quaker nurse and pacifist. Edith Pye trained as a nurse and midwife, and rose to become Superintendent of District Nurses in London. In 1908 she joined the Society of Friends and it is for her Quaker relief work that she is best known. During World War I, with her friend HILDA CLARK, she helped women and children war victims in France, organizing a maternity hospital within the war zone itself. Later the hospital was permanently established at Châlons, and Edith was awarded the Légion d'honneur. In 1919 she went to Vienna to help Hilda Clark in the stricken city, and in 1923 continued her relief work in the Ruhr. In 1927 she went to China for the Women's International League. Chairman of the Friends' Service Council France and Switzerland Committee, she was also concerned with the plight of refugees from Germany, as vice-chairman of the German Emergency Committee.

During the Spanish Civil War she organized the Friends' work in Spain, and was also tirelessly involved with the International Commission for the Assistance of Child Refugees, and in the Women's International League for Peace and Freedom. Her work with refugees continued in Britain during World War II and she argued passionately for the partial lifting of the Allied Blockade to avoid starvation in Europe, as a leading member of the Famine Relief Committee which lobbied the Ministry of Economic Warfare. She then turned her attention again to Europe, working especially in France and Greece from 1944 to 1951. A gentle but forceful and inspiring personality, she was respected internationally, and continued to work for peace and war relief until her very old age.

**Pyke, Margaret** (1893–1966). English birth-control campaigner. Born in Hampshire, a doctor's daughter, she was educated privately and graduated in history from Somerville College, Oxford. In 1918 she married Geoffrey Pyke, a brilliant educationalist, and with DR SUSAN ISAACA she ran a progressive school, the Malting House School, near Cambridge. Her husband died in 1929, and to support herself and her small son she accepted Lady GERTRUDE DENMAN's invitation to apply for the job of Secretary to the National Birth Control Association (which became the Family Planning Association in 1938). Her chief fight was to get local authorities to implement the Department of Health Circular of 1931, which allowed them to give contraception to married couples on health grounds. Ealing Council was the first to respond, instituting a monthly birth control session, but in 1932 Plymouth became the first City Council to hold a permanent clinic. By the time of Margaret Pyke's death there were 540 clinics in Britain. In 1954 she became Chairman of the Family Planning Association and was also active in the International Planned Parenthood Federation, visiting India on their behalf in 1959.

**Pym, Barbara (Mary Crampton)** (1913–80). British novelist. Born in Oswestry, Shropshire, Barbara Pym was educated at Liverpool College, Huyton, and St Hilda's College, Oxford. After graduating in 1934 she lived at home, where in her twenties she wrote her first novel, *Some Tame Gazelle*, which remained unpublished until 1950, and *Civil to Strangers* and *Crampton Hodnet*, both unpublished until after her death. She then went to Katowice, Poland, to teach English but returned before the outbreak of war. During the war she worked as a postal censor, and in 1943 joined the Women's Royal Naval Service, which eventually took her to Naples. After 1946 she worked for the International African Institute in London, as a research assistant.

During the 1950s she published a series of novels remarkable for their acute, ironic treatment of English life: spinsterhood, church and village gossip, unrequited love, loneliness, office intrigues. These include *Excellent Women* (1952), *Jane and Prudence* (1953), *Less Than Angels* (1955), *A Glass of Blessings* (1958) and *No Fond Return of Love* (1961). During the 1960s and 1970s her subjects and style fell out of fashion and her work was constantly rejected, but in 1977 she was singled out by Philip Larkin and David Cecil in a symposium on underrated writers in *The Times Literary Supplement*. Her reputation revived, and she published *Quartet in Autumn* (1977) and *The Sweet Dove Died* (1978). She had continued to work at the African Institute as editorial assistant on *Africa* from 1958 until 1974, when she retired to live with her sister near Oxford. In 1979 she was elected a fellow of the Royal Society of Literature. After her death from cancer more novels appeared: *A Few Green Leaves* and *Crampton Hodnet* (both 1980), *An Unsuitable Attachment* (1982) and *Civil to Strangers* (1987).

B. Pym: *A Very Private Eye* (1984)

# Q

**Qian Zhengying** (1923–). Chinese politician. She was born in the USA, but her family returned to China when she was a baby. Her father, a civil engineer who worked in water conservancy, encouraged her to become one of China's first women engineers. She became involved in revolutionary groups in 1937 in Shanghai, and two years after going to Datong University she became Secretary of an underground Communist Party group there (1941). From 1942 to 1947 she lived in the liberated zones, beginning her work with flood relief in 1944. During 40 years of practical experience she rose to become Minister of Water Conservancy in 1975 and also of Power since 1982, an extremely important position. She has been a member of the State Council since 1982.

**Quant, Mary** (1934–). British designer and businesswoman. Born in London, she had a disjointed education at numerous schools before enrolling at Goldsmiths' College of Art. She began designing in 1955, when she opened her shop Bazaar in Chelsea, with two partners; one of them was Alexander Plunket-Greene, whom she later married in 1957. Beginning with single garments made up overnight and sold the next day, they soon employed seamstresses, and their success eventually led them to adopt mass production. During the 1960s Quant became internationally famous for her casual clothes and spicy colours, and especially for her popularization of the mini-skirt. In 1965 she had her first American show, and in 1966, having helped to make London a centre of fashion, she was awarded the OBE. She won many awards and at this stage was producing over 20 collections a year. After 1970 the pace slowed and she became a member of the fashion establishment, rather than a radical innovator; she was made a member of the Design Council (1971), an adviser to the British-American Bicentennial Liaison Committee (1973), and a consultant to the Victoria and Albert Museum (1976–8). In 1973 she was the focus of an exhibition, 'Mary Quant's London', at the London Museum. Quant then moved from clothes to cosmetics, building a huge franchise business which became a part of the Max Factor empire, and she also gave her name to household textiles, linen and interior decorations.

M. Quant: *Quant by Quant* (1966)

**Questiaux** [née Valayer], **Nicole (Françoise)** (1931–). French politician. Born in Nantes, the daughter of an engineer, she married Paul Questiaux in 1951; they have two children. She graduated in politics from the University of Paris, studied at the École Nationale d'Administration (1953–5), and became an *auditeur* to the Council of State in 1955, and then a full member of the Council (1963–74). Her special area of concern was with administrative disputes, and problems relating to the elderly. In 1971 she was prominent in the launching of the new Socialist Party, becoming a member in 1979 of its executive committee and of the left-wing group Comité d'Etudes Régionales' Economiques et Sociales (CERES). After the inauguration of François Mitterand she was Minister of State for National Solidarity, 1981–2. Other women ministers in recent years have included YVETTE ROUDY (Women's Rights), Edith Cresson (Industry), Edwige Alice (Youth) and Georgina Dufoix (Social Affairs).

# R

Rābi'ah al-'Adawiyyah (712–801). Arabian religious scholar. A Sunnite Moslem from the al-Atik tribe, she had a hard childhood in a large peasant family, and was later abducted and sold as a slave. She fled to a desert hermitage and later lived in a hut in Basra, where she renounced the world and its attractions, devoting her life to the service of God. She rejected all offers of marriage and entered the path of *zahid* ('asceticism'). She is said to have performed many miracles, and she is the subject of many stories; she was also witty and outspoken and received many distinguished scholars and visitors. In her verses and teaching she developed the Sufi theme of mystical love, and her writings greatly influenced reformers such as al Ghazālī, three centuries later. With the development of Sufism within Islam, women were given the opportunity to attain the rank of sainthood, and the dignity conferred on women was equal to that of men. Rābi'ah died at the age of 89, and is buried in Basra.

M. Smith: *Rabia the Mystic* (1928)

Rachel [pseud. of Elisa Felix] (1821–58). French tragedienne. She was the daughter of a poor Jewish merchant, and during her harsh childhood she sang on the streets of Lyons and Paris for money. Her talent was soon noticed and for a time she studied at Saint-Aulaire's drama school and, briefly, at the Conservatoire d'Art Dramatique. Her father, eager to make money from her talent, forced her to seek work, and she appeared in *La vendéenne* by Pierre Dupont at the Gymnase-Théâtre in 1837. Janin, the famous and influential dramatic critic of the *Journal des débats*, championed her, and she joined the Comédie-Française in 1838. She went on to play all the female roles in the plays of Corneille and Racine. Although she was successful in a revival of Ponce-Denis Lebrun's *Marie Stuart* and in Eugène Scribe and Gabriel-Marie Legouve's *Adrienne Lecouvreur* (1849), she received most acclaim for her classical roles. She toured Europe, and played in London, the USA and Russia. She established a tradition of tragic acting that has never been surpassed, and, though not particularly beautiful, her intense fiery passion made her the most celebrated actress of her day. Early hardship, overwork during her career, and a spectacular succession of amorous intrigues aggravated a tubercular condition, and she died when she was 38.

B. Falk: *Rachel the Immortal* (1935)

Radcliffe [née Ward], Mrs (Ann) (1764–1823). English novelist. Born in London, she received a typical 'feminine education' in music, drawing and literature at the school in Bath run by the writers Harriet and Sophia Lee. In 1787 she married William Radcliffe, the future Editor of the *English Chronicle*, and began writing for her own amusement. The first of her nine Gothic romances was *The Castles of Athlin and Dumbayne* (1789), but the rest of her books are set in the Alps or the Pyrenees; they are all marked by superb evocation of landscape, twisting plots, romantic heroes and practical heroines, and strong supernatural elements disappointingly explained at the end. Her best-known books are *A Sicilian Romance* (1791), *The Mysteries of Udolpho* (1794) and *The Italian* (1796). In 1797, at the height of her fame, she stopped writing and retired to her estates near Leicester.

Radegund (518–87). German saint and queen. The daughter of the pagan King Berthaire of Thuringia, Radegund was carried off by the invading Frankish King Lothair I when she was only 12. He educated her as a Christian and married her six years later. Radegund bore his cruelty and infidelities patiently, but when Lothair murdered her brother she left him. At Noyon she induced a bishop to take the risk of making her a deaconess. In 557 she built the monastery of the Holy Cross at Poitiers, which became a great centre for learning. 12 years later she obtained for her convent, from Emperor Justin II, a large fragment of the true cross, which inspired Venantus Fortunatus to write his famous *Vexilla legis*.

A close friendship developed between her and Fortunatus, who became the nuns' Chaplain. He wrote of St Radegund: 'human eloquence is struck almost dumb by the piety, self-denial, charity, sweetness, humility, uprightness, faith and fervour in which she lived'.

F. Brittain: *St Radegund* (1925)

**Rainer, Yvonne** (1934–). American choreographer and film-maker. She moved from San Francisco to New York in 1956, and studied under MARTHA GRAHAM and Merce Cunningham. She began choreographic work in 1961, and in 1962 became a founder member of the experimental Judson Dance Theater. She concentrated on natural movement and form, often using modern or popular music, for example in *My Body's House* (1964), *The Mind is a Muscle* (1966–8), *Rose Fractions* (1969) and *Continuous Project. Altered Daily* (1970). She moved from using visual material in dance to exploring, emotion, psychology and sexuality in films which she wrote, directed and edited herself, deliberately fragmenting the narrative and breaking down identification with the characters to explore inter-relations and situations. *Journeys from Berlin/1971* was an ambitious international co-production made in England, the USA and Berlin; in it she related psychic depression to political repression in the postwar Federal German Republic (it was the result of a West German grant which enabled her to live in Berlin as visiting artist). She has made several short films, including *Vollyball, Hand Movie, Rhode Island Red, Trio Film, Line* (1967–9), *Lives of Performers* (1972), *Film about a Woman Who . . .* (1974), *Kristina Talking Pictures*

(1976) in addition to *Journeys from Berlin/1971* (1980).

Y. Rainer: *Work 1961–73* (1974)

**Rainey** [née Pridgett], **'Ma' (Gertrude Malissa)** (1886–1939). American blues singer. She was born in Georgia. She came from a show business family and first sang in public in a school show at the Columbus Opera House when she was 12.

In 1904 she married William 'Pa' Rainey, a dancing comedian, and they toured as a joint act with the Rabbit Foot Minstrels. She claimed that she first heard a blues lament while touring with a tent show in Missouri and included it in her act, arousing an immediate response. She continued touring with Tolliver's Circus but at the age of 37 her fame was suddenly increased when she began to record with Paramount. She made 90 recordings between 1923 and 1928. For a time she toured with her own 'Georgia' Jazz Band, also playing in the North and winning the rare title of 'Madame'.

Ma's stage acts were spectacular, and her singing style influenced BESSIE SMITH and all succeeding blues performers. Her career was hit by the Depression, and she retired in 1933 to keep house for her brother and also to run her two theatres in Rome, Georgia.

S.R. Lieb: *Mother of the Blues: a study of Ma Rainey* (1981)

**Rainier, Priaulx** (1903–86). South African-English composer. She studied the violin at the South African College of Music, Cape Town, and in 1920 won a scholarship to the Royal Academy of Music, London; she was Professor of composition at the latter from 1943 to 1961. The work which established her reputation as a composer was her First String Quartet, written in 1939, the year of a three-month period of study with NADIA BOULANGER. Such early works as the *Barbaric Dance Suite* (1949) for piano reflect her origins in their evocation of Zulu rhythms and melodies. In the 1950s she moved to St Ives, Cornwall, where her friendship with BARBARA HEPWORTH and Ben Nicholson influenced the more abstract direction her style was to take, for instance in the orchestral suite *Aequora lunae* (1967, dedicated to Hepworth). The settings of Donne in *Cycle for Declamation* (1953, for solo voice) and of EDITH SITWELL in *The Bee Oracles* (1969, for tenor or baritone and instrumental ensemble) were both commissioned by Peter Pears, who also gave the première of her *Requiem* (poems by David Gascoigne) at the 1956 Aldeburgh Festival. Other significant works include the dance concerto *Phala-phala* (1960, written for Boult's tenth anniversary with the London Philharmonic Orchestra), the oboe quartet *Quanta* (1962), the Cello Concerto (1964), the Violin Duo (1977, commissioned by Yehudi Menuhin and first performed at the Edinburgh Festival), and the Concertante Duo for oboe, clarinet and chamber orchestra (1981).

**Ramabai, Pandita** (1858–c1920). Indian feminist. She was a pioneer of the Women's Rights Movement in India and was also active in the Social Reform Movement that was sweeping the country into a new era. Pandita Ramabai committed herself specifically to creating alternative ways of living for women, campaigning for their education and for a change in their role and status. Despite public censure from conservative sectors, she had a wide audience in her appeals to the government to provide facilities for woman to gain entry into the fields of education and medicine. She came under further attack when she married a man of her choice from another caste. After her husband's death she was converted to Christianity.

She wrote a book on women, *Stridharma niti*, and visited England and the USA lecturing on the condition of Indian women, forming societies which pledged to collect and contribute money for a home for widows. In England she taught Sanskrit at Cheltenham Ladies' College. It was while she was abroad that she wrote her second book, *The High Caste Hindu Woman*. In 1882 she founded the Sharada Sadan, a home for widows, many of whom were aged between nine and twelve.

**Rambert,** Dame **Marie** [Rambam, Cyvia] (1888–1982). English choreographer, dancer and teacher. She was born in Warsaw, the daughter of an intellectual book-seller, and sent to study medicine at the Sorbonne after the Warsaw Uprising (1905). She was impressed by the performances of ANNA PAVLOVA and ISADORA DUNCAN and began to study dance. She gave private concerts, and in 1910

attended the Dalcroze Summer School in Geneva, and then the Academy of Eurhythmics in Dresden, where she became a teacher. She assisted Nijinsky with the choreography for *Sacre du printemps*, joined Dyagilev's Ballets Russes in 1912, and accompanied them on their South American tour (1913).

In 1917 Marie Rambert arrived in London, gaining immediate attention with her own ballet *La pomme d'or*. In 1918 she became a British subject when she married playwright Ashley Dukes, who created the tiny Mercury Theatre at Notting Hill Gate, London. Here she established a school in 1920, while continuing her own studies with Enrico Cecchetti and Astafieva. In 1926 she founded the Ballet Rambert. The year 1930 included the first season of the Ballet Rambert at the Lyric Theatre, Hammersmith, London, with TAMARA KARSAVINA as guest artist, and the foundation of the influential Ballet Club, where classical training was combined with the encouragement of young designers and choreographers, including Ashton, Tudor and Morrice. Rambert's influence equalled that of NINETTE DE VALOIS; in the words of Agnes de Mille 'the polarisation of these two fanatic females . . . on opposite sides of London produced a heat of creativity that generated genius'. Marie directed the Ballet Rambert for 30 years, through regular London seasons, provincial tours, wartime tours, and visits to the Middle and Far East, Europe and Scandinavia. The company was re-organized in 1966 as a modern dance company, achieving new influence on the spread of contemporary dance.

In 1972 Rambert became Vice-President of the Royal Academy of Dancing, and continued to take a keen interest. Both her daughters became dancers and Angela Ellis now directs the School at the Mercury Theatre. Marie Rambert had a reputation for gaiety and unpredictability as well as for her inspirational ability; until her late seventies she was notorious for turning cartwheels in unexpected places. Among her honours were the Légion d'Honneur (1957) and the DBE (1962).
M. Rambert: *Quicksilver* (1972)

**Rambouillet,** (Catherine de Vivonne) Marquise de (1588–1665). French saloniste. Born in Rome, the daughter of the French ambassador Jean de Vivonne and his Italian wife, she was married at the age of 12 to Charles d'Angennes, who was later Marquis de Rambouillet. She disliked the vulgarity of French as opposed to Italian society, and from about 1610 she invited cultured friends, intellectuals and aristocrats to her town house, the Hôtel de Rambouillet. From about 1617 these gatherings evolved into the first great French salon, which continued to flourish until her death. Kind, sophisticated and serious without being pedantic, Catherine exercised a great influence on contemporary French literature, although she herself published nothing. With her daughter, Julie d'Angennes, she received writers such as Malherbe, Saint-Evremond, La Rochefoucauld, MADELEINE DE SCUDÉRY, the Marquise de SÉVIGNÉ and Corneille. She set a standard for precise and elegant diction and spelling which, at its extreme, led Molière to satirize her salon in his first comedy of manners, *Les précieuses ridicules* (1659). She also influenced taste and fashion, countering convention in her original plans for her house, which was elegantly decorated in blue, with the rooms opening into each other uninterrupted by a central staircase.

**Rame, Franca** (1929–). Italian actress, director and author. A member of the famous Rame family of professional comedians, Franca toured northern Italy with them as a child. Her family had been associated with itinerant theatre since the commedia dell' arte of the 17th century and had developed highly flexible techniques of improvisation, known as *recitare al soggetto*, through which they interpreted, or 'translated' classic authors from Shakespeare to Ibsen for local audiences. She met Dario Fo while he was an architecture student in Milan and she was working in commercial theatre, resenting being cast merely as a 'beauty'. They married in 1954 and in 1956 formed their own company, forging one of the most significant collaborations in modern European theatre, a leading force in political avant-garde drama for over 20 years. Franca polished Dario's drafts of his political satires such as *Accidental Death of an Anarchist*, and taught the company traditional improvisatory tech-

niques. They played in unconventional locations, charging low prices and giving most of the proceeds to political causes.

In the 1970s, Franca established Soccorso Rosso, a movement for the rights of political prisoners which eventually dealt with over 800 cases. Accused of involvement with terrorist organizations, she wrote a book on this subject, *Don't Tell Me about Arches. Tell Me About your Prisons*, and the famous dramatic monologues such as *I, Ulrike*, and *A Mother*. After 1977 she became increasingly concerned with women's issues, and began working separately from Fo, playing her collection of dramatic monologues (collectively called *All Home, Bed and Church*) over a thousand times, in 152 different productions in 32 countries. In 1983 she began to tour with a second show, the three-piece farce *Open Couple*. Although she continued to collaborate with Fo, their work took them different ways and the partnership was formally broken in 1987.

**Ramphele, Mamphela** (1948–). South African doctor and activist. Born in the Northern Transvaal, she qualified in medicine at the University of Natal. In 1975 she founded the Zanempilo Health Clinic at King William's Town, a project established by the Black Community Programmes. She was closely associated with Mapetla Mohapi and Steve Biko, both of whom died in police custody. Detained under the Internal Security Act in 1977 and banned from carrying on her work at the clinic, she was removed to a remote district in the Northern Transvaal. In 1977 she became an itinerant doctor with a community health project at Trichardsdal and in 1978 founded the Ithuseng Community Health Centre. In 1984 she joined the faculty of the University of Cape Town and is co-author with Frances Wilson of *Children in South Africa* (1987) and of the Second Carnegie Inquiry into Poverty and Development in South Africa.

**Rand** [née Bignal], **Mary (Denise)** (1940–). English athlete, the first British woman to win an Olympic gold medal in athletics. She was born in Wells, Somerset, and by the time she was 17 proved her all-round ability by setting a national record (4046 points) in the pentathlon. The next year, 1958, she gained a silver medal in the Commonwealth

Games long jump and came seventh in the European pentathlon championships. In the 1960 Olympics she led the long jump qualifiers with a British record of 20'9¼", but an unusual attack of nerves brought her to ninth place in the finals; in hurdles she was fourth.

A few months after the birth of her daughter in 1962, she began to reach the peak of her form. She won a bronze medal in the European long jump, shared in the world relay record in 1963, then at the 1964 Tokyo Olympics made the greatest series of long jumps on record. Her world record jump of 22'2¼" gained the gold medal, but the worst of her six jumps was little less at 21'6¼" (this record is still unbeaten, and is thus very longstanding by modern athletic standards). She won a silver medal at the pentathlon and second place on the world's all-time list with 5035 points, then a bronze medal by contributing to the British team's third place in the 4 × 100 metres relay. She was created MBE.

In 1966 she was below her true form but won a gold medal in the Commonwealth Games long jump. Injury prevented her inclusion in the 1968 British Olympic team and she retired. Her second marriage in 1969 was to the Olympic decathlon champion Bill Toomey, an American. Mary held UK records of 10.6 seconds for 100 yards, and 10.9 seconds for 80 metres hurdles, as well as for high jump, long jump and pentathlon, an outstanding range of quality and versatility.

**Rankin,** Dame **Annabelle** (1908–86). Australian politician. Born in Brisbane, the daughter of a colonel, she was educated in Toowomba, Queensland. Her public career really began during World War II when she was a YWCA Assistant Commissioner and was placed in charge of welfare work for the women's services. After the war she organized the Junior Red Cross in Queensland, and in 1946 she was elected to the Senate. She acted as a member of various committees on broadcasting (1947) and public works (1950), was Opposition Whip (1947–9), becoming Vice-President of the Queensland Liberal Party in 1949, and from 1951 to 1966 held the position of a Government Whip. In 1966, after 20 years as a Member of Parliament, Annabelle Rankin became the first woman to control a federal department,

when she became Minister of Housing (1966–71). She then became Australia's first woman ambassador, when she held the post of High Commissioner to New Zealand from 1971 to 1975. Although officially retired, she remained a very influential figure until her death.

**Rankin, Jeanette (Pickering)** (1880–1973). American pacifist, feminist and politician. Born in Montana, she was the eldest of seven children of a rancher and was educated largely by her school teacher mother. She graduated in biology in 1902 from Montana University, but later studied at the New York School of Philanthropy (1908–9), becoming a social worker in Seattle. Here she joined the suffrage battle, campaigning in Washington State (1910), California (1911) and Montana (1912–14), becoming a field secretary for the National American Women's Suffrage Association, 1913.

In 1916 she ran successfully as Republican candidate for Montana, and in 1917 became the first woman to enter the House of Representatives. Here she sponsored protective legislation for women and children, but she lost her seat through her pacifism, which led her to vote against entry into World War I. In 1919, with JANE ADDAMS and FLORENCE KELLEY, she attended the Congress of the International Concil of Women, and between 1920 and 1924 became Secretary of Kelley's National Consumers' League, and worked for the Women's International League for Peace and Freedom. After moving to Georgia in 1928 she became an organizer for the National Council for the Prevention of War (1929–39).

In 1940 she was again elected to Congress, casting the only vote against entry into World War II after Pearl Harbour, her pacifist stance again losing her seat in 1942. After the war she studied the peace movement abroad, being particularly influenced by Gandhi, and during the 1950s she questioned constantly the USA's role in developing countries and opposed its involvement in Korea. In the 1960s her feminism led to an attempt to start a women's communal farm in Georgia, and her pacifism to vehement opposition to the Vietnam War: in 1968 she led the Jeanette

Rankin Brigade in a protest march in Washington.

H. Josephson: *First Lady in Congress: Jeanette Rankin* (1974)

**Ransome-Kuti, Fumilayo** (1900–). Nigerian feminist. She was born in Abeokuta and educated at the Anglican Church primary and secondary schools, before going to England to study domestic science at Wincham Hall College. On her return she began teaching, and campaigning for women's rights, especially the enfranchisement of women in Nigeria and the abolition of oppressive taxation against the market women in Egbaland. The University of Ibadan honoured her with a doctorate in law and she also holds a chieftaincy title. She is married and has four children.

**Rāteb, Aisha** (1928–). Egyptian politician. Educated at the Faculty of Law in Cairo, where she became a junior lecturer, she eventually rose to become the first Professor of International Law at Cairo University. In 1971 she became Minister of Social Affairs, the second woman to hold such a post (following Dr Hikmat Abū Zaid), remaining until 1977, when she added Insurance to her portfolio. In 1973 she became Chairman of the Legislative Affairs Committee, and in 1978 the Egyptian Minister of Foreign Affairs. From 1979–81 she was Ambassador to Denmark, and to Germany from 1981–84.

**Rathbone, Eleanor** (1872–1946). British reformer, feminist and politician. Born into a famous Liverpool merchant family with a Quaker background, noted for its philanthropy, Eleanor was the eighth of ten children. Her father, William Rathbone, was Liberal MP for the city and her childhood was divided between Liverpool and London. After Kensington High School she read Classics at Somerville College, Oxford. Returning home in 1896 she became a visitor for the Liverpool Central Relief Society and secretary of the Liverpool Women's Industrial Council, and worked on a major dock labour inquiry. From 1897 she was also the leading speaker for the local Women's Suffrage Society. In 1902 she met Elizabeth Macadam, warden of the Victoria Women's settlement, her companion until her death. Her research led to two important analyses of

family economics, *How the Casual Labourer Lives* (1909) and *The Conditions of Widows under the Poor Law in Liverpool* (1913). In 1909 she became the first woman member of Liverpool City Council.

During World War I she administered 'Service Separation Allowances' and in 1918 her Family Endowment Committee published its pamphlet *Equal Pay and the Family*. This was linked to her work for the women's movement: she succeeded MILLICENT FAWCETT in 1919 as President of the National Union of Societies for Equal Citizenship, the new form of the old National Union of Women's Suffrage Societies. In 1922 she stood unsuccessfully as an independent parliamentary candidate for East Toxteth. Her main priority continued to be family economics, powerfully analysed in *The Disinherited Family* (1924) and much later in *The Case for Family Allowances* (1940), which influenced the eventual legislation of 1945.

In 1928 she was deeply affected by Kathleen Mayo's book *Mother India* and after she was elected independent MP for the Combined English Universities she widened her concern for women to take in issues in India, expressing her views in works such as *Child Marriage: The Indian Minotaur* (1934). During the 1930s she firmly opposed British foreign policy on Abyssinia and the Spanish Civil war (which she visited in 1936 with the Duchess of Atholl and MAUDE ROYDEN) and the isolation of Russia, and argued passionately against appeasement in *War Can Be Averted* (1937). During World War II she worked with displaced persons in Europe and her concern for Jewish refugees led to her last great commitment, the Zionist cause. A Fellow of the Royal Statistical Society, she was awarded honorary degrees by Liverpool University in 1931 and Oxford in 1938.

M. Stocks: *Eleanor Rathbone: a Biography* (1949)

**Ratia, Armi** (1912–79). Finnish designer and businesswoman. Born in Karelia, she qualified in 1935 from the influential Art Industry Central School and went on to study in Germany, particularly in Tübingen at a textile manufacturer's. From 1935 to 1939 she also ran her own weaving firm. During World War II she worked for the Ministry of Defence, and from 1942 to 1949 for an American advertising company.

In 1944 she had been among the 4 million

refugees fleeing from the Soviet occupation of Karelia, and on their arrival in Helsinki her husband Viljo Ratia bought an old oil-cloth factory. From 1949 to 1951 they worked there together, and in 1951 founded Marimekko, which became one of the most famous Finnish design firms, producing textiles, clothes, upholstery and even bags and toys, often with simple colours and striking abstract patterns. Armi Ratia was Managing Director until 1969, when she and her husband separated, and resumed control from 1971 until her death. Marimekko was exporting to over 20 countries by the 1970s and Ratia was awarded the American Nieman Marcus Award in 1968, and later the highest Finnish honour, the Order of the White Rose.

**Ratushinskaya, Irina** (1954–). Russian poet, resident in America. Widely acclaimed as the finest Russian poet since Pasternak, Irina Ratushinskaya was born into a Polish family at Odessa, but her parents were concerned that she should be accepted as fully Russian, and forbade her grandparents to teach her Polish. Her belief in God caused trouble at school, but she was allowed to study physics and mathematics at the University of Odessa in 1971, and after working as a schoolteacher she became assistant lecturer at the Odessa Pedagogical Institute. She lost her job after refusing to serve on an examinations committee which involved accepting a quota for Jewish students.

In 1979 she married physicist and human rights activist Igor Gerashzenko and moved to Kiev. They were refused permission to emigrate and in 1982 were arrested for demonstrating on behalf of Andrei Sakharov. For this, and for her poetry, Irina was convicted of anti-Soviet agitation and propaganda, and sentenced in March 1983 to seven years' hard labour and five years' internal exile, the first woman to be given such a hard sentence. She served four years, including 138 days in freezing punishment cells, where she wrote 150 poems on bars of soap with charred matchsticks, washing them away once memorized. Many different groups in the West, political and literary, campaigned for her release and in September 1986 she and her husband were allowed three-month visas to the UK for treatment for her glaucoma and

heart trouble. She remained in Britain and was stripped of Soviet citizenship.

Ratushinskaya had written poetry since the age of 14; her cool, serene poetry tells of survival in the face of great odds and is influenced by AKHMATOVA, Mandelstam, Pasternak and TSVETAYEVA. Her poetry appeared in Samizdat publications and in European Russian journals, and was translated in *Poems* (1984) and *No I'm Not Afraid* (1986). In 1987, as part of the Poetry Live Festival, she read to 4000 people in the Albert Hall, London. Since her release she has travelled widely in the West, speaking on behalf of political prisoners, and in June 1987 became Poet-in-Residence at Northwestern University, Chicago. The title of her account of prison life (*Grey is the Colour of Hope*, 1988) refers to the grey uniform worn by inmates of 'the small zone' for the specially dangerous.

**Rau, Dhanvanthi Rama** (1893–1987). Indian social worker. She was born into an aristocratic family and was educated at St Mary's High School, Hubli, and at the University of Madras – she was one of the first Indian women to attend college. She then lectured in English at Queen Mary's College, Madras (1917–21). She married Sir Bengal Rama Rau, a leading Indian diplomat, and began to work for social reform. She was Secretary of the All-India Child Marriage Abolition League (1927–8), a member of the International Alliance for Suffrage and Equal Citizenship (1932–8) and President of the All-India Women's Conference at the time of independence (1946–7). Her chief concern became the world family planning movement. She worked for the Family Planning Association of India from 1949 to 1963, and was President of the International Planned Parenthood Association from 1963 to 1971. She published her memoirs in 1977.

Dhanvanthi's daughter, Santha Rama Rau (1923–), is famous as a novelist and writer, and her grand-daughter Aisha Wayle (1944–) continues the tradition of independent action, since she was the first woman to own a London investment company, after working as a financial director for Rothschild's.

D.R. Rau: *An Inheritance* (1987)

**Ravera, Camilla** (1889–). Italian socialist and feminist. She was born in Acqui, into a middle-class family in which the father, a radical atheist, exercised a strong influence. She later moved with her family to Turin and began to teach from 1908 to 1909 and to read Marxist writings. After witnessing the *settimana rossa* in 1914, World War I, the fight for work and the Turinese uprising of August 1917, she joined the Socialist Party. Subsequently, as an active participant in the group Ordine nuovo she joined the Italian Communist Party from its inception. In the daily newspaper *Ordine nuove* she ran the column 'Tribuna delle donne' (it held the most advanced position on the feminist question to be found within the revolutionary movement) and she became Editor of *La compagna*. In the autumn of 1922 she first met Zetkin, then Lenin and began to acquire an important organizational role in Italy. After the fascist repression of 1922–3, she co-ordinated clandestine work first under the name Silvia and later as Micheli. In 1927 she moved her nucleus, the 'Ufficio stampa e propoganda', to Lugano, and in 1929 she and Togliatti moved to Moscow to work in the Comintern.

As a result of her support for a change in policy and the reconstitution of an Italian centre in the Communist Party she re-entered Italy clandestinely in 1930. She was caught, arrested and found guilty by a special tribunal; imprisoned until 1935, she was then held in internal exile until 1943. Like Terracini she opposed the German-Soviet pact and the official line on World War II and was therefore excluded from the leadership until 1945, when she resumed political work. Elected to the Chamber of Deputies she was an active campaigner for women's rights, and in honour of her integrity and achievements she was nominated a life-senator. Ravera's publications include *La donna italiana dal primo al secondo Risorgimento* (1951); her account of the rise of fascism, *Diario di trenti anni, 1913–43* (1974); and the *Breve storia del movimento femminile in Italia* (1978).

**Read, Mary** (1690–1720). English soldier and pirate. The daughter of a sea captain, she was brought up by her mother and was disguised as a boy to obtain inheritance by posing as heir to her father's wealthy mother. Still dressed as a boy she became a servant at an inn, then footboy to a French noblewoman, and then 'powder-monkey' on a warship, where she remained for about six years. Eventually she deserted and enlisted in an infantry regiment in Flanders, fighting the French and soon transferring to the cavalry as a Light Dragoon. She became infatuated with a Flemish trooper, revealed her sex and married him, to the astonishment of the rest of the regiment, whose officers provided them with money to open a tavern near Breda, in Brabant. After the sudden death of her husband she re-enlisted in Holland, but after a short time she left and joined a ship bound for the West Indies. The ship was captured by English pirates and she joined their crew until 1717, when a general pardon issued by George I allowed her to return to a respectable life on land. In 1718 she joined a privateer at Providence, in New England, which was eventually captured by Jack Rackham and ANNE BONNEY. The two women became deeply attached to each other, and may have been lovers, although Mary apparently soon became infatuated with an English sailor, Peter Hines. After their eventual capture off Jamaica, Mary was sentenced to death. Although reprieved on the grounds of pregnancy, she died of fever in prison at St Jago de la Vega.

F. Strong: *Mary Read: The Pirate Wench* (1934)

**Reading** [née Charnaud], **Stella**, Dowager Marchioness of (1894–1971). British voluntary organizer. Born in Constantinople [now Istanbul] and educated privately, she worked for the British Red Cross during World War I. In 1925 she went to India as a member of the Viceroy's Staff, and she married Lord Reading in 1931. In 1931 she headed a Personal Service Loan to help victims of unemployment. From 1935, after the death of her husband, she devoted herself to voluntary work, serving on a number of government commissions and advisory bodies. In 1938 she was appointed by the Home Secretary as Chairman of the Women's Voluntary Service, founded to promote the recruitment of women into civil defence. During World War II she took over the massive administration of evacuation, rationing, and care for air-raid victims.

After the war the service was continued, becoming the Women's Royal Voluntary Service in 1966, caring for the old and underprivileged. Energetic and forceful, one of the last of the leisure-class philanthropists, she was also interested in international affairs and was Chairman of the Advisory Council on Commonwealth Immigration (1962–5). She was created DBE in 1941 and made a life peeress, as Baroness Swanborough, in 1958.

**Récamier** [née Bernard], **(Jeanne-Françoise-Julie-Adelaide),** Madame de (1777–1849). French salon hostess. Born at Lyons, the daughter of a banker, she was educated in a convent until the age of 15 when she came to Paris. The following year she married a rich, elderly banker Jacques Récamier. Very beautiful, charming, faithful and sensitive, during her life she was the object of much passionate devotion from writers such as Benjamin Constant, but she is thought to have had only platonic relationships with her many admirers. She soon became a fashionable hostess and her salon attracted both politicians and literary figures.

Her Royalist friends, such as Bernadotte, made her unpopular with Napoleon who exiled her from Paris in 1805. She stayed with her close friend Madame de STAEL (who portrayed her in *Corinne*) in Geneva, and went on to Rome and Naples, returning only after the Battle of Waterloo in 1815. The Récamier fortune had been greatly reduced and after 1819 she lived in Paris in rooms at the convent of l'Abbaye-aux-Bois. She continued to hold her salon, which in her later years revolved largely around the famous diplomat and writer Châteaubriand, who used to read aloud from his autobiographical *Memoires d'outre tombe*, which were published after his death. He died in 1848, and Madame de Récamier, who had become totally blind, died ten months later. A famous portrait of her by David, painted in 1800, hangs in the Louvre.

M. Trouncer: *Madame Récamier* (1949)

**Redgrave, Vanessa** (1937–). English actress. Born into a theatrical family, she is the daughter of Sir Michael Redgrave and Rachel Kempson. She was educated at Queensgate School, London, and the Central School of Speech and Drama, and made her stage debut in 1957. She appeared with her father in *A Touch of the Sun* (1958) and her first great success came as Stella Dean in Robert Bolt's *The Tiger and the Horse* (1960). She then confirmed her reputation with fine performances as Rosalind in *As You Like it* at Stratford in 1962 and in Ibsen's *Lady from the Sea* and Chekhov's *The Seagull* in 1964. Since then she has performed many major roles, her recent plays including *Ghosts* (1986) and O'Neill's *A Touch of the Poet* (1988).

She had appeared in a minor film role in 1958, but in 1966 began a new career in the cinema with films such as *Morgan* (1966), *Isadora* (1968) and *Mary Queen of Scots* (1971). All these won her Academy Award nominations, and she received an Oscar for her performance in *Julia* (1977). Later films include *The Bostonians* (1984), *Wetherby* (1985) and *Prick Up Your Ears* (1986).

Redgrave's political views are of the extreme left, and she was reprimanded for making a fiery anti-Zionist speech at the Award ceremony. She has been active in Trotskyist sects since the late 1960s and with her brother Corin was a prominent member of the Workers' Revolutionary Party (for whom she stood as a candidate in the 1974 and 1979 general elections) until expelled after an internal dispute.

She was married to the director Tony Richardson, but they were divorced in 1967. Their daughters Natasha and Joely have both made notable film debuts. In 1969 she had a son, with the actor Franco Nero.

**Reibey** [née Haydock], **Mary** (1777–1855). Australian businesswoman. Born in Bury, Lancashire, she was orphaned when she was a child, and brought up by her grandmother. In 1790 she was sentenced to seven years transportation to Australia for horse-stealing; aged only 13, she had disguised herself as a boy, calling herself James Burrow. She arrived in Sydney in 1792, was sent as nursemaid to the family of Major Francis Grose, and in 1794 married Thomas Reibey, an Irishman working for the East India Company. Reibey became a prosperous independent trader in grain, and then in general imports, trading up the Australian coast but also to the Pacific, China and India. Mary kept a hotel, looked after their seven children and ran the business during his voyages, proving tough and very competitive when she took it over after his death in 1811. She opened new warehouses, bought more ships and invested in property, and was accepted as a leader of society in Sydney, and fêted on a return visit to Lancashire in 1820.

During the late 1820s Mary withdrew from active trading and concentrated on her city properties and new building ventures in Sydney, living on her investments and becoming a noted philanthropist and religious worker. Her colourful past was uncomfortably revived when she was confused with MARGARET CATCHPOLE, whose life story was published in 1845. She eventually retired to the suburb of Newtown, and her three sons became prosperous merchants in their turn.

**Reiniger, Lotte** (1899–1981). German pioneer of film animation. In 1919 she developed animation techniques using silhouette figures made of cardboard, tin and paper. Collaborating with her husband, Carl Koch, she made the first full-length animated film, *The Adventures of Prince Achmed* (1926). Their work in England between 1936 and 1939 included *Tochter*, with music by Benjamin Britten. After working in Italy and Berlin, they settled in England in 1950 and directed many animated television films together until his death in 1963. She retired, but in the late 1970s made a new series of silhouette folk tales, including *Aucassin and Nicolette* and *The Rose and the Ring*, and continued to lecture extensively in Europe and the USA.

**Reisner, Larissa Mikhailovna** (1895–1926). Russian revolutionary and writer. Born in Lublin (now in Poland), Larissa was the daughter of a socialist law professor. She grew up in St Petersburg but the family moved to Berlin to avoid unrest in 1903, returning in 1907. After studying at a gymnasium Larissa entered the University of St Petersburg in 1913. In 1915–16 she published a satirical anti-war magazine, *Rudin*, and when this was censored wrote for Gorky's journal *Chronicle*. In 1918 she joined the Bolshevik party and fought as a soldier and intelligence officer on the Eastern Front and with the Volga Military Flotilla, becoming the Red Army's first woman political commissar. Her articles on her experiences were published as *The Front* (1924). In 1921 she became the first Soviet ambassador to Afghanistan and in 1923 worked in Berlin and Hamburg for the Comintern: these adventures are described in *Afghanistan* and *Hamburg at the Barricades* (both 1925). In the same year she wrote *Coal, Iron and Lively People*, about her travels through industrial regions of the Urals, Siberia and Byelorussia as correspondent for *Izvestia*. Her writing is notable for its combination of acute observation, political analysis and imaginative use of language. She died of typhus, in the Kremlin Hospital, aged 32.

C. Porter: *Larissa Reisner* (1988)

**Rekha** (1953?–). Indian film star. Rekha is the daughter of acting parents: her father, Gemini Ganeshan, was one of the stars of the southern Indian cinema, known as 'Kadar Manan' ('King of Romance'), and her mother was a leading actress in Madras. In 1968 the entrepreneurial Pal brothers took her to Bombay, where she was signed on by the director Mohan Segal to make *Sawan Bhadon*. An overnight hit, it made her a national star but her youth (either 13 or 15 depending on the source), her southern background, and her embarrassment at her buxom country image made this a difficult time for her. Gradually she has developed into India's highest paid star, enigmatic, glamorous, passionate, making over 100 films in which she has proved her versatility, her roles varying from carefree tomboy to jealous mistress, from the heroine of a historical epic to a gang-raped housewife. In 1982 she won the National Award for her portrayal of a courtesan in *Umrao Jaan*. Although a commercial star, she is admired by leading directors like Yash Chopra and Shyam Benegal, who sees her as a capable, disciplined actress with immense range, ability and mastery of precise detail.

Rekha is also unusual in Indian cinema for her flamboyant life-style and her long-held, highly publicized, self-proclaimed hopeless passion for the great star Amitabh Bachan. Her looks and style are copied throughout India, and she brought out a book on yoga, exercises and beauty called *Rekha's Mind and Body Temple* (1983). In 1985 she decided to give up the cinema and left for Los Angeles, giving a 13-city sell-out tour of songs and dances, but she soon returned to the screen and in 1987 made the remarkable *Aurat* ('Woman').

**Renaud, Madeleine** (1903–). French actress. After training at the Conservatoire d'Art Dramatique she joined the Comédie-Française in 1921, and achieved almost immediate fame with her performance as Agnès in Molière's *Ecole des femmes*. She played both classical and modern roles and remained a leading actress in the company for 25 years. In 1940 she married the actor Jean-Louis Barrault, who had been engaged as a director at the Comédie, and who extended its range to include plays such as Claudel's *Le soulier de satin*, in which Madeleine appeared. The following year they both left the company and formed the small touring Compagnie Renaud-Barrault, which gradually acquired a remarkable repertoire of classical, experimental and mime plays. Renaud took the lead in most of these, including Camus' *L'état de siège* (1948), Sardou's *Madame sans-gêne* (1957) and, most memorably, in Beckett's *Oh les beaux jours!* (1963). Later plays in which she took leading roles included *Pas Moi* (1976), *Wings* (1979), and *Savannah Bay* (1983. She has also acted in films, including *Vent debout* (1922), *Le ciel est à vous* (1944) and the film version of Marguerite Duras' *Des journées entières dans les arbres* (1976).

**Renger, Annemarie** (1919–). German politician. She was born in Leipzig, and in 1938 married Emil Renger, who was killed in World War II; they had one son. After the war she joined the Social Democratic Party (SPD) and became private secretary to Dr Kurt Schumacher from 1945 to 1952. The following year she was elected to the Bundestag, and became Chairwoman of the SPD Federal Women's Committee, campaigning for women's rights especially in the area of housing and consumer law. In 1965 she was married again, to Alexander Renger Loncarevic (he died in 1973), but her political career was not interrupted. She was a member of the SPD Parliamentary Group (1969–72), and from 1972 to 1976 was President of the Bundestag; afterwards she became joint Vice-president. In 1977 Renger became a member of the Committee for Foreign Relations, and for ten years she was also a member of the Consultative Assembly of the Council of Europe and of the Assembly of the Western European Union. During the same period she was Vice-President of the International Council of Social Democratic Women of the Socialist International (1972–6).

**Renzi, Anna** (*c*1620–1660 or later). Italian soprano. Born in Rome, she was a pupil of Filiberto Laurenzi and in 1640 sang in a performance of his opera *Il favorito del principe* at the French embassy there, having appeared in other works while still in her teens. Later that year she left for Venice with Laurenzi, with whom she remained associated until 1644. Venetian opera was still in its infancy (operatic activity was largely centred on the wealthier courts, and Venice did not have one), and her arrival was well timed to coincide with the establishment of the first public opera houses in the city. She soon came into contact with the members of the Accademia degli Incogniti, founded by Loredan, who published a fable describing how Apollo would have excluded her from Parnassus to avoid the jealousy of the Muses. This academy was closely linked to the Accademia degli Unisoni, founded by Giulio Strozzi (adoptive father of BARBARA STROZZI), who was so impressed by her that he published an encomium entitled *Le glorie della signora Anna Renzi romana* (1644). This volume is the main biographical source for her, and its verses are lavish in their praise of her many attributes as a performer; it was also intended to assert that Venice could now vie with operatic activity elsewhere in Italy. Her most important roles included Deidamia in Sacrati's *La finta pazza* (1641; for the opening of the Teatro Novissimo) and Archimene in his *Bellerofonte* (1642), Aretusa in Laurenzi's *La finta savia* (1643) and, most notably, Octavia in Monteverdi's *L'incoronazione di Poppea* (1643). She was the dedicatee or Orazio Tarditi's *Canzonette amorose* (1642) and Alessandro Leardini's *Argiope* (1645). Having heard her in Giovanni Rovetta's *Ercole in Lidia* (1645), John Evelyn invited her to dinner, describing both events in his diary. Comparatively little is known of Renzi from the 1650s onwards: she appeared at the Innsbruck court in 1653–4 and 1655, in the title role of Cesti's *Cleopatra* and as Dorisbe in his *Argia*, the latter at a performance for Queen Christina of Sweden. She was back in Venice in 1657, and an archival reference suggests that she was in Innsbruck again in 1660, the last documented date for her.

**Rhondda,** Lady Margaret (Haig Thomas) (1883–1958). Welsh publisher. She was born in South Wales, the daughter of an industrialist, and educated privately, and in London and St Andrews. After three London seasons she spent one year at Somerville College, Oxford, but left to marry Humphrey Mackworth in 1908. They were divorced in 1923. She joined the Women's Social and Political Union as a militant suffragette, was imprisoned and went on hunger-strike. She became her father's business associate and visited the USA, being rescued from the sinking of the *Lusitania* in 1916. She succeeded to the Viscountcy in 1918, became an influential businesswoman, and successfully obtained royal permission to attend the House of Lords. In 1920 she founded the journal *Time and Tide*, taking over as Editor in 1926, and attracting contributors such as George Bernard Shaw, G.K. Chesterton, REBECCA WEST, and WINIFRED HOLTBY. Although the paper moved from left-wing feminism to conservative individualism, she made it a leading weekly for over 30 years. After her death, it was found that her devotion to the publication had cost her over £250,000 in subsidies.

M. Thomas: *This was my World* (1933)

**Rhys, Jean** [pseud. of Gwen Williams] (1894–1979). British novelist. She was the daughter of a doctor in Dominica and was educated at the Convent of the Faithful Virgin in Roseau. In 1910 she accompanied an aunt to England, where she briefly went to school in Cambridge, and then to Tree's Academy, and later to the Royal Academy of Dramatic Art. After the death of her father, she had to earn her own living, and she changed her name to Jean Rhys and went into vaudeville. In 1919 she married Max Hamer, a Dutch poet and translator, and went to live in Vienna, Budapest and finally Paris. There she met James Joyce, Ernest Hemingway, the poet H.D., DJUNA BARNES, and, most important, Ford Madox Ford, who became her literary mentor. Her relationship with Ford and his wife is portrayed in her first novel, *Quartet* (1928).

She wrote three more novels before World War II, all depicting women duped or betrayed by the men they love or struggling to survive alone, as in *Good Morning Midnight* (1939). During this period she also worked as a translator, a tutor and a fashion model. She divorced and returned to England in 1934, and later remarried. She then lapsed into obscurity until the publication of her last novel, *The wide Sargasso Sea* (1966), which told the story of Mr Rochester's first wife, Charlotte, in Charlotte BRONTE's *Jane Eyre* and which was partly set in the Caribbean of her childhood. At the end of her life she divided her time between a remote cottage in Devon and London. Her autobiography, *Smile Please*, was unfinished, but was published posthumously in 1980.

L. James: *Jean Rhys* (1978)

**Ricard** [née Betenfeld], **Marthe** (1889–1982). French feminist. She was born in a small village in the eastern provinces while they were still occupied by Germany in the aftermath of the Franco-Prussian War. Always a pioneer, in 1911 she qualified as a pilot, and following the death of her first husband ( a grocer, Henri Richer) at the Battle of Verdun, she began to work for the French secret service. In San Sebastian she reputedly gained vital information, especially about submarine movements, from a military attaché, Baron von Krohn, whom she had made her lover. After World War I she was decorated with the Cross of the Légion d'Honneur.

Her second marriage was to Thomas Crompton, an Englishman, but after he died she returned to France, and during World War II worked for the Résistance. Her third marriage was to a Frenchman, Ricard. After the liberation she was elected a city councillor in Paris and launched a major campaign against legalized prostitution, objecting to the double standard of morality and to a system which exploited women as sexual 'slaves'. This resulted in the closure of Paris brothels in 1945, and in legislation covering the whole country in 1946. Nearly 30 years later Ricard suggested that some form of authorized prostitution should be reintroduced since street prostitution was still resulting in exploitation.

**Rich, Adrienne (Cecile)** (1929–). American poet and feminist. Born in Baltimore, she graduated from Radcliffe College in 1951, and while she was still a student her work was included in the Yale Younger Poets series on the recommendation of W.H. Auden, with *A Change of the World* (1951). During the 1950s her poetry was stylized and formal. She married Alfred Conrad and had three sons, describing her difficult experience of childbirth and motherhood 20 years later in *Of Woman Born* (1976). Her next two collections, *The Diamond Cutters* (1955) and *Snapshot of a Daughter-in-Law* (1963); both won awards, and during the 1960s her poetry became more closely identified with the student and anti-war movement, particularly with *Leaflets* (1969). She then moved towards the politics of private life and the crisis of identity, with *The Will to Change* (1971) and *Diving into the Wreck* (1973); this led her to adopt a feminist position, so that when she was awarded the National Book Award in 1974 she rejected it as an individual, but with ALICE WALKER and Audrey Rich accepted it on behalf of all women.

Since the mid-1970s her name has been synonymous with radical feminism, through her explanation of history, social oppression and private consciousness in *Of Woman Born* (1976), *Women and Honour: some Notes on Lying* (1977) and the selections of essays *On Lives, Secrets and Silence* (1979) and *Blood, Bread and Poetry* (1986), as well as in the poems in *The Dream of a Common Language* (1978), *A Wild Patience Has Taken Me This Far* (1981) and *The Fact of a Doorframe* (1984). She has taught at various American universities since the mid-1960s and has been on the staff at Smith College since 1979.

**Richards,** [née Swallow], **Ellen (Henrietta)** (1842–1911). American sanitary chemist and ecologist. Brought up on a farm, Ellen was an only child and was taught mainly by her parents. She entered Vassar College at the age of 25 and graduated in 1870. She then applied to the Massachusetts Institute of Technology (MIT) and was admitted as a special student of chemistry, without charge, as the president did not want formally to admit a woman. When she obtained her degree in 1873, Ellen became the first woman science graduate in the USA and the first woman to graduate from MIT. Women were formally admitted in 1876. In 1875 Ellen married Robert Richards, a professor of mining engineering, and they contributed to each other's work.

Not allowed to take a doctorate, Ellen established and organized a Women's Laboratory at MIT and was active in other organizations promoting education for women, particularly in science. In 1884 a laboratory for sanitary chemistry was set up at MIT, and Ellen became the first woman faculty member as an instructor, a post she held for the next 27 years. She taught the analysis of water, sewage, and air, and undertook a survey of the waters of Massachusetts, taking over 40,000 samples. She did consultancy work, particularly in food analysis, and published numerous textbooks. *Food Materials and their Adulterations* (1885) influenced the passage of the Pure Food and Drug Acts.

Having effectively launched the science of ecology, Ellen moved on to apply her knowledge to daily life. From 1890 she formed the home economics movement, establishing public kitchens, attempting popular education in nutrition and running courses. She also founded the *Journal of Home Economics*. In 1910 she was awarded an honorary DSc from Smith College in Massachusetts and appointed to the council of the National Educational Association.

R. Clarke: *Ellen Swallow: the Woman who founded Ecology* (1977)

**Richardson, Dorothy (Miller)** (1873–1957). English novelist. Born in Abingdon, Berkshire, she was educated in local day schools and grew up as the rebellious child in a household of girls, ruled by an authoritarian father who was a devotee of scientific nationalism. After her father's bankruptcy in 1893 she cared for her invalid mother until she committed suicide in 1895. Dorothy moved to London and took various jobs to maintain her independence, working as a dentist's assistant, teacher and clerk. She associated with radical feminist and socialist groups, and was particularly influenced by Fabian principles. She had a love affair with the writer H.G. Wells, and a subsequent miscarriage in 1907 drove her to the edge of collapse. Wells encouraged her to write and she ultimately chose a form entirely different from his abstract, political fiction, later depicting him in *Pilgrimage* as Hypo Wilson. In 1917 she married the artist Alan Odle.

She began writing in 1913, her first books being studies of the Quakers and George Fox (1914). Her first novel, *Painted Roofs* (1915), was followed by ten more, culminating in *Clear Horizon* (1935). She added a final section, *Dimple Hill*, and the books were collected as *Pilgrimage* in 1938. This work, which took 25 years to write, is a spiritual autobiography of the heroine Miriam Henderson, recalling every detail of her daily life and thought, in a new style which the critic May Sinclair christened 'stream of consciousness' in 1918. During the 1930s Richardson also worked as a translator, but she continued revising *Pilgrimage* until 1951 and the augmented manuscript was published as *March Moonlight* in 1967. She has been linked with VIRGINIA WOOLF in creating a distinctive female aesthetic which sought to break away from the old patterns of literature in an attempt to find adequate expression for women's inner consciousness. Richardson eventually left London to settle in Cornwall.

G. Hanscombe: *Art of Life: Dorothy Richardson and the Development of Feminist Consciousness* (1982)

**Richardson, Henry Handel** [pseud. of Ethel Florence Lindesay Robertson] (1870–1946). Australian novelist. Born in Melbourne, Victoria, she was the daughter of a doctor who had emigrated from Ireland during the 1850 gold rush; after her father died in 1879 she and her sister were brought up in country villages by her mother, who became a postmistress after her husband's death. Her youth was not a happy one. She was educated at the Presbyterian Ladies' College, Melbourne (described in *The Getting of Wisdom*, 1910). Her mother managed to save to send her to the Leipzig Conservatoire in 1887 to study piano, and she at once felt at home intellectually, becoming interested in German Romantic literature and later in the works of Nietzsche and Freud. In 1895 she married John George Robertson, whom she had met as a student, in Dublin, and from 1896 to 1904 they lived in Strasbourg, where John taught at the university. She wrote articles and in 1897

started writing her first novel, *Maurice Guest*, based on her student experiences with a heroine modelled on ELEANOR DUSE; it was eventually published in 1908, and was the first novel published in England to treat homosexuality openly.

By then her husband had been appointed the first Professor of Germanic and Scandinavian Languages at London University, where he remained until his death (in 1933). In London she became increasingly solitary, concentrating on her writing. After *The Getting of Wisdom* she travelled to Australia in 1912 to gather information for *The Fortunes of Richard Mahony*, her great trilogy about life in the goldfields, inspired by her father's life, and for *Australia Felix* (1917), *The Way Home* (1925) and *Ultima Thule* (1929). During the 1930s she wrote a collection of stories and a fine novel, *Young Cosima* (1939). Her description of her early life, *Myself when Young*, appeared after her death in 1948. She is considered by some critics to be the finest Australian novelist.

K. McLeod: *Dorothy Richardson* (1985)

**Richardson, Katy** [Kathleen] (1864–1927). British mountaineer. After first visiting Zermatt at 16, Katy made 116 major ascents between 1882 and 1893, 6 of them being pioneer first ascents and 14 first ascents by a woman. Despite her slight figure she had great physical endurance; she climbed in skirts and insisted on taking bread, jam and tea. In 1888, with Emile Rey and J.J. Bich, she climbed the Aiguille de Bionnassay and traversed the eastern ridge to the Dôme du Gouter, previously considered impossible. Her last five years climbing were with the Frenchwoman, Mary Paillon, with whom she lived at Oullins, nr Lyons.

**Richier, Germaine** (1904–59). French sculptor. She was born at Grans, near Arles, the daughter of a vineyard owner. Her family moved to Montpellier, where she attended the Ecole des Beaux Arts in 1922 against her parents' wishes. She then studied privately under Bourdelle in Paris between 1925 and 1929, established her own studio on the Avenue du Marne, and married the Swiss sculptor Otto Banninger. In 1936 she won the Blumenthal Prize at the Petit Palais exhibition and in 1937 obtained a Diploma of Honour. She was included in the 'Women Artists of Europe' exhibition at the Jeu de Paume in 1936, together with SUZANNE VALADON and MARIE LAURENCIN. During this period she worked on historical and classical figures, forceful and finely modelled. After the outbreak of World War II she fled from Paris to Switzerland, and then back to the South of France. The themes and techniques of her work changed. Her sculpture became brooding and sinister, as in *Storm*, and in works based on the insect life which had fascinated her since her childhood in the Midi, such as the huge *Praying Mantis*, or *Spider*. In the 1950s her sculptures developed into sinister artefacts, incorporating wood, bronze, skulls and other materials, as in *The Devil with Claws* (1952) or *The Batman* (1956), and she frequently set her work against painted backgrounds, or added colour, and mosaics of glass. Her unnerving, suggestive style is equally evident in the illustrations she engraved for Rimbaud's *Illuminations* in 1951, or for the poems of René de Solier, who had become her second husband in 1955. Before her death, after a lingering illness from cancer, she had been recognized internationally as one of the major sculptors of the century.

Arts Club of Chicago: *Germaine Richier* (1966)

**Ride, Sally Kristen** (1951–). American astronaut. Born in Encino, California, the elder of two girls, whose father taught political science, her sporting tomboy pursuits were at first channelled into tennis training, and she rose to the position of 18th nationally. Although she considered a career in tennis, she had developed an interest in science at Westlake School for Girls, and studied English and physics at Stanford University.

Her graduate work on x-ray astronomy and free-electron lasers resulted in a PhD in 1978. On impulse she applied to NASA, which had only previously recruited from all-male military test-pilots; six of the 35 chosen that year were women. After training, which for her included gaining a pilot's licence, she was On-orbit Capsule Communicator (Capcom) for space shuttles 2 and 3. She was part of a team designing a mechanical manipulator arm, and in that capacity, and also as a flight engineer, was selected to fly in Space Shuttle 7 on 18 June 1983. There were many

feminists among spectators, but Ride, while recognizing the significance of being the first American woman in space, emphasized her presence there as a scientist rather than as a woman. After the flight her comment was 'I'm sure it was the most fun that I'll ever have in my life.'

In 1982 Ride married a fellow astronaut, Steven Hawley. After 1983 she carried out liaison work for NASA, and was a member of the Presidential Commission on the Space Shuttle investigating the explosion of the shuttle flight *Discovery*, which exploded after take-off in February 1986 with the death of all the crew, including astronaut Judith Resnaik and teacher Christa McAuliffe, chosen to be the first civilian in space.

**Riding** [Reichenthal], **Laura** (1901–). American poet. She was born in New York. Her father was an Austrian émigré whose unsuccessful business interests meant that Laura's primary education was often interrupted. However, she attended high school in Brooklyn and won three scholarships to Cornell University. There she began writing poetry, married a history lecturer Louis Gottschalt, and left her studies to accompany him to the University of Illinois. In 1925 they were divorced and, encouraged by a prize from the Southern Fugitive Group of poets in Nashville, Laura left for Europe. She took the name Riding in 1926 and published her first collection *The Close Chaplet* the same year. She remained abroad for 13 years, living in Egypt, England, Majorca and France, and collections of poetry appeared in rapid succession until 1935. After the publication of her *Collected Poems* in 1938 she wrote no more verse. Her poetry is difficult and austere. During these years she also wrote satiric prose, producing some enjoyable fiction such as *Progress of Stories* (1935) and *Lives of Wives* (1939). She wrote *A Survey of Modernist Poetry* (1927) and *Against Anthologies* (1928) with Robert Graves, with whom she lived in Majorca, and was associated with him in establishing the Seizen Press and *Epilogue* magazine.

In 1939 Riding returned to the USA and in 1941 married Schuyler Jackson, editor of *Time*. She renounced poetry and turned to linguistics; together the Jacksons planned to write a working dictionary of English and a thesaurus which would reflect her strong ideological conviction that the expression of 'truth' is related to linguistic purity. They supported themselves as fruit farmers in Wabasso, Florida, and Laura remained there after her husband's death in 1968. She received a Guggenheim Fellowship in 1973, which allowed her to work on their joint project on language: *Rational meaning: a new Foundation for the Definition of Words*. Her *Selected Writings* were published in 1977, and her *Collected Poems* in 1982.

T.P. Wexler: *Riding's Pursuit of Truth* (1977)

**Rie** [née Gomperz] **Lucie** 1902–). British potter. Born in Austria, the daughter of a professor, she was educated at the Vienna Gymnasium and the Kunstwerbe Schule, and she opened a pottery studio and workshop in 1927. She won gold medals at the Brussels Exhibition in 1935 and at the Milan Triennale (1936), and was already admired for her elegant, simple shapes and varied subtle glazes when she arrived in the UK in 1938. She established a studio in 1939 and has influenced a generation of British potters. From 1960 she taught at the Camberwell Art School in London.

Her delicate pottery and stoneware are found in collections throughout the world, and she has had several major exhibitions, from an Arts Council retrospective in 1967 to a Retrospective at the Victoria and Albert Museum in 1982. She received the OBE in 1968, was made Doctor of the Royal Academy of Arts in 1969 and CBE in 1981.

T. Birks: *Lucie Rie* (1987)

**Riefenstahl, Leni** [Helene] **(Bertha Amalie)** (1902–). German actress, film maker and photographer. After studying fine art at the Berlin Academy, she received a ballet training and danced in Max Reinhardt's theatre company. The first film in which she appeared was *Der heilige Berg/Peaks of Destiny* (1926), made by her mentor, Arnold Fanck. She formed her own production company in 1931 and directed *Das blaue Licht/The Blue Light* (1932), which led Hitler to invite her to film the Nazi Party rallies at Nuremberg in 1934, although she was not a party member. She agreed but insisted on complete artistic and production control, and that she would undertake no further projects for the party. She now

describes *Triumph des Willens/Triumph of the Will* as a documentary and not a propaganda film; it is technically remarkable for its angling, moving shots and editing patterns. She agreed to film the 1938 Olympic Games in Berlin with the same control: supervising the editing, sound-mixing, and printing of the two-part film – *Olympiad: Fest der Völker/Festival of the Nations and Olympiad: Fest der Schönheit/Festival of Beauty* (1938). She defied an order from Goebbels to remove footage of the American black athlete, Jesse Owens, who dominates the first part. The film won the Grand Prize at the Venice International Film Festival in 1938.

Preparations for filming Von Kleist's *Penthesilea* were halted by the outbreak of World War II. Against constant difficulties she filmed *Tiefland* in Spain, but the footage was impounded by the French and she was interned for almost four years until cleared of Nazi involvement. The incomplete film was released in 1954 to critical acclaim. A skiing comedy, *The Red Devils*, to star De Sica and the unknown BRIGITTE BARDOT, and to have an additional 3D version, lost backing after the Austrian opposition press accused the government of backing 'one of Hitler's favourites'. Further projects also fell through and she began to work as a stills photographer for European magazines. A book of her photographs published after a visit to Africa, *The Last of the Nuba* (1973), gave her a new reputation. Her other recent books include *People of the Kau* (1976), *Coral Gardens* (1978) and *Mein Afrika* (1982). She remains unique for her pioneering work as Germany's only woman director during the 1930s, for resisting manipulation, and for her colossal reputation gained from two films, in spite of suppression and ill fortune over the last 40 years.

D.B. Hinton: *The Films of Leni Riefenstahl* (1978)

**Riley, Bridget (Louise)** (1931–). English artist. Born in London, she was educated at Taplow and at Cheltenham Ladies' College, before attending Goldsmiths College of Art, London (1949–52). She then moved on to the Royal College of Art and was one of an innovative generation which included Frank Auerbach and Peter Blake. She left in 1955, spent a year teaching in the Convent of the Sacred Heart at Roehampton (1957–8) and two years travelling to Spain, France and Italy. She also taught part-time at Loughborough Art School, Hornsey College and Croydon College of Art. She was included in a Young Contemporaries exhibition in 1955 and her work caused an immediate sensation when she first exhibited alone in 1962 at Gallery One, and she became identified with the 'Op art' movement of the 1960s. She was influenced by Vasarely, and her creation of three-dimensional effects with colour and geometric or intertwined arrangements of channels, discs and squares reflect meticulous research and design, although she describes herself as working with nature, a 'dynamism of vital forces'. Her reputation was further established by a touring exhibition in 1967. Further large retrospectives toured the USA and Europe in 1970–2; America, Australia and Japan in 1978–80, and the UK in 1984–5. She has won several awards and her paintings hang in many major collections.

**Ringgold** [née Jones], **Faith** (1934–). American artist. Born and educated in New York, she was married to Robert Wallace between 1950 and 1954, and taught art in New York schools between 1955 and 1972. In 1962 she married Burdelle Ringgold. She has lectured and written extensively on Black and African art, teaching at the Museum of Natural History in New York, and organizing exhibitions throughout the USA. Her own art is explicitly social and political, ranging from her vivid murals of the late 1960s, such as *Die, The Flag is Bleeding* and *Postage Stamp to Commemorate the Advent of Black Power*, to the soft sculptures and sewn masks of her feminist series, *The Family of Woman*, in the 1970s.

**Ristori, Adelaide** (1822–1906). Italian actress. A member of a theatrical family, she was born in Cividale del Friuli, where her parents were performing. She acted from the age of 3, and at 14 was noted in Silvio Pellico's version of *Francesca da Rimini*. She joined the company Reale Sarda in 1837, becoming their leading juvenile actress. by the time she was 24 she had changed to a larger company, and her repertoire included

leading parts in plays such as Shakespeare's *Romeo and Juliet,* Goldoni's *La locandiera,* Scribe's *Adrienne Lecouvreur,* Alfieri's *Antigone* and Schiller's *Maria Stuart* (first acted when she was 18 and one of her most famous roles). In 1846 she married a Roman nobleman Giuliano Capranica del Grillo, and retired briefly from the stage, but returned in 1853, and in 1855 moved to Paris where she became an instant favourite and a serious rival to RACHEL.

She toured England, Spain and the USA (from 1866), adding to her repertoire parts such as Legouvé's Medea, Racine's Phèdre and Shakespeare's Lady Macbeth. On returning to Italy in 1858 she was banned by the Austrian police for her recitations of patriotic poems. She continued to enthral audiences with her technical skill and dignified presence, combined with a sense of restrained power and profound emotion, until her final performance of *Maria Stuart* in New York in 1885. After her retirement she published her fascinating memoirs, *Ricordi e studi artistici* (1887).

**Roberts, Eirlys (Rhiwen Cadwalader)** (1911–). English consumer campaigner. The daughter of a doctor, she was educated at Clapham High School, London, and then obtained a Classics degree at Girton College, Cambridge. She became a journalist, working as a sub-editor in Amalgamated Press, and married John Cullen in 1941. At the end of the war she worked for military and then political intelligence (1943–5) and was part of a United Nations Mission to Albania (1945–7). On her return she moved to the Information Division of the Treasury, where she remained for ten years.

In 1957 Eirlys Roberts founded the Consumers' Association, acting as Head of the Research and Editorial Division from 1958 to 1973, and as Editor of the pioneering magazine *Which?* from 1961 to 1977. Introducing detailed reports on products in a clear, accessible style, and campaigning constantly for greater safety and efficiency standards and for more public accountability, she brought the journal up to a circulation of 7 million. From 1973 to 1978 she was also part-time Director of the Bureau of European Consumer Organizations in Brussels, and was a member of the Royal Commission on the Press from 1974 to 1977. Since 1978 she has been Chairman of the Research Institute for Consumer Affairs and of an Environment and Consumer Protection sub-committee of the European Economic Community. She received the OBE in 1971, and was created CBE in 1977.

**Robins, Elizabeth** (1862–1952). American actress, playwright and novelist. Originally intended by her father to have a career as a doctor, Elizabeth studied medicine at Vassar, but at length persuaded her father to allow her to act. She toured the US with Laurence Barrett and Edwin Booth, and, with the money she earned, paid for the education of her younger brother Raymond, who became a noted social reformer.

In 1889 she went to England, where JANET ACHURCH's performance of Nora in *The Doll's House* that year was a revelation – 'less like a play than a personal meeting'. Determined not to act the parts ordinarily provided by the West End theatre, she and Marion Lea secured the performing rights of *Hedda Gabler* and commissioned Edmund Gosse and William Archer to translate it. Turned down by commercial managements, they raised £300 and produced it themselves. She then learnt Norwegian and, having persuaded Ibsen to give her the performing rights of *The Master Builder*, translated and produced it herself, playing Hilda Wangel (1893). There followed Rebecca West in *Rosmersholm*, Agnes in *Brand* (both 1893), Asta in *Little Eyolf* (1896) and Ella Rentheim in *John Gabriel Borkman* (1897).

This last was the opening production of the New Century Theatre, intended for experimental plays and as a means to release actresses from the restrictions of the actor-manager's theatre. But the venture was a financial failure and Elizabeth turned instead to writing short stories and novels under the pseudonym C.E. Raymond. Her private life was dramatic and adventurous: in 1900 she almost died on a journey to Alaska to find her brother, then a lay preacher in the wilderness. An active feminist, one of the organizers of the Actresses Franchise League, she was a member of the board of the WSPU and, working with her sister-in-law MARGARET DREIER ROBINS, created strong links between the British movement and the Women's

Trade Union League of America. She was co-founder and President of the Women's Writers Suffrage League from 1908, and her highly influential play *Votes for Women!*, which she adapted into the novel *The Convert*, was performed at the Royal Court Theatre in 1907. Her other novels include *The Magnetic North* (1904) and *Come and Find Me* (1908). Several essays were included in *Way Stations* (1913), and her polemic *Ancilla's Share: An Indictment of Sex* was published anonymously in 1924.

E. Robins: *Ibsen and the Actress* (1928)
────── : *Theatre and Friendship* (1932)
────── : *Both Sides of the Curtain* (1940)

**Robins, Margaret Dreier** (1868–1945). American reformer. Born in Brooklyn, New York, into a prosperous German émigré family, she was educated privately and undertook her philanthropic work first with the Brooklyn Hospital, and then as a member of the State Charities Aid Association. As Chairman of the Women's Municipal League, she conducted a campaign for the registration of employment agencies (1903–4), and in 1904 she joined the Women's Trade Union League (WTUL). The following year she married Raymond Robins the brother of ELIZABETH ROBINS, an idealist deeply involved in religious and political reform and unionism, and they moved to Chicago where she began work at the Hull House settlement with JANE ADDAMS.

In 1907 she became president of both the Chicago and of the National WTUL, and was involved with ROSE SCHNEIDERMAN in organizing the effective garment workers' strikes in New York, Philadelphia and Chicago between 1909 and 1911. Her particular aim was organization, and she worked as a forceful and energetic campaigner, travelling widely. She acted on the education committee of the American Federation of Labor (AFL), on the board of the Chicago Fellowship of Labor (1906–17) and on the State Unemployment Commission. She supported the Progressive party in 1916 but was later an active Republican, until won over to Roosevelt's New Deal policies in 1933. Her other affiliations were the suffrage movement and the pacifist groups of the 1920s. Determined to fight for the interests of working women, she resigned from the WTUL in 1922 to act briefly as President of the International Federation of Working Women. She then moved to Florida, where she continued her voluntary work until her old age.

M. Dreier: *Margaret Dreier Robins: her Life, Letters and Work* (1950)

**Robinson** [née Maurice], **Joan Violet** (1903–86). English economist. She was born in London into a progressive academic liberal family – her grandfather was the Christian Socialist F.D. Maurice, and her father, Major General Sir Frederick Maurice, became Principal of Queen Mary's College, London, while her mother was the daughter of Howard March, Professor of Surgery and Master of Downing College, Cambridge. Joan herself won a scholarship to Girton College, Cambridge, from St Paul's Girls' School, graduating in economics in 1925. In 1926 she married the economist Austin Robinson, and after a brief period in India they returned to Cambridge, where Joan became an assistant lecturer in 1931, a university lecturer in 1937, Reader in 1949, and Professor from 1965 until her formal retirement in 1971.

In the late 1920s and early 1930s she was part of a close group of Cambridge economists, and was particularly influenced by Richard Kahn and Maynard Keynes. Her first book, *The Economics of imperfect Competition*, was published in 1933, and in 1937 she brought out her *Introduction to the Theory of Employment* which gave a clear account of Keynes's thinking in this area (his *General Theory* had been published the previous year). During the latter part of the decade, she became interested in combining the Keynesian insight with Marxist principles, and her influential and highly personal *Essay on Marxian Economics* appeared in 1942.

In 1952 she wrote an introduction to ROSA LUXEMBURG's *Accumulation of Capital* (1913), and four years later published her own major work under the same title. Her later books develop several of its themes: *Exercises in Economic Analysis* (1960), *Essays in the Theory of Economic Growth* (1962) and *Economic Heresies* (1971). Her concern for students, as a teacher who had lectured in many countries, led her to write a plea for progressive social science teaching, *Freedom and Necessity* (1970), and a rather

difficult *Introduction to Modern Economics* with John Eatwell in 1973. On the side of the radical left since the 1930s, Joan Robinson remained a tough, witty personality whose influence on 20th-century economic theory has been lively and significant.

**Rochefort, Christiane** (1917–). French writer. She was born and educated in Paris. She studied at the Sorbonne and followed courses in medicine and psychiatry at the School of Medicine. Her career has been varied: she has been an algebra teacher, an office worker, a journalist and the *chargée de presse* at the Cannes Film Festival; she has also worked at the Cinémathèque in Paris. In 1958 her first novel, *Le repos du guerrier*, was published; it won the Prix de la Nouvelle Vague and was an immediate success, although its eroticism shocked many readers. It was later made into a film by Roger Vadim (1962). Her next novel, *Les petits enfants du siècle* (1961), which was awarded the Prix Populiste, is a humorous and ironic portrayal of working-class family life on a Parisian council estate, showing the de-humanizing effect of the French system of social planning. *Les stances à Sophie* (1963), in which Rochefort again uses ironic humour, shows a woman's alienation in the prison created by her husband's tyranny and by the bourgeois, materialistic values of society – Rochefort said that this book was inspired by her own four years' experience of marriage. In 1970 Moshé Mizrahi made a film based on *Les stances à Sophie*. Other works by Rochefort include *Une rose pour Morrison* (1966), dedicated to Bob Dylan, *Printemps au parking* (1969) and *C'est bizarre l'écriture* (essay, 1970). In *Archaos ou le jardin étincelant* (1972), she creates a utopia run by women and children which presents an alternative to patriarchy, and *Les enfants d'abord* (1976) is a theoretical essay on infants and young children. She has also translated John Lennon's *In his own Write*, which was published under the title *En flagrant délire*. Her recent books include *Quand tu vas chez les femmes* (1982).

Although Rochefort's novels reflect her opposition to oppression in society, language and culture, her sense of humour and her use of slang and popular speech prevent her novels from seeming abstract or didactic.

**Rodnina, Irina** (1949–). Russian ice-skater. Irina has, with different partners, won more world figure-skating pairs titles than any other competitor. Between 1969 and 1972 she won the world title with Aleksiy Ulanov, and from 1973 to 1978, six times with Aleksander Zaitsev, to total ten successive wins. In 1972, with Ulanov, she won a gold medal at the Sapporo Olympics and the pair succeeded the Protopopovs as champions. The partnership ended when Ulanov married the silver medallist Lyudmila Smirnova, and Zaitsev was chosen as a replacement partner for Irina after a nationwide search. Irina was the dominant skater and continued · to undertake technically-difficult figures. In less than a year she and Zaitsev achieved a brilliantly co-ordinated partnership and had 12 full scores in the world championship. They married in 1975 and won Olympic gold medals in 1976 and 1980. Irina's three successive golds make a record matching that of Gillis Grafström and SONJA HENJE. Irina retired in 1980 after having her first child.

**Roland, Manon (Marie-Jeanne Phlipon)** (1754–93). French democratic leader. Born in Paris, the daughter of a jeweller, she was a lonely and precocious child and was educated at the convent of Neuve St Etienne. An ardent admirer of Rousseau, she was drawn into local politics when managing her father's shop after his death. In 1780 she married Roland de la Platière, and they moved first to Amiens and eventually to Lyons where he was inspector of factories. In 1789 they both became involved in revolutionary politics and returned to Paris, where Manon's salon became the centre of democratic discussion, attended by Brissot, Petion, Clavière, and the deputy Buzot to whom she became deeply but platonically attached. She inspired much of their policy, being especially influential while Roland was Minister of the Interior in 1792. She hated Robespierre and especially Danton, whom she blamed for the September massacres, and allied her considerable intellect and influence to the Girondin party. When they fell, in May 1793, she was imprisoned in Ste Pélagie, where she wrote her *Mémoires* and her eloquent *Appel à l'impartiale posterité*

(published in 1795). On 8 November 1793, dressed in white, she faced the Revolutionary Tribunal but was not allowed to speak in her own defence. Mounting the guillotine the same day, her last reported cry was 'O liberty; what crimes are committed in thy name!'. Her husband committed suicide on learning of her death.

G. May: *Madame Roland and the Age of Revolution* (1970)

**Roldan, Luisa** (1656–1704). Spanish sculptor. Born in Seville, the daughter of a sculptor who trained all his children in the art, she and her two sisters assisted in the family workshop. In 1671 she married the sculptor Luis de los Arcos, and they worked together, executing commissions for Cadiz Cathedral during the 1680s. In 1692 Luisa was appointed sculptor to the court at Madrid, serving first Charles II and then Philip V, but she was never financially well-rewarded. A thorough professional, who worked hard to obtain her commissions, her life was hard and difficult. Her best-known work is probably the emotive sculpture of St Catherine.

**Roosevelt, (Anna) Eleanor** (1884–1962). American reformer. Niece of Theodore Roosevelt, she lost both her parents by the time she was ten and she was educated in private schools in the USA and England. At the age of 17 she worked as a volunteer in settlement schools and joined the National Consumers' Council, but in 1905 she married her cousin Franklin. They had six children, their third son dying in infancy. She supported Franklin in his political career, especially after he was paralysed by polio in 1921, and in 1917 became an energetic organizer of voluntary service for the war effort. Becoming increasingly committed to the causes of women's and minority rights, in 1920 she began working for the League of Labor voters, in 1922 joined the Women's Trade Union League (WTUL), and from 1922 to 1928 organized the Women's Division of the Democratic State Committee. She lobbied for her husband for Governor of New York, then in 1932, for President. Partly because of his disability she undertook nationwide tours on behalf of his New Deal policy in 1933.

Although united publicly, the couple had

become increasingly estranged after his affair with Lucy Mercer in 1918, and from the mid-1920s Eleanor lived chiefly with two women friends, Marian Dickerman and Nancy Cook, founding a school and managing a craft factory with them. In 1936 she started her syndicated newspaper column 'My Day', and worked for civil rights and other reform causes, both as an intermediary at the White House, and as a public campaigner in the press, radio and lectures. During the 1930s she also wrote books for children, including *When you grow up to vote*. During World War II she insisted on the representation of women on major committees, and visited troops in the Pacific and Caribbean.

In 1945, after Franklin's death, Truman appointed her as delegate to the United Nations, where her part in drafting and pressing through the Declaration of Human Rights in 1948 was recognized by a standing ovation. During the 1950s she worked with liberal and left-wing reform groups, and opposed McCarthyism. She canvassed for Adlai Stevenson in 1952 and 1956, resigning her UN post when Eisenhower was elected in 1953. Her last public position was on the Commission on the Status of Women (1961–2).

E. Roosevelt: *This is My Story* (1937)
——: *This I Remember* (1949)
——: *Autobiography* (1961)
J. Lash: *Eleanor and Franklin* (1971)
——: *Eleanor: the Years Alone* (1972)

**Roper, Margaret** (1505–44). English scholar. The daughter of Sir Thomas More, she was educated by him with her two sisters Elizabeth and Cecilia and her brother John. Her mother died about 1511. She was noted for her learning in Greek, Latin, philosophy, astronomy, mathematics and music. She also translated Erasmus's *Treatise on the Lord's Prayer*, won the admiration of contemporary scholars, and was compared to the learned Alice Cooke, Roger Bacon's mother. She was apparently gentle, charming and affectionate.

When she was about 20 she married William Roper and settled in Kent. She was a staunch defender and supporter of her father during his imprisonment in the Tower of London and was briefly imprisoned herself. After his execution she recovered his head, although this was forbidden by

law, and it is buried in St Dunstan's Church, Canterbury. She had two sons and three daughters.

E.E. Reynolds: *Margaret Roper* (1966)

**Rosenberg, Anna** (1902–83). American management consultant and politician. One of the most influential women in the United States from the 1930s to the 1950s, Anna Lederer was born in Budapest and went to New York with her family in 1912. She became involved in politics after her marriage to Julius Rosenberg in 1919, when she worked on local New York City campaigns. In 1924 she started a public relations agency which she ran until the end of her life: her clients included politicians and companies, and ranged from F.D. Roosevelt to Studebaker Inc., from General Foods to the Encyclopedia Britannica.

In 1934 she was appointed assistant to Nathan Strauss, Regional Director of the National Recovery Administration, and took over as Director in 1935. From 1935 to 1945 she was also successively Regional Director of the Social Security Board, the Defence, Health and Welfare Services and the War Manpower Commission. In 1944 and 1945 she acted as personal representative in Europe of Presidents Roosevelt and Truman, and from 1946 to 1950 was a member of the American Commission to UNESCO. In 1950 she was appointed Assistant Secretary of Defense, in the face of anti-semitic opposition and of charges of communist sympathies. In this post she was instrumental in the drafting programmes for the Korean War, and in the recruitment of women to the military.

After 1953, she returned to her public relations firm, mediating in the major transit strike in New York in 1960, and during the 1960s was an influential member of many organizations including the New York City Board of Education and the United Nations Association, and a powerful voice in urban action and civil rights programmes. She divorced Rosenberg in 1962 to marry Paul Hoffman, the former administrator of the Marshall Plan. Her many awards included the Medal of Freedom (1945), the medallion of the City of New York (1966), and several honorary degrees.

**Rosenberg** [née Greenglass], **Ethel** (1915–53). American socialist and alleged spy.

Born on the lower East Side of New York City of Austrian–Russian parentage, she was educated locally. Although a gifted student and promising actress, she took a secretarial job with a shipping company in 1931. In 1935 she was fired for being on the strike committee of the Ladies' Apparel Shipping Clerks' Union; although later reinstated she transferred to work for the Bell Telephone Company.

In 1936 she met an engineering student Julius Rosenberg, who was a Communist, and they married in 1939. Both were involved in labour and anti-fascist activities. In 1945 Julius lost his job with the Signals Corps for his political views, and tried unsuccessfully to go into partnership with his brother-in-law, David Greenglass. In 1950 Greenglass, then under suspicion of spying, claimed to have been recruited to pass on atomic secrets by Rosenberg. Julius was arrested in July, Ethel in August; her sister-in-law later claimed that Ethel had been the typist in the transaction. On this evidence alone she was convicted of conspiracy with her husband in March 1951. She spent two years as the only woman prisoner in Sing Sing, an experience evoked in passionate letters to her husband and sons. She was executed with Julius in 1953, despite worldwide appeals for clemency.

V. Gardner: *The Rosenberg Story* (1954)

**Ross, Diana** (1944–). American singer. Born into a poor family in Detroit, she began singing with two school friends in the 1950s and after they left school they began to work for the local record company, Tamla Motown, as The Supremes. Their first two hits, *Where did our Love go?* and *Baby Love*, were followed by a string of commercial successes, and at the end of the 1960s they also made some records protesting at conditions in the black areas of American cities, like *I'm livin' in Shame*. In 1969, already an international star, Ross went solo, and added to her musical achievements by winning an Academy Award for her performance as BILLIE HOLIDAY in *Lady Sings the Blues* (1973). She has also made the films *Mahogany* (1975) and *The Wiz* (1978). She remained one of the most successful and influential American singers, her later successes including *Reflections* (1978) and *Muscles* (1982). She was married to Robert

Silberstein from 1971 until their divorce in 1975 and has three daughters. In 1985 she married Arne Naes Jnr, a Norwegian shipping tycoon and mountaineer.

**Rossetti, Christina** [pseud. Ellen Alleyne] (1830–94). English poet. Her father was a political refugee from Naples who became a teacher of Italian in London and her mother was half-English, a former governess. Christina, the youngest child of the family, was educated at home and her first poetry was published privately, when she was 12 and 17. Her work appeared under the name of Ellen Alleyne in 1850 with that of her brother Dante Gabriel in the Pre-Raphaelite Brotherhood's journal *The Germ*.

At this period the family's poverty was increased by the father's illness. Christina gave Italian lessons and tried to open schools in Camden Town, London, and in Frome, Somerset (1853). A devout High Church Anglican, she used religious difficulties to provide the ostensible grounds for breaking her engagements to the painter James Collinson, and later to the translator Charles Cayley, to whom she remained devoted. Eventually she retreated into a recluse-like invalidism, contracting Grave's Disease in 1873. Outwardly shy and passive, her poetry, both religious and natural, reveals a passionate, sensuous, visionary spirit. It includes narratives such as *Goblin Market* (1862) and the *The Prince's Progress* (1866), but the most remarkable works are lyrics and sonnets such as the 'Monna Innominata' series. That she was not totally isolated is revealed by her concern for social issues, such as poverty, unemployment and prostitution, which she treats in the religious commentaries written towards the end of her life.

G. Battiscombe: *Christina Rossetti* (1981)

**Roswitha of Gandersheim.** *See* HROTSVITHA.

**Rothschild, Miriam (Louisa)** (1908–). English zoologist and parasitologist. Miriam's father, Baron Rothschild, objected to higher education for girls so she was educated at home. However, she published more than 200 natural history and science papers and catalogued her father's 10,000 species of fleas in five illustrated volumes.

She married Captain George Lane, and they had four children and adopted two. At the same time she co-authored *Fleas, flukes and Cuckoos* (1952). The *Catalogue of the Rothschild Collection of Fleas* appeared in six volumes between 1953–1983. In 1968 she was awarded an honorary Fellowship at Oxford, and an Hon. DSc degree and appointed to the Chair of Biology at London University. She was a Trustee of the British Museum of Natural History from 1967 to 1975. Miriam Rothschild was the first to analyse the flea's jumping mechanism, and in 1977 hosted the first International Flea Conference at her country home in Northamptonshire. In the 1980s she has received several further honorary degrees and was Romaine Lecturer at Oxford in 1985.

**Rothwell, Evelyn** (1911–). English oboist. A pupil of Leon Goossens, she joined the Covent Garden touring orchestra in 1931. She then played in the Scottish Orchestra (1933–6), the Glyndebourne Festival Orchestra (1934–9) and the London Symphony Orchestra (1935–9). Her notable career as a soloist includes the first performances of many works that were written for her by such composers as ELIZABETH MACONCHY, Edmund Rubbra and Gordon Jacob. In 1939 she married the conductor John Barbirolli. She has written several books on oboe technique and repertoire, and was appointed a Professor at the Royal Academy of Music, London, in 1971.

H. Atkins and P. Cotes: *The Barbirollis: A Musical Marriage* (1983)

**Roudy, Yvette** (1929–). French politician. A prominent feminist activist and writer, in 1963 she translated Betty Friedan's *The Feminine Mystique* and subsequently became more involved with French feminist groups, becoming Secretary of the Mouvement Démocratique Féminin in 1964. She is leader of the women's division of the French Socialist Party. She was a long-term ally of François Mitterand, being a member of his Convention of Republican Institutions in 1965. In 1969 she wrote *La réussite de la femme* and in 1975 *La femme en marge*. In 1979 she was elected as deputy to the European Parliament in Strasbourg. After the inauguration of Mitterand as President in 1981, she was named Secretary of State for Women's Rights, was made minister in 1985, and was elected Socialist Deputy for Calvados in 1986. Her recent books include *Les métiers et les cajoints* (2nd edn, 1981) and *A cause d'elles* (1985).

**Rowbotham, Sheila** (1943–). English historian, feminist and socialist. Born in Leeds, she was educated at a Methodist school in Filey, Yorkshire, and at St Hilda's College, Oxford. She then taught in technical and further education colleges and in a comprehensive school before concentrating on adult education for the Workers' Educational Association. Since the early 1960s she has been an active socialist and was on the editorial committee of the left-wing journal *Black Dwarf*. Her pamphlet *Women's Liberation and the New Politics* (1970) laid down the fundamental approaches and demands of the emerging British Women's Movement. Her radical commitment and its relation to feminism are interestingly described in the provocative book *Beyond the Fragments*, which she wrote with Hilary Wainwright and Lynne Segal in 1979, and which provoked socialist and feminist conferences all over Britain.

Best-known as a historian, Rowbotham's chief works are *Woman, Resistance and Revolution*, *Women's Consciousness, Man's World* and *Hidden from History: 308 Years of Women's Oppression and the Fight against it* (all published in 1973). She has since written a study of Stella Browne, the birth-control campaigner, *A New World for Women* (1971); *Socialism and the New Life* (with J. Weeks, 1977); and edited *Dutiful Daughters*, a collection of biographical reminiscences (with J. McCrindle, 1977). Her collected writings were published in *Dreams and Dilemmas* (1983) and *Friends of Alice Wheeldon* appeared in 1986.

**Royden, (Agnes) Maude** (1876–1956). British suffragette and preacher. The younger daughter of shipowner Sir Thomas Royden, Mayor of Liverpool in the 1860s, Maude was educated at Cheltenham Ladies' College, and read history at Lady Margaret Hall, Oxford, graduating in 1899. On returning to Liverpool she worked at the Victoria Women's Settlement for three years but then moved to South Luffenham, Rutland, as parish worker with the Rev. Hudson Shaw, with whom she was to be linked for the rest of her life. She also worked as a lecturer for Oxford University extension classes. A committed feminist, she joined the NUWSS in 1908, was an energetic campaigner and speaker and edited the journal *The Common Cause* in 1912–14. Even at 'this stage she was more concerned with the religious and ethical aspects of the women's movement than with their political goals.

Unable to preach in the Anglican church (of which she remained a member) she became assistant preacher at the City Temple, London, from 1917 to 1920. In 1920 she was one of the founders of the Interdenominational Fellowship Services in Kensington Town Hall. The Fellowship Guild took over Eccleston Square Church as their Guildhouse in 1921, and Maude remained one of the Guild's leaders, with Percy Dearmer and Martin Shaw, until 1936, when she left to devote herself to campaigning for world peace. During the 1920s and 1930s, despite lingering illnesses, she travelled and preached on tours in Britain, America, Australia, New Zealand, India and China. A spontaneous, inspiring speaker with a stirring voice, her outspoken views on moral, political and social issues inevitably aroused controversy. In the 1930s she organized the 'Peace Army', but publicly renounced her pacifism during World War II. She was made a Companion of Honour in 1930, and received honorary degrees from the universities of Glasgow in 1931 and Liverpool in 1935. In 1944 she married the octogenarian Hudson Shaw, two months before his death. She wrote of their 43 years of love and work, and of the intense, platonic early relationship of the trio which included Shaw's first wife, in *A Threefold Chord* (1947).

**Royer, Clemence (Augustine)** (1830–1902). French scholar. After the death of her father in 1849 she was educated in England, but returned to France in her late teens. An outstanding scholar, she became a well-known political economist, and gave lectures during the 1850s in France and Switzerland. She published studies of Comte's writings, but was also interested in the evolutionary theories of Lamarck and was the first French translator of Darwin's book *On the Origin of Species by Means of* *Natural Selection* in 1869. She wrote her own book on social evolution, a powerful, controversial work *L'origine de l'homme et des sociétés* and contributed to the journal *La fronde*. Her intellectual stature was openly applauded, but although her admission to the Académie Française was often discussed it was never carried out. Renan called her 'almost a man of genius'.

**Rubinstein, Helena** (1882–1965). American beautician and businesswoman. She was born in Kraków, the daughter of a prosperous merchant family with a tradition in medical work. She was persuaded to study medicine in Kraków, and then Zürich, but emigrated to Australia in 1902. It is alleged that her Polish face cream seemed so appropriate to the Australian climate that she sent home for the recipe, went straight into business, taking courses in dermatology at the same time, advertised widely and made sufficient money in two years to depart for Europe, leaving her sisters in charge in Melbourne. Her business prospered; she opened salons in London (1908), Paris (1912) and New York (1915). After World War I she expanded her interests until she was running laboratories, factories and training schools throughout the world.

H. Rubinstein: *My Life for Beauty* (1965)

**Rudkin, Margaret (Fogarty)** (1897–1967). American businesswoman and baker. Born in New York City and educated in Flushing, she married Henry Rudkin, a broker in the office where she worked, in 1923. In 1929 they moved to Fairfield, Connecticut. She started baking when she was 40, as part of a health cure recommended by the local doctor for her children's asthma, and then provided loaves for neighbours, selling the surplus in local stores. The next year, 1938, she launched her bakery company, rapidly expanding output to 4000 loaves a week, and moving to a local town. Her Pepperidge Farm products, which soon included pastry and confectionary, were known for their high quality ingredients, using stone-ground flour and avoiding synthetic additives. Her husband became marketing manager, and they developed a multi-million-dollar concern. In 1963 she published the very popular *Margaret Rudkin Pepperidge Farm Cookbook*.

**Rudolph, Wilma (Glodean)** (1940–). American athlete. Born in St Bethlehem. Tennessee, Wilma's family was poor: she was the fifth of eight children, and there were eleven more children by a former marriage. Severe illness at four left one leg useless, but with family help with her physiotherapy she could walk by the age of eight, and was able to discard her special shoe when she was eleven.

At school she was so good at basketball and track that at the age of 16 she entered the 1956 Olympics and helped the American team win a bronze medal in the relay. She went on to Tennessee State University.

It was in the 1960 Olympics that her three gold medals, in the 100 metres, the 200 metres and the relay, combined with her tall graceful running, caused her to be nicknamed 'the black gazelle'. She was the third woman ever to win the Sullivan Memorial Trophy, and was invited to race in the usually all-male Millrose Games in New York's Madison Square Garden.

Wilma married William Ward; they had four children. She became a teacher, coach, and director of a youth foundation.

L. Jacobs: *Wilma Rudolph : Run for Glory* (1975)

**Ruffin, Josephine (St Pierre)** (1842–1924). Black American leader and clubwoman. Born in Boston, of mixed descent, she was educated in Salem until the end of black segregation meant that she could attend school in Boston. In 1858 she married George Ruffin, with whom she visited England, returning during the Civil War. George rose as a lawyer, becoming Boston's first black municipal judge in 1883. They had five children and Josephine was an active worker for Black rights, welfare movements and women's suffrage. Through her activities she met Julia Ward Howe and LUCY STONE. In 1874 she organized the Women's Era Club, and in 1895 helped to establish the National Federation of Afro-American Women, which became the National Association of Coloured Women in 1896. She also wrote for the weekly *Boston Courant* and was a member of the New England Women's Press Association. In 1900, after fierce debate, a colour bar was applied to keep the Era Club out of the General Federation of Women's Clubs. Josephine Ruffin continued to campaign,

founding the Boston branch of the National Association for the Advancement of Colored People (NAACP), and working for other community organizations.

**Rukeyser, Muriel** (1913–80). American poet, feminist and political activist. She was educated in New York, and then at Vassar College and Columbia University for two summer sessions in 1931 and 1932, when she also enrolled at the Roosevelt School of Aviation. Her first volume of poetry, *Theory of Flight*, appeared in 1935, when she was 22. During the 1930s she became involved in various political struggles; in 1933 she travelled to Alabama to the Scottsboro trials, and was jailed briefly for associating with blacks, and in 1936 she went to West Virginia to document the mistreatment and the effects of silicosis among tunnel workers in the mining areas. In her collection *U.S.1* (1938) she includes committee transcripts in her poems based on these experiences. She produced collections in rapid succession during the 1940s and 1950s, and these reinforced the impression of her as a sensuous, tough, experimental poet. She also wrote biographies and children's books. She became Vice-President of the House of Photography in New York (1946–60), and taught at Sarah Lawrence College in 1946 and 1956, but resisted being held to a particular job. In the 1960s she began a new career as a translator, working especially on the poetry of Octavio Paz and of Gunnar Ekelöf; she wrote her only novel, *The Orgy*, in 1965. She became a stong supporter of the anti-war movement, was jailed for her protest activities and later visited Hanoi. She made a further trip to South Korea, to protest against government harassment of the poet Kim Chi-Ha. From 1967 she was a member of the Board of Directors of the Teachers–Writers Collaborative, New York, and in 1975–6 was the President of the American Society for Poets, Playwrights, Editors, Essayists and Novelists (PEN). Her *Collected Poems* appeared in 1979.

**Russell** [née Black], **Dora (Winifred)** (1894–1986). English feminist. The daughter of Sir Frederick Black, a distinguished civil servant, she was educated at Sutton High School, and in 1912, after a few months in Germany, she went to Girton College,

Cambridge, where she obtained a first class degree and a fellowship. In 1917 she went to New York as secretary to her father when he was Chairman of the British Mission. On her return she moved in radical socialist and feminist circles. In 1919 she became the mistress of Bertrand Russell, whom she had first met three years earlier, and they visited the USSR together the following year, and spent a year at Peking [Beijing] University in 1921. They married that year, as soon as Bertrand's divorce from his first wife Alys came through; Dora was already pregnant, and they eventually had a son and a daughter. They wrote *The Prospects of Industrial Civilisation* together in 1923.

In 1924 she stood unsuccessfully as Labour candidate for Chelsea. One of the early campaigners for birth control and maternity leave, she worked with colleagues such as MARGARET SANGER and MARIE STOPES and founded the Workers' Birth Control Group (1924). In 1925 she published *Hypatia: or Women and Knowledge*, which attacked marriage and advocated sexual freedom, becoming a best-seller after the *Sunday Express* demanded it be banned. In 1927 the Russells founded Beacon Hill School, near Petersfield, which Dora ran until 1939, continuing alone after Russell left in 1935. They had had an open marriage and she already had a son and a daughter with an American, Griffin Barry, as well as other emotional involvements. She married Pat Grace in 1940.

During World War II Dora Russell worked for the Ministry of Information, chiefly in the Soviet Relations Division. Afterwards she continued to work for liberal causes, having been a founder member of the National Council for Civil Liberties, and in the 1950s was active in the Campaign for Nuclear Disarmament. In 1958 she inspired the Women's Caravan of Peace, from the UK across Europe, to protest at the Cold War. She also continued her interest in education, keeping abreast of new ideas and developments. Her many publications include *The Right to be Happy* (1927), attacking sexual taboos, and *In Defence of Children* (1932), about her permissive educational approach. In 1983 she published a book begun and abandoned in the 1930s for lack of encouragement, *The Religion of the Machine Age*, about the blight of technology she had analysed in her visits to both the USA and the USSR. A pacifist and feminist to the end, in 1983 she led a CND rally in her wheelchair, and took part in a demonstration at a Cornish RAF base a few months before her death.

D. Russell: *The Tamarisk Tree* (1974, 1980) [2 vols]

**Russell, Dorothy** (1895–1983). British pathologist. Born in Sydney, Dorothy Russell went to England at the age of eight after her parents died. She was educated at the Perse School for Girls, Cambridge, and achieved a first class degree at Girton in 1918. Brought in by the government recruitment of women into medicine in World War I, she trained at the London Hospital, graduating in 1922, when she began her research with the famous pathologist H.M. Turnbull, into the pathology of Bright's disease. As she specialized in neuropathology, an innovatory field in Britain, she went to study in Boston and Montreal on a Rockefeller Fellowship (1928–9), returning to the London Hospital and then working on the staff of the Medical Research Council from 1933 to 1946. During World War II she was made Head of Pathology in the Neurosurgical Department of the Nuffield Military Hospital in Oxford, where she began her fruitful collaboration with Hugh Cairns. After the war, in 1946, she succeeded Turnbull as Professor of Morbid Anatomy at the London Medical College, retiring in 1960 but holding the position of Professor Emeritus until her death. The holder of numerous awards for her original research and contributions to the knowledge and treatment of diseases of the brain, such as the use of tissue culture in the study of brain tumours, her publications are regarded as classic works, especially her *Observations on the Pathology of Hydrocephalus* (1946) and *Pathology of Tumours of the Nervous System* (with L. Rubenstein, 1959).

**Rutherford, Dame Margaret** (1892–1972). English actress. Born in London and educated in Wimbledon and Sussex, she taught piano and elocution before training for the stage at the Old Vic, where she first appeared in 1925. She established a reputation in repertory and on the London stage, especially in Gielgud's *Spring Meeting* (1938). Among numerous roles she played Lady Bracknell in *The Importance of Being*

*Earnest* (1947, 1957) and Mrs Malaprop in *The Rivals* (1966). She also became extremely popular with a wider public through her many comedy character parts in films, and especially as AGATHA CHRISTIE's Miss Marple. She was created DBE in 1967. She won an Academy Award for her performance in *The VIPs* (1963).

M. Rutherford: *Margaret Rutherford: an Autobiography* (1972)

**Ruysch, Rachel** (1664–1750). Dutch painter. She was born in Amsterdam. Her father was a professor of anatomy and botany and an amateur painter, and at the age of 15 she was apprenticed to the leading flower painter Willelm van Aelst (supposedly a rejected suitor of MARIA VAN OOSTERWYCK). Her early works, detailed scientific studies of insects and flowers, already had an exotic quality. She began to specialize in flower painting, and continued this work after her marriage in 1701 to the painter Juriaen Pool, although they had ten children. In 1701 they became members of the painters' guild in The Hague. In 1708 Rachel was invited by the Elector Palatine to be painter to his court at Düsseldorf; she returned to Holland in 1716. A slow but relatively prolific worker, she acquired an immense reputation, charging high prices for her works, and giving paintings as dowries to her daughters. Over 100 of her works have survived to demonstrate her sumptuous talent.

M.H. Grant: *Rachel Ruysch* (1956)

**Ryder, Sue** [Baroness Ryder of Warsaw in Poland and Cavendish in the County of Suffolk] (1923–). English philanthropist. The youngest of nine children of an English country gentleman, she was educated at Benenden School, Kent. During World War II she joined the First Aid Nursing Yeomanry (FANY) and also worked with the Special Operations Executive, which organized the work of agents assisting partisan groups in occupied Europe. After the war she became involved in relief work in North Africa and Italy, and in 1953 opened a home in Cavendish, Suffolk, for victims of the concentration camps, as part of her Mission for the Relief of Suffering. A devout Catholic, she soon extended her organization to include the physically and mentally ill, and it eventually became the Sue Ryder Foundation for the Sick and Disabled of All Age Groups. In 1959 she married the disabled war hero, Group Captain Leonard Cheshire, VC, and together they established the Cheshire Homes for the chronically ill. They have two children.

Ryder homes exist in the UK, and also in Poland, Yugoslavia and Italy, and Sue Ryder holds decorations from the first two countries. She received the OBE in 1957, CMG in 1976 and in 1979 was made Baroness Ryder of Warsaw in Poland and Cavendish in the County of Suffolk.

S. Ryder: *And the Morrow is Theirs* (1975)
——— : *Child of My Love* (1986)

**Rye, Maria (Susan)** (1829–1903). English feminist and reformer. Born in London, Maria was the oldest of nine children of a solicitor, a scholarly, liberal man. She was educated at home and became involved in local parish charity work from the age of 16. A pioneering feminist, she became Secretary of the committee to promote the Married Women's Property Bill, introduced in 1856. She also joined the Society for Promoting the Employment of Women, and was a member of the Langham Place Group which included BARBARA BODICHON, JESSIE BOUCHERETT, and others. In 1859 she opened a law stationers' business in Lincoln's Inn to employ middle-class girls. She was involved in other ventures such as the founding of the Victoria Press with EMILY FAITHFUL, and the Telegraph School, which taught girls how to operate the new technology, with ISA CRAIG. So many women applied for work through the Employment Society and the Telegraph School that Rye decided to get sponsorship for an emigration plan, and in 1861, with Jane Lewin, she founded the Female Middle Class Emigration Society, whose aims she outlined in *Emigration of Educated Women* (1861). For the next eight years she helped countless women settle in Australia, New Zealand and Canada.

On her journeys to supervise the welfare of her new colonists, she was horrified by the shipboard conditions, the high mortality rate and the consequent number of orphans, and thus diverted her attention to the problem of destitute children. She visited a home for children in New York, and when she returned to England in 1868 she founded a home for pauper children in Peckham, London. Many of the children were sent to Canada, where Rye also ran a home, and where they were later found jobs and accommodation. She influenced the founding of the Church of England Waifs and Strays Society in 1891 and this venutre became her main occupation in 1895. At that time she claimed she had been responsible for sending 4000 children to Canada. She retired to Hemel Hempstead with her sister for the last eight years of her life. In the course of her work she won a reputation for her independence, stubbornness and fierce, sometimes controversial, Protestant convictions. Her reputation as a philanthropist has been countered by accusations that she was an unscrupulous profiteer, who never visited her protégés in their new homes, and who caused much unhappiness by dividing families.

# S

**Saadawi, Nawal el.** *See* EL SAADAWI, NAWAL.

**Saarinen, Aline (Milton Bernstein)** (1914–72). American art critic and media personality. She was born in New York City. Her parents encouraged her interest in art which had been stimulated by a visit to Europe at the age of nine. After graduating from Vassar College in 1935 she married Joseph Louchheim, a public official. Although she had two children she studied at the Institute of Fine Arts, specializing in the history of architecture, and graduated in 1941. In 1944 she joined *Art News*, becoming Managing Director from 1946 to 1948 and composing the text for the popular *5000 Years of Art: a Pictorial History*. She also wrote for the *New York Times* from 1947 and became a well-known critic.

In 1954, having been divorced three years earlier, Aline married the architect Eero Saarinen, remaining an associate art critic for the *New York Times* but concentrating on publicity for her husband's firm. After his death she published *Eero Saarinen and his work* (1962).

The study of major American collectors, *The Proud Possessors* (1958), had made her reputation, and in 1963 she became an art critic for NBC Television, making some fine documentaries, and becoming an influential mentor of planning and design. In 1964, when she reputedly turned down an offer to become Ambassador to Finland, she became a correspondent on NBC News, surprising the public by her forceful views on issues such as birth-control and abortion which she developed in her show *For Women Only*. In 1971 she became the first woman to head an overseas television news bureau, when she took over NBC's Paris office.

**Sabalsajaray, Nibuya** (1951–74). Uruguayan unionist. The daughter of a poor family, she qualified as a teacher and became a union leader. In 1974 she was involved in a major demonstration against the dictatorship, was arrested, tortured and died 2 days later, aged only 23. She is now revered as one of the martyrs of the state's repressive policy towards the unions in the early 1970s.

**Sabin, Florence (Rene)** (1871–1953). American doctor and public health worker. Born in Central City, Colorado, where her father had unsuccessfully joined the Gold Rush, Florence was brought up by relatives after the death of her mother. She studied music, attended Smith College, and became a teacher in order to raise money to enter Johns Hopkins University Medical School in 1897. She was the first woman to graduate from there and to teach there. While still studying she made a model of the brain with a laboratory manual: *An Atlas of the Medulla and Mid-brain* was published in 1901.

In 1900 she gained her MD and became a research member of the anatomy department. She won a $1000 prize for the first comprehensive study of the lymphatic system, using pigs, and in 1916 gave the Harvey Memorial Lecture on this subject. In 1917 she became a full professor of histology and continued her research into the processes of the blood-cell.

From 1925 to 1938 she set up and headed the Department of Cellular Studies at Rockefeller Institute for Medical Research, working on blood in relation to tuberculosis. She became President of the American Association of Anatomists, and the first woman elected to the National Academy of Sciences. In 1929 she was received at the

White House by President J. Edgar Hoover. Her awards included 15 honorary degrees.

At the age of 73 Florence retired to Denver, where she fought for and saw passed the Sabin Health Bills, which gave Colorado one of the best public health programmes in the USA. She instituted a mass TB x-ray survey which resulted in halving the city's death rate from TB within two years. She also achieved a 90 per cent drop in the number of cases of syphilis.

M.K. Phelan: *The Story of Dr Florence Sabin: probing the Unknown* (1969)

**Sablière.** *See* DE LA SABLIÈRE.

**Sabuco, Oliva** (1562–1625). Spanish scholar. Oliva's name appears on the title page of the seven-volume *Nueva filosofía de la naturaleza del hombre, no conocida ni alcanzada de los grandes filósofos antiguos, la quae mejora la vida y salud humana*, published in 1587, a collection of philosophical dialogues covering medicine, astronomy, mathematics, politics and other subjects, designed to show that the emotions are more to be trusted than the reason, which holds the capacity for evil. In 1900 a biographer of Sabuco claimed that the dialogues were actually the work of her father, Miguel. Although this view is now generally accepted, some feminist historians disagree.

**Sacajawea** (*c*1786–1812). American-Indian guide. A member of the Shoshoni (Snake) Tribe, she was sold as a slave in 1800 and by 1804 was working in a French Canadian household. Her master, Toussaint Charbonneau, was employed as interpreter to the Lewis and Clark expedition to find a westward continental route. He took Sacajawea and her baby with him. She acted as interpreter, and liaised for the expedition with the Shoshoni, now led by her brother. She returned in 1806. In 1810 she and Charbonneau tried to settle in St Louis, but she was homesick and they soon returned to Dakota, where they remained until her death. One of the great heroines of the West, in popular legend she is mistakenly represented as the chief guide to Lewis and Clark.

N. Frazier: *Sacajawea: the Girl Nobody Knows* (1967)

**Sachs, Nelly** (1891–1970). German-Jewish poet and playwright. She was born and brought up in Berlin, the only daughter of a wealthy Jewish industrialist. She was educated by private tutors and studied music and dance. She did not attend university. She read voraciously, particularly the German Romantics and a range of mystical writers. In 1940 she fled from Germany with the help of Selma Lagerlöf with whom she had corresponded since childhood, and she and her mother settled in Sweden. The rest of her family died in concentration camps. Life in Sweden was difficult and Sachs supported herself and her mother by translating Swedish poetry into German. Her loneliness and agony at the plight of the Jews in her homeland turned her from an imitative nature lyricist into a powerful poet. Her first two collections, *In den Wohnungen des Todes*, published in East Germany in 1946, and *Sternverdunkelung* (1949) dealt with the suffering of the death camps and the tragedy of European Jewry during the Hitler regime. Her next two books, *Und niemand weiss weiter* (1957) and *Flucht und Verwandlung* (1959) continued the theme, but linked it to the eternal rhythms of natural change, influenced by the prophetic literature of the Cabala, the Bible and Hasidic literature. Still relatively unknown in the West, she was awarded the Nobel Prize with the poet Shmuel Agnon in 1966.

**Sackville-West, Vita** [Victoria] (1892–1962). English writer. Born at Knole, Kent, the daughter of the third Baron Sackville, she was educated privately. She loved writing as a child and had completed eight novels and five plays by the age of 18. In 1913 she married the civil servant Harold Nicolson, accompanying him on his posting to Constantinople, but later remaining in England during his times abroad. Their remarkable marriage endured despite Vita's passionate affair with Violet Trefusis between 1918 and 1921 and Nicolson's own homosexual attachments.

She always resented the fact that only a male heir could inherit Knole and her love for the family home is evident in *Knole and the Sackvilles* (1922). After her early novel *Heritage* she published a book each year, beginning with the symbolic *Dragon in Shallow Waters* (1921) and the poetic short stories in *The Heir* (1922). She also wrote poetry, and was awarded the Hawthornden Prize for her long poem *The Land* (1926). At this time her closest friend was VIRGINIA WOOLF, who dedicated *Orlando* to her in 1928. Her best-known later novels included *All Passion Spent* (1931), and her non-fiction ranged from the biographies *Joan of Arc* (1936), *St Teresa of Avila* and *St Thérèse of Lisieux* (1943) to several books on gardening. With Nicolson she created one of the most perfect English gardens at Sissinghurst, Kent, where they moved in 1930 after Nicolson retired from the diplomatic service. Her last novel was *No Signposts in the Sea* (1961). She had two sons.

V. Glendinning: *Vita* (1983)

**Saenger von Mossau, (Maria) Renata** (1680–1749). German witch. Renata became a member of a convent at Unter-Zell at the age of 19; she lived a life of apparent piety and rose to become Sub-Prioress by 1740. In 1746 a nun at the convent, Sister Cecilia, contracted a convulsive illness in which she claimed to be haunted by poltergeists and demons, and several other members of the community also became subject to fits. One of them died; on her deathbed she had denounced Renata as a veteran Satanist, accomplished in the arts of black magic. The convent was exorcised and the supposedly possessed nuns duly 'rolled on the ground howling and snapping like mad cats'. Renata's room was searched and poisons, ointments and strange robes were found.

She then confessed her 'tale of blackest infamy' to a Benedictine confessor, providing gruesome details of her relationship with Satan and other spirits. She also provided a new biography, according to which she had been vowed to the Devil at the age of seven, had been taught occult law and the arts of poison as a child, and had been a prostitute at the age of 12 and baptized as 'Maria' in a Satanist mass at 14. She claimed to have become a skilled chemist, preferring the poison recently developed by TOFANA of Naples, and that she had entered the convent solely to sow strife among the 'Brides of Christ'. Despite her penitence she was convicted of sorcery, heresy and apostasy and handed to the secular courts who ordered her to be beheaded and then to be burnt on a pyre in June 1749.

Renata's story is interesting, in that it combines the element of mass hysteria often associated with witchcraft accusations in small or closed communities with a graphic account of black magic practices, although it is hard to know if these were invented for the trial alone. The last witch to be executed in Germany was Anna Maria Swaegel, 25 years later (1775), and the last official execution of a witch in Europe was that of Anna Goddi who was hanged in Switzerland in 1782.

**Sagan, Françoise** [pseud. of Françoise Quoirez] (1935–). French writer. She was born at Cajarc in the Lot region of France and received a convent education in Paris. After failing an examination at the end of an introductory year at the Sorbonne, she cut short a summer holiday with her family and returned to Paris to write, in four weeks, her first novel *Bonjour tristesse* (1954) which was published when she was 18. She chose her pseudonym from a character in Proust, the Princesse de Sagan. She was awarded the Prix des Critiques for *Bonjour tristesse* which rapidly became a best-seller and brought her international fame. It was translated into many languages and, like other novels by Sagan, was made into a film. *Bonjour tristesse* was the first of many successful books such as *Un certain sourire* (1956), *Aimez-vous Brahms?* (1959), and *La chamade* (1965). She has written the scenario for the ballet *Le rendezvous manqué/Broken Date* in collaboration with Michel Magne, with whom she has also written popular songs (*La valse*, *De toute manière*). Her plays include *Château en Suède* (1959), *L'Echarde* (1966) and *Zaphorie* (1973). She worked with the film director Claude Chabrol on the script for the film *Landru/Bluebeard* and made her own film adaptation of her novel *Dans un mois, dans un an*. More recent works include *Le chien couchant* (1980) and *Un orage immobile* (1983).

Sagan has attracted as much publicity through her flamboyant life-style as through her writing. Her writing is not politically committed and she is not a technical innovator; her popular appeal lies in her gift for analysing, in her pessimistic love stories, feelings of solitude and disillusion which reflect a certain 'mal du siècle'.

F. Sagan: *Responses* (Eng. trans. 1979)

Sagan [née Schlesinger], **Leontine** (1899–1974). Austrian film director and actress. She was born in Vienna and trained with Max Reinhardt as a stage actress. She became renowned internationally with her first film, *Mädchen in Uniform* (1931), which was made in Germany with an all-female cast. It was the first German film ever to be produced co-operatively, giving shares (of possible profits) and not salaries to the cast and crew. Based on Christa Winsloe's novel, *Yesterday and Today*, it dealt with repressed homosexuality and anti-authoritarian values in a boarding school for the girls of military families. A new ending was imposed for its release in Germany and it was later banned by Goebbels as 'unhealthy'. The film created an uproar because of its frank handling of a Lesbian theme and Sagan went to England to direct a film for Alexander Korda, *Men of Tomorrow* (1932). She was instrumental in the development of the South African theatre during World War II and was co-founder of the National Theatre in Johannesburg.

**St Denis** [Dennis], **Ruth** (1877–1968). American dancer. She was the daughter of a New Jersey farmer and inventor and received little formal education but was encouraged in intellectual pursuits. She began her dancing career in vaudeville and lavish Broadway spectaculars. In 1898 she appeared in *The Ballet Girls*. She changed her name and spent several seasons with David Belasco, travelling through Europe and the USA.

She modelled her image on posters advertising 'Egyptian Deities' cigarettes and developed an obsession to 'dance Egypt'. Her next interest, in Hindu dance, led to her first success, *Radha* (1906). This was followed by *The Incense*, and *Cobras* which she took to London, Paris and Germany in 1909. Although she was not an innovatory or technically authentic dancer, her exotic oriental settings attracted a wide audience. Her works include *The Green Nautch*, *Yogi* and *Egypta*. In 1914 she married Ted Shawn, a dancer with her company, and their stormy association continued until 1931. Together they founded the influential Denishawn School in Los Angeles. In later years she concentrated on Christian themes, founding the Church of the Divine Dance in Hollywood in 1947, and producing religious, patriotic works such as *Freedom* (1955). She still performed as a soloist until late in life.

R. St Denis: *An Unfinished Life* (1939)
S. Shelton: *Divine Dancer* (1981)

**Salavarrieta, Pola** [Policarpa; 'La Pola'] (*c*1790–1817). Colombian spy. Born in a Creole family in the province of New Granada, she moved with her family to the town of Aguadas 1802, on the route from Cartagena to Santa Fé de Bogotá. In 1813 the colony declared independence from Spain, but was recaptured in 1816. La Pola became an active member of the resistance. In late 1816, trained as a seamstress, she found work in the houses of Spanish royalist women in Bogotá, passing on information to the rebels and setting up a network of contacts and safe routes. She was discovered, captured and shot in the public square as a republican agent in November 1817. Her execution aroused a wave of public sympathy and she became a legendary heroine of patriotic resistance. She was one of some 50 women agents executed during the rebellion.

**Sallé, Marie** (1707–56). French ballerina. Born into a family of touring players, she studied at the Paris Opéra school. A child prodigy, at the age of nine she danced at John Rich's Theatre, Lincoln's Inn Fields, London. She is alleged to have replaced Prévost at a performance at the Opéra at the age of 14, and she danced regularly in London and Paris between 1716 and 1727. She made her official debut at the Opéra in 1727, but she left the company twice, frustrated at lack of opportunity. Her performance in *Pygmalion* (1734) at the Drury Lane Theatre, London, caused a sensation when she replaced the usual complicated costume with a Grecian style muslin shift and left her hair unbound. During this visit she also danced in *Bacchus and Ariane*, and arranged *divertissements* for Handel's operas; he composed *Terpsichore* as a ballet for her.

In 1735 Sallé returned to the Opéra, in the absence of her great rival MARIE-ANNE CAMARGO, and appeared in the first performance of *Les Indes galantes*. A naturally graceful dancer and delicate mime artist, she captured leading roles during the next five years and became a great favourite at court. She retired in 1740 with a court pension. After 5 years in seclusion she re-emerged to star in 20 court ballets (1745–7) at Versailles and a further 4 at Fontainebleau (1752). Sallé was a pioneering, unconventional dancer, famed for expressive dramatic characterization, and she was a friend of many leading intellectuals and artists.

P. Migel: *The Ballerinas from the Court of Louis XIV to Pavlova* (1972)

**Salote** (1900–65). Queen of Tonga, Polynesia. She reigned over the Pacific Islands group from 1918. Born in Nukualoja and educated in New Zealand she was an ardent Methodist. She married Prince Uiliami Tungi in 1917 with whom she had three sons. In 1953 she came to England for the coronation of ELIZABETH II and won enormous popularity and affection by driving in an open carriage through the pouring rain. She was awarded the distinction of Dame Grand Cross of the Order of St Michael and St George in 1965.

**Salt,** Dame **Barbara** (1904–75). English diplomat. She was educated at Seaford in Sussex and then attended universities in Munich and Cologne. During World War II she acted as Vice-Consul in Tangier (1942–6) before joining the UN Department of the Foreign Office as a temporary First Secretary. In 1950 she was sent as First Secretary (commercial) to Moscow, and the following year held a similar position in Washington, being promoted to Counsellor in 1955. From 1957 to 1960 Barbara Salt was Counsellor and Consul-General in Tel Aviv. In 1960 she went as Deputy Head of the British delegation to the Geneva disarmament conference and in 1961 moved to New York as the representative for the UK on the Economic and Social Council of the UN.

She was appointed Ambassador to Israel in 1962, the first British woman ambassador, but a severe illness which resulted in the loss of both legs meant that she was unable to take up the post. She still remained a senior woman in the diplomatic service, leading several major delegations during the 1970s and becoming head of the Special Operations Executive section at the Foreign and Commonwealth Office from 1967 until her retirement in 1972. She was made CBE in 1959 and DBE in 1963.

**Sammuramat** [Semiramis] (*fl c*800 BC). Assyrian queen. The wife of King Shamsi-Ada V (824–810 BC) and the mother of King Adad-nirari (810–772 BC), Sammuramat appears to have been very influential during the reign of her son, particularly in developing the cult of the god Nabu. She has been connected by historians with the legend of Semiramis, developed in the *Bibliotheca historica* of Diodorus Siculus, who describes her as the daughter of a goddess, who became a powerful ruler after her royal husband's death, irrigating the land of Babylon and greatly expanding her territories, leading campaigns as far away as India. She allegedly ruled for 42 years until her son overthrew her, and is the subject of more stories than any other figure in Assyrian history.

**Samoilova, Konkordiya** (1876–1921). Russian socialist. Born in Siberia, the daughter of a priest, she became a student in St Petersburg [now Leningrad]. In 1897 she organized a demonstration after the suicide of Maria Vetrovna, who set fire to herself in her cell in Peter-Paul prison in protest at her treatment. She became a political activist, participating in the great demonstrations of 1901, and working under cover as 'Natasha' from 1903. She was imprisoned in 1903–4 and then worked in the Caucasus, attempting to win workers' wives to the radical movement. In 1905 she married a lawyer, who died in 1918.

Samoilova was an editor of *Pravda* from its foundation in 1912, and in 1913 was one of the six editors of the new journal *Rabotnitsa* ('Woman Worker'); she was arrested with the whole editorial board on the eve of International Woman's Day in 1914. In 1917 the journal was revived as part of the attempt to mobilize women in the Bolshevik revolution. With ALEXANDRA KOLLONTAI, ANGELIKA BALABANOFF, Elena Stasova (the Party Secretary) and Inessa Armand (organizer of the Zhenotdel, the department of women's labour), she was one of the great women leaders of the Bolshevik period.

**Sampson, Agnes** (*d* 1592). Scottish witch. A lay-healer from Haddington, nr Edinburgh, Agnes Sampson was brought to trial after having been named along with about 70 other people by another accused woman, Geillis Duncan, and described as being the 'eldest witch of them al'. After severe torture she confessed. She told of meetings she had led at North Berwick on Hallowe'en, when 200 people danced in a circle by the sea and the Devil appeared to them. They celebrated black mass and on the Devil's instructions plotted the death of the king and queen through sorcery and poison. Agnes was interrogated by James VI, who was deeply interested in the occult. She was executed with many of her fellow defendants.

It is generally accepted that some conspiracy was involved, probably plotted by the Earl of Bothwell, who aimed to seize the throne. Her trial, like that of Margery Jourdemain a century earlier, illustrated the long-standing association between sorcery and treason. Later Scottish witch-trials seem to have resulted more from dissension within the community or a Puritanical disapproval of individual behaviour. However, many Scottish and English witches, like Sampson, Elizabeth Southern (tried in 1613), Eleanor Gowdie ('Queen of Scottish Witches' who confessed in 1662), or Jane Weir who was charged with incest and satanism in 1670, proclaimed their allegiance as witches with great pride, and appear to have been active practitioners rather than mere victims.

**Sampson, Deborah** (1760–1827). American soldier. An adventurous girl, she dressed in men's clothing so as to have greater freedom, and to earn money enlisted as a soldier in the rebel army in the wars against the British. She engaged in many skirmishes against British and American Tory soldiers, and was wounded in action. Her identity was eventually discovered in 1783. She received an honourable discharge and married Benjamin Gannett, with whom she had three children. Her much-embellished biography, *The Female Review* by Herbert Mann, appeared in 1786 and she toured the theatres of New England and New York State, appearing in uniform on stage.

**Sand, George** [pseud. of Amandine Aurore Lucie Dupin], Baronne Dudevant (1804–76). French writer. An illegitimate daughter of Marshal de Saxe, she spent her early childhood with her grandmother at the château of Nohant. She was educated at a convent boarding school and returned to Nohant in 1820, marrying Baron Dudevant two years later. She found Nohant and married life stifling and in 1831 she left her husband, taking her two children with her to Paris. There she outraged bourgeois society by her unconventional ways (she wore trousers and smoked cigars in public) and by her love affairs – with Jules Sandeau (a writer from whose name her pseudonym was derived, and with whom she collaborated on newspaper articles and on one novel) and with the Romantic poet, Alfred de Musset. Her literary output was prolific and her novels defend both sensual and idealistic love: *Indiana* (1832); *Valentine* (1832); *Lélia* (1833); *Mauprat* (1838). *Lélia* created a sensation for its erotic candour. From the time of her relationship with Chopin, which lasted ten years, her private life became quieter and she turned her interest to politics. In *Le meunier d'Angibault* (1845) she exalts the working man while in *Consuelo* (1842) she preaches a pantheistic religion. In 1848 she supported the Revolution and wrote *Lettres au peuple* but retreated to Nohant at the time of the June insurrection. Here she wrote a series of pastoral novels including *La petite Fadette* (1849). Under the Second Empire, George Sand became a *grande dame* in the village of Nohant – entertaining writers and artists, presiding over village fêtes and bestowing alms. In 1854 her autobiography, *L'histoire de ma vie*, was published. Although her exalted style and outspoken views on conventional marriage now seem dated she was hailed as a great writer by many contemporary critics and writers.

C. Cate: *George Sand: a Biography* (1975)

**Sandel, Cora** (1880–1974). Norwegian novelist. Cora Sandel was born in Christiania (now Oslo) into an upper-class family, who moved when she was 12 to the port of Tromsö in the far north. Later she studied art with the painter Harriet Backer and in 1905 left for Paris, where she lived for the next 15 years. In 1913 she married the Swedish sculptor Anders Jonsson. They had a son in 1917 and moved to Sweden in 1921 but were divorced in 1926. To support herself Cora began to write, producing the famous 'Alberta Trilogy', *Alberta and Jaceb* (1926), *Alberta and Freedom* (1931) and *Alberta Alone* (1935), a powerful study of a woman's growth to self-knowledge and independence in northern Norway and Paris. Her later works reveal her deep instinctive feminism, her experimental boldness and her sensitivity to harsh social realities. They include *Krane's Cafe* (1945) and *Kjop ikke Dondi* (*The Leech*, 1958). She also published several collections of short stories. Her work was translated into English in the 1960s and has since been acclaimed by feminist critics and writers.

**Sandes, Flora** (1876–1956). English nurse and soldier. The daughter of a clergyman, she worked as a secretary in London but through service with St John's Ambulance Brigade she had the chance to go to Serbia with a nursing unit in 1914. Attached first to the Serbian Red Cross and then to the 2nd Infantry Regiment, she became an active soldier against the Bulgarians. She endured seven years of mountain warfare and frontline battles, returning briefly to England after a severe wound in 1916. She was decorated for conspicuous bravery, idolized by the troops and remained with the army, becoming a Captain in 1926. In 1927 she married a Russian emigré and lived in France and Belgrade. After internment by the Germans and her husband's death in 1941 she retired to Suffolk.

A. Burgess: *The Lovely Sergeant* (1963)

**Sanger, Margaret (Higgins)** (1883–1966). American birth control campaigner. Born in Corning, New York, Margaret was the sixth of 11 children of a stone-mason. After attending Claverack College in Hudson she trained as a nurse at White Plains Hospital. In 1902 she married an architect, William Sanger; they had three children but were eventually divorced in 1920. In 1912 she worked as a nurse in New York's Lower East Side and lectured on health to young mothers. She became deeply distressed at the connections she saw between poverty, unchecked childbirth, infant and maternal death, and backstreet abortions. She wrote for the left-wing paper *The Call* (including

an article on venereal disease that was suppressed by the government) and was friendly with radicals such as EMMA GOLDMAN. In 1913 she went to Paris, where she met Malthusian reformers, and on her return distributed a pamphlet, *Family Limitation*, which was prosecuted because Comstock's Law of 1873 prevented 'obscene' material being sent by post; she also began to publish the journal *Women Rebel*, which later became *Birth Control Review*. The case against her was dismissed in 1916, after she had been forced to flee to the UK to escape prosecution. In Europe she met MARIE STOPES and ALETTA JACOBS and apparently fell in love with the sexologist Havelock Ellis.

Returning to New York, she opened a clinic in Brooklyn; it was soon closed down and she was sentenced to 30 days in a workhouse for causing a 'public nuisance'. She persevered, and founded the American Birth Control League in 1921, remaining as President until 1928. Her second husband (from 1922) J. Noah Slee supported her work; she organized the first World Population Conference in Geneva in 1927 and created a national lobby group which pressed for changes in legislation throughout the 1930s. By 1932 over 80 clinics were operating in the USA. She retired from active leadership in 1938, after winning a limited victory in a court decision which allowed doctors to prescribe contraceptives for medical reasons, but she continued to lecture and was the first President of the International Planned Parenthood Federation in 1953, going on to work for birth control in India and the Far East. Her many books include *What every Mother should know* (1917), *Woman and the New Race* (1920), and *My Fight for Birth Control* (1931).

M. Sanger: *An Autobiography* (1938)

**Santamaria, Haydee** (1931–). Cuban revolutionary. While living in Havana with her brother Abel she became involved in the insurrection against Batista in 1952 and took part in the desperate attack on the Moncada barracks in 1953, in which 70 students were killed. Haydee was imprisoned and was brought terrible evidence (eyes and testicles) of the torture and death of her brother and her fiancé in an effort to make her talk. After her release she supported the underground movement in Havana and then fought with the guerillas in the Sierra Maestra, where she was a close friend of Che Guevara. She also worked under cover, obtaining money and arms in the USA.

After Castro's successful coup in January 1959 she was active in establishing the new regime. By the 1970s she had been involved in numerous organizations: she ran a student scholarship scheme, and was a member of the Central Party Committee, President of the Latin American Organization of Solidarity, and Director of the Casa de los Americas, a cultural institute. She married Armando Hart and they had seven children, five of them adopted from other countries. To many people at home and overseas Haydee became a symbol of the courage and achievement of the Cuban revolution.

**Sappho** (*b* *c*613 BC). Greek poet. The daughter of an aristocratic family from Lesbos, she lived in exile in Sicily during her childhood but returned to Mytilene in Lesbos, where she was married at an early age to Cercylas and had a daughter Cleis about whom she writes lovingly. Her poetry, written in the Lesbian vernacular, is full of idyllic scenes of the Greek society at peace: rural life, religious festivals, and weddings. A woman's life is also her favourite theme: love and the subsequent feelings of hatred and passion, jealousy and joy, pleasure and pain are described with great intensity in a rhythm and sound of immediate appeal. A circle of young girls, perhaps a cult in honour of Aphrodite and the Muses, formed around her to be taught music and poetry and they were the subject and audience of many lyrics which were full of affection and at times openly erotic. Little else is known of her life or death, although centuries later stories that she had thrown herself over a cliff for love of a man called Phaon were circulated. Her poetry was collected in nine books.

Sappho, and the slightly senior Alcaeus, were the first to create the personal, subjective lyric, which was later developed by the Roman poets such as Catullus and is still popular. Later Greek women poets whose works have survived include ERINNA and Jelessilla, and also Corinna and Praxilla, of the 5th century.

H.T. Wharton: *Sappho* (1979)

**Sarabhai, Anusyabehn** (1885–1972). Indian trade unionist. Born in Ahmedabad into a wealthy family, she was orphaned at the age of 10 and at 12 underwent an arranged marriage which was later annulled. In 1911 she went to England, where she studied at the London School of Economics and was greatly impressed by Fabian socialism and by the suffrage movement. She returned to India and undertook social work among the mill workers, starting classes for their children in 1914 and in 1917 chairing a meeting on their behalf at which the first labour strike in India was called. She was closely associated with Gandhi in his Ahmedabad strike of 1918. She also founded several craft unions which in 1920 combined to form the Textile Labour Association. She continued to supervise its activities, negotiating, and mediating in disputes. She was highly revered as a social worker and philanthropist.

**Saragossa, La** [Agostina] (1786–1857). Spanish heroine. In the defence of Saragossa against the French invaders in 1808 the 18-year-old Agostina was conspicuous for her bravery, especially in rescuing the wounded under constant fire and in nursing them without rest. The city surrendered after the death of 50,000 defenders in the second siege (1808–9). She became a symbol of national pride, courage and liberty and was immortalized in poetry and in painting, notably by Goya.

One version of her story describes how in the heat of the battle 'an unknown maiden issued from the Church of Nostra Donna de Pillas, habited in white raiment, a cross suspended from her neck, her dark hair dishelleved and her eyes sparkling with supernatural lustre'. She refused any reward, asking only to retain the military rank of Engineer and to bear the arms of Saragossa.

**Sarashina** (*c*1008–60). Japanese diarist. The daughter of a minor noble, Fujiwara Takasue, she seems to have lived on the fringe of court society. She was married and had two children, but little is known of her life except what can be gleaned from her diary *Sarashina Nikki*, a witty, gentle account, written just before her death, of journeys from Shimosa to Kyoto in 1021, and of other events, emotions and dreams which had remained in her memory. It has become one of the classics of Japanese literature.

I.I. Morris (trans.): *As I crossed a Bridge of Dreams* (1961)

**Sarraute, Nathalie** (1902–). French novelist. Born in Ivanovno-Voznesensk, Russia, she went with her family to France in 1904, although she frequently returned to Russia as a child. From 1908 onwards she was educated in Paris, graduating in literature and law, spending a year in Oxford (1920–21) and then studying sociology in Berlin. From 1922 until 1939 she practised law in Paris. Her first published work was *Tropismes* (1938), a series of sketches of bourgeois life, which shows an interest in psychology and in the subtle relations between conventions and behaviour. Called the first anti-novel, it reveals the influence of VIRGINIA WOOLF. From 1940 she devoted herself to writing, producing essays, and another novel *Portrait d'un inconnu* (1948). This book, with *Martereau* (1953) and *Le planétarium* (1959), established the symbolic, experimental, fragmented structure of the *nouveau roman*. She has also written radio plays, reviews and critical essays collected in *L'ève du soupçon*. Her other works include *Entre la vie et la mort* (1968) and *Vous les entendez* (1972), *Disent les imbéciles* (1976), *Elle est là* (1978) and *Enfance* (1983). For a long time she was at the centre of Parisian cultural life, and engaged in rivalry and controversy with SIMONE DE BEAUVOIR.

Y. Belaval and M. Cranaki: *Nathalie Sarraute* (1965)

**Sartain, Emily** (1841–1927). American art teacher. The daughter of an artist, she was born and educated in Philadelphia, showed early artistic ability and attended Pennsylvania Academy of Fine Art (1864–70) before spending four years travelling in Europe. On her return to the USA, she continued to work as a painter and engraver, becoming art editor of the magazine *Our Continent*. In 1886 she was appointed Principal of the Philadelphia School of Design for Women, remaining in her position until succeeded by her niece Harriet in 1920. Highly influential and progressive, she encouraged the teaching of industrial design to women and influenced the artistic taste of her generation. She retired to California.

**Sauvé, Jeanne (Benoit)** (1922–). Canadian journalist and politician. Born in Prud'homme, Saskatchewan, she was educated at universities in Ottawa and Paris, and acted as National President of Jeunesse Etudiante Catholique in Montreal from 1942 to 1947. In 1948 she married Maurice Sauvé and went to London as a student and as a teacher of French. She then worked briefly as assistant to the Director of the Youth section of UNESCO in Paris in 1951. Returning to Canada she made her career as a journalist and broadcaster for CBC and other networks from 1952 to 1972, and held increasingly important positions: Vice-President of the Canadian Institute of Public Affairs (1962–4), then President (1964); General Secretary of the Union des Artistes et Auteurs de Canada (1966–77); Director of Bushnell Communications and of EKAC Radio, Montreal (1969–72).

In 1972 Jeanne Sauvé was elected Member of Parliament for Montreal–Ahuntsic, and immediately became Secretary of State for Science and Technology. In 1974–5 she was Minister of Environment and then (1975–9) Minister of Communications. From 1980 to 1984 she was Speaker of the House of Commons. As Speaker she had to control an often difficult house but managed to push through several major reforms in parliamentary practice. In December 1983 she was made Governor General of Canada, again the first woman to hold this post. She is known as an outspoken speaker on behalf of women's rights.

Other notable women in Canadian politics in the 1980s include Flora Macdonald, currently Minister for Communications, Barbara McDougall, Minister for the Status of Women, Patricia Carney, Minister of International Trade and Monique Vezina, Minister of Supply and Services.

**Sayers, Dorothy L(eigh)** (1893–1957). English writer of detective stories. Born in Oxford, she was educated at the Godolphin School, Salisbury, and Somerville College, Oxford, where in 1915 she took a First in modern languages. After teaching for a year, she went into advertising until 1931, a profession she enjoyed enormously and in which she invented a number of witty slogans for companies such as Guinness. In 1924 she bore an illegitimate son whom she always claimed to be adopted. She married Captain Oswald ('Mac') Fleming in 1926.

She decided to supplement her income by writing detective stories, which she did with great success between 1923 (*Whose Body?*) and 1937 (*Busman's Honeymoon*). She created the famous character Lord Peter Wimsey, and in some of the later books the independent, semi-autobiographical Harriet Vane. The latter half of her career was devoted to the writing of religious drama such as *The Man Born to be King* (1941–2) and *The Zeal of the House* (1957), which was written for the Canterbury Festival, and to translation (Dante's *Inferno*, 1949, and *Purgatorio*, 1955, with commentaries). She also became involved in 'missionary' social work.

R.E. Hone: *Dorothy L. Sayers, a Literary Biography* (1979)

**Sayers, Peig** (1873–1958). Irish storyteller. Born at Dunquin, on the tip of the Kerry peninsula, she worked as a servant in Dingle before her marriage was arranged to Padraig O'Guithin, when she moved to the Great Blasket Island for 40 years. She became famous for her stories, learnt from her father, and in the 1920s over 375 stories and 40 folksongs were collected from her for the Irish Folklore Commission. In 1936 her haunting autobiography, dictated to her son, was published. It became an Irish classic, was was translated into English in 1962, and was followed by a second instalment in 1970, translated into English in 1973. Her husband died, her son was killed in a fall and her surviving children emigrated. After the mainland resettlement of the tiny island community she lived in a hospital in Dingle.

P. Sayers: *Reflections of an old Woman* (1962)
———: *Peig* (1973)

**Sayyidah.** *See* ARWĀ.

**Scharlieb** [née Bird], Dame **Mary (Ann)** (1845–1930). English doctor. Mary married before she was 20 and in 1866 left England for India where her husband was practising as a barrister. Becoming aware of the

unnecessary suffering of women in childbirth, she entered the Medical School of Madras with three other women and spent three years there, despite the superintendent's view of the 'undesirability and folly of educating women to be doctors'. She returned to the UK to take a degree from the Royal Free Hospital in London.

Mary alternated her professional life between England and India. She became a skilled abdominal surgeon, but maintained her belief that women doctors should confine themselves to the ample scope of midwifery, gynaecology and paediatrics. ELIZABETH GARRETT ANDERSON helped her to begin private practice in England and then obtain the Chief Surgeon post at the New Hospital after her own retirement. Mary also gained practical experience in Vienna, founded the Victoria Hospital for Caste and Gosha women and lectured at Madras Medical College.

During World War I she helped to form a Women's Medical Service for India, and was made first OBE, then DBE. In 1920 she became one of the first women magistrates in England. Her beliefs were Anglo-Catholic but she strongly respected Indian traditions. Her *Reminiscences* (1924) show her motive of service as an ideal.

M. Scharlieb: *Reminiscences* (1924)

**Scherchen, Tona** (1938–). French composer. Daughter of the conductor Hermann Scherchen and composer Hsiao Shusien, Tona Scherchen spent her teenage years in China where she studied Chinese classical music and the Chinese lute. In 1961 she returned to Europe and studied composition with Ligeti, Messiaen and Henze, winning the Premier Prix du Conservatoire National Súperieur de Musique de Paris in 1964. She also worked with Schaeffer at the Groupe de Recherches Musicales. From 1968 she lived in Europe and lectured widely, including a spell as guest Professor in Basle for music ethnology, 1969–71. She moved to the USA in 1979, returning to Paris in 1985. Since the 1970s she has also worked as a freelance radio producer, and in New York (1981–4) as a sound engineer, beginning to conduct and produce her own works, assuming the artistic direction and co-ordination of her two recent large multi-media works. The originality of her work has been described as a perfect integration of

*Marie-Jeanne Roland*

*Christina Rossetta*

*George Sand*

*Dorothy L. Sayers*

technique with elements of Western and Eastern philosophy, combining the rational and the imaginative in a highly personal language.

Scherchen's international career opened with *Tzang* for chamber orchestra (1966), which won the Gaudeamus Foundation's first prize in 1967; *Wai* (1966–7, for mezzo and string quartet), commissioned for the Donaueschingen Festival and premièred in 1968 by Cathy Berberian; *Shen* (1968), for the 1969 Holland Festival; and *Tzi* (1969–70, for choir *a cappella*), with a Strobel Foundation grant. Then followed the orchestral work *Khouang* (1966–8), which was premièred in 1972 in Strasbourg and has since been played in London, Paris, Berlin, Geneva and elsewhere. Its success led to numerous commissions, including the major works *Vague-T'ao* (1974–5), *Oeil de chat* (1976), *Tao* (1971, perf. 1976) and *L'illégitime* (1985–6). Her chamber orchestra works include *Bien* (1972–3), *'S . . .'* (1975), *L'invitation au voyage* (1977; for Pierre Boulez and Ensemble InterContemporain) and *Lô* (1978–9), which brought her the Koussevitzky Prize 'in recognition of her valuable contribution to the music of our time'.

Scherchen has also written many smaller pieces including *Tzoue* (1970), *Tzing* (1979), *Radar* (1980, a piano solo first performed at the New York International Composer festival, and a turning point in her work), and *Fuite* (1987), for electronic tape and small ensemble. During the 1980s she has turned more to electronic music; *Eclats-obscurs* (1982), *Man Ray* (music for the film, 1983), *Spacelight* and *Fou-Fou* (1987), and has concentrated on the large multi-media projects *Between '86* (1978–86), and *Cancer, Solstice '83* (1983–87). She has also participated in visual arts exhibitions in both New York and Paris and has worked on *Joujou 12*, a sound sculpture project.

**Schiaparelli, Elsa** (1890–1973). French couturier. Born in Rome, after World War I she worked in the USA as a translator and film script writer, before moving to Paris in the early 1920s. Here she made an impact with her modernistic knitwear designs, producing her work first from a Left Bank hotel-room, then a showroom in the Rue de la Paix, and finally a grand salon on the Place Vendome. Her designs were variously considered very inventive, with a flair for colour and texture, opportunistic, amusing, and outrageous. They were the first to feature padded shoulders (1931–2), zip fastenings, and synthetic fabrics and her best designs combined elegance with a slightly surreal exotic appeal. Always evasive about her age, she became a French subject in 1931. She also worked in the USA from 1939.

E. Schiaparelli: *Shocking Life* (1954)

**Schlafly, Phyllis** (1924–). American anti-feminist campaigner. She was born in St Louis; her father lost his job in 1930 and her mother, a librarian, had to support the family throughout the Depression. Educated at the Sacred Heart City House, in 1941 she went to Washington University and worked at nights testing explosives to pay her way. She won a Fellowship at Radcliffe where she gained an MA in government, then from 1945 to 1949 worked as a researcher in St Louis banks and became involved in Republican politics. She married Fred Schlafly in 1949; they have six children. Since the 1950s she has run for Congress twice and has been a delegate to every Republican convention.

In 1964 she caused a stir by the publication of her book *A Choice not an Echo*, which accused an elite group of running the Republican party, and in the next few years she wrote five books with Chester Ward on strategic defence policy, demanding that the USA obtain a powerful first-strike capacity in order to combat the Communist menace.

Since 1972 she has attacked the feminist movement with equal zeal. The basic argument of her book *The Power of the Positive Woman* (1977) was that women as a class are essentially different from men and should therefore not compete, and that the Equal Rights Amendment (ERA) was redundant, since so much legislation already existed to enable women to succeed if they wished. She has also attacked homosexuality, divorce, abortion, extramarital sex and socialism. Working from her home in Illinois she has built up a powerful lobby group with thousands of members, and her 'Stop ERA' campaign effectively blocked the amendment. She has been a syndicated columnist for the Copley News Service since 1976, and has also broadcast for CBS and Cable News. Her latest work has been on *Child Abuse in the Classroom* (1984).

C. Felsenthal: *Sweetheart of the Silent Majority: the Biography of Phyllis Schlafly* (1981)

**Schmidt, Auguste** (1833–1902). German feminist and educationalist. She became Head of the Women's Teacher Training College in Leipzig, and her pupils included several later leaders of the German feminist movement including CLARA ZETKIN. However, she stressed the sanctity of marriage and believed true fulfilment for women lay in 'the capacity for self-sacrifice' and in moral leadership. She became Head of the Allgemeiner Deutscher Frauenverein (General German Women's Association) in 1888, and first President of the Bund Deutscher Frauenverein (Federation of German Women's Associations) in 1894. A conservative, she disliked the radicals' campaign against the Civil Code but she did encourage women's involvement with charity work and in 1896–7 declared that her organization wished to increase employment opportunities and to improve the status of women in the law and in civil affairs. She was replaced as President in 1899 by MARIE STRITT.

**Schneiderman, Rose** (1882–1972). American trade unionist. She was born in Russian Poland; the family emigrated to the USA in 1890. She was educated in Hebrew, Russian and American schools. Her father, a tailor, died in 1892, and although her mother sewed and took lodgers Rose spent much time in institutions. From 13 she worked in a shop, then a cap factory where she organized the first women's branch of the Jewish Socialist Hat and Cap Makers' Union in 1903. A dynamic, fierce speaker, after 1908 she worked chiefly with the Women's Trade Union League, becoming New York organizer in 1910, co-ordinating the garment workers' strikes (1909–14), and then acting as national organizer for the International Ladies Garment Workers' Union (1915–16). She united working women and middle class reformers. A strong feminist, she was an organizer and speaker for the National American Women's Association from 1913, one of the founders of the International Congress of Working Women (1919), and organ-izer of the Bryn Mawr Summer Schools for women workers from 1921. At the same time, as a member of the New York Labor Party, she stood unsuccessfully for the Senate in 1920.

After World War I, Schneiderman fought for education and protective legislation, especially the eight-hour day and minimum wage, acting as President of the New York Women's Trade Union League (WTUL) (1918–49), and of the National League from 1926. A friend of ELEANOR ROOSEVELT, during Franklin's presidency she was the only woman in the National Recovery Administration (1933–5), and from 1937 to 1943 was Secretary of the New York State Department of Labor.

R. Schneiderman: *All for one* (1967)

**Scholtz-Klink, Gertrud** (1902–). German Nazi women's leader. Her first husband died in 1930 and she began working for the Nazi Party in Baden. She rose to prominence after 1931 as leader of the Baden German Woman's Order, which merged into the Nazi Women's Group, and in 1934 became head of the whole group, being given the title of Reichsfrauenführerin ('National Women's Leader'). She stabilized the movement, previously riven by disputes, because she accepted without question the importance of the unity of the Party. She was then 32, the mother of a large family, appealing both to youth and to family virtues (she eventually had 3 marriages and 11 children). She also had superb executive and delegatory skills, and she became co-opted on to numerous bodies, such as the Red Cross, the Labour Office, the National Council of Experts on Population and Racial Policy, and the Academy of German Law. She addressed foreign delegations and spoke on tours abroad (in 1939 she went to the UK billed as 'The Perfect Nazi Woman'). Her office was responsible for directing all female organizations in the Third Reich and for publishing propaganda about women's role in the home and in the state; and although some historians feel it may have had less influence than the propaganda suggests, the Nazi Women's Order certainly did not question many of the inhuman policies of the regime during World War II and was hated by working women in the factories. At the end of the war, Scholtz-Klink was also involved in forming 'women's battalions' to fight in the final defence of Germany.

She was rumoured to have committed suicide in April 1945 in Stuttgart, but had actually fled and was recaptured in 1948 with her husband General Heissmajer near Baden, where she was working under an assumed name. She was imprisoned for 18 months by the French occupying forces for living under a false name, and tried in Tübingen as a war criminal, but given only a light sentence, which she was deemed to have served already. In 1950 the new German government banned her from public office, and from teaching, journalism and other professions, and restricted her to her district. Her autobiographical account of this period was published in 1978 as *Die Frau im Dritten Reich*.

Koonz: *Mothers in the Fatherland* (1988)

**Schrader, Catharina Geertuida** (1656–1745). German–Dutch midwife. Born in Bentheim, Germany, the eldest daughter of a court tailor, Catharina married a local surgeon, Ernst Cramer in 1683. Three years later they moved to Hallum, Friesland and after her husband's death in 1692 she began work as a midwife to support her six children. Moving to the nearby town of Dokkum, she built up a large practice, and over the next 18 years attended over 100 births a year. She was remarried in 1713 to Thomas Hight, a gold- and silversmith and Mayor of Dokkum, but although her attendances dropped for a time, she returned to midwifery full-time after Hight's death in 1721, specializing in complicated deliveries. Her *Notebook* stresses traditional skills, the avoidance of instruments, and highly developed techniques of manual intervention in difficult births. She despaired of the low level of contemporary midwifery, and often co-operated with male doctors and surgeons. By the time she retired at the age of 88 she had attended 3060 deliveries, including 64 twins and 3 triplets.

**Schreiber, Adele** (*d* 1957). Austrian feminist and politician. Born in Vienna, the daughter of a doctor, she was a rebellious child who left Austria to take a job in Berlin where she married another doctor, and became a correspondent for the *Frankfurter Zeitung*. She was a founder member of the International Women's Suffrage Alliance in 1904 and in 1910 founded the German Association for the Rights of Mothers and Children, while she herself opened a centre for unmarried mothers. After World War I and the enfranchisement of women in 1919 she was one of the members of the first Reichstag of the Weimar Republic, holding her seat as a member of the Social Democratic Party. She continued to work for the rights of women, as Chairman of a committee which introduced a bill abolishing regulated prostitution, as the author of several books such as *Mutterschaft* and *Das Buch von Kinde* and as the editor of women's journals. She was also the President of the German Red Cross.

Adele Schreiber left Germany when Hitler achieved control and lived in exile, first in the UK and then in Switzerland, near Zurich, from 1947. She spoke five languages fluently and lectured in Europe and the USA and she was also Vice-President of the International Alliance of Women, of whose history, *Journey towards Freedom*, she was co-author in 1956.

**Schreiner, Olive** (1855–1920). South African novelist, rationalist, and feminist. She was born at the remote Wittebergen Mission Station, Cape of Good Hope, the sixth of 12 children of an idealistic German Methodist minister and his energetic English wife. She had no formal education, but read widely, loved nature and enjoyed her solitary meditations which turned her into a 'free-thinker', to the horror of her family. Her lack of education prevented her realizing her wish to become a doctor and at 15 she became a governess to a Boer family living near the Karoo desert. She began writing *Story of an African Farm* but could find no publisher in South Africa and in 1881 left for the UK to try there. She endured intense loneliness and poverty, before George Meredith helped her revise the novel for Chapman and Hall, for whom he was chief reader. On publication in 1884 it received both praise and hostility, especially for its fervent denunciation of the oppression of women and its attack on Christianity. (Early editions of the book were published under the pseudonym Ralph Iron.) Olive became friendly with progressive intellectual circles in London and met Havelock Ellis, with whom she had an intense but platonic relationship. She disliked England however, and returned to South Africa in 1889.

She published little more fiction during her lifetime, apart from the allegories *Dreams* (1891), *Dream Life and Real Life* (1893) and the polemical, pro-Boer *Trooper Peter Halket of Mashonaland* (1897), but after her death her husband published an early work, *Ondine*, and her last novel *From Man to Man*. Both contain haunting portraits of frustrated women. In 1894 she married Samuel Cronwright, a farmer and lawyer, and a former member of the South African parliament. They campaigned together for suffrage, for racial justice and for the Boer cause, and were interned during the Boer War, when she wrote her massive and influential study *Women and Labour* (1911). She returned to the UK in 1913 and was active in the peace movement. She died there seven years later, but she is buried on a hill in South Africa.

R. First and A. Scott: *Olive Schreiner* (1980)

**Schröder, Louise** (1887–1957). German socialist leader. Born in Altona, daughter of a socialist builder, she was educated locally and in Hamburg before working for an insurance company. She joined the Socialist Party in 1910 and made a reputation as a brilliant speaker. She was elected to the Weimar Assembly (1919) and to the Reichstag (1920) but in 1933 she was dismissed by the Nazis and continually harassed. She spent World War II in Berlin and after the war she renewed her work for the Socialist Party, becoming Deputy Chairman, and Deputy Mayor of Berlin in 1946. In 1947 she took over as Acting Lord Mayor when Russian intervention blocked Reuter's election. Energetic and dedicated, despite serious illness she became an international figure during the blockade and was nicknamed 'Mother of Berlin'. She was a member of the Bundestag from 1949 and a delegate to the Council of Europe.

**Schumann [née Wieck], Clara (Josephine)** (1819–96). German pianist, composer and teacher. Daughter of the composer Friedrich Wieck, who gave her a rigorous musical training, she made her debut as a pianist in Leipzig at the age of nine and was taken on her first concert tour in 1831–2. By the time she was 16 she was renown-

ed throughout Europe; honours accorded her included an appointment as *Kammervirtuosin* to the Austrian court, election to the Gesellschaft der Musikfreunde (both 1838) and the admiration of Goethe, Mendelssohn, Chopin, Paganini and (later) Liszt.

She had known Robert Schumann, a pupil of her father's, since childhood; they were married in 1840, though only after legal proceedings had ruled in their favour against parental opposition. Her concern not to disturb her husband's work threatened to disrupt her own career, especially with the advent, in quick succession, of their eight children (the fourth died in infancy). She continued to tour, however, going to Copenhagen in 1842 and Russia in 1844, returning to composition at home intermittently. The first of many visits to England took place in 1856, the last in 1888, with another Russian tour in 1864. During the years of Robert's deteriorating health and after his death (1856), Brahms was an increasingly devoted companion; she assiduously promoted the music of both composers in her recitals, also being among the first to perform Chopin's music in Germany. She admitted to less ambition as a composer (she wrote nothing after 1853), despite having written an effective Piano Concerto (1836) and Piano Trio (1847) as well as many piano pieces and songs.

She was particularly sought after as a teacher, having taught at the Leipzig Conservatory and privately in Dresden and Düsseldorf in the 1840s and being appointed principal piano teacher at the Hoch Conservatory, Frankfurt, in 1878.

Brahms assisted her in preparing the first complete edition of Robert's works (1881–93), and she also edited his correspondence of 1827–40 (published 1885).

B. Harding: *Concerto: the Story of Clara Schumann* (1961)

K. Stephenson: *Clara Schumann* (1969)

**Schumann, Elisabeth** (1888–1952). German soprano. Having studied singing in Dresden, Berlin and Hamburg, she made her operatic debut at the Hamburg Stadttheater as the Shepherd in Wagner's *Tannhäuser* in 1909. It was at the insistence of Richard Strauss, who had just been contracted as conductor of the Vienna Staatsoper, that she left Hamburg to become a member of the Vienna company in 1919. She had already been identified as an ideal interpreter of his music: she had appeared in Hamburg as Sophie in the second performance of *Der Rosenkavalier* in 1911, a role with which she became particularly closely associated; his esteem is exemplified in the dedication to her of his *Six Songs*, op. 68 (1918; settings of Brentano), and *Five Songs of the Orient*, op. 77 (1928), and also in his joining her for a recital tour of the USA in 1921. She was especially acclaimed as Sophie at the Metropolitan Opera, New York (1914), and during her first visit to England (1924); she appeared frequently at Covent Garden until 1931. Equally successful as a Mozartian, she underpinned her mercurial quality of voice with vivacious acting abilities that equipped her perfectly for such roles as Susanna (*The Marriage of Figaro*), Despina (*Così fan tutte*) and Zerlina (*Don Giovanni*).

Her reputation as a recitalist endures through her numerous recordings of lieder, especially those of Schubert, Schumann and Strauss, many of them with her second husband Karl Alwin as pianist (her first husband was Walther Puritz, an architect, and her third, Hans Kruegger, a dermatologist). Initially distressed by the unsympathetic atmosphere in Vienna (notorious for its hostile audiences), she overcame this to win an immense following, principally for her performances in works by Mozart and Strauss and also encompassing such roles as Micaela in Bizet's *Carmen*, Eva in Wagner's *Die Meistersinger*, Adele in Johann Strauss's *Die Fledermaus* (in which she caused a sensation through her imitation of a canary's trill), Laura in Korngold's *Der Ring des Polycrates* and Yvonne in Krenek's *Jonny spielt auf*. As a result of the Anschluss, she left Austria in 1938 and was thereafter based in New York, becoming an American citizen in 1944. She continued to teach and perform until the late 1940s, notably at the first Edinburgh Festival (1947), and in 1948 published a book entitled *German Song*.

**Schwartz, Anna Jacobson** (1915–). Anna Schwartz, as the collaborator with Milton Friedman in numerous articles, and in their *A Monetary History of the United States 1867–1960* (1963) and *Monetary Statistics* (1970), has exerted great influence on the economic approach and the attitude to money supply,

of American, British and other governments.

She was born in New York, and took degrees at Barnard and Columbia universities. Her research has been conducted at Columbia and at the National Bureau of Economic Research. Apart from her work on banking and monetarism, she is distinguished for her studies in economic history. She has also written on the international monetary system, on the gold standard and on international lending and in 1981–2 was Staff Director of the US Commission on the Role of Gold in the Domestic and International Monetary Systems.

**Schwarzkopf, (Olga Maria) Elisabeth (Friedrike)** (1915–). German soprano. Born in Jarotschin, Posen [now Poznań] province, the daughter of a Classics teacher, she studied at the Berlin Hochschule für Musik from 1934. In 1938 she joined the Berlin Städtische Oper, making her debut in *Parsifal* and soon undertaking major supporting roles, appearing as Zerbinetta in *Ariadne auf Naxos* (1941). She studied lieder with Maria Ivogün and gave a much acclaimed recital in Berlin in 1942. After World War II she became principal singer with the Vienna Staatsoper, and also took leading roles at Covent Garden in London (first appearing in 1947 as Donna Elvira and as Marzelline in *Fidelio*). She sang at La Scala, Milan, from 1949 and with the San Francisco Opera from 1955. In 1951 she created the role of Anne Trulove in Stravinsky's *The Rake's Progress* and that year took part in the Bayreuth Festival on its reopening after World War II. She also appeared at the Salzburg Festival nearly every year from 1949 to 1964. In addition to her appearances in opera (she was particularly acclaimed for such roles as Fiordiligi in *Così fan tutte* and the Countess in *The Marriage of Figaro*) she was noted for her lieder recitals and her concerts, which included works from Bach to Tippett. Her farewell recital tour of the USA occurred in 1975. She also made many superb recordings, especially with her husband Walter Legge, the artistic director of EMI records, whom she married in 1953.

In recent years, while continuing to give occasional recitals, she has been noted for her superb master-classes, for example at the Juilliard School in 1976 with Legge. In

1981 she enthralled a wide audience with master-classes filmed for British television.

**Schwimmer, Rosika** (1877–1948). Hungarian feminist and pacifist. Born in Budapest, after an early career as a musician she became a journalist and in her twenties took a prominent part in the feminist movement in Hungary. She organized a trades union for women, was a leader of the Women's Suffragist Society and edited a pacifist feminist journal, *A No* ('The Woman'), for 13 years. In 1909 Count Andrássy appointed her to the National Board of Child Welfare.

In 1914 she was working in London as a correspondent for several European newspapers and became deeply involved in the peace movement there and in the USA, signing the petition to President Wilson demanding an International Peace Conference, attending the International Congress of Women at The Hague in 1915, visiting Norway, Sweden and Denmark and becoming a Vice-President of the Women's International League for Peace and Freedom, of which JANE ADDAMS was President. Her most famous and ill-fated achievement was to persuade Henry Ford to sponsor a 'peace ship', the *SS Oscar II*, to visit the enemy nations on a pilgrimage in 1915. This inspired much ridicule, and Rosika left the ship in Christiania [now Oslo] before the expedition eventually broke up in Stockholm.

In October 1918 she returned to Hungary where she was elected to the National Council of Fifteen under Karolyi and was appointed Minister to Switzerland, the world's first woman ambassador. She resigned in 1919 when Béla Kun came to power and in 1920, with her life now in danger under the Horthy dictatorship, she was smuggled out on a boat down the Danube to the USA. There she found herself labelled a Bolshevik spy and in 1929 the Supreme Court refused her American citizenship because she said she would not bear arms in the event of war. In 1933 she launched a campaign for world citizenship for stateless people and in the late 1930s campaigned energetically against the fascism of Italy and Germany. Her feminism remained strong and and in 1935, supported by MARY BEARD, she proposed the establishment of a World Centre of Women's Archives. She lived in New York with her sister and in the year of her death, at the age of 81, was nominated for the Nobel Peace Prize.

**Scott, Charlotte Angas** (1858–1931). English mathematician. Born in Lincoln, after a private education she went to Girton College, Cambridge, where she was eighth on the Tripos list but as a woman was not allowed formal admission to a degree. While lecturing at Girton she gained a degree and then a DSc from the University of London.

In 1885 she was invited to the USA to inaugurate mathematics at the newly-established Bryn Mawr College. As a professor she published more than 30 papers in the developing field of algebraic geometry, with analysis of singularities for algebraic curves. She was elected Vice-president of the American Mathematical Society in 1906. In 1925 she retired and returned to Cambridge, England.

**Scott, Elizabeth Whitworth** (1898–1972). English architect. Although she was the daughter of a doctor, her family had a traditional connection with architecture, her grandfather being the great Victorian architect Sir Gilbert Scott. Educated at a private school in Bournemouth, she trained at the Architectural Association School, gaining her diploma in 1924. She worked in Welwyn Garden City, London and Cheltenham. Her most notable achievement was the design for the Shakespeare Memorial Theatre, Stratford-upon-Avon, which was chosen from 22 designs in 1928, and which she built in partnership with Maurice Chesterton. Her other work included extensions to Newnham College, Cambridge.

**Scott**, Lady **Margaret** (1875–?). English golfer. Lady Margaret was born in Wiltshire, where she learned to play golf on a course laid out in the grounds of her home, Stowell Park. Her father was Earl of Eldon. Her brothers, Osmund, Denys and Michael Scott, were all good at golf. Women had taken part in golf tournaments since the 16th century, but in 1893 the Ladies' Golf Union was formed and Lady Margaret was British Ladies' Champion for the first three years

(1893–5), after which she retired from competitive golf. Although she was supple and her backswing was in good form, ladies' courses were separate and the standards not comparable with today's. Her title helped make the game respectable for other women. On her marriage she became Lady Hamilton Russell.

**Scott, Rose** (1847–1925). Australian feminist. Born in Glendon, New South Wales, she lived in Sydney from 1879, and in 1891 founded the Womanhood Suffrage League, becoming its Secretary. She worked initially with the Marxist, Dora Montefiore, who later became a militant suffragette in England, and VIDA GOLDSTEIN who left to form her own Women's Federation. Rose lobbied energetically, not only for the franchise, but also for protective legislation, shorter hours for shop assistants, the raising of the age of consent, and social purity. She refused all offers of marriage, saying 'life is too short to waste on the admiration of one man'. She refused to stand for Parliament, although she organized the League for Political Education after the franchise was granted, becoming its President in 1910. She was also President of the Peace Society from 1907 and remained a convinced pacifist during World War I.

**Scott** [née Hopkins], **Sheila (Christine)** (1927-1988). English aviator. Born in Worcester, after leaving school she worked as a VAD nurse, and then acted in small parts in films and repertory companies. Between 1945 and 1950 she was married to Rupert Bellamy. In 1959 she started flying and to her surprise won the first races she entered, in an old RAF biplane, and won the 1960 De Havilland Trophy.

From 1964 she attempted and won many flying records; by 1971 she had set up some 100 internal or world records and won over 50 trophies. In 1965 she completed the longest ever consecutive solo flight of 31,000 miles round the world, in 189 flying hours. She was awarded the Harmon Trophy in 1967 and made OBE in 1968. Two more solo round-the-world flights followed, notably the first solo light aircraft flight, equator to equator, over the North Pole in 1971. NASA, the American space agency, monitored her mental and physical reactions

and also measured air pollution along her route for the five-week journey.

Between flights, much time was taken up with glamorous public appearances to raise money for the next attempt at record breaking. Sheila was the founder and first Governor of the British section of the Ninety Nines, and founder of the British Balloon and Airships Club.

S. Scott: *I Must Fly* (1968)
———— : *On Top of the World* (1973)
———— : *Barefoot in the Sky* (1974)

**Scott-Brown** [née Lakofski], **Denise** (1931–). American architect. Born in Northern Rhodesia, she emigrated to the USA in 1958, having been educated in South Africa at the University of Witwatersrand and in London at the Architectural Association School, where she gained a diploma in tropical architecture in 1956. In the USA she taught at the University of Pennsylvania (1960–65) and the University of California (1965–8). Since 1967 she has worked in private practice with Venturi and Ranch while continuing to hold visiting professorships at various institutions. She is particularly known for her city and traffic studies in New Jersey, Philadelphia, Miami and Washington, and especially for her large-scale designs for renewal of deprived urban areas. She has written widely on social conditions and their relation to architecture and planning. She has been the subject of both admiration and hostility, as a radical reformer in her profession. Her numerous projects in the 1980s have included the centre city plan for Memphis, and the New Building at Seattle Art Museum.

R.H. Bletter: *Venturi, Ranch & Scott-Brown: A Generation of Architecture* (1984)

**Scudder, Ida (Sophia)** (1870–1960). American medical missionary. Born in India into a family of medical missionaries, she was educated in the USA at the Woman's Medical College of Pennsylvania and Cornell University Medical School, from which she graduated in 1899.

She returned to India and developed the Mary Taber Schell Memorial Hospital (begun in 1902) and founded the Vellore Christian Medical College (1918). Her aim was to train Indian women to become doctors and to serve medical needs where purdah was customary. She also established a nursing school and other hospital and health services. Her niece, Ida Belle Scudder, joined her work at Vellore in the 1930s.

On her 88th birthday Ida Sophia was given an award by Cornell University for her contributions to medical education, public health, and international understanding.

D.C. Wilson: *Dr Ida: the Story of Dr Ida Scudder of Vellore* (1960)

**Scudéry, Madeleine de** (1607–1701). French writer. Madeleine de Scudéry first came to Paris in 1639 and frequented the famous salon of the Marquise de RAMBOUILLET. Eventually she started a salon of her own which, like the Hôtel de Rambouillet, became associated with the cult of *préciosité* – excessive refinement in manners and expression. In collaboration with her brother Georges, she began writing novels, the most famous being *Artamène, ou le grand Cyrus* (1649–53) – a vast tome which first appeared in parts, and whose last five volumes she wrote unaided. The work was an immediate success in France and was translated into many languages. Her novels consist of long, meandering tales with numerous digressions, linked to a central love story, and they contain portraits of contemporary figures disguised as characters from another age. When her brother left Paris she continued to write. Her two principal works are *Clélie* (1654), a ten-volume novel which contains the famous *Carte du tendre* (a guide to friendship *à la précieuse*), and *Amalida, ou l'esclave riche* (1660–63). Molière satirized her in his play *Les précieuses ridicules* (first performed in 1659). As the works of Molière and Boileau became popular, Madeleine de Scudéry found that her public had diminished. Her last novel, *Mathilde d'Aguilan*, was published in 1667 and was followed only by essays, treatises and occasional verses.

D. McDougall: *Madeleine de Scudéry* (1938)

**Seacole, Mary (Jane)** (1805–81). Jamaican nurse and businesswoman. Born in Kingston, Jamaica, Mary Grant learned Creole medical arts and hotel-keeping from her mother, a free black woman; of her father, a Scottish army officer, little is known. Her early travels included two visits to England, to which she always felt strong allegiance.

Her brief marriage to Edwin Horatio Seacole in 1836 ended with his death; thereafter she always lived independently. She rebuilt her hotel after the great Kingston fire of 1843, and gained excellent field training in medicine during two epidemics of cholera and one of yellow fever, in the latter case being asked to take charge of nursing arrangements at Up-Park Military Camp. She once made a post-mortem dissection of a baby who had died of cholera to try and learn more about the disease. She had followed her brother Edward to New Granada (now Colombia and Panama), where she led a colourful life among coarse adventurers, establishing hotels at Cruces, Gorgona and Escribanos, travelling, nursing, and briefly trying gold prospecting.

On hearing of the Crimean war she obtained references and was keen to offer her services to the British army, but on voyaging to England she received only official rebuffs, apparently because of her colour. She therefore paid for her own 3000-mile journey to the Crimea, trying to recoup her expenses by setting up as a sutler with a distant relative, Mr Day. The British Hotel which she built and ran at Spring Hill near Balaclava became a centre for both officers and soldiers; there she prohibited drunkenness and gambling. She used her nursing skills more directly than did FLORENCE NIGHTINGALE, whom she met several times; 'Mother' or 'Aunty' Seacole tended wounds on the battlefields under gunfire, as well as relieving symptoms of jaundice, dysentery, frostbite and other suffering.

The abrupt ending of the war in 1856 left her in debt, but she was acclaimed by *The Times*, *Punch*, and the *Illustrated London News*, and subscriptions were raised to release her from bankruptcy. Her lively autobiography was a best-seller; she conveys 'how hard the right woman had to struggle to convey herself to the right place'. Her later life was spent in Jamaica and London.

M. Seacole: *The Wonderful adventures of Mrs. Seacole in many lands* (1857; ed. Z. Alexander and A. Dewjee, 1984)

**Seaman, Elizabeth (Cochrane)** [pseud.: Nelly Bly] (1867–1922). American journalist. Born at Cochran Mills, Pennsylvania, she was educated at home and at school in Indiana until her family moved to Pittsburgh in 1881. She got her first job in journalism after sending an impassioned letter to the *Pittsburgh Dispatch* in response to an article, 'What Girls are Good For', which restricted women to housework and family. She wrote a series on working girls, before becoming Society and Arts Editor. Her pseudonym was taken from a popular Stephen Foster song.

In 1887 she went to Mexico with her mother and sent back a series of articles on social conditions there, collected in *Six Months in Mexico* (1885). On her return she moved to the *New York World*, and her exposé of the treatment of the insane (*Ten Days in a Mad-House*), was achieved by getting herself committed to the asylum at Blackwell's Island. She also wrote stories on slum life, sweat-shops, and minor crime using the same undercover techniques. She achieved world fame in 1890 when her editor sent her on a world tour, attempting to beat the fictional 80-day record of Jules Verne's Phineas Fogg. Nelly took only 72 days, travelling by boat, train and horse, stopping *en route* to interview Verne in France and describing her adventures in *Nelly Bly's Book: Around the World in Seventy-two Days* (1890).

In 1895 she married an elderly tycoon, Robert Seaman, 50 years her senior. He died in 1904 and she tried to run his business, but lengthy lawsuits with corrupt employees absorbed most of her fortune. She returned to journalism in 1919, but was less successful; at her death she was working for the *New York Journal*.

T. Lister: *Nelly Bly: First Woman of the News* (1978)

**Secord** [née Ingersoll], **Laura** (1775–1868). Canadian heroine. Born in Massachusetts, she went to Upper Canada [now Ontario] with her Loyalist parents after the American Revolution. There she married Sergeant James Secord, who joined the militia in the war of 1812 against the USA. In 1813, when the Americans invaded the Niagara Peninsula and soldiers were billeted in her house in Queenstown, she overheard talk about plans for a surprise attack on Beaver Dams. She crept through American lines and walked 19 miles to warn the militia commander Lieutenant James Fitzgibbon. Although he had already learned of the attack, Laura Secord was acclaimed as a heroine. (She is immortalized in the name of a leading brand of Canadian chocolate.)

**Seghers** [née Reiling], **Anna** [pseud. of Netty Radvanyi] (1900–83). German writer. Born in Mainz, the daughter of an art dealer, she studied art history at Heidelberg and Cologne and in 1924 submitted a thesis on Rembrandt's treatment of Judaism. In 1925 she married the Communist Laslo Radvanyi, and joined the Communist Party in 1929, the year after the publication of her first novel, about a fishermen's revolt, *Der Aufstand der Fischer von St Barbara*, which won the prestigious Kleist Prize. In 1933 she was arrested but escaped to Paris with her two children. She was an active supporter of the Republicans in the Spanish Civil War and after the German occupation of France in 1941 moved to Mexico, returning to East Berlin in 1947. She travelled widely, to the USSR, China and South America, and received several awards.

All her novels deal with oppression and the fight for justice, and they include *The Seventh Cross* (1942; Ger. trans. 1962), about an escape from a pre-war concentration camp; *Transit* (1943; in Eng.), about German refugees en route from France to America; *Die Toten bleiben jung* (1949), a political novel about inter-war Germany; and *Die Entscheidung* (1959), about life under socialism; her later works include *Die Überfahrt* (1971). Other writings include essays, criticism and short stories. She was a greatly respected figure in the post-war intellectual life of East Germany and was President of the Association of German Writers.

**Sei Shonagon** (*c*966–1013). Japanese writer. The daughter of a poet, Kiyohara no Motosuke, she became Lady-in-waiting to the Empress Sadako, who presided over a frivolous and witty court. Her life and style contrast with the serious tone of her contemporary SHIKIBU MURASAKI. Her chief work is *Makura no sashi* (*c*1000–15), a 'pillow book' or series of impressions, anecdotes, diary entries and written observations arranged by mood, such as 'annoying', 'amusing'. It is vivid, sarcastic, poetic and frank, and full of outspoken opinions.

I.I. Morris (trans.): *The Pillow Book of Sei Shonagon*

**Semenova, Ekaterina** (1786–1849). Russian actress. At the age of 10 she began studying at the St Petersburg Theatre School under the actor Dmitrevsky, and made her first appearance at 17, gradually becoming a leading actress in the plays of Ozerov, Racine, Shakespeare and Schiller. Her coaches included Prince Sharkovsky, the dramatist and imperial theatre director, and Gnedich, the poet. She was much admired for her great beauty, fine deep voice, and passionate if erratic acting, and is celebrated in some of Pushkin's poems. Her great rivalry with the French tragedienne, Madame George, then very popular in Russia, was widely publicised, and in 1820 she left the stage, convinced she was no longer the leading actress. She returned in 1822, creating a sensation in *Phèdre* the following year, but in 1826 she married Prince Ivan Gagarin, and thereafter played only in the private theatres of Moscow and St Petersburg [now Leningrad].

**Semiramis.** *See* SAMMURAMAT.

**Seneghun, Queen of.** *See* YOKO, Madam.

**Senesh, Hannah** (1921–44). Hungarian heroine. Born into a Jewish family in Hungary, she fiercely opposed the rise of fascism in Europe during her late teens. At the beginning of World War II she emigrated to Israel. She joined a commando unit dedicated to bringing Jews out of the occupied territories. After parachuting into Yugoslavia in 1944 she managed to reach Hungary but was captured and eventually executed after suffering severe torture.

H. Senesh: *Life and Diary* (1945; Eng. trans., 1971)

**Serao, Matilde** (1857–1927). Italian journalist and novelist. Born in Patras, Greece, of a Greek ' father and Neapolitan mother, Matilde graduated as a teacher at the Scuola Normale, Naples, and began writing articles in 1876–8 while working in a telegraph office. Her first novel was *Cuore Infermo* (1881). She then joined the Rome newspaper *Capitan Fracassa*, and contributed to several leading periodicals. Popular success came with the doom-laden, romantic novel *Fantasia* (1882), and with her brilliant, realistic reporting of Naples life, collected in *Il ventre di Napoli*

(1884). In 1885 she married the writer Edoardo Scarfoglio, and published her *Conquista di Roma*, a vivid novel about a provincial politician overwhelmed by Roman society. This theme was continued, with a provincial journalist as protagonist, in *Vita e Avventure di Riccardo Joanna* (1887). The novel reflected the failure of Serao and Scarfoglio to establish their own paper *Il Corriere di Roma*, although they eventually moved to Naples, and started *Il Corriere di Napoli*. Matilde Serao remained a prolific writer of novels and stories, including *All'erta sentinella* (1889), the famous *Il Paese di Cuccagna* (1891), *Suor Giovanna della Croce* (1901) and *Ella nar Ripose* (1914).

**Seton, Elizabeth Ann** [Mother Seton] (1774–1821). American founder. Born into a distinguished colonial family, Elizabeth lost her mother while still a young child. From an early age she showed great concern for the poor and sick, gaining the title of Protestant Sister of Charity, and her writings were of a spiritual nature.

She married a wealthy young merchant, William Seton, in 1794. The loss of his fortune so wrecked his health that they travelled to Italy, but he died there in 1803, leaving the family destitute. Elizabeth became attracted to Catholicism and she was received into the Catholic Church two years after her return to New York. Her new faith meant she was rejected by friends and family and unable to earn a living. She was invited by a priest to open a school in Baltimore, which soon attracted students and young teachers; the latter took simple vows as the Sisters of St Joseph. In 1809 she moved to New Maryland and here adopted for her teaching sisters the rule of the Sisters of Charity of St Vincent de Paul. She herself was appointed Superior but maintained legal guardianship of her children. In addition to training teachers and preparing textbooks, Mother Seton translated religious books, wrote spiritual treatises, and visited the poor and the sick. Above all, she has been described as laying the foundations of the American parochial school system.

R. Seton: *Memoirs, Letters and Journals of Elizabeth Seton* (1869)
J.F. Hindman: *Elizabeth Ann Seton* (1976)
M. Celeste: *Elizabeth Ann Seton* (1980)

**Séverine** [pseud. of Caroline [née Rémy] Guebhard] (1855–1929). French journalist. An extremely innovative and influential journalist, she wrote in Jules Valles' *Le Reveil*, and in other journals such as *Gil Blas*, *La France* and *Le matin* in the late 1870s and early 1880s, and from 1886 to 1888 edited the *Cri du peuple*. She revolutionized journalism: she was the first to conduct investigative interviews designed to reveal the personality, the first woman reporter to go down a mine, and was a tireless campaigner on behalf of the poor and oppressed. She later worked freelance after her views were found too individualistic, and gradually found herself blacked by leading papers because of her outspoken articles on abortion and sexual violence. Several of her socialist and feminist articles were collected in *Pages rouges* (1893), *Pages mystiques* (1895) and *Vers la lumière* (1900). In 1900 she wrote on behalf of women's suffrage in Marguerite Durand's *La fronde*. Her strong socialist leanings after World War I led her to join Communist groups briefly in 1920: When *Paris-soir* was launched in 1923 she wrote its first editorial.

Séverine: *Line* (1921)
E. Le Garrec: *Séverine, une Rebelle* (1982)

**Sévigné** *See* DE SÉVIGNÉ.

**Sexton, Anne (Harvey)** (1928–74). American poet. She was born in Newton, Massachusetts. Like SYLVIA PLATH, she grew up in Wellesley but after graduating from Garland Junior College she married Alfred Sexton in 1948; they had two daughters. She worked occasionally as a model in Boston, and began writing. She met Plath at one of Robert Lowell's poetry classes at Boston University and they became close friends, sharing similar preoccupations with death and influencing each other's work.

Her first collection, *To Bedlam and Part Way Back*, was published in 1960 and was based on her own experience of breakdown, attempted suicide and treatment. She then won a scholarship to Radcliffe College and continued to produce highly personal poetry in *All my Pretty Ones* (1962). By the late 1960s her reputation was established, despite her inner unhappiness. She

published *Live or Die* (1966) which won a Pulitzer Prize, obtained a Guggenheim award in 1969, published *Love Poems* (1969) and got a job as a lecturer in creative writing at Boston University (1969–72), followed by a professorship. Her next collections, *Transformations* (1971) and *The Book of Folly* (1972), explored less personal themes, especially political situations, but she returned to the confessional mode in *The Death Notebooks* (1974) and *The Awful Rowing toward God* (1975). During these years her marriage had collapsed and she was frequently depressed. Her divorce came shortly before her suicide. In 1976 her daughter Linda edited her final poems in *45 Mercy Street*.

L. Sexton, ed.: *Anne Sexton: a Self Portrait in Letters* (1977)

**Shabanova, Anna (Nikitichna)** (1848–1932). Russian doctor and feminist. From an upper-class family and well educated, she was briefly connected with radical activities through establishing a dressmaking collective, the Ivanova Workshop in Moscow, in 1866. After six months in prison she became a medical student in Helsinki, one of the first students at the new Women's Medical Academy. She taught and wrote about children's diseases and became involved with philanthropic feminist circles. In 1895 she became the leader of the Mutual Philanthropic Society with Nadezhda Filosova, and in 1905 established a suffrage division, the Electoral Department, which she led until 1917. The Society organized campaigns concerned with charitable work, education, and social problems, and tried to unite women's organizations to affiliate to the International Council of Women. She also campaigned with another doctor, Mariya Pokrovskaya (the leader of the Women's Progressive Party), against legalized prostitution, but she did not encourage militant suffrage campaigns. During World War I she organized voluntary agencies and worked with the War Industries Committee, welcoming Emmeline PANKHURST (who had called for similar mobilization of feminists in the UK) when she was sent by Lloyd-George to Moscow in 1914. After the Revolution, with its acceptance of the principles of female equality, Shabanova returned to her work on paediatrics, publishing her last work on the subject in 1926.

**Shafiq, Dori'a** (1910–75). Egyptian feminist. A member of an upper-class family and a noted beauty, she insisted on continuing her education after finishing ' school. She obtained a doctorate from the Sorbonne and then returned to Egypt to lead the emerging feminist movement. She founded Bint-E-Nil ('Daughters of the Nile') to campaign for women's rights. In 1951 she led a march of 1500 women who forced their way into the Egyptian parliament demanding the vote, which was eventually granted in 1956. She also trained in guerilla warfare and was actively involved in the nationalist campaign against the British during the Suez crisis. In later years she continued to campaign for greater democracy, and her open opposition to President Nasser meant that she had to live in seclusion in Cairo. She was married to Naur Raqai, a lawyer, and had two daughters. She died at the age of 65, falling from her sixth-floor flat in Cairo.

**Shagrat al-Durr** (*d* 1258). Arabian queen. She was bought as a Turkoman slave by the Caliph of Baghdad, Sālih Ayyub, who later married her and ruled with her in Egypt. She acted as his Regent when he was away on campaigns during the Crusades. Both fled to Mansûra in the Nile Delta to arrange their defence against the French in 1249. Sālih Ayyub died, but Shagrat concealed the event, forged his signature and collected an army which defeated and captured Louis IX of France. She then handed over to her son Turan Shah, but the army reinstated her as Sultan, a most unusual position for a woman. She retired when it was clear that the Caliphate disapproved, but kept power by marrying her successor, the soldier Aibak, whom she eventually had murdered in 1257. Unable to conceal the crime, she was beaten to death by harem slaves on the orders of Aibak's previous wife (whom she had banished) and son, and her body was flung on a rubbish tip before being placed in her tomb, which still exists.

**Sh'arawi, Huda** (1882–1947). Egyptian women's rights worker. Born in Minia into a wealthy household, she was educated in Turkish and French, these being the preferred languages of the elite. She learned Arabic by herself. In 1910 she opened a school for girls, offering them a general education rather than a vocational training such as midwifery. During the nationalist demonstrations in Egypt against the British, she organized hundreds of women to participate. The first women's association in Egypt was formed in 1920 with Huda Sh'arawi as its head. In 1923 she went to Rome as the Egyptian representative to the International Conference of Women. She established the Women's Union in 1924, and founded the journal *Egyptian Woman*, which was published both in Arabic and French to acquaint all women with the goals of the Union. The first secondary school for girls was opened in 1927 and co-educational university classes were held from 1929. After 1929 all Huda's speeches were delivered in Arabic. She attended the international women's conferences in 1935 and 1939. In 1944 she helped to set up the All Arab Federation of Women and in 1945 called for the abolition of all atomic weapons.

**Shaw,    Anna    (Howard)**    (1847–1919). American minister and suffragist. Born in Newcastle-upon-Tyne, England, into a Unitarian family who moved to America when she was three, Anna grew up in Lawrence, Massachusetts, and at 15 began teaching in a new frontier school. At the end of the Civil War, living with her sister's family in Big Rapids, she heard a Universalist woman preacher, Marianna Thompson, and decided that this was her vocation. After studying in the local high school she gave her first sermon in 1870 and was licensed as a Methodist preacher in 1871. She spent two years at Albion College and then entered the divinity school of Boston University in 1876, supporting herself by 'substitute preaching' until saved from virtual starvation by the Women's Foreign Missionary Society, and graduating in 1878. As pastor in East Dennis, Cape Cod, she fought hard against the Methodist authorities before leaving the Methodist Episcopal Church, being finally ordained as the first woman minister in the Methodist Protestant Church in 1880.

In 1883 she changed course and studied medicine, again at Boston, graduating in 1886, but her struggles had convinced her that the principal battle was for suffrage, and as a lecturer she became one of the movement's most influential women, a close associate of SUSAN B. ANTHONY and LUCY STONE, speaking throughout the whole of the United States. She eventually became President of the National American Woman Suffrage Association in 1904, after CARRIE CATT, but her leadership was marred by poor judgement and by her rifts with other members and with male supporters. In November 1915 she resigned and Catt became President again. During World War I she chaired the Women's Committee of the Council of National Defense, and shortly before her death campaigned for Woodrow Wilson's peace treaty and for the League of Nations. She died just as the long-fought for suffrage amendment was about to be finally ratified.

**Sheehy-Skeffington, Hannah** (1877–1946). Irish patriot and feminist. The daughter of David Sheehy, MP for South Meath, she was born in Kenturk, County Cork, and educated in Dublin. She obtained an MA from the National University of Ireland, and became a teacher. She was a founder member of the Irish Association of Women Graduates in 1901, joined the Irish Women's Suffrage and Local Government Association, and helped to found the militant Irish Women's Franchise League with CONSTANCE MARKIEWICZ in 1908. She took part in the Irish contingent in the great suffrage marches in London in the summer of 1910, and led many deputations in Dublin. In 1912 she was arrested and spent two months in prison for protesting against the exclusion of women from the Home Rule Bill, and went on hunger-strike in sympathy with the English suffragists who were being denied political status. By 1913 she had become Chairwoman of the Irish Franchise League and had been dismissed from her lectureship in German at the Rathmines School of Commerce because of her militant suffrage activities.

During World War I she became more involved with Irish nationalism than with the suffrage fight. In 1903 she married the radical journalist, Francis Skeffington, and they adopted the joint surname of Sheehy-Skeffington. In 1916 he was arrested, having witnessed the shooting of an unarmed boy by British soldiers. He was shot without trial

the next morning. An enquiry by a Royal Commission led to criticism of the officer involved, but Hannah never forgave the British. In 1919 she petitioned President Wilson at the Peace Conference on behalf of Irish women, to intervene in Ireland, and she travelled throughout the USA raising funds for the IRA. She spent the rest of her life in Dublin, where she was involved in local politics and became a town councillor.

**Sheepshanks, Mary** (1872–1958). English educationist, feminist and pacifist. The eldest daughter of the 13 children of the Bishop of Norwich, Mary was a lifelong unbeliever. Educated at Liverpool Girls' High School and Newnham College, Cambridge, she became a social worker, 1894–7, in Southwark and Stepney. From 1897 to 1913 she was Vice-Principal, but de facto Principal, of the radical and experimental Morley (Evening) College for Working Men and Women. In 1907 she became a public speaker for the non-violent wing of the Women's Suffrage movement and in 1913 she toured Belgium, Austria, Germany, Czechoslovakia and Russian Poland, lecturing in French and German on women's emancipation. A convinced pacifist, she played the key role in keeping alive the world-wide woman's movement as an internationalist ideal, editing and distributing the monthly *Ius Suffragii* via neutral countries across 'enemy' frontiers. After the war she became the first secretary of the Fight the Famine Committee (later Save the Children Fund), and then the International Secretary, based in Geneva, of the Women's International League for Peace and Freedom, founded by JANE ADDAMS. In 1929 she organized, under its auspices, the first international scientific conference on Modern Methods of Warfare and the Protection of Civilians. In 1930–31 she courageously investigated and publicized Polish atrocities in the Ukraine – 'the bullied had become the bullies'. Able, immensely public-spirited, a fascinating talker but often a 'difficult' colleague, Mary Sheepshanks suffered all her life from a lack of personal confidence and she was forgotten for a generation after her death. Her unpublished memoirs, *The Long Day's Task*, are held in the Fawcett Library and testify to her life of humanist feminism and pacifism as well as to her sense of indebtedness to all her women friends.

S. Oldfield: *Spinsters of this Parish – The life and times of F.M. Mayor and Mary Sheepshanks* (1984)

**Sheldon** [née French], **May** (1848–1936). American traveller. She belonged to a wealthy, cultured family, probably Southern, with Boston connections. She travelled widely with her family and was educated in Italy. By 1886 she had married a businessman, Eli Lemon Sheldon, and managed her own publishing firm, Saxon and Company. In 1886 she published her own translation of Gustave Flaubert's *Salammbô* and in 1889 a novel, *Herbert Severence*, from which some reconstruction of her own background is possible. Her heroine is a feminist, stating 'personal independence to a capable woman is a trait no sacrifice is too severe to make to secure'.

In 1891 May set off for Africa, leaving her husband in Naples. She proposed to study native customs and collect handicrafts and weapons in the Masai country, as well as to demonstrate that women can travel as well as men. Travelling in a palanquin carried by Zanzibaris, on ceremonial occasions she wore a court gown, artificial jewels and a blonde wig to impress tribal chiefs. She became known as Bébé Bwana, Swahili for 'Lady Boss'. She made several descents into the crater containing Lake Chala and circumnavigated it in a pontoon. On her return Lake Chala was the subject of her address to the British Association in Cardiff. In 1892 her husband died; she published *Sultan to Sultan*, describing adventures such as a python sleeping on her palanquin, and in the same year was elected among the first women Fellows of the Royal Geographical Society.

In 1894 she made a safari to the Belgian Congo and was granted facilities for research by King Leopold. For work here and for raising money in the USA for the Belgian Red Cross during World War I she was made a Chevalier de l'Ordre de la Couronne by King Albert of Belgium. She died in London.

**Shelley, Mary Wollstonecraft Godwin** (1797–1851). English novelist. She was born in London, the daughter of William Godwin and MARY WOLLSTONECRAFT. Her mother died after her birth. Brought up by a difficult, jealous stepmother she received no formal education, but read widely and was deeply influenced by Godwin's rationalism. At the age of 16 she met Shelley and they eloped to the Continent. They were disowned by Godwin, but eventually married, after the suicide of Harriet, Shelley's wife, in 1816. Mary's most famous book, *Frankenstein: or The modern Prometheus* was written while touring the Alps with Byron and Shelley, following Byron's suggestion that they should each write a ghost story.

The Shelleys' first son died, and after living for a year at Marlow, they left England in 1818, staying in various Italian cities, especially Pisa. Their baby Clara died in 1818, and the following summer their young son William also died after a sudden illness, plunging Mary into a deep depression. In July 1822 Shelley was drowned at Lerici. After spending some months with the Leigh Hunts at Genoa, Mary returned to England, determined not to re-marry, but to work as a professional writer to support her last child, Percy. She worked incessantly, producing short stories, travel books, biographies, reviews and six novels, including *Valperga* (1823); *The Last Man* (1826), a gloomy vision of the destruction of humanity by plague in the 21st century; *Lodore* (1835) and *Falkner* (1837), both defences of Shelley. When their financial circumstances improved after 1838, she began editing Shelley's works. After the death of Shelley's father in 1840 she started a biography of her husband, but her health was now poor and the work remained incomplete at her death.

M. Leighton: *Shelley's Mary: a Life of Mary Godwin Shelley* (1973)

**Sheppard** [née Malcolm], **Kate (Wilson)** (1848–1934). New Zealand feminist. Born in Islay, Scotland, she emigrated to New Zealand in the late 1860s and married a businessman and Christchurch City Councillor, Walter Sheppard. A feminist from her youth she concentrated first on physical emancipation, taking up cycling and dress reform, and then on equal status within marriage. She joined the Women's Christian Temperance Union and, after lobbying unsuccessfully for protective legislation for women and children, decided that the vote must be obtained before women would be able to exert any public influence. She led the Union into the franchise campaign between 1885 and 1890, published numerous pamphlets, such as *Ten Reasons why the Women of New Zealand should Vote*, and organized lectures, petitions and energetic parliamentary lobbies in the early 1890s, which resulted in the granting of the vote in September 1894.

She visited England and met international suffragists, and on her return to New Zealand in 1896 became the first President of the National Council of Women; one of the aims of the Council, the acceptance of women as parliamentary candidates, was eventually achieved in 1919. (The first woman to be elected, Elizabeth McCombs, did not enter Parliament until 1933, 40 years after the vote was granted.) She continued to work for women's rights at home and abroad, becoming honorary Vice-president of the International Council of Women in 1909. She wrote a brief history of her campaigns, *Women's Suffrage in New Zealand*, in 1907.

**Sheridan** [née Frewen]**, Clare (Consuelo)** (1885–1970). Irish sculptor, traveller and writer. She was born in London. Her father was Irish, and through her American mother she was the cousin of Sir Winston Churchill. Educated in Sussex, County Cork, at Paris and in Germany, she seemed set for a society life, especially after her marriage to the stockbroker William Sheridan in 1910. But after the death of her second daughter Elizabeth she began to work as a sculptor, turning professional after her husband was killed in 1915. A successful portraitist, she accepted an unexpected invitation from the Soviet Trade Delegation in 1920 to visit Moscow, and completed busts of Zinoviev, Kamenev, Lenin and Trotsky. Ostracized on her return to London she left for the USA, writing of her experiences in *Russian Diaries* (1921).

Her next career was as a traveller, exploring Mexico, and as a journalist for the *New York World*. She returned to Europe to cover the Irish Civil War, and won respect as a war correspondent for her reporting of the evacuation of Smyrna in the Greek–Turkish War. She interviewed Atatürk and other leaders, explored the southern USSR on a motorcycle, moved to Constantinople [now Istanbul] in 1926 (*Turkish Kaleidoscope*, 1926) and then lived briefly in Algeria. She continued to write and to work as a sculptor, turning from modelling to carving after the death of her son Dick in 1937, and spending some time working on an Indian reservation in the Rockies (*Redskin Interlude*, 1938). Her portraits include busts of politicians and cultural leaders, such as Gandhi and Lifar, but she produced some fine religious works when she settled in Galway after World War II and became a Roman Catholic.

C. Sheridan: *To the Four Winds* (1957)

**Shub, Esther** (1894–1959). Russian film editor and compilation specialist. She was born in the Ukraine and in 1922 she was hired to work in the emerging Soviet film industry; in the course of five years she worked as an editor on 200 foreign films and 10 Russian films. In 1927 she wrote and edited a compilation film for the anniversary of the February Revolution, *The Fall of the Romanov Dynasty*, covering the years 1912 to 1917, including footage from the Czar's own family films. She also wrote and edited a compilation film to celebrate the October Revolution, covering the years 1917 to 1927, *The Great Road* (1927). Sergei Eisenstein consulted her material when he made *October*. Shub also edited footage on Tolstoy, *The Russia of Nicholas II and Leo Tolstoy* (1928). She subsequently produced *Spain* (1939), *Twenty Years of Soviet Cinema* (1940) and *Across the Araks* (1947). Her films remain among the finest examples of creative editing in compilation films.

**Siddons** [née Kemble]**, Sarah** (1755–1831). English actress. Eldest of the 12 children of the actor Roger Kemble, she acted with her father's touring players and began her professional acting career at 18 with William Siddons, whom she married in 1773, against her parents' wishes. Success in the provincial theatre brought her to the attention of David Garrick, who engaged her for a season at Drury Lane Theatre, London (1775–6). She was a failure and returned to the provinces: Manchester (1776–7), Bath and Bristol (1777–81), at Richard Brinsley Sheridan's request, and played a considerable variety of parts. She returned to Drury Lane in 1782 to triumph as Isabella in Garrick's version of

*The Fatal Marriage.* She played her first Shakespearean characters in London in 1783, and played Lady Macbeth, her most outstanding role, for the first time in 1785. Among other parts that she made her own were Volumnia (1788), the Queen in *Hamlet* (1796), Mrs Haller in *The Stranger* (1798), Elvira in *Pizarro* (1799), and Hermione in *A Winter's Tale* (1801–2). In 1803 she moved with her brother John Kemble to Covent Garden and appeared regularly from 1806 until her retirement in 1812, after a farewell performance of *Macbeth*.

Sarah Siddons was an extremely dignified, statuesque woman, with a deep resonant voice and ample gestures. Hazlitt wrote of her, 'She was tragedy personified', and of her performance of the sleepwalking scene in *Macbeth*, it was said that one could 'smell the blood'. Byron, Haydon, Erskine, Leigh Hunt and Horace Walpole all praised her. Dr Johnson called her 'a prodigious fine woman'. She was also 'thrillingly passionate' – reeling on stage as Volumnia, for example, as though drunk with her son's glory. There is a statue of her by Chantrey in Westminster Abbey and a portrait by Sir Joshua Reynolds called *The Tragic Muse* at Dulwich. Her strong personality and uncompromising approach did not escape criticism. Her shrewd business sense was regarded as avarice and her dislike of publicity as unapproachability. At the end of her career she grew stout and her acting manner was thought outmoded and monotonous. Whilst pursuing her career, Sarah Siddons also bore seven children, two daughters dying in infancy and two sons and a daughter surviving her.

R. Manvell: *Sarah Siddons: Portrait of an Artist* (1971)

**Siebold, Charlotte Heidenreich von** (1788–1859). German doctor. Her father died when she was young and Charlotte was adopted by her stepfather, Damian Siebold. Both her parents were doctors and she worked with her mother, JOSEPHA VON SIEBOLD. Charlotte gained her doctorate at the University of Giessen in 1817 after defending her thesis on ectopic pregnancy. She married a military surgeon in 1829. She assisted at the births of eminent people in various countries, including the future English queen, VICTORIA.

**Siebold** [née Henning], **(Regina) Josepha von** (1771–1849). German doctor. She was trained to manage her uncle's large agricultural estates. After her marriage she had a daughter, CHARLOTTE HEIDENREICH VON SIEBOLD, and was widowed while young. In 1795 she married Damian Siebold, a doctor, and worked as a midwife and his assistant. Her husband became mentally incapable of continuing his practice, so Josepha studied obstetrics in Würzburg under her brother-in-law. In 1807 the Archducal Medical College at Darmstadt granted her permission to practise obstetrics and pox vaccination, but she had difficulty in obtaining payment from her patients. In 1815 she gained her doctorate in obstetrics from the University of Giessen, the first woman to be granted this title by a German university. She continued to run a charitable practice. Her daughter assisted her.

**Sigurdsen, Gertrud** (1923–). Swedish politician. Sigurdsen's political career began in the Confederation of Swedish Trade Unions, where she was a Secretary for 15 years from 1949. In 1964 she became Information Secretary, and joined the Executive of the Social Democratic Party in 1968, being elected a Member of Parliament the following year. By 1973 she was Minister for International Development Assistance, and in 1976 a member of the Committee on Foreign Affairs, of which she was Vice-Chair in 1979–82. She became Minister for Public Health in 1982, and in 1985 was confirmed as Minister for Health and Social Affairs. Other women prominent in recent Swedish politics have been Anita Gradin, Minister for Foreign Trade, Karin Ahrland, Minister for Public Health (1981–2), and Anna-Greta Leijon, Minister of Sexual Equality.

**Sillanpää, Miina** (1866–1952). Finnish politician and feminist. A strong feminist, she became a Member of Parliament when the country was still ruled by Russia in 1907, and remained an MP for 40 years. After World War I she became a City Councillor in Helsinki and edited a trade union paper called *Working Women*. In 1927 she became the first woman minister, in the Department of Social Affairs, and in 1931 became Chairwoman of the Social Democratic Women's League. She was the Speaker of

Parliament from 1936 to 1947. Her main concerns were with improving the social conditions of working-class women and single parents. At the end of her life she became involved in the co-operative movement.

**Sills, Beverly** [Silverstein, Belle] (1929–). American soprano. She studied in New York, having sung in a radio programme at the age of three, and appeared in productions of Gilbert and Sullivan. Her professional debut was in 1947, with the Philadelphia Civic Opera. After joining the New York City Opera Company in 1955 she sang many leading roles, though it was in 1966, as Cleopatra in Handel's *Giulio Cesare*, that she first came to wide public attention. This success was followed by invitations to the major European opera houses, including the Vienna Staatsoper (1967, Queen of the Night), La Scala, Milan (1969, in Rossini's *Le siège de Corinth*) and Covent Garden (1970, in the title role of Donizetti's *Lucia di Lammermoor*). Her debut at New York's Metropolitan was in 1975, and in 1979 she was appointed Director of the New York City Opera, retiring from the stage the following year. Among her roles, Massenet's Manon was one of her most distinguished. She published her autobiography *Bubbles: a Self-Portrait* in 1976 (revised in 1981 as *Bubbles: an Encore*).

**Simone, Nina** (1933–). American jazz singer. Born Eunice Kathleen Wayman, in Tryon, North Carolina, she was one of eight talented children of musical parents. Like many black American singers (including JESSYE NORMAN), she was inspired as a child by hearing MARIAN ANDERSON sing, and she herself began singing with her local church. At high school she was recognized as an accomplished pianist, and developed her own jazz piano style, influenced by folk blues. She graduated at 17 and moved to Philadelphia, where she taught piano and accompanied local singers. This was followed by two years at the Juilliard School of Music. In New York the talent scout Joyce Selznic heard her sing and obtained her a long-term contract with the record division of Columbia. Simone worked as a singer and pianist in Atlantic City in 1954 and then appeared at the Apollo Theatre, Harlem, and during the late 1950s and 1960s

she became known for her black protest songs like *Blacklash Blues* with Langston Hughes, *Turning Point* and *Wish I Knew How it would feel to be free*. She went on to make many fine albums, which established her as one of America's leading popular singers.

**Simpson, Mrs.** *See* WINDSOR, Duchess of.

**Sipilä** [née Sipilä], **Helvi (Linnea)** (1915–). Finnish lawyer. Born in Helsinki, she attended university there and in 1939 married Sauli Sipilä; they have four children. From 1941 to 1942 she was an acting judge in rural district courts, and then a secretary in the Ministry of Supply (1942–3) before taking legal posts in the superior courts and running her own law office from 1943 to 1972, only the second woman in Finland to do so. In 1969 she was a member of the Council of Human Rights at Strasbourg. She was Chairman of the Finnish Refugee Council (1965–72), and was a member of the Finnish deputation to the UN General Assembly from 1966 to 1971, chairing the UN Commission on the Stature of Women. From 1973 to 1982 she was Assistant Secretary-General for Social Development and Humanitarian Affairs and was general secretary of the UN Women's Year in 1975.

**Sirani, Elisabetta** (1638–65). Italian artist. She was born in Bologna, daughter of a painter. Her own listed works from the age of 17 amount to over 150 paintings on a wide range of subjects, religious, allegorical, mythological, and portraits; she is also recorded as a poet. Her father was persuaded by a family friend, Count Malvasia, to train her as an artist, and she had achieved public recognition in Bologna by the age of 16. She supported her family when her father could no longer work, gaining many important private commissions but achieving fame with her painting for the nave of San Girolamo in 1658. She apparently opened her studio to other women whom she accepted as pupils. At the age of 27 she died, amid rumours of poisoning, and was given an enormous civic funeral which included a catafalque representing the Temple of Fame with an effigy of the artist at work. She was buried next to the honoured painter, Guido Reni, the chief influence upon her style, and her friend Malvasia wrote an adulatory biography. Several of her paintings feature legendary women such as *Salome*, *Mary Magdalen*, and *Portia wounding her Thigh*.

E. Tufts: *Our hidden Heritage* (1974)

**Sirikit** (1932– ), Queen of Thailand. The daughter of Prince Chandaburi Suranth, Sirikit was educated in Europe and in 1950 married King Bhumibol Adulayadej, who had succeeded to the Thai throne four years earlier. Their son, the Crown Prince, was born in 1952 and they also have three daughters. In the 1960s Sirikit became known internationally for her great style and charm, stealing the limelight on foreign tours to North America, Europe, Asia and the Pacific, and being described as 'one of the world's most beautiful women'. Since 1970, however, the Thai royal family have devoted themselves to domestic affairs, and Sirikit has been particularly involved in campaigns for employment of the poor, organizing and supporting 10,000 artisans, many of them women, producing silks, silver-ware and traditional handicrafts. The scheme has been immensely successful, with a growing work schedule and a flourishing export business: an FAO medal was struck in honour of her achievements. She is also an active supporter of the Thai National Council of Women.

**Sitwell, Dame Edith** (1877–1964). English poet. Born in Scarborough, daughter of the noted eccentric Sir George Sitwell, she spent an unhappy, lonely childhood at the family home, Renishaw Hall, Derbyshire. A keen reader of poetry, she was inspired at the age of 17 by Swinburne and the French Symbolists. She first contributed poems to the *Daily Mirror* and in 1915 produced the anthology *Wheels*. During the 1920s, with her brothers Osbert and Sacheverell, she became a noted London literary figure, gaining notoriety with her original, musical collection *Façade* (1923), set to music by William Walton, and *Bucolic Comedies* (1923). Her vision deepened during the 1930s, beginning with *Gold Coast Customs* (1929), and after World War II her work shows still more depth of feeling, especially *The Shadow of Cain* (1947) which recognizes the horror of an atomic age.

She was also a critic and a biographer, her subjects including *The English Eccentrics* (1933) and ELIZABETH I. She herself loved publicity, appearing in exotic costumes and jewellery, but she was also noted for her generosity to other poets and artists. She was created DBE in 1954, and received many awards and honorary degrees.

E. Sitwell: *Taken Care of: an Autobiography* (1965)
V. Glendinning: *A Unicorn among Lions* (1981)

**Skram** [née Alver], **Bertha (Amalie)** (1847–1905). Norwegian-Danish novelist and feminist. She was born in Bergen. Her bankrupt father deserted the family when she was young. In 1864 she married Berent Muller, a sea captain, sailing the world with him until their divorce in 1878. She then lived in southern Norway, contributing criticism and short stories to periodicals. In 1884 she married the Danish author, Asjoborn Skram, and moved to Copenhagen.

Over the next ten years Skram wrote a series of frank novels concerned with the situation of women, especially their sexual problems, such as *Constance Ring* (1885), *Lucie* (1888), *Fru Ines* (1891), and *Foraadt* (1892), which won her much notoriety. But her best known work was the gloomy tetralogy *Hellemyrsfolket* (1887–98), the tragedy of a peasant family's decline. Her last novels, equally deterministic and pessimistic, focus on problems of heredity. In 1900, after her second divorce, she suffered a serious breakdown, and much of her very unhappy later life was spent in hospital.

**Slessor, Mary (Mitchell)** (1848–1919). Scottish missionary. Born in Aberdeen, she spent her early life working in a factory, devoting her spare time to the church. In 1876 she sailed to the Calabar coast of West Africa as a missionary with the United Presbyterian Church. The necessity of supporting her family at home made her seek a station of her own where she could live in the simplest possible way. She wanted to work with tribes who seemed to need her help most, first the people of the Okoyong and then the slave-dealing Aros. Mary's primary aim was not to win converts but to tackle tribal abuses, such as twin murder, human sacrifice and drunkenness, and to encourage trade between the coast and interior. She established her authority so successfully that the government invested her with the powers of a magistrate.

W.P. Livingstone: *Mary Slessor of Calabar: Pioneer Missionary* (1916, reprinted 1984)

**Slick, Grace (Wing)** (1939–). American rock singer. Born in Chicago, she was brought up in Palo Alto, California. She studied at Finch College (1957–8) and the University of Miami (1958–9). She married the film-maker Jerry Slick in 1961 (divorced 1970) and they played together in a San Francisco band, The Great Society. This group often supported the Jefferson Airplane in concerts and in 1966 Grace left and became Airplane's lead singer. Her extraordinary voice helped them to greater fame with *Surrealistic Pillow* (1967) and *Crown of Creation* (1968). One of the leading bands in the USA, it was also closely connected with the West Coast hippie culture and the protest against the Vietnam War. When Grace had a daughter, China, by Paul Kantner, a leading member of the group, the event had world-wide news coverage.

After more records, including *Sunfighter* (1971), she made a solo album, *Manhole* (1973), and then in 1974 with Kantner formed a slightly different touring group, Jefferson Starship, whose greatest successes were *Red Octopus* (1975) and *Spitfire* (1976). She was forced to leave the group in 1978 because of her alcoholism but returned in 1981 (despite her problems and two operations to her throat) to make the best-selling album *Modern Things*, and is still their lead singer, as on the hit single *Nothing's Gonna Stop Us* (1987). Her own solo albums include *Welcome to the Wrecking Ball* (1981). In 1976 she married Skip Johnson, and she still lives in San Francisco.

**Smedley, Agnes** (1890–1950). American writer. Born in Missouri into an agricultural labourer's family, she was brought up in poverty in the mining towns of Colorado. At the age of 16 she looked after the family following her mother's death, sold papers, worked in a tobacco factory, peddled books and struggled for education. In 1911 she went to Tempe Normal College, Arizona, and after a brief and disastrous marriage to Ernest Brundin, continued her studies at San Diego Normal School, and taught

typing. After losing her job because of involvement in the Free Speech Movement she went to New York, wrote articles for the socialist newspaper *The Call*, and for *Birth Control Review*. She became involved with Indian anti-British nationalist politics and was imprisoned for six months in 1918. Her short stories, *Cell Mates*, describe this experience.

Her years of depression in Europe after 1919 were ended by psychoanalysis and by the writing of her magnificent fictive autobiography *Daughter of Earth* (1928). She had planned to visit India, but eventually went to China in 1928 as special correspondent for the *Frankfurter Allgemeine Zeitung* until 1932, and later for the *Manchester Guardian* (1938–41).

Her first book on China, *Chinese Destinies*, was published in 1933, her second, *China's Red Army Marches*, was completed during a long convalescence in Russia in the same year, and her description of the war against Japan, *China Fights Back*, was published in 1938. While in China, Agnes Smedley campaigned for health care and the freedom of writers from persecution by the Kuomintang, worked behind battle lines and raised funds for medical supplies for the Red Army. She was a close friend of the writer DING LING.

In September 1940 she left for Hong Kong, and then returned to the USA for medical treatment. She continued to campaign for the Chinese war effort, wrote the *Battle Hymn of China* (1943), and her biography of Chu Ten, *The Great Road*. She lived in a writers' colony in New York State until, after persecution as a 'Russian spy' in 1949, she decided to return to China. She died in London, after an operation, but her remains were buried near Peking.

J.S. MacKinnon: *Agnes Smedley: The Life and Times of an American Radical* (1987)

**Smith, Bessie** (1898–1937). American blues singer. Born in Chattanooga, Tennessee, she began singing as a child and at 12 toured with 'MA' RAINEY in the Rabbit Foot Minstrels. She continued to tour the cities of the South with the Florida Cotton Pickers and her own Liberty Belles until the pianist Clarence Williams took her to New York to record for Columbia in 1923. With her first record, *Downhearted Blues*, which sold 2 million copies, she established herself among the most powerful and moving blues interpreters. She recorded with major artists such as Louis Armstrong and Benny Goodman throughout the 1920s and toured in her own shows with her husband Jackie Gee, whom she married in 1923, becoming one of the highest-paid artists of the day. Her records allegedly saved Columbia from bankruptcy. In 1929 she appeared in *St Louis Blues*, a tough, ironic film which was banned for its realism and is now preserved in the Museum of Modern Art, New York. As the Depression made people long for more sentimental escapist music, and as her increasing alcoholism made her an unreliable performer, her popularity waned. Her marriage collapsed and she was often impoverished and unemployed. In 1937 she was touring in Mississippi, when the truck in which she was travelling overnight to the next engagement crashed. Unable to gain admission to a white hospital she was rushed to the Afro-American Hospital in Clarksdale but died after an operation. The delay in treatment is the subject of Edward Albee's play *The Death of Bessie Smith* (1959).

Her 159 recordings, including classics such as *Nobody knows you when you're down and out*, *Backwater Blues* and *St Louis Blues*, won her the title 'Empress of the Blues'.

C. Albertson: *Bessie Smith* (1972)

**Smith, Maggie** [Margaret] **(Natalie)** (1934–). British actress. Born in Ilford, Essex, Maggie Smith was educated at Oxford High School and studied at the Oxford Playhouse School. Her first stage appearance was with OUDS (Oxford University Dramatic Society) in 1952, and in 1956 she appeared in New York with the *New Faces Revue*, making her London debut the next year in the revue *Share My Lettuce*. During the 1959–60 season she joined the Old Vic company and in the 1960s acted in London and in the provinces, playing both classical and modern roles and winning several awards. In 1964 she joined the National Theatre where her parts ranged from Desdemona to Olivier's Othello, to Hilda Wangel in *The Master Builder*, Myra in *Hay Fever* and the title role in *Miss Julie*. In 1970 she was awarded the CBE. Her reputation grew still higher in the 1970s, with

performances such as Hedda Gabler, and Amanda in *Private Lives*. In 1976 she played her first season with the Stratford Festival Theatre, Ontario, as Cleopatra, Millamant, and Masha in *Three Sisters*, returning in future years as Titania (1977), Lady Macbeth (1978), and as Virginia Woolf in Edna O'Brien's *Virginia* (1980). In the 1980s she has given a series of remarkable stage performances: in *The Way of the World* (1985), as Jocasta in Cocteau's *The Infernal Machine* (1986), in Schaffer's *Lettice and Lovage* and Poliakoff's *Coming In To Land* (1987). She has also had a distinguished career in films such as *The Pumpkin Eater* (1964), *The Prime of Miss Jean Brodie* (1968), *Travels with My Aunt* (1972), *California Suite* (1977), *Death on the Nile* (1978) and *Quartet* (1981). Her recent films include *A Private Function* (1986) and *A Room with a View* (1986).

She has been married twice, to Robert Stephens (1967–75), and to Beverley Cross since 1975.

**Smith, Margaret Chase** (1897–). American politician. Born in Skowhegan, Maine, she was educated at the local high school and became a teacher at the age of 19. After three years she changed to office work. On her marriage to Clyde Smith in 1930 she moved into politics, becoming a member of the Republican State Committee for Maine (1930–36). After her husband's death in 1940 she succeeded to his seat in Congress, having worked as his secretary for four years. She soon established her own position and in 1948 was elected to the Senate; she was re-elected in 1954, 1960 and 1966. A nominee for President at the Republican National Convention in 1964, she came second to Barry Goldwater. A diligent hardworking senator, she was eventually defeated at the age of 74.

During the 1970s Margaret Chase Smith was Visiting Professor at many American universities and lectured widely across the USA. She is the author of *Gallant Women* (1968), which looks at the tradition of independent women in American public life, of which she herself is a part, and contains biographies of ANNE HUTCHINSON, DOLLEY MADISON, HARRIET TUBMAN, CLARA STONE, LUCY BARTON, ELIZABETH BLACKWELL, SUSAN B. ANTHONY, Anne Sullivan (*see* KELLER, HELEN), AMELIA

EARHART, ALTHEA GIBSON, FRANCES PERKINS and ELEANOR ROOSEVELT. She has also been a nationally syndicated newspaper columnist.

M. Chase Smith: *Declaration of Conscience* (1972)

**Smith** [née Spear], **Mary Ellen** (1862–1933). Canadian politician. Born in Tavistock, Devon, she married a Methodist theological student Ralph Smith from Newcastle in 1883, and they emigrated to Canada eight years later. They settled in Nanaimo, British Columbia, where Ralph became a prominent local politician, and was elected Minister of Finance in the state legislature in 1916. He died the following year and Mary took his seat. She remained in the legislature until 1928 and was briefly a Minister without portfolio (1921–2), and thereby became the first woman in the British Empire to reach cabinet rank.

**Smith, Sophia** (1796–1870). American philanthropist. Born in Hartfield, Massachusetts, into an old settler family, she was educated locally. She never married; she became deaf at 40 and lived a retired life with her sister and brother. After their deaths she inherited her brother's stock-exchange fortune and took the advice of a local clergyman, who suggested she should leave it to a college for women. In 1868 she finally decided to do so and plans were drawn up by Amherst professors. Her will declares a belief that education for women would mean that 'as teachers, as writers, as mothers, as members of society, their power for good will be incalculably enlarged'. She died after a stroke, and Smith College, the first women's college to be established by a woman, was opened in 1875.

E.D. Hanscombe and H.E. Green: *Sophia Smith and the Beginnings of Smith College* (1925)

**Smith, Stevie (Florence Margaret)** (1902–71). English poet. Born in Hull, she moved to London with her mother, sister and aunt after her father deserted the family, and was educated at Palmers Green and at North London Collegiate School. After her mother's death she lived with her aunt, who was known as 'The Lion of Hull', and worked as secretary to Neville Pearson of Newnes Publishing Company from 1923 to 1953, then left to look after her aunt.

Her highly individual poetry, combining sharp wit with bitter irony and pathos, illustrated by comic line drawings, began to appear in the 1930s, with *A Good Time was had by All* (1937), and *Tender Any to One* (1938). After two more collections, she produced her best-known volume, *Not Waving but Drowning*, in 1957. She also wrote three quasi-autobiographical novels, *Novel on Yellow Paper* (1936), *Over the Frontier* (1938) and *The Holiday* (1950).

During the 1960s she became a popular poetry reader, even attending a pop-poetry festival in Brussels, and she made many recordings and broadcasts for the BBC. An unconventional character, with a disconcerting sense of humour, she was awarded the Queen's Gold Medal for Poetry in 1969.

K. Dick: *Ivy and Stevie* (1971)
J. Barbera & W. McBrien: *Stevie* (1985)

**Smithson** [née Gill], **Alison** (1928– ). English architect. Born in Sheffield, she was educated in Edinburgh and Durham, where she studied at the School of Architecture. She married the architect Peter Smithson in 1949; they have three children. Theirs is one of the most famous modern British partnerships, and their work, which is associated with the Independent Group and Team 10, was covered in many exhibitions during the 1960s and 1970s. They are responsible for three of the most influential buildings in England since World War II: Hunstanton Secondary School, Norfolk (1949–54), the Economist Building, London (1964) and the housing complex at Robin Hood Gardens, London (1972). They share all credit and all criticism of their designs, and both are also prolific writers on architecture, in books such as *Without Rhetoric: an Architectural Aesthetic 1955–72* (1973). Alison also found time to write a novel, *Portrait of the Female Mind as a Young Girl* (1966). She has also written a great deal about celebrations, especially Christmas, and she gave two exhibitions, entitled *Twenty-four Doors to Christmas* (1979) and *Christmas and Hogmanay* (1980–81). Outspoken and forceful, she is constantly involved in debates about the directions taken by modern architecture.

**Smyth,** Dame **Ethel (Mary)** (1858–1944). English composer and suffragette. Despite opposition towards a career in music from her family, who were steeped in the traditions of the army, navy and church, she studied at the Leipzig Conservatory and in Berlin, where her talents were noticed and encouraged by Brahms, CLARA SCHUMANN and Joachim. Her debut as a composer in England was in 1890, though it was with the performance of her Mass in D at the Albert Hall (1893) that she was recognized as the first significant English woman composer. She set about arranging performances of her music with characteristic vigour, finding Germany more receptive to opera, so that her first three operas received their premières there: *Fantasio* (Weimar, 1898), *Der Wald* (Berlin, 1902) and *The Wreckers* (originally to a French libretto, *Les naufrageurs*, by her close friend H.B. Brewster and first produced in German as *Standrecht*, Leipzig, 1906). *The Wreckers* remains among her most successful works and was conducted by Bruno Walter in London in 1910.

The difficulties she had experienced in getting her work accepted drew her to the suffrage movement, for which she wrote the *March of the Women* (1911), sung throughout London at this time. She was among those to be imprisoned for throwing stones at a cabinet minister's window, and took great delight in conducting the battle-song with a toothbrush in Holloway Prison.

She finished her next opera (*The Boatswain's Mate*; première London, 1916) on a visit to Egypt, its libretto containing overtones of the women's cause. This was followed by two one-act operas, *Fête galante* (Birmingham, 1923) and *Entente cordiale* (London, 1925). Her orchestral works include the overture *Antony and Cleopatra* (1890) and a concerto for violin and horn (1927); she also wrote several choral works and some chamber music. Among the occasions at which she appeared as a conductor was the unveiling of the statue of Emmeline PANKHURST (with the Metropolitan Police Band).

Smyth's literary output brought her almost as much distinction as her composing. She wrote a two-volume autobiography, *Impressions that Remained* (1919), and eight other books, largely autobiographical. These highly entertaining volumes chronicle her musical career as well

as her 'twin passions' for friendship and sport; her vast array of women friends included the Empress Eugénie, Princess Edmond de Polignac and VIRGINIA WOOLF. She received an honorary DMus from Durham University and was made a DBE in 1922.

L. Collis: *Impetuous Heart* (1985)

**Smythe, Pat** [Patricia] (1928–). English horsewoman and show jumper. Born in East Sheen, from the age of four she rode ponies in Richmond Park; at eight she joined the Mid-Surrey Drag Hunt and Surrey Union Hounds. Her father's death, the family's move to Gloucestershire and her evacuation during World War II, meant she had to pay her way early: she helped run her mother's guest-house, made delivery rounds with a pony and trap and worked on local farms.

At the age of 14 she acquired Finality, and in 1946 performed well at her first International Show at White City. As a result she was invited to join the British show jumping team under Harry Llewellyn for their first tour abroad. In 1950 at the Horse of the Year Show she tied first with him in a famous jump-off. Her next horses were Leona, Prince Hal and Tosca; on these she won repeatedly at White City and the Harringay Horse of the Year Show. There were successive Continental, then North American tours with the British team: in Paris in 1950 she set a European record height of 6' 10⅞" for women riders.

Between 1952 and 1962 she won the British Show Jumping Association championships a record eight times and was made OBE, and won the European championships four times. Show jumping had become so popular a spectator sport, partly through Pat's influence, that women were admitted to Olympic show jumping events for the first time in 1956. Riding Flanagan, she helped the British team win a bronze medal. She retired soon after the less successful Rome Olympics, married the Swiss lawyer Sam Koechlin in 1963, and had two daughters. She continued to train horses with care and success.

P. Smythe: *Jump for Joy* (1954)

**Snell, Hannah** (1723–92). English soldier. The daughter of a hosier from Worcester, and the grand-daughter of a professional soldier who died at Malplaquet, she was orphaned at the age of 17 and went to live with her sister in Wapping, London. In 1743 she married a Dutch sailor, James Summs, who deserted her after several months. Leaving her baby behind, and disguising herself as a man, she went to seek him. In Coventry she joined a foot regiment, marching against the Stuart rebellion in Scotland. She later claimed to have been publicly flogged in Carlyle, apparently for protecting a girl from her sergeant's advances, a punishment which led her to desert and head south again. At Portsmouth she joined a fleet heading for the East Indies, as assistant cook. The fleet was engaged in an attack on Mauritius and Hannah was an active participant in the assault on the French troops at Pondicherry on the Madras coast. She still managed to hide her identity, treating her wounds in secrecy, and returned to Europe as a sailor. At Lisbon she learnt of her husband's execution.

Arriving at Gravesend in 1750 she abandoned her disguise and made a profitable career out of selling her lavishly embroidered story *The Female Soldier: or The surprising Adventures of Hannah Snell* (1750), and appearing in uniform at the Royalty Theatre and Sadler's Wells. She was also granted a King's pension and a Chelsea outpatient's annuity in recognition of her wounds received at Pondicherry. She set herself up in an inn, *The Female Warrior*, in Wapping, married a second husband, Samuel Eyles, in 1759, and after his death a third, Richard Habgood, in 1772. She spent her last days in the asylum for the insane, Bethlehem Hospital.

**Sokolow, Anna** (1915–). American choreographer and teacher. She studied with MARTHA GRAHAM, and at the New York Metropolitan Opera Ballet School and Bennington School of Dance. She danced with Martha Graham's company in 1930–39, becoming a young star of the decade. She also danced with several other troupes and taught in Israel and Mexico, and in Europe. In 1934 she began to work as a choreographer with her own group. In musicals such as *Street Scene* she often used jazz scores. Her early work is concerned with social themes, but *Rooms* (1955), *Lyric Suite*

(1953), *Dreams* (1961) and *Steps of Silence* (1968) gained her a reputation for sensitive exploration of the loneliness of modern existence.

**Solntseva, Yulia** (1901–). Russian film director. Initially a film actress, she appeared in *Earth/Soil* (1930) and became assistant to its director, Alexander Dovzhenko (*d* 1956); they were later married.

She made her first film as associate director to Dovzhenko in 1939 (*Schors*). In 1943 she co-directed the documentary *The Fight for our Soviet Ukraine/Ukraine in Flames*. She worked on all stages of Dovzhenko's planned trilogy on a Ukrainian village and released the films after his death. She continued to work as a director.

**Solomon, Flora** (1895–1984). Russian–British welfare organizer. Born Flora Benenson in Pinsk, Russia, Flora grew up at Baku, on the Caspian Sea, where her father was an oil magnate. She was educated in Germany, returning at 16 to her father's St Petersburg mansion. In summer 1914 she was in Germany with her father, who needed plastic surgery after his mistress attacked him with vitriol, when war broke out. The family moved to England, and Flora married Colonel Harold Solomon in 1919. They lived in Jerusalem, where Solomon was a colonial servant, until he was injured in a riding accident in 1924. On their return to England they became part of the Kensington intelligentsia: W.H. Auden tutored their son, and Flora's circle included Ethel Snowden, Ellen Wilkinson and Margaret Bondfield. She became a socialist, despite her husband's conservative politics. From 1927 until the mid-1930s she was also embroiled in a stormy affair with Alexander Kerensky, the exiled Russian Prime Minister and revolutionary.

In 1929 the Wall Street crash ruined her family's fortune, and the following year Harold died. She met the store owner Simon Marks at a dinner party and, influenced by Bondfield's work with the shop-workers, she accused him of neglecting his staff: he offered her the job of improving working conditions at Marks & Spencer. There she established a highly progressive and radical Welfare Committee which introduced canteens, sickness and maternity benefits, health care, holidays and other benefits. In 1939 she also set up communal restaurants, backed by Marks, and was asked by the government to extend these on a national basis, creating the famous wartime British Restaurants. In 1945 she received the MBE. She remained at Marks & Spencer as a consultant but in 1948 became adviser to the Ministry of Labour in Israel, concerned with welfare provision for refugees. She continued to visit Israel in later years. Her son, Peter Benenson, was to be the founder of Amnesty International.

F. Solomon: *Baku to Baker Street: The Memoirs of Flora Solomon* (1984)

**Somerville, Edith (Anna Oenone)** (1858–1949). Irish novelist. She was born in Corfu, but returned to Drishane, County Cork, where her family belonged to the élite of Anglo-Irish society. She was educated at Alexandra College, Dublin and studied painting in London, Paris and Düsseldorf, becoming a magazine illustrator but also exhibiting in London, Dublin, and eventually New York (1929). In 1886 she met her cousin Violet Martin and they began a literary partnership as 'Somerville and Ross' with *An Irish Cousin* (1889); they completed 14 works together, of which the best known are *The Real Charlotte* (1894) and *Some Experiences of an Irish RM* (1899). Edith felt that the collaboration continued after Violet's death in 1915, and published many more works under their joint names including *Irish Memories* (1917) and *The Big House at Inver* (1925).

Edith was a forceful and courageous character, the first woman Master of Fox-hounds in 1903 and Master of the West Carberry pack from 1912 to 1919; she was a staunch feminist, President of the Munster Women's Franchise League and a close friend of ETHEL SMYTH. She was a founder member of the Irish Academy of Letters in 1933.

M. Collis: *Somerville and Ross: a Biography* (1968)

**Somerville [née Fairfax], Mary (Greig)** (1780–1872). British mathematician. She was born in Jedburgh, Scotland. Her father was a naval officer and she was allowed to run wild as a child. She had one year's boarding education at the age of ten, but found it repressive rather than instructive.

At 15 she saw algebraic symbols and became interested; she studied algebra, Euclid, and Classics. She was disapproved of by her immediate family who thought education for girls was unnecessary, although she received some support in her classical studies from her uncle. She married her cousin, Samuel Greig, who was hostile to intellectual women. He and one of their two children died within three years. Mary was then free to study mathematics and after winning a prize in a journal for solving a problem on diaphiantine equations, she bought a small library of mathematical texts, at the age of 33. In 1812 she married another cousin, William Somerville (a surgeon), who encouraged her work and introduced her to intellectual circles in London.

In 1826 she presented a paper to the Royal Society, *The Magnetic Properties of the Violet Rays of the Solar Spectrum*. Lord Brougham asked her to prepare an English edition of Laplace's *La mécanique céleste*. Her lucid translation, which also included original commentaries, brought much acclaim: she was elected an honorary member of the Royal Astronomical Society at the same time as CAROLINE HERSCHEL, her bust was placed in the Great Hall of the Royal Society, and she was given a government pension of £200, which was later raised to £300 a year. *The Connection of the Physical Sciences, Physical Geography, On Curves and Surfaces of Higher Orders* and *Molecular and Microscopic Science* were four major works which followed, together with numerous other papers.

Her signature was the first on J.S. Mill's petition to Parliament for women's suffrage.

M. Somerville: *Personal Recollections of Mary Somerville* (1874)
E.C. Patterson: *Mary Somerville and the Cultivation of Science* (1983)

**Sontag, Henriette (Gertrud Walpurgis), Countess Rossi** (1806–54). German soprano. She received her first musical instruction from her mother, an actress and singer, and made her first public appearance (in Kotzebue's *Die Beuchte*) at the age of five. After her father's death the family moved to Prague, where she was accepted at the conservatory, despite her youth, in 1815. She made her formal debut as the Princess in Boieldieu's *Jean de Paris* in 1821. Weber chose her to create the title role of *Euryanthe* (Vienna, 1823), a success followed by appearing with KAROLINE UNGER in the première of Beethoven's *Missa solemnis* and Ninth Symphony (1824). She excelled in Rossini roles, in which she made triumphant debuts at Berlin (1825), Paris (1826) and London (1828). It was in Berlin (where she is reputed to have excited interest through being the first woman to skate on the Spree) that the term 'Sontag fever' gained general currency, and she was similarly idolized elsewhere. Her secret marriage to Count Rossi, a Sardinian diplomat, prevented her from pursuing her operatic career until 1849, when the abdication of the King of Sardinia terminated her husband's livelihood, whereupon she promptly accepted engagements to sing in England, appearing in Rossini, Donizetti and Mozart roles and in the première of Halévy's *La tempesta* (1850). She died of cholera during a tour of Mexico. Goethe's poem *Neue Siren* was inspired by her.

E. Pirchan: *Henriette Sontag* (1946)

**Sontag, Susan** (1933–). American critic. Educated at the University of California, Berkeley, and at Chicago, where she obtained a BA, she then gained an MA at Harvard and won travel scholarships to St Anne's College, Oxford, and the University of Paris. After the late 1950s she taught at several American universities, including the City College of New York and Sarah Lawrence College (1959–60), Columbia University (1960–64) and Rutgers University (1964–5). Since then she has been a professional writer. Her first novel, *The Benefactor*, appeared in 1963, but she made her name with a series of philosophical essays on film, music and politics, which appeared in journals such as the *New York Review of Books* and *The New Yorker* before being collected in *Against Interpretation* (1966), and her role as one of the 'new intellectuals' was confirmed by *The Style of Radical Will* (1969). She had continued to write novels and short stories, but during the 1970s exerted most influence as a film-maker and critic. She wrote and directed four films herself: *Duet for Cannibals* (1969), *Brother Carl* (1971), *Promised Lands* (1974) and *Unguided Tour* (1983). Her book *On Photography* (1976)

proved a great critical success.

The discovery that she had cancer prompted the fascinating series of essays *Illness as Metaphor* (1978) and she has since written the short stories *I, etcetera* (1978) and the collection of essays *Under the Sign of Saturn* (1980). Her contribution to modern American culture has been recognized by many awards, and she became a member of the American Academy of Arts and Letters in 1976.

**Soong Ching Ling** (1893–1981). Chinese revolutionary and stateswoman. She was born in Shanghai and was educated there and in the USA at the Wesleyan College for Women, Georgia. On her return to China in 1913 she took the place of her elder sister Ai-Ling, who married a prominent Hong Kong businessman, as secretary to Dr Sun Yat-sen, leader of the Nationalist Party (Kuomintang), whom she married two years later despite the difference in their ages. In May 1921 after several years in exile in Japan Dr Sun became President of the Republic of China until ousted by a warlord the following year. After his death in March 1925, Soong Ching Ling devoted the rest of her life to the furtherance of the ideals they had shared on creating a new China. She broke with the Kuomintang over their anti-Communist policy, and left China to spend two years in the USSR (1927–9). In 1927 her sister SOONG MEI-LING married Chiang Kai-shek, leader of the right wing of the Nationalist Party whose policies Soong Ching Ling increasingly opposed.

During World War II she organized the China Defence League to raise funds for medical relief and child welfare, and kept links with the Chinese Communist Party. After the People's Republic was set up in 1949 she often undertook political and ceremonial duties and was prominent in the women's movement, in promoting child welfare, and in international relations. She was awarded the Stalin Peace Prize in 1950, and became honorary President of the Women's Federation of China in 1957. In her later years she lived quietly in Shanghai. During her last illness in May 1981 she was admitted to the Communist Party and given the title of Honorary President of the People's Republic.

R. Eunson: *The Soong Sisters* (1975)

**Soong Mei-ling** (1901–). Chinese states-woman. Soong Mei-ling was the fourth child of the famous Soong family whose father was a Methodist missionary and busi-nessman in Shanghai. She was educated in the USA from 1908 to 1917. Through her sister SOONG CHING LING she met Chiang Kai-shek who was to become the leader of the Nationalist Party (Kuomintang). After their marriage in 1927 she worked closely with her husband as his secretary and English interpreter. She took a leading role in the New Life Movement which encouraged moral reform based on traditional Chinese virtues, and held one or two government positions during the 1930s.

During World War II she became very influential, both as a propagandist for the Nationalist cause (she made a highly successful tour of the USA in 1942–3) and as adviser to her husband, who was by then the head of the government. Her influence waned after the war and she did not hold any official positions after the Nationalists fled to Taiwan. She continued to visit the USA, both for private reasons and as a goodwill ambassador for Chiang Kai-shek. She has lived in the USA since her husband's death in 1975.

E. Eunson: *The Soong Sisters* (1975)

**Sophia,** Electress of Hanover (1630–1714). German scholar. The twelfth child of Frederick V and Elizabeth Stuart (daughter of James I of England), Sophia married Ernest Augustus, Duke of Brunswick, in 1658. He became Elector of Hanover in 1692, and died six years later. By the British Act of Settlement of 1701 their son George became King of England. Like her sister Elizabeth of Bohemia (to whom Descartes dedicated his *Principia Philosophia* in 1644), Sophia was a distinguished scholar and an influential patron; a close friend of Leibniz, she corre-sponded with many scholars, including Fran-cis Mercury von Helmont, colleague of ANNE FINCH CONWAY.

**Sorabji, Cornelia** (1866–1954). Indian lawyer. The first woman in India to practise law, she came from a distinguished liberal family and was the first girl student in Decca College, Poona. Despite the hostility of male students and suspicions of the staff she came head of the degree list, but the automatic scholarship to a British university was withdrawn because of her sex. She then got a fellowship at Gujarat College, Ahmadebad, and while still in her teens became a lecturer in English language and literature. Eventually friends arranged a scholarship for her to Somerville College, Oxford, in 1888. She also studied law at Lincoln's Inn, and Jowett, the Vice-chancellor of Oxford, who became her close friend, ordered a special Congregational Decree in 1893 which allowed her to become the first woman to sit for the advanced examination, the BCL (Bachelor of Civil Law). Not until 30 years later were women admitted to the English Bar. (See HELENA NORMANTON.)

Sorabji submitted a plan to the India Office for protection of the legal rights of women in purdah who were wards of court, and in 1904 she was appointed legal adviser on behalf of such women in Bihar, Orissa and Assam. She continued this work until 1923 when she settled in Calcutta to practise as a barrister. She also wrote many studies of Indian life. Her own experiences as a lawyer are described in *India Calling* (1934) and *India Recalled* (1936). Her younger sister, Susie, was a great educational reformer.

C. Sorabji: *The Memoirs of Cornelia Sorabji* (1934)

**Sorel, Agnes** (1422–50). French; the mistress of Charles VII. A low-ranking member of the household of Isabella of Lorraine, queen of Sicily, she probably met the king in the summer of 1443 and became his mistress in 1444, possibly bearing a daughter in that year. She exercised considerable influence on his actions during the continuing campaigns against the English and her name was coupled with that of Pierre de Breze, who became the king's Chief Adviser until her death. Although she promoted her own family, and was accused of immorality and extravagance (she is credited with making diamonds fashionable at court), she was also said to be calm, shrewd and sensible. She gained the name of 'Dame de Beauté' from the estates of Beauté-sur-Marne which the king gave her. Her power gained her many enemies, and her death at 28 was said to have been due to poisoning. In 1451 the great financier Jacques Coeur was arrested and later imprisoned and fined for causing her death, but the charge was almost certainly manufactured.

F. Hamel: *The Lady of Beauty* (1912)

**Sorma [Zaremba], Agnes (Martha Karoline)** (1865–1927). German actress. A child actress, she moved from provincial repertory to the new Deutsches Theater in Berlin in 1883. After winning popularity in juvenile parts she became respected as a serious actress in plays by Grillparzer and as Shakespeare's tragic heroines. From 1890 to 1894 she was at the Berliner Theater, and in 1897 made her first appearance in New York. She toured Europe and Scandinavia, and was admired for her modern as well as classic roles, especially Nora in Ibsen's *The Doll's House* and the title role of Shaw's *Candida*. Beautiful and charming with a capacity to move audiences, she was called by Hauptmann the 'Queen of Grace' and was admired by Thomas Mann. From 1904 to 1907 she worked with the great director Max Reinhardt in Berlin, adding older roles such as Hermione in *The Winter's Tale* and Mrs Alving in *Ghosts* in 1906. During World War I she took a company to entertain troops at the front, and afterwards lived in Berlin until the death of her mother and her husband, when she went to join her son in the USA. She died in Arizona.

**Southcott, Joanna** (1750–1814). English religious fanatic. A farmer's daughter from Devon, Joanna Southcott was a servant for much of her life. Originally a Methodist, in 1792 she began to prophesy and claimed to be the woman who is described in *The Revelation* as divinely chosen to warn the world of the imminence of the second coming of Jesus Christ. She was invited to London and 14,000 seals (writings signed by Joanna and by the recipient and sealed) were issued.

At the age of 64, she announced that she was to bear, by virgin birth, the second Christ. She died shortly afterwards and an autopsy disclosed no sign of pregnancy. At that time there were reputed to be 100,000 Southcottians, although their numbers dwindled rapidly after her death. Joanna's numerous books include *Strange Effects of*

*Faith* and *True Explanation of the Bible* (1804).

J.K. Hopkins: *A Woman to Deliver Her People: Joanna Southcott* (1982)

**Spark, Muriel (Sarah)** (1917–). British novelist. Muriel Spark was born in Edinburgh, where her Jewish father was an engineer: her mother, Sarah, had been a suffragette. She went to James Gillespie's Girls' School and Heriot Watt College, but she ran away from school to marry at 18, moving to Rhodesia and returning to England in 1944 with her son after her marriage broke down. After a year working in Intelligence, she became a freelance writer and editor, her various jobs including a difficult time as General Secretary of the Poetry Society. She was Editor of *The Poetry Review*, 1947–9. Her first books in the early 1950s were critical studies of Wordsworth, Mary Shelley and John Masefield, and a collection of poetry, *The Fanfarlo and other Verse* (1952). In 1950 she won a short-story competition in the *Observer*, but her first novel, *The Comforters*, was not published until 1957, by which time she had been converted to the Roman Catholic Church. Her novels over the next 30 years were to win her the accolade of being the contemporary upholder, with Graham Greene, of the tradition of the English Catholic novel, and one of the most innovative and original novelists in Britain – cutting yet hilarious, serious yet absurd. Her books include *The Ballad of Peckham Rye* (1960), *The Prime of Miss Jean Brodie* (1961: later filmed, starring MAGGIE SMITH), *The Girls of Slender Means* (1963), *The Mandelbaum Gate* (1968), *The Abbess of Crewe* (1974), *Territorial Rights* (1976), *Loitering with Intent* (1981), *The Only Problem* (1984) and *A Far Cry from Kensington* (1988). Her collected stories appeared in 1967, with a second volume in 1987.

In 1961 she left England, moving first to New York and then, in 1966, to Rome.

**Spence, Catherine (Helen)** (1825–1910). Australian reformer and feminist. Born near Melrose, Scotland, she was the daughter of a banker who emigrated to South Australia in 1840, after the failure of his wheat speculations. She became a governess and the first successful woman novelist in Australia, publishing anonymously *Clara Morison: a Tale of South Australia during* *the Gold Fever* (1854) and *Tender and True: a Colonial Tale* (1856). She continued to write fiction for the next 30 years, including *Mr Hogarth's Will* (1865), *The Author's Daughter* (1868), *An Agnostic's Progress* (1884) and *A Week in the Future* (1889). She also became a well-known journalist and literary critic for newspapers in South Australia and Victoria, and in the major British reviews such as the *Cornhill* and *Fortnightly*, although after 1880 her work was sometimes criticized as being too radical and feminist.

She became involved in reform work in the 1870s, working especially with destitute children, and was a member of the newly-founded State Children's Council in 1886. She herself cared for three successive families of orphans. She campaigned for better educational facilities, especially for girls, and wrote innovative textbooks such as *The Laws We Live Under* (1880). She also fought for proportional representation, publishing *A Plea for Pure Democracy* as early as 1861 and returning to the subject 30 years later, when a campaign, inspired by her, was launched by the emergent Labour Party in 1892–3.

In 1891 Spence became Vice-president of the Women's Suffrage League of South Australia. She continued to work for the national and international women's movement after suffrage was obtained in South Australia in 1894. At the Chicago World Fair in 1893 she addressed a series of conferences which combined most of her interests: Charities and Corrections, Proportional Representation, Peace, Single Tax and Women's Rights. After touring the USA and the UK as a preacher and lecturer she returned to Australia, founding the Effective Voting League in 1895. In 1897 she ran unsuccessfully for the Federal Convention, the first woman to stand for an elected political seat. She continued to campaign for voting changes at every election until her death.

C.H. Spence: *Autobiography* (1910)

**Spencer, Anna (Garlin)** (1851–1931). American feminist, minister and reformer. Born in Attleboro, Massachusetts, into a distinguished New England family, she was educated privately and began teaching in Providence, Rhode Island, in 1870 and writing for the local newspaper. In 1878 she married a Unitarian clergyman, William Spencer. Already a noted public speaker on social issues, she began to preach in the Unitarian churches in Massachusetts and New York State, eventually being ordained in 1891. She remained a highly successful minister in Providence until 1905.

A tireless charity worker, a member of the American Purity Alliance and a feminist, after the turn of the century she became a leader of the New York Society for Ethical Culture, a director of the New York School of Philanthropy (which became the School of Social Work) and a lecturer at numerous colleges, including the University of Chicago and Teacher's College, Columbia University, and was Professor of Sociology and Ethics at Meadville Theological School. She was a prolific writer, her most significant work being *Woman's Share in Social Culture* (1912), which outlined the role of women in industry, the arts and public life from primitive to modern times. She also wrote *The Family and its Members* (1923).

**Spessivtseva, Olga (Alexandrovna)** (1895–1980). Russian ballerina. She was born in Rostov, the daughter of an opera singer, and was brought up in an orphanage at St Petersburg [now Leningrad]. She went to the Imperial Academy of Dancing with her sister Zinaida and her brother Alexander, with whom she also danced at the Mariinsky Theatre. She was taught by Fokin and AGRIPPINA VAGANOVA, and graduated in 1913. She danced Aurora in 1915 and was a ballerina by the age of 23. A romantic, ethereal dancer with a great tragic talent, she was a superb Giselle and Odette–Odile.

In 1916 she toured the USA with Dyagilev and partnered Nijinsky in the *Blue Bird* and *Le Spectre de la Rose*. The following year she returned to Russia but left in 1921, rejoining Dyagilev's company in London as guest ballerina in *The Sleeping Princess*. She returned again to Russia to take classic roles at the Mariinsky Theatre, but finally left, with Balanchin and ALEXANDRA DANILOVA, in 1924. After dancing at the Paris Opéra she took the title role in Balanchin's *La chatte* with Dyagilev's company in 1927. In 1932 she danced *Giselle* with Dolin for the Carmargo Society,

London. She toured South America and in 1934 joined the Dandré company. She moved to the USA in 1939. A nervous breakdown led to her hospitalization in 1943, and 20 years later her friends obtained a place for her at the Tolstoy Farm, a Russian settlement in New York State.

A. Dolin: *The Sleeping Ballerina* (1966)

**Spiridonova, Mariya** (1880–*c*1930). Russian revolutionary terrorist. The eldest daughter of the prosperous Tambov family, she joined the Socialist Revolutionary Party at 19 and became a member of the Central Committee. In 1906 she assassinated the repressive General Luzhenovsky on a railway station. She was assaulted and tortured by the soldiers who captured her and her treatment became a matter of international outrage, leading to demonstrations in Trafalgar Square, London. She was exiled to Siberia, where she organized a co-operative commune in the Mattsev hard-labour settlement in 1908. She later returned to Russia but was exiled again in 1916, after a campaign of dynamiting prisons.

I. Steinberg: *Spiridonova – Revolutionary Terrorist* (1935)

**Spry, Constance** (1886–1960). British flower arranger and cook. She was born in Derby and brought up in Ireland. She worked for the Ministry of Aircraft Production during World War I and was later Principal of an adult education school. She began professional flower arranging in the 1920s and in 1929 opened a shop in London which eventually moved to South Audley Street, where she founded her school of floristry in the 1930s. After World War II she helped start the Cordon Bleu Cookery School in London, and ran an exclusive domestic finishing school at Winkfield Place, Windsor, which embodied the 'Ideal Home' aspirations of the 1950s. A talented and committed designer, Constance Spry supervised floral decorations at royal weddings and opera galas, and advised on the decorations for the coronation of Elizabeth II (1953). She lectured in the UK, the USA and Australia and published 13 books on flowers and cookery.

E. Coxhead: *Constance Spry* (1975)

**Staël.** *See* DE STAËL.

**Stampa, Gaspara** (1523–54). Italian poet. Born in Padua, the daughter of a jewel merchant, she studied classics, history, philosophy and music. After her father's death she and her brother and sister moved to Venice, where she was quickly acclaimed as the Venetian Sappho. Her magnificent, deeply emotional Petrarchan sonnets follow the progress of her love for the Venetian aristocrat Collaltino de Collatro, whom she met in 1549. In 1552 he rejected her, and after unsuccessful attempts to distract herself with other lovers she died in 1554, perhaps by suicide. Suggestions that she was a courtesan seem to be belied by the passionate fidelity of her *Rime*, which were published by her sister Cassandra in 1554.

**Stanhope, Lady Hester (Lucy)** (1776–1839). English traveller. Born into the aristocratic Chatham family, Hester was the eldest of six children. Her eccentric socialist father called her 'the best logician I ever saw' and favoured her; she became a tall commanding figure. In 1802 she went to live with her uncle, William Pitt, then Prime Minister, and applied energy and enterprise to becoming his hostess and companion.

On his death in 1806, Pitt caused Parliament to settle on Hester £1200 a year, but she missed her powerful position. Intrigues did not satisfy her and in 1810 she left England and never returned. She employed a doctor, Charles Meryon, who accompanied her on most travels, and a maid, Mrs Fry, who remained with her till around 1820. In Gibraltar she acquired a young lover, Michael Crawford Bruce, who stayed with her until 1814; adopting masculine mores, Hester refused to accept him as a husband. From Malta she went to Greece then Constantinople [now Istanbul], where she plotted unsuccessfully to undermine Napoleon Buonaparte. In a shipwreck between Rhodes and Egypt she lost her luggage and thereafter always wore Turkish or Arabian male dress 'for its splendour and convenience'. Despite being one of the first English travellers among the tribes of Egypt and Syria, she approached governors, emirs and pashas as an equal and was generally granted their protection and sumptuous hospitality. Sometimes she adventured alone; in 1813, dressed as a Bedouin, she marched with their tribe through the desert

Lady Hester Stanhope

Marie Stopes

Harriet Tubman

Marie Tussaud

to Palmyra. She wrote 'I have been crowned Queen of the Desert, under the triumphal arch at Palmyra'.

From 1814 she spent more time living in a disused monastery and less on travels to Baalbeck and Tripoli. She tried to excavate treasure at Ashkela and became revered and influential despite her lack of success. From 1817 she lived at another deserted monastery, Dar Djoun, where she built secret rooms to shelter the local Druses from need and persecution during Ottoman oppression. Becoming a recluse, she studied the occult, smoked a chibouke and believed she could become Queen of the Jews. She withstood barbaric threats by the local Emir Beshyr, including dead bodies of her servants left at her gates, but when Palmerston stopped her pension, she walled herself into her house in protest on behalf of herself and her refugees, and died in poverty. Charles Meryon's *Memoirs* (3 vols, 1845) and *Travels* (3 vols, 1846) contain much of her writing, showing her as an archetypal adventurer.

M. Armstrong: *Lady Hester Stanhope* (2/1970)
Cleveland, Duchess of: *Life and Letters of Lady Hester Stanhope* (1914)

**Stanton, Elizabeth Cady** (1815–1902). American suffrage worker. She was born in Johnstown, Massachusetts, where she was educated before attending EMMA WILLARD's Troy Female Seminary (1830–2). She studied law with her father and her experience of his office led to a concern for the property and custody rights of women. After 1832 she was involved in a long, intense relationship with her brother-in-law Edward Bayard, but her interest in the suffrage movement led to her meeting Henry Stanton, reformer and journalist, whom she married in 1840. They had seven children between 1842 and 1859.

In 1840, attending the London anti-slavery convention, she met LUCRETIA MOTT, and after her return, living in Johnstown, Boston (1842–5) and then in Seneca Falls, she supported abolitionist, temperance and women's rights campaigns, eventually organizing (with Mott) the first women's rights convention in 1848. She contributed to the New York *Tribune* and to AMELIA BLOOMER's temperance paper *The Lily*, and through Bloomer met SUSAN B.

ANTHONY, her co-worker for the rest of her life. In 1852–3 she ran the Women's State Temperance Society, but her views on divorce were considered too radical and in 1854 she proceeded to found the New York Suffrage Society and also addressed the state legislature on married women's property rights. During the Civil War she diverted her organization into the Women's Loyal League, but after the war she demanded that the amendment giving voting rights to blacks should cover women as well. This stand, with her views as expressed in *The Revolution*, a weekly feminist journal she edited with Anthony, and her support of radicals like VICTORIA CLAFLIN WOODHULL, alienated many supporters. In 1869, when she was the first President of the National Woman's Suffrage Association, a more conservative group, under LUCY STONE, broke away to found the American Women's Suffrage Association.

From 1869 to 1881 she lectured across the country on family life, child care and education; with SUSAN B. ANTHONY and Matilda Gage she compiled the *History of Women's Suffrage* (1881–6) and in 1888 she organized the International Council of Women in Washington, DC. From 1890 to 1892 she was the first President of the reconciled wings of the suffrage movement, which were now combined in the National American Woman's Suffrage Association. Her pamphlets *The Degradation of Disenfranchisement* and *The Solitude of Self* (1892) had enormous influence. After her husband's death in 1887 she moved to New York. She continued to campaign and write, and turned her radical criticism to religion and the equality of women in the church, publishing the *Women's Bible* (1895–8). Her remarkable autobiography *Eighty Years and More* appeared in 1898.

L. Banner: *Elizabeth Cady Stanton* (1980)

**Stark, Dame Freya (Madeline)** (1893–). British traveller and writer. Born in Paris while her parents were studying art, by the age of five Freya spoke English, French and Italian. Her youth was varied, combining the practical and the intellectual; she worked in a matting factory in Italy with her mother, and suffered her scalp being caught in the machinery when she was 12, but also associated with artists and intellectuals. She attended Bedford College, London. She nursed on the Italian front during World War I and found relaxation in climbing mountains such as the Matterhorn and Monte Rosa, in spite of illnesses. She acted as arbitrator between her estranged parents, and made her own home at L'Arma, then at Asola in Italy.

She had first begun to learn Arabic in London and continued her studies with an Italian monk; in 1928 she was ready for her first journey to the Lebanon. She also travelled to Canada and elsewhere, but successive expeditions took her further east and further into the world of the Arab nomad. From Baghdad she explored the interior of Iraq and Iran, including the remote mountains of Luristan, described in *The Valley of the Assassins* (1934). *The Southern Gates of Arabia* (1938) and *A Winter in Arabia* (1940) describe travels in Southern Arabia, particularly the Hadhramaut. In 1943 she was briefly married to Stewart Perowne, a writer.

During World War II Freya was able to contribute intelligence to the British Government through her close knowledge of Arabia. Her war experiences were described in *West is East* (1945). She continued to travel in the East and write many more travel books, notable for their reflective quality, as was her autobiography. In 1972 she was created DBE; she also journeyed to Afghanistan. In 1976, aged 83, she travelled down the Euphrates.

F. Stark: *Traveller's Prelude* (1950)
———: *Beyond Euphrates* (1951)
———: *The Coast of Incense* (1953)
———: *Dust in the Lion's Paw* (1961)

**Starr, Belle** (1848–89). American outlaw heroine. She was born in Carthage, Missouri, the daughter of a pioneer farmer and saloon keeper. Her brother Edward, a member of the Quantrill gang, was killed by Union troops in 1863. After the family moved to Texas other members of the gang, such as the Younger brothers and Jesse James, took refuge at their farm. Belle worked in Dallas saloons, and had a daughter, Pearl Younger, in 1869; she then eloped with the outlaw Jim Reed and their son Edward was born in Los Angeles in 1872. Returning to Texas, the couple were involved in a famous stagecoach hold-up near Austin. Reed died after a gunfight within a year.

After a colourful life in Dallas, Belle moved to Oklahoma, marrying Cherokee Sam Starr in 1880. Their cabin near Fort Smith, Arkansas, became a hideout for Jesse James and other bandits raiding on the Chisholm Trail. Belle was reputed to be the master-mind of a gang of horse thieves, but due to her legal skills, although charged four times, she was imprisoned only once, briefly, in 1883. In 1885 her elopement with John Middleton was ended by his drowning. Two years later Sam Starr was shot; her last lover was the young Cherokee Jim July. In 1889, during one of her sensational court appearances in Fort Smith, she was shot in the back, allegedly by her son Edward Reed.

B. Roscoe: *Belle Starr* (1941)

**Stasova, Elena Dmitrievna** (1873–1966). Russian revolutionary feminist. Born in St Petersburg, Elena was the daughter of a prominent lawyer and niece of one of the leaders of the Russian women's movement, NADEZHDA STASOVA. Her father, defence counsel at major political trials, was twice arrested, in the 1860s and 1870s. After she graduated from the Gymnasium she worked with N.K. Krupskaia in weekend schools for workers and joined the St Petersburg League of Struggle for the Emancipation of the Working Class in 1898. From 1901, as an agent of *Iskra* (The Spark) she worked throughout Russia, and then in Geneva (1905–6). After returning to Russia she was an organizer in Tbilisi from 1907 to 1912, was arrested many times and exiled to Yeneseysk Province (1913–16). As Secretary of the Central Committee, in February 1917 she helped to plan and lead the October uprising.

After the Revolution Elena became an increasingly important Party official on the Central Committee and in regional government in the Caucasus. In 1921 she began working for the Comintern and was Deputy Chair of the International Organization for Aid to Revolutionaries from 1927 to 1937. In 1932 at the Amsterdam Anti-War Conference she was elected to the World Committee against War and Fascism, helping to found the Women's Committee in 1934. From 1938 to 1946 she edited *International Literature* and continued to write influential articles and memoirs after her retirement. A member of the Central Executive Committee of the USSR, she was awarded four Orders of Lenin and is buried in Red Square.

**Stasova, Nadezhda** (1822–95). Russian feminist. The daughter of a famous architect and a member of one of St Petersburg's leading families, Nadezhda with TRUBNIKOVA and FILOSOVA was one of the leaders of the women's movement in Russia from the 1860s to the 1890s. In 1859 'The female triumvirate' founded a philanthropic society to provide cheap housing, workshops, schools and kindergartens, and in 1863, since they were also interested in publishing and journalism, they established the Publishing Artel, an association of women translators. From 1859–61 women had begun attending courses at the University of St Petersburg, and in 1868 (after Eugenia Konradi's first petition of 1867) Trubnikova, Stasova and Filosova presented to the rector of the University a petition signed by 4000 women. Women were formally admitted in 1869, general courses were specially introduced soon after, and Stasova later became the first director of the Bestuzehv Advanced Courses. Until her death she chaired the society for Assistance to Graduates of Science Courses. She also worked for the Children's Aid Society, and organized some of the first children's nurseries in Russia. Her niece ELENA STASOVA was a prominent feminist revolutionary.

**Stead, Christina (Ellen)** (1902–83). Australian novelist. Born in Rockdale, Sydney, New South Wales, she was the daughter of English immigrants. Her mother died when she was a baby, and her father, a naturalist working for the Australian Fisheries, was a dominant influence. This has led people to see a 'strong biological base' in her fiction. She was educated in Sydney, and trained at Sydney University Teachers' College, graduating in 1922. She worked there as a demonstrator, and in Sydney schools until 1924 but disliked the work and became a secretary for three years until emigrating to Europe in 1928, working as a clerk in London and then as a secretary in a Paris bank. Here she started to write, and her first collection of stories, the lively and bizarre *Salzburg Tales* and her short novel, *Seven poor Men of Sydney*, appeared in 1934.

The following year she married William Blech, an American financier, better known as the writer, economist and socialist William Blake. Their marriage was very egalitarian and they lived briefly in Spain, moving to New York at the threat of civil war. Here she published *The Beauties and Furies* (1936) and *House of all Nations* (1938), before writing *The Man who loved Children* (1940), a semi-autobiographical novel about the unconscious domination of a flamboyant father. During World War II she worked as a writer for MGM and taught at New York University. But her time thereafter was mostly devoted to writing, and she produced eight more novels, variations on the theme of sexual power and politics, from *Letty Fox: her Luck* (1946) to *Miss Herbert (the Surburban Wife)* (1976). During the 1950s she also worked as an editor and translator from the French. On her husband's death in 1968 she returned to Australia, where she became a Fellow in Creative Arts at the Australian National University, Canberra.

R.G. Geering: *Stead* (1969)

**Steel, Dorothy (Dyne)** (1884–1965). English croquet player. Although a minority sport, croquet has had open championships since 1867, and Dorothy Steel has been the outstanding player of all time. Between 1919 and 1939 she won the Women's Championship 15 times, and more notably, won the Open Croquet Championship 4 times (1925, 1933, 1935–6), an event only ever won by 2 other women. She also had four wins in the Beddow Cup, forerunner of the President's Cup, which she won twice. 5 Open Doubles and 7 Mixed Doubles titles brought her total to 31 titles. She played in the MacRobertson Trophy for England in 1925, 1928 and 1937, and as always was noted for the apparent ease of her strokes and her upright, sideways stance.

**Stein, Edith** (1891–1942). German nun. Born into a Jewish family in Breslau, Edith studied philosophy at the universities of Breslau and Göttingen. In 1922, after reading a biography of TERESA OF AVILA, she was baptized a Catholic and for eight years taught at a convent school at Speyer, where she acquired a reputation for ascetic living, rising early, wearing patched linen clothes, and kneeling through three masses daily. In 1934, after the

Nazis banned Jews from academic posts, she entered a Carmelite convent in Cologne, taking the name of Sister Teresa Benedicta of the Cross. After pogroms against the Jews in 1938 she was sent to Echt in the Netherlands and although she tried to transfer to a Swiss convent when the Germans invaded the Netherlands, she was arrested with an older nun, Rosa. They died in the gas chamber at Auschwitz in August 1942. Her last words to Rosa before departure were 'Come, we are going for our people.'

Edith Stein was hailed as a martyr by the Catholic community and was beatified by Pope Paul II in May 1987 in Cologne. The move was disliked by many of her own family and aroused fierce controversy among both Jews and Catholics. Her words were taken to refer to her Jewish origins and it was argued that she could not be beatified as a Christian martyr when she had died as a Jew.

**Stein, Gertrude** (1874–1946). American writer. Born in Allegheny, Pennsylvania, she spent her early years in Vienna and Paris and then in Oakland and San Francisco. From 1893 to 1897 she was at Radcliffe College, where she studied philosophy under William James and became interested in experimental psychology, before moving on to Johns Hopkins University to do advanced work on brain anatomy. She took no degrees and left medicine in 1902, partly because of a tangled love affair. A private income allowed her to join her brother Leo in Paris, where they established an informal literary and artistic salon among a group of friends which included Picasso, Matisse and Braque. In 1907 she began sharing an apartment with Alice B. Toklas, a friend from San Francisco, and their close relationship lasted until Stein's death. Alice kept house and 'talked to the wives of geniuses' while Stein dominated conversation among the men. In the 1920s their group also included writers such as Fitzgerald and Hemingway.

She had been writing for some time, and *Three Lives* (1909), the first work for which she could find a publisher, attempted to view its subjects from all perspectives and to find techniques other than straightforward narrative to explore inner meaning. Other 'narrative' works, which although experimental are easily followed, are *The*

*Autobiography of Alice B. Toklas* (1933) and *Wars I Have Seen* (1945). Before World War I her only other published work was *Portrait of Mabel Dodge* (1912) and the highly experimental *Tender Buttons* (1914). During the war she and Alice helped with the American aid effort.

In the 1920s and 1930s Stein's reputation grew. She was very prolific, writing fiction, plays, verse and prose poems and portraits, which demonstrated her exploration of language in terms of grammar, punctuation and parts of speech and of formal literary structure. She also wrote non-fiction such as the celebrated *Autobiography*, which became a best seller, a book on Picasso in 1938, and critical works which also explain the basis of her own work: *Composition as Explanation* (1926), *Narration* (1935), *Lectures in America* (1935) and *What are Masterpieces?* (1940). *Lectures* followed her only return visit to the USA, when her opera *Four Saints in Three Acts*, with music by Virgil Thomson, was performed and she gave a lecture tour.

Devoted to France, Stein and Toklas remained there during World War II, staying in the village of Culoz during the Occupation. They became great favourites of the American soldiers after the liberation of France in 1944, and this closeness is evoked in Stein's novel *Brewsie and Willie* (1946). After the war she planned to return to the USA but died of cancer before she was able to leave. Alice B. Toklas survived her by 20 years and wrote *Staying on Alone* in 1973. Stein's achievement has often been questioned, but she was an original, forthright and courageous person, who undoubtedly influenced the literary experiments of the next generation. Many of her uncollected pieces were edited after her death.

G. Stein: *The Autobiography of Alice B. Toklas* (1933)
——: *Everybody's Autobiography* (1937)
E. Sprigg: *Stein: Her Life and Work* (1957)

**Steinem, Gloria** (1934–). American feminist and writer. Born in Toledo, Ohio, she was the top graduate from Smith College in 1956 and spent the following two years in India on a research fellowship. On her return she worked for her own research service in Cambridge, Massachusetts, and from 1960 worked as freelance journalist for many national journals. In 1968 she became the Contributing Editor and Political Editor of the *New York Magazine*, which she helped to found. During the 1960s she had emerged as a leading figure in the New Women's Movement in the USA and was also involved in other radical protest campaigns, particularly against the Vietnam War and against racism; she was Treasurer of the Committee for the Legal Defence of ANGELA DAVIS, and a firm supporter of crusading politicians such as SHIRLEY CHISHOLM. In 1970 she was a co-founder of the Women's Action Alliance and the following year she convened the National Women's Political Concerns and founded *Ms Magazine*, with Patricia Carbine, as a supplement to the *New York Magazine*. It went solo in 1972 and within a year had reached a circulation of 350,000, reporting on issues such as abortion and day-care, legal rights in marriage and divorce, and the Equal Rights Amendment, as well as more personal topics and profiles on leading women in various fields. Steinem continued to be one of America's leading liberal feminists and published a controversial study of the image of MARILYN MONROE, *Marilyn*, in 1986.

**Stepanova, Varvara** (1894–1958). Russian artist. Stepanova was born in Kovno, and after studying at home attended the Kazan Art School, 1911, and the Stroganov School of Arts and Crafts, Moscow, 1913–14. In 1911 she married the artist Alexander Rodchenko: they had one daughter. They settled in Moscow, and were associated with the Russian Cubo-Futurists, and the Constructivist movement. She became Vice-Director of the Art and Literature Department, Izo Narkompros, and a member of Inhuk, the Institute of Artistic Culture, in 1920. The following year she was a signatory, with Rodchenko, of the *Productivist Manifesto*, and they collaborated together on the magazine *Lef* from 1923 to 1928.

Like Rodchenko, Stepanova also worked on theatre and costume design, and applied her art to textile design (she was Director of Textile Department, Vkhutemas, 1924–5), as well as to posters, magazines and cinema during the 1920s and 1930s, and was included in two exhibitions of the decorative arts (Art Deco) in Paris (1925) and in Moscow (textile design, 1929), and also exhibited as one of the

Artists of the Soviet Theatre (Moscow, 1935). In the late 1940s and 1950s she continued to work on poster and magazine design.

**Stevens, May** (1924–). American artist. Born in Boston, she studied at Massachusetts College of Art, at the Arts Students' League, New York (1948), and then at the Académie Julien in Paris (1948). She had her first individual exhibition in Paris (1951). She married the artist Rudolf Baranik and from 1953 to 1957 taught at New York High School of Music and Art, then at Parson's School of Design and the School of Visual Arts. She was also visiting artist at several American universities.

From 1967 her work has been mainly associated with her Big Daddy series, which employs the figure of a pugnacious man, often with a bulldog, to convey a political, anti-authoritarian, feminist polemic, described by Lucy Lippard as 'a controlled but powerful rage against imperialism'. She was included in the International Feminist Exhibition in the Netherlands, 1979–80, and has continued to exhibit widely, her recent awards including a Guggenheim Fellowship in 1986.

**Stevens, Nettie (Maria)** (1861–1912). American biologist and geneticist. Born in Cavendish, Vermont, Nettie worked as a librarian for a time before going to Stanford University, aged 35, to study physiology. During summers spent at the Hopkins' Seaside Laboratory at Pacific Grove, California, she became interested in research rather than teaching and published an article on the life cycle of *Boveria*, a protozoan parasite of sea cucumbers.

The rest of her career was spent in successive research posts at Bryn Mawr College, where she worked at three main areas of biology. Her thesis was concerned with the morphology of ciliate protozoa; later she became interested in cytology, and with the geneticist Thomas Hunt Morgan worked on the regenerative processes of the Hydroid *Tubularia*. Her most important work dealt with chromosomes and their relation to Mendel's rediscovered laws of heredity. Using the beetle *Tenebrio molitor*, she correctly inferred that an egg fertilized by an X-carrying sperm produced a female embryo, and that the Y-sperm produced a male. This discovery, made independently by Edmund Wilson, was crucial in genetics and sex determination. Nettie continued to extend this work to cover other species, publishing her results in clear, terse articles; she also taught.

**Stevenson, May.** See CASSAT, MARY.

**Stewart, Ella Winter** (1898–1980). Australian radical journalist. She was born in Melbourne, of German Jewish parents who changed their name from Wertheimer to Winter on arriving in London in 1910. She studied at the London School of Economics, became a Fabian socialist, and accompanied the American delegation to the Versailles Peace Conference, where she met the journalist Lincoln Steffens (d 1936). They married in 1924 and settled in California. In 1930 Ella visited the USSR and wrote Red Virtue, on Russian women after the Revolution. She campaigned during the 1930s on behalf of migrant workers, unionists, Jewish refugees and Spanish loyalists, and against fascist movements in the USA. In 1944 she went to the USSR for the New York Post (described in her book, I Saw the Russian People). After 1945 she worked for the Peace Congress and settled in London to escape McCarthy's persecution.

Her second husband (from 1938), Donald Stewart, was a Hollywood scriptwriter.

E.W. Stewart: And Not to Yield (1963)

**Stobart, Kathy (Florence)** [Kathleen] (1925–). British jazz saxophonist. The first female modern jazz musician to obtain recognition, Kathy plays tenor, soprano and baritone saxophone. She was born in South Shields, where she played in town bands from the age of 14, and went to London in 1942. For the next 40 years she played with leading British and American jazz musicians, notably Art Pepper, Jimmy Skidmore and Dill Jones. Eventually, in 1974, she formed her own Kathy Stobart Quintet. She topped the bill at the first British Women's Jazz Festival in 1982 and the Women's Big Band 'Gail Force' in 1986 and has in recent years obtained a wider audience in the United States, on the record Jazz Women: a Feminist Retrospective. Other important jazz women today include American Carla Bley, an avant-garde jazz composer, and British Barbara Thompson, who heads the European ensemble Paraphernalia.

**Stöcker, Helene** (1869–1943). German feminist. Born in Elberfeld, the oldest of eight children in a strict Calvinist family, she trained as a teacher and studied in Berlin from 1896. There she met MINNA CAUER and became involved in the fight for better educational opportunities for women, and other feminist campaigns, and contributed to radical journals such as Die Frauenbewegung. She briefly edited her own magazine and was among the founders of the Deutscher Verband für Frauenstimmrecht (German Union for Women's Suffrage) in 1902. In 1900 she went to Bern to prepare her doctorate on German literary life in the 18th century, often working in Munich where she knew RICARDA HUCH. She was also a friend of LOU ANDREAS-SALOME.

Influenced by Nietzsche's writings which she saw not as misogynistic, but as promoting unfettered individualism, she insisted, unlike all her contemporaries, that married as well as single women should find fulfilment in professional and public life as well as in the family. Within the movement for the abolition of prostitution and the removal of the double standard of morality, she was unusual in asserting that women should have the capacity to express their sexuality and emotion, rather than that men should show greater restraint. Her own unhappy affair with a married teacher from Glasgow University is described in her novel Liebe (1922). In 1904 having broken with the more conservative Internationale Abolitionistische Föderation Deutscher Zweig (International Federation for the Abolition of State Regulated Prostitution), she established the Bund für Mutterschutz und Sexualreform (League for the Protection of Motherhood and Sexual Reform) which later became known as the Mutterschutz League, notorious for its advocation of free love. Under Stöcker's leadership it produced a journal and pamphlets, petitioned for welfare for unmarried mothers and arranged lectures on eugenics and birth control. In 1908 Stöcker supported her radical followers, such as MARIE STRITT and Camilla Jellinek, in their arguments for the legalization of abortion.

This led to disagreements with the moderates, including ADELE SCHREIBER (1910–14), and Stöcker's 'free marriage' to Dr Bruce Springer was revealed. The League collapsed amid a series of much-publicized law suits. The permissive idealism of the Mutterschutz horrified contemporary society and was soon swamped by conservative reaction within the women's movement.

During World War I Stöcker joined the small group of pacifist feminists, and after the war she continued to campaign with LIDA HEYMANN and ANITA AUGSBURG, editing *Die Neue Generation*, and reviving the Mutterschutz League. In 1933, gravely ill, she fled to Czechoslovakia and then to Switzerland. In 1938 she went to London, then to the USA, via Sweden, Russia and Japan. She died in the USA.

**Stocks, Mary** [Baroness Stocks of Kensington and Chelsea] (1891–1975). English educationalist. Born in London, into an intellectual doctor's family, she was educated at St Paul's Girls' School until she was 16, and at 19 entered the London School of Economics, graduating with a first-class degree. In 1907, while still at school, she took part in the famous 'Mud March' of suffragettes, and continued to be an active member of the constitutionalist, rather than militant, branch of the suffrage movement. In 1913 she married John Stocks, an Oxford don. During World War I Mary lectured on economics at the London School of Economics and at King's College for Women.

In 1924 they moved to Manchester, where John Stocks was Professor of Philosophy and Mary lectured in the university extra-mural department and for the Workers' Educational Association (WEA). (She later became Deputy-President and wrote a history of the WEA.) She was also deeply involved with the university settlement and with community associations, and helped found the first provincial birth control clinic. In 1936 they moved to Liverpool on Stock's appointment as Vice-chancellor of the university, but after his death in 1937 Mary returned to London. In 1938 she became both General Secretary of the London Council of Social Service and Principal of Westfield College,

where her unorthodox and lively rule continued until 1951. She was also a member of several government committees, including the Unemployment Insurance Committee, and gained a national reputation on the BBC radio programmes *The Brains Trust* and *Any Questions?*. Her writings include a biography of her friend Eleanor Rathbone.

In 1966 she was created a life peeress. She moved to the cross benches in 1974 to protest against Wilson's leadership.

M. Stocks: *My Commonplace Book* (1970)

**Stone, Constance** (1856–1902). Australian doctor and feminist. Educated at the Presbyterian Ladies College, Melbourne, she was determined to become a doctor, and travelled to the Women's Medical College in Philadelphia to qualify. The first woman to practise as a doctor in Victoria, she took the lead in other areas, being elected to the local school board, running the Victoria Vigilance Society, campaigning for the age of consent (and therefore of legal prostitution) to be raised to 16, and being involved in philanthropic projects such as the establishment of the Queen Victoria Hospital for the Melbourne poor.

**Stone, Lucy** (1818–93). American feminist. Born in West Brookfield, Massachusetts, into an old settler family, she rebelled against her father's strict views on women's position and demanded a college education like her brothers. Her father refused and she educated herself, becoming a schoolteacher at 16; her posts included Mount Holyoke Female Seminary. Her feminism was encouraged by her denial of a vote in the Congregational community there. She managed to save enough to enrol at Oberlin College in 1843 and eventually received some financial help from her father. She was a contemporary at Oberlin of ANTOINETTE BROWN BLACKWELL and she gained a reputation as an outspoken radical feminist and abolitionist. After her graduation in 1847 she began speaking on women's rights and in 1848 also became a speaker for the Anti-Slavery Society; she travelled the country during the early 1850s, often swaying hostile audiences by her eloquence.

From 1850 she became involved with the organization of the women's rights movement. In 1855 she married the reformer Henry Brown Blackwell, a champion of feminism. She retained her maiden name and they issued a joint statement on the legal disabilities of women in marriage. They lived in New Jersey, and Lucy campaigned for 'no taxation without representation' and for suffrage. In 1866 she became a member of the executive of the newly-formed American Equal Rights Association and then of the American Woman's Suffrage Association, the more conservative wing of the movement which broke away from SUSAN B. ANTHONY and ELIZABETH CADY STANTON's National Woman's Suffrage Association in 1870. She began to edit (and largely financed) the *Woman's Journal*, which remained the official organ of the national suffrage association for 50 years, being edited after her death by her daughter Alice Stone Blackwell. She and Henry also organized the Massachusett's Woman's Suffrage Association and continued to lecture and to draft model legislation to improve women's status. She remained on the executive when the American Woman's Suffrage Association and the National Woman's Suffrage Association were reunited as the National American Women's Suffrage Alliance). After her final lecture, for the World Columbian Exposition in Chicago in 1893, her health collapsed. In 1921 a women's rights organization, the Lucy Stone League, was created in her memory and in 1930 the first biography of her was written by her daughter Alice.

E.R. Hays: *Morning Star: a Biography of Lucy Stone* (1961)

**Stopes, Marie (Charlotte Carmichael)** (1880–1958). British birth control campaigner. Born in Edinburgh, the elder daughter of a leisured scholar and his feminist wife who was a pioneer in higher education for women, Marie was brought up in London and educated at home until the age of 12. She then went to St George's School in Edinburgh and later to the North London Collegiate School. A brilliant scholar, she went on to University College London where she obtained simultaneous degrees in geology, geography and botany. After a year's research she went to Munich, obtained a PhD in 1904, and was the first

woman to join the science faculty at Manchester University the same year. She became known as an expert on fossil plants, spending 1907 to 1908 researching in Japan, becoming a Fellow of University College London and publishing *Ancient Plants* (1910) and a two-volume catalogue, *Cretaceous Flora* (1913–15). She later published classic works, *The Constitution of Coal* (1918) and *Fuel* (1935).

In 1911, still recovering from a romance with a Japanese professor, she met and married a Canadian botanist, Reginald Ruggles Gates, in Montreal. The inadequacy of their sexual life caused her to read widely on the subject and after their marriage was annulled on the grounds of non-consummation in 1916, she concentrated on campaigning for birth control and sex education. Unlike MARGARET SANGER and ALETTA JACOBS, who saw their contraception campaign as an attack on poverty, she felt it was an aid to sexual fulfilment through reducing the fear of pregnancy. In 1918 she married Humphrey Verdon Roe, an aircraft manufacturer, and they campaigned together. Stopes's books *Married Love* and *Wise Parenthood* (both 1918) caused an uproar, sold millions of copies and were translated into 13 languages. Her other books were also best-sellers, including *Radiant Motherhood* (1920), *Contraception: its History, Theory and Practice* (1923) and *Enduring Passion* (1928).

In 1921, with her husband, she started a birth-control clinic in Islington against much opposition, especially from the medical establishment and the Catholic Church. In 1922 Halliday Sutherland, a public-health doctor, accused Stopes of committing a 'monstrous crime' in giving the public information to prevent conception, which deserved prosecution of the kind that had been faced by previous reformers such as ANNIE BESANT. In a long libel suit against him she won on Appeal but lost in the House of Lords. Her many legal battles and forceful statements undoubtedly publicized her cause. After World War II she campaigned for birth control in the Far East. She also developed semi-mystical literary interests and wrote several volumes of verse. Argumentative, demanding, courageous and idealistic, she lived at her house,

Norbury Park, in Surrey, maintaining up to her death that she would live to be 120.

R. Hall: *Marie Stopes* (1977)

**Storni, Alfonsina** (1892–1938). Argentinian feminist poet. Born in Switzerland, she had an adventurous youth as a travelling actress before she became a teacher and journalist in Argentina. Her poetry is marked by frank sexual desire, emotional desolation, and a resentment of the insensitivity and physical dominance of men, encapsulated in the ideology of *machismo*. Her books include *El dulce dano* (1918), *Languidez* (1920), *Ocre* (1925), *Avant-garde el mundo de siete pozos* (1934) and *Mascarillo y trébol* (1938). At the age of 46 she learnt that she had cancer and drowned herself.

R. Phillips: *Alfonsina Storni: from Poetess to Poet* (1975)

**Stowe** [née Jennings], **Emily (Howard)** (1831–1903). Canadian doctor and feminist. Emily was born in South Norwich, Upper Canada [now Ontario]. She became a schoolteacher and married John Stowe before attending the New York College of Medicine for Women, from which she gained her MD in 1867. She returned to Canada and began a long fight to be admitted to the College of Physicians and Surgeons in Ontario, which she achieved in 1880. She was the first woman authorized to practise medicine in Canada. Emily was a leading female suffragist and in 1893 organized the Dominion Woman Suffrage Association, of which she became the first President.

**Stowe, Harriet (Elizabeth) Beecher** (1811–96). American novelist. She was born in Lichfield, Connecticut. Her mother died when she was five and she was sent to her sister CATHARINE BEECHER's Connecticut Female Seminary, Hartford, in 1824. In 1832 she joined Catharine as a teacher at her college in Cincinnati. Here her earlier impressions of slavery were sharpened by the proximity of the South, across the Ohio River, and by the frequent news of runaways. In 1836 she married the Reverend Calvin Ellis Stowe and during the next few years had many pregnancies and seven surviving children. Although often ill and depressed she persevered with her writing, contributing sketches to the *Western*

*Monthly Magazine*. Her first published work was the prize-winning tale *A New England Sketch* (1834) and her second, *The Mayflower: or Sketches of Scenes and Characters among the Descendants of the Pilgrims*, appeared in 1843. Despite her liberal background these sketches are sentimental and conventional, demonstrating the sanctity of the home and of women's place there.

In 1850 the Stowes moved to Brunswick, Maine, where her horror at the passing of the Fugitive Slave Law prompted her to write *Uncle Tom's Cabin: or Life among the Lowly* (1852), which she wrote very rapidly, almost in a trance. Its powerful emotional plot and stylized characters, combined with good documentary realism, caught the American imagination and conscience. By the end of 1853 it had sold over 300,000 copies, and 3 million before the Civil War; it aroused as much hostility as admiration. From then on Harriet became a full-time writer, contributing to reviews such as the *Atlantic Monthly* and producing 11 more works of fiction and 23 assorted books of biography, children's tales and school geography. Although *Dred* returns to the subject of slavery, most of these later books are domestic or religious in theme; they include *A Reply on behalf of the Women of America* (1863), *The American Woman's Home* (1869), *Woman in sacred History* (1873) and *Our famous Women* (1884).

During these later years she lived in Andover, Massachusetts, and then Hartford, Connecticut, and Mandarin, Florida. She visited the UK three times and toured the Continent. While in London she became friendly with GEORGE ELIOT and Lady NOEL BYRON, in whose defence she wrote *Lady Byron Vindicated* in 1870.

F. Wilson: *Crusader in Crinoline: the Life of Stowe* (1941)

**Strachey** [née Costelloe], **Ray** [Rachel] (1887–1940). English feminist. She was educated at Kensington High School and Newnham College, Cambridge, and then at Bryn Mawr College in the USA. In 1911 she married Oliver, the brother of Lytton Strachey. Their sister Philippa was a noted suffragette and Ray was an active but not militant participant in the later suffrage movement, being Parliamentary Secretary of the National Union of Women's Suffrage

Society, lobbying Parliament and editing the *Women's Leader*; during World War I she was Chairman of the Women's Services Bureau. In 1917 she attended a conference in Paris to discuss the position of women war-workers. After World War I she was involved in many different organizations. She was President of the Society of Women Welders, Secretary of the committee to open the legal profession to women, a member of the committee dealing with women in the civil service, and Secretary of the Women's Employment Federation. She stood for Parliament as an Independent candidate three times (1918, 1922, 1923) and worked for a while as secretary to NANCY ASTOR. She continued to campaign on women's issues and from 1933 to 1936 was the first Chairman of the Save the Children Fund Nursery Schools' Committee. Today she is best known for her books, which include lives of FRANCES WILLARD and MILLICENT FAWCETT and the classic work *The Cause: a Brief History of the Women's Movement* (1928).

**Streep, Meryl (Mary Louise)** (1949–). American film actress. Meryl Streep has established herself as one of the most accomplished film actresses of the 1980s, gaining world-wide recognition in relatively few films. She was born in Summit, New Jersey, educated at Bernardville High School, and while still at Vassar College she appeared on the New York stage in *The Playboy of Seville* in 1969. She graduated in 1971, and later attended Yale Drama School. After small parts in theatre and television she made her film debut in *Julia* (1977) with JANE FONDA and VANESSA REDGRAVE, but it was her haunting portrayal of Linda in *The Deerhunter* (1978) which established her place in modern cinema. This was followed by *Kramer v. Kramer* (1979), *Manhattan* (1979), *The French Lieutenant's Woman* (1981), *Sophie's Choice* (1982), the anti-nuclear film based on the life of Karen Silkwood (1983), David Hare's *Plenty* (1985) and the film adaptation of KAREN BLIXEN's *Out of Africa* (1986). To all of these parts she has brought a combination of shyness and passion, and an outstanding control of technique, accent and mood. She married Don Gummar in 1978.

N. Smurthwaite: *The Meryl Streep Story* (1985)

**Streisand, Barb(a)ra (Joan)** (1942–). American singer and actress. Born in Brooklyn and educated at Erasmus Hall High School, she began her singing career as a night-club performer and in off-Broadway revues in 1961, appearing in New York and Detroit, and moving into musical comedy in *I Can Get It for You Wholesale* in 1962. In 1963 she married the actor Elliot Gould (they were divorced in 1971) and began recording with Columbia records. A big stage success, *Funny Girl* (New York, 1964) was followed by an award-winning television show which was shown in several countries from Sweden to the Philippines in 1966. Her record sales soared, she was acclaimed as a great new star and has sustained her reputation ever since. During the 1960s and 1970s she also became a successful film actress with the witty and moving performance as another Brooklyn star, FANNY BRICE, in *Funny Girl* (1968), which won her an Academy Award, followed by *Hello Dolly!* (1969), *On a Clear Day You Can See Forever* (1970), *The Owl and the Pussycat* (1971) and the zany comedy *What's Up Doc?* (1972). Her later films include *The Way We Were* (1973) and *A Star is Born* (1977). In 1983 she directed and produced the immensely successful *Yentl*, and has also directed *Nuts* (1988).

J. Spender: *Streisand: the Woman and the Legend* (1982)

**Stritt, Marie** (1856–1928). German feminist. In 1891 she joined the women's group Reform, founded by Hedwig Kessler, which demanded complete educational equality with men, and became its leader in 1895. She joined MINNA CAUER and ANITA AUGSBURG on the radical side of the Bund Deutscher Frauenvereine (Federation of German Women's Associations), and was elected President in 1899. She worked for the abolition of regulated prostitution, influenced by JOSEPHINE BUTLER, whom she had met in London, and was a leader of the suffrage movement after the turn of the century, being President of the Deutscher Reichsverband für Frauenstimmrecht (German Imperial Suffrage Union). During these years she was one of the leading radicals in HELENE STÖCKER's Bund für Mutterschutz und Sexualreform (League for the Protection of Motherhood and Sexual Reform), usually known as the

Mutterschutz League, which campaigned for a new morality, birth control, free love and the legalization of abortion. She was ousted by the right wing of the movement from her leadership of the Bund Deutscher Frauenvereine (Federation of German Women's Associations) in 1910, to be replaced by the conservative GERTRUDE BAUMER, but she never widely allied herself with the radical pacifist left-wingers. During the 1920s she lived in Dresden and took an active part in local politics.

**Strong, Anna (Louise)** (1885–1970). American radical journalist. The daughter of a clergyman, she was born in Friend, Nebraska. She studied in Germany for a year before graduating from Bryn Mawr College in 1903 and taking a PhD at Chicago. A militant radical journalist, she became deeply involved in labour issues and developed a passionate commitment to Communism. In 1921 her first visit to the USSR, as correspondent with the American Friends Relief Mission, resulted in *The First Time in History* (1924), which attracted wide attention. (Another radical American journalist was Louise Bryant, who visited Russia immediately after the revolution in 1917 and published *Mirrors of Moscow* in 1923.) Strong's next work was *China's Millions* (1928), a partisan account of Chiang Kai-shek's break with Moscow. She became Editor of *Moscow News* for Americans working in the USSR and remained there until 1949, when she was deported, accused of spying. Although her rights were restored, she went to live in China, which she had often visited and where she was friendly with Mao and Chou En-lai, and settled in Peking in 1958. She was an honorary member of the Red Guards during the Cultural Revolution.

D. Nies: *Seven Women: Portraits from the American Radical Tradition* (1977)

**Strozzi, Barbara** (1619–1664 or later). Italian composer and singer. She was the daughter of Isabella Griega (or Garzoni), servant to the writer Giulio Strozzi, an influential member of Venetian society and founder of the Accademia degli Unisoni (1637). Chiefly remembered as a librettist (notably for Monteverdi and Cavalli), he adopted Barbara and was probably her natural father; the first

documented mention of her is in his will of 1628. The academy met at the Strozzi household, and Barbara soon became not only its leading singer but one of its most colourful personalities (women were not traditionally accepted as members of such academies, but she was acknowledged to be its guiding spirit and hostess). Its published papers, the *Veglie de' Signori Unisoni* (1638), are dedicated to her and provoked a series of satires that brought her considerable notoriety for the libertine attitudes associated with the academy.

Strozzi's connections with musical and literary circles resulted in several works being written for her, notably two of Fontei's *Bizzarrie poetiche* (1635 and 1636), the first consisting entirely and the second predominantly of Giulio Strozzi's poems. In 1644 she published her own collection of madrigals, also settings of her father's texts. Her second published work, the *Cantate, ariette e duetti* (1651), includes a tribute to Cavalli, who was her teacher; his influence is indeed evident both here and in her later works, all of them vocal and reflecting her expertise as a singer. Among her finest works is the large-scale cantata *Lagrime mie* from the first of two sets entitled *Diporti di Euterpe* (1659). She published eight volumes altogether, the last of which is a volume of solo arias (1664). Many 17th-century Italian composers produced similar collections of secular vocal music, and (apart from the slightly older FRANCESCA CACCINI), Strozzi is the only known woman among them.

**Stuart [Barry], Miranda** [pseud.: James Barry] (?1795–1865). British doctor. Although 'James Barry' had a long and distinguished career as a military doctor in the British colonies, ending as Inspector-General of all British hospitals in Canada, it was the discovery after death that she was a woman that made her famous.

The facts of her early life are not certain; she may have been Miranda Stuart or Miranda Stuart Barry. She was orphaned and she entered Edinburgh College at about the age of 15 as a 'frail-looking young man'. She gained her MD in 1812. In 1813 she entered military service and was made Staff Surgeon in Canada. She served in South Africa, the West Indies and the Crimea. She performed at least one caesarian section;

made controversially strict administrative decisions about health care, sanitary conditions, and the diet of the sick; and presented a significant report on a plant from the Cape of Good Hope which treated syphilis and gonorrhoea.

It is thought that her real sex was known to one physician and probably to the highest army command. The Registrar-General heard rumours at her death and ordered an autopsy. When she was found to be a woman her previously-arranged military funeral was countermanded. Although she may have been reared as a boy, she probably masqueraded as a man in order to practise medicine, thus becoming the first woman MD in the UK.

J. Rose: *The Perfect Gentleman* (1977)

**Suggia, Guilhermina** (1888–1950). Portuguese cellist. Having had lessons from her father, she was appearing in public concerts (as a soloist and in string quartets) and was leading the cello section of the Orpheon Portuense, Oporto, before she had reached her teens. In 1904 she continued her studies with Klengel in Leipzig, where she joined the Gewandhaus Orchestra the following year and appeared as a soloist under Nikisch. Her liaison with Casals (1906–12) led to her being called 'Mme P. Casals-Suggia' in some advertisements, though they never married. Concerts in England, where she lived for some years, included piano trios with JELLY D'ARÁNYI and Fanny Davies. Her final appearance, after a period of retirement in Portugal, was at the Edinburgh Festival of 1949. Augustus John's portrait of her has contributed to her lasting reputation.

**Sullerot** [née Hammel], **Evelyne (Annie Henriette)** (1924–). French sociologist and journalist. Born in Montrou, she was educated at Compiègne, Royan and Uzès, and then at the universities of Paris and Aix-en-Provence. She married François Sullerot in 1946 and they have four children. A lecturer from 1947 to 1949, she was founder of the French movement for family planning in 1955 and its Secretary until 1958; she has remained honorary President. She established a centre for the study of mass communications in 1960 and she has taught at the Institut Français de la Presse since

1963. She has been an adviser to the European Economic Community since 1960 and to the International Labour Organization since 1970, and is a member of the French Economic and Social Council. A traditional feminist, she is the author of many books including *La vie des femmes* (1964), *Demain les femmes* (1965), *Histoire et sociologie du travail féminin* (1968), *La femme dans le monde moderne* (1970), *Les françaises au travail* (1973) and *Histoire et mythologie de l'amour* (1976). She is the editor of *Le fait féminin,* the proceedings of a colloquium of medical and behavioural scientists in 1978.

**Summerskill, Edith (Clara)** [Baroness Summerskill of Kenwood] (1901–80). English politician. She was born in London and educated at King's College, London, and Charing Cross Hospital, qualifying as a doctor at the age of 23. In 1924 she married Dr Jeffrey Samuel and they later shared a practice. Her work as a doctor among London's poor and with the Socialist Medical Association increased her political commitment. From 1934 to 1941 she was a member of Middlesex County Council and in 1934 also stood as Labour candidate at Putney, reducing the Conservative majority by 18,000. An unsuccessful candidate at Bury in 1935, she captured West Fulham in an important by-election in 1938.

Her main concerns were with preventive medicine, national insurance and women's rights (equal pay, birth control, wages for housework, property rights, painless childbirth). In the 1930s she travelled to Spain at the request of the Republican government, to study the condition of women and children; she also examined welfare and maternity services in the USA, Italy and the USSR. In 1945 she became Under-Secretary at the Ministry of Food, and was responsible for the Clean Milk Act in 1949 ('my finest hour'). She was Minister of National Insurance in 1950–51. A member of the National Executive from 1944, she was Chairman of the Labour Party in 1954–5. From 1955 to 1961 she represented Warrington and she took a prominent part in all debates on social security as a member of the Shadow Cabinet until 1957. With boundless energy she protected women's rights in many controversial areas; just tax of prostitutes' earnings, legal rights in polygamous marriages, and the interpretation of the co-habitation rule.

During the 1950s she was President of the Married Women's Association and she saw a successful result of her campaigns, with the Married Woman's Property Act (1964), and the Matrimonial Homes Act (1967). She also campaigned against professional boxing (*The Ignoble Art*, 1956) and smoking. In 1961 she was created a life peeress, and in 1966 was made a Companion of Honour. Her daughter, Shirley Summerskill, is also a doctor and an influential Labour MP.

E. Summerskill: *A Woman's World* (1967)

**Sutherland, Dame Joan** (1926–). Australian soprano. She was educated in Sydney, receiving piano and singing lessons from her mother. Her professional debut, as Dido, was in a concert performance of Purcell's *Dido and Aeneas* (1947). Competition awards enabled her to continue her studies in London at the Royal College of Music and Opera School. Her first auditions at Covent Garden were unsuccessful, but she joined the company in 1952 and in 1955 was chosen to create the role of Jenifer in Tippett's *The Midsummer Marriage*. With the immense success of her performance in Donizetti's *Lucia di Lammermoor* (Covent Garden, 1959) her international career was initiated: she made her American debut the following year, and in 1961 repeated the role of Lucia for her first appearances at the Metropolitan, New York, and at La Scala, Milan. Although primarily associated with similar coloratura roles in 19th-century Italian and French operas, notably Bellini's Norma, she has also been acclaimed for her performances of Handel. In 1954 she married Richard Bonynge, whose training did much to develop her technique; he became her regular accompanist and conductor. They settled in Switzerland in 1960 and have continued to tour widely, having a particularly successful Australian season in 1965–6 (with their own specially formed opera company) and being invited to appear at the opening of the South Korean cultural centre in 1978. She was made CBE in 1961 and DBE in 1979.

B. Adams: *La Stupenda: a Biography of Joan Sutherland* (1981)

N. Major: *Joan Sutherland: the Authorized Biography* (1987) [incl. discography]

**Suzman** [née Gavronsky], **Helen** (1917–). South African Liberal politician. Born in Germiston in the Transvaal, she was the daughter of a Lithuanian immigrant, and was educated at a convent and then at the University of Witwatersrand. She worked as a statistician for the War Supplies Board from 1941 to 1944, before becoming a lecturer in economics and economic history at Witwatersrand (1944–52) and at the same time undertaking voluntary social work. In 1937 she had married Dr Moses Suzman and they have two daughters. She became Member of Parliament for the United Party in 1953 and was a co-founder of the Progressive Party in 1959. At first the party's only MP, she had virtually alone to combat hostility from the white community in her fight against apartheid, and her struggle won her the UN Human Rights Award in 1978 and the Medallion of Heroism in 1980. Her later campaigns have been for an investigation of the torture and death of activists in police custody.

**Svolou, Maria** (*d* 1976). Greek feminist and Communist socialist. At an early age she made an impact in public life as an active member of the women's movement in Greece. For years, as Secretary of the League for Women's Rights, she worked devotedly for the emancipation of Greek women, writing articles on their unequal treatment, fighting against prostitution and instigating the creation of evening schools for working women. She then obtained a post in the Ministry of Economics and as an Inspector of Labour took great interest in working-class women and for the first time revealed their appalling housing and working conditions.

From 1911 to 1936 she was in the forefront of political activities against Fascism and in favour of the peace movement. She was Editor of the magazine *Woman's Struggle* and gave many open lectures on pressing social problems. From 1936 to 1940 – a period of Metaxas's dictatorship – she followed her husband Alexander Svolous, a professor of law, into exile because of their left-wing political views.

In 1940 she served as a volunteer nurse during the Greek–Albanian War and later in the Red Cross, organizing communal meals for children during the German occupation. She fought in the resistance against the Germans and for a year was a member of the National Council, the independent government set up in the mountains of free Greece.

In 1948, after the civil war in Greece which followed the withdrawal of the Germans, she was again sent into exile because of her Communist sympathies. On her return she was twice elected MP for the Greek Leftist Party and was a member of its Central Committee.

**Swanson, Gloria** (1899–1983). American film actress. The highest paid star of the silent screen (earning $20,000 a week), Gloria travelled around as a child, picking up an education in Chicago, Florida, Puerto Rico and elsewhere. She was 'discovered' while working as a shop-girl in Chicago and after acting in Keystone comedies from 1916, a contract with de Mille took her to Hollywood at the age of 18. An early pin-up, she featured in endless bathing sequences, in comedies of sexual manners like *Don't Change Your Husband, Why Change Your Wife*, and in portraits of unhappy sophisticated women. Her own life was rarely out of the gossip columns, and in 1926 with her lover Joseph P. Kennedy, she formed Swanson Productions, losing a fortune backing von Stroheim's *Queen Kelly*, which gave her one of her most powerful roles. Her flamboyant style went out of fashion in the 1930s and she retreated into a bitter retirement, making a triumphant comeback in Wilder's *Sunset Boulevard* as Norma Desmond, a regal aging star watching her own movies (a clip from *Queen Kelly*) and declaring 'I'm still big, it's the pictures that get small.

She had six husbands, one a French marquis, Henri de la Falaise. Her last marriage, to writer William Duffy, ended in divorce in 1981.

**Swanwick** [née Sickert], **Helena (Maria Lucy)** (1864–1939). British suffrage worker and pacifist. Born in Munich, the daughter of the artist and cartoonist Oswald Sickert,

she moved to England in 1868. She was educated in France from 1872 to 1876 and then at Notting Hill School in London. Her family's friends included the Burne Joneses, William Morris, Oscar Wilde and George Bernard Shaw. After graduating in Moral Sciences from Girton College in 1885 she became a psychology lecturer at Westfield College, London. In 1888 she married Frederick Swanwick, lecturer, and later Professor of Mathematics, at Owens College, Manchester. There she worked as a journalist and lecturer and was active in working-men's clubs, the Co-operative Guild and the Women's Trade Union Council. After 1900 she joined the North of England Suffrage Society, advocating constitutional as opposed to militant tactics. In 1909 she became Editor of *The Common Cause* but returned to free-lance writing in 1912, contributing to *The Manchester Guardian, The Observer, The Nation,* and *The Daily News.* In 1913 she attended the International Suffrage Congress in Budapest and published *The Future of the Women's Movement.*

Her violent opposition to World War I led her to join first the Union of Democratic Control (UDC) and then the Independent Labour Party, and she was President of the British branch of the Women's International League for Peace. She worked for the UDC until 1928, writing *Builders of Peace* (1924) and editing the journal *Foreign Affairs* (1924–7). After the war she was adviser to the Labour Party on international affairs and was a delegate to the League of Nations in 1924 and 1929; she became Vice-president of the League of Nations Union. During the 1930s she was a passionate advocate of pacifism and disarmament in Women's International League pamphlets and in works such as *Collective Insecurity* (1937). She died after the outbreak of World War II, in November 1939, following an overdose of sleeping pills.

H. Swanwick: *I have been young* (1935)

**Sylva, Carmen.** *See* ELISABETH OF ROMANIA.

**Syrkius** [née Niemirowska], **Helena** (1900–82). Polish architect. Born in Warsaw, she studied architecture at the Institute of Technology there (1918–23), but went on to devote two years to humanities and philosophy. In 1926 she married Simon Syrkius, who was her partner until his death in 1964. Together they became a major force in Polish and international avant-garde architectural design. In the 1920s and 1930s they were influenced by the Futurist and modernist movements, reflecting their approach in the journal *Praesens*, in which a functionalist approach attempts to relate architecture to social concerns. Helena worked for the Underground Polish Government during World War II and afterwards was head of the committee devoted to the rebuilding of Warsaw. In 1949 she moved to the Institute of Architecture and Town Planning at Warsaw, rising to Professor Emeritus in 1970. Simon and Helena Syrkius's ideas about the linking of social and environmental factors are highlighted in the Kolo Housing Development (1947–9), which was designated a historical monument in 1978. Helena was also an influential writer and theorist and a leading member of the Congrès Internationaux d'Architecture Moderne. During the 1970s she received many awards in Poland.

**Szold, Henrietta** (1860–1945). American Zionist leader. Born in Baltimore, Henrietta was the eldest of eight daughters of a Hungarian immigrant who had been a revolutionary in Vienna in 1848. Three of her sisters died in childhood. In 1877 she graduated from Baltimore's Western Female High School, and then taught English, French, German and Classics at a fashionable girls' school nearby for 15 years.

After the anti-semitic pogroms of the 1880s, thousands of Russian Jews fled to the USA. Szold became concerned at the difficulties they faced in adjusting to the new culture and in 1889 she founded a school in Baltimore to teach the language, customs and trades of the USA. During the next decade the school had 5000 pupils, and similar institutions were founded in other cities. She was also involved with Jewish discussion groups and was the Editorial Secretary of the Jewish publication society from 1893 to 1916. She visited Palestine, and returned a committed Zionist, becoming Secretary of the Federation of American Zionists in 1910 and organizing the women's body, Hadasseh, in 1912; their first task was to raise funds for medical units to be sent to Jerusalem. In 1918 Szold became Education Director of the newly-formed Zionist Organization of America. She visited Palestine two years later, and remained there for most of the rest of her life, although she never officially emigrated. During the 1920s and 1930s she arranged passages for many immigrants, and helped the work of the Youth Aliyah, which sent Jewish children out of fascist Germany. Shortly before World War II she became the first President of the League of Jewish Women. She paid her last visit to the USA in 1937.

I. Fineman: *Woman of Valor: the Life of Henrietta Szold* (1961)

# T

**Tabei, Junko** (1939–). Japanese mountaineer. Tabei was the first of four women who have now reached the top of Mount Everest (8864 metres) on separate expeditions. A slight woman (149 cm tall), she had a three-year old daughter at the time when she undertook to be deputy leader of an all-women Japanese expedition to Everest, and on 16 May 1975 reached the top with a male Sherpa. In the same year a Tibetan woman, Phanthog, also reached the summit.

**Taglioni, Marie** (1804–84). Italian ballerina. Born in Stockholm, she lived in Paris with her mother while her father, dancer and choreographer Filippo Taglioni, was on tour. She studied with Coulon at the Paris Opéra. Her father considered her unready for the debut prepared by him in Vienna and he subjected her to gruelling coaching before her first appearance in 1822. She instantly caught public attention as a poetic, wistful dancer.

From 1827 she danced at the Opéra, especially in works choreographed by her father such as *La sylphide,* and the *Ballet of the Nuns* in *Robert le diable.* She excelled in such supernatural ballets but could also adapt her style to other roles, such as Gitana. Taglioni was idolized in Paris (where her rivalry with FANNY ELSSLER was a *cause célèbre*); in London, where she appeared in the great *Pas de quatre* of 1845; and in St Petersburg [now Leningrad] (1837–42) where Czar Nicholas I was a professed admirer, and at a farewell banquet a pair of her ballet shoes was eaten 'cooked and served with a special sauce'. She is the subject of many other stories: in Russia she was held up by bandits and made to dance on furs laid in the road. In 1832 she married the Comte de Voisins; they were later divorced.

She had an illegitimate child but her lover died in Russia at the height of her fame.

Taglioni travelled back to Paris via Poland and Austria and retired to Lake Como in 1847. She returned to France in 1858 to be principal teacher at the Opéra, especially coaching the talented 16-year-old Emma Livry, for whom she created the ballet *Papillon*; Emma died when her dress caught fire at rehearsal. Towards the end of her life Taglioni opened a school in London but went to Marseilles in 1880, where she died in the same year as her great rival Fanny Elssler. Taglioni remains the prototype of the romantic ballerina.

A. Levinson: *Marie Taglioni* (1977)

**Tailleferre, Germaine** (1892–1984). French composer. She is known primarily as the only woman member of Les Six, a group of French composers (Auric, Durey, Honegger, Milhaud, Poulenc and Tailleferre) who, inspired by the examples of Satie and Cocteau, achieved notoriety in the 1920s for their rebellion against the aesthetic of romanticism. Most of them went to the Paris Conservatoire, where (despite parental opposition to a career in music) Tailleferre studied from 1904, winning three *premiers prix*. For their first collective concert (1917), which included Tailleferre's String Quartet, they were known as Les Nouveaux Jeunes, acquiring their more familiar label in 1920, when a review mentioned 'Les six français' alongside the Russian Five. During the group's short-lived hey-day, her music was well-received. She wrote several ballets and comic operas, some orchestral music, of which the *Pastorale* and *Ballade* (1922, for piano and orchestra) were particularly popular, as well as chamber music, pieces for two pianos and songs. Notable performances include the première of her ballet *Le marchand d'oiseaux* by the Ballets Suédois (Paris, 1923) and that of her Piano Concertino by the British Women's Symphony Orchestra with Cortot as soloist; Thibaud and Cortot included her Violin Sonata in their recitals. When Les Six dispersed, however, Tailleferre's productivity declined. Among her few later works, the Clarinet Sonata (1958) ventures into serial techniques, though most of her output captures the light-heartedness of the 1920s. She lived in the USA between 1942 and 1946. She published her *Mémoires à l'emporte pièce* in 1974.

**Talbot, Elizabeth,** Countess of Shrewsbury [Bess of Hardwick] (1518–1608). English aristocrat. The fourth daughter of a Derbyshire squire, John Hardwick, she married a local man, Robert Barlow, at the age of 14 but was widowed a year later, acquiring a considerable amount of land. She did not marry again until 1549, when she became the wife of Sir William Cavendish; six of their children survived to adulthood. Cavendish died after he had begun building Chatsworth; Elizabeth again inherited and again ensured that she kept her lands for her heirs in the settlement accompanying her next marriage, to Sir William Loe. He too died, she inherited, and was now so wealthy that she was courted by and married to the Earl of Shrewsbury. In 1568 he became the custodian of Mary, Queen of Scots, on behalf of ELIZABETH I, and remained so for 16 years, despite his wife's rash move in marrying her daughter Elizabeth Cavendish to Mary's brother-in-law, the Earl of Lennox; this led to her imprisonment in the Tower for three months. She later adopted her grand-daughter by this marriage, Arabella Stuart.

In 1583 Bess left her husband, with whom she had long been on bad terms, and settled at Chatsworth, building many houses in Derbyshire. After Shrewsbury's death in 1591 she created a new house at Hardwick, where she died 11 years after its completion in 1597. She was a stubborn, independent character, renowned for her territorial greed, her commercial astuteness, and her love of intrigue. She was one of the most assertive women in a vigorous age.

D. Durant: *Bess of Hardwick* (1977)

**Tallien, Thérésia de Cabarrus** (1773–1835). French political adventuress. Daughter of a Spanish banker, at 15 she married the Marquis de Fontenay and was presented at the court of Louis XV. In the 1780s she began to take an interest in liberal politics, and when her husband fled at the outbreak of the French Revolution in 1789 she resumed her maiden name, spoke before the Convention and obtained a divorce in 1791. Three years later she took refuge in Bordeaux and although arrested as the former wife of an emigré aristocrat, she ingratiated herself with the Commissary of the Convention, Tallien, became his mistress and through her influence obtained the release of many prisoners. She accompanied him when he was recalled to Paris, only to be imprisoned on Robespierre's orders first in La Force, then Carmes where she met JOSEPHINE DE BEAUHARNAIS. Tallien joined the conspiracy to oust Robespierre and in 1795 Thérésia was released and acclaimed as 'Notre Dame de Thermidor'. The couple were married, but divorced in 1802.

Her salon became the centre of Directoire society. Tallien's power waned and after a brief flirtation with Napoleon, she moved first to the powerful Barras, then to the millionaire-speculator Ouvrard and finally, attempting to gain respectability, she married the Comte de Caraman in 1805. The death of his father (allegedly from rage at the match) elevated her quickly to Princesse de Chimay, and she spent the rest of her life on their estates, which became part of Holland after the Battle of Waterloo. She bore ten children during her various liaisons.

L. Gastine: *Madame Tallien* (1930)

**Tamiris** [née Becker], **Helen** (1905–66). American dancer and choreographer. The daughter of Russian parents from the New York East Side, she showed early promise and received lessons from Irene Lewisohn at the Henry Street Settlement. From the age of 15 until 19 she danced with the Metropolitan Opera Ballet, including a season in South America, and then changed her name to Tamiris 'the ruthless queen who banishes all obstacles'. She left the Metropolitan to study with Fokin and performed in *Casanova*. After a short spell at the Duncan Studio, she danced in Chicago night clubs and revue, creating her own concert programme, based on contemporary jazz culture, spirituals and folk music, as in *Dance Moods* (1927). In 1928 she toured Salzburg, Paris and Berlin, returned to the USA the following year and created a series of social protest dances such as *Revolutionary March* and *Dance of the City*. She founded her own company, helped to found the Dance Repertory Theatre (1930–31) and worked for the Federal Theatre Project. From 1930 to 1945 she directed the School of American Dance.

During the 1930s her work emphasized social themes: *Cycle of Unrest*; *Manhattan*; *How Long, Brethren* (1937); and *Adelante* (on the Spanish Civil War) 1939. Her most affirmative work was the *Walt Whitman Suite* (1934). She continued to explore American themes with the *Liberty Song* (1941), and became a successful Broadway choreographer with *Annie get your Gun* (1946), *Inside USA* (1948) and *Plain and Fancy* (1955). From 1960 to 1963 she directed the Tamiris-Nagrin dance company with her husband.

**Tamyris** (*fl* 6th century BC). Scythian Queen. The ruler of the Massagetae tribe in Persia [now Iran], she was a famous warrior queen. According to Herodotus she opposed Cyrus the Great, who had wished to obtain her kingdom by marriage with her. She refused him, sent her armies to stop his invasion, and after the death of her son, the military leader, led her troops in battle. She defeated Cyrus, and to avenge her son, killed him.

**Tanaka, Kinuyo** (1910–77). Japanese film actress. One of the greatest actresses in Japanese cinema, Kinuyo Tanaka was born in Shinomoseki City, went to school in Osaka until 1919, and studied the musical instrument chikuzen-biwa. She had a brief career in musical theatre, with the Biwa Shojo Kafeti Girls revue in Osaka from 1920 to 1923, and in 1924 joined the Shochiku Kamata Film Company, one of the most influential studios of the time, to make her first film, *Genroku Onna* ('Women of Genroku'). She became the most celebrated star of silent films, playing a variety of parts, from innocent girls to prostitutes. In 1929 she

married the director Hiroshi Shimizu, but they were divorced the same year.

Tanaka appeared in the first Japanese talkie, *Madame to Nyobo* ('Madame and wife', 1931) and her soft voice brought her still more admirers. She obtained critical recognition for her brilliant performance as a blind woman in *Okoto to Sasuke* (1935) and in 1940 she made *Osaka Elegy*, the first of several films with the director Kenji Mizoguchi; it is for their long association that she is best known. Her most famous roles include Oharu in *Sai* ('The life of Oharu', 1952), the potter's wife in *Ogetsu Monogari* (1953) and the mother in *Sansho the Bailiff* (1954). She broke with Mizoguchi because she wanted to direct, and so became one of Japan's few women producers, directing six films between 1953 and 1962, beginning with *Love Letters* (1953). She continued to act in films and on television throughout the 1960s and 1970s and her portrayal of an ageing prostitute in *Sandakan No. 8* (1974) won her the Kinema Jumpo Prize, the Japanese film industry's highest award, and the Best Actress award at the Berlin Festival in 1975. Her career in films thus spanned 50 years, from her early melodramas to her late realistic films.

**Tarbell, Ida (Minerva)** (1857–1944). American journalist. Born in Pennsylvania, she graduated from Allegheny College in 1880, one of only five women students, and after teaching in an Ohio seminary worked for *The Chautauquan*, a home-study teaching guide, from 1883 to 1891. She then spent three years in Paris, studying at the Sorbonne and Collège de France, writing features and interviews for *McClures*. Her articles on Napoleon Buonaparte, republished in book form in 1895, brought national fame and were followed by biographies of Madame Roland (1896) and Abraham Lincoln (1900). From 1894 she was Assistant Editor of *McClures*, where she began publishing her aggressive *History of the Standard Oil Company* in 1902.

With a group of investigative journalists, dubbed 'muckrakers' by Theodore Roosevelt, she collectively owned and edited the *American Magazine* from 1906 to 1915, campaigning against corruption and big business interests. From 1915 to 1932 she was a travelling lecturer. An influential commentator, in 1919 she was a member of

President Wilson's Industrial Conference, and later of Harding's Unemployment Conference. Although in 1912 in *The Business of being a Woman* she did not support the suffrage movement, she was always a social feminist and was a member of the National Women's Mobilization Committee for Human Needs (1933–8).

I.M. Tarbell: *All in the Day's Work* (1939)

**Tate, Phyllis (Margaret)** (1911–87). English composer. She studied at the Royal Academy of Music, London (1928–32), where she was a composition pupil of Harry Farjeon. During the 1920s and 1930s she produced a considerable amount of light music under various assumed names. Most of her early works, including the one-act opera *The Policeman's Serenade* (performed while she was a student), were destroyed after World War II. The work with which she first reached a wide public was the Concerto for alto saxophone and strings (1944), commissioned by the BBC. Her Sonata for clarinet and cello, given its première in London in 1947, was chosen for inclusion in the 1952 festival of the International Society for Contemporary Music. After writing several more instrumental works, notably the String Quartet in F (1952, rev. 1982 as Movements for String Quartet), she was drawn increasingly to vocal music, resulting in the successful production of her two-act opera *The Lodger* (1960), based on the story of Jack the Ripper. Not a prolific composer, she concentrated on small-scale forms, as in *The Lady of Shalott* for tenor (1956) and the choral *Secular Requiem* (1967), both with unusual instrumental combinations. Among her most substantial choral works is *St Martha and the Dragon* (1976), a setting of Charles Causley's poem. Her commitment to writing music that is readily assimilated also led her to write highly effective music for young performers, notably the operettas *Twice in a Blue Moon* (1969) and *Scarecrow* (1982). She was the first woman to serve on the management committee of the Performing Right Society's Members' Fund (1976–81).

**Tauber-Arp, Sophie** (1889–1943). Swiss artist. Born in Davos, she trained in Munich and at the Hamburg Kunstgewerbeschule, specializing in decorative art. She became a member of an avant-garde group of craftsmen and artists in 1915, and later taught weaving and embroidery in Zürich, from 1916 to 1929. She also studied dance and the new theories of movement of Laban (*See* MARY WIGMAN), and joined the group of Dadaists (including Jean Arp, Janco Ball, Tristan Tzara) in their entertainments of poetry, dance and music at the Cabaret Voltaire in the Spiegelgasse. Although controversial and successful, the group broke up by 1919. In 1918 Sophie had created marionettes for Gozzi's *Le roi cerf* and she continued to be interested in theatre and design, but her painting became increasingly abstract and geometric. She published *Dessin et arts textils* in 1927 with Blanche Gauchat. In 1928 the Arps moved to Paris, where they lived until 1940, and here Sophie produced some of her finest paintings and wood reliefs. During World War II they moved to Grasse, sharing their home with SONIA DELAUNAY. They returned to Switzerland in 1942. Sophie died in an accident due to a faulty heating system in their Zürich hotel.

**Taussig, Helen Brooke** (1898–1986). American doctor. Born into an academic Boston family, Helen attended Radcliffe College, the University of California and others before obtaining her MD at Johns Hopkins University School of Medicine in 1927. In 1930 she was put in charge of the cardiac clinic of the Harriet Lane Home for Invalid Children and held this post until her retirement in 1963, specializing in congenital malformations of the heart.

Her first work at the clinic was on acute rheumatic fever, where she found the causes of cardiac enlargement and showed that a child could outgrow this. Her major work, however, was with Alfred Blalock, as co-developer on the clinical side of the 'blue baby' operation in 1944. She had observed that many cyanotic infants died of lack of oxygen rather than heart failure, and suggested the insertion of a blood vessel between the subclavian and pulmonary arteries. The child's dramatic change from blue to pink on the operating table established the validity of the operation, which brought them many honours including the Lasker Award.

In her book *Congenital Malformations of the Heart* (2/1960–61) she was the first to demonstrate that changes in the heart and lungs could be diagnosed by x-rays and the fluoroscope. In 1959 she was promoted from instructor to become the first woman appointed a full Professor in the Johns Hopkins Medical School. In 1962 she heard of an unusual malformation occurring in Germany and went there to investigate; by doing so she was able to alert American doctors of the dangers of thalidomide.

**Taylor, Annie R.** (1855–?1920). English traveller and missionary. Born in Egremont, Cheshire, Annie heard a missionary lecture when she was 13 and decided to dedicate her life to missionary work. She visited slums in Brighton and London, and, despite family opposition, at 28 she sailed to Shanghai with the China Inland Mission. For three years she was posted around the Yangtze River [now Chang Jiang] then to Lanchow [now Lanzhou] near the Tibetan border, and found that as a single woman she could move freely among Chinese women, urging them to study the Bible, influence their menfolk and unbind their feet.

She recovered from an illness in Australia, and then went to Darjeeling, where with the Mission's approval she worked among Tibetans and studied their language. In Sikkim she had converted a Tibetan youth, Pontso, to Christianity and took him as her servant on the 2092 km journey to Tibet which took seven months. She crossed Tibet through wild and magnificent country and at various times she was ambushed, robbed, encountered wolves, was beleaguered by ice and snow and suffered her horse dying under her, but her writing was more concerned with 'claiming the country for the Master'. At Lhasa she was sent back by a military chief and could not proceed to Darjeeling. The return journey was even more dangerous.

On her return to London, Annie was lionised. She gave lectures, and then formed a 'Tibetan Pioneer Band' of nine others, all men, to return to Darjeeling. This group was not successful, and Annie moved to Yatung and opened a shop. Her journey to Lhasa helped the British government to establish trade relations with Tibet and she worked as a nurse for the Younghusband mission when it passed through to Lhasa in 1904. Before

1909 Annie returned to England in poor health; her end is unknown.

A.R. Taylor: *Diary* in *William Carey's Travel and Adventure in Tibet* (1902)

**Taylor, Elizabeth** (1912–75). British novelist. Born Elizabeth Coles in Reading, Berkshire, and educated at the local Abbey School, she wrote secretly from an early age. After working as a governess and in a library, she married a businessman, John Taylor; they had two children and settled in Penn, Buckinghamshire. Much of her fiction is set in this middle-class, commuter society which she explores with sensitivity and wit. The best-known of her 12 novels include her first, *At Mrs Lippincott's* (1945), the best-seller *A Wreath of Roses* (1949), *Angel* (1957) and *Mrs Palfrey at the Claremont* (1971). She also wrote short stories for leading magazines such as *The New Yorker, Harper's* and *Vogue*, which were collected in four volumes between 1954 and 1972. Her reputation, high during her life, has soared again recently, and she has sometimes been described as a modern Jane Austen.

**Taylor, Elizabeth** (1932–). American actress. She was born in London and her American parents returned to Los Angeles in 1939. Elizabeth became a child performer in *There's one born every Minute* (1942), which she followed with films such as *Lassie Come Home* (1943) and *National Velvet* (1944), growing up, in cinematic terms, in *Little Women* (1949), *Father of the Bride* (1950) and *Ivanhoe* (1952). In 1950 she was briefly married to Nick Hilton, then to Michael Wilding (1952–7), and in 1957 to Mike Todd, who died in an air crash in 1958; she married the singer Eddie Fisher in 1959.

During the late 1950s she had made films such as *Raintree Country* (1957), *Cat on a Hot Tin Roof* (1958) and *Suddenly last Summer* (1959). She won an Academy Award for *Butterfield 8* in 1960. She attracted endless publicity, especially during the filming of *Cleopatra* (1963), after which she married her co-star Richard Burton. With him she made *The Taming of the Shrew* and *Dr Faustus* (both 1967) as well as the abrasive *Who's afraid of Virginia Woolf?* (1965). One of her best roles, a study of neurosis and suppressed sexuality, was in

John Houston's film of CARSON MCCULLERS's novel *Reflections in a Golden Eye* (1967). One of the most public marriages of the century ended in 1976. She subsequently married the American politician John Warner, from whom she separated in 1981. She continued to act, most recently in the American–Russian co-production of *The Bluebird*. On Broadway in 1981 and in London in 1982 she appeared on stage, amid much publicity, in LILLIAN HELLMAN's *The Little Foxes*.

She has continued to appear in films, such as *Between Friends* (1983), but has fought a much publicized battle against overweight and drugs, and has campaigned widely for humanitarian causes, especially AIDS research. In 1986 she received the Lifetime Achievement Award from the Film Society in New York, and in 1987 was awarded the French Légion d'honneur by François Mitterand, for her distinguished film career.

**Taylor, Harriet** (1808–58). English feminist. While married to a 'drysalter and wholesale druggist' in London, Harriet Taylor met John Stuart Mill in 1830. They became deeply attached to each other and spent much time together, a situation fully accepted by her husband, although it caused deep disapproval in the Mill family. Her husband died in 1849 and the couple were married in 1851. Harriet influenced Mill's ideas, particularly on the issues of social justice and personal liberty, for example as expressed in the chapter 'Probable Future of the Labouring Classes' in *Principles of Political Economy* (1848). In 1851 she published an article, 'The Enfranchisement of Women', in *The Westminster Review*, which explores women's claims to equality, and the 'female' intuitive nature of women, and defends the movement for political and legal emancipation against recent hostile arguments. When Mill eventually published *On the Subjection of Women* in 1869 he claimed that it was mostly due to Harriet's genius. They worked together in London, but in 1858 Mill's poor health made them decide to winter in the south of France. Harriet's health had also been poor for many years and on the journey she fell ill and died at Avignon. Mill bought a house there and spent six months of each year there, in her memory, for most of his life.

**Teerling** [née Benninck], **Levina** (1515–76). Flemish artist. The daughter of miniature painter Simon Benninck, she was born in Bruges, and studied there with her father. She married George Teerling and together they came to the court of Henry VIII in London. There Levina was given a fee as a court painter, a £40 annuity which was reduced to £10 in the reign of Edward VI and returned to its full amount by ELIZABETH I in 1559. She painted several portraits of Elizabeth after 1551, although attributions to her remain doubtful. A famous figure in her day, she became an English citizen in 1566; she died in Stepney.

**Te Kanawa, Kiri** (1944–). New Zealand soprano. Born into a Maori background on the North Island of New Zealand, she was adopted by a couple in Gisborne who gave her the name of Kiri, the Maori word for Bell. She was given a Roman Catholic education. Her singing was encouraged and she won many prizes; by the time she left New Zealand in 1966, she had a flourishing career entertaining in night clubs. She was accepted at the London Opera Centre without audition. Early appearances in England include those with Northern Opera and the Chelsea Opera Group. In 1970 she joined the Royal Opera Company, being cast as a Flower Maiden in Wagner's *Parsifal* and as Xenia in Musorgsky's *Boris Godunov*. In was in 1971, when she appeared as the Countess in Mozart's *Marriage of Figaro*, however, that her exceptional talent was recognized. She was immediately invited to sing the same role in Lyons (1971), San Francisco (1972) and Glyndebourne (1973). The lavish praise already accorded her was further endorsed by her debut at the Metropolitan Opera, New York, as Desdemona in Verdi's *Otello* (1974). Particularly well suited to Mozart and Verdi, she brings vibrant tone and a simple yet dignified stage presence equally to such roles as Mimi (Puccini's *La Bohème*), Tatyana (Tchaikovsky's *Eugene Onegin*), Marguerite (Gounod's *Faust*) and Micaela (Bizet's *Carmen*). She has appeared in most of the major opera centres in Europe, the USA and Australia. Besides her many recordings, she has reached a still wider audience through her performances of filmed opera, notably as Donna Elvira in Joseph Losey's production of Mozart's *Don Giovanni*. At the wedding of

Prince Charles and Lady Diana Spencer (1981) she sang 'Let the bright seraphim' from Handel's oratorio *Samson*, and in 1982 she was created a DBE.

D. Fingleton: *Kiri: a Biography* (1982)

**Telessilla** (5th century BC). Greek poet from Argos. She wrote hymns and patriotic songs, but is mainly remembered as a saviour of her city during a siege by the Spartans. While all the men were away fighting, Telessilla moved the women, through the power of her heroic verses, to take up arms and defend their city. Thus inspired they attacked and drove away the enemy. In gratitude for what she had done, her fellow citizens dedicated a statue to her in the temple of Aphrodite. The fragments of her poetry which survive are mostly hymns to Apollo and Artemis.

**Tempest,** Dame **Marie** [pseud. of Mary Susan Etherington] (1864–1942). English actress and singer. She trained as a singer and began her stage career in musical comedy but in 1899 she began to perform in dramatic roles. After London successes in comedy she toured the world as Kitty in *The Marriage of Kitty* (1902) and on her return to London became renowned for her playing of elegant middle-aged women. Her 'small, exquisite talent' (Agate) was best displayed as Judith Bliss in *Hay Fever* (1925), a part written especially for her by Noel Coward. She was made DBE in 1937.

H. Bolitho: *Marie Tempest* (1937)

**Tencin.** *See* DE TENCIN.

**Teng Ying-Ch'ao.** *See* DENG YINGCHAO.

**Tennant, May** [Margaret] **(Mary Edith)** (1869–1946). Irish reformer. Born in County Dublin, the daughter of a public service lawyer, she went to London in 1887, worked as secretary to Lady EMILY DILKE and became Treasurer of the Women's Trade Union League (WTUL). Her work for the Royal Commission on Labour in 1891 led to her appointment as the first woman factory inspector where she concentrated on illegal overtime, bad sanitation and safety and in 1895 sat on a departmental committee on dangerous trades. She married the committee chairman, Liberal MP Harold

Tennant, the following year. She later became Chairman of the Industrial Law Committee, a member of the Royal Commission on Divorce and adviser on women's welfare to the Ministry of Munitions (1914–18). Like GERTRUDE TUCKWELL, in later life she turned to problems of women's health, particularly maternal mortality.

V. Markham: *May Tennant* (1949)

**Te Puea,** Princess (1884–1952). Maori leader. Te Puea was born at Whatiwhatihoe in the Waikato, daughter of Tahuna Herangi and Princess Tiahuia, and grand-daughter of King Tawhiao. Her grandfather had placed a ban on his people attending official New Zealand schools after Maori lands were confiscated in the 1860s, but at 11 Te Puea went to Mercer School, then to Mangere and Parnell. After her mother's death when she was 15, she became the centre of attention in her tribe, arousing much disapproval among the elders, until she rescued King Mahuta from stampeding horses and gained the respect of the tribe. She then became even more outspoken and dominant at tribal meetings and determined to improve conditions for her people. In the 1920s, in Ngarnwahia, she persuaded Waikato craftsmen to give their labour free to create carved meeting houses and develop long-forgotten arts. She also inspired the revival of Maori agriculture, working on the land herself, and encouraged social reform, founding organizations for women and children. Her national stature was recognized by the award of the CBE. She was married to Rewi Tumoko Katipa.

**Teresa, Mother** [Gonxha Bejaxhia, Agnes] (1910–). Yugoslavian founder. Born of Albanian parents in Skopje, she decided, while still at school, that she wanted to work as a missionary among the poor of Bengal. In 1929, as Sister Teresa, she joined the congregation of Loreto nuns in Calcutta and taught at their school for girls for nearly 20 years. On 10 September 1946 in the train to Darjeeling, Mother Teresa received a clear call from God to leave the convent and help the poor while living among them. Two years later she started her work in the slums of Calcutta and set up the new congregation of the Missionaries of Charity; this new order has now spread throughout India and centres have been established in a number of other countries. The basic belief underlying Mother Teresa's work is that by serving the poor, Jesus is being served; the sisters are first of all religious, not social workers or nurses. Her book *Gift from God* appeared in 1975. In 1979 she received the Nobel Peace Prize, and in 1985 the Presidential Medal of Freedom in the USA.

D. Doig: *Mother Teresa: her People and her Work* (1976)

**Teresa of Ávila** [De Cepeda y Ahumada, Teresa] (1515–82). Spanish saint and founder. She was descended from an old well-to-do Spanish family. In 1533 she entered the local Carmelite convent but without any strong sense of vocation. At first she suffered serious ill-health, but she persevered with prayer and made deep progress in contemplation, and frequently experienced ecstasy and mystical visions.

In order to lead a more mortified life, Teresa wanted to found a house where the primitive rule of the Carmelite order would be strictly observed. Against much opposition, she succeeded in opening St Joseph's at Ávila in 1562, a small, poor, strictly enclosed and highly-disciplined community with daily mental prayer as part of the rule. During the next 20 years Teresa travelled throughout Spain, frequently in conditions of great hardship, and founded another 17 convents. Under her influence reform also spread to the men of the order.

St Teresa is the classical example of a person who combined the life of religious contemplation with intense activity and commonsense efficiency in practical affairs. Her writings include her spiritual autobiography (up to 1562, completed 1565), the *Way of Perfection, Book of Foundations* and *The Interior Castle*. With St Catherine of Siena, she was one of the first two women ever to be officially declared doctors of the Church.

V. Sackville-West: *The Eagle and the Dove* (1943)

**Teresa of Lisieux** [Martin, Thérèse] (1873–97). French Carmelite nun and saint. The youngest daughter of Louis Martin, a devout watchmaker of Alençon, Teresa's early religious inclinations grew in intensity from the time of her mother's death when she was four. At the age of 15 she joined two of her sisters at the Carmelite convent of Lisieux in

Normandy. The remaining nine years of her life were uneventful, similar to the lives of numberless other young nuns, until she died of tuberculosis at the age of 24.

In 1895 Sister Teresa had been told to write the recollections of her childhood, and she afterwards added an account of her later life. A heavily-edited version of this was published posthumously as *Histoire d'une âme*. It was an immediate and sensational success. Canonized in 1925, Teresa gained her extraordinary popularity by showing that sainthood is attainable by anybody, however ordinary, by following her 'little way' of 'spiritual childhood, the way of trust and absolute self-surrender'. In 1947 she was joined with Joan of Arc as patroness of France.

M. Furlong: *Thérèse of Lisieux* (1987)

**Tereshkova (Nikolayeva), Valentina (Vladimorovna)** (1937–). Russian cosmonaut. She was born on a farm in the village of Maslennikovo. Her father, a tractor driver, was killed in World War II. She worked first in a tyre factory, then followed her mother and sister into the textile trade. In 1959 she took up parachute jumping as a sport and became proficient; she was also an active member of Comsomol (Young Communist League). After Yuri Gagarin's first space flight in 1961, she wrote to the authorities volunteering herself.

An arduous physical and technical training culminated in her becoming the first woman in space on 16 June 1963. Her spaceship, Vostok VI, completed 48 orbits, travelling 1.2 million miles in three days before returning to earth. President Krushchev commented on the West's 'bourgeois' notion that woman is the weaker sex, pointing out that Valentina had been in flight longer than all four American astronauts combined. She was named Hero of the Soviet Union and received the Order of Lenin and Gold Star Medal.

Four months later she married a fellow cosmonaut, Andrian Nikolayev, and in 1964 had a daughter, Yelena. She continued as an aerospace engineer in the space programme, travelled abroad to lecture on her flight, became a member of the Presidium (1974), Chairwoman of the Soviet Women's Committee (1977) and Head of the Union of

Soviet Societies for Friendship with Foreign Countries in 1987.

M. Sharpe: '*It is I, Sea Gull*': *Valentina Tereshkova, First Woman in Space* (1974)

**Terry**, Dame **(Alice) Ellen** (1847–1928). English actress. She was born in Coventry, the third of eleven children of actor parents. Her first stage appearance was at the Princess Theatre, London, in *A Winter's Tale* at the age of eight. After a period in the provinces she returned to the Haymarket Theatre, London, but left in the middle of a run to marry the painter, G.F. Watts, in 1864. He was 27 years her senior. The marriage broke up ten months later. After a brief London season in which she acted with Henry Irving in *Katharine and Petrucchio*, between 1868 and 1874 she lived in the country with Edward Godwin, by whom she had two children, Edith and Edward Gordon Craig.

Pressed by debt, she returned to the stage to a brilliant success in *The Wandering Heir* by Charles Reade (1874). Subsequently she joined the Bancrofts at The Prince of Wales Theatre, giving a notable performance as Portia. Divorced from Watts in 1877, she married her second husband, Charles Kelly [pseud. for Wardell], but separated from him within three years. In 1878 Irving engaged her as his leading lady – a partnership that lasted until 1902. During this period she played the parts that established her reputation: Beatrice (considered her masterpiece), Portia, Desdemona, Viola, and Lady Teazle. Only her portrayal of Lady Macbeth divided critical opinion.

Ellen Terry became a manager herself in 1903, playing in Shakespeare and Ibsen's *Vikings*, directed by her son in 1906. Barrie and Shaw both wrote parts for her (in *Alice Sit-by-the-Fire*, and *Captain Brassbound's Conversion*), but the last phase of her career lost direction. In 1907 she made another unsuccessful marriage lasting only two years to the American actor James Carew. Ellen Terry's freshness, vitality, natural gentleness and command of mood made her more of a national figure than any previous actress, and she was acclaimed in the USA on seven long tours but her private life scandalized conventional society, both her children being illegitimate. Although worried by failing eyesight and by financial problems, she continued to appear until 1925. Her *Memoirs* were published in 1908 and her correspondence with Shaw in 1929.

J. Melville: *Ellen and Edy* (1988)

**Tescon, Trinidad** (1848–1928). Filipina freedom fighter; active during the Philippine Revolution. Born in San Miguel de Mayumo, in 1895 she joined the soldiers of Andres Bonifacio, the Katipunan. She fought with the soldiers led by General Llanera and attacked the town of San Miguel. In the battle of Zaragoza, where she fought under the command of General Soliman, she was badly wounded. After recovering she was involved in other confrontations with the Spanish and fought under the command of General del Pilar. She was also involved in organizing women to nurse the sick and the injured, and is considered the first person to start Red Cross work in the Philippines. After she set up her makeshift hospital in the fort of Biak-na-Bota, the soldiers lovingly called her '*Ina ng Biak-Na-Bota*' (Mother of Biak-Na-Bota). Trinidad's group of nurses extended into the southern provinces after the Revolution and her work was recognized by the International Red Cross. After her death she was buried in the Veterans' Tomb in Manila.

**Tetrazzini, Luisa** (1871–1940). Italian soprano. She studied singing with her sister Eva (1862–1938, wife of the conductor Campanini), making her operatic debut in Florence (1890) as Inès in Meyerbeer's *L'Africaine*. After touring throughout Italy to increasing acclaim, she was invited as far afield as St Petersburg [now Leningrad] and Buenos Aires. Her Covent Garden debut was in 1907, as Violetta in *La traviata*, a triumph followed by regular appearances there between 1908 and 1912 in the coloratura roles for which she is renowned. Having sung at San Francisco in 1904, she returned to the USA for her New York debut (Manhattan Opera House, 1908), repeating the role of Violetta for her Metropolitan debut in 1911 with equal success. Other roles for which she is celebrated include Donizetti's Lucia and Gilda in *Rigoletto*. Her career was interrupted by World War I, though she continued to make concert tours until 1934, giving her final performance in London. She published two books, *My Life in Song* (1921) and *How to Sing* (1923). After her retirement from the concert platform she was active as a teacher in Milan.

**Teyte**, Dame **Maggie** (1888–1976). English soprano. She studied at the Royal College of Music, London, and in Paris (1903–7) with Jean de Reszke. She made her formal operatic debut as Tyrcis in Offenbach's *Myriam et Daphné* (Monte Carlo, 1907) and the following year appeared in Paris as Mélisande, having been chosen by Debussy to succeed MARY GARDEN in this role. Operatic debuts in London (1910) and Chicago (1911) drew her to increased public attention. From 1922 she sang with the Beecham Opera Company (later the British National Opera Company) in operas ranging from Mozart's to Puccini's, though it is chiefly as an interpreter of French song that she is remembered. Having been accompanied by Debussy in her early recitals, she brought a distinctive insight to his songs in particular, as testified in the recordings she made with Alfred Cortot and Gerald Moore. She was made a Chevalier of the Légion d'Honneur in 1957 and a DBE in 1958.

G. O'Connor: *The Pursuit of Perfection: a Life of Maggie Teyte* (1979)

**Tharp, Twyla** (1942–). American choreographer. She was born in Portland, Indiana, studied at Pomona College, the American Ballet Theatre School, and graduated from Barnard College, New York. After dancing with the Paul Taylor Dance Company (1963–5) she founded her own troupe and began choreography with her first work *Tank Dive*. Until 1972 she concentrated on unaccompanied works performed by ensembles and large groups outside conventional theatre settings. Her major works include *Re-moves* (1966), *Forevermore* (1967), *Generation* (1978) and *Medley* (1969). The vitality and spontaneity of the choreography often disguises the highly-disciplined structure of her work.

Since 1971 Twyla Tharp has gained wider popularity with her jazz settings, for example *Eight Jelly Rolls* (1971), *Bix Pieces*, *Sue's Leg* (1975, music by Fats Waller) and *Ocean's Motion* (1975, music by Chuck Berry). Tharp is unusual among modern dance choreographers in that she has created works for ballet companies as well as for her own troupe (*Deuce Coupe* for the Joffrey Ballet in 1973 and *Push Comes to Shove* for Baryshnikov and American Ballet Theatre in 1976). Works from recent years include *Amadeus* (1984) and *White Nights* (1985). Her relaxed but highly virtuoso style, deriving much of its inspiration from social dance, marks her as one of the most original and innovatory contemporary choreographers.

**Thatcher** [née Roberts], **Margaret (Hilda)** (1925–). English politician. Born in Grantham, Lincolnshire, she was the younger daughter of Alfred Roberts, a prominent grocer in the town, twice mayor, a Methodist lay preacher who encouraged Margaret's intellectual ambitions. She attended the local Kesteven and Grantham Girls' School, where she was head girl, and won an exhibition to Somerville College, Oxford, where she studied chemistry, one of her tutors being DOROTHY HODGKIN. At university she made an impact on student politics, becoming President of the University Conservative Association.

After her graduation in 1947 she worked as a research chemist for a plastics firm in Colchester, and for J. Lyons and Co., but pursued her political career, making her first run as a candidate in Dartford in 1949 where she managed to cut back a large Labour majority. Here she met Denis Thatcher, manager of a family paint business, whom she married in 1951. Margaret left her job and began studying law, taking her Bar Finals in 1953 after an unusually short time, and that year also gave birth to twins, a son and a daughter. She then went into legal practice, specializing in taxation, until she eventually obtained a seat in Parliament, for Finchley, London, in 1959. She has remained in this constituency, which became Barnet Finchley in 1974, ever since.

From 1961 to 1964 she was Joint Parliamentary Secretary for the Ministry of Pensions and National Insurance, and during the Conservative period in opposition became spokesman for education, holding the equivalent Cabinet post, Secretary of State for Education and

Science on their return to power. After the Conservative defeat in the 1974 elections she ran against Edward Heath, and was elected Leader of the Conservative Party. In May 1979 she led her party to victory and became the UK's first woman Prime Minister. A keen monetarist, influenced by economists such as Milton Friedman, she introduced a policy of attacking inflation by reducing the money supply, reductions in public spending, and high interest rates. The inflation rate dropped, but there was a decline in industrial investment and subsequent unemployment of over 3 million by 1982. She continued to dominate her cabinet, despite internal dissension, and her determined stand there, as well as her hard-line attitude towards the USSR over the invasion of Afghanistan, won her the title of 'The Iron Lady'. She adopted an equally firm approach to the invasion of the Falkland Islands by Argentina in 1982. Her quick military response was widely supported in Britain. In the 1983 General Election she again led her party to victory. Her second term was marked by increased public spending cuts, confrontations with major unions and increased restraints on local government power including the abolition of the Greater London Council. While the City thrived in those years, manufacturing industry declined, although inflation was reduced to an annual level of 3.5%, in contrast to the 24% of 1979. She also encouraged wide-scale privatization programmes, which led to the creation of several major public companies, such as British Telecom, British Gas and British Airways.

In 1987 Margaret Thatcher became the first Prime Minister this century to win three consecutive terms: the Cabinet is regarded as very much under her control and 'Thatcherism' has become an accepted term of political ideology. With the economic and labour policies firmly established, the Conservative programme is now directed to controversial reforms such as the replacement of the national household rating system by a Poll Tax, and radical changes in the education and health services. On the international scene Mrs Thatcher is determined to effect changes in the EEC budgeting arrangements, and is regarded as an 'elder stateswoman', having built close links with President Reagan, François Mitterand and Mikhail Gorbachev.

**Theano** (*fl* 6th century BC). Greek philosopher. Theano was probably the most distinguished of the group of women associated with the Pythagorean school of philosophy. The first was Aristoclea, the teacher of Pythagoras at Delphi. Theano was a mathematician, who became a leading teacher with Pythagoras, and eventually married him. Her work was supposedly concerned largely with the virtue of moderation in the ethics of personal life, and education, although she was also an expert on medicine. Other women in this group include Damo, Pythagoras's daughter, whose chief concern was with the education of women, and Theoclea, who became a high priestess. In the 5th century Pythagorean women were associated with the origins of the Platonic school, Diotima, as a teacher of Socrates, and Perictyone, whose work *On Wisdom* is mentioned by Aristotle.

**Theodora** (497–548). Byzantine empress. The daughter of Acacious, the bear-keeper of the Hippodrome in Constantinople, her childhood is described in Procopius's *Secret History* (*Anecdota*). Orphaned at the age of 4, she followed her sister into the theatre as a dresser and at 15 was a popular dancer and mime, famous for her beauty and her flair for making people laugh. She became the mistress of Hecebolus, an administrative official, and followed him to Cyrene in the north of Africa, but soon left him and returned home through Egypt. Here she met the Monophysite patriarch Timothy, who was probably responsible for her religious education; she was also greatly influenced by the learned patriarch of Antioch, Severus, then in exile in Alexandria.

On her return to Constantinople she lived modestly as a wool spinner. Justinian, heir to the Byzantine throne, fell in love with her; he altered the law to allow a marriage between such divergent classes, married her in 525 and made her Empress when he succeeded in 527. Her skill and authority were immediately evident in administrative, religious and political affairs. Dedicated to her husband, she shared his vision of the empire, helped to plan his great building schemes and participated in Councils of State, 'always apologizing for taking the liberty to talk, being a woman'. She was consulted on legislation and received foreign envoys and ambassadors, an Imperial duty. Her influence was exercised at critical moments, as when she persuaded Justinian to stay in the capital rather than flee during the Nika Revolt of 532, thus allowing Belisarius to suppress the riots. She also had a significant effect on his religious policies, relaxing state persecution of the Monophysites, appeasing them by allowing the return of the exiled bishops and summoning a conciliatory conference in Constantinople.

Theodora was unique in her time for her devotion to causes concerning justice for women and she brought about changes in legislation to improve their status. Divorce laws were altered, daughters were given the right of inheritance, wives could keep their dowry as their own property and children were protected from being sold as slaves for their parents' debts. In 535 an edict made the activities of pimps a crime and banished brothel keepers from the major cities, while Theodora, at her own expense, bought the freedom of girls who had been sold into prostitution and looked after their welfare.

A woman of powerful and controversial character, she was dedicated to her friends and her particular causes but was merciless to opponents and jealous of rivals. Deeply engaged in all the issues of her time, she left the stamp of her personality on a great period of Byzantine history. Justinian was left distraught after her death from cancer and little effective legislation was passed during the 17 years in which he survived her.

A. Bridge: *Theodora: a Portrait* (1978)

**Theodoropoulou, Avra** (1880–1963). Greek; the founder of the League for Women's Rights. A professional pianist and music teacher for 52 years, she was also a music critic and writer. Parallel to her successful career as a musician, Avra developed a lifelong commitment to the social activities of the emerging women's movement in Greece. She founded the School for Working Women (1911) and a league called The Soldier's Sister (1918), as well as the League for Women's Rights (1920). As President of the League for 37 years she proved a superb administrator and an effective organizer of campaigns for women's equality. She was admired for her penetrating mind, originality of thought and

democratic approach to the problems she handled. With other members of the League she founded orphanages, an evening school for girls, the Papastrateio School of Crafts, and holiday camps for working women. She put forward many innovative proposals at conferences of the International Union of Women.

The wife of a famous Greek poet and writer, Agis Theros, she is also remembered as a hospitable, generous, and intellectual hostess who ran a salon in her home in Athens, where all her ideals about equality between men and women were reflected.

**Thoc-me-tony.** *See* WINNEMUCCA, SARAH.

**Thomas, Martha Carey** (1857–1935). American educator and feminist. Born in Baltimore, she was the eldest of ten children. Her parents were Quakers and both her mother and aunt were militant feminists. Badly burned in an accident, during her long convalescence she read widely. She was educated at private schools, graduated from Cornell University in 1877, and was admitted to Johns Hopkins University as a graduate by special vote. However, she was barred from attending seminars, and in 1879 she went to study philology at Leipzig. As a woman, her degree was refused here and at Göttingen, but she was granted a doctorate with distinction in Zürich in 1882.

In 1884 she became Dean and Professor of English at the newly-opened Bryn Mawr College for Women, where she designed a very advanced and academically-demanding curriculum, and created a prestigious graduate school. Although her autocratic rule, elitism and cutting remarks were often resented, she remained President of Bryn Mawr from 1894 until 1922. After her retirement she retained the title of President Emeritus and continued to live at Bryn Mawr, remaining active in college affairs. In 1915 she founded the first college school of social work, and in the 1920s ran summer schools for women workers. Thomas also pressed for women's entry into the professions, (including their acceptance by Johns Hopkins Medical School), campaigned for the suffrage, and was an active member of the League to Enforce Peace.

E. Finch: *Carey Thomas of Bryn Mawr* (1947)

**Thompson, Dorothy** (1894–1961). American journalist and feminist leader. Born in Lancaster, New York, she was educated in Chicago and then at Syracuse University, where she graduated in 1914, and at the University of Vienna, where she remained until 1915. On her return to the USA she directed publicity for the suffrage campaign in northern New York State, and after the suffrage was won, she worked· briefly as a social worker, before becoming foreign correspondent for the *Philadelphia Public Ledger* and *New York Evening Post* in 1920. From 1924 to 1928 she was chief of their Central European Service in Berlin, and she remained there as a free-lance journalist until her outspoken condemnation of the Nazi regime after 1933 led to her expulsion. She became political columnist for the *New York Herald Tribune* until 1941 and later syndicated her articles, reaching millions of readers each week, and arousing controversy by her views on such issues as the Polish elections in 1947 and the civil rights of Arabs in Palestine in 1951. She was married three times, to Josef Bad, Sinclair Lewis and the sculptor Maxim Kopf.

D. Thompson: *The Courage to be Happy* (1957)

**Thompson, Mary Harris** (1829–95). American doctor. Mary was born in upstate New York and became a teacher; there is no record of her wanting to be a doctor until she was over 30. In 1863 she enrolled at the New England Female Medical College while Dr Zakrezewska was in charge, and subsequently served a year in the New York Infirmary. Civil war prevented her from studying in Europe, and she went to Chicago where she was the leading woman doctor for more than 30 years.

In 1865 she opened the Chicago Hospital for Women and Children; it was renamed the Mary Thompson Hospital of Chicago after her death. In 1869 she enrolled at Chicago Medical College, and was the only woman to receive her MD from there since they rescinded admission of women soon after. She was co-founder of the Women's Hospital Medical College in 1870, but this was burnt down in a fire in 1871. In 1873 larger premises were converted, and she became Professor of clinical obstetrics and diseases of women, in which capacity she performed major surgical operations. In 1874 she founded a nurses' training school. She was a member of state medical societies and was elected to the American Medical Association in 1886.

**Thorndike**, Dame **Sybil** (1882–1976). English actress and tragedienne. She was the daughter of a canon of Rochester Cathedral. Her early theatrical experience was varied; she toured England and the USA with one of Ben Greet's companies and spent two seasons (1908–9 and 1911–13) with ANNIE HORNIMAN in Manchester. She married actor-director Lewis Casson in 1908; they had three children. In 1914 she joined the first Old Vic company and took leading roles in 12 of Shakespeare's plays, as well as male roles in others. Her most outstanding performance was as St Joan in Shaw's play in 1924, but over a long career she played a vast range of classical and modern parts, among the most notable being her Volumnia, Judith in *Granite* (1928), and Miss Moffat in *The Corn is Green* (1938). Sybil Thorndike has been called the SARAH SIDDONS of her generation: her acting style combined regality with simplicity, intense warmth and serenity. She was created DBE in 1931 and CH in 1970.

S. Morley: *Sybil Thorndike: a Life in the Theatre* (1977)

**Thrale** [Piozzi; née Salisbury], **Hester Lynch** (1741–1821). English intellectual. Born in Bodvel, Caernarvonshire, she was the daughter of John Salisbury, a fiery-tempered landowner who failed in his attempt to make a fortune in Nova Scotia and Ireland. Her mother arranged her marriage to Henry Thrale, the owner of Southwark brewery, in 1713, and her father's intense disapproval is said to have caused his fatal heart-attack. It was an unhappy marriage, which involved 12 pregnancies (5 daughters survived), but Mrs Thrale established a small salon in Streatham, London, and met Dr Johnson, who became a close friend. He lived in the household for some time, and they travelled together to Wales in 1774 and France in 1775. She also introduced FANNY BURNEY to literary society.

After Thrale's death in 1781, she fell in love with an Italian music teacher, Gabriel Piozzi; she called off the romance in 1782 because of family and friends' disapproval but became so ill that in 1784 he was summoned back from Italy and they married at once. Their life appears to have been extremely happy. They lived in Italy until 1787, and then in England until Piozzi's death in 1809. A tiny, spirited woman, who impressed everyone she met, her only writings, apart from travel and personal reminiscences published in 1789 and 1801, were the very popular *Anecdotes of the late Samuel Johnson* (1786). Her *Autobiography* and other works were edited by A. Hayward in 1861.

J.L. Clifford: *Hester Lynch Piozzi – Mrs Thrale* (1941)

**Tibbles, Susette (La Flèsche)** (1854–1903). American campaigner for Indian rights. She was born in Nebraska, the grandaughter of a French fur trader. Her father was chief of the Omaha Indian tribe from 1853 to 1888. Susette grew up on a reservation on the Missouri River, was educated in mission schools, and after attending the Elisabeth Institute, New Jersey, returned to the Omaha as a schoolteacher in 1879. In 1879 after the trial of Standing Bear, a chief who had been arrested when leading their remnants of his Ponca tribe back to the homelands, she went on a tour of the Eastern states as his interpreter, accompanying the journalist Thomas Henry Tibbles who lectured on the case, and whom she married in 1881. Their campaign drew supporters, including HELEN HUNT JACKSON, and influenced the passing of the Dawes Act in 1887, which granted land rights and citizenship to Indians. Susette visited England in 1886 and lectured widely on Indian women and culture. After spending some time in Washington, DC, the Tibbles returned to Nebraska, and to the Omaha tribe.

**Tilley, Vesta** [pseud. of Matilda Alice Powles] (1864–1952). English music hall star and male impersonator. Born in Worcester, she first appeared at the age of four in her father's music hall. She toured with him as 'Harry Ball the Tramp Musician and the Great Little Tilley', and adopted permanently the costume of top hat and tails at the age of five. She made her first appearance in London in 1874 and became a popular attraction by the time she was 16. Known as the 'London Idol' she was an impeccable performer who carefully researched all her roles, from soldier to priest. Her career was long and successful and she appeared in the first Royal Command Performance in 1912. Her most famous songs included *Burlington Bertie*, *Following in Father's Footsteps*, *After the Ball*, *The Army of Today's All Right*, and *Algy – The Piccadilly Johnny with the Little Glass Eye*. After 1898 she also toured the USA and was well-received in both New York and Chicago.

In 1890 she married a music hall owner, Walter de Frece, who was knighted in 1919, and later became a Member of Parliament. She retired 30 years later, receiving a rapturous farewell at the Coliseum, where a book was presented by ELLEN TERRY containing two million autographs. She spent her long retirement in England and the South of France, dying in Monte Carlo at the age of 88.

S. Maitland: *Vesta Tilley* (1986)

**Tillion, Germaine (Marie Rosine)** (1907–). French ethnologist. Born in Allègre, Haute Loire, the daughter of a scholarly lawyer, she was educated in Clermont-Ferrand and in Paris, taking further degrees at the Ecole du Louvre in oriental languages. She undertook several field trips to Aurès (1934–40), and from 1940 to 1942 was a commandant in the Résistance group at the Musée de l'Homme. In 1942 she was arrested and spent three years in Ravensbruck. She was later made an Officer of the Légion d'Honneur, and received the Croix de Guerre and Rosette de la Résistance. After the war she worked on enquiries into the German war crimes, and into the Soviet concentration camps (from 1951) and she took part in an enquiry into Algerian detention centres in 1957. In the same year she became the Director of Studies at the École Pratique des Hautes Etudes, holding a chair in ethnography, and has undertaken studies for the United Nations in East and North Africa, especially of many nomadic tribes. Her best-known works include *L'Algérie en 1957*, *Les ennemis complémentaires* (1978), *Le harem et les cousins* (1966) and *Ravensbruck* (1973). She holds strong socialist views.

**Ting Ling.** *See* DING LING.

**Tituba** (*fl c*1690). American witch. Tituba was the slave of the Reverend Samuel Parris of Salem, Massachusetts; she and her husband came from Spanish settlements in the West Indies. During 1691–2 a small group of girls and women, including Elizabeth Parris, aged 9, Abigail Williams, 11, and Anne Putnam, 12, used to meet every evening to hear Tituba's enthralling stories of voodoo rituals, prophecy and spirit life. It seems to have been a harmless circle, the only magic being some amateur fortune-telling and herbal-healing, but the three young girls worked themselves gradually into a state of hysteria and accused Tituba and two local old beggar-women of being witches. Tituba was tried, but made such a show of remorse and gave such vivid accounts of her supposed satanic activities that she was acquitted as a true penitent. A Puritan settlement, Salem was the scene of many notorious witch-trials during this period, successors to the Puritan mid-century trials which had taken place in England, especially during the Commonwealth under witch-finders such as Matthew Hopkins.

**Tofana** (*d* ?*c*1720). Italian poisoner. Living in Palermo, Sicily, at the end of the 17th century, she invented a medicine called the 'Mana of St Nicholas of Bari' which was sold in small phials and credited with miraculous healing powers. It turned out to be a deadly poison, probably an arsenic mixture. Early accounts say that it was much sought after by harassed women anxious to get rid of their husbands and in 1659, after a suspicious increase in the local death rate, a secret society was discovered, run by a woman called Spara. She and several companions were executed but Tofana fled to a convent. Years later, in 1709, she was taken from her asylum by force and confessed to being implicated in the death of over 600 people, although the claim could not be proved. Some accounts say she lived until 1730, others that she was strangled on the spot. The poison, called *Aqua tofana*, was that used later by the Marquise DE BRINVILLIERS.

**Tomaszewicz-Dobrska, Anna** (1854–1918). Polish doctor. Anna decided in her early teens to practise medicine, despite the objections of her family. From 1871 to 1877 she studied in Zürich, then did brief periods of postgraduate work in Vienna, Berlin, and Petrograd [now Leningrad] before returning to Warsaw. She married a doctor and began her practice: she was the second Polish woman to become a doctor, and the first to practise in Poland. Overcoming opposition to her sex from the establishment in Petrograd, in 1882 Anna was made Chief of Lying-In Hospital No.2 in Warsaw, where she remained until it closed in 1911. She also undertook private practice and social work. Anna was a founding member of the Society of Polish Culture and an advocate of women's rights.

**Topham, Mirabel** [pseud.: Hope Hillier] (?–1980). English racecourse owner. Her father was manager of the Haymarket Theatre, London, and in her youth, as Hope Hillier, she was one of the Gaiety Girls. In 1922 she married Arthur Topham, whose family had held the lease of Aintree racecourse (home of the Grand National, the world's most famous steeplechase) since 1843. Elected to the board in 1935, she took full charge of the company in 1936. She purchased the racecourse outright in 1949. There followed years of family disagreements and legal battles with bookmakers, and with the BBC over broadcasting rights, which she negotiated in a tough, tactless and obstinate fashion, gaining a reputation as a national 'character'. In the 1970s she entered into a deal with Ladbrokes but the racecourse was eventually sold to the Walton Group in 1973 for £3 million.

**Torvill, Jayne** (1957–). British ice-skater. Jayne Torvill grew up in Nottingham, where her parents ran a sweet shop. As a girl she spent every spare moment at the local ice rink and soon became a national prizewinner. She was freed from her job by grants from the City of Nottingham, and with her partner Christopher Dean she has since trained mostly at the ultra-modern centre in Oberstdorf, West Germany. They won the European and World ice-dance championships in 1981, 1982 and 1983. In the last year, at Helsinki and at Budapest they received a record number of 'sixes' from the judges (the 'perfect' score), and then, at the 1984 Olympics in Sarajevo, they received 19 'sixes' in all, for their interpretation in the compulsory dances, and for their free-skating programme: this was the first time a six had been awarded in Olympic history. They also revolutionized ice-dancing (which used to be considered a form of ballroom dancing) by their bold, innovative chorcography, developing dramatic narrative dances to modern and classical music, such as the tale of the anguished lovers performed to Ravel's *Bolero*, and they further upset some traditionalists by using only one piece of music instead of the conventional four.

Since 1984 Torvill and Dean have been professional skaters, touring the world in ice-shows.

**Toumanova, Tamara** (1919–). Russian-French ballerina. She was born nr Shanghai after her parents had left Russia. She studied in Paris with Preobrajenska and made her debut at the Paris Opéra aged nine in *L'éventail de Jeanne*. She joined the Ballet Russe de Monte Carlo in 1932 as one of the three 'baby ballerinas' with Riabouchinska and Baronova. She became famous in Balanchin's *La concurrence* and *Cotillon*, which revealed her superb technique, and Massin's *The Top*. In 1936 she danced the Beloved opposite Massin as the Poet in his *Symphonie fantastique* and in 1938 moved with Massin and Danilova to Blum's company.

Toumanova appeared in the Broadway musical *Stars in Your Eyes* the following year but rejoined De Basil to tour Australia. In 1941 Balanchin choreographed *Balustrade* for her, and during the 1940s she appeared as guest artist with many companies, including the American Ballet Theatre, and the Paris Opéra, where she created the title role in *Phèdre* (Cocteau/Lifar), in 1950. She also danced at La Scala, at Sadler's Wells, and with the London Festival Ballet. She appeared in several films including *Tonight We Sing* (1953), in which she played Pavlova, Gene Kelly's *Invitation to the Dance* (1956) and Hitchcock's *The Torn Curtain* (1966).

**Trimmer, Sarah** (1741–1810). English educationalist. She was born at Ipswich, daughter of the artist John Kirby. She proved to be a gifted student; at 18 she married James Trimmer and then educated her 12 children herself. In 1782, inspired by

ANNA BARBAULD, she published *An Easy Introduction to the Knowledge of Nature*, followed by a similar guide to scripture. She organized Sunday schools for poor children and adults. In 1786 she was asked to advise Queen Charlotte on the foundation of Sunday schools, and her works on this subject included *Reflection upon the Education of Children in Charity Schools* (1792) and *The Economy of Charity* (1801). She founded a school of industry in Brentford, edited two educational magazines, introduced picture books for pre-school children, and wrote children's books such as *Fabulous Histories* (1786). Her educational schemes were influential in maintaining the dominance of the church in popular education at a time when Jacobin radicalism seemed threatening.

S. Trimmer: *Some Account of the Life and Writings of Mrs Trimmer* (1814)

**Tristan, Flora (Célestine Thérèse)** (1803–44). French socialist. Flora Tristan's father was a Peruvian Spanish colonel and her uncle was President of Peru, yet she was brought up in poverty in Paris by her widowed French mother. In 1821 she married her employer, the painter and engraver André Chazel, but left him in 1824, initiating a long battle over custody of their children. She was unable to obtain a divorce, which had been suppressed in France in 1816. From 1825 to 1830 she worked as governess to an English family. In 1830 she went to Peru, in a vain attempt to persuade her uncle to support the family. Eight years later the frank revelations in her autobiography, *Peregrinations d'une paria*, provoked her husband to attempt murder, for which he was sentenced to 22 years hard labour. Their grandson was Paul Gauguin.

On returning to France in 1834 she wrote various feminist tracts. A great admirer of MARY WOLLSTONECRAFT, she was first influenced by the libertarian philosophy of Fourier, and then by the social reformism of Robert Owen, whom she met in 1837. She continued to write, publishing the novel *Mephis* in 1838. During a long visit to England she studied Chartism and made a detailed analysis of social conditions which resulted in her *Promenades des Londres* (1840) which describes early Chartism and British working life. Her travels had crystallized her strong socialist and feminist views and in 1843 she published her *Union ouvrière*. This is the first proposal for a Socialist International, advocating the uniting of all artisan clubs into a single international union, and the establishment of educational and welfare centres on a co-operative basis, as 'Workers' Palaces'. She was a strong champion of women's rights to education and employment, and the conclusion to her book stresses the right to work, to organize, to acquire education and the need to establish the equality of the sexes. She died of typhoid in Bordeaux while travelling around France to publicize her ideas. The workers of the city collected funds for her tombstone, which is inscribed *Liberté–Egalité–Fraternité–Solidarité.*

C.N. Gattey: *Gauguin's Astonishing Grandmother: a Biography of Flora Tristan* (1970)
J.A. Schneider: *Flora Tristan* (1980)

**Trivulzio, Cristina** [Countess of Belgioso] (1808–71). Italian revolutionary. She was born in Milan. In 1831, after participating in a failed revolt against Austria, she went to Paris to work as a propagandist, writing articles and pamphlets campaigning for political justice and constitutional democracy in Italy, and greatly influencing senior statesmen such as Lafayette and Thierry. From 1835 to 1843 she held a famous salon in Paris, and in 1843 founded the *Gazetta Italiana*. She also wrote, mostly in French, contributing to the *Constitutionnel*, and the *Revue des deux mondes*. Between 1842 and 1846 she published a four-volume study, *Essai sur la formation du dogme Catholique*. In the early 1840s she returned to Italy where she organized and financed a legion of volunteers in Naples, which she led to Milan, where she took part in the disturbances of 1848. The following year she was in Rome, tending the wounded rebels during the siege by the French.

When the revolution was defeated she fled first to France, then Turin (where she founded the newspaper *Italia* in 1850) and to Greece, where she stayed with a friend, another socialist aristocrat, the Duchesse de Plaisance. She bought a home in Cappadocia and lived there for five years, until she was badly injured in an assassination attempt, after which she returned to Europe. She never ceased to agitate, preach and write in the cause of Italian unity, founding several short-lived newspapers for the purpose. She was allowed to return to Milan in 1855, and in 1857 her confiscated property was returned to her. She wrote reminiscences, including *Souvenirs d'exil* (1850), and Turkish sketches in *Emina* (1856) and *Scènes de la vie turque* (1858). Her last work was *Réflexions sur l'état de l'Italie et sur son avenir* (1863). A memorable figure, even in her youth her appearance was striking; 'looking like a ghost, with huge black eyes, a white emaciated face and skeletal body'.

**Trollope, Frances** (1780–1863). British author. Frances Milton, a clergyman's daughter, was born at Stapleton, near Bristol. After her mother died and her father re-married, she moved to London as house-keeper to her brother Henry, and in 1809 she married the irascible Thomas Anthony Trollope who failed as a lawyer and then as a farmer, before trying to repair his fortunes by setting up a bazaar for 'fancy goods' in Cincinnati, Ohio, in 1827. After three years this scheme failed too, as did his next property investment in London, and the Trollopes with their six children became dependent on Frances's earnings as a writer. Her book *Domestic Manners of the Americans* (1831), a witty, critical and lively account of her reflections during her time in the United States was an immediate success in Britain (although it upset many Americans), and despite the fact that she had not begun writing until she was 52, she went on to publish over 100 books.

Frances's son Henry died in 1834, and her husband in 1835, but she weathered family tragedy and financial troubles, travelling and writing about Belgium, Paris and Austria during the 1830s and also began writing fiction, with *Tremordyn Cliff* (1835). Her most enduring novels are *The Vicar of Wrexhill* (1837), *Widow Barnaby* (1838), and the more personal *The Lottery of Marriage* (1849) and *The Life and Adventures of a Clever Woman* (1852). Her books were successful enough to support her family, including her son, the future novelist Anthony Trollope. She continued to travel, and settled in the British community in Florence in 1843, with her son Tom (later a friend of GEORGE ELIOT), where she died in 1863.

J. Johnston: *The Life, Manners and Travels of Fanny Trollope* (1979)

**Trotula** [Trotta; Trocta] (*fl* 11th century). Italian doctor. Trotula lived in Salerno (which has an old-established medical school). She was married to the doctor John Platearius, and their son Matteo also became a doctor.

Trotula wrote numerous medical works, extant as copied manuscripts and incorporated later into printed books including: *Regimen sanctatis salernitatum; De passinibus mulierum* (on gynaecology); and *Experimentarius Medicinae*. Her treatise on gynaecology was the first complete compendium and so practical that it was used for hundreds of years, offering many practical solutions to problems of menstruation, sterility or paediatrics. Her methods of surgery of the perineum were classic.

**Trubnikova, Mariya (Vasilevna)** (1835–97). Russian feminist and educationalist. She was born in Chita, Siberia, the daughter of an exiled Decembrist and his French wife, and was brought up by her grandmother and aunt after her parents' deaths. She had a superb education and as a young girl became interested in the ideas of Proudhon, Blanc and the German Romantics. At 19 she married Constantin Trubnikov, and they moved to Moscow where they edited a liberal journal, ran a famous radical salon, and corresponded with European feminists such as Jenny d'Hericourt, JOSEPHINE BUTLER and Marie Goegg.

With her close friends Nadezhda Stasova and Anna Filosova, both liberal aristocrats, she began the first feminist social movement of the 1860s. They were known as 'the triumvirate'. Their first venture was a society for cheap accommodation for poor women in 1859, followed by dressmaking workshops, communal kitchens and a school. They also became involved in the Sunday School movement, the provision of education for the working classes, and founded a women's publishing co-operative in 1863 to provide educated women with work writing, copying, editing and translating. In 1868 she and Stasova joined Eugenia Konradi in petitioning the Ministry of Education for the creation of a women's university, and their pressure eventually led to the opening of the extremely popular Alarchinskii courses in St Petersburg [now Leningrad] in 1869 (attended by SOFYA PEROVSKAYA and others) and the Vladimir courses in Moscow in 1870.

In 1869 Trubnikova left her husband and went abroad, and although she later returned, illness and financial problems forced her to withdraw from feminist activities after 1881. She spent some time in a mental hospital before her death. Stasova, however, continued to help women students throughout her life, and Anna Filosova, after abandoning her efforts during the turmoil and persecution of the 1880s, became active during the 1890s in uniting the women's clubs in Russia, and linking them to the international franchise movement.

**Truth, Sojourner** [Van Wagener, Isabella] (1777–1883). American abolitionist. She was born a slave and belonged to several owners before working on a farm in New York State (1810-26). Here she had at least eight children by a fellow slave Thomas, but in 1827 she fled to another farm owned by the Van Wagener family. She successfuly fought a legal battle to obtain the freedom of her son, illegally sold to an Alabama planter, and after receiving her own freedom moved to New York as Isabella van Wagener.

During the next 15 years she worked in the city, becoming involved with various visionary groups, until in 1843 she was commanded by voices to leave and take the name Sojourner Truth. She spoke at revival meetings in the Eastern states, and in 1847 met leading abolitionists in Northampton, Massachusetts. In 1850 she went west, selling her biography, *The Narrative of Sojourner Truth*, drawing huge crowds by her dramatic lectures on slavery and, increasingly, on the suffrage issue. She eventually settled in Battle Creek, Michigan, worked for union causes, was received by Lincoln in 1864, and became a worker for the Freedman's Relief Association. Her last campaigns were for land grants and a 'Negro state', and she encouraged Negro emigration to the Midwest. When she finally retired in 1875, aged nearly 100, she continued to receive visitors from all over the USA.

H. Pauli: *Her Name was Sojourner Truth* (1962)

**Tsvetayeva, Marina (Ivanovna)** [Cvetaeva] (1892–1941). Russian poet. Tsvetayeva was born in Moscow, where her father was a professor of art history. A child prodigy, she wrote from the age of six and her first collection of poems *Vecherniy albon* ('Evening album') appeared in 1910 and received enthusiastic reviews. Two more collections followed, *Volshebny fonar* ('Magic lantern') in 1912 and *Iz dvukh knig* ('From two books') in 1913. The style is accomplished but imitatory.

In 1911 she married Sergey Efran, a Moscow intellectual, and became influenced by Symbolist poets such as Aleksandr Blok and ANNA AKHMATOVA, as is clear in *Versty I* (1922). She travelled, studied in Paris and was a violent opponent of the Revolution. During the Civil War her husband fought for the Whites, and she joined him in exile in Berlin, Prague and Paris from 1922. She published several major collections in rapid succession, including *Romeslo* ('Craft') in 1923 and *Poste Rossii* ('After Russia') in 1928 and was one of the leading emigré writers, creating an original blend of traditional Russian diction and folk themes with experimental structures and themes of modern alienation. She also wrote several long narrative poems, both auto-biographical reminiscences and historical epics. Her personal loneliness amid the emigré community and her hatred of fascism made her return to the Soviet Union in 1939. There she was banned from publishing and shunned as a reactionary by literary circles. During World War II she was evacuated to Yelabuga, and, after hearing of the deaths of some close relatives, she committed suicide in 1941. Since the 'cultural thaw' in the mid-1950s her work has been widely admired in the USSR.

S. Kerlinsky: *Marina Cvetaeva; her Life and Art* (1966)

**Tubman, Harriet Ross** [Araminta] (1821–1913). American abolitionist. Born a slave in Maryland, as a girl she worked as a field hand. In 1844 she married John Tubman, but they soon separated. When her owner died in 1849 and she was threatened with sale to the Deep South, she escaped to Philadelphia. In December 1850 she returned to Baltimore and helped her sister and two children to escape, fetching her brother's family in 1851. She became active in the 'underground railway' helping up to 300 fugitives to reach the northern states and Canada. During the early 1850s she lived in Ontario where she acted as adviser to John Brown but in 1858 moved to Auburn, New York, where she also settled her parents who had been rescued from the South. She became a noted speaker in the abolitionist and women's rights movements, and during the Civil War worked as cook, laundress, nurse, scout and spy for the Union army. In 1869 she married Nelson Davies and worked with him founding freedmen schools, teaching and preaching. A deeply religious, energetic activist, she also founded a home for elderly black people in Auburn, partly financed by the sale of Sarah Bradford's biography *Harriet Tubman, the Moses of Her People* (1886).

E. Conrad: *Harriet Tubman* (1943)

**Tucker** [Abuza]**, Sophie** (1884–1966). American music-hall singer. Different versions of her life place her birth in Boston or in Russia, from where her Jewish family emigrated to the USA when she was three months old. Her parents opened a kosher restaurant in Hartford, Connecticut, where she began to sing. In 1906, after a brief marriage (at 16) to a brewer's drayman, Louis Tuck, she went to New York, where she adopted Tucker as her stage name. For her early vaudeville acts she blacked-up and called herself a 'red-hot momma', singing sentimental ballads, 'torch songs' and blues. She took part briefly in the Ziegfeld Follies in 1909, achieved fame in 1911 with her defiant song *Some of these Days* and by 1914 was topping the bill at the Palace Theatre. She toured the USA and crossed the Atlantic, to meet with great success in London at the Palladium (1922) and at provincial British theatres. A tireless professional, in 1925 she was estimated to be giving seven performances a day.

Known as 'the last of the red hot mommas' Jack Yellen wrote *My Yiddisher Mama* especially for her in 1925. She appeared in the early sound film *Honky Tonk* (1929), starred at a Royal Command Peformance in London in 1939 and entertained the

troops during World War II. Her stage career lasted 62 years; she was still performing at the age of 78, delivering sentimental ballads and comic suggestive songs with equal gusto. She also raised millions of dollars for charity, particularly Jewish welfare work.
M. Freedland: *Sophie* (1978)

**Tuckwell, Gertrude** (1861–1951). English trade unionist. Born in Oxford, she was educated at home by her father, the 'Radical parson' and Master of New College School. She worked as a teacher in elementary schools in London (1885–92), before becoming secretary to her aunt, Lady EMILY DILKE, and working for the Women's Trade Union League (of which she was President from 1904, until it was taken over by the TUC in 1921). She published *The State and its Children* (1894) and *Women in Industry* (1908). Together with MARY MACARTHUR, ADELAIDE ANDERSON and others she led campaigns against white lead poisoning and sweated trades, organizing the Sweated Goods Exhibition (1906) which prompted the Trade Boards Act of 1909.

After World War I, although still an active unionist and Labour Party member, she pursued other social reforms, particularly taking up Macarthur's work on maternity. Her activities included being first woman Justice of the Peace for the County of London (1920), membership of the Royal Commission on National Health Insurance (1924–6), founding the Maternal Mortality Committee (1927), being President of the Women Sanitary Inspectors and the National Association of Probation Officers, and sitting on the Central Committee on Women's Training and Employment.

**Tudor, Mary.** *See* MARY I.

**Tudor-Hart; Edith** (1908–78). Austrian–British photographer. Edith Suschitzky grew up in Austria and studied at the Dessau Bauhaus. She also trained as a Montessori teacher and an interest in children was to be a lifelong feature of her career as a photographer. She became known as a 'Modernist' photographer before she fled to London from Austria in 1933 and her series *Mit Bildern aus dem Wiener Montessori Kinderheim* appeared in the 1920s. (Her brother Wolf was also to become a well-known photographer in

Britain, and Valerie Williams, in *Women Photographers* (1987), notes that several other European women who fled from Nazi Europe also became prominent photographers, including Gerti Deutsch, Lotte Meiner-Graf and Edith Kaye.)

A political and anti-fascist activist, Edith saw photography as a medium for conveying new social ideas. She married Alex Tudor-Hart, a member of a well-known radical and artistic family, who practised as a doctor in the mining town of Rhondda, South Wales. She began to work for magazines like *The Listener*, *The Social Scene* and *Design Today*, concentrating on issues like refugees from the Spanish Civil War, or industrial decline in Britain's north-east, and took photographs to illustrate Margery Spring-Rice's *Working Class Wives*. From the late 1930s her work concentrated more on social needs such as housing policy and the care of disabled children. Her own son, Tommy, became an incurable schizophrenic as a child, and this personal tragedy darkened her hitherto idyllic view of childhood: notable series of childhood pictures appeared in *Picture Post* (1949) and in the HMSO publication *Moving and Growing* (1952).

Edith Tudor-Hart was one of the most remarkable of a group of left-wing documentary women photographers, and her pictures can be linked to the earlier work of Nora Smyth, as well as to that of Helen Muspratt and Margaret Monck, and to later *Picture Post* photographers such as Grace Robertson, each of whom created a distinct personal vision of life in British society.

**Tullis, Julie** (1939–86). English mountaineer. Julie Palau was born in Surrey of a Spanish father and German mother. An adventurous childhood included evacuation to rural Norfolk during 1943–5. At 17 she began rock-climbing at High Rocks near Tunbridge Wells, where she met Terry Tullis, whom she married in 1959. They ran a shop and a café, taught climbing, and had two children.

In 1974 Julie returned to personal climbing, frequently in North Wales. She was attracted to the aesthetic and non-competitive aspects of climbing as well as the challenge. A strong influence was the Budokan martial arts club where she became a black belt in karate and aikido. The positive attitudes and harmony she found through budo extended to her other activities such as the teaching of climbing to handicapped young people and offenders. In 1974 came her first climbing expedition, in the Peruvian Andes. Climbing in Yosemite followed, but 1982 marked the start of her Himalayan career and a climbing partnership with Kurt Diemberger as his sound recordist and filming assistant. Nanga Parbat was followed by a K2 expedition on which they reached 8000 metres and called themselves 'The highest film team in the world'. They frequently climbed alpine-style, as on Broad Peak where they reached the summit, making Julie, at the age of 45, the first British woman to climb an 8000-metre Himalayan mountain. In 1985 she became the first British woman to climb on an Everest expedition, and that year she and Diemberger spent a total of 52 days above 20,000 feet. K2 had become her 'mountain of mountains', and in 1986 she and Diemberger returned to it for the third time. They reached the summit but Julie died of cerebral oedema when their descent was delayed by storms.

J. Tullis: *Clouds from Both Sides* (1986)

**Turitscheva, Ludmila** (1952–). Russian gymnast. Ludmila began gymnastics in 1965 and joined the Russian team the next year. By 1970 she had great technical competence and poise; she won the world title, and in 1971 the European title.

At the 1972 Munich Olympics she beat OLGA KORBUT in the combined exercises and won the gold medal. At the European championships in London in 1973 Olga Korbut retired with an injured leg, and Ludmila won every gold medal for apparatus work as well as that for combined exercises. She regards public service as an important responsibility for all athletes and often gives displays at factories and clubs.

**Tussaud** [née Grasholtz], **Marie** (1761–1850). Swiss wax-modeller and business-woman. The posthumous daughter of a German soldier, she spent her childhood in Bern with her widowed mother who was housekeeper to her brother Philippe Curtius, a wax-modeller. In 1770 they went with Curtius to Paris, where he founded the *Cabinet de cire* (1780), a famous wax museum in the Palais Royal, and the *Caverne des grands valeurs* (1783), the

original of the 'Chamber of Horrors'. Marie was a skilled modeller by the time she was 17, but from 1780 until the Revolution she was art tutor at Versailles to Louis XVI's sister Elizabeth: during this time she modelled *The Royal Family at Dinner*.

In 1789 both uncle and niece hastily proved themselves 'patriots', although three of her brothers were apparently in the Swiss Guard and died defending the Tuileries in 1792. Marie herself took death masks of many guillotine victims, often of her former friends such as MARIE ANTOINETTE and Louis XVI; others included Marat, Robespierre and CHARLOTTE CORDAY. All were displayed in the museum. When Curtius was guillotined in 1794 Marie inherited the business. Even a brief imprisonment proved no drawback to her career, for she made an influential friend in her fellow prisoner JOSEPHINE DE BEAUHARNAIS. In 1795 she married the engineer Francis Tussaud and they had two children, but her unhappy home life and declining business persuaded her to emigrate to England in 1802.

Marie Tussaud toured the British Isles with her exhibition for 33 years, continually increasing her range of models, especially topical portraits of famous people. She also collected evocative objects, including an original guillotine knife for the Chamber of Horrors, and specializing in anything connected with Napoleon, such as his carriage built for the Moscow campaign and captured after Waterloo. She had numerous adventures, losing many models in a shipwreck in the Irish Sea, and nearly having her show burned to the ground during the Bristol riots of 1831. In 1834 she established a permanent exhibition in Baker Street, London, and worked there until eight years before her death, when she divided the business between her two sons.

A. Leslie and P. Chapman: *Madame Tussaud, Waxworker Extraordinary* (1979)

**Twining, Louisa** (1820–1912). British reformer and feminist. Louisa was the youngest daughter of Robert Twining, head of the old-established family tea firm in the Strand, London. In the 1840s she began work among the poor, and helped her father, who was one of the managers of King's College Hospital and supervisor of the local Public Dispensary, to establish a church nursing sisterhood in the neighbourhood: she herself became a Lady of Grace of the Order of St John of Jerusalem. In the 1850s she also helped and preached in the Strand workhouse, and visited workhouses across Britain. A member of the National Association for the Promotion of Social Science, she became secretary of their Workhouse Visiting Society in 1858 and published *Workhouses and Women's Work* in the same year. In 1861 she established a hostel for workhouse girls in domestic service. The two main concerns of her life were Poor Law reform and the extension of women's influence in local government. In 1879 she became secretary of the Association for Promoting Trained Nursing in Workhouse Infirmaries, and from 1884–90 acted as a Poor Law Guardian in Kensington. In 1890 she moved to Tunbridge Wells, where she was also a Poor Law Guardian in 1893–6. President of the Women's Local Government society, and a keen supporter of the suffrage movement, she described her ideas in *Recollections of Life and Work* (1895) and *Workhouses and Pauperism* (1898). Her sister Elizabeth (1805–89) was also an active reformer who originated 'Mothers' Meetings' in London, and was one of the founders of Bedford College.

**Tzavella, Moscho** (1760–1803). Greek heroine. A woman of outstanding courage, she was descended from a historic family of guerilla fighters and leaders of peasant armies against the Turkish conquerors. When Ali Pasha, the Albanian ruler of western Greece, attacked her mountain village of Souli, which was the only place that still resisted the Turkish occupation, Moscho led the women of the village against the enemy. Armed only with sticks and stones, the women forced the Pasha's powerful army to retreat and to give up any attempt to seize the village.

For her bravery, Moscho was given the title of Kapetanios ('Captain'), and was allowed to take part in the village councils of war, advising the guerillas on military tactics and attacks.

**Tz'u-hsi** [Hsiao-ch'in] (1835–1908). Empress of China. She was the child of a minor Manchu family. Her father was a clerk in government service, and later a provincial administrator. In 1851 Tz'u-hsi was selected as a low-ranking concubine of the Emperor Hs'en Feng, rising in status in 1854 and in 1856 when she bore his only son. She also worked as his secretary, learning about the administration of the state. When the Emperor died in 1861 her son succeeded and a regency council of eight elders was elected, but as no decrees could be passed without the seal being approved by the Dowager Empress she became the effective ruler, and soon achieved the status of co-regent with Tz'uan, the late Emperor's chief wife, ruling with the help of his brother Prince Kung. They enforced unity and peace, finally suppressing the Taiping Rebellion in the South (1850–64) and the Nien Rebellion in North China, and a final Moslem revolt in Yunnan was crushed in 1873. They also began the gradual Westernization of China, establishing schools of foreign languages, creating modern customs' services and reforming the army and navy. Meanwhile Tz'u-hsi increased her personal power (since Tz'uan was not interested in state affairs), and she refused to give up the regency in 1873, when her son came of age, or on his death in 1875 when she flouted all the laws of succession and made her adopted nephew the new heir. In 1881 Tz'uan died, perhaps poisoned, and Tz'u-hsi ruled alone, finally removing Kung in 1884.

She continued to rule until 1889 when she officially handed over control, but kept herself well-informed while she retired to her summer palace, which was rebuilt between 1886 and 1890, using much-needed funds designed for the creation of a new navy. She also made a fortune from selling posts and promotions. During the 1890s the Chinese were defeated by the Japanese, and that blow to morale led the Emperor to implement a series of reforms designed to minimize bureaucratic corruption. Tz'u-hsi led the conservative opposition, achieved a coup, revoked the reforms, executed the leaders and resumed the regency. During the Boxer Rebellion which brought retaliation from foreign powers after the riots of 1900, she fled from Peking [Beijing], but returned in 1901 on terms laid down by the Western powers and began, as a gesture of appeasement, to implement the 1898 reforms. As well as administrative changes, these included several edicts which affected women, ending foot-binding, allowing inter-marriage between Manchu and Chinese, and opening state schools to girls. The traditional civil service examinations were ended after many centuries, railways were built, opium growing was suppressed, and the end of the power of the Manchu dynasty was heralded by her agreement to a constitution. When she was dying, her nephew the Emperor Kuang-hsu, whose whole career she had dominated, also died, allegedly poisoned at her command.

Tz'u-hsi had always created her own opportunities, and although largely self-taught she became a fine calligrapher, and patron of the arts. Fascinating glimpses of life in her court were given by a lady-in-waiting, Princess Der Ling, in *Two Years in the Forbidden City* (1911). She had considerably greater effective power than Queen Victoria (whom she greatly admired): she loved money and power and worked ruthlessly to secure them, playing with great skill on the ambitions of her followers.

# U

**Ulanova, Galina** (1910–). Russian ballerina. Born in St Petersburg [now Leningrad], she was the daughter of two dancers at the Mariinsky Theatre. She studied with her mother and then with AGRIPPINA VAGANOVA. She made her debut at the Kirov Theatre in 1928 in *Chopiniana*. She gave her first performance of *Giselle*, regarded as the supreme modern interpretation, in 1932, and created many new roles, notably Maria in Zacharov's *Fountain of Bakchisarai* (1934), and Juliet in Lavrovsky's *Romeo and Juliet* (1940). In 1944 she joined the Bolshoi Ballet, and continued to interpret Lavrovsky, appearing as Tao-Hoa in *Red Poppy* (1949), and Katerina in *Stone Flower* (1954). She first appeared in the West in 1945 in Vienna and in 1956 visited the UK. After 1959 she danced only occasionally, giving her farewell performance in 1962. She became ballet mistress of the Bolshoi and played an important part in coaching young dancers, especially Maximova. Her influence on Soviet ballet has been enormous. She was honoured as People's Artist of the USSR, and awarded the Lenin Prize in 1957.

G. Ulanova: *The Making of a Ballerina*

**Ullmann, Liv** (1939–). Norwegian actress. Born in Tokyo, where her father was stationed as an engineer, she moved to Canada during World War II and went to Norway after her father's death. There she worked in provincial theatre before moving into films and on to the Oslo stage. She is especially associated with Ingmar Bergman, with whom she lived for five years and who is the father of her daughter. Although she has since made some American films he has directed her best work, mostly introspective studies of emotional tension: *Persona* (1966), *Hour of the Wolf* and *Shame* (1968),

*The Passion of Anna/Passion* (1969), *Cries and Whispers* (1972), *Face to Face* (1976) and *Autumn Sonata* (1978). *Scenes from a Marriage* (1973) was a Bergman television series which examined the strains, weaknesses and desires of a professional woman caught in a conventional relationship. Her recent films include *Dangerous Moves* (1985) and *Moscow Adieu* (1986) and she has also appeared more on the stage, particularly in the plays of Ibsen and Brecht.

L. Ullmann: *Changing* (1977)
———: *Choices* (1984)

**Underhill, Evelyn** (1875–1941). English mystic. Born in Wolverhampton, the daughter of a barrister, Evelyn was educated at King's College, London, and travelled much on the Continent. In 1907 she married Hubert Stuart Moore, a barrister and childhood friend. The year of her marriage witnessed her final conversion to the Christian faith. Her spiritual struggles at this time led her to study the mystics and then to write *Mysticism* (1911), a book which became a standard work because of its comprehensive approach to religious experience. Through this book she made the acquaintance of Baron Friedrich van Hügel and put herself under his spiritual guidance. Among her books of this period were *The Path of Eternal Wisdom* (1911), *The Spiral Way* (1912), and a number of other books on mysticism. In 1921 she was appointed lecturer on the Philosophy of Religion at Manchester College, Oxford. In 1927 she was made a Fellow of King's College, London. During World War I she had worked for the Admiralty but in 1939 she became a pacifist and wrote *The Church and War* (1940).

M. Cropper: *Evelyn Underhill* (1958)

**Underhill** [née O'Brien], **Miriam** (*c*1900–). American mountaineer. She was born in New England. In 1914 she was taken to Chamonix and Zermatt; she climbed the Breithorn in 1921 but began serious climbing on the Riffelhorn in 1924. After gaining further experience in New England and the Dolomites, in 1927 her guides introduced her to the Torre Grande in the Dolomites, where she pioneered what became known as the Via Miriam. The next year she made the first traverse of the Grépon led by a woman, then with Robert Underhill and guides, the first complete traverse of the Aiguille du Diable. In 1930 she skiied down Mont Rosa.

She was becoming known as the greatest American woman climber. Miriam began a three-year period of climbs without men, including the Aiguille du Peigne and the traverse of the Grépon (with Jo (Winifred) Marples and Alice Damesme). In 1931 the weather defeated her attempt on the Matterhorn but she climbed the Jungfrau. On 12 August 1932, with Damesme, she achieved the first women-only ascent of the Matterhorn. That autumn Miriam married Robert Underhill. They did not return to climb in the Alps until 19 years later, with their two sons; Miriam made a third ascent of the Matterhorn.

M. Underhill: *Give Me The Hills* (1956)

**Undset, Sigrid** (1882–1949). Norwegian novelist. Born in Kalundborg, Zeeland, Denmark, Sigrid Undset concentrated in her early novels, such as *Jenny* (1911), on the problems facing contemporary women, but it was when she turned to history, with the rich, detailed picture of 14th-century Norway in *Kristin Lavransdatter* (1920–22), that her concern for women's fulfilment was most successfully expressed. In the 1920s she was converted to Roman Catholicism, and her faith is evident in her later works such as the novel *Olav Andansson*, set in the 13th century (4 vols, 1925–7), *Gymadenia* (1929) and *Den trofaste hastra* (1936). Almost all her work has been translated into English.

**Unger, Karoline** (1803–77). Austrian contralto. She studied singing with Joseph Mozatti and Ugo Bassi, continuing her tuition with Aloysia Weber and J.M. Vogl and in Milan with D. Roncini. She made her debut as Dorabella in Mozart's *Così fan tutte* (Vienna, 1821). The performance that assured her place in musical history, however, was the première (with HENRIETTE SONTAG) of Beethoven's *Missa solemnis* and Ninth Symphony (Vienna, 1824); it was Unger who turned the deaf Beethoven around to face the audience so that he could at least see the applause. She spent most of her career from 1825 in Italy, where she enjoyed remarkable success (particularly given the dubious reputation of Austrian singers in Italy at the time). Among the composers to write operas for her were Donizetti (*Parisina*, 1833; *Belisario*, 1836; and *Maria di Rudenz*, 1838), Bellini (*La straniera*, 1829), Mercadante (*Le due illustri rivali*, 1838) and Pacini (*Niobe*, 1826). She was acclaimed for her Donizetti roles (*Maria Stuarda*, *Lucia di Lammermoor* and *Lucrezia Borgia*) as well as for her interpretations of lieder by Mozart and Schubert. She retired from the stage in 1843.

# V

**Vaganova, Agrippina** (1879–1951). Russian ballet teacher. She graduated from St Petersburg Imperial Theatre School in 1897, and danced at the Mariinsky Theatre, achieving ballerina status in 1915. Best-known for her technical virtuosity she became a superb classical teacher, beginning at the School of Russian Ballet in 1919, and then teaching at the Leningrad Choreographic School from 1921 to 1951. She developed her own teaching style, explained in her book *Basic Principles of Classical Ballet* (1948), which forms the basis of ballet training in Russia and in many schools in the West. The exceptional virtuosity of Soviet technique is grounded on her system of training. Among her pupils were NATALYA DUDINSKAYA and GALINA ULANOVA. In 1957 the Leningrad school was renamed Vaganova School in her honour. She was honoured as People's Artist of the USSR.

**Valadon, Suzanne (Marie Clementine)** (1865–1938). French painter. An illegitimate child, she was born in Bessines, Haute-Vienne. Her mother, who was a seamstress, took her to Paris. Suzanne received little formal education but worked instead at a series of jobs such as apprentice dressmaker, vegetable seller, waitress and groom in a livery stables; by the age of 16 she was a circus acrobat until a fall from a trapeze ended her career. She then modelled for the artist Puvis de Chavannes, who became her lover. She bore a son, Maurice, whose birth certificate was signed by Miguel Utrillo. She also modelled for Renoir and from 1887 for Toulouse-Lautrec. They encouraged her own work and introduced her to Degas, who gave her enthusiastic support and arranged her first exhibitions. Her works of the early 1890s are mostly portraits, for example of her current

lover Erik Satie, but she soon began making prints, and incorporating elements of style from the Breton 'primitives'.

In 1896 she married her wealthy lover, banker Paul Mousis, who built a house for her, but she continued to paint. She eventually returned to Montmartre, hoping to teach Maurice to paint as a therapy in his alcoholism cure. She met his young friend André Utter, and in 1909 she left her husband to live with him. They were married in 1914 and exhibited as a trio with Utrillo. Her work became increasingly strong and individualistic with bold outlines and raw colours. She painted still lifes, landscapes, portraits, sensuous nudes and unusual genre scenes, producing an extraordinary range of work, from *Adam and Eve* (1909) to *The Black Venus* (1919) or *The Family of André Utter* (1921). Her work was exhibited at avant-garde galleries and during the 1920s and 1930s was included in major group shows in France and abroad; in the 1930s she also exhibited in the Salon des Femmes Modernes.

J. Storm: *The Valadon Drama* (1959)

**Valette, Aline** (1850–99). French socialist. She was born in Paris, where she became a school-teacher and Secretary of the newly - formed Teachers' Union in 1878. She married a lawyer, was widowed, and became a journalist, publishing an extremely successful home-management book, *La journée de la petite ménagère* (1883). A charity worker, and one of the first voluntary labour inspectors in Paris during the 1880s, she joined a socialist study group: she was a founder member with EUGENIE POTONIE-PIERRE of the Federation Française des Sociétés Feministes in 1892, and a member of the National Council of the Parti Ouvrier Français in 1893. Valette fought for the rights of women workers, despite her inner conviction that their most glorious role was as mothers and home-makers. She died of tuberculosis in Arcachon.

**Vallayer-Coster, Anne** (1744–1818). French still life painter. The daughter of a goldsmith, she spent her childhood at the Gobelins tapestry factory where her father worked. The family moved to Paris when she was ten. Her earliest existing work dates from 1767 although she undoubtedly painted before then. In 1770 she was unanimously accepted into the Académie Royale with her *Allegory of the Visual Arts* and *Allegory of Music*. She had many wealthy patrons, who may have commissioned tapestry designs from her as well as paintings, and she was extremely prolific and versatile. 450 works are attributed to her, ranging from flower paintings to symbolic arrangements and 'banquet pieces'. One of the finest French still life painters, she was greatly admired even in her own day. In 1781 she married the lawyer Jean Pierre Coster and MARIE ANTOINETTE arranged for her to be given apartments in the Louvre. She remained in Paris during the Revolution, but painted less after 1800.

**Valle, Inger (Louise Andvig)** (1921–). Norwegian politician. Born in Oslo, she was educated at Commercial College and also studied law. In 1951 she was appointed to the Price Directorate and when this became the Consumer Council in 1958 she became head of its legal and economic section, remaining there until 1971. A member of the Labour Party, she was also involved in local government as a member of Baerum Municipal Council (1967–71). In 1971 she became Minister of Family and Consumer Affairs, adding Government Administration to her portfolio in 1972. She then transferred to the Ministry of Justice in 1973; she was reappointed in 1976 and 1979, but in the latter year she was transferred to the Ministry of Local Government and Labour.

**Valois, Ninette de.** *See* DE VALOIS, NINETTE.

**Vanderbilt-Cooper, Gloria (Morgan)** (1924–). American actress, writer and designer. Born in New York City, an heiress labelled the 'poor little rich girl' in a custody suit when she was ten, Gloria travelled Europe with her mother and after attending private schools in the USA, left at the age of 17 to marry her first husband Pasquale di Cicco. Three years later she ran away with the conductor Leopold Stokowski, who was 40 years her senior, and in their ten-year marriage they had two sons. She also established herself as a painter, completely self-taught, and exhibited widely throughout the USA from 1948 to 1971. After her divorce in 1955 she studied acting, appearing on Broadway in *The Time of Your Life* and following this with many stage and television appearances and occasional film performances. In 1956 she had married Sidney Lumet, the producer; but from 1963 to his death in 1978 she was married to Wyatt Cooper, with whom she had two more sons. She also published plays, poems and short stories.

In the late 1960s she began her career as a designer, starting with puzzles, cards and candles and moving to fabrics and household goods and eventually turning to fashion in the late 1970s, attaching her name to the internationally produced Gloria Vanderbilt jeans. Wealth and contacts are not the only reasons for her extraordinary career. She is an obsessive worker and still keeps mainly to a stringent routine. Her autobiography describes her lifelong search for identity.

G. Vanderbilt-Cooper: *Woman to Woman* (1979)
————: *Once Upon A Time* (1985)

**van Grippenberg, Baroness Alexandra** (1859–1913). Finnish feminist. A member of the temperance movement, she joined the Finsk Kvinnoførening (Finnish Women's Association) when it was founded in 1884 and soon became one of its leaders. During the 1890s she led a broad-based campaign for educational, professional and political equality, property rights, divorce reform and the abolition of state-regulated prostitution, in contrast to the specific and militant suffrage campaign led by LUCINA HAGMAN. In 1883 she attended the Women's Congress in Washington, DC, organized by SUSAN B. ANTHONY which led to the formation of the International Council of Women in 1889. She became Vice-president of the Council and concentrated on its policy of educating women for participation in politics after the granting of the franchise in Finland in 1906. In 1909 she was elected to the Finnish Diet and argued strongly against protective legislation on the grounds that it was illogical, if the principle demanded was that of total equality. In 1912 she founded the Finnish National Council of Women, but died shortly after being elected its first President.

**van Oosterwyck, Maria** (1630–93). Dutch painter. The daughter of a Protestant minister, she trained as an artist and allegedly chose to remain single so that she could devote herself to art. A painstaking worker, she left only a few paintings but those that remain, such as *Vanities* (1668), a symbolic still life, and the more usual flower-paintings, are among the finest examples of their kind. She was an innovative painter, adapting formal conventions to unusual effect. She is also reputed to have given lessons in painting to her servants.

**van Praagh,** Dame **Peggy** [Margaret] (1910–). British ballet director and teacher. She began dancing at an early age and studied under Craske, Sokolova, Agnes de Mille, and TAMARA KARSAVINA. She danced with the Ballet Rambert (1933–8), with De Mille's Modern Group, and joined Anthony Tudor's newly-founded London Ballet in 1938. She worked on the lunch-hour ballets at the Arts Theatre, London (1940–41), before joining the Sadler's Wells Ballet (1941–6). She was Ballet Mistress from 1946 to 1951 and Assistant Director to NINETTE DE VALOIS from 1951 to 1955. For a period she worked as a freelance teacher and producer, directing for different companies and for BBC television. In 1959 she was Guest Director for the last season of the Borovansky Ballet in Australia, and stayed on to become Artistic Director of the new Australian Ballet (1963–74 and 1975–9). An influential figure in Australian dance performance and education, she is also a member of the Victoria Council of the Arts. She was awarded the OBE in 1966, and created DBE in 1970.

P. Van Praagh: *How I became a Ballet Dancer* (1954)

**van Schurman, Anna Maria** (1607–78). Dutch philologist. She was born in Cologne, but her family moved to Utrecht to escape persecution as members of the Reformed Church. She was educated at home with her brothers in Classics, mathematics, geography and astronomy, and also produced remarkable paintings and engravings. When she was in her late twenties, Gijsbert Voetius, Rector of Utrecht University, arranged a cubicle so that she could attend his lectures on theology and oriental languages without being seen. She studied Hebrew, Arabic, and Ethiopian, in which she composed a grammar. In the mid-1630s she turned to theology, writing a treatise, *On the End of Life,* and the *Amica dissertatio*, which discussed the suitability of education for Christian women, asserting that it should be valued for its own sake but need not affect traditional social roles. She acquired an international reputation, and corresponded with a network of learned women in Europe.

After the deaths of the elderly aunts whom she had looked after for several years, she became a follower of Jean de Labadie. In 1673 she joined his religious community and retracted her *dissertatio*, claiming that loving fellowship was more important than learning. She subsequently wrote an autobiography entitled *Euklerion* ('Choice of a Better Part').

V. Birch: *Anna van Schurman: Scholar, Artist, Saint* (1909)
J. Irwin: 'Anna Maria van Schurman', *Female Scholars,* ed. J. Brink (1980)

**Varda, Agnes** (1928–). French film director. Born in Brussels to Greek-French parents, she was raised in France, studying at the Sorbonne and the Ecole du Louvre. She first became interested in theatre and cinema while working for the Théâtre National Populaire as their official photographer. After founding a film-making co-operative in 1954 with Alain Resnais as producer, she made her first film, *La pointe courte.* It was later considered to be a precursor of the New Wave movement of young French directors. Her reputation was established with *Cléo de 5 à 7/Cleo from 5 to 7* (1961) and *Le bonheur* (1965) which won the Best Film Award at the Cannes Film Festival. After some documentary work and an episode in the film *Loin de Vietnam* (1967), she made two shorts and a feature film in the USA in 1968 which reflected her growing interest in the political left and feminism, shown in her film, *L'une chante, l'autre pas/One sings, the Other does not* (1977) and *Vagabonde* (1985) which won the Golden Lion at the Venice Film Festival.

**Varnhagen von Ense, Rahel Levin** (1771–1833). German salon hostess. Born in Berlin, into an affluent family, she was the sister of Ludwig Robert who became a well-known playwright. At the turn of the century she held a salon in Berlin, which became a meeting place for leaders of the Romantic movement, but in 1806 she lost her fortune and her *soirées* ceased. She had experienced unhappy love affairs with the Count von Finckenstein and the diplomat Raphael d'Unquijo, but in 1808 she met the soldier, diplomat and writer Karl Varnhagen von Ense, 14 years her junior. She converted to Christianity and they were married in 1814. They lived in Karlsruhe until 1819 when they returned to Berlin, and made their home a fashionable centre of literary life. Rahel's salon attracted scholars and writers such as Heine, Humboldt, Arnim, Gutzkow and Laube. After her death, her husband published some of her writing in *Rahel: Ein Buch des Andenkens für ihre Freunde* (1834); her correspondence has also been published. During her life she had argued persuasively for the education and employment of women, opposing the current belief in their intellectual and moral inferiority. Her life has fascinated other intellectual feminists such as ELLEN KEY and HANNAH ARENDT, who both wrote portraits of her.

H. Arendt: *Rahel Varnhagen* (1975)

**Vaughan,** Dame **Janet (Maria)** (1899–). British doctor and university Principal. Janet Vaughan was born in Clifton, Bristol, and was educated at home until the age of 15 when she was sent to North Foreland Lodge. She studied medicine at Somerville College, Oxford and University College Hospital, London. She worked as an assistant clinical pathologist at University College Hospital from 1927 to 1929. Her experience of the terrible poverty around Euston, 'women giving birth with nothing but newspapers to lie on', turned her into a lifelong socialist. In 1929 she received a year's Rockefeller Travelling Fellowship to study in Boston, and in 1930 she married David Gourlay. They had two daughters, but her promising medical career continued – as a Beit Memorial Fellow

(1930–34), a Leverhulme Fellow of the Royal College of Physicians) (1934–5) and as a Clinical Pathologist at the British Post-Graduate Medical School (1935–9). Her book *The Anaemias* was published in 1934. During the Spanish Civil War she was active in Spanish Medical Aid to the International Brigade and was one of a team which introduced to Britain the Spanish method of storing blood for transfusion. She used these methods as Director of the North West London Blood Supply Depot throughout World War II, from 1939 to 1945. In 1945, before the war ended, she was one of the first doctors sent from Britain to work with the survivors of the Nazi concentration camps, her job being to develop treatment for extreme cases of starvation.

Janet Vaughan became Principal of Somerville College, Oxford, in the autumn of 1945, remaining Principal until her retirement in 1967, when she was made an Honorary Fellow. She became a leader in the study of the effects of radiation, and in 1950 was appointed Director of the Medical Research Unit for Research on Bone-Seeking Isotopes, and her later books (in addition to many scientific papers) include *The Physiology of Bone* (1970, 1975, 1981) and *The Effects of Irradiation on the Skeleton* (1973). She has held several other public positions, as a member of the Royal Commission on Equal Pay (1945–6), Chairman of Oxford Regional Hospital Board (1950–51), a member of the Phillips Committee on the Economics and Problems of the Provision for Old Age (1953) and of the Commonwealth Scholarship Commission (since 1964), and as a Trustee of the Nuffield Foundation. Since 1960 she has received many honorary degrees and fellowships, the most recent being awarded by Girton College, Cambridge, in 1986.

**Vaughan, Sarah (Lois)** (1924–). American jazz singer. Sarah Vaughan was born in Newark, New Jersey. Her father was a carpenter and her mother a laundress and from the age of seven she sang with them in the choir at Mount Zion Baptist Church. She also learnt piano and continued her music studies during the 1930s. When she won an amateur contest at the Apollo Theatre, Harlem, she was recognized by Billy Eckstine, the Earl Hines band vocalist, who obtained her a job with the band, and she made her professional debut at the Apollo in 1943. Even at the age of 19 she was acclaimed for her rare musicianship, and joined Eckstine when he founded his own band, cutting her first record in 1944 (for a fee of $20 a side). In the 1940s she was associated with the 'Bebop' music of Eckstine, Charlie Parker and Dizzy Gillespie, and from 1946 played in night clubs like the Café Society in Greenwich Village. In 1947 she married the trumpeter George Treadwell, who helped to build her career, and by 1950 was an international star, touring over the next three decades throughout the USA and Europe, being nicknamed either 'Sassy' or 'the Divine Sarah', after SARAH BERNHARDT. Her rich voice, use of vibrato and keen sense of structure are captured on a series of notable albums and singles including *I'll Wait and Pray*, *Tenderly*, *My Funny Valentine*, *A Foggy Day*, *Alone Again* (*Naturally*), *The Summer Knows* and *Rainy Days and Mondays*. Among many awards, she received a Grammy Award in 1983. She has been married three times and has one daughter.

**Vecsei** [née Hollo], **Eva** (1930–). Canadian architect. Born in Vienna, of Hungarian descent, she was educated at the University of Technical Sciences, Budapest (1948–52), and on graduating married the architect Andrei Vecsei. After working in Budapest on a large housing project she emigrated to Canada in 1957, and worked for a partnership in Montreal for 12 years. While in her thirties she became project designer for a huge commercial complex, Place Bonaventure (called the largest building in the world), opened in 1967. From her own office she has since designed another vast project, 'La Cité', which is a total development of a 7-acre site, completed in 1977. In the 1980s she has designed several large developments in Montreal and in 1983 was awarded the *Canadian Architect* award of excellence.

**Veil** [née Jacob], **Simone** (1927–). French lawyer and politician. Born in Nice, she was the daughter of a Jewish architect, André Jacob. In 1944 she was sent with her family to Auschwitz and only she and one sister survived. After World War II she married Antoine Veil and had three children, while studying law at the Institut d'Etudes Politiques in Paris. She entered the Ministry

of Justice as an Attaché (1957–9) and then became an Assistant (1959–65). Her special interests were in penal policy, especially probation and rehabilitation, and later in reform of the adoption law. In 1970 she was appointed Secretary-General of the Conseil Supérieur de la Magistrature, a body supervising the judiciary and advising the President on important legal matters. From 1972 to 1974 she was also on the administrative council of ORTF, the national radio and television service.

In 1974 Simone Veil was appointed Minister of Health by Giscard d'Estaing. She immediately introduced legislation making contraception more easily available and then, in a series of dramatic debates, successfully defended a bill to liberalize the abortion laws. In 1977–8 her post was changed to Minister of Health and Social Security and in 1978–9 to Health and Family Affairs. In 1979 she became a member of the European Parliament, of which she was President until January 1982, when she refused to stand for re-election because of dissension among her supporters. Since 1982 she has chaired the Legal Affairs Committee and since 1984 the Liberal and Democratic Group.

**Vestris, Lucia (Elisabetta)** (1797–1856). English actress and theatre manager. The daughter of an Italian engraver, Bartolozzi, she married the French ballet dancer Armand Vestris when she was 16. He deserted her in 1820. She made her career as a singer, specializing in burlesque or high comedy. With curly hair and dark eyes, she excelled at spirited 'breeches' roles such as MacHeath in *The Beggar's Opera*, following her first great success in 1817 in *Giovanni in London*, a burlesque of Mozart's *Don Giovanni*. She played for several years in Paris and was established as a leading London actress, playing at both Covent Garden and Drury Lane.

In 1830 she became a theatre manager, taking over the Olympic and presenting a series of successful farces and burlesques. She made her fortune and in 1838 married another manager, Charles Mathews with whom, after a visit to New York, she ran Covent Garden and then the Lyceum. An autocratic director, known as 'Madame' to her company, she reformed theatrical management and insisted on improvements in scenery, historical accuracy in costume and real props. It was she who introduced the box-set with ceiling in 1832. Unfortunately Mathews was a heavy drinker and a bad financial manager, and after years of great respectability their enterprise was on the verge of financial collapse at the time of Madame Vestris's death.

L.J. Williams: *Madame Vestris* (1973)

**Viardot** [née García]**, Pauline** (1821–1910). French-Spanish mezzo-soprano. The daughter of the celebrated tenor Manuel García, who died when she was 11, she was nevertheless influenced by his methods through the vocal training she received from her mother. She was a piano pupil of Liszt and studied composition with Reicha, but is remembered primarily as a singer. Although her success could not rival that of her sister MARIA MALIBRAN, she is equally important historically, especially in that her intelligence and integrity contributed to the raising of the status of singers. She married Louis Viardot, manager of the Théâtre-Italien, in 1840, and their household became one of the most important artistic centres in Paris, such figures as GEORGE SAND, Musset, Chopin, Berlioz, Gounod and Gustav Doré being among the regular visitors.

She made her London debut as Rossini's Desdemona in 1839, a role she repeated in Paris the same year. A visit to St Petersburg [now Leningrad] in 1843 brought her into contact with Russian music, which she introduced to the West, also being among the first Westerners to sing it in the original language. Meyerbeer wrote the role of Fidès in *Le prophète* for her, its première bringing her to increased public attention. Other roles she created include Saint-Saëns' Dalila (the opera is dedicated to her, as are Schumann's *Liederkreis* and several songs by Fauré) and Gounod's Sapho, while she was also acclaimed for her performances of Gluck's Orpheus and in operas by Meyerbeer and Halévy. She sang the solo in the première of Brahms's *Alto Rhapsody* (1870).

After her retirement from the stage she remained active as a teacher (she taught at the Paris Conservatoire, 1871–5) and composer. Her compositions are mostly vocal, including the operettas *Le dernier sorcier* and *L'ogre* for which Turgenyev (one of her most ardent admirers) supplied the librettos. Many of her published songs are settings of Russian poems, and she arranged a number of Chopin's mazurkas as songs.

A. Fitzlyon: *The Price of Genius: a Life of Pauline Viardot* (1964)

**Victoria (Alexandrina)** (1819–1901). English queen. She was the only child of the Duke of Kent, who was the fourth son of George III. He had married Princess Mary Louisa Victoria of Saxe-Coburg-Gotha, specifically to produce an heir. He died when Victoria was eight months old and she was brought up by her mother very frugally at Kensington Palace. She was recognized as heir to the throne when George IV died in 1830 and succeeded her uncle, William IV, in 1837. She immediately asserted her independence from her mother, her governess Louise Lehzen, and her uncle Leopold. Her early actions were rash and threatened her popularity, for example her persecution of the Tory lady-in-waiting Lady Fiona Hastings, whom she insisted should be examined for pregnancy and who later died, and her refusal to dismiss the Whig ladies of the bedchamber in courtesy to the incoming Prime Minister Sir Robert Peel in 1839, which forced Melbourne to remain in office.

In 1840 she married her cousin, Prince Albert of Saxe-Coburg-Gotha, and the first of her nine children was born that year. Her descendants later ruled in Sweden, Denmark, Norway, Spain, Greece and Russia, and 37 great-grandchildren had been born by the time of her death. Albert's influence on Victoria's private and political life was considerable. In 1841 he reconciled her to the Tories and to Peel, whom she came to like greatly; he increased the popularity of the monarchy through sponsorship of the Royal Exhibition in 1851 and influenced the formation of the coalition government in 1852. Her own preferences and actions were still influential, for example her dislike of Palmerston, which led to his temporary dismissal in 1851. During the Crimean War Victoria's keen support of the army, her institution of the Victoria Cross for bravery, and later her wholehearted support of FLORENCE NIGHTINGALE, managed to suppress any suspicion that Albert had made her 'pro-Russian'.

Victoria and Albert spent much time out of London; Osborne on the Isle of Wight, was built between 1845 and 1851, and Balmoral was leased in 1848 and bought four years later. After Albert died in 1861, Victoria suffered a nervous collapse leading to two years of severe depression. She spent much time in seclusion at Balmoral, becoming reliant on a few old friends, such as Albert's gillie, John Brown. She did not appear in public until 1864, or open Parliament until 1866, but Disraeli gradually won her confidence and coaxed her back into public view. He became her favourite, especially after he obtained for her the title of Empress of India in 1876. She was correspondingly hard on Gladstone during his periods of power (1868–74, 1880–85, 1886, 1892–4), opposing many of his policies, particularly Irish Home Rule. Victoria insisted upon lengthy consultation and intervened in some important issues, but by the end of her life the transition of the monarchy to an almost formal ceremonial position in the State was complete.

Her last years were more calm and lonely, and she experienced difficulty with the Prince of Wales, to whom she had always denied effective independence; but her popularity increased and national Jubilees were celebrated in 1887 and 1897, the 50th and 60th years of her reign. She died at Osborne, but was buried beside Albert at Frogmore near Windsor.

Victoria's personality is expressed not only in the style of her life, but also in her many sketchbooks (she was a talented artist), and in her writings. From about the age of 13 to her death she kept a vivid and detailed journal; she was also a copious letter writer, both on political subjects as in her letters to Gladstone and Palmerston, and on social affairs, reform movements or domestic life, as in the many letters she wrote to her eldest daughter Victoria after she married the Crown Prince of Prussia in 1858. She created the sense of an accessible monarch by publishing *Leaves from the Journal of our Life in the Highlands* (1868) and *More Leaves* (1884).

S. Weinraub: *Victoria* (1987)
C. Woodham Smith: *Queen Victoria: her Life and Times* (1972)

**Vigée-Lebrun, Marie (Elisabeth Louise)** (1755–1842). French painter. Born in Paris, the daughter of a pastel portraitist, she began drawing while a child and, although educated in a convent, she took art lessons from her father's friends during vacations. After his death in 1770, she began making portraits in oils to pay for her brother's schooling; these portraits included several aristocrats. In 1775 she married the rich art dealer, J.B.P. Lebrun, and achieved fame with portraits of academicians, including Lebruyère, and Fleury, and courtiers such as Count Orlov and the Comtesse de Brionne. In 1779 she painted the first of eight portraits of MARIE ANTOINETTE, who became a close friend and influenced her election to the Académie Royale in 1783.

In 1789 at the outbreak of the French Revolution she fled to Italy with her daughter, achieving great success in Florence, Rome (where she met ANGELICA KAUFFMAN), and Naples where she painted portraits of the royal family and EMMA HAMILTON. She then moved north to Turin, Vienna and St Petersburg [now Leningrad], spending six successful years at the court of CATHERINE II before returning to Paris via Potsdam in 1805. Here she lived separately from her husband, although they shared a house. She continued her independent career, visiting England, where she painted portraits of the Prince of Wales and Lord Byron (1801–4) and Switzerland where she painted *Madame de Staël as Corinne* (see STAËL). She settled in Paris where she continued to work, at a slower rate, until the end of her life. Her husband died in 1813, her daughter in 1818. Vigée-Lebrun was enormously prolific, being credited with 900 paintings, all of a high standard. She also had a reputation for her friendliness, energy and wit.

E. Vigée-Lebrun: *Memoirs* [Eng. trans., L. Strachey] (1904)

**Vionnet, Madeleine** (1877–1975). French fashion designer. The daughter of a plumber and a café proprietor, she was apprenticed to a dressmaker at the age of 14 and then trained in London and Paris, where she opened her own shop just before World War I. In 1919 she reopened it and the House of Vionnet had a dominant influence on the appearance of women for the next 20 years, revolutionizing design by cutting clothes on the bias, pioneering 'handkerchief point' skirts, and using soft flowing materials such as crêpe and silk. Vionnet was equally progressive as an employer, providing social services and facilities such as clinics and gymnasiums for her employees. Her shop closed in 1939.

**Vitti, Monica** [pseud. of Maria Luisa Ceciarelli] (1931–). Italian actress. She was born in Rome. After appearing in amateur productions, she studied at the National Academy of Dramatic Art in Rome until 1953 and then acted in classical roles and also made a considerable reputation in comedy and revue. During the mid-1950s she belonged to a theatre group directed by Antonioni, appearing as Sally Bowles in his version of *I am a Camera* (1957). Her international reputation was made in his films *L'avventura* (1960), *La notte/The Night* (1961), *L'eclisse/Eclipse* (1962) and *Il deserto rosso/Red Desert* (1964). She also appeared in comedies such as the British film *Modesty Blaise* (1966) and in dramatic films such as Jancsó's *La pacifista* (1970), but then concentrated on working in Italy, where she became increasingly famous and respected as an expert in quick-moving zany comedy.

**Vlachou, Helene** (1911–). Greek newspaper owner. Helene Vlachou inherited from her father, a famous journalist and democratic patriot, the management of *Kathimerini*, an independent daily newspaper with 70,000 sales and of *Messinvrine*. When the military junta took over she refused to submit to censorship and in 1967 ceased all publication. After widespread public protests she was placed under house-arrest, but she disguised herself and escaped to London on a forged passport. Until 1974 she was an energetic organizer of the Greek opposition in exile and after the junta was deposed she returned to Greece. She restarted publication of *Kathimerini* and became a member of parliament.

H. Vlachou: *House Arrest* (1970)

**Voisin, La** [Monvoisin, Catherine Deshayes] (d 1684). French witch. Brought into prominence in the DE BRINVILLIERS trial in 1677, La Voisin was a midwife and fortune-teller whose clients included the

Marquise DE MONTESPAN, and other leading aristocrats. She was tried with others in a special court known as the *chambre ardente*. Eventually convicted of selling poisons and charms, she was burnt alive in 1684.

**von Arnim, Bettina** (1785–1859). German Romantic writer. Bettina was born in Frankfurt-am-Main, the daughter of a rich Italian merchant, Pietro Brentano. Her mother Maximiliane von La Roche had been one of Goethe's early loves, and her grandmother Sophie von La Roche (1730–1807) was a well-known novelist, author of the highly successful novel in letters *Fräulein von Sternheim* (1771).

After her mother died in 1793 she was educated in a convent in Fritzlar, but also spent time with her grandmother at Offenbach, and from 1803–6 lived in Marburg: as a child she met Goethe, and knew his mother well. In 1811 she married the physicist and writer Achim von Arnim, who had collaborated with her brother Clemens von Brentano, a leading Romantic writer, on the collection of folk-lyrics *Des Knaben Wunderhorn* (1805–8). The von Arnims were at the centre of the German Romantic movement, and divided their time between Berlin and their estate at Wiepersdorf, where Bettina brought up their seven children: one of their daughters, Gisela, later married Hermann Grimm.

Wayward and brilliant, Bettina was celebrated for her lively wit, impulsive charm and imaginative intensity and after her husband died in 1831 she began her own career as a writer. Her most famous book is *Goethe's Briefwechsel mit einem Kinde* (1835), a blend of fact and fiction based on her childhood correspondence with Goethe and his mother, which was extremely popular in Germany and in America, where it was translated in 1837. She also wrote a biography of her friend the poetess and nun Karoline von Gunderode, who had committed suicide in 1806, and a memoir of her brother Clemens. Increasingly progressive and liberal in her views she was fired by the plight of the Silesian weavers to write a lengthy appeal on behalf of the oppressed, *Dies Buch gehört dem König* (1849) which also incorporated her demands for working-class rights as a whole, for the emancipation of the Jews and the abolition of capital punishment.

**von Suttner** [née Kinsky], **Bertha Felicie Sophie** (1843–1914). Austrian novelist and pacifist. Her father, Count Franz Kinsky, died soon after her birth in Prague. Well educated and widely travelled, after the loss of the family fortune she trained as a singer but worked as a secretary to Alfred Nobel, the dynamite manufacturer in 1868. She then became governess to the Von Suttner family in Vienna. In 1877 she eloped with Baron Arthur von Suttner to the Caucasus. He worked as an engineer, while she taught and began to write novels and short stories.

After returning to Austria in 1885 her novels reflected her concern for the position of women and for the peace movement; in 1886 she lectured to the London International Peace Association. In 1889 the publication of her great pacifist work, *Die Waffen nieder* (translated as *Lay down your Arms!*), caused controversy throughout Europe. It prompted Nobel to found his Peace Prize; Von Suttner was the first woman recipient in 1905. She wrote more novels, but was chiefly involved in pacifist work, founding the International Peace League, and editing its journal from 1894 to 1900. Her last book, *Memoiren,* appeared in 1911. She died in Vienna just before the outbreak of World War I.

B. Kempf: *Suffragette for Peace: the Life of Bertha von Suttner* (1972)

**von Trapp,** Baroness **Maria** (1905–86). Austrian singer. A 20-year-old novice nun in the Tyrolean Alps, Maria was sent as governess to the seven children of Baron Georg von Trapp in 1926. They married in 1927 and had three more children. Both were determined opponents of Nazism and fled Austria when the Germans invaded, crossing the Alps on foot before travelling to the United States. They arrived destitute, and turned their love of music to professional use, becoming famous as the touring Trapp Family Singers. Adopting Tyrolean costume, they performed a repertoire ranging from folksongs to Gregorian chants and English madrigals. Although they bought a house in Vermont, which later became a skiing hotel and music centre, they continued to tour until 1957. Maria's book *The Trapp Family Singers* was the basis for the 1959 Rodgers and Hammerstein musical *The Sound of Music,* later an Oscar-winning film. When their hotel was destroyed by fire in 1980, she built a new hotel, and ran it until her retirement in 1985. The large family flourished, and at her death she left 50 great-great-grandchildren.

**von Trotta, Margarethe** (1942–). German film director. One of Germany's leading contemporary directors, Margarethe was born in Berlin and studied languages in Munich and Paris, before training as an actress. After a stage career in the 1960s she has worked entirely in television and film. In 1969 she appeared in Fassbinder's *Götter der Pest,* and in 1970 began her collaboration with her husband, director Volker Schlondorff, appearing in several of his films, such as *Baal* (1970) and *Strohfeuer* (1972). She co-directed and co-wrote *The Lost Honour of Katharina Blum* (1975), which was followed by her sole direction of *The Second Awakening* (1977), *Sisters, or the Balance of Happiness* (1979), *Sheer Madness* (1983) and *Rosa Luxemburg* (1986). All her films focus on women's lives and relationships, whether exceptional and fiercely political, like ROSA LUXEMBURG or Christine Enslinn (the inspiration for *Marianne and Julianne*, 1981), or leading apparently everyday lives. Her works often explore subconscious impulses through the use of dream sequences and flashbacks.

**von Westphalen, Jenny** [Julia Joan Bertha] (1814–81). German; wife of Karl Marx. She came from a wealthy conservative family, her brother being Minister of the Interior in Prussia in the 1850s. She became engaged to Karl Marx, four years her junior, in 1836 and married him in 1843, despite family opposition. She went into exile with him, first to Paris and then to Brussels and London. After her dowry was spent, their life was one of extreme poverty, despite earnings from political journalism and the generosity of Engels. She bore six children, three of whom died young. Their three remaining daughters were Jenny, who married a Frenchman, Paul Longuet, and died in 1883; Laura, who married Paul Lafargue, the French socialist, and died with him in a mutual suicide pact in 1911; and ELEANOR MARX-AVELING, who became a prominent British trade unionist. Jenny Marx also worked as her husband's secretary, and helped with the administrative work of the Socialist International.

**Vreeland, Diana (Dalziel)** (c1901–). American fashion journalist. She was born in Paris of English parents who emigrated to the USA at the start of World War I. In 1924 she married the New York banker Thomas Reed Vreeland, and they had two children. They lived in Albany, New York, and then in Paris until 1935. On her return to the USA she began working as a fashion editor for *Harper's Bazaar*, acquiring fame and notoriety with her 'Why don't you?' column, with suggestions like 'Why don't you wash your child's hair in champagne?' or 'Cut your old ermine wrap into a bathrobe?'. In 1962 she moved to *Vogue*, where she was Editor-in-chief until 1971 and is still a consultant editor. On her retirement she was appointed special consultant to the Metropolitan Museum's Costume Institute, where she arranged elaborate and meticulously-detailed exhibitions illustrating the history of fashion and design. Always extravangantly dressed she has been described as 'the high priestess of style'.
D. Vreeland: *D.V.* (1984)

**Vyroubova, Nina** (1921–). Russian-French ballerina. She was born in Gurzuf and she was taught by her mother and made a solo debut in *Coppélia* in 1937. From 1945 to 1947 she was a member of the Ballet des Champs Elysées where she created a number of exciting roles for Roland Petit, such as *Les forains*. Moving to the Opéra, she danced the Queen in Lifar's *Blanche-Neige,* and excelled in *Les Indes galantes* (1952) and *Noces fantastiques* (1955). Her repertoire also included classic roles such as Giselle and Aurora. In 1956 she left the Opéra for the De Cuevas Ballet, and continued to create leading roles until the late 1960s, for example in Van Dijk's *Abraxas* (1965). She then taught at the Opéra and at her own school until 1980, when she became Professor of Classical Dance at the Conservatoire Nationale de Troyes. Her unusual range and ability for classic as well as lyrical roles have ensured a lasting reputation.

# W

**Wagner** [née Liszt], **(Francesca Gaetana) Cosima** (1837–1930). German; wife of Richard Wagner. A daughter of Franz Liszt and Countess MARIE D'AGOULT (second of three children born of that liaison), she had an unstable childhood, her loyalties constantly divided. She was educated in France and was sent in her teens to Berlin to live with the Bülow family; this was at Liszt's instigation, as a means of reducing maternal influence. She inherited both literary talent from her mother and precocious musicianship from her father. In her youth she played Beethoven's piano sonatas and Liszt's compositions, inspiring the comment from Hans von Bülow, 'This is not talent, it is genius'; he advocated a career as a pianist for her, but this was vetoed by Liszt. As a writer her first publications were translations from German into French for the *Revue germanique*; she also worked on texts for Bülow's compositions, including a synopsis of the *Oresteia* for a projected symphony.

Cosima married Hans von Bülow in 1857; they had two daughters. From their honeymoon onwards she came into increasing contact with Wagner, to whom her husband was devoted to a degree verging on idolatry. By 1863 she and Wagner had declared their love for each other; shortly after Wagner was summoned to Munich by Ludwig II in 1864, Hans and Cosima followed at Wagner's behest. An anonymous article (by Wagner, with Cosima's assistance) attacking Ludwig's cabinet caused public hostility towards Wagner to escalate, and he was obliged to leave Bavaria; he eventually settled at Triebschen, nr Lucerne. Cosima finally left Bülow to join him there in 1868, having already borne him two daughters, Isolde (*b* 1865) and Eva (*b* 1867). The birth of their son Siegfried (1869) is celebrated in Wagner's *Siegfried Idyll,* first performed on the staircase of their home as a present to Cosima. She married Wagner in August 1870, a month after her divorce from Bülow had been secured. The rest of her life was one of total sacrifice to Wagner, which she regarded as both duty and recompense in itself. From 1869 until Wagner's death in 1883 she kept diaries which, along with his autobiography (written down by Cosima to his dictation and dedicated to her), remain standard source material; their unabridged publication was not possible until 1974, when a court decision lifted the embargo imposed on them by her daughter Eva Chamberlain's will. Cosima's letters to Nietzsche, written with apparently less of an eye on posterity, were published in 1938–40.

After Wagner's death Cosima assumed directorship of the Bayreuth Festival (until 1906, when Siegfried took over). Her tenure was characterized by rigid adherence to what she deemed to be Wagner's wishes in details of production and stage direction as well as in all musical aspects, which she carried through against considerable opposition. She also amassed a great deal of Wagner's correspondence. Blind during her last decade, she died at the age of 92.

A. Hunt Sokoloff: *Cosima Wagner: a Biography* (1969)
G. Skelton: *Richard and Cosima Wagner: Biography of a Marriage* (1981)

**Waitz, Grete** (1953–). Norwegian athlete. Grete Andersen, born in Oslo, was spotted at the age of 11 by the Olympic javelin champion Pedersen, who recruited her for his track team. It became clear that her strength was distance running. She took part in the 1972 Olympic Games at 1500 metres, which was at that time the longest women's Olympic run. She continued to compete well at 1500 and

3000 metres in international competitions, setting a record of 8 minutes 46.6 seconds at 3000 metres in 1975, but like other women endurance runners found the distances too short to realize her full potential. She married Jack Nilsen in 1975 and together they took the name Waitz. He became her coach and helped to persuade her to accept an invitation from the New York Runners' Club to run in the 1978 New York Marathon. She finished in 2 hours, 32 minutes and 30 seconds, a new women's world record by more than 2 minutes. Waitz won the New York marathon in 1979 and 1980, but in 1981 she was forced to drop out because of a stress fracture in her right foot which also stopped her competing in the European Championships in Athens in 1982. However, she won in New York in 1982 and in London equalled the world's best time (set by Allison Roe of New Zealand in 1981 in New York). But, as she predicted, this only lasted one day as Joan Benoit of the USA ran a new world best in Boston 24 hours later. Waitz also won the gold medal five times in the World Cross-Country Championships (1978–83). The marathon was finally included in the women's events at the 1984 Olympic Games, where Waitz won the silver medal. She refused a stipend from the Norwegian Amateur Athletic Association because she did not want to feel under pressure to perform, and became consultant to a sporting goods company.

**Wald, Lillian D.** (1867–1940). American public health nurse. Born in Cincinnati, Ohio, Lillian had a happy, cultured childhood as the third of four children. She was refused entrance to Vassar College at the age of 16 because she was too young. At 22 she felt 'the need of serious, definite work' and entered the training school for nurses of the New York Hospital. In 1893, while organizing home nursing classes for immigrant families, the sight of a sick woman in a squalid tenement on the Lower East Side determined her to move to a tenement in the area in order to identify with the problems she was tackling.

Lillian founded the Henry Street Nurses Settlement. By 1913 it had developed into the Henry Street Visiting Nurses Service with 92 nurses making 200,000 visits annually. She made the service fully professional, independent of religious or official ties; Henry Street also became a community centre.

She was a co-founder of the National Child Labor Committee in 1904; her suggestion to Theodore Roosevelt led to the forming of the Children's Bureau as part of the Department of Labor in 1912. She was surprised to find that her work with vocational training and education of retarded children led her to politics and child welfare legislation.

In 1910 she established a Department of Nursing and Health at Columbia University, and the Town and Country Nursing Service under the Red Cross. Having coined the term 'public health nursing', she became first President of its national organization. During World War I Lillian had hoped that mediation would prevail; after the war she founded the League of Free Nations Association. She was chairman of the Nurses Emergency Council during the 1918 influenza epidemic. She travelled often, sometimes with JANE ADDAMS, and was noted in her social work for maintaining warm personal relations with opponents as well as allies.

L. Wald: *The House on Henry Street* (1915)
R.L. Duffus: *Lillian Wald: Neighbor and Crusader* (1938)

**Walker, Alice Malsenior** (1944–). American novelist. Born in Eatonton, Georgia, the eighth child of a family of sharecroppers, Alice Walker reached Spelman College at 17 and in 1963 went on to Sarah Lawrence College, graduating in 1966. She became a caseworker in the New York City Welfare Department for some months, before joining the civil rights movement and working for voter legislation. She moved on to teach black studies, and lectured at Jackson State College (1968–9). After a spell as writer in residence at Tongalou College she became a full-time writer. She later became a consulting editor of *MS* and *Freedomways*. Her writing talent was already recognized by the late 1960s, and she received a Charles Merrill Fellowship in 1967, and a National Foundation for the Arts Award in fiction (1969–70). She is the author of three volumes of poetry and two collections of stories *In Love and Trouble* (1973) and *You can't keep a good Woman down*. Her first novel *The Third Life of*

*Grange Copeland* (1970), and her second *Meridian* (1976), widely acclaimed, build on her own experiences during the civil rights movement. In 1979 she published *Good Night Willie Lee, I'll see you in the Morning*, and her recent works include *You Can't Keep a Good Woman Down* (1981), *The Color Purple* (1982), which won the American Book Award and Pulitzer Prize in 1983 and was made into an Oscar winning film, and *In Search of Our Mothers' Gardens* (1983). These essays include discussion of ZORA NEALE HURSTON, and develop the idea of 'womanist writing', a phrase wider than 'feminist' which she derives from the black custom of describing independent, wilful girls as 'womanish'.

**Walker, Lucy** (1836–1916). English mountaineer. Lucy's father and brother were practised alpinists, and she climbed regularly in the Alps from the age of 22, always with the guide Melchior Anderegg. With the ascent of Albels, they established a climbing partnership of 98 expeditions in 22 years, notable summits being Dufourspitze of Monte Rosa (4557.6 metres); Finsterarhorn in 1862; Rimpfischhorn in 1864; then a pioneer ascent of Balmhorn with her father and brother Horace later that year.

On 20 July 1871 she became the first woman to climb the Matterhorn. This success publicized her earlier first female ascent of the Weisshorn and Lyskamm, for Lucy was unassuming and her exploits little-known. She was stocky, generally climbed in a white print dress and liked to eat sponge cake and drink champagne on a climb, and was not a feminist. She lived in Liverpool, but continued to visit the Alps each year. She became one of the first members of the Ladies' Alpine Club (founded 1907), and at 76 in 1912 became its second President.

**Walker, Mary Edwards** (1832–1919). American doctor. She was born in Oswego, New York, the daughter of a teacher and physician. She graduated from Syracuse Medical College in 1855 and practised in Columbus, Ohio, and in New York State. At the outbreak of the American Civil War she volunteered, and worked in tent hospitals in Virginia until she was appointed an official army surgeon in 1863. She took risks crossing Confederate lines to attend civilians and was imprisoned for four months in 1864, but was eventually awarded a Congressional Medal of Honour.

After she resigned from the army, she worked for a New York newspaper, becoming one of the first woman journalists in the USA. She also wrote two books, *Hit* (1871), and *Unmasked or The Science of Immorality* (1878). Mary was noted for her eccentricity in dress. When she first practised medicine she wore trousers and a tunic. While in the army she wore officer's uniform. After the Civil War she appeared on public occasions in men's full evening dress and a silk top hat, but she wore her hair in curls to show she was a woman. She was arrested several times for 'masquerading in men's clothes'. In 1897 she founded a colony for women called Adamless Eden, and lectured widely on women's rights.

C. Snyder: *Dr Mary Walker* (1962)

**Walker, Sarah Breedlove** (1867–1919). American pioneer businesswoman. The daughter of poor negro sharecroppers, she was born in Delta, Louisiana, orphaned at the age of six and brought up by an older sister. At 14 she married C.J. Walker, but was a widow at 20 and moved to St Louis, Missouri, where she became a washerwoman, brought up her daughter and studied at night school. In 1905 she had the idea of developing hair products, especially straighteners, for black women. She worked on preparation for a year in St Louis, then moved to Denver and travelled for five years, building up a huge mail order business. She now called herself Madam C.J. Walker, and in 1908 set up an office in Pittsburgh. In 1910 she founded laboratories in Indianapolis and a training school for the famous Walker Agents, who numbered about 2000 and covered the whole of the USA. A good employer, she organized social clubs and sponsored philanthropic and educational work by her employees. She supported the National Association for the Advancement of Coloured People, founded scholarships and endowed old people's homes. Rising from extreme poverty, she made a vast fortune and owned property in New York and Indianapolis, and a luxurious estate 'Villa Lewaro' on the Hudson River.

**Wallace, Lila Acheson** (1889–1984). American businesswoman and patron. Born in Virden, Manitoba, the daughter of a Presbyterian minister, Lila Acheson was educated in Nashville and graduated from the University of Oregon in 1917, when she became a teacher at Eatonville, Washington. Her experience of running a YWCA summer school led to a job as full-time YWCA organizer in New Jersey from 1919 to 1921, and she also ran a Presbyterian social service scheme, and set up day-care centres for the Inter-Church World Movement in several states.

In 1921 she married De Witt Wallace, and shortly afterwards they moved to New York where they launched the *Reader's Digest* 'from a basement under a speakeasy in Greenwich Village'. Its instant success was to continue for the next 60 years, until it had reached a 30-million subscription by the 1980s and was translated into 17 languages. Lila was involved as an editor, manager (introducing model welfare schemes) and, from the 1930s, as a buyer of art for the *Digest* headquarters in Pleasantville. The immense art collection, principally Impressionist and post-Impressionist paintings, became one of the finest in the United States. She became a major patron of the arts and a benefactor to social causes, allegedly donating over $60 million. Her trusteeships included the Metropolitan Museum of Art, the New York Zoological Society and the Juilliard School of Music. At the Metropolitan Museum she was largely responsible for the restoration of the Great Hall, and for the modernization of 32 galleries in the Egyptian wing. Her other notable contributions to restoration included the Boscobel mansion, Manet's house and gardens at Giverny, and the moving of the Abu Simbel temples on the Nile. Her energy was boundless and her personality unique: as another of her great passions was gardening, she insisted that the *Digest* offices were full of flowers, and even that flowers should be arranged in the Metropolitan Museum's Great Hall in perpetuity.

Lila and De Witt Wallace were co-chairmen of the *Reader's Digest* from 1965 to 1973 and retained joint ownership until De Witt's death in 1981, after which she became the sole proprietor. Her many honours included the Theodore Roosevelt Award, 1954, the US Medal of Freedom, 1972, and the French Légion d'honneur. She died at Mount Kisco, New York.

**Wallace, Nellie** (1870–1948). English music hall comic. Born in Glasgow, the daughter of actors, she first appeared as a clog dancer at the age of 12 and then toured in a dance act with her two sisters. She married an actor, Bill Liddie, and after a disastrous attempt at serious acting she moved back to music hall and pantomime, taking over as principal girl from Ada Reeve in *Jack and Jill* in Manchester in 1895. She did not appear in London until 1903, but by 1910 she was a recognized star, billed as 'The Essence of Eccentricity'. Extremely funny, artfully grotesque and suggestive, she toured England and the USA with equal success, turning to revue after World War I. She was one of the very few great women pantomime dames throughout the 1920s and 1930s. During World War II she worked with the Entertainments National Service Association (ENSA). She collapsed in the wings after appearing in a Royal Variety Show, where she had sung *A Boy's Best Friend is his Mother*, and died shortly afterwards.

**Wallādah bint al-Mustakfi** (*fl* 11th century). Hispano-Arabic poet. Her father was Caliph of Córdova between 1023 and 1131; historians believe that her mother was an Ethiopian Christian slave. During a rebellion her father was poisoned and her family lost power but at the age of about 30 she inherited a fortune and began to live an independent life. She abandoned the veil, ran a salon for leading writers and artists, and was the great passion of the famous Arab poet, Ibn Zaydūn, although their long relationship was troubled by gossip, slander and intrigue. She was a fine poet in her own right, and her surviving poems form part of a verse correspondence with her lover.

**Walpurgis, Maria Antonia.** *See* MARIA ANTONIA WALPURGIS.

**Walters, Barbara** (1931–). American newscaster. Born in Brookline, Massachusetts, the daughter of an impresario, she graduated from Sarah Lawrence College in 1953 and soon began writing and producing for television. In 1961 she joined the *Today Show* as a writer and remained for 14 years, as a panel member from 1963 to 1974 and as co-host from 1974 to 1976. In 1976 she moved to ABC to 'co-author' the evening news programme, and to produce a series of special assignments and to chair the syndicated programme *Not for Women Only*. Her most famous assignments have included aggressive interviews with individuals including Sadat, Prince Philip and Fidel Castro. She has won numerous awards, and was named one of *Harper's* ten Women of Accomplishment in 1967 and 1971, and one of the 200 Leaders of the Future by *Time* in 1974. Her popularity continues: in both 1982 and 1984 Gallup Polls showed she was one of the women most admired by the American people.

**Walters, Ethel** (1900–). American jazz singer. Born in Chester, Pennsylvania, she sang in church choirs as a child, worked as a maid and gained entrance to the Baltimore and Philadelphia theatres by winning a local talent contest. In 1917 she became a popular New York singer and after touring widely won a national reputation with her records and numerous revue appearances. She visited Europe in 1930, had recording sessions with Duke Ellington and Benny Goodman, and then took her own show on the road with her husband Eddie Mallory until 1939. She worked in cabaret, films and theatre in the 1950s and 1960s, continuing to work after a heart attack in 1964. She was also a dedicated religious campaigner.

E. Walters: *His Eye on the Sparrow* (1951)

**Walters, 'Skittles'** [Catherine] (1839–c1900). English courtesan. Born in Liverpool, she went to London and became a successful prostitute. Her name came later from a reply to an insult from some drunken guardsmen that 'if they didn't hold their bloody row, she'd knock them down like a row of bloody skittles'. The poet laureate Alfred Austen paid tribute to her appearance in Rotten Row where 'though scowling matrons stamping steeds restrain, she flaunts propriety with flapping mane'. In 1862 a letter to *The Times* complained that her appearance in Hyde Park attracted as much attention as the international exhibition at the nearby Science Museum. She became a famous London character, enhancing her glamorous reputation by eloping to the USA with the married Aubrey de Vere Beauclerk, then to Paris as mistress of the Marquess of Hartington, who paid her £2000 per year. In France the young poet

Wilfred Scawen Blunt fell madly in love with her and they became close lifelong friends. She is the subject of his sonnet sequence *Esther* (1892) and of many early love lyrics. In London the Prince of Wales attended her fashionable Sunday parties. She was vivacious, splendidly witty and daring (being among the first to take up roller-skating in the 1880s), and was also highly cultured, intelligent and well-read.

C. Pearl: *The Girl with the Swandown Seat* (1957)

**Wang Guangmei** (1922–). Chinese politician. Wang Guangmei was born in America, but returned to China as a child and went to school in Beijing and Tianjin. She studied physics at Furen University from 1939 to 1943, followed by postgraduate research at Yanjing University. In 1946 she was an interpreter for the Communists in the vital mediation talks with the Kuomintang and went on to work for the Central Committee Foreign Affairs Department in Yan'an. She married the politician Lin Shaoqi in 1948.

During the 1950s and 1960s she worked with her husband, touring Indonesia, Burma, Cambodia and Vietnam in 1963, and Pakistan and Afghanistan in 1966, setting in motion four anti-corruption investigations which were later described as 'the Taoynan Experience' and credited as a 'crime'. She was elected Deputy for Hebei province in 1964 and 1966 and at the start of the Cultural Revolution she was sent to direct the movement at Qinhua University. However, she was criticized for suppressing the students' revolutionary fervour and was publicly tried by the Red Guards three times in 1967. For the next decade she was in disgrace but she reappeared in 1979 to be elected a member of the Fifth Central Committee, and to become Director of the Foreign Affairs Bureau at the Academy of Social Sciences.

**Ward**, Dame **Barbara** [Baroness Jackson of Lodsworth] (1914–81). English economist. Born in Sussex, she was educated at a convent in Felixstowe, the Lycée Molière and the Sorbonne in Paris, and Jugenheim in Germany. She graduated in politics, philosophy and economics from Somerville College, Oxford, in 1935. From 1936 to 1939 she taught as a university extension lecturer until she became Assistant Editor of *The*

*Economist*, specializing in international affairs, at the age of 25. During World War II she lectured for the Ministry of Information and afterwards held various academic posts. She began lecturing in the USA in 1942 and was later Visiting Scholar at Harvard (1957–68) and Schweitzer Professor of International Economic Development at Columbia University (1968–1973). In 1967 she was appointed to the Vatican Commission for Justice and Peace, and in 1971 became the first woman to address the Vatican Council in Rome. Between 1973 and 1980 she was President of the International Institute for Environment and Development, remaining Chairman from 1980 to 1981. Her husband, Robert Jackson, was a UN official.

Barbara Ward wrote 16 books, beginning with *The International Share-out* (1938), and including *The rich and poor Nations* (1962), *Spaceship Earth* (1966), and her three major works with René Dubos: *Only one Earth* (1970), *The Home of Man* (1976) and *Progress for a small Planet* (1979). Throughout her career she argued for justice to the world's poor, for a fair balance between developed nations and the Third World, and for an equitable and rational use of natural resources. An active lobbyist as well as writer, she was instrumental in persuading the UN to launch its current clean water and sanitation programmes. Described as 'one of the most brilliant contributors to economic and political thought since the 1930s', she received several honours, including the Jawarharlal Nehru Award for international understanding (1974). She was created DBE in 1974 and a life peer in 1976, taking the title Baroness Jackson of Lodsworth.

**Ward, Dorothy** (1891–1987). British pantomime star. Born and educated in Birmingham, Dorothy first went on stage at 15 as Zenobia in *Bluebird* at the Alexandra, Birmingham, appearing a year later in the West End. A spectacular success in music hall, comedy and revues, she became famous as one of the greatest of pantomime's 'principal boys', notably in *Jack and the Beanstalk* at the London Hippodrome in 1922, playing opposite George Robey as Dame Trot. Red-haired, with long legs and a dazzling smile she toured in variety in Britain and abroad,

accompanied by a children's troupe, 'Dorothy Ward's Tiny Tots'. Her songs included *Take me back to dear old Blighty*, *The Sheik of Araby* and *A shanty in old Shanty Town*. She often appeared with her husband, Shaun Glenville, as principal boy and Dame. Her admirers included Lloyd George and Winston Churchill and during World War II, touring with ENSA, she was known as 'Mademoiselle from the Maginot Line'. She retired in 1957, making her last stage appearance just before her 70th birthday at the Old Pavilion, Liverpool. She died aged 96.

**Ward** [née Arnold], Mrs **Humphrey (Mary Augusta)** (1851–1920). English novelist and anti-suffrage leader. Born in Hobart, Tasmania, she was the grand-daughter of Dr Arnold, founder of Rugby School, and niece of the poet Matthew Arnold. She returned to England with her family in 1856 and was educated in private boarding schools until she was 16, continuing her studies on her own in Oxford, where her parents lived. In 1872 she married Thomas Humphrey Ward.

She was friendly with leading intellectuals of the day and began to write by contributing to the *Dictionary of Christian Biography* in 1877. She believed in the need for higher education for women and in 1879 became Secretary to Somerville College, Oxford. In 1881 she moved to London and wrote for *The Times*, *Pall Mall Gazette* and *Macmillan's Magazine*. After publishing a children's story, *Mitty and Olly* (1881), she began writing novels for adults, starting with the instant best-seller *Robert Elsmere* (1883), about the agonies of religious doubt and the duty to resist. Altogether she wrote 25 novels, 3 plays and 9 non-fiction works. In 1890 she founded a social settlement at University Hall, Gordon Square, and pressed for women to become more involved in social work. Her novels of the next few years, including *Marcella* (1894), *Sir George Tressady* (1896), and *Lady Rose's Daughter* (1903), are concerned with the need to help the poor, but she saw suffering as an inevitable and not a political problem.

Although sensitive to women's distress – in childbirth, as impoverished mothers, even as frustrated intellectuals deprived of educational and professional opportunities –

Ward resisted any radical solution. She had actively opposed the franchise movement from 1889 onwards and in 1908 became first President of the Anti-Suffrage League, which published the monthly *Anti-Suffrage Review*. She criticised suffragettes in several of her novels, most notably *Diana Mallory* (1908), *Delia Blanchflower* (1915), and *Cousin Philip* (1919). As a book reviewer she was also noticeably hard on other women writers, and she often provoked public controversy. At the same time she was concerned to promote the charitable activities of women, founding the Local Government Advancement Committee in 1911. She was appointed as one of the first seven women magistrates in 1920. She published *A Writer's Recollections* in 1918.

E. Huws Jones: *Mrs Ward* (1973)

**Ward**, Dame **Irene**. English politician. Daughter of an architect, she was born and educated in Newcastle, where she worked as a secretary and became an active member of the Northern Conservative Association. In 1924 and 1927 she was an unsuccessful candidate in elections in Morpeth, and in 1931 defeated MARGARET BONDFIELD in Wallsend. An energetic MP, she campaigned fiercely for constituency and other interests, including shipbuilding, the fishing industry, pensioners, nurses and midwives. During the 1930s she was a member of the government delegation to the League of Nations, and from 1939 to 1945 was on the Ministry of Labour Committee dealing with the call-up of women. In 1943 she visited China.

Irene Ward lost her seat in 1945, but was returned for Tynemouth from 1950 to 1974. The longest-serving woman member of the House of Commons, she was responsible for four Acts of Parliament; she was notorious for her back-bench heckling. She was created Vice-president of the Royal College of Nursing for her services to nursing, DBE (1951) and Companion of Honour (1973).

**Ward, Mary (Joan)** (1585–1645). English Catholic founder. She was born in Yorkshire; she joined a religious community in St Omer in 1606. She worked in St Omer, founding a school for English girls and schools for the poor, extending these to Liège, Cologne and Trèves. On returning to England she founded a lay organization like the Dutch *béguines*, the 'English ladies', whose members would work in the community, especially in improving the education of women, and would be subject directly to the Pope rather than to the local bishops. In 1621 the English Catholic leaders appealed to Pope Gregory XV to order the dissolution of the group, on the grounds that women were temperamentally unsuited to such pastoral work and that their visits to people's homes would cause scandal and bring the Church into disrepute. Mary meanwhile appealed to the Pope herself, and founded schools in Italy and, after 1625, in Germany, Austria and Hungary. Although the case had been reviewed in 1624 by Pope Urban VIII, her order was finally suppressed in 1629. When Mary continued with her work she was arrested as a heretic, but she worked in Rome until her return to England in 1639.

M. Chambers: *Life of Mary Ward* (1885)

**Warnock**, Baroness **(Helen) Mary** (1924–). British philosopher. Mary Wilson, the youngest in a large family (her father, a houseman at Winchester College, died before she was born), was educated at St Swithun's, Winchester and took a degree in Classics at Lady Margaret Hall, Oxford. She married the philosopher Geoffrey Warnock in 1949, the year in which she became Tutor in Philosophy at St Hugh's College, Oxford, where she remained until 1966: the Warnocks had five children between 1950 and 1961. In the 1960s Mary Warnock became known for her books *Modern Ethics* (1960), *Sartre* (1963) and *Existentialism* (1966, 1970). She was Headmistress of Oxford High School for six years from 1966 and then moved back into academic life as a Research Fellow at Lady Margaret Hall (1972–6) and St Hugh's (1976–84), and is now Mistress of Girton College, Cambridge.

Her interest in ethics and education, and her frankness, tact and open-minded sensitivity to complex issues, made her an excellent leader of government commissions and enquiries: into Special Education in the mid-1970s, on animal experiments (1979–86), on Environmental Pollution (1979–84) and, most notably, on the Committee of Enquiry into Human Fertilization (1982–4), which produced the Guidelines of the *Warnock Report*. Animated and alert, her varied concerns are reflected in her later books, *Imagin-*

*ation* (1976), *Schools of Thought* (1977), *Education: A Way Forward* (1979), *A Question of Life* (1985) and *Memory* (1987).

**Warwick** [née Maynard], **Daisy (Frances Evelyn Greville)**, Countess of (1861–1938). English socialite and socialist. Born in Mayfair, London, she inherited the large estates of her grandfather, Viscount Maynard, when she was four. She was educated privately and grew up to be a famous beauty, marrying Charles Greville, Lord Brooke, heir to the fourth Earl of Warwick, in 1881. He succeeded his father in 1893. Enormously wealthy and very popular, she was a member of the 'Marlborough House Set' which surrounded the Prince of Wales, with whom she had a long affair during the 1890s.

In 1895 she gave a wildly extravagant ball at Warwick Castle, and the fierce criticism of it in the socialist paper *The Clarion* led her to meet the editor, Robert Blatchford. Gradually she became a socialist. She had already been very influenced by the reforming journalist W.T. Stead, and had initiated charitable schemes, such as a needlework school to help rural unemployment in Essex, a shop and workshop in Bond Street, London, and a home for crippled children in Warwick. In the late 1890s she started a school for rural children, established hostels in Warwick for agricultural women and an agricultural association, eventually founding a college for the association at Studely Castle, Warwickshire. From 1899 she ran the *Women's Agricultural Times*.

In 1904 she joined the Social Democratic Federation, campaigned and lectured in London, and supported industrial action such as the 1912 dock strike. She opposed World War I although she still undertook Red Cross and charity work, and published her views in *A Woman and the War* (1916). After the war she joined the Labour Party and stood unsuccessfully as a candidate against her relative, Sir Anthony Eden, for Warwick and Leamington in the 1923 election. After her husband's death in 1923 she lost her income and made a living chiefly from her writing. Since the 1890s she had published several books and pamphlets on subjects ranging from the history of Warwick Castle (1903) to William Morris

(1912). She now turned to autobiography with *Life's Ebb and Flow* (1929) and *Afterthought* (1931). She published a novel, *Branch Line* (1932), and a natural history book, *Nature's Quest* (1934). She is remembered as a lively, warm-hearted and eccentric character.

M. Blunden: *The Countess of Warwick: a Biography* (1967)

**Webb, Beatrice (Potter)** (1858–1943). English socialist. Born at Standish House, nr Gloucester, daughter of a railway magnate, she was brought up in liberal political and intellectual circles. She was educated privately, developing her ideas through wide reading, travel, and contacts with family friends, especially Herbert Spencer. At 18 she became a debutante but when her mother died six years later she became her father's business associate. During 1883–4 an inconclusive love affair with Joseph Chamberlain sharpened her interest in reform, and she became a visitor with the Charity Organization Society and a rent collector in London, before working with Booth on the survey *Life and Labour of the People of London* (1887). She published her research into East End dock life and other studies, and gave evidence to the House of Lords Committee on the Sweating System (1888–9).

While working on *The Co-operative Movement in Great Britain* (1891), she met the Fabian theorist, Sidney Webb. They were married in 1892, beginning a remarkable partnership in which they produced over 100 books, pamphlets and articles, and became the most influential researchers and propagandists of the labour movement. Their first major works were the *History of Trade Unionism* (1894) and *Industrial Democracy* (1897). They were also involved in founding the London School of Economics (1895). After a tour of the USA and the Dominions (1898), they embarked on the massive nine-volume *English Local Government* (1906–29).

In 1905 Beatrice was appointed to the Royal Commission on the Poor Laws, drafting an influential Minority Report (1909) with George Lansbury and two others, which was followed by a nation-wide campaign advocating a new system of social insurance. The Webbs moved into active politics, supporting the new Labour Party. In 1913 they founded the *New Statesman*. During World War I Beatrice wrote her classic *Wages of Men and Women – should they be Equal?* In 1922 her husband became an MP and held ministerial appointments in both the early Labour Governments. After he left office they visited the USSR (1932) and the resulting *Soviet Communism: a New Civilisation* (1935) saw the final abandonment of their gradualist approach. Beatrice then worked on her autobiography, following the earlier *My Apprenticeship* (1926), with *Our Partnership* which was published posthumously in 1948.

R. Adam and K. Muggeridge: *Beatrice Webb: a Life, 1858–1943* (1967)

**Webb, Catherine** (1859–1947). English co-operative leader. Her father was a coppersmith and a director of the Co-operative Wholesale Society and her mother was a remarkably independent woman whose interests were astronomy and polar exploration. In 1886 Catherine founded the Battersea branch of the Women's Co-operative Guild in London, and lectured throughout England on behalf of the Guild during the 1890s. She later became a member of the Central Board of the Co-operative Union. *Industrial Co-operation*, which she edited in 1904, became the standard text about the movement and in 1927 she wrote a history of the Women's Guild called *Woman with a Basket*. Later she became involved with adult education, being a lecturer and then a governor of Morley College, in south London.

**Weber.** German family of musicians, daughters of Fridolin Weber (1733–79) and Caecilia Stumm (1727–93). The composer Carl Maria von Weber was their first cousin.

(1) **Josepha** (1759–1819). Soprano. She studied with Righini and sang professionally from the 1780s, joining Schikaneder's opera company in Vienna in 1790. She knew Mozart (through her first husband as well as her sisters) and created the role of the Queen of the Night, in *The Magic Flute*, which was designed for her remarkable vocal agility and range; Mozart also wrote the aria *Schon lacht der holde Frühling* (1789) for her. Her second husband, Sebastian Mayer, was the

first Pizarro in Beethoven's *Fidelio*.

(2) **Aloysia** (1761–1839). Soprano. She is remembered primarily for her connection with Mozart, whose advances she rejected some four years before his marriage to her sister (3) Constanze. He had given her some singing lessons (1777–8) and wrote admiringly of her voice in letters to his father. Several of his arias were written for her, as well as the part of Madam Herz in *Der Schauspieldirektor*. She made her debut in an opera by Philidor (Vienna, 1779) and appeared regularly in Vienna until 1792, being one of the few singers to be retained when the new Italian opera company took over from the German. In 1795 she left her husband (the painter Joseph Lange, who painted a well-known portrait of Mozart) to accompany Constanze on concert tours.

(3) **Constanze.** *See* MOZART, CONSTANZE.

**Weber, Helene** (1881–1962). German politician. Born in North Rhine-Westphalia, she spent five years teaching in state primary schools before studying history at Bonn and Grenoble. She then established a reputation as a campaigning social worker and in 1916 took over the new school of social welfare in Cologne, organized by the German Catholic Women's Federation (of which she later became President). In 1919 she joined the Prussian Ministry of Social Welfare, with special responsibility for youth, and from 1924 to 1933 was a representative of the Zentrum party, until dismissed by the Nazis. After World War II she became a member of the Christian Democratic Party and was elected to the North Rhine-Westphalia assembly in 1946. She later became Chairman of the women's committee in the Bundestag and in 1957 was awarded the Grosse Bundeverdienstyrenz, the highest civilian award. She exerted great influence over the organization of social work and campaigned effectively for legislation for the equal status of women.

**Weber, Lois** (1882–1939). American film director and actress. She came to Hollywood in 1907 with her husband, the actor Phillips Smalley. Working for Gaumont, they directed, wrote and starred in a number of films and experimented with early-sound-on-cylinder talking pictures. After moving to

Edwin S. Porter's Rex Company, they worked with him writing, editing and directing all the Rex releases. Placed in charge of production, they formed their own company of players. Their products are characterized by elements of serious social drama, marked by Lois Weber's personal interest in them. In 1913 she was elected Mayor of Universal City. A year later she directed a rare comedy about studio life, *The Career of Waterloo Peterson*, using many Universal characters. During a year away from Universal, she made the film *Hypocrites* (1915) which caused a sensation by featuring a nude girl (possibly acted by Weber herself) as 'The Naked Truth'. Returning to Universal as a noted and controversial director, she made *Where are my Children?* (1916), which advocated birth control but called abortion a crime. She formed her own studio and company in 1917 and became renowned for supervising everything down to the most minute detail. She returned to Universal, making two features with Billie Dove. She made her last film, *White Heat*, in 1934. The same year she led a campaign to introduce visual aids into teaching. She died almost penniless in Hollywood.

**Wedgwood,** Dame **(Cicely) Veronica** (1910–). British historian. The daughter of Sir Ralph Wedgwood, she was educated privately and obtained a first-class degree in modern history from Lady Margaret Hall, Oxford, in 1931. During the 1930s and 1940s she established a reputation for scholarship which was at once original, meticulously researched and immensely readable, with books such as *Straford* (1935), *The Thirty Years War* (1938), *Oliver Cromwell* (1939), *William the Silent* (1944) and *Richelieu and the French Monarchy* (1949). Among notable later works are *The King's Peace* and *The King's War* (1955 and 1958) and *The Great Rebellion* (1966). In 1984 she published the first volume of *The Spoils of Time*. She is remarkable among historians of her generation for her appreciation of the wider European context of English history, and for her elegant literary style; in contrast to the often arid debates of modern academic scholarship, she maintains a distinctive narrative approach.

A Fellow of the Royal Historical Society, C.V. Wedgwood was a member of the Royal Commission on Historical Manuscripts from 1953 to 1978. She was also President of the English Association in the 1950s and of the English Centre of International PEN, 1951–7. She served on the Arts Council, 1958–61, and on its Literature Panel, 1965–7, and has been an adviser to the Victoria and Albert Museum and a Trustee of the National Gallery. Her awards and honorary degrees are numerous, including the Goethe Medal, 1958, Membership of the American Academy of Arts and Letters, 1966, and of Arts and Sciences, 1973. In Britain she received the CBE in 1956, the OM in 1969 and was made a Dame of the British Empire in 1968. Her collected essays, entitled *History and Hope*, were published in 1988.

**Wei Fu-Jen** (*c*272–350). Chinese artist. She was born during the Chin dynasty and married Li Chun, the Governor of Anhui province. She became a highly honoured calligrapher. Her own work was lost in the anarchic period which followed but she was the teacher of the greatest Chinese calligrapher, Wang Hsi-Chih, and her own fame is celebrated in the *Book of One Hundred Beauties*.

**Weigel, Helene** (1901–71). German actress and theatre director. Born in Vienna, she was educated in a militant feminist school. At the age of 18 she worked at the Neues Theater, Frankfurt, moving to the Berlin Staatstheater in 1923. During 1925–6 she worked at the Deutsches Theater, where she met Bertholt Brecht. Their son Stefan was born in 1926 and they married two years later, after the collapse of his first marriage. Always on the political left, their fight against fascism, expressed in *Die Mutter/The Mother* (1932), led them to flee the Nazi regime in 1933. They lived in Switzerland, Denmark, and Sweden, where *Mutter Courage/Mother Courage* was written in 1939, with Dumb Katrin as a role for the non-Swedish-speaking Helene. From Finland, they journeyed across the USSR, finally settling in California. During six years in the USA, Weigel had only one ten-second silent part in a Hollywood film.

In 1947, pressured by anti-communist feeling in the USA, they returned to Europe, where Helene played Antigone (1948) and the following year gave a sensational performance in *Mother Courage* in East Berlin. The East German government offered them the Deutsches Theater, where they built up the Berliner Ensemble, eventually moving to their own building in 1954. A magnificent actress, Helene Weigel specialized in the main Brecht roles, Vlassova, Mother Courage, Senora Carrara and Volumnia, continuing the impetus of their remarkable partnership after his death in 1956. Her last performance was the lead in *Mother Courage* a few weeks before she died.

**Weil, Simone** (1903–43). French philosophical writer. She was born and brought up in Paris and educated at the Lycée Henri IV (where she was greatly influenced by the philosopher, Alain) and at the Ecole Normale Superieure, where she was one of the first women to be admitted. From an early age she developed a sympathy with the poor which was never to leave her. She was profoundly interested by Marx but never joined the Communist Party. After graduating in 1931 she taught philosophy at a girls' school in Le Puy but was dismissed after demonstrating with strikers in front of the school. She also taught at Bourges and St Quentin, interspersing this with periods of hard manual labour on farms and at the Renault factory to experience the life of the working class. In 1936 she served in the Republican forces in the Spanish Civil War.

During Easter 1938 she had her first mystical experiences. Although she revered the sacraments of Catholicism, she was never baptized and preferred to identify herself with the poor and powerless outside the church. Her writings, published posthumously, demonstrate her religious thought and include: *La Pesanteur et la Grâce/Gravity and Grace* (1947, Eng. trans. 1952); *Attente de Dieu/Waiting on God* (1950, Eng. trans. 1951); *Gateway to God* (1957), an English selection of her writings.

With deep reluctance, Simone left France in 1942 during World War II and joined the Free French forces in London. Here she wrote *L'Enracinement/The Need for Roots* (1949, Eng. trans. 1952), a study of the reciprocal duties of the individual and the state. She died of tuberculosis, exacerbated by her refusal to eat more than the rations allowed in occupied France. Her

*Notebooks* were published between 1952 and 1955.

S. Petrement: *Simone Weil: a Life* (1976)

**Weinstein, Hannah** (1911–84). American film producer and activist. Hannah Dormer grew up in New York, and was a journalist on the *New York Herald Tribune* from 1918 to 1937. She then worked for the La Guardia campaign staff (and later worked for F.D. Roosevelt and Henry Wallace). In 1938 she married the reporter Peter Weinstein. Her career in films began in Paris in 1950, her first production being *Fait-divers à Paris* (1952), and she moved into television in London, making over 400 films and series, including the *Robin Hood* series, on which she defiantly employed McCarthy blacked writers such as Ring Lardner. In the late 1960s she was appalled by the almost total exclusion of black and female technicians and managers in the American film industry and founded Third World Cinema in 1971, with 40% of stock owned by the East Harlem Community Organization. Her films there included *Claudine* (1972), *Greased Lightning* (1976) and *Stir Crazy* (1980). In 1982 she was awarded the Women in Film Lifetime Award, and in 1984 the Liberty Hill Upton Sinclair Award, presented to her daughters shortly after her death. A lifelong activist, she was also a leading campaigner against the war in Vietnam in the 1970s.

**Weir, Judith** (1954–). Scottish composer. Born into a musical family from Aberdeenshire, she went to school in London and became a composition pupil of John Tavener. In 1973 she spent a term at the Massachusetts Institute of Technology, where she received instruction from Barry Vercoe on computer-generated methods of composition. She then enrolled at King's College, Cambridge (1973–6), where she studied composition with Robin Holloway, and in 1975, on a Koussevitsky Fellowship, went to Tanglewood for further tuition from Gunther Schuller. On her return to England she worked as composer-in-residence at the Southern Arts Association (1976–9) and then taught at Glasgow University (1979–82). From 1983 to 1985 she was back in Cambridge on a creative arts fellowship at Trinity College, thereafter being based in London.

Weir first came to attention when her

orchestral piece *Where the Shining Trumpets Blow* (1973) was performed by the Philharmonia Orchestra in London, though her wind quintet *Out of the Air* (1975), which won a prize from the Greater London Arts Association in 1976, is generally regarded as her first mature work. She continued to write effectively for small ensembles in such works as *Several Concertos* (1980; for flute, cello and piano) and *Music for 247 Strings* (1981; for violin and piano). Among her few works using electronic sound is *Spij döbrze* ('Pleasant dreams'; for double bass and tape), which received its première in Poland as part of the International Society for Contemporary Music festival in 1983. Her orchestral commissions include *Isti Mirant Stella* (1981), first performed at the St Magnus Festival, Orkney, and *Ballad* (1981), with solo baritone. The piece that pointed towards the increasingly dramatic direction that Weir's music took from the early 1980s was *Thread!* (1981; for narrator and eight instrumentalists), a humorous interpretation of the Bayeux Tapestry whose text (by Weir) and music deftly combine levity with seriousness. Her first opera, *The Black Spider* (1984), suitable for performance by schoolchildren, was followed by *The Consolations of Scholarship* (1985), a music-drama based on Chinese theatre of the Yuan dynasty (1279–1368). The enthusiastic reception accorded *A Night at the Chinese Opera* (1987), commissioned by the BBC and first performed at the Cheltenham Festival by Kent Opera, has confirmed her reputation as one of the most individual British composers of her generation.

**Weiss, Louise** (1893–1983). French feminist and journalist. Louise Weiss was born in Arras, France, and educated at Oxford University and the Sorbonne, Paris. During World War I she ran a military hospital in Brittany, and in 1918 she founded *L'Europe Nouvelle*, one of the most influential political weeklies in France during the 1920s. In the 1930s she formed the feminist group La Femme Nouvelle, working full-time for the women's suffrage movement from 1934, causing a national stir in 1936 when she chained herself with other women across the rue Royale (wearing a Molyneux evening gown). She declined the bait of a cabinet post, continuing to fight for the vote (eventually obtained in 1944) and for other causes, such

as eliminating 'obey' from the French marriage vows.

As a member of the French Resistance during World War II, Weiss ran the illicit paper *La Nouvelle République*. From 1945 until her old age, she wrote and directed documentaries for French television, and also achieved fame as a writer. Her novel *La Marseillaise* won the Literature Prize of the French Academy in 1947, and her series of travel books from 1948 to 1960 won wide acclaim. In 1974 she caused more outrage to the establishment by proposing herself as a member of the French Academy, an unheard-of step, and a protest against the exclusion of women.

A committed pacifist, in 1971 she founded the Institute for the Science of Peace, Strasbourg. At the age of 83 she was a delegate to UNESCO, and in 1979 became the oldest member of the European Parliament, remaining fiercely energetic until her death at the age of 90. Her memoirs include *Tempête sur l'occident 1945–1975* (1976), and the six volumes of *Mémoires d'une Européenne* (1970–76).

**Weldon, Fay** (1931–). British novelist, playwright and feminist. Fay Weldon is one of Britain's most popular and provocative writers. Her parents emigrated to New Zealand and were divorced when she was five, so she and her sister were brought up by their mother and grandmother: 'It never occurred to me that women were supported by men'. She was educated at Christchurch Girls' School. They returned to England after the war and Fay obtained an MA in Economics at St Andrew's University, London. After various casual jobs, a brief unhappy first marriage and the birth of her eldest son, she married Ron Weldon, a musician: they have three sons. She worked as an advertising copywriter (for much of the time for Ogilvy, Benson & Mather) and was responsible for the enduring slogan 'Go to work on an egg', but she also began writing plays for television and radio; she has now written over 50 original plays and adaptations (including the first of the *Upstairs, Downstairs* scripts) and is particularly remembered for her television version of *Pride and Prejudice* as well as her own plays, such as *Lives and Loves of A She-Devil* (1985) and *The Heart of the Country* (1987). Fay Weldon's novels and stories, which can swing from realism to satirical fantasy, are biting analyses of the lives of women and the battle of the sexes, but they also convey a concern for society generally, for the abuses of power and the exploitation of nature, and suggest an interest in a more mystical vision of life. The best-known of her many books include *The Fat Woman's Joke* (1967), *Down Among the Women* (1971), *Female Friends* (1975), *Praxis* (1978), *Puffball* (1980), *The President's Child* (1982) and *Life and Loves of a She-Devil* (1984).

She has also been prominent on behalf of authors, campaigning energetically for causes such as the Public Lending Right and the Minimum Terms Agreement, and was an outspoken critic of publishers' exploitation of writers when she was Chair of the Judges for the Booker McConnell Prize 1983. An entertaining speaker, as well as writer, she has a gift for conveying serious, hard-hitting ideas with wit and imagination.

**Wells-Barnett, Ida B.** (1862–1931). American journalist and reformer. Born a slave in Holly Springs, Missouri, she was educated at the local freedmen's school and became a teacher when orphaned at the age of 14. In 1883 she moved to Memphis, continuing to teach and doing some writing. She lost her teaching contract in 1891 because of complaints about facilities for blacks and devoted herself to exposing their conditions in her Memphis newspaper *Free Speech*. In 1892 she was driven from town after describing the lynching of three black grocers by white businessmen as due to competition and not revenge for rape. She became a reporter for the New York newspaper *Age*. She campaigned widely against lynching, visiting the British Isles between 1893 and 1894.

She then moved to Chicago and organized protests against black exclusion from the World Columbian Exposition. She married the lawyer, Ferdinand Barnett, by whom she had four children. Her campaigns continued and in 1895 she published *A Red Record*, a statistical study of lynching. She also fought other civil rights battles, becoming first President of the Negro Fellowship League in 1900, a co-founder of the National Association for the Advancement of Colored People in 1909 (which she felt was insufficiently militant), and Chair-

man of the Chicago Equal Rights League (1915). She worked as a probation officer and organized legal aid for people such as the victims of the 1918 Race Riots. From 1900 she spoke on behalf of women's suffrage, organizing the first black suffrage association, the Alpha Suffrage Club of Chicago.

A.M. Duster, ed.: *Crusade for Justice: the Autobiography of Ida B. Wells* (1970)

**Welty, Eudora** (1909–). American novelist. She was born in Jackson, Mississippi, where she has remained for most of her life apart from periods at the Mississippi State College for Women in Columbus (1926–7), the University of Wisconsin (1929) and the Columbia School of Advertising, New York (1930–31). She tried to find a job in New York but the encroaching Depression drove her back to Jackson, where she worked for an agency, travelling all over the state and talking to many different kinds of people who later figure in her stories. She also wanted to be a photographer and was employed by the government to take photographs of Mississippi during the mid-1930s. Some of these have been published in *One Time, one Place: Mississippi in the Depression: a Snapshot Album* (1971).

In 1936 she began publishing her short stories, the first to appear being *Death of a Travelling Salesman*, and her first collection appeared in 1941. She went on to write *A Robber Bridegroom* (1942), *The Wide Net and Other Stories* (1943), *Delta Wedding* (1946) and *The Golden Apples* (1949), establishing a reputation as a writer whose subjects are the South and its tensions, but who is above all a superb and sympathetic creator of character, however grotesque. Her last collection of stories, *The Bride of Innisfallen*, appeared in 1954 and she has written three more novels, *The Ponder Heart* (1954), *Losing Battles* (1970) and *The Optimist's Daughter* (1972), which won the Pulitzer Prize.

Welty is also an accomplished reviewer and critic. During World War II she was a staff member on *The New York Times Book Review*. She has written several pieces on fiction and her selected essays and reviews were reprinted in *The Eye of the Story* (1978). During the 1970s she received many American honours, particularly from Southern universities. In 1980 she was awarded the National Medal for literature and the Presidential Medal of Freedom, and in 1984 the Commonwealth Award for Distinguished Service in literature. She is still an active lecturer, and is on the advisory board of the Center for Southern Culture.

E. Welty: *One Writer's Beginnings* (1984)

**Wenying, Wu** (1932–). Chinese politician. Born in Nantong, Jiangsu Province, Wu began to work in the textile industry at the age of 14 and was named a model worker in Changzhou City in 1950. From this she progressed to being a Deputy Secretary of Changzhou Municipal Textile Bureau Party Committee, Deputy Head of Changzhou Cotton Mill and secretary of its party committee. In 1960–63 she studied industrial management at the Shanghai East China textile industry academy. She was made Deputy Secretary of Changzhou Municipal Party Committee and head of its Organization Department after the fall of the 'gang of four' in 1977, and was Mayor of Changzhou before moving to Peking. From 1982 to 1985 she was an alternate member of the CCP central committee and in 1983 became Minister of the Textile Industry – the largest textile industry, numerically, in the world. She became a full member of the Central Committee in 1985 and led textile delegations to West Germany, Belgium, New Zealand and Burma in 1985, and to Britain and Bulgaria in 1986.

**Wertmuller** [von Elgg]**, Lina (Arcangela Felice Assunta)** (1928–). Italian film director. After graduating from Rome's Theatre Academy, she toured Europe with a puppet show and then worked for ten years in the theatre as actress, playwright and director. Her first job in films was as assistant to Federico Fellini on *8½* (1963). She wrote and directed her first film, *I basilischi/The Lizards* in the same year. In 1965 she began her long association with Giancarlo Giannini, an actor she had first directed in the theatre; he was a partner in her production company and her most frequent leading actor. Her fifth film, *Mimi metallurgio ferito nell'onore/The Seduction of Mimi* (1972) won her the best director award at the Cannes Film Festival. Her reputation was substantiated by *Film*

*d'amore e d'anarchia/Love and Anarchy* (1973); *Tutto a posto e niente in ordine/All Screwed Up* (1974); *Travolti da un insolito destino nell'azzurro Mare d'Agosto/Swept Away* (1974); and *Pasqualino settebellezze/Seven Beauties* (1976). *Seven Beauties* was an enormous success in the USA and won her an exclusive contract with Warner Bros. to direct four films in English, at least two in the USA. In 1977 she completed the first film, *The end of the World in our usual Bed in a Night full of Rain*, with Candice Bergen and Giannini, but it received disappointing reviews. The contract was cancelled and she returned to independent work making *Revenge* in 1979. Obviously influenced by Fellini's love of excess and sexual mores, her work is often linked with other Italian directors who attempt to inject political allegory into personal relationship. She works closely with her husband, Enrico Job, a sculptor and conceptual artist, who is her business partner and regular set designer.

**West, Mae** (1892–1980). American comedienne. The daughter of Brooklyn boxer turned detective 'Battling Jack West', she often went to vaudeville shows with her Bavarian mother and started imitating the stars, in church socials, at the age of five. She made her debut as a dancer at the age of seven and played child parts with stock companies. Sexuality was always part of Mae West's humour, from her appearance at 14 as 'The Baby Vamp'. In 1911 she married vaudeville actor Frank Wallace, living with him briefly before pursuing an independent career. They were not divorced until 1943. She developed her own act, with comic monologues, provocative dresses and an adaptation of the new black dance 'The Shimmy' and by 1918 was causing riots and selling out theatres wherever she appeared.

During the 1920s Mae West became a Broadway star, notorious for shows such as *Sex*. This was the result of Mae's serious investigations into sexuality in the works of Freud, Jung, Adler and Havelock Ellis, combined with her own experience. It ran for a year but was then closed down by the police and Mae spent a week in prison. Her second play, *The Drag*, about homosexuality, ran for only two weeks in 1927, but she followed it with successes like *The Wicked Age* and *Diamond Lil*. After five more plays she arrived in Hollywood in 1932, and achieved instant fame starring with George Raft in *Night After Night*, for which she wrote her own dialogue, *She done him Wrong* (1933) and *I'm no Angel* (1935) established her success. By 1934 she was earning the second highest salary in the USA, investing her money in property in Los Angeles. Towards the end of the decade, bowing to pressure from moral crusaders, her films became less outrageous and less successful, and she stopped filmmaking in 1943. She returned to the stage with her own script about the Empress of Russia, *Catherine was Great* (1944) and continued to appear on Broadway until 1952. She then toured with a cabaret act including nine 'musclemen' in loincloths, made records and returned to the screen only twice, in 1970 for a vast fee in Gore Vidal's *Myra Breckinridge*, and in 1978 in *Sextette*. As she herself said 'Too much of a good thing can be wonderful'.

M. West: *Goodness had Nothing to do with It* (1959)
———: *Mae West on Sex, Health and ESP* (1975)

**West,** Dame **Rebecca** [pseud. of Cicily Fairfield Andrews] (1892–1983). British novelist and journalist. She was born in County Kerry, Ireland. Her father was a soldier and war correspondent and after his death in 1902 she moved with her mother to Edinburgh, where she was educated at George Watson's Ladies' College. She then studied drama and made several stage appearances, notably in Ibsen's *Rosmersholm*, from whose heroine she took her pseudonym. In 1911 she turned to writing, joining the staff of *Freewoman*, a feminist paper her mother had forbidden her to read, and then moving on to the socialist *Clarion* as a political writer in 1912. She was a determined suffragist and clung to her independence, despite her affair with the novelist H.G. Wells and the birth of their son Anthony in 1914.

In 1916 her first full-length book, *Henry James*, appeared but she then turned to fiction with *Return of the Soldier* (1918). Her early novels and stories are rather self-conscious and not tightly structured, but she left 20 years between *The Thinking Reed* (1936) and *The Fountain Overflows* (1956) which, together with *The Birds fall down* (1966), presents a superb picture of the frustration of women's life at the turn of the century.

If anything, Rebecca West has been more famous as a critic and as a journalist, contributing to newspapers such as *The New Statesman* and later *The Daily Telegraph* in the UK, and *The New Republic* and *The New Yorker* in the USA. Her early essays (1911–1917) are collected in *The Young Rebecca* (1982). Despite outspoken pronouncements against marriage, she and the banker Henry Maxwell Andrews were married in 1930. In 1937 they visited Yugoslavia, a trip which resulted in the two-volume travel diary *Black Lamb and Grey Falcon*, written during a long convalescence in 1941; it was enormously controversial at the time. During World War II she supervised BBC broadcasts to Yugoslavia. In 1945 she was acclaimed as a brilliant reporter for her coverage of the trial of William Joyce ('Lord Haw-Haw'), later published as *The Meaning of Treason* (1949) and revised in 1965 to include studies of Philby, Burgess and Maclean, and Blake. She explored similar themes in the essays *A Train of Powder* (1955). Her last critical work was *McLuhan and the Future of Literature* (1969), but she has continued to contribute occasional pieces: *1900*, a historical study, was published in 1982. One of the century's most outspoken and talented women of letters, she was created OBE in 1949 and DBE in 1959.

V. Glendinning: *Rebecca West* (1986)

**Wethered, Joyce** [Lady Heathcoat-Amory] (1901–). English golfer. Born in Surrey, Joyce came from a golfing family and at the age of 19 became English Ladies' Champion, holding the title five times. She was British Ladies' Champion four times between 1922 and 1929. One informal event she made famous was the Worplesdon Mixed Foursomes which started in 1921; she and her brother Roger were defeated, but in subsequent years Joyce won eight times with various partners. Her last appearance at the event was in 1948 when she was beaten in the final. In 1935 she was temporarily deprived of her amateur status for working in a sports shop; she also toured the USA, beating the young 'Babe' Zaharias both times they met.

Joyce is often regarded as the finest woman golfer of all time. The uniquely straight flight of her ball belied her pale, apparently frail appearance and retiring manner.

J. Wethered: *Golfing Memories and Methods* (1933)

**Wharton, Edith (Newbold)** (1862–1937). American novelist. Born in New York City, she led a privileged existence travelling in Italy, Spain and France as a child and was educated privately, her literary interests being regarded as an eccentricity. At the age of 23 she married another upper-class socialite Edward Wharton, and they set up house in Newport, Rhode Island; they moved to Europe in 1907. The marriage was a disaster (her husband was mentally unstable), and finally ended in 1913. During World War I she remained in Europe, organizing American relief for refugees, running a workroom for unemployed women, subsidizing refugees' meals in her restaurants, and organizing the Children of Flanders Rescue Committee for 600 orphans fleeing from Belgium. She received the Cross of the Légion d'Honneur in 1916 and the Order of Leopold in 1919. Although she stayed abroad for many years, her novels are chiefly concerned with American society.

Edith Wharton wrote constantly and her first published work, a book of verses, appeared when she was 16. She began by contributing to *Scribner's* magazine, issuing collections of her stories in 1899 and in 1901. Her first fiction was not published until she was in her late thirties. After that she produced virtually a book a year until her death, including 20 novels, 10 collections of short stories, and works on interior design, houses, travel and the theory of writing. She was a close friend of another expatriate, Henry James, and her style is often compared to his, but her work is far more concerned with social manners and realistic depiction of behaviour rather than complex moral problems. Her best novels are *Ethan Frome* (1911), *The House of Mirth* (1905), *The Reef* (1912) and *The Age of Innocence* (1920). They deal with the tensions which spring up between conventional expectations, moral imperatives and personal desires. The fiction after 1920 is more satirical and, on the whole less successful. In 1921 and 1935 she won the Pulitzer Prize and in 1930 became a member of the American Academy of Arts and Letters. She was the first woman to receive

an honorary LittD from Yale in 1923. She died in France, at her villa outside Paris.

R.W.B. Louis: *Wharton: a Biography* (1975)

**Wheatley, Phillis** (*c*1753–84). American poet. Born in Africa, possibly in Senegal, she was taken in a slave ship to Boston at the age of eight and bought by John Wheatley, a prosperous tailor, to be a servant for his wife. They educated her and treated her kindly. She soon mastered English and Latin, and read widely, especially the contemporary Augustan poets and the Classics. Her friends arranged the publication of several occasional poems and in 1773 her *Poems on various Subjects, Religious and Moral* appeared, mostly didactic verses but with a clear note of individual faith and hope. In the same year she was sent to England for her health, with Wheatley's son Nathaniel, and was a popular figure in London society. After she returned to the USA, the Wheatleys died. In 1778, after trying to support herself, she married John Peters, a free negro. She lost touch with her old circle of friends, the marriage was not happy and two of her three children died. When her husband was imprisoned for debt she went out to work as a servant. She died alone and in poverty at the age of 31, her last child dying with her.

S. Graham: *The Story of Phillis Wheatley* (1949)

**Whitbread, Fatima** (1961–). British athlete. Of Cypriot extraction, born in Hackney, London, she was adopted at 12. With the help of her adoptive mother, a famous British international athlete, she has been successful in javelin throwing, a sport for which, at only 5ft 5ins (1.67m), she is said to be too small. She started competing in major events in 1975; in 1978 at the Commonwealth Games she came sixth, and first in 1979 at the European Junior Championships. Until 1983, she was number two in the British team to Tessa Sanderson. In the 1983 World Championships she won a silver medal, then a gold at the European Cup, and was voted 'Woman Athlete of the Year'. In 1984 she was a member of the British Olympic team in Los Angeles and, despite having undergone an operation on her womb shortly before the Games, won the bronze medal. (Tessa Sanderson took the gold with a throw of 69.56 metres). In August 1986, despite the tension of her rivalry with Tessa Sanderson, she broke the women's world javelin record at the European Athletics Championships in Stuttgart at an amazing 77.44 metres in the qualifying round. During that year she threw the javelin over 70 metres 22 times in 12 competitions, a unique record.

In June 1987 she was awarded the MBE. Immensely popular with the public and the media, Whitbread has been said to bring 'personality' to the javelin and her strong stand against drug abuse both in and out of sport has also won respect.

**White, Maude Valérie** (1855–1937). English composer and writer. She studied at the Royal Academy of Music, London (1876–9), becoming the first woman to win the Mendelssohn Scholarship in 1879. Dogged by ill-health throughout her life, she had to resign the scholarship in 1881, but took advantage of travels in Europe and South America (in search of a suitable climate) in developing her skills as a linguist. Primarily a composer of songs (she wrote about 200), she translated many of the texts herself (including poems by Hugo and Heine) as well as a number of books; English poets she set include Shelley and Byron. She also wrote music for a ballet, *The Enchanted Heart* (1913), and some instrumental works. She published two autobiographical books, *Friends and Memories* (1914) and *My Indian Summer* (1932).

**Whiting, Sarah (Frances)** (1847–1927). American physicist and astronomer. Born in Wyoming, New Jersey, Sarah was precocious in Greek, Latin and mathematics, and assisted her father in preparing demonstrations for his classes in physics. After attending Ingham University she taught Classics and mathematics, meanwhile going to scientific lectures in New York.

In 1876 she was appointed Professor of Physics in the all-female faculty of the new Wellesley College. She attended physics classes at the Massachusetts Institute of Technology as a guest. In 1880 she introduced 'applied physics' (astronomy) at Wellesley, meeting the need for a college observatory through the gift of a friend, Mrs John G. Whitin. The observatory, housing a 12″ telescope and spectrascopic laboratory,

was finished in 1900 and enlarged in 1906. As Director of the Whitin Observatory, Sarah was an outstanding teacher rather than researcher. She retired from physics in 1912 and astronomy in 1916.

**Whitney, Anne** (1821–1915). American sculptor. Born in Watertown, Massachusetts, the youngest of seven children, she grew up in a liberal Unitarian community and was educated at home and in private schools. From 1847 to 1849 she ran a school in Salem. A keen abolitionist and feminist, she was also a writer, her *Poems* being published in 1859. About 1855 she began making portrait busts of members of her family and in 1858 went to study art and sculpture in New York and Philadelphia, and anatomy in a Brooklyn hospital. Her first exhibition was held in 1860 at the National Academy of Design. Her sculptures were often polemical, illustrating themes related to the liberation of blacks and women, such as *Lady Godiva* (1864) and *Africa* (1865). In 1867 she went to Rome for four years. She characterized society there in the person of a beggar woman in her *Roma* (1869), which caused such a furore in the Papal Court that the piece was moved to France. In 1871 she returned to the USA and worked largely on public statuary; in 1875 she won a certificate for a memorial to Charles Sumner in Boston, but the commission was revoked when it was realized that Whitney was a woman. However, she completed the piece in 1902 and it is now outside Harvard Law School. In 1876 she settled in Boston, where she remained for the next 20 years, producing portrait busts of leading intellectuals and also of reformers such as LUCY STONE, HARRIET BEECHER STOWE, FRANCES WILLARD and HARRIET MARTINEAU.

**Whitney, Mary Watson** (1847–1921). American astronomer. Mary went to Vassar College in 1865, its opening year; she was proficient in mathematics but majored in astronomy under MARIA MITCHELL. Because of the death of her father and elder brother, she took a teaching post near her family, but joined Mitchell and a group of former students to observe a solar eclipse. She was then invited to join Professor Benjamin Peirce's abstruse course on quarternions (although Harvard was not officially open to women) and took a postgraduate course on celestial mechanics.

After gaining her master's degree from Vassar and spending three years in Zürich, Mary became Mitchell's private assistant (1881) and succeeded her as Director of Vassar College Observatory and Professor of Astronomy in 1888. Her research programme included observation of double stars, asteroids and comets.

She retired in 1910 due to partial paralysis. Mary actively promoted the cause of women's education, and said before her death, 'I hope when I get to heaven I shall not find the women playing second fiddle'.

**Wightman** [née Hotchkiss], **Hazel** (1886–1974). American lawn tennis player. Hazel got up at dawn when she started playing tennis at the age of 16, because after 8 a.m. the courts were reserved for men. She won her first American title in 1909, the women's singles, and won 47 more before 1954, including three more singles wins (1910, 1911, 1919).

It was in doubles that her ability to smash and volley, combined with her persistence as a competitor, brought her most success. She and HELEN WILLS N. MOODY were never beaten when they played together. They won the Wimbledon doubles in 1924 and the American title six times.

Hazel married George Wightman and they had five children. Although continuing to play competitively, which she did until retiring from veterans' competitions at the age of 74, Hazel now added a role as advocate of tennis, particularly by inaugurating the prestigious Wightman Cup competition in 1923. She presented a tall silver vase as the trophy of matches between American and British women. Although the Wightman Cup remains an important competition, it lost some status after the introduction of open tennis, and of the Bonne Belle Cup between Australia and the USA in 1972. Hazel played doubles in the first Wightman Cup match and on three other occasions, as well as captaining the team several times. She believed that 'tennis needs courage', and in her book *Better Tennis* (1934) referred to the game as 'a channel of intensified life'.

**Wigman, Mary** [Wiegmann, Marie] (1896–1973). German dancer, choreographer and teacher. In 1911 she began to study with Emile Jaques-Dalcroze. She then worked with Rudolf von Laban in Munich and Zürich, where she became his assistant. In 1919 she gave solo recitals in Zürich and Hamburg, and opened her own school in Dresden in 1920. This became the centre of the Central European dance style, which cultivated a masculine, angular style of movement as an individual expression of psychological truth. The ballet critic and historian, Haskell, called it 'the school of the clenched fist and the flat feet'. In works such as *Dance of Sorrows* Wigman encouraged exploration of frenzy, nightmare and neurosis. She taught many influential dancers, including HANYA HOLM. She danced in London in 1928, and the USA in 1930 and had a distinguished solo career until 1942. After World War II she taught in Leipzig, moving to West Berlin in 1949. Her work has been the greatest influence on modern dance in Europe.

M. Wigman: *The Language of Dance* (Eng. trans., 1976)

**Wilding, Dorothy** (1893–1976). British portrait photographer. The youngest of a large family, Dorothy was sent at the age of four to live with relations in the south of England. Determined to be independent and to pursue an artistic career, she chose photography and began as a 'pupil retoucher' at Walter Barnet's studio in Knightsbridge, around 1911, and worked for other London photographers before opening her studio in George Street, Portman Square, in 1914. She lived at one end of the studio and supported herself by retouching work until her business became self-supporting in the 1930s. Dorothy was in a tradition of women studio photographers, such as the Victorian Alice Hughes, the Edwardian Lallie Charles and Madame Yevonde (Edith Middleton). Her style was influenced by the postcards of actors and actresses popular before World War I, and among the celebrities she herself photographed were POLA NEGRI, Diana Wynyard, Fay Compton and TALLULAH BANKHEAD. A lively, natural personality who put her subjects at ease, her stylish, classical portraits with their flowing lines were extremely successful. She later opened a fashionable studio in New York, on 56th Street, designed in collaboration with her husband, Rufus Leighton-Pearce, and continued to work as a photographer until 1957.

**Wilhelmina** (1880–1962). Queen of the Netherlands. She was the daughter of King William III, and she succeeded to the throne at the age of ten, with her mother, Queen Emma, acting as Regent. Her adult reign began in 1898, at the start of the Boer War. In 1900 she married Duke Henry of Mecklenberg-Schwerin, initially an unpopular choice. Her only child, JULIANA, was born in 1909 and her husband died in 1934.

With the onset of World War II, in 1939 Wilhelmina proposed Dutch neutrality, as she had during World War I, and offered to mediate for peace, but the Netherlands were invaded by Germany in May 1940. She sent her daughter and grandchildren to England, and after attempting to join the Dutch forces in Zeeland was forced by kidnap threats to escape on a British destroyer. In England she headed the Dutch government in exile and broadcast constantly to the Netherlands until able to return in July 1945. Three years later, due to illness and strain, she abdicated after her golden jubilee celebrations in favour of Juliana. Queen for 50 years, she was shrewd, practical and influential as a ruler, as well as acting as a symbol of Dutch endurance during World War II. Her memoirs, *Lonely but not alone*, were published in 1958.

**Wilkinson, Ellen (Cicely)** ['Red Ellen'] (1891–1947). English trade-unionist, politician and feminist. The third of four children of a Lancashire cotton-worker, she grew up in a family committed to the labour movement, and like her mother and grandmother became a member of the Manchester and Salford Co-operative Society. From her local school she won a history scholarship to Manchester University, and graduated second in her class in 1913. In the same year she began working for the National Union of Women's Suffrage Societies, and was also a much-admired speaker for the Independent Labour Party. By 1915 she was appointed a national women's organizer for the Amalgamated Union of Co-operative Employees, for whom she worked tirelessly, campaigning particularly on behalf of lower-paid groups such as the laundry workers until 1925. Inspired by Sylvia PANKHURST, she led the women's movement to a wider concern for working women.

From 1920 to 1924 she was a member of the newly-established Communist Party of Great Britain and visited the USSR in 1921. She was an unsuccessful Labour candidate for Ashton-under-Lyme in 1923, but won a seat for Middlesborough (1924–31). The first woman Labour MP, she was nicknamed 'Red Ellen' (for the colour of her hair as much as her politics). She continued to work for the Labour movement, fund-raising in the USA for miners' families during the General Strike of 1926, and travelled to many countries including India and Germany, where she spoke against fascism, and wrote several books, including *Clash* (1929) and *Why Fascism?* (1934, with Edward Conze). She became Labour MP for Jarrow in 1935 and in 1936 led the famous hunger march to London for much of the route. She later described the cruel effects of unemployment in her depressed constituency in *The Town that was Murdered* (1939). In Parliament she pressed through the Hire-Purchase Bill in 1938. From 1940 she worked as Parliamentary Secretary to the Ministry of Pensions, and then to the Ministry of Home Security, with especial responsibility for civil defence. Following the Labour Party victory in 1945 she was made Minister of Education, and one of her last acts was to ensure the implementation of the Education Act of 1944, although she did not fully support the principle of comprehensive education.

B.D. Vernon: *Ellen Wilkinson 1891–1947* (1982)

**Willard, Emma (Hart)** (1787–1870). American educator. Born in Berlin, Connecticut, a member of a large, locally important family, she was educated in the district school and attended Berlin Academy (1802–3). She combined teaching with further study until 1807 when she became Head of the Female Academy, Middlebury, Vermont. In 1809 she left to marry Dr John Willard (*d*1825). She continued to study, completing the curriculum of Middlebury College, but was not allowed to attend classes or obtain a degree. In 1814 financial pressures led her to open the Middlebury Female Seminary with a new curriculum containing mathematics, philosophy, and geometry. In 1818 she petitioned Governor Clinton and the New York State Legislature to support her *Plan for Improving Female Education* (1919). She moved to Waterford, where her school was chartered but not funded by the Legislature, and finally to Troy, New York, at the invitation of the town.

From 1821 to 1838 she ran the Troy Female Seminary, effectively the first women's college, training many influential school teachers; she also wrote best-selling textbooks. She took a trip to Europe in 1830, and used the proceeds of her *Journal and Letters from France and Great Britain* to help found a women's college in Athens, Greece. In 1838 she was remarried, to Dr Christopher Yates, but was divorced in 1843. She left the seminary, and began campaigning with Henry Barnard, the educationalist, for more public schools, better conditions, buildings, and equal opportunities for women teachers. In 1854 she represented the USA at the World's Educational Convention in London. Despite her pioneering educational work, her views on the position of women were very conservative.

A. Lutz: *Emma Willard, Pioneer Educator* (1964)

**Willard, Frances (Elizabeth Candine)** (1839–98). American temperance and suffrage leader. She was born in Churchville, New York. Her parents were school teachers who moved to Ohio and then Wisconsin, where she lived a rather lonely pioneer life until the age of 18. She attended Milwaukee Female College (1857) and Northwestern Female College (Evanston) (1858–9). She became a Methodist, and taught in a local school in 1860, followed by Pittsburgh Female College (1863–4), and Tenessee Wesleyan Seminary (1866–7). Between 1868 and 1870 she travelled to Europe, spending time at the Sorbonne and the Collège de France.

In 1871 she became President of the new Evanston College for Ladies, then Dean of Women and Professor of Aesthetics after the merger with Northwestern University in 1873. The following year she resigned, refused all teaching offers and, influenced by the current revivalist crusade, became President of the Chicago Women's Christian Temperance Union; she was National President from 1881 until her death. She was a vigorous leader and her campaigns drew many women into politics for the first time. A radical Christian socialist, she linked temperance to the suffrage and populist movements, and also campaigned for women's legal rights and better working conditions. In 1882 she helped re-organize the Prohibition party, conducting a nationwide tour in 1883. In 1888 she became President of the National Council of Women, pressing for social reform, and in 1891 President of the World Women's Christian Temperance Union (WCTU). She toured England (1892–3) and continued to campaign and write. Her many articles and books include *Women and Temperance* (1883) and her autobiography, *Glimpses of Fifty Years* (1889).

**Williams, Betty** (1943–). Irish peace campaigner. Born in Belfast and educated at St Dominic's Grammar School, Betty married Ralph Williams in 1961 and they had a son and a daughter. She was living in Andersonstown, a republican area of Belfast, when in 1976 she witnessed the tragedy in which the three Maguire children were killed when struck by a getaway car used by a gunman. She was so horrified that she went from door to door begging neighbours to join her to stop the violence, quickly collecting 200 people, one of the first being MAIREAD CORRIGAN. A week later 10,000 people, Protestant and Catholic, marched through Belfast, as part of the Peace Movement. Further rallies followed in Belfast and throughout Northern Ireland, arousing much support in Britain and abroad, especially from Norway, Germany and the United States. Betty Williams was awarded the Nobel Peace Prize in 1976, with Mairead Corrigan. In the late 1970s the movement began to concentrate on small group work within the commupity, after attacking the established politicians. After setting up a 'Peace Assembly' for formal discussion, Betty Williams resigned from the Executive Committee in 1978, but remained involved, and spoke about the Irish troubles at home and abroad. In February 1980, Betty ceased to be associated with the Peace Movement after a dispute, and in 1982 she married Jim Perkins, in Florida.

**Williams, Cicely (Delphine)** (1893–). English

public health doctor. Due to the scarcity of male students caused by World War I, Cicely was able to obtain her medical education at Oxford and London. She joined the Colonial Medical Service and spent seven years in public health work on the Gold Coast [now Ghana] where she was the first person to describe the disease kwashiorkor. During 12 years in Malaya she lectured in paediatrics at the College of Medicine, Singapore, and was senior specialist in child health for the government.

During World War II she was held prisoner by the Japanese, afterwards returning to England to become Head of the Child Health Department at the Institute of Social Medicine, Oxford. There followed a post with the World Health Organization as Head of the Maternal and Child Health Section from 1948 to 1951. She fought propaganda on feeding condensed milk to babies, and her emphasis was on educating mothers and on family planning. She was Senior Lecturer in Nutrition at London University (1953–5) and adviser in the training programme of the Family Planning Association from 1964 to 1967.

A. Dally: *Cicely: the Story of a Doctor* (1968)

**Williams, Grace (Mary)** (1906–77). Welsh composer. She studied at University College, Cardiff, and from 1926 at the Royal College of Music, London, where she was a pupil of Vaughan Williams until 1932; she received further tuition from Egon Wellesz in Vienna (1930–31). She then taught at various schools in London, also producing some educational programmes for the BBC. After her return to Wales in 1946, she concentrated increasingly on composition, coming to occupy a crucial place in the history of music in Wales, though not seeking to extend her influence elsewhere. She is primarily associated with vocal and orchestral music, to which she brought a distinctively national voice, as evident in *Penillion for Orchestra* (1955), *Ballads for Orchestra* (1968) and the *Missa cambrensis* (1971). Another trait of her music shows the influence of Britten, a close friend and correspondent in her early years. She also wrote a one-act opera, *The Parlour* (1961), for which she derived a libretto from Guy de Maupassant's *En famille*; two symphonies (1943 and 1956, the first of which she

withdrew); and concertos for violin (1950) and trumpet (1963).

M. Boyd: *Grace Williams* (1980)

**Williams** [née Scruggs; Burleigh], **Mary Lou** [Elfrieda] (1910–81). American jazz pianist. Born in Atlanta, Georgia, she moved to Pittsburgh with her mother and sister in 1914. She started playing the piano in public at an early age, leaving school to tour under her stepfather's name as Mary Lou Burleigh. In 1925 she joined the group led by saxophonist John Williams, whom she later married, and in 1927 became leader of his group when he moved to another band. She arranged for Andy Kirk's band from 1929 to 1942, recorded with him, and eventually became a solo pianist. She also arranged for Benny Goodman, Louis Armstrong, Earl Hines, Tommy Dorsey, and Duke Ellington. After divorcing Williams, she married trumpeter Harold Baker and worked with him in Duke Ellington's band. Her chief composition during the 1940s was the *Zodiac Suite* (1946).

During the 1940s and 1950s she lived and worked in both New York and California and was a patron of young artists such as Miles Davis and Charlie Parker; she also spent two years in England from 1952 to 1954. She retired from music between 1954 and 1957 after a religious conversion, returning to be recognized as a leading jazz composer and brilliant technical performer. She was also very concerned with the study of religion, and with the work of the Bel Canto Charity Organization. In the 1970s, encouraged by Peter O'Brien, a young priest who became her manager and confidant, she composed long religious pieces, including several masses – one commissioned by the Vatican. In 1977 she gave a concert with the avant-garde pianist Cecil Taylor. She received several honorary degrees, and held a Guggenheim Fellowship in 1972.

**Williams, Shirley (Vivien Teresa Brittain)** (1930–). English politician. She was born in Chelsea into a prominent intellectual family. Her father, Professor Sir George Catlin, taught political science, and was a Labour candidate in the 1930s, and her mother was the socialist feminist VERA BRITTAIN. She attended schools in London, and was evacuated during World War II to St Paul,

Minnesota (1940–43). From St Paul's Girls' School, London, she went to Somerville College, Oxford. A member of the Labour League of Youth, in 1948 she became first woman Chairman of the Labour Club. After graduating she worked in factories and as a waitress until taking up a year's fellowship at Columbia University, New York, in 1952. Here she met Bernard Williams whom she married in 1955 (dissolved 1974).

On returning to England, Shirley Williams worked as a journalist, first on the *Daily Mirror* and later the *Financial Times* until 1958. During this period she stood as Labour candidate for Harwich (1954 and 1955) being nicknamed 'the schoolgirl candidate', and contested Southampton Test (1959), before becoming MP for Hitchin (1964–74), and Hertford and Stevenage (1974–9). During the 1960s she was General Secretary of the Fabian Society (1960–64) and held a number of posts: Parliamentary Private Secretary and Minister of Health (1964–6); Ministry of Labour (1966–7); Minister of State for Education and Science (1967–9); Home Office (1969–70). A devout Catholic, she voted against liberalizing divorce and against changes in the abortion laws in the late 1960s.

After a decade of achievement, the 1970s proved more difficult. During the Labour opposition she was spokesman on Social Services, Home Affairs and Prices and Consumer Protection. She then became Secretary of State for Prices and Consumer Protection (1974–6), followed by Education and Science, and Paymaster General (1976–9). As Education Minister she conducted a vigorous campaign for comprehensive education, but also cut teacher training places by 40 per cent. She lost her seat in the 1979 election. From 1970 Shirley Williams had been a member of the Labour Party National Executive. She resigned in 1981 after disagreements with Michael Foot and Anthony Wedgwood Benn and formed the Social Democratic Party (SDP) with David Owen, Roy Jenkins and Bill Rogers, becoming President of the SDP in 1982. From 1979–85 she was Professorial Fellow at the Policy Studies Institute, London. In a by-election in November 1981 she became the Social Democratic Party MP for Crosby but lost the seat in 1983. Her book, *Politics is for People*,

appeared in 1981, and *A Job To Live* in 1985. In 1987 she married Professor Richard Neustadt, a Harvard political economist.

**Winchilsea** [née Kingsmith], **Anne Finch** Countess of (1661–1720). English poet. Born nr Southampton and educated at home, in 1683 she became Maid of Honour to Mary of Modena, wife of James II. The following year she married Heneage Finch, who became Earl of Winchilsea in 1712. In 1690, after the Stuart downfall, she and her husband retired to their estates at Eastwell, Kent; Anne wrote poems and blank verse dramas which were circulated among her friends. Her Pindaric ode, *The Spleen* (1709), won her a wide reputation but later readers, especially Wordsworth and other 19th-century Romantics, preferred her meditative nature poetry. In several poems she defends women's right to escape domesticity, to acquire education and to write for the public.

**Windeyer** [née Bolton], **Mary (Elizabeth)** [Lady Windeyer] (1836–1912). Australian feminist. The daughter of a clergyman, she married a barrister, William Windeyer, in 1857 at Hexham. As he rose to prominence in the law and in politics, she persuaded him to support women's interests; as Attorney General (1878–9) he introduced and carried the Married Women's Property Act. From an early involvement in charitable organizations, she became drawn into the women's rights movement, and was a prominent member of the Women's Christian Temperance Union. In 1888 she helped to organize a Women's Industrial Exhibition, and supported the right to information on birth control; her husband upheld an appeal against conviction for obscenity for selling ANNIE BESANT's *Law of Population*. She campaigned for higher education for women and was a member of the feminist Dawn Club, founded by LOUISA LAWSON. The Windeyers were closely associated with the founding of the Women's College, as part of Sydney University in 1891. In that year she also became the first President of the Womanhood Suffrage League with ROSE SCOTT as Secretary. In 1895 she was a founder and first President of the Women's

Hospital, Sydney, and she remained an active campaigner into old age.

**Windsor, Wallis Warfield,** Duchess of (1896–). American; wife of Edward VIII, Duke of Windsor. Born in Blue Ridge Summit, Pennsylvania, she went to Oldfields, a private school in Maryland, and then became a debutante in Baltimore in 1914. A lively and extremely fashionable society belle, she first married Earl Winfield Spencer, and after her divorce from him married Ernest Aldrich Simpson in 1928.

In June 1931 she met Edward, Prince of Wales, and in the same year was presented at the British court. The couple formed part of a smart international set and their close association provoked widespread gossip in the press in the USA and Europe, although such stories were censored in the UK for a long time. In January 1936 Edward succeeded to the throne and in October Wallis Simpson obtained a divorce. Anxiety in the Cabinet grew, as the possibility of their marriage was rumoured; she was unacceptable to the Royal family as a commoner and as a twice-divorced woman. On 13 November the King told Baldwin, the Prime Minister, that he intended to marry her, and that if he could not do so and remain king, he would abdicate. On 3 December this was announced in the press and in Parliament, and although Edward had been considering the compromise of marrying Wallis without raising her to the status of queen, the public revelation forced his hand. He abdicated on 10 December. The couple married in France in June 1937, but although George VI allowed Edward, now titled Duke of Windsor, to be styled HRH, Wallis was openly snubbed by exclusion from that honour, a slight which caused great distress.

No attempt at reconciliation was made by the British royal family until 1967 when ELIZABETH II invited the Windsors to the unveiling of a memorial to Queen Mary.

They lived in the South of France from 1938, and from 1940 to 1945 in the Bahamas where the Duke was Governor, and then returned to Paris, where the Duchess continued to live reclusively after her husband's death in 1972. Her memoirs, *The Heart has its Reasons*, appeared in 1956. When she died in 1986 her body was taken to England to be buried next to the Duke at Frogmore. Her fabulous collection of jewels, many of them presents from the Duke, were auctioned by Sothebys in Paris in April 1987, raising over £31 million for the Pasteur Institute.

**Winnemucca, Sarah** [Thoc-me-tony] (1844–91). American Indian leader. The daughter of a Piute Chief, given the Indian name Thoc-me-tony ('Shell-flower'), in 1850 she was taken by her grandfather from Nevada to work in California. She learned English and Spanish, and when she returned and lived with the family of a stage-coach company agent she was baptized 'Sarah'. During the 1860s the Piutes were driven into reservations and Sarah acted as their interpreter at Camp McDermott from 1868 to 1871 and then on a reservation in Oregon. In 1876 she was dismissed, and during the Bannock wars of 1878 she persuaded the Piutes not to fight and acted as an army guide. She went on to lecture widely in the East about the ill-treatment of her people, campaigning on their behalf in Washington (1880), and returned to the West to teach at an Indian school in Vancouver. There she married a Lieutenant Hopkins (her previous two brief marriages had failed) and he accompanied her on a further lecture tour (1882–3). In 1883 Sarah published *Life Among the Piutes*, which was a success, and the following year a bill was passed granting land to her tribe. The next two years she spent teaching in Nevada, before ill-health drove her to retire to her sister's home in Montana, where she died of consumption at the age of 47.

K. Gehan: *Sarah Winnemucca* (1975)

**Wittig, Monique** (1935–). French feminist novelist. A radical lesbian, she was one of the prime movers in the rejection by avant-garde French women writers of what they felt to be an alien male language. Her first novel was *L'opopomax* (1964) and her second *Les guérillères* (1969), a utopian allegory of female warrior resistance. In the same year, two other influential works appeared intent on destroying 'male language', MARGUERITE DURAS' *Détruire dit-elle*, and Joyce Mansour's poetry *Phallus et momies*. In Wittig's works, grammar is literally fragmented on the page, for example 'tu m//es tu m//es (à l'aide m/a Sappho). . .'.

In 1970 Wittig joined CHRISTIANE ROCHEFORT in a much publicized protest which horrified the French bourgeoisie, the attempt to place a wreath on the tomb of the unknown soldier in Paris inscribed 'to the unknown wife of the soldier'. She was a member of the Gemines Rouges, and founder (and for a short time from 1970 spokeswoman) of the separatist group Feministes Révolutionnaires, which organized spectacular demonstrations such as the 'Day for Denouncing Crimes Against Women'. She then became disillusioned with the divisions between the psychoanalytic and socialist radical feminist sects, and has remained outside organized groups. She published Le corps lesbien (1973) and Brouillon pour un dictionnaire des amants (1976) and in 1977 contributed with very different feminists, SIMONE DE BEAUVOIR and the socialist economist, Christine Delphy, to the new journal Questions feministes.

**Woffington, Peg** [Margaret] (c1714–60). Irish actress. She sang in the streets as a child and first appeared on stage at the age of ten as Polly in The Beggar's Opera. After a successful career in Dublin she moved to London in 1740. A noted beauty, unusually tall and with a harsh voice, independent and bold, Peg Woffington was notorious for her numerous sexual liaisons, particularly her ménage à trois with Charles Macklin and David Garrick. She was renowned for 'breeches' parts, especially Sir Harry Wildair in The Constant Couple. Her attempts at tragic roles were unsuccessful (Francis Gentleman called her 'the screech owl of tragedy') but her excellence in comedy was unrivalled, notably as Millimant. She dominated the stage at Drury Lane between 1740 and 1746, in Dublin between 1747 and 1754, and at Covent Garden between 1754 and 1757. She was taken ill while appearing as Rosalind in a benefit performance in May 1757 and she died three years later. Her Memoires were published in 1760.

J. Dunbar: Peg Woffington and her World (1968)

**Wolf, Christa** (1929–). East German novelist. Born in Landsberg [now in Poland], she moved with her family to Mecklenburg in 1945. Her years growing up in Nazi Germany are movingly evoked in her fourth novel Kindheitsmuster/A Model Childhood (1976; Eng. trans. 1982). She studied literature at the universities of Leipzig and Jena, and then worked as an editor for various publishers and literary journals, including Neue Deutsche Literatur and as a critic for the Mitteldeutscher Verlag and the Verlag Neues Leben. She is married, and lives with her family in East Berlin.

Wolf acquired her reputation as East Germany's finest woman writer in the 1960s, with a novella Moskauer Novelle (1961), Der geteilte Himmel/Divided Heaven (1963; Eng. trans. 1976) about a woman's socialist commitment and difficult decision not to join her lover in the West, and the remarkable Nachdenken über Christa T/The Quest for Christa T (1966; Eng. trans. 1970). This was banned from publication and then severely criticized for five years because of its disillusionment with the corruption of the original idealistic vision of a new society in East Germany. It became a best-seller when published in West Germany in 1970. Her other works include the stories in Unter den Linden (1974), and the critical essays in Lesen und Schreiben/The Reader and the Writer (1972; Eng. trans. 1978), whose subjects include ANNA SEGHERS and INGEBORG BACHMANN. Apart from the Heinrich Mann Prize, which was awarded to her for Der geteilte Himmel, she has received the Literary Prize of the City of Halle (1961) and the National Prize for Art and Literature of the German Democratic Republic (1964). Her recent works include the novel Kassandra and Vorlesungen und Störfall, written in response to the Chernobyl disaster in 1985.

**Wollstonecraft (Godwin), Mary** (1759–97). English feminist and radical. She was born in Hoxton, near London, of Irish parents. Her father was a drunkard and wife-beater who tried unsuccessfully to farm in Yorkshire and Wales. Mary was largely self-educated and in 1778 began work as a companion in Bath. After her mother's death in 1782 she started a school in Newington Green with her friend Fanny Blood and met many liberal nonconformists; the school failed and

Tz'u-hsi

Marie Vigée-Lebrun

Mary Wollstonecraft

Virginia Woolf

Fanny left and later died in childbirth in Lisbon, while Mary was hurrying to nurse her.

In 1787 she published *Thoughts on the Education of Daughters*, and took a post as governess to Lord Kingsborough's family. But by 1790 she was back in London, working for the publisher Johnson, reading manuscripts, writing articles and translating. She became a member of a radical intellectual group which included Paine, Godwin and Fuseli, to whom she was deeply attached. Her work at this time includes *Mary (A Fiction)* (1788) and *The Female Reader* (1789), followed by the remarkable *History and Moral View of the Origins and Progress of the French Revolution*. In 1792 she went to Paris and began her love affair with the American Gilbert Imlay, following him to Le Havre, where their daughter Fanny was born in 1794. She returned with him to England and travelled on business to Norway for him, but, unable to accept his infidelity, attempted suicide at Putney Bridge in 1795.

During 1796 she worked for Johnson again and met William Godwin, and despite objections of principle they married when she became pregnant. She died of puerperal fever ten days after the birth of their daughter Mary (later MARY SHELLEY). Her *Vindication of the Rights of Women* challenges Rousseau's notions of female inferiority, arguing for equality of education, employment for single women, and companionship with men. It caused a scandal, linked by critics to her own unconventional life, but has become a seminal work in the tradition of liberal feminism.

C. Tomalin: *The Life and Death of Mary Wollstonecraft* (1978)

**Wood,** Mrs **Henry** (pen name of Ellen Wood) (1814–87). British novelist. The popular Victorian novelist 'Mrs Henry Wood', was born Ellen Price, in Worcester. The daughter of a prosperous glove manufacturer, she was brought up by her maternal grandmother and was educated at home since a curvature of the spine affected her health; she remained a semi-invalid for most of her life, and often wrote her novels lying on a sofa. She married Henry Wood, son of a banking and shipping family and a member of the consular service,

and for the next 20 years lived largely in the Dauphiné, France. There she began to write stories for *Bentley's Miscellany* and the *New Monthly Magazine*.

After the Woods returned and settled in Norwood in 1860 she earned her first money from her writing, with the novel *Danesbury House* (1869); which won £100 from the Scottish Temperance League. The famous *East Lynne* appeared the following year in the *New Monthly Magazine* and then as a book; after a dazzling review in *The Times*, it sold over 500,000 copies by 1900, was widely translated and often dramatized. Her next novels, *Mrs Halliburton's Troubles* and *The Channings* (1862) confirmed her success. In the same decade she wrote *The Shadow of Ashlydyat* (1863), *Lord Oakburn's Daughters* (1864), *Lady Adelaide's Oath* (1867, an anonymous novel attacking trade unions and strikes), *A Life's Secret* (1867) and *Roland Yorke* (1869).

In 1866 Henry Wood died, but with her son Charles she founded and edited *Argosy* in 1867, continuing the fine, less melodramatic 'Johnny Ludlow' stories for this magazine from 1868. She was to write another 20 books before her death, the most successful being *Within the Maze* (1872) and *Edina* (1876). A devout Anglican, and an ultraconservative, her novels were liked for their melodramatic plots and for the social realism of their backgrounds, and although they are imbued with an almost punitive morality they offer interesting glimpses of the desires and suppressed anger of contemporary women.

**Woodhull** [née Claflin], **Victoria** (1838–1927). American feminist, journalist and financier. She was the seventh child of Buck [Reuben] and Roxanna Claflin and was born in Homer, Ohio. The family had to leave town when Buck was suspected of arson after a fire at their mill. They moved around Ohio with a travelling medicine and fortune-telling show; Victoria and her sister TENNESSEE CELESTE CLAFLIN gave demonstrations of clairvoyance, influenced by their fanatically spiritualist mother. Victoria took the lead in the stage career of the two sisters and claimed later to have had visions since the age of three and to have seen the spirit of the orator Demosthenes. In 1853 at the age of 15 she married Dr Canning Woodhull, an alcoholic, but although she had a son and a daughter she returned to the family show. She worked with Tennessee as a clairvoyant in Cincinnati and Chicago. In 1866 she divorced Woodhull and probably married Colonel James Blood.

In 1868 the two sisters moved to New York. Through promises of spiritualist help to contact his newly-dead wife, they influenced the millionaire, Cornelius Vanderbilt, to set them up as the first professional women stockbrokers. They were extremely successful. Victoria then became involved in Pantarchy, a socialist group run by Stephen Andrews advocating free love and communal children and property. In 1870 the two sisters began proselytizing these views, campaigning for equal rights, a single morality and legalized prostitution in Woodhull and Claflin's Weekly which ran from 1870 to 1876. Victoria became drawn into the women's movement. In 1871 she appealed for suffrage to the Senate Judiciary Committee, and the defence of her outspoken views by SUSAN B. ANTHONY and ELIZABETH CADY STANTON led to their break with the more conservative LUCY STONE in 1872. After a subsequent split in the movement, in which Victoria was defeated for the leadership of the National Woman Suffrage Association, she was named the first woman nominee for President by the Equal Rights Party. In the same year the sisters published the first English translation of the Communist Manifesto in their journal. They were also the subject of a more personal scandal. In defence of their attack on the double standard of morality, they had published in the Weekly an account of a love affair between the prominent Rev Henry Ward Beecher (brother of HARRIET BEECHER STOWE) and the wife of Theodore Tilton, a suffragist friend of Victoria. They were arrested for issuing an obscene publication and spent some time in prison, but were acquitted the following year.

The next few years were quieter although the Weekly continued. In 1877, perhaps sponsored by the Vanderbilt family to avoid challenges to Cornelius's will, they moved to London. There Victoria met John Biddulph Martin in 1881, and after overcoming objections from his family they married in 1883.

Victoria became a noted society hostess but also continued to work for women's rights and joined the PANKHURST suffrage campaigns. She moved to a more conservative position, publishing a journal on eugenics, The Humanitarian (1892–1910) with her daughter Zulu Maud Woodhull. Among her other publications were Stirpiculture, or the Scientific Propagation of The Human Race (1888); Humanitarian Money (1892); and with Tennessee, The Human Body the Temple of God (1890). Among the most colourful figures in the women's rights movement the sisters continued to cause a sensation on their later visits to the USA. Both outlived their husbands and enjoyed an affluent old age.

J. Johnston: Mrs Satan: the Incredible Saga of Victoria Woodhull (1967)

Woolf [née Stephen], (Adeline) Virginia (1882–1941). English writer. She was born at Hyde Park Gate, London, the daughter of Julia (née Jackson) and Sir Leslie Stephen. Her adolescence and early adult life were greatly affected by the deaths of her mother, her step-sister Stella and her elder brother Thoby. After her father's death in 1904 she, her sister (the painter VANESSA BELL) and two brothers set up house in Bloomsbury. Here they got to know, among others, Clive Bell, Leonard Woolf and Lytton Strachey. In 1912 she married Woolf and in 1915 her first novel, The Voyage Out, was published. Apart from this and Night and Day (1919), all her work was published by the Hogarth Press, which she and Leonard set up in 1917, and which also issued work by writers such as T.S. Eliot and KATHERINE MANSFIELD. After her marriage her time was divided between London, where she knew most of the famous literary figures of her time, and Sussex – first at Asham House and after 1919 at Monk's House, Rodmell, Lewes.

Despite intermittent nervous breakdowns she produced a great variety of novels, stories, criticism and other work. Although she was never actively involved in feminism, her two non-fiction works, A Room of One's Own (1929) and the anti-war Three Guineas (1938), are deeply concerned with the problems obstructing women's achievement and commitment. Her fiction is famous for its allusive style and innovative technique, particularly To the Lighthouse (1927) and The Waves (1931). Under the pressure of finishing the last of her nine novels, *Between the Acts* (1941), and of World War II, she drowned herself in March 1941.

Q. Bell: *Virginia Woolf: a Biography* (1972)

**Wootton,** Baroness **Barbara (Frances)** (1897–1988). British social scientist. Barbara Adam studied for her degree at Cambridge University and in 1917 married J.W. Wootton, who was killed in action in the same year. She was appointed Director of Studies in Economics at Girton in 1920, but became increasingly interested in labour affairs and worked as a researcher for the Trades Union Congress and the Labour Party from 1922. In 1926, at an extremely young age, she became Principal of Morley College for Working Men and Women in London, and was Director of Studies in Adult Education for the University of London in 1927–44. After the war she was promoted to Reader, then Professor of Social Studies, 1948–52, and remained a research fellow until her retirement from the University in 1957.

In 1935 she married G.P. Wright (who died in 1964). She published several books which display her clear thought and social and educational commitment: *Twos and Threes* (1933), *Plan or No Plan* (1934), *London's Burning* (1936), *Lament for Economics* (1938), *Freedom Under Planning* (1945), *Testament for Social Science* (1950) and *Social Foundations of Wage Policy* (1955). She also took an increasingly public role, as a member of Royal Commissions on Workmen's Compensation (1938), the Press (1947), the Civil Service (1954) and as a Governor of the BBC (1950–56) and Chairman of the Metropolitan Juvenile Courts (1946–62).

In 1958 she was made a life peer, taking the title of Baroness Wootton of Abinger, after her home at Abinger Common, near Dorking in Surrey. She continued to publish, with *Social Science and Social Pathology* (1959) and *Crime and the Criminal Law* (1963). In the 1960s and 1970s criminal justice and penal policy became her chief concern, as a member of the Departmental Committee on Criminal Statistics (1963–7), the Advisory Council on the Penal System (1966–74) and on the Misuse of Drugs (1971–4). This is regarded as her most important and influential area of work, continuing up to the book written in her eightieth year, *Crime and Penal Policy*

(1978); she also wrote generally in *Contemporary Britain* (1971) and questioned economic policy in *Incomes Policy: An Inquest and a Proposal* (1974).

B. Wootton: *In A World I Never Made* (1967)
————: *Reflections on Fifty Years Experience* (1978)

**Wordsworth, Dorothy** (1771–1855). English diarist. Born in Cockermouth, Westmoreland, where her father was agent of the Latimer family, Dorothy was sent away to cousins in Halifax when her mother died in 1777. She remained there for ten years, being educated chiefly at a local day school. After an unhappy few months with her grandparents at Penrith, at the end of 1788 she went to live with her uncle, William Cookson, in Norfolk until 1794 when a legacy allowed her to take a house in Dorset with her brother William who was 18 months older. She was devoted to William and became his companion through life, both before and after his marriage.

In Dorset they met Coleridge, moving to live near him at Nether Stowey in 1797, and after a long visit to Germany (1798–9) finally settled in the Lake District at Grasmere. She lived there or at Rydal for the rest of her life, although she paid many visits to friends and relations. In 1803, with Wordsworth and Coleridge she made a six-week trip to Scotland, revising her *Recollections of a Tour in Scotland* after a return visit in 1820, (eventually published 1874). Dorothy kept detailed journals, which were not only source books for her brother but also vivid documents of her own thoughts and her response to nature, and of local country life. They were published 30 years after her death.

In April 1829 an illness ruined her previously robust health, and she gradually became increasingly mentally confused; during her last 20 years almost her only calm period followed the shock of William's death in 1850.

R. Gittings and J. Manton: *Dorothy Wordsworth* (1985)
D. Wordsworth: *Journals,* ed. M. Moorman (1971)

**Workman, Fanny** (1859–1925). American traveller and mountaineer. Born in Worcester, Massachusetts, the daughter of a former governor of the state, Fanny Bullock was educated in New England, Paris and Dresden. In 1881 she married William Hunter Workman, a local doctor. With him she moved to Europe for the sake of his health, then undertook a series of cycling tours between 1895 and 1899. *Algerian Memories* (1895), *Sketches Awheel in fin de siècle Iberia* (1897) and *Through Town and Jungle: 14,000 Miles Awheel among the Temples and Peoples of the Indian Plain* (1904) are three of her nine travel books, notable for observation and photographs, but perhaps lacking in humanity. With her cycling, sensible clothes and belief in female suffrage, Fanny was an extreme example of the Victorian 'New Woman'. Her daughter Rachel was educated in England and was not included on the journeys or mentioned in the books.

After a final cycling tour in Java, Fanny (aged 40) and William (aged 52) became pioneer Himalayan explorers. They explored successively the Chogo Lungma glacier in the Lesser Karakoram, the Nun Kun Massif, the Hispar glacier and Siachen or Rose glacier, as well as naming and surveying numerous peaks. In 1906 Fanny established an altitude record for a woman, of 6930 metres on Pinnacle Peak. She is pictured in the snow with her ice axe, displaying a 'Votes for Women' poster. She survived adventures such as falling into a crevasse and losing her famous topi down a mountain, but although the expeditions were well organized, many heights, names and surveys they competitively established have since been discredited. Fanny's appreciation of mountains is evident in her later books, such as *In the Ice World of the Himalaya* (1900) and *The Call of the Snowy Hispar* (1910), and from her frequent lectures. In November 1905 she was the first woman to address the Royal Geographical Society since ISABELLA BIRD BISHOP in 1897, and thereafter reported findings regularly. She suffered an eight-year-long illness before her death.

**Wright, Frances** (1795–1852). Scottish-American radical. Born in Dundee, Scotland, she was orphaned when she was two-and-a-half. After being educated in London she returned to Scotland. She first visited the USA in 1818 with her sister Camilla, preferring this to a European Grand Tour, and the following year her play *Altdorf*, about the Swiss independence

movement, was produced in New York. Her impressions of the visit were described after her return in *Views of Society and Manners in America* (1821), and her independent materialist philosophy was outlined in *A few Days in Athens* (1822). The former book led to a friendship with Lafayette. She travelled to the USA with him in 1824–5 and discussed the problem of slavery with Madison and Jefferson. She decided to settle there and in 1825 began her first social experiment, providing funds for a settlement of slaves in Nashoba, western Tennessee, which was seen as a step to their gradual emancipation and colonization outside the USA. One group did settle in Haiti in 1830.

In 1828 she began editing the *New Harmony Gazette* with Robert Dale Owen. A bold free-thinker she lectured in public, a shocking precedent, speaking not only against slavery but also on free state education, and on the repressive nature of religion and marriage, advocating a 'free union' instead of a legal contract. Despite an abusive reception in many places she persevered and in 1829 edited the *Free Enquirer* in New York, published her *Course of Popular Lectures* and joined the Working Men's Club.

From 1829 to 1835 she lived in Europe, and after Camilla's death in 1831 she married William Philquepal d'Arusmont, a Frenchman who had worked with her in the USA. They had one daughter but were later divorced. In 1836 Frances returned to the USA and undertook new lecture tours, opposing monopolies, attacking the banking system and fighting slavery. She also wrote for the Boston *Investigator* and edited the *Manual of American Principles*. After 1838 the issues she raised grew still more controversial and included birth control, the legal and social emancipation of women, the equal distribution of property and communitarian living. She died in Cincinnati, after breaking her hip in a fall. Her courageous example, as much as her ideas, influenced women to claim greater independence.

C.M. Eckhardt: *Fanny Wright: Rebel in America* (1984)

**Wright** [née Lowenfeld], **Helena (Rosa)** (1888–1982). English birth control campaigner. She was born in Brixton,

London. Her father was a poor Polish immigrant who built and owned the Apollo Theatre and made an immense fortune. Educated under DOROTHEA BEALE at Cheltenham Ladies' College, Helena resisted all pressures to remain an elegant society debutante and decided to become a doctor. She trained at the Royal Free Hospital Medical School for Women, joined the Royal Army medical corps and worked at Bethnal Green Hospital during World War I. There she met Henry Wright, a surgeon, whom she subsequently married.

Helena had long been determined on a missionary career and after training as a gynaecologist she departed for China with her husband and two sons; she taught gynaecology at Shantung Christian University from 1922 to 1927. The family then returned home on the Trans-Siberian Railway. *The Times* Obituary suggests that to cope with the problem of her four-month baby sleeping in the luggage rack, she 'invented' disposable nappies.

In Berlin she became interested in new birth-control methods, such as the experimental intra-uterine device, and on her return to England joined one of the first free London clinics in Kensington, where she gave sexual counselling advice as well as help with contraception. She was a founder of the National Birth Control Council in 1930 (later the Family Planning Association or FPA), and was a leading member of the International Planned Parenthood Federation, where she fought particularly for high standards of service and the specialized training of doctors. In 1930 she wrote a best-selling book, *The Sex Factor in Marriage*. She retired from working in FPA clinics in 1958, practised privately and trained overseas students studying family planning in Britain, since she was already well known for her teaching in Commonwealth countries, particularly India and Sri Lanka. In 1968, now aged 80, she published another progressive work *Sex and Society*. She remained a teacher, broadcaster, and well-known public figure, always open to new ideas and views, until her death at 94.

**Wright, Judith** (1915–). Australian poet. Born near Armidale, Judith Wright was brought up in the sheep farming district of New South Wales, and was educated through a correspondence school and at the New England Girls' School. After attending Sydney University she spent a year in Europe, before working as a secretary, 1938–42. She then joined the University of Queensland (1945–8) as a statistician, and it is in the Queensland mountains that she has written most of her work although lecturing in several Australian Universities since 1949. With a fine lyric gift she explores the relationship of modern Australia to its past, and has also given a voice to essential female feelings about sexuality and identity. Among her collections of poetry are *The Moving Image* (1946), *Woman to Man* (1950), *The Gateway* (1953), *Birds* (1960), *Alive* (1972), *The Double Tree* (1978) and *Phantom Dwellings* (1985). A volume of collected poetry appeared in 1970.

She also edited *The Oxford Book of Australian Verse* in 1954 and *New Land, New Language* (1957), and has done much to establish the tradition of Australian poetry. Her prose works include the historical memoir *The Generations of Men* (1955), *Preoccupations in Australian Poetry* (1964), *The Coral Battleground* (1977) and *We Call for a Treaty* (1985). She has also written children's books and numerous articles, and a collection of short stories, *The Nature of Love* (1966).

**Wu Chao** [Wu Hau] (625–705). Chinese empress. The daughter of a general, and reputedly very beautiful, she was summoned to the palace of the Emperor T'ai Tsung as a junior concubine at the age of 13. By the time of his death in 649 she was involved with his heir Kao Tsung, who brought her back from the convent to which the concubines traditionally retired at their lord's death. By the time she was 30 she had had a son, had displaced the childless empress and ousted all the statesmen who disliked her elevation to that rank. Ruthlessly ambitious, she is said to have had all the other concubines killed, and she savagely removed all opposition including members of her own and the Imperial family. She had four sons and one daughter. She entirely dominated her husband, who let her take over the administration and employ her own loyal officials, such as the military leaders who successfully ended the war with Korea.

In 683 Kao Tsung died, but as soon as her authority was threatened by the new Emperor (her son Chung) and his wife Wei, Wu Chao deposed and exiled Chung and continued to govern, with her second son Jui as official ruler. In 690 she finally usurped the throne; although this was counter to all tradition, there was no 'revolt. She ruled supreme for 15 years, although she recalled Chung to be her heir in 698. Her long period of power, extending for half a century from 655, established peace and prosperity, the unification of the T'ang Empire, the replacement of aristocratic military control by a scholarly meritocratic bureaucracy, and high cultural achievement, symbolized by the magnificent buildings in the capital. In the later years, after Kao's death, she became infamous for her favourites and this eventually led to her downfall. The first, a pedlar, Hsuen Huai-i, was raised to the position of Abbot and Commander-in-Chief before his extravagance led her to have him killed in 696. He was succeeded by the notorious Chang brothers, dilettante courtiers whose power over the ailing Empress finally led to a revolt on the part of the leading ministers, in which they were killed. Wu Chao was persuaded to retire to her summer palace, where she died ten months later at the age of 80. The most indomitable of Chinese women, her extaordinary rule was long underrated by misogynic historians.

C.I. Fitzgerald: *The Empress Wu* (2/1968)

**Wynette [Pugh], Tammy** (1942–). American country singer. She was born near Tupelo, Mississippi; her father died when she was a baby and she was brought up on her grandparents' farm while her mother undertook war work. She hoped for a career in singing but married at 17 and had three children before she separated from her husband in 1962. Her last child suffered from spinal meningitis and to pay the medical bills Tammy worked as a beautician and began singing on local radio and television shows and working in clubs. Her breakthrough came in 1966 with *Apartment No. 9* and her series of hits then included classic songs such as *D–I–V–O–R–C–E* and *Stand by Your Man* (1968); the latter is also the title of her autobiography, published in 1979. From 1968 to 1975 she was married to the singer George Jones and they recorded together despite a notoriously tempestuous relationship. Her own successes and her unique lamenting voice kept her at the top of her profession throughout the 1970s. Her *Greatest Hits* album alone remained in the best-selling charts for over a year and earned over a million dollars.

# X

**Xiang Jingyu** (1895–1928). Chinese revolutionary and feminist. She was born into a prosperous liberal family in Hunan province and educated at a girls' school in Zhangsha where she became influenced by the revolutionary movement. She was a friend of Mao and Cai Hseng (*d*1931). After her graduation in 1916 she opened a girls' school, campaigned against footbinding and feudal marriage and led student demonstrations in the 4th May movement in 1919. In the same year, with Mao and others, she arranged a work study programme in France. She cut her hair, starting the vogue for bobbed hair among intellectuals. In 1920, working in a textile mill in Montargis, she studied Marx, and co-founded the Chinese Communist Party. After marrying Cai Hseng, she wrote *A thesis on the Emancipation and Transformation of Women*.

She was elected to the Central Committee in 1922 and became the first Director of the Communist Party women's department, which she herself established. Leaving her baby with her sister, she organized among working women and visited Moscow. After Xiang Kai Shek's 'White Terror' campaign against the Communists in 1927 she insisted on staying in Hunan, organizing unions and running an underground newspaper. She was arrested and executed in May 1928, gagged to prevent her final speech.

**Xie Xide** (1921–). Chinese physicist and university administrator. Xie Xide was born in South China, but grew up in Beijing, where her father was a professor of physics. In 1937, at the start of the Japanese invasion, the family moved to the distant cities of Wuhan and Changsa, where she spent three years recovering from tuberculosis. From 1942 to 1946 she studied at Xiamen University and became a physics teacher in the University of Shanghai during the turbulent period of conflict between the Communists and the Kuomintang. In 1947 she went to Smith College, Massachusetts, and in 1949 to MIT where in 1951 she completed her PhD (on electrons in compressed gases). The following year, in England, she married Cao Tianqin, whom she had met in Beijing, but who was now working in Cambridge. They returned to Shanghai, where she was to teach at Fudan University until 1977. Soon established as one of China's leading physicists, she published *Semi-conductor Physics* (1958) and *Solid Physics* (1962) and numerous papers, was made a professor in 1962, and became Deputy Director of the Institute of Technical Physics, Shanghai.

During the Cultural Revolution she lost her job; she was publicly humiliated and separated from her husband. Re-instated in 1974, she began to concentrate on her research on surface physics, and on educational projects, founding the Modern Physics Institute in 1977. Her many honours include membership of the Chinese Academy of Sciences and of the Praesidium. She was Vice-President of Fudan University, 1978–83, and is now President, and was one of 11 women elected to the Central Committee of the Chinese Communist Party in 1982. During the 1980s her work was recognized internationally, with honorary degrees from American, British and Japanese universities.

# Y

**Yalow** [née Sussman], **Rosalyn** (1921–). American physicist in medicine. She was born in New York City; her mother was German and both of her parents had received only elementary education. Rosalyn was interested in mathematics and chemistry, but specialized in physics at Hunter College. She worked as a typist, then took an assistantship in physics at the College of Engineering of the University of Illinois, where she was the only woman in a faculty of 400. In 1943 she married Aaron Yalow, who was in the same department and later became a Professor of physics. Rosalyn gained her PhD in nuclear physics in 1945.

Returning to New York, she volunteered to work in a laboratory in order to gain experience in medical applications of radioisotopes. She also continued teaching at Hunter College, then became a consultant at Bronx V.A. Hospital. Here she began a 22-year partnership with Solomon Berson; they measured insulin in the body and from 1959 developed the new method of radioimmuno-assay. This made possible the precise measurement of substances in the blood such as drugs, hormones, and enzymes.

In 1977 they were awarded the Nobel Prize for medicine, Rosalyn being the second woman to receive it. At the Nobel Prize address she talked of discrimination against women: 'The world cannot afford the loss of the talents of half its people if we are to solve the many problems which beset us.' She has held the chair at the Department of Clinical Sciences of the Montefiore Hospital in the Bronx, New York, and holds numerous honorary degrees and awards including the Georg Charles de Henesy Nuclear Medicine Pioneer Award 1986.

**Yates, Frances Amelia** (1899–1981). British cultural historian. Born in London, Frances Yates was the daughter of a naval architect and was educated at Glasgow and Liverpool. She graduated with first-class honours in French from University College, London, in 1924, taking her MA two years later, and continued her research privately, with some teaching at the North London Collegiate School from 1926 to 1939. Her first book, *John Florio*, appeared in 1934. During the first year of the war she was an ambulance attendant in London, but in 1941 became a research assistant at the Warburg Institute, her base for most of her career. She worked there as lecturer and editor of publications, 1944–56, and was then made Reader in the History of the Renaissance, 1956–67.

At the Warburg, she concentrated on 16th-century England, France and Italy, bringing vivid imaginative insight to her study of the period, particularly to its symbolism, ritual and hermetic traditions. Her best-known works include *The French Academies of the Sixteenth Century* (1947), *Giordano Bruno and the Hermetic Tradition* (1964), the acknowledged classic *The Art of Memory* (1966), *The Rosicrucian Enlightenment* (1972) and *Shakespeare's Last Plays* (1975). Her last work was *The Occult Philosophy in the Elizabethan Age* (1979).

After her retirement she continued to write and lecture widely in Britain and America in the 1970s, receiving many honorary fellowships and awards including the Wolfson History Award in 1973 and the Galileo Prize in 1978. She received the OBE in 1972 and was made a Dame of the British Empire in 1977.

**Yeager, Jeana** (1952–). American aviator. Born and brought up in Fort Worth, Texas, Jeana qualified as an engineer and moved to

California, where she worked on commercial rockets for Project Private Enterprise. She spent 14 years in engineering design drafting and in her spare time tried sky-diving and helicopter flying before turning to fixed-wing aircraft, building up 1000 flying hours on general aviation and experimental planes, gaining several records for flight distance and speed. She met Dick Rutan at an air-show in China in 1980 and they settled in Mojave, the site of his brother Brian Rutan's aircraft factory, where *Voyager* was designed. In 1986, with Dick Rutan, she completed the first non-stop flight around the world without refuelling in the tiny *Voyager*, a feather-weight aircraft using the latest airfoil tech-nology, navigational aids and weather satellite links. The 25,012 miles took them 9 days, spent in a cabin the size of a telephone box, deafened by the engines and slammed against the walls by turbulence.

J. Yeager and D. Rutan: *Voyager: the Flying Adventure of a Lifetime* (1988)

**Yermolova, Maria Nikolaijevna** (1853–1928). Russian actress. She was the daughter of a prompter at the Maly Theatre in Moscow; she trained at a drama school and made her first appearance at the Maly in 1870 in the title role of Lessing's *Emilia Galotti*. She was unusual in her inter-pretation of tragic heroines as active and independent women rather than passive victims. Her famous roles included Judith in Gutzkov's *Uriel Acosta* (1879), Schiller's *Maria Stuart* (1886), Klarchen in Goethe's *Egmont* (1888) and Racine's *Phèdre* (1890), but she was especially remembered for her performance in Schiller's *Die Jungfrau von Orleans* (1884).

She was a woman of longstanding liberal sympathies; her performance of Lope de Vega's historical drama, *Fuenteovejuna*, about the struggle of the Spanish peasantry against oppression, which she selected for her benefit in 1876, caused so much enthusiasm that it was banned. She supported the 1917 Revolution, and in 1920 at the celebration of her 50 years on the stage she was awarded the title of People's Artist of the Republic. Two years after her death, a studio of the Maly Theatre was named after her, later becoming the well-known Yermolova Theatre. Stanislavsky called her the greatest actress he had ever known.

**Yoko,** Madam, Queen of Seneghun (*c*1849–1906). Sierra Leone leader. Madam Yoko's third husband was a powerful Mendeland chieftain, and as his head wife she became involved with local politics. A skilful diplomat, she took his place as Chief on his death in 1878. Through local alliances she developed a large confederacy and nego-tiated with the British for protection, using them in the late 1880s to destroy her final political rival, Kamanda. She then became officially described as Queen of Seneghun, and she further extended her territories after her support of the British in suppressing the Hut Tax insurrection in 1898. Madam Yoko was only one of several remarkable women rulers who owed their position to the government at this time, although she disliked missionaries and refused Christian conversion. Through political manoeuvring and continual minor warfare she continued to dominate the chiefs of the Kpa confederacy. In 1906 she was rumoured to have committed suicide because she was unable to face the weakness of old age.

**Yonge, Charlotte (Mary)** (1823–1901). English novelist. She was born in Otterbourne, near Winchester, where she lived for the rest of her life. Her father was a country gentleman and she was brought up very austerely but given a sound classical education. Greatly influenced by John Keble, who prepared her for confirmation and examined all her writing, she later became a leading apologist of the Oxford Movement, the High Church faction in the Anglican Church led by Pusey and Newman. Apart from a single trip to Paris in 1869, she remained at home for the rest of her life, involving herself in parish life and teaching at the school and Sunday school.

Always an inveterate writer, she shocked her family when she began writing for juvenile magazines in 1842 but they agreed to let her continue if all proceeds went to missionary causes. Altogether she produced over 160 titles, especially novels of upper class family life, full of self-sacrificing heroines and noble lovers. Among the most successful were *The Heir of Radclyffe* (1853), *The Daisy Chain* (1856), and the historical novels *The Prince and the Page* (1865) and *The Dove in the Eagle's Nest*. She was also an editor, biographer, historian and translator; she edited the children's journal, *The Monthly Packet*, from 1851 to 1890, (acting as assistant until 1895) and two Sunday school journals, *The Monthly Paper* (1860–75) and *Mothers in Council* (1890–1900). She firmly opposed Catholicism, feminism, socialism and other threats to Victorian decencies.

G. Battiscombe: *Charlotte Mary Yonge: an Uneventful Life* (1943)

**Yosano** [née Otori], **Akiko** (1878–1942). Japanese poet. She was born at Sakai, nr Osaka, the daughter of a confectioner. In 1900 she began sending her work to Yosano Hiroshi, the poetry editor of *Myojo* ('Morning star'). He arranged publication of her first collection of 400 poems, chiefly lyrical poems of passionate love, entitled *Midaregami* ('Tangled hair') in 1901 and they married that year. Her later work verged on the sentimental, but she was extremely influential in Japan in breaking the literary ban against women expressing their emotions in print, which had prevailed for centuries.

**Young** [née Baker], **Janet**, Baroness (1926–). English politician. The daughter of an Oxford don, she was educated in Oxford, spent four years with an American family in Yale during World War II, and returned to take a degree at St Anne's College in philosophy, politics and economics. In 1950 she married another don, Geoffrey Young, and they had three daughters. From 1957 to 1972 she was a member of Oxford City Council, an alderman and leader of the Conservative Group from 1967. She hoped to stand for Parliament but was offered a life peerage by Prime Minister Edward Heath in 1971. She became the first conservative woman to be a Whip in the House of Lords in 1972, and was Under-Secretary of State for Education (1973–4). When MARGARET THATCHER (an old friend) became Conservative leader in 1975 Baroness Young was made Vice-chairman of the Party. After the Conservative victory in 1979 she entered the Cabinet as Minister of State in the Department of Education and Science. From 1981–3 she was Leader of the House of Lords and became Minister of State for the Foreign and Commonwealth office in 1983.

**Yourcenar,    Marguerite** [pseud. of Marguerite de Crayencour] (1903–87). French-American novelist, poet, critic and translator. She was born in Brussels and her mother died a week after her birth. She was brought up by her father, a wealthy leisured scholar. Educated at home, she was reading Racine and Aristophanes at the age of eight. At 16 her father had her first volume of verse published privately, and together they made up her anagrammatic *nom de plume*. She became a Classical scholar before writing her first novel in 1929, and many of her works have classical themes, such as *La nouvelle Eurydice* (1931). She became a well-known novelist during the 1930s, but the family fortune left to her by her father was lost during World War II and at the suggestion of her friend, translator Grace Frick, she emigrated to America where she taught and lectured. She settled in Maine in 1950 and became an American citizen, although she continued to write in French. During the 1950s she published several major essays and became interested in varieties of religious experience, reflected in her *Préface à Gita-Gavinda* (1958) and her anthology of American spirituals, *Fleuve profande, sombre rivière* (1964). She achieved international stature as a novelist with *Les mémoires d'Hadrien* (1951), she wrote much of the novel in Greek to improve her identification with the character. She also translated works by VIRGINIA WOOLF and Henry James into French. In 1977 she published her *Souvenirs pieux*. Her later works included *Comme l'eau qui coule* (1982) and *Le temps, ce grand sculpteur* (1983). These were translated, as were her *Oriental Tales* (1986), and the study *Mishima: A Vision of the Void* (1987). Her last work to appear in English was *Two Lives and a Dream* (1987).

In 1980 Yourcenar became the first woman to be elected to the Académie Française in its 345 years and she was given French citizenship by presidential decree.

# Z

**Zakrzewska, Marie Elizabeth** (1829–1902). American doctor of German birth. Marie came from a Polish family and was brought up in poverty. She became assistant to the Director of the Royal Hospital Charité in Berlin (Prussia), and succeeded to his position when she was only 22; adverse criticism that she was too young for the responsibility caused her to emigrate to the USA.

Marie helped ELIZABETH BLACKWELL at her first dispensary in New York. Recognizing her ability, Elizabeth encouraged her to study medicine; she was one of the first four women to be admitted to Cleveland in 1854, and gained her MD in 1856. With the Blackwell sisters, Marie helped to run the new New York Infirmary, introducing the keeping of patients' records and taking over administration while Elizabeth Blackwell was in England.

After two years' free service, Marie left for Boston in 1859 to raise money for the Infirmary. Here she was active in causes such as setting up lunchrooms for working women and the poor, projects for Jewish people, abolition of slavery, and the rights of blacks. She became a friend of the radical Karl Heinzen. She was Professor of Obstetrics and Diseases of Women at the New England Female Medical College, but resigned when she felt unable to raise the standards, and felt the lack of a hospital for clinical work. In 1863 she founded the New England Hospital for Women and Children, the first in the USA with a school for nurses and a social service organization. From a 10-bed hospital it grew into a large organization which she headed for nearly 40 years. In 1878 she founded the New England Hospital Medical Society (the first formed by a woman), and became its President.

A.G. Vietor: *A Woman's Quest: the Life of Marie Elizabeth Zakrzewska* (1924)

**Zambelli, Carlotta** (1875–1968). Italian ballerina. She was born in Milan and studied at La Scala. She made her debut at the Paris Opéra in 1894, becoming principal dancer in 1898. She was the last foreign ballerina to appear at the Mariinsky Theatre (1901). Renowned for her brilliant technique and witty, vivacious interpretation, she created many leading roles such as in *La ronde des saisons* (1905); and her classical repertoire included an outstanding interpretation of Swanilda in *Coppélia*. After leading the Opéra company for 40 years she retired as a dancer in 1930, to direct the school. She had succeeded Rosita Mauri as teacher of the *classe de perfectionnement* in 1920, and also taught privately. Known as an energetic, severe but kindly teacher, she finally retired in 1950 after 60 years in ballet. She was the first person to enter the Légion d'Honneur for dance, being made a Chevalier in 1926 and an Officier in 1956.

I. Guest: *Carlotta Zambelli* (1969)

**Zapolska, Gabriela** [pseud. of Gabriela Kerwin-Piotrowska] (1860–1921). Polish novelist and dramatist. Born in Kiwerce, the daughter of a nobleman and a ballerina, she was educated in a convent in Lvov. After divorcing her husband in 1880, she became an actress and toured Poland. Between 1890 and 1895 she worked with Antoine's Théâtre Libre in Paris.

During the 1880s she began writing novels and short stories about the predicament of women, including *Malaszka* (1883), *Janka* (1895), *Fin-de-siècle Istka* (1897) and *Z pamiętrikow mlodej mezatki* ('Memoirs of a newly-wed-woman') (1899). Adopting French naturalistic models, she shocked contemporaries by her exposure of bourgeois hypocrisy, and treatment of subjects such as free love and prostitution. She later adapted her work to the stage; her bitingly sharp satire *Moralnosc pani Dulskiej* ('The morality of Mrs Dulska') (1907) has become a classic of Polish theatre.

**Zasulich, Vera** (1849–1919). Russian revolutionary. The youngest of three daughters of an impoverished landowner, after her father's death in 1852 she spent an unhappy childhood with various relatives. After attending a Moscow boarding school, at the age of 17 she went to St Petersburg [now Leningrad] where she worked as a clerk, becoming involved in the radical movement, running a bookbinding and weaving collective and conducting literacy classes. In 1869 she was arrested and imprisoned for five years in the Litovski fortress. In 1873 she took medical courses in Khar'kov, where she joined the Kiev insurgents and worked with the underground press. In 1878, outraged by the actions of the hated governor of St Petersburg, General Trepov, who had ordered a political prisoner to be flogged for not removing his cap in his presence, she demanded an audience, smuggled a pistol under her coat and shot him in front of a room full of petitioners. It was the first act of political violence by the conspiratorial movement. The jury refused to condemn her and she was acquitted; although the Czar ordered her re-arrest, friends smuggled her to Switzerland.

In 1879 she returned to Russia and joined The Black Repartition, the propagandist rather than activist wing. In 1880 she was sent back to Switzerland, whjere she was co-founder of the Emancipation of Labour group in 1883. She spent the next 20 years writing and translating. She later joined the Russian Social Democratic Labour Party and in 1905 returned to Russia where she worked as a translator.

**Zauditu (Judith)** (1876–1930). Ethiopian empress. The daughter of Menelik II, she was a child bride, but her first husband Aria Selassi died in 1888 and after the death of her second husband she married Ras Gugsa Wolie in 1902. He was the nephew of her step-mother, Taitu, who dominated the court from 1906 until Menelik's death in 1913 and who then supported Zauditu's claim to the throne. However, Zauditu did not succeed until the death of Menelik's grandson Iyasu V in 1916, and then only on condition that she renounce Gugsa Wolie, and authority was virtually handed over to the young Ras Tafari Makonnen (Haile Selassi). In February 1917 she was crowned Empress in Addis Ababa.

She reigned until 1928 when, despite her attempts to raise a protective force, Haile Selassi staged a successful coup. In 1930 her husband tried to lead a revolt in the northern provinces and Zauditu collapsed and died on learning the news of his capture and execution. Rumours surround her death, which was variously attributed to diabetes, severe mental stress and a broken heart. 25 years later Haile Selassi's new constitution debarred women from being independent monarchs.

**Zayas y Sofomayor, María de** (1590–c1660). Spanish novelist. Born in Madrid, she lived in Saragossa, and became famous with two collections of novels *Novelas amorosas y exemplares* (1637) and *Parle segunda des sarao y entretenimientos honestos* (1674). The first all have happy, the second tragic, endings, and form a sequence linked by the device of entertaining an elderly woman. Her style is marked by a love of sensation, melodrama and horror, but she defended women against the charges of inferiority and argued for their right to education. A noted scholar, she was also an admired poet and playwright.

**Zell [née Schutz], Katharine** (1497–1562). German Protestant. She lived in Strasbourg where she married a priest, Matthew Zell, in 1527. He was excommunicated because of the marriage (which was forbidden by the Roman Catholic Church) and Katharine spoke publicly in his defence, although reminded of St Paul's order that women should be silent in church. An energetic and spirited woman, she visited the sick and the imprisoned, gave shelter to Protestant refugees and took part in the affairs of the town. She also edited a small religious songbook in 1534 and wrote letters which were circulated within the Protestant community.

**Zeng Xiaoying** (1929–). Chinese conductor. She began performing in public when she was 14. She studied medicine at Jinling

Girls' College, Nanking, where she joined a revolutionary studies group opposed to the Kuomintang government. In 1948 she gave up her studies, moved to communist-liberated areas and spent four years in a song-and-dance troupe, teaching theory of music, conducting classes and orchestras and composing folksongs and operettas. In 1952 she was chosen to study at the Central Conservatory of Music and then sent to the Moscow Conservatory. She returned to lecture, teach and conduct, soon becoming nationally recognized. In 1977 she became principal conductor at the Central Opera Theatre, Beijing [Peking]. She is the first woman to become a conductor in China.

**Zenobia (Septimia)** [Bat Zabbai] (*d* 274). Syrian queen. Of Arabian descent, she married Odenathus, who ruled Palmyra under Roman protection. After his death and that of his heir, her stepson Herodes, both of which she was suspected of engineering (*c*268), she took power in the name of her son Vaballathus [Wahballat], called herself Queen of Palmyra and defeated a Roman army sent against her. Zenobia went on to capture Egypt in 269, then Asia Minor (270), and declared her independence, calling her son Augustus. In 271 the Emperor Aurelian retaliated and defeated her armies at Antioch and Emesa. Zenobia and her son were taken prisoner in 272 and after a brief truce were recaptured the following year. They were exhibited in Aurelian's triumphal procession in Rome in 274, but Zenobia was granted a pension and a villa at Tibur and apparently married a Roman senator. She became a figure of legend, because of her beauty and her ruthless ambition, both in Roman and in Arabic tradition.

G.H. Macurdy: *Vassal Queens in the Roman Empire* (1937)

**Zetkin** [née Eissner], **Clara** (1857–1933). German Communist leader and feminist. Born in Wiederau, she was the daughter of a village schoolteacher and was one of the first women to train as a teacher at the Leipzig Teacher's College for Women, run by the feminist AUGUSTE SCHMIDT. There she became a socialist, joining the new German Social Democratic Party in 1881, and met foreign revolutionaries, including the

Russian Ossip Zetkin, whom she married in Paris in 1882. They had two children and lived in Paris and Switzerland, mixing with international socialist leaders including Lenin. Clara became increasingly concerned about the legal rights of women and children. In 1889 she returned to Germany as one of the few women delegates to the Second Socialist International and she organized a social democratic women's movement, speaking throughout the country. From 1892 until 1916 she edited the paper *Gleichheit* ('Equality'). In 1907 she was a founder of the International Socialist Women's Congress.

With ROSA LUXEMBURG and Liebknecht she was one of the few Social Democrats to oppose World War I. In 1914 Clara was gaoled as a pacifist but she helped to organize the peace conference in Berne in 1915, and in 1916 to form the Spartacus League, then the Independent Social Democratic Party (1917). After the Russian Revolution she was one of the founders of the German Communist Party (1918). After Rosa's death Clara continued the struggle. In 1921 she became a member of the Executive Committee of the Communist International and also headed the International Women's Secretariat. She served as a Communist member of the Reichstag from 1920 to 1932, although she spent many of these years in the USSR. She presided over the Reichstag's last opening in 1932 before its destruction by fire.

Her reminiscences of Lenin, a lifelong friend, were published in 1929. She spent her last years in the USSR and died in a clinic there, but she never lost influence in Germany, where she continued to fight against persecution of the Left. Clara Zetkin was a fine Marxist theoretician as well as a polemical writer and activist. As a feminist, however, she believed that the participation of women in the labour force and legal equality would automatically lead to their political and social emancipation.

**Zetterling, Mai** (1925–). Swedish film director and actress. She trained at the Royal Dramatic Theatre School in Stockholm and made her stage debut and first film at the age of 16. Her performance in Alf Sjöberg's *Hets/Torment* (USA)/*Frenzy* (UK) in 1944 attracted considerable attention. She made a contract with Rank and made her first British film, *Frieda*, in 1946. She worked both in films and in the theatre in the UK, Sweden and the USA, including a leading role in Ingmar Bergman's *Musik i Mörker/Night is my Future* (1947). In the early 1960s she directed four documentary films for BBC television. In 1963 she made *The War Game*, which she wrote with her husband, David Hughes, winning first prize at the Venice Film Festival. She returned to Sweden to direct her next four films, *Loving Couples* (1964), *Night Games* (1965), *Doktor Glas* (1967) and *The Girls* (1968). Her subsequent work included *Vincent the Dutchman* (1972), and *Visions of Eight*, a documentary about weight lifting in the official film of the 1972 Munich Olympic Games and several other films, such as *Scrubbers* (1983) and *Amorosa* (1986). Mai Zetterling has also written a number of novels.

M. Zetterling: *All Those Tomorrows* (1985)

**Zhang Jie** (1937–). Chinese writer. The daughter of a teacher, Zhang was born in Beijing, and as a child loved fairy tales and fables, especially the European stories of the Grimm brothers and Hans Christian Andersen. She studied economics at the People's University, 1956–60, and worked for a State Bureau before transferring to the Beijing Film Studio as a scriptwriter. In 1978 her short story *The Music of the Forests* won a major prize: she continued to work at the Film Studio as an editor and director but became increasingly well known for her fiction, including the novel *Leaden Winds* (1981) which was officially named the most popular novel in China. She has also written a short novel, *The Ark*, and many short stories. In 1985 she became a member of the Secretariat of the Writers' Association, and was also appointed vice-chair of the Commission for the Protection of Writers' Legal Rights and Welfare. In 1987 a collection of her stories was published in translation, *As Long as Nothing Happens, Nothing Will*.

**Zhang Ruifang** (1918–). Chinese film actress. Zhang Ruifang began acting at the age of 19 when she was a student in Beijing. After the outbreak of the Chinese-Japanese War, she joined a student drama troupe and in 1938 became a member of the Communist Party.

During the next decade, in Chonqing, she created many roles which led to her becoming China's most popular actress, and from 1949 to 1966 she starred in numerous feature films including the famous comedy *Li Shuang-shuang* in the early 1960s. In 1957 she was a delegate to the Afro-Asian Solidarity Conference in Cairo, and also visited Japan. In 1967, she was branded as one of the 'black line people' and imprisoned for two years. After the change of policy in 1973, she was elected a member of the National Committee and returned to the screen, as the heroine of *The Roaring River*. By 1980 she had become head of the Shanghai Drama Troupe and in 1982 headed the delegation to the First Manila Film Festival, and represented China at the New Youth International Film Festival in India the following year. In 1985, her reputation still at its height, she was elected vice-chair of the Shanghai Branch of the Chinese Communist Party.

**Zhirkova, Lyudmila** (1944–81). Bulgarian politician. One of the most prominent women in the Soviet bloc, she was the daughter of the Bulgarian President Toder Zhirkov, who had been party leader since 1954. She studied history at Sofia University and then spent a year at St Anthony's College, Oxford, writing her thesis on British policy in the Balkans before World War I. In 1971, aged 27, she was elected to the Bulgarian Committee of Arts and Culture, becoming Chairman in 1975, a post of ministerial rank. She sponsored a huge cultural centre in Sofia and promoted the belief in 'New Socialist Man', her personal philosophy combining Marxism with elements of European and oriental thought. She also acted as First Lady after her mother's death in 1971, accompanying Zhirkov on most foreign visits, and she became a member of the Party Politburo in 1979. Her position and influence before her early death were compared to those of ELENA CEAUSESCU.

**Zubaidah** (*d* 831). Arabian queen. The grandaughter of the famous Caliph of Baghdad, al-Mansūr, she married her cousin Harūn al-Rashīd. Harūn's court became legendary for its luxury (it was said Zubaidah would have table-ware only of gold and silver encrusted with jewels), and for his intrigues and affairs; it is described in many stories in *The Thousand and One Nights* which present the queen as forceful and glamorous. Zubaidah herself was a noted patron of poetry and music. Harūn al-Rashīd ruled from 786 to 809. After some years she had a son, al-Amīn, whom she brought up closely with his step-brother, Harūn's child by a Persian slave. After her husband died civil war broke out between the two sons and although Zubaidah tried to mediate, al-Amīn was killed escaping from besieged Baghdad. Zubaidah's refusal to take revenge, and her generosity to her stepson and his young wife Burān ushered in a period of peace. She herself lived in retirement and her last public appearance was her sixth pilgrimage to Mecca. She is famous not only for the building-work and gardens she commissioned in Baghdad, but also for her improvement of the wells and water supply on the 900-mile route from Iraq to Mecca. Several cities were named Zubaidiyah after her.

**Zucchi, Virginia** (1849–1930). Italian ballerina. She was born in Parma. She

studied in Milan and began her career in 1884 touring minor Italian theatres. Her performance in Padua in 1873 led to her engagement at La Scala in 1874 where she starred in Manzetti's *Rolla* (1875) and the opera *La gioconda* (1876). She then appeared in Berlin in *La fille mal gardée* and at Covent Garden, London.

In 1885 Zucchi went to St Petersburg [now Leningrad] as visiting ballerina at the Livadia summer theatre and was received so enthusiastically that she was engaged by the Imperial Theatre, making a sensational debut in *Fille de Pharaon*. She paid repeated visits to Russia over the next seven years, dancing in Moscow as well as St Petersburg, and establishing the powerful Italian influence over Russian ballet. A virtuoso technician, she became famous for her passionate interpretation of Petipa's work. In 1889 she returned to France, appearing in Nice, Monte Carlo (1893–6) and occasionally in Milan. She opened a school in Monte Carlo, where she taught until her death; she died in Nice.

I. Guest: *The Divine Virginia* (1977)

# SUBJECT INDEX

The following index has been arranged by subject and includes all of the women on whom entries appear in the *Dictionary*. In each of the four subject areas there are further divisions into primary fields within that area and in some instances a further subdivision has been made. Entries are arranged alphabetically by surname and each entry includes the date(s) of birth (and death) as well as the country/place of the woman's major activity during her lifetime. In some instances where a woman has been active in more than one area, her name will appear more than once, under the relevant headings.

## SUBJECT INDEX CATEGORIES

### A. PUBLIC LIFE

1. **Politics: establishment and opposition**
   1. Royalty
   2. Pre-20th century: the politics of influence, court, aristocracy
   3. 20th century: elected politicians, diplomats, civil servants
   4. Revolutionaries, radicals, nationalists

2. **Religion**

3. **Social reform**
   1. Education
   2. Health care: medicine, nursing, birth control, psychoanalysis
   3. Welfare and philanthropy
   4. Organized labour and unions
   5. Minority rights, abolitionists, pressure groups

4. **Other professions and occupations**
   1. Finance, commerce and industry
   2. Law
   3. Architecture and planning
   4. Communications: journalism, publishing, broadcasting

5. **Women's rights**

### B. CULTURAL LIFE

1. **Scholarship and research**
   1. Humanities and social sciences
   2. Mathematics, pure and applied sciences, medicine

2. **Arts and entertainment**
   1. Cinema
   2. Dance
   3. Literature
   4. Music
   5. Photography
   6. Theatre and music hall
   7. Visual arts
   8. Other: salon hostesses and patrons

3. **Domestic arts, fashion and cosmetics**

# C. PHYSICAL ACHIEVEMENTS

1. Competitive sport

2. Exploration and travel

3. Other pioneering exploits

# D. DYNAMIC CHARACTERS

1. National heroines

2. Soldiers and spies

3. Frontierswomen and pioneers

4. Beauties, lovers and society leaders

5. Occult practitioners, witches and mediums

6. Criminals: pirates, pickpockets and poisoners

## A. PUBLIC LIFE

### 1. Politics: establishment and opposition

*A1.1 Royalty*
Adelaide (931–99; Holy Roman Empire)
Aelgifu (*c*1010–40; England/Denmark/Norway)
Aethelflaed (*d* 918; Mercia)
Agnes of Courtenay (*c*1136–*c*1186; Palestine)
Agnes of Poitou (1024–77; Holy Roman Empire)
Agrippina I (14 BC–33 AD; Rome)
Agrippina II (15–59 AD; Rome)
Al-Khaizurān (*d* 790; Arabia)
Amina (1560–1610; Nigeria)
'Anastasia' (1901–84; USSR)
Anne (1665–1714; England)
Anne, Princess Royal (1950–; UK)
Anne of Austria (1601–66; France)
Anne of Brittany (1477–1514; Brittany/France)
Arwā (1052–1137; Yemen)
Asmā (*c*1028–84; Yemen)
Athaliah (*d* 837 BC; Judah)
Balthild (*c*630–80; France)
Beatrix (1938–; Netherlands)
Berenice II (*d* 80 BC; Egypt)
Blanche of Castile (1188–1252; France)
Boleyn, Anne (1507–36; England)
Boudicca (*d* 62; England)
Brunhilda (*d* 613; Austrasia/Burgundy)
Catherine II (1729–96; Russia)
Catherine of Aragon (1485–1536; Spain/England)
Cleopatra VII (69–30 BC; Egypt)
Clotilda (470–545; Frankish kingdom)
Corner, Caterina (1454–1510; Cyprus/Venice)
Cynethryth (*fl* 8th century; Mercia)
d'Albret, Jeanne (1528–72; Navarre)
d'Este, Isabella (1474–1539; Mantua)
Diana, Princess of Wales (1961–; UK)
Diane of France (1538–1619; France)

Dido (*fl c*800 BC; Carthage)
Drummond, Annabella (*c*1350–1402; Scotland)
Eadburgh (*fl* 800; Wessex/Frankish kingdom)
Eleanor of Aquitaine (1122–1202; France/England)
Elisabeth of Romania (1843–1916; Romania)
Elizabeth, Queen Mother (1900–; UK)
Elizabeth I (1533–1603; England/Ireland)
Elizabeth II (1926–; UK)
Elizabeth of Portugal (1271–1336; Portugal)
Elizabeth of Russia (1709–62; Russia)
Eugénie (1826–1920; France)
Faustina, Anna Galeria (*c*125–76; Rome)
Fredegund (*d* 597; Neustria)
Galla Placidia (?390–450; Rome)
Gauhar Shad (*c*1378–1459; Persia/Afghanistan)
Giovanna I (1326–82; Naples)
Grace (Kelly), Princess of Monaco (1929–82; USA/Monaco)
Hatshepsut (1503–1482 BC; Egypt)
'Iffat (1910–; Saudi Arabia)
Irene of Athens (*fl* 8th century; Byzantine empire)
Isabella I (1451–1504; Spain)
Jadwiga (1374–99; Poland)
Jezebel (*c*9th century BC)
Julia Domna (*d* AD 217; Rome)
Julia Maesa (*d c*226; Rome)
Juliana (1909–; Netherlands)
Livia, Drusilla (*c*55 BC–29 AD; Rome)
Louise of Savoy (1476–1531; France)
Margaret (1353–1412; Denmark/Norway/Sweden)
Margaret of Anjou (1430–82; France/England)
Margrethe II (1940–; Denmark)
Maria Theresa (1717–80; Austria)
Marie Antoinette (1755–93; France)
Mary, Queen of Scots (1542–87; France/Scotland/England)
Mary I (1516–58; England)
Mary II (1662–94; England/Holland)
Matilda (1046–1115; Tuscany)
Medici, Catherine de (1519–89; Florence/France)
Médicis, Marie de (1573–1642; France)

## A1.4  Revolutionaries, radicals, nationalists

## 2.  Religion

Clare of Assisi (c1194–1253; Assisi)
Deborah (fl 12thc BC; Israel)
de Marillac, Louise (1591–1660; France)
Eddy, Mary Baker (1821–1910; USA)
Elizabeth of Hungary (1207–31; Hungary)
Estaugh, Elizabeth (c1680–1762; New Jersey)
Fatimah (c606–632; Arabia)
Fell, Margaret (1614–1702; England)
Gertrud von Helfta (1256–1302; Saxony)
Guyard, Marie (1599–1672; France/Canada)
Guyon, Jeanne Marie (1648–1717; France)
Hadewijch (fl late 12th or early 13th century; Brabant)
Héloïse (1101–64; France)
Herrade of Landsburg (d 1195; Alsace)
Hilda of Whitby (616–80; Durham/Whitby)
Hildegarde of Bingen (1098–1178; Bingen)
Hrotsvitha of Gandersheim (c935–72; Saxony)
Huntingdon, Selina (1707–91; England)
Hutchinson, Anne (1591–1643; New England)
Joan (d858; Rome)
Julian of Norwich (1342–1443; England)
Kempe, Margery (c1373–after 1438; England)
Khadijah (c564–619; Arabia)
Lal-Ded (fl late 14th century; India)
Lee, 'Mother' Ann (1736–84; USA)
Lioba (d782; Wessex/Frankish kingdom)
McLaren, Agnes (1837–1913; UK/France)
McPherson, Aimée Semple (1890–1944; USA)
Martin, Emma (1812–51; UK)
Mary (1st century BC–1st century AD; Palestine)
Mechtild of Magdeburg (1210–82; Saxony)
Neuman, Theresa (1898–1962; Austria)
Olga (890–969; Russia)
Pulcheria (399–453; Byzantine empire)
Rābi'ah al-'Adawiyyah (712–801; Arabia)
Radegund (518–87; Frankish kingdom)
Royden, Maude (1876–1956; UK)
Seton, Elizabeth Ann (1774–1821; USA)
Shaw, Anna (1847–1919; USA)
Slessor, Mary (1848–1919; West Africa)
Southcott, Joanna (1750–1814; UK)
Stein, Edith (1891–1942; Poland)
Teresa, Mother (1910–; India)
Teresa of Ávila (1515–82; Spain)
Teresa of Lisieux (1873–97; France)
Underhill, Evelyn (1875–1941; UK)
Ward, Mary (1585–1645; England)
Weil, Simone (1903–43; France)
Zell, Katharine (1497–1562; Strasbourg)

# 3. Social reform

## A3.1.  Education

Ashton-Warner, Sylvia (1905–84; New Zealand)
Astell, Mary (1668–1731; England)
Barbauld, Anna Letitia Aikin (1743–1825; UK)
Beale, Dorothea (1831–1906; UK)
Beecher, Catharine (1800–78; USA)
Bethune, Mary McCleod (1875–1955; USA)
Blow, Susan (1843–1916; USA)
Bose Abala (1865–1951; India)
Buss, Frances Mary (1827–94; UK)
Chapone, Hester (1727–1801; England)
Clough, Anne Jemima (1820–92; UK)
Cousins, Margaret (1878–1954; UK/India)

Dalrymple, Learmonth White (1827–1906; New Zealand)
Davies, Emily (1830–1921; UK)
de Maintenon, Françoise (1635–1719; France)
Edgeworth, Maria (1767–1849; UK)
Hani, Motoko (1873–1957; Japan)
Hollingworth, Leta (1886–1939; USA)
Isaacs, Susan (1885–1948; UK)
Kairi, Evanthia (1797–1866; Greece)
Kartini, Adjeng (1879–1904; Java)
Kehajia, Kalliopi (1839–1905; Greece)
Laskaridou, Aikaterini (1842–1916; Greece)
McMillan, Margaret (1860–1931; UK)
Makin, Bathshua (1608–75; England)
Montessori, Maria (1870–1952; Italy)
More, Hannah (1745–1835; UK)
Peabody, Elizabeth Palmer (1804–94; USA)
Rau, Dhanvanthi Rama (1893–1987; India)
Sartain, Emily (1841–1927; USA)
Schmidt, Auguste (1833–1902; Germany)
Sheepshanks, Mary (1872–1958; UK)
Smith, Sophia (1796–1870; USA)
Stocks, Mary (1891–1975; UK)
Thomas, Martha Carey (1857–1935; USA)
Trimmer, Sarah (1741–1810; England)
Trubnikova, Mariya (1835–97; Russia)
Warnock, Mary (1924–; UK)
Willard, Emma (1787–1870; USA)

## A3.2.  Health care: medicine, nursing, birth control, psychoanalysis

Anderson, Elizabeth Garrett (1836–1917; UK)
André, Valérie (1922–; France/Vietnam)
Andreas-Salomé, Lou (1861–1937; Russia/Germany)
Baker, Josephine (i) (1873–1945; USA)
Barnes, Josephine (1912–; UK)
Barton, Clara (1821–1912; USA)
Besant, Annie (1847–1933; UK/India)
Blackwell, Elizabeth (1821–1910; UK/USA)
Blackwell, Emily (1826–1910; UK/USA)
Boivin, Marie (1773–1847; France)
Bourgeois, Louyse (1563–1636; France)
Cavell, Edith (1865–1915; UK/Belgium)
Cellier, Elizabeth (fl 1680s; England)
Clark, Hilda (1881–1955; UK)
Clisby, Harriet (1830–1931; Australia)
Deutsch, Helene (1884–1982; Poland/USA)
Dix, Dorothea (1802–87; USA)
du Coudray, Angélique (1712–89; France)
Durocher, Marie (1809–93; France/Brazil)
Erxleben, Dorothea (1715–62; Prussia)
Fabiola (?d 399; Rome)
Fenwick, Ethel (1857–1947; UK)
Fleming, Amalia (1909?–86; Greece/UK)
Fowler, Lydia Folger (1822–79; USA/UK)
Freud, Anna (1895–1982; Austria/UK)
Hamilton, Alice (1869–1970; USA)
Hobbs, Lucy (1833–c1900; USA)
Horney, Karen (1885–1952; Germany/USA)
Hugonnai-Wartha, Vilma (1847–1922; Hungary)
Hunt, Harriot (1805–75; USA)
Inglis, Elsie (1864–1917; UK)
Jacobi, Mary Putnam (1842–1906; USA)
Jacobs, Aletta (1851–1929; Netherlands)
Jex-Blake, Sophia (1840–1912; UK)
Kendrick, Pearl Luella (1890–1980; USA)
Kitzinger, Sheila (1929–; UK/USA)

Klein, Melaine (1882–1960; Austria/UK)
Lachapelle, Marie (1769–1821; France)
McLaren, Agnes (1837–1913; UK/France)
Milner, Marion (1900–; UK)
Murray, Lilian (1871–1959; UK)
Murrell, Christine (1874–1933; UK)
Nayar, Shushila (1914–; India)
Necker, Suzanne (1739–1817; Switzerland/France)
Nightingale, Florence (1820–1910; UK/Crimea)
Payne, Sylvia (1880–1974; UK)
Pechey-Phipson, Edith (1845–1908; UK)
Preston, Anne (1813–72; USA)
Pye, Edith (1876–1965; UK, Europe)
Pyke, Margaret (1893–1966; UK)
Ramphele, Mamphela (1948–; South Africa)
Russell, Dora (1894–1986; UK)
Russell, Dorothy (1895–1983; UK)
Sabin, Florence (1871–1953; USA)
Sanger, Margaret (1883–1966; USA)
Scharlieb, Mary (1845–1930; UK/India)
Schrader, Catharina Geertuida (1656–1745; Netherlands)
Scudder, Ida (1870–1960; USA/India)
Seacole, Mary (1805–81; Jamaica)
Shabanova, Anna (1848–1932; USSR)
Siebold, Charlotte Heidenreich von (1788–1859; Hesse-
    Darmstadt)
Siebold, Josepha von (1771–1849; Hesse-Darmstadt)
Stopes, Marie (1880–1958; UK)
Stowe, Emily (1831–1903; Canada)
Stuart, Miranda (?1795–1865; UK/Canada)
Taussig, Helen Brooke (1898–; USA)
Thompson, Mary Harris (1829–95; USA)
Tomaszewicz-Dobrska, Anna (1854–1918; Poland)
Trotula (fl 11th century; Salerno)
Vaughan, Janet (1899–; UK)
Wald, Lillian D. (1867–1940; USA)
Walker, Mary Edwards (1832–1919; USA)
Williams, Cicely (1893–; UK/Gold Coast/Malaya)
Wright, Helena (1888–1982; UK)
Zakrzewska, Marie (1829–1902; Prussia/USA)

## A3.3  Welfare and philanthropy

Abbott, Edith (1876–1957; USA)
Addams, Jane (1860–1935; USA)
Arenal, Concepción (1820–93; Spain)
Baden-Powell, Olave (1889–1977; UK)
Black, Clementina (1853–1922; UK)
Burdett-Coutts, Angela (1814–1906; UK)
Butler, Josephine (1828–1906; UK)
Carpenter, Mary (1807–77; UK)
Chattopadhyay, Kamaladevi (1903–; India)
Chisholm, Caroline (1808–77; UK/Australia)
Cons, Emma (1838–1912; UK)
Day, Dorothy (1897–1980; USA)
Denman, Gertrude (1884–1954; UK)
Dix, Dorothea (1802–87; USA)
Dodge, Grace (1856–1914; USA)
Franklin, Jane (1791–1875; UK/Tasmania)
Fry, Elizabeth (1780–1845; UK)
Fry, Margery (1874–1958; UK)
Goldmark, Josephine (1877–1950; USA)
Hill, Octavia (1838–1912; UK)
Hoodless, Adelaide (1857–1910; Australia)
Jebb, Eglantyne (1876–1928; UK)
Keller, Helen (1880–1968; USA)
Kelley, Florence (1859–1932; USA)
Lathrop, Julia (1858–1932; USA)
Loeb, Sophie Irene (1876–1929; USA)

Lowell, Josephine Shaw (1843–1905; USA)
Nation, Carry (1846–1911; USA)
Pizzey, Erin (1939–; UK)
Pye, Edith (1876–1965; UK/Europe)
Reading, Stella (1894–1971; UK)
Roosevelt, Eleanor (1884–1962; USA)
Ryder, Sue (1923–; UK)
Rye, Maria (1829–1903; UK)
Sheepshanks, Mary (1872–1958; UK/Europe)
Solomon, Flora (1895–1984; USSR/UK)
Spence, Catherine (1825–1910; Australia)
Szold, Henrietta (1860–1945; USA/Palestine)
Te Puea, Princess (1884–1952; New Zealand)
Twining, Louisa (1820–1912; UK)
Willard, Frances (1839–98; USA)
Wootton, Barbara (1897–1988; UK)
Wright, Frances (1795–1852; UK/USA)

## A3.4  Organized labour and unions

Ahern, Lizzie (1877–1969; Australia)
Anderson, Mary (ii) (1872–1964; USA)
Bennett, Louie (1870–1956; UK/Republic of Ireland)
Besant, Annie (1847–1933; UK/India)
Black, Clementina (1854–1922; UK)
Bondfield, Margaret (1873–1953; UK)
Cole, Margaret (1893–1980; UK)
Davies, Margaret (1861–1944; UK)
Day, Dorothy (1897–1980; USA)
Dean, Brenda (1943–; UK)
Dilke, Emily (1840–1904; UK)
Flynn, Elizabeth Gurley (1890–1964; USA)
Goldman, Emma (1869–1940; Russia/USA)
Goldmark, Josephine (1877–1950; USA)
Hamilton, Alice (1869–1970; USA)
Hancock, Florence (1893–1974; UK)
Hicks, Amie (1839 or 1840–1917; UK)
Jones, Mary (1830–1930; USA)
Kehew, Mary Morton (1859–1918; USA)
Kelley, Florence (1859–1932; USA)
Kenney, Annie (1879–1953; UK)
Kuliscioff, Anna (1854–1925; Russia/Italy)
Lathrop, Julia (1858–1932; USA)
Lease, Mary (1850–1933; USA)
Lee, Jennie (1904–; UK)
Loughlin, Anne (1894–1979; UK)
Luxemburg, Rosa (1870–1919; Poland/Germany)
MacArthur, Mary (1880–1921; UK)
Martindale, Hilda (1875–1952; UK)
Marx-Aveling, Eleanor (1856–1908; UK)
Mink, Paule (1839–1900; France)
Molony, Helena (1884–1967; Republic of Ireland)
Morison, Harriet (1862–1925; New Zealand)
Mozzoni, Anna Maria (1837–1920; Italy)
Noce, Teresa (1900–; Italy)
Pankhurst, Adela Constantia (1885–1961; UK/Australia)
Pankhurst, Sylvia (1882–1960; UK/Ethiopia)
Paterson, Emma (1848–86; UK)
Patterson, Marie (1934–; UK)
Pedersen, Helga (1911–; Denmark)
Phillips, Marion (1881–1932; UK)
Popp, Adelheid (1869–1939; Austria)
Robins, Margaret Dreier (1868–1945; USA)
Samoilova, Konkordiya (1876–1921; USSR)
Sarabhai, Anusyabehn (1885–1972; India)
Schneiderman, Rose (1882–1972; USA)
Stewart, Ella Winter (1898–1980; USA/UK)
Strong, Anna (1885–1970; USA/USSR/China)
Tennant, May (1869–1946; UK)

Tuckwell, Gertrude (1861–1951; UK)
Valette, Aline (1850–99; France)
Warwick, Daisy (1861–1938; UK)
Webb, Beatrice (1858–1943; UK)
Webb, Catherine (1859–1947; UK)
Wilkinson, Ellen (1891–1947; UK)
Wright, Frances (1795–1852; UK/USA)
Zetkin, Clara (1857–1933; Germany)

*A3.5 Minority rights, abolitionists, pressure groups*

Bates, Daisy (1861–1951; Australia)
Bethune, Mary McCleod (1875–1955; USA)
Bonner, Yelena (1923–; USSR)
Brant, Molly (1736–96; USA)
Caldicott, Helen (1938–; Australia)
Carson, Rachel (1907–64; USA)
Chapman, Maria (1806–85; USA)
Child, Lydia Maria (1802–80; USA)
Chisholm Shirley (1924–; USA)
Clark, Hilda (1881–1955; UK)
Corrigan, Mairead (1944–; N. Ireland)
First, Ruth (1925–82; South Africa)
Fleming, Amalia (1909?–86; Greece/UK)
Grimké, Angelina Emily (1805–79; USA)
Grimké, Sarah Moore (1792–1873; USA)
Hamer, Fannie (1918–77; USA)
Harper, Frances (1825–1911; USA)
Hurston, Zora Neale (1901–60; USA)
Jackson, Helen Hunt (1830–85; USA)
Jacobs, Aletta (1851–1929; Netherlands)
King, Coretta Scott (1922–; USA)
Menchu, Rigoberta (1951 ; Guatemala)
Mott, Lucretia (1793–1880; USA)
Rame, Franca (1929–; Italy)
Roberts, Eirlys (1911–; UK)
Ruffin, Josephine (1842–1924; USA)
Schwimmer, Rosika (1877–1948; Hungary)
Stowe, Harriet Beecher (1811–96; USA)
Swanwick, Helena (1864–1939; UK)
Szold, Henrietta (1860–1945; USA/Palestine)
Te Puea (1884–1952; New Zealand)
Tibbles, Susette (1854–1903; USA)
Truth, Sojourner (1777–1883; USA)
Tubman, Harriet Ross (1821–1913; USA)
von Suttner, Bertha Felicie Sophie (1843–1914; Austria)
Ward, Barbara (1914–81; UK)
Wells-Barnett, Ida B. (1862–1931; USA)
Williams, Betty (1943–; Northern Ireland)
Winnemucca, Sarah (1844–91; USA)

## 4. Other professions and occupations

*A4.1 Finance, commerce and industry*

Arden, Elizabeth (c1884–1966; Canada/USA)
Ashley, Laura (1925–85; UK)
Ayer, Harriet Hubbard (1849–1903; USA)
Bateman, Hester (1709–94; England)
Benetton, Giuliana (1938–; Italy)
Burdett-Coutts, Angela (1814–1906; UK)
Chanel, Coco (c1883–1971; France)
Danieli, Cecilia (1943–; USA)
Follett, Mary (1868–1933; USA)
Green, Hetty (1834–1916; USA)
Hurst, Margery (1914–; UK)
Lansing, Sherry (1944–; USA)
Lauder, Estee (1908–; USA)

Lawrence, Mary (1928–; USA)
Lukens, Rebecca Webb (1794–1854; USA)
Macarthur, Elizabeth (1767–1850; Australia)
Okwei, Omu (1872–1943; Nigeria)
Pinckney, Eliza (1723–93; USA)
Pinkham, Lydia E. (1819–83; USA)
Quant, Mary (1934–; UK)
Ratia, Armi (1912–79; Finland)
Reibey, Mary (1777–1855; Australia)
Rosenberg, Anna (1902–83; USA)
Rubinstein, Helena (1882–1965; Australia/UK/France/ USA)
Rudkin, Margaret (1897–1967; USA)
Schiaparelli, Elsa (1890–1973; USA/France)
Topham, Mirabel (?–1980; UK)
Tussaud, Marie (1761–1850; Switzerland/France/UK)
Walker, Sarah Breedlove (1867–1919; USA)
Wallace, Lila Acheson (1889–1984; USA)
Woodhull, Victoria (1838–1927; USA/UK)

*A4.2 Law*

Abiertas, Josepha (1894–1929)
Abzug, Bella (1920–; USA)
Alakija, Aduke (1921–; Nigeria)
Benjamin, Hilde (1902–; GDR)
Bradwell, Myra (1831–94; USA)
Butler-Sloss, Elizabeth (1923–; UK)
d'Andrea, Novella (*d* 1333; Italy)
Gerin-Lajoie, Marie (1867–1945; Canada)
Halimi, Gisèle (1927–; France)
Harris, Patricia (1924–85; USA)
Heilbron, Rose (1914–; UK)
Lane, Elizabeth (1905–; UK)
McGill, Helen (1871–1947; Canada)
Mentschikoff, Soia (1915–84; USA)
Murphy, Emily (1886–1933; Canada)
Mussey, Ellen Spencer (1850–1936; USA)
Normanton, Helena (1883–1957; UK)
O'Connor, Sandra (1930–; USA)
Pedersen, Helga (1911–; Denmark)
Rāteb, Aisha (1928–; Egypt)
Sipilä, Helvi (1915–; Finland)
Sorabji, Cornelia (1866–1954; India)
Veil, Simone (1927–; France)
Wootton, Barbara (1897–1988; UK)

*A4.3 Architecture, planning*

Antonakakis, Suzana (1935–; Greece)
Aulenti, Gae (1927–; Italy)
Bethune, Louise (1856–1913; USA)
Clifford, Anne (1590–1676; England/Wales)
Colvin, Brenda (1897–1981; UK)
Crowe, Sylvia (1901–; UK)
Drew, Jane (1911–; UK)
Gray, Eileen (1879–1976; UK)
Loughlin, Anne (1894–1979; UK)
Scott, Elizabeth Whitworth (1898–1972; UK)
Scott-Brown, Denise (1931–; USA)
Smithson, Alison (1928–; UK)
Syrkius, Helena (1900–82; Poland)
Vecsei, Eva (1930–; Canada)

*A4.4 Communications: journalism, publishing, broadcasting*

Beach, Sylvia (1887–1962; USA/France)
Bourke-White, Margaret (1904–71; USA)

Brown, Helen Gurley (1927–; USA)
Callil, Carmen (1938–; Australia/UK)
Child, Lydia Maria (1802–80; USA)
Cobbe, Frances Power (1822–1904; UK)
Conran, Shirley (1932–; UK)
Eisner, Lotte (1896–1983; Germany)
Faithful, Emily (1835–95; UK)
Fallaci, Oriana (1930–; Italy)
Frederick, Pauline (c1920–; USA)
Giroud, Françoise (1916–; France)
Gordon-Lazareff, Hélène (1909–88; France)
Graham, Katharine (1917–; USA)
Hale, Sarah Josepha (1788–1879; USA)
Hopper, Hedda (1890–1966; USA)
Lejeune C.A. (1897–1973; UK)
Linton, Eliza Lynn (1822–98; UK)
Martineau, Harriet (1802–76; UK)
Mitford, Jessica (1917–; UK/USA)
Morris, Jan (1926–; UK)
Parturier, Françoise (1919–; France)
Rhondda, Margaret (1883–1958; UK)
Saarinen, Aline (1914–72; USA)
Seaman, Elizabeth (1867–1922; USA)
Séverine (1855–1929; France)
Sheridan, Clare (1885–1970; Republic of Ireland)
Sontag, Susan (1933–; USA)
Steinem, Gloria (1934–; USA)
Stewart, Ella Winter (1898–1980; USA/UK)
Strong, Anna (1885–1970; USA/USSR/China)
Tarbell, Ida (1857–1944; USA)
Thompson, Dorothy (1894–1961; USA)
Vlachou, Helene (1911–; Greece)
Vreeland, Diana (c1901–; USA)
Walters, Barbara (1931–; USA)
Weiss, Louise (1893–1983; France)
Wells-Barnett, Ida B. (1862–1931; USA)
West, Rebecca (1892–1983; UK)

## 5. Women's rights

Abbott, Edith (1876–1957)
Abzug, Bella (1920–; USA)
Addams, Jane (1860–1935; USA)
Ahern, Lizzie (1877–1969; Australia)
Alcott, Louisa May (1832–88; USA)
Aleramo, Sibilla (1876–1960; Italy)
Aliberty, Soteria (1847–1929; Greece)
Al-Sa'īd' Amīnah (1914–; Egypt)
Anderson, Elizabeth Garrett (1836–1917; UK)
Anthony, Susan, B. (1820–1906; USA)
Aptheker, Bettina (1944–; USA)
Armand, Inesse (1874–1920; USSR)
Ashby, Margery Corbett (1882–1981; UK)
Astell, Mary (1668–1731; England)
Auclert, Hubertine (1848–1914; France)
Augspurg, Anita (1857–1943; Germany/Switzerland)
Ayrton, Hertha (1854–1923; UK)
Bajer, Matilde (1840–1934; Denmark)
Balch, Emily Greene (1867–1961; USA)
Barnes, Djuna (1892–1982; USA)
Barney, Natalie (1876–1972; USA/France)
Baumer, Gertrude (1873–1954; Germany/FGR)
Beale, Dorothea (1831–1906; UK)
Beard, Mary Ritter (1876–1958; USA)
Becker, Lydia Ernestine (1827–90; UK)
Belmont, Alva (1853–1933; USA)
Bennett, Louie (1870–1956; UK/Republic of Ireland)

Bernard, Jessie (1903–; USA)
Besant, Annie (1847–1933; UK/India)
Billington-Greig, Teresa (1877–1964; UK)
Blackburn, Helen (1842–1903; UK)
Blackwell, Elizabeth (1821–1910; UK/USA)
Blackwell, Emily (1826–1910; UK/USA)
Blatch, Harriet Stanton (1856–1940; USA)
Bloomer, Amelia (1818–94; USA)
Bodichon, Barbara (1827–91; UK)
Bol Poel, Martha (1877–1956; Belgium)
Bondfield, Margaret (1873–1953; UK)
Bose, Abala (1865–1951; India)
Boucherett, Jessie (1825–1905; UK)
Braun, Lily (1865–1916; Germany)
Bremer, Fredrika (1801–65; Sweden)
Brittain, Vera (1893–1970; UK)
Brown, Helen Gurley (1927–; USA)
Brown Blackwell, Antoinette-Louisa (1825–1921; USA)
Buss, Frances Mary (1827–94; UK)
Butler, Josephine (1828–1906; UK)
Byron, Noel (1792–1860; UK)
Catt, Carrie (1859–1947; USA)
Cauer, Minna (1841–1922; Germany)
Chattopadhyay, Kamaldevi (1903–; India)
Chen Tiejun (1904–28; China)
Chicago, Judy (1939–; USA)
Child, Lydia Maria (1802–80; USA)
Cixous, Hélène (1937–; France)
Claflin, Tennessee (1846–1923; USA/UK)
Clisby, Harriet (1830–1931; Australia/USA/Switzerland)
Clough, Anne Jemima (1820–92; UK)
Cobbe, Frances Power (1822–1904; UK)
Collet, Clara (1860–1948; UK)
Collett, Camilla (1813–95; Norway)
Cons, Emma (1839–1912; UK)
Courtney, Kathleen (1878–1974; UK)
Cousins, Margaret (1878–1954; UK/India)
Craig, Isa (1831–1903; UK)
Dalrymple, Learmonth White (1827–1906; New Zealand)
Daly, Mary (1928–; USA)
Darling, Flora (1840–1910; USA)
Daubie, Julie-Victoire (1824–74; France)
Davies, Emily (1830–1921; UK)
Davies, Margaret (1861–1944; UK)
Davison, Emily (1872–1913; UK)
de Beauvoir, Simone (1908–86; France)
de Gournay, Marie le Jars (1566–1645; France)
de Méricourt, Théroigne (1762–1817; France)
de Pisan, Christine (1364–1430; France)
Deraismes, Maria (1828–94; France)
Deroin, Jeanne (c1810–94; France)
Despard, Charlotte (1844–1939; UK)
Dexter, Caroline (1819–84; Australia)
d'Hericourt, Jenny (fl 19th century; France)
Drummond, Flora (1869–1949; UK)
Dugdale, Henrietta (1826–1918; Australia)
Durand, Marguerite (1864–1936; France)
Eastman, Crystal (1881–1928; USA)
El Saadawi, Nawal (1930–; Egypt)
Enoki, Miswo (1939–; Japan)
Espin, Vilma (1930–; Cuba)
Faithful, Emily (1835–95; UK)
Fawcett, Millicent Garrett (1847–1929; UK)
Figes, Eva (1932–; UK)
Figuero, Aña (1908–70; Chile)
Filosova, Anna (1837–1912; USSR)
Firestone, Shulamith (1945–; Canada/USA)
Fonda, Jane (1937–; USA)

Schreiber, Adele (d 1957; Austria/Germany/Switzerland)
Schreiner, Olive (1855–1920; South Africa)
Schwimmer, Rosika (1877–1948; Hungary)
Scott, Rose (1847–1925; Australia)
Séverine (1855–1929; France)
Shabanova, Anna (1848–1932; USSR)
Shafiq, Dori'a (1910–75; Egypt)
Sh'arawi, Huda (1882–1947; Egypt)
Shaw, Anna (1847–1919; USA)
Sheehy-Skeffington, Hannah (1877–1946; UK)
Sheepshanks, Mary (1872–1958; UK)
Sheppard, Kate (1848–1934; New Zealand)
Skram, Bertha (1847–1905; Norway)
Smedley, Agnes (1890–1950; USA/China)
Smith, Margaret Chase (1897–; USA)
Smith, Mary Ellen (1862–1933; Canada)
Smith, Sophia (1796–1870; USA)
Somerville, Edith (1858–1949; UK)
Spence, Catherine (1825–1910; Australia)
Spencer, Anna (1851–1931; USA)
Stanton, Elizabeth Cady (1815–1902; USA)
Stasova, Elena (1873–1966; USSR)
Stasova, Nadezhda (1822–95; Russia)
Steinem, Gloria (1934–; USA)
Stöcker, Helene (1869–1943; Germany/USA)
Stone, Lucy (1818–93; USA)
Stopes, Marie (1880–1958; UK)
Storni, Alfonsina (1892–1938; Argentina)
Stowe, Emily (1831–1903; Canada)
Strachey, Ray (1887–1940; UK)
Stritt, Marie (1856–1928; Germany)
Sullerot, Evelyne (1924–; France)
Summerskill, Edith (1901–80; UK)
Svolou, Maria (d 1976; Greece)
Swanwick, Helena (1864–1939; UK)
Taylor, Harriet (1808–58; UK)
Tennant, May (1869–1946; UK)
Theodoropoulou, Avra (1880–1963; Greece)
Thomas, Martha Carey (1857–1935; USA)
Tillion, Germaine (1907–; France)
Tristan, Flora (1803–44; France)
Trubnikova, Mariya (1835–97; Russia)
Truth, Sojourner (1777–1883, USA)
Twining, Louisa (1820–1912; UK)
Valette, Aline (1850–99; France)
van Grippenberg, Alexandra (1859–1913; Finland)
Webb, Catherine (1859–1947; UK)
Weber, Helene (1881–1962; FDR)
Weiss, Louise (1893–1983; France)
Wilkinson, Ellen (1891–1947; UK)
Willard, Emma (1787–1870; USA)
Willard, Frances (1839–98; USA)
Windeyer, Mary (1836–1912; Australia)
Wittig, Monique (1935–; France)
Wollstonecraft, Mary (1759–97; UK)
Woodhull, Victoria (1838–1927; USA/UK)
Wright, Frances (1795–1852; UK/USA)
Wright, Helena (1888–1982; UK)
Zetkin, Clara (1857–1933; Germany)

Anscombe, Elizabeth (1919–; UK)
Aptheker, Bettina (1944–; USA)
Arendt, Hannah (1906–75; Germany/USA)
Arete of Cyrene (mid-4th century BC; Greece)
Beard, Mary Ritter (1876–1958; USA)
Benedict, Ruth (1887–1948; USA)
Bernard, Jessie (1903–; USA)
Boserup, Esther Talke (1910–; Denmark)
Carter, Elizabeth (1717–1806; England)
Cixous, Hélène (1937–; France)
Cole, Margaret (1893–1980; UK)
Collet, Clara (1860–1948; UK)
Comnena, Anna (1083–1153; Byzantine empire)
Daly, Mary (1928–; USA)
d'Andrea, Novella (d 1333; Bologna)
d'Aragona, Tullia (1510–56; Florence)
de Beauvoir, Simone (1908–86; France)
de Pisan, Christine (1364–1430; France)
Eady, Dorothy (1904–81; UK/Egypt)
Elstob, Elizabeth (1683–1756; England)
Fletcher, Alice Cunningham (1838–1923; USA)
Franco, Veronica (1546–91; Italy)
Galindo, Beatriz (1474–1534; Spain)
Garnett, Constance (1861–1946; UK)
Groza, Maria (1918–; Romania)
Hamilton, Edith (1865–1963; USA)
Harrison, Jane (1850–1928; UK)
Hawkes, Jacquetta (1919–; UK)
Herbert, Mary (1561–1621; England)
Jesenská, Miléna (1890–1944; Czechoslovakia)
Kreps, Juanita (1921–; USA)
Kristeva, Julia (1941–; France)
Langer, Susanne Knauth (1895–1985; USA)
Leakey, Mary (1913–; UK/Tasmania)
Macaulay, Catharine Graham (1731–91; England)
Masham, Damaris (1658–1708; England)
Mead, Margaret (1901–78; USA)
Morata, Olympia Fulvia (1526–55; Ferrara/Heidelberg)
Murray, Margaret (1863–1963; UK/India)
Myrdal, Alva (1902–86; Sweden)
Nogarola, Isotta (1418–66; Verona/Venice)
Oakley, Ann (1944–; UK)
Ossoli, Margaret Fuller (1810–50; USA/Italy)
Pan Chao (c45–115AD; China)
Pardo Bazán, Emilia (1851–1921; Spain)
Parr, Catherine (1512–48; England)
Power, Eileen (1899–1940; UK)
Robinson, Joan Violet (1903–86; UK)
Roper, Margaret (1505–44; England)
Royer, Clemence (1830–1902; France)
Sabuco, Oliva (1562–1625; Spain)
Schwartz, Anna Jacobson (1915–; USA)
Sontag, Susan (1933–; USA)
Sophia, Electress of Hanover (1630–1714; Germany)
Theano (fl 6th century BC; Greece)
Tillion, Germaine (1907–; France)
van Schurman, Anna Maria (1607–78; Netherlands)
Ward, Barbara (1914–81; UK)
Warnock, Mary (1924–; UK)
Wedgwood, Veronica (1910–; UK)
Wootton, Barbara (1897–1988; UK)
Yates, Frances Amelia (1899–1981; UK)

## B. CULTURAL LIFE

### 1. Scholarship and research

*B1.1  Humanities and social sciences*

Abdel Rahman, Aisha (c1920–; Egypt)
Ahrweiler, Hélène (1916–; France)

*B1.2  Mathematics, pure and applied sciences, medicine*

Abbott, Maude (1869–1940; Canada)
Adamson, Joy (1910–80; Kenya)
Agassiz, Elizabeth Cary (1822–1907; USA)

## 2. Arts and entertainment

### B2.1 Cinema

Holland, Agnieszka (1948–; Poland)
Hopper, Hedda (1890–1966; USA)
Horne, Lena (1917–; USA)
Jakubowska, Wanda (1907–; Poland)
Kael, Pauline (1919–; USA)
Kaplan, Nelly (1931–; France)
Kelly, Grace (see Grace, Princess of Monaco)
Kyo, Machiko (1924–; Japan)
Lansing, Sherry (1944–; USA)
Lejeune, C.A. (1897–1973; UK)
Loden, Barbara (1934–80; USA)
Loos, Anita (1893–1981; USA)
Loren, Sophia (1934–; Italy/USA)
Love, Bessie (1898–1986; USA)
Lupino, Ida (1918–; UK/USA)
MacLaine, Shirley (1934–; USA)
Magnani, Anna (1908–73; Italy/USA)
Mangolte, Babette (c1945–; France)
Masina, Giulietta (1920–; Italy)
Mercouri, Melina (1923–; Greece)
Mészarós, Márta (1931ᵣ; Hungary)
Minnelli, Liza (1946–; USA)
Monroe, Marilyn (1926–62; USA)
Moreau, Jeanne (1928–; France)
Negri, Pola (1894–1987; Poland/Germany/USA)
Nielsen, Asta (1883–1972; Denmark/Germany)
Patil, Smita (1955–86; India)
Pickford, Mary (1893–1979; USA)
Reiniger, Lotte (1899–1981; Germany/UK)
Rekha (1953?; India)
Riefenstahl, Leni (1902–81; Germany)
Sagan, Leontine (1899–1974; Austria/South Africa)
Shub, Esther (1894–1959; USSR)
Smith, Maggie (1934–; UK)
Solntseva, Yulia (1901–; USSR)
Streep, Meryl (1949–; USA)
Swanson, Gloria (1899–1983; USA)
Tanaka, Kinuyo (1910–77; Japan)
Taylor, Elizabeth (1932–; USA)
Ullman, Liv (1939–; Norway)
Varda, Agnes (1928–; France)
Vitti, Monica (1931–; Italy)
von Trotta, Margarethe (1942–; Germany)
Weber, Lois (1882–1939; USA)
Weinstein, Hannah (1911–84; USA)
Wertmuller, Lina (1928–; Italy)
West, Mae (1892–1980; USA)
Zetterling, Mai (1925–; Sweden/UK/USA)
Zhang Ruifang (1918–; China)

## B2.2 Dance

Amaya, Carmen (1913–63; Spain)
Argentenita, La (1895–1945; Argentina/Spain)
Argentina, La (1888–1936; Argentina/Spain)
Baker, Josephine (ii) (1906–75; USA/France)
Bausch, Pina (1940–; Germany)
Beriosova, Svetlana (1932–; USSR/USA/UK)
Cerrito, Fanny (1817–1909; Italy/UK/France)
Chase, Lucia (1907–86; USA)
Chauviré, Yvette (1917–; France)
Cullberg, Brigit (1908–; Sweden/USA)
Cupis de Camargo, Marie-Anne (1710–70; France)
Danilova, Alexandra (1904–; USSR/France/USA)
de Valois, Ninette (1898–; UK)
Dudinskaya, Natalya (1912–; USSR)
Duncan, Isadora (?1879–1927; USA/France)
Elssler, Fanny (1810–84; Austria/France)

Farrell, Suzanne (1945–; USA)
Fonteyn, Margot (1919–; UK)
Fuller, Loie (1862–1928; USA)
Graham, Martha (1894–; USA)
Grahn, Lucille (1819–1907; Denmark/France/Germany)
Grey, Beryl (1927–; UK)
Grisi, Carlotta (1819–99; Italy/France)
Halprin, Ann (1920–; USA)
Holm, Hanya (1895–; Germany/USA)
Humphrey, Doris (1895–1958; USA)
Jamison, Judith (1943–; USA)
Karsavina, Tamara (1885–c1955; Russia/UK)
Kschessinskaya, Mathilde (1872–1971; Russia/France)
Lee, 'Gypsy Rose' (1914–70; USA)
Lopokova, Lydia (1892–1981; Russia/UK)
Lyn, Gillian (UK/USA)
McBride, Patricia (1942–; USA)
Makarova, Natalia (1940–; USSR)
Markova, Alicia (1910–; UK/France/USA)
Maywood, Augusta (1825–76; USA/France)
Montez, Lola (1818–61; UK/Europe/USA)
Nijinska, Bronislava (1891–1972; Russia/France/USA)
Pavlova, Anna (1882–1931; Russia/UK)
Primus, Pearl (1919–; West Indies/USA/Nigeria)
Rainer, Yvonne (1934–; USA)
Rambert, Marie (1888–1982; UK)
St Denis, Ruth (1877–1968; USA)
Sallé, Marie (1707–56; France)
Sokolow, Anna (1915–; USA)
Spessivtseva, Olga (1895–1980; Russia/France/USA)
Taglioni, Marie (1804–84; France)
Tamiris, Helen (1905–66; USA)
Tharp, Twyla (1942–; USA)
Toumanova, Tamara (1919–; France)
Ulanova, Galina (1910–; USSR)
Vaganova, Agrippina (1879–1951; USSR)
van Praagh, Peggy (1910–; UK/Australia)
Vyroubova, Nina (1921–; USSR/France)
Wigman, Mary (1896–1973; FGR)
Zambelli, Carlotta (1875–1968; Italy/France)
Zucchi, Virginia (1849–1930; Italy/Russia/France)

## B2.3 Literature

Acosta de Samper, Soledad (1833–1903; Colombia)
Adams, Abigail (1744–1818; USA)
Adcock, Fleur (1934–; New Zealand/UK)
Adivar, Halide (1883–1964; Turkey)
Aguilar, Grace (1816–47; UK)
Agustini, Delmira (1890–1914; Uruguay)
Aidoo, Ama Ata (1942–; Ghana)
Ainianos, Aganice (1838–92; Greece)
Akhmadulina, Bella Akhatovna (1937–; USSR)
Akhmatova, Anna (1889–1967; USSR)
Alcott, Louisa May (1832–88; USA)
Aleramo, Sibilla (1876–1960; Italy)
Alexander, Cecil Frances (1818–95; UK)
Al-Khansā (600–670; Arabia)
Al-Mala 'ikah, Nazik (1923–; Iraq)
Andreas-Salomé, Lou (1861–1937; Russia/Germany)
Angelou, Maya (1928–; USA)
Ariyoshi, Sawako (1921–84; Japan)
Ashford, 'Daisy' (1881–1972; UK)
Atwood, Margaret (1939–; Canada)
Austen, Jane (1775–1817; England)
Bā, Mariama (1929–81; Senegal)
Bachmann, Ingeborg (1926–73; Austria)
Bagryana, Elisaveta (1893–; Bulgaria)
Baillie, Joanna (1762–1851; UK)

B2.4  Music

(a)  Classical and modern: performers, composers etc

Walters, Ethel (1900–; USA)
Williams, Mary Lou (1910–81; USA)
Wynette, Tammy (1942–; USA)


**B2.5  Photography**

Abbott, Berenice (1898–; USA)
Arbus, Diane (1923–71; USA)
Bourke-White, Margaret (1904–71; USA)
Cameron, Julia Margaret (1815–79; UK)
Cunningham, Imogen (1883–1976; USA)
Lange, Dorothea (1895–1965; USA)
Tudor-Hart, Edith (1908–78; Austria/UK)
Wilding, Dorothy (1893–1976; UK)


**B2.6  Theatre and music hall**

Achurch, Janet (1864–1916; UK)
Anderson, Judith (1898–; Australia/USA)
Anderson, Mary (i) (1859–1940; USA)
Andreini, Isabella (1562–1604; Italy)
Andzhaparidzi, Vera (1900–; USSR)
Ashcroft, Peggy (1907–; UK)
Babanova, Maria Ivanovna (1900–; USSR)
Baker, Sarah (1736–1816; England)
Barry, Elizabeth (1658–1713; England)
Baylis, Lilian (1874–1937; UK)
Béjart, Madeleine (1618–72; France)
Berghaus, Ruth (1927–; GDR)
Bernhardt, Sarah (1844–1923; France/UK)
Bloom, Claire (1931–; UK)
Bracegirdle, Anne (1663–1748; England)
Brice, Fanny (1891–1951; USA)
Bryant, Hazel (1939–83; USA)
Calamity Jane (1852–1903; USA)
Campbell, (Mrs) Patrick (1865–1940; UK)
Carney, Kate (1868–1950; UK)
Casarès, Maria (1922–; Spain/France)
Champmeslé, Marie Desmares (1642–98; France)
Churchill, Caryl (1938–; UK)
Cibber, Susanna (1714–66; England)
Clairon, Claire (1723–1803; France)
Clive, Kitty (1711–85; England)
Cons, Emma (1838–1912; UK)
Crawford, Cheryl (1962–86; USA)
Cushman, Charlotte Saunders (1816–76; USA)
Dench, Judi (1934–; UK)
Draper, Ruth (1904–56; USA)
Drouet, Juliette (1806–83; France)
Dumesnil, Marie-Françoise (1713–1803; France)
Duse, Eleanora (1858–1924; Italy)
Enters, Angna (1907–; USA)
Espert, Nuria (1935–; Spain)
Evans, Edith (1888–1976; UK)
Faucit, Helena (1817–98; UK)
Feuillère, Edwige (1907–; France)
Fields, Gracie (1898–1979; UK/USA)
Fiske, Minnie Maddern (1865–1932; USA)
Genée, Adeline (1878–1970; Denmark/UK)
Goodbody, Buzz (1946–75; UK)
Gwyn, Nell (1650–87; England)
Hayes, Helen (1900–; USA)
Holden, Joan (USA)
Horniman, Annie (1860–1937; UK)
Inchbald, Elizabeth (1753–1821; UK)

Jackson, Glenda (1936–; UK)
Janauschek, Francesca (1830–1904; Czechoslovakia/Germany/USA)
Karatza, Rallou (c1778–1830; Romania/Greece)
Karinska, Barbara (1886–1983; USSR/France/USA)
Kemble, Fanny (1809–93; UK/USA)
Knipper-Chekhova, Olga (1870–1959; USSR)
Langtry, Lily (1853–1929; UK)
Lecouvreur, Adrienne (1692–1730; France)
Leigh, Vivien (1913–67; UK)
Lillie, Beatrice (1898–; Canada/UK)
Littlewood, Joan (1914–; UK/France)
Lloyd, Marie (1870–1922; UK)
Lundequist, Gerda (1871–1959; Sweden)
Lyn, Gillian (UK/USA)
MacBride, Maud (1866–1953; UK/Republic of Ireland)
Malina, Judith (1926–; USA/France)
Melmoth, Charlotte (1749–1823; USA)
Menken, Adah Isaacs (1835–68; USA/France)
Merman, Ethel (1908?–84; USA)
Midler, Bette (1945–; USA)
Minnelli, Liza (1946–; USA/UK)
Mistinguett (1873–1956; France)
Mnouchkine, Ariane (1939–; France)
Modjeska, Helena (1844–1909; Poland/USA)
Nazimova, Alla (1879–1945; Russia/USA)
Neuber, Frederika (1697–1760; Saxony)
Paxinou, Katina (1900–; Greece/USA/UK)
Pritchard, Hannah (1711–68; UK)
Rachel (1821–58; France)
Rame, Franca (1929–; Italy)
Redgrave, Vanessa (1937–; UK)
Renaud, Madeleine (1903–; France)
Ristori, Adelaide (1822–1906; Italy)
Robins, Elizabeth (1862–1952; UK/USA)
Rutherford, Margaret (1892–1972; UK)
Semenova, Ekaterina (1786–1849; Russia)
Siddons, Sarah (1755–1831; UK)
Smith, Maggie (1934–; UK/Canada)
Sorma, Agnes (1865–1927; Germany)
Tempest, Marie (1864–1942; UK)
Terry, Ellen (1847–1928; UK)
Thorndike, Sybil (1882–1976; UK)
Tilley, Vesta (1864–1952; UK)
Tucker, Sophie (1884–1966; USA)
Vestris, Lucia (1797–1856; UK)
Wallace, Nellie (1870–1948; UK)
Ward, Dorothy (1891–1987; UK)
Weigel, Helene (1901–71; Germany/USA/GDR)
Woffington, Peg (c1714–60; UK)
Yermolova, Maria (1853–1928; USSR)


**B2.7  Visual arts**

Abakanowicz, Magdalena (1930–; Poland)
Anguissola, Sofonisba (c1535–1625; Italy/Spain)
Attwell, Mabel Lucie (1879–1964; UK)
Bashkirtseff, Marie (1860–84; France)
Beale, Mary (1632–99; England)
Bell, Vanessa (1879–1961; UK)
Benoist, Marie (1768–1826; France)
Bonheur, Rosa (1822–99; France)
Brooks, Romaine (1874–1970; Italy/France)
Butler, Elizabeth (1850–1933; UK/Republic of Ireland)
Carr, Emily (1871–1945; Canada)
Carriera, Rosalba (1675–1757; Rome/Venice)
Cassat, Mary (1855–1926; USA/France)
Charpentier, Constance (1767–1841; France)

Cheron, Sophie (1648–1711; France)
Chicago, Judy (1939–; USA)
Claudel, Camille (1864–1943; France)
Damer, Anne Seymour (1749–1828; UK)
Delaunay, Sonia (1885–1979; France)
Exter, Alexandra (1882–1949; USSR/France)
Fini, Leonor (1908–; Argentina/France)
Fontana, Lavinia (1552–1614; Bologna/Rome)
Frankenthaler, Helen (1928–; USA)
Frink, Elisabeth (1930–; UK)
Gentileschi, Artemisia (1593–c1653; Florence/Rome/
    Naples)
Goncharova, Natalia (1881–1962; Russia/France)
Hemessen, Caterina van (1528–87; Antwerp/Spain)
Hepworth, Barbara (1903–75; UK)
Herrade of Landsburg (d 1195; Alsace)
Hesse, Eva (1936–70; USA)
Hicks, Sheila (1934–; USA/France)
Hodgkins, Frances (1869–1947; New Zealand)
Hoffman, Malvina (1887–1966; USA)
Hosmer, Harriet (1830–1908; USA)
John, Gwen (1876–1939; UK/France)
Kahlo, Frida (1910–54; Mexico/USA)
Kalvak, Helen (1901–84; Canada)
Kauffman, Angelica (1741–1807); Switzerland/England/
    Rome)
Knight, Laura (1877–1970; UK)
Kollwitz, Käthe (1867–1945; Germany)
Krasner, Lee (1908–84; USA)
Kuan, Fu-Jen (1212–1319; China)
Labille-Guiard, Adelaide (1749–1803; France)
Laurencin, Marie (1886–1956; France/Spain)
Lewis, Edmonia (1845–? after 1909; USA/Italy)
Leyster, Judith (1609–60; Netherlands)
Lisiewska, Anna (1721–82; Prussia/Stuttgart/Mannheim)
Merian, Maria Sibylla (1647–1717; Germany/Netherlands)
Modersohn-Becker, Paula (1876–1907; Germany/France)
Moillon, Louise (1615–75; France)
Morisot, Berthe (1841–95; France)
Moses, Anna (1860–1961; USA)
Munter, Gabriele (1877–1962; Germany/Sweden)
Nevelson, Louise (1899–; USA)
O'Keeffe, Georgia (1887–1986; USA)
Oppenheim, Meret (1913–; France/Switzerland)
Peeters, Clara (1594–after 1657; Netherlands)
Pereira, Irene (1907–71; USA)
Popova, Liubov (1889–1924; USSR)
Potter, Beatrix (1861–1943; UK)
Richier, Germaine (1904–59; France)
Rie, Lucie (1902–; Austria/UK)
Riley, Bridget (1931–; UK)
Ringgold, Faith (1934–; USA)
Roldan, Luisa (1656–1704; Spain)
Ruysch, Rachel (1664–1750; Netherlands)
Sartain, Emily (1841–1927; USA)
Sheridan, Clare (1885–1970; Republic of Ireland)
Sirani, Elisabetta (1638–65; Bologna)
Stepanova, Varvara (1894–1958; USSR)
Stevens, May (1924–; USA)
Tauber-Arp, Sophie (1889–1943; Switzerland/France)
Teerling, Levina (1515–76; Flanders/England)
Tussaud, Marie (1761–1850; Switzerland/France/UK)
Valadon, Suzanne (1865–1938; France)
Vallayer-Coster, Anne (1744–1818; France)
van Oosterwyck, Maria (1630–93; Netherlands)
Vigée-Lebrun, Marie (1755–1842; France)
Wei Fu-Jen (c272–350; China)
Whitney, Anne (1821–1915; USA)

*B2.8  Other: salon hostesses and patrons*

Aspasia of Miletos (5th century BC; Greece)
Barney, Natalie (1876–1972; USA)
Beach, Sylvia (1887–1962; USA/France)
Beaufort, Margaret (1443–1509; England)
Corner, Caterina (1454–1510; Cyprus/Venice)
Cushman, Charlotte Saunders (1816–76; USA)
Dandolo, Giovanna (fl 15th century; Venice)
de Lenclos, Ninon (1620–1705; France)
de Poitiers, Diane (1499–1566; France)
d'Este, Isabella (1474–1539; Mantua)
du Deffand (1697–1780; France)
Eleanor of Aquitaine (1122–1202; France/England)
Elizabeth I (1533–1603; England/Ireland)
Gardner, Isabella Stewart (1840–1924; USA)
Geoffrin, Marie-Thérèse Rodet de (1699–1777; France)
Guggenheim, Peggy (1898–1980; France/USA/Italy)
Horniman, Annie (1860–1937; UK)
Lespinasse, Julie de (1732–76; France)
Marguerite of Navarre (1492–1549; France)
Mavrokordatou, Alexandra (1605–84; Greece)
Montagu, Elizabeth (1720–1800; England)
Necker, Suzanne (1739–1817; Switzerland/France)
Ocampo, Victoria (1890–1978; Argentina)
Rambouillet (1588–1665; France)
Récamier (1777–1849; France)
Thrale, Hester Lynch (1741–1821; UK)
Varnhagen von Ense, Rahel Levin (1771–1833; Prussia)

## 3.  Domestic arts, fashion and cosmetics

Acton, Elizabeth (1799–1859; UK)
Arden, Elizabeth (c1884–1966; Canada/USA)
Ashley, Laura (1925–85; UK)
Ayer, Harriet Hubbard (1849–1903; USA)
Beeton, Isabella (1837–65; UK)
Bloomer, Amelia (1818–94; USA)
Chanel, Coco (c1883–1971; France)
Child, Julia (1912–; USA)
David, Elizabeth (UK)
Davis, Adele (1904–74; USA)
Denman, Gertrude (1884–1954; UK)
Farmer, Fannie Merritt (1857–1915; USA)
Fisher, Mary Frances Kennedy (1908–; USA)
Glasse, Hannah (1708–70; England)
Hamnett, Katherine (1952–; USA)
Head, Edith (1907–86; USA)
Hoodless, Adelaide (1857–1910; Canada)
Jekyll, Gertrude (1843–1932; UK)
Karinska, Barbara (1886–1983; USSR/France/USA)
Kawakubo, Rei (1942–; Japan)
Muir, Jean (?1931–; UK/USA)
Paston, Margaret (1423–84; England)
Post, Emily (1873–1960; USA)
Quant, Mary (1934–; UK)
Ratia, Armi (1912–79; Finland)
Richards, Ellen (1842–1911; USA)
Rubinstein, Helena (1882–1965; Australia/UK/France/
    USA)
Rudkin, Margaret (1897–1967; USA)
Saarinen, Aline (1914–72; USA)
Schiaparelli, Elsa (1890–1973; USA/France)
Spry, Constance (1886–1960; UK)
Vanderbilt-Cooper, Gloria (1924–; USA)
Vionnet, Madeleine (1877–1975; France)
Vreeland, Diana (c1901–; USA)

## C. PHYSICAL ACHIEVEMENTS

### 1. Competitive sport

Altwegg, Jeannette (1930–; UK)
Applebee, Constance (1883–1981; UK/USA)
Balas, Iolanda (1936–; Romania)
Belousova, Lyudmila (1935–; USSR)
Blankers-Koen, Fanny (1918–; Netherlands)
Bragina, Lyudmila (1943–; USSR)
Brough, Louise (1923–; USA)
Burton, Beryl (1937–; UK)
Caslavska, Vera (1942–; Czechoslovakia)
Chadwick, Florence (1919–; USA)
Connolly, 'Little Mo' (1934–69; USA)
Decker-Slaney, Mary (1958–; USA)
Didrikson, Babe (1914–56; USA)
Dod, Lottie (1871–1960; UK)
Douglass, Dorothea (1878–1960; UK)
Durack, Fanny (1894–1960; Australia)
Ederle, Gertrude (1906–; USA)
Fraser, Dawn (1937–; Australia)
Gibson, Althea (1927–; USA)
Heath, Sophia (1896–1936; USA/UK)
Henje, Sonja (1910–69; Norway/USA)
Heyhoe Flint, Rachel (1939–; UK)
Hopkins, Thelma (1936–; UK)
King, Billie-Jean (1943–; USA)
Koch, Marita (1957–; GDR)
Korbut, Olga (1955–; USSR)
Kristiansen, Ingrid (1956–; Norway)
Latynina, Larissa (1935–; USSR)
Legh, Alice Blanche (1855–1948; UK)
Lenglen, Suzanne (1899–1938; France)
Lloyd, Christine Evert (1954–; USA)
Lonsbrough, Anita (1941–; UK)
Lopez, Nancy (1957–; USA)
Moody, Helen N. Wills (1905–; USA)
Navratilova, Martina (1957–; Czechoslovakia/USA)
Okamoto, Ayako (1951–; Japan)
Peters, Mary (1939–; UK)
Pollard, Marjorie (1899–1982; UK)
Press, Tamara (1937–; USSR)
Rand, Mary (1940–; UK)
Rodnina, Irina (1949–; USSR)
Rudolph, Wilma (1940–;USA)
Scott, Margaret (1875–?; UK)
Smythe, Pat (1928–UK)
Steel, Dorothy (1884–1965; UK)
Torvill, Jayne (1957–; UK)
Turitscheva, Ludmila (1952–; USSR)
Waitz, Grete (1953–; Norway)
Wethered, Joyce (1901–; UK)
Whitbread, Fatima (1961–; UK)
Wightman, Hazel (1886–1974; USA)

### 2. Exploration and travel

Bell, Gertrude (1868–1926; UK/Arabia)
Bishop, Isabella (1831–1904; UK)
Blunt, Anne (1837–1917; UK/Arabia/Egypt)
Burton, Isabel (1831–96; UK)
Cable, Mildred (1878–1952; UK)
Cameron, Agnes Deans (1863–1912; Canada)
Coudreau, Octavie (c1870–c1910; France)
David-Neel, Alexandra (1869–1968; France)
Digby El Mezrab, Jane (1807–81; UK/Syria)

Eberhardt, Isabelle (1877–1904; USSR/Switzerland)
Fiennes, Celia (1662–1741; England)
Forbes, Joan Rosita (1893–1967; UK)
Franklin, Jane (1791–1875; UK/Tasmania)
Grimshaw, Beatrice (1871–1953; UK/Australia)
Kingsley, Mary (1862–1900; UK/Africa)
Marsden, Kate (1859–1931; UK)
Montagu, Mary Wortley (1689–1762; England)
North, Marianne (1830–90; UK)
Pfeiffer, Ida (d 1858; Austria)
Sheldon, May (1848–1936; USA/Africa)
Stanhope, Hester (1776–1839; England/Arabia)
Stark, Freya (1893–; UK/Italy/Arabia)
Taylor, Annie R. (1855–?1920; UK/China/Tibet)
Workman, Fanny (1859–1925; USA/UK)

### 3. Other pioneering exploits

*(a)  Aviation/space exploration*

Auriol, Jacqueline (1917–; France)
Bailey, Mary (1890–1960; UK)
Batten, Jean Gardner (1909–82; New Zealand)
Cochran, Jacqueline (1910–80; USA)
Earhart, Amelia (1898–1937; USA)
Heath, Sophia (1896–1936; USA/UK)
Johnson, Amy (1903–41; UK)
Markham, Beryl (1902–86; Kenya)
Ride, Sally Kristen (1951–; USA)
Scott, Sheila (1927–; UK)
Tereshkova, Valentina (1937–; USSR)
Yeager, Jeana (1952–; USA)

*(b)  Mountaineering*

Blum, Arlene (1945–; USA)
d'Angeville, Henriette (1795–1871; France)
Kogan, Claude (1919–59; France)
Le Blond, Elizabeth (1861–1934; UK)
Peck, Annie (1850–1935; USA)
Richardson, Katy (1864–1927; UK/France)
Tabei, Junko (1939–; Japan)
Tullis, Julie (1939–86; UK)
Underhill, Miriam (c1900–; USA)
Walker, Lucy (1836–1916; UK)
Workman, Fanny (1859–1925; USA/UK)

*(c)  Other*

Chojnowska-Liskiewicz, Krystyna (1936–; Poland)
Cintron, Conchita (1922–; Chile)
Francis, Clare (1946–; UK)
Hernandez, Angela (1949?–; Spain)
Oakley, Annie (1860–1926; USA)

## D. DYNAMIC CHARACTERS

### 1. National heroines

Bai, Lakshmi (1835–57; India)
Bouboulina, Laskarina (1772–1825; Greece)
Bouhired, Djamila (1935–; Algeria)
Boupacha, Djamila (1942–; Algeria)
Ch'iu Chin (?1879–1907; China)
Darling, Grace (1815–42; UK)
Deborah (fl 12thc BC; Israel)

## 2. Soldiers and spies *(see also 1)*

## 3. Frontierswomen and pioneers

## 4. Beauties, lovers and society leaders

## 5. Occult practitioners, witches and mediums

## 6. Criminals: pirates, pickpockets and poisoners